Collins
CANADIAN
DICTIONARY

HarperCollins Publishers
2 Bloor Street East,
20th floor,
Toronto,
Ontario,
Canada M4W 1A8

Second edition 2016

10 9 8 7 6 5 4 3

© HarperCollins Publishers 2011,
2016

ISBN 978-0-00-818462-9

Collins ® is a registered
trademark of HarperCollins
Publishers Limited

www.harpercollins.ca

A catalogue record for this book is
available from the British Library

Typeset by Market House Books
Ltd, Aylesbury, Great Britain

Printed in USA by Quad/Graphics

Acknowledgements
We would like to thank those
authors and publishers who
kindly gave permission for
copyright material to be used
in the Collins Corpus. We
would also like to thank Times
Newspapers Ltd for providing
valuable data.

CONTENTS

LIST OF CONTRIBUTORS

Senior Editor
Robert Pontisso

Editors
Lorna Gilmour
Robert Groves
Mary O'Neill

For the Publisher
Gerry Breslin
Michelle Fullerton

USING THIS DICTIONARY

Main entry words are printed in large bold type. All main entry words, including abbreviations and combining forms, appear in one alphabetical sequence, eg

> **abbreviate**
> **ABC**
> **abdicate**
> **abdomen**

Variant spellings are shown in full, eg

> **adrenalin, adrenaline**

Pronunciations are given in square brackets for words that are difficult or confusing; the word is respelt as it is pronounced, with the stressed syllable in bold type, eg

> **aegis** [ee-jiss]

Parts of speech are shown in italics as an abbreviation, eg

> **afflict** *v*

When a word can be used as more than one part of speech, the change of part of speech is shown after an arrow, eg

> **aim** *v* **1** point (a weapon or
> missile) or direct (a blow
> or remark) at a target... ▷ *n*
> **3** aiming

Parts of speech may be combined for words, eg

> **affront** *v, n* insult

Meanings of the word are separated by numbers, eg

> **absorb** *v* **1** soak up (a liquid)
> **2** take in **3** engage the interest
> of (someone)

Irregular parts or confusing forms of verbs, nouns, adjectives, and adverbs are shown in bold black, in smaller bold type than the main entry word, eg

> **begin** *v* **-ginning, -gan, -gun**
> **regret** *v* **-gretting, -gretted**
> **anniversary** *n, pl* **-ries**
> **busy** *adj* **busier, busiest**
> **well¹** *adv* **better, best**

Phrases and idioms are included immediately after meanings of the main entry word, eg

> **head** *n...adj...***go to someone's**
> **head** make someone drunk or
> conceited **head over heels** very
> much in love

Related words are shown in the same paragraph as the main entry word, eg

> **accelerate** *v* (cause to)
> move faster **acceleration** *n*
> **accelerator** *n* pedal in a motor
> vehicle to increase speed

Note: where the meaning of a related word is not given, it may be understood from the main entry word, or from another related word.

Compounds formed from the main entry word are shown in bold black in alphabetical order at the end of the paragraph, eg

> **ash**[1] *n*...**ashtray** *n* receptacle for tobacco ash and cigarette butts
> **Ash Wednesday** first day of Lent

Cross references, shown in bold black, refer the user to another entry where a full explanation or additional information is given, eg

> **alto** *n, pl* **-tos** *music* **1** short for **contralto**

ABBREVIATIONS USED IN THIS DICTIONARY

AD	anno Domini	*meteorol*	Meteorology
adj	adjective	*mil*	Military
adv	adverb	*n*	noun
anat	Anatomy	*N*	North
archit	Architecture	*naut*	Nautical
astrol	Astrology	*NZ*	New Zealand
Aust	Australia(n)	*offensive*	offensive
BC	before Christ	*orig.*	originally
biol	Biology	*photog*	Photography
Brit	British	*pl*	plural
Canad	Canadian	*prep*	preposition
chem	Chemistry	*pron*	pronoun
conj	conjunction	*psychol*	Psychology
E	East	*®*	Trademark
eg	for example	*RC*	Roman Catholic
esp.	especially	*S*	South
etc.	et cetera	*S Afr*	South Africa(n)
fem	feminine	*Scot*	Scottish
foll.	followed	*sing*	singular
geom	Geometry	*US*	United States
hist	History	*usu.*	usually
interj	interjection	*v*	verb
lit	Literary	*W*	West
masc	masculine	*Zool*	Zoology
med	Medicine		

Aa

a *adj* indefinite article, used before a noun being mentioned for the first time

AA 1 Alcoholics Anonymous 2 Automobile Association

aardvark *n* S African anteater with long ears and snout

AB 1 Alberta 2 able-bodied seaman

aback *adv* **taken aback** startled or disconcerted

abacus [ab-a-cuss] *n* beads on a wire frame, used for doing calculations

abalone [ab-a-**lone**-ee] *n* edible shellfish yielding mother-of-pearl

abandon *v* 1 desert or leave (one's wife, children, etc.) 2 give up (hope etc.) altogether ▷ *n* 3 freedom from inhibition **abandoned** *adj* 1 deserted 2 uninhibited **abandonment** *n*

abase *v* humiliate, degrade (oneself) **abasement** *n*

abashed *adj* embarrassed and ashamed

abate *v* diminish in strength **abatement** *n*

abattoir [ab-a-**twahr**] *n* slaughterhouse

abbess *n* nun in charge of a convent

abbey *n* dwelling place of, or a church belonging to, a community of monks or nuns

abbot *n* head of an abbey of monks

abbr., abbrev abbreviation

abbreviate *v* shorten (a word) by omitting some letters

abbreviation *n* shortened form of a word or words

ABC *n* 1 alphabet 2 rudiments of a subject

abdicate *v* give up (the throne or a responsibility) **abdication** *n*

abdomen *n* part of the body containing the stomach and intestines **abdominal** *adj*

abduct *v* carry off, kidnap **abduction** *n* **abductor** *n*

Aberdeen Angus *n* breed of cattle, orig. Scottish

aberration *n* 1 deviation from what is normal 2 mental lapse **aberrant** *adj* showing aberration **aberrance** *n*

abet *v* **abetting, abetted** assist or encourage in wrongdoing **abettor** *n*

abeyance *n* state of not being in use

abhor *v* **-horring, -horred** dislike strongly **abhorrence** *n* **abhorrent** *adj* hateful, loathsome

abide *v* 1 endure, put up with 2 *obsolete* stay or dwell: *abide with me* **abiding** *adj* lasting **abide by** *v* obey (the law, rules, etc.)

ability *n, pl* **-ties** 1 competence, power 2 talent

abject *adj* 1 utterly miserable 2 lacking all self-respect **abjectly** *adv* **abjectness** *n*

abjure *v* deny or renounce on oath **abjuration** *n*

ablative [ab-**lat**-iv] *n* case of nouns in Latin and other languages, indicating source,

a

agent, or instrument of action

ablaze adj burning fiercely

able adj capable, competent
ably adv **able-bodied** adj
strong and healthy

ablutions pl n act of washing

abnegate v give up, renounce
abnegation n

abnormal adj not normal
or usual **abnormally** adv
abnormality n

aboard adv, prep on, in, onto,
or into a ship, train, or aircraft

abode n home, dwelling

abolish v do away with
abolition n **abolitionist** n
person who wishes to do
away with something, esp.
slavery

abominate v detest or hate
abominable adj detestable,
very bad **abominably** adv
abomination n **abominable
snowman** large apelike
creature said to inhabit the
Himalayas

aborigine [ab-or-**rij**-in-ee],
aboriginal n original
inhabitant of a country or
region **Aborigine** original
inhabitant of Australia
aboriginal or **Aboriginal** adj

abort v **1** terminate (a
pregnancy) prematurely
2 give birth to a dead fetus
3 end prematurely and
unsuccessfully **abortion**
n **1** operation to terminate
a pregnancy **2** informal
something grotesque
abortionist n person who
performs abortions, esp.
illegally **abortive** adj
unsuccessful

abound v **1** be plentiful
2 overflow **abounding** adj

about prep **1** concerning,
on the subject of **2** in or
near a place ▷ adv **3** nearly,
approximately **4** nearby
about to 1 intending to **2** on
the point of: *about to give up*

hope **about turn** v mil turn
to face the opposite direction
about-turn n **1** turn to the
opposite direction **2** complete
change of attitude

above adv, prep **1** over or higher
than **2** greater than **3** superior
to **above board** in the open,
without dishonesty

abracadabra n supposedly
magic word

abrade v rub or scrape away

abrasion n scraped area on
the skin **abrasive** adj **1** harsh
and annoying in manner
2 causing abrasion ▷ n
3 substance for cleaning or
polishing by rubbing

abreast adj, adv side by side
abreast of up to date with

abridge v shorten by using
fewer words **abridgment** or
abridgement n

abroad adv **1** to or in a foreign
country **2** at large

abrogate v cancel (a law
or agreement) formally
abrogation n

abrupt adj **1** sudden,
unexpected **2** blunt and rude
abruptly adv **abruptness** n

abs pl n informal abdominal
muscles

abscess n inflamed swelling
containing pus

abscond v leave secretly

abseil [**ab**-sale] v esp. Brit
rappel

absent adj **1** not present
2 lacking **3** inattentive
▷ v **4** keep (oneself) away
absently adv **absence**
n **1** being away **2** lack
absentee n person who
should be present but is not
absenteeism n persistent
absence from work or
school **absent-minded**
adj inattentive or forgetful
absent-mindedly adv

absinthe n potent green
aniseed-flavoured liqueur

absolute adj 1 complete and utter 2 not limited, unconditional 3 pure: *absolute alcohol* **absolutely** adv 1 completely ▷ interj 2 certainly, yes **absolutism** n government by a ruler with unrestricted power

absolve v declare to be free from blame or sin **absolution** n

absorb v 1 soak up (a liquid) 2 take in 3 engage the interest of (someone) **absorption** n **absorbent** adj able to absorb liquid **absorbency** n

abstain v 1 choose to refrain 2 choose not to vote **abstainer** n **abstention** n abstaining, esp. from voting **abstinence** n abstaining, esp. from drinking alcohol **abstinent** adj

abstemious [ab-**steem**-ee-uss] adj sparing in the consumption of food or alcohol **abstemiously** adv **abstemiousness** n

abstract adj 1 existing as a quality or idea rather than a material object 2 theoretical 3 (of art) using patterns of shapes and colours rather than realistic likenesses ▷ n 4 summary 5 abstract work of art 6 abstract word or idea ▷ v 7 remove 8 summarize **abstracted** adj preoccupied **abstraction** n

abstruse adj not easy to understand

absurd adj incongruous or ridiculous **absurdly** adv **absurdity** n

abundant adj plentiful **abundantly** adv **abundance** n

abuse n 1 prolonged ill-treatment of someone 2 insulting comments 3 wrong use ▷ v 4 use wrongly 5 ill-treat violently 6 speak harshly and rudely to **abuser** n **abusive** adj **abusively** adv **abusiveness** n

abut v abutting, abutted adjoin, border on **abutment** n end support of a bridge or arch

abysmal adj informal extremely bad, awful **abysmally** adv

abyss n very deep hole or chasm

AC alternating current

a/c account

acacia [a-**kay**-sha] n tree or shrub with yellow or white flowers

academy n, pl -mies 1 society to advance arts or sciences 2 institution for specialized training 3 Scot secondary school **academic** adj 1 of an academy or university 2 of theoretical interest only ▷ n 3 lecturer or researcher at a university **academically** adv **academician** n member of an academy

acanthus n 1 prickly plant 2 ornamental carving in the shape of an acanthus leaf

accede v 1 consent or agree (to) 2 take up (an office or position)

accelerate v (cause to) move faster **acceleration** n **accelerator** n pedal in a motor vehicle to increase speed

accent n 1 distinctive style of pronunciation of a local, national, or social group 2 mark over a letter to show how it is pronounced 3 stress on a syllable or musical note ▷ v 4 place emphasis on

accentuate v stress, emphasize **accentuation** n

accept v 1 receive willingly 2 consider to be true 3 agree to **acceptance** n **acceptable** adj 1 satisfactory 2 tolerable **acceptably** adv **acceptability** n

access n 1 means of or

a

right to approach or enter ▷ v **2** obtain (data) from a computer **accessible** adj easy to approach or enter **accessibility** n

accession n taking up of an office or position

accessory n, pl **-ries** **1** supplementary part or object **2** person involved in a crime although not present when it is committed

accident n **1** mishap, usu. one causing injury or death **2** event happening by chance **accidental** adj **1** happening by accident ▷ n **2** music symbol indicating that a sharp, flat, or natural note is not a part of the key signature **accidentally** adv

acclaim v **1** applaud, praise ▷ n **2** applause **acclamation** n **1** acclaim **2** election without opposition to a public position

acclimatize v adapt to a new climate or environment **acclimatization** n

accolade n **1** award, honour, or praise **2** award of knighthood

accommodate v **1** provide with lodgings **2** have room for **3** do a favour for **4** get used to (something) **accommodating** adj obliging **accommodation** n house or room for living in

accompany v **-nying,** **-nied 1** go along with **2** occur with **3** provide a musical accompaniment for **accompaniment** n **1** something that accompanies **2** music supporting part that goes with a solo **accompanist** n

accomplice n person who helps another to commit a crime

accomplish v **1** manage to do **2** finish **accomplished** adj expert, proficient

accomplishment n **1** personal ability or skill **2** completion

accord n **1** agreement, harmony ▷ v **2** fit in with

accordance n **in accordance with** in conformity with

according adv **according to** **1** as stated by **2** in conformity with **accordingly** adv **1** in an appropriate manner **2** consequently

accordion n portable musical instrument played by moving the two sides apart and together, and pressing a keyboard or buttons to produce the notes **accordionist** n

accost v approach and speak to

account n **1** report, description **2** business arrangement making credit available **3** record of money received and paid out with the resulting balance **4** person's money held in a bank **5** importance, value ▷ v **6** judge to be **on account of** because of **accountable** adj responsible to someone or for something **accountability** n

accounting n skill or practice of maintaining and auditing business accounts **accountant** n person who maintains and audits business accounts **accountancy** n

accoutrements [ak-**koo**-trem-ments] pl n clothing and equipment

accredited adj authorized, officially recognized

accretion [ak-**kree**-shun] n **1** gradual growth **2** something added

accrue v **-cruing, -crued** increase gradually **accrual** n

accumulate v gather together in increasing quantity **accumulation**

n **accumulative** *adj*
accumulator *n* rechargeable electric battery
accurate *adj* exact, correct **accurately** *adv* **accuracy** *n*
accursed *adj* 1 under a curse 2 detestable
accusative *n* grammatical case indicating the direct object
accuse *v* 1 charge with wrongdoing 2 blame **accused** *n, adj* **accuser** *n* **accusing** *adj* **accusation** *n* **accusatory** *adj*
accustom *v* make used to **accustomed** *adj* 1 usual 2 used (to) 3 in the habit (of)
ace *n* 1 playing card with one spot on it 2 *informal* expert 3 *tennis* unreturnable serve ▷ *adj* 4 *informal* excellent
acerbic [ass-**sir**-bik] *adj* harsh or bitter **acerbity** *n*
acetate [**ass**-it-tate] *n* 1 *chem* salt or ester of acetic acid 2 Also **acetate rayon** synthetic textile fibre
acetic [ass-**see**-tik] *adj* of or involving vinegar **acetic acid** colourless liquid used to make vinegar
acetone [**ass**-it-tone] *n* colourless liquid used as a solvent
acetylene [ass-**set**-ill-een] *n* colourless flammable gas used in welding metals
ache *n* 1 dull continuous pain ▷ *v* 2 be in or cause continuous pain
achieve *v* gain by hard work or ability **achievement** *n* something accomplished
Achilles heel [ak-**kill**-eez] *n* small but fatal weakness **Achilles tendon** cord connecting the calf to the heel bone
achromatic *adj* 1 colourless 2 *music* with no sharps or flats
acid *n* 1 *chem* one of a class of compounds, corrosive

and sour when dissolved in water, that combine with a base to form a salt 2 *slang* LSD ▷ *adj* 3 containing acid 4 sour-tasting 5 sharp or sour in manner **acidic** *adj* **acidify** *v* **acidity** *n* **acidulous** *adj* 1 sharp 2 caustic **acid rain** rain containing acid from atmospheric pollution **acid reflux** regurgitation of stomach acid, causing heartburn **acid test** conclusive test of value
acknowledge *v* 1 admit, recognize 2 indicate recognition of (a person) 3 say one has received **acknowledgment** *or* **acknowledgement** *n*
acme [**ak**-mee] *n* highest point of achievement or excellence
acne [**ak**-nee] *n* pimply skin disease
acolyte *n* 1 follower or attendant 2 *Christianity* person who assists a priest
aconite *n* 1 poisonous plant with hoodlike flowers 2 poison obtained from this plant
acorn *n* nut of the oak tree
acoustic *adj* 1 of sound and hearing 2 (of a musical instrument) not electronically amplified **acoustics** *n* 1 science of sounds ▷ *pl n* 2 features of a room or building determining how sound is heard within it **acoustically** *adv*
acquaint *v* make familiar, inform **acquainted** *adj* **acquaintance** *n* 1 person known 2 personal knowledge
acquiesce [ak-wee-**ess**] *v* accept without complaining **acquiescence** *n* **acquiescent** *adj*
acquire *v* gain, get **acquirement** *n* **acquisition** *n* 1 act of getting 2 thing

acquired **acquisitive** *adj* eager to gain material possessions **acquisitiveness** *n*

acquit *v* **-quitting, -quitted** **1** declare innocent **2** conduct (oneself) in a particular way **acquittal** *n*

acre *n* measure of land, 4840 square yards **acreage** [ake-er-rij] *n* land area in acres

acrid [ak-rid] *adj* pungent, bitter **acridity** *n*

acrimony [ak-rim-mon-ee] *n* bitterness of speech or manner **acrimonious** *adj*

acrobat *n* person skilled in gymnastic feats requiring agility and balance **acrobatic** *adj* **acrobatics** *pl n* acrobatic feats

acronym *n* word formed from the initial letters of other words, such as NATO

acropolis [a-**crop**-pol-liss] *n* citadel of an ancient Greek city

across *adv, prep* **1** from side to side (of) **2** on or to the other side (of) **across the board** applying equally to all

acrostic *n* word puzzle in which the first or last letters of each line spell a word or saying

acrylic *n, adj* (synthetic fibre, paint, etc.) made from acrylic acid **acrylic acid** strong-smelling corrosive liquid

act *n* **1** thing done **2** law or decree **3** section of a play or opera **4** one of several short performances in a show **5** pretended attitude ▷ *v* **6** do something **7** behave in a particular way **8** perform in a play, film, etc. **act of God** unpredictable natural event **acting** *n* **1** art of an actor ▷ *adj* **2** temporarily performing the duties of **actor** (**actress**) *n* person

who acts in a play, film, etc.

actinium *n* radioactive chemical element

action *n* **1** process of doing **2** thing done **3** operating mechanism **4** lawsuit **5** minor battle **actionable** *adj* giving grounds for a lawsuit **action replay** rerun of an event on a television tape

active *adj* **1** busy, energetic **2** moving, working **3** *grammar* (of a verb) in a form indicating that the subject is performing the action, eg *threw* in *Kim threw the ball* **actively** *adv* **activity** *n* **1** active behaviour **2** leisure pursuit **activate** *v* make active **activation** *n* **activator** *n* **activist** *n* person who works energetically to achieve political or social goals **activism** *n*

actual *adj* existing in reality **actually** *adv* really, indeed **actuality** *n*

actuary *n, pl* **-aries** statistician who calculates insurance risks **actuarial** *adj*

actuate *v* activate (a device) **actuation** *n*

acuity [ak-**kew**-it-ee] *n* keenness of vision or thought

acumen [ak-yew-men] *n* ability to make good judgments

acupuncture *n* medical treatment involving the insertion of needles at various points on the body **acupuncturist** *n*

acute *adj* **1** severe or intense **2** keen, shrewd **3** sharp, sensitive **4** (of an angle) less than 90° ▷ *n* **5** accent (´) over a letter to indicate the quality or length of its sound, as in *café* **acutely** *adv* **acuteness** *n*

ad *n informal* advertisement

AD anno Domini

adage [**ad**-ij] *n* wise saying, proverb

adagio [ad-**dahj**-yo] *adv music* slowly and gracefully

adamant *adj* inflexibly determined **adamantly** *adv*

Adam's apple *n* projecting lump of thyroid cartilage at the front of the throat

adapt *v* alter for new use or new conditions **adaptable** *adj* **adaptability** *n* **adaptation** *n* 1 adapting 2 thing produced by adapting something **adaptor** *or* **adapter** *n* device for connecting several electrical appliances to a single socket

add *v* 1 combine (numbers or quantities) 2 join (to something) 3 say further

addendum *n, pl* **-da** 1 an addition 2 appendix to a book etc.

adder *n* 1 any of various harmless American snakes 2 *Brit* small poisonous snake

addict *n* 1 person who is unable to stop taking drugs 2 *informal* person devoted to something **addicted** *adj* **addiction** *n* **addictive** *adj* causing addiction

addition *n* 1 adding 2 thing added **in addition** besides, as well **additional** *adj* **additionally** *adv* **additive** *n* something added, esp. to foodstuffs

addle *v* make rotten or muddled

address *n* 1 place where a person lives 2 direction on a letter 3 location 4 formal public speech ▷ *v* 5 mark the destination, as on an envelope 6 speak to 7 give attention to (a problem, task, etc.) **addressee** *n* person addressed

adduce *v* cite as proof

adenoids [**ad**-in-oidz] *pl n* mass of tissue at the back of the nose **adenoidal** *adj* having a nasal voice caused by swollen adenoids

adept *adj, n* very skilful (person)

adequate *adj* 1 sufficient, enough 2 not outstanding **adequately** *adv* **adequacy** *n*

adhere *v* 1 stick to 2 be devoted to **adherence** *n* **adherent** *n* devotee, follower **adhesion** *n* 1 adhering 2 abnormal sticking together of parts of the body, as after surgery

adhesive *adj* 1 able to stick to things ▷ *n* 2 substance used to stick things together

ad hoc *adj, adv* for a particular occasion only

adieu [a-**dew**] *interj* farewell, goodbye

ad infinitum *adv Latin* endlessly

adipose *adj* of fat, fatty

adj. adjective

adjacent *adj* 1 near or next to 2 having a common boundary 3 *geom* (of a side in a right-angled triangle) lying between a specified angle and the right angle

adjective *n* word that adds information about a noun or pronoun **adjectival** *adj*

adjoin *v* be next to **adjoining** *adj*

adjourn *v* 1 close (a court) at the end of a session 2 postpone temporarily 3 *informal* go elsewhere **adjournment** *n*

adjudge *v* declare (to be)

adjudicate *v* 1 decide on (a dispute) 2 judge (a competition) **adjudication** *n* **adjudicator** *n*

adjunct *n* subordinate or additional person or thing

adjure *v* 1 command to do 2 appeal earnestly

adjust *v* 1 adapt to new conditions 2 alter slightly so as to be suitable **adjustable** *adj* **adjuster** *n* **adjustment** *n*

adjutant [aj-oo-tant] *n* army officer in charge of routine administration

ad-lib *v* -libbing, -libbed **1** improvise a speech etc. without preparation ▷ *n* **2** improvised remark

admin *n informal* administration

administer *v* **1** manage (business affairs) **2** dispense (justice) **3** give (medicine or treatment)

administrate *v* manage (an organization) **administration** *n* **administrative** *adj* **administrator** *n*

admiral *n* highest naval rank

admire *v* regard with esteem and approval **admirable** *adj* **admirably** *adv* **admiration** *n* **admirer** *n* **admiring** *adj* **admiringly** *adv*

admissible *adj* allowed to be brought in as evidence in court **admissibility** *n*

admission *n* **1** permission to enter **2** entrance fee **3** confession

admit *v* -mitting, -mitted **1** confess, acknowledge **2** concede the truth of **3** allow in **admittance** *n* permission to enter **admittedly** *adv* it must be agreed (that)

admixture *n* **1** mixture **2** ingredient

admonish *v* reprove sternly **admonition** *n* **admonitory** *adj*

ad nauseam [ad naw-zee-am] *adv Latin* to a boring or sickening extent

ado *n* fuss, trouble

adobe [ad-oh-bee] *n* sun-dried brick

adolescence *n* period between puberty and adulthood. **adolescent** *n, adj* (person) between puberty and adulthood

adopt *v* **1** take (someone else's child) as one's own **2** take up (a plan or principle) **adoption** *n* **adoptive** *adj* related by adoption

adore *v* **1** love intensely **2** worship **adorable** *adj* **adoration** *n* **adoring** *adj* **adoringly** *adv*

adorn *v* decorate, embellish **adornment** *n*

ADP automatic data processing

adrenal [ad-reen-al] *adj* near the kidney **adrenal glands** glands covering the top of the kidneys

adrenalin, adrenaline *n* hormone secreted by the adrenal glands in response to stress

adrift *adj, adv* **1** drifting **2** without clear purpose

adroit *adj* quick and skilful **adroitly** *adv* **adroitness** *n*

adsorb *v* (of a gas or vapour) condense and form a thin film on a surface **adsorbent** *adj* **adsorption** *n*

ADT Atlantic Daylight Time

adulation *n* uncritical admiration

adult *adj* **1** fully grown, mature ▷ *n* **2** adult person or animal. **adulthood** *n*

adulterate *v* make impure by addition **adulteration** *n*

adultery *n, pl* -teries sexual unfaithfulness of a husband or wife **adulterer** (**adulteress**) *n* **adulterous** *adj*

adumbrate *v* give a faint indication of **adumbration** *n*

adv. adverb

advance *v* **1** go or bring forward **2** further (a cause) **3** propose **4** lend (a sum of money) ▷ *n* **5** forward movement **6** improvement **7** loan **advances 8** approaches to a person with the hope of starting a romantic or

sexual relationship ▷ adj
9 previous **in advance**
ahead **advanced** adj **1** at a
late stage in development
2 not elementary ▷ n
3 green flashing traffic
signal that allows left turn
advancement n promotion

advantage n **1** more
favourable position or state
2 benefit or profit **3** tennis
point scored after deuce
take advantage of 1 use (an
opportunity) **2** use (a person)
unfairly **advantageous** adj
advantageously adv

advent n **1** arrival **2 Advent**
season of four weeks before
Christmas **Adventist** n
member of a Christian sect
that believes in the imminent
return of Christ

adventitious adj added or
appearing accidentally

adventure n exciting and
risky undertaking or exploit
adventurer (**adventuress**) n
1 person who seeks adventures
2 person who unscrupulously
seeks money or power
adventurous adj

adverb n word that adds
information about a verb,
adjective, or other adverb
adverbial adj **adverbially** adv

adversary [ad-verse-sair-
ree] n, pl **-saries** opponent or
enemy

adverse adj **1** antagonistic
or hostile **2** unfavourable
adversely adv **adversity** n
affliction or hardship

advertise v **1** present or
praise (goods or services)
to the public in order to
encourage sales **2** make (a
vacancy, event, etc.) known
publicly **advertisement** n
public announcement to sell
goods or publicize an event
advertiser n **advertising**
adj, n

advice n recommendation
as to what to do **advise**
v **1** offer advice to **2** notify
(someone) **adviser** or **advisor**
n **advisable** adj prudent,
sensible **advisability** n
advisory adj giving advice
advised adj considered,
thought-out: ill-advised
advisedly adv deliberately

advocaat n liqueur with a
raw egg base

advocate v **1** propose or
recommend ▷ n **2** person
who publicly supports a
cause **3** Scot barrister
advocacy n

adze n tool with an arched
blade set at right angles to the
handle

aegis [ee-jiss] n sponsorship,
protection

aeolian harp [ee-oh-lee-an]
n musical instrument that
produces sounds when the
wind passes over its strings

aeon n same as **eon**

aerate v put gas into (a
liquid), as when making a
fizzy drink. **aeration** n

aerial adj **1** in, from, or
operating in the air **2** relating
to aircraft ▷ n **3** metal pole
or wire for receiving or
transmitting radio or
TV signals

aerie n same as **eyrie**

aerobatics pl n stunt flying
aerobatic adj

aerobics pl n exercises
designed to increase the
amount of oxygen in the
blood **aerobic** adj

aerodrome n small airport

aerodynamics pl n (study of)
air flow, esp. around moving
solid objects **aerodynamic**
adj

aerofoil n part of an aircraft,
such as the wing, designed to
give lift

aerogram n airmail letter on

a single sheet of paper that seals to form an envelope

aeronautics n study or practice of aircraft flight **aeronautical** adj

aeroplane n Brit airplane

aerosol n pressurized can from which a substance can be dispensed as a fine spray

aerospace n earth's atmosphere and space beyond

aesthetic, esthetic [iss-thet-ik] adj relating to the appreciation of art and beauty **aesthetics** or **esthetics** n study of art, beauty, and good taste **aesthetically** or **esthetically** adv **aesthete** or **esthete** [ess-theet] n person who has or affects an extravagant love of art **aestheticism** or **estheticism** n

aether n same as **ether**

aetiology n same as **etiology**

afar adv from or at a great distance

affable adj friendly and easy to talk to **affably** adv **affability** n

affair n 1 event or happening 2 sexual relationship outside marriage 3 thing to be done or attended to **affairs** 4 personal or business interests 5 matters of public interest

affect[1] v 1 act on, influence 2 move (someone) emotionally **affecting** adj moving the feelings **affection** n fondness or love **affectionate** adj loving **affectionately** adv

affect[2] v 1 put on a show of 2 wear or use by preference **affectation** n show, pretence **affected** adj 1 full of affectation 2 pretended

affianced [af-fie-anst] adj old-fashioned engaged to be married

affidavit [af-fid-dave-it] n written statement made on oath

affiliate v (of a group) link up with a larger group **affiliation** n

affinity n, pl -ties 1 close connection or liking 2 close resemblance 3 chemical attraction

affirm v 1 assert, declare 2 uphold or confirm (an idea or belief) **affirmation** n **affirmative** n, adj (word or phrase) indicating agreement **affirmative action** provision of special opportunities in employment for a disadvantaged group

affix v 1 attach or fasten ▷ n 2 word or syllable added to a word to change its meaning

afflict v give pain or grief to **affliction** n

affluent adj wealthy **affluence** n wealth

afford v 1 have enough money to buy 2 be able to spare (the time etc.) 3 give or supply **affordable** adj

afforest v plant trees on **afforestation** n

affray n noisy fight, brawl

affront v, n insult

Afghan adj of Afghanistan or its language **Afghan hound** large slim dog with long silky hair

aficionado [af-fish-yo-**nah**-do] n, pl -**dos** enthusiastic fan of something or someone

afield adv, adj **far afield** far away

aflame adv, adj burning

afloat adv, adj 1 floating 2 at sea

afoot adv, adj happening, in operation

aforesaid adj referred to previously

aforethought adj premeditated: with malice aforethought

Afr. Africa(n)

afraid *adj* **1** frightened **2** regretful

afresh *adv* again, anew

African *adj* **1** of Africa ▷ *n* **2** person from Africa **African violet** house plant with pink or purple flowers and hairy leaves

Afrikaans *n* language used in S Africa, related to Dutch

Afrikaner *n* White S African whose mother tongue is Afrikaans

Afro *n, pl* **-ros** frizzy bushy hair style

Afro- *combining form* African: *Afro-Caribbean*

aft *adv* at or towards the rear of a ship or aircraft

after *prep* **1** following in time or place **2** in pursuit of **3** in imitation of ▷ *conj* **4** at a later time than ▷ *adv* **5** at a later time **afters** *pl n Brit informal* dessert

afterbirth *n* material expelled from the womb after childbirth

aftercare *n* **1** support given to a person discharged from a hospital or prison **2** regular care required to keep something in good condition

aftereffect *n* effect occurring some time after its cause

afterglow *n* **1** glow left after a source of light has gone **2** pleasant feeling left after an enjoyable experience

afterlife *n* life after death

aftermath *n* aftereffects collectively

afternoon *n* time between noon and evening

aftershave *n* lotion applied to the face after shaving

afterthought *n* **1** idea occurring later **2** something added later

afterwards, afterward *adv* later

Ag *chem* silver

again *adv* **1** once more **2** in addition

against *prep* **1** in opposition or contrast to **2** in contact with **3** in readiness for

agape *adj* **1** (of the mouth) wide open **2** (of a person) very surprised

agaric *n* fungus with gills on the underside of the cap, such as a mushroom

agate [ag-git] *n* semiprecious form of quartz with striped colouring

age *n* **1** length of time a person or thing has existed **2** time of life **3** latter part of human life **4** period of history **5** long time ▷ *v* **ageing** *or* **aging, aged 6** make or grow old **aged** *adj* **1** [ay-jid] old **2** [rhymes with **raged**] having the age of **ageing** *or* **aging** *n, adj* **ageless** *adj* **1** apparently never growing old **2** timeless **age-old** *adj* very old

agenda *n* list of things to be dealt with, esp. at a meeting

agent *n* **1** person acting on behalf of another **2** person or thing producing an effect **agency** *n* **1** organization providing a service **2** business or function of an agent **3** *old-fashioned* power or action by which something happens **agent general** diplomat who represents a Canadian province

agent provocateur [azh-on prov-vok-at-**tur**] *n, pl* **agents provocateurs** [azh-on prov-vok-at-**tur**] person employed by the authorities to tempt people to commit illegal acts and so be discredited or punished

agglomerate *v* **1** gather into a mass ▷ *n* **2** confused mass **3** rock consisting of fused volcanic fragments

▷ *adj* **4** formed into a mass **agglomeration** *n*

agglutinate *v* stick with or as if with glue **agglutination** *n* **agglutinative** *adj*

aggrandize *v* make greater in size, power, or rank **aggrandizement** *n*

aggravate *v* **1** make worse **2** *informal* annoy **aggravating** *adj* **aggravation** *n*

aggregate *v* **1** gather into a mass ▷ *adj* **2** gathered into a mass **3** total or final ▷ *n* **4** total **5** rock consisting of a mixture of minerals **6** sand or gravel used to make concrete **aggregation** *n*

aggression *n* **1** unprovoked attack **2** hostile behaviour **aggressive** *adj* **1** full of anger or hostility **2** forceful or determined **aggressively** *adv* **aggressiveness** *n* **aggressor** *n*

aggrieved *adj* upset and angry

aggro *n slang* aggression

aghast *adj* amazed or shocked

agile *adj* **1** nimble, quick-moving **2** mentally quick **agilely** *adv* **agility** *n*

agitate *v* **1** disturb or excite **2** stir or shake (a liquid) **3** stir up public opinion for or against something **agitation** *n* **agitator** *n*

aglow *adj* glowing

AGM annual general meeting

agnostic *n* **1** person who believes that it is impossible to know whether God exists ▷ *adj* **2** of agnostics **agnosticism** *n*

ago *adv* in the past

agog *adj* eager or curious

agony *n, pl* **-nies** extreme physical or mental pain **agonize** *v* **1** (cause to) suffer agony **2** worry greatly **agonizing** *adj* **agony column** newspaper or magazine

feature offering advice on personal problems

agoraphobia *n* fear of open spaces **agoraphobic** *n, adj*

agrarian *adj* of land or agriculture **agrarianism** *n*

agree *v* **agreeing, agreed 1** be of the same opinion **2** consent **3** reach a joint decision **4** be consistent **5** (foll. by *with*) be suitable to one's health or digestion **agreeable** *adj* **1** willing **2** pleasant **agreeably** *adv* **agreement** *n* **1** agreeing **2** contract

agriculture *n* raising of crops and livestock **agricultural** *adj* **agriculturalist** *n*

agronomy [ag-ron-om-mee] *n* science of soil management and crop production **agronomist** *n*

aground *adv* onto the bottom of shallow water

ague [aig-yew] *n* periodic fever with shivering

ahead *adv* **1** in front **2** forwards

ahoy *interj* shout used at sea to attract attention

AI 1 artificial insemination **2** artificial intelligence

aid *v, n* help, support

aide *n* assistant

aide-de-camp [aid-de-kom] *n, pl* **aides-de-camp** [aid-de-kom] military officer serving as personal assistant to a senior

AIDS acquired immunodeficiency syndrome, a viral disease that destroys the body's ability to fight infection

ail *v* **1** trouble, afflict **2** be ill **ailing** *adj* sickly **ailment** *n* illness

aileron [ale-er-on] *n* movable flap on an aircraft wing which controls rolling

aim *v* **1** point (a weapon or missile) or direct (a blow or remark) at a target

2 propose or intend ▷ *n*
3 aiming **4** intention, purpose
aimless *adj* without purpose
aimlessly *adv*
ain't *not standard* **1** am not **2** is
not **3** are not **4** has not **5** have
not
air *n* **1** mixture of gases
forming the earth's
atmosphere **2** space above
the ground, sky **3** breeze
4 tune **5** quality or manner
airs 6 affected manners
▷ *v* **7** expose to air to dry or
ventilate **8** make known
publicly **on the air** in
the act of broadcasting on
radio or television **airy** *adj*
1 well-ventilated **2** jaunty,
nonchalant **airily** *adv*
airiness *n* **airless** *adj* stuffy
airing *n* **1** exposure to air
for drying or ventilation
2 exposure to public debate
air base centre from which
military aircraft operate
air bed inflatable mattress
airborne *adj* **1** carried by
air **2** (of aircraft) in flight
air brake brake worked by
compressed air **airbrush**
n atomizer spraying paint
by compressed air **air
conditioning** system that
controls the temperature
and humidity of the air in
a building **aircraft** *n* any
machine that flies, such as
an airplane **aircraft carrier**
warship from which aircraft
operate **airfield** *n* place
where aircraft can land and
take off **air force** branch of
the armed forces responsible
for air warfare **air gun** gun
discharged by the force of
compressed air **airlift** *n*
1 transport of troops or cargo
by aircraft when other routes
are blocked ▷ *v* **2** transport
by airlift **airline** *n* company
providing scheduled flights

for passengers and cargo
airliner *n* large passenger
aircraft **airlock** *n* **1** air bubble
obstructing the flow of liquid
in a pipe **2** airtight chamber
airmail *n* **1** system of sending
mail by aircraft **2** mail
sent in this way **airman**
(**airwoman**) *n* member
of the air force **airplane**
n powered flying vehicle
with fixed wings **airplay** *n*
broadcast performances (of
a record) on radio **airport** *n*
airfield for civilian aircraft,
with facilities for aircraft
maintenance and passengers
air raid attack by aircraft
airship *n* lighter-than-air
flying machine with means
of propulsion **airsick** *adj*
nauseated from travelling
in an aircraft **airspace** *n*
atmosphere above a country,
regarded as its territory
airstrip *n* strip of ground
where aircraft can take off
and land **airtight** *adj* not
allowing the passage of air
airworthy *adj* (of aircraft) fit
to fly **airworthiness** *n*
Airedale *n* large rough-coated
terrier dog
aisle [rhymes with **mile**]
n passageway separating
seating areas in a church,
theatre, etc., or row of shelves
in a supermarket
ajar *adj, adv* (of a door)
partly open
akimbo *adv* **with arms
akimbo** with hands on hips
and elbows outwards
akin *adj* similar, related
Al *chem* aluminum
alabaster *n* soft white
translucent stone
à la carte *adj, adv* (of a menu)
having dishes individually
priced
alack *interj obsolete* cry of
grief or sorrow

alacrity n speed, eagerness

à la mode adj fashionable

alarm n 1 sudden fear caused by awareness of danger 2 warning sound 3 device that gives this 4 alarm clock ▷ v 5 frighten **alarming** adj **alarmist** n person who alarms others needlessly **alarm clock** clock which sounds at a set time to wake someone up

alas adv unfortunately, regrettably

albatross n large sea bird with very long wings

albeit conj although

albino n, pl **-nos** person or animal with white skin and hair and pink eyes **albinism** n

album n 1 book with blank pages for keeping photographs or stamps in 2 long-playing record

albumen n egg white

albumin, albumen n protein found in blood plasma, egg white, milk, and muscle **albuminous** adj

alchemy n medieval form of chemistry concerned with trying to turn base metals into gold and to find the elixir of life **alchemist** n

alcohol n 1 colourless flammable liquid present in intoxicating drinks 2 intoxicating drinks generally **alcoholic** adj 1 of alcohol ▷ n 2 person addicted to alcohol **alcoholism** n addiction to alcohol

alcove n recess in the wall of a room

aldehyde n one of a group of chemical compounds derived from alcohol by oxidation

alder n tree related to the birch

alderman n member of a municipal council

ale n kind of beer

aleatory adj dependent on chance

alert adj 1 watchful, attentive ▷ n 2 warning of danger ▷ v 3 warn of danger 4 make (someone) aware of (a fact) **on the alert** watchful **alertness** n

alfalfa n kind of plant used as fodder

alfresco adv, adj in the open air

algae [al-jee] pl n plants which live in or near water and have no true stems, leaves, or roots

algebra n branch of mathematics using symbols to represent numbers **algebraic** adj

ALGOL n computers computer programming language designed for mathematical and scientific purposes

Algonquin, Algonkin n member of a North American Indian people formerly living along the St Lawrence and Ottawa Rivers in Canada

algorithm n logical arithmetical or computational procedure for solving a problem

alias adv 1 also known as: William Bonney, alias Billy the Kid ▷ n 2 false name

alibi n 1 plea of being somewhere else when a crime was committed 2 informal excuse

alien adj 1 foreign 2 repugnant (to) 3 from another world ▷ n 4 foreigner 5 being from another world **alienable** adj law able to be transferred to another owner **alienate** v cause to become hostile **alienation** n

alight¹ v 1 step out of (a vehicle) 2 land

alight² adj 1 burning 2 lit up

align [a-line] v 1 place in a line 2 make or bring (a person or group) into agreement with the policy of another **alignment** n

alike adj **1** like, similar ▷ adv **2** in the same way

alimentary adj of nutrition **alimentary canal** food passage in the body

alimony n allowance paid under a court order to a separated or divorced spouse

A-line adj (of a skirt) slightly flared

aliquot adj **1** of or denoting an exact divisor of a number ▷ n **2** exact divisor

alive adj **1** living, in existence **2** lively **alive to** aware of **alive with** swarming with

alkali [alk-a-lie] n substance which combines with acid and neutralizes it to form a salt **alkaline** adj **alkalinity** n **alkaloid** n any of a group of organic compounds containing nitrogen

all adj **1** whole quantity or number (of) ▷ adv **2** wholly, entirely **3** (in the score of games) each ▷ n **4** whole **5** everything, everyone **all-Canadian** adj composed exclusively of Canadians **all in** adj **1** exhausted **2** (of wrestling) with no style prohibited ▷ adv **3** with all expenses included **all right** adj **1** adequate, satisfactory **2** unharmed ▷ interj **3** expression of approval or agreement **all-rounder** n person with ability in many fields **all-terrain vehicle** motor vehicle with large tires for travel over rough land

Allah n name of God in Islam

allay v reduce (fear or anger) or relieve (pain or grief)

allege v state without proof **alleged** adj **allegedly** adv **allegation** n thing alleged

allegiance n loyalty to a person, country, or cause

allegory n, pl **-ries** story with an underlying meaning as well as the literal one **allegorical** adj **allegorically** adv **allegorize** v

allegretto adv music fairly quickly or briskly

allegro adv music in a brisk lively manner

allergy n, pl **-gies** extreme sensitivity to a substance, which causes the body to react to any contact with it **allergic** adj **1** having or caused by an allergy **2** informal having an aversion (to): allergic to work **allergen** [al-ler-jen] n substance capable of causing an allergic reaction

alleviate v lessen (pain or suffering) **alleviation** n

alley n **1** narrow street or path **2** long narrow enclosure in which tenpin bowling or skittles is played

alley-oop n basketball high pass to a teammate who jumps to catch it and immediately attempts to score

alliance n **1** state of being allied **2** formal relationship between countries or groups for a shared purpose

alligator n reptile of the crocodile family, found in the southern US and China

alliteration n use of the same sound at the start of consecutive words **alliterative** adj

allocate v allot or assign **allocation** n

allophone n Canadian whose native language is neither French nor English

allot v **-lotting, -lotted** assign as a share or for a particular purpose **allotment** n **1** distribution **2** portion allotted **3** small piece of public land rented to grow vegetables on

allotrope n any of two or more physical forms in which an element can exist **allotropic** adj

allow v 1 permit 2 acknowledge (a point or claim) 3 set aside **allow for** take into account **allowable** adj **allowance** n 1 amount of money given at regular intervals 2 amount permitted **make allowances for 1** be lenient towards (someone) because he or she has special problems 2 take into account

alloy n 1 mixture of two or more metals ▷v 2 mix (metals)

allspice n spice made from the berries of a tropical American tree

allude v (foll. by to) refer indirectly to **allusion** n indirect reference **allusive** adj

allure v 1 entice or attract ▷n 2 attractiveness **allurement** n **alluring** adj

alluvium n fertile soil deposited by flowing water **alluvial** adj

ally n, pl -lies 1 country or person having an agreement to support another ▷v -lying, -lied 2 ally oneself with join as an ally **allied** adj

alma mater n one's former school, university, or college

almanac n yearly calendar with detailed information on anniversaries, phases of the moon, etc.

almighty adj 1 having absolute power 2 informal very great ▷n 3 **the Almighty** God

almond n edible oval-shaped nut which grows on a small tree

almoner n person who distributes alms

almost adv very nearly

alms [ahmz] pl n old-fashioned gifts to the poor **almshouse** n formerly, a house financed by charity, offering accommodation to the poor

aloe n 1 plant with fleshy spiny leaves **aloes** 2 bitter drug made from aloe leaves

aloft adv 1 in the air 2 in a ship's rigging

alone adj, adv without anyone or anything else

along prep 1 over part or all the length of ▷ adv 2 forward 3 in company with others: come along for the ride **alongside** adv, prep beside

aloof adj distant or haughty in manner **aloofness** n

alopecia [al-loh-pee-sha] n loss of hair

aloud adv in an audible voice

alpaca n 1 Peruvian llama 2 its wool 3 cloth made from this

alpenstock n iron-tipped staff used by climbers

alphabet n set of letters used in writing a language **alphabetical** adj in the conventional order of the letters of an alphabet **alphabetically** adv **alphabetize** v put in alphabetical order **alphabetization** n

alpine adj 1 of high mountains 2 **Alpine** of the Alps, a high mountain range in S central Europe ▷ n 3 mountain plant

already adv 1 before this time 2 sooner than expected

Alsatian n large wolflike dog

also adv 1 in addition 2 too **also-ran** n loser in a race, competition, or election

alt. combining form informal alternative: alt. rock

Alta. Alberta

altar n 1 raised structure on which sacrifices are offered and religious rites are performed **2** table used for Communion in Christian churches **altarpiece** n work of art above and behind the altar in some Christian churches

alter v make or become different **alteration** n

altercation n heated argument

alter ego n **1** second self **2** very close friend

alternate v **1** (cause to) occur by turns ▷ adj **2** occurring by turns **3** every second one of a series: *alternate Fridays* **alternately** adv **alternation** n **alternative** n **1** one of two choices ▷ adj **2** able to be done or used instead of something else **3** (of medicine, lifestyle, etc.) not conventional **alternatively** adv **alternator** n electric generator for producing alternating current **alternating current** electric current that reverses direction at frequent regular intervals

although conj despite the fact that

altimeter [al-**tim**-it-er] n instrument that measures altitude

altitude n height above sea level

alto n, pl **-tos** music **1** short for **contralto 2** (singer with) the highest adult male voice **3** instrument with the second-highest pitch in its group

altogether adv **1** entirely **2** on the whole **3** in total

altruism n unselfish concern for the welfare of others **altruist** n **altruistic** adj **altruistically** adv

aluminum, aluminium n light nonrusting silvery-white metal

alumnus [al-**lumm**-nuss] n, pl **-ni** [-nie] graduate of a college **alumna** [al-**lumm**-na] n fem, pl **-nae** [-nee]

always adv **1** at all times **2** for ever

alyssum n garden plant with small yellow or white flowers

am v see **be**

AM amplitude modulation

a.m. before noon

amalgam n **1** blend or combination **2** alloy of mercury and another metal

amalgamate v combine or unite **amalgamation** n

amanuensis [am-man-yew-en-siss] n, pl **-ses** [-seez] person who writes from dictation

amaranth n **1** imaginary flower that never fades **2** lily-like plant with red, green, or purple flowers

amaryllis n lily-like plant with large red or white flowers

amass v collect or accumulate

amateur n **1** person who performs a sport or activity as a pastime rather than as a profession **2** person unskilled in something ▷ adj **3** not professional **amateurish** adj lacking skill **amateurishly** adv

amatory adj relating to romantic or sexual love

amaut, amowt n a hood on an Inuit woman's parka for carrying a child

amaze v surprise greatly, astound **amazing** adj **amazingly** adv **amazement** n

Amazon n **1** legendary female warrior **2** tall strong woman **Amazonian** adj

ambassador n senior diplomat who represents his or her country in another country **ambassadorial** adj **ambassadorship** n

amber n **1** yellowish translucent fossil resin ▷ adj **2** brownish-yellow

a

ambergris [**am**-ber-greece] n waxy substance secreted by the sperm whale, used in making perfumes

ambidextrous adj able to use both hands with equal ease

ambience n atmosphere of a place

ambient adj surrounding

ambiguous adj 1 having more than one possible meaning 2 uncertain **ambiguously** adv **ambiguity** n

ambit n limits or boundary

ambition n 1 desire for success 2 something so desired, goal **ambitious** adj **ambitiously** adv **ambitiousness** n

ambivalence [am-**biv**-a-lenss] n state of feeling two conflicting emotions at the same time **ambivalent** adj **ambivalently** adv

amble v 1 walk at a leisurely pace ▷ n 2 leisurely walk or pace

ambrosia n 1 myth food of the gods 2 anything delightful to taste or smell **ambrosial** adj

ambulance n motor vehicle designed to carry the sick or injured

ambush n 1 act of waiting in a concealed position to make an attack 2 attack from a concealed position ▷ v 3 attack from a concealed position

ameliorate [am-**meal**-lee-yor-rate] v make (something) better **amelioration** n **ameliorative** adj

amen interj so be it: used at the end of a prayer

amenable adj likely or willing to cooperate **amenability** n

amend v correct or improve (something) **amendment** n

amends pl n **make amends for** compensate for

amenity n, pl -ties useful or enjoyable facility

American adj 1 of the United States of America or the North, Central, or South American continents ▷ n 2 American person **Americanism** n expression or custom peculiar to people in the US

amethyst [**am**-myth-ist] n bluish-violet variety of quartz used as a gemstone

amiable adj friendly, pleasant-natured **amiably** adv **amiability** n

amicable adj friendly **amicably** adv **amicability** n

amid, amidst prep in the middle of, among **amidships** adv at or towards the middle of a ship

amino acid [am-**mean**-oh] n organic compound found in protein

amiss adv 1 wrongly, badly ▷ adj 2 wrong, faulty **take something amiss** be offended by something

amity n friendship

ammeter n instrument for measuring electric current

ammonia n 1 pungent alkaline gas containing hydrogen and nitrogen 2 solution of this in water

ammonite n fossilized spiral shell of an extinct sea creature

ammunition n 1 any projectile that can be fired from or as a weapon 2 facts that can be used in an argument

amnesia n loss of memory **amnesiac** adj, n

amnesty n, pl -ties general pardon for offences against a government

amniocentesis n, pl -ses removal of amniotic fluid to test for possible abnormalities in a fetus

amniotic fluid n fluid surrounding a fetus in the womb

amoeba [am-**mee**-ba] *n, pl* -**bae**, -**bas** microscopic single-celled animal able to change its shape

amok *adv* **run amok** run about in a violent frenzy

among, amongst *prep* **1** in the midst of **2** in the group or number of **3** to each of: *divide it among yourselves*

amoral [eh-**mor**-ral] *adj* without moral standards **amorality** *n*

amorous *adj* feeling, showing, or relating to sexual love. **amorously** *adv* **amorousness** *n*

amorphous *adj* without distinct shape

amortize *v* pay off (a debt) gradually by periodic transfers to a sinking fund **amortization** *n*

amount *n* **1** extent or quantity ▷ *v* **2** (foll. by *to*) be equal to or add up to

amour *n* (illicit) love affair

amp *n* **1** ampere **2** *informal* amplifier

ampere [am-**pair**] *n* unit of electric current

ampersand *n* the character (&), meaning *and*

amphetamine [am-**fet**-am-in] *n* drug used as a stimulant

amphibian *n* **1** animal that lives on land but breeds in water **2** vehicle that can travel both on land and water **amphibious** *adj* living or operating both on land and in water

amphitheatre *n* open oval or circular building with tiers of seats rising round an arena

amphora *n, pl* -**phorae**, -**phoras** two-handled ancient Greek or Roman jar

ample *adj* **1** more than sufficient **2** large **amply** *adv*

amplify *v* -**fying**, -**fied** **1** increase the strength of (a current or sound signal) **2** explain in more detail **3** increase the size or effect of **amplification** *n* **amplifier** *n* device used to amplify a current or sound signal

amplitude *n* **1** greatness of extent **2** breadth or scope

amplitude modulation method of sending information by varying the size of the peaks and troughs of the carrier wave to suit the input signal

ampoule *n* small sealed glass vessel containing liquid for injection

amputate *v* cut off (a limb etc.) for medical reasons **amputation** *n*

amuck *adv* same as **amok**

amulet *n* something carried or worn as a charm against evil

amuse *v* **1** entertain or divert **2** cause to laugh or smile **amusing** *adj* **amusement** *n* **1** state of being amused **2** something that amuses

an *adj* form of **a** used before vowels, and sometimes before h: *an hour*

anabolic steroid *n* synthetic steroid hormone used by athletes to stimulate muscle growth

anachronism [an-**nak**-kron-iz-zum] *n* person or thing placed in the wrong historical period or seeming to belong to another time **anachronistic** *adj*

anaconda *n* large S American snake which kills by constriction

anaemia *n* same as **anemia**

anaesthetic *n, adj* same as **anesthetic**

anagram *n* word or phrase made by rearranging the letters of another word or phrase

anal [**ain**-al] adj of the anus
analgesic [an-nal-**jeez**-ik] n, adj (drug) relieving pain **analgesia** n absence of pain
analogy [an-**nal**-a-jee] n, pl **-gies 1** similarity in some respects **2** comparison made to show such a similarity **analogical** adj **analogically** adv **analogize** v use or show analogy **analogue** [**an**-nal-log] n something that is analogous to something else ▷ adj displaying information by means of a dial **analogous** [an-**nal**-log-uss] adj similar in some respects
analysis [an-**nal**-liss-iss] n, pl **-ses** [-seez] **1** separation of a whole into its components for study and interpretation **2** psychoanalysis **analyse** [**an**-nal-lize] v **1** make an analysis of (something) **2** psychoanalyse **analyst** [**an**-nal-list] n person skilled in analysis **analytical** or **analytic** adj **analytically** adv
anarchy [**an**-ark-ee] n **1** lawlessness and disorder **2** lack of government in a state **anarchic** adj **anarchism** n doctrine advocating the abolition of government **anarchist** n person who believes in anarchism **anarchistic** adj
anathema [an-**nath**-im-a] n detested person or thing **anathematize** v curse (a person or thing)
anatomy n, pl **-mies 1** science of the structure of the body **2** physical structure **3** person's body: *a delicate part of his anatomy* **4** detailed analysis **anatomical** adj **anatomically** adv **anatomist** n expert in anatomy
ancestor n **1** person from whom one is descended **2** forerunner **ancestral** adj

ancestry n lineage or descent
anchor n **1** heavy hooked device attached to a boat by a cable and dropped overboard to fasten the ship to the sea bottom ▷ v **2** fasten with or as if with an anchor **anchorage** n place where boats can be anchored
anchorman n **1** broadcaster in a central studio who links up and presents items from outside camera units and other studios **2** last person to compete in a relay team
anchorite n religious recluse
anchovy [**an**-chov-ee] n, pl **-vies** small strong-tasting fish
ancient adj **1** dating from very long ago **2** very old ▷ n **3** person who lived long ago
ancillary adj **1** auxiliary, supplementary **2** subsidiary
and conj **1** in addition to **2** as a consequence **3** then, afterwards
andante [an-**dan**-tay] adv music moderately slowly
andiron n iron stand for supporting logs in a fireplace
androgynous adj having both male and female characteristics
android n robot resembling a human
anecdote n short amusing account of an incident **anecdotal** adj
anemia, anaemia [an-**neem**-ee-a] n deficiency in the number of red blood cells **anemic** or **anaemic** adj **1** having anemia **2** pale and sickly **3** lacking vitality
anemometer n instrument for recording wind speed
anemone [an-**nem**-on-ee] n plant with white, purple, or red flowers
aneroid barometer n device for measuring air pressure, consisting of a partially

evacuated chamber in which variations in pressure cause a pointer on the lid to move

anesthetic, anaesthetic [an-niss-**thet**-ik] n, adj (substance) causing loss of sensation **anesthesia** or **anaesthesia** [an-niss-**theez**-ee-a] n loss of sensation **anesthetist** or **anaesthetist** [an-**neess**-thet-ist] n doctor trained to administer anesthetics **anesthetize** or **anaesthetize** v

aneurysm, aneurism [an-new-riz-zum] n permanent swelling of a blood vessel

anew adv 1 once more 2 in a different way

angel n 1 spiritual being believed to be an attendant or messenger of God 2 very kind person **angelic** adj **angelically** adv

angelica [an-**jell**-ik-a] n 1 aromatic plant 2 its candied stalks, used in cookery

Angelus [an-jell-uss] n (in the Roman Catholic Church) 1 prayers recited in the morning, at midday, and in the evening 2 bell signalling the times of these prayers

anger n 1 fierce displeasure 2 extreme annoyance 3 rage, wrath ▷ v 4 make (someone) angry **angry** adj 1 full of anger 2 inflamed: an angry wound **angrily** adv

angina [an-**jine**-a] n heart disorder causing sudden severe chest pains (Also **angina pectoris**)

angle[1] n 1 space between or shape formed by two lines or surfaces that meet 2 divergence between these, measured in degrees 3 corner 4 point of view ▷ v 5 bend or place (something) at an angle

angle[2] v 1 fish with a hook and line 2 try to get by hinting

angler n **angling** n

Anglican n, adj (member) of the Church of England **Anglicanism** n

anglicize v make English in outlook, form, etc. **Anglicism** n expression or custom peculiar to the English

Anglo- combining form English or British: Anglo-French **Anglo** n an English-speaking person

Anglo-Saxon n 1 member of any of the W Germanic tribes which settled in England from the fifth century AD 2 language of the Anglo-Saxons ▷ adj 3 of the Anglo-Saxons or their language

angora n 1 variety of goat, cat, or rabbit with long silky hair 2 hair of the angora goat or rabbit 3 cloth made from this hair

Angostura Bitters pl n ® bitter tonic, used as a flavouring in alcoholic drinks

angst n feeling of anxiety

angstrom n unit of length used to measure wavelengths

anguish n great mental or physical pain **anguished** adj

angular adj 1 (of a person) lean and bony 2 having angles 3 measured by an angle **angularity** n

anhydrous adj chem containing no water

aniline n colourless oily liquid obtained from coal tar and used for making dyes, plastics, and explosives

animadversion n criticism or censure

animal n 1 living creature having specialized sense organs and the power of voluntary motion, esp. one other than a human being 2 quadruped ▷ adj 3 of animals 4 sensual, physical **animalcule** n microscopic animal

a

animate v **1** give life to
2 enliven **3** motivate **4** make a
cartoon film of ▷ adj **5** having
life **animated** adj **animation**
n **1** life, vigour **2** technique
of making cartoon films
animator n

animism n belief that natural
objects possess souls **animist**
n, adj **animistic** adj

animosity n, pl **-ties** hostility,
hatred

animus n hatred, animosity

anion [an-eye-on] n ion with
negative charge

anise [an-niss] n plant with
liquorice-flavoured seeds

aniseed n liquorice-flavoured
seeds of the anise

ankle n joint between the foot
and leg **anklet** n ornamental
chain worn round the ankle

annals pl n yearly records of
events **annalist** n

anneal v toughen (metal or
glass) by heating and slow
cooling

annelid n worm with a
segmented body, such as an
earthworm

annex v **1** seize (territory)
2 take (something) without
permission **3** join or add
(something) to something
larger ▷ n **4** extension to a
building **5** nearby building
used as an extension
annexation n

annihilate v destroy utterly
annihilation n

anniversary n, pl **-ries**
1 date on which something
occurred in a previous year
2 celebration of this

anno Domini adv Latin
(indicating years numbered
from the supposed year of the
birth of Christ) in the year of
our Lord

annotate v add notes to (a
written work) **annotation** n

announce v **1** make
known publicly **2** proclaim
announcement n
announcer n person who
introduces radio or television
programmes

annoy v irritate or displease
annoyance n

annual adj **1** happening once
a year **2** lasting for a year
▷ n **3** plant that completes
its life-cycle in a year
4 book published each year
annually adv

annuity n, pl **-ties** fixed sum
paid every year

annul v **-nulling, -nulled**
make (something, esp.
a marriage) invalid
annulment n

annular [an-new-lar] adj ring-
shaped

Annunciation n
Christianity angel Gabriel's
announcement to the Virgin
Mary of her conception of
Christ

anode n *electricity* positive
electrode in a battery, valve,
etc. **anodize** v coat (metal)
with a protective oxide film
by electrolysis

anodyne n **1** something that
relieves pain or distress ▷ adj
2 relieving pain or distress

anoint v smear with oil as a
sign of consecration

anomaly [an-nom-a-lee] n, pl
-lies something that deviates
from the normal, irregularity
anomalous adj

anon adv obsolete in a short
time, soon

anon. anonymous

anonymous adj **1** by someone
whose name is not known
2 having no known name
anonymously adv **anonymity**
n

anorak n waterproof hooded
jacket

anorexia n psychological
disorder characterized by fear

of becoming fat and refusal to eat (Also **anorexia nervosa**) **anorexic** adj, n

another adj, pron **1** one more **2** a different (one)

answer v **1** give an answer (to) **2** respond or react **3** be responsible to (a person) ▷ n **4** reply to a question, request, letter, etc. **5** solution to a problem **6** reaction or response **answerable** adj (foll. by for or to) responsible for or accountable to **answering machine** device for answering a telephone automatically and recording messages

ant n small insect living in highly organized colonies **anteater** n mammal which feeds on ants by means of a long sticky tongue **ant hill** mound built by ants around their nest

antagonist n opponent or adversary **antagonism** n open opposition or hostility **antagonistic** adj **antagonize** v arouse hostility in, annoy

Antarctic n **1 the Antarctic** area around the South Pole ▷ adj **2** of this region

ante n **1** player's stake in poker ▷ v **-teing, -ted** or **-teed 2** place (one's stake) in poker

ante- prefix before in time or position: antedate; antechamber

antecedent n **1** thing coming before something else ▷ adj **2** preceding, prior

antedate v precede in time

antediluvian adj **1** of the time before the biblical Flood **2** old-fashioned

antelope n deerlike mammal with long legs and horns

antenatal adj during pregnancy, before birth

antenna n **1** pl **-nae** insect's feeler **2** pl **-nas** aerial

anterior adj **1** to the front **2** earlier

anteroom n small room leading into a larger one, often used as a waiting room

anthem n **1** song of loyalty, esp. to a country **2** piece of music for a choir, usu. set to words from the Bible

anther n part of a flower's stamen containing pollen

anthology n, pl **-gies** collection of poems or other literary pieces by various authors **anthologist** n

anthracite n hard coal burning slowly with little smoke or flame but intense heat

anthrax n dangerous disease of cattle and sheep, communicable to humans

anthropoid adj **1** like a human ▷ n **2** ape, such as a chimpanzee, resembling a human

anthropology n study of human origins, institutions, and beliefs **anthropological** adj **anthropologist** n

anthropomorphic adj attributing human form or personality to a god, animal, or object **anthropomorphism** n

anti- prefix **1** against, opposed to: anti-war **2** opposite to: anticlimax **3** counteracting: antifreeze

anti-aircraft adj for defence against aircraft attack

antibiotic n **1** chemical substance capable of destroying bacteria ▷ adj **2** of antibiotics

antibody n, pl **-bodies** protein produced in the blood, which destroys bacteria

anticipate v **1** foresee and act in advance of **2** look forward to **3** expect **anticipation** n **anticipatory** adj

anticlimax n disappointing conclusion to a series of events

anticlockwise adv, adj in the opposite direction to the rotation of the hands of a clock

antics pl n absurd acts or postures

anticyclone n area of moving air of high pressure in which the winds rotate outwards

antidote n substance that counteracts a poison

antifreeze n liquid added to water to lower its freezing point, used in automobile radiators

antigen [an-ti-jen] n substance, usu. a toxin, causing the blood to produce antibodies

antihero n, pl -roes central character in a book, film, etc. who lacks the traditional heroic virtues

antihistamine n drug used to treat allergies

antimacassar n cloth put over a chair-back to prevent soiling

antimony [an-tim-mon-ee] n brittle silvery-white metallic element

antipathy [an-tip-a-thee] n dislike, hostility **antipathetic** adj

antiperspirant n substance used to reduce or prevent sweating

antiphon n hymn sung in alternate parts by two groups of singers **antiphonal** adj

antipodes [an-tip-pod-deez] pl n any two places diametrically opposite one another on the earth's surface **the Antipodes** Australia and New Zealand **antipodean** adj

antipyretic adj 1 reducing fever ▷ n 2 drug that reduces fever

antique n 1 object of an earlier period, valued for its beauty, workmanship, or age ▷ adj 2 made in an earlier period 3 old-fashioned **antiquarian** adj of or relating to antiquities or rare books **antiquary** n student or collector of antiques or ancient works of art **antiquated** adj out-of-date **antiquity** n 1 great age 2 ancient times 3 object dating from ancient times

antiracism n policy of challenging racism and promoting racial tolerance

antirrhinum n two-lipped flower of various colours

anti-Semitism n prejudice against Jews **anti-Semitic** adj

antiseptic adj 1 preventing infection by killing germs ▷ n 2 antiseptic substance

antisocial adj 1 avoiding the company of other people 2 (of behaviour) harmful to society

antistatic adj reducing the effects of static electricity

antithesis [an-tith-iss-iss] n, pl -ses [-seez] 1 exact opposite 2 placing together of contrasting ideas or words to produce an effect of balance **antithetical** adj

antitoxin n (serum containing) an antibody that acts against a toxin

antivirus adj protecting computers from viruses

antler n branching horn of male deer

antonym n word that means the opposite of another

anus [ain-uss] n opening at the end of the alimentary canal, through which feces are discharged

anvil n heavy iron block on which a smith hammers metal into shape

anxiety n, pl -ties state of being anxious

anxious *adj* **1** worried and tense **2** intensely desiring **anxiously** *adv*

any *adj, pron* **1** one or some, no matter which ▷ *adv* **2** at all: *it isn't any worse* **anybody** *pron* anyone **anyhow** *adv* anyway **anyone** *pron* **1** any person **2** person of any importance **anything** *pron* **anyway** *adv* **1** at any rate, nevertheless **2** in any manner **anywhere** *adv* in, at, or to any place

Anzac *n* (in World War 1) a soldier serving with the Australian and New Zealand Army Corps

aorta [eh-**or**-ta] *n, pl* **-tas**, **-tae** main artery of the body, carrying oxygen-rich blood from the heart **aortic** *or* **aortal** *adj*

apace *adv lit* swiftly

apart *adv* **1** to or in pieces **2** to or at a distance **3** individual, distinct

apartheid *n* former official government policy of racial segregation in S Africa

apartment *n* set of rooms for living in which are part of a larger building

apathy *n* lack of interest or enthusiasm **apathetic** *adj* **apathetically** *adv*

ape *n* **1** tailless monkey such as the chimpanzee or gorilla **2** stupid, clumsy, or ugly man ▷ *v* **3** imitate **apish** *adj*

aperient [ap-**peer**-ee-ent] *adj* **1** mildly laxative ▷ *n* **2** mild laxative

aperitif [ap-per-rit-**teef**] *n* alcoholic drink taken before a meal

aperture *n* opening or hole

apex *n* highest point

APEX Advance Purchase Excursion: reduced fare for journeys booked a specified period in advance

aphasia *n* disorder of the central nervous system that affects the ability to speak and understand words

aphid [**eh**-fid], **aphis** [**eh**-fiss] *n* small insect which sucks the sap from plants

aphorism *n* short wise saying **aphoristic** *adj*

aphrodisiac [af-roh-**diz**-zee-ak] *adj* **1** arousing sexual desire ▷ *n* **2** aphrodisiac substance

apiary [**ape**-ee-yar-ee] *n, pl* **-ries** place where bees are kept **apiarist** *n* beekeeper **apiculture** *n* breeding and care of bees

apiece *adv* each: *they were given two apples apiece*

aplomb [ap-**plom**] *n* calm self-possession

apocalypse *n* **1** end of the world **2** event of great destruction **the Apocalypse** book of Revelation, last book of the New Testament **apocalyptic** *adj*

Apocrypha [ap-**pok**-rif-fa] *pl n* **the Apocrypha** collective name for the 14 books of the Old Testament which are not accepted as part of the Hebrew scriptures **apocryphal** *adj* (of a story) of questionable authenticity

apogee [**ap**-oh-jee] *n* **1** point of the moon's or a satellite's orbit farthest from the earth **2** highest point

apology *n, pl* **-gies** **1** expression of regret for wrongdoing **2** (foll. by *for*) poor example of **3** formal written defence of a cause **apologetic** *adj* making an apology **apologetically** *adv* **apologetics** *n* branch of theology concerned with the reasoned defence of Christianity **apologist** *n* person who formally defends a cause **apologize** *v* make an apology

apophthegm [ap-poth-em] n
short wise saying

apoplexy n med stroke
apoplectic adj 1 of apoplexy
2 informal furious

apostasy [ap-**poss**-stass-ee]
n, pl -sies abandonment of
one's religious faith or other
belief **apostate** [ap-**poss**-
state] n, adj

a posteriori [eh poss-steer-
ee-or-rye] adj logic involving
reasoning from effect to cause

Apostle n 1 one of the twelve
disciples chosen by Christ to
preach the Gospel 2 apostle
ardent supporter of a cause or
movement **apostolic** adj

apostrophe [ap-**poss**-trof-fee]
n 1 punctuation mark (')
showing the omission of a
letter or letters in a word (eg
don't) or forming the possessive
(eg Jill's coat) 2 digression from
a speech to address an
imaginary or absent person or
thing **apostrophize** v
address an apostrophe to

apothecary n, pl -caries
obsolete pharmacist

apotheosis [ap-poth-ee-**oh**-
siss] n, pl -ses [-seez]
1 elevation to the rank of a god
2 perfect example

app n computer program
designed for a particular
purpose

appal v -palling, -palled
dismay, terrify **appalling** adj
dreadful, terrible

apparatus n equipment for a
particular purpose

apparel [ap-**par**-rel] n
old-fashioned clothing

apparent adj 1 readily seen,
obvious 2 seeming as opposed
to real **apparently** adv

apparition n ghost or
ghostlike figure

appeal v 1 make an earnest
request 2 be attractive

3 request a review of a lower
court's decision by a higher
court ▷ n 4 earnest request
5 attractiveness 6 request for a
review of a lower court's
decision by a higher court
appealing adj

appear v 1 become visible or
present 2 seem 3 be seen in
public **appearance** n 1 sudden
arrival of someone or
something 2 way a person or
thing looks

appease v 1 pacify (a person)
by yielding to his or her
demands 2 satisfy or relieve (a
feeling) **appeasement** n

appellant n person who makes
an appeal to a higher court

appellation n name, title

append v join on, add
appendage n thing joined on
or added

appendicitis n inflammation
of the appendix

appendix n, pl -dixes, -dices
1 separate additional material
at the end of a book 2 anat
short closed tube attached to
the large intestine

appertain v (foll. by to)
1 belong to 2 be connected with

appetite n desire or
inclination, esp. for food or
drink **appetizer** n 1 first
course of a meal 2 thing eaten
or drunk to increase the
appetite **appetizing** adj
stimulating the appetite
appetizingly adv

applaud v 1 show approval of
by clapping one's hands
2 approve strongly **applause**
n approval shown by clapping
one's hands

apple n round firm fleshy fruit
that grows on trees **apple-pie
order** informal perfect order
apple polisher informal
sycophant or toady

appliance n device with a
specific function

appliqué [ap-**plee**-kay] n kind of decoration in which one material is cut out and attached to another

apply v -**plying**, -**plied** 1 make a formal request 2 put to practical use 3 put onto a surface 4 be relevant or appropriate **apply oneself** concentrate one's efforts **applicable** adj relevant **applicably** adv **applicability** n **applicant** n person who applies for something **application** n 1 formal request 2 act of applying something to a particular use 3 concentrated effort 4 act of putting something onto a surface **applied** adj (of a skill, science, etc.) put to practical use

appoint v 1 assign to a job or position 2 fix or decide: appoint a time 3 equip or furnish **appointment** n 1 arrangement to meet a person 2 act of placing someone in a job 3 the job itself **appointments** 4 fixtures or fittings

apportion v divide out in shares **apportionment** n

apposite adj suitable, apt **appositeness** n **apposition** n grammatical construction in which two nouns or phrases referring to the same thing are placed one after another without a conjunction: my son the doctor

appraise v estimate the value or quality of **appraisal** n

appreciate v 1 value highly 2 be aware of and understand 3 be grateful for 4 rise in value **appreciable** adj enough to be noticed **appreciably** adv **appreciation** n act of appreciating **appreciative** adj feeling or showing appreciation

apprehend v 1 seize, arrest 2 understand **apprehension** n 1 dread, anxiety 2 arrest 3 understanding **apprehensive** adj fearful or anxious

apprentice n 1 someone working for a skilled person for a fixed period in order to learn his or her trade ▷ v 2 take or place (someone) as an apprentice **apprenticeship** n

apprise v make aware (of)

appro n **on appro** informal on approval

approach v 1 come near or nearer (to) 2 make a proposal or suggestion to 3 begin to deal with (a matter) ▷ n 4 approaching or means of approaching 5 approximation **approachable** adj **approachability** n

approbation n approval

appropriate adj 1 suitable, fitting ▷ v 2 take for oneself 3 put aside for a particular purpose **appropriately** adv **appropriateness** n **appropriation** n

approve v 1 consider good or right 2 authorize, agree to **approval** n 1 favourable opinion 2 consent **on approval** (of goods) with an option to be returned without payment if unsatisfactory

approx. approximate(ly)

approximate adj 1 almost but not quite exact ▷ v 2 come close to 3 be almost the same as **approximately** adv **approximation** n

appurtenance n minor or additional feature

Apr. April

après-ski [ap-ray-**skee**] n social activities after a day's skiing

apricot n 1 yellowish-orange juicy fruit like a small peach.

a

▷ *adj* **2** yellowish-orange

April *n* fourth month of the year **April fool** victim of a practical joke played on April 1 (**April Fools' Day**)

a priori [eh pry-**or**-rye] *adj* involving reasoning from cause to effect

apron *n* **1** garment worn over the front of the body to protect the clothes **2** part of a stage in front of the curtain **3** area at an airport or hangar for manoeuvring and loading aircraft

apropos [ap-prop-**poh**] *adj, adv* appropriate(ly) **apropos of** with regard to

apse *n* arched or domed recess, esp. in a church

apt *adj* **1** having a specified tendency **2** suitable **3** quick to learn **aptly** *adv* **aptness** *n* **aptitude** *n* natural ability

AQ al-Qaeda

aqualung *n* mouthpiece attached to air cylinders, worn for underwater swimming

aquamarine *n* **1** greenish-blue gemstone ▷ *adj* **2** greenish-blue

aquaplane *n* **1** board on which a person stands to be towed by a motorboat ▷ *v* **2** ride on an aquaplane **3** (of a motor vehicle) skim uncontrollably on a thin film of water

aquarium *n, pl* **aquariums, aquaria 1** tank in which fish and other underwater creatures are kept **2** building containing such tanks

aquatic *adj* **1** living in or near water **2** done in or on water **aquatics** *pl n* water sports

aquatint *n* print like a watercolour, produced by etching copper

aqua vitae [ak-wa **vee**-tie] *n obsolete* brandy

aqueduct *n* structure carrying water across a valley or river

aqueous *adj* of, like, or containing water

aquiline *adj* **1** of or like an eagle **2** (of a nose) curved like an eagle's beak

Ar *chem* argon

Arab *n* **1** member of a Semitic people originally from Arabia ▷ *adj* **2** of the Arabs **Arabian** *adj* of Arabia or the Arabs **Arabic** *n* **1** language of the Arabs ▷ *adj* **2** of Arabic, Arabs, or Arabia

arabesque [ar-ab-**besk**] *n* **1** ballet position in which one leg is raised behind and the arms are extended **2** elaborate ornamental design

arable *adj* suitable for growing crops on

arachnid [ar-**rak**-nid] *n* eight-legged invertebrate, such as a spider, scorpion, tick, or mite

Aran *adj* (of sweaters etc.) knitted in a complicated pattern traditional to the Aran Islands, usu. with natural unbleached wool

arbiter *n* **1** person empowered to judge in a dispute **2** person with influential opinions about something **arbitrary** *adj* based on personal choice or chance, rather than reason **arbitrarily** *adv* **arbitrate** *v* settle (a dispute) by arbitration **arbitration** *n* hearing and settling of a dispute by an impartial referee chosen by both sides **arbitrator** *n*

arboreal [ahr-**bore**-ee-al] *adj* of or living in trees

arboretum [ahr-bore-**ee**-tum] *n, pl* -**ta** place where rare trees or shrubs are cultivated

arboriculture *n* cultivation of trees or shrubs

arbour *n* glade sheltered by trees

arc *n* **1** part of a circle or other

curve **2** luminous discharge of electricity across a small gap between two electrodes ▷ v **3** form an arc

arcade n **1** row of arches on pillars **2** covered passageway, usu. lined with shops **3** set of arches

arcane adj mysterious and secret

arch¹ n **1** curved structure supporting a bridge or roof **2** something curved **3** curved lower part of the foot ▷ v **4** (cause to) form an arch **archway** n passageway under an arch

arch² adj **1** superior, knowing **2** coyly playful **archly** adv **archness** n

arch- combining form chief, principal: archenemy

archaeology, archeology n study of ancient cultures from their physical remains **archaeological** or **archeological** adj **archaeologist** or **archeologist** n

archaic [ark-**kay**-ik] adj **1** ancient **2** out-of-date **archaically** adv **archaism** [ark-kay-iz-zum] n archaic word or phrase **archaistic** adj

archangel [ark-ain-jell] n chief angel

archbishop n chief bishop

archdeacon n priest ranking just below a bishop **archdeaconry** n

archdiocese n diocese of an archbishop

archery n art or sport of shooting with a bow and arrow **archer** n

archetype [ark-i-type] n **1** original model **2** perfect specimen **archetypal** adj

archiepiscopal adj of an archbishop

archipelago [ark-ee-**pel**-a-go] n, pl -gos **1** group of islands **2** sea full of small islands **archipelagic** adj

architect n person qualified to design and supervise the construction of buildings **architecture** n **1** style of building **2** designing and construction of buildings **architectural** adj

architrave n archit **1** beam that rests on columns **2** moulding round a doorway or window

archive [**ark**-ive] n **1** often pl collection of records or documents **2** place where these are kept **archival** adj **archivist** [**ark**-iv-ist] n person in charge of archives

Arctic n **1 the Arctic** area around the North Pole ▷ adj **2** of this region **3 arctic** informal very cold **arctic hare** large hare with white fur in winter **arctic willow** low-growing shrub of Canadian tundra

ardent adj **1** passionate **2** eager, zealous **ardently** adv **ardency** n **ardour** n **1** passion **2** enthusiasm, zeal

arduous adj hard to accomplish, strenuous **arduously** adv **arduousness** n

are¹ v see **be**

are² n unit of measure, 100 square metres

area n **1** part or region **2** size of a two-dimensional surface **3** subject field **4** small sunken yard giving access to a basement

arena n **1** seated enclosure for sports events **2** area of a Roman amphitheatre where gladiators fought **3** sphere of intense activity

aren't are not

areola n, pl -lae, -las small circular area, such as the coloured ring around the human nipple

argon n inert gas found in the air

argot [ahr-go] n slang or jargon

argue v -guing, -gued 1 try to prove by giving reasons 2 debate 3 quarrel, dispute **arguable** adj **arguably** adv **argument** n 1 point presented for or against something 2 discussion 3 quarrel **argumentation** n process of reasoning methodically **argumentative** adj given to arguing

aria [ah-ree-a] n elaborate song for solo voice, esp. one from an opera

arid adj 1 parched, dry 2 uninteresting **aridity** n

aright adv rightly

arise v arising, arose, arisen 1 come about 2 come into notice 3 get up

aristocracy n, pl -cies 1 highest social class 2 government by this class **aristocrat** n member of the aristocracy **aristocratic** adj **aristocratically** adv

arithmetic n 1 calculation by or of numbers ▷ adj 2 of arithmetic **arithmetical** adj **arithmetically** adv **arithmetician** n

ark n 1 Bible boat built by Noah, which survived the Flood 2 **Ark** Judaism chest containing the writings of Jewish Law

arm¹ n 1 upper limb from the shoulder to the wrist 2 sleeve of a garment 3 side of a chair **armful** n as much as an arm can hold **armchair** n upholstered chair with side supports for the arms **armhole** n opening in a garment through which the arm passes **armpit** n hollow under the arm at the shoulder

arm² v 1 supply with weapons 2 prepare (a bomb etc.) for use

arms pl n 1 weapons 2 military exploits 3 heraldic emblem

armament n 1 military weapons 2 preparation for war

armada n large number of warships

armadillo n, pl -los small S American mammal covered in strong bony plates

Armageddon n 1 Bible final battle between good and evil at the end of the world 2 catastrophic conflict

armature n revolving structure in an electric motor or generator, wound with coils carrying the current

armistice [arm-miss-stiss] n suspension of fighting

armour, armor n 1 metal clothing formerly worn to protect the body in battle 2 metal plating of tanks, warships, etc. **armourer** or **armorer** n maker, repairer, or keeper of arms or armour **armoury** or **armory** n place where weapons are stored **armorial** adj relating to heraldry

army n, pl -mies 1 military force that fights on land 2 great number

aroma n pleasant smell **aromatic** adj

aromatherapy n massage with fragrant oils to relieve tension

arose v past tense of **arise**

around prep, adv 1 on all sides (of) 2 from place to place (in) 3 somewhere in or near 4 approximately

arouse v 1 awaken 2 stimulate, make active

arpeggio [arp-**pej**-ee-oh] n, pl -**gios** music notes of a chord played or sung in quick succession

arr. 1 arranged (by) 2 arrival 3 arrive(d)

arraign [ar-**rain**] v 1 indict (a

person) on a charge **2** accuse **arraignment** n

arrange v **1** plan **2** agree **3** put in order **4** adapt (music) for performance in a certain way **arrangement** n

arrant adj utter, downright

arras n tapestry wall-hanging

array n **1** impressive display or collection **2** orderly arrangement, esp. of troops **3** poetic rich clothing ▷ v **4** arrange in order **5** dress in rich clothing

arrears pl n money owed **in arrears** late in paying a debt

arrest v **1** take (a person) into custody **2** stop the movement or development of **3** catch and hold (the attention) ▷ n **4** act of taking a person into custody **5** slowing or stopping **arresting** adj attracting attention, striking

arrive v **1** reach a place or destination **2** happen, come **3** informal be born **4** informal attain success **arrival** n **1** arriving **2** person or thing that has just arrived

arrogant adj proud and overbearing **arrogantly** adv **arrogance** n

arrogate v claim or seize without justification

arrow n **1** pointed shaft shot from a bow **2** arrow-shaped sign or symbol used to show direction **arrowhead** n pointed tip of an arrow

arrowroot n nutritious starch obtained from the root of a W Indian plant

arse n taboo buttocks or anus **arsehole** n taboo **1** anus **2** stupid or annoying person

arsenal n place where arms and ammunition are made or stored

arsenic n **1** toxic grey element **2** highly poisonous compound of this **arsenical** adj

arson n crime of intentionally setting property on fire **arsonist** n

art n **1** creation of works of beauty, esp. paintings or sculpture **2** works of art collectively **3** skill **arts 4** nonscientific branches of knowledge **artful** adj cunning, wily **artfully** adv **artfulness** n **artist** n **1** person who produces works of art, esp. paintings or sculpture **2** person skilled at something **3** artiste **artiste** n professional entertainer such as a singer or dancer **artistic** adj **artistically** adv **artistry** n artistic skill **artless** adj **1** free from deceit or cunning **2** natural, unpretentious **artlessly** adv **artlessness** n **arty** adj informal having an affected interest in art

artefact, artifact n something made by man

arteriosclerosis [art-ear-ee-oh-skler-**oh**-siss] n hardening of the arteries

artery n, pl -teries **1** one of the tubes carrying blood from the heart **2** major road or means of communication **arterial** adj **1** of an artery **2** (of a route) major

artesian well [art-**tee**-zhan] n well bored vertically so that the water is forced to the surface by natural pressure

arthritis n painful inflammation of a joint or joints **arthritic** adj, n

arthropod n animal, such as a spider or insect, with jointed limbs and a segmented body

artichoke n thistle-like plant with a flower cooked as a vegetable.

article n **1** item or object **2** written piece in a magazine or newspaper **3** clause in a document **4** grammar any of

a

the words *the*, *a*, or *an* **articled** *adj* bound by a written contract: *an articled clerk*

articulate *adj* **1** able to express oneself clearly and coherently **2** *zool* having joints **3** (of speech) clear, distinct ▷ *v* **4** speak or say clearly and coherently **articulately** *adv* **articulated** *adj* jointed **articulation** *n*

artifice *n* **1** clever trick **2** cleverness, skill **artificer** [art-**tiff**-iss-er] *n* craftsman **artificial** *adj* **1** man-made, not occurring naturally **2** made in imitation of something natural **3** not sincere **artificial insemination** introduction of semen into the womb by means other than sexual intercourse **artificial intelligence** branch of computer science aiming to produce machines which can imitate intelligent human behaviour **artificial respiration** method of restarting a person's breathing after it has stopped **artificially** *adv* **artificiality** *n*

artillery *n* **1** large-calibre guns **2** branch of the army who use these

artisan *n* skilled worker, craftsman

arum lily [**air**-rum] *n* plant with a white funnel-shaped leaf surrounding a spike of flowers

as *conj* **1** while, when **2** in the way that **3** that which: *do as you are told* **4** since, seeing that **5** for instance ▷ *adv, conj* **6** used to indicate amount or extent in comparisons: *he is as tall as you* ▷ *prep* **7** in the role of, being: *as a mother, I am concerned*

As *chem* arsenic

asafoetida *n* strong-smelling plant resin used as a spice in Eastern cookery

a.s.a.p. as soon as possible

asbestos *n* fibrous mineral which does not burn **asbestosis** *n* lung disease caused by inhalation of asbestos fibre

ascend *v* go or move up **ascension** *n* ascending **ascent** *n* **1** ascending **2** upward slope **ascendant** *adj* dominant or influential ▷ *n* **in the ascendant** increasing in power or influence **ascendancy** *n* condition of being dominant

ascertain *v* find out definitely **ascertainable** *adj* **ascertainment** *n*

ascetic [ass-**set**-tik] *n* **1** person who abstains from worldly pleasures and comforts ▷ *adj* **2** abstaining from worldly pleasures and comforts **ascetically** *adv* **asceticism** *n*

ascorbic acid [ass-**core**-bik] *n* vitamin C

ascribe *v* attribute, as to a particular origin **ascribable** *adj* **ascription** *n*

aseptic [eh-**sep**-tik] *adj* germ-free **asepsis** [eh-**sep**-siss] *n* aseptic condition

asexual [eh-**sek**-shoo-al] *adj* without sex **asexually** *adv*

ash[1] *n* **1** powdery substance left when something is burnt **ashes 2** remains after burning, esp. of a human body after cremation **ashen** *adj* pale with shock **ashtray** *n* receptacle for tobacco ash and cigarette butts **Ash Wednesday** first day of Lent

ash[2] *n* tree with grey bark

ashamed *adj* feeling shame

ashlar *n* square block of hewn stone used in building

ashore *adv* towards or on land

ashram *n* religious retreat where a Hindu holy man lives

Asian *adj* **1** of the continent of Asia or any of its peoples or languages ▷ *n* **2** person from Asia or a descendant of one **Asiatic** *adj*

aside *adv* **1** to one side **2** out of other people's hearing: *he took me aside to tell me his plans* ▷ *n* **3** remark not meant to be heard by everyone present

asinine [**ass**-in-nine] *adj* stupid, idiotic **asininity** *n*

ask *v* **1** say or write (something) in a form that requires an answer **2** make a request or demand **3** invite

askance [ass-**kanss**] *adv* **look askance at 1** look at with an oblique glance **2** regard with suspicion

askew *adv, adj* to one side, crooked

aslant *adv, prep* at a slant (to), slanting (across)

asleep *adj* **1** sleeping **2** (of limbs) numb

asp *n* small poisonous snake

asparagus *n* plant whose shoots are cooked as a vegetable

aspect *n* **1** feature or element **2** appearance or look **3** position facing a particular direction

aspen *n* kind of poplar tree

asperity [ass-**per**-rit-ee] *n* roughness of temper

aspersion *n* **cast aspersions on** make derogatory remarks about

asphalt *n* **1** black hard tarlike substance used for road surfaces etc. ▷ *v* **2** cover with asphalt

asphodel *n* plant with clusters of yellow or white flowers

asphyxia [ass-**fix**-ee-a] *n* suffocation **asphyxiate** *v* suffocate **asphyxiation** *n*

aspic *n* savoury jelly used to coat meat, eggs, fish, etc.

aspidistra *n* plant with long tapered leaves

aspirate *phonetics* ▷ *v* **1** pronounce with an *h* sound ▷ *n* **2** an *h* sound

aspire *v* (foll. by *to*) yearn (for), hope (to do or be) **aspirant** *n* person who aspires **aspiration** *n* strong desire or aim

aspirin *n* **1** drug used to relieve pain and fever **2** tablet of this

ass *n* **1** donkey **2** stupid person

assagai *n* same as **assegai**

assail *v* attack violently **assailant** *n*

assassin *n* person who murders a prominent person **assassinate** *v* murder (a prominent person) **assassination** *n*

assault *n* **1** violent attack ▷ *v* **2** attack violently **assault course** series of obstacles used in military training

assay *n* **1** analysis of a substance, esp. a metal, to ascertain its purity ▷ *v* **2** make such an analysis

assegai *n* slender spear used in S Africa

assemble *v* **1** collect or congregate **2** put together the parts of (a machine) **assemblage** *n* **1** collection or group **2** assembling **assembly** *n* **1** assembling **2** assembled group **assembly line** sequence of machines and workers in a factory assembling a product

assent *n* **1** agreement or consent ▷ *v* **2** agree or consent

assert *v* **1** declare forcefully **2** insist upon (one's rights etc.) **assert oneself** speak and act forcefully **assertion** *n* **assertive** *adj* **assertively** *adv*

assess *v* **1** judge the worth or importance of **2** estimate the value of (income or property) for taxation purposes **assessment** *n* **assessor** *n*

asset *n* **1** valuable or useful

person or thing **assets**
2 property that a person or
firm can sell, esp. to pay debts
asseverate v declare
solemnly **asseveration** n
assiduous adj diligent and
persevering **assiduously** adv
assiduity n
assign v **1** appoint (someone)
to a job or task **2** allot (a task)
3 attribute **assignation** [ass-
sig-**nay**-shun] n **1** assigning
2 secret arrangement to meet
assignment n **1** assigning
2 task assigned
assimilate v **1** learn and
understand (information)
2 absorb or be absorbed or
incorporated **assimilable** adj
assimilation n
assist v give help or support
assistance n **assistant** n
1 helper ▷ adj **2** junior or
deputy
assizes pl n court sessions
formerly held in each county
of England and Wales
associate v **1** connect in
the mind **2** mix socially ▷ n
3 partner in business **4** friend
or companion ▷ adj **5** having
partial rights or subordinate
status: associate member
association n **1** associating
2 society or club
assonance n rhyming
of vowel sounds but not
consonants, as in time and
light **assonant** adj
assorted adj consisting of
various types mixed together
assortment n assorted
mixture
assuage [ass-**wage**] v relieve
(pain, grief, thirst, etc.)
assume v **1** take to be true
without proof **2** pretend: I
assumed indifference **3** take upon
oneself: he assumed command
assumption n **1** assuming
2 thing assumed **assumptive**
adj

assure v **1** promise or
guarantee **2** convince **3** make
(something) certain **4** insure
against loss of life **assured**
adj **1** confident **2** certain
to happen **assuredly** adv
definitely **assurance** n
assuring or being assured
AST Atlantic Standard Time
aster n plant with daisy-like
flowers
asterisk n **1** star-shaped
symbol (*) used in printing
to indicate a footnote etc. ▷ v
2 mark with an asterisk
astern adv **1** at or towards the
stern of a ship **2** backwards
asteroid n any of the small
planets that orbit the sun
between Mars and Jupiter
asthma [**ass**-ma] n illness
causing difficulty in
breathing **asthmatic** adj, n
astigmatism [eh-**stig**-mat-
tiz-zum] n inability of a
lens, esp. of the eye, to focus
properly **astigmatic** adj
astir adj **1** out of bed **2** in
motion
astonish v surprise greatly
astonishment n
astound v overwhelm with
amazement **astounding** adj
astrakhan n **1** dark curly
fleece of lambs from
Astrakhan in Russia **2** fabric
resembling this
astral adj **1** of stars **2** of the
spirit world
astray adv off the right path
astride adv, prep with a leg on
either side (of)
astringent adj **1** severe or
harsh **2** causing contraction
of body tissue **3** checking
the flow of blood from a cut
▷ n **4** astringent substance
astringency n
astrolabe n instrument
formerly used to measure the
altitude of stars and planets
astrology n study of the

alleged influence of the stars, planets, and moon on human affairs **astrologer** n **astrological** adj

astronaut n person trained for travelling in space

astronautics n science and technology of space flight **astronautical** adj

astronomy n scientific study of heavenly bodies **astronomer** n **astronomical** adj 1 of astronomy 2 very large **astronomically** adv

astrophysics n science of the physical and chemical properties of stars, planets, etc. **astrophysical** adj **astrophysicist** n

Astroturf n ® artificial grass

astute adj perceptive or shrewd **astutely** adv **astuteness** n

asunder adv into parts or pieces

asylum n 1 refuge or sanctuary 2 old name for a psychiatric hospital

asymmetry n lack of symmetry **asymmetrical** or **asymmetric** adj

asymptote [ass-im-tote] n straight line closely approached by but never met by a curve

at prep 1 indicating position in space or time 2 towards 3 engaged in 4 in exchange for: *it's selling at two pounds* 5 indicating the cause of an emotion: *shocked at his rudeness*

atavism [at-a-viz-zum] n recurrence of a trait present in distant ancestors **atavistic** adj

ataxia n lack of muscular coordination **ataxic** adj

at-bat baseball ▷ n 1 turn to bat resulting in the batter making an out or a hit ▷ adv 2 Also **at bat** (of a batter) about to bat

ate v past tense of **eat**

atheism [aith-ee-iz-zum] n belief that there is no God **atheist** n **atheistic** adj

atherosclerosis n, pl **-ses** disease in which deposits of fat cause the walls of the arteries to thicken

athlete n person trained in or good at athletics **athletic** adj 1 physically fit or strong 2 of an athlete or athletics **athletics** pl n track and field sports such as running, jumping, throwing, etc. **athletically** adv **athleticism** n

athwart prep 1 across ▷ adv 2 transversely

atigi n a type of parka worn by the Inuit

Atlantic Daylight Time n one of the standard times used in North America, three hours behind Greenwich Mean Time Abbreviation: **ADT**

Atlantic Standard Time n one of the standard times used in North America, four hours behind Greenwich Mean Time Abbreviation: **AST**

atlas n book of maps

atmosphere n 1 mass of gases surrounding a heavenly body, esp. the earth 2 prevailing tone or mood (of a place etc.) 3 unit of pressure **atmospheric** adj **atmospherics** pl n radio interference due to electrical disturbance in the atmosphere

atoll n ring-shaped coral island enclosing a lagoon

atom n 1 smallest unit of matter which can take part in a chemical reaction 2 very small amount **atomic** adj 1 of atoms 2 of or using atomic bombs or atomic energy **atomic bomb** or **atom bomb**

bomb in which the energy is provided by nuclear fission **atomic energy** nuclear energy **atomic number** number of protons in the nucleus of an atom **atomic weight** ratio of the mass per atom of an element to one twelfth of the mass of a carbon atom **atomize** v reduce to atoms or small particles **atomizer** n device for discharging a liquid in a fine spray

atonal [eh-**tone**-al] adj (of music) not written in an established key **atonality** n

atone v make amends (for sin or wrongdoing) **atonement** n

atop prep on top of

atrium n, pl **atria 1** upper chamber of either half of the heart **2** central hall extending through several storeys of a modern building **3** main courtyard of an ancient Roman house

atrocious adj **1** extremely cruel or wicked **2** horrifying or shocking **3** informal very bad **atrociously** adv **atrocity** n **1** wickedness **2** act of cruelty

atrophy [**at**-trof-fee] n, pl -**phies 1** wasting away of an organ or part ▷ v -**phying**, -**phied 2** (cause to) waste away

attach v **1** join, fasten, or connect **2** attribute or ascribe: *he attaches great importance to his looks* **attached** adj (foll. by to) fond of **attachment** n

attaché [at-**tash**-shay] n specialist attached to a diplomatic mission **attaché case** flat rectangular briefcase for papers

attack v **1** launch a physical assault (against) **2** criticize **3** set about (a job or problem) with vigour **4** affect adversely ▷ n **5** act of attacking **6** sudden bout of illness **attacker** n

attain v **1** achieve or accomplish (a task or aim) **2** reach **attainment** n accomplishment **attainable** adj **attainability** n

attar n fragrant oil made from roses

attempt v **1** try, make an effort ▷ n **2** effort or endeavour

attend v **1** be present at **2** look after **3** pay attention **4** apply oneself (to) **attendance** n **1** attending **2** number attending **attendant** n **1** person who assists, guides, or provides a service ▷ adj **2** accompanying **attention** n **1** concentrated direction of the mind **2** consideration **3** care **4** alert position in military drill **attentive** adj **1** giving attention **2** considerately helpful **attentively** adv **attentiveness** n

attenuate v **1** weaken **2** make or become thin **attenuation** n

attest v affirm the truth of, be proof of **attestation** n

attic n space or room within the roof of a house

attire n **1** fine or formal clothes ▷ v **2** clothe

attitude n **1** way of thinking and behaving **2** posture of the body

attorney n person legally appointed to act for another, esp. a lawyer

attract v **1** arouse the interest or admiration of **2** draw (something) closer by exerting a force on it **attraction** n **1** power to attract **2** something that attracts **attractive** adj **attractively** adv **attractiveness** n

attribute v **1** (usu. foll. by to) regard as belonging to or produced by ▷ n **2** quality or feature representative of a person or thing **attributable**

adj **attribution** *n* **attributive** *adj grammar* (of an adjective) preceding the noun modified

attrition *n* constant wearing down to weaken or destroy: *war of attrition*

attune *v* adjust or accustom (a person or thing)

atypical [eh-**tip**-ik-al] *adj* not typical

Au *chem* gold

aubergine [**oh**-bur-zheen] *n* *Brit* eggplant

aubrietia [aw-**bree**-sha] *n* trailing plant with purple flowers

auburn *adj*, *n* (of hair) reddish-brown

auction *n* **1** public sale in which articles are sold to the highest bidder ▷ *v* **2** sell by auction **auctioneer** *n* person who conducts an auction

audacious *adj* **1** recklessly bold or daring **2** impudent **audaciously** *adv* **audacity** *n*

audible *adj* loud enough to hear **audibly** *adv* **audibility** *n*

audience *n* **1** group of spectators or listeners **2** formal interview

audio *adj* **1** of sound or hearing **2** of or for the transmission or reproduction of sound **audiotypist** *n* typist trained to type from a dictating machine **audiovisual** *adj* (esp. of teaching aids) involving both sight and hearing

audit *n* **1** official examination of business accounts ▷ *v* **2** examine (business accounts) officially **auditor** *n*

audition *n* **1** test of a performer's ability for a particular role or job ▷ *v* **2** test or be tested in an audition

auditorium *n*, *pl* **-toriums**, **-toria** building for public gatherings or meetings

auditory *adj* of or relating to hearing

au fait [oh **fay**] *adj French* **1** fully informed **2** expert

Aug. August

auger *n* carpenter's tool for boring holes

aught *pron old-fashioned* anything

augment *v* increase or enlarge **augmentation** *n*

au gratin [oh **grat**-tan] *adj* covered and cooked with breadcrumbs and sometimes cheese

augur *v* be a sign of (future events) **augury** *n* **1** foretelling of the future **2** omen

august *adj* dignified and imposing

August *n* eighth month of the year

auk *n* northern sea bird with short wings and black-and-white plumage

aunt *n* **1** father's or mother's sister **2** wife of parent's sibling **auntie** *or* **aunty** *n informal* aunt **Aunt Sally 1** figure used in fairgrounds as a target **2** target of abuse or criticism

au pair *n* young foreign woman who does housework in return for board and lodging

aura *n* distinctive air or quality of a person or thing

aural *adj* of or using the ears or hearing **aurally** *adv*

aureole, aureola *n* halo

au revoir [oh rev-**vwahr**] *interj French* goodbye

auricle *n* **1** upper chamber of the heart **2** outer part of the ear **auricular** *adj*

aurochs *n*, *pl* **aurochs** recently extinct European wild ox

aurora *n*, *pl* **-ras**, **-rae** bands of light sometimes seen in the sky in polar regions **aurora australis** aurora seen near the South Pole **aurora borealis** aurora seen near the North Pole

auscultation n listening to the internal sounds of the body, usu. with a stethoscope, to help with diagnosis

auspices [aw-spiss-siz] pl n **under the auspices of** with the support and approval of

auspicious adj showing signs of future success, favourable **auspiciously** adv

Aussie n, adj informal Australian

austere adj 1 stern or severe 2 ascetic 3 severely simple or plain **austerely** adv **austerity** n

Australasian n, adj (person) from Australia, New Zealand, and neighbouring islands

Australian n, adj (person) from Australia

autarchy [aw-tar-kee] n absolute power or autocracy

autarky [aw-tar-kee] n policy of economic self-sufficiency

authentic adj known to be real, genuine **authentically** adv **authenticity** n **authenticate** v establish as genuine **authentication** n

author n 1 writer of a book etc. 2 originator or creator **authoress** n fem **authorship** n

authority n, pl -ties 1 power to command or control others 2 often pl person or group having this power 3 expert in a particular field **authoritarian** n, adj (person) insisting on strict obedience to authority **authoritative** adj 1 recognized as being reliable: the authoritative book on Shakespeare 2 possessing authority **authoritatively** adv **authorize** v 1 give authority to 2 give permission for **authorization** n

autism n psychiatry disorder, usu. of children, characterized by lack of response to people and limited ability to communicate **autistic** adj

auto- combining form self-: autobiography

autobiography n, pl -phies account of a person's life written by that person **autobiographical** adj **autobiographically** adv

autocrat n 1 absolute ruler 2 dictatorial person **autocratic** adj **autocratically** adv **autocracy** n government by an autocrat

autocross n motor-racing over a rough course

Autocue n ® electronic television prompting device displaying a speaker's script, unseen by the audience

autogiro, autogyro n, pl -ros self-propelled aircraft resembling a helicopter but with an unpowered rotor

autograph n 1 handwritten signature of a (famous) person ▷ v 2 write one's signature on or in

automate v make (a manufacturing process) automatic

automatic adj 1 (of a device) operating mechanically by itself 2 (of a process) performed by automatic equipment 3 done without conscious thought 4 (of a firearm) self-loading ▷ n 5 self-loading firearm 6 vehicle with automatic transmission **automatic transmission** transmission system in a motor vehicle in which the gears change automatically **automatically** adv **automation** n use of automatic devices in industrial production

automaton n 1 robot 2 person who acts mechanically

automobile *n* motor vehicle designed to carry a small number of people

autonomy *n* self-government **autonomous** *adj*

autopsy *n, pl* **-sies** examination of a corpse to determine the cause of death

autoroute *n* expressway

autosuggestion *n* process in which a person unconsciously influences his or her own behaviour or beliefs

autumn *n* fall **autumnal** *adj* **autumnally** *adv*

auxiliary *adj* **1** secondary or supplementary **2** supporting ▷ *n, pl* **-ries 3** person or thing that supplements or supports **auxiliary verb** verb used to form the tense, voice, or mood of another, such as *will* in *I will go*

avail *v* **1** be of use or advantage (to) ▷ *n* **2** use or advantage: *to no avail* **avail oneself of** make use of

available *adj* obtainable or accessible **availability** *n*

avalanche *n* **1** mass of snow or ice falling down a mountain **2** sudden overwhelming quantity of anything

avant-garde [av-ong-**gard**] *n* **1** group of innovators, esp. in the arts ▷ *adj* **2** innovative and progressive

avarice [**av**-a-riss] *n* greed for wealth **avaricious** *adj*

avast *interj naut* stop

avatar *n Hinduism* appearance of a god in animal or human form

Ave. Avenue

avenge *v* take revenge in retaliation for (harm done) or on behalf of (a person harmed) **avenger** *n*

avenue *n* **1** wide street **2** road between two rows of trees **3** way of approach

aver [av-**vur**] *v* **averring**,

averred state to be true **averment** *n*

average *n* **1** typical or normal amount or quality **2** result obtained by adding quantities together and dividing the total by the number of quantities ▷ *adj* **3** usual or typical **4** calculated as an average ▷ *v* **5** calculate the average of **6** amount to as an average

averse *adj* (usu. foll. by *to*) disinclined or unwilling **aversion** *n* **1** strong dislike **2** person or thing disliked

avert *v* **1** turn away **2** ward off

avg. average

aviary *n, pl* **aviaries** large cage or enclosure for birds

aviation *n* art of flying aircraft **aviator** *n*

avid *adj* **1** keen or enthusiastic **2** greedy (for) **avidly** *adv* **avidity** *n*

avocado *n, pl* **-dos** pear-shaped tropical fruit with a leathery green skin and yellowish-green flesh

avocation *n old-fashioned* **1** occupation **2** hobby

avocet *n* long-legged wading bird with a long slender upward-curving bill

avoid *v* **1** refrain from **2** prevent from happening **3** keep away from **avoidable** *adj* **avoidance** *n*

avoirdupois [av-er-de-**poise**] *n* system of weights based on pounds and ounces

avow *v* **1** state or affirm **2** admit openly **avowal** *n* **avowed** *adj* **avowedly** *adv*

avuncular *adj* friendly, helpful, and caring towards someone younger

await *v* **1** wait for **2** be in store for

awake *adj* **1** not sleeping **2** alert ▷ *v* **awaking, awoke, awoken 3** emerge or rouse from sleep **4** (cause to) become alert

awaken v awake **awakening** n start of a feeling or awareness

award v **1** give (something, such as a prize) formally ▷ n **2** something awarded, such as a prize

aware adj having knowledge, informed **awareness** n

awash adv washed over by water

away adv **1** from a place: go away **2** to another place: put that gun away **3** out of existence: fade away **4** continuously: laughing away ▷ adj **5** not present **6** distant: two miles away **7** sports played on an opponent's ground

awe n **1** wonder and respect mixed with dread ▷ v **2** fill with awe **awesome** adj **1** inspiring awe **2** slang excellent or wonderful **awestruck** adj filled with awe

awful adj **1** very bad or unpleasant **2** obsolete inspiring awe **3** informal very great **awfully** adv **1** in an unpleasant way **2** informal very

awhile adv for a time

awkward adj **1** clumsy or ungainly **2** embarrassed **3** difficult to use, handle, or deal with **4** inconvenient **awkwardly** adv **awkwardness** n

awl n pointed tool for piercing wood, leather, etc.

awning n canvas roof supported by a frame to give protection against the weather

awoke v past tense of **awake** ▶ **awoken** v past participle of **awake**

AWOL adj mil absent without leave

awry [a-**rye**] adv, adj **1** with a twist to one side, askew **2** amiss

axe n **1** tool with a sharp blade for felling trees or chopping wood **2** informal dismissal from employment etc. ▷ v **3** informal dismiss (employees), restrict (expenditure), or terminate (a project)

axil n angle where the stalk of a leaf joins a stem

axiom n **1** generally accepted principle **2** self-evident statement **axiomatic** adj **1** containing axioms **2** self-evident

axis n, pl **axes 1** (imaginary) line round which a body can rotate or about which an object or geometrical figure is symmetrical **2** one of two fixed lines on a graph, against which quantities or positions are measured **axial** adj **axially** adv

axle n shaft on which a wheel or pair of wheels turn

ayatollah n Islamic religious leader in Iran

aye, ay interj **1** yes ▷ n **2** affirmative vote or voter

azalea [az-**zale**-ee-ya] n garden shrub grown for its showy flowers

azimuth n **1** arc of the sky between the zenith and the horizon **2** horizontal angle of a bearing measured clockwise from the north

Aztec n, adj (person) of the Indian race ruling Mexico before the Spanish conquest in the 16th century

azure adj, n (of) the colour of a clear blue sky

Bb

BA Bachelor of Arts

baa *v* **baaing, baaed 1** make the cry of a sheep ▷ *n* **2** cry made by a sheep

babble *v* **1** talk excitedly or foolishly **2** (of streams) make a low murmuring sound ▷ *n* **3** incoherent or foolish talk

babe *n* baby

babel [**babe**-el] *n* confused mixture of noises or voices

babiche *n* thongs or lacings of rawhide

baboon *n* large monkey with a pointed face and a long tail

baby *n, pl* **-bies 1** very young child or animal **2** *slang* sweetheart ▷ *adj* **3** comparatively small of its type **babyish** *adj* **baby beef 1** young beef animal **2** its meat **baby carriage** small hand-pushed carriage for a baby **baby-sit** *v* take care of a child while the parents are out **baby-sitter** *n*

baccarat [**back**-a-rah] *n* card game involving gambling

bacchanalia *pl n* drunken revelry or orgy

bachelor *n* **1** unmarried man **2** person who holds the lowest university degree

bacillus [bass-**ill**-luss] *n, pl* **-li** [-lie] rod-shaped bacterium

back *n* **1** rear part of the human body, from the neck to the pelvis **2** part or side of an object opposite the front **3** part of anything less often seen or used **4** *ball games* defensive player or position ▷ *v* **5** (cause to) move backwards **6** provide money for (a person or enterprise) **7** bet on the success of **8** (foll. by *onto*) have the back facing towards ▷ *adj* **9** situated behind **10** owing from an earlier date ▷ *adv* **11** at, to, or towards the rear **12** to or towards the original starting point or condition **back bacon** sweet pickled bacon cut from the loin **backbench** *adj Canad, Brit, Aust, & NZ* relating to a backbencher or backbenchers **backbencher** *n* Member of Parliament who does not hold office in the government or opposition **backbiting** *n* spiteful talk about an absent person **backbone** *n* **1** spinal column **2** strength of character **back channel** secret or unofficial intermediary or means of communication **backchat** *n informal* answering back, esp. impudently **backcheck** *v hockey* (of a forward) return to the defensive area and check attacking opponents **backcloth** *or* **backdrop** *n* painted curtain at the back of a stage set **backdate** *v* make (a document) effective from an earlier date **backer** *n* person who gives financial support **backfire** *v* **1** (of a plan) fail to have the desired effect **2** (of an engine) make a loud noise like an explosion **back forty 1** area

b

of farm most remote from a farmhouse **2** any remote area **background** n **1** events or circumstances that help to explain something **2** person's social class, education, or experience **3** space behind the chief figures in a picture **backhand** n tennis etc. stroke played with the back of the hand facing the direction of the stroke **backhanded** adj sarcastic: a backhanded compliment **backhouse** n outhouse **backing** n **1** support **2** musical accompaniment for a pop singer **backlash** n sudden and adverse reaction **backlog** n accumulation of things to be dealt with **backpack** n rucksack **backside** n informal buttocks **backslide** v relapse into former bad habits **backslider** n **backstage** adv, adj behind the stage in a theatre **backstroke** n swimming stroke performed on the back **backtrack** v **1** return by the same route by which one has come **2** retract or reverse one's opinion or policy **back up** v support **backup** n **1** support or reinforcement **2** reserve or substitute **backward** adj **1** directed towards the rear **2** slow in physical, material, or intellectual development **backwardness** n **backwards** adv **1** towards the rear **2** with the back foremost **3** in the reverse of the usual direction **backwash** n **1** water washed backwards by the motion of a boat **2** repercussion **backwater** n isolated or backward place or condition **backwoods** pl n remote sparsely populated area **backgammon** n game played with counters and dice

bacon n salted or smoked pig meat

bacteria pl n, sing. **-rium** large group of microorganisms, many of which cause disease **bacterial** adj **bacteriology** n study of bacteria **bacteriologist** n

bad adj **worse, worst 1** of poor quality **2** lacking skill or talent **3** harmful **4** immoral or evil **5** naughty or mischievous **6** rotten or decayed **7** severe or unpleasant **badly** adv **badness** n **badlands** pl n barren, rocky region in western N America

bade v a past tense of **bid**

badge n emblem worn to show membership, rank, etc.

badger n **1** nocturnal burrowing mammal with a black and white head ▷ v **2** pester or harass

badinage [bad-in-nahzh] n playful and witty conversation

badminton n game played with a racket and shuttlecock, which is hit over a high net

baffle v perplex or puzzle **bafflement** n

bag n **1** flexible container with an opening at one end **2** offensive ugly or bad-tempered woman **bags 3** informal (foll. by of) lots of ▷ v **bagging, bagged 4** put into a bag **5** (cause to) bulge **6** capture or kill **baggy** adj (of clothes) hanging loosely **bagman** n informal person who solicits money for a political party

bagatelle n **1** something of little value **2** board game in which balls are struck into holes

baggage n suitcases packed for a journey

bagpipes pl n musical wind instrument with reed pipes

and an inflatable bag

bail¹ *n law* **1** money deposited with a court as security for a person's reappearance in court ▷ *v* **2** pay bail for (a person)

bail², **bale** *v* (foll. by *out*) remove (water) from (a boat) **bail on** *v slang* leave or abandon a person or thing **bail out** or **bale out** *v* **1** *informal* help (a person or organization) out of a predicament **2** make an emergency parachute jump from an aircraft

bailey *n* outermost wall or court of a castle

bailiff *n* **1** sheriff's officer who serves writs and summonses **2** court official **3** landlord's agent

bairn *n Scot* child

bait *n* **1** piece of food on a hook or in a trap to attract fish or animals ▷ *v* **2** put a piece of food on or in (a hook or trap) **3** persecute or tease

baize *n* woollen fabric used to cover billiard and card tables

bake *v* **1** cook by dry heat as in an oven **2** make or become hardened by heat **baker** *n* person whose business is to make or sell bread, cakes, etc. **baker's dozen** thirteen **bakery** *n, pl* **-eries** place where bread, cakes, etc. are baked or sold **baking powder** powdered mixture used in baking instead of yeast

bakeapple *n* cloudberry

Balaclava, **Balaclava helmet** *n* close-fitting woollen hood that covers the ears and neck

balalaika *n* guitar-like musical instrument with a triangular body

balance *n* **1** stability of mind or body **2** state of being in balance **3** harmony in the parts of a whole **4** something that remains **5** difference between the credits and debits of an account **6** weighing device ▷ *v* **7** weigh on a balance **8** remain steady **9** equalize in weight, amount, etc. **10** consider or compare

balcony *n, pl* **-nies 1** platform on the outside of a building with a rail along the outer edge **2** upper tier of seats in a theatre or cinema

bald *adj* **1** having little or no hair on the scalp **2** (of a tire) having a worn tread **3** without unnecessary words **balding** *adj* becoming bald **baldness** *n* **bald prairie** part of prairie without trees

balderdash *n* stupid talk

bale¹ *n* **1** large bundle of hay or goods tightly bound together ▷ *v* **2** make or put into bales

bale² *v* same as **bail²**

baleful *adj* vindictive or menacing **balefully** *adv*

balk, **baulk** *v* **1** be reluctant to (do something) **2** thwart or hinder

Balkan *adj* of any of the countries of the Balkan Peninsula: Romania, Bulgaria, Albania, Greece, the former Yugoslavia, and the European part of Turkey

ball¹ *n* **1** round or nearly round object, esp. one used in games **2** single delivery of the ball in a game **3** *baseball* ball pitched outside the strike zone and not swung at by the batter **balls** *taboo, slang* **4** testicles **5** nonsense ▷ *v* **6** form into a ball **ball bearings** steel balls between moving parts of a machine to reduce friction **ball cock** device with a floating ball and a valve for regulating the flow of water **ballpoint** or **ballpoint pen** *n* pen with a tiny ball bearing as a writing point

ball² n formal social function for dancing **ballroom** n

ballad n 1 narrative poem or song 2 slow sentimental song

ballast n substance, such as sand, used to stabilize a ship when it is not carrying cargo

ballet n 1 classical style of expressive dancing based on conventional steps 2 theatrical performance of this **ballerina** n female ballet dancer

ballistics n study of the flight of projectiles, such as bullets **ballistic missile** missile guided automatically in flight but which falls freely at its target

balloon n 1 inflatable rubber bag used as a plaything 2 large bag inflated with air or gas, designed to carry passengers in a basket underneath ▷ v 3 fly in a balloon 4 swell or increase rapidly in size **balloonist** n

ballot n 1 method of voting secretly 2 actual vote or paper indicating a person's choice ▷ v -**loting**, -**loted** 3 vote or ask for a vote from **ballot box**

ballyhoo n exaggerated fuss

balm n 1 aromatic substance used for healing and soothing 2 anything that comforts or soothes

balmy adj **balmier, balmiest** 1 (of weather) mild and pleasant 2 same as **barmy**

baloney n informal nonsense

balsa [**bawl**-sa] n tropical American tree that yields light wood

balsam n 1 soothing ointment 2 flowering plant

baluster n set of posts supporting a rail **balustrade** n ornamental rail supported by balusters

bamboo n tall treelike tropical grass with hollow stems

bamboozle v informal 1 cheat or mislead 2 confuse, puzzle

ban v **banning, banned** 1 prohibit or forbid officially ▷ n 2 official prohibition

banal [ban-**nahl**] adj ordinary and unoriginal **banality** n

banana n yellow crescent-shaped fruit

band¹ n 1 group of musicians playing together 2 group of people having a common purpose 3 community of Canadian Indians recognized by federal government **bandsman** n **bandstand** n roofed outdoor platform for a band **band together** v unite

band² n 1 strip of material, used to hold objects together 2 physics range of frequencies or wavelengths between two limits **bandwidth** n the range of frequencies used in a telecommunications signal

bandage n 1 piece of material used to cover a wound ▷ v 2 cover with a bandage

bandanna, bandana n large brightly coloured handkerchief

b. and b., B and B bed and breakfast

bandit n robber, esp. a member of an armed gang **banditry** n

bandoleer, bandolier n shoulder belt for holding cartridges

bandwagon n **climb on the bandwagon** or **jump on the bandwagon** join a party or movement that seems assured of success

bandy adj -**dier**, -**diest** 1 having legs curved outwards at the knees ▷ v -**dying**, -**died** 2 exchange (words) in a heated manner 3 circulate (a name, rumour, etc.)

bane n person or thing that causes misery or distress **baneful** adj

bang n 1 short loud explosive noise 2 hard blow or loud knock ▷ v 3 hit or knock, esp. with a loud noise 4 close (a door) noisily ▷ adv 5 with a sudden impact 6 precisely

banger n 1 slang sausage 2 informal old decrepit automobile 3 firework that explodes loudly

bangle n bracelet worn round the arm or the ankle

banish v 1 send (someone) into exile 2 dismiss from one's thoughts **banishment** n

banisters pl n railing supported by posts on a staircase

banjo n, pl **-jos**, **-joes** guitar-like musical instrument with a circular body

bank[1] n 1 institution offering services, such as the safekeeping and lending of money 2 any supply, store, or reserve ▷ v 3 deposit (cash or cheques) in a bank **banker** n manager or owner of a bank **banking** n **bank machine** machine that allows users to withdraw or deposit money at a bank **banknote** n piece of paper money **bank on** v rely on

bank[2] n 1 raised mass, esp. of earth 2 sloping ground at the side of a river ▷ v 3 form into a bank 4 cause (an aircraft) or (of an aircraft) to tip to one side on turning (of an aircraft)

bank[3] n row of switches, keys, etc. on a machine

bankrupt n 1 person declared by a court to be unable to pay his or her debts ▷ adj 2 financially ruined ▷ v 3 make bankrupt **bankruptcy** n

banner n 1 long strip of cloth displaying a slogan, advertisement, etc. 2 placard carried in a demonstration or procession

bannisters pl n same as **banisters**

banns pl n public declaration, esp. in a church, of an intended marriage

banquet n elaborate formal dinner

banshee n (in Irish folklore) female spirit whose wailing warns of impending death

bantam n 1 small chicken ▷ adj 2 sports under 15 years of age **bantamweight** n boxer weighing up to 118lb (professional) or 54kg (amateur)

banter v 1 tease jokingly ▷ n 2 teasing or joking conversation

Bantu n group of languages of Africa

banyan n Indian tree whose branches grow down into the soil forming additional trunks

baptism n Christian religious ceremony in which a person is immersed in or sprinkled with water as a sign of purification and acceptance into the Church **baptismal** adj **baptize** v perform baptism on

Baptist n member of a Protestant denomination that believes in adult baptism by immersion

bar[1] n 1 rigid length of metal, wood, etc. 2 solid, usu. rectangular block, of any material 3 anything that obstructs or prevents 4 counter or room where drinks are served 5 heating element in an electric fire 6 music group of beats repeated throughout a piece of music ▷ v **barring**, **barred** 7 secure with a bar 8 ban or forbid 9 obstruct ▷ prep 10 Also

b

barring except for **the bar** lawyers collectively **barman** (**barmaid**) *n*

bar² *n* unit of atmospheric pressure

barachois *n* (in the Atlantic Provinces) a shallow lagoon formed by a sand bar

barb *n* **1** point facing in the opposite direction to the main point of a fish-hook etc. **2** cutting remark **barbed** *adj* **barbed wire** strong wire with protruding sharp points

barbarian *n* member of a primitive or uncivilized people **barbaric** *adj* cruel or brutal **barbarism** *n* condition of being backward or ignorant **barbarity** *n* **1** state of being barbaric or barbarous **2** vicious act **barbarous** *adj* **1** uncivilized **2** brutal or cruel

barbecue *n* **1** grill on which food is cooked over hot charcoal, usu. outdoors **2** outdoor party at which barbecued food is served ▷ *v* **3** cook (food) on a barbecue

barber *n* person who cuts men's hair

barbiturate *n* drug used as a sedative

bard *n lit* poet **the Bard** William Shakespeare

bare *adj* **1** unclothed **2** without the natural or usual covering **3** unembellished, simple **4** just sufficient ▷ *v* **5** uncover **bareback** *adj, adv* (of horse-riding) without a saddle **bare-bones** *adj* basic, containing only the essential elements **barefaced** *adj* shameless or impudent **barefoot** or **barefooted** *adj, adv* with feet uncovered **barely** *adv* only just **bareness** *n*

bargain *n* **1** agreement establishing what each party will give, receive, or perform in a transaction **2** something bought or offered at a low price ▷ *v* **3** negotiate the terms of an agreement **bargain for** *v* anticipate or take into account

barge *n* **1** flat-bottomed boat used to transport freight ▷ *v* **2** *informal* push violently **barge in** or **barge into** *v* interrupt rudely

barista *n* person who makes and sells coffee in a coffee bar

baritone *n* (singer with) the second lowest adult male voice

barium [**bare**-ee-um] *n* soft white metallic element

bark¹ *n* **1** loud harsh cry of a dog ▷ *v* **2** (of a dog) make its typical cry **3** shout in an angry tone

bark² *n* tough outer layer of a tree

barley *n* tall grasslike plant cultivated for grain

barmy *adj* -**mier**, -**miest** *slang* insane

barn *n* large building on a farm used for storing grain **barnstorm** *v* tour rural districts putting on shows or making speeches in a political campaign

barnacle *n* shellfish that lives attached to objects under water

barometer *n* instrument for measuring atmospheric pressure **barometric** *adj*

baron *n* **1** member of the lowest rank of nobility **2** powerful businessman **baroness** *n fem* **baronial** *adj*

baronet *n* commoner who holds the lowest hereditary British title **baronetcy** *n*

baroque [bar-**rock**] *n* **1** highly ornate style of art and architecture from the late 16th to the early 18th century

▷ *adj* **2** extremely complicated, rich, and elaborate

barque [**bark**] *n* sailing ship, esp. one with three masts

barrack *v* criticize loudly or shout against (a team or speaker)

barracks *pl n* building used to accommodate military personnel

barracuda [bar-rack-**kew**-da] *n* predatory tropical sea fish

barrage [**bar**-rahzh] *n* **1** continuous delivery of questions, complaints, etc. **2** continuous artillery fire **3** artificial barrier across a river

barrel *n* **1** cylindrical container with rounded sides and flat ends **2** tube in a firearm through which the bullet is fired **barrel organ** musical instrument played by turning a handle

barren *adj* **1** (of land) unable to support the growth of crops, fruit, etc. **2** (of a woman or female animal) incapable of producing offspring **barrenness** *n* **Barren Lands** or **Barren Grounds** sparsely inhabited tundra region in Canada

barricade *n* **1** barrier, esp. one erected hastily for defence ▷ *v* **2** erect a barricade across (an entrance)

barrier *n* anything that prevents access or progress

barrister *n* lawyer who pleads in court

barrister and solicitor *n Canad* lawyer empowered to plead in court, advise clients, draw up documents, etc.

barrow[1] *n* **1** wheelbarrow **2** movable stall, used esp. by street vendors

barrow[2] *n* mound of earth placed over a prehistoric tomb

barter *v* **1** trade (goods) in exchange for other goods ▷ *n* **2** trade by the exchange of goods

basalt [**bass**-awlt] *n* dark volcanic rock **basaltic** *adj*

bascule *n* drawbridge that operates by a counterbalanced weight

base[1] *n* **1** bottom or supporting part of anything **2** fundamental part **3** centre of operations, organization, or supply **4** starting point **5** *baseball* any of three corners of the baseball diamond which batters must reach before returning to home plate to score a run ▷ *v* **6** (foll. by *on* or *upon*) use as a basis (for) **7** (foll. by *at* or *in*) station, post, or place **base hit** hit that enables the batter to run to at least one base **baseless** *adj* **basement** *n* partly or wholly underground storey of a building **baserunner** *n baseball* member of the batting team who is on a base or running between bases

base[2] *adj* **1** dishonourable or immoral **2** of inferior quality **basely** *adv* **baseness** *n*

baseball *n* **1** N American team game played with a bat and ball **2** ball used for this **baseball diamond** part of the playing field delimited by home plate and the three bases

bash *informal* ▷ *v* **1** hit violently or forcefully ▷ *n* **2** heavy blow

bashful *adj* shy or modest **bashfully** *adv* **bashfulness** *n*

basic *adj* **1** of or forming a base or basis **2** elementary or simple **basics** *pl n* fundamental principles, facts, etc. **basically** *adv*

BASIC *n* computer programming language that uses common English words

b

basil n aromatic herb used in cooking

basilica n rectangular church with a rounded end and two aisles

basilisk n legendary serpent said to kill by its breath or glance

basin n 1 round open container 2 sink for washing the hands and face 3 sheltered area of water where boats may be moored 4 catchment area of a river

basis n, pl -ses fundamental principles etc. from which something is started or developed

bask v lie in or be exposed to (pleasant warmth)

basket n 1 container made of interwoven strips of wood or cane 2 basketball metal hoop with netting mounted on a tall pole, serving as the goal **basketwork** n

basketball n 1 game in which two teams of five players bounce a rubber ball and try to place it in a high hoop called the basket to score points 2 ball used for this

Basque n, adj (member or language) of a people living in the W Pyrenees in France and Spain

bas-relief n sculpture in which the figures stand out slightly from the background

bass¹ [base] n 1 (singer with) the lowest adult male voice ▷ adj 2 of the lowest range of musical notes

bass² n edible sea fish

basset hound n smooth-haired dog with short legs and long ears

bassoon n large woodwind instrument

basswood n tall shade tree with heart-shaped leaves

bastard n 1 person born of parents not married to each other 2 offensive obnoxious or despicable person **bastardize** v debase or corrupt **bastardy** n

baste¹ v moisten (meat) during cooking with hot fat

baste² v sew with loose temporary stitches

bastion n 1 projecting part of a fortification 2 thing or person regarded as defending a principle

bat¹ n 1 any of various types of club used to hit the ball in certain sports ▷ v **batting, batted** 2 strike with or as if with a bat **batting average** baseball number of hits divided by times at bat, expressed as a decimal with three places

bat² n nocturnal mouselike flying animal

batch n group of people or things dealt with at the same time

bated adj **with bated breath** in suspense or fear

bath n 1 large container in which to wash the body 2 act of washing in such a container **baths** 3 public swimming pool ▷ v 4 wash in a bath **bathroom** n room with a bath, sink, and usu. a toilet

bathe v 1 swim in open water 2 apply liquid to (the skin or a wound) in order to cleanse or soothe 3 (foll. by in) fill (with): bathed in sunlight **bather** n

bathos [bay-thoss] n sudden change in speech or writing from a serious subject to a trivial one

bathyscaph, bathyscaphe n deep-sea diving vessel for observation

batik [bat-teek] n 1 process of printing fabric using wax to cover areas not to be dyed 2 fabric printed in this way

baton *n* **1** thin stick used by the conductor of an orchestra **2** short bar transferred in a relay race **3** policeman's truncheon

battalion *n* army unit consisting of three or more companies

batten[1] *n* strip of wood fixed to something, esp. to hold it in place **batten down** *v* secure with a batten

batten[2] **batten on** *v* thrive at the expense of (someone else)

batter[1] *v* **1** hit repeatedly ▷ *n* **2** *baseball* member of the batting team who is currently at bat **battering ram** large beam used to break down fortifications

batter[2] *n* mixture of flour, eggs, and milk, used in cooking

battery *n, pl* -**teries 1** device that produces electricity in a flashlight, radio, etc. **2** group of heavy guns operating as a single unit **3** series of cages for intensive rearing of poultry

battle *n* **1** fight between large armed forces **2** conflict or struggle ▷ *v* **3** struggle **battle-axe** *n* **1** *informal* domineering woman **2** large heavy axe **battleship** *n* heavily armoured warship

battlement *n* wall with gaps for shooting through

batty *adj* -**tier**, -**tiest** *slang* **1** crazy **2** eccentric

bauble *n* trinket of little value

baulk *v* same as **balk**

bauxite *n* claylike substance from which aluminum is obtained

bawdy *adj* **bawdier**, **bawdiest** (of writing etc.) containing humorous references to sex **bawdiness** *n*

bawl *v* shout or weep noisily

bay[1] *n* wide curving coastline

bay[2] *n* **1** recess in a wall **2** area in which vehicles may park or unload

bay[3] *v* (of a hound or wolf) howl in deep prolonged tones

bay[4] *n* Mediterranean laurel tree **bay leaf** dried leaf of a laurel, used in cooking

bay[5] *adj, n* reddish-brown (horse)

bayonet *n* **1** sharp blade that can be fixed to the end of a rifle ▷ *v* -**neting**, -**neted** **2** stab with a bayonet

bazaar *n* **1** sale in aid of charity **2** market area, esp. in Eastern countries

bazooka *n* rocket launcher that fires a projectile capable of piercing armour

BBC British Broadcasting Corporation

BC 1 before Christ **2** British Columbia

be *v, present sing. 1st person* **am** *2nd person* **are** *3rd person* **is** *present pl.* **are** *past sing. 1st person* **was** *2nd person* **were** *3rd person* **was** *past pl* **were** *present participle* **being** *past participle* **been 1** exist or live **2** used as a linking between the subject of a sentence and its complement: *John is a musician* **3** forms the progressive present tense: *the man is running* **4** forms the passive voice of all transitive verbs: *a good film is being shown on television tonight*

beach *n* **1** area of sand or pebbles on a shore ▷ *v* **2** run or haul (a boat) onto a beach **beachcomber** *n* **1** person who searches shore debris for anything of worth **2** (in British Columbia) person who is paid for salvaging loose logs for logging companies **beachhead** *n* beach captured by an attacking army on which troops can be landed

beacon *n* fire or light on a hill or tower, used as a warning

bead n **1** small ball of plastic etc., pierced for threading on a string to form a necklace etc. **2** small drop of moisture **beaded** adj **beading** n strip of moulding used for edging furniture **beady** adj small, round, and glittering: *beady eyes*

beagle n small hunting dog with short legs and drooping ears

beak n **1** projecting horny jaws of a bird **2** slang nose **beaky** adj

beaker n **1** large drinking cup **2** lipped glass container used in laboratories

beam n **1** broad smile **2** ray of light **3** narrow flow of electromagnetic radiation or particles **4** long thick piece of wood, metal, etc., used in building ▷ v **5** smile broadly **6** divert or aim (a radio signal, light, etc.) in a certain direction

bean n seed or pod of various plants, eaten as a vegetable or used to make coffee etc.

bear[1] v **bearing, bore, borne** **1** support or hold up **2** bring: *to bear gifts* **3** passive **born** give birth to **4** produce as by natural growth **5** tolerate or endure **6** hold in the mind **7** show or be marked with **8** move in a specified direction **bearable** adj **bearer** n **bear out** v show to be truthful

bear[2] n large heavy mammal with a long shaggy coat **bearskin** n tall fur helmet worn by some British soldiers

beard n hair growing on the lower parts of a man's face **bearded** adj

bearing n **1** relevance (to) **2** part of a machine that supports another part, esp. one that reduces friction **3** person's general social conduct **bearings 4** sense of one's own relative position

beast n **1** large wild animal **2** brutal or uncivilized person **beastly** adj unpleasant or disagreeable

beat v **beating, beat, beaten** or **beat 1** hit hard and repeatedly **2** move (wings) up and down **3** throb rhythmically **4** stir or mix vigorously **5** overcome or defeat ▷ n **6** regular throb **7** assigned route, as of a policeman **8** basic rhythmic unit in a piece of music **beater** n **beat up** v injure (someone) by repeated blows or kicks

beatify [bee-**at**-if-fie] v **-fying, -fied** RC Church declare (a dead person) to be among the blessed in heaven **beatific** adj displaying great happiness **beatification** n **beatitude** n supreme blessedness

beau [boh] n, pl **beaus, beaux** dandy

Beaufort scale n scale for measuring the speed of wind

beauty n, pl **-ties 1** combination of all the qualities of a person or thing that delight the senses and mind **2** very attractive woman **3** informal something outstanding of its kind **beautiful** adj **1** possessing beauty **2** very pleasant **beautifully** adv **beautify** v make or become beautiful **beautification** n **beautician** n person whose profession is to give beauty treatments

beaver n **1** amphibious rodent with a big flat tail **2 Beaver** Beaver Scout **beaver away** v work industriously **beaver lodge** rounded structure of mud, sticks, and stones built by beavers as a den **Beaver Scout** member of a junior branch of the Boy Scouts

becalmed *adj* (of a sailing ship) motionless through lack of wind

became *v* past tense of **become**

because *conj* on account of the fact that **because of** on account of

beck *n* **at someone's beck and call** subject to someone's slightest whim

beckon *v* summon with a gesture

become *v* -coming, -came, -come 1 come to be 2 (foll. by *of*) happen to 3 suit **becoming** *adj* 1 attractive or pleasing 2 appropriate or proper

bed *n* 1 piece of furniture on which to sleep 2 garden plot 3 bottom of a river, lake, or sea 4 layer of rock ▷ *v* **bedding, bedded** 5 have sexual intercourse with **go to bed with** have sexual intercourse with **bedding** *n* sheets and covers that are used on a bed **bed down** *v* go to or put into a place to sleep or rest **bedpan** *n* shallow bowl used as a toilet by bedridden people **bedridden** *adj* confined to bed because of illness or old age **bedrock** *n* 1 solid rock beneath the surface soil 2 basic facts or principles **bedroom** *n* **bedsit** or **bedsitter** *n* furnished sitting room with a bed

bedevil [bid-**dev**-ill] *v* -**illing, -illed** harass or torment

bedlam *n* noisy confused situation

bedraggled *adj* untidy, wet, or dirty

bee *n* insect that makes wax and honey **beehive** *n* structure in which bees live **beeswax** *n* wax secreted by bees, used in polishes etc.

beech *n* European tree with a smooth greyish bark

beef *n* 1 flesh of a cow, bull, or ox ▷ *v* 2 *informal* complain **beefy** *adj* 1 like beef 2 *informal* strong and muscular 3 *informal* fleshy, obese **beefalo** *n* cross between bison and other cattle **beefeater** *n* yeoman warder at the Tower of London

been *v* past participle of **be**

beep *n* 1 high-pitched sound, like that of an automobile horn ▷ *v* 2 (cause to) make this noise **beeper** *n*

beer *n* alcoholic drink brewed from malt and hops **beery** *adj* **beer parlour** tavern

beet *n* plant with an edible root and leaves **beetroot** *n* type of beet plant with a dark red root

beetle *n* 1 insect with a hard wing cover on its back ▷ *v* 2 *informal* scuttle or scurry

befall *v* old-fashioned happen to (someone)

befit *v* be appropriate or suitable for **befitting** *adj*

before *conj* 1 earlier than the time when 2 rather than ▷ *prep* 3 preceding in space or time 4 in the presence of 5 in preference to ▷ *adv* 6 at an earlier time, previously 7 in front **beforehand** *adv* in advance

befriend *v* be a friend to

beg *v* **begging, begged** 1 solicit (for money or food), esp. in the street 2 ask formally or humbly **beggar** *n* **beggarly** *adj*

began *v* past tense of **begin**

beget *v* -**getting, -got** or -**gat, -gotten** or -**got** 1 cause or create 2 father

begin *v* -**ginning, -gan, -gun** 1 start 2 bring or come into being **beginner** *n* person who has just started learning to do something **beginning** *n*

begonia *n* tropical plant with waxy flowers

b

begrudge v grudge

beguile [big-**gile**] v **1** cheat or mislead **2** charm or amuse **beguiling** adj

begun v past participle of **begin**

behalf n **on behalf of** in the interest of or for the benefit of

behave v **1** act or function in a particular way **2** conduct (oneself) properly **behaviour** or **behavior** n

behead v remove the head from

beheld v past of **behold**

behest n order or earnest request

behind prep **1** at the back of **2** responsible for or causing **3** supporting ▷ adv **4** in or to a position further back **5** remaining after someone's departure **6** in arrears **7** late ▷ n **8** informal buttocks

behold v old-fashioned look (at), observe **beholder** n

beholden adj indebted or obliged

behove v old-fashioned be necessary or fitting for

beige adj pale brown

being v **1** present participle of **be** ▷ n **2** existence **3** something that exists or is thought to exist **4** human being, person

belabour, belabor v attack verbally or physically

belated adj late or too late **belatedly** adv

belch v **1** expel wind from the stomach noisily through the mouth **2** expel or be expelled forcefully: smoke belched from the factory ▷ n **3** act of belching

beleaguered adj **1** besieged **2** surrounded or beset

belfry n, pl -**fries** part of a tower where bells are hung

belie v show to be untrue

belief n **1** trust or confidence

2 opinion **3** principle etc. accepted as true **4** religious faith **believe** v **1** accept as true or real **2** think, assume, or suppose **3** (foll. by in) be convinced of the truth or existence of **believable** adj **believer** n

belittle v treat as having little value or importance

bell n **1** hollow, usu. metal, cup-shaped instrument that emits a ringing sound when struck **2** device that rings or buzzes as a signal

belladonna n (drug obtained from) deadly nightshade

belle n beautiful woman

bellicose adj warlike and aggressive

belligerent adj **1** hostile and aggressive **2** engaged in war ▷ n **3** person or country engaged in war **belligerence** n

bellow v **1** make a low deep cry like that of a bull **2** shout in a loud deep voice ▷ n **3** loud deep roar

bellows pl n instrument for pumping a stream of air into something

belly n, pl -**lies 1** part of the body of a vertebrate which contains the intestines **2** stomach **3** front, lower, or inner part of something **4 go belly up** informal fail utterly; die ▷ v -**lying**, -**lied 5** (cause to) swell out **bellyful** n slang more than one can tolerate

belong v (foll. by to) **1** be the property of **2** (foll. by to) be a part of **3** have a proper or usual place **belongings** pl n personal possessions

beloved adj **1** dearly loved ▷ n **2** person dearly loved

below prep, adv at or to a position lower than, under

belt n **1** band of cloth, leather,

etc., worn usu. around the waist **2** long narrow area **3** circular strip of rubber that drives moving parts in a machine **4** area where a specific thing is found ▷ *v* **5** fasten with a belt **6** *slang* hit very hard

bemoan *v* express sorrow or dissatisfaction about

bemused *adj* puzzled or confused

bench *n* **1** long seat **2** judge or magistrate sitting in court **3** long narrow work table **bencher** *n* governing member of a provincial law society **bench mark 1** mark on a fixed object, used as a reference point in surveying **2** criterion by which to measure something

bend *v* **bending, bent 1** (cause to) form a curve **2** (often foll. by *down* etc.) incline the body ▷ *n* **3** curved part **bends 4** *informal* decompression sickness **bendy** *adj*

beneath *adv, prep* **1** below **2** not worthy of

Benedictine *n, adj* (monk or nun) of the order of Saint Benedict

benediction *n* prayer for divine blessing

benefit *n* **1** something helpful, beneficial, or advantageous **2** payment made by a government to a poor, ill, or unemployed person ▷ *v* -**fiting,** -**fited 3** do or receive good **beneficial** *adj* advantageous **beneficiary** *n* person who gains or benefits **benefactor** (**benefactress**) *n* someone who supports a person or institution by giving money **benefaction** *n* **beneficent** [bin-**eff**-iss-ent] *adj* charitable or generous **beneficence** *n*

benevolent *adj* kind and helpful **benevolently** *adv* **benevolence** *n*

benighted *adj* ignorant or uncultured

benign [bin-**nine**] *adj* **1** showing kindliness **2** (of a tumour) not malignant **benignly** *adv*

bent *v* **1** past of **bend** ▷ *adj* **2** curved **3** *slang* dishonest ▷ *n* **4** personal inclination or aptitude **bent on** determined to pursue (a course of action)

bento, bento box *n* thin lightweight box divided into compartments, which contain small separate dishes comprising a Japanese meal

benzene *n* flammable poisonous liquid used as a solvent, fuel, etc.

bequeath *v* dispose of (property) as in a will **bequest** *n* legal gift of money or property by someone who has died

berate *v* scold harshly

bereaved *adj* having recently lost someone close through death **bereavement** *n*

bereft *adj* (foll. by *of*) deprived

beret [**ber**-ray] *n* round flat close-fitting brimless cap

bergamot *n* small Asian tree with sour pear-shaped fruit

beriberi *n* tropical disease caused by vitamin B deficiency

berry *n, pl* -**ries** small soft stoneless fruit

berserk *adj* **go berserk** become violent or destructive

berth *n* **1** bunk in a ship or train **2** place assigned to a ship at a mooring ▷ *v* **3** dock (a vessel)

beryl *n* hard transparent mineral

beseech *v* -**seeching,** -**sought** *or* -**seeched** ask (someone) earnestly

beset *v* trouble or harass constantly

b

beside *prep* **1** at, by, or to the side of **2** as compared with **beside oneself** overwhelmed or overwrought **besides** *adv, prep* in addition

besiege *v* **1** surround with military forces **2** overwhelm, as with requests

besom *n* broom made of twigs

besotted *adj* infatuated

besought *v* past of **beseech**

bespeak *v* indicate or suggest **bespoke** *adj* (of clothes) made to the customer's specifications

best *adj* **1** most excellent of a particular group etc. ▷ *adv* **2** in a manner surpassing all others ▷ *n* **3** most outstanding or excellent person, thing, or group in a category **best man** groom's attendant at a wedding **best seller** book or other product that has sold in great numbers

bestial *adj* **1** brutal or savage **2** of or like a beast **bestiality** *n*

bestir *v* cause (oneself) to become active

bestow *v* present (a gift) or confer (an honour) **bestowal** *n*

bestride *v* have or put a leg on either side of

bet *n* **1** agreement that money will be paid to someone who correctly predicts the outcome of an event **2** stake risked ▷ *v* **betting, bet** or **betted 3** make or place (a bet) **4** *informal* predict (a certain outcome)

betel [bee-tl] *n* Asian climbing plant, the leaves and nuts of which can be chewed

bête noire [bet nwahr] *n, pl* **bêtes noires** person or thing that one particularly dislikes

betide *v* happen (to)

betoken *v* indicate or signify

betray *v* **1** hand over or expose (one's nation etc.) treacherously to an enemy **2** disclose (a secret or confidence) treacherously **3** reveal unintentionally **betrayal** *n* **betrayer** *n*

betrothed *adj* engaged to be married **betrothal** *n*

better *adj* **1** more excellent than others **2** improved or fully recovered in health ▷ *adv* **3** in a more excellent manner **4** in or to a greater degree ▷ *pl n* **5** one's superiors ▷ *v* **6** improve upon

between *prep* **1** at a point intermediate to two other points in space, time, etc. **2** indicating a linked relation or comparison **3** indicating alternatives ▷ *adv* **4** between one specified thing and another

betwixt *prep, adv old-fashioned* between

bevel *n* **1** slanting edge ▷ *v* **-elling, -elled 2** cut a bevel on (a piece of timber etc.)

beverage *n* drink **beverage room** tavern

bevy *n, pl* **bevies** flock or group

bewail *v* express great sorrow over

beware *v* be on one's guard (against)

bewilder *v* confuse utterly **bewildering** *adj* **bewilderment** *n*

bewitch *v* **1** attract and fascinate **2** cast a spell over **bewitching** *adj*

beyond *prep* **1** at or to a point on the other side of **2** outside the limits or scope of ▷ *adv* **3** at or to the far side of something

bi- *combining form* twice or two: *bifocal*

biannual *adj* occurring twice a year **biannually** *adv*

bias *n* **1** mental tendency, esp. prejudice **2** diagonal cut across the weave of a fabric **3** *bowls* weight on one side of a bowl that causes it to run in a curve ▷ *v* **-asing, -ased** *or* **-assing, -assed 4** cause to have a bias **biased** *or* **biassed** *adj*

bib *n* **1** piece of cloth or plastic worn under a child's chin to protect his or her clothes when eating **2** upper front part of dungarees etc.

Bible *n* **1** sacred writings of the Christian and Jewish religions **2 bible** book regarded as authoritative **biblical** *adj*

bibliography *n, pl* **-phies 1** list of books on a subject **2** list of sources used in a book etc. **bibliographer** *n*

bibliophile *n* person who collects or is fond of books

bibulous *adj* addicted to alcohol

bicarbonate *n* salt of carbonic acid **bicarbonate of soda** powder used in baking or as medicine

bicentenary *n, pl* **-naries** 200th anniversary

biceps *n* large muscle in the upper arm

bicker *v* argue over petty matters

bicultural *adj* having or relating to two cultures, esp. English and French **biculturalism** *n*

bicycle *n* vehicle with two wheels, one behind the other, pedalled by the rider

bid *v* **bidding, bade, bidden 1** offer (a sum of money) in an attempt to buy something **2** *past* **bid** say (a greeting etc.) **3** command ▷ *n* **4** offer of a sum of money **5** attempt **bidder** *n* **biddable** *adj* obedient **bidding** *n* command

bide *v* **bide one's time** wait patiently for an opportunity

bidet [**bee**-day] *n* low basin for washing the genital area

biennial *adj* **1** occurring every two years ▷ *n* **2** plant that completes its life cycle in two years

bier *n* stand on which a coffin rests before burial

bifocals *pl n* pair of spectacles with each lens in two parts, the upper for distance and the lower for reading

big *adj* **bigger, biggest 1** of considerable size, height, number, or capacity **2** important through having wealth etc. **3** elder **4** generous, magnanimous **5** (of wine) full-bodied, with a strong aroma and flavour ▷ *adv* **6** on a grand scale **Bigfoot** *n* legendary hairy, human-like monster in Pacific NW of N America **big league 1** highest league in a professional sport, esp. baseball **2** highest class in any sphere of activity **big shot** *or* **bigwig** *n informal* important person

bigamy *n* crime of marrying a person while still legally married to someone else **bigamist** *n* **bigamous** *adj*

bigot *n* person who is intolerant, esp. regarding religion or race **bigoted** *adj* **bigotry** *n*

bijou [**bee**-zhoo] *adj* small but tasteful

bike *n informal* bicycle or motorcycle

bikini *n* woman's brief two-piece swimming costume

bilateral *adj* affecting or undertaken by two parties

bile *n* bitter yellow fluid secreted by the liver **bilious** *adj* sick, nauseous

bilge *n* **1** *informal* nonsense **2** ship's bottom, where dirty water collects

bilingual *adj* speaking, or written in, two languages **bilingualism** *adj*

bill¹ *n* **1** statement of money

owed for goods or services supplied **2** draft of a proposed new law **3** piece of paper money **4** poster **5** list of events, such as a theatre programme ▷ v **6** send or present a bill to **7** advertise by posters **billable** adj referring to time worked, esp. by a lawyer, for which a client will be expected to pay

bill² n bird's beak

billabong n Aust stagnant pool in an intermittent stream

billboard n large outdoor board for displaying advertisements

billet v -**leting**, -**leted 1** assign a lodging to (a soldier) ▷ n **2** civilian accommodation for a soldier

billet-doux [bill-ay-**doo**] n, pl **billets-doux** love letter

billhook n tool with a hooked blade, used for chopping etc.

billiards n game played on a table with balls and a cue

billion n **1** one thousand million **2** Brit formerly, one million million **billionth** adj

billow n **1** large sea wave ▷ v **2** rise up or swell out

billy, billycan n, pl -**lies**, -**lycans** metal can or pot for cooking on a camp fire

bimbo n slang attractive but empty-headed young person, esp. a woman

bin n container for garbage or for storing grain, coal, etc.

binary [**bine**-a-ree] adj **1** composed of two parts **2** math, computers of or expressed in a counting system with only two digits, o and 1

bind v **binding**, **bound 1** make or become secure with or as if with a rope **2** place (someone) under obligation **3** enclose and fasten (the pages of a book) between covers ▷ n **4** informal annoying situation **binder** n firm cover for holding loose

sheets of paper together

binding n **1** book cover **2** strip of cloth used as edging

bindweed n flowering plant that twines around a support

binge n informal bout of excessive eating or drinking

bingo n gambling game in which numbers are called out and covered by the players on their individual cards

binoculars pl n telescope made for both eyes **binocular** adj involving both eyes

binomial n, adj (mathematical expression) consisting of two terms

bio- combining form life or living organisms: biology

biochemistry n study of the chemistry of living things **biochemist** n

biodegradable adj capable of being decomposed by natural means

biodiesel n diesel oil derived from renewable biological resources

biography n, pl -**phies** account of a person's life by another **biographical** adj **biographer** n

biology n study of living organisms **biological** adj **biologist** n

bionic adj having a part of the body that is operated electronically

biopsy n, pl -**sies** examination of tissue from a living body

bioterrorism n use of viruses, bacteria, etc. by terrorists **bioterrorist** n

biped [**bye**-ped] n animal with two feet

biplane n airplane with two sets of wings

birch n **1** tree with thin peeling bark **2** birch rod or twigs used, esp. formerly, for flogging offenders

bird n **1** creature with feathers

and wings, the female of which lays eggs **2** *slang* young woman

birdie *n golf* score of one stroke under par for a hole

biretta *n* stiff square cap worn by the Catholic clergy

birth *n* **1** childbirth **2** act of being born **3** ancestry **give birth to** *v* bear (offspring) **birth control** any method of contraception **birthday** *n* anniversary of the day of one's birth **birthmark** *n* blemish on the skin formed before birth **birthright** *n* privileges or possessions that someone is entitled to as soon as he or she is born

biscuit *n* **1** small cake of bread made with soda or baking powder **2** *Brit* cookie or thin cracker

bisect *v* divide into two equal parts

bisexual *adj* sexually attracted to both men and women **bisexuality** *n*

bishop *n* **1** member of the clergy who governs a diocese **2** piece at chess **bishopric** *n* diocese or office of a bishop

bismuth *n* pinkish-white metallic element

bison *n, pl* **-son** large hairy animal of the cattle family

bistro *n, pl* **-tros** small restaurant

bit[1] *n* small piece, portion, or quantity **a bit** rather, somewhat **bit by bit** gradually

bit[2] *n* **1** metal mouthpiece on a bridle **2** cutting or drilling part of a tool

bit[3] *v* past tense of **bite**

bit[4] *n* smallest unit of information held in a computer's memory, either o or 1

bitch *n* **1** female dog, fox, or wolf **2** *offensive* spiteful

woman ▷ *v* **3** *informal* complain or grumble **bitchy** *adj* **bitchiness** *n*

bite *v* **biting, bit, bitten** **1** cut off, puncture, or tear as with the teeth or fangs **2** take firm hold of or act effectively upon ▷ *n* **3** act of biting **4** wound or sting inflicted by biting **5** snack **biter** *n* **biting** *adj* **1** piercing or keen **2** sarcastic

bitter *adj* **1** having a sharp unpleasant taste **2** showing or caused by hostility or resentment **3** extremely cold ▷ *n* **4** beer with a slightly bitter taste **bitters** **5** bitter-tasting alcoholic drink. **bitterly** *adv* **bitterness** *n*

bittern *n* wading bird like a heron

bivalve *n* marine mollusc with a double shell

bivouac *n* **1** temporary camp in the open air ▷ *v* **-acking, -acked** **2** camp in a bivouac

bizarre *adj* odd or unusual

blab *v* **blabbing, blabbed** **1** reveal (secrets) indiscreetly **2** chatter thoughtlessly

black *adj* **1** of the darkest colour, like jet or coal **2** Black dark-skinned **3** without hope **4** angry or resentful: *black looks* **5** unpleasant in a macabre manner: *black comedy* ▷ *n* **6** darkest colour **7** Black member of a dark-skinned race, esp. of African origin **8** complete darkness ▷ *v* **9** make black **blackness** *n* **blacken** *v* **1** make or become black **2** defame or slander **blackball** *v* exclude from a group **blackbird** *n* common American or European thrush **blackboard** *n* hard black surface used for writing on with chalk **blackhead** *n* small black spot on the skin **blacklist** *n* list of people or organizations considered untrustworthy etc. **black magic** magic used for evil purposes **blackmail** *n* **1** act of attempting to extort money by threats ▷ *v* **2** (attempt to) obtain money by blackmail **black market** illegal trade in goods or currencies **black out** *v* **1** extinguish (lights) **2** lose consciousness or memory temporarily **blackout** *n* **1** extinguishing of all light as a precaution against an air attack **2** momentary loss of consciousness or memory **black sheep** person who is regarded as a disgrace by his or her family **blacksmith** *n* person who works iron with a furnace, anvil, etc.

BlackBerry *n* ® hand-held wireless device incorporating e-mail, browser, and mobile-phone functions

bladder *n* **1** sac in the body where urine is held **2** hollow bag which may be filled with air or liquid

blade *n* **1** cutting edge of a weapon or tool **2** thin flattish part of a propeller, oar, etc. **3** leaf of grass

blame *v* **1** consider (someone) responsible for ▷ *n* **2** responsibility for something that is wrong **blameless** *adj* **blameworthy** *adj* deserving blame

blanch *v* **1** become pale **2** prepare (vegetables etc.) by plunging them in boiling water

blancmange [blam-**monzh**] *n* jelly-like dessert made with milk

bland *adj* dull and uninteresting **blandly** *adv*

blandishments *pl n* persuasive flattery

blank *adj* **1** not written on **2** showing no interest, feeling, or understanding ▷ *n* **3** empty space **4** cartridge containing no bullet **blankly** *adv* **blank verse** unrhymed verse

blanket *n* **1** thick covering for a bed **2** concealing cover, as of snow ▷ *v* **3** cover as with a blanket

blare *v* **1** sound loudly and harshly ▷ *n* **2** loud harsh noise

blarney *n* flattering talk

blasé [**blah**-zay] *adj* indifferent or bored through familiarity

blaspheme *v* speak disrespectfully of (God or sacred things) **blasphemy** *n* **blasphemous** *adj* **blasphemer** *n*

blast *n* **1** explosion **2** sudden strong gust of air or wind **3** sudden loud sound, as of a trumpet ▷ *v* **5** blow up (a rock etc.) with explosives **blastoff** *n* launching of a rocket

blatant [**blay**-tant] *adj* glaringly obvious **blatantly** *adv*

blaze[1] *n* **1** strong fire or flame **2** very bright light ▷ *v* **3** burn or shine brightly

blaze[2] *n* mark made on a tree to indicate a route

blazer *n* lightweight jacket, esp. in the colours of a school etc.

blazon *v* proclaim publicly

bleach *v* **1** make or become white or colourless ▷ *n* **2** bleaching agent

bleak *adj* **1** exposed and barren **2** offering little hope

bleary *adj* -**rier**, -**riest** with eyes dimmed, as by tears or tiredness **blearily** *adv*

bleat *v, n* (utter) the plaintive cry of a sheep, goat, or calf

bleed *v* **bleeding, bled 1** lose blood **2** draw blood from (a person or animal) **3** *informal* obtain money by extortion

bleep *n* **1** short high-pitched

sound made by an electrical device ▷ v **2** make a bleeping sound

blemish n **1** defect or stain ▷ v **2** spoil or tarnish

blench v shy away, as in fear

blend v **1** mix or mingle (components) **2** look good together ▷ n **3** mixture **blender** n kitchen appliance for mixing food or liquid at high speed

bless v **1** make holy by means of a religious rite **2** call upon God to protect **3** endow with health, talent, etc. **blessed** adj holy **blessing** n **1** prayer for God's favour **2** happy event

blew v past tense of **blow²**

blight n **1** withering plant disease **2** person or thing that spoils or prevents growth ▷ v **3** frustrate or disappoint **blighter** n informal irritating person

blimp n small airship

blind adj **1** unable to see **2** unable or unwilling to understand **3** not determined by reason: blind hatred ▷ v **4** deprive of sight **5** deprive of good sense, reason, or judgment ▷ n **6** covering for a window **7** something that serves to conceal the truth **blinders** pl n leather flaps on a horse's bridle to prevent sideways vision **blindly** adv **blindness** n **blindfold** v **1** prevent (a person) from seeing by covering the eyes ▷ n **2** piece of cloth used to cover the eyes **blind trust** arrangement in which a public official's personal wealth is managed by another person

blink v **1** close and immediately reopen (the eyes) **2** shine intermittently ▷ n **3** act of blinking **on the blink** slang not working properly

blip n small light which flashes on and off regularly on equipment such as a radar screen

bliss n perfect happiness **blissful** adj **blissfully** adv

blister n **1** small bubble on the skin **2** swelling, as on a painted surface ▷ v **3** (cause to) have blisters **blistering** adj **1** (of weather) very hot **2** (of criticism) extremely harsh

blithe adj casual and indifferent **blithely** adv

blitz n **1** violent and sustained attack by aircraft **2** football defensive charge on the quarterback **3** intensive attack or concerted effort ▷ v **4** attack suddenly and intensively

blizzard n blinding storm of wind and snow

bloated adj swollen up with liquid or gas

bloater n salted smoked herring

blob n **1** soft mass or drop **2** indistinct or shapeless form

bloc n people or countries combined by a common interest

block n **1** large solid piece of wood, stone, etc. **2** large building of offices, apartments, etc. **3** group of buildings enclosed by intersecting streets **4** obstruction or hindrance **5** slang person's head ▷ v **6** obstruct or impede by introducing an obstacle **blockage** n **blockhead** n stupid person **block heater** electrical device for keeping engine of motor vehicle warm **block letter** plain capital letter

blockade n **1** action that prevents goods from reaching a place ▷ v **2** impose a blockade on

Bloc Québécois n Canad
federal party advocating
autonomy for Quebec
blog n 1 short for **weblog** ▷ v
blogging, blogged 2 write
such a blog **blogger** n
bloke n informal man
blonde, blond adj, n fair-
haired (person)
blood n 1 red fluid that flows
around the body 2 race or
ancestry **in cold blood** done
deliberately **bloodless** adj
bloody adj 1 covered with
blood 2 marked by much
killing ▷ adj, adv 3 slang
extreme or extremely ▷ v
4 stain with blood **bloody-
minded** adj deliberately
unhelpful **blood bath**
massacre **bloodhound** n
large dog used for tracking
bloodshed n slaughter or
killing **bloodshot** adj (of
eyes) inflamed **blood sport**
sport involving the killing
of animals **bloodstream** n
flow of blood round the body
bloodsucker n 1 animal that
sucks blood 2 informal person
who extorts money from
other people **bloodthirsty** adj
taking pleasure in violence ·
bloom n 1 blossom on a
flowering plant 2 youthful
or healthy glow ▷ v 3 bear
flowers 4 be in a healthy
glowing condition
bloop v baseball 1 hit the ball
just beyond the infield ▷ n
2 (as modifier): a bloop single
blooper n 1 informal blunder or
stupid mistake 2 baseball ball
hit just beyond the infield
blossom n 1 flowers of a plant
▷ v 2 (of plants) flower 3 come
to a promising stage
blot n 1 spot or stain
2 something that spoils or
stains ▷ v **blotting, blotted**
3 cause a blemish in or on
4 soak up (ink) by using

blotting paper **blotter** n
blot out v darken or hide
completely **blotting paper**
soft absorbent paper for
soaking up ink
blotch n discoloured area or
stain **blotchy** adj
blotto adj slang extremely
drunk
blouse n woman's shirtlike
garment
blow[1] v **blowing, blew,
blown** 1 (of air, the wind, etc.)
move 2 move or be carried
as if by the wind 3 expel (air
etc.) through the mouth
or nose 4 cause (a musical
instrument) to sound by
forcing air into it 5 burn out
(a fuse etc.) 6 slang spend
(money) freely **blower** n
blowy adj windy **blow-dry**
v style (the hair) with a
hand-held dryer **blowout** n
1 sudden loss of air in a tire
2 escape of oil or gas from
a well 3 slang filling meal
blow up v 1 explode 2 fill
with air 3 informal enlarge (a
photograph) 4 informal lose
one's temper
blow[2] n 1 hard hit 2 sudden
setback 3 attacking action
blown v past participle of
blow[2]
blowzy, blowsy adj fat,
untidy, and red-faced
blubber v 1 sob without
restraint ▷ n 2 fat of whales,
seals, etc.
bludgeon n 1 short thick club
▷ v 2 hit with a bludgeon
3 force or bully
blue n 1 colour of a clear
unclouded sky 2 short for
blue line blues 3 feeling
of depression 4 sad slow
music like jazz ▷ adj **bluer,
bluest** 5 of the colour blue
6 depressed 7 pornographic
out of the blue unexpectedly
bluish adj **bluebell** n flower

with blue bell-shaped flowers
bluebottle n large fly with
a dark-blue body **blue-
collar** adj denoting manual
industrial workers **blue jay**
N American bird with bright
blue feathers **blue line** ice
hockey line drawn midway
between the centre of the rink
and each goal **blueprint** n
1 photographic print of a plan
2 description of how a plan is
expected to work **blue-sky**
v theorize about something
that may not lead to any
practical application

bluff¹ v 1 pretend to be
confident in order to
influence (someone) ▷ n 2 act
of bluffing

bluff² n 1 steep cliff or bank
▷ adj 2 good-naturedly frank
and hearty

blunder n 1 clumsy mistake
▷ v 2 make a blunder 3 act
clumsily

blunderbuss n obsolete gun
with a wide muzzle

blunt adj 1 lacking sharpness
2 (of people, speech,
etc.) straightforward or
uncomplicated ▷ v 3 make
less sharp **bluntly** adv

blur v blurring, blurred
1 make or become vague or
less distinct ▷ n 2 something
vague, hazy, or indistinct
blurry adj

blurb n promotional
description, as on the jacket
of a book

blurt v (foll. by out) utter
suddenly and involuntarily

blush v 1 become red
in the face, esp. from
embarrassment or shame ▷ n
2 reddening of the face

bluster v 1 speak loudly or in
a bullying way ▷ n 2 empty
threats or protests **blustery**
adj (of weather) rough and
windy

BO informal body odour

boa constrictor n large snake
that kills its prey by crushing

boar n 1 uncastrated male pig
2 wild pig

board n 1 long flat piece of
wood 2 smaller flat piece of
rigid material for a specific
purpose: ironing board 3 group
of people who administer a
company, trust, etc. 4 meals
provided for money **boards**
5 wooden barrier around
the surface of an ice hockey
rink ▷ v 6 go aboard (a train,
airplane, etc.) 7 cover with
boards 8 receive meals and
lodgings in return for money
on board on or in a ship,
airplane, etc. **boarder** n pupil
who lives at school during
the school term **boarding**
n ice hockey illegal bodycheck
of a player into the boards
boarding house private
house that provides meals
and accommodation for
paying guests **boardroom**
n room where the board of a
company meets

boast v 1 speak too proudly
about one's talents etc.
2 possess (something to be
proud of) ▷ n 3 boasting
statement **boastful** adj

boat n small vehicle for
travelling across water
boater n flat straw hat
boating n **boatswain**,
bo's'n, or **bosun** [boh-sn] n
ship's officer in charge of the
equipment

bob¹ v bobbing, bobbed
1 move up and down
repeatedly ▷ n 2 short abrupt
movement

bob² n 1 hair style in which the
hair is cut level with the chin
▷ v bobbing, bobbed 2 cut
(the hair) in a bob

bobbin n reel on which thread
is wound

bobble n small ball of material, usu. for decoration

bobby n, pl **-bies** informal policeman

bobsleigh n **1** sledge used for racing ▷ v **2** ride on a bobsleigh

bode v be an omen of (good or ill)

bodice n upper part of a dress

bodkin n blunt large-eyed needle

body n, pl **bodies 1** entire physical structure of an animal or human **2** trunk or torso **3** corpse **4** group regarded as a single entity **5** main part of anything **6** woman's one-piece undergarment **bodily** adj **1** relating to the body ▷ adv **2** by taking hold of the body **bodycheck** sports ▷ n **1** use of the body to block an opposing player ▷ v **2** make a bodycheck **bodyguard** n person or group of people employed to protect someone **body mass index** measure used to gauge whether a person is overweight: a person's weight in kilograms divided by the square of his or her height in metres **bodywork** n outer shell of a motor vehicle

Boer n descendant of the Dutch settlers in S Africa

bog n **1** wet spongy ground **2** slang toilet **boggy** adj **bog down** v **bogging, bogged** impede physically or mentally

bogan n sluggish side stream

bogey n **1** something that worries or annoys **2** golf score of one stroke over par on a hole

boggle v be surprised, confused, or alarmed

bogus [boh-guss] adj not genuine

bogy n, pl **-gies** same as **bogey**

bohemian n, adj (person) leading an unconventional life

boil[1] v **1** (cause to) change from a liquid to a vapour so quickly that bubbles are formed **2** cook by the process of boiling ▷ n **3** state or action of boiling **boiler** n piece of equipment which provides hot water **boilerplate** v incorporate standard material in a text automatically

boil[2] n red pus-filled swelling on the skin

boisterous adj noisy and lively **boisterously** adv

bold adj **1** confident and fearless **2** immodest or impudent **boldly** adv **boldness** n

bole n tree trunk

bolero n, pl **-ros 1** short open jacket **2** traditional Spanish dance

bollard n short thick post used to prevent the passage of motor vehicles

boloney n same as **baloney**

Bolshevik n Russian Communist **bolshie** or **bolshy** adj informal difficult or rebellious

bolster v **1** support or strengthen ▷ n **2** long narrow pillow

bolt n **1** sliding metal bar for fastening a door etc. **2** metal pin which screws into a nut **3** flash (of lightning) ▷ v **4** fasten with a bolt **5** eat hurriedly **6** run away suddenly **bolt upright** stiff and rigid **bolt hole** place of escape

bomb n **1** container fitted with explosive material ▷ v **2** attack with bombs **3** move very quickly **the bomb** nuclear bomb **bomber** n **1** aircraft that drops bombs **2** person who throws or puts a bomb in a particular

bombard v 1 attack with heavy gunfire or bombs 2 attack verbally, esp. with questions **bombardment** n **bombshell** n shocking or unwelcome surprise

bombastic adj using pompous language

bona fide [bone-a **fide**-ee] adj real or genuine

bonanza n sudden good luck or wealth

bond n 1 something that binds or fastens 2 feeling of friendship etc. that unites two people or a group of people 3 (often pl) something that restrains or imprisons 4 written or spoken agreement 5 finance certificate of debt issued to raise funds ▷ v 6 bind **bonded** adj

bondage n slavery

bone n 1 any of the hard parts in the body that form the skeleton ▷ v 2 remove the bones from (meat for cooking etc.) **boneless** adj **bony** adj 1 having many bones 2 thin or emaciated **bone-dry** adj completely dry **bone-idle** adj extremely lazy

bonfire n large outdoor fire

bongo n, pl -gos, -goes small drum played with the fingers

bonhomie [bon-om-ee] n happy friendliness

bonk v informal 1 have sex with 2 hit **bonking** n

bonnet n Brit 1 hood of automobile 2 hat which ties under the chin

bonny adj -nier, -niest Scot beautiful

bonsai n, pl -sai ornamental miniature tree or shrub

bonspiel n curling match

bonus n something given, paid, or received above what is due or expected

boo interj 1 shout of disapproval ▷ v **booing,**

booed 2 shout 'boo' to show disapproval

boob n slang 1 foolish mistake 2 female breast

booby n, pl -bies foolish person **booby prize** prize given for the lowest score in a competition **booby trap** 1 hidden bomb primed to be set off by an unsuspecting victim 2 trap for an unsuspecting person, intended as a joke

boogie v informal dance quickly to pop music

book n 1 number of printed pages bound together between covers 2 written work 3 number of tickets, stamps, etc. fastened together **books** 4 record of transactions of a business or society ▷ v 5 reserve (a place, passage, etc.) in advance 6 record the name of (a person) in a book or on a list **bookie** n informal short for **bookmaker** ▸ **booklet** n thin book with paper covers **book-keeping** n systematic recording of business transactions **bookmaker** n person whose occupation is taking bets **bookworm** n person devoted to reading

bookmark v computers store (a website) so that one can return to it easily

boom[1] v 1 make a loud deep echoing sound 2 prosper vigorously and rapidly ▷ n 3 loud deep echoing sound 4 rapid increase 5 period of high economic growth

boom[2] n 1 pole to which the foot of a sail is attached 2 pole carrying an overhead microphone 3 barrier across a waterway

boomerang n 1 curved wooden missile which returns to the thrower ▷ v 2 (of a plan) recoil unexpectedly

boon n something helpful or beneficial

boondoggle n informal unnecessary work

boor n rude or insensitive person **boorish** adj

boost n 1 encouragement or help 2 increase ▷ v 3 improve 4 increase **booster** n small additional injection of a vaccine

boot[1] n 1 shoe that covers the whole foot and the lower part of the leg 2 Brit trunk of automobile 3 informal kick ▷ v 4 informal kick 5 start up (a computer) **bootee** n baby's soft shoe

boot[2] n **to boot** in addition

booth n 1 small partly enclosed cubicle 2 stall where goods are sold

bootleg v -**legging**, -**legged** 1 make, carry, or sell (illicit goods) ▷ adj 2 produced, distributed, or sold illicitly **bootlegger** n

booty n, pl -**ties** valuable articles obtained as plunder

booze v, n informal (consume) alcoholic drink **boozy** adj **boozer** n informal 1 person who is fond of drinking 2 pub **booze-up** n informal drinking spree

bop v **bopping, bopped** informal dance to pop music

borax n white mineral used in making glass

border n 1 dividing line between regions 2 band around or along the edge of something ▷ v 3 provide with a border 4 be nearly the same as: his stupidity borders on madness

bore[1] v 1 make (a hole) with a drill etc. ▷ n 2 (diameter of) the hollow of a gun barrel

bore[2] v 1 make weary by being dull or repetitious ▷ n 2 dull

or repetitious person or thing **boredom** n

bore[3] n tidal wave in a narrow estuary

bore[4] v past tense of **bear**[1]

boreal adj northern

born v 1 a past participle of **bear**[1] ▷ adj 2 possessing certain qualities from birth: a born musician

borne v a past participle of **bear**[1]

boron n chemical element used in hardening steel

borough n town or district with its own council

borrow v 1 obtain (something) temporarily 2 adopt (ideas etc.) from another source **borrower** n

borstal n prison for young criminals

borzoi n tall dog with a long silky coat

bosh n informal empty talk, nonsense

Bosnian n, adj (person) from Bosnia

bosom n 1 chest of a person, esp. the female breasts ▷ adj 2 very dear: a bosom friend

boss[1] n person in charge of or employing others ▷ v **boss around** or **about** be domineering towards **bossy** adj

boss[2] n raised knob or stud

botany n study of plants **botanical** or **botanic** adj **botanist** n

botch v 1 spoil through clumsiness ▷ n 2 Also **botch-up** badly done piece of work

both adj, pron two considered together

bother v 1 take the time or trouble 1 give annoyance or trouble to 2 pester ▷ n 4 trouble, fuss, or difficulty **bothersome** adj

bottle n 1 container for holding liquids ▷ v 2 put in a

bottle **bottleneck** n narrow stretch of road where traffic is held up **bottle up** v restrain (powerful emotion)

bottom n 1 lowest, deepest, or farthest removed part of a thing 2 buttocks ▷ adj 3 lowest or last **bottomless** adj

botulism n severe food poisoning

boudoir [boo-dwahr] n woman's bedroom or private sitting room

bougainvillea n climbing plant with red or purple flowers

bough n large branch of a tree

bought v past of **buy**

boulder n large rounded rock

boulevard n 1 wide street 2 grass strip between sidewalk and road

bounce v 1 (of a ball etc.) rebound from an impact 2 slang (of a cheque) be returned uncashed owing to a lack of funds in the account ▷ n 3 act of rebounding 4 springiness 5 informal vitality or vigour **bouncer** n person employed at a disco etc. to remove unwanted people **bouncing** adj vigorous and robust

bound[1] v 1 past of **bind** ▷ adj 2 destined or certain 3 compelled or obliged

bound[2] v 1 move forwards by jumps ▷ n 2 jump upwards or forwards

bound[3] v 1 form a boundary of ▷ pl n 2 limit: his ignorance knows no bounds **boundary** n dividing line that indicates the farthest limit

bound[4] adj going or intending to go towards: homeward bound

bounty n, pl -ties 1 generosity 2 generous gift or reward **bountiful** or **bounteous** adj

bouquet n 1 bunch of flowers 2 aroma of wine

bourbon [bur-bn] n whiskey made from corn

bourgeois [boor-zhwah] adj, n offensive middle-class (person)

bout n 1 period of activity or illness 2 boxing or wrestling match

boutique n small clothes shop

bovine adj 1 relating to cattle 2 rather slow and stupid

bow[1] v 1 lower (one's head) or bend (one's knee or body) as a sign of respect or shame 2 comply or accept ▷ n 3 movement made when bowing

bow[2] n 1 knot with two loops and loose ends 2 long stick stretched with horsehair for playing stringed instruments 3 weapon for shooting arrows **bow-legged** adj bandy

bow[3] n front end of a ship

bowdlerize v remove words regarded as indecent from (a play etc.) **bowdlerization** n

bowel n 1 intestine, esp. the large intestine **bowels** 2 innermost part

bower n shady leafy shelter

bowl[1] n 1 round container with an open top 2 hollow part of an object

bowl[2] n 1 large heavy ball **bowls** 2 game played on smooth grass with wooden bowls ▷ v 3 cricket send (a ball) towards the batsman **bowler** n **bowling** n game in which bowls are rolled at a group of pins

bowler n stiff felt hat with a rounded crown

box[1] n 1 container with a flat base and sides 2 separate compartment in a theatre, stable, etc. 3 informal television ▷ v 4 put into a box **box office** place where theatre or cinema tickets are sold

box[2] v fight (an opponent) in a boxing match **boxer** n 1 man

box | 66

who participates in the sport of boxing **2** medium-sized dog similar to a bulldog **boxing** n sport of fighting with the fists **boxer shorts** or **boxers** men's underpants shaped like shorts but with a front opening

box³ n evergreen tree with shiny leaves

boy n male child **boyish** adj **boyhood** n **boyfriend** n woman's male companion

boycott v **1** refuse to deal with or engage in ▷ n **2** instance of boycotting

BQ Bloc Québécois

Br chem bromine

bra n woman's undergarment for supporting the breasts

brace n **1** object fastened to something to straighten or support it **2** appliance of metal bands and wires for correcting uneven teeth **3** pair, esp. of game birds **braces 4** Brit suspenders ▷ v **5** steady or prepare (oneself) for something unpleasant **6** strengthen or fit with a brace **bracing** adj refreshing and invigorating

bracelet n ornamental chain for the wrist

bracken n large fern

bracket n **1** pair of characters used to enclose a section of writing **2** group falling within certain defined limits **3** support fixed to a wall ▷ v -eting, -eted **4** put in brackets **5** class together

brackish adj (of water) slightly salty

bract n leaf at the base of a flower

brag v **bragging, bragged** speak arrogantly and boastfully **braggart** n

Brahman, Brahmin n member of the highest Hindu caste

braid v **1** interweave (hair, thread, etc.) ▷ n **2** length of hair, etc. that has been braided **3** narrow ornamental tape of woven silk etc.

Braille n system of writing for the blind, consisting of raised dots interpreted by touch

brain n **1** soft mass of nervous tissue in the head **2** intellectual ability ▷ v **3** hit (someone) hard on the head **brainless** adj stupid **brainy** adj informal clever **brainchild** n idea produced by creative thought **brainwash** v force (a person) to change his or her beliefs, esp. by methods based on isolation, pain, sleeplessness, etc. **brainwave** n sudden idea

braise v stew slowly in a covered pan

brake n **1** device for slowing or stopping a vehicle ▷ v **2** slow down or stop by using a brake

bramble n prickly shrub that produces blackberries

bran n husks of cereal grain

branch n **1** secondary stem of a tree **2** offshoot or subsidiary part of something larger or more complex ▷ v **3** (of stems, roots, etc.) grow and diverge (from another part) **branch out** v expand one's interests

brand n **1** particular product **2** particular kind or variety **3** identifying mark burnt onto the skin of an animal ▷ v **4** mark with a brand **5** denounce or stigmatize **brand-new** adj absolutely new

brandish v wave (a weapon etc.) in a threatening way

brandy n, pl -dies alcoholic spirit distilled from wine

brash adj self-confident and aggressive **brashness** n

brass n **1** alloy of copper and zinc **2** group of wind instruments made of brass

brassy adj **1** like brass, esp. in colour **2** insolent or brazen

brasserie n **1** restaurant specializing in food and beer **2** (in Quebec) pub

brassiere n bra

brat n unruly child

bravado n showy display of self-confidence

brave adj **1** having or showing courage, resolution, and daring ▷ n **2** North American Indian warrior ▷ v **3** confront with resolution or courage **bravery** n

bravo interj well done!

brawl n **1** rough fight ▷ v **2** fight noisily

brawn n **1** physical strength **2** pressed meat from the head of a pig or calf **brawny** adj

bray v **1** (of a donkey) utter its loud harsh sound ▷ n **2** donkey's loud harsh sound

brazen adj **1** shameless and bold **brazenly** adv

brazier [bray-zee-er] n container for burning charcoal or coal

breach n **1** breaking or violation of a promise etc. **2** gap or break ▷ v **3** break (a promise etc.) **4** make a gap in

bread n **1** food made of baked flour and water **2** slang money **breadwinner** n person whose earnings support a family

breadth n extent of something from side to side

break v **breaking, broke, broken 1** separate or become separated into two or more pieces **2** damage or become damaged so as to be inoperative **3** fail to observe (an agreement etc.) **4** disclose or be disclosed: he broke the news **5** bring or come to an end: the good weather broke at last **6** weaken or be weakened, as in spirit **7** cut through or penetrate **8** improve on or surpass: break a record **9** (of the male voice) become permanently deeper at puberty ▷ n **10** act or result of breaking **11** gap or interruption in continuity **12** informal fortunate opportunity **breakable** adj **breakage** n **breaker** n large wave **break camp** v leave one's camping place **break down** v **1** cease to function **2** yield to strong emotion **4** analyse **breakdown** n **1** act or instance of breaking down **2** nervous breakdown **3** analysis **break even** v make neither a profit nor a loss **break-in** n illegal entering of a building, esp. by thieves **breakneck** adj fast and dangerous **break off** v **1** sever or detach **2** end (a relationship etc.) **break out** v begin or arise suddenly **breakthrough** n important development or discovery **break trail** v force a path through snow or bush **break-up** n thawing of ice in lakes and rivers in springtime **break up** v **1** (cause to) separate **2** (of a relationship) come to an end **3** (of a school) close for the holidays **breakwater** n wall that extends into the sea to protect a harbour or beach from the force of waves

breakfast v, n (eat) the first meal of the day

breast n **1** either of the two soft fleshy milk-secreting glands on a woman's chest **2** chest ▷ v **3** meet at breast level: she breasted the finishing line **breaststroke** n swimming stroke performed on the front

breath n **1** taking in and letting out of air during breathing **2** air taken in and

b

let out during breathing
breathless *adj* **breathtaking**
adj causing awe or excitement
breathe *v* **1** take in oxygen
and give out carbon dioxide
2 whisper **breather** *n informal*
short rest **breathing** *n*
Breathalyzer *n* ® device
for estimating the amount
of alcohol in the breath
breathalyze *v*
bred *v* past of **breed**
breech *n* **1** buttocks **2** part of
a firearm behind the barrel
breech delivery birth of baby
with the feet or buttocks
appearing first
breeches *pl n* trousers
extending to just below the
knee
breed *v* **breeding**, **bred**
1 produce new or improved
strains of (domestic animals
or plants) **2** bear (offspring)
3 produce or be produced: *breed
trouble* ▷ *n* **4** group of animals
etc. within a species **5** kind or
sort **breeder** *n* **breeding** *n*
result of good upbringing or
training
breeze *n* **1** gentle wind ▷ *v*
2 move quickly or casually
breezy *adj* **1** windy **2** casual or
carefree
brethren *pl n old-fashioned*
(used in religious contexts)
brothers
Breton *adj* **1** of Brittany ▷ *n*
2 person from Brittany
3 language of Brittany
breviary *n, pl* **-aries** book of
prayers to be recited daily by a
Roman Catholic priest
brevity *n* shortness
brew *v* **1** make (beer, ale,
etc.) by steeping, boiling,
and fermentation **2** prepare
(a drink) by infusing **3** be
impending or forming ▷ *n*
4 beverage produced by
brewing **brewer** *n* **brewery**
n **1** company that brews beer

etc. **2** place where beer etc. is
brewed
briar *n* wild rose with long
thorny stems
bribe *n* **1** anything offered
or given to someone to gain
favour, influence, etc. ▷ *v*
2 give (someone) a bribe
bribery *n*
bric-a-brac *n* miscellaneous
small ornamental objects
brick *n* **1** (rectangular block of)
baked clay used in building
▷ *v* **2** build, enclose, or fill
with bricks **bricklayer** *n*
person who builds with bricks
bride *n* woman who has just
been or is about to be married
bridal *adj* **bridegroom** *n* man
who has just been or is about
to be married **bridesmaid** *n*
girl who attends a bride at her
wedding
bridge[1] *n* **1** structure for
crossing a river etc. **2** platform
from which a ship is steered
or controlled **3** upper part of
the nose **4** dental plate with
artificial teeth that is secured
to natural teeth **5** piece of
wood supporting the strings
of a violin etc. ▷ *v* **6** build
a bridge over (something)
bridgehead *n* fortified
position at the end of a bridge
nearest the enemy
bridge[2] *n* card game based on
whist
bridle *n* **1** headgear for
controlling a horse ▷ *v*
2 show anger or indignation
3 restrain **bridle path** path
suitable for riding or leading
horses
brief *adj* **1** short in duration
▷ *n* **2** condensed statement
or written synopsis **3** set of
instructions **briefs 4** men's
or women's underpants
▷ *v* **5** give information and
instructions to (a person)
briefly *adv* **briefcase** *n* small

flat case for carrying papers, books, etc.

brier n same as **briar**

brig n two-masted square-rigged ship

brigade n 1 army unit smaller than a division 2 group of people organized for a certain task **brigadier** n high-ranking army officer

brigand n bandit

brigantine n two-masted sailing ship

bright adj 1 emitting or reflecting much light 2 (of colours) intense 3 clever **brightly** adv **brightness** n **brighten** v

brilliant adj 1 shining with light 2 splendid 3 extremely clever **brilliance** or **brilliancy** n

brim n 1 projecting edge of a hat 2 upper rim of a cup etc. ▷ v **brimming, brimmed** 3 be full to the brim

brimstone n obsolete sulfur

brindled adj brown streaked with another colour

brine n salt water **briny** adj very salty **the briny** informal the sea

bring v **bringing, brought** 1 carry, convey, or take to a designated place or person 2 cause to happen 3 law put forward (charges) officially **bring about** v cause to happen **bring down** v present (a budget) in a legislature **bring off** v succeed in achieving **bring out** v 1 publish or have (a book) published 2 reveal or cause to be seen **bring up** v 1 rear (a child) 2 mention 3 vomit (food)

brink n edge of a steep place

brisk adj lively and quick **briskly** adv

brisket n beef from the breast of a cow

bristle n 1 short stiff hair ▷ v 2 (cause to) stand up like bristles 3 show anger **bristly** adj

Brit n informal British person

British adj 1 of Great Britain or the British Commonwealth ▷ pl n 2 people of Great Britain

Briton n native or inhabitant of Britain

brittle adj hard but easily broken **brittleness** n

broach v 1 introduce (a topic) for discussion 2 open (a bottle or barrel)

broad adj 1 having great breadth or width 2 not detailed 3 extensive: broad support 4 vulgar or coarse 5 strongly marked: a broad Yorkshire accent **broadly** adv **broaden** v **broadband** n telecommunication transmission technique using a wide range of frequencies

broadleaf n evergreen tree with large glossy leaves

broad-minded adj tolerant

broadside n 1 strong verbal or written attack 2 naval firing of all the guns on one side of a ship at once

broadcast n 1 programme or announcement on radio or television ▷ v 2 transmit (a programme or announcement) on radio or television 3 make widely known **broadcaster** n **broadcasting** n

brocade n rich woven fabric with a raised design

broccoli n type of cabbage with greenish flower heads

brochure n booklet that contains information about a product or service

brogue¹ n sturdy walking shoe

brogue² n strong accent, esp. Irish

broil v grill

broke v 1 past tense of **break**

▷ adj **2** informal having no money

broken v **1** past participle of **break** ▷ adj **2** fractured or smashed **3** (of the speech of a foreigner) imperfectly spoken: broken English **brokenhearted** adj overwhelmed by grief

broker n agent who buys or sells shares, securities, etc.

brolly n, pl -**lies** informal umbrella

bromance n informal close, non-sexual friendship between two men

bromide n chemical compound used in medicine and photography

bromine n toxic liquid element

bronchus [bronk-uss] n, pl **bronchi** [bronk-eye] either of the two branches of the windpipe **bronchial** adj **bronchitis** n inflammation of the bronchi

bronco n, pl -**cos** wild or partially tamed pony

brontosaurus n very large plant-eating four-footed dinosaur

bronze n **1** alloy of copper and tin **2** statue, medal, etc. made of bronze ▷ adj **3** made of, or coloured like, bronze ▷ v **4** (of the skin) make or become brown

brooch n ornament with a pin for attaching to clothes

brood n **1** number of birds produced at one hatching **2** all the children of a family ▷ v **3** think long and morbidly **broody** adj **1** moody and sullen **2** (of a hen) wishing to hatch eggs

brook[1] n small stream

brook[2] v bear or tolerate

broom n **1** long-handled sweeping brush **2** yellow-flowered shrub **broomball** n hockey game similar to hockey, played with a large ball that the players hit with brooms

broomstick n handle of a broom

broth n soup, usu. containing vegetables

brothel n house where men pay to have sex with prostitutes

brother n **1** boy or man with the same parents as another person **2** member of a male religious order **brotherly** adj **brotherhood** n **1** fellowship **2** association, such as a trade union **brother-in-law** n **1** brother of one's husband or wife **2** husband of one's sibling

brought v past of **bring**

brow n **1** forehead **2** eyebrow **3** top of a hill

browbeat v frighten (someone) with threats

brown n **1** colour of earth or wood ▷ adj **2** of the colour brown ▷ v **3** make or become brown **brownish** adj **browned-off** adj informal bored and depressed

Brownie Guide, Brownie n junior Girl Guide

browse v **1** look through (a book or articles for sale) in a casual manner **2** nibble on young shoots or leaves ▷ n **3** instance of browsing **4** shoots and leaves used as food by wild animals **browser** n computers software package that enables a user to read hypertext, esp. on the internet

bruise n **1** discoloured area on the skin caused by an injury ▷ v **2** cause a bruise on **bruiser** n strong tough person

brunch n informal breakfast and lunch combined

brunette n girl or woman with brown hair

brunt n main force or shock of a blow, attack, etc.

brush[1] n **1** device made of bristles, wires, etc. used for cleaning, painting, etc. **2** brief unpleasant encounter **3** fox's tail ▷ v **4** apply, remove, clean, etc. with a brush **5** touch lightly and briefly **brush off** v *slang* dismiss or ignore (someone) **brush up** v refresh one's knowledge of (a subject)

brush² n thick growth of shrubs

brusque *adj* blunt or curt in manner or speech **brusquely** *adv* **brusqueness** n

Brussels sprout n vegetable like a tiny cabbage

brute n **1** brutal person **2** animal other than man ▷ *adj* **3** wholly instinctive or physical, like that of an animal **4** without reason **brutish** *adj* of or like an animal **brutal** *adj* cruel and vicious **brutally** *adv* **brutality** n **brutalize** v

BSc Bachelor of Science

BSE bovine spongiform encephalopathy

bubble n **1** ball of air in a liquid ▷ v **2** form bubbles **3** move or flow with a gurgling sound **bubbly** *adj* **1** excited and lively **2** full of bubbles **bubble over** v express an emotion freely

bubonic plague [bew-**bonn**-ik] n acute infectious disease characterized by swellings

buccaneer n pirate

buck¹ n **1** male of certain animals, such as the deer and hare ▷ v **2** (of a horse etc.) jump with legs stiff and back arched **buck up** v make or become more cheerful

buck² n *slang* dollar

buck³ n **pass the buck** *informal* shift blame or responsibility onto someone else

bucket n open-topped round container with a handle **bucketful** n **bucket down** v -**eting**, -**eted** rain heavily

buckle n **1** metal clasp for fastening a belt or strap ▷ v **2** fasten or be fastened with

a buckle **3** (cause to) bend out of shape through pressure or heat **buckle down** v apply oneself with determination

buckram n coarse stiffened cloth

buckshee *adj slang* free

buckteeth *pl* n projecting upper front teeth **buck-toothed** *adj*

buckwheat n small black grain used for making flour

bucolic [bew-**koll**-ik] *adj* rustic

bud n **1** swelling on a tree or plant that develops into a leaf or flower ▷ v **budding**, **budded 2** produce buds **3** develop or grow: *a budding actor*

Buddhism n eastern religion founded by Buddha **Buddhist** n, *adj*

buddleia n shrub with purple or yellow flowers

buddy n, *pl* -**dies** *informal* friend

budge v move slightly

budgerigar n small brightly coloured Aust. bird

budget n **1** financial plan for a period of time **2** money allocated for a specific purpose ▷ v -**eting**, -**eted 3** plan the expenditure of (money or time) ▷ *adj* **4** cheap **budgetary** *adj*

budgie n *informal* short for **budgerigar**

buff¹ *adj* **1** dull yellowish-brown ▷ v **2** rub with soft material **in the buff** *informal* naked

buff² n *informal* expert on a given subject

buffalo n **1** type of cattle **2** bison **buffalo jump** (formerly) place where bison were stampeded over a cliff

buffer n something that lessens shock or protects from damaging impact, circumstances, etc.

buffet¹ [buff-ay] *n*
1 refreshment bar **2** meal
at which guests serve
themselves

buffet² [buff-it] *v* **-feting,
-feted** knock against or about

buffoon *n* clown or fool
buffoonery *n*

bug *n* **1** small insect **2** *informal*
minor illness **3** small mistake
in a computer program
4 concealed microphone ▷ *v*
bugging, bugged 5 *informal*
irritate (someone) **6** conceal
a microphone in (a room or
phone) **buggy** *adj informal
computers* containing errors or
faults

bugbear *n* thing that causes
obsessive anxiety

bugger *n* **1** *taboo slang*
unpleasant or difficult
person or thing **2** person who
practises buggery ▷ *v* **3** *slang*
tire **4** practise buggery with
buggery *n* anal intercourse

bugle *n* instrument like a
small trumpet **bugler** *n*

build *v* **building, built
1** make, construct, or form
by joining parts or materials
▷ *n* **2** shape of the body
builder *n* **building** *n*
structure with walls and
a roof **build-up** *n* gradual
increase **built-up** *adj* having
many buildings

bulb *n* **1** glass part of an electric
lamp **2** onion-shaped root
which grows into a flower
or plant **bulbous** *adj* round
and fat

bulge *n* **1** swelling on a
normally flat surface **2** sudden
increase in number ▷ *v*
3 swell outwards **bulging** *adj*

bulimia *n* disorder
characterized by compulsive
overeating followed by
vomiting

bulk *n* **1** great size or volume
2 main part **in bulk** in large
quantities **bulky** *adj*

bulkhead *n* partition in a ship
or airplane

bull¹ *n* male of some animals,
such as cattle, elephants, and
whales **bullock** *n* castrated
bull **bulldog** *n* sturdy thickset
dog with a broad head and a
muscular body **bulldozer** *n*
powerful tractor for moving
earth **bulldoze** *v* **bullfight**
n public show in which a
matador kills a bull **bull's-
eye** *n* central disc of a target

bull² *n* papal decree

bull³ *n* *informal* complete
nonsense

bullet *n* small piece of metal
fired from a gun

bulletin *n* short official report
or announcement

bullion *n* gold or silver in the
form of bars

bully *n, pl* **-lies 1** person
who hurts, persecutes, or
intimidates a weaker person
▷ *v* **-lying, -lied 2** hurt,
intimidate, or persecute (a
weaker person)

bulrush *n* tall stiff reed

bulwark *n* **1** wall used as a
fortification **2** person or thing
acting as a defence

bum¹ *n* *slang* buttocks or anus

bum² *n* *informal* person who
avoids work, idler

bumble *v* speak, do, or move in
a clumsy way **bumbling** *adj, n*

bumblebee *n* large hairy bee

bump *v* **1** knock or strike with
a jolt **2** travel in jerks and
jolts ▷ *n* **3** (dull thud from) an
impact or collision **4** raised
uneven part **bumper** *n* **1** bar
on the front and back of a
vehicle to protect against
damage ▷ *adj* **2** unusually
large or abundant **bump off** *v*
informal murder

bumph, bumf *n* *informal*
official documents or forms

bumpkin _n_ awkward simple country person

bumptious _adj_ offensively self-assertive

bun _n_ 1 small round cake 2 hair gathered into a bun shape **buns** 3 _slang_ the buttocks

bunch _n_ 1 number of things growing, fastened, or grouped together 2 group: _a bunch of boys_ ▷ _v_ 3 group or be grouped together in a bunch

bundle _n_ 1 number of things gathered loosely together ▷ _v_ 2 cause to go roughly or unceremoniously **bundle up** _v_ make into a bundle

bung _n_ 1 stopper for a cask etc. ▷ _v_ 2 (foll. by _up_) _informal_ close with a bung

bungalow _n_ one-storey house

bungle _v_ spoil through incompetence **bungler** _n_ **bungling** _adj, n_

bunion _n_ inflamed swelling on the big toe

bunk[1] _n_ narrow shelflike bed **bunk bed** one of a pair of beds constructed one above the other

bunk[2] _n_ same as **bunkum**

bunk[3] _n_ **do a bunk** _slang_ leave a place without telling anyone

bunker _n_ 1 sandy hollow on a golf course 2 underground shelter 3 large storage container for coal etc.

bunkum _n_ nonsense

bunny _n, pl_ **-nies** child's word for a rabbit

Bunsen burner _n_ gas burner used in laboratories

bunt _baseball_ ▷ _v_ 1 tap the ball with the bat without swinging it ▷ _n_ 2 gentle hit made without swinging the bat

bunting _n_ decorative flags

buoy _n_ 1 floating marker anchored in the sea ▷ _v_ 2 prevent from sinking 3 encourage or hearten

buoyant _adj_ 1 able to float 2 cheerful or resilient **buoyancy** _n_

bur _n_ same as **burr**[1]

burble _v_ 1 make a bubbling sound 2 talk quickly and excitedly

burden[1] _n_ 1 heavy load 2 something difficult to cope with ▷ _v_ 3 put a burden on 4 oppress **burdensome** _adj_

burden[2] _n_ theme of a speech etc.

bureau _n, pl_ **-reaus, -reaux** 1 office that provides a service 2 writing desk with shelves and drawers

bureaucracy _n, pl_ **-cies** 1 administrative system based on complex rules and procedures 2 excessive adherence to complex procedures **bureaucrat** _n_ **bureaucratic** _adj_

burgeon _v_ develop or grow rapidly

burgh _n_ Scottish borough

burglar _n_ person who enters a building to commit a crime, esp. theft **burglary** _n_ **burglarize** _v_

burgundy _n_ 1 type of French wine ▷ _adj_ 2 dark purplish-red

burial _n_ burying of a dead body

burlesque _n_ artistic work which satirizes a subject by caricature

burly _adj_ **-lier, -liest** (of a person) broad and strong

burn[1] _v_ **burning, burnt** _or_ **burned** 1 be or set on fire 2 destroy or be destroyed by fire 3 damage, injure, or mark by heat 4 feel strong emotion 5 record data on (a compact disc) ▷ _n_ 6 injury or mark caused by fire or exposure to heat

burn[2] _n_ Scot small stream

burning _adj_ 1 intense 2 urgent or crucial

b

burnish v make smooth and shiny by rubbing

burp v, n informal belch

burr[1] n head of a plant with prickles or hooks

burr[2] n 1 soft trilling sound given to the letter (r) in some English dialects 2 whirring sound

burrow n 1 hole dug in the ground by a rabbit etc. ▷ v 2 dig holes in the ground

bursar n treasurer of a school, college, or university **bursary** n scholarship

burst v bursting, burst 1 (cause to) break open or apart noisily and suddenly 2 come or go suddenly and forcibly 3 be full to the point of breaking open ▷ n 4 instance of breaking open suddenly 5 sudden and violent outbreak or occurrence **burst into** v give vent to (an emotion) suddenly

bury v burying, buried 1 place in a grave 2 place in the earth and cover with soil 3 conceal or hide

bus n 1 large motor vehicle for carrying passengers ▷ v bussing, bussed 2 travel or transport by bus

busby n, pl -bies tall fur hat worn by certain soldiers

bush n 1 dense woody plant, smaller than a tree 2 wild uncultivated part of a country **bushed** adj 1 tired out 2 mentally disturbed from living in isolation **bushy** adj (of hair) thick and shaggy **bushbaby** n small tree-living mammal with large eyes **bush-league** adj informal inferior or lacking sophistication **bush pilot** pilot who flies in northern or remote areas

bushel n unit of measure equal to eight gallons

business n 1 purchase and sale of goods and services 2 commercial establishment 3 trade or profession 4 proper concern or responsibility 5 affair: *it's a dreadful business* **businesslike** adj **businessman** (**businesswoman**) n

busker n street entertainer **busk** v act as a busker

bust[1] n 1 woman's bosom 2 sculpture of the head and shoulders

bust[2] informal ▷ v busting, bust or busted 1 break 2 (of the police) raid (a place) or arrest (someone) ▷ adj 3 broken **go bust** become bankrupt

bustle[1] v 1 hurry with a show of activity or energy ▷ n 2 energetic and noisy activity **bustling** adj

bustle[2] n hist cushion worn by women to hold out their dress below the waist at the back

busy adj busier, busiest 1 actively employed 2 full of activity ▷ v busying, busied 3 keep (someone) busy **busily** adv **busybody** n meddlesome or nosy person

but conj 1 contrary to expectation 2 in contrast 3 other than 4 without it happening ▷ prep 5 except ▷ adv 6 only **but for** were it not for

butane [bew-tane] n gas used for fuel

butch adj slang markedly or aggressively masculine

butcher n 1 person who sells the meat of slaughtered animals 2 brutal murderer ▷ v 3 slaughter (animals) for meat 4 kill (people) brutally or indiscriminately **butchery** n

butler n chief male servant

butt[1] n 1 thick end of something 2 unused end of a

cigar or cigarette **3** *informal* the buttocks

butt² *n* person or thing that is the target of ridicule

butt³ *v* strike with the head or horns **butt in** *v* interrupt a conversation

butt⁴ *n* large cask

butte *n* steep, often flat-topped hill in W Canada

butter *n* **1** edible fatty solid made from cream by churning ▷ *v* **2** put butter on **buttery** *adj* **butter tart** small tart with sugar and butter filling **butter up** *v* flatter

buttercup *n* small yellow flower

butterfingers *n informal* person who drops things by mistake

butterfly *n* **1** insect with brightly coloured wings **2** swimming stroke in which both arms move together in a forward circular action

buttermilk *n* sourish milk that remains after the butter has been separated from milk

butterscotch *n* kind of hard brittle toffee

buttock *n* either of the two fleshy masses that form the human rump

button *n* **1** small hard object sewn to clothing to fasten it **2** knob that operates a piece of equipment when pressed ▷ *v* **3** fasten with buttons **buttonhole** *n* **1** slit in a garment through which a button is passed **2** flower worn on a lapel ▷ *v* **3** detain (someone) in conversation

buttress *n* **1** structure to support a wall ▷ *v* **2** support with a buttress

buxom *adj* (of a woman) healthily plump and full-bosomed

buy *v* **buying, bought** **1** acquire by paying money for

2 bribe **3** *slang* accept as true ▷ *n* **4** thing acquired through payment **buyer** *n* **1** customer **2** person employed to buy merchandise

buzz *n* **1** rapidly vibrating humming sound **2** *informal* sense of excitement ▷ *v* **3** make a humming sound **4** be filled with an air of excitement **buzzer** *n* **buzz around** *v* move around quickly and busily **buzz word** jargon word which becomes fashionably popular

buzzard *n* bird of prey of the hawk family

by *adv* **1** near **2** past ▷ *prep* **3** used to indicate the person responsible for a creative work: *an opera by Verdi* **4** used to indicate a means used: *I go home by bus* **5** past **6** not later than **7** during **8** near **9** placed between measurements: *a plank fourteen inches by seven* **by and by** presently **by and large** in general

bye, bye-bye *interj informal* goodbye

by-election *n* election held during parliament to fill a vacant seat

bygone *adj* **1** past or former

bylaw, bye-law *n* rule made by a local authority

bypass *n* **1** main road built to avoid a city **2** operation to divert blood flow away from a damaged part of the heart ▷ *v* **3** go round or avoid

by-product *n* secondary or incidental product of a process

bystander *n* person present but not involved

byte *n* *computers* group of bits processed as one unit of data

byway *n* side road

byword *n* person or thing regarded as a perfect example of something

Cc

C 1 *chem* carbon 2 Celsius 3 centigrade

c. 1 cent 2 century 3 circa 4 copyright

Ca *chem* calcium

ca. circa

CAA Canadian Automobile Association

cab *n* 1 taxi 2 enclosed driver's compartment on a train, truck, etc. **cabbie** *n informal* taxi driver

cabal [kab-**bal**] *n* 1 small group of political plotters 2 secret plot

cabaret [**kab**-a-ray] *n* dancing and singing show in a nightclub

cabbage *n* vegetable with a large head of green leaves

caber *n* tree trunk tossed in competition at Highland games

cabin *n* 1 compartment in a ship or aircraft 2 small hut **cabin cruiser** motorboat with a cabin

cabinet *n* 1 piece of furniture with drawers or shelves 2 **Cabinet** committee of senior government ministers **cabinet-maker** *n* person who makes fine furniture

cable *n* 1 strong thick rope 2 bundle of wires that carries electricity or telegraph messages 3 telegram sent abroad ▷ *v* 4 send (a message) to (someone) by cable **cable car** vehicle pulled up a steep slope by a moving cable **cable television** television

service conveyed by cable to subscribers

caboodle *n* **the whole caboodle** *informal* the whole lot

cacao [kak-**kah**-oh] *n* tropical tree with seed pods from which chocolate and cocoa are made

cache [**kash**] *n* 1 hiding place, esp. for supplies and provisions 2 hidden store of weapons or treasure

cachet [**kash**-shay] *n* 1 prestige, distinction 2 distinctive mark

cackle *v* 1 laugh or chatter shrilly 2 (of a hen) squawk with shrill broken notes ▷ *n* 3 cackling noise

cacophony [kak-**koff**-on-ee] *n* harsh discordant sound **cacophonous** *adj*

cactus *n, pl* **-tuses, -ti** fleshy desert plant with spines but no leaves

cad *n old-fashioned* dishonourable man **caddish** *adj*

cadaver [kad-**dav**-ver] *n* corpse **cadaverous** *adj* 1 deathly pale 2 gaunt

caddie, caddy *n, pl* **-dies** 1 person who carries a golfer's clubs ▷ *v* **-dying, -died** 2 act as a caddie

caddis fly *n* insect whose larva (**caddis worm**) lives underwater in a protective case of sand and stones

caddy *n, pl* **-dies** small box for tea

cadence [**kade**-enss] *n* **1** rise and fall in the pitch of a voice **2** close of a musical phrase

cadenza *n* complex passage for a soloist in a piece of music

cadet *n* young person training for the armed forces or police

cadge *v* get (something) from someone by taking advantage of his or her generosity **cadger** *n*

cadmium *n* bluish-white metallic element used in alloys

cadre [**kah**-der] *n* (member of) a group of selected trained people forming the core of a military unit, Communist Party, etc.

caecum [**seek**-um] *n, pl* **-ca** pouch at the beginning of the large intestine

Caesarean section [sa-**zair**-ee-an] *n* surgical incision into the womb to deliver a baby

caesium *n* same as **cesium**

café *n* small or inexpensive restaurant serving light refreshments **cafeteria** *n* self-service restaurant

caffeine *n* stimulant found in tea and coffee

caftan *n* same as **kaftan**

cage *n* **1** enclosure of bars or wires, for keeping animals or birds **2** enclosed platform of a elevator, esp. in a mine **caged** *adj* kept in a cage

cagey *adj* **cagier, cagiest 1** not frank **2** wary **caginess** *n*

cagoule [kag-**gool**] *n* lightweight hooded waterproof jacket

cahoots *pl n* **in cahoots** *informal* conspiring together

cairn *n* mound of stones erected as a memorial or marker **cairn terrier** small rough-haired terrier

cairngorm *n* yellow or brownish quartz gemstone

caisse populaire [**kayss** pop-oo-**layr**] *n Canad* (in Quebec and other French-speaking communities) financial institution run cooperatively, similar to a credit union

caisson [**kay**-son] *n* watertight chamber used to carry out construction work under water

cajole *v* persuade by flattery **cajolery** *n*

cake *n* **1** sweet food baked from a mixture of flour, eggs, etc. **2** flat compact mass ▷ *v* **3** form into a hardened mass or crust

calabash *n* type of large gourd

calamine *n* pink powder consisting chiefly of zinc oxide, used in skin lotions and ointments

calamity *n, pl* **-ties** disaster **calamitous** *adj*

calcify *v* **-fying, -fied** harden by the depositing of calcium salts **calcification** *n*

calcium *n* silvery-white metallic element found in bones, teeth, limestone, and chalk

calculate *v* **1** solve (a problem) mathematically **2** estimate **3** plan deliberately **calculable** *adj* **calculating** *adj* selfishly scheming **calculation** *n* **calculator** *n* small electronic device for making calculations

calculus *n, pl* **-luses 1** branch of mathematics dealing with infinitesimal changes to a variable number or quantity **2** *pathol* stone

Caledonian *adj* of Scotland

calendar *n* **1** chart showing a year divided into months, weeks, and days **2** system for determining the beginning, length, and division of years **3** schedule of events or appointments

calendula *n* marigold

calf[1] *n, pl* **calves 1** young cow, bull, elephant, whale, or seal **2** leather made from calf skin **calve** *v* give birth to a calf **calf love** adolescent infatuation

calf[2] *n, pl* **calves** back of the leg between the ankle and knee

calibre [kal-lib-ber] *n* **1** ability, personal worth **2** diameter of the bore of a gun or of a shell or bullet **calibrate** *v* **1** mark the scale or check the accuracy of (a measuring instrument) **2** measure the calibre of **calibration** *n*

calico *n, pl* -**coes**, -**co** plain white cotton cloth

caliph *n hist* Muslim ruler

call *v* **1** name **2** shout to attract attention **3** telephone **4** ask to come **5** (often foll. by *on*) visit **6** arrange (a meeting, strike, etc.) ▷ *n* **7** shout **8** animal's or bird's cry **9** telephone communication **10** visit **11** summons or invitation **12** need, demand **caller** *n* **calling** *n* vocation or profession **callbox** *Brit* telephone booth **call for** *v* need, demand **call off** *v* cancel **call up** *v* **1** summon to serve in the armed forces **2** evoke

calligraphy *n* (art of) beautiful handwriting **calligrapher** *n*

calliper *n* **1** *usu pl* metal splint for the leg **2** instrument for measuring diameters

callisthenics *pl n* light keep-fit exercises **callisthenic** *adj*

callous *adj* showing no concern for other people's feelings **calloused** *adj* covered in calluses **callously** *adv* **callousness** *n*

callow *adj* immature and inexperienced

callus *n, pl* -**luses** area of thick hardened skin

calm *adj* **1** not showing or feeling agitation or excitement **2** not ruffled by the wind **3** windless ▷ *n* **4** peaceful state ▷ *v* **5** make or become calm **calmly** *adv* **calmness** *n*

calorie *n* **1** unit of heat **2** unit of measurement for the energy value of food **calorific** *adj* of calories or heat

calumny *n, pl* -**nies** slander **calumniate** *v* slander

calypso *n, pl* -**sos** West Indian song with improvised topical lyrics

calyx *n, pl* **calyxes**, **calyces** outer leaves that protect the bud of a flower

cam *n* device which converts rotary motion to to-and-fro motion **camshaft** *n* part of an engine consisting of a rod to which cams are fixed

camaraderie *n* comradeship

camber *n* slight upward curve to the centre of a surface

cambric *n* fine white linen fabric

camcorder *n* combined portable video camera and recorder

came *v* past tense of **come**

camel *n* **1** humped mammal of Asia and Africa ▷ *adj* **2** fawn-coloured

camellia [kam-**meal**-ya] *n* evergreen ornamental shrub with roselike white, pink, or red flowers

Camembert [**kam**-mem-bare] *n* soft creamy French cheese

cameo *n, pl* **cameos 1** brooch or ring with a profile head carved in relief **2** small, brief part in a film or television play performed by a well-known actor or actress

camera *n* apparatus used for taking photographs **in camera** in private

cameraman n photographer, esp. for television or cinema

camisole n woman's bodice-like garment

camomile n aromatic plant, used to make herbal tea

camouflage [kam-moo-flahzh] n 1 use of natural surroundings or artificial aids to conceal or disguise something ▷ v 2 conceal or disguise by camouflage

camp[1] n 1 (place for) temporary lodgings consisting of tents, huts, or cabins 2 group supporting a particular doctrine ▷ v 3 stay in a camp **camper** n

camp[2] adj informal 1 homosexual 2 consciously artificial or affected **camp it up** informal behave in a camp way

campaign n 1 series of coordinated activities designed to achieve a goal ▷ v 2 conduct or take part in a campaign

campanology n art of ringing bells **campanologist** n

campanula n plant with blue or white bell-shaped flowers

camphor n aromatic crystalline substance used medicinally and in mothballs **camphorated** adj

campion n white or pink wild flower

campus n, pl -puses grounds of a college or university

can[1] v, past **could** 1 be able 2 be allowed

can[2] n 1 metal container for liquid or foods ▷ v **canning**, **canned** 2 put (something) in a can **canned** adj 1 preserved in a can 2 (of music etc.) prerecorded **cannery** n factory where food is canned

Canada Day July 1st, anniversary of establishment of Confederation in 1867

Canada goose large greyish-brown N American goose

Canada jay N American bird with grey, white-tipped feathers

Canadarm n extension of spacecraft to fetch and deploy objects

Canadian n, adj (native) of Canada **Canadianize** v make or become Canadian

canal n 1 artificial watercourse 2 duct in the body

canapé [kan-nap-pay] n small piece of bread or toast spread with a savoury topping

canary n, pl -ries small yellow songbird often kept as a pet

canasta n card game like rummy, played with two packs

cancan n lively high-kicking dance performed by a female group

cancel v -celling, -celled 1 postpone indefinitely 2 cross out 3 mark (a cheque or stamp) to prevent reuse **cancellation** n **cancel out** v counterbalance or neutralize

cancer n 1 serious disease caused by a malignant growth or tumour 2 malignant growth or tumour **cancerous** adj

candela [kan-dee-la] n unit of luminous intensity

candelabrum n, pl -bra ornamental candleholder for several candles

candid adj frank and outspoken **candidly** adv

candidate n 1 person seeking a job or position 2 person taking an examination **candidacy** or **candidature** n

candle n stick of wax enclosing a wick, which is burned to produce light **candlestick** n holder for a candle **candlewick** n cotton

fabric with a tufted surface
candour, candor *n* frankness
CANDU *n* ® type of nuclear reactor pioneered in Canada
candy *n, pl* **-dies** shaped piece of food consisting mainly of sugar **candied** *adj* coated with sugar **candyfloss** *n* light fluffy mass of spun sugar on a stick **candy-striped** *adj* having coloured stripes on a white background
cane *n* **1** stem of the bamboo or similar plant **2** slender walking stick **3** flexible rod used to beat someone ▷ *v* **4** beat with a cane
canine [**kay**-nine] *adj* of or like a dog **canine tooth** sharp pointed tooth between the incisors and the molars
canister *n* metal container
canker *n* **1** ulceration or ulcerous disease **2** something that spreads and corrupts ▷ *v* **3** infect or become infected with canker **cankerous** *adj*
cannabis *n* drug obtained from the hemp plant
cannelloni *pl n* tubular pieces of pasta filled with meat etc.
cannibal *n* **1** person who eats human flesh **2** animal that eats others of its own kind **cannibalism** *n* **cannibalize** *v* use parts from (one machine) to repair another
cannon[1] *n* large gun on wheels **cannonade** *n* continuous heavy gunfire **cannonball** *n* heavy metal ball fired from a cannon
cannon[2] *n* **1** billiard stroke in which the cue ball hits two balls successively ▷ *v* **2** make this stroke **3** rebound, collide
cannot can not
canny *adj* **-nier, -niest** shrewd and cautious **cannily** *adv*
canoe *n* **1** light narrow boat propelled by a paddle or paddles **canoeing** *n* **canoeist** *n*
canola *n* rapeseed oil
canon[1] *n* **1** Church law or decree **2** general rule or principle **3** set of writings accepted as genuine **canonical** *adj* **canonize** *v* declare (a person) officially to be a saint **canonization** *n*
canon[2] *n* priest serving in a cathedral
canoodle *v slang* kiss and cuddle
canopy *n, pl* **-pies 1** covering above a throne, bed, etc. **2** any large or wide covering **canopied** *adj*
cant[1] *n* **1** insincere talk **2** specialized vocabulary of a particular group
cant[2] *v, n* tilt or slope
can't can not
cantaloupe, cantaloup *n* kind of melon with sweet orange flesh
cantankerous *adj* bad-tempered, quarrelsome
cantata [kan-**tah**-ta] *n* musical work consisting of arias, duets, and choruses
canteen *n* **1** restaurant attached to a workplace **2** case of cutlery
canter *n* **1** horse's gait between a trot and a gallop ▷ *v* **2** (cause to) move at a canter
canticle *n* short hymn with words from the Bible
cantilever *n* beam or girder fixed at one end only
canto [**kan**-toe] *n, pl* **-tos** main division of a long poem
canton *n* political division of a country, esp. Switzerland
cantonment [kan-**toon**-ment] *n* military camp
cantor *n* man employed to lead services in a synagogue
Canuck *n, adj informal* Canadian
canvas *n* **1** heavy coarse cloth

used for sails and tents, and for painting on **2** a painting on canvas

canvass *v* **1** try to get votes or support (from) **2** determine the opinions of (people) by conducting a survey ▷ *n* **3** canvassing

canyon *n* deep steep-sided valley

cap *n* **1** soft close-fitting covering for the head **2** small lid **3** small explosive device used in a toy gun ▷ *v* **capping, capped 4** cover or top with something **5** select (a player) for a national team **6** impose an upper limit on (a tax) **7** outdo

capable *adj* **1** (foll. by *of*) having the ability or skill to do something **2** competent and efficient **capably** *adv* **capability** *n*

capacity *n, pl* **-ties 1** ability to contain, absorb, or hold **2** maximum amount that can be contained or produced **3** physical or mental ability **4** position or function **capacious** *adj* roomy **capacitance** *n* (measure of) the ability of a system to store electric charge **capacitor** *n* device for storing electric charge

caparisoned [kap-**par**-risssond] *adj* magnificently decorated or dressed

cape[1] *n* short cloak

cape[2] *n* large piece of land jutting into the sea

capelin [**kap**-ill-in] *n* small food fish of the N Atlantic and Pacific

caper[1] *n* **1** high-spirited prank ▷ *v* **2** skip or dance about

caper[2] *n* pickled flower bud of a Mediterranean shrub used in sauces

capercaillie, capercailzie [kap-per-**kale**-yee] *n* large

black European grouse

capillary [kap-**pill**-a-ree] *n, pl* **-laries** very fine blood vessel

capital *n* **1** chief town of a country **2** accumulated wealth **3** wealth used to produce more wealth **4** large letter, as used at the beginning of a name or sentence **5** top part of a pillar ▷ *adj* **6** involving or punishable by death **7** chief or principal **8** *old-fashioned* excellent **capitalism** *n* economic system based on the private ownership of industry **capitalist** *adj* **1** based on or supporting capitalism ▷ *n* **2** supporter of capitalism **3** person who owns capital **capitalize** *v* **1** convert into or provide with capital **2** write or print (text) in capital letters **capitalize on** *v* take advantage of (a situation)

capitation *n* charge or grant of a fixed amount per person

capitulate *v* surrender on agreed terms **capitulation** *n*

capon [**kay**-pon] *n* castrated cock fowl fattened for eating

cappuccino [kap-poo-**cheen**-oh] *n, pl* **-nos** coffee with steamed milk

caprice [kap-**reess**] *n* whim **capricious** *adj* changeable **capriciously** *adv*

capsicum *n* kind of pepper used as a vegetable or as a spice

capsize *v* overturn accidentally

capstan *n* rotating cylinder on which a rope etc. is wound

capsule *n* **1** soluble case containing a dose of medicine **2** seed vessel of a plant **3** detachable crew compartment of a spacecraft

captain *n* **1** leader of a team or group **2** commander of a ship or civil aircraft **3** middle-ranking naval officer **4** junior

officer in the armed forces ▷ v
5 be captain of **captaincy** n

caption n **1** title or explanation
accompanying an illustration
▷ v **2** provide with a caption

captious adj tending to make
trivial criticisms **captiously**
adv **captiousness** n

captivate v fascinate or
enchant **captivating** adj
captivation n

captive n **1** person kept in
confinement ▷ adj **2** kept
in confinement **3** (of an
audience) unable to leave
captivity n

captor n person who captures
a person or animal

capture v **1** take prisoner
2 gain control over **3** succeed
in representing (something
elusive) artistically ▷ n
4 capturing

capybara n very large S
American rodent

car n **1** motor vehicle designed
to carry a small number
of people **2** passenger
compartment of a cable
car, elevator, etc. **3** railway
carriage **car park** area or
building reserved for parking
cars

carafe [kar-**raff**] n glass bottle
for serving water or wine

caramel n **1** chewy candy
made from sugar and milk
2 burnt sugar used for
colouring and flavouring
food **caramelize** v turn into
caramel

carapace n hard upper shell
of tortoises and crustaceans

carat n **1** unit of weight of
precious stones **2** measure of
the purity of gold in an alloy

caravan n **1** group travelling
together for safety in the
East **2** Brit large enclosed
vehicle for living in, able to
be towed by an automobile or
horse

caraway n plant whose seeds
are used as a spice

carb n informal short for
carbohydrate

carbide n compound of carbon
with a metal

carbine n light automatic rifle

carbohydrate n any of a large
group of energy-producing
compounds in food, such as
sugars and starches

carbolic, carbolic acid n
disinfectant derived from
coal tar

carbon n nonmetallic element
occurring as charcoal,
graphite, and diamond,
found in all organic matter
carbonate n salt or ester of
carbonic acid **carbonated**
adj containing carbon dioxide
carbonize v **1** turn into carbon
as a result of heating **2** coat
with carbon **carbon copy**
1 copy made with carbon
paper **2** very similar person
or thing **carbon dioxide**
colourless gas exhaled by
people and animals **carbon
footprint** measure of the
carbon dioxide produced by
an individual or organization
carbonic acid weak acid
formed from carbon dioxide
and water **carbon-neutral**
adj not affecting the overall
volume of carbon dioxide
in the atmosphere **carbon
offset** act which compensates
for carbon emissions of
an individual or company
carbon paper paper covered
with a dark waxy pigment,
used to make a duplicate of
something as it is typed or
written

Carborundum n ® compound
of silicon and carbon, used for
grinding and polishing

carboy n large bottle with a
protective casing

carbuncle n **1** inflamed boil

2 rounded garnet cut without facets

carburetor *n* device which mixes gasoline and air in an internal-combustion engine

carcass, carcase *n* dead body or skeleton of an animal

carcinogen *n* substance producing cancer **carcinogenic** *adj* **carcinoma** *n* malignant tumour, cancer

card[1] *n* **1** piece of thick stiff paper or cardboard used for identification, reference, or sending greetings or messages **2** one of a set of cards with a printed pattern, used for playing games **3** small rectangle of stiff plastic for use as a credit card or banker's card **4** *old-fashioned* witty or eccentric person **cards 5** any card game, or card games in general **cardboard** *n* thin stiff board made from paper pulp **cardholder** *n* person who owns a credit or debit card **cardsharp** *or* **cardsharper** *n* professional card player who cheats

card[2] *n* machine or tool for combing wool before spinning **carder** *n*

cardiac *adj* of the heart **cardiograph** *n* instrument which records heart movements **cardiogram** *n* record of heart movements **cardiology** *n* study of the heart and its diseases **cardiologist** *n* **cardiovascular** *adj* of the heart and the blood vessels

cardigan *n* knitted jacket

cardinal *n* **1** one of the high-ranking clergymen of the RC Church who elect the Pope and act as his counsellors ▷ *adj* **2** chief, principal **3** deep red **cardinal number** number denoting quantity but not order in a group, for example one, two, or three **cardinal point** one of the four main points of the compass

care *v* **1** be concerned **2** have regard or liking for **3** have a desire for **4** look after ▷ *n* **5** serious attention **6** protection or supervision **7** worry, anxiety **8** caution **careful** *adj* **carefully** *adv* **carefulness** *n* **careless** *adj* **carelessly** *adv* **carelessness** *n* **carefree** *adj* without worry or responsibility **caretaker** *n* person employed to look after a place **careworn** *adj* showing signs of worry

careen *v* tilt over to one side

career *n* **1** profession or occupation **2** course through life ▷ *v* **3** rush in an uncontrolled way **careerist** *n* person who seeks advancement by any possible means

caress *n* **1** gentle affectionate touch or embrace ▷ *v* **2** touch gently and affectionately

caret [**kar**-rett] *n* symbol (∧) showing the place in written or printed matter where something is to be inserted

cargo *n, pl* -**goes** goods carried by a ship, aircraft, etc. **cargo pants** *or* **cargo trousers** loose trousers with a large pocket on each leg

caribou *n* N American reindeer

caricature *n* **1** likeness of a person which exaggerates features for comic effect ▷ *v* **2** portray by a caricature

caries [**care**-reez] *n* tooth decay

carillon [kar-**rill**-yon] *n* **1** set of bells played by keyboard or mechanically **2** tune played on this

carmine *adj* vivid red

carnage *n* slaughter

carnal *adj* of a sexual or

sensual nature **carnal knowledge** sexual intercourse

carnation n cultivated plant with sweet-scented white, pink, or red flowers

carnival n festive period with processions and entertainment

carnivore n flesh-eating animal **carnivorous** adj

carob n Mediterranean tree with edible pods used as a chocolate substitute

carol n 1 joyful religious song sung at Christmas ▷ v -olling, -olled 2 sing carols 3 sing joyfully

carotid [kar-**rot**-id] adj, n (of) one of the two arteries supplying blood to the head

carouse v have a merry drinking party **carousal** n merry drinking party

carousel [kar-roo-**sell**] n 1 revolving conveyor 2 merry-go-round

carp¹ n freshwater fish

carp² v complain or find fault

carpel n female reproductive organ of a flowering plant

carpenter n person who makes or repairs wooden structures **carpentry** n

carpet n 1 heavy fabric for covering a floor ▷ v **carpeting, carpeted** 2 cover with a carpet **on the carpet** informal being reprimanded

carpus n, pl -pi set of eight small bones forming the wrist

carriage n 1 one of the sections of a train for passengers 2 person's bearing 3 four-wheeled horse-drawn vehicle 4 moving part of a machine that supports and shifts another part 5 act or cost of conveying goods **carriageway** n part of a road along which traffic passes in one direction

carrier n 1 person or thing that carries something 2 person or animal that does not show symptoms of a disease but can transmit it to others **carrier pigeon** homing pigeon used for carrying messages

carrion n dead and rotting flesh

carrot n 1 long tapering orange root vegetable 2 incentive **carroty** adj reddish

carry v -rying, -ried 1 take (something) from one place to another, transport 2 have on one's person 3 transmit 4 have as a penalty or result 5 bear (the head, body, etc.) in a specified manner 6 win acceptance for (a bill or motion) 7 (of sound) travel over a distance **carryall** n large strong travelling bag **carry on** v 1 continue or persevere 2 informal fuss unnecessarily **carry-on** adj (of luggage) to be taken inside the cabin of an aircraft by a passenger **carry out** v perform or complete

cart n 1 open two-wheeled horse-drawn vehicle for carrying goods or passengers ▷ v 2 carry in a cart 3 carry with effort **carthorse** n large heavily built horse **cartwheel** n 1 sideways somersault supported by the arms with the legs outstretched 2 large spoked wheel of a cart

carte blanche n French complete authority

cartel n association of competing firms formed to fix prices

cartilage [**kar**-till-ij] n firm elastic tissue forming part of the skeleton **cartilaginous** adj

cartography n map making **cartographer** n **cartographic** adj

carton n container made of cardboard or waxed paper

cartoon n 1 humorous or satirical drawing 2 sequence of these telling a story 3 film made by photographing a series of drawings which give the illusion of movement when projected 4 preliminary sketch for a painting **cartoonist** n

cartridge n 1 casing containing an explosive charge for a firearm 2 sealed container of film, tape, etc. 3 unit in the pick-up of a record player holding the stylus **cartridge paper** strong thick paper

carve v 1 cut 2 form (an object or design) by cutting, esp. in stone or wood 3 slice (meat) into pieces **carving** n

caryatid [kar-ree-**at**-id] n supporting column in the shape of a female figure

CAS Canad Children's Aid Society: organization providing help for abused or homeless children

Casanova n promiscuous man

cascade n 1 waterfall 2 something that flows or falls like a waterfall ▷ v 3 fall in cascades

case¹ n 1 instance or example 2 matter for discussion 3 condition or state of affairs 4 set of arguments for an action or cause 5 person attended to by a doctor, solicitor, or social worker 6 lawsuit 7 grounds for a lawsuit 8 grammar form of a noun, pronoun, or adjective showing its relation to other words in the sentence **in case** so as to allow for eventualities

case² n 1 container or protective covering 2 container and its contents ▷ v 3 slang inspect (a building) with the intention of burgling it **case-harden** v harden (an iron alloy) by carbonizing the surface **case-hardened** adj made callous by experience

casement n window that is hinged on one side

cash n 1 banknotes and coins ▷ v 2 obtain cash for **cash in on** v informal gain profit or advantage from **cash register** till that displays and adds the prices of the goods sold

cashew n edible tropical American nut

cashier¹ n person responsible for handling cash in a bank or shop

cashier² v dismiss with dishonour from the armed forces

cashmere n 1 fine soft wool 2 fabric made from this

casing n protective case or covering

casino n, pl -nos public building or room where gambling is done

cask n barrel for holding alcoholic drink

casket n 1 small box for valuables 2 coffin

cassava n flour obtained from the roots of a tropical American plant, used to make tapioca

casserole n 1 covered dish in which food is cooked and served 2 food cooked in this way ▷ v 3 cook in a casserole

cassette n plastic case containing a reel of film or magnetic tape

cassock n long tunic worn by the clergy

cassowary n, pl -waries large flightless bird of Australia and New Guinea

cast n 1 actors in a play or

C

film collectively **2** something shaped by a mould while molten **3** mould used to shape something **4** rigid casing to help set a broken bone **5** quality or nature **6** slight squint in the eye ▷ v **casting, cast 7** select (actors) to play parts in a play or film **8** give (a vote) **9** let fall, shed **10** shape (molten material) in a mould **11** throw with force **12** direct (a glance) **castaway** n shipwrecked person **casting vote** deciding vote used by the chairman when the votes on each side are equal **cast-iron** adj **1** made of a hard but brittle type of iron **2** rigid or unchallengeable **cast-off** adj, n discarded (garment)

castanets pl n two small curved pieces of hollow wood clicked together in the hand, used esp. by Spanish dancers

caste n **1** one of the hereditary classes into which Hindu society is divided **2** social rank

castellated adj having battlements

caster sugar n Brit finely ground white sugar

castigate v criticize or scold severely **castigation** n

castle n **1** large fortified building **2** rook in chess

castor n small swivelled wheel fixed to a piece of furniture to allow it to be moved easily

castor oil n oil obtained from an Indian plant, used as a lubricant and purgative

castrate v **1** remove the testicles of **2** deprive of vigour or masculinity **castration** n

casual adj **1** appearing unconcerned **2** (of work or workers) occasional **3** shallow or superficial **4** for informal wear **5** happening by chance **casually** adv

casualty n, pl -ties **1** person killed or injured in an accident or war **2** anything lost or destroyed

casuistry n reasoning that is misleading or oversubtle **casuist** n

cat n **1** small domesticated furry mammal **2** related wild mammal, such as the lion or tiger **3** informal spiteful woman **catty** adj informal spiteful **catkin** n drooping flower spike of certain trees **catcall** n derisive whistle or cry **catgut** n strong cord used to string musical instruments **catnap** v, n doze **cat's paw** person used as a tool by another **catwalk** n narrow pathway or platform

cataclysm [kat-a-kliz-zum] n **1** violent upheaval **2** disaster, such as an earthquake **cataclysmic** adj

catacombs [kat-a-kooms] pl n underground burial place consisting of tunnels with recesses for tombs

catafalque [kat-a-falk] n raised platform on which a body lies in state before or during a funeral

catalepsy n trancelike state in which the body is rigid **cataleptic** adj

catalogue n **1** book containing details of items for sale **2** systematic list of items ▷ v **3** make such a list **4** enter (an item) in a catalogue

catalyst n substance that speeds up a chemical reaction without itself changing **catalyse** v speed up (a chemical reaction) by a catalyst **catalysis** n **catalytic** adj

catamaran n boat with twin parallel hulls

catapult n **1** Brit slingshot **2** device used to launch

aircraft from a warship ▷ *v* **3** launch as if from a catapult
cataract *n* **1** eye disease in which the lens becomes opaque **2** opaque area of an eye **3** waterfall
catarrh [kat-**tar**] *n* inflammation of a mucous membrane causing a flow of mucus **catarrhal** *adj*
catastrophe [kat-**ass**-trof-fee] *n* great and sudden disaster **catastrophic** *adj*
catch *v* **catching, caught** **1** seize or capture **2** surprise: *catch someone red-handed* **3** hit unexpectedly **4** be in time for **5** see or hear by chance or with difficulty **6** contract (a disease) **7** understand **8** entangle or become entangled **9** check (one's breath) suddenly **10** begin to burn ▷ *n* **11** catching **12** thing caught **13** device that fastens **14** *informal* concealed or unforeseen difficulty **catch it** *informal* be punished **catching** *adj* infectious **catchy** *adj* (of a tune) pleasant and easily remembered **catchment area** area served by a particular school or hospital **catch on** *v informal* **1** become popular **2** understand **catch out** *v informal* trap (someone) in an error or lie **catch phrase** *or* **catchword** *n* well-known and frequently used phrase or slogan **catch 22** inescapable dilemma
catechism [**kat**-ti-kiz-zum] *n* doctrine of a Christian Church in a series of questions and answers **catechize** *v* **1** instruct by using a catechism **2** question (someone) thoroughly **catechist** *n*
category *n, pl* **-ries** class or group **categorical** *adj* absolute or unconditional

categorically *adv* **categorize** *v* put in a category **categorization** *n*
cater *v* provide what is needed or wanted, esp. food or services **caterer** *n*
caterpillar *n* **1** wormlike larva of a moth or butterfly **2** ® endless track, driven by cogged wheels, used to propel a heavy vehicle.
caterwaul *v* wail, yowl
catharsis [kath-**thar**-siss] *n, pl* **-ses** release of strong suppressed emotions **cathartic** *adj*
cathedral *n* principal church of a diocese
Catherine wheel *n* rotating firework
catheter [**kath**-it-er] *n* tube inserted into a body cavity to drain fluid
cathode *n* negative electrode, by which electrons leave a circuit **cathode rays** stream of electrons from a cathode in a vacuum tube
catholic *adj* **1** (of tastes or interests) covering a wide range ▷ *n, adj* **2 Catholic** (member) of the Roman Catholic Church **Catholicism** *n*
cattle *pl n* domesticated cows, bulls, or oxen
Caucasoid *adj* of the light-skinned racial group of mankind
caucus *n, pl* **-cuses** **1** local committee or faction of a political party **2** political meeting to decide future plans
caught *v* past of **catch**
cauldron *n* large pot used for boiling
cauliflower *n* type of cabbage with an edible white flower head
caulk *v* stop up (cracks, esp. in a ship) with filler

causal *adj* **1** of or being a cause **2** of cause and effect **causally** *adv* **causality** *or* **causation** *n* relationship of cause and effect

cause *n* **1** aim or principle supported by a person or group **2** something that produces an effect **3** reason or motive ▷ *v* **4** be the cause of

cause célèbre [kawz sill-**leb**-ra] *n, pl* **causes célèbres** [kawz sill-**leb**-ra] controversial legal case or issue

causeway *n* raised road or path across water or marshland

caustic *adj* **1** capable of burning by chemical action **2** sarcastic or cutting ▷ *n* **3** caustic substance **caustically** *adv*

cauterize *v* burn (body tissue) with heat or a chemical to treat a wound **cauterization** *n*

caution *n* **1** care, attention to safety **2** warning ▷ *v* **3** warn or advise **cautionary** *adj* warning **cautious** *adj* showing caution **cautiously** *adv*

cavalcade *n* procession of people on horseback or in cars

cavalier *adj* **1** arrogant, offhand ▷ *n* **2 Cavalier** supporter of Charles I in the English Civil War

cavalry *n, pl* **-ries** mounted troops

cave *n* large hole in a hill or cliff **caving** *n* sport of exploring caves **cave in** *v* **1** collapse inwards **2** give in **caveman** *n* prehistoric cave dweller

caveat [kav-vee-at] *n* warning

cavern *n* large cave **cavernous** *adj*

caviar, caviare *n* salted sturgeon roe

cavil *v* **-illing, -illed 1** make petty objections ▷ *n* **2** petty objection

cavity *n, pl* **-ties 1** hole **2** decayed area in a tooth

cavort *v* prance, caper

caw *n* **1** cry of a crow, rook, or raven ▷ *v* **2** make this cry

cayenne pepper, cayenne *n* hot red spice made from capsicum seeds

cayman *n, pl* **-mans** S American reptile similar to an alligator

CB Citizens' Band

CBC Canadian Broadcasting Corporation

CBE Commander of the Order of the British Empire

cc cubic centimetre(s)

Cd *chem* cadmium

CD compact disc

CD-ROM compact disc read-only memory

CDT Central Daylight Time

cease *v* bring or come to an end **ceaseless** *adj* **ceaselessly** *adv* **cease-fire** *n* **1** order to stop firing **2** temporary truce

cedar *n* **1** large evergreen tree **2** its wood

cede *v* surrender (territory or legal rights)

cedilla *n* hooklike symbol (‚) placed under a letter *c* to show that it is pronounced *s*, not *k*

CEGEP [**see**-jep] *Canad* (in Quebec) Collège d'enseignement général et professionnel: a post-secondary educational institution providing university preparation and training for trades and professions

ceilidh [**kay**-lee] *n* informal social gathering for singing and dancing, esp. in Scotland

ceiling *n* **1** inner upper surface of a room **2** upper limit set on something

celandine *n* wild plant with yellow flowers

celebrate _v_ **1** hold festivities to mark (a happy event, anniversary, etc.) **2** perform (a religious ceremony) **celebrated** _adj_ famous **celebration** _n_ **celebrant** _n_ person who performs a religious ceremony **celebrity** _n_ **1** famous person **2** fame

celeriac [sill-**ler**-ee-ak] _n_ kind of celery with a large turnip-like root

celerity [sill-**ler**-rit-tee] _n_ swiftness

celery _n_ vegetable with crisp juicy edible stalks

celestial _adj_ **1** heavenly, divine **2** of the sky

celibate _adj_ **1** unmarried or abstaining from sex, esp. because of a religious vow of chastity ▷ _n_ **2** celibate person **celibacy** _n_

cell _n_ **1** smallest unit of an organism that is able to function independently **2** small room for a prisoner, monk, or nun **3** small compartment **4** small group operating as the core of a larger organization **5** device which generates electrical energy from a chemical reaction **cellular** _adj_ **1** of or consisting of cells **2** woven with an open texture **cell phone** _or_ **cellular phone** telephone operating by radio communication via a network of transmitters each serving a small area

cellar _n_ **1** underground room for storage **2** stock of wine

cello [**chell**-oh] _n, pl_ **-los** low-pitched instrument of the violin family **cellist** _n_

Cellophane _n_ ® thin transparent cellulose sheeting used as wrapping

celluloid _n_ **1** plastic formerly used to make photographic film **2** cinema or films generally

cellulose _n_ main constituent of plant cell walls, used in making plastics, paper, etc.

Celsius _adj_ of the temperature scale in which water freezes at 0° and boils at 100°

Celt [kelt] _n_ person who speaks a Celtic language **Celtic** [**kel**-tik, **sel**-tik] _n_ **1** group of languages including Gaelic and Welsh ▷ _adj_ **2** of the Celts or the Celtic languages

cement _n_ **1** fine grey powder mixed with water and sand to make mortar or concrete **2** adhesive **3** material used to fill teeth ▷ _v_ **4** join, bind, or cover with cement **5** make (a relationship) stronger

cemetery _n, pl_ **-teries** burial ground not attached to a church

cenotaph _n_ monument honouring soldiers who died in a war

censer _n_ container for burning incense

censor _v_ **1** ban or cut parts of (a film, book, etc.) considered obscene or otherwise unacceptable ▷ _n_ **2** official employed to examine and censor films, books, etc. **censorship** _n_ **censorial** _adj_ **censorious** _adj_ harshly critical

censure _n_ **1** severe disapproval ▷ _v_ **2** criticize severely

census _n, pl_ **-suses** official count, esp. of population

cent _n_ hundredth part of a monetary unit such as the dollar

centaur _n_ mythical creature resembling a horse with the head, arms, and torso of a man

centenary [sen-**teen**-a-ree] _n, pl_ **-naries** 100th anniversary or its celebration **centenarian** n person at least 100 years old **centennial** n centenary

centigrade adj same as **Celsius**

centigram, centigramme n hundredth part of a gram

centilitre n hundredth part of a litre

centimetre n hundredth part of a metre

centipede n small wormlike creature with many legs

central adj 1 of, at, or forming the centre 2 main or principal **centrally** adv **centrality** n **centralism** n principle of central control of a country or organization **centralize** v bring under central control **centralization** n **central heating** system for heating a building from one central source of heat

Central Daylight Time n one of the standard times used in North America, five hours behind Greenwich Mean Time Abbreviation: **CDT**

Central Standard Time n one of the standard times used in North America, six hours behind Greenwich Mean Time Abbreviation: **CST**

centre, center n 1 middle point or part 2 place for a specified activity 3 political party or group favouring moderation 4 *sports* player who plays in the middle of the field 5 *hockey* forward who plays between the two wingers ▷ v 6 move towards, put, or be at the centre **centre field** *baseball* part of the outfield between right field and left field **centre fielder** *baseball* fielder who covers centre field **centre on** v have as a centre or main theme **centrist** n, adj

(person) favouring political moderation **centrifugal** adj moving away from the centre **centrifuge** n machine which separates substances by centrifugal force **centripetal** adj moving towards the centre

centurion n Roman officer commanding 100 men

century n, pl **-ries** 1 period of 100 years 2 cricket score of 100

CEO chief executive officer

cephalopod [seff-a-loh-pod] n sea mollusc with a head and tentacles, such as the octopus

ceramic n 1 hard brittle material made by firing clay 2 object made of this **ceramics** 3 art of producing ceramic objects ▷ adj 4 made of ceramic 5 of ceramics

cereal n 1 grass plant with edible grain, such as wheat or rice 2 this grain 3 breakfast food made from this grain

cerebral [ser-rib-ral] adj 1 of the brain 2 intellectual **cerebrum** n main part of the human brain

ceremony n, pl **-nies** 1 formal act or ritual 2 formally polite behaviour **ceremonial** adj, n **ceremonially** adv **ceremonious** adj **ceremoniously** adv

cerise [ser-reess] adj cherry-red

certain adj 1 sure, without doubt 2 reliable or unerring 3 some but not much **certainly** adv **certainty** n 1 state of being sure 2 thing sure to happen

certificate n official document stating the details of a birth, death, etc.

certify v **-fying, -fied** 1 declare formally or officially 2 declare (someone) legally insane **certifiable** adj **certification** n

certitude n confidence, certainty

cerulean [ser-**rule**-ee-an] adj of a deep blue colour

cervix n, pl **cervixes, cervices** 1 narrow entrance of the womb 2 neck **cervical** [ser-vik-kl, ser-**vie**-kl] adj

cesium, caesium n silvery-white metallic element used in photocells

cessation n ceasing

cesspool, cesspit n covered tank or pit for sewage

cetacean [sit-**tay**-shun] n, adj (member) of the whale family

cf. compare

CFC chlorofluorocarbon

CFL Canadian Football League

CGI computer-generated image(s)

ch. 1 chapter 2 church

chafe v 1 make or become sore or worn by rubbing 2 make or be impatient or annoyed

chafer n large beetle

chaff n 1 grain husks 2 chopped hay and straw used to feed cattle 3 light-hearted teasing ▷ v 4 tease good-naturedly

chagrin [**shag**-grin] n 1 annoyance and embarrassment ▷ v 2 annoy and embarrass

chain n 1 flexible length of connected metal links 2 connected series of things or events 3 group of shops, hotels, etc. owned by one firm 4 unit of length equal to 22 yards **pull someone's chain** informal tease, mislead, or harass ▷ v 5 confine or fasten with or as if with a chain **chain reaction** series of events, each of which causes the next **chain-smoke** v smoke (cigarettes) continuously **chain-smoker** n

chair n 1 seat with a back, for one person 2 official position of authority 3 person holding this 4 professorship ▷ v 5 preside over (a meeting) **chair lift** series of chairs on a cable for carrying people, esp. skiers, up a slope **chairman, chairperson,** or **chairwoman** n person who presides over a meeting

chaise [**shaze**] n light horse-drawn carriage

chaise longue [**long**] n sofa with a back and single armrest

chalcedony [kal-**sed**-don-ee] n, pl -**nies** variety of quartz

chalet n 1 kind of Swiss wooden house 2 house like this, used as a holiday home

chalice [**chal**-liss] n large goblet

chalk n 1 soft white rock consisting of calcium carbonate 2 piece of this, often coloured, used for drawing and writing on blackboards ▷ v 3 draw or mark with chalk **chalky** adj

challenge v 1 invite (someone) to take part in a contest or fight 2 call (something) into question 3 order (someone) to stop and be identified 4 be difficult but stimulating to ▷ n 5 act of challenging **challenged** adj disabled as specified: physically challenged; mentally challenged **challenger** n

chamber n 1 hall used for formal meetings 2 legislative or judicial assembly 3 compartment or cavity 4 obsolete bedroom **chambers** 5 set of rooms used as offices by a barrister **chamberlain** n official who manages the household of a king or nobleman **chambermaid** n woman employed to clean bedrooms in a hotel **chamber music** classical music to be played by a small group of players **chamber pot** bowl

c

for urine, formerly used in bedrooms

chameleon [kam-**meal**-ee-yon] *n* small lizard that changes colour according to its surroundings

chamfer [**cham**-fer] *v* bevel the edge of

chamois [**sham**-wah] *n, pl* -**ois 1** small mountain antelope **2** [**sham**-ee] soft leather **3** [**sham**-ee] cloth of this

chamomile [**kam**-mo-mile] *n* same as **camomile**

champ[1] *v* **1** chew noisily **2** be impatient

champ[2] *n* short for **champion**

champagne *n* sparkling white French wine

champion *n* **1** overall winner of a competition **2** someone who defends a person or cause ▷ *v* **3** support ▷ *adj* **4** excellent **championship** *n*

chance *n* **1** likelihood, probability **2** opportunity **3** risk, gamble **4** unpredictable element that causes things to happen one way rather than another ▷ *v* **5** risk **6** happen by chance ▷ *adj* **7** accidental **chancy** *adj* risky

chancel *n* part of a church containing the altar and choir

chancellor *n* **1** state or legal officer of high rank **2** head of a university **chancellorship** *n*

Chancery *n* division of the British High Court of Justice

chandelier [shan-dill-**eer**] *n* hanging branched holder for lights

chandler *n* dealer, esp. in ships' supplies

change *n* **1** becoming different **2** variety or novelty **3** different set **4** balance received when the amount paid is more than the cost of a purchase **5** coins of low value ▷ *v* **6** make or become different

7 interchange or exchange **8** exchange (money) for its equivalent in a smaller denomination or different currency **9** put different clothes or coverings on **10** leave one vehicle and board another **changeable** *adj* changing often **changeling** *n* child believed to have been exchanged by fairies for another **change up** *baseball* slow pitch thrown like a fast pitch to deceive the batter

channel *n* **1** band of broadcasting frequencies **2** means of access or communication **3** broad strait connecting two areas of sea **4** course along which a river, shipping, etc. moves **5** groove ▷ *v* -**nelling, -nelled 6** direct or convey through a channel

chant *v* **1** sing or utter (a psalm or slogan) ▷ *n* **2** rhythmic or repetitious slogan **3** psalm with a short simple melody

chanter *n* (on bagpipes) pipe on which the melody is played

chaos *n* complete disorder or confusion **chaotic** *adj* **chaotically** *adv*

chap *n informal* man or boy

chapatti, chapati *n* (in Indian cookery) flat thin unleavened bread

chapel *n* **1** place of worship with its own altar, within a church **2** similar place of worship in a large house or institution **3** Nonconformist place of worship **4** section of a trade union in the print industry

chaperone [**shap**-per-rone] *n* **1** older person who accompanies and supervises a young person ▷ *v* **2** act as a chaperone to

chaplain *n* cleric attached to a chapel, military body, or institution **chaplaincy** *n*

chaplet *n* garland for the head

chapped *adj* (of the skin) raw and cracked, through exposure to cold

chapter *n* **1** division of a book **2** period in a life or history **3** branch of a society or club **4** group of canons of a cathedral

char¹ *v* **charring, charred** blacken by partial burning

char² *Brit informal* ▷ *n* **1** charwoman ▷ *v* **charring, charred 2** work as a charwoman

char³ *n Brit slang* tea

character *n* **1** combination of qualities distinguishing an individual **2** moral strength **3** reputation, esp. good reputation **4** person represented in a play, film, or story **5** notable or eccentric person **6** letter, numeral, or symbol used in writing or printing **characteristic** *n* **1** distinguishing feature or quality ▷ *adj* **2** distinguishing **characteristically** *adv* **characterize** *v* **1** be a characteristic of **2** describe the character of **characterization** *n*

charade [shar-**rahd**] *n* **1** absurd pretence **charades 2** game in which one team acts out a word, which the other team has to guess

charcoal *n* black substance formed by partially burning wood

charge *v* **1** ask as a price **2** enter a debit against (a person or an account) **3** accuse formally **4** assign a task to **5** make a rush or sudden attack (upon) **6** fill (a battery) with electricity **7** fill or load ▷ *n* **8** price charged **9** formal accusation **10** attack or rush **11** command or exhortation **12** custody **13** person or thing entrusted to someone's care **14** amount of electricity stored in a battery **in charge** in command **chargeable** *adj* **charger** *n* **1** device for charging an accumulator **2** horse used in battle

chargé d'affaires [shar-zhay daf-**fair**] *n*, *pl* **chargés d'affaires** head of a diplomatic mission in the absence of an ambassador or in a small or unimportant mission

chariot *n* two-wheeled horse-drawn vehicle used in ancient times in wars and races **charioteer** *n* chariot driver

charisma [kar-**rizz**-ma] *n* person's power to attract or influence people **charismatic** [kar-rizz-**mat**-ik] *adj*

charity *n*, *pl* **-ties 1** organization that helps those in need **2** giving of help, such as money or food, to those in need **3** help given **4** kindly attitude towards people **charitable** *adj* **charitably** *adv*

charlady *n* same as **charwoman**

charlatan [**shar**-lat-tan] *n* person who claims expertise that he or she does not have

charleston *n* lively dance of the 1920s

charm *n* **1** attractiveness **2** trinket worn on a bracelet **3** magic spell ▷ *v* **4** attract or delight **5** protect or influence as if by magic **6** influence by personal charm **charmer** *n* **charming** *adj* attractive

charnel house *n* building or vault for the bones of the dead

chart *n* **1** information shown in the form of a diagram, graph, or table **2** map to aid navigation ▷ *v* **3** plot the course of **4** make a chart of the charts *informal* weekly list of best-selling pop records

charter *n* 1 document granting or demanding certain rights 2 constitution of an organization 3 hire of transport for private use ▷ *v* 4 hire by charter 5 grant a charter to **chartered** *adj* officially qualified to practise a profession: *chartered accountant*

chartreuse [shar-**trerz**] *n* sweet-smelling green or yellow liqueur

charwoman *n* woman who is employed as a cleaner

chary [**chair**-ee] *adj* -rier, -riest cautious **charily** *adv*

chase[1] *v* 1 run after quickly in order to catch or drive away 2 *informal* hurry 3 *informal* try energetically to obtain ▷ *n* 4 chasing or pursuit **chaser** *n* drink drunk after another of a different kind

chase[2] *v* engrave or emboss (metal)

chasm [**kaz**-zum] *n* deep crack or ravine in the earth

chassis [**shass**-ee] *n, pl* -sis frame, wheels, and mechanical parts of a motor vehicle

chaste *adj* 1 refraining from sex outside marriage or altogether 2 (of style) simple **chastely** *adv* **chastity** *n*

chasten [**chase**-en] *v* 1 correct by punishment 2 subdue

chastise *v* 1 scold severely 2 punish by beating **chastisement** *n*

chasuble [**chazz**-yew-bl] *n* long sleeveless outer vestment worn by a priest while celebrating Mass

chat *v* chatting, chatted 1 talk in an easy familiar way ▷ *n* 2 easy familiar talk **chatty** *adj* **chattily** *adv*

chateau [**shat**-toe] *n, pl*

-teaux, -teaus French castle or country house

chatelaine [**shat**-tell-lane] *n* esp. formerly, mistress of a large house or castle

chattels *pl n* movable possessions

chatter *v* 1 talk about trivial matters rapidly and continuously 2 (of the teeth) rattle with cold or fear ▷ *n* 3 idle talk **chatterbox** *n* person who chatters incessantly

chauffeur *n* person employed to drive a car **chauffeuse** *n fem*

chauvinism [**show**-vin-iz-zum] *n* 1 irrational belief that one's own race, group, or sex is superior 2 fanatical patriotism **chauvinist** *n, adj* **chauvinistic** *adj*

cheap *adj* 1 low in price 2 of poor quality 3 of little value 4 mean, despicable **cheaply** *adv* **cheapen** *v* 1 make cheap or cheaper 2 degrade **cheap shot** *informal* cruel or critical remark directed at a person's known weakness **cheapskate** *n informal* miserly person

cheat *v* 1 act dishonestly to gain profit or advantage 2 deprive (someone) unfairly ▷ *n* 3 person who cheats 4 fraud or deception

check *v* 1 examine or investigate 2 stop or hinder 3 verify ▷ *n* 4 examination or investigation 5 stoppage or restraint 6 *US* cheque 7 pattern of squares or crossing lines 8 *chess* position of a king under attack **check in** *v* register one's arrival **checkmate** *n* 1 *chess* winning position in which an opponent's king is under attack and unable to escape 2 utter defeat ▷ *v* 3 *chess* place (an opponent's king) in checkmate **4** defeat **check out** v **1** pay the bill and leave a hotel **2** examine or investigate **3** informal have a look at **checkout** n counter in a supermarket, where customers pay **checkup** n general (medical) examination

checker n **1** piece used in Chinese checkers **checkers 2** game played on chessboard with flat, round pieces **checkered** adj **1** marked in squares **2** marked by varied fortunes: a checkered career

Cheddar n smooth firm cheese

cheek n **1** side of the face below the eye **2** informal impudence ▷ v **3** informal speak impudently to **cheeky** adj impudent **cheekily** adv **cheekiness** n

cheep n **1** young bird's high-pitched cry ▷ v **2** utter a cheep

cheer v **1** applaud or encourage with shouts **2** (often foll. by up) make or become happy or hopeful ▷ n **3** shout of applause or encouragement **cheerful** or **cheery** adj **cheerfully** or **cheerily** adv **cheerfulness** n **cheerless** adj gloomy

cheerio interj Brit informal goodbye

cheese n **1** food made from coagulated milk curd **2** shaped block of this **cheesy** adj **cheeseburger** n hamburger with cheese on it **cheesecake** n **1** dessert with a crumb base and a cream cheese filling **2** slang photographs of scantily clad women **cheesecloth** n loosely woven cotton cloth **cheesed off** bored or annoyed

cheetah n **1** swift spotted African animal of the cat family

chef n cook in a restaurant

chef-d'oeuvre [shay-**durv**] n, pl **chefs-d'oeuvre** masterpiece

chemical n **1** substance used in or resulting from a reaction involving changes to atoms or molecules ▷ adj **2** of chemistry or chemicals **chemically** adv

chemise [shem-**meez**] n woman's loose-fitting slip or dress

chemistry n science of the composition, properties, and reactions of substances **chemist** n **1** specialist in chemistry **2** Brit pharmacist

chemotherapy n treatment of disease by chemical means

chenille [shen-**neel**] n (fabric of) thick tufty yarn

cheque n written order to one's bank to pay money from one's account

chequer n same as **checker**

cherish v **1** care for **2** hold dear **3** cling to (an idea or feeling)

cheroot [sher-**root**] n cigar with both ends cut flat

cherry n, pl **-ries 1** small red or black fruit with a stone **2** tree bearing this ▷ adj **3** deep red

cherub n **1** angel, often represented as a winged child **2** sweet child **cherubic** [cher-**rew**-bik] adj

chervil n herb with an aniseed flavour

chess n game of skill for two players with 16 pieces each on a checkered board (**chessboard**) of 64 squares **chessman** n piece used in chess

chest n **1** front of the body, from the neck to the belly **2** large strong box **chest of drawers** piece of furniture consisting of drawers in a frame

chesterfield n sofa with high padded sides and back

chestnut *n* **1** reddish-brown edible nut **2** tree bearing this **3** horse of a reddish-brown colour **4** *informal* old joke ▷ *adj* **5** reddish-brown

cheval glass [shev-**val**] *n* full-length mirror mounted to swivel within a frame

chevron [**shev**-ron] *n* V-shaped pattern, esp. denoting rank

chew *v* grind (food etc.) between the teeth **chewy** *adj* requiring chewing **chewing gum** flavoured gum that is chewed but not swallowed

chianti [kee-**ant**-ee] *n* dry red Italian wine

chiaroscuro [kee-ah-roh-**skew**-roh] *n*, *pl* **-ros** distribution of light and shade in a picture

chic [**sheek**] *adj* **1** stylish or elegant ▷ *n* **2** stylishness

chick *n* young bird **chickadee** *n* small N American bird with a dark crown **chickpea** *n* edible pealike seed of an Asian plant **chickweed** *n* weed with small white flowers

chicken *n* **1** domestic fowl **2** flesh of this used as food **3** *slang* coward ▷ *adj* **4** cowardly **chicken feed** *slang* trifling amount of money **chicken out** *v informal* fail to do something through cowardice **chickenpox** *n* infectious disease with an itchy rash

chicory *n*, *pl* **-ries 1** plant whose leaves are used in salads **2** root of this plant, used as a coffee substitute

chide *v* **chiding, chided** *or* **chid, chid** *or* **chidden** rebuke

chief *n* **1** head of a group of people ▷ *adj* **2** principal, foremost **chiefly** *adv* **1** mainly **2** especially **chieftain** *n* leader of a tribe

chiffon [**shif**-fon] *n* thin gauzy fabric

chignon [**sheen**-yon] *n* knot of hair worn at the back of the head

chihuahua [chee-**wah**-wah] *n* tiny short-haired dog

chilblain *n* inflammation on the fingers or toes, caused by exposure to cold

child *n*, *pl* **children 1** young human being **2** son or daughter **childhood** *n* **childish** *adj* **1** immature or silly **2** of or like a child **childishly** *adv* **childless** *adj* **childlike** *adj* simple or innocent **childbirth** *n* giving birth to a child **child's play** very easy task

chile, chili *n* small hot-tasting red or green pepper used in cooking

chill *n* **1** feverish cold **2** unpleasant coldness ▷ *v* **3** make or become cold ▷ *adj* **4** cold **chilly** *adj* **1** cold **2** unfriendly **chilliness** *n* **chill out** *v informal* relax, esp. after energetic dancing at a rave

chime *n* **1** bell or set of bells **2** sound of this ▷ *v* **3** ring or be rung **4** produce (sounds) or indicate (the time) by chiming **5** be in agreement

chimera [kime-**meer**-a] *n* **1** illusory hope **2** fabled monster with a lion's head, goat's body, and serpent's tail

chimney *n* hollow vertical structure for carrying away smoke or steam **chimneypot** *n* short pipe on the top of a chimney **chimney sweep** person who cleans soot from chimneys

chimp *n informal* short for **chimpanzee**

chimpanzee *n* intelligent ape of central W Africa

chin *n* part of the face below the mouth

china *n* 1 fine earthenware or porcelain 2 cups, saucers, etc.

chinchilla *n* 1 S American rodent with soft grey fur 2 its fur

Chinese *adj* 1 of China or its people ▷ *n* 2 *pl* -**ese** person from China 3 any of the languages of China

chink¹ *n* cleft or crack

chink² *n* 1 light ringing sound ▷ *v* 2 make this sound

chinook *n* warm wind during winter in western N America

chintz *n* printed cotton fabric with a glazed finish

chip *n* 1 very thin slice of potato fried till crunchy 2 *Brit* French fried potato 3 tiny wafer of a semiconductor forming an integrated circuit 4 counter used to represent money in gambling 5 small piece broken off 6 mark left where a small piece has broken off ▷ *v* **chipping, chipped** 7 break small pieces from **have a chip on one's shoulder** *informal* bear a grudge **chip in** *v* 1 *informal* contribute (money) 2 interrupt with a remark

chipboard *n* thin board made of compressed wood particles

chipmunk *n* small striped N American squirrel

chipolata *n* *Brit* small sausage

chiropodist [kir-**rop**-pod-ist] *n* person who treats minor foot complaints **chiropody** *n*

chiropractic [kire-oh-**prak**-tik] *n* system of treating bodily disorders by manipulation of the spine **chiropractor** *n*

chirp, chirrup *v* 1 (of a bird or insect) make a short high-pitched sound ▷ *n* 2 this sound **chirpy** *adj informal* cheerful and lively

chisel *n* 1 metal tool with a sharp end for shaping wood or stone ▷ *v* -**elling, -elled** 2 carve or form with a chisel

chit *n* note or memorandum

chitchat *n* chat or gossip

chitterlings *pl n* pig's intestines cooked as food

chivalry *n* 1 courteous and considerate behaviour, esp. towards women 2 medieval system and principles of knighthood **chivalrous** *adj*

chive *n* herb with a mild onion flavour

chivvy *v* -**vying, -vied** *informal* urge to do something

chlorine *n* yellowish-green pungent gaseous element **chlorinate** *v* disinfect or purify (esp. water) with chlorine **chlorination** *n* **chloride** *n* compound of chlorine

chlorofluorocarbon *n* any of various gaseous compounds of chlorine, fluorine, and carbon, used in refrigerators and aerosol propellants, some of which cause a breakdown of ozone in the earth's atmosphere

chloroform *n* 1 strong-smelling liquid formerly used as an anesthetic ▷ *v* 2 make unconscious with chloroform

chlorophyll *n* green colouring matter in plants, which helps them convert sunlight into energy

chock *n* block or wedge used to prevent a heavy object from moving **chock-full** *or* **chock-a-block** *adj* completely full

chocolate *n* 1 food made from cacao seeds 2 candy or drink made from this ▷ *adj* 3 dark brown **chocolate bar** bar of sweetened chocolate, often with a filling such as nuts, raisins, caramel, etc.

choice *n* 1 choosing 2 opportunity or power

of choosing **3** thing or person chosen **4** possibilities from which to choose ▷ *adj* **5** of superior quality

choir *n* **1** organized group of singers, esp. in church **2** part of a church occupied by the choir

choke *v* **1** hinder or stop the breathing of (a person) by squeezing or blocking the windpipe **2** have trouble in breathing **3** block or clog up ▷ *n* **4** device controlling the amount of air that is mixed with the fuel in a gasoline engine **choker** *n* tight-fitting necklace **choke back** *v* suppress (anger, tears, etc.)

cholera [kol-ler-a] *n* dangerous infectious disease characterized by vomiting and diarrhea

choleric *adj* bad-tempered

cholesterol [kol-**lest**-er-oll] *n* fatty substance found in animal tissue

chomp *v* chew noisily

choose *v* choosing, chose, chosen **1** select from a number of alternatives **2** decide (to do something) **choosy** *adj informal* fussy, hard to please

chop[1] *v* chopping, chopped **1** cut with a blow from an axe or knife **2** cut into pieces **3** hit (an opponent) with a sharp blow ▷ *n* **4** sharp blow **5** slice of meat, usu. with a rib **chopper** *n* **1** small axe **2** *informal* helicopter **choppy** *adj* (of the sea) fairly rough

chop[2] *v* chopping, chopped ▸ **chop and change** change one's mind repeatedly

chops *pl n informal* jaws or cheeks

chopsticks *pl n* pair of thin sticks used to eat with by the Chinese and Japanese

chop suey *n* Chinese-style

dish of chopped meat and vegetables fried in soy sauce

choral *adj* of or for a choir

chorale [kor-**rahl**] *n* slow stately hymn tune

chord *n* **1** simultaneous sounding of three or more musical notes **2** *math* straight line joining two points on a curve

chore *n* routine task

choreography *n* steps and movements of a ballet or dance **choreographer** *n* **choreographic** *adj*

chorister *n* singer in a choir

chortle *v* **1** chuckle gleefully ▷ *n* **2** gleeful chuckle

chorus *n, pl* -ruses **1** large choir **2** group of singers or dancers who perform together **3** part of a song repeated after each verse **4** something expressed by many people at once ▷ *v* chorusing, chorused **5** sing or say together **in chorus** in unison

chose *v* past tense of **choose** ▸ **chosen** *v* past participle of **choose**

choux pastry [shoo] *n* very light pastry made with eggs

chow[1] *n* thick-coated dog with a curled tail, orig. from China

chow[2] *n informal* food

chowder *n* thick soup containing clams or fish

chow mein *n* Chinese dish consisting of chopped meat or vegetables fried with noodles

Christ *n* Jesus, regarded by Christians as the Messiah

christen *v* **1** baptize **2** give a name to **3** use for the first time **christening** *n*

Christendom *n* all Christian people or countries

Christian *n* **1** person who believes in and follows Christ ▷ *adj* **2** relating to Christ or Christianity **3** kind or good **Christianity** *n* religion based on the life and teachings of Christ **Christian name** person's first name **Christian Science** religious system which emphasizes spiritual healing

Christmas *n* 1 annual festival on Dec. 25 commemorating the birth of Christ 2 period around this time **Christmassy** *adj* **Christmas Day** Dec. 25 **Christmas Eve** Dec. 24 **Christmas tree** evergreen tree or imitation of one, decorated as part of Christmas celebrations

chromatic *adj* 1 of colour or colours 2 *music* (of a scale) proceeding by semitones **chromatically** *adv*

chromatography *n* separation and analysis of the components of a substance by slowly passing it through an adsorbing material

chrome, chromium *n* metallic element used in steel alloys and for electroplating

chromosome *n* microscopic gene-carrying body in the nucleus of a cell

chronic *adj* 1 lasting a long time 2 habitual: *a chronic smoker* 3 *informal* very bad **chronically** *adv*

chronicle *n* 1 record of events in chronological order ▷ *v* 2 record in or as if in a chronicle **chronicler** *n*

chronology *n, pl* -**gies** list or arrangement of events in order of occurrence **chronological** *adj* **chronologically** *adv*

chronometer *n* timepiece designed to be accurate in all conditions

chrysalis [**kriss**-a-liss] *n* insect in the stage between larva and adult, when it is in a cocoon

chrysanthemum *n* garden plant with bright showy flowers

chub *n* freshwater fish of the carp family

chubby *adj* -**bier**, -**biest** plump **chubbiness** *n*

chuck[1] *v* 1 *informal* throw 2 *informal* give up, reject 3 touch (someone) affectionately under the chin

chuck[2] *n* 1 cut of beef from the neck to the shoulder 2 device that holds a workpiece in a lathe or a tool in a drill **chuck wagon** wagon carrying cooking supplies for men working in the open

chuckle *v* 1 laugh softly ▷ *n* 2 soft laugh

chug *n* 1 short dull sound, as of an engine ▷ *v* **chugging, chugged** 2 operate or move with this sound

chum *informal* ▷ *n* close friend ▷ *v* **chumming, chummed** ▸ **chum up with** form a close friendship with **chummy** *adj*

chump *n informal* stupid person

chunk *n* 1 thick solid piece 2 considerable amount **chunky** *adj* 1 thick and short 2 with thick pieces

church *n* 1 building for public Christian worship 2 **Church** particular Christian denomination 3 **Church** Christians collectively 4 clergy **churchgoer** *n* person who attends church regularly **churchyard** *n* grounds round a church, used as a graveyard

churlish *adj* surly and rude

churn *n* 1 machine in which cream is shaken to make butter 2 large container for milk ▷ *v* 3 stir (cream) vigorously or make butter in a churn 4 move about violently **churn out** *v informal* produce (things) rapidly in large numbers

chute [**shoot**] n **1** steep channel down which things may be slid **2** waterfall or rapids **3** informal short for **parachute**

chutney n pickle made from fruit, vinegar, and spices

CIA US Central Intelligence Agency

cicada [sik-**kah**-da] n large insect that makes a high-pitched drone

cicatrix [**sik**-a-trix] n, pl -trices scar

CID Brit Criminal Investigation Department

cider n drink made from apples

cigar n roll of cured tobacco leaves for smoking **cigarette** n shredded tobacco in a thin paper cylinder for smoking

cilantro n plant widely cultivated for its aromatic seeds and leaves, used in flavouring food etc.

cinch [**sinch**] n informal **1** easy task **2** certainty

cinder n piece of incombustible material left after burning coal

cine camera n camera for taking moving pictures

cinema n **1** place for showing films **2** films collectively **cinematic** adj **cinematography** n technique of making films **cinematographer** n

cineraria n garden plant with daisy-like flowers

cinnamon n spice obtained from the bark of an Asian tree

cipher [**sife**-er] n **1** system of secret writing **2** unimportant person

circa [**sir**-ka] prep Latin about, approximately

circle n **1** perfectly round geometric figure, line, or shape **2** group of people sharing an interest or activity **3** theatre section of seats

above the main level of the auditorium ▷ v **4** move in a circle **5** surround **circlet** n circular ornament worn on the head **circular** adj **1** round **2** moving in a circle ▷ n **3** letter or notice for general distribution **circularity** n **circulate** v send, go, or move around **circulation** n **1** flow of blood around the body **2** number of copies of a newspaper or magazine sold **3** sending or moving around **circulatory** adj

circuit n **1** complete round or course **2** complete path through which an electric current can flow **3** periodical journey around a district, as made by judges **4** motor-racing track **circuitous** [sir-**kew**-it-uss] adj roundabout, indirect **circuitry** [**sir**-kit-tree] n electrical circuit(s)

circumcise v cut off the foreskin of **circumcision** n

circumference n **1** boundary of a specified area or shape, esp. of a circle **2** distance round this

circumflex n accent (^) over a vowel to show that it is pronounced in a particular way

circumlocution n indirect expression **circumlocutory** adj

circumnavigate v sail right round **circumnavigation** n

circumscribe v **1** restrict **2** draw a line round **circumscription** n

circumspect adj cautious, prudent **circumspectly** adv **circumspection** n

circumstance n usu pl occurrence or condition that accompanies or influences a person or event **circumstantial** adj **1** (of evidence) strongly suggesting something but not proving it **2** detailed **circumstantiate** v prove by giving details

circumvent v avoid or get round (a difficulty etc.) **circumvention** n

circus n, pl **-cuses** (performance given by) a travelling company of acrobats, clowns, performing animals, etc.

cirrhosis [sir-**roh**-siss] n liver disease

cirrus n, pl **-ri** high wispy cloud

cisco [**siss**-ko] n, pl **-coes** N American whitefish

cistern n water tank

citadel n fortress in a city

cite v **1** quote **2** bring forward as proof **citation** n

citizen n **1** native or naturalized member of a state or nation **2** inhabitant of a city or town **citizenship** n **Citizens' Band** range of radio frequencies for private communication by the public

citric acid n weak acid found in citrus fruits

citrus fruit n juicy, sharp-tasting fruit such as an orange, lemon, or lime

city n, pl **-ties** large or important town **the City** area of London as a financial centre

civet [**siv**-vit] n **1** spotted catlike African mammal **2** musky fluid from its glands used in perfume

civic adj of a city or citizens **civics** pl n study of the rights and responsibilities of citizenship

civil adj **1** relating to the citizens of a state as opposed to the armed forces or the Church **2** polite **civilly** adv **civility** n politeness **civilian** n, adj (person) not belonging to the armed forces **civil**

service public service **civil servant** public servant **civil war** war between people of the same country

civilize v **1** bring out of barbarism into a state of civilization **2** refine **civilization** n **1** high level of human cultural and social development **2** particular society which has reached this level

civvies pl n slang civilian clothes

Cl chem chlorine

clack n **1** sound made by two hard objects striking together ▷ v **2** (cause to) make this sound

clad v a past of **clothe**

cladding n material used for the outside facing of a building etc.

claim v **1** assert **2** demand as a right **3** call for or need ▷ n **4** assertion **5** demand for something as due **6** right **7** thing claimed **claimant** n

clairvoyance n power of perceiving things beyond the natural range of the senses **clairvoyant** n, adj

clam n **1.** edible shellfish with a hinged shell ▷ v **clamming**, **clammed 2 clam up** informal refuse to talk

clamber v climb awkwardly or with difficulty

clammy adj **-mier, -miest** unpleasantly moist and sticky **clamminess** n

clamour n **1** loud protest **2** loud persistent outcry or noise ▷ v **3** make a loud outcry or noise **clamorous** adj **clamour for** v demand noisily

clamp n **1** tool with movable jaws for holding things together tightly ▷ v **2** fasten with a clamp **clamp down on** v **1** become stricter about **2** suppress

clan *n* **1** group of families with a common ancestor **2** close group **clannish** *adj* (of a group) tending to exclude outsiders

clandestine *adj* secret, furtive

clang *n* **1** loud ringing sound ▷ *v* **2** (cause to) make this sound **clanger** *n informal* conspicuous mistake

clangour *n* loud continuous clanging sound **clangorous** *adj*

clank *n* **1** harsh metallic sound ▷ *v* **2** (cause to) make this sound

clap[1] *v* **clapping, clapped** **1** applaud by striking the palms of one's hands sharply together **2** put quickly or forcibly ▷ *n* **3** act or sound of clapping **4** sharp abrupt sound, esp. of thunder **clapped out** *slang* worn out **clapper** *n* piece of metal inside a bell, which causes it to sound when struck against the side **clapperboard** *n* pair of hinged boards clapped together during filming to aid synchronizing sound and picture **claptrap** *n* empty words

clap[2] *n slang* gonorrhea

claret [**klar**-rit] *n* dry red wine from Bordeaux

clarify *v* **-fying, -fied** make or become clear **clarification** *n*

clarinet *n* keyed woodwind instrument with a single reed **clarinettist** *n*

clarion *n* **1** obsolete high-pitched trumpet **2** its sound **clarion call** rousing appeal

clarity *n* clearness

clash *v* **1** come into conflict **2** (of events) coincide **3** (of colours) look unattractive together **4** (cause to) make a clashing sound ▷ *n* **5** conflict **6** loud harsh noise, esp. of things striking together

clasp *n* **1** device for fastening things **2** firm grasp or embrace ▷ *v* **3** grasp or embrace firmly **4** fasten with a clasp **clasp knife** knife whose blade folds into the handle

class *n* **1** social group of a particular rank **2** system of dividing society into such groups **3** group of people or things sharing a common characteristic **4** group of pupils or students taught together **5** standard of quality **6** *informal* excellence or elegance ▷ *v* **7** place in a class **classy** *adj informal* stylish, elegant **classify** *v* **1** arrange in classes **2** designate (information) as officially secret **classifiable** *adj* **classification** *n* **classroom** *n* room, esp. in a school, in which classes are conducted

classic *adj* **1** typical **2** of lasting significance because of excellence **3** characterized by simplicity and purity of form ▷ *n* **4** author, artist, or work of art of recognized excellence **classics** **5** study of ancient Greek and Roman literature and culture **classical** *adj* **1** traditional and standard **2** *music* denoting serious art music **3** of or influenced by ancient Greek and Roman culture **classically** *adv* **classicism** *n* artistic style showing regularity of form and emotional restraint **classicist** *n*

clatter *n* **1** rattling noise ▷ *v* **2** (cause to) make a rattling noise

clause *n* **1** part of a sentence, containing a verb **2** section in a legal document

claustrophobia *n* abnormal fear of confined spaces **claustrophobic** *adj*

clavichord n early keyboard instrument

clavicle n collarbone

claw n 1 sharp hooked nail of a bird or beast 2 similar part, such as a crab's pincer ▷ v 3 tear with claws or nails

clay n fine-grained earth, soft when moist and hardening when baked, used to make bricks and pottery **clayey** adj **clay pigeon** baked clay disc hurled into the air as a target for shooting

claymore n two-edged broadsword formerly used by Scottish Highlanders

CLC Canadian Labour Congress

clean adj 1 free from dirt or impurities 2 morally sound 3 without obscenity 4 not yet used 5 complete: a clean break 6 smooth and regular ▷ v 7 free from dirt ▷ adv 8 not standard completely **come clean** informal confess **cleaner** n **cleanly** adv **cleanliness** n **cleanse** v make clean **cleanser** n

clear adj 1 free from doubt or confusion 2 plain, distinct 3 transparent 4 free from darkness or obscurity, bright 5 free from obstruction 6 (of weather) free from clouds 7 without blemish or defect 8 (of money) net ▷ adv 9 clearly 10 completely 11 out of the way: stand clear of the gates ▷ v 12 make or become clear 13 pass by or over without touching 14 acquit 15 make as profit **clearly** adv **clearness** n **clearance** n 1 clearing 2 official permission **clearing** n area cleared of trees **clear off** v informal go away **clear out** v 1 empty 2 informal go away **clear-sighted** adj perceptive

cleat n 1 wedge 2 piece of wood or iron with two projecting ends round which ropes are fastened

cleave¹ v **cleaving, cleft, cleaved** or **clove, cleft, cleaved,** or **cloven** split apart **cleavage** n 1 space between a woman's breasts, as revealed by a low-cut dress 2 division, split **cleaver** n heavy butcher's knife

cleave² v cling or adhere

clef n music symbol at the beginning of a stave to show the pitch

cleft n 1 split or indentation ▷ v 2 a past of **cleave¹** ▶ **in a cleft stick** in a very difficult position

clematis n climbing plant with showy flowers

clement adj (of weather) mild **clemency** n mercy

clementine n small orange citrus fruit

clench v 1 close or squeeze (one's teeth or fist) firmly together 2 grasp firmly

clerestory [clear-store-ee] n, pl -ries row of windows at the top of a wall above an adjoining roof

clergy n priests and ministers as a group **clergyman** n

cleric n member of the clergy

clerical adj 1 of clerks or office work 2 of the clergy

clerk n employee in an office, bank, or court who keeps records, files, and accounts

clever adj 1 intelligent, quick at learning 2 showing skill **cleverly** adv **cleverness** n

cliché [klee-shay] n hackneyed expression or idea **clichéd** adj

click n 1 short slight sound ▷ v 2 (cause to) make this sound 3 informal become suddenly clear 4 informal (of two people) get on well 5 slang be a success 6 Also **click on** computers select a particular function by pressing a button on a mouse

client n 1 person who uses the services of a professional 2 customer 3 *computers* program or work station that requests data from a server
clientele [klee-on-**tell**] n clients collectively

cliff n steep rock face, esp. along the sea shore
cliffhanger n film, game, etc. which is exciting and full of suspense because its outcome is uncertain

climate n prevalent weather conditions of an area
climatic adj

climax n 1 most intense point of an experience, series of events, or story 2 orgasm ▷ v 3 reach a climax **climactic** adj

climb v 1 go up or ascend 2 rise ▷ n 3 place to be climbed
climber n **climb down** v retreat from an opinion or position

clime n lit region or its climate

clinch v 1 settle (an argument or agreement) decisively ▷ n 2 clinching **clincher** n informal something decisive

cling v **clinging**, **clung** hold fast or stick closely **clingfilm** n thin polythene wrapping

clinic n 1 place in which outpatients receive medical advice or treatment 2 private or specialized hospital
clinical adj 1 of a clinic 2 scientifically detached
clinically adv

clink¹ n 1 light sharp metallic sound ▷ v 2 (cause to) make such a sound

clink² n slang prison

clinker n fused coal residues from a fire or furnace

clinker-built adj (of a boat) made of overlapping planks

clip¹ v **clipping**, **clipped** 1 cut with shears or scissors 2 informal hit sharply ▷ n 3 short extract of a film 4 informal sharp blow **clippers** pl n tool for clipping **clipping** n something cut out, esp. an article from a newspaper

clip² n 1 device for attaching or holding things together ▷ v 2 attach or hold together with a clip

clipper n fast commercial sailing ship

clique [kleek] n small exclusive group **cliqueish** adj

clitoris [**klit**-or-iss] n small sexually sensitive part of the female genitals **clitoral** adj

cloak n 1 loose sleeveless outer garment ▷ v 2 cover or conceal
cloakroom n room where coats may be left temporarily

clobber v informal 1 batter 2 defeat utterly

cloche [klosh] n 1 cover to protect young plants 2 woman's close-fitting hat

clock n 1 instrument for showing the time 2 device with a dial for recording or measuring **clockwise** adv, adj in the direction in which the hands of a clock rotate
clock in, clock on, clock off, or **clock out** v register arrival at or departure from work on an automatic time recorder
clock up v reach (a total)
clockwork n mechanism similar to that of a clock, as in a wind-up toy

clod n 1 lump of earth 2 stupid person **cloddish** adj

clog v **clogging**, **clogged** 1 block ▷ n 2 wooden-soled shoe

cloisonné [klwah-**zon**-nay] n design made by filling in a wire outline with coloured enamel

cloister n covered pillared arcade, usu. in a monastery
cloistered adj sheltered

clone n 1 group of organisms

or cells reproduced asexually from a single plant or animal **2** *informal* person who closely resembles another ▷ *v* **3** produce as a clone

close[1] *v* **1** shut **2** prevent access to **3** finish **4** bring or come nearer together ▷ *n* **5** end **closed shop** place of work in which all workers must belong to a particular trade union

close[2] *adj* **1** near **2** intimate **3** careful, thorough **4** oppressive or stifling **5** secretive **6** compact, dense ▷ *adv* **7** closely or tightly ▷ *n* **8** street closed at one end **9** courtyard or quadrangle **closely** *adv* **closeness** *n* **close season** period when it is illegal to kill certain kinds of game and fish **close shave** *informal* narrow escape **close-up** *n* photograph or film taken at very close range

closer *n* **1** person or thing that closes **2** *baseball* relief pitcher brought in to make the final outs for the team with the lead

closet *n* **1** cupboard **2** small private room ▷ *adj* **3** private or secret ▷ *v* **closeting, closeted** **4** shut away in private, esp. for conference

closure *n* **1** closing or being closed **2** a resolution of a significant event or relationship in a person's life

clot *n* **1** soft thick lump formed from liquid **2** *informal* fool ▷ *v* **clotting, clotted 3** form clots

cloth *n* woven fabric

clothe *v* **clothing, clothed** or **clad 1** put clothes on **2** provide with clothes **clothes** *pl n* **1** articles of dress **clothesline** *n* piece of rope from which clean washing is hung to dry **clothing** *n* clothes collectively

cloud *n* **1** mass of condensed water vapour floating in the sky **2** floating mass of smoke, dust, etc. **3** *computers* internet server used to store data and services ▷ *v* **4** make or become cloudy **5** confuse **6** make gloomy or depressed **cloudless** *adj* **cloudy** *adj* **1** full of clouds **2** (of liquid) opaque **cloudberry** *n* creeping plant with yellowish fruit **cloudburst** *n* heavy fall of rain

clout *informal* ▷ *n* **1** blow **2** influence, power ▷ *v* **3** hit

clove[1] *n* **1** dried flower bud of a tropical tree, used as a spice **2** segment of a bulb of garlic

clove[2] *v* a past tense of **cleave**[1] ▶ **clove hitch** knot used to fasten a rope to a spar

cloven *v* a past participle of **cleave**[1] ▶ **cloven hoof** divided hoof of a sheep, goat, etc.

clover *n* plant with three-lobed leaves **in clover** in luxury

clown *n* **1** comic entertainer in a circus **2** amusing person **3** stupid person ▷ *v* **4** perform as a clown **5** behave foolishly **clownish** *adj*

cloy *v* sicken by an excess of something sweet or pleasurable

club *n* **1** association of people with common interests **2** building used by such a group **3** thick stick used as a weapon **4** bat or stick used in some games **5** playing card of the suit marked with black three-leaved symbols ▷ *v* **clubbing, clubbed 6** strike with a club **club together** combine resources for a common purpose

club foot *n* congenitally deformed foot

cluck *n* **1** low clicking noise made by a hen ▷ *v* **2** make this noise

clue *n* something that helps to solve a mystery or puzzle **not have a clue** be completely baffled **clueless** *adj* stupid

clump[1] *n* **1** cluster or mass ▷ *v* **2** form into a clump

clump[2] *v* **1** walk or tread heavily ▷ *n* **2** dull heavy tread

clumsy *adj* **-sier, -siest 1** lacking skill or physical coordination **2** badly made or done **clumsily** *adv* **clumsiness** *n*

clung *v* past of **cling**

clunk *n* **1** dull metallic sound ▷ *v* **2** make such a sound

cluster *n* **1** small close group ▷ *v* **2** (cause to) form a cluster

clutch[1] *v* **1** grasp tightly **2** try to seize ▷ *n* **3** tight grasp **4** device enabling two revolving shafts to be connected and disconnected

clutch[2] *n* **1** set of eggs laid at the same time **2** brood of chickens

clutter *v* **1** strew objects about (a place) in disorder ▷ *n* **2** disordered heap or mass of objects

cm centimetre(s)

Co *chem* cobalt

CO Commanding Officer

Co. **1** Company **2** County

co- *prefix* **1** together **2** joint or jointly: *coproduction*

c/o **1** care of **2** *book-keeping* carried over

coach *n* **1** long-distance bus **2** railway carriage **3** large four-wheeled horse-drawn carriage **4** trainer, tutor ▷ *v* **5** train or teach

coagulate [koh-**ag**-yew-late] *v* change from a liquid to a semisolid mass **coagulation** *n* **coagulant** *n* substance causing coagulation

coal *n* black mineral consisting mainly of carbon, used as fuel **coalfield** *n* area rich in coal

coalesce [koh-a-**less**] *v* come together, merge **coalescence** *n*

coalition [koh-a-**lish**-un] *n* temporary alliance, esp. between political parties

coarse *adj* **1** rough in texture **2** unrefined or indecent **coarsely** *adv* **coarseness** *n* **coarsen** *v* **coarse fish** *Brit* any freshwater fish not of the salmon family

coast *n* **1** sea shore ▷ *v* **2** move by momentum, without the use of power **coastal** *adj* **coaster** *n* **1** small ship **2** small mat placed under a glass **coastguard** *n* **1** organization which aids shipping and prevents smuggling **2** member of this **coastline** *n* outline of a coast

coat *n* **1** long outer garment with sleeves **2** animal's fur or hair **3** covering layer ▷ *v* **4** cover with a layer **coating** *n* covering layer **coat of arms** heraldic emblem of a family or institution

coax *v* **1** persuade gently **2** manipulate carefully and patiently

coaxial [koh-**ax**-ee-al] *adj* (of a cable) transmitting by means of two concentric conductors separated by an insulator

cob *n* **1** thickset type of horse **2** male swan **3** stalk of an ear of corn **4** round loaf of bread

cobalt *n* **1** metallic element **2** deep blue pigment made from it

cobber *n Aust informal* (used as a term of address between men) friend, mate

cobble *v* **1** put together roughly ▷ *n* **2** Also **cobblestone** round stone used for paving **cobbler** *n* shoe mender

cobra *n* venomous hooded snake of Asia and Africa

cobweb *n* spider's web

cocaine *n* addictive drug

used as a narcotic and local anesthetic

coccyx [**kok**-six] *n, pl* **coccyges** [kok-**sije**-eez] bone at the base of the spinal column

cochineal *n* scarlet dye obtained from a Mexican insect

cock *n* **1** male bird, esp. of the domestic fowl **2** stopcock **3** hammer of a gun ▷ *v* **4** draw back (the hammer of a gun) to firing position **5** lift and turn (part of the body) **cockerel** *n* young cock **cock-a-hoop** *adj* in high spirits **cock-and-bull story** improbable story **cockeyed** *adj informal* **1** askew **2** absurd

cockade *n* rosette or feather worn on a hat as a badge

cockatoo *n* crested parrot of Australia or the East Indies

cockatrice [**kok**-a-triss] *n* mythical animal like a small dragon

cockchafer *n* large flying beetle

cocker spaniel *n* small breed of spaniel

cockle *n* edible bivalve mollusc

Cockney *n* **1** native of the East End of London **2** Cockney dialect

cockpit *n* **1** pilot's compartment in an aircraft **2** driver's compartment in a racing car

cockroach *n* beetle-like insect which is a household pest

cocksure *adj* overconfident, arrogant

cocktail *n* **1** mixed alcoholic drink **2** appetizer of seafood or mixed fruits

cocky *adj* **cockier, cockiest** conceited and overconfident **cockily** *adv* **cockiness** *n*

cocoa *n* **1** powder made from the seed of the cacao tree **2** drink made from this powder

coconut *n* **1** large hard fruit of a type of palm tree **2** edible flesh of this fruit **coconut matting** coarse matting made from the fibrous husk of the coconut

cocoon *n* **1** silky sheath of a chrysalis **2** protective covering ▷ *v* **3** wrap or protect as if in a cocoon

cod *n* large food fish of the North Atlantic

COD cash on delivery

coda [**kode**-a] *n* final part of a musical composition

coddle *v* overprotect or pamper

code *n* **1** system of letters, symbols, or prearranged signals by which messages can be communicated secretly or briefly **2** set of principles or rules ▷ *v* **3** put into code **4** write computer programs **codify** [**kode**-if-fie] *v* organize (rules or procedures) systematically **codification** *n*

codeine [**kode**-een] *n* drug used as a painkiller

codex *n, pl* **codices** volume of manuscripts of an ancient text

codger *n informal* old man

codicil [**kode**-iss-ill] *n* addition to a will

coeducation *n* education of boys and girls together **coeducational** *adj*

coefficient *n math* number or constant placed before and multiplying a quantity

coelacanth [**seel**-a-kanth] *n* primitive marine fish

coeliac disease [**seel**-ee-ak] *n* disease which hampers digestion of food

coerce [koh-**urss**] *v* compel or force **coercion** *n* **coercive** *adj*

coeval [koh-**eev**-al] *adj, n* contemporary

coexist *v* exist together, esp. peacefully despite differences **coexistence** *n*

C of E Church of England
coffee n **1** drink made from the roasted and ground seeds of a tropical shrub **2** beanlike seeds of this shrub ▷ adj **3** light brown **coffee table** small low table
coffer n **1** chest for valuables **coffers 2** store of money
cofferdam n watertight enclosure pumped dry to enable construction work to be done
coffin n box in which a corpse is buried or cremated
cog n **1** one of a series of teeth on the rim of a gearwheel **2** unimportant person in a big organization
cogent [**koh**-jent] adj forcefully convincing **cogency** n **cogently** adv
cogitate [**koj**-it-tate] v think deeply, ponder **cogitation** n
cognac [**kon**-yak] n French brandy
cognate adj related, akin
cognition n act or experience of knowing or acquiring knowledge **cognitive** adj
cognizance n knowledge, perception **cognizant** adj
cognoscenti [kon-yo-**shen**-tee] pl n connoisseurs
cohabit v live together without being married **cohabitation** n
cohere v **1** stick together **2** be logically connected and consistent **coherence** n **coherent** adj **1** capable of intelligible speech **2** logical and consistent **coherently** adv **cohesion** n tendency to unite **cohesive** adj
cohort n **1** band of associates **2** tenth part of a Roman legion
coiffure n hairstyle **coiffeur** (**coiffeuse**) n hairdresser
coil v **1** wind or be wound in loops **2** move in a winding course ▷ n **3** something coiled

4 single loop of this **5** Brit contraceptive device inserted in the womb
coin n **1** piece of metal money **2** metal currency collectively ▷ v **3** invent (a word or phrase) **coin it in** informal make money rapidly **coinage** n **1** coining **2** coins collectively **3** word or phrase coined
coincide v **1** happen at the same time **2** agree or correspond exactly **coincidence** n **1** occurrence of simultaneous or apparently connected events **2** coinciding **coincident** adj **coincidental** adj **coincidentally** adv
coir n coconut husk fibre
coition [koh-**ish**-un], **coitus** [**koh**-it-uss] n sexual intercourse **coital** adj
coke[1] n solid fuel left after gas has been distilled from coal
coke[2] n slang cocaine
col n high mountain pass
cola n soft drink flavoured with an extract from the nuts of a tropical tree
colander n perforated bowl for straining or rinsing foods
cold adj **1** lacking heat **2** lacking affection or enthusiasm **3** (of a colour) giving an impression of coldness **4** slang unconscious: out cold ▷ n **5** lack of heat **6** illness characterized by catarrh and sneezing **coldly** adv **coldness** n **cold-blooded** adj **1** having a body temperature that varies with that of the surroundings **2** callous or cruel **cold cream** creamy preparation for softening and cleansing the skin **cold feet** slang fear **cold-shoulder** v treat (someone) with indifference **cold war** political hostility between countries without actual warfare

coleslaw n salad dish of shredded raw cabbage in a dressing

coley n codlike food fish of the N Atlantic

colic n severe pains in the stomach and bowels **colicky** adj

colitis [koh-**lie**-tiss] n inflammation of the colon

collaborate v 1 work with another on a project 2 cooperate with an enemy invader **collaboration** n **collaborative** adj **collaborator** n

collage [kol-**lahzh**] n 1 art form in which various materials or objects are glued onto a surface 2 picture made in this way

collapse v 1 fall down or in suddenly 2 fail completely 3 fold compactly ▷ n 4 act of collapsing 5 sudden failure or breakdown **collapsible** adj

collar n 1 part of a garment round the neck 2 band put round an animal's neck 3 cut of meat from an animal's neck 4 band round a pipe, rod, or shaft ▷ v informal 5 seize, arrest 6 catch in order to speak to 7 take for oneself **collarbone** n bone joining the shoulder blade to the breast bone

collate v compare carefully **collation** n 1 collating 2 light meal **collator** n

collateral n security pledged for the repayment of a loan

colleague n fellow worker, esp. in a profession

collect[1] v 1 gather or be gathered together 2 accumulate (stamps etc.) as a hobby 3 fetch **collected** adj calm and controlled **collection** n 1 collecting 2 things collected **collector** n **collective** adj 1 of or done by a group, combined ▷ n 2 group of people working together on an enterprise and sharing the benefits from it **collectively** adv

collect[2] n short prayer

colleen n Irish girl

college n 1 place of higher education 2 group of people of the same profession or with special duties **collegiate** adj

collide v 1 crash together violently 2 conflict **collision** n

collie n silky-coated sheepdog

colliery n, pl -lieries coal mine **collier** n 1 coal miner 2 coal ship

collocate v (of words) occur together regularly **collocation** n

colloid n suspension of particles in a solution

collop n small slice of meat

colloquial adj suitable for informal speech or writing **colloquialism** n colloquial expression

colloquy n, pl -quies conversation or conference

collusion n secret agreement for a fraudulent purpose **collude** v act in collusion

collywobbles pl n slang 1 nervousness 2 upset stomach

cologne n perfumed toilet water

colon[1] n punctuation mark (:)

colon[2] n part of the large intestine connected to the rectum

colonel n senior commissioned army or air-force officer

colonnade n row of columns

colony n, pl -nies 1 group of people who settle in a new country but remain subject to their parent state 2 territory occupied by a colony 3 group of people or animals of the same kind living together **colonial** adj, n (inhabitant) of a colony **colonialism** n policy of acquiring and maintaining colonies **colonist** n settler in a colony **colonize** v make into a colony **colonization** n

colophon n publisher's emblem

Colorado beetle n black-and-yellow beetle that is a serious pest of potatoes

coloration n colouring

colossal adj huge

colossus n, pl **-si**, **-suses** 1 huge statue 2 huge or important person or thing

colostomy n, pl **-mies** operation to form an opening from the colon onto the surface of the body, for emptying the bowel

colour n 1 appearance of things as a result of reflecting light 2 paint or pigment 3 complexion **colours** 4 flag 5 sports badge or symbol denoting membership of a team ▷ v 6 apply or give colour to 7 influence or distort 8 blush **Coloured** adj 1 offensive non-White 2 (in S Africa) of mixed race **colourful** adj 1 with bright or varied colours 2 vivid or distinctive **colourfully** adv **colourless** adj **colour-blind** adj unable to distinguish between certain colours

colt n young male horse

columbine n garden flower with five spurred petals

column n 1 pillar 2 vertical arrangement of numbers 3 long narrow formation of troops 4 vertical division of a newspaper page 5 regular feature in a newspaper **columnist** n journalist writing a regular feature for a newspaper

coma n state of deep unconsciousness **comatose** adj 1 in a coma 2 sound asleep

comb n 1 toothed implement for arranging the hair 2 cock's crest 3 honeycomb ▷ v 4 use a comb on 5 search with great care

combat v **-bating**, **-bated**, n fight, struggle **combatant** n **combative** adj

combine v 1 join together ▷ n 2 association of people or firms for a common purpose **combination** n 1 combining 2 people or things combined 3 set of numbers that opens a special lock **combinations** 4 one-piece undergarment with long sleeves and legs **combine harvester** machine which reaps and threshes grain in one operation

combustion n process of burning **combustible** adj burning easily

come v **coming**, **came**, **come** 1 move towards a place, arrive 2 occur 3 be available 4 reach a specified point or condition 5 originate (from) 6 become **come across** v 1 meet or find by accident 2 (foll. by as) give an impression (of being) **comeback** n informal 1 return to a former position 2 retort **comedown** n 1 decline in status 2 disappointment **comeuppance** n informal deserved punishment

comedy n, pl **-dies** humorous play, film, or programme **comedian** (**comedienne**) n entertainer who tells jokes

comely adj **-lier**, **-liest** old-fashioned good-looking

comestibles pl n food

comet n heavenly body with a long luminous tail

comfort n 1 physical ease or wellbeing 2 relief from suffering 3 person or thing that brings ease ▷ v 4 give

comfort to **comfortable**
adj 1 giving comfort 2 free
from pain 3 informal well-off
financially **comfortably** adv
comforter n

comfrey n tall plant with
bell-shaped flowers

comfy adj -fier, -fiest informal
comfortable

comic adj 1 humorous, funny
2 relating to comedy ▷ n
3 comedian 4 magazine
consisting of strip cartoons
comical adj amusing
comically adv

comma n punctuation mark
(,)

command v 1 order 2 have
authority over 3 deserve and
get 4 look down over ▷ n
5 authoritative instruction
that something must be done
6 authority to command
7 knowledge, mastery
8 military or naval unit
with a specific function
commandant n officer
commanding a military group
commandeer v seize for
military use **commander** n
1 military officer in command
of a group or operation
2 middle-ranking naval
officer **commander-in-
chief** n supreme commander
commandment n divine
command

commando n, pl -dos, -does
(member of) a military unit
trained for swift raids in
enemy territory

commemorate v honour
or keep alive the memory
of **commemoration** n
commemorative adj

commence v begin
commencement n

commend v 1 praise
2 recommend 3 entrust
commendable adj
commendably adv
commendation n

commensurable adj
measurable by the same
standard **commensurability**
n

commensurate adj
corresponding in degree, size,
or value

comment n 1 remark
2 gossip 3 explanatory note
▷ v 4 make a comment or
comments **commentary**
n 1 spoken accompaniment
to a broadcast or film
2 explanatory notes
commentate v provide a
commentary **commentator**
n

commerce n 1 buying and
selling, trade 2 dealings
commercial adj 1 of
commerce 2 (of television or
radio) paid for by advertisers
3 having profit as the
main aim ▷ n 4 television
or radio advertisement
commercialize v
make commercial
commercialization n

commiserate v (foll. by with)
express pity or sympathy (for)
commiseration n

commissar n official
responsible for political
education in Communist
countries

commissariat n military
department in charge of food
supplies

commission n 1 order for a
piece of work, esp. a work of
art 2 duty or task given to
someone 3 percentage paid
to a salesperson for each
sale made 4 group of people
appointed to perform certain
duties 5 committing 6 mil
rank or authority officially
given to an officer 7 delegated
authority ▷ v 8 place an order
for 9 mil give a commission
to 10 grant authority to **out
of commission** not working

commissioner n 1 appointed official in a government department 2 member of a commission

commissionaire n uniformed doorman at a hotel, theatre, etc.

commit v -mitting, -mitted 1 perform (a crime or error) 2 pledge to a cause or course of action 3 send (someone) to prison or hospital **committal** n sending of someone for trial, etc. **commitment** n 1 dedication to a cause 2 responsibility or promise that hinders freedom of action

committee n group of people appointed to perform a specified service or function

commode n 1 seat with a compartment holding a chamber pot 2 chest of drawers

commodious adj roomy

commodity n, pl -ities article of trade

commodore n 1 senior naval or air-force officer 2 president of a yacht club

common adj 1 occurring often 2 belonging to two or more people 3 public, general 4 low-class ▷ n 5 area of grassy land belonging to a community **commons** 6 ordinary people 7 **Commons** House of Commons **commonly** adv **commoner** n Brit person who does not belong to the nobility **common-law** adj (of a relationship) regarded as marriage through being long-standing **Common Market** European Community **commonplace** adj 1 ordinary, everyday ▷ n 2 trite remark **common sense** sound practical understanding **commonwealth** n 1 republic 2 **Commonwealth** federation

of independent states that used to be ruled by Britain

commotion n noisy disturbance

commune[1] n group of people living together, sharing property and responsibilities **communal** adj shared **communally** adv

commune[2] v (foll. by with) experience strong emotion (for) **communion** n 1 sharing of thoughts or feelings 2 **Communion** Christian ritual of sharing consecrated bread and wine 3 religious group with shared beliefs and practices

communicate v 1 make known, reveal (information, thoughts, or feelings) 2 (of rooms) have a connecting door **communicable** adj (of a disease) able to be passed on **communicant** n person who receives Communion **communication** n 1 communicating 2 thing communicated **communications** 3 means of travelling or sending messages **communicative** adj willing to talk

communiqué [kom-**mune**-ik-kay] n official announcement

communism n 1 doctrine that all property and means of production should be shared by the people 2 **Communism** political and social system of state control of the economy and society in some countries **communist** n, adj

community n, pl -ties 1 all the people living in one district 2 group having shared interests or origins 3 society, the public **community centre** building used by a community for activities

commute v 1 travel daily to

and from work **2** reduce (a sentence) to a less severe one

commuter *n* person who commutes to and from work

commutator *n* device used to change alternating electric current into direct current

compact[1] *adj* **1** closely packed **2** neatly arranged **3** concise, brief ▷ *n* **4** small flat case containing a mirror and face powder ▷ *v* **5** pack closely together **compactly** *adv* **compactness** *n* **compact disc** small digital audio disc on which the sound is read by an optical laser system

compact[2] *n* agreement, contract

companion *n* person who associates with or accompanies another **companionable** *adj* friendly **companionship** *n*

companionway *n* ladder linking the decks of a ship

company *n, pl* **-nies 1** business firm **2** group of actors **3** small unit of troops **4** crew of a ship **5** companionship **6** gathering of people **7** guest or guests **8** associates

compare *v* **1** examine (things) to find the resemblances or differences **2** declare to be like **3** be worthy of comparison **comparable** *adj* **comparability** *n* **comparative** *adj* **1** relative **2** involving comparison **3** *grammar* denoting the form of an adjective or adverb indicating *more* ▷ *n* **4** *grammar* comparative form of a word **comparatively** *adv* **comparison** *n*

compartment *n* **1** separate section **2** section of a railway carriage

compass *n* **1** instrument for showing direction, with a needle that points north

2 range **compasses 3** hinged instrument for drawing circles

compassion *n* pity, sympathy **compassionate** *adj*

compatible *adj* able to exist, work, or be used together **compatibility** *n*

compatriot *n* fellow countryman or countrywoman

compeer *n* equal, companion

compel *v* **-pelling, -pelled** force (to be or do) **compelling** *adj* **1** convincing **2** arousing strong interest

compendium *n, pl* **-diums, -dia** selection of different table games in one container **compendious** *adj* brief but inclusive

compensate *v* **1** make amends to (someone), esp. for injury or loss **2** (foll. by *for*) cancel out a bad effect **compensation** *n* **compensatory** *adj*

compère *n Brit* **1** person who presents a stage, radio, or television show ▷ *v* **2** be the compère of

compete *v* **1** take part in (a contest or competition) **2** strive (to achieve something or be successful) **competition** *n* **1** competing **2** event in which people compete **3** people against whom one competes **competitive** *adj* **competitor** *n*

competent *adj* having sufficient skill or knowledge **competently** *adv* **competence** *n*

compile *v* collect and arrange (information), esp. to form a book **compilation** *n* **compiler** *n*

complacent *adj* self-satisfied **complacently** *adv* **complacency** *n*

complain v 1 express resentment or displeasure 2 state that one is suffering from pain or illness **complaint** n 1 complaining 2 mild illness **complainant** n plaintiff

complaisant [kom-**play**-zant] adj obliging, willing to please **complaisance** n

complement n 1 thing that completes something 2 complete amount or number 3 grammar word or words added after a verb to complete the meaning ▷ v 4 make complete **complementary** adj

complete adj 1 thorough 2 perfect in quality or kind 3 finished 4 having all the necessary parts ▷ v 5 finish 6 make whole or perfect **completely** adv **completeness** n wholeness **completion** n finishing

complex adj 1 made up of parts 2 complicated ▷ n 3 whole made up of parts 4 group of unconscious feelings that influences behaviour **complexity** n

complexion n 1 natural appearance of the skin of the face 2 character or nature

complicate v make or become complex or difficult to deal with **complication** n

complicity n fact of being an accomplice, esp. in a crime

compliment n 1 expression of praise **compliments** 2 formal greetings ▷ v 3 praise **complimentary** adj 1 expressing praise 2 free of charge

compline n last service of the day in the Roman Catholic Church

comply v -plying, -plied act in accordance (with a rule,

order, or request) **compliance** n **compliant** adj

component n 1 part of a whole ▷ adj 2 being a component

comport v behave (oneself) in a specified way

compose v 1 put together 2 be the component parts of 3 create (music or literature) 4 arrange in order 5 calm (oneself) **composer** n

composite adj made up of separate parts

composition n 1 way that something is put together or arranged 2 musical work 3 essay 4 act of composing

compositor n person who arranges type for printing

compos mentis adj Latin sane

compost n decayed plants used as a fertilizer

composure n calmness

compote n fruit stewed in syrup

compound¹ n, adj 1 (thing, esp. chemical) made up of two or more combined parts or elements ▷ v 2 combine or make by combining 3 intensify, make worse

compound² n fenced enclosure containing buildings

comprehend v understand **comprehensible** adj **comprehension** n **comprehensive** adj of broad scope, fully inclusive

compress v 1 squeeze together 2 condense ▷ n 3 pad applied to stop bleeding or cool inflammation **compressible** adj **compression** n **compressor** n device that compresses a gas

comprise v be made up of, constitute

compromise [**kom**-prom-mize] n 1 settlement reached by concessions on each side ▷ v **2** settle a dispute by making concessions **3** put in a dishonourable position

comptroller n (in titles) financial controller

compulsion n **1** irresistible impulse **2** compelling or being compelled **compulsive** adj **compulsively** adv **compulsory** adj required by rules or laws, obligatory

compunction n feeling of guilt or remorse

compute v calculate, esp. using a computer **computation** n **computer** n electronic machine that stores and processes data **computerize** v **1** equip with a computer **2** perform or operate by computer **computerization** n

comrade n **1** fellow member of a union or socialist political party **2** companion **comradeship** n

con¹ informal ▷ v **conning, conned 1** deceive or swindle (someone) by gaining his or her trust ▷ n **2** such a deception or swindle

con² n **pros and cons** see **pro¹**

concatenation n linked series of events

concave adj curving inwards **concavity** n

conceal v **1** cover and hide **2** keep secret **concealment** n

concede v **1** admit to be true **2** grant as a right **3** acknowledge defeat in (a contest or argument)

conceit n **1** too high an opinion of oneself **2** lit far-fetched or clever comparison **conceited** adj

conceive v **1** imagine or think **2** form in the mind **3** become pregnant **conceivable** adj imaginable or possible **conceivably** adv

concentrate v **1** fix one's

attention or efforts (on) **2** bring or come together in large numbers in one place **3** make (a substance) stronger ▷ n **4** concentrated substance **concentration** n **1** concentrating **2** concentrated substance **concentration camp** prison camp for civilian prisoners, esp. in Nazi Germany

concentric adj having the same centre

concept n abstract or general idea **conceptual** adj of or based on concepts **conceptualize** v form a concept of

conception n **1** general idea **2** act of conceiving

concern n **1** anxiety **2** something that concerns a person **3** business or firm ▷ v **4** worry **5** involve or interest **6** be relevant or important to **concerned** adj **1** interested or involved **2** anxious **concerning** prep about, regarding

concert n musical entertainment **in concert 1** working together **2** (of musicians) performing live **concerted** adj done together

concertina n **1** small musical instrument similar to an accordion ▷ v **-naing, -naed 2** collapse or fold up like a concertina

concerto [kon-**chair**-toe] n, pl **-tos, -ti** large-scale composition for a solo instrument and orchestra

concession n **1** grant **2** reduction in price for a specified category of people **3** conceding **4** thing conceded **5** land division in township survey **concessionary** adj **concession road** one of a series of roads separating concessions in township

c

conch *n* **1** marine mollusc with a large spiral shell **2** its shell

concierge [kon-see-**airzh**] *n* (in France) caretaker of an apartment block

conciliate *v* overcome the hostility of **conciliation** *n* **conciliator** *n* **conciliatory** *adj*

concise *adj* brief and to the point **concisely** *adv* **concision** *or* **conciseness** *n*

conclave *n* **1** secret meeting **2** private meeting of cardinals to elect a new pope

conclude *v* **1** decide by reasoning **2** end, finish **3** arrange or settle finally **conclusion** *n* **1** decision or opinion **2** ending **3** outcome **conclusive** *adj* ending doubt, convincing **conclusively** *adv*

concoct *v* **1** make by combining ingredients **2** make up (a story or plan) **concoction** *n*

concomitant *adj* accompanying

concord *n* state of peaceful agreement, harmony **concordance** *n* **1** similarity or consistency **2** index of words in a book **concordant** *adj* agreeing

concourse *n* **1** large open public place where people can gather **2** crowd

concrete *n* **1** mixture of sand, gravel, and cement, used in building ▷ *adj* **2** made of concrete **3** particular, specific **4** real or solid, not abstract

concubine [kon-kew-bine] *n* **1** woman living with a man as his wife, but not married to him **2** secondary wife in polygamous societies **concubinage** *n*

concupiscence [kon-kew-**piss**-enss] *n* lust **concupiscent** *adj*

concur *v* **-curring,** **-curred** agree, be in accord

concurrence *n* **concurrent** *adj* **concurrently** *adv* at the same time

concussion *n* brain injury caused by a blow or fall **concuss** *v* affect with concussion

condemn *v* **1** express disapproval of **2** sentence **3** doom **4** declare unfit for use **condemnation** *n* **condemnatory** *adj*

condense *v* **1** express in fewer words **2** concentrate, make more dense **3** turn from gas into liquid **condensation** *n* **condenser** *n electricity* capacitor

condescend *v* **1** behave patronizingly towards **2** do something as if it were beneath one's dignity **condescension** *n*

condiment *n* relish or seasoning for food

condition *n* **1** particular state of being **2** necessary requirement for something else to happen **3** restriction or qualification **4** state of health, physical fitness **5** ailment **conditions 6** circumstances ▷ *v* **7** accustom **8** make fit or healthy **9** subject to a condition **on condition that** only if **conditional** *adj* dependent on circumstances **conditioner** *n* thick liquid used when washing to make hair or clothes feel softer

condo *n, pl* **-dos** *informal* condominium building or apartment

condole *v* express sympathy (with someone) **condolence** *n*

condom *n* rubber sheath worn on the penis or in the vagina during sexual intercourse to prevent conception or infection

condominium *n* apartment

building in which each apartment is individually owned

condone v overlook or forgive (an offence or wrongdoing)

condor n large vulture of S America

conducive adj (foll. by to) likely to produce (a result)

conduct n 1 behaviour 2 management ▷ v 3 carry out 4 behave (oneself) 5 direct (musicians) by moving the hands or a baton 6 lead, guide 7 transmit (heat or electricity) **conduction** n transmission of heat or electricity **conductive** adj able to conduct heat or electricity **conductivity** n **conductor** n 1 person who conducts musicians 2 (**conductress**) official on a bus who collects fares 3 official on a passenger train 4 something that conducts electricity or heat

conduit [kon-dew-it] n channel or tube for fluid or cables

cone n 1 hollow or solid object with a circular base, tapering to a point 2 scaly fruit of a conifer tree

coney n same as **cony**

confabulation, informal **confab** n conversation

confection n 1 any sweet food 2 elaborate article of clothing **confectioner** n maker or seller of confectionery **confectionery** n candies and cakes

confederate n 1 member of a confederacy 2 accomplice ▷ v 3 unite in a confederacy ▷ adj 4 united, allied **confederacy** n union of states or people for a common purpose **confederation** n 1 alliance of political units 2 **Confederation** federation of Canada inaugurated in 1867

confer v -ferring, -ferred 1 discuss together 2 give **conference** n meeting for discussion **conferment** n formal giving

confess v 1 admit (a fault or crime) 2 admit to be true 3 declare (one's sins) to God or a priest, in hope of forgiveness **confession** n 1 confessing 2 thing confessed **confessional** n small stall in which a priest hears confessions **confessor** n priest who hears confessions

confetti n small bits of coloured paper thrown at weddings

confidant n person confided in **confidante** n fem

confide v (foll. by in) 1 tell (something) in confidence (to) 2 entrust **confidence** n 1 trust 2 self-assurance 3 something confided, secret **in confidence** as a secret **confidence game** same as **con**[1] ▷ **confident** adj feeling or showing self-assurance **confidently** adv **confidential** adj 1 private or secret 2 entrusted with another's secret affairs **confidentially** adv **confidentiality** n

configuration n 1 arrangement of parts 2 shape

confine v 1 keep within bounds 2 restrict the free movement of **confines** pl n boundaries, limits **confinement** n 1 being confined 2 period of childbirth

confirm v 1 prove to be true 2 reaffirm or strengthen 3 administer the rite of confirmation to **confirmation** n 1 confirming 2 something that confirms 3 Christianity rite which admits a baptized person

to full church membership
confirmed adj long-established in a habit or condition
confiscate v seize (property) by authority **confiscation** n
conflagration n great destructive fire
conflate v combine or blend into a whole **conflation** n
conflict n 1 disagreement 2 struggle or fight ▷ v 3 be incompatible
confluence n place where two rivers join **confluent** adj
conform v 1 comply with accepted standards, rules, or customs 2 be like or in accordance with **conformist** n person who conforms, esp. excessively **conformity** n
confound v 1 astound, bewilder 2 confuse **confounded** adj informal damned
confront v come or bring face to face with **confrontation** n serious argument
confuse v 1 mix up, mistake (one thing) for another 2 perplex or disconcert 3 make unclear **confusion** n
confute v prove wrong **confutation** n
conga n 1 dance performed by a number of people in single file 2 large single-headed drum played with the hands
congeal v (of a liquid) coagulate, solidify
congenial adj 1 pleasant, agreeable 2 of similar disposition or tastes **congenially** adv **congeniality** n
congenital adj (of a condition) existing from birth **congenitally** adv
conger n large sea eel
congested adj 1 too full 2 clogged or blocked **congestion** n

conglomerate n 1 large corporation comprising many companies 2 mass composed of several different things ▷ v 3 form into a mass ▷ adj 4 made up of several different things **conglomeration** n
congratulate v express one's pleasure to (a person) at his or her good fortune or success **congratulations** pl n **congratulatory** adj
congregate v gather together in or as a crowd **congregation** n assembled group of worshippers **congregational** adj **Congregationalism** n Protestant denomination in which each church is self-governing **Congregationalist** n, adj
congress n 1 formal meeting for discussion 2 **Congress** federal parliament of the US **congressional** adj **Congressman** or **Congresswoman** n member of the US Congress
congruent adj 1 agreeing or corresponding 2 geom identical in shape and size **congruence** n
conic adj of a cone **conical** adj cone-shaped
conifer n cone-bearing tree, such as the fir or pine **coniferous** adj
conjecture n, v guess **conjectural** adj
conjoined twins pl n the technical name for **Siamese twins**
conjugal [kon-jew-gal] adj of marriage
conjugate [kon-jew-gate] v give the inflections of (a verb) **conjugation** n complete set of inflections of a verb
conjunction n 1 combination 2 simultaneous occurrence of events 3 part of speech joining

words, phrases, or clauses

conjunctivitis n inflammation of the membrane covering the eyeball and inner eyelid **conjunctiva** n this membrane

conjure v perform tricks that appear to be magic **conjure up** v produce as if by magic **conjurer** or **conjuror** n

conk n slang head or nose **conk out** v informal (of a machine) break down

conker n informal horse chestnut

connect v 1 join together 2 associate in the mind **connection** or **connexion** n 1 association 2 link or bond 3 opportunity to transfer from one public vehicle to another 4 influential acquaintance **connective** adj **connectivity** n

conning tower n raised observation tower containing the periscope on a submarine

connive v 1 (foll. by at) give assent to (wrongdoing) by ignoring it 2 conspire **connivance** n

connoisseur [kon-noss-**sir**] n person with special knowledge of the arts, food, or drink

connote v imply in addition to the literal meaning **connotation** n

connubial [kon-**new**-bee-al] adj of marriage

conquer v 1 defeat 2 overcome 3 take (a place) by force **conqueror** n **conquest** n 1 conquering 2 person or thing conquered

consanguineous adj related by birth **consanguinity** n

conscience n sense of right or wrong as regards thoughts and actions **conscientious** adj 1 painstaking 2 governed by conscience **conscientious objector** person who refuses

to serve in the armed forces on moral or religious grounds **conscientiously** adv

conscious adj 1 alert and awake 2 aware 3 deliberate, intentional **consciously** adv **consciousness** n

conscript v 1 enrol (someone) for compulsory military service ▷ n 2 conscripted person **conscription** n

consecrate v 1 make sacred 2 dedicate to a specific purpose **consecration** n

consecutive adj in unbroken succession **consecutively** adv

consensus n general agreement

consent n 1 permission, agreement ▷ v 2 permit, agree (to)

consequence n 1 result, effect 2 importance **consequent** adj resulting **consequently** adv 1 therefore 2 as a result **consequential** adj important

conservative adj 1 opposing change 2 cautious 3 conventional in style 4 **Conservative** of or supporting the Progressive Conservative Party, the most conservative of the three main political parties ▷ n 5 one who wishes to preserve political institutions against change 6 one opposed to hasty changes or innovations 7 **Conservative** supporter or member of the Progressive Conservative Party **conservatism** n

conservatoire [kon-**serv**-a-twahr] n school of music

conservatory n, pl -ries 1 greenhouse 2 conservatoire

conserve v 1 protect from harm, decay, or loss 2 preserve (fruit) with sugar ▷ n 3 fruit preserved by cooking in sugar **conservancy** n environmental conservation

conservation n 1 protection of natural resources and the environment 2 conserving **conservationist** n

consider v 1 be of the opinion that 2 think about 3 be considerate of 4 discuss 5 examine **considerable** adj 1 fairly large 2 much **considerably** adv **considerate** adj thoughtful towards others **considerately** adv **consideration** n 1 careful thought 2 fact that must be considered 3 kindness 4 payment for a service **considering** prep taking (a specified fact) into account

consign v 1 deposit 2 entrust 3 address or deliver (goods) **consignment** n shipment of goods

consist v **consist in** have as its main or only feature **consist of** be made up of

consistency n, pl -cies 1 degree of thickness or smoothness 2 being consistent **consistent** adj 1 unchanging, constant 2 in agreement **consistently** adv

console[1] v comfort in distress **consolation** n 1 consoling 2 person or thing that consoles

console[2] n 1 panel of controls for electronic equipment 2 cabinet for a television or audio equipment 3 ornamental wall bracket 4 part of an organ containing the pedals, stops, and keys

consolidate v 1 make or become stronger or more stable 2 combine into a whole **consolidation** n

consommé [kon-**som**-may] n thin clear meat soup

consonant n 1 speech sound made by partially or completely blocking the breath stream 2 letter representing this ▷ adj 3 (foll. by with) agreeing (with) **consonance** n

consort v 1 (foll. by with) keep company (with) ▷ n 2 husband or wife of a monarch

consortium n, pl -tia association of business firms

conspectus n survey or summary

conspicuous adj 1 clearly visible 2 striking **conspicuously** adv

conspire v 1 plan a crime together in secret 2 act together as if by design **conspiracy** n 1 conspiring 2 plan made by conspiring **conspirator** n **conspiratorial** adj

constable n police officer of the lowest rank **constabulary** n police force of an area

constant adj 1 continuous 2 unchanging 3 faithful ▷ n 4 unvarying quantity 5 something unchanging **constantly** adv **constancy** n

constellation n group of stars

consternation n anxiety, dismay, or confusion

constipation n difficulty in defecating **constipated** adj having constipation

constituent n 1 member of a constituency 2 component part ▷ adj 3 forming part of a whole **constituency** n 1 area represented by a Member of Parliament 2 voters in such an area

constitute v form, compose **constitution** n 1 principles on which a state is governed 2 physical condition 3 structure **constitutional** adj 1 of a constitution 2 in accordance with a political constitution ▷ n 3 walk taken for exercise **constitutionally** adv

constrain v 1 force, compel 2 restrain or confine **constraint** n 1 compulsion or restraint 2 forced unnatural manner

constrict v make narrower or tighter, esp. by squeezing **constriction** n **constrictive** adj **constrictor** n 1 large snake that squeezes its prey to death 2 muscle that constricts

construct v build or put together **construction** n 1 constructing 2 thing constructed 3 interpretation 4 grammar way in which words are arranged in a sentence, clause, or phrase **constructive** adj (of advice, criticism, etc.) useful and helpful **constructively** adv

construe v -struing, -strued 1 interpret 2 analyse grammatically

consul n 1 official representing a state in a foreign country 2 one of the two chief magistrates in ancient Rome **consular** adj **consulate** n position or offices of a consul **consulship** n

consult v go to for information or advice **consultant** n Brit 1 specialist doctor with a senior position in a hospital 2 specialist who gives professional advice **consultancy** n work or position of a consultant **consultation** n (meeting for) consulting **consultative** adj giving advice

consume v 1 eat or drink 2 use up 3 destroy 4 obsess **consumer** n person who buys goods or uses services **consumption** n 1 consuming 2 amount consumed 3 old-fashioned tuberculosis **consumptive** adj, n (person)

having tuberculosis

consummate v [kon-sume-mate] 1 make (a marriage) legal by sexual intercourse 2 complete or fulfil ▷ adj [kon-sum-mit] 3 supremely skilled 4 perfect **consummation** n

cont. continued

contact n 1 communicating 2 touching 3 useful acquaintance 4 connection between two electrical conductors in a circuit ▷ v 5 get in touch with **contact lens** lens fitting over the eyeball to correct defective vision

contagion n 1 passing on of disease by contact 2 contagious disease 3 spreading of a harmful influence **contagious** adj spreading by contact, catching

contain v 1 hold or be capable of holding 2 consist of 3 control, restrain **container** n 1 receptacle used to hold something 2 large standard-sized box for transporting cargo by truck or ship **containment** n prevention of the spread of something harmful

contaminate v 1 pollute, make impure 2 make radioactive **contaminant** n contaminating substance **contamination** n

contemplate v 1 think deeply (about) 2 consider as a possibility 3 gaze at **contemplation** n **contemplative** adj **contemplatively** adv

contemporary adj 1 present-day, modern 2 living or occurring at the same time ▷ n, pl -raries 3 person or thing living at the same time or of approximately the same age as another

contemporaneous adj

contempt n 1 attitude of scornful disregard 2 open disrespect for the authority of a court **contemptible** adj deserving contempt **contemptuous** adj showing contempt **contemptuously** adv

contend v 1 (foll. by with) deal with 2 assert 3 compete **contender** n competitor **contention** n 1 disagreement or dispute 2 point asserted in argument **contentious** adj 1 causing dispute 2 quarrelsome

content¹ n 1 meaning or substance of a book etc. 2 amount of a substance in a mixture **contents** 3 what something contains 4 list of chapters at the front of a book

content² adj 1 satisfied with things as they are ▷ v 2 make (someone) content ▷ n 3 peace of mind **contented** adj **contentment** n

contest n 1 competition or struggle ▷ v 2 dispute 3 fight or compete for **contestant** n

context n 1 circumstances of an event or fact 2 words before and after a word or passage that contribute to its meaning **contextual** adj

contiguous adj very near or touching **contiguity** n

continent¹ n one of the earth's large masses of land **the Continent** Brit mainland of Europe **continental** adj **continental breakfast** light breakfast of rolls, coffee, etc.

continent² adj 1 able to control one's urination and defecation 2 sexually chaste **continence** n

contingent adj 1 (foll. by on) dependent on (something uncertain) ▷ n 2 group of people, esp. soldiers, that is part of a larger group **contingency** n something that may happen

continue v -tinuing, -tinued 1 (cause to) remain in a condition or place 2 carry on (doing something) 3 resume **continual** adj 1 constant 2 frequently recurring **continually** adv **continuance** n continuing **continuation** n 1 continuing 2 part added **continuity** n smooth development or sequence **continuous** adj continuing uninterrupted **continuously** adv

continuo n, pl -tinuos music continuous bass part, usually played on a keyboard instrument

continuum n, pl -tinua, -tinuums continuous series

contort v twist out of normal shape **contortion** n **contortionist** n performer who contorts his or her body to entertain

contour n 1 outline 2 Also **contour line** line on a map joining places of the same height

contra- prefix against or contrasting: contraflow

contraband adj, n smuggled (goods)

contraception n prevention of pregnancy by artificial means **contraceptive** n 1 device used or pill taken to prevent pregnancy ▷ adj 2 preventing pregnancy

contract n 1 formal agreement ▷ v 2 make a formal agreement (to do something) 3 make or become smaller or shorter 4 catch (an illness) **contraction** n **contractor** n firm that supplies materials or labour, esp. for building **contractual** adj

contradict v 1 declare the

opposite of (a statement) to be true **2** be at variance with **contradiction** n **contradictory** adj

contralto n, pl **-tos** (singer with) lowest female voice

contraption n strange-looking device

contrapuntal adj music of or in counterpoint

contrary adj **1** opposed, completely different **2** perverse, obstinate ▷ n **3** complete opposite ▷ adv **4** in opposition **contrarily** adv **contrariness** n **contrariwise** adv conversely

contrast n **1** striking difference **2** something showing this ▷ v **3** compare or be compared in order to show differences **4** (foll. by with) be very different (from) **contrastive** adj

contravene v break (a rule or law) **contravention** n

contretemps [kon-tra-tahn] n, pl **-temps** embarrassing minor disagreement

contribute v **1** give to a common purpose or fund **2** (foll. by to) help (something) to occur **contribution** n **contributor** n **contributory** adj

contrite adj guilty and regretful **contritely** adv **contrition** n

contrive v **1** make happen **2** invent and construct **contrivance** n **1** device **2** plan **3** contriving **contrived** adj planned, artificial

control n **1** power to direct something **2** curb or check **3** standard of comparison in an experiment **controls** **4** instruments used to operate a machine ▷ v **-trolling,** **-trolled 5** have power over **6** limit or restrain **7** regulate **controllable** adj **controller** n

controversy n, pl **-sies** fierce argument or debate **controversial** adj causing controversy

contumacy [kon-tume-mass-ee] n obstinate disobedience **contumacious** [kon-tume-may-shuss] adj

contumely [kon-tume-mill-ee] n scornful or insulting treatment

contusion n bruise

conundrum n riddle

conurbation n large urban area formed by the growth and merging of towns

convalesce v recover health after an illness or operation **convalescence** n **convalescent** adj, n

convection n transmission of heat in liquids or gases by the circulation of currents **convector** n heater which emits hot air

convene v gather or summon for a formal meeting **convener** or **convenor** n person who calls a meeting

convenient adj **1** suitable or opportune **2** easy to use **3** nearby **conveniently** adv **convenience** n **1** quality of being convenient **2** convenient thing **3** Brit public lavatory **convenience store** small shop open long hours

convent n **1** building where nuns live **2** school run by nuns

convention n **1** widely accepted view of proper behaviour **2** formal agreement **3** assembly or meeting **conventional** adj **1** (slavishly) following the accepted customs **2** customary **3** (of weapons or warfare) not nuclear **conventionally** adv **conventionality** n

converge v move towards the same point **convergence** n

conversant adj **conversant with** having knowledge or experience of

converse[1] v have a conversation **conversation** n informal talk **conversational** adj **conversationalist** n person with a specified ability at conversation

converse[2] adj, n opposite or contrary **conversely** adv

convert v **1** change in form, character, or function **2** cause to change in opinion or belief **3** sports score (a touchdown, goal, etc.) after receiving a pass ▷ n **4** converted person **conversion** n (thing resulting from) a converting or being converted **converter** or **convertor** n **convertible** adj **1** capable of being converted ▷ n **2** automobile with a folding or removable roof

convex adj curving outwards **convexity** n

convey v **1** communicate (information) **2** carry, transport **conveyance** n **1** old-fashioned vehicle **2** transfer of the legal title to property **conveyancing** n branch of law dealing with the transfer of ownership of property **conveyor belt** continuous moving belt for transporting things, esp. in a factory

convict v **1** declare guilty ▷ n **2** person serving a prison sentence **conviction** n **1** firm belief **2** instance of being convicted

convince v persuade by evidence or argument **convincing** adj **convincingly** adv

convivial adj sociable, lively **conviviality** n

convoke v call together **convocation** n **1** convoking **2** large formal meeting

convoluted adj **1** coiled, twisted **2** (of an argument or sentence) complex and hard to understand **convolution** n

convolvulus n twining plant with funnel-shaped flowers

convoy n group of vehicles or ships travelling together

convulse v **1** (of muscles) undergo violent spasms **2** informal be overcome (with laughter or rage) **convulsion** n **1** violent muscular spasm **convulsions 2** uncontrollable laughter **convulsive** adj **convulsively** adv

cony n, pl **conies 1** rabbit **2** rabbit fur

coo v **cooing, cooed 1** (of a dove or pigeon) make a soft murmuring sound ▷ n **2** cooing sound

cooee interj call to attract attention

cook v **1** prepare (food) by heating **2** (of food) be cooked **3** informal falsify (accounts etc.) ▷ n **4** person who cooks food **cooker** n **1** apparatus for cooking heated by gas or electricity **2** apple suitable for cooking **cookery** n art of cooking **cook up** v informal devise (a story or scheme)

cookie n **1** small flat or slightly raised cake **2** computers piece of data downloaded to a computer by a website, containing the user's preferences for use when revisiting that website **toss one's cookies** or **lose one's cookies** slang vomit

cool adj **1** moderately cold **2** calm and unemotional **3** indifferent or unfriendly **4** informal sophisticated or excellent **5** informal (of a large sum of money) without exaggeration: a cool ten thousand ▷ v **6** make or become cool ▷ n **7** coolness **8** slang calmness, composure

coolly *adv* **coolness** *n* **coolant** *n* fluid used to cool machinery while it is working **cooler** *n* **1** container for making or keeping things cool **2** *slang* prison

coolie *n old-fashioned, offensive* unskilled Oriental labourer

coomb, coombe *n* valley

coop *n* cage or pen for poultry **coop up** *v* confine in a restricted place

co-op *n* **1** cooperative society **2** shop run by one

cooper *n* person who makes or repairs barrels or casks

cooperate *v* work or act together **cooperation** *n* **cooperative** *adj* **1** willing to cooperate **2** (of an enterprise) owned and managed collectively ▷ *n* **3** cooperative organization

co-opt *v* add (someone) to a group by the agreement of the existing members **co-option** *n*

coordinate *v* **1** bring together and cause to work together efficiently ▷ *n* **2** *math* any of a set of numbers defining the location of a point **coordinates** **3** garments designed to be worn together **coordination** *n* **coordinator** *n*

coot *n* small black water bird

cop *slang* ▷ *n* **1** policeman ▷ *v* **copping, copped 2 cop it** get into trouble or be punished **cop out** *v* avoid taking responsibility or committing oneself

cope[1] *v* deal successfully (with)

cope[2] *n* large ceremonial cloak worn by some Christian priests

coping *n* sloping top row of a wall **coping stone**

copious [kope-ee-uss] *adj* abundant, plentiful **copiously** *adv*

copper[1] *n* **1** soft reddish-brown metal **2** copper or bronze coin **3** large metal container used to boil water **copper-bottomed** *adj* financially reliable **copperplate** *n* fine handwriting style

copper[2] *n slang* policeman

coppice, copse *n* dense growth of small trees and undergrowth

copra *n* dried oil-yielding kernel of the coconut

copulate *v* have sexual intercourse **copulation** *n*

copy *n, pl* **copies 1** thing made to look exactly like another **2** single specimen of a book etc. **3** material for printing ▷ *v* **copying, copied 4** make a copy of **5** act or try to be like another **copyright** *n* **1** exclusive legal right to reproduce and control a book, work of art, etc. ▷ *v* **2** take out a copyright on ▷ *adj* **3** protected by copyright **copywriter** *n* person who writes advertising copy

coquette *n* woman who flirts **coquettish** *adj* **coquetry** *n*

coracle *n* small round boat of wicker covered with skins

coral *n* **1** hard substance formed from the skeletons of very small sea animals ▷ *adj* **2** made of coral **3** orange-pink

corbel *n* stone or timber support projecting from a wall

cord *n* **1** thin rope or thick string **2** cordlike structure in the body **3** corduroy **cords 4** corduroy trousers ▷ *adj* **5** (of fabric) ribbed

cordial *adj* **1** warm and friendly **2** strong: *cordial dislike* ▷ *n* **3** drink with a fruit base **cordially** *adv* **cordiality** *n*

cordite *n* explosive used in guns and bombs

cordon *n* **1** chain of police,

soldiers, etc. guarding an area **2** fruit tree grown as a single stem **cordon off** v form a cordon round

cordon bleu [**bluh**] adj (of cookery or cooks) of the highest standard

corduroy n cotton fabric with a velvety ribbed surface

core n **1** central part of certain fruits, containing the seeds **2** central or essential part ▷ v **3** remove the core from

co-respondent n person with whom someone being sued for divorce is claimed to have committed adultery

corgi n short-legged sturdy dog

coriander n plant with aromatic seeds and leaves used for flavouring

cork n **1** thick light bark of a Mediterranean oak **2** piece of this used as a stopper ▷ v **3** stop up with a cork **corkage** n restaurant's charge for serving wine bought elsewhere **corkscrew** n tool for extracting corks from bottles

corm n bulblike underground stem of certain plants

cormorant n large dark-coloured long-necked sea bird

corn[1] n **1** tall plant bearing kernels on cobs enclosed in husks **2** grain of this plant used for food or fodder **3** cereal grass or grain **4** slang something unoriginal or oversentimental **corny** adj slang unoriginal or oversentimental **cornflakes** pl n breakfast cereal of toasted corn flakes **cornflour** n finely ground corn **cornflower** n plant with blue flowers

corn[2] n painful hard skin on the foot or toe

cornea [**korn**-ee-a] n, pl -neas, -neae transparent membrane covering the eyeball **corneal** adj

corned beef n beef preserved in salt

cornelian n reddish semiprecious stone

corner n **1** area or angle where two converging lines or surfaces meet **2** place where two streets meet **3** sharp bend in a road **4** remote or inaccessible place **5** sports free kick or shot from the corner of the field ▷ v **6** (of a vehicle) turn a corner **7** force into a difficult or inescapable position **8** obtain a monopoly of **cornerstone** n indispensable part or basis

cornet n **1** brass instrument similar to the trumpet **2** cone-shaped ice-cream wafer

cornice [**korn**-iss] n decorative moulding round the top of a wall

Cornish adj **1** of Cornwall in SW England ▷ pl n **2** people of Cornwall ▷ n **3** Celtic language of Cornwall

cornucopia [korn-yew-**kope**-ee-a] n **1** great abundance **2** symbol of plenty, consisting of a horn overflowing with fruit and flowers

corolla n petals of a flower collectively

corollary [kor-**oll**-a-ree] n, pl -laries idea, fact, or proposition which is the natural result of something else

corona [kor-**rone**-a] n, pl -nas, -nae ring of light round the moon or sun

coronary [**kor**-ron-a-ree] adj **1** of the arteries surrounding the heart ▷ n, pl -naries **2** coronary thrombosis **coronary thrombosis** condition in which the flow of blood to the heart is blocked by a blood clot

coronation n ceremony of crowning a monarch

coroner n official responsible for the investigation of violent, sudden, or suspicious deaths

coronet n small crown

corpora n plural of **corpus**

corporeal[1] adj of the body **corporal punishment** physical punishment, such as caning

corporal[2] n non-commissioned officer below sergeant

corporation n 1 large business or company 2 city or town council 3 informal large paunch **corporate** adj 1 relating to business corporations 2 shared by a group

corporeal [kore-**pore**-ee-al] adj physical or tangible

corps [kore] n, pl **corps** 1 military unit with a specific function 2 organized body of people

corpse n dead body

corpulent adj fat or plump **corpulence** n

corpus n, pl **corpora** collection of writings, esp. by a single author

corpuscle n red or white blood cell

corral n 1 enclosure for cattle or horses ▷ v **-ralling, -ralled** 2 put in a corral

correct adj 1 free from error, true 2 in accordance with accepted standards ▷ v 3 put right 4 indicate the errors in 5 rebuke or punish **correctly** adv **correctness** n **correction** n 1 correcting something 2 alteration correcting something **corrective** n, adj (thing) intended or tending to correct

correlate v 1 place or be placed in a mutual relationship ▷ n 2 either of two things mutually related **correlation** n **correlative** adj, n

correspond v 1 be consistent or compatible (with) 2 be similar (to) 3 communicate (with) by letter **corresponding** adj **correspondingly** adv **correspondence** n 1 communication by letters 2 letters so exchanged 3 relationship or similarity **correspondent** n 1 writer of letters 2 person employed by a newspaper etc. to report on a special subject or from a foreign country

corridor n 1 passage in a building or train 2 strip of land or air space providing access through foreign territory

corrigendum [kor-rij-**end**-um] n, pl **-da** thing to be corrected

corroborate v support (a fact or opinion) by giving proof **corroboration** n **corroborative** adj

corrode v eat or be eaten away by chemical action **corrosion** n **corrosive** adj

corrugate v fold into alternate grooves and ridges **corrugated** adj **corrugation** n

corrupt adj 1 open to or involving bribery 2 morally wrong 3 (of a text or data) made unreliable by errors or alterations ▷ v 4 make corrupt **corruptly** adv **corruption** n **corruptible** adj

corsage [kor-**sahzh**] n small bouquet worn on the bodice of a dress

corsair n 1 pirate 2 pirate ship

corset n close-fitting undergarment worn to support or shape the torso

cortege [kor-**tayzh**] n funeral procession

cortex n, pl **-tices** anat outer layer of the brain or other internal organ **cortical** *adj*

cortisone *n* steroid hormone used to treat various diseases

corundum *n* hard mineral used as an abrasive

coruscate *v* sparkle **coruscation** *n*

corvette *n* lightly armed escort warship

cos *math* cosine

cosh *n* **1** heavy blunt weapon ▷ *v* **2** hit with a cosh

cosine [**koh**-sine] *n* (in trigonometry) ratio of the length of the adjacent side to that of the hypotenuse in a right-angled triangle

cosmetic *n* **1** preparation used to improve the appearance of a person's skin ▷ *adj* **2** improving the appearance only

cosmic *adj* of the whole universe **cosmic rays** electromagnetic radiation from outer space

cosmonaut *n* Russian name for **astronaut**

cosmopolitan *adj* **1** composed of people or elements from many countries **2** having lived and travelled in many countries ▷ *n* **3** cosmopolitan person **cosmopolitanism** *n*

cosmos *n* the universe **cosmology** *n* study of the origin and nature of the universe **cosmological** *adj*

Cossack *n* member of a S Russian people famous as horsemen

cosset *v* **cosseting, cosseted** pamper or pet

cost *n* **1** amount of money, time, labour, etc. required for something **costs 2** expenses of a lawsuit ▷ *v* **costing, cost 3** have as its cost **4** involve the loss or sacrifice of **5** estimate the cost of **costly** *adj* **1** expensive **2** involving great loss or sacrifice **costliness** *n*

costive *adj* having or causing constipation

costume *n* **1** style of dress of a particular place or time, or for a particular activity **2** clothes worn by an actor or performer **costumier** *n* maker or seller of costumes **costume jewellery** inexpensive artificial jewellery

cosy *adj* **-sier, -siest 1** snug and warm **2** intimate, friendly ▷ *n, pl* **cosies 3** cover to keep a teapot etc. hot **cosily** *adv* **cosiness** *n*

cot *n Brit* **1** child's bed with high sides **2** small portable bed

coterie [**kote**-er-ee] *n* exclusive group, clique

cotoneaster [kot-tone-ee-**ass**-ter] *n* garden shrub with red berries

cottage *n* small house in the country **cottage cheese** soft mild white cheese **cottage industry** craft industry in which employees work at home **cottage pie** dish of minced meat topped with mashed potato

cotter *n* pin or wedge used to secure machine parts

cotton *n* **1** white downy fibre covering the seeds of a tropical plant **2** thread or cloth made of this **cottony** *adj* **cotton batting** *or* **cotton wool** fluffy cotton used for surgical dressings etc. **cotton on (to)** *v informal* understand

cotyledon [kot-ill-**ee**-don] *n* first leaf of a plant embryo

couch *n* **1** piece of upholstered furniture for seating more than one person ▷ *v* **2** express in a particular way

couchette [koo-**shett**] *n* bed converted from seats in a train

couch grass *n* quickly spreading grassy weed

cougar [**koo**-gar] *n* puma

cough v 1 expel air from the lungs abruptly and noisily. ▷ n 2 act or sound of coughing 3 illness which causes coughing

could v past tense of **can**[1]

couldn't could not

coulee [**koo**-lay] n ravine cut by water in western N America

coulomb [**koo**-lom] n unit of electric charge

coulter [**kole**-ter] n blade at the front of a plowshare

council n 1 group meeting for discussion or consultation 2 local governing body of a town or county **councillor** n member of a council

counsel n 1 advice or guidance 2 barrister or barristers ▷ v **-selling, -selled** 3 give guidance to 4 urge or recommend **counsellor** n

count[1] v 1 say numbers in order 2 find the total of 3 be important 4 regard as 5 take into account ▷ n 6 number reached by counting 7 counting 8 law one of a number of charges **countless** adj too many to be counted **count on** v 1 expect 2 rely on

count[2] n European nobleman **countess** n fem

countdown n counting backwards to zero of the seconds before an event

countenance n 1 (expression of) the face ▷ v 2 support or tolerate

counter[1] n 1 long flat surface in a bank or shop, on which business is transacted 2 small flat disc used in board games

counter[2] v 1 oppose, retaliate against ▷ adv 2 in the opposite direction 3 in direct contrast ▷ n 4 opposing or retaliatory action

counter- prefix 1 against, opposite: counterbalance 2 retaliatory, rival: counter-revolution; counterclaim

counteract v neutralize or act against **counteraction** n

counterattack v, n attack in response to an attack

counterbalance n 1 weight or force balancing or neutralizing another ▷ v 2 act as a counterbalance to

counterblast n aggressive response to a verbal attack

counterfeit adj 1 fake, forged ▷ n 2 fake, forgery ▷ v 3 fake, forge

counterfoil n Brit part of a cheque or receipt kept as a record

countermand v cancel (a previous order)

counterpane n bed covering

counterpart n person or thing complementary to or corresponding to another

counterpoint n music technique of combining melodies

counterpoise n, v counterbalance

counterproductive adj having an effect opposite to the one intended

countersign v sign (a document already signed by another) as confirmation

countersink v drive (a screw) into a shaped hole so that its head is below the surface

countertenor n male alto

counterterrorism n activities intended to prevent terrorism **counterterrorist** adj

country n, pl **-tries** 1 nation 2 nation's territory 3 nation's people 4 rural areas as opposed to town **countrified** adj rustic in manner or appearance **country and western** popular music based on N American White folk music **countryman**

(**countrywoman**) *n*
1 compatriot **2** person who lives in the country **countryside** *n* rural areas

county *n, pl* **-ties** division of a country

coup [koo] *n* **1** successful action **2** coup d'état

coup de grace [**koo** de **grahss**] *n* final or decisive action

coup d'état [**koo** day-**tah**] *n* sudden violent overthrow of a government

coupé [**koo**-pay] *n* sporty automobile with two doors and a sloping fixed roof

couple *n* **1** two people who are married or romantically involved **2** two partners in a dance or game ▷ *v* **3** connect, associate **4** *lit* have sexual intercourse **a couple 1** a pair **2** *informal* a few **couplet** *n* two consecutive lines of verse, usu. rhyming and of the same metre **coupling** *n* device for connecting things, such as railway carriages

coupon *n* **1** piece of paper entitling the holder to a discount or gift **2** detachable order form **3** football pools entry form

courage *n* ability to face danger or pain without fear **courageous** *adj* **courageously** *adv*

coureur de bois [koo-rir-di-**bwah**] *n, pl* **coureurs de bois** [koo-rir] French Canadian or Métis woodsman

courgette *n Brit* zucchini

courier *n* **1** person who looks after and guides travellers **2** person paid to deliver urgent messages

course *n* **1** series of lessons or medical treatment **2** onward movement in space or time **3** direction or route of movement **4** area where

golf is played or a race is run **5** any of the successive parts of a meal **6** continuous layer of masonry at one level in a building **7** mode of conduct or action **8** natural development of events ▷ *v* **9** (of liquid) run swiftly **10** hunt with hounds that follow the quarry by sight and not scent **of course** naturally

court *n* **1** body which decides legal cases **2** place where it meets **3** marked area for playing a racket game **4** courtyard **5** residence, household, or retinue of a sovereign ▷ *v* **6** *old-fashioned* try to win (someone) as a spouse **7** try to win (someone's favour) **8** invite: *court disaster* **courtier** *n* attendant at a royal court **courtly** *adj* ceremoniously polite **courtliness** *n* **courtship** *n* courting of an intended spouse or mate **court martial** court for trying naval or military offences **court shoe** woman's low-cut shoe without straps or laces **courtyard** *n* paved space enclosed by buildings or walls

courtesan [kor-tiz-**zan**] *n hist* mistress or high-class prostitute

courtesy *n, pl* **-sies** **1** politeness, good manners **2** courteous act **courtesy of** or **by courtesy of** by permission of **courteous** *adj* polite **courteously** *adv*

cousin *n* child of one's uncle or aunt

couturier *n* person who designs women's fashion clothes

cove *n* small bay or inlet

coven [**kuv**-ven] *n* meeting of witches

covenant [**kuv**-ven-ant] *n* **1** formal agreement, esp. to

cover v **1** place or spread or be placed or spread over **2** screen or conceal **3** travel over **4** protect from loss or risk by insurance **5** keep a gun aimed at **6** include **7** report (an event) for a newspaper **8** be enough to pay for ▷ n **9** anything which covers **10** outside of a book or magazine **11** pretext or disguise **12** shelter or protection **13** insurance **coverage** n amount or extent covered **coverlet** n bed cover

covert adj **1** secret, concealed ▷ n **2** thicket giving shelter to game birds or animals **covertly** adv

covet v **coveting, coveted** long to possess (what belongs to someone else) **covetous** adj **covetousness** n

covey [**kuv**-vee] n small flock of grouse or partridge

cow[1] n mature female of cattle and of certain other animals, such as the elephant or whale **cowboy** n **1** ranch worker who herds and tends cattle, usu. on horseback **2** informal irresponsible or unscrupulous worker

cow[2] v intimidate, subdue

coward n person who lacks courage **cowardly** adj **cowardice** n lack of courage

cower v cringe or shrink in fear

cowl n **1** loose hood **2** monk's hooded robe **3** cover on a chimney to increase ventilation

cowling n cover on an engine

cowrie n brightly marked sea shell

cowslip n fragrant wild primrose

cox n **1** coxswain ▷ v **2** act as cox of (a boat)

coxswain [**kok**-sn] n person who steers a rowing boat

coy adj affectedly shy or modest **coyly** adv **coyness** n

coyote [koy-**ote**-ee] n prairie wolf of N America

coypu n beaver-like aquatic rodent, bred for its fur

cozen v cheat or trick

CP Canadian Pacific

Cr chem chromium

crab n edible shellfish with ten legs, the first pair modified into pincers

crab apple n small sour apple

crabbed adj **1** (of handwriting) hard to read **2** Also **crabby** bad-tempered

crack v **1** break or split partially **2** break with a sharp noise **3** (cause to) make a sharp noise **4** break down or yield under strain **5** hit suddenly **6** tell (a joke) **7** solve (a code or problem) **8** (of the voice) become harsh or change pitch suddenly ▷ n **9** narrow gap **10** sudden sharp noise **11** sharp blow **12** informal gibe or joke **13** slang pure highly addictive form of cocaine ▷ adj **14** informal excellent, first-rate: a crack shot

cracker n **1** thin dry biscuit **2** decorated cardboard tube, pulled apart with a bang, containing a paper hat and a motto or toy **3** small explosive firework **crackers** adj slang crazy **cracking** adj first-class **crackdown** n severe disciplinary or repressive measure **crack down on** v take severe measures against **crackpot** adj, n informal eccentric (person)

crackle v **1** make small sharp popping noises ▷ n **2** crackling sound **crackling** n **1** crackle **2** crisp skin of roast pork

cradle n **1** baby's bed on

rockers **2** place where
something originated
3 supporting structure ▷ *v*
4 hold gently as if in a cradle

craft[1] *n* **1** skilled trade **2** skill or
ability **3** cunning **crafty** *adj*
skilled in deception **craftily**
adv **craftiness** *n* **craftsman**
(**craftswoman**) *n* skilled
worker **craftsmanship** *n*

craft[2] *n, pl* **craft** boat, ship,
aircraft, or spaceship

crag *n* steep rugged rock
craggy *adj*

cram *v* **cramming, crammed**
1 force into too small a space
2 fill too full **3** study hard just
before an examination

cramp *n* **1** painful muscular
contraction **2** clamp for
holding masonry or timber
together ▷ *v* **3** confine or
restrict

crampon *n* spiked plate
strapped to a boot for
climbing on ice

cranberry *n* sour edible red
berry

crane *n* **1** machine for lifting
and moving heavy weights
2 wading bird with long legs,
neck, and bill ▷ *v* **3** stretch
(one's neck) to see something

crane fly *n* long-legged insect
with slender wings

cranium *n, pl* **-niums, -nia**
skull **cranial** *adj*

crank *n* **1** arm projecting at
right angles from a shaft, for
transmitting or converting
motion **2** *informal* eccentric
person ▷ *v* **3** start (an engine)
with a crank **cranky** *adj*
1 eccentric **2** bad-tempered
crankshaft *n* shaft driven by
a crank

cranny *n, pl* **-nies** small
opening, chink

crepe *n* same as **crepe**

craps *n* gambling game played
with two dice

crash *n* **1** collision involving a

vehicle or vehicles **2** sudden
loud smashing noise
3 financial collapse ▷ *v*
4 (cause to) collide violently
with a vehicle, a stationary
object, or the ground **5** (cause
to) make a loud smashing
noise **6** (cause to) fall with
a crash **7** collapse or fail
financially ▷ *adj* **8** requiring
or using great effort to achieve
results quickly: *a crash course*

crash helmet protective
helmet worn by a motorcyclist

crash-land *v* land (an
aircraft) in an emergency,
causing it damage **crash-
landing** *n*

crass *adj* grossly stupid
crassly *adv* **crassness** *n*

crate *n* large wooden
container for packing goods

crater *n* **1** bowl-shaped cavity
made by the impact of a
meteorite or an explosion
2 mouth of a volcano

cravat *n* man's scarf worn like
a tie

crave *v* **1** desire intensely **2** beg
or plead for **craving** *n*

craven *adj* cowardly

craw *n* **1** bird's crop **2** animal's
stomach

crawfish *n* same as **crayfish**

crawl *v* **1** move on one's hands
and knees **2** move very slowly
3 act in a servile manner
4 be or feel as if covered
with crawling creatures ▷ *n*
5 crawling motion or pace
6 overarm swimming stroke
crawler *n*

crayfish *n* edible freshwater
shellfish like a lobster

crayon *n* **1** stick or pencil
of coloured wax or clay ▷ *v*
2 draw or colour with a crayon

craze *n* short-lived fashion
or enthusiasm **crazed** *adj*
1 demented **2** (of porcelain)
having fine cracks **crazy** *adj*
informal **1** ridiculous **2** (foll. by

about) very fond (of) **3** insane
craziness *n* **crazy paving**
paving made of irregularly
shaped slabs of stone
creak *v, n* (make) a harsh
squeaking sound **creaky** *adj*
cream *n* **1** fatty part of milk
2 something, esp. a food or
cosmetic, resembling cream
in consistency **3** best part (of
something) ▷ *adj* **4** yellowish-
white ▷ *v* **5** beat to a creamy
consistency **6** (foll. by *off*) take
the best part from **creamy** *adj*
cream cheese rich soft white
cheese
crease *n* **1** line made by folding
or pressing **2** *hockey* small area
in front of goal net ▷ *v* **3** make
or develop creases
create *v* **1** bring into being
2 appoint to a new rank or
position **3** *slang* make an angry
fuss **creation** *n* **creative**
adj imaginative or inventive
creativity *n* **creator** *n*
creature *n* person, animal, or
being
crèche *n* day nursery for very
young children
credence [**kreed**-enss] *n*
belief in the truth or accuracy
of a statement
credentials *pl n* document
giving evidence of the bearer's
identity or qualifications
credible *adj* **1** believable
2 trustworthy **credibly** *adv*
credibility *n*
credit *n* **1** system of allowing
customers to take goods and
pay later **2** reputation for
trustworthiness in paying
debts **3** money at one's
disposal in a bank account
4 side of an account book on
which such sums are entered
5 (source or cause of) praise
or approval **6** influence or
reputation based on the
good opinion of others
7 belief or trust **credits**

8 list of people responsible
for the production of a film,
programme, or record ▷ *v*
crediting, credited 9 enter
as a credit in an account
10 (foll. by *with*) attribute
(to) **11** believe **creditable** *adj*
praiseworthy **creditably** *adv*
creditor *n* person to whom
money is owed **credit card**
card allowing a person to
buy on credit **credit crunch**
period during which there
is a sudden reduction in the
availability of credit (from
banks etc.)
credo *n, pl* -**dos** creed
credulous *adj* too willing to
believe **credulity** *n*
creed *n* statement or system
of (Christian) beliefs or
principles
creek *n* **1** narrow inlet or bay
2 small stream
creel *n* wicker basket used by
anglers
creep *v* **creeping, crept**
1 move with stealthy slow
movements **2** crawl with the
body near to the ground **3** (of a
plant) grow along the ground
or over a surface ▷ *n* **4** *slang*
obnoxious or servile person
creeps 5 feeling of fear or
disgust **creeper** *n* creeping
plant **creepy** *adj informal*
causing a feeling of fear or
disgust
cremate *v* burn (a corpse)
to ash **cremation** *n*
crematorium *n* building
where corpses are cremated
crenellated *adj* having
battlements **crenellation** *n*
creole *n* **1** language developed
from a mixture of languages
2 Creole native-born W
Indian or Latin American of
mixed European and African
descent
creosote *n* **1** dark oily liquid
distilled from coal tar and

used for preserving wood ▷ v
2 treat with creosote
crepe [**krayp**] n **1** fabric or
rubber with a crinkled texture
2 very thin pancake **crepe
paper** paper with a crinkled
texture
crept v past of **creep**
crepuscular adj of or like
twilight
crescendo [krish-**end**-oh] n,
pl -**dos** gradual increase in
loudness, esp. in music
crescent n **1** (shape of) the
moon as seen in its first or
last quarter **2** crescent-shaped
street
cress n plant with strong-
tasting leaves, used in salads
crest n **1** top of a mountain,
hill, or wave **2** tuft or growth
on a bird's or animal's head
3 heraldic device used on
a coat of arms, notepaper,
and elsewhere **crested** adj
crestfallen adj disheartened
cretin n **1** obsolete person
with physical and mental
disability caused by a thyroid
deficiency **2** informal, offensive
stupid person **cretinous** adj
cretonne n heavy printed
cotton fabric used in
furnishings
crevasse n deep open chasm,
esp. in a glacier
crevice n narrow fissure or
crack
crew n **1** people who man a
ship or aircraft **2** group of
people working together
3 informal any group of people
▷ v **4** serve as a crew member
on **crew cut** man's closely
cropped haircut
crewel n fine worsted yarn
used in embroidery
crib n **1** child's bed usu. with
barred sides **2** barred rack
used for fodder **3** plagiarism
4 translation or list of
answers used by students,

often illicitly ▷ v **cribbing,
cribbed 5** confine in small
space **6** copy (someone's
work) dishonestly **crib death**
unexplained death of a baby
while asleep
cribbage n card game for two
to four players
crick n **1** muscle spasm or
cramp, esp. in the back or
neck ▷ v **2** cause a crick in
cricket[1] n outdoor game
played with bats, a ball, and
wickets by two teams of
eleven **cricketer** n
cricket[2] n chirping insect like
a grasshopper
crime n **1** unlawful act
2 unlawful acts collectively
3 informal disgraceful act
criminal n **1** person guilty
of a crime ▷ adj **2** of crime
criminally adv **criminality** n
criminology n study of crime
criminologist n
crimp v fold or press into
ridges
crimson adj deep red
cringe v **1** flinch or shrink
2 behave in a servile or timid
way
crinkle v, n wrinkle, twist, or
fold
crinoline n hooped petticoat
cripple n offensive **1** person
who is lame or disabled ▷ v
2 make a cripple of (someone)
3 damage (something)
crisis n, pl -**ses 1** crucial stage,
turning point **2** time of acute
trouble or danger
crisp adj **1** fresh and firm
2 dry and brittle **3** clean and
neat **4** (of weather) cold but
invigorating **5** brisk and
lively ▷ n **6** Brit potato chip
crisply adv **crispness** n
crispy adj **crispbread** n thin
dry biscuit
crisscross v **1** move in,
mark with, or consist of a
crosswise pattern ▷ adj **2** (of

lines) crossing in different directions

criterion n, pl **-ria** standard of judgment

critic n 1 professional judge of any of the arts 2 person who finds fault **critical** adj 1 very important or dangerous 2 seriously ill 3 fault-finding 4 discerning 5 of a critic or criticism **critically** adv **criticism** n 1 fault-finding 2 evaluation of a work of art **criticize** v find fault with **critique** n critical essay

croak v 1 (of a frog or crow) give a low hoarse cry 2 utter or speak with a croak ▷ n 3 low hoarse cry **croaky** adj hoarse

Croatian [kroh-**ay**-shun], **Croat** [**kroh**-at] adj 1 of Croatia ▷ n 2 person from Croatia 3 dialect of Serbo-Croat spoken in Croatia

crochet [**kroh**-shay] n 1 handicraft like knitting, done with a single hooked needle ▷ v 2 do or make such work

crock n 1 earthenware jar or pot 2 informal old or decrepit person or thing **crockery** n earthenware or china dishes

crocodile n 1 large amphibious tropical reptile 2 line of children walking two by two **crocodile tears** insincere grief

crocus n, pl **-cuses** small plant with yellow, white, or purple flowers in spring

croft n small farm worked by the occupier in Scotland **crofter** n

croissant [**krwah**-son] n rich flaky crescent-shaped roll

cromlech n circle of prehistoric standing stones

crone n witchlike old woman

crony n, pl **-nies** close friend

crook n 1 informal criminal 2 bent or curved part 3 hooked pole **crooked** adj 1 bent or twisted 2 set at an angle 3 informal dishonest

croon v hum, sing, or speak in a soft low tone **crooner** n

crop n 1 cultivated plant 2 season's total yield of produce 3 group of things appearing at one time 4 hunting whip 5 pouch in a bird's gullet 6 short haircut ▷ v **cropping, cropped** 7 cut short 8 produce or harvest as a crop 9 (of animals) feed on (grass etc.) **cropper** n **come a cropper** informal have a disastrous failure or heavy fall

crop-top n short T-shirt or vest that reveals the wearer's midriff **crop up** v informal happen unexpectedly

croquet [**kroh**-kay] n game in which balls are hit through hoops

croquette [kroh-**kett**] n fried cake of potato, meat, or fish

crosier n same as **crozier**

cross v 1 move or go across (something) 2 meet and pass 3 draw a cross or lines through (something) 4 mark with lines across 5 place (one's arms or legs) crosswise 6 make the sign of the cross on (oneself) 7 thwart or oppose 8 interbreed or cross-fertilize ▷ n 9 structure, symbol, or mark of two intersecting lines 10 such a structure of wood as a means of execution 11 representation of the Cross as an emblem of Christianity 12 mixture of two things 13 affliction ▷ adj 14 angry, in a bad mood 15 lying or placed across **the Cross** Christianity the cross on which Christ was crucified **crossing** n 1 place where a street etc. may be crossed 2 place where things cross 3 journey across

water **crossly** *adv* **crossness**
n **crossbar** *n* horizontal
bar across goalposts or
on a bicycle **crossbow** *n*
bow fixed across a wooden
stock **crossbred** *adj* bred
from two different types of
animal or plant **crossbreed**
n crossbred animal or plant
crosscheck *v* **1** check the
accuracy of (something) by
using a different method
2 *hockey* illegally check an
opponent forcefully with
the shaft of the stick held
between the hands ▷ *n* **3** act
of crosschecking **cross-
country** *adj, adv* by way
of open country or fields
cross-examine *v* question
(a witness in court) to check
his or her testimony **cross-
examination** *n* **cross-eyed**
adj with eyes turning inwards
cross-fertilize *v* fertilize (an
animal or plant) from one
of a different kind **cross-
fertilization** *n* **crossfire**
n gunfire crossing another
line of fire **cross-ply** *adj* (of a
tire) having the fabric cords
in the outer casing running
diagonally **cross-purposes**
pl n **at cross-purposes**
misunderstanding each other
cross-reference *n* reference
within a text to another part
crossroads *n* place where
roads intersect **cross section**
1 (diagram of) a surface made
by cutting across something
2 representative sample
crosswalk *n* place marked
where pedestrians may
cross a road **crosswise** *adj,
adv* **1** transverse(ly) **2** in the
shape of a cross **crossword
puzzle** *or* **crossword** *n* puzzle
in which words suggested by
clues are written into a grid of
squares
crotch *n* fork between the legs

crotchet *n Brit* quarter note
crotchety *adj informal* bad-
tempered
crouch *v* **1** bend low with the
legs and body close ▷ *n* **2** this
position
croup[1] [**kroop**] *n* throat
disease of children, with a
cough
croup[2] [**kroop**] *n* hind quarters
of a horse
croupier [**kroop**-ee-ay] *n*
person who collects bets
and pays out winnings at a
gambling table
crouton *n* small piece of fried
or toasted bread served in
soup
crow[1] *n* large black bird with a
harsh call **as the crow flies**
in a straight line **crow's feet**
wrinkles at the corners of the
eyes **crow's nest** lookout
platform high on a ship's
mast
crow[2] *v* **1** (of a cock) utter
a shrill squawking sound
2 boast of one's superiority
3 (of a baby) utter cries of
pleasure ▷ *n* **4** cock's cry
crowbar *n* iron bar used as a
lever
crowd *n* **1** large group of people
or things **2** particular group
of people ▷ *v* **3** flock together
4 fill or occupy fully
crown *n* **1** monarch's
headdress **2** wreath for the
head **3** highest point of
something arched or curved
4 artificial cover for a broken
or decayed tooth **5** former
British coin worth twenty-
five pence ▷ *v* **6** put a crown
on the head of (someone)
to proclaim him or her
monarch **7** form or put on
the top of **8** put the finishing
touch to (a series of events)
9 *informal* hit on the head
the Crown power of the
monarchy **crown attorney**

lawyer who represents a government at a trial **crown corporation** business owned by a government but run like a private company **crown prince** (**crown princess**) heir to the throne

crozier n bishop's hooked staff

cruces n a plural of **crux**

crucial adj very important, critical **crucially** adv

crucible n pot in which metals are melted

crucify v -fying, -fied 1 put to death by fastening to a cross 2 treat cruelly 3 informal ridicule publicly **crucifix** n model of Christ on the Cross **crucifixion** n crucifying **the Crucifixion** Christianity 1 crucifying of Christ 2 representation of this **cruciform** adj cross-shaped

crude adj 1 rough and simple 2 tasteless or vulgar 3 in a natural or unrefined state **crudely** adv **crudity** n

cruel adj 1 delighting in others' pain 2 causing pain or suffering **cruelly** adv **cruelty** n

cruet n small container for salt, pepper, etc. at table

cruise n 1 voyage for pleasure ▷ v 2 sail about for pleasure 3 (of a vehicle, aircraft, or ship) travel at a moderate and economical speed **cruiser** n 1 motorboat with a cabin 2 fast warship 3 police patrol car **cruise missile** low-flying guided missile

crumb n 1 small fragment of bread or other dry food 2 small bit

crumble v 1 break into fragments 2 fall apart or decay ▷ n 3 pudding of stewed fruit with a crumbly topping **crumbly** adj

crummy adj -mier, -miest slang 1 inferior 2 squalid

crumpet n 1 round soft yeast cake eaten buttered 2 slang sexually attractive women collectively

crumple v 1 crush and crease 2 collapse **crumpled** adj

crunch v 1 crush (food) noisily with the teeth 2 (cause to) make a crisp or brittle sound ▷ n 3 crunching sound 4 informal critical moment **crunchy** adj

crupper n strap that passes from the back of a saddle under a horse's tail

crusade n 1 medieval Christian war to recover the Holy Land from the Muslims 2 vigorous campaign in favour of a cause ▷ v 3 take part in a crusade **crusader** n

crush v 1 compress so as to break, injure, or crumple 2 break into small pieces 3 defeat utterly ▷ n 4 dense crowd 5 informal infatuation 6 drink made by crushing fruit

crust n 1 hard outer part of something, esp. bread ▷ v 2 cover with or form a crust **crusty** adj 1 having a crust 2 irritable

crustacean n hard-shelled, usu. aquatic animal with several pairs of legs, such as the crab or lobster

crutch n 1 staff with a rest for the armpit, used by a lame person 2 support 3 crotch

crux n, pl **cruxes**, **cruces** crucial or decisive point

cry v **crying**, **cried** 1 shed tears 2 call or utter loudly 3 appeal urgently (for) ▷ n, pl **cries** 4 fit of weeping 5 loud utterance 6 urgent appeal **crybaby** n person who cries too readily

cryogenics n branch of physics concerned with very low temperatures **cryogenic** adj

crypt n vault, esp. one under a church **cryptic** adj obscure in meaning **cryptically** adv **cryptogram** n message in code **cryptography** n art of writing in and deciphering codes

cryptogam n plant that reproduces by spores, not seeds

crystal n 1 glasslike mineral 2 very clear and brilliant glass 3 tumblers, vases, etc. made of such glass 4 (single grain of a) symmetrically shaped solid formed naturally by some substances ▷ adj 5 bright and clear **crystalline** adj 1 of or like crystal or crystals 2 clear **crystallize** v 1 make or become definite 2 form into crystals 3 preserve (fruit) in sugar **crystallization** n **crystal meth** informal highly addictive drug with dangerous side effects

CSIS Canadian Security and Intelligence Service

CST Central Standard Time

CTV Canadian Television (Network Ltd.)

Cu chem copper

cu. cubic

cub n 1 young of certain mammals, such as the lion 2 **Cub** Cub Scout ▷ v **cubbing, cubbed** 3 give birth to (cubs) **Cub Scout** member of a junior branch of the Boy Scouts

cubbyhole n small enclosed space or room

cube n 1 solid with six equal square sides 2 product obtained by multiplying a number by itself twice ▷ v 3 find the cube of (a number) 4 cut into cubes **cubic** adj 1 having three dimensions 2 cube-shaped **cubism** n style of art in which objects are represented by geometrical

shapes **cubist** n, adj **cube root** number whose cube is a given number

cubicle n enclosed part of a large room, screened for privacy

cuckold n 1 man whose spouse has committed adultery ▷ v 2 make a cuckold of

cuckoo n 1 migratory bird with a characteristic two-note call, which lays its eggs in the nests of other birds ▷ adj 2 informal crazy

cucumber n long green-skinned fleshy fruit used in salads

cud n partially digested food which a ruminant brings back into its mouth to chew again **chew the cud** reflect or ponder

cuddle v 1 hug fondly 2 nestle ▷ n 3 fond hug **cuddly** adj

cudgel n short thick stick used as a weapon

cue¹ n 1 signal to an actor or musician to begin speaking or playing 2 signal or reminder ▷ v **cueing, cued** 3 give a cue to (someone)

cue² n 1 long tapering stick used in billiards, snooker, or pool ▷ v **cueing, cued** 2 strike (a ball) with a cue

cuff¹ n end of a sleeve **off the cuff** informal impromptu **cuff link** one of a pair of decorative fastenings for shirt cuffs

cuff² v 1 strike with an open hand ▷ n 2 blow with an open hand

cuisine [quiz-zeen] n style of cooking

cul-de-sac n road with one end blocked off

culinary adj of the kitchen or cookery

cull v 1 gather, select 2 remove or kill (inferior or surplus animals) from a herd ▷ n 3 culling

culminate v reach the highest point or climax **culmination** n

culottes pl n women's flared trousers cut to look like a skirt

culpable adj deserving blame **culpability** n

culprit n person guilty of an offence or misdeed

cult n 1 specific system of worship 2 devotion to a person, idea, or activity 3 popular fashion

cultivate v 1 prepare (land) to grow crops 2 grow (plants) 3 develop or improve (something) 4 try to develop a friendship with (someone) **cultivated** adj cultured or well-educated **cultivation** n

culture n 1 ideas, customs, and art of a particular society 2 particular society 3 developed understanding of the arts 4 cultivation of plants or rearing of animals 5 growth of bacteria for study **cultural** adj **cultured** adj showing culture **cultured pearl** pearl artificially grown in an oyster shell

culvert n drain under a road or railway

cumbersome adj awkward or unwieldy

cumin, cummin n aromatic seeds of a Mediterranean plant, used in cooking

cummerbund n broad sash worn round the waist

cumulative [kew-myew-la-tiv] adj increasing steadily

cumulus [kew-myew-luss] n, pl -li cloud shaped in heaped-up rounded masses

cuneiform [kew-nif-form] n 1 ancient system of writing using wedge-shaped characters ▷ adj 2 written in cuneiform

cunning adj 1 clever at deceiving 2 ingenious ▷ n 3 cleverness at deceiving 4 ingenuity **cunningly** adv

cup n 1 small bowl-shaped drinking container with a handle 2 contents of a cup 3 cup-shaped trophy given as a prize 4 hollow rounded shape 5 mixed drink with fruit juice or wine as a base ▷ v **cupping, cupped** 6 form (one's hands) into the shape of a cup 7 hold in cupped hands **cupful** n

cupboard n piece of furniture or recess with a door, for storage

cupidity [kew-pid-it-ee] n greed for wealth or possessions

cupola [kew-pol-la] n domed roof or ceiling

cur n 1 mongrel dog 2 contemptible person

curaçao [kew-rah-so] n orange-flavoured liqueur

curare [kew-rah-ree] n poisonous resin of a S American tree, used as a muscle relaxant in medicine

curate n cleric who assists a parish priest **curacy** [kew-rah-see] n work or position of a curate

curative adj 1 able to cure ▷ n 2 something curative

curator n person in charge of a museum or art gallery **curatorship** n

curb n 1 check or restraint 2 edge of sidewalk ▷ v 3 restrain

curd n coagulated milk **curdle** v turn into curd, coagulate

cure v 1 heal (an ailment or problem) 2 restore to health 3 preserve by salting, smoking, or drying ▷ n 4 restoration to health 5 medical treatment 6 remedy or solution **curable** adj

curet, curette n 1 surgical instrument for scraping

tissue from body cavities ▷ v -**retting**, -**retted** **2** scrape with a curet **curettage** n

curfew n **1** law ordering people to stay indoors after a specific time at night **2** time set as a deadline by such a law

curie n standard unit of radioactivity

curio [**kew-ree-oh**] n, pl -**rios** strange or rare thing valued as a collector's item

curious adj **1** eager to know **2** eager to find out private details **3** unusual or peculiar **curiously** adv **curiosity** n **1** eagerness to know **2** eagerness to find out private details **3** strange or rare thing

curium [**kew-ree-um**] n artificial radioactive element produced from plutonium

curl v **1** twist (hair) or (of hair) be twisted into coils **2** twist into a spiral or curve ▷ n **3** coil of hair **4** spiral or curved shape **curly** adj **curling** n game like bowls, played with heavy stones on ice

curlew n long-billed wading bird

curmudgeon n bad-tempered or mean person

currant n **1** dried grape **2** small round berry, such as a redcurrant

current adj **1** of the immediate present **2** most recent, up-to-date **3** commonly accepted ▷ n **4** flow of water or air in one direction **5** flow of electricity **6** general trend **currently** adv **currency** n **1** money in use in a particular country **2** state of being current

curriculum n, pl -**la**, -**lums** specified course of study **curriculum vitae** [**vee-tie**] outline of someone's educational and professional history, prepared for job applications

curry[1] n, pl -**ries** **1** dish of meat or vegetables in a hot or mild spicy sauce ▷ v -**rying**, -**ried** **2** prepare (food) with curry powder **curry powder** mixture of spices for making curry

curry[2] v -**rying**, -**ried** groom (a horse) with a currycomb **curry favour** ingratiate oneself, esp. with one's superiors **currycomb** n ridged comb for grooming a horse

curse v **1** say profane or obscene things (to) **2** utter a curse against ▷ n **3** profane or obscene expression, usu. of anger **4** call to a supernatural power for harm to come to a person **5** affliction, misfortune **cursed** adj hateful

cursive n, adj (handwriting) done with joined letters

cursor n movable point of light that shows a specific position on a visual display unit

cursory adj hasty and superficial **cursorily** adv

curt adj (of speech) impolitely brief **curtly** adv **curtness** n

curtail v **1** cut short **2** restrict **curtailment** n

curtain n **1** piece of cloth hung at a window or opening as a screen **2** hanging cloth separating the audience and the stage in a theatre **3** end of a scene or act, marked by the fall or closing of the curtain **4** thing(s) forming a barrier or screen ▷ v **5** conceal with a curtain **6** provide with curtains

curtsy, curtsey n, pl -**sies**, -**seys 1** woman's gesture of respect made by bending the knees and bowing the head ▷ v -**sying**, -**sied** or -**seying**, -**seyed 2** make a curtsy

curve n 1 continuously bending line with no straight parts ▷ v 2 bend into or move in a curve **curvy** adj **curvaceous** adj informal (of a woman) having a shapely body **curvature** n state or degree of being curved **curvilinear** adj consisting of or bounded by a curve

cushion n 1 bag filled with soft material, to make a seat more comfortable 2 something that provides comfort or absorbs shock ▷ v 3 protect from injury or shock 4 lessen the effects of

cushy adj **cushier**, **cushiest** informal easy: a cushy job

cusp n 1 pointed end, esp. on a tooth 2 astrol division between houses or signs of the zodiac

cuss informal ▷ n 1 curse, oath 2 annoying person ▷ v 3 swear (at) **cussed** [**kuss**-id] adj informal obstinate

custard n dish or sauce made of sweetened milk thickened with eggs or cornflour

custody n 1 guardianship 2 imprisonment prior to being tried **custodial** adj **custodian** n person in charge of a public building or museum collection

custom n 1 long-established activity or action 2 usual habit 3 regular use of a shop or business **customs** 4 duty charged on imports or exports 5 government department which collects these 6 area at a port, airport, or border where baggage and freight are examined for dutiable goods **customary** adj 1 usual 2 established by custom **customarily** adv **customer** n person who buys goods or services **customize** v modify (something) according to a customer's individual requirements **custom-built** or **custom-made** adj made to the specifications of an individual customer

cut v **cutting**, **cut** 1 open up, penetrate, wound, or divide with a sharp instrument 2 divide 3 intersect 4 trim or shape by cutting 5 abridge 6 reduce 7 informal snub (a person) 8 informal absent oneself from (classes) ▷ n 9 stroke or incision made by cutting 10 piece cut off 11 reduction 12 abridgment 13 style in which hair or a garment is cut 14 informal share, esp. of profits **cutter** n 1 person or tool that cuts 2 any of various small fast boats **cutting** n 1 piece cut from a plant for rooting or grafting 2 article cut from a newspaper or magazine 3 passage cut through high ground for a road or railway ▷ adj 4 keen, piercing 5 (of a remark) hurtful **cutting edge** leading position in any field **cut in** v 1 interrupt 2 obstruct another vehicle in overtaking it

cutthroat adj 1 fierce or relentless ▷ n 2 murderer

cutaneous [kew-**tane**-ee-uss] adj of the skin

cute adj 1 appealing or attractive 2 informal clever or shrewd **cutely** adv **cuteness** n

cuticle [**kew**-tik-kl] n skin at the base of a fingernail or toenail

cutlass n short curved one-edged sword

cutlery n knives, forks, and spoons, used for eating **cutler** n maker or seller of cutlery

cutlet n small piece of meat grilled or fried

cuttlefish n sea mollusc like a squid

CV curriculum vitae

cwt. hundredweight

cyanide n extremely

poisonous chemical compound

cyanosis n blueness of the skin, caused by a deficiency of oxygen in the blood

cyber- combining form computers: cyberspace

cybernetics n branch of science in which electronic and mechanical systems are studied and compared to biological systems

cyberspace n place said to contain all the data stored in computers

cyclamen [sik-la-men] n plant with red, pink, or white flowers having turned-back petals

cycle n 1 bicycle 2 motorcycle 3 recurrent series of events 4 time taken for one such series ▷ v 5 ride a cycle **cyclic** or **cyclical** adj occurring in cycles **cyclist** n person who rides a cycle

cyclone n violent wind moving clockwise round a central area **cyclonic** adj

cyclotron n apparatus which accelerates charged particles by means of a strong vertical magnetic field

cygnet n young swan

cylinder n 1 solid or hollow body with straight sides

and circular ends 2 chamber within which the piston moves in an internal-combustion engine **cylindrical** adj

cymbal n percussion instrument consisting of a brass plate which is struck against another or hit with a stick

cynic [sin-ik] n person who believes that people always act selfishly **cynical** adj **cynically** adv **cynicism** n

cynosure [sin-oh-zyure] n centre of attention

cypher n same as **cipher**

cypress n evergreen tree with very dark foliage

Cypriot n, adj (person) from Cyprus

cyst [sist] n (abnormal) sac in the body containing fluid or soft matter **cystic** adj **cystitis** [siss-tite-iss] n inflammation of the bladder

cytology [site-ol-a-jee] n study of plant and animal cells **cytological** adj **cytologist** n

czar [zahr] n same as **tsar**

Czech adj 1 of the Czech Republic ▷ n 2 person from the Czech Republic 3 language of the Czech Republic

Dd

d *physics* density

D *chem* deuterium

d. 1 died 2 *Brit* old penny

dab¹ *v* **dabbing, dabbed** 1 pat lightly 2 apply with short tapping strokes ▷ *n* 3 small amount of something soft or moist 4 light tap or stroke **dab hand** *informal* person who is particularly good at something

dab² *n* small flatfish

dabble *v* 1 deal in something superficially 2 splash about **dabbler** *n*

dace *n* small freshwater fish

dachshund *n* dog with a long body and short legs

dactyl *n* metrical foot of three syllables, one long followed by two short **dactylic** *adj*

dad *n informal* father

daddy *n, pl* **-dies** *informal* father

daddy-longlegs *n informal* crane fly

dado [**day**-doe] *n, pl* **-does, -dos** lower part of an interior wall that is decorated differently from the upper part

daffodil *n* spring plant with yellow trumpet-shaped flowers

daft *adj informal* foolish or crazy

dagger *n* short stabbing weapon with a pointed blade

dago [**day**-go] *n offensive* Spanish or other Latin person

daguerreotype [dag-**gair**-

oh-type] *n* type of early photograph produced on chemically treated silver

dahlia [**day**-lya] *n* garden plant with showy flowers

daily *adj* 1 occurring every day or every weekday ▷ *adv* 2 every day ▷ *n, pl* **-lies** 3 daily newspaper 4 *Brit informal* charwoman

dainty *adj* **-tier, -tiest** delicate or elegant **daintily** *adv*

daiquiri [**dak**-eer-ee] *n* iced drink containing rum, lime juice, and sugar

dairy *n, pl* **dairies** 1 place for the processing or sale of milk and its products 2 food containing milk or milk products: *I can't eat dairy* ▷ *adj* 3 of milk or its products

dais [**day**-iss] *n* raised platform in a hall

daisy *n, pl* **-sies** flower with a yellow centre and white petals **daisywheel** *n* flat disc in a word processor with radiating spokes for printing letters

Dalai Lama *n* chief lama and (until 1959) ruler of Tibet

dale *n* valley

dally *v* **-lying, -lied** 1 dawdle 2 (foll. by *with*) amuse oneself (with) **dalliance** *n* flirtation

Dalmatian *n* large dog with a white coat and black spots

dam¹ *n* 1 barrier built across a river to create a lake 2 lake created by this ▷ *v* **damming, dammed** 3 restrict by a dam

dam | 144

dam² n female parent of an animal
damage v 1 harm ▷ n 2 injury or harm to a person or thing 3 informal cost: what's the damage? **damages** 4 money to be paid as compensation for injury or loss
damask n fabric with a pattern woven into it, used for tablecloths etc.
dame n 1 slang woman 2 **Dame** title of a woman who has been awarded the Order of the British Empire or another order of chivalry
damn interj 1 slang exclamation of annoyance ▷ adv, adj 2 Also **damned** slang extreme or extremely ▷ v 3 declare to be bad or worthless 4 swear (at) 5 (of God) condemn to hell 6 prove (someone) guilty: damning evidence **damnable** adj annoying **damnably** adv **damnation** n
damp adj 1 slightly wet ▷ n 2 slight wetness, moisture ▷ v 3 make damp 4 (foll. by down) reduce the force of (feelings or actions) **damply** adv **dampness** n **dampen** v damp **damper** n 1 depressing influence 2 movable plate to regulate the draft in a fire or furnace 3 pad in a piano that deadens the vibration of each string
damsel n obsolete young woman
damson n small blue-black plumlike fruit
dance v 1 move the feet and body rhythmically in time to music 2 perform (a particular kind of dance) 3 skip or leap 4 move rhythmically ▷ n 5 social meeting arranged for dancing 6 series of steps and movements in time to music **dancer** n
D and C surgery dilat(at)ion

and curettage: an operation in which the neck of the womb is stretched and the lining of the womb is scraped, for example to remove diseased tissue
dandelion n yellow-flowered wild plant
dander n **get one's dander up** slang become angry
dandle v move (a child) up and down on one's knee
dandruff n loose scales of dry dead skin shed from the scalp
dandy n, pl -dies 1 man who is greatly concerned with the elegance of his appearance ▷ adj -dier, -diest 2 informal very good or fine **dandified** adj
danger n 1 state of being vulnerable to injury or loss 2 person or thing that may cause injury 3 likelihood that something unpleasant will happen **dangerous** adj **dangerously** adv
dangle v 1 hang freely 2 display as an enticement
dank adj unpleasantly damp and chilly
daphne n shrub with small bell-shaped flowers
dapper adj (of a man) neat in appearance and slight in build
dappled adj marked with spots of a different colour **dapple-grey** n horse having a grey coat with spots of a different colour
dare v 1 be courageous enough to try (to do something) 2 challenge to do something risky ▷ n 3 challenge **daring** adj 1 willing to take risks ▷ n 2 courage to do dangerous things **daringly** adv **daredevil** adj, n reckless (person)
daren't dare not
dark adj 1 having little or no

light **2** (of a colour) reflecting little light **3** (of hair or skin) brown or black **4** gloomy or sinister **5** secret: *keep it dark* ▷ *n* **6** absence of light **7** night **darkly** *adv* **darkness** *n* **darken** *v* **dark horse** person who reveals unexpected talents **darkroom** *n* darkened room for processing film

darling *n* **1** much-loved person **2** favourite: *the darling of the gossip columns* ▷ *adj* **3** beloved

darn[1] *v* **1** mend (a garment) with a series of interwoven stitches ▷ *n* **2** patch of darned work

darn[2] *interj, adv, adj, v* *euphemistic* damn

dart *n* **1** small narrow pointed missile that is thrown or shot, esp. in the game of darts **2** sudden quick movement **3** tuck made in dressmaking **darts 4** indoor game in which darts are thrown at a circular numbered board (**dartboard**) ▷ *v* **5** move or throw quickly and suddenly

Darwinism *n* theory of the origin of animal and plant species by evolution **Darwinian** or **Darwinist** *adj, n*

dash *v* **1** move hastily **2** throw or strike violently **3** frustrate (someone's hopes) ▷ *n* **4** sudden quick movement **5** small amount **6** mixture of style and courage **7** punctuation mark (–) showing a change of subject **8** longer symbol used in Morse code **dashing** *adj* **1** lively **2** stylish **dashboard** *n* instrument panel in an automobile, boat, or aircraft

dastardly *adj* mean and cowardly

data *n* **1** series of observations, measurements, or facts **2** numbers, digits, etc. operated on by a computer

database *n* store of information that can be easily handled by a computer **data capture** process for converting information into a form that can be handled by a computer

data processing series of operations performed on data, esp. by a computer, to extract or interpret information

date[1] *n* **1** specified day of the month **2** particular day or year when an event happened **3** *informal* appointment, esp. with a person of the opposite sex **4** *informal* this person ▷ *v* **5** mark with the date **6** assign a date of occurrence to **7** (foll. by *from*) originate from (a date): *this house dates from the 16th century* **8** make or become old-fashioned **dated** *adj*

date[2] *n* dark-brown sweet-tasting fruit of the date palm **date palm** tall palm grown in tropical regions for its fruit

dative *n* (in certain languages) the form of the noun that expresses the indirect object

daub *v* smear or spread quickly or clumsily

daughter *n* **1** female child **2** woman who comes from a certain place or is connected with a certain thing: *daughter of the church* **daughterly** *adj* **daughter-in-law** *n, pl* **daughters-in-law** wife of one's child

daunt *v* intimidate or dishearten **daunting** *adj* **dauntless** *adj* fearless

dauphin [**daw**-fin] *n* (formerly) eldest son of the king of France

davenport *n* **1** small writing table with drawers **2** large couch

davit [**dav**-vit] *n* crane, usu. one of a pair, at a ship's side, for lowering and hoisting boats

Davy lamp *n* miner's lamp designed to prevent it from igniting gas

dawdle *v* **1** be slow or lag behind **2** waste time **dawdler** *n*

dawn *n* **1** daybreak **2** beginning (of something) ▷ *v* **3** begin to grow light **4** begin to develop or appear **5** (foll. by *on* or *upon*) become apparent (to)

day *n* **1** period of 24 hours **2** period of light between sunrise and sunset **3** part of a day occupied with regular activity, esp. work **4** period or point in time **5** day of special observance **6** time of success **daybreak** *n* time in the morning when light first appears **daydream** *n* **1** pleasant fantasy indulged in while awake ▷ *v* **2** indulge in idle fantasy **daydreamer** *n* **daylight** *n* light from the sun **day release** system in which workers go to college one day a week **day-to-day** *adj* routine

daze *v* **1** stun, esp. by a blow or shock ▷ *n* **2** state of confusion or shock

dazzle *v* **1** impress greatly **2** blind temporarily by sudden excessive light ▷ *n* **3** bright light that dazzles **dazzling** *adj* **dazzlingly** *adv*

dB, db decibel(s)

DC direct current

DCM Distinguished Conduct Medal

DD Doctor of Divinity

D-day *n* day selected for the start of some operation, esp. the Allied invasion of Europe in 1944

DDT kind of insecticide

de- *prefix* **1** *indicating* removal: *deforest* **2** *indicating* reversal: *decode* **3** *indicating* departure: *decamp*

deacon *n Christianity*

1 ordained minister ranking immediately below a priest **2** (in some Protestant churches) lay official who assists the minister **deaconess** *n fem*

dead *adj* **1** no longer alive **2** no longer in use **3** numb: *my leg has gone dead* **4** complete: *a dead stop* **5** *informal* very tired **6** (of a place) lacking activity ▷ *n* **7** period during which coldness or darkness is most intense: *the dead of night* ▷ *adv* **8** extremely **9** suddenly: *stop dead* **the dead** dead people **dead beat** *informal* exhausted **dead set against** completely opposed to **deaden** *v* **1** make less sensitive or lively **2** make less resonant **deadly** *adj* **-lier, -liest 1** likely to cause death **2** *informal* extremely boring ▷ *adv* **3** extremely **deadly nightshade** plant with poisonous black berries **deadbeat** *n informal* lazy useless person **dead end 1** road with one end blocked off **2** situation in which further progress is impossible **deadhead 1** *informal* person who does not pay on a bus, to get into a sports game, etc. **2** *slang* dull, unenterprising person **3** *informal* train, bus, etc. travelling empty **4** log sticking out of water and hindering navigation **dead heat** tie for first place between two participants in a contest **dead letter** law or rule that is no longer enforced **deadline** *n* time limit **deadlock** *n* **1** point in a dispute at which further progress is impossible ▷ *v* **2** bring to a deadlock **deadpan** *adj*, *adv* showing no emotion or expression **dead reckoning** method of establishing one's position using the distance and direction travelled **dead weight** heavy weight

deaf adj unable to hear **deaf to** refusing to listen to or take notice of **deafen** v make deaf, esp. temporarily **deafness** n

deal[1] n **1** transaction or agreement or treatment: a fair deal **3** large amount ▷ v **dealing, dealt** [delt] **4** distribute **5** inflict (a blow) on **6** cards give out (cards) to the players **dealer** n **dealings** pl n transactions or business relations **deal in** v engage in commercially **deal with** v **1** take action on **2** be concerned with

deal[2] n plank of fir or pine wood

dean n **1** chief administrative official of a college or university faculty **2** chief administrator of a cathedral **deanery** n **1** office or residence of a dean **2** parishes of a dean

dear n **1** someone regarded with affection ▷ adj **2** beloved **3** costly **dearly** adv **dearness** n

dearth [dirth] n inadequate amount, scarcity

death n **1** permanent end of all functions of life in a person or animal **2** instance of this **3** ending, destruction **deathly** adj, adv like death: deathly quiet; deathly pale **death duty** Brit tax paid on property left at death **death's-head** n human skull or a representation of one **deathtrap** n place or vehicle considered very unsafe **deathwatch beetle** beetle that bores into wood and makes a tapping sound

deb n informal debutante

debacle [day-**bah**-kl] n disastrous collapse or defeat

debar v exclude or bar

debase v lower in value, quality, or character **debasement** n

debate n **1** discussion ▷ v **2** discuss, esp. in a formal assembly **3** consider (a course of action) **in debate** in doubt, uncertain **debatable** adj not absolutely certain

debauched adj immoral, sexually corrupt **debauchery** n

debenture n long-term bond, bearing fixed interest, issued by a company or a government agency

debilitate v weaken **debilitation** n **debility** n weakness, infirmity

debit n **1** acknowledgment of a sum owing by entry on the left side of an account ▷ v **debiting, debited 2** record as a debit **3** charge with a debt

debonair adj **1** suave or refined **2** carefree

debouch v move out from a narrow place to a wider one

debrief v receive a report from (a soldier, diplomat, etc.) after an event **debriefing** n

debris [**deb**-ree] n fragments of something destroyed

debt n **1** something owed, esp. money **2** state of owing something **debtor** n

debunk v informal expose the pretensions or falseness of

debut [**day**-byoo] n first public appearance of a performer **debutante** [**day**-byoo-tont] n young upper-class woman making her first formal appearance in society

Dec. December

deca- combining form ten

decade n period of ten years

decadence [**dek**-a-denss] n state of deterioration of morality or culture **decadent** adj

decaffeinated [dee-**kaf**-fin-ate-id] adj (of tea or coffee) with caffeine removed

decagon n geometric figure

with ten sides **decagonal** adj
decahedron [dek-a-**hee**-dron]
n solid figure with ten faces
Decalogue n the Ten
Commandments
decamp v depart secretly or
suddenly
decant v 1 pour (a liquid) from
one container to another
2 rehouse (people) while their
homes are being refurbished
decanter n stoppered bottle
for wine or spirits
decapitate v behead
decapitation n
decarbonize v remove carbon
from (an internal-combustion
engine) **decarbonization** n
decathlon n athletic contest
with ten events
decay v 1 rot 2 become weaker
or more corrupt ▷ n 3 process
of decaying 4 state brought
about by this process
decease n formal death
deceased adj formal dead **the
deceased** person who has
recently died
deceive v 1 mislead by lying
2 be unfaithful to (one's
sexual partner) **deceiver** n
deceit n behaviour intended
to deceive **deceitful** adj
decelerate v slow down
deceleration n
December n twelfth month of
the year
decennial adj 1 lasting for ten
years 2 happening every ten
years
decent adj 1 of an acceptable
standard or quality 2 polite or
respectable 3 fitting or proper
4 conforming to conventions
of sexual behaviour 5 informal
kind **decently** adv **decency** n
decentralize v reorganize
into smaller local units
decentralization n
deception n 1 deceiving
2 something that
deceives, trick **deceptive**

adj likely or designed to
deceive **deceptively** adv
deceptiveness n
deci- combining form one tenth
decibel n unit for measuring
the intensity of sound
decide v 1 (cause to) reach a
decision 2 settle (a contest
or question) **decided** adj
1 unmistakable 2 determined
decidedly adv **decision** n
1 judgment, conclusion, or
resolution 2 act of making
up one's mind 3 firmness
of purpose **decisive** adj
1 indisputable: a decisive win
2 having the ability to make
(quick) decisions **decisively**
adv **decisiveness** n
deciduous adj (of a tree)
shedding its leaves annually
decimal n 1 fraction written
in the form of a dot followed
by one or more numbers
▷ adj 2 relating to or using
powers of ten 3 expressed
as a decimal **decimalize** v
change (a system or number)
to the decimal system
decimalization n **decimal
currency** system of currency
in which the units are parts or
powers of ten **decimal point**
dot between the unit and the
fraction of a number in the
decimal system **decimal
system** number system
with a base of ten, in which
numbers are expressed by
combinations of the digits 0
to 9
decimate v destroy or
kill a large proportion of
decimation n
decipher v 1 decode 2 make
out the meaning of (poor
handwriting) **decipherable**
adj
deck n 1 area of a ship that
forms a floor 2 similar area
in a bus 3 platform that
supports the turntable and

pick-up of a record player ▷ *v* **4** decorate **deck chair** folding chair made of canvas over a wooden frame **decking** *n* wooden platform in a garden **deck out** *v* dress (oneself) or decorate (a room)

declaim *v* **1** speak loudly and dramatically **2** protest loudly **declamation** *n* **declamatory** *adj*

declare *v* **1** state firmly and forcefully **2** announce officially **3** acknowledge for tax purposes **declaration** *n* **declaratory** *adj*

decline *v* **1** become smaller, weaker, or less important **2** say that one is unwilling to give, accept, or do (something) **3** *grammar* list the inflections of (a noun, pronoun, or adjective) ▷ *n* **4** gradual deterioration **5** movement downwards **6** diminution **declension** *n grammar* changes in the form of nouns, pronouns, or adjectives to show case, number, and gender

declivity *n, pl* **-ties** downward slope **declivitous** *adj*

declutch *v* disengage the clutch of a motor vehicle

decoct *v* extract the essence from (a substance) by boiling **decoction** *n*

decode *v* convert from code into ordinary language **decoder** *n*

décolleté [day-**kol**-tay] *adj* (of a woman's garment) having a low neckline

decompose *v* be broken down through chemical or bacterial action **decomposition** *n*

decompress *v* **1** free from pressure **2** return (a diver) to normal atmospheric pressure **decompression** *n*

decongestant *n* drug that relieves nasal congestion

decontaminate *v* render harmless by the removal of poisons, radioactivity, etc. **decontamination** *n*

decor [**day**-core] *n* decorative scheme of a room or house

decorate *v* **1** ornament **2** paint or wallpaper (a room) **3** award a (military) medal to **decoration** *n* **decorative** *adj* **decorator** *n*

decorous [**dek**-a-russ] *adj* polite, calm, and sensible in behaviour **decorously** *adv* **decorousness** *n* **decorum** [dik-**core**-um] *n* decorous behaviour

decoy *n* **1** person or thing used to lure someone into danger **2** image of a bird or animal, used to lure game within shooting range ▷ *v* **3** lure into danger by means of a decoy

decrease *v* **1** diminish ▷ *n* **2** lessening **3** amount by which something has been diminished

decree *n* **1** law made by someone in authority **2** court judgment ▷ *v* **3** order by decree

decrepit *adj* weakened or worn out by age or long use **decrepitude** *n*

decry *v* **-crying, -cried** express disapproval of

decrypt *v* decode (a message)

dedicate *v* **1** commit (oneself or one's time) wholly to a special purpose or cause **2** inscribe or address (a book etc.) to someone as a tribute **dedicated** *adj* devoted to a particular purpose or cause **dedication** *n*

deduce *v* reach (a conclusion) by reasoning from evidence **deducible** *adj*

deduct *v* subtract

deduction *n* **1** deducting **2** something that is deducted **3** deducing **4** conclusion

d

reached by deducing
deductive adj
deed n **1** something that is
done **2** legal document
deem v have as an opinion
deep adj **1** extending or
situated far down, inwards,
backwards, or sideways
2 of a specified dimension
downwards, inwards, or
backwards **3** coming from or
penetrating to a great depth
4 difficult to understand **5** of
great intensity **6** (foll. by *in*)
immersed (in) **7** (of a colour)
strong or dark **8** low in pitch
the deep *poetic* the sea **deeply**
adv profoundly or intensely
deepen v **deepfreeze** n same
as **freezer**
deer n, pl **deer** hoofed
mammal with antlers in the
male **deerstalker** n cloth hat
with peaks back and front and
earflaps
deface v spoil the surface or
appearance of **defacement** n
de facto adv **1** in fact ▷ adj
2 existing in fact, whether
legally recognized or not
defame v attack the good
reputation of **defamation** n
defamatory [dif-**fam**-a-
tree] adj
default n **1** failure to do
something **2** *computers*
instruction to a computer
to select a particular option
unless the user specifies
otherwise ▷ v **3** fail to fulfil
an obligation **in default of** in
the absence of **defaulter** n
defeat v **1** overcome **2** thwart
▷ n **3** defeating or being
defeated **defeatism** n ready
acceptance or expectation of
defeat **defeatist** n, adj
defecate v discharge waste
from the body through the
anus **defecation** n
defect n **1** imperfection ▷ v
2 desert one's cause or country

to join the opposing forces
defective adj having a flaw
defection n **defector** n
defence esp. US **defense** n
1 resistance to attack **2** plea
in support of something **3** a
country's military resources
4 defendant's case in a court
of law **defenceless** adj
defend v **1** protect from harm
or danger **2** support in the face
of criticism, esp. by argument
3 represent (a defendant) in
court **4** protect (a title) against
a challenge **defendant** n
person accused of a crime
defender n **defensible** adj
capable of being defended
because believed to be right
defensibility n **defensive**
adj **1** intended for defence
2 overanxious to protect
oneself against (threatened)
criticism **defensively** adv
defer[1] v **-ferring, -ferred**
delay (something) until a
future time **deferment** or
deferral n
defer[2] v **-ferring, -ferred** (foll.
by *to*) comply with the wishes
(of) **deference** n **1** compliance
with the wishes of another
2 respect **deferential** adj
deferentially adv
deficient adj **1** lacking some
essential **2** inadequate
in quality or quantity
deficiency n **1** lack **2** state
of being deficient **deficit** n
amount by which a sum of
money is too small
defile[1] v desecrate
defilement n
defile[2] n narrow pass or valley
define v **1** describe the nature
of **2** state precisely the
meaning of **3** show clearly
the outline of **definable**
adj **definite** adj **1** firm, clear,
and precise **2** having precise
limits **3** known for certain
definitely adv **definition** n

1 statement of the meaning of a word or phrase **2** quality of being clear and distinct **definitive** *adj* **1** providing an unquestionable conclusion **2** being the best example of something

deflate *v* **1** (cause to) collapse through the release of gas **2** take away the self-esteem or conceit from **3** *economics* cause deflation of (an economy) **deflation** *n* **1** *economics* reduction in economic activity resulting in lower output and investment **2** feeling of sadness following excitement **deflationary** *adj*

deflect *v* (cause to) turn aside from a course **deflection** *n* **deflector** *n*

deflower *v lit* deprive (a woman) of her virginity

defoliate *v* deprive (a plant) of its leaves **defoliant** *n* **defoliation** *n*

deforest *v* clear of trees **deforestation** *n*

deform *v* **1** cause to be misshapen **2** make ugly **deformation** *n* **deformity** *n*

defraud *v* take away or withhold money, rights, etc. from (a person) by fraud

defray *v* provide money for (costs or expenses)

defrock *v* deprive (a priest) of priestly status

defrost *v* **1** make or become free of frost or ice **2** thaw (frozen food) by removing it from a freezer

deft *adj* quick and skilful in movement **deftly** *adv* **deftness** *n*

defunct *adj* no longer existing or operative

defuse *v* **1** remove the triggering device from (an explosive device) **2** remove the tension from (a situation)

defy *v* **-fying, -fied 1** resist openly and boldly **2** elude, esp. in a baffling way: *defy description* **defiance** *n* open resistance to authority or opposition **defiant** *adj*

degenerate *adj* **1** having deteriorated to a lower mental, moral, or physical level ▷ *n* **2** degenerate person ▷ *v* **3** become degenerate **degeneracy** *n* degenerate behaviour **degeneration** *n*

degrade *v* **1** reduce to dishonour or disgrace **2** reduce in status or quality **3** *chem* decompose into smaller molecules **degradation** *n*

degree *n* **1** stage in a scale of relative amount or intensity **2** academic award given by a university or college on successful completion of a course **3** unit of measurement for temperature or angles

dehumanize *v* **1** deprive of human qualities **2** make (an activity) mechanical or routine **dehumanization** *n*

dehydrate *v* **1** cause to lose water **2** deprive the body of (someone) of water **dehydration** *n*

de-ice *v* free of ice **de-icer** *n*

deify [**day**-if-fie] *v* **-fying, -fied** treat or worship as a god **deification** *n*

deign [**dane**] *v* think it worthy of oneself (to do something), condescend

deity [**day**-it-ee] *n, pl* **-ties 1** god or goddess **2** state of being divine

déjà vu [**day**-zhah **voo**] *n* feeling of having experienced before something that is actually happening now

dejected *adj* in low spirits **dejectedly** *adv* **dejection** *n*

de jure *adv, adj* according to law

deke *ice hockey* ▷ *n* **1** feigned move which draws an

d

opponent out of position ▷ *v*
2 feign a move

delay *v* **1** put off to a later time
2 slow up or cause to be late
▷ *n* **3** act of delaying **4** interval
of time between events

delectable *adj* very attractive
delectation *n formal* great
pleasure

delegate *n* **1** person chosen
to act for others, esp. at a
meeting ▷ *v* **2** entrust (duties
or powers) to another person
3 appoint as a delegate
delegation *n* **1** group of
people appointed as delegates
2 delegating

delete *v* remove (something
written or printed) **deletion**
n

deleterious [del-lit-**eer**-ee-
uss] *adj* harmful, injurious

deli *n* delicatessen

deliberate *adj* **1** carefully
thought out in advance
2 careful and unhurried ▷ *v*
3 consider (something) deeply
deliberately *adv* **deliberation**
n **deliberative** *adj* for the
purpose of deliberating: *a
deliberative assembly*

delicate *adj* **1** fine or subtle
in quality or workmanship
2 having a fragile beauty **3** (of
a taste etc.) pleasantly subtle
4 easily damaged **5** requiring
tact **delicately** *adv* **delicacy** *n*
1 being delicate **2** something
particularly good to eat

delicatessen *n* shop selling
imported or unusual foods,
already cooked or prepared

delicious *adj* very appealing,
esp. to taste or smell
deliciously *adv*

delight *n* **1** great pleasure ▷ *v*
2 please greatly **3** (foll. by
in) take great pleasure (in)
delightful *adj* **delightfully**
adv

delimit *v* mark or prescribe
the limits of **delimitation** *n*

delineate [dill-**lin**-ee-ate] *v*
1 show by drawing **2** describe
in words **delineation** *n*

delinquent *n* **1** someone,
esp. a young person, who
repeatedly breaks the law
▷ *adj* **2** repeatedly breaking
the law **delinquency** *n*

delirium *n* **1** state of
excitement and mental
confusion, often with
hallucinations **2** violent
excitement **delirious** *adj*
deliriously *adv*

deliver *v* **1** carry (goods etc.)
to a destination **2** hand over
3 aid in the birth of **4** release
or rescue **5** present (a speech
etc.) **6** strike (a blow) suddenly
deliverance *n* rescue from
danger or captivity **delivery** *n*
1 act of delivering **2** something
that is delivered **3** act of giving
birth to a child **4** style, esp. in
public speaking

dell *n* small wooded hollow

Delphic *adj* ambiguous, like
the ancient Greek oracle at
Delphi

delphinium *n* plant with
spikes of blue flowers

delta *n* **1** fourth letter of the
Greek alphabet **2** flat area
at the mouth of some rivers
where the main stream splits
up into several tributaries

delude *v* deceive **delusion**
n **1** mistaken idea or belief
2 state of being deluded
delusive *adj*

deluge [**del**-lyooj] *n* **1** great
flood of water **2** torrential rain
3 overwhelming number ▷ *v*
4 flood **5** overwhelm

de luxe *adj* **1** rich or
sumptuous **2** superior in
quality

delve *v* research deeply or
intensively (for information)

demagogue *n* political
agitator who appeals to the
prejudice and passions of

the mob **demagogic** adj
demagogy n

demand v **1** ask for forcefully
2 require as just, urgent,
etc. **3** claim as a right ▷ n
4 forceful request **5** economics
willingness and ability to
purchase goods and services
demands 6 something that
requires special effort or
sacrifice **demanding** adj
requiring a lot of time or
effort

demarcation n
establishment of limits or
boundaries, esp. between the
work performed by different
trade unions

demean v lower (someone) in
dignity, character, or status

demeanour n way a person
behaves

demented adj mad
dementedly adv **dementia**
[dim-**men**-sha] n state of
serious mental deterioration

demerara sugar n brown
crystallized cane sugar

demerit n flaw, disadvantage

demesne [dim-**mane**] n
1 land surrounding a house
2 law possession of one's
own property or land

demi- combining form half

demijohn n large bottle with
a short neck, often encased in
wicker

demilitarize v remove
the military forces from
demilitarization n

demimonde n **1** (esp. in
the 19th century) class of
women considered to be
outside respectable society,
because of promiscuity
2 group considered not wholly
respectable

demise n **1** formal death
2 eventual failure (of
something successful)

demo n informal
demonstration, organized

expression of public opinion

demob v informal demobilize

demobilize v release from the
armed forces **demobilization**
n

democracy n, pl **-cies**
1 government by the people or
their elected representatives
2 state governed in this way
3 social equality **democrat**
n **1** advocate of democracy
2 Democrat member or
supporter of the Democratic
Party in the US **democratic**
adj **1** connected with
democracy **2** upholding
democracy **3 Democratic** of
the Democratic Party, the
more liberal of the two main
political parties in the US
democratically adv

demography n study
of human populations
demographer n
demographic adj

demolish v **1** tear down or
break up (buildings) **2** put
an end to (an argument etc.)
demolisher n **demolition** n

demon n **1** evil spirit **2** person
extremely skilful in or
devoted to a given activity
demonic adj **demoniacal** or
demoniac adj **1** appearing
to be possessed by a devil
2 frenzied **demoniacally**
adv **demonology** n study of
demons

demonstrate v **1** show
or prove by reasoning
or evidence **2** reveal the
existence of **3** display and
explain the workings of
4 show support or protest
by public parades or rallies
demonstrable adj able to be
proved **demonstrably** adv
demonstration n **1** organized
expression of public opinion
2 explanation or experiment
showing how something
works **3** proof **demonstrative**

adj tending to express one's feelings unreservedly **demonstratively** *adv* **demonstrator** *n* **1** person who demonstrates machines, products, etc. **2** person who takes part in a public demonstration

demoralize *v* undermine the morale of **demoralization** *n*

demote *v* reduce in status or rank **demotion** *n*

demur *v* -murring, -murred show reluctance **without demur** without objecting

demure *adj* quiet, reserved, and rather shy **demurely** *adv* **demureness** *n*

den *n* **1** home of a wild animal **2** small secluded room in a home **3** place where people indulge in criminal or immoral activities: *den of iniquity*

denationalize *v* transfer (an industry) from public to private ownership **denationalization** *n*

denature *v* **1** change the nature of **2** make (alcohol) unfit to drink

denigrate *v* criticize unfairly **denigration** *n* **denigrator** *n*

denim *n* **1** hard-wearing cotton fabric **denims 2** jeans made of denim

denizen *n* inhabitant

denominate *v* give a specific name to **denomination** *n* **1** group having a distinctive interpretation of a religious faith **2** grade or unit of value, measure, etc. **denominational** *adj* **denominator** *n* divisor of a fraction

denote *v* **1** be a sign of **2** have as a literal meaning **denotation** *n*

denouement [day-**noo**-mon] *n* final outcome or solution, esp. in a play or book

denounce *v* **1** speak violently against **2** give information against **denunciation** *n* open condemnation

dense *adj* **1** closely packed **2** difficult to see through **3** stupid **densely** *adv* **density** *n* **1** degree to which something is filled or occupied **2** *physics* measure of the compactness of a substance, expressed as its mass per unit volume

dent *n* **1** hollow in a surface, as made by a blow ▷ *v* **2** make a dent in

dental *adj* of or relating to the teeth or dentistry **dental floss** waxed thread used to remove food particles from between the teeth **dentifrice** [**den**-tif-riss] *n* paste or powder for cleaning the teeth **dentine** [**den**-teen] *n* calcified tissue comprising the bulk of a tooth **denture** *n* **1** artificial tooth **dentures 2** set of artificial teeth

dentist *n* person qualified to practise dentistry **dentistry** *n* branch of medicine concerned with the teeth and gums

denude *v* (foll. by *of*) remove the covering or protection from **denudation** *n*

deny *v* -nying, -nied **1** declare to be untrue **2** refuse to give or allow **3** refuse to acknowledge **deniable** *adj* **denial** *n* **1** denying **2** statement that something is not true

deodorize *v* remove or disguise the smell of **deodorization** *n* **deodorant** *n* substance applied to the body to mask the smell of perspiration

dep. 1 department **2** departure

depart *v* **1** leave **2** differ **departed** *adj* euphemistic dead **the departed** dead people **departure** *n*

department n
1 specialized division
of a large organization
2 major subdivision of
the administration of a
government **departmental**
adj **department store** large
shop selling many kinds of
goods

depend v (foll. by on or
upon) 1 put trust (in) 2 be
influenced or determined
(by) 3 rely (on) for income
or support **dependable**
adj **dependably** adv
dependability n **dependant**
n person who depends on
another for financial support
dependence n state of being
dependent **dependency** n
1 territory subject to a state
on which it does not border
2 overreliance on another
person or a drug **dependent**
adj depending on a person or
thing for support

depict v 1 give a picture of
2 describe in words **depiction**
n

depilatory [dip-**pill**-a-tree]
adj, n, pl -**ries** (substance)
designed to remove unwanted
hair

deplete v 1 use up 2 reduce in
number **depletion** n

deplore v express or feel
strong disapproval of
deplorable adj very bad

deploy v organize (troops or
resources) into a position
ready for immediate action
deployment n

depopulate v cause to
be reduced in population
depopulation n

deport v remove forcibly from
a country **deport oneself**
behave oneself in a specified
manner **deportation** n
deportee n **deportment** n
manner in which a person
behaves

depose v 1 remove from an
office or position of power
2 law make a statement on
oath

deposit v 1 put down
2 entrust for safekeeping,
esp. to a bank 3 lay down
naturally ▷ n 4 entrusting
of money to a bank 5 money
entrusted 6 money given in
part payment or as security
7 accumulation of sediments,
minerals, etc. **depositary** n
person to whom something
is entrusted for safety
depositor n **depository** n
store for furniture etc.

deposition n 1 law sworn
statement of a witness used
in court in his or her absence
2 deposing 3 depositing
4 something deposited

depot [**dee**-poh, **dep**-oh] n
1 building used for storage
2 building for the storage and
servicing of buses or railway
engines 3 bus or railway
station

deprave v make morally bad
depravity n moral corruption

deprecate v express
disapproval of, protest against
deprecation n **deprecatory**
adj

depreciate v 1 decline in
value or price 2 criticize
depreciation n **depreciatory**
adj

depredation n plundering

depress v 1 lower the spirits
of (someone) 2 lower (prices
or wages) 3 push down
depressing adj **depressingly**
adv **depressant** n drug which
reduces nervous activity
depression n 1 mental
state in which a person
has feelings of gloom and
inadequacy 2 economic
condition in which there is a
lot of unemployment and low
output and investment 3 area

of low air pressure **4** sunken place **depressive** adj tending to cause depression

deprive v (foll. by *of*) prevent from (possessing or enjoying) **deprivation** n **deprived** adj lacking adequate living conditions, education, etc.

depth n **1** distance downwards, backwards, or inwards **2** intensity of emotion **3** profundity of character or thought **4** intensity of colour **depth charge** bomb used to attack submarines by exploding at a preset depth of water

depute v appoint (someone) to act on one's behalf **deputation** n body of people appointed to represent others **deputize** v act as a deputy **deputy** n person appointed to act on behalf of another

derail v cause (a train) to go off the rails **derailment** n

derange v **1** make insane **2** throw into disorder **derangement** n

derby n, pl -bies **1** sporting event between teams from the same area **2** bowler hat **the Derby** annual horse race run at Epsom Downs

deregulate v remove regulations or controls from **deregulation** n

derelict adj **1** deserted or abandoned **2** falling into ruins ▷ n **3** social outcast, vagrant **dereliction** n **1** wilful neglect (of duty) **2** state of being abandoned

deride v speak of or treat with contempt or ridicule **derision** n **derisive** adj mocking or scornful **derisory** adj so small or inadequate that it is not worth serious consideration

de rigueur [de rig-**gur**] adj required by fashion

derive v (foll. by *from*) draw or be drawn (from) in origin **derivation** n **derivative** adj, n

dermatitis n inflammation of the skin

dermatology n branch of medicine concerned with the skin **dermatologist** n

derogatory [dir-**rog**-a-tree] adj intentionally offensive

derrick n **1** simple crane **2** framework erected over an oil well

dervish n member of a Muslim religious order noted for a frenzied whirling dance

descant n *music* tune played or sung above a basic melody

descend v **1** move down (a slope etc.) **2** move to a lower level, pitch, etc. **3** (foll. by *to*) stoop to (unworthy behaviour) **4** (foll. by *on*) visit unexpectedly **be descended from** be connected by a blood relationship to **descendant** n person or animal descended from an individual, race, or species **descendent** adj descending **descent** n **1** act of descending **2** downward slope **3** derivation from an ancestor

describe v **1** give an account of (something or someone) in words **2** trace the outline of (a circle etc.) **description** n **1** statement that describes something or someone **2** sort: *reptiles of every description* **descriptive** adj **descriptively** adv

descry v -scrying, -scried **1** catch sight of **2** discover by looking carefully

desecrate v violate the sacred character of (an object or place) **desecration** n

desegregate v end racial segregation in **desegregation** n

desert[1] n region that has little or no vegetation

because of low rainfall

desert² v **1** abandon (a person or place) without intending to return **2** mil abscond from (a post or duty) with no intention of returning **deserter** n **desertion** n

deserts pl n **get one's just deserts** get the punishment one deserves

deserve v be entitled to or worthy of **deserved** adj rightfully earned **deservedly** adv **deserving** adj worthy, esp. of praise or help

deshabille n same as **dishabille**

desiccate v remove most of the water from **desiccation** n

design v **1** work out the structure or form of (something), as by making a sketch or plans **2** plan and make artistically **3** intend for a specific purpose ▷ n **4** preliminary drawing **5** arrangement or features of an artistic or decorative work **6** art of designing **7** intention: by design **designedly** adv by intention **designer** n **1** person who draws up original sketches or plans from which things are made ▷ adj **2** designed by a well-known designer **3** fashionable or trendy: designer stubble **designing** adj crafty, cunning

designate [**dez**-zig-nate] v **1** give a name to **2** select (someone) for an office or duty ▷ adj **3** appointed but not yet in office **designation** n name

desire v **1** long for ▷ n **2** strong feeling of wanting something **3** sexual appetite **4** person or thing desired **desirable** adj **1** worth having **2** arousing sexual desire **desirability** n **desirous of** [diz-**zire**-uss] having a desire for

desist v (foll. by from) stop or abstain (from)

desk n **1** piece of furniture with a writing surface and usually drawers **2** service counter in a public building **3** section of a newspaper covering a specific subject: the news desk **desktop** adj denoting a computer system small enough to use at a desk ▷ n main screen display on computer

desolate adj **1** uninhabited and bleak **2** without hope ▷ v **3** lay waste **4** make (a person) very sad **desolation** n

despair n **1** total loss of hope ▷ v **2** lose hope

despatch v, n same as **dispatch**

desperado n, pl -does, -dos reckless person ready to commit any violent illegal act

desperate adj **1** careless of danger, as from despair **2** (of an action) undertaken as a last resort **3** having a great need or desire **desperately** adv **desperation** n

despise v look down on with contempt **despicable** adj worthy of being despised **despicably** adv

despite prep in spite of

despoil v formal plunder **despoliation** n

despondent adj dejected or depressed **despondently** adv **despondency** n

despot n person in power who acts tyrannically **despotic** adj **despotically** adv **despotism** n tyrannical government or behaviour

dessert n sweet course served at the end of a meal **dessertspoon** n spoon between a tablespoon and a teaspoon in size

destination n place to which someone or something is going

destine [**dess**-tin] v set apart

(for a certain purpose)

destiny *n, pl* **-nies 1** future destined for a person or thing **2 Destiny** the power that predetermines the course of events

destitute *adj* totally impoverished **destitution** *n*

destroy *v* **1** ruin **2** put an end to **3** kill (an animal) **destroyer** *n* **1** small heavily armed warship **2** person or thing that destroys **destructible** *adj* **destruction** *n* **1** destroying or being destroyed **2** cause of ruin **destructive** *adj* **1** causing destruction **2** intending to discredit someone, without positive suggestions: *destructive criticism* **destructively** *adv*

desuetude [diss-**syoo**-it-tude] *n* condition of not being in use

desultory [**dez**-zl-tree] *adj* **1** changing fitfully from one thing to another **2** random **desultorily** *adv*

detach *v* disengage and separate **detachable** *adj* **detached** *adj* **1** standing apart **2** showing no emotional involvement **detachment** *n* **1** aloofness **2** small group of soldiers

detail *n* **1** item that is considered separately **2** unimportant item **3** treatment of particulars **4** (*chiefly*) *mil* personnel assigned a specific duty ▷ *v* **5** list fully

detain *v* **1** delay (someone) **2** hold (someone) in custody **detainee** *n* **detainment** *n*

detect *v* **1** notice **2** discover the existence or presence of **detectable** *adj* **detection** *n* **detective** *n* policeman or private agent who investigates crime **detector**

n instrument used to find something: *smoke detector*

detente [day-**tont**] *n* easing of tension between nations

detention *n* **1** imprisonment **2** form of punishment in which a pupil is detained after school

deter *v* **-terring, -terred** discourage (someone) from doing something by instilling fear or doubt **deterrent** *n* **1** something that deters **2** weapon, esp. nuclear, to deter attack by another nation ▷ *adj* **3** tending to deter

detergent *n* **1** chemical cleansing agent ▷ *adj* **2** having cleansing power

deteriorate *v* become worse **deterioration** *n*

determine *v* **1** settle (an argument or a question) conclusively **2** find out the facts about (something) **3** fix in scope, extent, etc. **4** make a decision to do something **determinant** *n* factor that determines **determinate** *adj* definitely limited or fixed **determination** *n* **1** condition of being determined or resolute **2** act of determining **determined** *adj* firmly decided, unable to be persuaded **determinedly** *adv* **determiner** *n grammar* word that determines the object to which a noun phrase refers: *all* **determinism** *n* theory that human choice is not free, but decided by past events **determinist** *n, adj*

detest *v* dislike intensely **detestable** *adj* **detestation** *n*

dethrone *v* remove from a throne or deprive of high position

detonate *v* cause (an explosive device) to explode or (of an explosive device) explode **detonation** *n*

detonator n small amount of explosive, or a device, used to set off an explosion

detour n deviation from a direct route or course of action

detox v, n informal (undergo) treatment to rid the body of poisonous substances

detract v (foll. by *from*) lessen the value of, diminish **detractor** n **detraction** n

detriment n disadvantage or damage **detrimental** adj **detrimentally** adv

detritus [dit-**trite**-uss] n loose mass of stones or silt worn away from rocks, debris **detrital** adj

de trop [de **troh**] adj 1 not wanted 2 in the way

deuce [**dyewss**] n 1 tennis score of forty all 2 playing card or dice with two spots

deuterium n isotope of hydrogen twice as heavy as the normal atom

Deutschmark [**doytch**-mark], **Deutsche Mark** [**doytch**-a] n former monetary unit of Germany

devalue v -valuing, -valued 1 reduce the exchange value of (a currency) 2 reduce the value of (something or someone) **devaluation** n

devastate v damage (a place) severely or destroy it **devastated** adj shocked and extremely upset **devastation** n

develop v 1 grow or bring to a later, more elaborate, or more advanced stage 2 come or bring into existence 3 improve the value or change the use of (land) 4 treat (a photographic plate or film) to produce a visible image **developer** n 1 person who develops property 2 chemical used to develop photographs or films **development** n

developing country poor or nonindustrial country that is seeking to develop its resources by industrialization

deviate v 1 differ from others in belief or thought 2 turn aside from a course of action **deviation** n **deviant** n, adj (person) deviating from what is considered acceptable behaviour **deviance** n

device n 1 machine or tool used for a specific task 2 scheme or trick

devil n 1 evil spirit 2 person regarded as wicked 3 person: *poor devil* 4 person regarded as daring 5 informal something difficult or annoying ▷ v -illing, -illed 6 prepare (food) with a highly flavoured spiced mixture 7 do routine literary work, esp. for a lawyer or author **the Devil** Christianity chief spirit of evil and enemy of God **devilish** adj 1 of or like the devil ▷ adv 2 Also **devilishly** informal extremely **devilment** n mischievous conduct **devilry** n 1 reckless fun 2 wickedness **devil-may-care** adj happy-go-lucky **devil's advocate** person who takes an opposing or unpopular point of view for the sake of argument

devious adj 1 not sincere or straightforward 2 indirect **deviously** adv **deviousness** n

devise v work out (something) in one's mind

devoid adj (foll. by *of*) destitute (of) or free (from)

devolve v (foll. by *on* or *upon* or *to*) pass (power or duties) or (of power or duties) be passed to a successor or substitute **devolution** n transfer of authority from a central government to regional governments

devote v apply or dedicate

to some cause **devoted** adj feeling loyalty or devotion **devotedly** adv **devotee** [dev-vote-**tee**] n **1** person ardently enthusiastic about something **2** zealous follower of a religion **devotion** n **1** strong affection for or loyalty to a cause or person **2** religious zeal or piety **devotions 3** prayers **devotional** adj

devour v **1** eat up greedily **2** engulf and destroy **3** read or look at avidly **devouring** adj

devout adj deeply religious **devoutly** adv

dew n drops of water condensed on a cool surface at night from vapour in the air **dewy** adj

dewclaw n nonfunctional claw on a dog's leg

dewlap n loose fold of skin hanging under the throat in dogs, cattle, etc.

dexterity n **1** skill in using one's hands **2** mental quickness **dexterous** adj **dexterously** adv

dextrose n glucose occurring in fruit, honey, and the blood of animals

dg decigram

diabetes [die-a-**beet**-eez] n disorder in which an abnormal amount of urine containing an excess of sugar is excreted **diabetic** n, adj

diabolic adj **1** of the devil **2** extremely cruel **diabolical** adj informal extremely bad **diabolically** adv **diabolism** n witchcraft, devil worship

diaconate n position or period of office of a deacon **diaconal** adj

diacritic n sign above or below a letter or character to indicate phonetic value or stress

diadem n old-fashioned crown

diaeresis n, pl **-ses** same as **dieresis**

diagnosis [die-ag-**no**-siss] n, pl **-ses** [-seez] discovery and identification of diseases from the examination of symptoms **diagnose** v **diagnostic** adj

diagonal adj **1** from corner to corner **2** slanting ▷ n **3** diagonal line **diagonally** adv

diagram n sketch demonstrating the form or workings of something **diagrammatic** adj **diagrammatically** adv

dial n **1** face of a clock or watch **2** graduated disc on a measuring instrument **3** control on a radio or television used to change the station **4** numbered disc on the front of some telephones ▷ v **dialling, dialled 5** try to establish a telephone connection with (someone) by operating the dial or buttons on a telephone

dialect n form of a language spoken in a particular area **dialectal** adj

dialectic n logical debate by question and answer to resolve differences between two views **dialectical** adj

dialogue n **1** conversation between two people **2** discussion between representatives of two nations or groups **dialogue box** small window on a computer screen prompting the user to enter information

dialysis [die-**al**-iss-iss] n med filtering of blood through a membrane to remove waste products

diamanté [die-a-**man**-tee] adj decorated with artificial jewels or sequins

diameter n (length of) a

straight line through the centre of a circle or sphere **diametric** or **diametrical** adj **1** of a diameter **2** completely opposed: *the diametric opposite* **diametrically** adv

diamond n **1** usually colourless, exceptionally hard precious stone **2** geom figure with four sides of equal length forming two acute and two obtuse angles **3** playing card marked with red diamond-shaped symbols **diamond wedding** sixtieth anniversary of a wedding

diaper n piece of absorbent material fastened round a baby's lower torso to absorb urine and feces

diaphanous [die-**af**-fan-ous] adj fine and almost transparent

diaphragm [die-a-fram] n **1** muscular partition that separates the abdominal cavity and chest cavity **2** contraceptive device placed over the neck of the womb

diarrhea, diarrhoea [die-a-**ree**-a] n frequent discharge of abnormally liquid feces

diary n, pl -**ries** (book for) a record of daily events, appointments, or observations **diarist** n

diatribe n bitter critical attack

dibble n small hand tool used to make holes in the ground for seeds or plants

dice n, pl **dice 1** small cube each of whose sides has a different number of spots (1 to 6), used in games of chance ▷ v **2** cut (food) into small cubes **dice with death** take a risk **dicey** adj informal dangerous or risky

dichotomy [die-**kot**-a-mee] n, pl -**mies** division into two opposed groups or parts

dicky¹ n, pl **dickies 1** false shirt front **dicky-bird** n child's word for a bird

dicky² adj **dickier, dickiest** informal shaky or weak: *a dicky heart*

Dictaphone n ® tape recorder for recording dictation for subsequent typing

dictate v **1** say aloud for another person to transcribe **2** give (commands) authoritatively ▷ n **3** authoritative command **4** guiding principle **dictation** n **dictator** n **1** ruler who has complete power **2** tyrannical person **dictatorship** n **dictatorial** adj like a dictator, tyrannical **dictatorially** adv

diction n manner of pronouncing words and sounds

dictionary n, pl -**aries 1** book that consists of an alphabetical list of words with their meanings **2** reference book listing terms and giving information about a particular subject

dictum n, pl -**tums, -ta 1** formal statement **2** popular saying

did v past tense of **do**

didactic adj intended to instruct **didactically** adv

diddle v informal swindle

didn't did not

die¹ v **dying, died 1** (of a person, animal, or plant) cease all biological activity permanently **2** (of something inanimate) cease to exist or function **be dying for** informal be eager for **die-hard** n person who resists change

die² n **1** shaped block used to cut or form metal **2** casting mould

dieresis [die-**air**-iss-iss] n, pl -**ses** [-seez] mark (¨) placed over a vowel to show that it is pronounced separately from

d

the preceding one, as in *Noël*

diesel *n* **1** diesel engine
2 vehicle driven by a diesel
engine **3** *informal* diesel oil
diesel engine internal-
combustion engine in which
oil is ignited by compression
diesel oil fuel obtained from
petroleum distillation

diet¹ *n* **1** food that a person
or animal regularly eats
2 specific allowance of food,
to control weight or for health
reasons ▷ *v* **3** follow a special
diet so as to lose weight ▷ *adj*
4 (of food or drink) suitable
for eating with a weight-
reduction diet **dietary**
adj **dietary fibre** fibrous
substances in fruit and
vegetables that aid digestion
dieter *n* **dietetic** *adj*
prepared for special dietary
requirements **dietetics** *pl*
n study of food intake and
preparation **dietician** *n*
person who specializes in
dietetics

diet² *n* parliament of some
countries

differ *v* **1** be unlike **2** disagree
difference *n* **1** state or
quality of being unlike
2 disagreement **3** remainder
left after subtraction
different *adj* **1** unlike
2 unusual **differently** *adv*

differential *adj* **1** of or using
a difference **2** *math* involving
differentials ▷ *n* **3** factor that
differentiates between two
comparable things **4** *math*
slight difference between
values in a scale **5** difference
between rates of pay for
different types of labour
differential calculus branch
of calculus concerned with
derivatives and differentials
differential gear mechanism
in a road vehicle that allows
one driving wheel to rotate

faster than the other when
cornering **differentiate**
v **1** perceive or show the
difference (between) **2** make
(one thing) distinct from
other such things **3** *math*
determine the derivative
of (a function or variable)
differentiation *n*

difficult *adj* **1** requiring effort
or skill to do or understand
2 not easily pleased
difficulty *n*

diffident *adj* lacking self-
confidence **diffidence** *n*
diffidently *adv*

diffract *v* cause to undergo
diffraction **diffraction** *n*
physics **1** deviation in the
direction of a wave at the
edge of an obstacle in its path
2 formation of light and dark
fringes by the passage of light
through a small aperture

diffuse *v* **1** spread in all
directions ▷ *adj* **2** widely
spread **3** lacking conciseness
diffusely *adv* **diffusion** *n*

dig *v* **digging, dug** (often
foll. by *up*) **1** cut into, break
up, and turn over or remove
(earth etc.), esp. with a spade
2 (foll. by *out* or *up*) find by
effort or searching **3** (foll. by
in or *into*) thrust or jab ▷ *n*
4 act of digging **5** thrust
or poke **6** cutting remark
7 archaeological excavation
digs 8 *informal* lodgings
digger *n*

digest *v* **1** subject to a process
of digestion **2** absorb mentally
▷ *n* **3** methodical compilation
of information, often a
condensed one **digestible**
adj **digestion** *n* process of
breaking down food into
easily absorbed substances
digestive *adj*

digit [**dij**-it] *n* **1** finger or toe
2 numeral from 0 to 9 **digital**
adj displaying information

as numbers rather than with a dial: *digital clock* **digital recording** sound-recording process that converts audio or analogue signals into a series of pulses **digitally** *adv* **digitate** *adj* **1** (of leaves) shaped like a hand **2** (of animals) having digits **digitized** *adj computers* recorded or stored in digital form

digitalis *n* drug made from foxglove leaves, used as a heart stimulant

dignity *n, pl* **-ties 1** serious, calm, and controlled behaviour or manner **2** quality of being worthy of honour **3** sense of self-importance **dignify** *v* **-fying, -fied** give dignity to **dignitary** *n* person of high official position

digress *v* depart from the main subject in speech or writing **digression** *n* **digressive** *adj*

dike *n* same as **dyke**

dilapidated *adj* (of a building) having fallen into ruin **dilapidation** *n*

dilate *v* make or become wider or larger **dilation** *or* **dilatation** *n*

dilatory [**dill**-a-tree] *adj* tending or intended to waste time

dildo *n, pl* **-dos** object used as a substitute for an erect penis

dilemma *n* situation offering a choice between two equally undesirable alternatives

dilettante [dill-it-**tan**-tee] *n* person whose interest in a subject, esp. art, is superficial rather than serious **dilettantism** *n*

diligent *adj* **1** careful and persevering in carrying out duties **2** carried out with care and perseverance **diligently** *adv* **diligence** *n*

dill *n* sweet-smelling herb used for flavouring

dilly-dally *v* **-lying, -lied** *informal* dawdle or waste time

dilute *v* **1** make (a liquid) less concentrated, esp. by adding water **2** make (a quality etc.) weaker in force **dilution** *n*

diluvial, diluvian *adj* of a flood, esp. the great Flood described in the Old Testament

dim *adj* **dimmer, dimmest 1** badly illuminated **2** not clearly seen **3** mentally dull ▷ *v* **dimming, dimmed 4** make or become dim **take a dim view of** disapprove of **dimly** *adv* **dimness** *n* **dimmer** *n* device for dimming an electric light

dime *n* coin of Canada and the US, worth ten cents

dimension *n* **1** aspect or factor: *a new dimension to politics* **dimensions 2** scope or extent **3** measurement of the size of something in a particular direction

diminish *v* make or become smaller, fewer, or less **diminution** *n* **diminutive** *adj* **1** very small ▷ *n* **2** word or affix which implies smallness or unimportance **diminutiveness** *n*

diminuendo *n music* gradual decrease in loudness

dimple *n* **1** small natural dent, esp. in the cheeks or chin ▷ *v* **2** produce dimples by smiling

din *n* **1** loud discordant confused noise ▷ *v* **dinning, dinned 2** instil (something) into someone by constant repetition

dinar [**dee**-nahr] *n* monetary unit of various Balkan, Middle Eastern, and North African countries

dine *v* eat dinner **diner** *n* **1** person eating a meal **2** small cheap restaurant **dining car** railway coach in which meals are served **dining room** room where meals are eaten

ding-dong n **1** sound of a bell **2** informal violent exchange of blows or words

dinghy [**ding**-ee] n, pl -**ghies** small boat, powered by sails, oars, or an outboard motor

dingle n small wooded dell

dingo n, pl -**goes** wild dog of Australia

dingy [**din**-jee] adj -**gier**, -**giest** dirty-looking, dull **dinginess** n

dinkum adj Aust & NZ informal genuine or right

dinky adj -**kier**, -**kiest** informal small and neat

dinner n **1** main meal of the day, taken either in the evening or at midday **2** official banquet **dinner jacket** man's semiformal evening jacket, usu. black

dinosaur n extinct prehistoric reptile, often of gigantic size

dint n **by dint of** by means of

diocese [**die**-a-siss] n district under the jurisdiction of a bishop **diocesan** adj

diode n semiconductor device for converting alternating current to direct current

dioptre [die-**op**-ter] n unit for measuring the refractive power of a lens

dioxide n oxide containing two oxygen atoms per molecule

dip v **dipping**, **dipped 1** plunge quickly or briefly into a liquid **2** slope downwards **3** switch (automobile headlights) from the main to the lower beam **4** lower briefly ▷ n **5** act of dipping **6** brief swim **7** liquid chemical in which farm animals are dipped to rid them of insects **8** depression, esp. in a landscape **9** creamy

mixture into which pieces of food are dipped before being eaten **dip into** v read passages at random from (a book or journal)

diphtheria [dif-**theer**-ya] n contagious disease producing fever and difficulty in breathing and swallowing

diphthong n union of two vowel sounds in a single compound sound

diploma n document conferring a qualification or recording successful completion of a course of study

diplomacy n **1** conduct of the relations between nations by peaceful means **2** tact or skill in dealing with people **diplomat** n official engaged in diplomacy **diplomatic** adj **1** of or relating to diplomacy **2** tactful in dealing with people **diplomatically** adv

dipper n **1** ladle used for dipping **2** Also **ousel, ouzel** European songbird that lives by a river

dipsomania n compulsive craving for alcohol **dipsomaniac** n, adj

dipsy-doodle Canad informal ▷ v -**dling**, -**dled 1** hockey evade defenders by using swerves, feints, stickhandling, etc. ▷ n **2** an evasive movement of this sort

diptych [**dip**-tik] n painting on two hinged panels

dire adj **1** desperate or urgent **2** indicating disaster

direct adj **1** (of a route) shortest, straight **2** without anyone or anything intervening **3** honest, frank ▷ adv **4** in a direct manner ▷ v **5** conduct or control the affairs of **6** give orders with authority to (a person or group) **7** tell (someone) the way to a place **8** address (a letter, package, remarks, etc.) **9** provide guidance to (actors, cameramen, etc.) in (a play or film) **directly** adv **1** in a direct manner **2** at once ▷ conj **3** as soon as **directness** n **direction** n **1** course or line along which a person or thing moves, points, or lies **2** management or guidance **directions 3** instructions for doing something or for reaching a place **directional** adj **directive** n instruction, order **director** n **1** person or thing that directs or controls **2** member of the governing board of a business etc. **3** person responsible for the artistic and technical aspects of the making of a film etc. **directorial** adj **directorship** n **directorate** n **1** board of directors **2** position of director **directory** n **1** book listing names, addresses, and telephone numbers of individuals and firms **2** computers area of a disk containing the names and locations of the files it currently holds

dirge n slow sad song of mourning

dirigible [dir-rij-jib-bl] adj **1** able to be steered ▷ n **2** airship

dirk n dagger, formerly worn by Scottish Highlanders

dirndl n (dress with) full gathered skirt

dirt n **1** unclean substance, filth **2** loose earth or soil **3** obscene speech or writing **4** informal scandal, harmful gossip **dirt track** racetrack made of packed earth or cinders

dirty adj **dirtier, dirtiest 1** covered or marked with dirt **2** unfair or dishonest **3** obscene **4** displaying dislike or anger: a dirty look ▷ v **dirtying, dirtied 5** make dirty **dirtiness** n

dis- prefix **1** indicating reversal: disconnect **2** indicating negation or lack: dissimilar; disgrace **3** indicating removal or release: disembowel

disable v make ineffective, unfit, or incapable **disabled** adj lacking one or more physical powers, such as the ability to walk **disablement** n **disability** n **1** condition of being physically or mentally impaired **2** something that disables someone

disabuse v (foll. by of) rid (someone) of a mistaken idea

disadvantage n unfavourable circumstance, thing, or situation **disadvantageous** adj **disadvantaged** adj socially or economically deprived

disaffected adj having lost loyalty to or affection for someone or something **disaffection** n

disagree v -**greeing, -greed 1** have different opinions **2** fail to correspond **3** (foll. by with) cause physical discomfort (to): curry disagrees with me **disagreement** n **disagreeable** adj **1** (of a person) bad-tempered or disobliging **2** unpleasant **disagreeably** adv

disallow v reject as untrue or invalid

disappear v **1** cease to be visible **2** cease to exist **disappearance** n

disappoint v fail to meet the expectations or hopes of **disappointment** n **1** feeling of being disappointed **2** person or thing that disappoints

disapprobation n disapproval

disapprove v (foll. by of)

consider wrong or bad
disapproval n

disarm v 1 deprive of weapons
2 win the confidence or
affection of 3 (of a nation)
decrease the size of one's
armed forces **disarmament**
n **disarming** adj removing
hostility or suspicion
disarmingly adv

disarrange v throw into
disorder **disarrangement** n

disarray n 1 confusion and
lack of discipline 2 extreme
untidiness

disaster n 1 occurrence that
causes great distress or
destruction 2 project etc.
that fails **disastrous** adj
disastrously adv

disavow v deny connection
with or responsibility for
(something) **disavowal** n

disband v (cause to) cease to
function as a group or unit

disbelieve v 1 reject as false
2 (foll. by in) have no faith (in)
disbelief n

disburse v pay out
disbursement n

disc n 1 flat circular object
2 gramophone record 3 anat
circular flat structure in
the body, esp. between the
vertebrae 4 computers same
as **disk** ▸ **disc jockey** person
who introduces and plays pop
records on a radio programme
or at a disco

discard v get rid of
(something or someone) as
useless or undesirable

discern v see or be aware
of (something) clearly
discernible adj **discerning**
adj having or showing good
judgment **discernment** n

discharge v 1 release, allow
to go 2 dismiss (someone)
from duty or employment
3 fire (a gun) 4 pour forth,
emit 5 meet the demands of

(an obligation etc.) 6 relieve
oneself of (a responsibility or
debt) ▸ n 7 something that
is discharged 8 dismissal
from duty or employment
9 pouring forth of a fluid,
emission

disciple [diss-**sipe**-pl] n
follower of the doctrines of a
teacher, esp. Jesus Christ

discipline n 1 practice of
imposing strict rules of
behaviour on other people
2 ability to behave and work
in a controlled manner
3 branch of learning ▸ v
4 (attempt to) improve the
behaviour of (oneself or
another) by training or rules
5 punish **disciplinarian** n
person who practises strict
discipline **disciplinary** adj

disclaim v deny
(responsibility for or
knowledge of something)
disclaimer n repudiation,
denial

disclose v 1 make known
2 allow to be seen **disclosure**
n

disco n, pl -cos 1 occasion at
which people dance to pop
records 2 place where such
dances are held 3 mobile
equipment for providing
music for a disco

discolour v change in colour,
stain **discoloration** n

discomfit v make uneasy or
confused **discomfiture** n

discomfort n inconvenience,
distress, or mild pain

discommode v cause
inconvenience to
discommodious adj

disconcert v disturb the
confidence or self-possession
of

disconnect v 1 undo or break
the connection between
(two things) 2 stop the
supply of (electricity or gas)

of ▷ *n* **3** lack of a connection; disconnection: *a disconnect between political discourse and the public* **disconnected** *adj* (of speech or ideas) not logically connected **disconnection** *n*

disconsolate *adj* sad beyond comfort **disconsolately** *adv*

discontent *n* lack of contentment, as with one's lot in life **discontented** *adj* **discontentedly** *adv*

discontinue *v* **-uing, -ued** come or bring to an end **discontinuous** *adj* characterized by interruptions **discontinuity** *n* lack of smooth or unbroken development

discord *n* **1** lack of agreement or harmony between people **2** harsh confused sounds **discordant** *adj* **discordance** *n*

discotheque *n* full name for **disco**

discount *v* **1** leave (something) out of account as being unreliable, prejudiced, or irrelevant **2** deduct (an amount) from the price of something ▷ *n* **3** deduction from the full price of something

discourage *v* **1** deprive of the will to persist in something **2** oppose by expressing disapproval **discouragement** *n*

discourse *n* **1** conversation **2** formal treatment of a subject in speech or writing ▷ *v* **3** (foll. by *on*) speak or write (about) at length

discourteous *adj* showing bad manners **discourteously** *adv* **discourtesy** *n*

discover *v* **1** be the first to find or to find out about **2** learn about for the first time **3** find after study or search **discoverer** *n* **discovery** *n*

1 act of discovering **2** person, place, or thing that has been discovered

discredit *v* **1** damage the reputation of (someone) **2** cause (an idea) to be disbelieved or distrusted ▷ *n* **3** (something that causes) damage to someone's reputation **discreditable** *adj* bringing discredit

discreet *adj* **1** careful to avoid embarrassment, esp. by keeping confidences secret **2** unobtrusive **discreetly** *adv*

discrepancy *n, pl* **-cies** conflict or variation between facts, figures, or claims

discrete *adj* separate or distinct

discretion [diss-**kresh**-on] *n* **1** quality of behaving in a discreet way **2** freedom or authority to make judgments and to act as one sees fit **discretionary** *adj*

discriminate *v* **1** (foll. by *against* or *in favour of*) single out a particular person or group for special disfavour or favour **2** (foll. by *between* or *among*) recognize or understand the difference (between) **discriminating** *adj* showing good taste and judgment **discrimination** *n* **discriminatory** *adj* based on prejudice

discursive *adj* passing from one topic to another

discus *n* disc-shaped object with a heavy middle, thrown in sports competitions

discuss *v* **1** consider (something) by talking it over **2** treat (a subject) in speech or writing **discussion** *n*

disdain *n* **1** feeling of superiority and dislike ▷ *v* **2** refuse with disdain **disdainful** *adj* **disdainfully** *adv*

disease *n* illness, sickness
 diseased *adj*
disembark *v* (cause to) land
 from a ship, aircraft, or bus
 disembarkation *n*
disembodied *adj* **1** lacking
 a body **2** seeming not to be
 attached to or coming from
 anyone
disembowel *v* **-elling, -elled**
 remove the entrails of
disenchanted *adj*
 disappointed
 and disillusioned
 (with something)
 disenchantment *n*
disenfranchise *v* deprive
 (a person) of the right to
 vote or of other rights of
 citizenship
disengage *v* release from a
 connection **disengagement** *n*
disentangle *v* release from
 entanglement or confusion
 disentanglement *n*
disfavour *n* disapproval or
 dislike
disfigure *v* spoil the
 appearance or shape of
 disfigurement *n*
disfranchise *v* same as
 disenfranchise
disgorge *v* **1** vomit **2** discharge
 (contents)
disgrace *n* **1** condition of
 shame, loss of reputation, or
 dishonour **2** shameful person
 or thing ▷ *v* **3** bring shame
 upon (oneself or others)
 disgraceful *adj* **disgracefully**
 adv
disgruntled *adj* sulky
 or discontented
 disgruntlement *n*
disguise *v* **1** change the
 appearance or manner in
 order to conceal the identity
 of (someone or something)
 2 misrepresent (something)
 in order to obscure its actual
 nature or meaning ▷ *n*
 3 mask, costume, or manner

that disguises **4** state of being
 disguised
disgust *n* **1** great loathing or
 distaste ▷ *v* **2** sicken, fill with
 loathing
dish *n* **1** shallow container
 used for holding or serving
 food **2** portion or variety of
 food **3** short for **dish aerial**
 4 *informal* attractive person
 dish aerial aerial consisting
 of a concave disc-shaped
 reflector **dishcloth** *n* cloth
 for washing dishes **dish out**
 v informal distribute **dish up** *v*
 informal serve (food)
dishabille [diss-a-**beel**] *n* state
 of being partly dressed
dishearten *v* weaken or
 destroy the hope, courage, or
 enthusiasm of
dishevelled *adj* (of a person's
 hair, clothes, or general
 appearance) disordered and
 untidy
dishonest *adj* not honest
 or fair **dishonestly** *adv*
 dishonesty *n*
dishonour *v* **1** treat with
 disrespect ▷ *n* **2** lack of respect
 3 state of shame or disgrace
 4 something that causes a loss
 of honour **dishonourable** *adj*
 dishonourably *adv*
disillusion *v* **1** destroy the
 illusions or false ideas of ▷ *n*
 2 Also **disillusionment** state
 of being disillusioned
disincentive *n* something
 that acts as a deterrent
disinclined *adj* unwilling or
 reluctant **disinclination** *n*
disinfect *v* rid of harmful
 germs, esp. by chemical
 means **disinfectant** *n*
 substance that destroys
 harmful germs **disinfection** *n*
disinformation *n* false
 information intended to
 mislead
disingenuous *adj* not sincere
 disingenuously *adv*

disinherit v law deprive (an heir) of inheritance **disinheritance** n

disintegrate v break up into fragments **disintegration** n

disinter v -terring, -terred 1 dig up 2 reveal, make known

disinterested adj free from bias or involvement **disinterest** n

disjointed adj 1 having no coherence 2 disconnected

disk n computers storage device, consisting of a stack of plates coated with a magnetic layer, which rotates rapidly as a single unit

dislike v 1 consider unpleasant or disagreeable ▷ n 2 feeling of not liking something or someone

dislocate v 1 displace (a bone or joint) from its normal position 2 disrupt or shift out of place **dislocation** n

dislodge v remove (something) from a previously fixed position

disloyal adj not loyal, deserting one's allegiance **disloyalty** n

dismal adj 1 causing gloom or depression 2 informal of poor quality **dismally** adv

dismantle v take apart piece by piece

dismay v 1 fill with alarm or depression ▷ n 2 alarm mixed with sadness

dismember v 1 remove the limbs of 2 cut to pieces **dismemberment** n

dismiss v 1 remove (an employee) from a job 2 allow (someone) to leave 3 put out of one's mind 4 (of a judge) state that (a case) will not be brought to trial **dismissal** n **dismissive** adj scornful, contemptuous

dismount v get off a horse or a bicycle

disobey v neglect or refuse to obey **disobedient** adj **disobedience** n

disobliging adj unwilling to help

disorder n 1 state of untidiness and disorganization 2 public violence or rioting 3 an illness **disordered** adj untidy **disorderly** adj 1 very untidy, disorganized 2 uncontrolled, unruly

disorganize v disrupt the arrangement or system of **disorganization** n

disorientate, disorient v cause (someone) to lose his or her bearings **disorientation** n

disown v deny any connection with (someone)

disparage v speak contemptuously of **disparagement** n

disparate adj utterly different in kind **disparity** n

dispassionate adj uninfluenced by emotion **dispassionately** adv

dispatch v 1 send off to a destination or to perform a task 2 carry out (a duty or a task) with speed 3 old-fashioned kill ▷ n 4 official communication or report, sent in haste 5 report sent to a newspaper by a correspondent **dispatch rider** motorcyclist who carries dispatches

dispel v -pelling, -pelled disperse or drive away

dispense v 1 distribute in portions 2 prepare and distribute (medicine) 3 administer (the law etc.) **dispensable** adj not essential **dispensation** n 1 act of dispensing 2 exemption from an obligation 3 administrative system **dispenser** n **dispensary** n place where medicine is dispensed

dispense with v **1** do away with **2** manage without

disperse v **1** scatter over a wide area **2** (cause to) leave a gathering **dispersal** or **dispersion** n

dispirit v make downhearted

displace v **1** move from the usual location **2** remove from office **displacement** n **displaced person** person forced from his or her home or country, esp. by war or revolution

display v **1** make visible or noticeable ▷ n **2** act of displaying **3** something displayed **4** exhibition

displease v annoy **displeasure** n

disport v **disport oneself** indulge oneself in pleasure

dispose v place in a particular way **disposable** adj **1** designed to be thrown away after use **2** available for use if needed: *disposable assets* **disposal** n getting rid of something **at one's disposal** available for use **disposed** adj **1** willing (to do something) **2** inclined as specified (towards someone or something): *well disposed* **disposition** n **1** person's usual temperament **2** tendency **3** arrangement **dispose of** v **1** throw away **2** give or sell to another **3** deal with (a problem, etc.) **4** kill

dispossess v (foll. by *of*) deprive (someone) of (a possession) **dispossession** n

disproportion n lack of proportion or equality **disproportionate** adj **disproportionately** adv

disprove v show (an assertion or claim) to be incorrect

dispute n **1** disagreement between workers and their employers **2** argument ▷ v **3** argue about (something) **4** doubt the validity of **5** fight over possession of **disputation** n *formal* argument

disqualify v -**fying**, -**fied** **1** debar from a contest **2** make ineligible **disqualification** n

disquiet n **1** feeling of anxiety ▷ v **2** make (someone) anxious **disquietude** n anxiety, uneasiness

disregard v **1** give little or no attention to ▷ n **2** lack of attention or respect

disrepair n condition of being worn out or in poor working order

disrepute n loss or lack of good reputation **disreputable** adj having or causing a bad reputation

disrespect n lack of respect **disrespectful** adj **disrespectfully** adv

disrobe v undress

disrupt v interrupt the progress of **disruption** n **disruptive** adj

dissatisfied adj not pleased, disappointed **dissatisfaction** n

dissect v **1** cut open (a dead body) to examine it **2** examine critically and minutely **dissection** n

dissemble v conceal one's real motives or emotions by pretence

disseminate v scatter about **dissemination** n

dissent v **1** disagree **2** *Christianity* reject the doctrines of an established church ▷ n **3** disagreement **4** *Christianity* separation from an established church **dissension** n **dissenter** n

dissertation n **1** written thesis, usu. required for a higher university degree **2** long formal speech

disservice n bad turn or wrong

dissident n 1 person who disagrees, esp. with the government ▷ adj 2 disagreeing **dissidence** n

dissimilar adj not alike, different **dissimilarity** n

dissimulate v conceal one's real feelings by pretence **dissimulation** n

dissipate v 1 waste or squander 2 scatter **dissipated** adj showing signs of overindulging in alcohol and other pleasures **dissipation** n

dissociate v regard or treat as separate **dissociate oneself from** deny or break a connection with **dissociation** n

dissolute adj leading an immoral life

dissolve v 1 (cause to) become liquid 2 bring to an end 3 dismiss (a meeting, Parliament, etc.) 4 collapse emotionally **dissolution** n 1 destruction by breaking up and dispersing 2 termination of a meeting, assembly, or legal relationship

dissonance n 1 discordant combination of sounds 2 lack of agreement or consistency **dissonant** adj

dissuade v deter (someone) by persuasion from a course of action, policy, etc. **dissuasion** n

distaff n rod on which wool, flax, etc. is wound for spinning **distaff side** female side of a family

distance n 1 space between two points 2 state of being apart 3 distant place 4 remoteness in manner **distance oneself from** separate oneself mentally from **distant** adj 1 far apart 2 separated by a specified distance 3 remote in manner **distantly** adv

distaste n dislike, aversion **distasteful** adj unpleasant or offensive

distemper[1] n highly contagious disease of animals, esp. dogs

distemper[2] n paint mixed with water, glue, etc., which is used for painting walls

distend v expand by pressure from within **distension** n

distil v -tilling, -tilled 1 subject to or obtain by distillation 2 give off (a substance) in drops 3 extract the essence of **distillation** n 1 process of evaporating a liquid and condensing its vapour 2 Also **distillate** concentrated essence **distiller** n person or company that makes spirits **distillery** n place where alcoholic drinks are made by distillation

distinct adj 1 not the same 2 clearly seen, heard, or recognized 3 clear and definite: a distinct possibility of rain **distinctly** adv **distinction** n 1 act of distinguishing 2 distinguishing feature 3 state of being different 4 special honour, recognition, or fame **distinctive** adj easily recognizable **distinctively** adv **distinctiveness** n

distinguish v 1 (foll. by between or among) make, show, or recognize a difference (between or among) 2 be a distinctive feature of 3 perceive **distinguishable** adj **distinguished** adj 1 noble or dignified in appearance 2 highly respected

distort v 1 alter or misrepresent (facts) 2 twist out of shape **distortion** n

distract v 1 draw the attention

of (a person) away from something **2** confuse, trouble **3** entertain **distraction** n

distrait [diss-**tray**] adj absent-minded or abstracted

distraught [diss-**trawt**] adj extremely anxious or agitated

distress n **1** extreme unhappiness or worry **2** great physical pain **3** financial trouble ▷ v **4** upset badly **distressed** adj **1** much troubled **2** in financial difficulties **distressing** adj **distressingly** adv

distribute v **1** hand out or deliver (leaflets, etc.) **2** share (something) among the members of a particular group **distribution** n **1** act of distributing **2** arrangement or spread of anything over an area, period of time, etc. **distributor** n **1** wholesaler who distributes goods to retailers in a specific area **2** device in a gasoline engine that sends the electric current to the spark plugs

district n area of land regarded as an administrative or geographical unit

distrust v **1** regard as untrustworthy ▷ n **2** suspicion or doubt **distrustful** adj

disturb v **1** intrude on **2** disarrange **3** worry, make anxious **disturbance** n **disturbing** adj **disturbingly** adv **disturbed** adj psychiatry emotionally upset, troubled, or maladjusted

disunite v cause disagreement among **disunity** n

disuse n condition of being unused **disused** adj

ditch n **1** narrow channel dug in the earth for drainage or irrigation ▷ v **2** slang abandon

dither v **1** be uncertain or indecisive ▷ n **2** state of

indecision or agitation **ditherer** n **dithery** adj

ditto n, pl **-tos 1** the same ▷ adv **2** in the same way

ditty n, pl **-ties** short simple poem or song

diuretic [die-yoor-**et**-ik] n drug that increases the flow of urine

diurnal [die-**urn**-al] adj happening during the day or daily

divan n **1** backless sofa or couch **2** low backless bed

dive v **diving, dived 1** plunge headfirst into water **2** (of a submarine or diver) submerge under water **3** fly in a steep nose-down descending path **4** move quickly in a specified direction **5** (foll. by in or into) start (doing something) enthusiastically ▷ n **6** act of diving **7** steep nose-down descent **8** slang disreputable bar or club **diver** n **1** person who works or explores underwater **2** person who dives for sport **dive bomber** military aircraft designed to release bombs during a dive

diverge v **1** separate and go in different directions **2** deviate (from a prescribed course) **divergence** n **divergent** adj

divers adj old-fashioned various

diverse adj **1** having variety **2** different in kind **diversity** n **1** quality of being different or varied **2** range of difference **diversify** v **diversification** n

divert v **1** change the direction of (traffic) **2** distract the attention of **3** entertain **diversion** n **1** something that distracts someone's attention **2** an entertainment **diversionary** adj

divest v **1** strip (of clothes) **2** dispossess or deprive

divide v **1** separate into parts **2** share or be shared out in parts **3** (cause to) disagree **4** keep apart, be a boundary between **5** calculate how many times (one number) can be contained in (another) ▷ *n* **6** division, split **dividend** *n* **1** sum of money representing part of the profit made, paid by a company to its shareholders **2** bonus **divider** *n* **1** screen used to divide a room into separate areas ▷ *pl n* **2** compasses with two pointed arms, used for measuring or dividing lines

divine *adj* **1** of God or a god **2** godlike **3** *informal* splendid ▷ *v* **4** discover (something) by intuition or guessing **divinely** *adv* **divination** *n* art of discovering future events, as though by supernatural powers **divinity** *n* **1** theology **2** state of being divine **3** god **divining rod** forked twig said to move when held over ground in which water or metal is to be found

division *n* **1** act of dividing or sharing out **2** one of the parts into which something is divided **3** difference of opinion **4** mathematical operation of dividing **divisional** *adj* of a division in an organization **divisible** *adj* **divisibility** *n* **divisive** [div-**vice**-iv] *adj* tending to cause disagreement **divisor** *n* number to be divided into another number

divorce *n* **1** legal ending of a marriage **2** separation, esp. one that is total ▷ *v* **3** separate or be separated by divorce **4** remove or separate **divorcé** (**divorcée**) *n* person who is divorced

divulge *v* make known, disclose **divulgence** *n*

Dixie *n* southern states of the US

dizzy *adj* **-zier**, **-ziest 1** having or causing a whirling sensation **2** mentally confused ▷ *v* **-zying**, **-zied 3** make dizzy **dizzily** *adv* **dizziness** *n*

DJ 1 disc jockey **2** dinner jacket

dl decilitre

dm decimetre

DNA *n* deoxyribonucleic acid, the main constituent of the chromosomes of all living things

do *v* **does, doing, did, done 1** perform or complete (a deed or action) **2** be suitable, suffice **3** provide, serve: *this place doesn't do lunch on Sundays* **4** make tidy, elegant, or ready: *do one's hair* **5** improve: *that hat does nothing for you* **6** find the answer to (a problem or puzzle) **7** cause or produce: *complaints do nothing to help* **8** give or render: *do me a favour* **9** work at, esp. as a course of study or a job **10** travel (a distance) **11** *informal* cheat or rob **12** used to form questions: *do you agree?* **13** used to intensify positive statements and commands: *I do like your new house; do hurry!* **14** used to form negative statements and commands: *do not leave me here alone!* **15** used to replace an earlier verb: *he likes you as much as I do* ▷ *n, pl* **dos, do's 16** *informal* festive gathering or party **do away with** *v* **1** kill **2** get rid of **do-it-yourself** *n* practice of constructing and repairing things oneself, esp. as a hobby **do up** *v* **1** fasten **2** renovate **do with** *v* find useful or benefit from **do without** *v* manage without

Doberman, Doberman pinscher *n* large slender dog with a glossy black-and-tan coat

docile *adj* (of a person or

animal) easily managed **docilely** *adv* **docility** *n*

dock[1] *n* **1** enclosed area of water where ships are loaded, unloaded, or repaired ▷ *v* **2** moor or be moored at dock **3** link (two spacecraft) or (of two spacecraft) be linked together in space **docker** *n* person employed in the loading or unloading of ships **dockyard** *n* place with docks and equipment where ships are built or repaired

dock[2] *v* **1** deduct (an amount) from (a person's wages) **2** remove part of (an animal's tail) by cutting through the bone

dock[3] *n* enclosed space in a court of law where the accused person sits or stands

dock[4] *n* weed with broad leaves

docket *n* **1** piece of paper accompanying a package or other delivery, stating contents, delivery instructions, etc. ▷ *v* **2** fix a docket to (a package etc.)

doctor *n* **1** person licensed to practise medicine **2** person who has been awarded a doctorate ▷ *v* **3** make different in order to deceive **4** poison or drug (food or drink) **5** *informal* castrate or sterilize (a cat, dog, etc.) **doctoral** *adj* **doctorate** *n* highest academic degree in any field of knowledge

doctrine [**dock**-trin] *n* **1** body of teachings of a religious, political, or philosophical group **2** principle or body of principles that is taught or advocated **doctrinal** *adj* of or related to doctrine **doctrinaire** *adj* stubbornly insistent on the application of a theory without regard to practicality

document *n* **1** piece of paper, booklet, etc. providing information, esp. of an official nature ▷ *v* **2** record or report (something) in detail **3** support (a claim) with evidence **documentation** *n*

documentary *n, pl* -**ries 1** film or television programme presenting the facts about a particular subject ▷ *adj* **2** of or based on documents

dodder *v* move unsteadily **dodderer** *n* **doddery** *adj*

dodecagon [doe-**deck**-a-gon] *n* geometric figure with twelve sides

dodge *v* **1** avoid (a blow, being seen, etc.) by moving suddenly **2** evade by cleverness or trickery ▷ *n* **3** plan contrived to deceive **4** sudden evasive movement **dodger** *n* **dodgy** *adj informal* **1** difficult or dangerous **2** untrustworthy

Dodgem *n* ® electrically propelled vehicle driven and bumped against similar vehicles in a rink at a funfair

dodo *n, pl* **dodos, dodoes** large flightless extinct bird

doe *n* female deer, hare, or rabbit

does *v* third person singular of the present tense of **do**

doesn't does not

doff *v* take off or lift (one's hat) as a mark of respect

dog *n* **1** domesticated four-legged meat-eating mammal occurring in many different breeds **2** any other member of the dog family, such as the dingo or coyote **3** male of animals of the dog family **4** *informal* fellow, chap: *you lucky dog!* ▷ *v* **dogging, dogged** **5** follow (someone) closely **6** trouble or plague **go to the dogs** go to ruin physically or morally **let sleeping dogs lie** leave things undisturbed

dogged [dog-gid] *adj* obstinately determined **doggedly** *adv* **doggedness** *n* **doggy** *or* **doggie** *n* child's word for a dog **dogcart** *n* light horse-drawn two-wheeled vehicle **dog collar** 1 collar for a dog 2 *informal* clerical collar **dog-eared** *adj* 1 (of a book) having pages folded down at the corner 2 shabby or worn **dogfight** *n* 1 close-quarters combat between fighter aircraft 2 any rough fight **dogfish** *n* small shark **doghouse** *n* kennel **in the doghouse** *informal* in disfavour **dogleg** *n* sharp bend **dog rose** wild rose with pink or white flowers **dogsbody** *n informal* person who carries out menial tasks for others **dogsled** *n* sled drawn by dogs **dog-tired** *adj informal* exhausted

doge [doje] *n* (formerly) chief magistrate of Venice or Genoa

doggerel *n* poorly written, usually comic verse

doggo *adv* **lie doggo** *informal* hide and keep quiet

dogma *n* doctrine or system of doctrines proclaimed by authority as true **dogmatic** *adj* (of a statement or opinion) 1 forcibly asserted as if unchallengeable 2 (of a person) prone to making such statements **dogmatically** *adv* **dogmatism** *n*

doily *n, pl* -lies decorative mat of lace or lacelike paper, laid on plates

doldrums *pl n* 1 depressed state of mind 2 state of inactivity

dole *n* 1 *informal* money received from the state while out of work ▷ *v* 2 (foll. by *out*) distribute (something), esp. in small portions

doleful *adj* dreary or mournful **dolefully** *adv* **dolefulness** *n*

doll *n* 1 small model of a human being, used as a toy 2 *slang* girl or young woman, esp. a pretty one

dollar *n* standard monetary unit of Canada, the US, and various other countries

dollop *n informal* semisolid lump

dolly *n, pl* -lies 1 child's word for a doll 2 wheeled support on which a camera may be moved

dolman sleeve *n* sleeve that is very wide at the armhole and tapers to a tight wrist

dolmen *n* prehistoric monument consisting of a horizontal stone supported by vertical stones

dolomite *n* mineral consisting of calcium magnesium carbonate

dolorous *adj* causing or involving pain or sorrow

dolphin *n* sea mammal of the whale family, with a beaklike snout

dolt *n* stupid person **doltish** *adj*

domain *n* 1 field of knowledge or activity 2 land under one ruler or government

dome *n* 1 rounded roof built on a circular base 2 something shaped like this **domed** *adj*

domestic *adj* 1 of the home or family 2 home-loving 3 (of an animal) bred or kept as a pet or for the supply of food 4 of one's own country or a specific country: *domestic and foreign affairs* ▷ *n* 5 household servant **domestically** *adv* **domesticity** *n* **domesticate** *v* 1 bring or keep (wild animals or plants) under control or cultivation 2 accustom (someone) to home life **domestication** *n* **domestic**

science study of household skills

domicile [dom-miss-ile] n person's regular dwelling place **domiciliary** adj

dominant adj 1 having authority or influence 2 main or chief: the dominant topic of the day **dominance** n

dominate v 1 control or govern 2 tower above (surroundings) 3 be the most important of (a particular set of people or things) **domination** n

domineering adj acting arrogantly or tyrannically

Dominican n 1 friar or nun of an order founded by Saint Dominic ▷ adj 2 of the Dominican order

dominion n 1 rule or authority 2 land governed by one ruler or government 3 formerly, self-governing division of the British Empire

domino n, pl -noes 1 small rectangular block marked with dots, used in dominoes **dominoes** 2 game in which dominoes with matching halves are laid together

don[1] v donning, donned put on (clothing)

don[2] n 1 Brit member of the teaching staff at a university or college 2 Spanish gentleman or nobleman **donnish** adj resembling a university don

donair n snack of doner kebab meat served with a sweet sauce

donate v give (something), esp. to a charity **donation** n 1 act of donating 2 a contribution **donor** n 1 med person who gives blood, organs, etc. for use in the treatment of another person 2 person who makes a donation

done v past participle of **do**

doner kebab n grilled minced lamb served in a split slice of unleavened bread

donkey n long-eared member of the horse family **donkey jacket** man's thick hip-length jacket with a waterproof panel across the shoulders **donkey's years** informal a long time **donkey-work** n 1 groundwork 2 drudgery

don't do not

doodle v 1 scribble or draw aimlessly ▷ n 2 shape or picture drawn aimlessly

doom n 1 death or a terrible fate ▷ v 2 destine or condemn to death or a terrible fate **doomsday** n 1 Christianity day on which the Last Judgment will occur 2 any dreaded day

door n 1 hinged or sliding panel for closing the entrance to a room, cupboard, etc. 2 entrance **doormat** n 1 mat, placed at an entrance, for wiping dirt from shoes 2 informal person who offers little resistance to ill-treatment **doorway** n opening into a building or room

dope n 1 slang illegal drug, usu. cannabis 2 drug, esp. one administered to a racehorse etc. to affect its performance 3 informal slow-witted person 4 confidential information ▷ v 5 administer a drug to **dopey** or **dopy** adj 1 half-asleep 2 slang silly

dormant adj temporarily quiet, inactive, or not being used **dormancy** n

dormer (window) n window that projects from a sloping roof

dormitory n, pl -ries large room, esp. at a school, containing several beds

dormouse n small rodent resembling a mouse with a furry tail

dorsal adj of or on the back

dory *n, pl* **-ries** spiny-finned sea fish

dose *n* **1** specific quantity of a medicine taken at one time **2** *informal* something unpleasant to experience ▷ *v* **3** administer a dose to (someone) **dosage** *n* size of a dose

doss *v* **doss down** *Brit slang* sleep, esp. on a makeshift bed **dosshouse** *n Brit slang* cheap lodging house for homeless people

dossier [**doss**-ee-ay] *n* collection of papers with information about a subject or person

dot *n* **1** small round mark **2** shorter symbol used in Morse code ▷ *v* **dotting, dotted 3** mark with a dot **4** scatter or intersperse **on the dot** at exactly the arranged time **dotty** *adj slang* slightly mad **dottiness** *n*

dote *v* **dote on** love to an excessive or foolish degree **dotage** [**dote**-ij] *n* feebleness of mind as a result of old age **dotard** [**dote**-ard] *n* person who is feeble-minded through old age

double *adj* **1** as much again in size, strength, number, etc. **2** composed of two equal or similar parts **3** designed for two users **4** folded in two ▷ *adv* **5** twice over, twofold ▷ *n* **6** twice the number, amount, size, etc. **7** duplicate or counterpart, esp. a person who closely resembles another **8** *baseball* hit that enables the batter to run to second base **doubles 9** game between two pairs of players ▷ *v* **10** make or become twice as much **11** bend or fold (material etc.) **12** play two parts **13** turn sharply **at the double** quickly or immediately **doubly** *adv*

double agent spy employed simultaneously by two opposing sides **double bass** stringed instrument, largest and lowest member of the violin family **double chin** fold of fat under the chin **double cream** thick cream with a high fat content **double-cross** *v* **1** cheat or betray ▷ *n* **2** instance of double-crossing **double-dealing** *n* treacherous or deceitful behaviour **double-decker** *n* **1** bus with two passenger decks one on top of the other **2** *informal* sandwich made from three slices of bread with two fillings **double-double** *n Canad* cup of coffee with two helpings of cream and sugar **double Dutch** *informal* incomprehensible talk, gibberish **double glazing** two panes of glass in a window, fitted to reduce heat loss **double-header** *n sports* two games played consecutively on the same day at the same venue **double take** (esp. in comedy) delayed reaction by a person to a remark or situation **double talk** deceptive or ambiguous talk

double entendre [**doob**-bl on-**tond**-ra] *n* word or phrase that can be interpreted in two ways, esp. with one meaning that is rude

doublet [**dub**-lit] *n* (formerly) man's close-fitting jacket, with or without sleeves

doubloon *n* former Spanish gold coin

doubt *n* **1** uncertainty about the truth, facts, or existence of something **2** unresolved difficulty or point ▷ *v* **3** be inclined to disbelieve (a

fact or story) **4** distrust or
be suspicious of (a person)
doubter n **doubtful** adj
1 unlikely **2** feeling doubt
doubtfully adv **doubtless** adv
1 certainly **2** probably

douche [**doosh**] n
1 (instrument for applying) a
stream of water directed onto
or into the body for cleansing
or medical purposes ▷ v
2 cleanse or treat by means of
a douche

dough n **1** thick mixture of
flour and water or milk, used
for making bread **2** slang
money **doughnut** n small
cake of sweetened dough
cooked in hot fat

doughty [**dowt**-ee] adj **-tier,
-tiest** hardy or resolute

dour [**doo**-er] adj sullen and
unfriendly **dourness** n

douse [rhymes with **mouse**]
v **1** drench with water or other
liquid **2** put out (a light)

dove n **1** bird with a heavy
body, small head, and short
legs **2** politics person opposed
to war **dovecote** or **dovecot** n
structure for housing pigeons

dovetail n **1** joint containing
wedge-shaped tenons ▷ v **2** fit
together neatly

dowager n widow possessing
property or a title obtained
from her husband

dowdy adj **-dier, -diest**
shabby or old-fashioned
dowdily adv **dowdiness** n

dowel n wooden or metal
peg that fits into two
corresponding holes to join
two adjacent parts

dower n life interest in a
part of her husband's estate
allotted to a widow by law

down[1] prep **1** from a higher
to a lower position in or on
2 at a lower or further level
or position on, in, or along
▷ adv **3** at or to a lower position

or level **4** used to indicate
lowering or destruction:
knock down **5** used with several
verbs to indicate intensity
or completion: calm down
6 immediately: cash down **7** on
paper: write this down **8** lower
in price **9** from an earlier to a
later time ▷ adj **10** depressed,
sad ▷ v **11** informal drink, esp.
quickly **have a down on**
informal bear ill will towards

download v transfer (data)
from the memory of one
computer to that of another

downtown n the central or
lower part of a city, especially
the main commercial area

down under informal Australia
or New Zealand **downward**
adj **1** descending from a higher
to a lower level, condition, or
position ▷ adv **2** downwards

downwards adv from a higher
to a lower place, level, etc.

down-and-out adj **1** without
any means of livelihood ▷ n
2 person who is destitute and,
often, homeless **downbeat**
adj informal **1** gloomy **2** relaxed

downcast adj **1** dejected
2 directed downwards

downfall n **1** sudden loss
of position or reputation
2 cause of this **downgrade**
v reduce in importance or
value **downhearted** adj sad
and discouraged **downhill**
adj **1** going or sloping down
▷ adv **2** towards the bottom
of a hill **downpour** n heavy
fall of rain **downright** adj,
adv extreme(ly) **downstairs**
adv **1** to or on a lower floor
▷ n **2** lower or ground floor
down-to-earth adj sensible
or practical **downtrodden**
adj oppressed and lacking the
will to resist

down[2] n soft fine feathers or
hair **downy** adj

downs pl n rolling upland,

esp. in the chalk areas of S England

Down's syndrome n genetic disorder characterized by learning difficulties and physical differences such as a broad face

dowry n, pl **-ries** property brought by a woman to her husband at marriage

dowse [rhymes with **cows**] v search for underground water or minerals using a divining rod

doxology n, pl **-gies** short hymn of praise to God

doyen [**doy**-en] n senior member of a group, profession, or society **doyenne** [doy-**en**] n fem

doze v 1 sleep lightly or intermittently ▷ n 2 short sleep **dozy** adj 1 drowsy 2 informal stupid **doze off** v fall into a light sleep

dozen adj, n twelve **dozenth** adj, n

Dr 1 Doctor 2 Drive

drab adj **drabber**, **drabbest** 1 dull or dingy 2 cheerless or dreary **drabness** n

drachma n, pl **-mas**, **-mae** former standard monetary unit of Greece

draconian adj harsh or severe

draft[1] n 1 preliminary outline of a book, speech, etc. 2 written order for payment of money by a bank 3 US selection for compulsory military service ▷ v 4 write a preliminary outline of a book, speech, etc. 5 detach (personnel) from one place to another 6 US select for compulsory military service

draft[2], **draught** n 1 current of air, esp. in an enclosed space 2 act of pulling a load by a vehicle or animal 3 portion of liquid to be drunk, esp. medicine 4 instance of

drinking **drafty** adj exposed to drafts of air **draftsman** n person employed to prepare detailed scale drawings of machinery, buildings, etc.

draftsmanship n **draft beer** beer stored in a cask

drag v **dragging**, **dragged** 1 pull with force, esp. along the ground 2 trail on the ground 3 (foll. by along or to) bring (oneself or someone else) with effort or difficulty 4 (foll. by on or out) last, prolong, or be prolonged tediously 5 search (a river) with a dragnet or hook ▷ n 6 person or thing that slows up progress 7 informal tedious person or thing 8 slang women's clothes worn by a man

dragnet n net used to scour the bottom of a pond or river, when searching for something

drag race race in which specially built automobiles or motorcycles are timed over a measured course

dragon n 1 mythical fire-breathing monster with a scaly body, wings, claws, and a long tail 2 informal fierce woman **dragonfly** n, pl **-flies** brightly coloured insect with a long slender body and two pairs of wings

dragoon n 1 heavily armed cavalryman ▷ v 2 coerce or force

drain n 1 pipe or channel that carries off water or sewage 2 cause of continuous diminution of resources or energy ▷ v 3 draw off or remove liquid from 4 flow away or filter off 5 drink the entire contents of (a glass or cup) 6 make constant demands on (resources, energy, etc.) 7 exhaust (someone) physically and emotionally **drainage**

n **1** process or method of draining **2** system of drains

drake *n* male duck

dram *n* **1** small amount of spirits, esp. whisky **2** one sixteenth of an ounce

drama *n* **1** a work to be performed by actors **2** art of the writing or production of plays **3** situation that is highly emotional, turbulent, or tragic **dramatic** *adj* **1** of or like drama **2** striking or effective **dramatically** *adv* **dramatist** *n* playwright **dramatize** *v* **1** put into dramatic form **2** express (something) in a dramatic or exaggerated way **dramatization** *n*

drank *v* past tense of **drink**

drape *v* **1** cover with material, usu. in folds **2** place casually and loosely ▷ *n* **3** curtain **draper** *n* *Brit* dealer in fabrics and sewing materials **drapery** *n* **1** fabric or clothing arranged and draped **2** fabrics and cloth collectively **draperies 3** curtains

drastic *adj* sudden and extreme

draught *n* **1** same as **draft²** **draughts 2** *Brit* checkers

draw *v* **drawing, drew, drawn 1** depict or sketch (a figure, picture, etc.) in lines, with a pencil or pen **2** cause (a person or thing) to move out, as from a drawer, holster, etc. **3** move in a specified direction **4** arouse the interest or attention of **5** formulate or derive: *draw conclusions* **6** take from a source: *draw money from the bank* **7** (of two teams or contestants) finish a game with an equal number of points ▷ *n* **8** raffle or lottery **9** contest or game ending in a tie **10** event, act, etc. that attracts a large audience **drawer** *n* boxlike container

in a chest, table, etc. made for sliding in and out **drawers** *old-fashioned* undergarment worn below the waist

drawing *n* **1** picture or plan made by means of lines on a surface **2** art of making drawings **drawing pin** short tack with a broad smooth head **drawing room** *old-fashioned* room where visitors are received and entertained

drawback *n* disadvantage

drawbridge *n* bridge that may be raised to prevent access or to enable vessels to pass **draw out** *v* **1** extend **2** encourage (a person) to talk freely **drawstring** *n* cord run through a hem around an opening, so that when it is pulled tighter, the opening closes **draw up** *v* **1** (of a vehicle) come to a halt **2** formulate and write out (a contract)

drawl *v* **1** speak slowly, esp. prolonging the vowel sounds ▷ *n* **2** drawling manner of speech

drawn *v* **1** past participle of **draw** ▷ *adj* **2** haggard, tired, or tense in appearance

dray *n* low cart used for carrying heavy loads

dread *v* **1** anticipate with apprehension or terror ▷ *n* **2** great fear **dreadful** *adj* **1** extremely disagreeable, shocking, or bad **2** extreme **dreadfully** *adv*

dreadlocks *pl n* hair worn in the Rastafarian style of tightly curled strands

dream *n* **1** mental activity, usu. an imagined series of events, occurring during sleep **2** cherished hope **3** *informal* something wonderful ▷ *v* **dreaming, dreamt** *or* **dreamed 4** experience (a dream) **5** (foll. by *of* or *about*) have an image (of) or fantasy (about) **6** (foll. by *of*) consider the possibility (of) **dream catcher** webbed hoop used by some N American native peoples as a charm to catch good dreams and block bad ones **dreamer** *n* **dreamy** *adj* **1** vague or impractical **2** *informal* wonderful **dreamily** *adv*

dreary *adj* **drearier, dreariest** dull or boring **drearily** *adv* **dreariness** *n*

dredge¹ *v* remove (silt or mud) from (a river bed etc.) **dredger** *n* boat fitted with machinery for dredging

dredge² *v* sprinkle (food) with flour etc.

dregs *pl n* **1** solid particles that settle at the bottom of some liquids **2** most despised elements: *the dregs of society*

drench *v* make completely wet **drenching** *n*

dress *n* **1** one-piece garment for a woman or girl, consisting of a skirt and bodice and sometimes sleeves **2** complete style of clothing ▷ *v* **3** put clothes on **4** put on formal clothes **5** apply protective covering to (a wound) **6** arrange or prepare **dressing** *n* **1** sauce for salad **2** covering for a wound **dressing-down** *n informal* severe scolding **dressing gown** robe worn before dressing **dressing room** room used for changing clothes, esp. backstage in a theatre **dressy** *adj* (of clothes) elegant **dressiness** *n* **dress circle** first gallery in a theatre **dressmaker** *n* person who makes clothes for women **dressmaking** *n* **dress rehearsal** last rehearsal of a play, using costumes, lighting, etc., as for the first night

dressage [**dress**-ahzh] *n* training of a horse to perform manoeuvres in response to the rider's body signals

dresser¹ *n* set of shelves, usu. with cupboards, for storing or displaying dishes

dresser² *n theatre* person employed to assist actors with their costumes

drew *v* past tense of **draw**

drey *n* squirrel's nest

dribble *v* **1** (allow to) flow in drops **2** allow saliva to trickle from the mouth **3** propel (a ball) by repeatedly tapping it with the foot, hand, or a stick ▷ *n* **4** small quantity of liquid falling in drops **dribbler** *n*

dried *v* past of **dry**

drier *adj* **1** comparative of **dry** ▷ *n* **2** same as **dryer**

driest *adj* superlative of **dry**

drift *v* **1** be carried along by currents of air or water **2** move aimlessly from one place or activity to another ▷ *n* **3** something piled up by the wind or current, such as a snowdrift **4** general movement or development **5** main point of an argument or speech **drifter** *n* person who moves aimlessly from place to place or job to job **driftwood** *n* wood floating on or washed ashore by the sea

drill¹ *n* **1** tool or machine for boring holes **2** strict and often repetitive training **3** *informal* correct procedure ▷ *v* **4** pierce, bore, or cut (a hole) in (material) (as if) with a drill **5** teach by rigorous exercises and training

drill² *n* **1** machine for sowing seed in rows **2** small furrow for seed

drill³ *n* hard-wearing cotton cloth

drily *adv* same as **dryly**

drink *v* **drinking, drank, drunk 1** swallow (a liquid) **2** consume alcohol, esp. to excess ▷ *n* **3** liquid suitable for drinking **4** portion of liquid for drinking **5** alcohol or its habitual or excessive consumption **drinkable** *adj* **drinker** *n* **drink in** *v* pay close attention to **drink to** *v* drink a toast to

drip *v* **dripping, dripped 1** fall or let fall in drops ▷ *n* **2** falling of drops of liquid **3** sound made by falling drops **4** *informal* weak or foolish person **5** *med* apparatus for the administration of a solution drop by drop into a vein **drip-dry** *adj* denoting clothing that will dry free of creases if hung up when wet

dripping *n* fat that comes from meat while it is being roasted or fried

drive *v* **driving, drove, driven 1** guide the movement of (a vehicle) **2** transport or be transported in a vehicle **3** goad into a specified state **4** push or propel **5** *sports* hit (a ball) very hard and straight ▷ *n* **6** journey in a driven vehicle **7** road for vehicles, esp. a private road leading to a house **8** united effort towards a common goal: *an investment drive* **9** energy, ambition, or initiative **10** *psychol* motive or interest: *sex drive* **11** means by which force, motion, etc. is transmitted in a mechanism **driver** *n* **1** person who drives a vehicle **2** *golf* club used for tee shots **drive at** *v informal* intend or mean: *what are you driving at?* **drive-in** *adj, n* (denoting) a public facility used by patrons in their automobiles

drivel *n* **1** foolish talk ▷ *v*

-elling, -elled 2 speak foolishly

drizzle *n* **1** very light rain ▷ *v* **2** rain lightly **drizzly** *adj*

droll *adj* quaintly amusing **drolly** *adv* **drollery** *n*

dromedary [drom-mid-er-ee] *n, pl* **-daries** camel with a single hump

drone¹ *n* male bee

drone² *v, n* (make) a monotonous low dull sound **drone on** *v* talk for a long time in a monotonous tone

drool *v* **1** (foll. by *over*) show excessive enthusiasm (for) or pleasure (in) **2** allow saliva to flow from the mouth

droop *v* sag, as from weakness **droopy** *adj*

drop *v* **dropping, dropped 1** (allow to) fall vertically **2** decrease in amount, strength, or value **3** mention casually **4** discontinue (an activity) ▷ *n* **5** small quantity of liquid forming a round shape **6** very small quantity of liquid **7** act of falling **8** decrease in amount or value **9** vertical distance that anything may fall **drops** **10** liquid medication applied drop by drop **droplet** *n* **droppings** *pl n* feces of certain animals, such as rabbits or birds **drop in** *or* **drop by** *v* pay someone a casual visit **drop off** *v* **1** grow smaller or less **2** *informal* fall asleep **dropout** *n* **1** person who rejects conventional society **2** person who fails to complete a course of study **drop out of** *v* abandon or withdraw from (a school, job, etc.)

dropsy *n* illness in which watery fluid collects in the body

dross *n* **1** scum formed on the surfaces of molten metals **2** worthless matter

drought *n* prolonged shortage of rainfall

drove[1] *v* past tense of **drive**

drove[2] *n* **1** moving herd of livestock **2** moving crowd of people **drover** *n* person who drives sheep or cattle

drown *v* **1** die or kill by immersion in liquid **2** forget (one's sorrows) temporarily by drinking alcohol **3** drench thoroughly **4** render (a sound) inaudible by making a loud noise

drowse *v* be sleepy, dull, or sluggish **drowsy** *adj* **drowsily** *adv* **drowsiness** *n*

drubbing *n* utter defeat, as in a contest

drudge *n* **1** person who works hard at wearisome menial tasks ▷ *v* **2** toil at such tasks **drudgery** *n*

drug *n* **1** substance used in the treatment or prevention of disease **2** chemical substance, esp. a narcotic, taken for the effect it produces ▷ *v* **drugging, drugged 3** administer a drug to (a person or animal) in order to induce sleepiness or unconsciousness **4** mix a drug with (food or drink) **drugstore** *n* pharmacy where a wide variety of goods is available

Druid *n* member of an ancient order of Celtic priests **Druidic** or **Druidical** *adj*

drum *n* **1** percussion instrument sounded by striking a skin stretched across the opening of a hollow cylinder **2** cylindrical object or container ▷ *v* **drumming, drummed 3** play (music) on a drum **4** tap rhythmically or regularly **drummer** *n* **drum into** *v* instil into (someone) by constant repetition **drumstick** *n* **1** stick used for playing a drum **2** lower joint of the leg of a cooked fowl **drum up** *v* obtain (support) by solicitation or canvassing

drunk *v* **1** past participle of **drink** ▷ *adj* **2** intoxicated with alcohol to the extent of losing control over normal functions **3** overwhelmed by a strong influence or emotion ▷ *n* **4** person who is drunk **drunkard** *n* person who is frequently or habitually drunk **drunken** *adj* **1** drunk **2** caused by or relating to alcoholic intoxication **drunkenly** *adv* **drunkenness** *n*

dry *adj* **drier, driest** or **dryer, dryest 1** lacking moisture **2** having little or no rainfall **3** *informal* thirsty **4** (of wine) not sweet **5** uninteresting: *a dry book* **6** (of humour) subtle and sarcastic **7** prohibiting the sale of alcohol: *a dry area* ▷ *v* **drying, dried 8** make or become dry **9** preserve (food) by removing the moisture **dryly** *adv* **dryness** *n* **dryer** *n* apparatus for removing moisture **dry-clean** *v* clean (clothes etc.) with a solvent other than water **dry-cleaner** *n* **dry-cleaning** *n* **dry out** *v* **1** make or become dry **2** (cause to) undergo treatment for alcoholism or drug addiction **dry rot** crumbling and drying of timber, caused by certain fungi **dry run** *informal* rehearsal

dryad *n* wood nymph

DSc Doctor of Science

dual *adj* **1** relating to or denoting two **2** twofold **duality** *n* **dual carriageway** *Brit* road on which traffic travelling in opposite directions is separated by a central strip of turf or concrete

dub[1] *v* **dubbing, dubbed** give (a person or place) a name or nickname

dub[2] *v* **dubbing, dubbed** 1 provide (a film) with a new soundtrack, esp. in a different language 2 provide (a film or tape) with a soundtrack

dubbin *n* greasy preparation applied to leather to soften and waterproof it

dubious [dew-bee-uss] *adj* feeling or causing doubt **dubiously** *adv* **dubiety** [dew-by-it-ee] *n*

ducal [duke-al] *adj* of a duke

ducat [duck-it] *n* former European gold or silver coin

duchess *n* 1 woman who holds the rank of duke in her own right 2 wife or widow of a duke

duchy *n, pl* **duchies** territory of a duke or duchess

duck[1] *n* 1 water bird with short legs, webbed feet, and a broad blunt bill 2 female of this bird 3 flesh of this bird, used as food 4 *cricket* score of nothing **duckling** *n* young duck

duck[2] *v* 1 move (the head or body) quickly downwards, to escape observation or to dodge a blow 2 plunge suddenly into water 3 *informal* dodge or escape (a duty etc.)

duct *n* 1 tube, pipe, or canal by means of which a fluid or gas is conveyed 2 bodily passage conveying secretions or excretions **ductile** *adj* 1 (of metal) able to be shaped into sheets or wires 2 easily influenced **ductility** *n*

dud *informal* ▷ *n* 1 person or thing that proves ineffectual ▷ *adj* 2 bad or useless

dude *n US informal* 1 man, chap 2 *old-fashioned* dandy

dudgeon *n* **in high dudgeon** angry or resentful

due *adj* 1 expected or scheduled to be present or arrive 2 owed as a debt 3 fitting, proper ▷ *n* 4 something that is owed, required, or due **dues** 5 charges for membership of a club or organization ▷ *adv* 6 directly or exactly: *due north* **due to** attributable to or caused by

duel *n* 1 formal prearranged combat with deadly weapons between two people, to settle a quarrel ▷ *v* **duelling, duelled** 2 fight in a duel **duellist** *n*

duenna *n* (esp. in Spain) elderly woman acting as chaperone to a young woman

duet *n* piece of music for two performers

duffel, duffle *n* coat made of heavy woollen cloth

duffer *n informal* dull or incompetent person

dug[1] *v* past of **dig**

dug[2] *n* teat or udder

dugong *n* whalelike mammal found in tropical waters

dugout *n* 1 canoe made by hollowing out a log 2 (at a sports ground) covered bench where managers and substitutes sit 3 *mil* covered excavation dug to provide shelter

duke *n* 1 nobleman of the highest rank 2 prince or ruler of a small principality or duchy **dukedom** *n*

dulcet [dull-sit] *adj* (of a sound) soothing or pleasant

dulcimer *n* tuned percussion instrument consisting of a set of strings stretched over a sounding board and struck with hammers

dull *adj* 1 uninteresting 2 stupid 3 (of a pain) not acute or intense 4 (of weather) not bright or clear 5 lacking in spirit 6 (of a blade) lacking

sharpness ▷ v **7** make or become dull **dullness** n **dully** adv **dullard** n dull or stupid person

duly adv **1** in a proper manner **2** at the proper time

dumb adj **1** offensive lacking the power to speak **2** silent **3** informal stupid **dumbly** adv **dumbness** n **dumbbell** n exercising weight consisting of a short bar with a heavy ball or disc at either end **dumbfounded** adj speechless with amazement **dumb show** meaningful gestures without speech

dumdum n soft-nosed bullet that expands on impact and inflicts extensive wounds

dummy n, pl -**mies 1** figure representing the human form, used for displaying clothes etc. **2** copy of an object, often lacking some essential feature of the original **3** slang stupid person ▷ adj **4** imitation or substitute **dummy run** practice, rehearsal

dump v **1** drop or let fall heavily or in a mass **2** informal abandon (something or someone) **3** dispose of (nuclear waste) **4** market (goods) in bulk and at low prices, esp. abroad ▷ n **5** place where waste materials are dumped **6** informal dirty unattractive place **7** mil place where weapons or supplies are stored **down in the dumps** in a state of depression **dumpy** adj short and plump

dumpling n **1** small ball of dough cooked and served with stew **2** round pastry case filled with fruit

dun adj brownish-grey

dunce n person who is stupid or slow to learn

dunderhead n slow-witted person

dune n mound or ridge of drifted sand

dung n excrement of animals

dungarees pl n trousers with a bib attached

dungeon n underground prison cell

dunk v **1** dip (a cookie etc.) into liquid before eating it **2** submerge (something) in liquid **3** basketball drop (the ball) through the hoop with the hands above the rim ▷ n **4** basketball scoring shot in which a player drops the ball through the hoop with the hands above the rim **5** see **slam dunk**

duo n, pl **duos 1** pair of performers **2** informal pair of closely connected people

duodecimal adj reckoned in twelves or twelfths

duodenum [dew-oh-**deen**-um] n, pl -**na**, -**nums** first part of the small intestine, just below the stomach **duodenal** adj

dupe v **1** deceive or cheat ▷ n **2** person who is easily deceived

duple adj music having two beats in a bar

duplex adj **1** twofold ▷ n **2** house divided into two separate dwellings **3** either dwelling

duplicate adj **1** copied exactly from an original ▷ n **2** exact copy ▷ v **3** make a replica of **4** do again (something that has already been done) **duplication** n **duplicator** n

duplicity n deception or double-dealing

durable adj long-lasting **durables** or **durable goods** pl n goods that require infrequent replacement **durability** n

duration n length of time that something lasts

duress n compulsion by use of force or threats

during prep throughout or within the limit of (a period of time)

dusk n time just before nightfall, when it is almost dark **dusky** adj 1 dark in colour 2 shadowy **duskiness** n

dust n 1 dry fine powdery material, such as particles of dirt ▷ v 2 remove dust from (furniture) by wiping 3 sprinkle (something) with dust or some other powdery substance **duster** n cloth used for dusting **dusty** adj covered with dust **dustbin** n Brit garbage can **dustbowl** n dry area in which the surface soil is exposed to wind erosion **dust jacket** or **dust cover** removable paper cover used to protect a book **dustman** n Brit garbage collector **dustpan** n short-handled hooded shovel into which dust is swept from floors

Dutch adj of the Netherlands, its inhabitants, or their language **go Dutch** informal share the expenses on an outing **Dutch courage** false courage gained from drinking alcohol

duty n, pl **-ties** 1 task that a person is bound to perform for moral or legal reasons 2 government tax, esp. on imports **on duty** at work **dutiable** adj (of goods) requiring payment of duty **dutiful** adj showing or resulting from a sense of duty **dutifully** adv

duvet [doo-vay] n quilt filled with down or artificial fibre

DVT deep-vein thrombosis

dwarf n, pl **dwarfs**, **dwarves** 1 undersized person 2 (in folklore) small ugly manlike creature, often possessing magical powers ▷ adj 3 denoting an animal or plant much below the average size for a species ▷ v 4 cause (someone or something) to seem small by being much larger

dwell v dwelling, dwelt or dwelled live as a permanent resident **dweller** n **dwelling** n place of residence **dwell on** or **dwell upon** v think, speak, or write at length about

dwindle v grow less in size, intensity, or number

dye n 1 staining or colouring substance 2 colour produced by dyeing ▷ v dyeing, dyed 3 colour or stain (fabric, hair, etc.) by the application of dye **dyer** n **dyed-in-the-wool** adj uncompromising or unchanging in attitude or opinion

dying v present participle of **die**[1]

dyke n 1 wall built to prevent flooding 2 ditch 3 offensive slang lesbian

dynamic adj 1 characterized by force of personality, ambition, and energy 2 of or concerned with energy or forces that produce motion **dynamically** adv **dynamism** n forcefulness of an energetic personality

dynamics n branch of mechanics concerned with the forces that change or produce the motions of bodies

dynamite n 1 high-explosive mixture containing nitroglycerin 2 informal spectacular or potentially dangerous person or thing ▷ v 3 mine or blow (something) up with dynamite

dynamo n, pl **-mos** device for converting mechanical

energy into electrical energy

dynasty *n, pl* **-ties** sequence of hereditary rulers **dynastic** *adj*

dysentery *n* infection of the intestine causing severe diarrhea

dysfunction *n med* disturbance or abnormality in the function of an organ or part

dyslexia *n* disorder causing impaired ability to read **dyslexic** *adj*

dysmenorrhea, dysmenorrhoea *n* painful menstruation

dyspepsia *n* indigestion **dyspeptic** *adj*

dystrophy [**diss**-trof-fee] *n* wasting of the body tissues, esp. the muscles

d

Ee

E East(ern)

e- *prefix* electronic: *e-mail*

each *adj, pron* every (one) taken separately

eager *adj* showing or feeling great desire, keen **eagerly** *adv* **eagerness** *n*

eagle *n* **1** large bird of prey with keen eyesight **2** *golf* score of two strokes under par for a hole **eaglet** *n* young eagle

ear¹ *n* **1** organ of hearing, esp. the external part of it **2** sensitivity to musical or other sounds **earache** *n* pain in the ear **eardrum** *n* thin piece of skin inside the ear which enables one to hear sounds **earmark** *v* **1** set (something) aside for a specific purpose ▷ *n* **2** distinguishing mark **earphone** *n* receiver for a radio etc. held to or put in the ear **earring** *n* ornament for the lobe of the ear **earshot** *n* hearing range

ear² *n* head of corn

earl *n* British nobleman ranking next below a marquess **earldom** *n*

early *adj, adv* **-lier, -liest** **1** before the expected or usual time **2** in the first part of a period **3** in a period far back in time

earn *v* **1** obtain by work or merit **2** (of investments etc.) gain (interest) **3** *baseball* score (a run) without the fielding side making an error **earner** *n* **earnings** *pl n* money earned

earnest¹ *adj* serious and sincere **in earnest** seriously **earnestly** *adv*

earnest² *n* part payment given in advance, esp. to confirm a contract

earth *n* **1** planet that we live on **2** land, the ground **3** soil **4** fox's hole **5** wire connecting an electrical apparatus with the earth ▷ *v* **6** connect (a circuit) to earth **earthen** *adj* made of baked clay or earth **earthenware** *n* pottery made of baked clay **earthly** *adj* conceivable or possible: *no earthly reason* **earthy** *adj* **1** coarse or crude **2** of or like earth **earthquake** *n* violent vibration of the earth's surface **earthwork** *n* fortification made of earth **earthworm** *n* worm which burrows in the soil

earwig *n* small insect with a pincer-like tail

ease *n* **1** freedom from difficulty, discomfort, or worry **2** rest or leisure: *at one's ease* ▷ *v* **3** give bodily or mental ease to **4** lessen (severity, tension, pain, etc.) **5** move carefully or gradually

easel *n* frame to support an artist's canvas or a blackboard

east *n* **1** part of the horizon where the sun rises **2** eastern lands or the orient ▷ *adj* **3** on, in, or near the east **4** (of the wind) from the east ▷ *adv* **5** in, to, or towards the east **easterly** *adj, adv* **1** to the east

2 (of a wind) from the east
eastern adj of, in, or from the east **eastward** adj, adv **eastwards** adv **East Coast** Atlantic Coast of N America
Easter n Christian spring festival commemorating the Resurrection of Jesus Christ **Easter egg** chocolate egg given at Easter
Eastern Daylight Time n one of the standard times used in North America, four hours behind Greenwich Mean Time Abbreviation: **EDT**
Eastern Standard Time n one of the standard times used in North America, five hours behind Greenwich Mean Time Abbreviation: **EST**
easy adj **easier, easiest 1** not needing much work or effort **2** free from pain, care, or anxiety **3** easy-going **easily** adv **easiness** n **easy chair** comfortable armchair **easy-going** adj relaxed in attitude, tolerant
eat v **eating, ate, eaten 1** take (food) into the mouth and swallow it **2** (foll. by away or up) destroy **3** have a meal **eatable** adj fit or suitable for eating
eau de Cologne [oh de kol-**lone**] n French light perfume
eaves pl n overhanging edges of a roof **eavestrough** n Canad gutter at the eaves of a building
eavesdrop v **-dropping, -dropped** listen secretly to a private conversation **eavesdropper** n **eavesdropping** n
ebb v **1** (of tide water) flow back **2** become weaker ▷ n **3** flowing back of the tide **at a low ebb** in a state of weakness
ebony n, pl **-onies 1** hard black wood ▷ adj **2** deep black
e-book n **1** electronic book ▷ v **2** book (airline tickets, appointments, etc.) on

the internet
ebullient adj overflowing with enthusiasm and excitement **ebullience** n
eccentric adj **1** odd or unconventional **2** (of circles) not having the same centre ▷ n **3** unconventional person **eccentrically** adv **eccentricity** n **1** unconventional behaviour **2** odd habit
ecclesiastic adj **1** Also **ecclesiastical** of the Christian Church or clergy ▷ n **2** clergyman
ECG 1 electrocardiogram **2** electrocardiograph
echelon [**esh**-a-lon] n **1** level of power or responsibility **2** mil formation in which units follow one another but are spaced out sideways to allow each a line of fire ahead
echo n, pl **-oes 1** repetition of sounds by reflection of sound waves off a surface **2** close imitation ▷ v **-oing, -oed 3** repeat or be repeated as an echo **4** imitate closely **echo sounder** sonar **echo sounding** use of sonar to navigate
e-cigarette n electronic vaporizer that simulates the effect of smoking
éclair n finger-shaped pastry filled with cream and covered with chocolate
éclat [ake-**lah**] n **1** brilliant success **2** splendour
eclectic adj selecting from various ideas or sources **eclecticism** n
eclipse n **1** temporary obscuring of one heavenly body by another ▷ v **2** surpass or outclass **ecliptic** n apparent path of the sun
eclogue n short poem on a rural theme
ecological adj **1** of ecology **2** intended to protect the environment **ecologically**

adv **ecology** *n* study of the relationships between living things and their environment **ecologist** *n*

e-commerce, ecommerce *n* business transactions done on the internet

economy *n, pl* **-mies 1** system of interrelationship of money, industry, and employment in a country **2** careful management of resources to avoid waste **economic** *adj* **1** of economics **2** profitable **economics** *n* **1** social science concerned with the production and consumption of goods and services ▷ *pl n* **2** financial aspects **economical** *adj* not wasteful, thrifty **economically** *adv* **economist** *n* specialist in economics **economize** *v* limit or reduce waste

ecosystem *n* system involving interactions between a community and its environment

ecru *adj* greyish-yellow

ecstasy *n* **1** state of intense delight **2** *slang* powerful drug that can produce hallucinations **ecstatic** *adj* **ecstatically** *adv*

ectoplasm *n spiritualism* substance that supposedly is emitted from the body of a medium during a trance

ECU European Currency Unit

ecumenical *adj* of the Christian Church throughout the world, esp. with regard to its unity

eczema [ek-sim-a] *n* skin disease causing intense itching

Edam *n* round Dutch cheese with a red rind

eddy *n, pl* **eddies 1** small whirling movement in air, water, etc. ▷ *v* **eddying, eddied 2** move in eddies

edelweiss [**ade**-el-vice] *n* alpine plant with white flowers

Eden *n* **1** *Bible* garden in which Adam and Eve were placed at the Creation **2** place of delight or contentment

edge *n* **1** border or line where something ends or begins **2** cutting side of a blade **3** sharpness of tone ▷ *v* **4** provide an edge or border for **5** push (one's way) gradually **have the edge on** have an advantage over **on edge** nervous or irritable **edgeways** *adv* with the edge forwards or uppermost **edging** *n* anything placed along an edge **edgy** *adj* nervous or irritable

edible *adj* fit to be eaten **edibility** *n*

edict [**ee**-dikt] *n* order issued by an authority

edifice [**ed**-if-iss] *n* large building

edify [**ed**-if-fie] *v* **-fying, -fied** improve morally by instruction **edification** *n*

edit *v* prepare (a book, film, etc.) for publication or broadcast **edition** *n* **1** form in which something is published **2** number of copies of a new publication printed at one time **editor** *n* **1** person who edits **2** person in overall charge of a newspaper or magazine **editorial** *adj* **1** of editing or editors ▷ *n* **2** newspaper article stating the opinion of the editor

EDT Eastern Daylight Time

educate *v* **1** teach **2** provide schooling for **education** *n* **educational** *adj* **educationally** *adv* **educationalist** *n* expert in the theory of education **educative** *adj* educating

Edwardian *adj* of the reign

of King Edward VII of Great Britain and Ireland (1901–10)

EEG electroencephalogram

eel n snakelike fish

eerie adj uncannily frightening or disturbing **eerily** adv

efface v 1 remove by rubbing 2 make (oneself) inconspicuous **effacement** n

effect n 1 change or result caused by someone or something 2 overall impression 3 condition of being operative: *the law comes into effect next month* **effects** 4 property 5 lighting, sounds, etc. to accompany a film or a broadcast ▷ v 6 cause to happen, accomplish **effective** adj 1 producing a desired result 2 impressive 3 operative **effectively** adv **effectual** adj successful in producing a desired result **effectually** adv

effeminate adj (of a man) displaying characteristics thought to be typical of a woman **effeminacy** n

effervescent adj (of a liquid) 1 giving off bubbles 2 (of a person) lively and enthusiastic **effervescence** n

effete [if-**feet**] adj powerless, feeble

efficacious adj producing the intended result, effective **efficacy** n

efficient adj functioning effectively with little waste of effort **efficiently** adv **efficiency** n

effigy [**ef**-fij-ee] n, pl **-gies** image or likeness of a person

efflorescence n flowering

effluent n liquid discharged as waste **effluence** n something that flows out **effluvium** n, pl **-via** unpleasant smell, as decaying matter or gaseous waste

effort n 1 physical or mental exertion 2 attempt **effortless** adj

effrontery n brazen impudence

effusion n unrestrained outburst **effusive** adj openly emotional, demonstrative **effusively** adv **effusiveness** n

EFTA European Free Trade Association

e.g. for example

egalitarian adj 1 upholding the equality of all people ▷ n 2 person who holds egalitarian beliefs **egalitarianism** n

egg[1] n 1 oval or round object laid by the females of birds and other creatures, containing a developing embryo 2 hen's egg used as food 3 Also **egg cell** ovum **egghead** n informal intellectual person **eggplant** n plant bearing egg-shaped purple fruit eaten as a vegetable

egg[2] v **egg on** encourage or incite, esp. to do wrong

eglantine n sweetbrier

ego n, pl **egos** 1 self-esteem 2 the self of an individual person **egoism** or **egotism** n 1 excessive concern for one's own interests 2 excessively high opinion of oneself **egoist** or **egotist** n **egoistic** or **egotistic** adj **egocentric** adj self-centred

egregious [ig-**greej**-uss] adj outstandingly bad

egress [**ee**-gress] n 1 way out 2 departure

egret [**ee**-grit] n lesser white heron

Egyptology n study of the culture of ancient Egypt

eider n Arctic duck **eiderdown** n quilt (orig. stuffed with eider feathers)

eight adj, n 1 one more than seven ▷ n 2 eight-oared boat

3 its crew **eighth** *adj, n* (of) number eight in a series **eighteen** *adj, n* eight and ten **eighteenth** *adj, n* **eighty** *adj, n* eight times ten **eightieth** *adj, n*

eisteddfod [ice-**sted**-fod] *n* Welsh festival with competitions in music and other performing arts

either *adj, pron* **1** one or the other (of two) **2** each of two ▷ *conj* **3** used preceding two or more possibilities joined by *or* ▷ *adv* **4** likewise: *I don't eat meat and he doesn't either*

ejaculate *v* **1** eject (semen) **2** utter abruptly **ejaculation** *n*

eject *v* force out, expel **ejection** *n* **ejector** *n*

eke *v* **eke out** **1** make (a supply) last by frugal use **2** make (a living) with difficulty

elaborate *adj* **1** with a lot of fine detail ▷ *v* **2** expand upon **elaboration** *n*

élan [ale-**an**] *n* style and vigour

eland [**eel**-and] *n* large antelope of southern Africa

elapse *v* (of time) pass by

elastic *adj* **1** resuming normal shape after distortion **2** adapting easily to change ▷ *n* **3** tape or fabric containing interwoven strands of flexible rubber **elasticity** *n*

elate *v* fill with high spirits or pride **elation** *n*

elbow *n* **1** joint between the upper arm and the forearm **2** part of a garment that covers this ▷ *v* **3** shove or strike with the elbow **elbow grease** vigorous physical labour **elbowroom** *n* sufficient room to move freely

elder¹ *adj* **1** older ▷ *n* **2** older person **3** (in certain Protestant Churches) lay officer **elderly** *adj* (fairly) old **eldest** *adj* oldest

elder² *n* small tree with white flowers and black berries

El Dorado [el dor-**rah**-doe] *n* fictitious country rich in gold

eldritch *adj Scot* weird, uncanny

elect *v* **1** choose by voting **2** decide (to do something) ▷ *adj* **3** appointed but not yet in office: *president elect* **election** *n* **1** choosing of representatives by voting **2** act of choosing **electioneer** *v* be active in a political election **elective** *adj* **1** chosen by election **2** optional **elector** *n* someone who has the right to vote in an election **electoral** *adj* **electorate** *n* people who have the right to vote

electricity *n* **1** form of energy associated with stationary or moving electrons or other charged particles **2** electric current or charge **electric** *adj* **1** produced by, producing, transmitting, or powered by electricity **2** exciting or tense **electrics** *pl n* electric appliances **electric chair** *US* chair in which criminals who have been sentenced to death are electrocuted **electric cord** flexible insulated cable that conducts electricity **electrical** *adj* using or concerning electricity **electrician** *n* person trained to install and repair electrical equipment **electrify** *v* **-fying, -fied** **1** adapt for operation by electric power **2** charge with electricity **3** startle or excite intensely **electrification** *n*

electro- *combining form* operated by or caused by electricity **electrocardiograph** *n* instrument for recording the electrical activity of the heart **electrocardiogram**

n tracing produced by this **electrodynamics** *n* branch of physics concerned with the interactions between electrical and mechanical forces **electroencephalograph** [ill-lek-tro-en-**sef**-a-loh-graf] *n* instrument for recording the electrical activity of the brain **electroencephalogram** *n* tracing produced by this **electromagnet** *n* magnet containing a coil of wire through which an electric current is passed **electromagnetic** *adj* **electromagnetism** *n* **electroplate** *v* coat with silver etc. by electrolysis

electrocute *v* kill or injure by electricity **electrocution** *n*

electrode *n* conductor through which an electric current enters or leaves a battery, vacuum tube, etc.

electrolysis [ill-lek-**troll**-iss-iss] *n* **1** conduction of electricity by an electrolyte, esp. to induce chemical change **2** destruction of living tissue such as hair roots by an electric current

electrolyte *n* solution or molten substance that conducts electricity **electrolytic** *adj*

electron *n* elementary particle in all atoms that has a negative electrical charge **electronic** *adj* **1** (of a device) dependent on the action of electrons **2** (of a process) using electronic devices **electronic mail** see **e-mail** ► **electronics** *n* technology concerned with the development of electronic devices and circuits **electron microscope** microscope that uses electrons, rather than light, to produce a magnified image **electron volt** unit of energy used in nuclear physics

elegant *adj* **1** tasteful in dress, style, or design **2** graceful **elegance** *n*

elegy [**el**-lij-ee] *n, pl* -**egies** mournful poem, esp. a lament for the dead **elegiac** *adj* mournful or plaintive

element *n* **1** component part **2** substance which cannot be separated into other substances by ordinary chemical techniques **3** distinguishable section of a social group: *liberal elements in Polish society* **4** heating wire in an electric kettle, stove, etc. **elements 5** basic principles of something **6** weather conditions, esp. wind, rain, and cold **in one's element** in a situation where one is happiest **elemental** *adj* **1** fundamental **2** of primitive natural forces or passions **elementary** *adj* simple and straightforward

elephant *n* huge four-footed thick-skinned animal with ivory tusks and a long trunk **elephantine** *adj* unwieldy, clumsy **elephantiasis** [el-lee-fan-**tie**-a-siss] *n* disease with hardening of the skin and enlargement of the legs etc.

elevate *v* **1** raise in rank or status **2** lift up **elevation** *n* **1** raising **2** scale drawing of one side of a building **3** height above sea level **elevator** *n* cage raised or lowered in a vertical shaft to transport people or goods

eleven *adj, n* **1** one more than ten ▷ *n* **2** *sports* team of eleven people **eleventh** *adj, n* (of) number eleven in a series **elevenses** *n informal* light mid-morning snack

elf *n, pl* **elves** (in folklore) small mischievous fairy **elfin** *adj* small and delicate

elicit *v* draw out (information) from someone

elide *v* omit (a vowel or syllable) from a spoken word **elision** *n*

eligible *adj* **1** qualified to be chosen **2** desirable as a spouse **eligibility** *n*

eliminate *v* get rid of **elimination** *n*

elite [ill-**eet**] *n* most powerful, rich, or gifted members of a group **elitism** *n* belief that society should be governed by a small group of superior people **elitist** *n*, *adj*

elixir [ill-**ix**-er] *n* liquid medicine in syrup

Elizabethan *adj* of the reign of Elizabeth I of England (1558–1603)

elk *n* large deer of N Europe and Asia

ellipse *n* oval shape **elliptical** *adj* **1** oval-shaped **2** (of speech or writing) obscure or ambiguous

ellipsis [ill-**lip**-siss] *n*, *pl* -**ses** omission of letters or words in a sentence

elm *n* tree with serrated leaves

elocution *n* art of speaking clearly in public

elongate [eel-**long**-gate] *v* make or become longer **elongation** *n*

elope *v* run away secretly to get married **elopement** *n*

eloquence *n* fluent powerful use of language **eloquent** *adj* **eloquently** *adv*

else *adv* **1** otherwise **2** besides **3** instead **elsewhere** *adv* in or to another place

elucidate *v* make (something difficult) clear, explain **elucidation** *n*

elude *v* **1** baffle **2** escape from by cleverness or quickness **elusive** *adj* difficult to catch or remember

elver *n* young eel

elves *n* plural of **elf**

emaciated [im-**mace**-ee-ate-id] *adj* abnormally thin **emaciation** *n*

e-mail, email *n* **1** Also **electronic mail** sending of messages between computer terminals ▷ *v* **2** communicate in this way

emanate [**em**-a-nate] *v* issue, proceed from a source **emanation** *n*

emancipate *v* free from social, political, or legal restraints **emancipation** *n*

emasculate *v* deprive of power **emasculation** *n*

embalm *v* preserve (a corpse) from decay by the use of chemicals etc. **embalmment** *n*

embankment *n* man-made ridge that carries a road or railway or holds back water

embargo *n*, *pl* -**goes 1** order stopping the movement of ships **2** legal stoppage of trade **3** ban ▷ *v* -**going, -goed 4** put an embargo on

embark *v* **1** board a ship or aircraft **2** (foll. by *on* or *upon*) begin (a new project) **embarkation** *n*

embarrass *v* cause to feel self-conscious or ashamed **embarrassed** *adj* **embarrassment** *n*

embassy *n*, *pl* -**sies 1** offices or official residence of an ambassador **2** ambassador and his staff

embattled *adj* having a lot of difficulties

embed *v* -**bedding, -bedded** fix firmly in something solid

embellish *v* **1** decorate **2** embroider (a story) **embellishment** *n*

ember *n* glowing piece of wood or coal in a dying fire

embezzle *v* steal money that has been entrusted to one

embezzlement n **embezzler** n

embitter v make bitter
embitterment n

emblazon [im-**blaze**-on] v
1 decorate with bright colours
2 proclaim or publicize

emblem n object or
representation that
symbolizes a quality, type, or
group **emblematic** adj

embody v -**bodying**, -**bodied**
1 be an example or expression
of **2** comprise, include
embodiment n

embolden v encourage
(someone)

embolism n blocking of a
blood vessel by a blood clot or
air bubble

emboss v mould or carve a
raised design on

embrace v **1** clasp in the
arms, hug **2** accept (an idea)
eagerly **3** comprise ▷ n **4** act of
embracing

embrasure n **1** door or window
having splayed sides so that
the opening is larger on the
inside **2** opening like this in
a fortified wall, for shooting
through

embrocation n lotion for
rubbing into the skin to
relieve pain

embroider v **1** decorate
with needlework **2** make (a
story) more interesting with
fictitious detail **embroidery** n

embroil v involve (a person) in
problems **embroilment** n

embryo [**em**-bree-oh] n, pl
-**bryos 1** unborn creature
in the early stages of
development **2** something
at an undeveloped stage
embryonic adj at an early
stage **embryology** n

emend v remove errors from
emendation n

emerald n **1** bright green
precious stone ▷ adj **2** bright
green

emerge v **1** come into view
2 (foll. by from) come out of
3 become known **emergence**
n **emergent** adj

emergency n, pl -**cies**
1 sudden unforeseen
occurrence needing
immediate action
▷ adj **2** for use in an
emergency: emergency exit

emeritus [im-**mer**-rit-uss]
adj retired, but retaining
an honorary title: emeritus
professor

emery n hard mineral used
for smoothing and polishing
emery board cardboard strip
coated with crushed emery,
for filing the nails

emetic [im-**met**-ik] n
1 substance that causes
vomiting ▷ adj **2** causing
vomiting

emigrate v go and settle in
another country **emigrant** n
emigration n

émigré [**em**-mig-gray] n
someone who has left his
native country for political
reasons

eminent adj distinguished,
well-known **eminently**
adv **eminence** n **1** position
of superiority or fame
2 Eminence title of a cardinal

emir [em-**meer**] n Muslim
ruler **emirate** n his country

emissary n, pl -**saries** agent
sent on a mission by a
government

emit v **emitting**, **emitted**
1 give out (heat, light, or a
smell) **2** utter **emission** n

emollient adj **1** softening,
soothing ▷ n **2** substance
which softens or soothes
something

emolument n formal payment
for work, salary

emoji [im-**moh**-jee] n image
used in electronic messages

emoticon [i-**mote**-i-kon] n

symbol depicting a smile or other facial expression, used in electronic messages

emotion n strong feeling **emotional** adj readily affected by or appealing to the emotions **emotive** adj tending to arouse emotion

empathy n power of imaginatively entering into and understanding another's feelings

emperor n ruler of an empire **empress** n fem

emphasis n, pl -ses 1 special importance or significance given to something, such as an idea 2 stress on a word or phrase in speech **emphasize** v **emphatic** adj showing emphasis **emphatically** adv

emphysema [em-fiss-**see**-ma] n condition in which the air sacs of the lungs are grossly enlarged, causing breathlessness

empire n 1 group of territories under the rule of one state or person 2 large organization that is directed by one person or group

empirical adj relying on experiment or experience, not on theory **empirically** adv **empiricism** n doctrine that all knowledge derives from experience **empiricist** n

emplacement n prepared position for a gun

employ v 1 hire (a person) 2 provide work or occupation for 3 use ▷ n 4 state of being employed: in someone's employ **employee** n **employer** n **employment** n 1 state of being employed 2 work done by a person to earn money

emporium n old-fashioned large general shop

empower v enable, authorize

empress n see **emperor**

empty adj -tier, -tiest

1 containing nothing 2 unoccupied 3 without purpose or value 4 (of words) insincere ▷ v -tying, -tied 5 make or become empty **empties** pl n empty boxes, bottles, etc. **emptiness** n

emu n large Aust. flightless bird with long legs

emulate v attempt to equal or surpass by imitating **emulation** n

emulsion n 1 light-sensitive coating on photographic film 2 type of water-based paint ▷ v 3 paint with emulsion paint **emulsify** v -**fying**, -**fied** make into an emulsion **emulsifier** n

enable v provide (a person) with the means, opportunity, or authority (to do something)

enact v 1 establish by law 2 represent as in a play **enactment** n

enamel n 1 glasslike coating applied to metal etc. to preserve the surface 2 hard white coating on a tooth ▷ v -**elling**, -**elled** 3 cover with enamel

enamoured adj inspired with love

en bloc adv French as a body or a whole, all together

encamp v set up in a camp **encampment** n

encapsulate v 1 abridge 2 enclose as in a capsule

encephalitis [en-sef-a-**lite**-iss] n inflammation of the brain

encephalogram n short for **electroencephalogram**

enchant v bewitch or delight **enchantment** n **enchanter** n **enchantress** n fem

enchilada [en-chill-**lah**-duh] n Mexican dish consisting of a tortilla filled with meat, served with chili sauce **the whole enchilada** slang the

encircle v form a circle around **encirclement** n

enclave n part of a country entirely surrounded by foreign territory

enclose v 1 surround completely 2 include along with something else **enclosure** n

encomium n, pl -**miums**, -**mia** formal expression of praise

encompass v 1 surround 2 include comprehensively

encore interj 1 again, once more ▷ n 2 extra performance due to enthusiastic demand

encounter v 1 meet unexpectedly 2 be faced with ▷ n 3 unexpected meeting 4 contest

encourage v 1 inspire with confidence 2 spur on **encouragement** n

encroach v intrude gradually on a person's rights or land **encroachment** n

encrust v cover with a layer of something

encrypt v put (a message) into code

encumber v hamper or burden **encumbrance** n impediment

encyclical [en-**sik**-lik-kl] n letter sent by the Pope to all bishops

encyclopedia, encyclopaedia n book or set of books containing facts about many subjects, usually in alphabetical order **encyclopedic** or **encyclopaedic** adj comprehensive

end n 1 furthest point or part 2 limit 3 last part of something 4 act of bringing or coming to a finish 5 fragment 6 lit death 7 destruction 8 purpose 9 sports either of the two defended areas of a playing field ▷ v 10 bring or come to a finish **make ends meet** have just enough money for one's needs **ending** n **endless** adj

endways adv having the end forwards or upwards

endanger v put in danger

endear v cause to be liked **endearing** adj **endearment** n affectionate word or phrase

endeavour v 1 try ▷ n 2 effort

endemic adj present within a localized area or peculiar to a particular group of people

endive n curly-leaved plant used in salads

endocrine adj relating to the glands which secrete hormones directly into the bloodstream

endogenous [en-**dodge**-in-uss] adj originating from within

endorse v 1 give approval to 2 sign the back of (a cheque) 3 record a conviction on (a driving licence) **endorsement** n

endow v provide permanent income for **endowed with** provided with **endowment** n

endure v 1 bear (hardship) patiently 2 last for a long time **endurable** adj **endurance** n act or power of enduring

enema [en-im-a] n medicine injected into the rectum to empty the bowels

enemy n, pl -**mies** hostile person or nation, opponent

energy n, pl -**gies** 1 capacity for intense activity 2 capacity to do work and overcome resistance 3 source of power, such as electricity **energetic** adj **energetically** adv **energize** v give vigour to **energy drink** soft drink supposed to boost the drinker's energy levels

enervate v weaken, deprive of vigour **enervation** n

enfant terrible [on-fon ter-**reeb**-la] *n, pl* **enfants terribles** *French* clever but unconventional or indiscreet person

enfeeble *v* weaken **enfeeblement** *n*

enfold *v* **1** cover by wrapping something around **2** embrace

enforce *v* **1** impose obedience (to a law etc.) **2** impose (a condition) **enforceable** *adj* **enforcement** *n* **enforcer** *n* **1** person who enforces something **2** *hockey* tough player meant to intimidate the opposition and protect teammates

enfranchise *v* grant (a person) the right to vote **enfranchisement** *n*

engage *v* **1** take part, participate **2** involve (a person or his or her attention) intensely **3** employ (a person) **4** bring (a mechanism) into operation **5** *mil* begin a battle with **engaged** *adj* **1** pledged to be married **2** in use **engagement** *n* **engaging** *adj* charming

engender *v* produce, cause to occur

engine *n* **1** any machine which converts energy into mechanical work **2** railway locomotive **engineer** *n* **1** person trained in any branch of engineering ▷ *v* **2** plan in a clever manner **3** design or construct as an engineer **engineering** *n* profession of applying scientific principles to the design and construction of engines, automobiles, buildings, or machines

English *n* **1** language of Britain, the US, Canada, most parts of the Commonwealth, and certain other countries ▷ *adj* **2** relating to England

the English the people of England **English muffin** small, round, flat baked yeast roll, usually served toasted and split

engrave *v* **1** carve (a design) onto a hard surface **2** fix deeply in the mind **engraver** *n* **engraving** *n* print made from an engraved plate

engross [en-**groce**] *v* occupy the attention of (a person) completely

engulf *v* cover or surround completely

enhance *v* increase in quality, value, or attractiveness **enhancement** *n*

enigma *n* puzzling thing or person **enigmatic** *adj* **enigmatically** *adv*

enjoin *v* order (someone) to do something

enjoy *v* **1** receive pleasure from **2** have or experience something: *enjoy excellent health* **enjoy oneself** have a good time **enjoyable** *adj* **enjoyment** *n*

enlarge *v* **1** make or grow larger **2** (foll. by *on* or *upon*) speak or write about in greater detail **enlargement** *n*

enlighten *v* give information to **enlightenment** *n*

enlist *v* **1** enter the armed forces **2** obtain the support of **enlistment** *n*

enliven *v* make lively or cheerful

en masse *adv French* in a group, all together

enmesh *v* entangle

enmity *n, pl* -**ties** ill will, hatred

ennoble *v* make noble, elevate **ennoblement** *n*

ennui [on-**nwee**] *n* boredom, dissatisfaction

enormous *adj* very big, vast **enormity** *n, pl* -**ties 1** great wickedness **2** gross offence

3 *informal* great size

enough *adj* **1** as much or as many as necessary ▷ *n* **2** sufficient quantity ▷ *adv* **3** sufficiently **4** just adequately

en passant [on pass-on] *adv French* in passing, by the way

enquire *v* same as **inquire** ► **enquiry** *n*

enrapture *v* fill with delight

enrich *v* **1** improve in quality **2** make rich

enrol *v* **-rolling, -rolled** (cause to) become a member **enrolment** *n*

en route *adv French* on the way

ensconce *v* settle firmly or comfortably

ensemble [on-**som**-bl] *n* **1** all the parts of something taken together **2** complete outfit of clothes **3** company of actors or dancers **4** *music* group of musicians playing together

enshrine *v* cherish or treasure

ensign *n* **1** naval flag **2** banner **3** *US* naval officer

ensilage *n* **1** process of storing green fodder in a silo **2** silage

enslave *v* make a slave of (someone) **enslavement** *n*

ensnare *v* catch in or as if in a snare

ensue *v* come next, result

en suite *adv French* as part of a set or single unit

ensure *v* **1** make certain or sure **2** make safe or protect

entail *v* bring about or impose inevitably

entangle *v* catch or involve in or as if in a tangle **entanglement** *n*

entente [on-**tont**] *n* friendly understanding between nations

enter *v* **1** come or go in **2** join **3** become involved or take part (in) **4** record (an item) in a journal etc. **5** begin: *enter upon a new career* **entrance**

n **1** way into a place **2** act of entering **3** right of entering

entrant *n* person who enters a university, contest, etc.

entry *n, pl* **-tries 1** entrance **2** entering **3** item entered in a journal etc.

enteric [en-**ter**-ik] *adj* intestinal **enteritis** [en-ter-**rite**-iss] *n* inflammation of the intestine, causing diarrhea

enterprise *n* **1** company or firm **2** bold or difficult undertaking **3** boldness and energy **enterprising** *adj* full of boldness and initiative

entertain *v* **1** amuse **2** receive as a guest **3** consider (an idea) **entertainer** *n* **entertainment** *n*

enthral [en-**thrawl**] *v* **-thralling, -thralled** hold the attention of **enthralling** *adj* **enthralment** *n*

enthusiasm *n* ardent interest, eagerness **enthuse** *v* (cause to) show enthusiasm **enthusiast** *n* ardent supporter of something **enthusiastic** *adj* **enthusiastically** *adv*

entice *v* attract by exciting hope or desire, tempt **enticement** *n*

entire *adj* **1** complete **2** unbroken or undivided **entirely** *adv* **entirety** *n*

entitle *v* **1** give a right to **2** give a title to **entitlement** *n*

entity *n, pl* **-ties** separate distinct thing

entomology *n* study of insects **entomological** *adj* **entomologist** *n*

entourage [on-**toor**-ahzh] *n* group of people who assist an important person

entrails *pl n* **1** intestines **2** innermost parts of something

entrance[1] *n* see **enter**

entrance² v **1** delight **2** put into a trance

entreat v ask earnestly **entreaty** n, pl **-ties** earnest request

entrée [on-tray] n **1** right of admission **2** main course of a meal **3** dish served before a main course

entrench v **1** establish firmly **2** establish in a fortified position with trenches **entrenchment** n

entrepreneur n business person who attempts to make a profit by risk and initiative

entropy [en-trop-ee] n formal lack of organization

entrust v put into the care or protection of

entwine v twist together or around

enumerate v name one by one **enumeration** n

enunciate v **1** pronounce clearly **2** proclaim **enunciation** n

envelop v **enveloping, enveloped** wrap up, enclose **envelopment** n

envelope n folded gummed paper cover for a letter

environment [en-vire-on-ment] n external conditions and surroundings in which people, animals, or plants live **environmental** adj **environmentalist** n person concerned with the protection of the natural environment

environs pl n surrounding area, esp. of a town

envisage v **1** visualize **2** conceive of as a possibility

envoy n **1** messenger **2** diplomatic minister ranking below an ambassador

envy v **-vying, -vied 1** grudge (another's good fortune, success, or qualities) ▷ n **2** bitter contemplation of another's good fortune

enviable adj arousing envy, fortunate **envious** adj full of envy

enzyme n any of a group of complex proteins that act as catalysts in specific biochemical reactions

Eolithic adj of the early part of the Stone Age

eon, aeon [ee-on] n immeasurably long period of time

EPA Environmental Protection Agency

epaulette n shoulder ornament on a uniform

ephemeral adj short-lived

epic n **1** long poem, book, or film about heroic events or actions ▷ adj **2** very impressive or ambitious

epicentre n point on the earth's surface immediately above the origin of an earthquake

epicure n person who enjoys good food and drink **epicurism** n **epicurean** adj **1** devoted to sensual pleasures, esp. food and drink ▷ n **2** epicure **epicureanism** n

epidemic n **1** widespread occurrence of a disease **2** rapid spread of something

epidermis n outer layer of the skin

epidural [ep-pid-**dure**-al] adj, n (of) spinal anesthetic injected to relieve pain during childbirth

epiglottis n thin flap that covers the opening of the larynx during swallowing

epigram n short witty remark or poem **epigrammatic** adj

epigraph n **1** quotation at the start of a book **2** inscription

epilepsy n disorder of the nervous system causing loss of consciousness and sometimes convulsions **epileptic** n offensive **1** person who has epilepsy ▷ *adj* **2** of or having epilepsy

epilogue *n* short speech or poem at the end of a literary work, esp. a play

Epiphany *n* Christian festival held on January 6 commemorating the manifestation of Christ to the Magi

episcopal [ip-**piss**-kop-al] *adj* of or governed by bishops **episcopalian** *n* **1** member of an episcopal Church ▷ *adj* **2** advocating Church government by bishops

episode *n* **1** incident in a series of incidents **2** section of a serialized book, television programme, etc. **episodic** *adj* occurring at irregular intervals

epistemology [ip-iss-stem-ol-a-jee] *n* study of the source, nature, and limitations of knowledge **epistemological** *adj* **epistemologist** *n*

epistle *n* letter, esp. of an apostle **epistolary** *adj*

epitaph *n* **1** commemorative inscription on a tomb **2** commemorative speech or passage

epithet *n* descriptive word or name

epitome [ip-**pit**-a-mee] *n* typical example **epitomize** *v* be the epitome of

epoch [**ee**-pok] *n* period of notable events **epoch-making** *adj* extremely important

eponymous [ip-**pon**-im-uss] *adj* after whom a book, play, etc. is named

equable [**ek**-wab-bl] *adj* even-tempered **equably** *adv*

equal *adj* **1** identical in size, quantity, degree, etc. **2** having identical rights or status **3** evenly balanced **4** (foll. by *to*) having the necessary ability (for) ▷ *n* **5** person or thing equal to another ▷ *v* **equalling, equalled 6** be equal to **equally** *adv* **equality** *n* state of being equal **equalize** *v* **1** make or become equal **2** reach the same score as one's opponent **equalization** *n* **equal opportunity** nondiscrimination as to sex, race, etc. in employment

equanimity *n* calmness of mind

equate *v* make or regard as equivalent **equation** *n* **1** mathematical statement that two expressions are equal **2** act of equating

equator *n* imaginary circle round the earth, equidistant from the poles **equatorial** *adj*

equerry [**ek**-kwer-ee] *n, pl* -ries officer who acts as an attendant to a member of a royal family

equestrian *adj* of horses and riding

equidistant *adj* equally distant

equilateral *adj* having equal sides

equilibrium *n, pl* -ria steadiness or stability

equine *adj* of or like a horse

equinox *n* time of year when day and night are of equal length **equinoctial** *adj*

equip *v* **equipping, equipped** provide with what is needed **equipment** *n* **1** set of tools or devices used for a particular purpose **2** equipping

equipoise *n* perfect balance

equity *n, pl* -ties **1** fairness **2** legal system, founded on the principles of natural justice, that supplements common law **equities 3** interest of ordinary shareholders in a company **equitable** *adj* fair, just **equitably** *adv*

equivalent n 1 something having the same function as something else ▷ adj 2 equal in value 3 having the same meaning or result **equivalence** n

equivocal adj 1 ambiguous 2 deliberately misleading 3 of doubtful character or sincerity **equivocally** adv **equivocate** v use equivocal words to mislead people **equivocation** n

ER Queen Elizabeth

era n period of time considered as distinctive

ERA baseball earned run average: rating of a pitcher's performance, equal to the number of earned runs allowed per nine innings pitched

eradicate v destroy completely **eradication** n

erase v 1 rub out 2 remove **eraser** n object for erasing something written **erasure** n 1 erasing 2 place or mark where something has been erased

ere prep, conj poetic before

e-reader n portable device that allows users to download and read texts in electronic form

erect v 1 build 2 set up ▷ adj 3 upright 4 (of the penis, clitoris, or nipples) rigid as a result of sexual excitement **erectile** adj capable of becoming erect from sexual excitement **erection** n

erg n unit of work or energy

ergonomics n study of the relationship between workers and their environment **ergonomic** adj

ergot n 1 fungal disease of cereal 2 dried fungus used in medicine

ermine n 1 stoat in northern regions 2 its white winter fur

erode v wear away **erosion** n

erogenous [ir-**roj**-in-uss] adj sexually sensitive or arousing

erotic adj relating to sexual pleasure or desire **eroticism** n **erotica** n sexual literature or art

err v formal make a mistake **erratum** n, pl -ta error in writing or printing **erroneous** adj incorrect, mistaken **error** n something considered to be wrong or incorrect

errand n short trip to do something for someone

errant adj behaving in a manner considered to be unacceptable

erratic adj irregular or unpredictable **erratically** adv

ersatz [**air**-zats] adj made in imitation: ersatz coffee

erstwhile adj former

erudite [**air**-rude-ite] adj having great academic knowledge **erudition** n

erupt v 1 eject (steam, water, or volcanic material) violently 2 (of a blemish) appear on the skin 3 burst forth suddenly and violently **eruption** n

erysipelas n acute skin infection causing purplish patches

escalate v increase in extent or intensity **escalation** n

escalator n moving staircase

escalope [**ess**-kal-lop] n thin slice of meat, esp. veal

escape v 1 get free (of) 2 avoid: escape attention 3 (of a gas, liquid, etc.) leak gradually 4 be forgotten by: the figure escapes me ▷ n 5 act of escaping 6 means of relaxation or relief **escapade** n mischievous adventure **escapee** n person who has escaped **escapism** n taking refuge in fantasy to avoid unpleasant reality **escapologist** n entertainer who specializes in freeing himself or herself from confinement **escapology** n

escarpment n steep face of

a ridge or mountain

eschew [iss-**chew**] v abstain from, avoid

escort n 1 people or vehicles accompanying another person for protection or as an honour 2 person who accompanies a person of the opposite sex to a social event ▷ v 3 act as an escort to

escudo [ess-**kyoo**-doe] n, pl -**dos** former monetary unit of Portugal

escutcheon n shield with a coat of arms **blot on one's escutcheon** stain on one's honour

Eskimo n old-fashioned, offensive a name applied to the Inuit and Yupik peoples

esoteric [ee-so-**ter**-rik] adj understood by only a small number of people with special knowledge

ESP extrasensory perception

esp. especially

espadrille [**ess**-pad-drill] n light canvas shoe with a braided cord sole

espalier [ess-**pal**-yer] n 1 shrub or fruit tree trained to grow flat 2 trellis for this

esparto n, pl -**tos** grass used for making rope etc.

especial adj formal special **especially** adv particularly

Esperanto n universal artificial language

espionage [**ess**-pyon-ahzh] n spying

esplanade n wide open road used as a public promenade

espouse v adopt or give support to (a cause etc.) **espousal** n

espresso n, pl -**sos** strong coffee made by forcing steam or boiling water through ground coffee beans

esprit [ess-**pree**] n spirit, liveliness **esprit de corps** [de **core**] pride in and loyalty to a group

espy v **espying, espied** catch sight of

Esq. esquire

esquire n courtesy title placed after a man's name

essay n 1 short literary composition 2 short piece of writing on a subject done as an exercise by a student ▷ v 3 attempt **essayist** n

essence n 1 most important feature of a thing which determines its identity 2 concentrated extract obtained by distillation: vanilla essence **essential** adj 1 vitally important 2 fundamental ▷ n 3 something essential **essentially** adv

EST Eastern Standard Time

establish v 1 set up on a permanent basis 2 make secure or permanent in a certain place, job, etc. 3 prove 4 cause to be accepted **establishment** n 1 act of establishing 2 commercial or other institution **the Establishment** group of people having authority within a society

estate n 1 landed property 2 large area of property development, esp. of new houses or factories 3 property of a deceased person **estate agent** Brit real estate agent **estate car** Brit station wagon

esteem v 1 think highly of 2 judge or consider ▷ n 3 high regard

ester n chem compound produced by the reaction between an acid and an alcohol

esthetic n, adj same as **aesthetic**

estimate v 1 calculate roughly 2 form an opinion about ▷ n 3 approximate calculation

4 opinion **5** statement from a workman etc. of the likely charge for a job **estimable** *adj* worthy of respect **estimation** *n* judgment, opinion

estranged *adj* **1** no longer living with one's spouse **2** having lost someone's affection and loyalty **estrangement** *n*

estuary *n, pl* **-aries** mouth of a river

ETA estimated time of arrival

etc. et cetera

et cetera [et **set**-ra] *n, v* **1** and the rest, and others **2** or the like **etceteras** *pl n* miscellaneous extra things or people

etch *v* **1** wear away or cut the surface of (metal, glass, etc.) with acid **2** imprint vividly (on someone's mind) **etching** *n*

eternal *adj* **1** without beginning or end **2** unchanging **eternally** *adv* **eternity** *n* **1** infinite time **2** timeless existence after death **eternity ring** ring given as a token of lasting affection

ether *n* **1** colourless sweet-smelling liquid used as an anesthetic **2** region above the clouds **ethereal** [eth-**eer**-ee-al] *adj* extremely delicate

ethic *n* **1** moral principle **ethics 2** code of behaviour **3** study of morals **ethical** *adj* **ethically** *adv*

ethnic *adj* **1** relating to a people or group that shares a culture, religion, or language **2** belonging or relating to such a group, esp. one that is a minority group in a particular place **ethnic cleansing** practice, by the dominant ethnic group in an area, of removing other ethnic groups by expulsion or extermination

ethnology *n* study of human races **ethnological** *adj* **ethnologist** *n*

ethos [**eeth**-oss] *n* distinctive spirit and attitudes of a people, culture, etc.

ethyl [**eth**-ill] *adj* of, consisting of, or containing the hydrocarbon group C_2 H_5 **ethylene** *n* poisonous gas used as an anesthetic and as fuel

etiolate [**ee**-tee-oh-late] *v* **1** become pale and weak **2** *botany* whiten through lack of sunlight

etiology *n* study of the causes of diseases

etiquette *n* conventional code of conduct

étude [**ay**-tewd] *n* short musical composition for a solo instrument, esp. intended as a technical exercise

etymology *n, pl* **-gies** study of the sources and development of words **etymological** *adj* **etymologist** *n*

EU European Union

eucalyptus, eucalypt *n* tree, mainly grown in Australia, that provides timber and gum

Eucharist [**yew**-kar-ist] *n* **1** Christian sacrament commemorating Christ's Last Supper **2** consecrated elements of bread and wine **Eucharistic** *adj*

eugenics [yew-**jen**-iks] *n* study of methods of improving the human race

eulogy *n, pl* **-gies** speech or writing in praise of a person **eulogize** *v* praise (a person or thing) highly in speech or writing **eulogist** *n* **eulogistic** *adj*

eunuch *n* castrated man, esp. (formerly) a guard in a harem

euphemism *n* inoffensive word or phrase substituted

for one considered offensive or upsetting **euphemistic** adj **euphemistically** adv

euphony n, pl **-nies** pleasing sound **euphonious** adj pleasing to the ear **euphonium** n brass musical instrument, tenor tuba

euphoria n sense of elation **euphoric** adj

Eurasian adj **1** of Europe and Asia **2** of mixed European and Asian parentage ▷ n **3** person of Eurasian parentage

eureka [yew-**reek**-a] interj exclamation of triumph at finding something

European n, adj (person) from Europe **European Union** association of a number of European nations for trade, etc.

Eustachian tube n passage leading from the ear to the throat

euthanasia n act of killing someone painlessly, esp. to relieve his or her suffering

evacuate v **1** send (someone) away from a place of danger **2** empty **evacuation** n **evacuee** n

evade v **1** get away from or avoid **2** elude **evasion** n **evasive** adj not straightforward: an evasive answer **evasively** adv

evaluate v find or judge the value of **evaluation** n

evanescent adj quickly fading away **evanescence** n

evangelical adj **1** of or according to gospel teaching **2** of certain Protestant sects which maintain the doctrine of salvation by faith ▷ n **3** member of an evangelical sect **evangelicalism** n

evangelist n **1** writer of one of the four gospels **2** travelling preacher **evangelism** n teaching and spreading of the Christian gospel **evangelize** v preach the gospel **evangelization** n

evaporate v **1** change from a liquid or solid to a vapour **2** disappear **evaporation** n **evaporated milk** thick unsweetened canned milk

eve n **1** evening or day before some special event **2** period immediately before an event **evensong** n evening prayer

even adj **1** flat or smooth **2** (foll. by with) on the same level (as) **3** constant **4** calm **5** equally balanced **6** divisible by two ▷ adv **7** equally **8** simply **9** nevertheless ▷ v **10** make even

evening n **1** end of the day or early part of the night **2** concluding period

even-strength adj hockey (of a goal etc.) occurring when both teams have the same number of players on the ice

event n **1** anything that takes place **2** actual outcome **3** contest in a sporting programme **eventful** adj full of exciting incidents **eventing** n riding competitions, usually involving cross-country, jumping, and dressage **eventual** adj ultimate **eventually** adv **eventuality** n possible event

ever adv **1** at any time **2** always **evergreen** n, adj (tree or shrub) having leaves throughout the year **everlasting** adj **evermore** adv all time to come

every adj **1** each without exception **2** all possible **everybody** pron every person **everyday** adj usual or ordinary **everyone** pron every person **everything** pron **everywhere** adv in all places

evict v legally expel (someone)

from his or her home
eviction n

evidence n 1 ground for
belief or disbelief 2 matter
produced before a lawcourt
to prove or disprove a point
▷ v 3 demonstrate, prove
in evidence on display
evident adj easily noticed or
understood **evidently** adv
evidential adj of, serving
as, or based on evidence
evidentially adv
evil n 1 wickedness 2 wicked
deed ▷ adj 3 morally bad
4 harmful 5 very unpleasant
evilly adv **evildoer** n wicked
person
evince v make evident
eviscerate v disembowel
evisceration n
evoke v call or summon up
(a memory, feeling, etc.)
evocation n **evocative** adj
evolve v 1 develop gradually
2 (of an animal or plant
species) undergo evolution
evolution n gradual change
in the characteristics of
living things over successive
generations, esp. to a more
complex form **evolutionary**
adj
ewe n female sheep
ewer n large jug with a wide
mouth
ex n informal former wife or
husband
ex- prefix 1 out of, outside, from:
exodus 2 former: ex-wife
exacerbate [ig-**zass**-er-
bate] v make (pain, emotion,
or a situation) worse
exacerbation n
exact adj 1 correct and
complete in every detail
2 precise, as opposed to
approximate ▷ v 3 demand
(payment or obedience)
exactly adv precisely, in
every respect **exactness** or
exactitude n **exacting** adj

making rigorous or excessive
demands
exaggerate v 1 regard or
represent as greater than is
true 2 make greater or more
noticeable **exaggeratedly** adv
exaggeration n
exalt v 1 praise highly
2 elevate in rank **exaltation**
n 1 feeling of great joy 2 act of
praising highly
exam n short for **examination**
examine v 1 inspect carefully
2 test the knowledge of
3 formally question someone
on oath **examination**
n 1 examining 2 test of a
candidate's knowledge or skill
examinee n **examiner** n
example n 1 specimen typical
of its group 3 person or
thing worthy of imitation
4 punishment regarded as a
warning to others
exasperate v cause great
irritation to **exasperation** n
excavate v 1 unearth buried
objects from (a piece of land)
methodically to learn about
the past 2 make (a hole)
in solid matter by digging
excavation n **excavator**
n large machine used for
digging
exceed v 1 be greater than 2 go
beyond (a limit) **exceedingly**
adv very
excel v -**celling**, -**celled** 1 be
superior to 2 be outstandingly
good at something **excellent**
adj very good **excellence**
n **Excellency** n title
used to address a high-
ranking official, such as an
ambassador
except prep 1 (sometimes
foll. by for) other than, not
including ▷ v 2 not include
except that with the
exception that **excepting** prep
except **exception** n thing that
is excluded from or does not

conform to the general rule
exceptionable adj causing
offence **exceptional** adj 1 not
ordinary 2 much above the
average

excerpt n passage taken from
a book, speech, etc.

excess n 1 state or act of
exceeding the permitted
limits 2 immoderate amount
3 amount by which a thing
exceeds the permitted limits
excessive adj **excessively** adv

exchange v 1 give or receive
(something) in return for
something else ▷ n 2 act of
exchanging 3 thing given or
received in place of another
4 centre in which telephone
lines are interconnected
5 finance place where
securities or commodities are
traded 6 finance transfer of
sums of money of equal value
between different currencies
exchangeable adj

Exchequer n Brit government
department in charge of state
money

excise[1] n tax on goods
produced for the home
market

excise[2] v cut out or away
excision n

excite v 1 arouse to strong
emotion 2 arouse or evoke (an
emotion) 3 arouse sexually
excitement n **excitable** adj
easily excited **excitability** n

exclaim v speak suddenly,
cry out **exclamation**
n **exclamation mark**
punctuation mark (!)
used after exclamations
exclamatory adj

exclude v 1 leave out of
consideration 2 keep
out, leave out **exclusion**
n **exclusive** adj 1 catering
for a privileged minority
2 not shared 3 excluding
everything else ▷ n 4 story

reported in only one
newspaper **exclusively** adv
exclusiveness or **exclusivity**
n

excommunicate v exclude
from membership and the
sacraments of the Church
excommunication n

excoriate v 1 censure severely
2 strip skin from **excoriation**
n

excrement n waste matter
discharged from the body

excrescence n lump or
growth on the surface of an
animal or plant

excrete v discharge (waste
matter) from the body
excretion n **excreta** [ik-
skree-ta] n excrement
excretory adj

excruciating adj 1 agonizing
2 very intense **excruciatingly**
adv

exculpate v free from blame
or guilt

excursion n short journey,
esp. for pleasure

excuse n 1 explanation offered
to excuse (a fault etc.) ▷ v
2 put forward a reason or
justification for (a fault
etc.) 3 forgive (a person) or
overlook (a fault etc.) 4 make
allowances for 5 exempt
6 allow to leave **excusable** adj

ex-directory adj not listed
in a telephone directory by
request

execrable [eks-sik-rab-bl] adj
of very poor quality

execute v 1 put (a condemned
person) to death 2 perform
(a plan or action) 3 produce
(a work of art) 4 render (a
legal document) effective,
as by signing **execution**
n **executioner** n person
employed to execute
criminals **executor**
(**executrix**) n person
appointed to perform the

instructions of a will

executive *n* **1** person or group in an administrative position **2** branch of government responsible for carrying out laws etc. ▷ *adj* **3** having the function of carrying out plans, orders, laws, etc.

exegesis [eks-sij-**jee**-siss] *n*, *pl* **-ses** explanation of a text, esp. of the Bible

exemplar *n* **1** example **2** person or thing to be copied, model **exemplary** *adj* **1** being a good example **2** serving as a warning

exemplify *v* **-fying, -fied** **1** be an example of **2** show an example of **exemplification** *n*

exempt *adj* **1** not subject to an obligation etc. ▷ *v* **2** release from an obligation etc. **exemption** *n*

exequies [**eks**-sik-wiz] *pl n* funeral rites

exercise *n* **1** activity to train the body or mind **2** set of movements or tasks designed to improve or test a person's ability **3** performance of a function ▷ *v* **4** take exercise or perform exercises **5** make use of: *to exercise one's rights*

exert *v* use (influence, authority, etc.) forcefully or effectively **exert oneself** make a special effort **exertion** *n*

exeunt [**eks**-see-unt] *Latin* they go out: used as a stage direction

exfoliate *v* scrub away dead skin cells, esp. by washing with an abrasive lotion

ex gratia [eks **gray**-sha] *adj* given as a favour where no legal obligation exists

exhale *v* breathe out **exhalation** *n*

exhaust *v* **1** tire out **2** use up **3** discuss (a subject)

thoroughly ▷ *n* **4** gases ejected from an engine as waste products **5** pipe through which an engine's exhaust fumes pass **exhaustible** *adj* **exhaustion** *n* **1** extreme tiredness **2** exhausting **exhaustive** *adj* comprehensive **exhaustively** *adv*

exhibit *v* **1** show (a quality) **2** display to the public ▷ *n* **3** object exhibited to the public **4** *law* document or object produced in court as evidence **exhibitor** *n* **exhibition** *n* **1** public display of art, skills, etc. **2** exhibiting **exhibitionism** *n* **1** compulsive desire to draw attention to oneself **2** compulsive desire to display one's genitals in public **exhibitionist** *n*

exhilarate *v* make lively and cheerful **exhilaration** *n*

exhort *v* urge earnestly **exhortation** *n*

exhume [ig-**zyume**] *v* dig up (something buried, esp. a corpse) **exhumation** *n*

exigency *n*, *pl* **-cies** urgent demand or need **exigent** *adj*

exiguous *adj* scanty, meagre

exile *n* **1** prolonged, usu. enforced, absence from one's country **2** person banished or living away from his or her country ▷ *v* **3** expel from one's country

exist *v* **1** have being or reality **2** eke out a living **3** live **existence** *n* **existent** *adj*

existential *adj* of or relating to existence, esp. human existence **existentialism** *n* philosophical movement stressing the personal experience and responsibility of the individual, who is seen as a free agent **existentialist** *adj*, *n*

exit *n* **1** way out **2** going out

3 actor's going off stage ▷ v
4 go out **5** go offstage: used
as a stage direction

exocrine adj relating to a
gland, such as the sweat
gland, that secretes externally
through a duct

exodus [**eks**-so-duss] n
departure of a large number of
people **the Exodus** departure
of the Israelites from Egypt

ex officio [**eks** off-**fish**-ee-
oh] adv, adj Latin by right of
position or office

exonerate v free from
blame or a criminal charge
exoneration n

exorbitant adj (of prices,
demands, etc.) excessive,
immoderate **exorbitantly**
adv

exorcize v (attempt to) expel
(evil spirits) by prayers and
religious rites **exorcism** n
exorcist n

exotic adj **1** having a strange
allure or beauty **2** originating
in a foreign country ▷ n
3 non-native plant **exotically**
adv **exotica** pl n (collection of)
exotic objects

expand v **1** make or become
larger **2** spread out **3** (foll. by
on) enlarge (on) **4** become
more relaxed, friendly,
and talkative **expansion**
n **expanse** n uninterrupted
wide area **expansive** adj
1 friendly and talkative **2** wide
or extensive

expatiate [iks-**pay**-shee-ate]
v (foll. by on) speak or write at
great length (on) **expatiation**
n

expatriate [eks-**pat**-ree-it]
n **1** person living outside his
or her native country ▷ adj
2 living outside one's native
country **expatriation** n

expect v **1** regard as probable
2 look forward to, await
3 require as an obligation

expectation n **1** act or state
of expecting **2** something
looked forward to **3** attitude
of anticipation or hope

expectancy n **1** something
expected on the basis of an
average: *life expectancy* **2** feeling
of anticipation **expectant**
adj **1** expecting or hopeful
2 pregnant **expectantly** adv

expectorate v spit out
(phlegm etc.) **expectoration**
n **expectorant** n medicine
that helps to bring up phlegm
from the respiratory passages

expedient [iks-**pee**-dee-
ent] n **1** something that
achieves a particular purpose
▷ adj **2** suitable to the
circumstances, appropriate
expediency n

expedite v hasten the
progress of **expedition** n
1 organized journey, esp. for
exploration **2** people and
equipment comprising an
expedition **3** pleasure trip or
excursion **expeditionary** adj
relating to an expedition, esp.
a military one **expeditious**
adj prompt, speedy

expel v **-pelling, -pelled**
1 dismiss from a school etc.
permanently **2** drive out with
force **expulsion** n

expend v spend, use up
expendable adj able to be
sacrificed to achieve an
objective **expenditure** n
1 something expended, esp.
money **2** amount expended
expense n **1** cost **2** (cause
of) spending **expenses**
3 charges, outlay incurred
expensive adj high-priced

experience n **1** direct personal
participation **2** particular
incident, feeling, etc. that
a person has undergone
3 accumulated knowledge ▷ v
4 participate in **5** be affected
by (an emotion) **experienced**

adj skilful from extensive participation

experiment *n* **1** test to provide evidence to prove or disprove a theory **2** attempt at something new ▷ *v* **3** make an experiment **experimental** *adj* **experimentally** *adv* **experimentation** *n*

expert *n* **1** person with extensive skill or knowledge in a particular field ▷ *adj* **2** skilful or knowledgeable **expertise** [eks-per-**teez**] *n* special skill or knowledge

expiate *v* make amends for **expiation** *n*

expire *v* **1** finish or run out **2** *lit* die **3** breathe out **expiration** *n* **expiry** *n* end, esp. of a contract period

explain *v* **1** make clear and intelligible **2** account for **explanation** *n* **explanatory** *adj*

expletive [iks-**plee**-tiv] *n* swearword

explicable *adj* able to be explained **explicate** *v formal* explain **explication** *n*

explicit *adj* **1** precisely and clearly expressed **2** shown in realistic detail **explicitly** *adv*

explode *v* **1** burst with great violence, blow up **2** react suddenly with emotion **3** increase rapidly **4** show (a theory etc.) to be baseless **explosion** *n* **explosive** *adj* **1** tending to explode ▷ *n* **2** substance that causes explosions

exploit *v* **1** take advantage of for one's own purposes **2** make the best use of ▷ *n* **3** notable feat or deed **exploitation** *n* **exploiter** *n*

explore *v* **1** travel into (unfamiliar regions), esp. for scientific purposes **2** investigate **exploration** *n* **exploratory** *adj* **explorer** *n*

expo *n informal* exposition, large public exhibition

exponent *n* **1** person who advocates an idea, cause, etc. **2** skilful performer, esp. a musician **exponential** *adj informal* very rapid **exponentially** *adv*

export *n* **1** selling or shipping of goods to a foreign country **2** product shipped or sold to a foreign country ▷ *v* **3** sell or ship (goods) to a foreign country **exporter** *n*

expose *v* **1** uncover or reveal **2** make vulnerable, leave unprotected **3** subject (a photographic film) to light **expose oneself** display one's sexual organs in public **exposure** *n* **1** exposing **2** lack of shelter from the weather, esp. the cold **3** appearance before the public, as on television

exposé [iks-**pose**-ay] *n* bringing of a crime, scandal, etc. to public notice

exposition *n* see **expound**

expostulate *v* (foll. by *with*) reason (with), esp. to dissuade **expostulation** *n*

expound *v* explain in detail **exposition** *n* **1** explanation **2** large public exhibition

express *v* **1** put into words **2** show (an emotion) **3** indicate by a symbol or formula **4** squeeze out (juice etc.) ▷ *adj* **5** explicitly stated **6** (of a purpose) particular **7** of or for rapid transportation of people, mail, etc. ▷ *n* **8** fast train or bus stopping at only a few stations ▷ *adv* **9** by express delivery **expression** *n* **1** expressing **2** word or phrase **3** showing or communication of emotion **4** look on the face that indicates mood **5** *math* variable, function, or some combination of

these **expressionless** adj
expressive adj
expressionism n early 20th-
century artistic movement
which sought to express
emotions rather than
represent the physical world
expressionist n, adj
expropriate v deprive
an owner of (property)
expropriation n
expunge [iks-**sponge**] v
delete, erase, blot out
expurgate [eks-per-gate] v
remove objectionable parts
from (a book etc.)
exquisite adj 1 of extreme
beauty or delicacy 2 intense in
feeling **exquisitely** adv
extant adj still existing
extemporize v speak,
perform, or compose without
preparation
extend v 1 increase in size
or scope 2 draw out or be
drawn out, stretch 3 last for
a certain time 4 (foll. by to)
include 5 offer: extend one's
sympathy **extendable** adj
extension n 1 continuation or
additional part of a building
etc. 2 additional telephone
connected to the same line
as another 3 extending
extensive adj 1 covering
a large area 2 very great
in effect: extensive damage
extensor n muscle that
extends a part of the body
extent n length, area, or size
of something
extenuate v make (an offence
or fault) less blameworthy
extenuation n
exterior n 1 part or surface
on the outside 2 outward
appearance ▷ adj 3 of, on,
or coming from the outside
exterminate v destroy
(animals or people)
completely **extermination** n
exterminator n

external adj of, situated on,
or coming from the outside
externally adv
extinct adj 1 having died out
2 (of a volcano) no longer
liable to erupt **extinction** n
extinguish v 1 put out (a fire
or light) 2 remove or destroy
entirely **extinguisher** n
extirpate [eks-ter-pate] v
destroy utterly
extol v -tolling, -tolled
praise highly
extort v get (something) by
force or threats **extortion** n
extortionate adj (of prices)
excessive
extra adj 1 additional 2 more
than usual ▷ n 3 additional
person or thing 4 something
for which an additional
charge is made 5 films actor
hired for crowd scenes ▷ adv
6 unusually or exceptionally
extra- prefix outside or beyond
an area or scope: extrasensory;
extraterritorial
extract v 1 pull out by force
2 remove 3 derive 4 copy out
(an article, passage, etc.) from
a publication ▷ n 5 something
extracted, such as a passage
from a book etc. 6 preparation
containing the concentrated
essence of a substance:
beef extract **extraction** n
extractor n
extradite v send (an accused
person) back to his or her own
country for trial **extradition**
n
extramural adj connected
with but outside the normal
courses of a university or
college
extraneous [iks-**train**-ee-
uss] adj irrelevant
extraordinary adj 1 very
unusual 2 (of a meeting)
specially called to deal
with a particular subject
extraordinarily adv

extrapolate [iks-**trap**-a-late] *v* **1** infer (something not known) from the known facts **2** *math* estimate (a value of a function or measurement) beyond the known values by the extension of a curve **extrapolation** *n*

extrasensory *adj* **extrasensory perception** supposed ability to obtain information other than through the normal senses

extravagant *adj* **1** spending money excessively **2** going beyond reasonable limits **extravagance** *n* **extravaganza** *n* elaborate and lavish entertainment, display, etc.

extreme *adj* **1** of a high or the highest degree or intensity **2** immoderate **3** severe **4** farthest or outermost ▷ *n* **5** either of the two limits of a scale or range **extremely** *adv* **extremist** *n* **1** person who favours immoderate methods ▷ *adj* **2** holding extreme opinions **extremity** *n, pl* **-ties** **1** farthest point **2** extreme condition, as of misfortune **extremities 3** hands and feet **extreme sport** sport with a high risk of injury or death

extricate *v* free from complication or difficulty **extrication** *n*

extrovert *adj* **1** lively and outgoing **2** concerned more with external reality than inner feelings ▷ *n* **3** extrovert person

extrude *v* squeeze or force out **extrusion** *n*

exuberant *adj* **1** high-spirited **2** growing luxuriantly **exuberance** *n*

exude *v* **1** make apparent by mood or behaviour: *exude confidence* **2** ooze out as sweat or sap

exult *v* be joyful or jubilant **exultation** *n* **exultant** *adj*

exurb *n* region outside a suburb, where rich commuters live

eye *n* **1** organ of sight **2** often *pl* ability to see **3** external part of an eye **4** attention: *his new shirt caught my eye* **5** ability to judge or appreciate: *a good eye for detail* **6** one end of a sewing needle **7** dark spot on a potato from which a stem grows **8** small area of calm at the centre of a hurricane ▷ *v* **eyeing** *or* **eying, eyed 9** look at carefully or warily **eyeless** *adj* **eyelet** *n* **1** small hole for a lace or cord to be passed through **2** ring that strengthens this **eyeball** *n* ball-shaped part of the eye **eyebrow** *n* line of hair on the bony ridge above the eye **eyeglass** *n* lens for aiding defective vision **eyelash** *n* short hair that grows out from the eyelid **eyelid** *n* fold of skin that covers the eye when it is closed **eyeliner** *n* cosmetic used to outline the eyes **eye-opener** *n informal* something startling or revealing **eye shadow** coloured cosmetic worn on the upper eyelids **eyesight** *n* ability to see **eyesore** *n* ugly object **eyetooth** *n* canine tooth **eyewash** *n informal* nonsense **eyewitness** *n* person who was present at an event and can describe what happened

eyrie *n* **1** nest of an eagle **2** high isolated place

Ff

f *music* forte

F 1 Fahrenheit 2 farad 3 *chem* fluorine

fable *n* 1 story with a moral 2 legend 3 lie **fabled** *adj* made famous in legend

fabric *n* 1 knitted or woven cloth 2 framework or structure **fabricate** *v* 1 make or build 2 make up (a story or lie) **fabrication** *n* **fabricator** *n*

fabulous *adj* 1 *informal* excellent 2 astounding 3 told of in fables **fabulously** *adv*

façade [fas-**sahd**] *n* 1 front of a building 2 (false) outward appearance

face *n* 1 front of the head 2 facial expression 3 distorted expression 4 front or main side 5 dial of a clock 6 exposed area of coal or ore in a mine 7 dignity, self-respect 8 outward appearance ▷ *v* 9 look or turn towards 10 be opposite 11 be confronted by 12 provide with a surface **faceless** *adj* impersonal, anonymous **facing** *n* 1 lining or covering for decoration or reinforcement **facings** 2 contrasting collar and cuffs on a jacket **face-lift** *n* operation to tighten facial skin, to remove wrinkles **face-saving** *adj* maintaining dignity or self-respect **face up to** *v* accept (an unpleasant fact or reality) **face value** apparent worth or meaning

facet *n* 1 surface of a cut gem 2 aspect

facetious [fas-**see**-shuss] *adj* funny or trying to be funny, esp. at inappropriate times **facetiousness** *n*

facia *n*, *pl* -**ciae** same as **fascia**

facial *adj* 1 of the face ▷ *n* 2 beauty treatment for the face

facile [**fas**-sile] *adj* superficial and showing lack of real thought

facilitate *v* make easy **facilitation** *n*

facility *n*, *pl* -**ties** 1 ability to do things easily or well **facilities** 2 means or equipment for an activity

facsimile [fak-**sim**-ill-ee] *n* exact copy

fact *n* 1 event or thing known to have happened or existed 2 provable truth **facts of life** details of sex and reproduction **factual** *adj*

faction *n* 1 (dissenting) minority group within a larger body 2 dissension **factious** *adj* of or producing factions

factitious *adj* artificial

factor *n* 1 element contributing to a result 2 *math* one of the integers multiplied together to give a given number 3 level on a scale: *factor 15 suntan cream* **factorial** *n* product of all the integers from one to a given number **factorize** *v* calculate the factors of (a number)

factory *n*, *pl* -**ries** building where goods are manufactured

factotum *n* person employed to do all sorts of work

faculty *n, pl* **-ties 1** physical or mental ability **2** department in a university or college

fad *n* **1** short-lived fashion **2** whim **faddy** *or* **faddish** *adj*

fade *v* **1** (cause to) lose brightness, colour, or strength **2** vanish slowly **fade-in** *or* **fade-out** *n* gradual increase or decrease, as of vision or sound in a film or broadcast

faeces *pl n* same as **feces**

fag¹ *n* **1** *informal* boring task **2** *Brit* young public schoolboy who does menial chores for a senior boy ▷ *v* **3** (often foll. by *out*) *informal* tire **4** do menial chores in a public school

fag² *n offensive* male homosexual

faggot *n offensive* male homosexual

Fahrenheit [**far**-ren-hite] *adj* of a temperature scale with the freezing point of water at 32° and the boiling point at 212°

faience [**fie**-ence] *n* tin-glazed earthenware

fail *v* **1** be unsuccessful **2** stop operating **3** be or judge to be below the required standard in a test **4** disappoint or be useless to (someone) **5** omit or be unable to do (something) **6** go bankrupt ▷ *n* **7** instance of not passing an exam or test **without fail 1** definitely **2** regularly **failing** *n* **1** weak point ▷ *prep* **2** in the absence of **failure** *n* **1** act or instance of failing **2** unsuccessful person or thing

fain *adv obsolete* gladly

faint *adj* **1** lacking clarity, brightness, or volume **2** lacking conviction or force **3** feeling dizzy or weak ▷ *v* **4** lose consciousness temporarily ▷ *n* **5** temporary loss of consciousness

fair¹ *adj* **1** unbiased and reasonable **2** light in colour **3** beautiful **4** quite good **5** unblemished **6** (of weather) fine ▷ *adv* **7** fairly **8** absolutely **fairly** *adv* **1** as deserved, reasonably **2** moderately **3** to a great degree or extent **fairness** *n* **fairway** *n golf* smooth area between the tee and the green

fair² *n* **1** travelling entertainment with stalls and machines to ride on, etc. **2** exhibition of commercial or industrial products **fairground** *n* open space used for a fair

Fair Isle *n* intricate multicoloured knitted pattern

fairy *n, pl* **fairies 1** imaginary small creature with magic powers **2** *offensive* male homosexual **fairy godmother** person who helps in time of trouble **fairyland** *n* **fairy light** small coloured light used as decoration **fairy tale** *or* **fairy story 1** story about fairies or magic **2** unbelievable story or explanation

fait accompli [**fate** ak-**kom**-plee] *n French* something already done that cannot be altered

faith *n* **1** strong belief, esp. without proof **2** religion **3** complete confidence or trust **4** allegiance to a person or cause **faithful** *adj* **1** loyal **2** firm in support **3** accurate **faithfully** *adv* **faithless** *adj* disloyal or dishonest

fake *v* **1** cause (something) to appear real or more valuable by fraud **2** pretend to have (an illness, emotion, etc.) ▷ *n* **3** person, thing, or act that is not genuine ▷ *adj* **4** not genuine **faker** *n*

fakir [**fay**-keer] *n* **1** member of any Islamic religious order **2** Hindu holy man

falcon *n* small bird of prey **falconry** *n* **1** art of training falcons **2** sport of hunting with falcons **falconer** *n*

fall *v* **falling, fell, fallen 1** drop from a higher to a lower place through the force of gravity **2** collapse to the ground **3** decrease in number or quality **4** slope downwards **5** die in battle **6** be captured **7** pass into a specified condition **8** (of the face) take on a sad expression **9** yield to temptation **10** occur ▷ *n* **11** falling **12** thing or amount that falls **13** decrease in value or number **14** decline in power or influence **15** season between summer and winter **16** capture or overthrow **falls 17** waterfall **fall for** *v* **1** fall in love with **2** be taken in by **fall guy** *informal* **1** victim of a confidence trick **2** scapegoat **fallout** *n* radioactive particles spread as a result of a nuclear explosion

fallacy *n, pl* -**cies 1** false belief **2** unsound reasoning **fallacious** *adj*

fallible *adj* liable to error **fallibility** *n*

Fallopian tube *n* either of a pair of tubes through which egg cells pass from the ovary to the womb

fallow[1] *adj* (of land) plowed but left unseeded to regain fertility

fallow[2] *adj* **fallow deer** reddish-brown deer with white spots in summer

false *adj* **1** not true or correct **2** not genuine but intended to seem so **3** deceptive or misleading **falsely** *adv* **falseness** *or* **falsity** *n* **falsehood** *n* **1** quality of being untrue **2** lie **falsify** *v* -**fying, -fied** alter fraudulently **falsification** *n*

falsetto *n, pl* -**tos** voice pitched higher than one's natural range

falter *v* **1** lose power momentarily **2** be unsure **3** utter hesitantly **4** move unsteadily

fame *n* state of being widely known or recognized **famed** *adj* famous

familiar *adj* **1** well-known **3** acquainted **4** too friendly **5** intimate, friendly ▷ *n* **6** friend **7** demon supposed to attend a witch **familiarly** *adv* **familiarity** *n* **familiarize** *v* acquaint fully with a particular subject **familiarization** *n*

family *n, pl* -**lies 1** group of parents and their children **2** one's spouse and children **3** one's children **4** group descended from a common ancestor **5** group of related objects or beings ▷ *adj* **6** suitable for parents and children together **familial** *adj* **family planning** control of the number of children in a family, esp. through contraception

famine *n* severe shortage of food

famished *adj* very hungry

famous *adj* very well-known **famously** *adv informal* excellently

fan[1] *n* **1** hand-held or mechanical object used to create a current of air for ventilation or cooling ▷ *v* **fanning, fanned 2** blow or cool with a fan **3** spread out like a fan **fan belt** belt that drives a cooling fan in an automobile engine

fan[2] *n informal* devotee of a pop star, sport, or hobby

fanbase n body of admirers of a particular pop singer, sports team, etc.

fanatic n person who is excessively enthusiastic about something **fanatical** adj **fanatically** adv **fanaticism** n

fancy adj **-cier, -ciest** 1 elaborate, not plain 2 (of prices) higher than usual ▷ n, pl **-cies** 3 sudden irrational liking or desire 4 uncontrolled imagination ▷ v **-cying, -cied** 5 informal have a wish for 6 picture in the imagination 7 suppose 8 Brit informal be sexually attracted to **fancy oneself** informal have a high opinion of oneself **fanciful** adj 1 not based on fact 2 excessively elaborate **fancifully** adv **fancy dress** party costume representing a historical figure, animal, etc. **fancy-free** adj not in love

fandango n, pl **-gos** lively Spanish dance

fanfare n short loud tune played on brass instruments

fang n 1 snake's tooth which injects poison 2 long pointed tooth

fantasy n, pl **-sies** 1 far-fetched idea 2 imagination unrestricted by reality 3 daydream 4 fiction with a large fantasy content **fantasize** v indulge in daydreams **fantasia** n musical composition of an improvised nature **fantastic** adj 1 informal very good 2 unrealistic or absurd 3 strange or difficult to believe **fantastically** adv

FAQ computers frequently asked question or questions

far adv **farther** or **further, farthest** or **furthest** 1 at, to, or from a great distance 2 at or to a remote time 3 very much ▷ adj 4 remote in space or time **Far East** East Asia **far-fetched** adj hard to believe **Far North** the Arctic

farad n unit of electrical capacitance

farce n 1 boisterous comedy 2 ludicrous situation **farcical** adj ludicrous **farcically** adv

fare n 1 charge for a passenger's journey 2 passenger 3 food provided ▷ v 4 get on (as specified): we fared badly **farewell** interj 1 goodbye ▷ n 2 act of saying goodbye and leaving

farinaceous adj mealy, starchy

farm n 1 area of land for growing crops or rearing livestock ▷ v 2 cultivate (land) 3 rear (stock) **farmer** n **farmers' market** market at which farm produce is sold directly to the public by the producer **farmhouse** n **farm out** v send (work) to be done by others **farmstead** n farm and its buildings **farmyard** n

farrago [far-**rah**-go] n, pl **-gos, -goes** jumbled mixture of things

farrier n person who shoes horses

farrow n 1 litter of pigs ▷ v 2 (of a sow) give birth

fart taboo ▷ n 1 emission of gas from the anus ▷ v 2 break wind

farther, farthest adv, adj see **far**

farthing n former British coin equivalent to a quarter of a penny

farthingale n obsolete hoop worn under skirts

fascia [**fay**-shya] n, pl **-ciae** 1 flat surface above a shop window 2 outer surface of a dashboard

fascinate v 1 attract and interest strongly 2 make

motionless from fear or awe
fascinating *adj* **fascination** *n*
fascism [fash-iz-zum] *n*
right-wing political system
characterized by state control
and extreme nationalism
fascist *adj, n*
fashion *n* **1** style in clothes,
esp. the latest style **2** manner
of doing something ▷ *v*
3 form or make into a
particular shape **fashionable**
adj currently popular
fashionably *adv*
fast¹ *adj* **1** (capable of) acting
or moving quickly **2** done
in or lasting a short time
3 allowing rapid movement
4 (of a clock) showing a time
later than the correct time
5 dissipated **6** firmly fixed
7 steadfast ▷ *adv* **8** quickly
9 tightly, firmly **10** soundly,
deeply **fast food** food, such
as hamburgers, prepared and
served very quickly **fast-
track** *adj* taking the quickest
but most competitive route to
success: *fast-track executives*
fast² *v* **1** go without food, esp.
for religious reasons ▷ *n*
2 period of fasting
fasten *v* **1** make or become
firmly fixed or joined **2** close
by fixing in place or locking
3 (foll. by *on*) direct (one's
attention) towards **fastener**
or **fastening** *n* device that
fastens
fastidious *adj* **1** very fussy
about details **2** easily
disgusted **fastidiously** *adv*
fastidiousness *n*
fastness *n* fortress, safe place
fat *n* **1** extra flesh on the body
2 oily substance obtained
from animals or plants ▷ *adj*
fatter, fattest 3 having
excess flesh on the body
4 containing much fat **5** thick
6 profitable **fatness** *n* **fatten**
v (cause to) become fat **fatty**

adj containing fat **fathead** *n*
informal fool **fat-headed** *adj*
fatal *adj* causing death or
ruin **fatally** *adv* **fatality** *n*
death caused by an accident
or disaster
fatalism *n* belief that all
events are predetermined
and man is powerless to
change his destiny **fatalist** *n*
fatalistic *adj*
fate *n* **1** power supposed
to predetermine events
2 inevitable fortune that
befalls a person or thing
fated *adj* **1** destined **2** doomed
to death or destruction
fateful *adj* having important,
usu. disastrous, consequences
father *n* **1** male parent **2** man
who originates or founds
something **3** title of some
priests **4 Father** God **fathers**
5 ancestors ▷ *v* **6** be the father
of (offspring) **fatherhood**
n **fatherless** *adj* **fatherly**
adj **father-in-law** *n* father
of one's husband or wife
fatherland *n* one's native
country
fathom *n* **1** unit of
measurement of the depth
of water, equal to six feet ▷ *v*
2 understand **fathomable** *adj*
fathomless *adj* too difficult to
fathom
fatigue [fat-**eeg**] *n* **1** physical
or mental exhaustion caused
by exertion **2** weakening
of a material due to stress
3 soldier's nonmilitary duty
▷ *v* **4** tire out
fatuous *adj* foolish **fatuously**
adv **fatuity** *n*
faucet *n* valve with handle,
plug, etc. to regulate or stop
flow of fluid
fault *n* **1** responsibility for
something wrong **2** mistake
3 defect or flaw **4** *geology*
break in layers of rock **5** *tennis,
squash, etc.* invalid serve ▷ *v*

6 criticize or find mistakes in **at fault** guilty of error **find fault with** seek out minor imperfections in **to a fault** excessively **faulty** *adj* **faultily** *adv* **faultless** *adj* **faultlessly** *adv*

faun *n* (in Roman legend) rural god with goat's horns and legs

fauna *n, pl* **-nas, -nae** animals of a given place or time

faux pas [**foe pah**] *n, pl* **faux pas** social blunder

favour *n* **1** goodwill, approval **2** act of goodwill or generosity **3** partiality ▷ *v* **4** prefer **5** regard or treat with especial kindness **6** support or advocate **7** *informal* resemble **favourable** *adj* **1** encouraging **2** giving consent **3** useful or beneficial **favourably** *adv* **favourite** *n* **1** preferred person or thing **2** *sports* competitor expected to win ▷ *adj* **3** most liked **favouritism** *n* practice of unfairly favouring one person or group

fawn[1] *n* **1** young deer ▷ *adj* **2** light yellowish-brown

fawn[2] *v* **1** (foll. by *on*) seek attention from (someone) by being obsequious **2** (of a dog) try to please by a show of extreme affection

fax *n* **1** electronic system for sending facsimiles of documents by telephone **2** document sent by this system ▷ *v* **3** send by this system

FBI *US* Federal Bureau of Investigation

FC Football Club

Fe *chem* iron

fealty *n obsolete* subordinate's loyalty to his ruler or lord

fear *n* **1** distress or alarm caused by impending danger or pain **2** cause of this ▷ *v* **3** be afraid of (something

or someone) **4** feel anxiety about (something) **fearful** *adj* **1** feeling fear **2** causing fear **3** *informal* very unpleasant **fearfully** *adv* **fearless** *adj* **fearlessly** *adv* **fearsome** *adj* terrifying

feasible *adj* able to be done, possible **feasibly** *adv* **feasibility** *n*

feast *n* **1** lavish meal **2** periodic religious celebration **3** something extremely pleasing ▷ *v* **4** eat a feast **5** (foll. by *on*) enjoy eating (something) **6** give a feast to **7** delight

feat *n* remarkable, skilful, or daring action

feather *n* **1** one of the barbed shafts forming the plumage of birds ▷ *v* **2** fit or cover with feathers **3** turn (an oar) edgeways **feather in one's cap** achievement one can be pleased with **feather one's nest** make one's life comfortable **feathered** *adj* **feathery** *adj* **featherbedding** *n* overprotection **featherweight** *n* **1** boxer weighing up to 126lb (professional) or 57kg (amateur) **2** insignificant person or thing

feature *n* **1** prominent or distinctive part **2** part of the face, such as the eyes **3** special article in a newspaper or magazine **4** main film in a cinema programme ▷ *v* **5** have as a feature or be a feature in **6** give prominence to **featureless** *adj*

Feb. February

febrile [**fee-brile**] *adj* feverish

February *n* second month

feces, faeces [**fee**-seez] *pl n* waste matter discharged from the anus **fecal** *or* **faecal** *adj*

feckless *adj* ineffectual or irresponsible

fecund *adj* fertile **fecundity** *n*

fed *v* past of **feed** ▸ **fed up** *informal* bored, dissatisfied

federal *adj* 1 of a system in which power is divided between one central government and several regional governments 2 of the central government of a federation **federalism** *n* **federalist** *n* **federate** *v* unite in a federation **federation** *n* 1 union of several states, provinces, etc. 2 association

fedora [fid-**or**-a] *n* man's soft hat with a brim

fee *n* 1 charge paid to be allowed to do something 2 payment for professional services

feeble *adj* 1 lacking physical or mental power 2 unconvincing **feebleness** *n* **feebly** *adv* **feeble-minded** *adj* mentally deficient

feed *v* **feeding, fed** 1 give food to 2 give (something) as food 3 eat 4 supply or prepare food for 5 supply (what is needed) ▸ *n* 6 act of feeding 7 food, esp. for babies or animals 8 *informal* meal **feeder** *n* 1 baby's bib 2 road or railway line linking outlying areas to the main traffic network **feedback** *n* 1 information received in response to something done 2 return of part of the output of an electrical circuit or loudspeaker to its source

feel *v* **feeling, felt** 1 have a physical or emotional sensation of 2 become aware of or examine by touch 3 believe ▸ *n* 4 act of feeling 5 way something feels 6 impression 7 sense of touch 8 instinctive aptitude **feeler** *n* 1 organ of touch in some animals 2 remark made to test others' opinion **feeling** *n* 1 emotional reaction 2 intuitive understanding 3 opinion 4 sympathy, understanding 5 ability to experience physical sensations 6 sensation experienced **feelings** 7 emotional sensitivities **feel like** wish for, want

feet *n* plural of **foot**

feign [**fane**] *v* pretend

feint[1] [**faint**] *n* 1 sham attack or blow meant to distract an opponent ▸ *v* 2 make a feint

feint[2] [**faint**] *n* narrow lines on ruled paper

feisty *adj informal* lively, resilient, and self-reliant

feldspar *n* hard mineral that is the main constituent of igneous rocks

felicity *n, pl* **-ties** 1 happiness 2 appropriate expression or style **felicitate** *v* congratulate **felicitation** *n* **felicitous** *adj*

feline *adj* 1 of cats 2 catlike ▸ *n* 3 animal of the cat family

fell[1] *v* past tense of **fall**

fell[2] *v* 1 knock down 2 cut down (a tree)

fell[3] *adj old-fashioned* fierce, terrible **one fell swoop** single action or occurrence

fell[4] *n* (in N England) a mountain, hill, or moor

felloe *n* (segment of) the rim of a wheel

fellow *n* 1 *informal* man or boy 2 comrade or associate 3 person in the same group or condition 4 member of a learned society or the governing body of a college ▸ *adj* 5 in the same group or condition **fellowship** *n* 1 sharing of aims or interests 2 group with shared aims or interests 3 feeling of friendliness 4 college research post

felon *n* person guilty of a felony **felony** *n, pl* **-nies**

serious crime **felonious** adj

felspar n same as **feldspar**

felt[1] v past of **feel**

felt[2] n matted fabric made by bonding fibres by pressure **felt-tip pen** pen with a writing point made from pressed fibres

fem. feminine

female adj **1** of the sex which bears offspring **2** (of plants) producing fruits ▷ n **3** female person or animal

feminine adj **1** of women **2** having qualities traditionally regarded as suitable for, or typical of, women **3** belonging to a particular class of grammatical inflection in some languages **femininity** n **feminism** n advocacy of equal rights for women **feminist** n, adj

femme fatale [fam fat-**tahl**] n, pl **femmes fatales** alluring woman who causes men distress

femur [**fee**-mer] n thighbone **femoral** adj of the thigh

fen n low-lying flat marshy land

fence n **1** barrier of posts linked by wire or wood, enclosing an area **2** slang dealer in stolen property ▷ v **3** enclose with or as if with a fence **4** fight with swords as a sport **5** avoid a question **fencing** n **1** sport of fighting with swords **2** material for making fences **fencer** n

fend v **fend for oneself** provide for oneself **fend off** v ward off

fender n **1** part of an automobile bodywork surrounding the wheels **2** soft but solid object hung over a ship's side to prevent damage when docking **3** low metal frame in front of a fireplace

feng shui [fung **shway**] n Chinese art of deciding the best design of a building, etc., in order to bring good luck

fennel n fragrant plant whose seeds, leaves, and root are used in cookery

fenugreek n Mediterranean plant grown for its pungent seeds

feral adj wild

ferment n **1** commotion, unrest ▷ v **2** undergo or cause to undergo fermentation **fermentation** n reaction in which an organic molecule splits into simpler substances, esp. conversion of sugar to alcohol

fern n flowerless plant with fine fronds

ferocious adj fierce, violent **ferocity** n

ferret n **1** tamed polecat used to catch rabbits or rats ▷ v **ferreting, ferreted 2** hunt with ferrets **3** search around **ferret out** v find by searching

ferric, ferrous adj of or containing iron

ferris wheel n large vertical fairground wheel with hanging seats for riding in

ferrule n metal cap to strengthen the end of a stick

ferry n, pl **-ries 1** boat for transporting people and vehicles ▷ v **-rying, -ried 2** carry by ferry **3** convey (goods or people) **ferryman** n

fertile adj **1** capable of producing young, crops, or vegetation **2** highly productive **fertility** n **fertilize** v **1** provide (an animal or plant) with sperm or pollen to bring about fertilization **2** supply (soil) with nutrients **fertilization** n **fertilizer** n

fervent, fervid adj intensely passionate and sincere

fervently adv **fervour** n intensity of feeling

fescue n pasture and lawn grass with stiff narrow leaves

festal adj festive

fester v 1 form or cause to form pus 2 rot, decay 3 become worse

festival n 1 organized series of special events or performances 2 day or period of celebration **festive** adj of or like a celebration **festivity** n, pl **-ties** 1 joyful celebration, merriment **festivities** 2 celebrations

festoon v hang decorations in loops

feta n white salty Greek cheese

fetch v 1 go after and bring back 2 be sold for 3 informal deal (a blow) **fetching** adj attractive **fetch up** v informal arrive or end up

fete, fête [fate] n 1 gala, bazaar, etc., usu. held outdoors ▷ v 2 honour or entertain regally

fetid adj stinking

fetish n 1 form of behaviour in which sexual pleasure is derived from looking at or handling an inanimate object 2 thing with which one is excessively concerned 3 object believed to have magical powers **fetishism** n **fetishist** n

fetlock n projection behind and above a horse's hoof

fetter n 1 chain or shackle for the foot **fetters** 2 restrictions ▷ v 3 restrict 4 bind in fetters

fettle n state of health or spirits

fetus [fee-tuss] n, pl **-tuses** embryo of a mammal in the later stages of development **fetal** adj

feud n 1 long bitter hostility between two people or groups ▷ v 2 carry on a feud

feudalism n medieval system in which vassals held land from a lord, and in return worked and fought for him **feudal** adj of or like feudalism

fever n 1 (illness causing) high body temperature 2 nervous excitement **fevered** adj **feverish** adj 1 suffering from fever 2 in a state of nervous excitement **feverishly** adv

few adj not many **a few** a small number **a good few** or **quite a few** several

fey adj 1 whimsically strange 2 clairvoyant

fez n, pl **fezzes** brimless tasselled cap, orig. from Turkey

ff music fortissimo

fiancé [fee-on-say] n man engaged to be married **fiancée** n fem

fiasco n, pl **-cos, -coes** ridiculous or humiliating failure

fiat [fee-at] n 1 arbitrary order 2 official permission

fib n 1 trivial lie ▷ v **fibbing, fibbed** 2 tell a fib **fibber** n

fibre n 1 thread that can be spun into yarn 2 threadlike animal or plant tissue 3 fibrous material in food 4 strength of character 5 essential substance or nature **fibrous** adj **fibreboard** n board made of compressed plant fibres **fibreglass** n material made of fine glass fibres **fibre optics** transmission of information by light along very thin flexible fibres of glass

fibroid [fibe-royd] n benign tumour derived from fibrous connective tissue **fibrositis** [fibe-roh-site-iss] n inflammation of muscle tissue, causing pain and stiffness

fibula [fib-yew-la] n, pl **-lae,**

-las slender outer bone of the lower leg **fibular** adj

fiche [feesh] n sheet of film for storing publications in miniaturized form

fickle adj changeable, inconstant **fickleness** n

fiction n 1 literary works of the imagination, such as novels 2 invented story **fictional** adj **fictionalize** v turn into fiction **fictitious** adj 1 not genuine 2 of or in fiction

fiddle n 1 violin 2 informal dishonest action or scheme ▷ v 3 play the violin 4 move or touch something restlessly 5 falsify (accounts) **fiddling** adj trivial **fiddly** adj awkward to do or use **fiddlehead** n edible coiled tip of young fern frond

fidelity n 1 faithfulness 2 accuracy in detail 3 quality of sound reproduction

fidget v 1 move about restlessly ▷ n 2 person who fidgets **fidgets** 3 restlessness **fidgety** adj

fiduciary [fid-yew-sheer-ee] adj 1 relating to a trust or trustee ▷ n, pl -aries 2 trustee

fief [feef] n hist land granted by a lord in return for war service

field n 1 enclosed piece of agricultural land 2 marked off area for sports 3 area rich in a specified natural resource 4 sphere of knowledge or activity 5 place away from the laboratory or classroom where practical work is done 6 all the competitors in a competition 7 all the competitors except the favourite 8 battlefield 9 area over which electric, gravitational, or magnetic force is exerted 10 background, as of a flag ▷ v 11 sports catch and return (a ball) 12 sports send a (player or team) on to the field 13 sports

play as a fielder 14 deal with (a question) successfully **fielder** n sports player whose task is to field the ball **field day** day or time of exciting activity **field events** throwing and jumping events in athletics **field glasses** binoculars **field hockey** game similar to hockey played on a field with a ball and curved sticks **field marshal** army officer of the highest rank **field sports** hunting, shooting, and fishing **fieldwork** n investigation made in the field as opposed to the classroom or the laboratory

fiend [feend] n 1 evil spirit 2 cruel or wicked person 3 informal person devoted to something: fresh-air fiend **fiendish** adj 1 cruel 2 informal cunning 3 informal very difficult **fiendishly** adv

fierce adj 1 wild or aggressive 2 intense 3 turbulent **fiercely** adv **fierceness** n

fiery [fire-ee] adj **fierier, fieriest** 1 consisting of or like fire 2 easily angered 3 (of food) very spicy

fiesta n religious festival, carnival

fife n small high-pitched flute

fifth, fifteen, fifteenth, fifty, fiftieth n, adj see **five**

fig n 1 soft pear-shaped fruit 2 tree bearing it

fight v **fighting, fought** 1 struggle (against) in battle or physical combat 2 struggle to overcome someone or obtain something 3 carry on (a battle or struggle) 4 make (a way) by fighting ▷ n 5 aggressive conflict between two (groups of) people 6 quarrel or contest 7 resistance 8 boxing match **fighter** n 1 boxer 2 determined person 3 aircraft designed to destroy other aircraft **fight off** v **1** repulse **2** struggle to avoid

figment n **figment of one's imagination** imaginary thing

figure n **1** numerical symbol **2** amount expressed in numbers **3** bodily shape **4** well-known person **5** representation in painting or sculpture of a human form **6** diagram or illustration **7** set of movements in dancing or skating **8** math any combination of lines, planes, points, or curves ▷ v **9** consider, conclude **10** (usu. foll. by in) be included (in) **11** calculate **figure of speech** expression in which words do not have their literal meaning **figurative** adj (of language) abstract, imaginative, or symbolic **figuratively** adv **figurine** n statuette **figurehead** n **1** nominal leader **2** carved bust at the bow of a ship **figure out** v solve or understand

filament n **1** fine wire in a light bulb that gives out light **2** fine thread

filbert n hazelnut

filch v steal (small amounts)

file¹ n **1** box or folder used to keep documents in order **2** documents in a file **3** information about a person or subject **4** line of people one behind the other **5** computers organized collection of related material ▷ v **6** place (a document) in a file **7** place (a legal document) on official record **8** bring a lawsuit, esp. for divorce **9** walk or march in a line **file sharing** sharing computer data on a network, esp. the internet

file² n **1** tool with a roughened blade for smoothing or

shaping ▷ v **2** shape or smooth with a file **filings** pl n shavings removed by a file

filial adj of or befitting a son or daughter

filibuster v **1** obstruct legislation by making long speeches ▷ n **2** act of filibustering **3** person who filibusters

filigree n **1** delicate ornamental work of gold or silver wire ▷ adj **2** made of filigree

Filipino adj **1** of the Philippines ▷ n **2** (**Filipina**) person from the Philippines

fill v **1** make or become full **2** occupy completely **3** plug (a gap) **4** satisfy (a need) **5** hold and perform the duties of (a position) **6** appoint to (a job or position) **one's fill** sufficient for one's needs or wants **filler** n substance that fills a gap or increases bulk

filling n **1** substance that fills a gap or cavity, esp. in a tooth ▷ adj **2** (of food) substantial and satisfying **filling station** garage selling gasoline, oil, etc.

fillet n **1** boneless piece of meat or fish ▷ v **filleting, filleted 2** remove the bones from

fillip n something that adds stimulation or enjoyment

filly n, pl -lies young female horse

film n **1** sequence of images projected on a screen, creating the illusion of movement **2** story told in such a sequence of images **3** thin strip of light-sensitive cellulose used to make photographic negatives and transparencies **4** thin sheet or layer ▷ v **5** photograph with a movie or video camera **6** make a film of (a scene, story, etc.) **7** cover or become covered with a thin layer ▷ *adj* **8** connected with cinema **filmy** *adj* very thin, delicate **film strip** set of pictures on a strip of film, projected separately as slides

filter *n* **1** material or device permitting fluid to pass but retaining solid particles **2** device that blocks certain frequencies of sound or light **3** traffic signal that allows vehicles to turn either left or right while the main signals are at red ▷ *v* **4** pass slowly or faintly **5** remove impurities from (a substance) with a filter **filtrate** *n* **1** filtered gas or liquid ▷ *v* **2** remove impurities with a filter **filtration** *n*

filth *n* **1** disgusting dirt **2** offensive material or language **filthy** *adj* **filthily** *adv* **filthiness** *n*

fin *n* **1** projection from a fish's body enabling it to balance and swim **2** vertical tailplane of an aircraft

finagle [fin-**nay**-gl] *v* get or achieve by craftiness or trickery

final *adj* **1** at the end **2** having no possibility of further change, action, or discussion ▷ *n* **3** deciding contest in a competition **finals** **4** last examinations in an educational course **finally** *adv* **finality** *n* **finalist** *n* competitor in a final **finalize** *v* put into final form **finale** [fin-**nah**-lee] *n* concluding part of a dramatic performance or musical work

finance *v* **1** provide or obtain funds for ▷ *n* **2** management of money **3** (provision of) funds **finances** **4** money resources **financial** *adj* **financially** *adv* **financier** *n* person involved in large-scale financial business **financial**

year twelve-month period used for financial calculations

finch *n* small songbird with a stout bill

find *v* **finding**, **found** **1** discover by chance **2** discover by search or effort **3** become aware of **4** consider to have a particular quality **5** experience (a particular feeling) **6** *law* pronounce (the defendant) guilty or not guilty **7** provide, esp. with difficulty ▷ *n* **8** person or thing found, esp. when valuable **finder** *n* **finding** *n* conclusion from an investigation **find out** *v* **1** gain knowledge of **2** detect (a crime, deception, etc.)

fine¹ *adj* **1** very good **2** in good health **3** acceptable **4** thin or slender **5** in small particles **6** subtle or abstruse: *a fine distinction* **7** of delicate workmanship **8** (of weather) clear and dry **finely** *adv* **fineness** *n* **finery** *n* showy clothing **fine art** art produced to appeal to the sense of beauty **fine-tune** *v* make small adjustments to (something) so that it works really well

fine² *n* **1** payment imposed as a penalty ▷ *v* **2** impose a fine on

finesse [fin-**ness**] *n* **1** delicate skill **2** subtlety and tact

finger *n* **1** one of the four long jointed parts of the hand **2** part of a glove that covers a finger **3** quantity of liquid in a glass as deep as a finger is wide ▷ *v* **4** touch or handle with the fingers **fingering** *n* technique of using the fingers in playing a musical instrument **fingerboard** *n* part of a stringed instrument on which the fingers are placed **fingerprint** *n* **1** impression of the ridges on the tip of the finger ▷ *v* **2** take the fingerprints of (someone)

finial n archit ornament at the apex of a gable or spire

finicky adj 1 excessively particular, fussy 2 overelaborate

finis n Latin end: used at the end of a book

finish v 1 bring to an end, stop 2 use up 3 bring to a desired or completed condition 4 put a surface texture on (wood, cloth, or metal) 5 defeat or destroy ▷ n 6 end, last part 7 death or defeat 8 surface texture

finite [**fine**-ite] adj having limits in space, time, or size

fiord n same as **fjord**

fir n pyramid-shaped tree with needle-like leaves and erect cones

fire n 1 state of combustion producing heat, flames, and smoke 2 uncontrolled destructive burning 3 burning coal or wood, or a gas or electric device, used to heat a room 4 shooting of guns 5 intense passion, ardour ▷ v 6 operate (a weapon) so that a bullet or missile is released 7 informal dismiss from employment 8 excite 9 bake (ceramics etc.) in a kiln **firearm** n rifle, pistol, or shotgun **firebrand** n person who causes unrest **firebreak** n strip of cleared land to stop the advance of a fire **firebug** n informal person who deliberately starts fires **firedamp** n explosive gas, composed mainly of methane, formed in mines **fire department** organized body of people whose job it is to put out fires **fire drill** rehearsal of procedures for escape from a fire **fire engine** vehicle with apparatus for extinguishing fires **fire escape** metal staircase or ladder down the outside of a building for escape in the event of fire **firefly** n beetle that glows in the dark **fireguard** n protective grating in front of a fire **fire hall** building housing fire department **fire irons** tongs, poker, and shovel for tending a domestic fire **fireman** n member of a fire brigade **fireplace** n recess in a room for a fire **firepower** n mil amount a weapon or unit can fire **fire station** building where fire-fighting vehicles and equipment are stationed **firewall** n computers computer that prevents unauthorized access to a computer network from the internet **firework** n 1 device containing chemicals that is ignited to produce spectacular explosions and coloured sparks **fireworks** 2 show of fireworks 3 informal outburst of temper **firing squad** group of soldiers ordered to execute an offender by shooting

firkin n small cask

firm[1] adj 1 not soft or yielding 2 securely in position 3 definite 4 determined, resolute ▷ adv 5 in an unyielding manner: hold firm ▷ v 6 make or become firm **firmly** adv **firmness** n

firm[2] n business company

firmament n lit sky, heavens

first adj 1 earliest in time or order 2 graded or ranked above all others ▷ n 3 person or thing coming before all others 4 outset, beginning 5 first-class honours degree at university 6 lowest forward gear in a motor vehicle ▷ adv 7 before anything else 8 for the first time **firstly** adv **first aid** immediate medical assistance given in an emergency **first-class** *adj* **1** of the highest quality **2** excellent **first-hand** *adj, adv* (obtained) directly from the original source **first mate** *or* **first officer** officer of a merchant ship second in command to the captain **First Minister** premier of a Canadian province or territory or the Canadian prime minister **First Nations** Canadian aboriginal communities **First Peoples** Indian, Inuit, and Métis in Canada **first person** *grammar* category of verbs and pronouns used by a speaker to refer to himself or herself **first-rate** *adj* excellent **first-strike** *adj* (of a nuclear missile) for use in an opening attack to destroy enemy weapons

firth *n* narrow inlet of the sea

fiscal *adj* of government finances, esp. taxes

fish *n, pl* **fish, fishes 1** cold-blooded vertebrate with gills, that lives in water **2** its flesh as food ▷ *v* **3** try to catch fish **4** try to catch fish in (a specified place) **5** (foll. by *for*) grope for and find with difficulty **6** (foll. by *for*) seek indirectly **fisherman** *n* person who catches fish for a living or for pleasure **fishery** *n, pl* **-eries** area of the sea used for fishing **fishy** *adj* **1** of or like fish **2** *informal* suspicious or questionable **fish finger** oblong piece of fish covered in breadcrumbs **fish meal** dried ground fish used as animal feed or fertilizer **fishmonger** *n Brit* seller of fish **fishnet** *n* open mesh fabric resembling netting **fishwife** *n* coarse scolding woman

fishplate *n* metal plate joining one rail to the next on a track

fission *n* **1** splitting **2** *biol* asexual reproduction involving a division into two or more equal parts **3** splitting of an atomic nucleus with the release of a large amount of energy **fissionable** *adj* **fissile** *adj* **1** capable of undergoing nuclear fission **2** tending to split

fissure [fish-er] *n* long narrow cleft or crack

fist *n* clenched hand **fisticuffs** *pl n* fighting with the fists

fistula [fist-yew-la] *n* long narrow ulcer

fit¹ *v* **fitting, fitted 1** be appropriate or suitable for **2** be of the correct size or shape (for) **3** adjust so as to make appropriate **4** try (clothes) on and note any adjustments needed **5** make competent or ready **6** correspond with the facts or circumstances ▷ *adj* **7** appropriate **8** in good health **9** worthy or deserving ▷ *n* **10** way in which something fits **fitness** *n* **fitter** *n* **1** person skilled in the installation and adjustment of machinery **2** person who fits garments **fitting** *adj* **1** appropriate, suitable ▷ *n* **2** accessory or part **3** trying on of clothes for size **fittings 4** furnishings and accessories in a building **fitment** *n* detachable part of the furnishings of a room **fit in** *v* **1** give a place or time to **2** belong or conform **fit out** *v* provide with the necessary equipment

fit² *n* **1** sudden attack or convulsion, such as an epileptic seizure **2** sudden short burst or spell

fitful *adj* occurring in irregular spells **fitfully** *adv*

five *adj, n* one more than four **fives** *n* ball game resembling squash but played with bats or the hands **fifth** *adj, n* (of) number five in a series **fifth column** group secretly helping the enemy **fifteen** *adj, n* five and ten **fifteenth** *adj, n* **fifty** *adj, n* five times ten **fiftieth** *adj, n*

fix *v* **1** make or become firm, stable, or secure **2** repair **3** place permanently **4** settle definitely **5** direct (the eyes etc.) steadily **6** *informal* unfairly influence the outcome of ▷ *n* **7** *informal* difficult situation **8** ascertaining of the position of a ship by radar etc. **9** *slang* injection of a narcotic drug **fixed** *adj* **fixedly** [**fix**-id-lee] *adv* steadily **fixation** *n* preoccupation, obsession **fixated** *adj* obsessed **fixative** *n* liquid used to preserve or hold things in place **fixer** *n* **1** solution used to make a photographic image permanent **2** *slang* person who arranges things **fixture** *n* **1** permanently fitted piece of household equipment **2** person whose presence seems permanent **3** sports match or the date fixed for it **fix up** *v* **1** arrange **2** provide (with)

fizz *v* **1** give off small bubbles **2** make a hissing or bubbling noise ▷ *n* **3** hissing or bubbling noise **4** releasing of small bubbles of gas by a liquid **5** effervescent drink **fizzy** *adj* **fizziness** *n*

fizzle *v* make a weak hissing or bubbling sound **fizzle out** *v informal* come to nothing, fail

fjord [fee-**ord**] *n* long narrow inlet of the sea between cliffs, esp. in Norway

flab *n informal* unsightly body fat

flabbergast *v* amaze utterly

flabby *adj* **-bier, -biest** **1** loose or limp **2** having flabby flesh **flabbiness** *n*

flaccid [**flas**-sid] *adj* soft and limp **flaccidity** *n*

flag[1] *n* **1** piece of cloth attached to a pole as an emblem or signal ▷ *v* **flagging, flagged** **2** mark with a flag or sticker **3** (often foll. by *down*) signal (a vehicle) to stop by waving the arm **flagpole** *or* **flagstaff** *n* pole for a flag **flagship** *n* **1** admiral's ship **2** most important product of an organization

flag[2] *v* **flagging, flagged** lose enthusiasm or vigour

flag[3], **flagstone** *n* flat paving-stone **flagged** *adj* paved with flagstones

flagellate [**flaj**-a-late] *v* whip **flagellation** *n* **flagellant** *n* person who whips himself, esp. in religious penance

flageolet [flaj-a-**let**] *n* small instrument like a recorder

flagon *n* **1** wide bottle for wine or cider **2** narrow-necked jug for liquid

flagrant [**flayg**-rant] *adj* openly outrageous **flagrantly** *adv* **flagrancy** *n*

flail *v* **1** wave about wildly **2** beat or thrash ▷ *n* **3** tool formerly used for threshing grain by hand

flair *n* **1** natural ability **2** stylishness

flak *n* **1** anti-aircraft fire **2** *informal* adverse criticism

flake *n* **1** small thin piece, esp. chipped off something ▷ *v* **2** peel off in flakes **flaky** *adj* **flake out** *v informal* collapse or fall asleep from exhaustion

flambé [**flahm**-bay] *v* **flambéing, flambéed** cook or serve (food) in flaming brandy

flamboyant *adj* **1** very bright

and showy **2** behaving in a very noticeable, extravagant way **flamboyance** *n*

flame *n* **1** luminous burning gas coming from burning material ▷ *v* **2** burn brightly **3** become bright red **old flame** *informal* former sweetheart

flamenco *n, pl* **-cos 1** rhythmical Spanish dance accompanied by a guitar and vocalist **2** music for this dance

flamingo *n, pl* **-gos, -goes** large pink wading bird with a long neck and legs

flammable *adj* easily set on fire **flammability** *n*

flan *n* **1** egg custard with caramelized topping **2** *Brit* open sweet or savoury tart

flange *n* projecting rim or collar **flanged** *adj*

flank *n* **1** part of the side between the hips and ribs **2** side of a body of troops ▷ *v* **3** be at or move along the side of

flannel *n* **1** soft woollen fabric for clothing **2** small piece of cloth for washing the face and hands **3** *informal* evasive talk **flannels 4** trousers made of flannel ▷ *v* **-nelling, -nelled 5** *informal* talk evasively **flannelette** *n* cotton imitation of flannel

flap *v* **flapping, flapped 1** move back and forwards or up and down ▷ *n* **2** action or sound of flapping **3** piece of something attached by one edge only **4** *informal* state of excitement or panic

flapjack *n* thin pancake

flare *v* **1** blaze with a sudden unsteady flame **2** *informal* (of temper, violence, or trouble) break out suddenly **3** (of a skirt or trousers) become wider towards the hem ▷ *n* **4** sudden unsteady flame

5 signal light **flares 6** flared trousers **flared** *adj* (of a skirt or trousers) becoming wider towards the hem

flash *n* **1** sudden burst of light or flame **2** sudden occurrence (of intuition or emotion) **3** very short time **4** brief unscheduled news announcement **5** *photog* small bulb that produces an intense flash of light ▷ *v* **6** (cause to) burst into flame **7** (cause to) emit light suddenly or intermittently **8** move very fast **9** come rapidly (to mind or view) **10** *informal* display ostentatiously **11** *slang* expose oneself indecently ▷ *adj* **12** Also **flashy** vulgarly showy **flasher** *n slang* man who exposes himself indecently **flashing** *n* watertight material used to cover joins in a roof **flashback** *n* scene in a book, play, or film, that shows earlier events **flash flood** sudden short-lived flood **flashlight** *n* small portable battery-powered lamp **flash point 1** critical point beyond which a situation will inevitably erupt into violence **2** lowest temperature at which vapour given off by a liquid can ignite

flask *n* **1** vacuum flask **2** flat bottle for carrying alcoholic drink in the pocket **3** narrow-necked bottle

flat¹ *adj* **flatter, flattest 1** level and horizontal **2** even, smooth **3** (of a tire) deflated **4** outright **5** fixed **6** without variation or emotion **7** (of a battery) with no electrical charge **8** (of a drink) no longer fizzy **9** *music* below the true pitch ▷ *adv* **10** in or into a flat position **11** exactly **12** completely, absolutely **13** *music* too low in pitch ▷ *n* **14** flat surface

15 *music* symbol lowering the pitch of a note by a semitone **16** punctured automobile tire **17** level ground **18** mudbank exposed at low tide **flat out** with maximum speed or effort **flatly** *adv* **flatness** *n* **flatten** *v* **flatfish** *n* sea fish, such as the sole, which has a flat body **flat racing** horse racing over level ground with no jumps **flatscreen** *n* slim lightweight TV set or computer with a flat screen

flat² *n* Brit apartment

flatter *v* **1** praise insincerely **2** show to advantage **3** make (a person) appear more attractive in a picture than in reality **flatterer** *n* **flattery** *n*

flatulent *adj* suffering from, or caused by, excess gas in the intestines **flatulence** *n*

flaunt *v* display (oneself or one's possessions) arrogantly

flautist [**flaw**-tist] *n* flute player

flavour *n* **1** distinctive taste **2** distinctive characteristic or quality ▷ *v* **3** give flavour to **flavouring** *n* substance used to flavour food **flavourless** *adj*

flaw *n* **1** imperfection or blemish **2** mistake that makes a plan or argument invalid **flawed** *adj* **flawless** *adj*

flax *n* **1** plant grown for its stem fibres and seeds **2** its fibres, spun into linen thread **flaxen** *adj* (of hair) pale yellow

flay *v* **1** strip the skin off, esp. by whipping **2** criticize severely

flea *n* small wingless jumping bloodsucking insect **flea market** market for cheap goods **fleapit** *n informal* shabby cinema or theatre

fleck *n* **1** small mark, streak, or speck ▷ *v* **2** speckle

fled *v* past of **flee**

fledged *adj* **1** (of young birds) able to fly **2** (of people) fully trained **fledgling** or **fledgeling** *n* **1** young bird ▷ *adj* **2** new, inexperienced

flee *v* **fleeing, fled** run away (from)

fleece *n* **1** sheep's coat of wool **2** sheepskin used as a lining for coats etc. ▷ *v* **3** defraud or overcharge **fleecy** *adj* made of or like fleece

fleet¹ *n* **1** number of warships organized as a unit **2** number of vehicles under the same ownership

fleet² *adj* swift in movement **fleeting** *adj* rapid and soon passing **fleetingly** *adv*

Flemish *n* **1** one of two official languages of Belgium ▷ *adj* **2** of Flanders, in Belgium

flesh *n* **1** soft part of a human or animal body **2** *informal* excess fat **3** meat of animals as opposed to fish or fowl **4** thick soft part of a fruit or vegetable **5** human body as opposed to the soul ▷ *adj* **6** yellowish-pink **in the flesh** actually present **one's own flesh and blood** one's family **fleshly** *adj* **1** carnal **2** worldly **fleshy** *adj* **1** plump **2** like flesh **flesh wound** wound affecting only superficial tissue

fleur-de-lis, fleur-de-lys [flur-de-**lee**] *n, pl* **fleurs-de-lis, fleurs-de-lys** heraldic lily with three petals

flew *v* past tense of **fly¹**

flex *v* **1** bend ▷ *n* **2** Brit electric cord **flexible** *adj* **1** easily bent **2** adaptable **flexibly** *adv* **flexibility** *n* **flexitime** *n* system permitting variation in starting and finishing times of work

flibbertigibbet *n* flighty gossiping person

flick *v* **1** touch or strike lightly ▷ *n* **2** tap or quick stroke **flicks**

3 *slang* the cinema **flick knife** knife with a spring-loaded blade which shoots out when a button is pressed **flick through** v look at (a book or magazine) quickly or idly

flicker v **1** shine unsteadily or intermittently **2** move quickly to and fro ▷ n **3** unsteady brief light **4** brief faint indication

flier n see **fly**[1]

flight[1] n **1** act or manner of flying through the air **2** journey by air **3** group of birds or aircraft flying together **4** aircraft flying on a scheduled journey **5** set of stairs between two landings **6** stabilizing feathers or plastic fins on an arrow or dart **flightless** adj (of certain birds or insects) unable to fly **flight deck 1** crew compartment in an airliner **2** runway deck on an aircraft carrier **flight recorder** electronic device in an aircraft storing information about its flight

flight[2] n act of running away

flighty adj **flightier**, **flightiest** frivolous and fickle

flimsy adj **-sier, -siest 1** not strong or substantial **2** thin **3** unconvincing, weak **flimsily** adv **flimsiness** n

flinch v draw back or wince, as from pain **flinch from** v shrink from, avoid

fling v **flinging, flung 1** throw, send, or move forcefully or hurriedly ▷ n **2** spell of self-indulgent enjoyment **3** brief romantic or sexual relationship **fling oneself into** (start to) do with great vigour

flint n **1** hard grey stone **2** piece of this **3** small piece of an iron alloy producing a spark when struck, as in a cigarette

lighter **flinty** adj **1** cruel **2** of or like flint

flip v **flipping, flipped 1** flick **2** turn (something) over **3** *slang* fly into an emotional state (Also **flip one's lid**) ▷ n **4** snap or tap **5** alcoholic drink containing beaten egg ▷ adj **6** *informal* flippant **flipper** n **1** limb of a sea animal adapted for swimming **2** one of a pair of paddle-like rubber devices worn on the feet to help in swimming **flip-flop** n rubber-soled sandal held on by a thong between the big toe and the next toe **flip side** less important side of a record **flip through** v look at (a book or magazine) quickly or idly

flippant adj treating serious things lightly **flippantly** adv **flippancy** n

flirt v **1** behave amorously without emotional commitment **2** consider lightly, toy (with) ▷ n **3** person who flirts **flirtation** n **flirtatious** adj

flit v **flitting, flitted 1** move lightly and rapidly **2** *informal* depart hurriedly and secretly ▷ n **3** act of flitting

flitch n side of bacon

flitter v, n same as **flutter**

float v **1** rest on the surface of liquid **2** move lightly and freely **3** move about aimlessly **4** launch (a company) **5** offer for sale on the stock market **6** allow (a currency) to fluctuate against other currencies ▷ n **7** inflatable object used to help people to swim **8** indicator on a fishing line that moves when a fish bites **9** small delivery vehicle **10** motor vehicle carrying a tableau in a parade **11** sum of money used for minor expenses or to provide change **floating** adj **1** moving about,

changing: *floating population*
2 (of a voter) not committed
to one party **flotation** *n*
launching or financing of a
business enterprise

flocculent *adj* like tufts of
wool

flock[1] *n* **1** number of animals
of one kind together **2** large
group of people **3** *Christianity*
congregation ▷ *v* **4** gather in
a crowd

flock[2] *n* **1** very small tufts of
wool giving a raised pattern
on wallpaper **2** wool or cotton
waste used as stuffing

floe *n* sheet of floating ice

flog *v* **flogging, flogged 1** beat
with a whip, stick, etc. **2** *slang*
sell **flogging** *n*

flood *n* **1** overflow of water
onto a normally dry area
2 large amount of water
3 rising of the tide ▷ *v* **4** cover
or become covered with water
5 fill to overflowing **6** come in
large numbers or quantities
floodgate *n* gate used to
control the flow of water
floodlight *n* **1** lamp that casts
a broad intense beam of light
▷ *v* **-lighting, -lit 2** illuminate
by floodlight

floor *n* **1** lower surface of a
room **2** level of a building
3 flat bottom surface **4** (right
to speak in) a legislative hall
▷ *v* **5** *informal* disconcert or
defeat **6** knock down **floored**
adj covered with a floor
flooring *n* material for floors
floor show entertainment in
a nightclub

floozy *n, pl* **-zies** *slang*
disreputable woman

flop *v* **flopping, flopped**
1 bend, fall, or collapse loosely
or carelessly **2** *informal* fail
▷ *n* **3** flopping movement
4 *informal* failure **floppy** *adj*
hanging downwards, loose
floppiness *n* **floppy disk**

computers flexible magnetic
disk that stores information

flora *n* plants of a given time
or place **floral** *adj* consisting
of or decorated with flowers

floret [**flaw**-ret] *n* small
flower forming part of a
composite flower head

floribunda *n* type of rose
whose flowers grow in large
clusters

florid *adj* **1** with a red or
flushed complexion **2** ornate

florin *n* former British coin
equivalent to ten pence

florist *n* seller of flowers

floss *n* fine silky fibres

flotilla *n* **1** fleet of small ships
2 small fleet

flotsam *n* floating wreckage
flotsam and jetsam 1 odds
and ends **2** homeless or
vagrant people

flounce[1] *v* **1** go with emphatic
movements ▷ *n* **2** flouncing
movement

flounce[2] *n* ornamental ruffle
on a garment

flounder[1] *v* **1** move with
difficulty, as in mud **2** behave
or speak in a bungling or
hesitating manner

flounder[2] *n* edible flatfish

flour *n* **1** powder made by
grinding grain, esp. wheat ▷ *v*
2 sprinkle with flour **floury**
adj **flouriness** *n*

flourish *v* **1** be active,
successful, or widespread **2** be
at the peak of development
3 wave (something)
dramatically ▷ *n* **4** dramatic
waving motion **5** ornamental
curly line in writing
6 extravagant action or part
flourishing *adj*

flout [rhymes with **out**] *v*
deliberately disobey (a rule,
law, etc.)

flow *v* (of liquid) **1** move
in a stream **2** (of blood
or electricity) circulate

3 proceed smoothly **4** hang loosely **5** be abundant ▷ *n* **6** act, rate, or manner of flowing **7** continuous stream or discharge **flow chart** diagram showing a sequence of operations in a process

flower *n* **1** part of a plant that produces seeds **2** plant grown for its colourful flowers **3** best or finest part ▷ *v* **4** produce flowers, bloom **5** come to prime condition **in flower** with flowers open **flowered** *adj* decorated with a floral design **flowery** *adj* **1** decorated with a floral design **2** (of language or style) elaborate **flowerbed** *n* piece of ground for growing flowers on

flown *v* past participle of **fly**[1]

fl. oz. fluid ounce(s)

flu *n* short for **influenza**

fluctuate *v* change frequently and erratically **fluctuation** *n*

flue *n* passage or pipe for smoke or hot air

fluent *adj* **1** able to speak or write with ease **2** spoken or written with ease **fluently** *adv* **fluency** *n*

fluff *n* **1** soft fibres **2** down **3** *informal* mistake ▷ *v* **4** make or become soft and light **5** *informal* make a mistake **fluffy** *adj*

fluid *n* **1** liquid ▷ *adj* **2** able to flow or change easily **fluidity** *n* **fluid ounce** one twentieth of a pint

fluke[1] *n* accidental stroke of luck **fluky** *adj*

fluke[2] *n* **1** flat triangular point of an anchor **2** lobe of a whale's tail

fluke[3] *n* parasitic worm

flume *n* narrow sloping channel for water

flummox *v* perplex or bewilder

flung *v* past of **fling**

flunk *v* *informal* fail

flunky, flunkey *n*, *pl* **flunkies, flunkeys** **1** manservant who wears a livery **2** servile person

fluorescence *n* emission of light from a substance bombarded by particles, such as electrons, or by radiation **fluorescent** *adj* **fluoresce** *v* exhibit fluorescence

fluoride *n* compound containing fluorine **fluoridate** *v* add fluoride to (water) as protection against tooth decay **fluoridation** *n*

fluorine *n* toxic yellow gas, most reactive of all the elements

fluorspar *n* mineral consisting of calcium fluoride

flurry *n*, *pl* **-ries 1** sudden commotion **2** squall or gust of rain, wind, or snow ▷ *v* **-rying, -ried 3** fluster

flush[1] *v* **1** blush **2** send water through (a toilet or pipe) so as to clean it **3** elate ▷ *n* **4** blush **5** rush of water **6** excitement or elation

flush[2] *adj* **1** level with the surrounding surface **2** *informal* having plenty of money

flush[3] *n* (in card games) hand all of one suit

flush[4] *v* drive out of a hiding place

fluster *v* **1** make nervous or upset ▷ *n* **2** nervous or upset state

flute *n* **1** wind instrument consisting of a tube with sound holes and a mouth hole in the side **2** decorative groove **3** tall thin wineglass **fluted** *adj* having decorative grooves **fluting** *n*

flutter *v* **1** wave rapidly **2** flap the wings **3** move quickly and irregularly **4** (of the heart) beat abnormally quickly ▷ *n* **5** flapping movement

6 nervous agitation **7** *informal* small bet **8** abnormally fast heartbeat

fluvial [**flew**-vee-al] *adj* of rivers

flux *n* **1** constant change or instability **2** flow or discharge **3** substance mixed with metal to assist in fusion

fly¹ *v* **flying, flew, flown 1** move through the air on wings or in an aircraft **2** control the flight of **3** float, flutter, display, or be displayed in the air **4** transport or be transported by air **5** move quickly or suddenly **6** (of time) pass rapidly **7** flee ▷ *n*, *pl* **flies 8** *often pl* fastening at the front of trousers **9** flap forming the entrance to a tent **flies 10** space above a stage, used for storage **flyer** *or* **flier** *n* **1** small advertising leaflet **2** aviator **fly ball** *baseball* ball that is hit high up into the air **flyleaf** *n* blank leaf at the beginning or end of a book **flyover** *n Brit* road passing over another by a bridge **flywheel** *n* heavy wheel regulating the speed of a machine

fly² *n, pl* **flies** two-winged insect, esp. the housefly **flyblown** *adj* covered with bluebottle eggs **flycatcher** *n* small insect-eating songbird **fly-fishing** *n* fishing with an artificial fly as a lure **flypaper** *n* paper with a sticky poisonous coating, used to kill flies **flyweight** *n* boxer weighing up to 112lb (professional) or 51kg (amateur)

flying *adj* hurried, brief **flying boat** aircraft fitted with floats instead of landing wheels **flying buttress** *archit* buttress supporting a wall by an arch **flying colours** conspicuous success: *pass with flying colours*

flying fish fish with winglike fins used for gliding above the water **flying fox** large fruit-eating bat **flying saucer** unidentified disc-shaped flying object, supposedly from outer space **flying squad** small group of police, soldiers, etc., ready to act quickly **flying start** very good start

FM frequency modulation

FN First Nation

foal *n* **1** young of a horse or related animal ▷ *v* **2** give birth to a foal

foam *n* **1** mass of small bubbles on a liquid **2** frothy saliva **3** light spongelike solid used for insulation, packing, etc. ▷ *v* **4** produce foam **foamy** *adj*

fob¹ *n* **1** short watch chain **2** small pocket in a waistcoat

fob² *v* **fobbing, fobbed** (foll. by *off*) **1** pretend to satisfy (a person) with lies or excuses **2** sell or pass off (something inferior) as valuable

fo'c's'le *n* same as **forecastle**

focus *v* **-cusing, -cused** *or* **-cussing, -cussed 1** adjust one's eyes or an instrument so that an image becomes clear **2** concentrate (on) ▷ *n*, *pl* **-cuses, -ci** [-sye] **3** point at which light or sound waves converge **4** state of an optical image when it is clearly defined **5** state of an instrument producing such an image **6** centre of interest or activity **focal** *adj* of or at a focus **focus group** group of people gathered by a market-research company to discuss and assess a product or service

fodder *n* feed for livestock

foe *n* enemy, opponent

foetid *adj* same as **fetid**

foetus *n, pl* **-tuses** same as **fetus**

fog *n* **1** mass of condensed water vapour in the lower air, often greatly reducing visibility ▷ v **fogging, fogged 2** cover with steam **foggy** adj **foghorn** n large horn sounded to warn ships in fog

fogy, fogey n, pl **-gies, -geys** old-fashioned person

foible n minor weakness, idiosyncrasy

foil¹ v ruin (someone's plan)

foil² n **1** metal in a thin sheet **2** anything which sets off another thing to advantage

foil³ n light slender flexible sword tipped with a button

foist v (usu. foll. by on) force or impose on

fold¹ v **1** bend so that one part covers another **2** interlace (the arms) **3** lit clasp (in the arms) **4** cooking mix gently **5** informal fail ▷ n **6** folded piece or part **7** mark, crease, or hollow made by folding **folder** n piece of folded cardboard for loose papers

fold² n **1** enclosure for sheep **2** church or its members

foliage n leaves **foliaceous** adj of or like leaves **foliate** adj **1** having leaves **2** leaflike **foliation** n process of producing leaves

folio n, pl **-lios 1** sheet of paper folded in half to make two leaves of a book **2** book made up of such sheets **3** page number

folk n **1** people in general **2** race of people **3** informal folk music **folks 4** relatives **folksy** adj simple and unpretentious **folk dance** traditional country dance **folklore** n traditional beliefs and stories of a people **folk song 1** song handed down among the common people **2** modern song like this **folk singer**

follicle n small cavity in the body, esp. one from which a hair grows

follow v **1** go or come after **2** be a logical or natural consequence of **3** keep to the course or track of **4** act in accordance with **5** accept the ideas or beliefs of **6** understand **7** have a keen interest in **8** choose to receive messages posted by (a blogger or microblogger) **follower** n disciple or supporter **following** adj **1** about to be mentioned **2** next in time ▷ n **3** group of supporters ▷ prep **4** as a result of **follow up** v **1** investigate **2** do a second, often similar, thing after (a first) **follow-up** n something done to reinforce an initial action

folly n, pl **-lies 1** foolishness **2** foolish action or idea **3** useless extravagant building

foment [foam-**ent**] v encourage or stir up (trouble) **fomentation** n

fond adj **1** tender, loving **2** unlikely to be realized: a fond hope **3** indulgent **fond of** having a liking for **fondly** adv **fondness** n

fondant n (sweet made from) flavoured paste of sugar and water

fondle v caress

fondue n Swiss dish typically of a hot melted cheese sauce into which pieces of bread are dipped

font n bowl in a church for baptismal water

fontanelle n soft membranous gap between the bones of a baby's skull

food n what one eats, solid nourishment **foodie** n informal gourmet **food group** category of food based on its nutritional content **foodstuff** n substance used as food

fool¹ n **1** person lacking sense or judgment **2** person made to appear ridiculous **3** hist jester, clown ▷ v **4** deceive (someone) **foolish** adj unwise, silly, or absurd **foolishly** adv **foolishness** n **foolery** n foolish behaviour **fool around** v act or play irresponsibly or aimlessly **foolproof** adj unable to fail

fool[2] n dessert of puréed fruit mixed with cream

foolhardy adj recklessly adventurous **foolhardiness** n

foolscap n size of paper, 13 or 13.5 by 16 or 17 inches (33 or 44 by 41 or 43 centimetres)

foot n, pl **feet 1** part of the leg below the ankle **2** unit of length of twelve inches (0.3048 metre) **3** lowest part of anything **4** unit of poetic rhythm **5** obsolete infantry **foot the bill** pay the entire cost **footage** n amount of film used **foot-and-mouth disease** infectious viral disease of sheep, cattle, etc. **footbridge** n bridge for pedestrians **footfall** n sound of a footstep **foothills** pl n hills at the foot of a mountain **foothold** n **1** small place giving a secure grip for the foot **2** secure position from which progress may be made **footlights** pl n lights across the front of a stage **footloose** adj free from ties **footman** n male servant in livery **footnote** n note printed at the foot of a page **footprint** n mark left by a foot **footsore** adj having sore or tired feet **footstep** n **1** step in walking **2** sound made by walking **footstool** n low stool used to rest the feet on while sitting **footwear** n anything worn to cover the feet **footwork** n skilful use of the feet, as in sport or dancing

football n **1** game played by two teams, each side attempting to kick, pass, or carry a ball across a goal line in order to score points **2** rugby **3** Brit soccer **footballer** n **football pools** Brit form of gambling on the results of football matches

footing n **1** secure grip by or for the feet **2** basis, foundation **3** relationship between people

footsie n informal flirtation involving the touching together of feet

fop n man excessively concerned with fashion **foppery** n **foppish** adj

for prep **1** intended to be received or used by **2** in order to help or benefit **3** representing: speaking for the opposition **4** because of: I could not see for the fog **5** over a span of (time or distance) **6** in the direction of: heading for the border **7** at a cost of **8** in favour of: vote for me ▷ conj **9** because **for it** informal liable for punishment or blame

forage [for-ridge] v **1** search about (for) ▷ n **2** food for cattle or horses

foray n **1** brief raid or attack **2** first attempt or new undertaking

forbear v cease or refrain (from doing something) **forbearance** n tolerance, patience **forbearing** adj

forbid v prohibit, refuse to allow **forbidden** adj **forbidding** adj severe, threatening

force n **1** strength or power **2** compulsion **3** physics influence tending to produce a change in a physical system **4** mental or moral strength **5** person or thing with strength or influence **6** vehemence or intensity **7** group of people organized for a particular task or duty **8** body of troops, police, etc.

▷ v **9** compel, make (someone) do something **10** acquire or produce through effort, strength, etc. **11** propel or drive **12** break open **13** impose or inflict **14** cause to grow at an increased rate **15** strain to the utmost **in force 1** having legal validity **2** in great numbers **forced** *adj* **1** compulsory **2** false or unnatural **3** due to an emergency **forceful** *adj* **1** emphatic **2** effective **forcefully** *adv* **forcefulness** *n* **forcible** *adj* **1** involving physical force or violence **2** strong and emphatic **forcibly** *adv*

forceps *pl n* surgical pincers

ford *n* **1** shallow place where a river may be crossed ▷ *v* **2** cross (a river) at a ford **fordable** *adj*

fore *adj* **1** in, at, or towards the front ▷ *n* **2** front part **to the fore** in a conspicuous position

fore- *prefix* **1** before in time or rank: *forefather* **2** at the front: *forecourt*

fore-and-aft *adj* located at both ends of a ship

forearm[1] *n* arm from the wrist to the elbow

forearm[2] *v* prepare beforehand

forebear *n* ancestor

foreboding *n* feeling that something bad is about to happen

forecast *v* **-casting, -cast** or **-casted 1** predict (weather, events, etc.) ▷ *n* **2** prediction

forecastle [foke-sl] *n* raised front part of a ship

foreclose *v* take possession of (property bought with borrowed money which has not been repaid) **foreclosure** *n*

forecourt *n* courtyard or open space in front of a building

forefather *n* ancestor

forefinger *n* finger next to the thumb

forefront *n* **1** most active or conspicuous position **2** very front

forego *v* same as **forgo**

foregoing *adj* going before, preceding **foregone conclusion** inevitable result

foreground *n* part of a view, esp. in a picture, nearest the observer

forehand *adj* **1** (of a stroke in tennis, squash, etc.) made with the palm of the hand forward ▷ *n* **2** such a stroke

forehead *n* part of the face above the eyebrows

foreign *adj* **1** not of, or in, one's own country **2** relating to or connected with other countries **3** unfamiliar, strange **4** in an abnormal place or position: *foreign matter* **foreigner** *n*

foreland *n* headland

forelock *n* lock of hair over the forehead

foreman *n* **1** person in charge of a group of workers **2** leader of a jury

foremast *n* mast nearest the bow of a ship

foremost *adj, adv* first in time, place, or importance

forename *n* first name

forenoon *n* morning

forensic [for-**ren**-sik] *adj* used in or connected with courts of law **forensic medicine** use of medical knowledge for the purposes of the law

foreplay *n* sexual stimulation before intercourse

forerunner *n* person or thing that goes before, precursor

foresee *v* see or know beforehand **foreseeable** *adj*

foreshadow *v* show or indicate beforehand

foreshore *n* part of the shore

between high- and low-tide marks

foreshorten v represent (an object) in a picture as shorter than it really is in accordance with perspective

foresight n ability to anticipate and provide for future needs

foreskin n fold of skin covering the tip of the penis

forest n large area with a thick growth of trees **forested** adj

forestry n science of planting and caring for trees **forester** n person skilled in forestry

forestall v prevent or guard against in advance

foretaste n early limited experience of something to come

foretell v tell or indicate beforehand

forethought n thoughtful planning for future events

forever adv 1 without end 2 at all times 3 informal for a long time

forewarn v warn beforehand

foreword n preface

forfeit [for-fit] n 1 thing lost or given up as a penalty for a fault or mistake ▷ v 2 lose as a forfeit ▷ adj 3 lost as a forfeit **forfeiture** n

forgather v meet together, assemble

forge[1] n 1 place where metal is worked, smithy 2 furnace for melting metal ▷ v 3 make a fraudulent imitation of (something) 4 shape (metal) by heating and hammering it 5 create (an alliance etc.)

forge[2] v advance steadily **forge ahead** v increase speed or take the lead

forgery n, pl -ries 1 something forged 2 act of making a fraudulent imitation **forger** n

forget v -getting, -got, -gotten 1 fail to remember

2 neglect 3 leave behind by mistake **forgetful** adj tending to forget **forgetfulness** n **forget-me-not** n plant with clusters of small blue flowers

forgive v cease to blame or hold resentment against, pardon **forgiveness** n

forgo v do without, give up

forgot v past tense of **forget** ▷ **forgotten** v past participle of **forget**

fork n 1 tool for eating food, with prongs and a handle 2 large similarly-shaped tool for digging or lifting 3 point where a road, river, etc. divides into branches 4 one of the branches ▷ v 5 branch 6 take one or other branch at a fork in the road 7 pick up, dig, etc. with a fork **forked** adj **fork-lift truck** vehicle with a forklike device at the front which can be raised or lowered to move loads **fork out** v informal pay

forlorn adj forsaken and unhappy **forlorn hope** hopeless enterprise **forlornly** adv

form n 1 shape or appearance 2 mode in which something appears 3 type or kind 4 printed document with spaces for details 5 physical or mental condition 6 previous record of an athlete, racehorse, etc. 7 class in school 8 procedure or etiquette 9 bench 10 hare's nest ▷ v 11 give a (particular) shape to or take a (particular) shape 12 come or bring into existence 13 make or be made 14 train 15 acquire or develop 16 be an element of **formless** adj **formation** n 1 forming 2 thing formed 3 structure or shape 4 arrangement of people or things acting

as a unit **formative** *adj*
1 shaping **2** of or relating to
development

formal *adj* **1** of or characterized
by established conventions
of ceremony and behaviour
2 of or for formal occasions
3 stiff in manner **4** organized
5 symmetrical **formally** *adv*
formality *n* **1** requirement
of custom or etiquette
2 necessary procedure without
real importance **formalize** *v*
make official or formal

formaldehyde [for-**mal**-de-
hide] *n* colourless pungent
gas used to make formalin
formalin *n* solution of
formaldehyde in water,
used as a disinfectant or a
preservative for biological
specimens

format *n* **1** size and shape of a
publication **2** style in which
something is arranged ▷ *v*
-**matting**, -**matted 3** arrange
in a format

former *adj* of an earlier time,
previous **the former** first
mentioned of two **formerly**
adv

Formica *n* ® kind of
laminated sheet used to make
heat-resistant surfaces

formic acid *n* acid derived
from ants

formidable *adj* **1** difficult
to overcome or manage
2 extremely impressive
formidably *adv*

formula *n, pl* -**las**, -**lae**
1 group of numbers, letters,
or symbols expressing a
scientific or mathematical
rule **2** set form of words used
in religion, law, etc. **3** method
or rule for doing or producing
something **4** specific category
of vehicle in motor racing
formulaic *adj* **formulate** *v*
plan or describe precisely and
clearly **formulation** *n*

fornicate *v* have sexual
intercourse without being
married **fornication** *n*
fornicator *n*

forsake *v* -**saking**, -**sook**,
-**saken 1** withdraw support
or friendship from **2** give up,
renounce

forsooth *adv obsolete* indeed

forswear *v* renounce or reject

forsythia [for-**syth**-ee-a] *n*
shrub with yellow flowers in
spring

fort *n* fortified building or
place **hold the fort** *informal*
keep things going during
someone's absence

forte[1] [**for**-tay] *n* thing at
which a person excels

forte[2] *adv music* loudly

forth *adv* forwards, out, or
away

forthcoming *adj* **1** about to
appear or happen **2** available
3 (of a person) communicative

forthright *adj* direct and
outspoken

forthwith *adv* at once

fortieth *adj, n* see **four**

fortify *v* -**fying**, -**fied 1** make
(a place) defensible, as by
building walls **2** strengthen
3 add alcohol to (wine) to
make sherry or port **4** add
vitamins etc. to (food)
fortification *n*

fortissimo *adv music* very
loudly

fortitude *n* courage in
adversity or pain

fortnight *n* two weeks
fortnightly *adv, adj*

FORTRAN *n computers*
programming language for
mathematical and scientific
purposes

fortress *n* large fort or
fortified town

fortuitous [for-**tyew**-it-uss]
adj happening by (lucky)
chance **fortuitously** *adv*
fortuity *n*

fortunate *adj* **1** having good luck **2** occurring by good luck **fortunately** *adv*

fortune *n* **1** luck, esp. when favourable **2** power regarded as influencing human destiny **3** wealth, large sum of money **fortunes 4** person's destiny **fortune-teller** *n* person who claims to predict the future of others

forty *adj, n* see **four**

forty-ninth parallel *n informal* border between Canada and the US

forum *n* meeting or medium for open discussion or debate

forward *adj* **1** directed or moving ahead **2** in, at, or near the front **3** presumptuous **4** well developed or advanced **5** relating to the future ▷ *n* **6** *sports* attacking player in various team games, such as hockey or soccer ▷ *v* **7** send (a letter etc.) on to an ultimate destination **8** advance or promote ▷ *adv* **9** forwards **forwardly** *adv* **forwardness** *n* **forwards** *adv* **1** towards or at a place further ahead in space or time **2** towards the front

fossil *n* hardened remains of a prehistoric animal or plant preserved in rock **fossilize** *v* **1** turn into a fossil **2** become out-of-date or inflexible **fossilization** *n* **fossil fuel** fuel, like coal and oil, found in the remains of prehistoric organisms

foster *v* **1** bring up (a child not one's own) **2** promote the growth or development of ▷ *adj* **3** of or involved in fostering a child

fought *v* past of **fight**

foul *adj* **1** loathsome or offensive **2** stinking or dirty **3** (of language) obscene or vulgar **4** unfair ▷ *n* **5** *sports* violation of the rules ▷ *v*

6 make dirty or polluted **7** make or become entangled or clogged **8** *sports* commit a foul against (an opponent) **fall foul of** come into conflict with **foully** *adv* **foulness** *n* **foul-mouthed** *adj* (habitually) using foul language **foul play** unfair conduct, esp. involving violence

found¹ *v* past of **find**

found² *v* **1** establish or bring into being **2** lay the foundation of **3** (foll. by *on* or *upon*) have a basis (in) **founder** *n* **foundation** *n* **1** basis or base **2** act of founding **3** institution supported by an endowment **4** cosmetic used as a base for make-up **foundations 5** part of a building or wall below the ground

found³ *v* **1** cast (metal or glass) by melting and setting in a mould **2** make (articles) by this method **founder** *n* **foundry** *n* place where metal is melted and cast

founder *v* **1** break down or fail **2** (of a ship) sink **3** stumble or fall

foundling *n* abandoned infant

fount *n* **1** *lit* fountain **2** source **3** set of printing type of one style and size

fountain *n* **1** pool or structure from which a jet or water spurts **2** jet of water **3** source **fountainhead** *n* source **fountain pen** pen supplied with ink from a container inside it

four *adj, n* **1** one more than three ▷ *n* **2** (crew of) four-oared rowing boat **on all fours** on hands and knees **fourth** *adj, n* **1** (of) number four in a series ▷ *n* **2** quarter **fourthly** *adv* **foursome** *n* group of four people

fourteen *adj, n* four and ten
fourteenth *adj, n* **forty** *adj, n*
four times ten **fortieth** *adj,
n* **fourth dimension** time
fourth estate the press **four-
letter word** short obscene word
referring to sex or excrement
four-poster *n* bed with four
posts supporting a canopy

fowl *n* **1** domestic cock or
hen **2** any bird used for
food or hunted as game ▷ *v*
3 hunt or snare wild birds
fowler *n*

fox *n* **1** reddish-brown bushy-
tailed animal of the dog
family **2** its fur **3** cunning
person ▷ *v* **4** *informal* perplex
or deceive **foxy** *adj* **foxglove**
n tall plant with purple or
white flowers **foxhole** *n mil*
small pit dug for protection
foxhound *n* dog bred for
hunting foxes **fox terrier**
small short-haired terrier
foxtrot *n* **1** ballroom dance
with slow and quick steps
2 music for this

foyer [**foy**-ay] *n* entrance hall
in a theatre, cinema, or hotel

fracas [**frak**-ah] *n, pl* -**cas**
noisy quarrel

fracking *n* extraction of oil or
gas by forcing liquid into rock
at high pressure

fraction *n* **1** numerical
quantity that is not a whole
number **2** fragment, piece
3 *chem* substance separated
by distillation **fractional** *adj*
fractionally *adv*

fractious *adj* easily upset and
angered

fracture *n* **1** breaking, esp. of a
bone ▷ *v* **2** break

fragile *adj* **1** easily broken or
damaged **2** in a weakened
physical state **fragility** *n*

fragment *n* **1** piece broken off
2 incomplete piece ▷ *v* **3** break
into pieces **fragmentary** *adj*
fragmentation *n*

fragrant *adj* sweet-smelling
fragrantly *adv* **fragrance** *n*
1 pleasant smell **2** perfume,
scent

frail *adj* **1** physically weak
2 easily damaged **frailty** *n*

frame *n* **1** structure giving
shape or support **2** enclosing
case or border, as round a
picture **3** person's build
4 individual exposure on a
strip of film **5** individual
game of snooker in a match
▷ *v* **6** put into a frame **7** put
together, construct **8** put into
words **9** *slang* incriminate (a
person) on a false charge
frame of mind mood, attitude
frame-up *n slang* false
incrimination **framework** *n*
supporting structure

franc *n* monetary unit of
Switzerland

franchise *n* **1** right to vote
2 authorization to sell a
company's goods

Franciscan *n, adj* (friar or nun)
of a Christian religious order
founded by St Francis of Assisi

francization *n* practice of
making French the main
language in the workplace,
esp. in Quebec

Franco- *combining form* of
France or the French

Francophone *n* native
speaker of French

frangipani [fran-jee-**pah**-nee]
n fragrant tropical American
shrub

frank *adj* **1** honest and
straightforward **2** outspoken
or blunt ▷ *v* **3** put a mark on
(a letter) to allow it delivery
▷ *n* **4** official mark on a letter
allowing delivery **frankly** *adv*
frankness *n*

frankfurter *n* smoked sausage

frankincense *n* aromatic gum
resin burned as incense

frantic *adj* **1** distracted with
rage, grief, joy, etc. **2** hurried

and disorganized **frantically**
adv

fraternal *adj* of a brother,
brotherly **fraternally**
adv **fraternity** *n* **1** group
of people with shared
interests, aims, etc.
2 brotherhood **3** male social
club at college **fraternize** *v*
associate on friendly terms
fraternization *n* **fratricide**
n **1** crime of killing one's
brother **2** person who does
this

Frau [rhymes with **how**] *n*
German title, equivalent to
Mrs **Fräulein** [**froy**-line] *n*
German title, equivalent to
Miss

fraud *n* **1** (criminal) deception,
swindle **2** person who acts in a
deceitful way **fraudulent** *adj*
fraudulence *n*

fraught [frawt] *adj* tense
or anxious **fraught with**
involving, filled with

fray¹ *v* **1** make or become
ragged at the edge **2** become
strained

fray² *n* noisy quarrel or conflict

frazzle *n informal* exhausted
state

freak *n* **1** abnormal person
or thing **2** person who is
excessively enthusiastic about
something ▷ *adj* **3** abnormal
freakish *adj* **freak out** *v slang*
(cause to) be in a heightened
emotional state

freckle *n* small brown spot on
the skin **freckled** *adj* marked
with freckles

free *adj* **freer, freest 1** able to
act at will, not compelled or
restrained **2** not subject (to)
3 independent **4** provided
without charge **5** generous,
lavish **6** not in use **7** (of a
person) not busy **8** not fixed
or joined ▷ *v* **freeing, freed**
9 release, liberate **10** remove
(obstacles, pain, etc.) from

11 make available or usable
freely *adv* **freedom** *n* being
free **freebooter** *n* pirate
free fall part of a parachute
descent before the parachute
opens **free-for-all** *n informal*
brawl **freehand** *adj* drawn
without guiding instruments
free hand unrestricted
freedom to act **freehold** *n*
tenure of land for life without
restrictions **freeholder** *n*
free house *Brit* public house
not bound to sell only one
brewer's products **freelance**
adj, n (of) self-employed
person doing specific
pieces of work for various
employers **freeloader** *n*
slang habitual scrounger
Freemason *n* member of a
secret fraternity pledged to
help each other **free-range**
adj kept or produced in
natural conditions **freeway** *n*
highway **freewheel** *v* travel
downhill on a bicycle without
pedalling

-free *adj combining form*
without: *a trouble-free journey*

freesia *n* plant with fragrant
tubular flowers

freeze *v* **freezing, froze,**
frozen 1 change from a liquid
to a solid by the reduction
of temperature, as water
to ice **2** preserve (food etc.)
by extreme cold **3** (cause
to) be very cold **4** become
motionless with fear, shock,
etc. **5** fix (prices or wages)
at a particular level **6** ban
the exchange or collection
of (loans, assets, etc.) ▷ *n*
7 period of very cold weather
8 freezing of prices or wages
freezer *n* insulated cabinet
for cold-storage of perishable
foods **freeze-dry** *v* preserve
(food) by rapid freezing and
drying in a vacuum **freeze-**
up *n* freezing of watercourses

and wetlands during fall and winter

freight [frate] n 1 commercial transport of goods 2 cargo transported 3 cost of this ▷ v 4 send by freight **freighter** n ship or aircraft for transporting goods

French n 1 language of France ▷ adj 2 of France, its people, or their language **French bread** white bread in a long thin crusty loaf **French dressing** salad dressing of oil and vinegar **French fries** thin strips of potato, fried **French horn** brass wind instrument with a coiled tube **French polish** shellac varnish for wood **French window** window extending to floor level, used as a door

frenetic [frin-**net**-ik] adj uncontrolled, excited **frenetically** adv

frenzy n, pl -zies 1 violent mental derangement 2 wild excitement **frenzied** adj **frenziedly** adv

frequent adj 1 happening often 2 habitual ▷ v 3 visit habitually **frequently** adv **frequency** n 1 rate of occurrence 2 physics number of times a wave repeats itself in a given time

fresco n, pl -coes, -cos watercolour painting done on wet plaster on a wall

fresh adj 1 newly made, acquired, etc. 2 novel, original 3 most recent 4 further, additional 5 (of food) not preserved 6 (of water) not salty 7 (of weather) brisk or invigorating 8 not tired 9 informal impudent **freshly** adv **freshness** n **freshen** v **freshman** or **fresher** n first-year student

fret[1] v **fretting, fretted** be worried **fretful** adj irritable

fret[2] n small bar on the fingerboard of a guitar etc. **fret saw** fine saw with a narrow blade, used for fretwork **fretwork** n decorative carving in wood

Freudian [**froy**-dee-an] adj of or relating to the psychoanalyst Sigmund Freud or his theories

friable [**fry**-a-bl] adj easily crumbled **friability** n

friar n member of a male Roman Catholic religious order **friary** n house of friars

fricassee n stewed meat served in a thick sauce

friction n 1 rubbing 2 resistance met with by a body moving over another 3 clash of wills or personalities **frictional** adj

Friday n sixth day of the week **Good Friday** Friday before Easter

fridge n short for **refrigerator**

fried v past of **fry**[1]

friend n 1 person whom one knows well and likes 2 supporter 3 **Friend** Quaker **friendly** adj 1 showing or expressing liking 2 not hostile, on the same side **-friendly** combining form good or easy for the person or thing specified: user-friendly **friendly fire** military firing by one's own side, esp when it harms one's own personnel **friendliness** n **friendless** adj **friendship** n

Friesian [**free**-zhan] n Brit Holstein

frieze [freeze] n ornamental band on a wall

frigate [**frig**-it] n medium-sized fast warship

fright n 1 sudden fear or alarm 2 sudden alarming shock 3 informal grotesque person **frighten** v 1 scare or terrify 2 force (someone) to do something from fear **frightening** adj **frightful** adj **1** horrifying **2** informal very great **frightfully** adv

frigid [frij-id] adj **1** (of a woman) sexually unresponsive **2** very cold **3** excessively formal **frigidly** adv **frigidity** n

frill n **1** gathered strip of fabric attached at one edge **frills 2** superfluous decorations or details **frilled** adj **frilly** adj

fringe n **1** hair cut short over the forehead **2** ornamental edge of hanging threads, tassels, etc. **3** outer edge **4** less important parts of an activity or group ▷ v **5** decorate with a fringe ▷ adj **6** (of theatre) unofficial or unconventional **fringed** adj **fringe benefit** benefit given in addition to a regular salary

frippery n, pl **-peries 1** useless ornamentation **2** trivia

frisk v **1** move or leap playfully **2** informal search (a person) for concealed weapons etc. **frisky** adj lively or high-spirited **friskily** adv

frisson [frees-sonn] n shiver of fear or excitement

fritter n piece of food fried in batter

fritter away v waste

frivolous adj **1** not serious or sensible **2** enjoyable but trivial **frivolously** adv **frivolity** n

frizz v form (hair) into stiff wiry curls **frizzy** adj

frizzle v cook or heat until crisp and shrivelled

frock n dress **frock coat** man's skirted coat as worn in the 19th century

frog n smooth-skinned tailless amphibian with long back legs used for jumping **frog in one's throat** phlegm on the vocal cords, hindering speech **frogman** n swimmer with

a rubber suit and breathing equipment for working underwater **frogmarch** v force (a resisting person) to move by holding his arms **frogspawn** n jelly-like substance containing frog's eggs

frolic v **-icking, -icked 1** run and play in a lively way ▷ n **2** lively and merry behaviour **frolicsome** adj playful

from prep indicating the point of departure, source, distance, cause, change of state, etc.

frond n long leaf or leaflike part of a fern, palm, or seaweed

front n **1** fore part **2** position directly before or ahead **3** seaside promenade **4** battle line or area **5** meteorol dividing line between two different air masses **6** outward aspect **7** informal cover for another, usu. criminal, activity **8** group with a common goal ▷ v **9** face (onto) **10** be the presenter of (a television show) ▷ adj **11** of or at the front **frontal** adj **frontage** n façade of a building

frontispiece n illustration facing the title page of a book

front bench parliamentary leaders of the government or opposition **front-bencher** n

front court basketball **1** half of the court into which a given team is attacking **2** centre and forwards of a team

frontrunner n informal person regarded as most likely to win a race, election, etc.

frontier n area of a country bordering on another

frost n **1** white frozen dew or mist **2** atmospheric temperature below freezing point ▷ v **3** become covered with frost **frosted** adj **1** (of glass) having a rough surface to make it opaque **2** covered with frosting **frosting** n sugar icing **frosty** adj **1** characterized or covered by frost **2** unfriendly **frostily** adv **frostiness** n **frostbite** n destruction of tissue, esp. of the fingers or ears, by cold **frostbitten** adj **frost boil** bulge in road caused by freezing

froth n **1** mass of small bubbles ▷ v **2** foam **frothy** adj

frown v **1** wrinkle one's brows in worry, anger, or thought **2** look disapprovingly (on) ▷ n **3** frowning expression

frowsy adj **-sier, -siest** dirty or unkempt

froze v past tense of **freeze** ▶ **frozen** v past participle of **freeze**

fructify v **-fying, -fied** (cause to) bear fruit **fructification** n

frugal [**froo**-gl] adj **1** thrifty, sparing **2** meagre and inexpensive **frugally** adv **frugality** n

fruit n **1** part of a plant containing seeds, esp. if edible **2** any plant product useful to man **3** often pl result of an action or effort ▷ v **4** bear fruit **fruiterer** n person who sells fruit **fruitful** adj useful or productive **fruitfully** adv **fruition** [froo-**ish**-on] n fulfilment of something worked for or desired **fruitless** adj useless or unproductive **fruitlessly** adv **fruity** adj **1** of or like fruit **2** (of a voice) mellow **3** informal mildly bawdy **fruit machine** coin-operated gambling machine

frump n dowdy woman **frumpy** adj

frustrate v **1** upset or anger **2** hinder or prevent **frustrated** adj **frustrating** adj **frustration** n

fry¹ v **frying, fried 1** cook or be cooked in fat or oil ▷ n, pl **fries 2** dish of fried food **3** social occasion at which fried food is eaten

fry² pl n young fishes **small fry** young or insignificant people

ft. 1 foot **2** feet

fuchsia [**fyew**-sha] n ornamental shrub with hanging flowers

fuddle v cause to be intoxicated or confused **fuddled** adj

fuddy-duddy n, pl **-dies**, adj informal old-fashioned (person)

fudge¹ n soft caramel-like candy

fudge² v avoid making a firm statement or decision

fuel n **1** substance burned or treated to produce heat or power **2** something that intensifies (a feeling etc.) ▷ v **fuelling, fuelled 3** provide with fuel

fug n hot stale atmosphere **fuggy** adj

fugitive [**fyew**-jit-iv] n **1** person who flees, esp. from arrest or pursuit ▷ adj **2** fleeing **3** transient

fugue [**fyewg**] n musical composition in which a theme is repeated in different parts

fulcrum n, pl **-crums, -cra** pivot about which a lever turns

fulfil v **-filling, -filled 1** bring about the achievement of (a desire or promise) **2** carry out (a request or order) **3** do what is required **fulfilment** n **fulfil oneself** v achieve one's potential

full adj **1** containing as much or as many as possible **2** abundant in supply **3** having had enough to eat **4** plump **5** complete, whole **6** (of a garment) of ample cut **7** (of a sound or flavour) rich and strong ▷ *adv* **8** completely **9** directly **10** very **fully** *adv* **fullness** *n* **in full** without shortening **full-blooded** *adj* vigorous or enthusiastic **full-blown** *adj* fully developed **full moon** phase of the moon when it is visible as a fully illuminated disc **full-scale** *adj* **1** (of a plan) of actual size **2** using all resources **full stop** punctuation mark (.) at the end of a sentence and after abbreviations

fulmar *n* Arctic sea bird

fulminate *v* (foll. by *against*) criticize angrily **fulmination** *n*

fulsome *adj* insincerely excessive

fumble *v* **1** handle awkwardly **2** say awkwardly

fume *v* **1** be very angry **2** give out smoke or vapour **3** treat with fumes ▷ *n* **4** *usu pl* pungent smoke or vapour

fumigate [**fyew**-mig-gate] *v* disinfect with fumes **fumigation** *n*

fun *n* enjoyment or amusement **make fun of** mock or tease **funny** *adj* **1** comical, humorous **2** odd **funny bone** part of the elbow where the nerve is near the surface **funnily** *adv*

function *n* **1** purpose something exists for **2** way something works **3** large or formal social event **4** *math* quantity whose value depends on the varying value of another **5** series of operations done by a computer ▷ *v* **6** operate or work **7** (foll. by *as*) fill the role of **functional** *adj* **1** of or as a function **2** practical rather than decorative **3** in working order **functionally** *adv* **functionary** *n* official

fund *n* **1** stock of money for a special purpose **2** supply or store **funds 3** money resources ▷ *v* **4** provide money to **funding** *n*

fundamental *adj* **1** essential or primary **2** basic **fundamentals** *pl n* **3** basic rules or facts **fundamentally** *adv* **fundamentalism** *n* literal or strict interpretation of a religion **fundamentalist** *n, adj*

funeral *n* ceremony of burying or cremating a dead person **funerary** *adj* of or for a funeral **funereal** [fyew-**neer**-ee-al] *adj* gloomy or sombre

funfair *n* entertainment with machines to ride on and stalls

fungus *n, pl* **-gi, -guses** plant without leaves, flowers, or roots, such as a mushroom or mould **fungal** *or* **fungous** *adj* **fungicide** *n* substance that destroys fungi

funicular [fyew-**nik**-yew-lar] *n* cable railway on a mountainside or cliff

funk[1] *n* style of dance music with a strong beat **funky** *adj* (of music) passionate or soulful

funk[2] *informal* ▷ *n* **1** nervous or fearful state ▷ *v* **2** avoid (doing something) through fear

funnel *n* **1** cone-shaped tube for pouring liquids into a narrow opening **2** chimney of a ship or locomotive ▷ *v* **-nelling, -nelled 3** (cause to) move through or as if through a funnel

fur *n* **1** soft hair of a mammal **2** animal skin with the fur left on **3** garment made of this **4** whitish coating on the tongue or inside a kettle ▷ *v* **5** cover or become covered with fur **furry** *adj* **furrier** *n* dealer in furs

furbish v smarten up

furious adj **1** very angry **2** violent or unrestrained **furiously** adv

furl v roll up and fasten (a sail, umbrella, or flag)

furlong n eighth of a mile

furlough [**fur**-loh] n leave of absence from military duty

furnace n enclosed chamber containing a very hot fire

furnish v **1** fit up (a house or room) with furniture **2** (foll. by *with*) supply, provide **furnishings** pl n furniture, carpets, and fittings **furniture** n large movable articles such as chairs and wardrobes

furore [fyew-**ror**-ee] n very excited or angry reaction

furrow n **1** trench made by a plow **2** groove ▷ v **3** make or become wrinkled **4** make furrows in

further adv **1** in addition **2** to a greater distance or extent ▷ adj **3** additional **4** more distant ▷ v **5** assist the progress of **furthest** adv **1** to the greatest distance or extent ▷ adj **2** most distant **furtherance** n **furthermore** adv besides **furthermost** adj most distant

furtive adj sly and secretive **furtively** adv

fury n, pl -ries **1** wild anger **2** uncontrolled violence

furze n gorse

fuse[1] n cord containing an explosive for detonating a bomb

fuse[2] v **1** join or combine **2** melt with heat **3** unite by melting **4** (cause to) fail as a result of a blown fuse ▷ n **5** safety device for electric circuits, containing a wire that melts and breaks the connection when the circuit is overloaded **fusible** adj

fusion n **1** melting **2** product of fusing **3** combination of two atoms with release of energy **4** popular music blending styles, esp. jazz and funk ▷ adj **5** of a style of cooking that combines traditional Western techniques and ingredients with those used in Eastern cuisine

fuselage [**fyew**-zill-lahzh] n body of an aircraft

fusilier [fyew-zill-**leer**] n soldier of certain regiments

fusillade [fyew-zill-**lade**] n **1** continuous discharge of firearms **2** outburst of criticism, questions, etc.

fuss n **1** needless activity or worry **2** complaint or objection **3** great display of attention ▷ v **4** make a fuss **fussy** adj **1** inclined to fuss **2** overparticular **3** overelaborate **fussily** adv **fussiness** n

fusty adj -tier, -tiest **1** stale-smelling **2** behind the times **fustiness** n

futile [**fyew**-tile] adj unsuccessful or useless **futility** n

futon [**foo**-tonn] n Japanese padded quilt, laid on the floor as a bed

future n **1** time to come **2** what will happen **3** prospects ▷ adj **4** yet to come or be **5** of or relating to time to come **6** (of a verb tense) indicating that the action specified has not yet taken place **futuristic** adj of a design appearing to belong to some future time

fuzz[1] n mass of fine or curly hairs or fibres **fuzzy** adj **1** of, like, or covered with fuzz **2** blurred or indistinct **3** (of hair) tightly curled **fuzzily** adv **fuzziness** n

fuzz[2] n slang police(man)

Gg

g 1 gram(s) **2** (acceleration due to) gravity

gab *n, v* gabbing, gabbed *informal* talk or chatter **gift of the gab** eloquence **gabby** *adj informal* talkative

gabardine, gaberdine *n* strong twill cloth used esp. for raincoats

gabble *v* **1** speak rapidly and indistinctly ▷ *n* **2** rapid indistinct speech

gable *n* triangular upper part of a wall between sloping roofs **gabled** *adj*

gad *v* gadding, gadded ▶ **gad about** *or* **gad around** go around in search of pleasure **gadabout** *n* pleasure-seeker

gadfly *n* **1** fly that bites cattle **2** constantly annoying person

gadget *n* small mechanical device or appliance **gadgetry** *n* gadgets

Gael [gayl] *n* Gaelic-speaker **Gaelic** [gal-lik] *n* **1** Celtic language of Ireland and the Scottish Highlands ▷ *adj* **2** of the Gaels or their language

gaff¹ *n* **1** stick with an iron hook for landing large fish ▷ *v* **2** hook or land (a fish) with a gaff

gaff² *n* **blow the gaff** *slang* divulge a secret

gaffe *n* social blunder

gaffer *n* **1** old man **2** *informal* foreman or boss

gag¹ *v* gagging, gagged **1** stop up the mouth of (a person) with cloth etc. **2** deprive of free speech **3** retch **4** choke ▷ *n* **5** cloth etc. put into or tied across the mouth

gag² *n informal* joke

gaga [gah-gah] *adj slang* **1** senile **2** crazy

gage *n* **1** thing given as security **2** formerly, something thrown down as a challenge to combat

gaggle *n* **1** flock of geese **2** *informal* disorderly crowd

gaiety *n* **1** cheerfulness **2** merrymaking **gaily** *adv* **1** merrily **2** colourfully

gain *v* **1** acquire or obtain **2** win in competition **3** increase or improve **4** reach **5** (of a watch or clock) be or become too fast ▷ *n* **6** profit **7** increase or improvement **gainful** *adj* useful or profitable **gainfully** *adv* **gain on** *or* **upon** *v* get nearer to or catch up with

gainsay *v* **-saying, -said** deny or contradict

gait *n* manner of walking

gaiter *n* cloth or leather covering for the lower leg

gala [gah-la] *n* **1** festival **2** competitive sporting event

galaxy *n, pl* **-axies 1** system of stars **2** gathering of famous people **galactic** *adj*

gale *n* **1** strong wind **2** *informal* loud outburst

gall¹ [gawl] *n* **1** *informal* impudence **2** bitter feeling **gall bladder** sac attached to the liver, storing bile **gallstone** *n* hard growth in the gall bladder or its ducts

gall² [gawl] *n* **1** sore caused by

chafing ▷ v **2** make sore by rubbing **3** annoy

gall³ [gawl] n abnormal outgrowth on a tree or plant

gallant adj **1** brave and noble **2** (of a man) attentive to women **gallantly** adv **gallantry** n

galleon n large three-masted sailing ship of the 15th–17th centuries

gallery n, pl -**ries 1** room or building for displaying works of art **2** balcony in a church, theatre, etc. **3** long narrow room for a specific purpose: shooting gallery **4** passage in a mine

galley n **1** kitchen of a ship or aircraft **2** hist ship propelled by oars, usu. rowed by slaves **galley proof** printer's proof in long slip form **galley slave 1** slave forced to row in a galley **2** informal drudge

Gallic adj **1** French **2** of ancient Gaul **Gallicism** n French word or idiom

gallium n soft grey metallic element used in semiconductors

gallivant v go about in search of pleasure

gallon n liquid measure of eight pints, equal to 4.55 litres

gallop n **1** horse's fastest pace **2** galloping ▷ v **galloping, galloped 3** go or ride at a gallop **4** move or progress rapidly

gallows n wooden structure used for hanging criminals

Gallup poll n public opinion poll carried out by questioning a cross section of the population

galore adv in plenty: presents galore

galoshes pl n waterproof overshoes

galumph v informal leap or move about clumsily

galvanic adj **1** of or producing an electric current generated by chemical means **2** informal stimulating or startling

galvanize v **1** stimulate into action **2** coat (metal) with zinc

gambit n **1** opening line or move intended to secure an advantage **2** chess opening move involving the sacrifice of a pawn

gamble v **1** play games of chance to win money **2** act on the expectation of something ▷ n **3** risky undertaking **4** bet or wager **gambler** n **gambling** n

gamboge [gam-boje] n gum resin used as a yellow pigment and purgative

gambol v -**bolling, -bolled 1** jump about playfully, frolic ▷ n **2** frolic

game n **1** amusement or pastime **2** contest for amusement **3** single period of play in a contest **4** scheme or trick **5** animals or birds hunted for sport or food **6** their flesh ▷ v **7** gamble ▷ adj **8** brave **9** willing **gamely** adv **gamer** n person who plays computer games **gaming** n gambling **gamekeeper** n person employed to breed game and prevent poaching **gameplan** n **1** strategy for playing a particular game **2** any plan or strategy **gamesmanship** n art of winning by cunning practices without actually cheating

gamete [gam-eet] n biol reproductive cell

gamine [gam-een] n slim boyish young woman

gamma n third letter of the Greek alphabet **gamma ray** electromagnetic ray of shorter wavelength and higher energy than x-rays

gammon *n* cured or smoked ham

gamut *n* whole range or scale (of music etc.)

gander *n* **1** male goose **2** *informal* quick look

gang *n* **1** (criminal) group **2** organized group of workmen **gangland** *n* criminal underworld **gang up** *v* form an alliance (against)

gangling *adj* lanky and awkward

ganglion *n* **1** group of nerve cells **2** small harmless tumour

gangplank *n* portable bridge for boarding or leaving a ship

gangrene *n* decay of body tissue as a result of disease or injury interrupting blood supply **gangrenous** *adj*

gangster *n* member of a criminal gang

gangway *n* **1** passage between rows of seats **2** gangplank

gannet *n* **1** large sea bird **2** *slang* greedy person

gantry *n*, *pl* **-tries** structure supporting something such as a crane or rocket

gaol [**jayl**] *n* same as **jail**

gap *n* **1** break or opening **2** interruption or interval **3** divergence or difference **gappy** *adj*

gape *v* **1** stare in wonder **2** open the mouth wide **3** be or become wide open **gaping** *adj*

garage *n* **1** building used to house automobiles **2** place for the refuelling and repair of automobiles ▷ *v* **3** put or keep an automobile in a garage

garb *n* **1** clothes ▷ *v* **2** clothe

garbage *n* waste matter **garbage can** large usu. cylindrical container for household rubbish **garbage collector** person whose job is to collect household rubbish

garble *v* jumble or distort (a story etc.)

garden *n* **1** piece of land for growing flowers, fruit, or vegetables **gardens 2** ornamental park ▷ *v* **3** cultivate a garden **gardener** *n* **gardening** *n* **garden centre** place selling plants and gardening equipment

gardenia [gar-**deen**-ya] *n* **1** large fragrant white waxy flower **2** shrub bearing this

gargantuan *adj* huge

gargle *v* **1** wash the throat with (a liquid) by breathing out slowly through the liquid ▷ *n* **2** act or sound of gargling **3** liquid used for gargling

gargoyle *n* waterspout carved in the form of a grotesque face, esp. on a church

garish *adj* crudely bright or colourful **garishly** *adv* **garishness** *n*

garland *n* **1** wreath of flowers worn or hung as a decoration ▷ *v* **2** decorate with garlands

garlic *n* pungent bulb of a plant of the onion family, used in cooking

garment *n* article of clothing

garner *v* collect or store

garnet *n* red semiprecious stone

garnish *v* **1** decorate (food) ▷ *n* **2** decoration for food

garret *n* attic in a house

garrison *n* **1** troops stationed in a town or fort **2** fortified place ▷ *v* **3** station troops in

garrotte *n* **1** Spanish method of execution by strangling **2** cord or wire used for this ▷ *v* **3** kill by this method

garrulous *adj* talkative **garrulously** *adv* **garrulity** *n*

garter *n* band worn round the leg to hold up a sock or stocking

gas *n*, *pl* **gases** or **gasses 1** airlike substance that is not liquid or solid **2** fossil fuel in the form of a gas, used for heating **3** gaseous anesthetic **4** gasoline **5** *informal* idle talk, boasting ▷ *v* **gassing, gassed 6** poison or render unconscious with gas **7** *informal* talk idly or boastfully **gassy** *adj* filled with gas **gaseous** *adj* of or like gas **gasbag** *n informal* person who talks too much **gas chamber** airtight room filled with poison gas to kill people or animals **gasholder** or **gasometer** [gas-**som**-it-er] *n* large tank for storing gas **gas mask** mask with a chemical filter to protect the wearer against poison gas

gash *v* **1** make a long deep cut in ▷ *n* **2** long deep cut

gasket *n* piece of rubber etc. placed between two metal surfaces to act as a seal

gasoline *n* inflammable liquid obtained from petroleum, used as fuel in internal-combustion engines **gasoline bomb** incendiary device consisting of a bottle filled with gasoline

gasp *v* **1** draw in breath sharply or with difficulty **2** utter breathlessly ▷ *n* **3** convulsive intake of breath

gastric *adj* of the stomach **gastritis** *n* inflammation of the stomach

gastroenteritis *n* inflammation of the stomach and intestines

gastronomy *n* art of good eating **gastronomic** *adj*

gastropod *n* mollusc, such as a snail, with a single flattened muscular foot

gate *n* **1** movable barrier, usu. hinged, in a wall or fence **2** opening with a gate **3** any entrance or way in **4** (entrance money paid by)

those attending a sporting event **gate-crash** *v* enter (a party) uninvited **gatehouse** *n* building at or above a gateway **gateway** *n* **1** entrance with a gate **2** means of access: *Bombay, gateway to India*

gâteau [**gat**-toe] *n, pl* **-teaux** [-toes] *Brit* rich elaborate cake

gather *v* **1** assemble **2** increase gradually **3** collect gradually **4** learn from information given **5** draw (material) into small tucks or folds **6** pick or harvest **gathers** *pl n* gathered folds in material **gathering** *n* assembly

gauche [gohsh] *adj* socially awkward **gaucheness** *n* **gaucherie** *n* **1** awkwardness **2** gauche act

gaucho [**gow**-choh] *n, pl* **-chos** S American cowboy

gaudy *adj* **gaudier, gaudiest** vulgarly bright or colourful **gaudily** *adv* **gaudiness** *n*

gauge [gayj] *v* **1** measure the amount or condition of **2** estimate or judge ▷ *n* **3** scale or standard of measurement **4** measuring instrument **5** distance between the rails of a railway track

gaunt *adj* **1** lean and haggard **2** (of a place) desolate or bleak **gauntness** *n*

gauntlet[1] *n* heavy glove with a long cuff **throw down the gauntlet** offer a challenge

gauntlet[2] *n* **run the gauntlet 1** be forced to run between, and be struck by, two rows of men, as a former military punishment **2** be exposed to criticism or unpleasant treatment

gauze *n* **1** transparent loosely-woven fabric **2** fine wire mesh **gauzy** *adj*

gave *v* past tense of **give**

gavel [**gahv**-el] *n* small hammer banged on a table

by a judge, auctioneer, or chairman to call for attention

gavotte *n* **1** old formal dance **2** music for this

gawk *v slang* stare stupidly **gawky** *adj* clumsy or awkward **gawkiness** *n*

gawp *v slang* stare stupidly

gay *adj* **1** homosexual **2** carefree and merry **3** colourful ▷ *n* **4** homosexual **gayness** *n* homosexuality

gaze *v* **1** look fixedly ▷ *n* **2** fixed look

gazebo [gaz-**zee**-boh] *n, pl* -**bos, -boes** summerhouse with a good view

gazelle *n* small graceful antelope

gazette *n* official publication containing announcements **gazetteer** *n* (part of) a book that lists and describes places

gazump *v* raise the price of a house after verbally agreeing it with (a prospective buyer)

GB 1 Great Britain **2** Also **Gb** gigabyte

GDP gross domestic product

gear *n* **1** set of toothed wheels connecting with another or with a rack to change the direction or speed of transmitted motion **2** mechanism for transmitting motion by gears **3** setting of a gear to suit engine speed: *first gear* **4** clothing or belongings **5** equipment ▷ *v* **6** adapt (one thing) to fit in with another **in** *or* **out of gear** with the gear mechanism engaged or disengaged **gearbox** *n* case enclosing a set of gears in a motor vehicle **gear up** *v* prepare for an activity

gecko *n, pl* **geckos, geckoes** small tropical lizard

geek *n informal* person who is knowledgeable and enthusiastic about a subject **geeky** *adj*

geese *n* plural of **goose**

geezer *n informal* (old or eccentric) man

Geiger counter [**guy**-ger] *n* instrument for detecting and measuring radiation

geisha [**gay**-sha] *n, pl* -**sha, -shas** (in Japan) professional female companion for men

gel [**jell**] *n* **1** jelly-like substance ▷ *v* **gelling, gelled 2** form a gel **3** *informal* take on a definite form

gelatin [**jel**-at-tin], **gelatine** *n* **1** substance made by boiling animal bones **2** edible jelly made of this **gelatinous** [jel-**at**-in-uss] *adj* of or like jelly

geld *v* castrate **gelding** *n* castrated horse

gelid [**jel**-lid] *adj* very cold

gelignite *n* type of dynamite used for blasting

gem *n* **1** precious stone or jewel **2** highly valued person or thing

gen *n informal* information **gen up on** *v* **genning, genned** *informal* make or become fully informed about

gendarme [**zhahn**-darm] *n* member of the French police force

gender *n* **1** state of being male or female, sex **2** *grammar* classification of nouns in certain languages as masculine, feminine, or neuter

gene [**jean**] *n* part of a cell which determines inherited characteristics

genealogy [jean-ee-**al**-a-gee] *n, pl* -**gies** (study of) the history and descent of a family or families **genealogical** *adj* **genealogist** *n*

genera [**jen**-er-a] *n* plural of **genus**

general *adj* **1** common or widespread **2** of or affecting all or most **3** not specific **4** including or dealing with various or miscellaneous items **5** highest in authority or rank: *general manager* **6** true in most cases ▷ *n* **7** very senior army officer **generally** *adv*

generality *n* **1** general principle **2** state of being general **generalize** *v* **1** draw general conclusions **2** speak in generalities **3** make widely known or used **generalization** *n* **general delivery** post office department where a traveller's letters are kept until called for **general election** election in which representatives are chosen for every constituency **general practitioner** nonspecialist doctor serving a local area

generate *v* produce or bring into being **generative** *adj* capable of producing **generator** *n* machine for converting mechanical energy into electrical energy

generation *n* **1** all the people born about the same time **2** average time between two generations (about 30 years) **3** generating

generic [jin-**ner**-ik] *adj* of a class, group, or genus **generically** *adv*

generous *adj* **1** free in giving **2** free from pettiness **3** plentiful **generously** *adv* **generosity** *n*

genesis [**jen**-iss-iss] *n, pl* **-eses** [-iss-eez] beginning or origin

genetic [jin-**net**-tik] *adj* of genes or genetics **genetics** *n* study of heredity and variation in organisms **geneticist** *n* **genetic engineering** alteration of the genetic structure of an organism for a particular purpose **genetic fingerprinting** use of a person's unique DNA pattern for identification

genial [**jean**-ee-al] *adj* cheerful and friendly

genially *adv* **geniality** *n*

genie [**jean**-ee] *n* (in fairy tales) a servant who appears by magic and grants wishes

genital *adj* of the sexual organs or reproduction **genitals** *or* **genitalia** [jen-it-**ail**-ya] *pl n* external sexual organs

genitive *adj, n* (of) the grammatical case indicating possession or association

genius [**jean**-yuss] *n* (person with) exceptional ability in a particular field

genocide [**jen**-no-side] *n* murder of a race of people

genome *n biol* full complement of genetic material within an organism

genre [**zhahn**-ra] *n* style of literary, musical, or artistic work

gent *n informal* **1** gentleman **gents** **2** men's public lavatory

genteel *adj* affectedly proper and polite **genteelly** *adv*

gentian [**jen**-shun] *n* mountain plant with deep blue flowers

gentile *adj, n* non-Jewish (person)

gentle *adj* **1** mild or kindly **2** not rough or severe **3** gradual **4** easily controlled, tame **5** noble or well-born **gentleness** *n* **gently** *adv* **gentleman** *n* **1** polite well-bred man **2** man of high social position **3** polite name for a man **gentlemanly** *adj* **gentlewoman** *n fem*

gentry *n* people just below the nobility in social rank **gentrification** *n* taking-over of a traditionally working-class area by middle-class incomers **gentrify** *v*

genuflect *v* bend the knee as a sign of reverence or deference **genuflection** *or* **genuflexion** *n*

genuine *adj* **1** not fake,

authentic **2** sincere **genuinely** adv **genuineness** n

genus [jean-uss] n, pl **genera**
1 group into which a family of animals or plants is divided **2** kind, type

geocentric adj **1** having the earth as a centre **2** measured as from the earth's centre

geode n cavity lined with crystals within a rock

geography n study of the earth's physical features, climate, population, etc. **geographer** n **geographical** or **geographic** adj **geographically** adv

geology n study of the earth's origin, structure, and composition **geological** adj **geologically** adv **geologist** n

geometry n branch of mathematics dealing with points, lines, curves, and surfaces **geometric** or **geometrical** adj **geometrically** adv **geometrician** n

geopolitics n **1** study of the effect of the geographical position of a country on its politics **2** global politics **geopolitical** adj

georgette [jor-**jet**] n fine silky fabric

Georgian adj **1** of the time of any of the kings of Britain called George, esp. 1714–1830 **2** of or from Georgia

geostationary adj (of a satellite) orbiting so as to remain over the same point of the earth's surface

geothermal adj of or using the heat in the earth's interior

geranium n cultivated plant with red, pink, or white flowers

gerbil [**jer**-bill] n burrowing desert rodent of Asia and Africa

geriatrics n branch of medicine dealing with old age and its diseases **geriatric** adj, n old (person)

germ n **1** microbe, esp. one causing disease **2** beginning from which something may develop **3** simple structure that can develop into a complete organism **germicide** n substance that kills germs **germicidal** adj

german adj **1** having the same parents: brother-german **2** being a first cousin: cousin-german

German adj **1** of Germany ▷ n **2** person from Germany **3** language of Germany, Austria, and parts of Switzerland **German measles** contagious disease accompanied by a cough, sore throat, and red spots **German shepherd dog** Alsatian

germane adj **germane to** relevant to

germinate v (cause to) sprout or begin to grow **germination** n **germinal** adj of or in the earliest stage of development

gerrymandering n division of voting constituencies in order to give an unfair advantage to one party

gerund [**jer**-rund] n noun formed from a verb: living

Gestapo n secret state police of Nazi Germany

gestation n **1** (period of) carrying of babies in the womb during pregnancy **2** developing of a plan or idea in the mind

gesticulate v make expressive movements of the hands and arms **gesticulation** n

gesture n **1** movement to convey meaning **2** thing said or done to show one's feelings ▷ v **3** gesticulate

get v **getting**, **got** **1** obtain

or receive **2** bring or fetch **3** contract (an illness) **4** (cause to) become as specified: *get wet* **5** understand **6** (often foll. by *to*) come (to) or arrive (at) **7** go on board (a plane, bus, etc.) **8** persuade **9** *informal* annoy **10** *informal* have the better of **11** be revenged on **12** receive a broadcast signal **13** prepare (a meal) **get across** *v* (cause to) be understood **get at** *v* **1** gain access to **2** imply or mean **3** criticize **getaway** *adj, n* (used in) escape **get by** *v* manage in spite of difficulties **get off** *v* (cause to) avoid the consequences of, or punishment for, an action **get off with** *v informal* start a romantic or sexual relationship with **get over** *v* recover from **get through** *v* **1** (cause to) succeed **2** contact by telephone **3** use up (money or supplies) **get through to** *v* make (a person) understand **get-up** *n informal* costume **get up to** *v* be involved in

geyser [**geez**-er] *n* **1** spring that discharges steam and hot water **2** *Brit* domestic gas water heater

ghastly *adj* -**lier**, -**liest** **1** *informal* very unpleasant **2** deathly pale **3** *informal* horrible **ghastliness** *n*

ghat *n* (in India) **1** steps leading down to a river **2** mountain pass

ghee [**gee**] *n* (in Indian cookery) clarified butter

gherkin *n* small pickled cucumber

ghetto *n, pl* -**tos**, -**toes** slum area inhabited by a deprived minority **ghetto-blaster** *n informal* large portable cassette-recorder

ghillie *n* same as **gillie**

ghost *n* **1** disembodied spirit of a dead person **2** faint trace ▷ *v* **3** ghostwrite **ghostly** *adj*

ghost town deserted town

ghostwrite *v* write (a book or article) on behalf of another person who is credited as the author **ghostwriter** *n*

ghoul [**gool**] *n* **1** person with morbid interests **2** demon that eats corpses **ghoulish** *adj*

GI *n informal* US soldier

giant *n* **1** mythical being of superhuman size **2** very large person or thing ▷ *adj* **3** huge **giantess** *n fem*

gibber [**jib**-ber] *v* speak or utter rapidly and unintelligibly **gibberish** *n* rapid unintelligible talk

gibbet [**jib**-bit] *n* gallows

gibbon [**gib**-bon] *n* agile tree-dwelling ape of S Asia

gibbous *adj* (of the moon) more than half but less than fully illuminated

gibe [**jibe**] *v, n* same as **jibe**[1]

giblets [**jib**-lets] *pl n* gizzard, liver, heart, and neck of a fowl

GIC *Canad* guaranteed investment certificate: certificate guaranteeing a fixed rate of interest on a sum deposited for a fixed term

giddy *adj* -**dier**, -**diest** **1** feeling unsteady on one's feet, as if about to faint **2** scatter-brained **giddily** *adv* **giddiness** *n*

gift *n* **1** present **2** natural talent ▷ *v* **3** present with **gifted** *adj* talented

gig[1] *n* **1** single performance by pop or jazz musicians ▷ *v* **gigging, gigged 2** play gigs

gig[2] *n* light two-wheeled horse-drawn carriage

gigantic *adj* enormous

giggle *v* **1** laugh nervously or foolishly ▷ *n* **2** such a laugh **giggly** *adj*

gigolo [**jig**-a-lo] *n, pl* -**los** man paid by an older woman to be her escort or lover

gigot n leg of lamb or mutton

gild v **gilding, gilded** or **gilt**
1 put a thin layer of gold on
2 make falsely attractive **gilt**
adj **1** gilded ▷ n **2** thin layer
of gold used as decoration
gilt-edged adj denoting
government stocks on which
interest payments and final
repayment are guaranteed

gill [**jill**] n liquid measure of
quarter of a pint, equal to
0.142 litres

gillie n (in Scotland) attendant
for hunting or fishing

gills [**gillz**] pl n breathing
organs in fish and other water
creatures

gimbals pl n set of pivoted
rings which allow nautical
instruments to remain
horizontal at sea

gimcrack [**jim**-krak] adj
1 showy but cheap **2** shoddy

gimlet [**gim**-let] n small tool
with a screwlike tip for boring
holes in wood **gimlet-eyed**
adj having a piercing glance

gimmick n something
designed to attract attention
or publicity **gimmickry**
n **gimmicky** adj

gin¹ n alcoholic drink flavoured
with juniper berries

gin² n **1** machine for separating
seeds from raw cotton **2** wire
noose used to trap small
animals

ginger n **1** root of a tropical
plant, used as a spice **2** light
orange-brown colour **gingery**
adj **ginger ale** or **ginger beer**
fizzy ginger-flavoured soft
drink **gingerbread** n moist
cake flavoured with ginger
ginger group group within a
larger group that agitates for
a more active policy **ginger
snap** hard ginger-flavoured
cookie

gingerly adv **1** cautiously ▷ adj
2 cautious

gingham n cotton cloth, usu.
checked or striped

gingivitis [jin-jiv-**vite**-iss] n
inflammation of the gums

ginkgo [**gink**-go] n, pl **-goes**
ornamental Chinese tree

ginseng [**jin**-seng] n (root of)
a plant believed to have tonic
and energy-giving properties

Gipsy n, pl **-sies** same as **Gypsy**

giraffe n African ruminant
mammal with a spotted
yellow skin and long neck and
legs

gird v **girding, girded** or **girt**
1 put a belt round **2** secure
with or as if with a belt
3 surround **gird (up) one's
loins** prepare for action

girder n large metal beam

girdle¹ n **1** woman's elastic
corset **2** belt **3** anat encircling
structure or part ▷ v
4 surround or encircle

girl n **1** female child **2** young
woman **girlhood** n **girlish**
adj **girlie** adj informal
featuring photographs
of naked or scantily clad
women **girlfriend** n **1** girl or
woman with whom a person
is romantically or sexually
involved **2** female friend

giro [**jire**-oh] n, pl **-ros** Brit
1 system of transferring
money within a post office
or bank directly from one
account to another **2** informal
social security payment
by giro cheque

girt v past of **gird**

girth n **1** measurement round
something **2** band round a
horse to hold the saddle
in position

gist [**jist**] n substance or
main point of a matter

give v **giving, gave, given**
1 present (something) to
another person **2** transfer
in exchange or payment
3 grant or provide **4** utter or

emît **5** perform or do: *give an interview* **6** organize or host **7** sacrifice or devote **8** concede **9** yield or break under pressure ▷ *n* **10** resilience or elasticity **give away** *v* **1** donate as a gift **2** reveal **3** hand over (a bride) formally to her spouse in a marriage ceremony **giveaway** *n* **1** unintentional disclosure ▷ *adj* **2** very cheap or free **give in** *v* admit defeat **give off** *v* emit **give out** *v* **1** distribute **2** emit **3** come to an end or fail **give over** *v* **1** set aside for a specific purpose **2** *informal* cease **give up** *v* **1** acknowledge defeat **2** abandon

gizzard *n* part of a bird's stomach

glacé [**glass**-say] *adj* crystallized or candied

glacier *n* slow-moving mass of ice formed by accumulated snow **glacial** *adj* **1** of ice or glaciers **2** very cold **3** unfriendly **glaciated** *adj* covered with or affected by glaciers **glaciation** *n*

glad *adj* **gladder, gladdest 1** pleased and happy **2** causing happiness **glad to** very willing to (do something) **the glad eye** *informal* an inviting or seductive glance **gladly** *adv* **gladness** *n* **gladden** *v* make glad **glad rags** *informal* best clothes

glade *n* open space in a forest

gladiator *n* (in ancient Rome) man trained to fight in arenas to provide entertainment

gladiolus *n, pl* **-lus, -li, -luses** garden plant with sword-shaped leaves

glamour *n* alluring charm or fascination **glamorous** *adj* alluring **glamorize** *v*

glance *n* **1** quick look ▷ *v* **2** look quickly **glancing** *adj* hitting at an oblique angle

glance off *v* strike and be deflected off (an object) at an oblique angle

gland *n* organ that produces and secretes substances in the body **glandular** *adj*

glanders *n* contagious disease of horses

glare *v* **1** stare angrily **2** be unpleasantly bright ▷ *n* **3** angry stare **4** unpleasant brightness **glaring** *adj* **1** conspicuous **2** unpleasantly bright **glaringly** *adv*

glasnost *n* policy of openness and accountability, developed in the USSR in the 1980s

glass *n* **1** hard brittle, usu. transparent substance made by melting sand **2** objects made of glass **3** tumbler **4** its contents **5** mirror **6** barometer **glasses 7** spectacles **glassy** *adj* **1** like glass **2** expressionless **glassiness** *n* **glasshouse** *n* **1** greenhouse **2** *informal* army prison **glass wool** fine glass fibres used for insulating

glaucoma *n* eye disease

glaze *v* **1** fit or cover with glass **2** cover with a glassy substance **3** become glassy ▷ *n* **4** transparent coating **5** substance used for this **glazier** *n* person who fits windows with glass

gleam *n* **1** small beam or glow of reflected light **2** brief or faint indication ▷ *v* **3** shine **gleaming** *adj*

glean *v* **1** gather (facts etc.) bit by bit **2** gather (the useful remnants of a crop) after harvesting **gleaner** *n*

glebe *n* land belonging to a parish church

glee *n* **1** triumph and delight **2** musical composition for three or more unaccompanied voices **gleeful** *adj* **gleefully** *adv*

glen n deep narrow valley

glib adj **glibber, glibbest** fluent but insincere or superficial **glibly** adv **glibness** n

glide v 1 move easily and smoothly 2 (of an aircraft) move without the use of engines ▷ n 3 smooth easy movement **glider** n aircraft without an engine which floats on air currents **gliding** n sport of flying gliders

glimmer v 1 shine faintly, flicker ▷ n 2 faint gleam 3 faint indication

glimpse n 1 brief or incomplete view ▷ v 2 catch a glimpse of

glint v 1 gleam brightly ▷ n 2 bright gleam

glissando n music slide between two notes in which all intermediate notes are played

glisten v gleam by reflecting light

glitch n sudden malfunction in an electronic system

glitter v 1 shine with bright flashes 2 be showy ▷ n 3 sparkle or brilliance 4 shiny powder used as decoration

glitzy adj **glitzier, glitziest** slang showily attractive

gloaming n twilight

gloat v (often foll. by over) look (at) or think (of) with smug or malicious pleasure

glob n rounded mass of thick fluid

global adj 1 worldwide 2 total or comprehensive **globally** adv **globalization** n process by which a company, etc., expands to operate internationally **global warming** increase in the planet's temperature believed to be caused by the greenhouse effect

globe n 1 sphere with a map of the earth on it 2 spherical object **the globe** the earth **globetrotter** n habitual worldwide traveller **globetrotting** n, adj

globule n small round drop **globular** adj

globulin n simple protein found in living tissue

glockenspiel n percussion instrument consisting of small metal bars played with hammers

gloom n 1 melancholy or depression 2 darkness **gloomy** adj **gloomily** adv

glory n, pl **-ries** 1 praise or honour 2 splendour 3 praiseworthy thing 4 adoration or worship ▷ v **-rying, -ried** 5 (foll. by in) take great pleasure in 6 (foll. by in) triumph or exalt **glorify** v 1 make (something) seem more important than it is 2 praise 3 worship (God) **glorification** n **glorious** adj 1 brilliantly beautiful 2 delightful 3 having or full of glory **gloriously** adv **glory hole** informal untidy cupboard or storeroom

gloss[1] n 1 surface shine or lustre 2 paint or cosmetic giving a shiny finish **glossy** adj 1 smooth and shiny 2 (of a magazine) printed on shiny paper **glossily** adv **glossiness** n **gloss over** v (try to) cover up or pass over (a fault or error)

gloss[2] n 1 explanatory comment added to the text of a book ▷ v 2 add glosses to

glossary n, pl **-ries** list of special or technical words with definitions

glottis n, pl **-tises, -tides** vocal cords and the space between them **glottal** adj

glove n covering for the hand with individual sheaths for each finger and the thumb

g

gloved adj covered by a glove

glove compartment small storage area in the dashboard of an automobile

glow n 1 light produced by a great heat 2 brightness of complexion 3 feeling of wellbeing ▷ v 4 produce a steady light without flames 5 shine 6 have a feeling of wellbeing or satisfaction 7 (of a colour) look warm **glow-worm** n insect giving out a green light

glower [rhymes with **power**] v, n scowl

gloxinia n tropical plant with large bell-shaped flowers

glucose n kind of sugar found in fruit

glue n 1 natural or synthetic sticky substance used as an adhesive ▷ v **glueing** or **gluing, glued** 2 fasten with glue 3 (foll. by to) pay full attention to: her eyes were glued to the TV **gluey** adj **glue-sniffing** n inhaling of glue fumes for intoxicating or hallucinating effects

glum adj **glummer, glummest** sullen or gloomy **glumly** adv

glut n 1 excessive supply ▷ v **glutting, glutted** 2 feed or fill to excess 3 oversupply

gluten [**gloo**-ten] n protein found in cereal grain

glutinous [**gloo**-tin-uss] adj sticky or gluey

glutton[1] n 1 greedy person 2 person with a great capacity for something **gluttonous** adj **gluttony** n

glutton[2] n wolverine

glycerin, glycerine n colourless sweet liquid used widely in chemistry and industry

glycerol n technical name for glycerin(e)

gm gram

GM genetically modified

GMT Greenwich Mean Time

gnarled adj rough, twisted, and knobbly

gnash v grind (the teeth) together in anger or pain

gnat n small biting two-winged fly

gnaw v **gnawing, gnawed, gnawed** or **gnawn** 1 bite or chew steadily 2 (foll. by at) cause constant distress (to)

gneiss n coarse-grained metamorphic rock

gnome n imaginary creature like a little old man

gnomic [**no**-mik] adj of pithy sayings

Gnosticism n religious movement believing in intuitive spiritual knowledge **Gnostic** n, adj

GNP gross national product

gnu [**noo**] n oxlike S African antelope

go v **going, went, gone** 1 move to or from a place 2 depart 3 make regular journeys 4 function 5 be, do, or become as specified 6 contribute to a result: it just goes to show 7 be allotted to a specific purpose or recipient 8 be sold 9 blend or harmonize 10 fail or break down 11 elapse 12 be got rid of 13 attend 14 reach or exceed certain limits: she's gone too far this time 15 be acceptable 16 carry authority ▷ n 17 attempt 18 verbal attack 19 turn 20 informal energy or vigour **make a go of** be successful at **go back on** v break (a promise etc.) **go-between** n intermediary **go for** v 1 choose 2 attack 3 apply to equally **go-getter** n energetically ambitious person **go-go dancer** scantily-dressed erotic dancer **go off** v 1 explode 2 ring or sound 3 informal stop liking **4** *informal* become stale or rotten **go out** *v* **1** go to social events **2** be romantically involved (with) **3** be extinguished **go over** *v* examine or check **go-slow** *n* deliberate slowing of work-rate as an industrial protest **go through** *v* **1** suffer or undergo **2** examine or search

goad *v* **1** provoke (someone) to take action, usu. in anger ▷ *n* **2** spur or incentive **3** spiked stick for driving cattle

goal *n* **1** *sports* posts through which the ball or puck has to be propelled to score **2** *sports* score made in this way **3** aim or purpose **goalie** *n informal* goalkeeper **goalkeeper** *n* player whose task is to stop shots entering the goal **goalpost** *n* one of the two posts supporting the crossbar of a goal **move the goalposts** change the aims of an activity to ensure the desired result

goat *n* sure-footed ruminant animal **get someone's goat** *slang* annoy someone **goatee** *n* small pointed beard

gob *n* **1** lump of a soft substance **2** *slang* mouth

gobbet *n* lump, esp. of food

gobble[1] *v* eat hastily and greedily

gobble[2] *n* **1** rapid gurgling cry of the male turkey ▷ *v* **2** make this noise

gobbledegook, gobbledygook *n* unintelligible (official) language or jargon

goblet *n* drinking cup

goblin *n* (in folklore) small malevolent creature

goby *n, pl* **-by, -bies** small spiny-finned fish

god *n* **1** spirit or being worshipped as having supernatural power **2** object of worship, idol **3 God** (in monotheistic religions) the Supreme Being, creator and ruler of the universe **goddess** *n fem* **the gods** top balcony in a theatre **godlike** *adj* **godly** *adj* devout or pious **godliness** *n* **god-fearing** *adj* pious and devout **godforsaken** *adj* desolate or dismal **godsend** *n* something unexpected but welcome

godetia *n* garden plant with showy flowers

godparent *n* person who promises at a person's baptism to look after his or her religious upbringing **godchild** *n* child for whom a person stands as godparent **goddaughter** *n* **godfather** *n* **1** male godparent **2** head of a criminal, esp. Mafia, organization **godmother** *n* **godson** *n*

goggle *v* stare with wide-open eyes **goggles** *pl n* protective spectacles

going *n* **1** departure **2** condition of the ground for walking or riding over **3** rate of travel ▷ *adj* **4** thriving **5** current or accepted **6** available **going-over** *n, pl* **goings-over** *informal* **1** investigation or examination **2** scolding or thrashing **goings-on** *pl n* mysterious or unacceptable events

goitre [**goy**-ter] *n* swelling of the thyroid gland in the neck

go-kart *n* small low-powered racing car

gold *n* **1** yellow precious metal **2** jewellery or coins made of this ▷ *adj* **3** made of gold **4** deep yellow **gold-digger** *n* **2** *informal* woman who uses her sexual attractions to get money from a man **goldeye** *n* edible N American fish, often smoked **goldfinch** *n* kind of finch, the male of which has yellow-and-black wings **goldfish** n orange fish kept in ponds or aquariums **gold leaf** thin gold sheet used for gilding **gold medal** medal given to the winner of a competition or race

golden adj **1** made of gold **2** gold-coloured **3** very successful or promising **golden eagle** large mountain eagle of the N hemisphere **golden handshake** informal payment to a departing employee **golden mean** middle course between extremes **golden rule** important principle **golden wedding** fiftieth wedding anniversary

golf n **1** outdoor game in which a ball is struck with clubs into a series of holes ▷ v **2** play golf **golfer** n

golliwog n soft black-faced male doll

gonad n organ producing reproductive cells, such as a testicle or ovary

gondola n **1** long narrow boat used in Venice **2** suspended cabin of a cable car, airship, etc. **gondolier** n person who rows a gondola

gone v past participle of **go** ▶ **goner** n informal person or thing beyond help or recovery

gong n **1** rimmed metal disc that produces a note when struck **2** slang medal

gonorrhea, gonorrhoea [gon-or-**ree**-a] n venereal disease with a discharge from the genitals

good adj **better, best** **1** giving pleasure **2** kindly **3** commendable **4** morally excellent **5** talented **6** well-behaved **7** beneficial **8** valid **9** reliable **10** financially

sound **11** complete or full ▷ n **12** benefit **13** positive moral qualities **goods** **14** merchandise **15** property **as good as** virtually **for good** permanently **goodness** n **goodly** adj considerable **goody** n, pl **-dies 1** enjoyable thing **2** informal hero in a book or film **goody-goody** adj, n smugly virtuous (person) **good-for-nothing** adj, n irresponsible or worthless (person) **Good Samaritan** person who helps another in distress **goodwill** n **1** kindly feeling **2** popularity and good reputation of a business

goodbye interj, n expression used on parting

gooey adj **gooier, gooiest** informal sticky and soft

goof informal ▷ n **1** mistake ▷ v **2** make a mistake

Google n **1** popular search engine on the internet ▷ v **2** **google** search for (something on the internet) using a search engine

goon n informal **1** stupid person **2** hired thug

goose n, pl **geese 1** web-footed bird like a large duck **2** female of this bird **goose flesh** or **goose pimples** bristling of the skin due to cold or fright **goose-step** v march with the legs high and without bending the knees

gooseberry n **1** edible yellowy-green berry **2** informal unwanted single person accompanying a couple

gopher [**go**-fer] n N American burrowing rodent

gore[1] n blood from a wound

gore[2] v pierce with horns

gorge n **1** deep narrow valley ▷ v **2** eat greedily **make one's gorge rise** cause feelings of disgust

gorgeous adj **1** strikingly

beautiful or attractive **2** *informal* very pleasant **gorgeously** *adv*

gorgon *n* terrifying or repulsive woman

Gorgonzola *n* sharp-flavoured blue-veined Italian cheese

gorilla *n* largest of the apes, found in Africa

gormless *adj informal* stupid

gorse *n* prickly yellow-flowered shrub

gory *adj* **gorier, goriest 1** horrific or bloodthirsty **2** involving bloodshed

goshawk *n* large hawk

gosling *n* young goose

gospel *n* **1** unquestionable truth **2 Gospel** any of the first four books of the New Testament

gossamer *n* **1** filmy cobweb **2** very fine fabric

gossip *n* **1** idle talk, esp. about other people **2** person who engages in gossip ▷ *v* **gossiping, gossiped 3** engage in gossip **gossipy** *adj*

got *v* past of **get** ▶ **have got** possess **have got to** need or be required to

Gothic *adj* **1** (of architecture) of or in the style common in Europe from the 12th–16th centuries, with pointed arches **2** of or in an 18th-century literary style characterized by gloom and the supernatural **3** in a heavy ornate script typeface

gouache *n* (painting using) watercolours mixed with glue

Gouda *n* mild-flavoured Dutch cheese

gouge [gowj] *v* **1** scoop or force out **2** cut (a hole or groove) in (something) ▷ *n* **3** chisel with a curved cutting edge **4** hole or groove

goulash [goo-lash] *n* rich stew seasoned with paprika

gourd [goord] *n* **1** fleshy fruit of a climbing plant **2** its dried shell, used as a container

gourmand [goor-mand] *n* person who is very keen on food and drink

gourmet [goorm-may] *n* connoisseur of food and drink

gout [gowt] *n* disease causing inflammation of the joints **gouty** *adj*

govern *v* **1** rule, direct, or control **2** exercise restraint over (temper etc.) **governable** *adj* **governance** *n* governing **governess** *n* woman teacher in a private household **government** *n* **1** executive policy-making body of a state **2** the state and its administration **3** system by which a country or state is ruled **governmental** *adj* **Government House** residence of Canadian governor general or lieutenant governor **governor** *n* **1** official governing a province or state **2** senior administrator of a society, institution, or prison **governor general** representative of the Crown in a Commonwealth dominion

gown *n* **1** woman's long formal dress **2** surgeon's overall **3** official robe worn by judges, clergymen, etc.

goy *n slang* Jewish word for a non-Jew

GP general practitioner

GPS Global Positioning System: a satellite-based navigation system

grab *v* **grabbing, grabbed 1** grasp suddenly, snatch ▷ *n* **2** sudden snatch

grace *n* **1** beauty and elegance **2** polite, kind behaviour **3** goodwill or favour **4** delay granted **5** courtesy or decency **6** short prayer of thanks for a meal **7 Grace** title of a duke, duchess, or archbishop ▷ v **8** add grace to **9** honour **graceful** adj **gracefully** adv **graceless** adj **gracious** adj **1** kind and courteous **2** condescendingly polite **3** elegant **graciously** adv **grace note** music note ornamenting a melody

grade n **1** place on a scale of quality, rank, or size **2** mark or rating **3** class in school ▷ v **4** arrange in grades **5** assign a grade to **make the grade** succeed **gradation** n **1** (stage in) a series of degrees or steps **2** arrangement in stages

gradient n (degree of) slope

gradual adj occurring, developing, or moving in small stages **gradually** adv

graduate n **1** person with a degree or diploma ▷ v **2** receive a degree or diploma **3** change by degrees **4** mark (a container etc.) with units of measurement **graduation** n

graffiti [graf-**fee**-tee] pl n words or drawings scribbled or sprayed on walls etc.

graft[1] n **1** shoot of a plant set in the stalk of another **2** surgical transplant of skin or tissue ▷ v **3** insert (a plant shoot) in another stalk **4** transplant (living tissue) surgically

graft[2] informal ▷ n **1** hard work **2** obtaining of money by misusing one's position ▷ v **3** work hard **grafter** n

grail n same as **Holy Grail**

grain n **1** seedlike fruit of a cereal plant **2** cereal plants in general **3** small hard particle **4** arrangement of fibres, as in wood **5** texture or pattern resulting from this **6** very small amount **go against the grain** be contrary to one's natural inclination **grainy** adj

gram, gramme n metric unit of mass equal to one thousandth of a kilogram

grammar n **1** branch of linguistics dealing with the form, function, and order of words **2** book on the rules of grammar **3** use of words **grammarian** n **grammatical** adj according to the rules of grammar **grammatically** adv **grammar school** esp. formerly, a secondary school providing an education with a strong academic bias

gramophone n record player

grampus n, pl **-puses** sea mammal

gran n informal grandmother

granary n, pl **-ries** building for storing threshed grain

grand adj **1** large or impressive, imposing **2** dignified or haughty **3** informal excellent **4** (of a total) final **5** chief ▷ n **6** grand piano **7** slang thousand pounds or dollars **grandchild** n child of one's child **granddaughter** n female grandchild **grandfather** n male grandparent **grandfather clock** tall standing clock with a pendulum and wooden case **grandmother** n female grandparent **grandparent** n parent of one's parent **grand piano** large harp-shaped piano with the strings set horizontally **grand slam** see **slam** ▸ **grandson** n male grandchild **grandstand** n terraced block of seats giving the best view at a sports ground

grandeur n **1** magnificence **2** nobility or dignity

grandiloquent adj using pompous language **grandiloquently** adv **grandiloquence** n

grandiose adj **1** imposing

2 pretentiously grand **grandiosity** n

grange n country house with farm buildings

granite [**gran**-nit] n very hard igneous rock often used in building

granivorous adj feeding on grain or seeds

granny, grannie n informal grandmother **granny apartment** apartment in or added to a house, suitable for an elderly parent

grant v **1** give formally **2** consent to fulfil (a request) **3** admit ▷ n **4** sum of money provided by a government for a specific purpose, such as education **take for granted 1** accept as true without proof **2** take advantage of without due appreciation

granule n small grain **granular** adj of or like grains **granulated** adj (of sugar) in coarse grains

grape n small juicy green or purple berry, eaten raw or used to produce wine, raisins, currants, or sultanas **grapevine** n **1** grape-bearing vine **2** informal unofficial way of spreading news

grapefruit n large round yellow citrus fruit

graph n drawing showing the relation of different numbers or quantities plotted against a set of axes

graphic adj **1** vividly descriptive **2** of or using drawing, painting, etc. **graphics** pl n diagrams, graphs, etc., esp. as used on a television programme or computer screen **graphically** adv

graphite n soft black form of carbon, used in pencil leads

graphology n study of

handwriting **graphologist** n

grapnel n tool with several hooks, used to grasp or secure things

grapple v **1** come to grips with (a person) **2** try to cope with (something difficult) **grappling iron** grapnel

grasp v **1** grip something firmly **2** understand ▷ n **3** grip or clasp **4** understanding **5** total rule or possession **grasping** adj greedy or avaricious

grass n **1** common type of plant with jointed stems and long narrow leaves, including cereals and bamboo **2** lawn **3** pasture land **4** slang marijuana ▷ v **5** cover with grass **grassy** adj **grasshopper** n jumping insect with long hind legs **grass roots** ordinary members of a group, as distinct from its leaders **grassroots** adj **grass widow** woman whose spouse is absent for a time

grate[1] n framework of metal bars for holding fuel in a fireplace **grating** n framework of metal bars covering an opening

grate[2] v **1** rub into small bits on a rough surface **2** scrape with a harsh rasping noise **3** annoy **grater** n **grating** adj **1** harsh or rasping **2** annoying

grateful adj feeling or showing thanks **gratefully** adv **gratefulness** n

gratify v -**fying, -fied 1** satisfy or please **2** indulge (a desire or whim) **gratification** n

gratis adv, adj free, for nothing

gratitude n feeling of being thankful for a favour or gift

gratuitous [grat-**tyoo**-it-uss] adj **1** unjustified: *gratuitous violence* **2** given free **gratuitously** adv

gratuity [grat-**tyoo**-it-ee]
n, pl **-ties** money given for
services rendered, tip

grave¹ *n* hole for burying a
corpse **gravestone** *n* stone
marking a grave **graveyard** *n*
cemetery

grave² *adj* **1** serious and
worrying **2** serious and
solemn **gravely** *adv*

grave³ [rhymes with
halve] *n* accent (`) over a
vowel to indicate a special
pronunciation

gravel *n* mixture of small
stones and coarse sand
gravelled *adj* covered with
gravel **gravelly** *adj* **1** covered
with gravel **2** rough-
sounding

graven [**grave**-en] *adj* carved
or engraved

gravid [**grav**-id] *adj med*
pregnant

gravitate *v* **1** be influenced
or drawn towards **2** *physics*
move by gravity **gravitation**
n **gravitational** *adj*

gravity *n, pl* **-ties 1** force of
attraction of one object for
another, esp. of objects to
the earth **2** seriousness or
importance **3** solemnity

gravy *n, pl* **-vies 1** juices from
meat in cooking **2** sauce made
from these

gray *adj US* same as **grey**

grayling *n* fish of the salmon
family

graze¹ *v* feed on grass **grazier**
n person who feeds cattle for
market

graze² *v* **1** touch lightly in
passing **2** scratch or scrape
the skin ▷ *n* **3** slight scratch
or scrape

grease *n* **1** soft melted animal
fat **2** any thick oily substance
▷ *v* **3** apply grease to **greasy**
adj **greasiness** *n* **grease gun**
appliance for injecting oil
or grease into machinery

greasepaint *n* theatrical
make-up

great *adj* **1** large in size
or number **2** extreme
3 important **4** pre-eminent
5 *informal* excellent **great-**
prefix one generation older or
younger than: *great-grandfather*
greatly *adv* **greatness** *n*
greatcoat *n* heavy overcoat
Great Dane very large
graceful dog

greave *n* piece of armour for
the shin

grebe *n* diving water bird

Grecian [**gree**-shan] *adj* of
ancient Greece

greed *n* excessive desire for
something, such as food or
money **greedy** *adj* **greedily**
adv **greediness** *n*

Greek *n* **1** language of Greece
2 person from Greece ▷ *adj*
3 of Greece, the Greeks, or the
Greek language

green *adj* **1** of a colour between
blue and yellow **2** covered
with grass or plants **3** unripe
4 of or concerned with
environmental issues
5 envious or jealous
6 immature or gullible ▷ *n*
7 colour between blue and
yellow **8** area of grass kept for
a special purpose **9** **Green**
person concerned with
environmental issues **greens**
10 green vegetables
greenness *n* **greenish** *or*
greeny *adj* **greenery** *n*
vegetation **green belt**
protected area of open country
around a town **greengage** *n*
sweet green plum
greengrocer *n Brit* shopkeeper
selling vegetables and fruit
greenhorn *n* novice
greenhouse *n* glass building
for rearing plants
greenhouse effect rise in the
temperature of the earth
caused by heat absorbed from

the sun being unable to leave the atmosphere **greenhouse gas** any gas that contributes to the greenhouse effect **green light 1** signal to go **2** permission to proceed with something **greenroom** n room for actors when offstage **greenshank** n large European sandpiper **green thumb** skill in gardening

greet v **1** meet with expressions of welcome **2** receive in a specified manner **3** be immediately noticeable to **greeting** n

gregarious adj **1** fond of company **2** (of animals) living in flocks or herds

gremlin n imaginary being blamed for mechanical malfunctions

grenade n small bomb thrown by hand or fired from a rifle **grenadier** n soldier of a regiment formerly trained to throw grenades

grenadine [gren-a-**deen**] n syrup made from pomegranates, used in cocktails

grew v past tense of **grow**

grey adj **1** of a colour between black and white **2** (of hair) partly turned white ▷ n **3** colour between black and white **4** grey or whitish horse **greyness** n **grey matter** informal brains **greyish** adj

greyhound n swift slender dog used in racing

grid n **1** network of horizontal and vertical lines, bars, etc. **2** national network of electricity supply cables

griddle n flat iron plate for cooking

gridiron n **1** frame of metal bars for grilling food **2** N American football field

grief n deep sadness **grieve** v (cause to) feel grief **grievance** n real or imaginary cause

for complaint **grievous** adj **1** very severe or painful **2** very serious

griffin n mythical monster with an eagle's head and wings and a lion's body

grill n **1** device on a cooker that radiates heat downwards **2** grilled food **3** gridiron ▷ v **4** cook under a grill **5** question relentlessly **grilling** n relentless questioning

grille, grill n grating over an opening

grilse [grills] n salmon on its first return from the sea to fresh water

grim adj **grimmer, grimmest 1** harsh and unpleasant **2** stern **3** disagreeable **grimly** adv **grimness** n

grimace n **1** ugly or distorted facial expression of pain, disgust, etc. ▷ v **2** make a grimace

grime n **1** ingrained dirt ▷ v **2** make very dirty **grimy** adj **griminess** n

grin v **grinning, grinned 1** smile broadly, showing the teeth ▷ n **2** broad smile

grind v **grinding, ground 1** crush or rub to a powder **2** smooth or sharpen by friction **3** scrape together with a harsh noise **4** (foll. by down) treat harshly so as to prevent resistance ▷ n **5** informal hard or tedious work **grind out** v produce in a routine or uninspired manner **grindstone** n stone used for grinding

grip n **1** firm hold or grasp **2** way in which something is grasped **3** control or understanding **4** travelling bag **5** handle ▷ v **gripping, gripped 6** grasp or hold tightly **7** hold the interest or attention of **gripping** adj

gripe v **1** informal complain

persistently ▷ *n* **2** sudden intense bowel pain **3** *informal* complaint

grisly *adj* **-lier, -liest** horrifying or ghastly

grist *n* grain for grinding **grist to one's mill** something which can be turned to advantage

gristle *n* cartilage in meat **gristly** *adj*

grit *n* **1** rough particles of sand **2** courage **3 Grit** *informal* member or supporter of Liberal Party **grits 3** meal consisting of coarsely ground grain ▷ *v* **gritting, gritted 4** spread grit on (an icy road) **5** clench or grind (the teeth) **gritty** *adj* **grittiness** *n*

grizzle *v informal* whine or complain

grizzled *adj* grey-haired

grizzly *n, pl* **-zlies** Also **grizzly bear** large American bear

groan *n* **1** deep sound of grief or pain **2** *informal* complaint ▷ *v* **3** utter a groan **4** *informal* complain

groat *n hist* fourpenny piece

grocer *n* shopkeeper selling foodstuffs **grocery** *n, pl* **-ceries 1** business or premises of a grocer **groceries 2** goods sold by a grocer

grog *n* spirit, usu. rum, and water

groggy *adj* **-gier, -giest** *informal* faint, shaky, or dizzy

groin *n* **1** place where the legs join the abdomen **2** edge made by the intersection of two vaults

grommet *n* **1** ring or eyelet **2** *med* tube inserted in the ear to drain fluid from the middle ear

groom *n* **1** person who looks after horses **2** bridegroom **3** officer in a royal household ▷ *v* **4** make or keep one's clothes and appearance neat

and tidy **5** brush or clean a horse **6** train (someone) for a future role

groove *n* **1** long narrow channel in a surface ▷ *v* **2** cut groove(s) in

grope *v* feel about or search uncertainly **groping** *n*

gross *adj* **1** outrageously wrong **2** vulgar **3** repulsively fat **4** total, without deductions ▷ *n* **5** twelve dozen ▷ *v* **6** make as total revenue before deductions **grossly** *adv* **grossness** *n*

grotesque [grow-**tesk**] *adj* **1** strangely distorted or bizarre **2** ugly ▷ *n* **3** grotesque person or thing **4** artistic style mixing distorted human, animal, and plant forms **grotesquely** *adv*

grotto *n, pl* **-toes, -tos** small picturesque cave

grotty *adj* **-tier, -tiest** *informal* nasty or in bad condition

grouch *informal* ▷ *v* **1** grumble ▷ *n* **2** grumble **3** persistent grumbler **grouchy** *adj*

ground¹ *n* **1** surface of the earth **2** soil **3** area used for a specific purpose: *rugby ground* **4** position in an argument or controversy **grounds 5** enclosed land round a house **6** reason or motive **7** coffee dregs **8** *electrical* Also **earth** *US & Canad* connection between an electrical circuit or device and the earth, which is at zero potential ▷ *v* **9** ban an aircraft or pilot from flying **10** forbid (a child) to go out as a punishment **11** run (a ship) aground **12** instruct in the basics **13** base **14** *US & Canad* connect (a circuit or electrical device) to a ground **15** *baseball* hit the ball along the ground **groundless** *adj* without reason **grounding** *n* basic knowledge of a subject

groundhog n marmot with a flat head on a very short neck, and short, rounded ears
groundnut n peanut
groundsheet n waterproof sheet put on the ground under a tent **groundsman** n person employed to maintain a sports ground or park **groundswell** n rapidly developing general feeling **groundwork** n preliminary work
ground² v past of **grind**
group n 1 number of people or things regarded as a unit 2 small band of musicians or singers ▷ v 3 place or form into a group
grouper n large edible sea fish
grouse¹ n 1 stocky game bird 2 its flesh
grouse² v 1 grumble or complain ▷ n 2 complaint
grout n 1 thin mortar ▷ v 2 fill up with grout
grove n small group of trees
grovel [grov-el] v -elling, -elled 1 behave humbly in order to win a superior's favour 2 crawl on the floor
grow v growing, grew, grown 1 develop physically 2 (of a plant) exist 3 cultivate (plants) 4 increase in size or degree 5 originate 6 become gradually: *it was growing dark* **growth** n 1 growing 2 increase 3 something grown or growing 4 tumour **grown-up** adj, n adult **grow-op** n Canad illegal scheme to grow marijuana plants **grow up** v mature
growl v 1 make a low rumbling sound 2 say in a gruff manner ▷ n 3 growling sound
groyne n wall built out from the shore to control erosion
grub n 1 legless insect larva 2 slang food ▷ v grubbing, grubbed 3 dig out or uproot 4 dig up the surface of (soil) 5 search

grubby adj -bier, -biest dirty **grubbiness** n
grudge v 1 be unwilling to give or allow ▷ n 2 resentment
gruel n thin porridge
gruelling adj exhausting or severe
gruesome adj causing horror and disgust
gruff adj rough or surly in manner or voice **gruffly** adv **gruffness** n
grumble v 1 complain 2 rumble ▷ n 3 complaint 4 rumble **grumbler** n **grumbling** adj, n
grumpy adj grumpier, grumpiest bad-tempered **grumpily** adv **grumpiness** n
grunge n 1 style of rock music with a fuzzy guitar sound 2 deliberately untidy and uncoordinated fashion style
grunt v 1 (esp. of pigs) make a low short gruff sound ▷ n 2 pig's sound 3 gruff noise
Gruyère [grew-yair] n hard yellow Swiss cheese with holes
gryphon n same as **griffin**
GST goods and services tax
G-string n small strip of cloth covering the genitals and attached to a waistband
GT gran turismo, used of a sports automobile
guano [gwa-no] n dried sea-bird manure
guarantee n 1 formal assurance, esp. in writing, that a product will meet certain standards 2 something that makes a specified condition or outcome certain ▷ v -teeing, -teed 4 ensure 5 give a guarantee 6 secure against risk etc. **guarantor** n person who gives or is bound by a guarantee
guard v 1 watch over to protect or to prevent escape ▷ n 2 person or group that

guards **3** official in charge of a train **4** protection **5** screen for enclosing anything dangerous **6** posture of defence in sports such as boxing or fencing **7** *basketball* player in the position furthest from the basket **guards 8 Guards** regiment with ceremonial duties **guardsman** *n* member of the Guards **guarded** *adj* cautious or noncommittal **guardedly** *adv* **guard against** *v* take precautions against

guardian *n* **1** keeper or protector **2** person legally responsible for a child or other vulnerable person **guardianship** *n*

guava [gwah-va] *n* yellow-skinned tropical American fruit

gudgeon *n* small European freshwater fish

Guernsey [gurn-zee] *n* **1** breed of dairy cattle **2 guernsey** seaman's knitted sweater

guerrilla, guerilla *n* member of an unofficial armed force fighting regular forces

guess *v* **1** estimate or draw a conclusion without proper knowledge **2** estimate correctly by guessing **3** suppose ▷ *n* **4** estimate or conclusion reached by guessing **guesswork** *n* process or results of guessing

guest *n* **1** person entertained at another's house or at another's expense **2** invited performer or speaker **3** customer at a hotel or restaurant **guesthouse** *n* boarding house

guff *n* *slang* nonsense

guffaw *n* **1** crude noisy laugh ▷ *v* **2** laugh in this way

guide *n* **1** person who shows the way **2** adviser **3** book of instruction or information **4** device for directing motion **5 Guide** member of an organization for girls equivalent to the Scouts ▷ *v* **6** act as a guide for **7** control, supervise, or influence **guidance** *n* leadership, instruction, or advice **guided missile** missile whose flight is controlled electronically **guide dog** dog trained to lead a blind person **guideline** *n* set principle for doing something

guild *n* **1** organization or club **2** *hist* society of men in the same trade or craft

guilder *n* former monetary unit of the Netherlands

guile [gile] *n* cunning or deceit **guileful** *adj* **guileless** *adj*

guillemot [gil-lee-mot] *n* black-and-white diving sea bird

guillotine *n* **1** machine for beheading people **2** device for cutting paper or sheet metal **3** method of preventing lengthy debate in parliament by fixing a time for taking the vote ▷ *v* **4** behead by guillotine **5** limit debate by the guillotine

guilt *n* **1** fact or state of having done wrong **2** remorse for wrongdoing **guiltless** *adj* innocent **guilty** *adj* **1** responsible for an offence or misdeed **2** feeling or showing guilt **guiltily** *adv*

guinea *n* **1** former British monetary unit worth 21 shillings (1.05 pounds) **2** former gold coin of this value **guinea fowl** bird related to the pheasant **guinea pig 1** tailless S American rodent **2** *informal* person used for experimentation

guise [rhymes with **size**] *n* false appearance

guitar *n* six-stringed instrument played by plucking or strumming **guitarist** *n*

gulch *n* deep narrow valley in western N America

gulf *n* **1** large deep bay **2** chasm **3** large difference in opinion or understanding

gull *n* long-winged sea bird

gullet *n* muscular tube through which food passes from the mouth to the stomach

gullible *adj* easily tricked **gullibility** *n*

gully *n, pl* **-lies** channel cut by running water

gulp *v* **1** swallow hastily **2** gasp ▷ *n* **3** gulping **4** thing gulped

gum[1] *n* firm flesh in which the teeth are set **gummy** *adj* toothless

gum[2] *n* **1** sticky substance obtained from certain trees **2** adhesive **3** gumdrop **4** chewing gum **5** gumtree ▷ *v* **gumming, gummed 6** stick with gum **gummy** *adj* **gumboots** *pl n* Wellington boots **gumdrop** *n* hard jelly-like candy **gumtree** *n* eucalypt tree

gumption *n informal* **1** resourcefulness **2** courage

gun *n* **1** weapon with a metal tube from which missiles are fired by explosion **2** device from which a substance is ejected under pressure ▷ *v* **gunning, gunned 3** cause (an engine) to run at high speed **jump the gun** see **jump** ▶ **gunner** *n* artillery soldier **gunnery** *n* use or science of large guns **gunboat** *n* small warship **gun dog** dog used to retrieve game **gun down** *v* shoot (a person) **gun for** *v* seek or pursue vigorously **gunman** *n* armed criminal **gunmetal** *n* **1** alloy of copper, tin, and zinc ▷ *adj* **2** dark grey **gunpowder** *n* explosive mixture of potassium nitrate, sulfur, and charcoal **gunrunning** *n* smuggling of guns and ammunition **gunrunner** *n* **gunshot** *n* shot or range of a gun

gunge *n informal* sticky unpleasant substance **gungy** *adj*

gunny *n* strong coarse fabric used for sacks

gunwale, gunnel [gun-nel] *n* top of a ship's side

guppy *n, pl* **-pies** small colourful aquarium fish

gurgle *v, n* (make) a bubbling noise

Gurkha *n* person, esp. a soldier, belonging to a Hindu people of Nepal

guru *n* **1** Indian spiritual teacher **2** leader or adviser

gush *v* **1** flow out suddenly and profusely **2** express admiration effusively ▷ *n* **3** sudden copious flow **4** effusiveness **gusher** *n* spurting oil well

gusset *n* piece of material sewn into a garment to strengthen it

gust *n* **1** sudden blast of wind ▷ *v* **2** blow in gusts **gusty** *adj*

gusto *n* enjoyment or zest

gut *n* **1** intestine **2** short for **catgut 3** *informal* fat stomach **guts 4** internal organs **5** *informal* courage ▷ *v* **gutting, gutted 6** remove the guts from **7** (of a fire) destroy the inside of (a building) ▷ *adj* **8** basic or instinctive: *gut reaction* **gutsy** *adj informal* **1** courageous **2** vigorous or robust: *a gutsy performance* **gutted** *adj informal* disappointed and upset

gutter *n* **1** shallow trough for carrying off water from a roof or roadside ▷ *v* **2** (of a candle) burn unsteadily, with wax running down the sides **the gutter** degraded or criminal environment **guttering** n material for gutters **gutter press** newspapers that rely on sensationalism

guttural [**gut**-ter-al] adj **1** (of a sound) produced at the back of the throat **2** (of a voice) harsh-sounding

guy¹ n **1** informal man or boy **2** Brit effigy of Guy Fawkes burnt on Nov. 5th (**Guy Fawkes Day**)

guy² n rope or chain to steady or secure something **guyrope** n

guzzle v eat or drink greedily

gybe [**jibe**] v **1** (of a fore-and-aft sail) swing suddenly from one side to the other **2** (of a boat) change course by gybing

gym n short for **gymnasium**, **gymnastics**

gymkhana [jim-**kah**-na] n horse-riding competition

gymnasium n large room with equipment for physical training **gymnast** n expert in gymnastics **gymnastic** adj **gymnastics** pl n exercises to develop strength and agility

gynecology, gynaecology [guy-nee-**kol**-la-jee] n branch of medicine dealing with diseases and conditions specific to women **gynecological** or **gynaecological** adj **gynecologist** or **gynaecologist** n

gypsophila n garden plant with small white flowers

gypsum n chalklike mineral used to make plaster of Paris

Gypsy n, pl **-sies** member of a travelling people found throughout Europe

gyrate [jire-**rate**] v rotate or spiral about a point or axis **gyration** n **gyratory** adj gyrating

gyrocompass n compass using a gyroscope

gyroscope [**jire**-oh-skohp] n disc rotating on an axis that can turn in any direction, used to keep navigation instruments steady **gyroscopic** adj

Hh

H *chem* hydrogen

habeas corpus [hay-bee-ass kor-puss] *n* writ ordering a prisoner to be brought before a court

haberdasher *n Brit* dealer in small articles used for sewing **haberdashery** *n*

habit *n* **1** established way of behaving **2** addiction to a drug **3** costume of a nun or monk **4** woman's riding costume **habitual** *adj* done regularly and repeatedly **habitually** *adv* **habituate** *v* accustom **habituation** *n* **habitué** [hab-it-yew-ay] *n* frequent visitor to a place

habitable *adj* fit to be lived in **habitant** *n* (descendant of) original French settler **habitat** *n* natural home of an animal or plant **habitation** *n* **1** dwelling place **2** occupation of a dwelling place

hacienda [hass-ee-end-a] *n* ranch or large estate in Latin America

hack¹ *v* **1** cut or chop (at) violently **2** utter a harsh dry cough **hacker** *n slang* computer enthusiast, esp. one who breaks into the computer system of a company or government

hack² *n* **1** horse kept for riding **2** *informal* (inferior) writer or journalist **hackwork** *n* dull repetitive work

hackles *pl n* hairs or feathers on the back of the neck of some animals and birds, which are raised in anger

hackney carriage *n* **1** taxi **2** coach or carriage for hire

hackneyed [hak-need] *adj* (of language) stale or trite because of overuse

hacksaw *n* small saw for cutting metal

had *v* past of **have**

haddock *n* large edible sea fish

Hades [hay-deez] *n Greek myth* underworld home of the dead

hadj *n* same as **hajj**

haematic *adj* same as **hematic**

haemoglobin *n* same as **hemoglobin**

haemophilia *n* same as **hemophilia**

haemorrhage *n* same as **hemorrhage**

haemorrhoids *pl n* same as **hemorrhoids**

haft *n* **1** handle of an axe, knife, or dagger ▷ *v* **2** provide with a haft

hag *n* **1** ugly old woman **2** witch **hag-ridden** *adj* distressed or worried

haggard *adj* looking tired and ill

haggis *n* Scottish dish made from sheep's offal, oatmeal, suet, and onion

haggle *v* bargain or wrangle over a price

hagiology *n, pl* -gies literature about the lives of the saints **hagiography** *n* writing of this **hagiographer** *n*

hail¹ n 1 (shower of) small pellets of ice 2 large amount of words, missiles, blows, etc. ▷ v 3 fall as or like hail **hailstone** n

hail² v 1 greet 2 call (out to) 3 acclaim, acknowledge **hail from** v come originally from

hair n 1 threadlike growth on the skin 2 such growths collectively, esp. on the head **hairy** adj 1 covered with hair 2 slang dangerous or exciting **hairiness** n **hairdo** n style in which a person's hair is cut and arranged **hairdresser** n person who cuts and styles hair **hairline** n 1 margin of hair at the top of the forehead ▷ adj 2 very fine or narrow **hairpin** n U-shaped wire used to hold the hair in place **hairpin bend** U-shaped bend in the road **hair-raising** adj terrifying **hairsplitting** n making of petty distinctions **hairspring** n very fine spring in a watch or clock

hajj n pilgrimage a Muslim makes to Mecca **hajji** n Muslim who has made a pilgrimage to Mecca

hake n edible fish of the cod family

halal n meat from animals slaughtered according to Muslim law

halberd n spear with an axe blade

halcyon [hal-see-on] adj peaceful and happy **halcyon days** time of peace and happiness

hale adj robust, healthy: hale and hearty

half n, pl **halves** 1 either of two equal parts 2 informal half-pint 3 half-price ticket ▷ adj 4 incomplete ▷ adv 5 to the extent of half 6 partially **half-baked** adj informal poorly planned **half-breed** n half-caste **half-brother** or **half-sister** n brother or sister related through one parent only **half-caste** n person with parents of different races **half-cocked** adj go off **half-cocked** fail because of inadequate preparation **half-hearted** adj unenthusiastic **half-life** n time taken for half the atoms in radioactive material to decay **half-nelson** n hold in wrestling in which one wrestler's arm is pinned behind his back by his opponent **half note** musical note half the length of a whole note **halfpenny** [hayp-nee] n former British coin worth half an old penny **half-pipe** n large U-shaped ramp used for skateboarding, snowboarding, etc. **half-timbered** adj having an exposed wooden frame filled in with plaster **half-time** n sports interval between two halves of a game **halftone** n illustration showing lights and shadows by means of very small dots **halfway** adv, adj at or to half the distance **halfwit** n foolish or feeble-minded person

halibut n large edible flatfish

halitosis n bad-smelling breath

hall n 1 (entrance) passage 2 large room or building belonging to a particular group or used for a particular purpose 3 large country house

hallelujah [hal-ee-loo-ya] interj exclamation of praise to God

hallmark n 1 mark indicating the standard of tested gold and silver 2 distinguishing feature ▷ v 3 stamp with a hallmark

hallo interj same as **hello**

hallowed *adj* regarded as holy

Hallowe'en *n* October 31, the eve of All Saints' Day

hallucinate *v* seem to see something that is not really there **hallucination** *n* experience of seeming to see something that is not really there **hallucinatory** *adj* **hallucinogen** *n* drug that causes hallucinations

halo [**hay**-loh] *n, pl* **-loes, -los** 1 disc of light round the head of a sacred figure 2 ring of light round the sun or moon

halogen [**hal**-oh-jen] *n chem* any of a group of nonmetallic elements including chlorine and iodine

halt *v* 1 stop ▷ *n* 2 temporary stop 3 minor railway station without a building **halting** *adj* hesitant: *halting speech*

halter *n* strap around a horse's head with a rope to lead it with **halterneck** *n* top or dress with a strap fastened at the back of the neck

halve *v* 1 cut in half 2 reduce to half 3 share

halves *n* plural of **half**

halyard *n* rope for raising a ship's sail or flag

ham *n* 1 smoked or salted meat from a pig's thigh 2 *informal* amateur radio operator 3 *informal* actor who overacts ▷ *v* **hamming, hammed** 4 **ham it up** *informal* overact **ham-fisted** or **ham-handed** *adj* clumsy

hamburger *n* flat round piece of minced beef, often served in a bread roll

hamlet *n* small village

hammer *n* 1 tool with a heavy head, used to drive in nails, beat metal, etc. 2 part of a gun which causes the bullet to be fired 3 metal ball on a wire, thrown as a sport 4 auctioneer's mallet 5 striking mechanism in a piano ▷ *v* 6 strike (as if) with a hammer 7 *informal* defeat **hammer and tongs** with great effort or energy

hammerhead *n* shark with a wide flattened head

hammertoe *n* condition in which the toe is permanently bent at the joint

hammock *n* hanging bed made of canvas or net

hamper[1] *v* make it difficult for (someone or something) to move or progress

hamper[2] *n* 1 large basket with a lid 2 selection of food and drink packed as a gift

hamster *n* small rodent with a short tail and cheek pouches

hamstring *n* 1 tendon at the back of the knee ▷ *v* 2 make it difficult for someone to take any action

hand *n* 1 end of the arm beyond the wrist 2 style of writing 3 applause 4 pointer on a dial 5 manual worker 6 cards dealt to a player in a card game 7 unit of four inches used to measure horses ▷ *v* 8 pass or give **at hand, on hand,** or **to hand** nearby **hand in glove** in close association **hands down** easily **have a hand in** be involved in **lend a hand** help **out of hand** beyond control **handful** *n* 1 the amount that can be held in the hand 2 small quantity or number 3 *informal* person or thing that is difficult to control **handbag** *n* purse **handbill** *n* small printed notice **handbook** *n* small reference or instruction book **handcuff** *n* 1 one of a linked pair of metal rings used for securing a prisoner ▷ *v* 2 put handcuffs on **handheld** *adj* 1 (of a computer) small enough to be held in the

h

hand ▷ n **2** computer small enough to be held in the hand **handicraft** n objects made by hand **handiwork** n work of a particular person **hand-out** n **1** thing given free **2** written information given out at a talk etc. **handprint** n mark left by the impression of a hand **hands-on** adj involving practical experience of equipment **handstand** n act of supporting the body on the hands in an upside-down position **handwriting** n (style of) writing by hand

handicap n **1** any physical or mental disability **2** something that makes progress difficult **3** contest in which the competitors are given advantages or disadvantages in an attempt to equalize their chances **4** disadvantage or advantage given ▷ v **5** make it difficult for (someone) to do something

handkerchief n small square of fabric used to wipe the nose

handle n **1** small lever used to open and close a door etc. **2** part of an object that is held so that it can be used ▷ v **3** hold, feel, or move with the hands **4** control or deal with **handler** n person who controls an animal **handlebars** pl n curved metal bar used to steer a cycle

handsome adj **1** attractive in appearance **2** large or generous: a handsome reward

handy adj **handier, handiest 1** convenient, useful **2** good at manual work **handily** adv **handiness** n **handyman** n man skilled at odd jobs

hang v **hanging, hung 1** attach or be attached at the top with the lower part free **2** past **hanged** suspend or be suspended by the neck

until dead **3** fasten to a wall **4** droop **get the hang of** informal understand **hanger** n curved piece of wood or hook for hanging clothes on **hang back** v hesitate **hangdog** adj sullen, dejected **hang-glider** n glider with a light framework from which the pilot hangs in a harness **hang-gliding** n **hangman** n person who executes people by hanging **hangover** n aftereffects of drinking too much alcohol **hang-up** n informal emotional or psychological problem **hang up** v end a telephone call

hangar n large shed for storing aircraft

hank n coil or skein, esp. of yarn

hanker v (foll. by after) crave, long for

hanky, hankie n, pl **hankies** informal handkerchief

hanky-panky n informal illicit sexual relations

hansom n formerly, a two-wheeled horse-drawn cab for hire

haphazard adj not organized or planned **haphazardly** adv

hapless adj unlucky

happen v **1** occur, take place **2** do by chance **happening** n occurrence, event

happy adj **-pier, -piest 1** glad or content **2** lucky or fortunate **3** willing **happily** adv **happiness** n **happy-go-lucky** adj carefree and cheerful

hara-kiri n Japanese ritual suicide by disembowelment

harangue v **1** address angrily or forcefully ▷ n **2** angry or forceful speech

harass v annoy or trouble constantly **harassed** adj **harassment** n

harbinger [**har**-binge-er] n person or thing that

announces the approach of something

harbour n **1** sheltered port ▷ v **2** give shelter or protection to **3** maintain secretly in the mind

hard adj **1** firm, solid, or rigid **2** difficult **3** requiring a lot of effort **4** unkind or unfeeling **5** difficult to bear **6** (of water) containing calcium salts which stop soap lathering freely **7** (of a drug) strong and addictive ▷ adv **8** with great energy or effort **9** carefully **10** intensely **hard of hearing** slightly deaf **hard up** informal short of money **harden** v **hardness** n **hardship** n **1** suffering **2** difficult circumstances **hard-bitten** adj tough **hardboard** n thin stiff board made of compressed sawdust and woodchips **hard-boiled** adj **1** (of eggs) boiled until solid **2** informal tough, unemotional **hard copy** computer output printed on paper **hard-core** adj (of pornography) showing sexual acts in explicit detail **hard drive** computers mechanism that handles the reading, writing, and storage of data on the hard disk **hard-headed** adj shrewd, practical **hard-hearted** adj unfeeling, unkind **hard sell** aggressive sales technique **hardware** n **1** metal tools or implements **2** machinery used in a computer system **3** military weapons **hardwood** n wood of a deciduous tree such as oak or ash

hardly adv **1** scarcely or not at all **2** with great difficulty

hardy adj -**dier**, -**diest** able to stand difficult conditions **hardiness** n

hare n **1** animal like a large rabbit, with longer legs and ears ▷ v **2** run fast **harebell** n blue bell-shaped flower **harebrained** adj foolish or impractical **harelip** n split in the upper lip

harem n (apartments of) a Muslim man's wives and concubines

haricot [har-rik-oh] n white bean which can be dried

hark v old-fashioned listen **hark back** v return (to an earlier subject)

harlequin n **1** stock comic character, with a diamond-patterned costume and mask ▷ adj **2** in varied colours

harlot n obsolete prostitute

harm v **1** injure physically, mentally, or morally ▷ n **2** physical, mental, or moral injury **harmful** adj **harmless** adj

harmony n, pl -**nies** **1** peaceful agreement and cooperation **2** combination of notes to make a pleasing sound **harmonious** adj **harmoniously** adv **harmonic** adj **1** of harmony **2** harmonious **harmonics** n science of musical sounds **harmonize** v fit in or go well with each other **harmonization** n **harmonica** n mouth organ **harmonium** n small organ

harness n **1** equipment for attaching a horse to a cart or plow **2** set of straps fastened round someone's body to attach something: *a parachute harness* ▷ v **3** put a harness on **4** control (something) in order to use its energy

harp n large triangular stringed instrument played with the fingers **harpist** n **harp on about** v talk about continuously

harpoon n **1** barbed spear attached to a rope used for hunting whales ▷ *v* **2** spear with a harpoon

harpsichord *n* stringed keyboard instrument

harpy *n, pl* **-pies** cruel or grasping woman

harridan *n* shrewish (old) woman

harrier *n* cross-country runner

harrow *n* **1** implement used to break up clods of soil ▷ *v* **2** draw a harrow over

harrowing *adj* very distressing

harry *v* **-rying, -ried** keep asking (someone) to do something, pester

harsh *adj* **1** unpleasant to the senses **2** severe or cruel **harshly** *adv* **harshness** *n*

hart *n* adult male deer

hartebeest *n* large African antelope

harum-scarum *adj* reckless

harvest *n* **1** (season for) the gathering of crops **2** crops gathered ▷ *v* **3** gather (a ripened crop) **harvester** *n*

has *v* third person singular of the present tense of **have** ▸ **has-been** *n informal* person who is no longer popular or successful

hash¹ *n* **1** dish of diced meat and vegetables **2** *informal* hashish **make a hash of** *informal* mess up or destroy

hash² *n* the character (#) **hashtag** *n* (on the Twitter website) word or phrase preceded by a hash, used to denote the topic of a post

hashish [hash-**eesh**] *n* drug made from the hemp plant, taken for its intoxicating effects

hasp *n* clasp which fits over a staple and is secured by a bolt or padlock, used as a fastening

hassle *informal* ▷ *n* **1** trouble or difficulty **2** nuisance ▷ *v* **3** cause annoyance or trouble to

hassock *n* cushion for kneeling on in church

haste *n* speed or hurry **make haste** hurry or rush **hasten** *v* (cause to) increase speed **hasty** *adj* (too) quick **hastily** *adv*

hat *n* covering for the head, often with a brim, usually worn to give protection from the weather **keep something under one's hat** keep something secret **hat trick** any three successive achievements, esp. in sport

hatch¹ *v* **1** (cause to) emerge from an egg **2** devise (a plot or plan) **hatchery** *n* place for hatching eggs

hatch² *n* **1** (hinged door covering) an opening in a floor or wall **2** opening in the wall between a kitchen and a dining area **3** door in an aircraft or spacecraft **hatchback** *n* automobile with a single lifting door in the rear **hatchway** *n* opening in the deck of a ship

hatchet *n* small axe **bury the hatchet** make peace **hatchet job** malicious verbal or written attack **hatchet man** *informal* person carrying out unpleasant tasks for an employer

hate *v* **1** dislike intensely **2** be unwilling (to do something) ▷ *n* **3** intense dislike **4** person or thing that is hated **hateful** *adj* causing or deserving hate **hatred** *n* intense dislike

haughty *adj* **-tier, -tiest** proud, arrogant **haughtily** *adv* **haughtiness** *n*

haul *v* **1** pull or drag with effort ▷ *n* **2** amount gained by effort or theft **long haul** something that takes a lot of time and effort to achieve **haulage** *n* (charge for) transporting goods **haulier** *n* firm or person that transports goods by road

haunch *n* human hip or fleshy hindquarter of an animal

haunt v 1 visit in the form of a ghost 2 remain in the thoughts or memory of ▷ n 3 place visited frequently **haunted** adj 1 visited by ghosts 2 worried **haunting** adj extremely beautiful or sad

haute couture [oat koo-**ture**] n French high fashion

hauteur [oat-**ur**] n haughtiness

have v has, having, had 1 hold, possess 2 experience or be affected with 3 be obliged (to do) 4 slang cheat or outwit 5 receive, take, or obtain 6 cause to be done 7 give birth to 8 used to form past tenses (with a past participle): I have gone; I had gone **have it out** informal settle by argument **have-not province** Canad province whose own tax revenue entitles it to receive payments from the federal government **have on** v informal trick or tease **have province** Canad province whose own tax revenue does not entitle it to receive payments from the federal government

haven n place of safety

haversack n canvas bag carried on the back or shoulder

havoc n disorder and confusion

haw n hawthorn berry

hawk¹ n 1 bird of prey with short rounded wings and a long tail 2 supporter or advocate of warlike policies **hawkish** or **hawklike** adj **hawk-eyed** adj having extremely good eyesight

hawk² v offer (goods) for sale in the street or door-to-door **hawker** n

hawser n large rope used on a ship

hawthorn n thorny shrub or tree

hay n grass cut and dried as fodder **hay fever** allergic reaction to pollen or dust **haystack** n large pile of stored hay **haywire** adj **go haywire** informal not function properly

hazard n 1 risk, danger ▷ v 2 put at danger 3 venture (a guess) **hazardous** adj

haze n mist, often caused by heat **hazy** adj 1 misty 2 vague

hazel n 1 bush producing nuts ▷ adj 2 (of eyes) greenish-brown **hazelnut** n

H-bomb n hydrogen bomb

he pron 1 male person or animal 2 person or animal of unspecified sex

He chem helium

head n 1 upper or front part of the body, containing the sense organs and the brain 2 upper or most forward part of anything 3 aptitude, intelligence 4 chief of a group or organization 5 person or animal considered as a unit 6 white froth on beer 7 headline or title 8 informal headache ▷ adj 9 chief, principal ▷ v 10 be at the top or front of 11 lead, direct 12 move (in a particular direction) 13 provide with a heading 14 hit (a ball) with the head **go to someone's head** make someone drunk or conceited **head over heels** very much in love **not make head nor tail of** not understand **off one's head** slang insane **header** n 1 action of striking a ball with the head 2 headlong dive **heading** n title written or printed at the top of a page **heads** adv informal with the side of a coin which has a portrait of a head on it uppermost **heady** adj

intoxicating or exciting
headache n 1 continuous pain
in the head 2 cause of worry
or annoyance **headboard**
n vertical board at the head
of a bed **head-hunter** n
person who sets out to recruit
someone from another
company for a particular
job **headland** n area of
land jutting out into the
sea **headlight** n powerful
light on the front of a vehicle
headline n 1 news summary
in large type in a newspaper
headlines 2 main points of
a news broadcast **headlong**
adv 1 head foremost 2 with
haste **head-on** adj, adv
1 front foremost 2 direct(ly)
and uncompromising(ly)
headphones pl n two small
loudspeakers held against the
ears by a strap **headquarters**
pl n centre from which
operations are directed
head start advantage in a
competition **headstone**
n gravestone **headstrong**
adj 1 self-willed 2 obstinate
headway n progress
headwind n wind blowing
against the course of an
aircraft or ship

heal v make or become well
healer n **health** n 1 normal
good condition of someone's
body 2 toast drunk in a
person's honour **healthy**
adj 1 having good health of
or producing good health
2 functioning well, sound
healthily adv **health food**
natural food, organically
grown and free from additives
heap n 1 pile of things lying
one on top of another 2 large
quantity ▷ v 3 gather into
a pile 4 (foll. by on) give
abundantly (to)
hear v **hearing, heard**
1 perceive (a sound) by ear

2 listen to 3 learn or be
informed 4 law try (a case)
hear! hear! exclamation
of approval or agreement
hearer n **hearing** n 1 ability
to hear 2 trial of a case **within
hearing** close enough to be
heard
hearken v obsolete listen
hearsay n 1 gossip 2 rumour
hearse n funeral vehicle used
to carry a casket
heart n 1 organ which pumps
blood round the body 2 centre
of emotions and affections
3 tenderness 4 enthusiasm
or courage 5 central or most
important part 6 figure
representing a heart 7 playing
card of the suit marked with
the figure of a heart **break
someone's heart** cause
someone great grief **by
heart** from memory **set
one's heart on something**
greatly desire something
take to heart get upset about
hearten v make cheerful,
encourage **heartless** adj
cruel **hearty** adj 1 friendly,
enthusiastic 2 substantial,
nourishing **heartily** adv
heartache n intense anguish
heart attack sudden severe
malfunction of the heart
heartbeat n one complete
pulsation of the heart
heartbreak n intense grief
heartburn n pain in the chest
caused by indigestion **heart
failure** sudden stopping
of the heartbeat **heartfelt**
adj felt sincerely or strongly
heart-rending adj causing
great sorrow **heart-throb** n
slang very attractive person
hearth n 1 floor of a fireplace
2 home
heat n 1 state of being hot
2 energy transferred as a
result of a difference in
temperature 3 hot weather

4 intensity of feeling **5** preliminary eliminating contest in a competition **6** readiness to mate in some female animals ▷ v **7** make hot **heated** adj angry **heatedly** adv **heater** n

heath n **1** area of open uncultivated land **2** low-growing evergreen shrub

heathen n **1** person not believing in an established religion, pagan ▷ adj **2** of or relating to heathen peoples

heather n shrub with small bell-shaped flowers growing on heaths and mountains

heave v **1** lift with effort **2** throw (something heavy) **3** utter (a sigh) **4** rise and fall **5** vomit ▷ n **6** act of heaving

heaven n **1** home of God **2** place or state of bliss **the heavens** sky **heavenly** adj **1** wonderful or divine **2** of or like heaven **3** of or occurring in space

heavy adj **-vier, -viest 1** of great weight **2** great in degree or amount **3** dense **4** difficult or severe **5** sorrowful **6** (of a situation) serious **heavily** adv **heaviness** n **heavy industry** large-scale production of raw material or machinery **heavy metal** very loud rock music featuring guitar riffs **heavyweight** n boxer weighing over 175lb (professional) or 81kg (amateur)

Hebrew n **1** ancient language of the Hebrews **2** its modern form, used in Israel **3** member of an ancient Semitic people ▷ adj **4** of this language or people

heckle v interrupt (a public speaker) with questions, taunts, and comments **heckler** n

hectare n one hundred ares or 10 000 square metres (2.471 acres)

hectic adj rushed or busy

hector v bully

hedge n **1** row of bushes forming a barrier or boundary ▷ v **2** be evasive or noncommittal **3** (foll. by against) protect oneself from (loss) **hedgerow** n bushes forming a hedge **hedge sparrow** small brownish songbird

hedgehog n small mammal with a protective covering of spines

hedonism n doctrine that pleasure is the most important thing in life **hedonist** n **hedonistic** adj

heed v pay close attention to **heedless** adj **heedless of** taking no notice of

heel[1] n **1** back part of the foot **2** part of a shoe supporting the heel **3** slang contemptible person ▷ v **4** make or replace the heel of

heel[2] v lean to one side

hefty adj **heftier, heftiest** large, heavy, or strong

hegemony [hig-**em**-on-ee] n political domination

Hegira n Mohammed's flight from Mecca to Medina in 622 AD

heifer [**hef**-fer] n young cow

height n **1** distance from base to top **2** distance above sea level **3** highest degree or topmost point **heighten** v make or become higher or more intense

heinous adj evil and shocking

heir n person entitled to inherit property or rank **heiress** n fem **heirloom** n object that has belonged to a family for generations

held v past of **hold**[1]

helicopter n aircraft lifted and propelled by rotating

overhead blades **heliport** *n* airport for helicopters

heliotrope *n* **1** plant with purple flowers ▷ *adj* **2** light purple

helium [**heel**-ee-um] *n* very light colourless odourless gas

helix [**heel**-iks] *n, pl* **helices, helixes** spiral **helical** *adj*

hell *n* **1** home of the wicked after death **2** place or state of wickedness, suffering, or punishment **hell for leather** at great speed **hellish** *adj* **hell-bent** *adj* intent

Hellenic *adj* of the (ancient) Greeks or their language

hello *interj* expression of greeting or surprise

helm *n* tiller or wheel for steering a ship

helmet *n* hard hat worn for protection

help *v* **1** make something easier, better, or quicker for (someone) **2** improve (a situation) **3** refrain from: *I can't help laughing* ▷ *n* **4** assistance or support **help oneself 1** serve oneself **2** *informal* steal something **helper** *n* **helpful** *adj* **helping** *n* single portion of food **helpless** *adj* weak or incapable **helplessly** *adv* **helpline** *n* telephone line set aside for callers to contact an organization for help with a problem **helpmate** or **helpmeet** *n* **1** companion and helper **2** husband or wife

helter-skelter *adj* **1** haphazard and careless ▷ *adv* **2** in a haphazard and careless manner ▷ *n* **3** high spiral slide at a fairground

hem *n* **1** border of cloth, folded under and stitched down ▷ *v* **hemming, hemmed 2** provide with a hem **hem in** *v* surround and prevent from moving **hemline** *n* level

to which the hem of a skirt hangs

hematic, haematic *adj* relating to or containing blood **hematology** or **haematology** *n* study of blood and its diseases

hemisphere *n* half of a sphere, esp. the earth **hemispherical** *adj*

hemlock *n* **1** poison derived from a plant with spotted stems and small white flowers **2** evergreen of pine family

hemoglobin, haemoglobin [hee-moh-**globe**-in] *n* protein found in red blood cells which carries oxygen

hemophilia, haemophilia *n* hereditary illness in which the blood does not clot **hemophiliac** *n*

hemorrhage, haemorrhage [**hem**-or-ij] *n* **1** heavy bleeding ▷ *v* **2** bleed heavily

hemorrhoids, haemorrhoids [**hem**-or-oydz] *pl n* swollen veins in the anus (Also **piles**)

hemp *n* **1** Asian plant **2** its fibre, used to make canvas and rope **3** narcotic drug obtained from hemp

hen *n* **1** female domestic fowl **2** female of any bird **henpecked** *adj* (of a man) dominated by his wife

hence *adv* **1** for this reason **2** from this time **henceforward** or **henceforth** *adv* from now on

henchman *n* attendant or follower

henna *n* **1** reddish dye made from a shrub or tree ▷ *v* **2** dye the hair with henna

henry *n, pl* **-ry, -ries, -rys** unit of electrical inductance

hepatic *adj* of the liver **hepatitis** *n* inflammation of the liver

heptagon *n* figure with seven sides **heptagonal** *adj*

heptathlon *n* athletic contest involving seven events

her *pron* **1** refers to a female person or animal or anything personified as feminine when the object of a sentence or clause ▷ *adj* **2** of, belonging to, or associated with her **herself** *pron* emphatic or reflexive form of **she**, **her**

herald *n* **1** person who announces important news **2** forerunner ▷ *v* **3** announce or signal the approach of **heraldry** *n* study of coats of arms and the histories of families **heraldic** *adj*

herb *n* plant used for flavouring in cookery, and in medicine **herbal** *adj* **herbalist** *n* person who grows or specializes in the use of medicinal herbs **herbaceous** *adj* (of a plant) soft-stemmed **herbaceous border** flower bed that contains perennials rather than annuals **herbicide** *n* chemical which destroys plants **herbivore** *n* animal that feeds on plants **herbivorous** [her-**biv**-or-uss] *adj*

herculean [her-kew-**lee**-an] *adj* requiring great strength or effort

herd *n* **1** group of animals feeding and living together **2** large crowd of people ▷ *v* **3** collect into a herd **herdsman** *n* man who looks after a herd of animals

here *adv* in, at, or to this place or point **hereabouts** *adv* near here **hereafter** *n* **1** life after death ▷ *adv* **2** in the future **hereby** *adv* by means of or as a result of this **herein** *adv* in this place, matter, or document **herewith** *adv* with this

heredity [hir-**red**-it-ee] *n* passing on of characteristics from one generation to another **hereditary** *adj* **1** passed on genetically from one generation to another **2** passed on by inheritance

heresy [**herr**-iss-ee] *n, pl* **-sies** opinion contrary to accepted opinion or belief **heretic** [**herr**-it-ik] *n* person who holds unorthodox opinions **heretical** [hir-**ret**-ik-al] *adj*

heritage *n* possessions, traditions, or conditions passed from one generation to another

hermaphrodite [her-**maf**-roe-dite] *n* person, animal, or plant that has both male and female reproductive organs

hermetic *adj* sealed so as to be airtight **hermetically** *adv*

hermit *n* person living in solitude, esp. for religious reasons **hermitage** *n* dwelling of a hermit

hernia *n* protrusion of (part of) an organ through the lining of the surrounding body cavity

hero *n, pl* **heroes 1** principal character in a film, book, play, etc. **2** man greatly admired for exceptional qualities or achievements **heroine** *n fem* **heroic** *adj* **1** courageous **2** of, like, or befitting a hero **heroics** *pl n* extravagant behaviour **heroically** *adv* **heroism** [**herr**-oh-izz-um] *n*

heroin *n* highly addictive drug derived from morphine

heron *n* long-legged wading bird **heronry** *n* place where herons breed

herpes [**her**-peez] *n* any of several inflammatory skin diseases, including shingles and cold sores

Herr [**hair**] *n, pl* **Herren**

German title of address equivalent to Mr

herring *n* important food fish of northern seas **herringbone** *n* pattern of zigzag lines **herring choker** *Canad slang* native or inhabitant of the Maritime Provinces

hertz *n*, *pl* **hertz** *physics* unit of frequency

hesitate *v* **1** be slow or uncertain in acting **2** pause during speech **3** be reluctant (to do something) **hesitation** *n* **hesitant** *adj* undecided or wavering **hesitantly** *adv* **hesitancy** *n*

hessian *n* coarse jute cloth

heterodox *adj* not orthodox **heterodoxy** *n*

heterogeneous [het-er-oh-**jean**-ee-uss] *adj* composed of diverse elements **heterogeneity** *n*

heterosexual *n*, *adj* (person) sexually attracted to members of the opposite sex **heterosexuality** *n*

heuristic [hew-**rist**-ik] *adj* involving learning by investigation

hew *v* **hewing, hewed, hewed** or **hewn** **1** chop or cut with an axe **2** carve from a substance

hexagon *n* figure with six sides **hexagonal** *adj*

hey *interj* **1** expression of surprise or for catching attention **2** exclamation used for emphasis at the end of a statement, or alone to seek repetition or confirmation of another person's statement

heyday *n* time of greatest success, prime

Hg *chem* mercury

hiatus [hie-**ay**-tuss] *n*, *pl* **-tuses, -tus** break in continuity

hibernate *v* (of an animal) pass the winter as if in a deep sleep **hibernation** *n*

Hibernia *n poetic* Ireland **Hibernian** *adj*

hibiscus *n*, *pl* **-cuses** tropical plant with large brightly coloured flowers

hiccup, hiccough *n* **1** spasm of the breathing organs with a sharp coughlike sound ▷ *v* **2** make a hiccup or hiccups

hick *n informal* unsophisticated country person

hickory *n*, *pl* **-ries** **1** N American nut-bearing tree **2** its tough wood

hide[1] *v* **hiding, hid, hidden** **1** conceal or obscure (oneself or an object) **2** keep secret ▷ *n* **3** place of concealment, esp. for a bird-watcher **hide-out** *n* hiding place

hide[2] *n* skin of an animal **hiding** *n slang* thrashing **hidebound** *adj* restricted by petty rules

hideous [**hid**-ee-uss] *adj* ugly, revolting **hideously** *adv*

hierarchy [**hire**-ark-ee] *n*, *pl* **-chies** system of people or things arranged in a graded order **hierarchical** *adj*

hieroglyphic [hire-oh-**gliff**-ik] *adj* **1** of a form of writing using picture symbols, as used in ancient Egypt ▷ *n* **2** Also **hieroglyph** symbol representing an object, idea, or sound **3** symbol that is difficult to decipher

hi-fi *n* **1** set of high-quality sound-reproducing equipment ▷ *adj* **2** short for **high-fidelity**

higgledy-piggledy *adv*, *adj* in confusion

high *adj* **1** tall, of greater than average height **2** far above ground or sea level **3** being at its peak **4** greater than usual in intensity or amount **5** of great importance, quality, or rank **6** (of a sound) acute in pitch **7** *informal* under the influence of alcohol or drugs **8** (of food) slightly decomposed ▷ *adv* **9** at or to a high level ▷ *n* **10** high level **11** *informal* (in names) high school: *Burlington High* **highly** *adv* **highly strung** nervous and easily upset **Highness** *n* title used to address or refer to a royal person **High Arctic** regions of Canada, esp. northern islands, within the Arctic Circle **highbrow** *n* **1** intellectual or scholar ▷ *adj* **2** appealing to highbrows **High Commission** embassy of one Commonwealth country in another **High Church** belonging to a section within the Anglican church stressing the importance of ceremony and ritual **higher education** education at colleges, universities, and polytechnics **high-fidelity** *adj* able to reproduce sound with little or no distortion **high-flown** *adj* (of ideas or speech) grand and elaborate **high-handed** *adj* overbearing and dogmatic **highlands** *pl n* area of relatively high ground **highlight** *n* **1** outstanding part or feature **2** light-toned area in a painting or photograph **3** lightened streak in the hair ▷ *v* **4** give emphasis to **high-maintenance** *adj* **1** (of equipment) requiring regular maintenance to keep it in working order **2** *informal* (of a person) requiring a lot of care and attention **high-rise** *adj* (of a building) having many storeys **high tea** *Brit* early evening meal consisting of a cooked dish, bread, cakes, and tea **high-tech** *adj* same as **hi-tech** ▶ **high time** latest possible time **highway** *n* main road for fast-moving

traffic **highwayman** *n* formerly, robber, usually on horseback, who robbed travellers at gunpoint

hijab *n* head covering worn by Muslim women

hijack *v* seize control of (a vehicle or aircraft) while travelling **hijacker** *n*

hike *v* **1** walk a long way (for pleasure) in the country **2** (foll. by *up*) pull (up) or raise **hiker** *n*

hilarious *adj* very funny **hilariously** *adv* **hilarity** *n*

hill *n* **1** raised part of the earth's surface, less high than a mountain **2** incline or slope **hilly** *adj* **hillock** *n* small hill **hillbilly** *n US* unsophisticated country person

hilt *n* handle of a sword or knife

him *pron* refers to a male person or animal or anything personified as masculine when the object of a sentence or clause **himself** *pron* emphatic or reflexive form of **he**, **him**

hind[1] *adj* **hinder**, **hindmost** situated at the back

hind[2] *n* female deer

hinder *v* obstruct the progress of **hindrance** *n*

Hinduism *n* dominant religion of India which involves the worship of many gods and a belief in reincarnation **Hindu** *n* **1** person who practises Hinduism ▷ *adj* **2** of Hinduism **Hindi** *n* language of N central India

hinge *n* **1** device for holding together two parts so that one can swing freely ▷ *v* **2** fit a hinge to **3** (foll. by *on*) depend (on)

hint *n* **1** indirect suggestion **2** piece of advice **3** small amount ▷ *v* **4** suggest indirectly

hinterland *n* land lying behind

a coast or near a city, esp. a port

hip¹ n either side of the body below the waist and above the thigh

hip² n fruit of the rose bush

hip-hop n pop-culture movement originating in the 1980s, comprising rap music, graffiti, and break dancing

hippie n (esp. in the late 1960s) person whose behaviour and dress imply a rejection of conventional values

hippo n, pl -pos informal hippopotamus

hippodrome n music hall, variety theatre, or circus

hippopotamus n, pl -muses, -mi large African mammal with thick wrinkled skin, living in rivers

hippy n, pl -pies same as **hippie**

hipster n informal person pursuing non-mainstream cultural trends

hire v 1 obtain temporary use of by payment 2 employ for wages ▷ n 3 act of hiring 4 payment for the use of something **hireling** n person who works only for wages **hire-purchase** n Brit instalment plan

hirsute [**her**-suit] adj hairy

his pron, adj (something) belonging to him

Hispanic adj of Spain or a Spanish-speaking country

hiss n 1 sound like that of a long s (as an exclamation of contempt) ▷ v 2 utter a hiss 3 show derision or anger towards

histamine [**hiss**-ta-meen] n substance released by the body tissues, causing allergic reactions

histogram n statistical graph in which the frequency of values is represented by vertical bars of varying heights and widths

histology n study of the tissues of an animal or plant

history n, pl -ries 1 (record or account of) past events and developments 2 study of these 3 record of someone's past 4 play that depicts historical events **historian** n writer of history **historic** adj famous or significant in history **historical** adj 1 based on history 2 occurring in the past **historically** adv

histrionic adj excessively dramatic **histrionics** pl n melodramatic behaviour

hit v **hitting, hit** 1 strike forcefully 2 come into violent contact with 3 affect adversely 4 reach (a point or place) 5 sports propel (a ball) by striking ▷ n 6 impact or blow 7 success 8 computers single visit to a website 9 sports act or instance of hitting (a ball) **hitter** n **hit it off** informal get on well together **hit the trail** or **hit the road** informal set out on a journey **hit-and-run** n 1 motor-vehicle accident in which the driver leaves the scene without stopping to give assistance or call the police 2 baseball play in which a base runner begins to run as the pitcher throws the ball to the batter **hit man** hired assassin **hit on** v 1 think of (an idea) 2 make sexual advances to **hit-or-miss** adj haphazard

hitch v 1 fasten with a loop or hook 2 pull up with a jerk 3 informal obtain (a lift) by hitchhiking ▷ n 4 slight difficulty **hitchhike** v travel by obtaining free lifts **hitchhiker** n

hi-tech adj using sophisticated technology

hither adv to or towards this place **hitherto** adv until this time

HIV human immunodeficiency virus

hive *n* structure in which bees live **hive of activity** place where people are very busy **hive off** *v* separate from a larger group

hives *n* disease causing itchy red or whitish patches on the skin

HM Her (*or* His) Majesty

HMCS Her (*or* His) Majesty's Canadian Ship

HMS Her (*or* His) Majesty's Service *or* Ship

hoard *n* **1** store hidden away for future use ▷ *v* **2** gather or accumulate **hoarder** *n*

hoarding *n* large board for displaying advertisements

hoarfrost *n* white ground frost

hoarse *adj* **1** (of a voice) rough and unclear **2** having a rough and unclear voice **hoarsely** *adv* **hoarseness** *n*

hoary *adj* **hoarier, hoariest** **1** grey or white (with age) **2** very old

hoax *n* **1** deception or trick ▷ *v* **2** deceive or play a trick upon **hoaxer** *n*

hob *n* flat top part of a cooker

hobble *v* **1** walk lamely **2** tie the legs of (a horse) together

hobby *n, pl* **-bies** activity pursued in one's spare time **hobbyhorse** *n* **1** favourite topic **2** toy horse

hobgoblin *n* mischievous goblin

hobnail *n* large-headed nail for boot soles

hobnob *v* **-nobbing, -nobbed** (foll. by *with*) socialize (with)

hobo *n, pl* **-bos** tramp or vagrant

hock[1] *n* joint in the leg of a horse or similar animal corresponding to the human ankle

hock[2] *n* white German wine

hock[3] *v* informal pawn **in hock** **1** pawned **2** in debt

hockey *n* **1** team game played on ice with a puck and long sticks **2** *esp. Brit* field hockey

hocus-pocus *n* trickery

hod *n* **1** open wooden box attached to a pole, for carrying bricks or mortar **2** type of coal scuttle

hoe *n* **1** long-handled tool used to loosen soil or to weed ▷ *v* **2** scrape or weed using a hoe

hog *n* **1** castrated male pig **2** informal greedy person ▷ *v* **hogging, hogged 3** informal take more than one's share of **hog line** curling line marked across the ice which must be passed by a played stone **hogshead** *n* large cask **hogwash** *n* informal nonsense

Hogmanay *n* (in Scotland) New Year's Eve

hoi polloi *n* the ordinary people

hoist *v* **1** raise or lift up ▷ *n* **2** device for lifting things

hoity-toity *adj* informal arrogant or haughty

hold[1] *v* **holding, held 1** keep or support in or using the hands or arms **2** consider to be as specified: *who are you holding responsible?* **3** maintain in a specified position or state **4** have the capacity for **5** informal wait, esp. on the telephone **6** own, possess **7** keep possession of **8** reserve (a room etc.) **9** restrain or keep back **10** not use **11** cause to take place: *hold a meeting* **12** (cause to) remain committed to (a promise etc.) **13** believe ▷ *n* **14** act or method of holding **15** influence **16** something held onto for support **holder** *n* **holding** *n* property, such as land or stocks and shares **holdall** *n* Brit carryall **hold-up** *n* **1** armed robbery **2** delay

hold² n cargo compartment in a ship or aircraft

hole n 1 area hollowed out in a solid 2 opening or hollow 3 animal's burrow 4 informal unattractive place 5 informal difficult situation 6 golf place into which the ball is to be played ▷ v 7 make holes in 8 hit (a golf ball) into a hole **holey** adj

holiday n 1 time spent away from home for rest or recreation 2 day or other period of rest from work or studies

holism n consideration of the complete person in the treatment of disease **holistic** adj

hollow adj 1 having a hole or space inside 2 (of sounds) as if echoing in a hollow place 3 without any real value or worth ▷ n 4 cavity or space 5 dip in the land ▷ v 6 form a hollow in

holly n evergreen tree with prickly leaves and red berries

hollyhock n tall garden plant with spikes of colourful flowers

holocaust n destruction or loss of life on a massive scale

hologram n three-dimensional photographic image

holograph n document handwritten by the author

holography n science of using lasers to produce holograms

Holstein n breed of black-and-white dairy cattle

holster n leather case for a pistol, hung from a belt

holy adj -lier, -liest 1 of or associated with God or a deity 2 devout or virtuous **holiness** n **holier-than-thou** adj self-righteous **Holy Communion** Christianity service in remembrance of the death and resurrection of Jesus Christ **Holy Grail** (in medieval legend) the bowl used by Jesus Christ at the Last Supper **Holy Spirit** or **Holy Ghost** Christianity one of the three aspects of God **Holy Week** Christianity week before Easter

homage n show of respect or honour towards something or someone

home n 1 place where one lives 2 institution to care for the elderly, infirm, etc. ▷ adj 3 of one's home, birthplace, or native country ▷ adv 4 to or at home ▷ v 5 (foll. by in, in on) direct or be directed onto (a point or target) **at home** at ease **bring home to** make clear to **home and dry** informal safe or successful **home-brew** n beer made at home **homeless** adj 1 having nowhere to live ▷ pl n 2 people who have nowhere to live **homelessness** n **homely** adj 1 unattractive 2 Brit simple, ordinary, and comfortable **home-made** adj made at home or on the premises **home page** computers introductory information about a website with hyperlinks to further pages **home plate** baseball base where hitter bats **homesick** adj depressed by absence from home **homesickness** n **homestead** n 1 house with outbuildings, esp. on a farm 2 hist land assigned to a N American settler **homesteader** n **home truths** unpleasant facts told to a person about himself or herself **homeward** adj, adv **homewards** adv **homework** n school work done at home

homeopathy [home-ee-**op**-ath-ee] n treatment of

disease by small doses of a drug that produces symptoms of the disease in healthy people **homeopath** n person who practises homeopathy **homeopathic** [home-ee-oh-**path**-ik] adj **homeopathically** adv

homicide n **1** killing of a human being **2** person who kills another **homicidal** adj

homily n, pl **-lies** speech telling people how they should behave

hominid n man or any extinct forerunner of man

homo- combining form same: homosexual

homogeneous [home-oh-**jean**-ee-uss] adj formed of similar parts **homogeneity** n **homogenize** v **1** make homogeneous **2** break up fat globules in (milk or cream) to distribute them evenly

homograph n word spelt the same as another

homologous [hom-**ol**-log-uss] adj having a related or similar position or structure

homonym n word with the same spelling or pronunciation as another, but with a different meaning

homophobia n hatred or fear of homosexuals **homophobic** adj

homophone n word with the same pronunciation as another

Homo sapiens [**hoe**-moh **sap**-ee-enz] n human beings as a species

homosexual n, adj (person) sexually attracted to members of the same sex **homosexuality** n

Hon. Honourable

hone v sharpen

honest adj **1** not cheating, lying, or stealing **2** genuine or sincere **3** gained or earned fairly **honestly** adv **honesty** n **1** quality of being honest **2** plant with silvery seed pods

honey n **1** sweet edible fluid made by bees from nectar **2** term of endearment **honeycomb** n waxy structure of hexagonal cells in which honey is stored **honeydew melon** melon with yellow skin and sweet pale flesh **honeymoon** n holiday taken by a newly married couple **honeysuckle** n climbing shrub with sweet-smelling flowers

honk n **1** sound made by an automobile horn **2** sound made by a goose ▷ v **3** (cause to) make this sound

honour, honor n **1** personal integrity **2** (award given out of) respect **3** pleasure or privilege **honours 4** rank or mark of the highest academic standard in a university degree course ▷ v **5** give praise and attention to **6** give an award to (someone) out of respect **7** keep (a promise) **8** accept or pay (a cheque or bill) **do the honours** act as host or hostess by pouring drinks or giving out food **honourable** or **honorable** adj **honourably** or **honorably** adv **honorary** adj **1** held or given only as an honour **2** holding a position or giving one's services without pay **honorific** adj showing respect

hood[1] n **1** head covering, often part of a coat etc. **2** folding roof of a convertible automobile or a baby carriage **3** metal cover over a vehicle's engine ▷ v **4** cover (as if) with a hood **hooded** adj **1** (of a garment) having a hood **2** (of eyes) having heavy eyelids that appear to be half closed

hood[2] n slang hoodlum

hoodlum n slang gangster, lawless youth

hoodoo n, pl -doos (person or thing that brings) bad luck

hoodwink v trick or deceive

hoof n, pl **hooves, hoofs** horny casing of the foot of a horse, deer, etc. **hoof it** informal walk

hoo-ha n fuss or commotion

hook n 1 curved piece of metal or plastic used to hang, hold, or pull something 2 short swinging punch ▷ v 3 fasten or catch (as if) with a hook **hooked** adj 1 shaped like a hook 2 caught 3 (foll. by on) slang addicted (to) **hooker** n slang prostitute **hook shot** basketball shot made by holding the ball to one's side with one hand and throwing it over one's head **hook-up** n linking of radio or television stations **hookworm** n parasitic worm with hooked mouth parts

hookah n oriental pipe in which smoke is drawn through water and a long tube

hooligan n rowdy young person **hooliganism** n

hoop n rigid circular band, used esp. as a child's toy or for animals to jump through in the circus **be put through the hoops** go through an ordeal or test **hooped** adj

hoopla n fairground game in which hoops are thrown over objects in an attempt to win them

hooray interj same as **hurrah**

hoot n 1 sound of an automobile horn 2 owl's cry or similar sound 3 cry of derision 4 informal amusing person or thing ▷ v 5 jeer or yell contemptuously at (someone) 6 sound (an automobile horn) 7 informal laugh **hooter** n 1 device that hoots 2 slang nose

Hoover n 1 ® vacuum cleaner ▷ v 2 **hoover** vacuum

hooves n a plural of **hoof**

hop¹ v **hopping, hopped** 1 jump on one foot 2 move in short jumps 3 informal move quickly ▷ n 4 instance of hopping 5 short journey, esp. by air 6 informal dance

hop² n 1 climbing plant with green conelike flowers used to give beer a bitter flavour **hops** 2 the dried flowers

hope v 1 want (something) to happen or be true ▷ n 2 expectation of something desired 3 thing that gives cause for hope or is desired **hopeful** adj 1 having, expressing, or inspiring hope ▷ n 2 person considered to be on the brink of success **hopefully** adv 1 in a hopeful manner 2 it is hoped **hopeless** adj

hopper n container for storing things such as grain or sand

hopscotch n children's game of hopping in a pattern drawn on the ground

horde n large crowd

horizon n 1 apparent line that divides the earth and the sky **horizons** 2 limits of scope, interest, or knowledge

horizontal adj 1 flat and level with the ground or with a line considered as a base ▷ n 2 horizontal plane, position, or line **horizontally** adv

hormone n 1 substance secreted by certain glands which stimulates certain organs of the body 2 synthetic substance with the same effect **hormonal** adj

horn n 1 one of a pair of bony growths on the heads of animals such as cows and antelopes 2 substance of which this is made 3 wind instrument with a tube or pipe of brass fitted with a mouthpiece **4** device on a vehicle sounded as a warning **horned** adj **horny** adj **1** of or like horn **2** slang sexually aroused **hornbeam** n tree with smooth grey bark **hornbill** n bird with a bony growth on its large beak **hornpipe** n (music for) a lively solo dance, traditionally associated with sailors

hornblende n mineral containing aluminum, calcium, sodium, magnesium, and iron

hornet n large wasp with a severe sting

horology n art or science of clock-making and measuring time

horoscope n **1** prediction of a person's future based on the positions of the planets, sun, and moon at his or her birth **2** diagram of the positions of these at a particular time and place

horrendous adj horrific

horror n (thing or person causing) terror or hatred **horrible** adj **1** disagreeable **2** causing horror **horribly** adv **horrid** adj **1** unpleasant or disagreeable **2** informal unkind **horrify** v **1** cause feelings of horror in **2** shock **horrific** adj particularly horrible

hors d'oeuvre [or **durv**] n appetizer served before a main meal

horse n **1** four-footed animal with hooves, a mane, and a tail, used for riding and pulling carts, etc. **2** piece of gymnastic equipment used for vaulting over **straight from the horse's mouth** from the most reliable source **horsy** adj **1** devoted to horses **2** like a horse **horse about** or **horse around** v informal play

roughly or boisterously **horse chestnut** tree with broad leaves, white or pink flowers, and large brown shiny nuts **horsefly** n large bloodsucking fly **horsehair** n hair from the tail or mane of a horse **horse laugh** harsh boisterous laugh **horseman** (**horsewoman**) n rider on a horse **horseplay** n rough or rowdy behaviour **horsepower** n unit of power (equivalent to 745.7 watts), used to measure the power of an engine **horseradish** n plant with a strong-tasting root, used to make a sauce **horseshoe** n protective U-shaped piece of iron nailed to a horse's hoof, often regarded as a symbol of good luck

horticulture n art or science of cultivating gardens **horticultural** adj **horticulturist** n

hosanna interj exclamation of praise to God

hose[1] n **1** flexible tube for conveying liquid or gas ▷ v **2** water with a hose **hoser** n slang beer-drinking country dweller

hose[2] n stockings, socks, and tights **hosiery** n stockings, socks, etc. collectively

hospice [**hoss**-piss] n nursing home for the terminally ill

hospital n institution for the care and treatment of sick or injured people **hospitalize** v send or admit for care in a hospital **hospitalization** n

hospitality n friendliness in welcoming strangers or guests **hospitable** adj welcoming **hospitably** adv

host[1] n **1** person who entertains another as a guest **2** place or country providing the facilities for an event **3** compère of a show **4** animal or plant on which a parasite lives ▷ *v* **5** be the host of **hostess** *n* woman who welcomes guests or visitors

host² *n* large number

Host *n Christianity* bread used in Holy Communion

hostage *n* person who is illegally held prisoner until certain demands are met by other people

hostel *n* building providing accommodation at a low cost for particular categories of people, such as homeless people

hostelry *n, pl* **-ries** *obsolete* tavern

hostile *adj* **1** unfriendly **2** of an enemy **3** (foll. by *to*) opposed (to) **hostility** *n* **1** unfriendly and aggressive feelings or behaviour **hostilities 2** acts of warfare

hot *adj* **hotter, hottest** **1** having a high temperature **2** giving or feeling heat **3** (of a temper) quick to flare up **4** (of a competition) intense **5** recent or new **6** liked very much: *a hot favourite* **7** spicy **8** *slang* stolen **in hot water** *informal* in trouble **hotly** *adv* **hotness** *n* **hotting** *n informal* practice of stealing fast automobiles and putting on a show of skilful but dangerous driving **hot air** *informal* empty talk **hotbed** *n* any place encouraging a particular activity: *a hotbed of vice* **hot-blooded** *adj* passionate or excitable **hot dog** hot sausage (esp. a frankfurter) in a bread roll **hotfoot** *v, adv informal* (go) as fast as possible **hotheaded** *adj* hasty, having a hot temper **hothouse** *n* heated greenhouse **hot line** direct telephone link for emergency use **hotplate** *n*

1 heated metal surface on an electric cooker **2** portable device for keeping food warm

hotchpotch *n* jumbled mixture

hotel *n* commercial establishment providing lodging and meals **hotelier** *n* owner or manager of a hotel

Hottentot *n* member of a race of people of southern Africa, now nearly extinct

hound *n* **1** hunting dog ▷ *v* **2** pursue relentlessly

hour *n* **1** twenty-fourth part of a day **2** sixty minutes **3** time of day **4** appointed time **hours** **5** period regularly appointed for work or business **hourly** *adj, adv* **1** (happening) every hour **2** frequent(ly) **hourglass** *n* device with two glass compartments, containing a quantity of sand that takes an hour to trickle from the top section to the bottom one

houri *n Islam* any of the beautiful nymphs of paradise

house *n* **1** building used as a dwelling **2** building for some specific purpose: *schoolhouse* **3** law-making body or the hall where it meets **4** family or dynasty **5** business firm **6** theatre audience or performance ▷ *v* **7** give accommodation to **8** cover or contain **get on like a house on fire** *informal* get on very well together **on the house** *informal* provided free by the management **housing** *n* **1** (providing of) houses **2** protective case or covering of a machine **house arrest** confinement to one's home rather than to prison **houseboat** *n* stationary boat used as a home **housebreaker** *n* burglar **housecoat** *n* woman's long loose robelike garment for casual wear **household** n all the people living in a house **householder** n person who owns or rents a house **housekeeper** n person employed to run someone else's household **housekeeping** n (money for) running a household **housemaid** n female servant who does housework **housetrain** v train (a domestic animal) to urinate and defecate outside **housewares** pl n US & Canad kitchenware and other utensils for use in the home **house-warming** n party to celebrate moving into a new home **housewife** n woman who runs her own household **housework** n work of running a house, such as cleaning, cooking, and shopping

House music, House n kind of disco music based on funk, with fragments of other recordings edited in electronically

hovel n small dirty dwelling

hover v 1 (of a bird etc.) remain suspended in one place in the air 2 loiter 3 be in a state of indecision **hovercraft** n vehicle which can travel over both land and sea on a cushion of air

how adv 1 in what way 2 by what means 3 in what condition 4 to what degree **however** adv 1 nevertheless 2 by whatever means 3 no matter how

howdah n canopied seat on an elephant's back

howitzer n cannon firing shells at a steep angle

howl v 1 utter a long loud cry ▷ n 2 such a cry 3 loud burst of laughter **howler** n informal stupid mistake

hoyden n wild or boisterous girl, tomboy

HP, hp 1 hire-purchase **2** horsepower

HQ headquarters

HRH Her (or His) Royal Highness

HST harmonized sales tax

HTML hypertext markup language: text description language used on the internet

hub n 1 centre of a wheel, through which the axle passes 2 central point of activity

hubbub n confused noise of many voices, uproar

hubby n, pl -bies informal husband

hubris [hew-briss] n pride, arrogance

huckster n person using aggressive methods of selling

huddle n 1 small group 2 informal impromptu conference ▷ v 3 heap or crowd closely together 4 hunch (oneself) as through cold

hue n colour

hue and cry n public outcry

huff n 1 passing mood of anger or resentment ▷ v 2 blow or puff heavily **huffy** adj **huffily** adv

hug v **hugging, hugged 1** clasp tightly in the arms, usually with affection 2 keep close to ▷ n 3 tight or fond embrace

huge adj very big **hugely** adv very much

huh interj exclamation of derision, bewilderment, or inquiry

hula n native dance of Hawaii

Hula-Hoop n ® plastic hoop swung round the body by wriggling the hips

hulk n 1 body of an abandoned ship 2 offensive large or unwieldy person or thing **hulking** adj bulky or unwieldy

hull n **1** main body of a boat **2** leaves round the stem of a strawberry, raspberry, or similar fruit **3** shell or husk of a fruit or seed ▷ v **4** remove the hulls from (fruit or seeds)

hullabaloo n, pl **-loos** loud confused noise or clamour

hum v **humming, hummed 1** make a low continuous vibrating sound **2** sing with closed lips **3** slang be very active ▷ n **4** humming sound **hummingbird** n very small N American bird whose powerful wings make a humming noise as they vibrate

human adj **1** of, concerning, or typical of people ▷ n **2** human being **humanity** n **1** human nature **2** mankind **3** kindness or mercy **humanities 4** study of literature, philosophy, and the arts **human being** man, woman, or child **humanly** adv by human powers or means **humanize** v make human or humane **humankind** n mankind

humane adj kind or merciful **humanely** adv

humanism n belief in human effort rather than religion **humanist** n **humanitarian** n, adj (person) with the interest of mankind at heart

humble adj **1** conscious of one's failings **2** modest, unpretentious **3** unimportant ▷ v **4** cause to become humble **5** humiliate **humbly** adv

humbug n **1** boiled candy flavoured with peppermint **2** nonsense **3** person or thing that deceives people

humdinger n slang excellent person or thing

humdrum adj commonplace and dull

humerus [hew-mer-uss] n, pl **-eri** bone from the shoulder to the elbow

humid adj (of the weather) damp and warm **humidity** n **humidify** v **humidifier** n device for increasing the amount of water vapour in the air in a room

humiliate v lower the dignity or hurt the pride of **humiliating** adj **humiliation** n

humility n quality of being humble

hummock n hillock

humour n **1** ability to say or perceive things that are amusing **2** situations, speech, or writings that are humorous **3** state of mind, mood **4** obsolete fluid in the body ▷ v **5** be kind and indulgent to **humorous** adj **humorously** adv **humorist** n person who acts, speaks, or writes in a humorous way

hump n **1** normal or deforming lump, esp. on the back **2** hillock **3** informal fit of sulking ▷ v **4** slang carry or heave **humpback** n person with an abnormal curvature of the spine **humpbacked** adj **hump-back bridge** road bridge with a sharp slope on either side

humus [hew-muss] n decomposing vegetable and animal mould in the soil

hunch n **1** informal feeling or suspicion not based on facts ▷ v **2** draw (one's shoulders) up or together **hunchback** n humpback

hundred adj, n ten times ten **hundredth** adj, n (of) number one hundred in a series **hundredfold** adj, adv **hundredweight** n unit of weight of 112 lbs (50.8 kg)

hung v **1** past of **hang** ▷ adj **2** (of a jury) unable to decide

3 (of a parliament) with no clear majority **hung over** *informal* suffering the effects of a hangover

hunger *n* **1** discomfort or weakness from lack of food **2** lack of food that causes suffering or death: *refugees dying of hunger* **3** desire or craving ▷ *v* **4** (foll. by *for*) want very much **hungry** *adj* desiring food **hungrily** *adv* **hunger strike** refusal of all food, as a means of protest

hunk *n* **1** large piece **2** *slang* sexually attractive man

hunt *v* **1** seek out (animals) to kill or capture for sport or food **2** search (for) ▷ *n* **3** act or instance of hunting **4** (party organized for) hunting wild animals for sport **hunter** *n* **1** man or animal that seeks out and kills or captures game **2** horse or dog bred for hunting **huntress** *n* *obsolete* woman who seeks out and kills or captures game **huntsman** *n* **1** man in charge of a pack of hounds **2** man who hunts

hurdle *n* **1** light barrier for jumping over **2** problem or difficulty **hurdles 3** race involving hurdles ▷ *v* **4** jump over (something) **hurdler** *n* person who races over hurdles

hurdy-gurdy *n, pl* -**dies** mechanical musical instrument, such as a barrel organ

hurl *v* **1** throw or utter violently **2** *slang* vomit **hurler** *n baseball* pitcher

hurling, hurley *n* Irish game resembling hockey

hurly-burly *n* loud confusion

hurrah, hurray *interj* exclamation of joy or applause

hurricane *n* very strong, often destructive wind or storm **hurricane lamp** kerosene

lamp with a glass covering

hurry *v* -**rying**, -**ried** **1** (cause to) move or act in great haste ▷ *n* **2** haste **3** eagerness **hurriedly** *adv*

hurt *v* **hurting, hurt 1** cause physical or mental pain to **2** wound the feelings of **3** *informal* feel pain ▷ *n* **4** physical or mental pain or suffering **hurtful** *adj*

hurtle *v* move rapidly or violently

husband *n* **1** male partner in marriage ▷ *v* **2** use economically **husbandry** *n* **1** farming **2** management of resources

hush *v* **1** make or be silent ▷ *n* **2** stillness or quietness **hush-hush** *adj informal* secret **hush up** *v* suppress information about

husk *n* **1** outer covering of certain seeds and fruits ▷ *v* **2** remove the husk from

husky¹ *adj* **huskier, huskiest 1** hoarse or dry in the throat **2** *informal* big and strong **huskily** *adv*

husky² *n, pl* **huskies** Arctic sledge dog with a thick coat and a curled tail

hussar [hoo-**zar**] *n hist* lightly armed cavalry soldier

hussy *n, pl* -**sies** brazen or promiscuous woman

hustings *pl n* proceedings at a parliamentary election

hustle *v* **1** push about, jostle **2** *slang* (of a prostitute) solicit ▷ *n* **3** lively activity or bustle

hut *n* small house or shelter

hutch *n* cage for small pet animals

hyacinth *n* sweet-smelling spring flower which grows from a bulb

hyaena *n* same as **hyena**

hybrid *n* **1** offspring of two plants or animals of different species **2** anything of mixed ancestry **3** vehicle powered by an internal-combustion engine and another source of power ▷ *adj* **4** of mixed ancestry **5** (of a vehicle) powered by more than one source

hydra *n* **1** mythical many-headed water serpent **2** any persistent problem **3** freshwater polyp

hydrangea *n* ornamental shrub with clusters of pink, blue, or white flowers

hydrant *n* outlet from a water main with a nozzle for a hose

hydrate *n* chemical compound of water with another substance

hydraulic *adj* operated by pressure forced through a pipe by a liquid such as water or oil **hydraulics** *n* study of the mechanical properties of fluids as they apply to practical engineering **hydraulically** *adv*

hydro *n* **1** hydroelectric power **2** electricity as supplied to residence, business, etc. **3 Hydro** hydroelectric power company

hydro- *combining form* **1** water **2** hydrogen

hydrocarbon *n* compound of hydrogen and carbon

hydrochloric acid *n* strong colourless acid used in many industrial and laboratory processes

hydrodynamics *n* science concerned with the mechanical properties of fluids

hydroelectric *adj* of the generation of electricity by the use of water

hydrofoil *n* fast light vessel with its hull raised out of the water on one or more pairs of fins

hydrogen *n* light flammable colourless gaseous element which combines with oxygen to form water **hydrogen bomb** atom bomb of enormous power in which energy is released by the fusion of hydrogen nuclei to give helium nuclei **hydrogen peroxide** colourless liquid used as a hair bleach and as an antiseptic

hydrolysis [hie-**drol**-iss-iss] *n* decomposition of a chemical compound reacting with water

hydrometer [hie-**drom**-it-er] *n* device for measuring the relative density of a liquid

hydropathy *n* method of treating disease by the use of large quantities of water both internally and externally

hydrophobia *n* **1** fear of water **2** rabies

hydroplane *n* light motorboat which skims the water

hydroponics *n* science of cultivating plants in water without using soil

hydrotherapy *n med* treatment of certain diseases by exercise in water

hydrous *adj* containing water

hyena, hyaena *n* scavenging doglike mammal of Africa and S Asia

hygiene *n* **1** principles and practice of health and cleanliness **2** study of these principles **hygienic** *adj* **hygienically** *adv*

hymen *n* membrane covering the opening of a girl's vagina, which breaks before puberty or at the first occurrence of sexual intercourse

hymn *n* Christian song of praise sung to God or a saint **hymnal** *adj* **1** of hymns ▷ *n* **2** Also **hymn book** book of hymns

hype *n* **1** intensive or

exaggerated publicity or sales promotion ▷ v **2** promote (a product) using intensive or exaggerated publicity

hyper adj informal overactive or overexcited

hyper- prefix over, above, excessively: hyperactive; hypercritical

hyperbola [hie-**per**-bol-a] n curve produced when a cone is cut by a plane at a steeper angle to its base than its side

hyperbole [hie-**per**-bol-ee] n deliberate exaggeration for effect **hyperbolic** adj

hyperlink n computers link from a hypertext file giving users instant access to related material in another file

hypermarket n huge self-service store

hypersensitive adj unduly vulnerable emotionally or physically

hypersonic adj having a speed of at least five times the speed of sound

hypertension n abnormally high blood pressure

hyphen n punctuation mark (-) indicating that two words or syllables are connected **hyphenate** v join with a hyphen **hyphenated** adj having two words or syllables joined by a hyphen **hyphenation** n

hypnosis n artificially induced state of relaxation in which the mind is more than usually receptive to suggestion **hypnotic** adj of or (as if) producing hypnosis **hypnotism** n **hypnotist** n **hypnotize** v induce hypnosis in (someone)

hypo- prefix below, less than: hypocrite; hypodermic

hypoallergenic adj (of cosmetics) not likely to cause an allergic reaction

hypochondria n undue preoccupation with one's health **hypochondriac** n

hypocrisy [hip-**ok**-rass-ee] n, pl -**sies** (instance of) pretence of having standards or beliefs that are contrary to one's real character or actual behaviour **hypocrite** [**hip**-oh-krit] n person who pretends to be what he or she is not **hypocritical** adj **hypocritically** adv

hypodermic adj, n (denoting) a syringe or needle used to inject a drug beneath the skin

hypotension n abnormally low blood pressure

hypotenuse [hie-**pot**-a-news] n side of a right-angled triangle opposite the right angle

hypothermia n condition in which a person's body temperature is reduced to a dangerously low level

hypothesis [hie-**poth**-iss-iss] n, pl -**ses** [-seez] suggested but unproved explanation of something **hypothetical** adj based on assumption rather than fact or reality **hypothetically** adv

hysterectomy n, pl -**mies** surgical removal of the womb

hysteria n state of uncontrolled excitement, anger, or panic **hysterical** adj **hysterically** adv **hysterics** pl n attack of hysteria

Hz hertz

Ii

I *pron* used by a speaker or writer to refer to himself or herself as the subject of a verb

iambic *adj* (of poetry) written in metrical units formed of one long and one short syllable

IBA Independent Broadcasting Authority

Iberian *adj* of Iberia, the peninsula of Spain and Portugal

ibex [ibe-eks] *n* wild goat with large backward-curving horns

ibid. (referring to a book, passage, etc. previously cited) in the same place

ibis [ibe-iss] *n* wading bird with long legs

ice *n* 1 frozen water 2 *Brit* portion of ice cream ▷ *v* 3 become covered with ice 4 cover with icing 5 cool with ice **break the ice** create a relaxed atmosphere, esp. between people meeting for the first time **iced** *adj* 1 served very cold 2 covered with icing **icy** *adj* 1 very cold 2 covered with ice 3 aloof and unfriendly **icily** *adv* **iciness** *n* **ice age** period when much of the earth's surface was covered in glaciers **iceberg** *n* large floating mass of ice **ice bridge** road of ice across a frozen watercourse or harbour **ice cap** mass of ice permanently covering an area **ice cream** sweet creamy frozen food **ice cube** small square block of ice added to a drink to cool it **ice floe** sheet of floating ice **ice hockey** *esp. Brit* hockey **ice lolly** flavoured ice on a stick **ice pick** axe-like tool for breaking ice **ice skate** boot with a steel blade fixed to the sole, to enable the wearer to glide over ice **ice-skate** *v* **ice-skater** *n*

ichthyology [ik-thi-**ol**-a-jee] *n* scientific study of fish

icicle *n* tapering spike of ice hanging where water has dripped

icing *n* mixture of sugar and water etc. used to cover and decorate cakes **icing sugar** finely ground sugar for making icing

icon *n* 1 picture of Christ or another religious figure, venerated in the Orthodox Church 2 picture on a computer screen representing a computer function that can be activated by moving the cursor over it

iconoclast *n* person who attacks established principles or ideas **iconoclastic** *adj*

id *n psychoanalysis* the mind's instinctive unconscious energies

idea *n* 1 plan or thought formed in the mind 2 thought of something: *the idea horrified her* 3 belief or opinion

ideal *n* 1 conception of something that is perfect 2 perfect person or thing ▷ *adj* 3 most suitable 4 perfect **ideally** *adv* **idealism** *n* tendency to seek perfection in everything **idealist** n **idealistic** adj **idealize** v regard or portray as perfect **idealization** n

idem pron, adj Latin the same: used to refer to a book, article, etc. already quoted

identical adj exactly the same **identically** adv

identify v **-fying, -fied 1** prove or recognize as being a certain person or thing **2** understand and sympathize with a person or group because one regards oneself as being similar or similarly situated **3** treat as being the same **identifiable** adj **identification** n

Identikit n ® set of pictures of parts of faces that can be built up to form a likeness of a person wanted by the police

identity n, pl **-ties 1** state of being a specified person or thing **2** individuality or personality **3** state of being the same **identity theft** crime of fraudulently setting up and using bank accounts and credit facilities in another person's name

ideogram, ideograph n picture, symbol, etc. representing an object rather than the sounds of its name

ideology n, pl **-gies** body of ideas and beliefs of a group, nation, etc. **ideological** adj **ideologist** n

idiocy n, pl **-cies** utter stupidity

idiom n **1** group of words which when used together have a different meaning from the component words: raining cats and dogs **2** way of expression natural or peculiar to a language or group **idiomatic** adj **idiomatically** adv

idiosyncrasy n, pl **-sies**

personal peculiarity of mind, habit, or behaviour

idiot n **1** foolish person **2** obsolete, offensive person with learning difficulties **idiotic** adj utterly stupid **idiotically** adv

idle adj **1** not doing anything **2** not being used **3** lazy **4** useful: idle thoughts ▷ v **5** (esp. foll. by away) waste (time) **6** (of an engine) run slowly with the gears disengaged **idleness** n **idler** n **idly** adv

idol [**ide**-ol] n **1** image of a god as an object of worship **2** object of excessive devotion **idolatry** [ide-**ol**-a-tree] n **1** worship of idols **2** excessive devotion or reverence **idolater** n **idolatrous** adj **idolize** v love or admire excessively

idyll [**id**-ill] n **1** scene or time of peace and happiness **2** description in literature of a picturesque or charming scene or episode, esp. of country life **idyllic** adj **idyllically** adv

i.e. that is to say

if conj **1** on the condition or supposition that **2** whether **3** even though ▷ n **4** uncertainty or doubt: I won't have any ifs or buts **iffy** adj informal doubtful, uncertain

igloo n, pl **-loos** dome-shaped Inuit house of snow and ice

igneous [**ig**-nee-uss] adj (of rocks) formed as molten rock cools and hardens

ignite v catch fire or set fire to **ignition** n **1** system that ignites the fuel-air mixture to start an engine **2** igniting

ignoble adj dishonourable **ignobly** adv

ignominy [**ig**-nom-in-ee] n humiliating disgrace **ignominious** adj **ignominiously** adv

ignoramus *n, pl* **-muses**
ignorant person
ignore *v* refuse to notice,
disregard deliberately
ignorance *n* lack of
knowledge **ignorant** *adj*
lacking knowledge rude
through lack of knowledge of
good manners **ignorantly** *adv*
iguana *n* large tropical
American lizard
ileum *n* lower part of the small
intestine **ileac** *adj*
ilk *n* **of that ilk** of the same
type
ill *adj* **1** not in good health
2 bad, evil **3** unfavourable:
an ill omen ▷ *n* **4** evil, harm
▷ *adv* **5** badly **6** hardly,
with difficulty: *I can ill
afford the expense* **ill at ease**
uncomfortable, unable to
relax **illness** *n* **ill-advised** *adj*
1 badly thought out **2** unwise
ill-disposed *adj* (often foll.
by *towards*) unfriendly or
unsympathetic **ill-fated**
adj doomed or unlucky
ill-gotten *adj* obtained
dishonestly **ill-health** *n*
condition of being unwell **ill-
mannered** *adj* rude **ill-treat**
v treat cruelly **ill will** unkind
feeling, hostility
illegal *adj* against the
law **illegally** *adv* **illegality** *n*
illegible *adj* unable to be read
or deciphered
illegitimate *adj* **1** born
to parents not married
to each other **2** unlawful
illegitimacy *n*
illicit *adj* **1** illegal **2** forbidden
or disapproved of by society
illiterate *adj* **1** unable to
read or write **2** uneducated,
ignorant **illiteracy** *n*
illogical *adj* **1** unreasonable
2 not logical **illogicality** *n*
illuminate *v* **1** light up **2** make
clear, explain **3** decorate
with lights **4** *hist* decorate (a

manuscript) with designs
of gold and bright colours.
illumination *n* **illuminating**
adj helping to explain
illusion *n* deceptive
appearance or belief
illusionist *n* conjurer
illusory *adj* false
illustrate *v* **1** explain by use
of examples **2** provide (a book
or text) with pictures **3** be
an example of **illustration**
n **1** picture or diagram
2 example **illustrative** *adj*
illustrator *n*
illustrious *adj* famous and
distinguished
IM instant messaging:
communication between two
or more people in real time
through the transmission of
electronic messages over a
computer network
image *n* **1** mental picture
of someone or something
2 impression people have of
a politician, organization,
etc. **3** simile or metaphor
4 representation of a person
or thing in art or literature
5 optical counterpart, as in
a mirror **6** double, copy ▷ *v*
7 make an image of **8** reflect
imagery *n* images collectively,
esp. in literature
imagine *v* **1** form a mental
image of **2** think, believe,
or guess **imaginable** *adj*
imaginary *adj* existing
only in the imagination
imagination *n* **1** ability to
make mental images of
things not present **2** creative
mental ability **imaginative**
adj **imaginatively** *adv*
imago [im-**may**-go] *n, pl*
imagoes, imagines [im-**maj**-
in-ees] sexually mature adult
insect
imam *n* **1** leader of prayers in a
mosque **2** title of some Islamic
leaders

IMAX ® [**eye**-max] n film projection process which produces an image ten times larger than standard

imbalance n lack of proportion

imbecile [imb-ess-eel] n 1 idiot ▷ adj 2 idiotic **imbecility** n

imbibe v 1 drink (esp. alcohol) 2 lit absorb (ideas etc.)

imbroglio [imb-**role**-ee-oh] n, pl -**ios** confusing and complicated situation

imbue v -buing, -bued (usu. foll. by with) fill or inspire with (ideals or principles)

IMF International Monetary Fund

imitate v 1 take as a model 2 mimic or copy **imitation** n 1 copy of an original 2 imitating **imitative** adj **imitator** n

immaculate adj 1 completely clean or tidy 2 completely flawless **immaculately** adv

immanent adj present within and throughout something **immanence** n

immaterial adj not important, not relevant

immature adj 1 not fully developed 2 lacking wisdom or stability because of youth **immaturity** n

immediate adj 1 occurring at once 2 next or nearest in time, space, or relationship **immediately** adv **immediacy** n

immemorial adj having existed or happened for longer than anyone can remember **immemorially** adv

immense adj huge or vast **immensely** adv **immensity** n

immerse v 1 plunge (something) into liquid 2 involve deeply: I immersed myself in my work **immersion** n immersing **immersion**

heater or **immerser** n electric heater contained in a domestic hot-water tank

immigrant n person who comes to a foreign country in order to settle there **immigration** n

imminent adj about to happen **imminently** adv **imminence** n

immobile adj 1 unable to move 2 not moving **immobility** n **immobilize** v make unable to move or work

immoderate adj excessive or unreasonable

immolate v kill as a sacrifice **immolation** n

immoral adj 1 morally wrong, corrupt 2 sexually depraved or promiscuous **immorality** n

immortal adj 1 living forever 2 famed for all time ▷ n 3 immortal being 4 person whose fame will last for all time **immortality** n **immortalize** v

immune adj 1 protected against a specific disease 2 secure (against) 3 exempt (from) **immunity** n 1 ability to resist disease 2 freedom from prosecution, tax, etc. **immunize** v make immune to a disease **immunization** n

immunodeficiency n deficiency in or breakdown of a person's immune system

immunology n study of immunity **immunological** adj **immunologist** n

immure v lit imprison

immutable [im-**mute**-a-bl] adj unchangeable **immutability** n

imp n 1 demon 2 mischievous child

impact n 1 strong effect 2 collision ▷ v 3 press firmly against or into **impaction** n

impair v weaken or damage **impaired** adj law influenced

by alcohol while driving a
motor vehicle **impairment** n

impala [imp-**ah**-la] n southern
African antelope

impale v pierce with a sharp
object **impalement** n

impalpable adj
1 imperceptible to the touch
2 difficult to understand

impart v 1 communicate
(information) 2 give: impart
flavour

impartial adj not favouring
one side or the other
impartially adv **impartiality**
n

impassable adj (of a road etc.)
impossible to travel over or
through

impasse [am-pass] n
situation in which progress is
impossible

impassioned adj full of
emotion

impassive adj showing no
emotion, calm **impassivity** n

impatient adj 1 irritable
at any delay or difficulty
2 restless to have or do
something **impatiently** adv
impatience n

impeach v charge with a
serious crime against the
state **impeachment** n

impeccable adj without fault,
excellent **impeccably** adv

impecunious adj penniless

impedance [imp-**eed**-anss]
n electricity measure of the
opposition to the flow of an
alternating current

impede v hinder in action
or progress **impediment** n
something that makes action,
speech, or progress difficult
impedimenta pl n objects
impeding progress, esp.
baggage or equipment

impel v -pelling, -pelled
drive (a person) to do
something

impending adj (esp. of

something bad) about to
happen

impenetrable adj
1 impossible to get through
2 impossible to understand

imperative adj 1 extremely
urgent, vital 2 grammar
denoting a mood of verbs used
in commands ▷ n 3 grammar
imperative mood

imperceptible adj too slight
or gradual to be noticed
imperceptibly adv

imperfect adj 1 having
faults or mistakes 2 not
complete 3 grammar denoting
a tense of verbs describing
continuous, incomplete, or
repeated past actions ▷ n
4 grammar imperfect tense
imperfection n

imperial adj 1 of an empire or
emperor 2 majestic 3 denoting
weights and measures
formerly official in Britain,
Canada, and other countries
of the Commonwealth
imperialism n rule by one
country over many others
imperialist n, adj

imperil v -illing, -illed
endanger

imperious adj used to being
obeyed, domineering

impersonal adj 1 not
influenced by emotion
2 lacking human warmth
or personality 3 grammar
(of a verb) without a
personal subject: it is snowing
impersonality n

impersonate v 1 pretend
to be (another person)
2 imitate the mannerisms of
(someone) **impersonation** n
impersonator n

impertinent adj disrespectful
or rude **impertinently** adv
impertinence n

imperturbable adj calm, not
excitable **imperturbability** n

impervious adj 1 not letting

(water etc.) through **2** not influenced by (a feeling, argument, etc.)

impetigo [imp-it-**tie**-go] *n* contagious skin disease

impetuous *adj* done or acting without thought, rash. **impetuously** *adv* **impetuosity** *n*

impetus [**imp**-it-uss] *n, pl* -**tuses 1** impulse **2** force with which a body moves

impinge *v* encroach (upon), affect or restrict

impious [**imp**-ee-uss] *adj* showing a lack of respect or reverence

impish *adj* mischievous

implacable *adj* **1** not to be appeased **2** unyielding **implacably** *adv* **implacability** *n*

implant *v* **1** fix firmly in the mind **2** insert or embed ▷ *n* **3** *med* anything implanted in the body, such as a tissue graft **implantation** *n*

implement *n* **1** tool or instrument ▷ *v* **2** carry out (instructions etc.) **implementation** *n*

implicate *v* show to be involved, esp. in a crime **implication** *n* something implied

implicit *adj* **1** expressed indirectly **2** absolute: *implicit belief* **implicitly** *adv*

implore *v* beg desperately

imply *v* -**plying**, -**plied 1** indicate by hinting, suggest **2** mean

impolitic *adj* unwise, ill-advised

imponderable *n, adj* (something) impossible to assess

import *v* **1** bring in (goods) from another country ▷ *n* **2** something imported **3** meaning **4** importance **importation** *n* **importer** *n*

important *adj* **1** of great significance or value **2** famous, powerful **importance** *n*

importunate *adj* persistent in making demands **importune** *v* persist in demands **importunity** *n*

impose *v* **1** force the acceptance of **2** take unfair advantage of **imposing** *adj* impressive **imposition** *n* unreasonable demand, burden

impossible *adj* **1** incapable of being done or experienced **2** absurd or unreasonable **impossibly** *adv* **impossibility** *n*

impostor *n* person who cheats or swindles by pretending to be someone else

impotent [**imp**-a-tent] *adj* **1** powerless **2** (of a man) incapable of sexual intercourse **impotence** *n* **impotently** *adv*

impound *v* take legal possession of, confiscate

impoverish *v* make poor or weak **impoverishment** *n*

impracticable *adj* incapable of being put into practice

impractical *adj* not sensible

imprecation *n* curse

impregnable *adj* impossible to break into **impregnability** *n*

impregnate *v* **1** saturate, spread all through **2** make pregnant **impregnation** *n*

impresario *n, pl* -**ios** person who runs theatre performances, concerts, etc.

impress *v* **1** affect strongly, usu. favourably **2** stress or emphasize **3** imprint or stamp **impression** *n* **1** (strong or favourable) effect **2** vague idea **3** impersonation for entertainment **4** mark made by pressing **impressionable**

adj easily influenced

impressionism *n* art style that gives a general effect or mood rather than form or structure **impressionist** *n* **impressionistic** *adj*

impressive *adj* making a strong impression, esp. through size, importance, or quality

imprimatur [imp-rim-**ah**-ter] *n* official approval to print a book

imprint *n* **1** mark made by printing or stamping **2** publisher's name and address on a book ▷ *v* **3** produce (a mark) by printing or stamping

imprison *v* put in prison **imprisonment** *n*

improbable *adj* unlikely **improbability** *n*

impromptu *adv, adj* without preparation, improvised

improper *adj* **1** indecent **2** incorrect or irregular **3** (of a fraction) with a numerator larger than the denominator, as in 5/3

impropriety [imp-roe-**pry**-a-tee] *n, pl* -**ties** improper behaviour

improve *v* make or become better **improvement** *n*

improvident *adj* not planning for future needs **improvidence** *n*

improvise *v* **1** make use of materials at hand **2** make up (a piece of music, speech, etc.) as one goes along **improvisation** *n*

impudent *adj* cheeky **impudently** *adv* **impudence** *n*

impugn [imp-**yoon**] *v* call in question, cast doubt on

impulse *n* **1** sudden urge to do something **2** short electrical signal passing along a wire or nerve or through the air **on impulse** suddenly and

without planning **impulsive** *adj* tending to act without thinking first **impulsively** *adv*

impunity [imp-**yoon**-it-ee] *n* **with impunity** without punishment or unpleasant consequences

impure *adj* **1** having unwanted substances mixed in **2** immoral or obscene **impurity** *n*

impute *v* attribute responsibility to **imputation** *n*

in *prep* **1** inside, within **2** during **3** at the end of (a period of time) **4** indicating a state, situation, or manner **5** into ▷ *adv* **6** in or into a particular place **7** at one's home or place of work **8** in office or power **9** in fashion ▷ *adj* **10** fashionable

inability *n* lack of means or skill to do something

inaccurate *adj* not correct **inaccuracy** *n*

inadequate *adj* **1** not enough **2** not good enough **inadequacy** *n*

inadvertent *adj* unintentional **inadvertently** *adv*

inalienable *adj* not able to be taken away: *an inalienable right*

inane *adj* senseless or silly **inanity** *n*

inanimate *adj* not living

inanition *n* exhaustion or weakness, as from lack of food

inappropriate *adj* not suitable

inarticulate *adj* unable to express oneself clearly or well

inasmuch as *conj* seeing that, because

inaugurate *v* **1** open or begin the use of, esp. with ceremony **2** formally establish (a new leader) in office **inaugural** *adj* **inauguration** *n*

inauspicious adj unlucky, suggesting an unfavourable outcome

inboard adj (of a boat's engine) inside the hull

inborn adj existing from birth, natural

inbox n (on a computer) folder in a mailbox in which incoming messages are stored and displayed

inbred adj 1 produced as a result of inbreeding 2 inborn or ingrained

inbreeding n breeding from closely related individuals

inbuilt adj present from the start

Inc. (of a company) incorporated

incalculable adj impossible to estimate, very great

in camera adv in private session

incandescent adj 1 glowing with heat 2 (of artificial light) produced by a glowing filament **incandescence** n

incantation n ritual chanting of magic words or sounds **incantatory** adj

incapable adj 1 (foll. by of) lacking the ability to 2 helpless

incapacitate v deprive of strength or ability, disable **incapacity** n

incarcerate v imprison **incarceration** n

incarnate adj 1 possessing human form 2 typified: stupidity incarnate **incarnation** n **Incarnation** n Christianity God's coming to earth in human form as Jesus Christ

incendiary [in-**send**-ee-ya-ree] adj 1 (of bombs etc.) designed to cause fires ▷ n, pl -**aries** 2 bomb designed to cause fires 3 fire raiser or arsonist

incense[1] v make very angry

incense[2] n 1 substance that gives off a sweet perfume when burned 2 its smoke

incentive n something that encourages effort or action

inception n beginning

incessant adj never stopping **incessantly** adv

incest n sexual intercourse between two people too closely related to marry **incestuous** adj

inch n 1 unit of length equal to one twelfth of a foot or 2.54 centimetres ▷ v 2 move very slowly

inchoate [in-**koe**-ate] adj just begun and not yet properly developed

incidence n extent or frequency of occurrence

incident n 1 (memorable) event 2 public disturbance

incidental adj 1 occurring as a minor part of or accompaniment to something else 2 happening by chance **incidentally** adv **incidental music** background music for a film or play

incinerate v burn to ashes **incineration** n **incinerator** n furnace for burning rubbish

incipient adj just starting to appear or happen

incise v cut into with a sharp tool **incision** n **incisive** adj direct and forceful **incisor** n cutting tooth

incite v stir up or provoke **incitement** n

incivility n, pl -**ties** rudeness

inclement adj (of weather) bad **inclemency** n

incline v 1 lean, slope 2 (cause to) have a certain disposition or tendency ▷ n 3 slope **inclination** n 1 liking, tendency, or preference 2 slope 3 degree of deviation from the horizontal or vertical

include v 1 have as (part of) the contents 2 put in as part of a set or group **inclusion** n **inclusive** adj including everything **inclusively** adv

incognito [in-kog-**nee**-toe] *adv, adj* **1** under an assumed identity ▷ *n, pl* **-tos 2** false identity

incoherent *adj* (of speech) unclear and impossible to understand **incoherence** *n* **incoherently** *adv*

income *n* amount of money earned from work, investments, etc. **income tax** personal tax levied on annual income

incoming *adj* **1** about to arrive **2** about to come into office

incommode *v* inconvenience

incommodious *adj* cramped

incommunicado *adj, adv* deprived of communication with other people

incomparable *adj* beyond comparison **incomparably** *adv*

incompatible *adj* inconsistent or conflicting **incompatibility** *n*

incompetent *adj* lacking the necessary ability to do something **incompetence** *n*

inconceivable *adj* impossible to imagine

inconclusive *adj* not giving a final decision or result

incongruous *adj* inappropriate or out of place **incongruously** *adv* **incongruity** *n*

inconsequential *adj* unimportant or irrelevant

inconsiderable *adj* **1** relatively small **2** insignificant

inconstant *adj* liable to change one's loyalties or opinions

incontinent *adj* not able to control one's bladder or bowels **incontinence** *n*

incontrovertible *adj* impossible to deny or disprove

inconvenience *n* **1** trouble or difficulty ▷ *v* **2** cause trouble or difficulty to **inconvenient** *adj*

incorporate *v* include or be included as part of a larger unit **incorporation** *n*

incorporeal *adj* without bodily existence

incorrigible *adj* beyond reform **incorrigibility** *n*

incorruptible *adj* **1** impossible to bribe or corrupt, honest **2** not subject to decay

increase *v* **1** make or become greater in size, number, etc. ▷ *n* **2** rise in number, size, etc. **3** amount by which something increases **increasingly** *adv* more and more

incredible *adj* **1** unbelievable **2** *informal* marvellous, amazing **incredibly** *adv*

incredulous *adj* not willing or able to believe something **incredulity** *n*

increment *n* increase in money or value, esp. a regular salary increase **incremental** *adj*

incriminate *v* make (someone) seem guilty of a crime **incriminating** *adj* **incrimination** *n*

incubate [in-cube-ate] *v* **1** (of birds) hatch eggs by sitting on them **2** grow (bacteria) **3** (of bacteria) remain inactive in an animal or person before causing disease **incubation** *n* **incubator** *n* **1** heated enclosed apparatus for rearing premature babies **2** apparatus for artificially hatching eggs

incubus [in-cube-uss] *n, pl* **-bi, -buses 1** demon believed to have sex with sleeping women **2** nightmare

inculcate *v* fix in someone's mind by constant repetition **inculcation** *n*

incumbent *adj* **1 it is incumbent on** it is the duty

of ▷ *n* **2** person holding a particular office or position **incumbency** *n*

incur *v* **-curring, -curred** bring (something unpleasant) upon oneself

incurable *adj* not able to be cured **incurably** *adv*

incurious *adj* showing no curiosity or interest

incursion *n* **1** sudden brief invasion **2** inroad

indebted *adj* **1** owing gratitude for help or favours **2** owing money **indebtedness** *n*

indecent *adj* **1** morally or sexually offensive **2** unsuitable or unseemly: *indecent haste* **indecently** *adv* **indecency** *n* **indecent assault** sexual attack which does not include rape **indecent exposure** showing of one's genitals in public

indecipherable *adj* impossible to read

indeed *adv* **1** really, certainly ▷ *interj* **2** showing surprise, doubt, etc.

indefatigable *adj* never getting tired **indefatigably** *adv*

indefensible *adj* **1** not justifiable **2** unable to be defended **indefensibly** *adv*

indefinite *adj* **1** without exact limits: *an indefinite period* **2** vague **indefinite article** *grammar* the word *a* or *an* **indefinitely** *adv*

indelible *adj* **1** impossible to erase or remove **2** producing indelible marks **indelibly** *adv*

indelicate *adj* embarrassing, tasteless **indelicacy** *n*

indemnify *v* **-ifying, -ified 1** give indemnity to **2** compensate **indemnification** *n*

indemnity *n, pl* **-ties 1** insurance against loss or damage **2** compensation for loss or damage suffered

indent *v* **1** start (a line of writing) further from the margin than the other lines **2** order (goods) using a special order form **indentation** *n* dent in a surface or edge

indenture *n* contract, esp. one binding an apprentice to his employer

independent *adj* **1** free from the control or influence of others **2** separate **3** financially self-reliant **4** capable of acting for oneself or on one's own ▷ *n* **5** politician who does not belong to any party **independently** *adv* **independence** *n*

in-depth *adj* detailed or thorough

indescribable *adj* too intense or extreme for words **indescribably** *adv*

indeterminate *adj* uncertain in extent, amount, or nature **indeterminacy** *n*

index *n, pl* **indexes**, *math* **indices** [in-diss-eez] **1** alphabetical list of names or subjects dealt with in a book **2** file or catalogue used to find things **3** pointer or indicator **4** *math* exponent ▷ *v* **5** provide (a book) with an index **6** enter in an index **7** make index-linked **index finger** finger next to the thumb **index-linked** *adj* (of pensions, wages, etc.) rising or falling in line with the cost of living

Indian *n, adj* **1** (person) from India **2** (person) descended from the original inhabitants of the American continents **Indian summer** period of warm sunny weather in fall

India rubber *n* eraser

indicate *v* **1** be a sign or symptom of **2** point out **3** state briefly **4** (of a measuring instrument) show a reading of **indication** n **indicative** [in-**dik**-a-tiv] adj **1** suggesting: clouds indicative of rain **2** grammar denoting a mood of verbs used to make a statement **indicator** n **1** something acting as a sign or indication **2** flashing light on a vehicle showing the driver's intention to turn **3** dial or gauge

indict [in-**dite**] v formally accuse of a crime **indictable** adj **indictment** n

indifferent adj **1** showing no interest or concern **2** of poor quality or low standard **indifference** n **indifferently** adv

indigenous [in-**dij**-in-uss] adj born in or natural to a country

indigent adj so poor as to lack necessities **indigence** n

indigestion n (discomfort or pain caused by) difficulty in digesting food **indigestible** adj

indignation n anger caused by something unfair or wrong **indignant** adj feeling or showing indignation **indignantly** adv

indignity n, pl -**ties** embarrassing or humiliating treatment

indigo n **1** deep violet-blue **2** dye of this colour

indirect adj **1** done or caused by someone or something else **2** not by a straight route **indirect object** grammar person or thing indirectly affected by an action, such as Sue in I bought Sue a book **indirect speech** report that gives the content of what someone said but not the actual words

indiscreet adj incautious or tactless in revealing secrets

indiscreetly adv **indiscretion** n

indiscriminate adj chosen or choosing without thought or care

indispensable adj impossible to do without

indisposed adj **1** unwell or ill **2** unwilling **indisposition** n

indisputable adj without doubt **indisputably** adv

indissoluble adj permanent

indium n soft silver-white metallic element

individual adj **1** characteristic of or meant for a single person or thing **2** separate or distinct **3** distinctive, unusual ▷ n **4** single person or thing **individually** adv singly **individualism** n principle of living one's life in one's own way **individualist** n **individualistic** adj **individuality** n distinctive character or personality

indoctrinate v teach (someone) to accept a doctrine or belief uncritically **indoctrination** n

Indo-European adj, n (of) a family of languages spoken in most of Europe and much of Asia, including English, Russian, and Hindi

indolent adj lazy **indolence** n

indomitable adj too strong to be defeated or discouraged **indomitably** adv

indoor adj inside a building **indoors** adv

indubitable [in-**dew**-bit-a-bl] adj beyond doubt, certain **indubitably** adv

induce v **1** persuade **2** cause **3** med bring on (labour) by the use of drugs etc. **inducement** n something that encourages someone to do something

induct v formally install someone, esp. a cleric, in office

induction n 1 reasoning process by which general conclusions are drawn from particular instances 2 process by which electrical or magnetic properties are produced by the proximity of an electrified or magnetic object 3 formal installing of a person into office **inductance** n **inductive** adj **induction coil** transformer for producing high voltage from a low voltage **induction course** training course to help familiarize someone with a new job

indulge v 1 allow oneself pleasure: *indulge in daydreaming* 2 allow (someone) to have or do everything he or she wants **indulgence** n 1 something allowed because it gives pleasure 2 act of indulging oneself or someone else 3 favourable or tolerant treatment **indulgent** adj **indulgently** adv

industrial adj of, used in, or employed in industry **industrialize** v develop large-scale industry in (a country or region) **industrial action** action such as a strike or work-to-rule, by which workers can protest about their conditions **industrial estate** Brit industrial park **industrial park** area of land set aside for factories and warehouses **industrial relations** relations between management and workers

industry n, pl **-tries** 1 manufacture of goods 2 branch of this: *the publishing industry* 3 quality of working hard **industrious** adj hard-working

inebriate adj, n habitually drunk (person) **inebriated**

adj drunk **inebriation** n drunkenness

inedible adj not fit to be eaten

ineffable adj too great for words **ineffably** adv

ineffectual adj having no effect or an inadequate effect

ineligible adj not qualified for or entitled to something

ineluctable adj impossible to avoid

inept adj clumsy, lacking skill **ineptitude** n

inequitable adj unfair

ineradicable adj impossible to remove

inert adj 1 without the power of motion or resistance 2 chemically unreactive **inertly** adv **inertness** n

inertia n 1 feeling of unwillingness to do anything 2 *physics* property by which a body remains still or continues to move unless a force is applied to it **inertial** adj

inescapable adj unavoidable

inestimable adj too great to be estimated **inestimably** adv

inevitable adj 1 unavoidable, sure to happen ▷ n 2 something inevitable **inevitably** adv **inevitability** n

inexorable adj 1 relentless 2 unavoidable **inexorably** adv

inexpert adj lacking skill

inexplicable adj impossible to explain **inexplicably** adv

in extremis adv Latin 1 in great difficulty 2 at the point of death

inextricable adj 1 impossible to escape from 2 impossible to disentangle or separate

infallible adj 1 never wrong 2 always successful **infallibly** adv **infallibility** n

infamous [in-fam-uss] adj well-known for something bad **infamously** adv **infamy** n

infant n very young child

infancy *n* **1** early childhood **2** early stage of development

infantile *adj* childish

infanticide *n* **1** murder of an infant **2** person guilty of this

infantry *n* foot soldiers

infatuate *v* inspire with intense unreasonable passion **infatuated** *adj* **infatuation** *n*

infect *v* **1** affect with a disease **2** affect with a feeling **infection** *n* **infectious** *adj* **1** (of a disease) spreading without actual contact **2** spreading from person to person: *infectious laughter*

infer *v* -ferring, -ferred work out from evidence **inference** *n*

inferior *adj* **1** lower in position, status, or quality ▷ *n* **2** person of lower position or status **inferiority** *n*

infernal *adj* **1** of hell **2** *informal* irritating **infernally** *adv*

inferno *n, pl* -nos intense raging fire

infertile *adj* **1** unable to produce offspring **2** (of soil) barren, not productive **infertility** *n*

infest *v* inhabit or overrun in unpleasantly large numbers **infestation** *n*

infidel *n* **1** person with no religion **2** person who rejects a particular religion, esp. Christianity or Islam

infidelity *n, pl* -ties sexual unfaithfulness to one's husband, wife, or lover

infield *n* baseball area covered by the home plate and three bases

infighting *n* quarrelling within a group

infiltrate *v* enter gradually and secretly **infiltration** *n* **infiltrator** *n*

infinite [in-fin-it] *adj* without any limit or end **infinitely** *adv*

infinitesimal *adj* extremely small

infinitive [in-fin-it-iv] *n grammar* form of a verb not showing tense, person, or number, such as *to sleep*

infinity *n* endless space, time, or number

infirm *adj* physically or mentally weak **infirmity** *n*

infirmary *n, pl* -ries hospital

inflame *v* make angry or excited **inflamed** *adj* (of part of the body) red and swollen because of infection **inflammation** *n* inflamed part of the body **inflammatory** *adj* likely to provoke anger

inflammable *adj* easily set on fire **inflammability** *n*

inflate *v* **1** expand by filling with air or gas **2** cause economic inflation in **inflatable** *adj* **1** able to be inflated ▷ *n* **2** plastic or rubber object which can be inflated

inflation *n* **1** increase in prices and fall in the value of money **2** inflating **inflationary** *adj*

inflection, inflexion *n* **1** change in the pitch of the voice **2** *grammar* change in the form of a word to show grammatical use

inflexible *adj* **1** obstinate or unyielding **2** fixed and unalterable **inflexibly** *adv* **inflexibility** *n*

inflict *v* impose (something unpleasant) on **infliction** *n*

inflorescence *n botany* arrangement of flowers on a stem

influence *n* **1** effect of one person or thing on another **2** (person with) the power to have such an effect ▷ *v* **3** have an effect on **influential** *adj* **influentially** *adv*

influenza *n* viral disease

causing muscle pains, fever, and catarrh

influx n 1 arrival or entry of many people or things 2 a flowing in

info n informal information

inform v 1 tell 2 give incriminating information to the police **informant** n person who gives information **information** n what is told, knowledge **information technology** use of computers and electronic technology to store and communicate information **informative** adj giving useful information **informer** n person who informs to the police

informal adj 1 relaxed and friendly 2 appropriate for everyday life or use **informally** adv **informality** n

infra dig adj informal beneath one's dignity

infrared adj of or using rays below the red end of the visible spectrum

infrastructure n basic facilities, services, and equipment needed for a country or organization to function properly

infringe v break (a law or agreement) **infringement** n

infuriate v make very angry

infuse v 1 fill with (an emotion or quality) 2 soak to extract flavour **infusion** n 1 infusing 2 liquid obtained by infusing

ingenious [in-**jean**-ee-uss] adj 1 clever at contriving 2 cleverly contrived **ingeniously** adv **ingenuity** [in-jen-**new**-it-ee] n

ingénue [an-**jay**-new] n naive or inexperienced young woman, esp. as a role played by an actress

ingenuous [in-**jen**-new-uss] adj unsophisticated and trusting **ingenuously** adv

ingest v take (food or drink) into the body **ingestion** n

inglorious adj dishonourable or shameful

ingot n oblong block of cast metal

ingrained adj (of a habit etc.) 1 deep-rooted 2 (of dirt) deeply fixed

ingratiate v bring (oneself) into favour (with) **ingratiating** adj **ingratiatingly** adv

ingredient n component of a mixture or compound

ingress n act or right of entering

ingrowing adj (of a toenail) growing abnormally into the flesh

inhabit v -habiting, -habited live in **inhabitable** adj **inhabitant** n

inhale v breathe in (air, smoke, etc.) **inhalation** n **inhalant** [in-**hale**-ant] n medical preparation inhaled to help breathing problems **inhaler** n container for an inhalant

inherent adj existing as an inseparable part **inherently** adv

inherit v -heriting, -herited 1 receive (money etc.) from someone who has died 2 receive (a characteristic) from parents etc. 3 receive from predecessors **inheritance** n **inheritor** n

inhibit v -hibiting, -hibited 1 restrain (an impulse or desire) 2 hinder or prevent (action) **inhibition** n feeling of fear or embarrassment that stops one from behaving naturally **inhibited** adj

inhospitable adj 1 not hospitable, unfriendly 2 difficult to live in, harsh

inhuman adj 1 cruel or brutal 2 not human

inhumane *adj* cruel or brutal **inhumanity** *n*

inimical *adj* unfavourable or hostile **inimically** *adv*

inimitable *adj* impossible to imitate, unique **inimitably** *adv*

iniquity *n, pl* -**ties 1** great injustice **2** wickedness **3** sin **iniquitous** *adj*

initial *adj* **1** first, at the beginning ▷ *n* **2** first letter, esp. of someone's name ▷ *v* -**tialling**, -**tialled 3** sign with one's initials **initially** *adv* first, originally

initiate *v* **1** begin or set going **2** admit (someone) into a closed group **3** instruct in the basics of something ▷ *n* **4** initiated person **initiation** *n* **initiator** *n* **initiatory** *adj*

initiative *n* **1** first step, commencing move **2** ability to act independently

inject *v* **1** put (a fluid) into the body with a syringe **2** introduce (a new element): *he injected some humour into the scene* **injection** *n*

injudicious *adj* showing poor judgment, unwise

injunction *n* court order not to do something

injure *v* **1** hurt physically or mentally **2** damage **injury** *n* **1** physical hurt **2** damage **injury time** *sports* time added at the end of a match to compensate for time spent treating injured players **injurious** *adj*

injustice *n* **1** unfairness **2** unfair treatment or action

ink *n* **1** coloured liquid used for writing or printing ▷ *v* **2** mark or cover with ink **inky** *adj* **1** dark or black **2** stained with ink

inkling *n* slight idea or suspicion

inlaid *adj* **1** set in another material so that the surface is smooth **2** made like this: *an inlaid table*

inland *adj, adv* in or towards the interior of a country, away from the sea

in-laws *pl n* relatives by marriage

inlay *n* inlaid substance or pattern

inlet *n* **1** narrow piece of water extending from the sea into the land **2** valve etc. through which liquid or gas enters

in loco parentis [par-**rent**-iss] *Latin* in place of a parent

inmate *n* person living in an institution such as a prison

inmost *adj* furthest inside, most secret

inn *n* **1** hotel **2** *Brit* pub or small hotel, esp. in the country **innkeeper** *n*

innards *pl n informal* **1** internal organs **2** working parts

innate *adj* being part of someone's nature, inborn

inner *adj* **1** happening or located within **2** of the mind or spirit: *inner peace* **innermost** *adj* **inner city** parts of a city near the centre, esp. when seen as poor or violent

innings *n* **1** *sports* player's or side's turn of batting **2** spell or turn

innocent *adj* **1** not guilty of a crime **2** without experience of evil **3** harmless ▷ *n* **4** innocent person, esp. a child **innocently** *adv* **innocence** *n*

innocuous *adj* harmless **innocuously** *adv*

innovate *v* introduce new ideas or methods **innovation** *n* **innovative** *adj* **innovator** *n*

innuendo *n, pl* -**does** indirect accusation

innumerable *adj* too many to be counted **innumerably** *adv*

innumerate *adj* having

no understanding of mathematics or science **innumeracy** n

inoculate v protect against disease by injecting with a vaccine **inoculation** n

inoperable adj med unable to be operated on without risk

inopportune adj badly timed

inordinate adj excessive

inorganic adj 1 not having the characteristics of living organisms 2 of or denoting chemical substances that do not contain carbon **inorganically** adv

inpatient n patient who stays in a hospital for treatment

input n 1 resources put into a project etc. 2 data fed into a computer ▷ v -**putting, -put** 3 enter (data) in a computer

inquest n official inquiry, esp. into a sudden death

inquire v seek information or ask about **inquirer** n **inquiry** n 1 question 2 investigation

inquisition n 1 thorough investigation 2 hist **Inquisition** organization within the Catholic Church for suppressing heresy **inquisitor** n **inquisitorial** adj

inquisitive adj too curious about other people's business **inquisitively** adv

inquorate adj without enough people present to make a quorum

inroads pl n **make inroads into** start affecting or reducing: my gambling has made inroads into my savings

insalubrious adj likely to cause ill-health

insane adj 1 mentally deranged 2 stupidly irresponsible **insanely** adv **insanity** n

insanitary adj dirty or unhealthy

insatiable [in-**saysh**-a-bl] adj impossible to satisfy

inscribe v write or carve words on **inscription** n words inscribed

inscrutable adj 1 mysterious or enigmatic 2 incomprehensible **inscrutably** adv **inscrutability** n

insect n small invertebrate animal with six legs, a segmented body, and usu. two or four wings **insecticide** n substance for killing insects **insectivorous** adj insect-eating

insecure adj 1 anxious or uncertain 2 not safe or firm

inseminate v implant semen into **insemination** n

insensate adj 1 without sensation, unconscious 2 unfeeling

insensible adj 1 unconscious 2 without feeling 3 not aware 4 imperceptible **insensibility** n

insensitive adj unaware of or ignoring other people's feelings **insensitivity** n

insert v 1 put inside or between ▷ n 2 something inserted **insertion** n

inset adj 1 decorated with something inserted ▷ n 2 small map or diagram within a larger one

inshore adj 1 close to the shore ▷ adj, adv 2 towards the shore

inside prep 1 in or to the interior of ▷ adj 2 of or on the inside 3 by or from someone within an organization: inside information ▷ adv 4 in or into the inside 5 slang in prison ▷ n 6 inner side, surface, or part **insides** 7 informal stomach and bowels **inside out** 1 with the interior facing outwards 2 thoroughly **insider** n member of a group who has exclusive knowledge about it

insidious adj subtle or unseen

but dangerous **insidiously** adv

insight n clear understanding

insignia [in-**sig**-nee-a] n, pl -**nias**, -**nia** badge or emblem of honour or office

insignificant adj not important **insignificance** n

insincere adj pretending what one does not feel **insincerely** adv **insincerity** n

insinuate v **1** suggest indirectly **2** work oneself into a position by gradual manoeuvres **insinuation** n

insipid adj lacking interest, spirit, or flavour **insipidity** n

insist v demand or state firmly **insistent** adj **1** making persistent demands **2** demanding attention **insistently** adv **insistence** n

in situ adv, adj Latin in its original position

insofar as adv to the extent that

insole n inner sole of a shoe or boot

insolent adj arrogantly rude **insolence** n **insolently** adv

insoluble adj **1** incapable of being solved **2** incapable of being dissolved

insolvent adj unable to pay one's debts **insolvency** n

insomnia n sleeplessness **insomniac** n

insouciant adj carefree and unconcerned **insouciance** n

inspect v check closely or officially **inspection** n **inspector** n **1** person who inspects **2** high-ranking police officer

inspire v **1** fill with enthusiasm, stimulate **2** arouse (an emotion) **inspiration** n **1** good idea **2** creative influence or stimulus **inspirational** adj

instability n lack of steadiness or reliability

install v **1** put in and prepare (equipment) for use **2** formally place (a person) in a position or rank **installation** n **1** installing **2** equipment installed **3** place containing equipment for a particular purpose: radar installation

instalment n any of the portions of a thing presented or a debt paid in successive parts **instalment plan** system of purchase by which the buyer pays for goods by instalments

instance n **1** particular example ▷ v **2** mention as an example **for instance** for example

instant n **1** very brief time **2** particular moment ▷ adj **3** immediate **4** (of foods) requiring little preparation **instantly** adv at once

instantaneous adj happening at once **instantaneously** adv

instead adv as a replacement or substitute

instep n **1** part of the foot forming the arch between the ankle and toes **2** part of a shoe etc. covering this

instigate v cause to happen, bring about **instigation** n **instigator** n

instil v -**stilling**, -**stilled** introduce (an idea etc.) gradually in someone's mind **instilment** n

instinct n inborn tendency to behave in a certain way **instinctive** adj **instinctively** adv

institute n **1** organization set up for a specific purpose, esp. teaching or research ▷ v **2** start or establish **institution** n **1** large important organization such as a university or bank **2** hospital etc.

for people with special needs **3** long-established custom **institutional** adj **institutionalize** v make unable to cope with life outside an institution

instruct v **1** order to do something **2** teach (someone) how to do something **3** brief (a solicitor or barrister) **instruction** n **1** order **2** teaching **instructions** **3** information on how to do or use something **instructive** adj informative or helpful **instructor** n

instrument n **1** tool used for particular work **2** object played to produce a musical sound **3** measuring device to show height, speed, etc. **4** informal person used by another **instrumental** adj **1** helping to cause **2** played by or composed for musical instruments **instrumentalist** n player of a musical instrument **instrumentation** n **1** set of instruments in an automobile etc. **2** arrangement of music for instruments

insubordinate adj not submissive to authority **insubordination** n

insufferable adj unbearable

insular adj **1** not open to new ideas, narrow-minded **2** of or like an island **insularity** n

insulate v **1** prevent or reduce the transfer of electricity, heat, sound, etc. by surrounding or lining with nonconductive material **2** isolate or set apart **insulation** n **insulator** n

insulin [in-syoo-lin] n hormone produced by the pancreas which controls the amount of sugar in the blood

insult v **1** behave rudely to, offend ▷ n **2** insulting remark or action **insulting** adj

insuperable adj impossible to overcome **insuperability** n **insuperably** adv

insupportable adj **1** incapable of being tolerated **2** indefensible

insurance n **1** agreement by which one makes regular payments to a company who pay an agreed sum if damage, loss, or death occurs **2** money paid by or for insurance **3** means of protection **insure** v protect by insurance **insurance policy** contract of insurance

insurgent adj **1** in revolt ▷ n **2** rebel **insurgence** n revolt

insurrection n rebellion

intact adj not changed or damaged in any way

intaglio [in-tah-lee-oh] n, pl **-lios**, **-li** (gem carved with) an engraved design

intake n **1** thing or quantity taken in **2** opening through which fluid or gas enters an engine, pipe, etc.

integer n positive or negative whole number or zero

integral adj **1** being an essential part of a whole ▷ n **2** math sum of a large number of very small quantities

integrate v **1** combine into a whole **2** amalgamate (a religious or racial group) into a community **integration** n **integrated circuit** tiny electronic circuit on a silicon chip

integrity n **1** honesty **2** quality of being sound or whole

integument n natural covering such as skin or rind

intellect n power of thinking and reasoning **intellectual** adj **1** of or appealing to the intellect **2** clever or intelligent ▷ n **3** intellectual person **intellectually** adv

intelligent adj 1 able to understand, learn, and think things out quickly 2 (of a computerized device) able to initiate or modify action in the light of ongoing events **intelligently** adv **intelligence** n 1 quality of being intelligent 2 collection of secret information 3 people or department collecting military information **intelligent design** theory that a sentient being designed and created the universe and all life

intelligentsia n intellectual or cultured classes

intelligible adj understandable **intelligibility** n

intemperate adj 1 uncontrolled 2 drinking alcohol to excess 3 extreme **intemperance** n

intend v 1 propose or plan (something or to do something) 2 have as one's purpose

intense adj 1 of great strength or degree 2 deeply emotional **intensity** n

intensify v -fying, -fied make or become more intense **intensification** n

intensive adj using or needing concentrated effort or resources **intensively** adv

intent n 1 intention ▷ adj 2 paying close attention **intently** adv **intentness** n **intent on** determined to

intention n something intended **intentional** adj deliberate **intentionally** adv

inter [in-**ter**] v -terring, -terred bury (a corpse) **interment** n burial (of a corpse)

inter- prefix between or among: *intercontinental*

interact v act on or in close relation with each other **interaction** n **interactive** adj

interbreed v breed within a related group

intercede v 1 plead in favour of 2 mediate **intercession** n **intercessor** n

intercept v seize or stop in transit **interception** n

interchange v 1 (cause to) exchange places ▷ n 2 highway junction **interchangeable** adj

inter-city adj (of a passenger service) travelling fast between cities

intercom n internal communication system with loudspeakers

intercontinental adj travelling between or linking continents

intercourse n 1 act of having sex 2 communication or dealings between people or groups

interdict, interdiction n formal order forbidding something

interdisciplinary adj involving more than one academic discipline

interest n 1 desire to know or hear more about something 2 hobby or subject that one enjoys 3 *often pl* advantage: *in one's own interests* 4 sum paid for use of borrowed money 5 right or share ▷ v 6 arouse the interest of **interested** adj 1 feeling or showing interest 2 involved in or affected by **interesting** adj **interestingly** adv

interface n 1 area where two things interact or link 2 circuit linking a computer and another device

interfaith adj relating to or involving different religions

interfere v 1 try to influence

other people's affairs where one is not involved or wanted **2** clash (with) **3** *euphemistic* abuse sexually **interfering** *adj* **interference** *n* **1** interfering **2** *radio* interruption of reception by atmospherics or unwanted signals

interferon *n* protein that stops the development of an invading virus

interim *adj* temporary or provisional

interior *n* **1** inside **2** inland region ▷ *adj* **3** inside, inner **4** mental or spiritual

interject *v* make (a remark) suddenly or as an interruption **interjection** *n*

interlace *v* join by lacing or weaving together

interlay *v* insert (layers) between

interlink *v* connect together

interlock *v* **1** join firmly together ▷ *adj* **2** closely knitted

interlocutor [in-ter-**lok**-yew-ter] *n* person who takes part in a conversation

interloper [**in**-ter-lope-er] *n* person in a place or situation where he or she has no right to be

interlude *n* short rest or break in an activity or event

intermarry *v* (of families, races, or religions) become linked by marriage **intermarriage** *n*

intermediate *adj* coming between two points or extremes **intermediary** *n* **1** person trying to create agreement between others **2** messenger

intermezzo [in-ter-**met**-so] *n, pl* -**zos**, -**zi** short piece of music, esp. one performed between the acts of an opera

interminable *adj* seemingly

endless because boring **interminably** *adv*

intermingle *v* mix together

intermission *n* interval between parts of a play, film, etc.

intermittent *adj* occurring at intervals **intermittently** *adv*

intern *v* **1** imprison, esp. during a war ▷ *n* **2** trainee doctor in a hospital **internment** *n* **internee** *n* person who has been interned

internal *adj* **1** of or on the inside **2** within a country or organization **3** spiritual or mental **internally** *adv* **internal-combustion engine** engine powered by the explosion of a fuel-and-air mixture within the cylinders

international *adj* **1** of or involving two or more countries ▷ *n* **2** game or match between teams of different countries **3** player in such a match **internationally** *adv*

internecine *adj* mutually destructive

internet *n* large international computer network

interplanetary *adj* of or linking planets

interplay *n* action and reaction of two things upon each other

interpolate [in-**ter**-pole-ate] *v* insert (a comment or passage) in (a conversation or text) **interpolation** *n*

interpose *v* **1** insert between or among things **2** say as an interruption **interposition** *n*

interpret *v* **1** explain the meaning of **2** convey the meaning of (a poem, song, etc.) in performance **3** translate orally from one language into another **interpretation** *n* **interpreter** *n*

interprovincial *adj* between

or involving two or more provinces

interregnum *n, pl* **-nums, -na** interval between reigns

interrogate *v* question closely **interrogation** *n* **interrogative** *adj* 1 questioning ▷ *n* 2 word used in asking a question, such as *how* or *why* **interrogator** *n*

interrupt *v* 1 break into (a conversation etc.) 2 temporarily stop (a process or activity) **interruption** *n*

intersect *v* 1 (of roads or lines) meet and cross 2 divide by passing across or through **intersection** *n*

interspersed *adj* scattered among, between, or on

interstate *adj* US between or involving two or more states

interstellar *adj* between or among stars

interstice [in-**ter**-stiss] *n* small crack or gap between things

intertwine *v* twist together or entwine

interval *n* 1 time between two particular moments or events 2 break between parts of a play, concert, etc. 3 difference in pitch between notes **at intervals** 1 repeatedly 2 with spaces left between

intervene *v* 1 involve oneself in a situation, esp. to prevent conflict 2 happen so as to stop something **intervention** *n*

interview *n* 1 formal discussion, esp. between a job-seeker and employer 2 questioning of a well-known person about his or her career, views, etc., by a reporter ▷ *v* 3 have an interview with **interviewee** *n* **interviewer** *n*

interwar *adj* of or during the period 1919–39

interweave *v* weave together

intestate *adj* not having

made a will **intestacy** *n*

intestine *n usu pl* lower part of the alimentary canal between the stomach and the anus **intestinal** *adj*

intimate[1] *adj* 1 having a close personal relationship 2 private 3 (of knowledge) extensive and detailed 4 *euphemistic* having sexual relations 5 having a friendly quiet atmosphere ▷ *n* 6 intimate friend **intimately** *adv* **intimacy** *n*

intimate[2] *v* 1 hint or suggest 2 announce **intimation** *n*

intimidate *v* subdue or influence by frightening **intimidation** *n* **intimidating** *adj*

into *prep* 1 to the inner part of 2 to the middle of 3 (up) against 4 used to indicate the result of a change: *he turned into a monster* 5 *math* used to indicate division: *three into six is two* 6 *informal* interested in

intolerable *adj* more than can be endured **intolerably** *adv*

intolerant *adj* narrow-minded or bigoted **intolerance** *n*

intonation *n* sound pattern produced by variations in the voice

intone *v* speak or recite in an unvarying tone of voice

intoxicate *v* 1 make drunk 2 excite to excess **intoxicant** *n, adj* (drink) capable of intoxicating **intoxication** *n*

intractable *adj* (of a person) 1 difficult to influence 2 (of a problem or illness) hard to solve or cure

intranet *n computers* internal network that makes use of internet technology

intransigent *adj* refusing to change one's attitude **intransigence** *n*

intransitive *adj* (of a verb) not

taking a direct object

intrauterine *adj* within the womb

intravenous [in-tra-**vee**-nuss] *adj* into a vein **intravenously** *adv*

intrepid *adj* fearless or bold **intrepidity** *n*

intricate *adj* **1** involved or complicated **2** full of fine detail **intricately** *adv* **intricacy** *n*

intrigue *v* **1** make interested or curious **2** plot secretly ▷ *n* **3** secret plotting **4** secret love affair **intriguing** *adj*

intrinsic *adj* part of the basic nature of **intrinsically** *adv*

introduce *v* **1** present (someone) by name (to another person) **2** present (a radio or television programme) **3** bring forward for discussion **4** bring into use **5** insert **introduction** *n* **1** introducing **2** preliminary part or treatment **3** presentation of one person to another **introductory** *adj* preliminary

introspection *n* examination of one's own thoughts and feelings **introspective** *adj*

introvert *n* person concerned more with his or her thoughts and feelings than with external reality **introverted** *adj* **introversion** *n*

intrude *v* come in or join in without being invited **intruder** *n* **intrusion** *n* **intrusive** *adj*

intuition *n* instinctive knowledge or insight without conscious reasoning **intuitive** *adj* **intuitively** *adv*

Inuit *n* **1** indigenous people of Northern Canada, Alaska, or Greenland **2** language of Inuit

Inuk *n* a member of any Inuit people

Inuktitut [in-**nook**-ti-toot] *n* language of Inuit

inundate *v* **1** flood **2** overwhelm **inundation** *n*

inure *v* accustom, esp. to hardship or danger

invade *v* **1** enter (a country) by military force **2** enter in large numbers **3** disturb (privacy etc.) **invader** *n*

invalid[1] *n* **1** disabled or chronically ill person ▷ *v* **2** dismiss from active service because of illness etc. **invalidity** *n*

invalid[2] *adj* **1** having no legal force **2** (of an argument etc.) not valid because based on a mistake **invalidate** *v* make or show to be invalid

invaluable *adj* priceless

invasion *n* **1** act of invading **2** intrusion

invective *n* abusive speech or writing

inveigh [in-**vay**] *v* (foll. by *against*) criticize (something) harshly

inveigle *v* coax or entice **inveiglement** *n*

invent *v* **1** think up or create (something new) **2** make up (a story, excuse, etc.) **invention** *n* **1** something invented **2** ability to invent **inventive** *adj* **1** resourceful **2** creative **inventiveness** *n* **inventor** *n*

inventory [**in**-ven-tree] *n, pl* **-tories** detailed list of goods or furnishings

inverse *adj* **1** opposite, inverted **2** *math* linking two variables in such a way that one increases as the other decreases **inversely** *adv*

invert *v* turn upside down or inside out **inversion** *n* **inverted commas** raised commas in writing to show where speech begins and ends

invertebrate *n* animal with no backbone

invest *v* spend (money, time, etc.) on something with

the expectation of profit **investment** n **1** money invested **2** something invested in **investor** n **invest in** v buy **invest with** v give (power or rights) to

investigate v **1** inquire into **2** examine **investigation** n **investigative** adj **investigator** n

investiture n formal installation of a person in an office or rank

inveterate adj **1** deep-rooted **2** confirmed in a habit or practice **inveteracy** n

invidious adj likely to cause resentment **invidiously** adv

invigilate [in-**vij**-il-late] v supervise examination candidates **invigilator** n

invigorate v give energy to or refresh

invincible adj unconquerable **invincibly** adv **invincibility** n

inviolable adj that must not be broken or violated

inviolate adj unharmed, unaffected

invisible adj not able to be seen **invisibly** adv **invisibility** n

invite v **1** request the company of **2** ask politely for **3** attract: *the plan invited criticism* ▷ n **4** informal invitation **inviting** adj **invitation** n

in vitro adj (of a biological process) happening outside the body in an artificial environment

invoice v, n (send) a bill for goods or services supplied

invoke v **1** put (a law or penalty) into operation **2** prompt or cause (a certain feeling) **3** call on (a god) for help, inspiration, etc. **invocation** n

involuntary adj **1** not done consciously **2** unintentional **involuntarily** adv

involve v **1** include as a necessary part **2** affect **3** implicate (a person) **4** make complicated **involved** adj **1** complicated **2** concerned in **involvement** n

invulnerable adj not able to be wounded or harmed

inward adj **1** internal **2** situated within **3** spiritual or mental ▷ adv **4** Also **inwards** towards the inside or middle **inwardly** adv

iodine n bluish-black element used in medicine, photography, and dyeing **iodize** v treat with iodine

ion n electrically charged atom **ionic** adj **ionize** v change into ions **ionization** n **ionosphere** n region of ionized air in the upper atmosphere which reflects radio waves

iota [eye-**oh**-ta] n **1** ninth letter in the Greek alphabet **2** very small amount

IOU n signed paper acknowledging debt

IPA International Phonetic Alphabet

iPod n ® pocket-sized device used to play digital music files

ipso facto adv Latin by that very fact

IQ intelligence quotient

IRA Irish Republican Army

irascible adj easily angered **irascibly** adv **irascibility** n

irate adj very angry

ire n lit anger

iridescent adj having shimmering changing colours like a rainbow **iridescence** n

iris n **1** circular membrane of the eye containing the pupil **2** plant with sword-shaped leaves and showy flowers

Irish adj of Ireland **Irish coffee** hot coffee mixed with whiskey and topped with cream

irk v irritate or annoy **irksome** adj tiresome

iron n 1 metallic element widely used for structural and engineering purposes 2 tool made of iron 3 appliance used, when heated, to press clothes or fabric 4 metal-headed golf club **irons 5** fetters or chains ▷ adj 6 made of iron 7 inflexible: an iron will ▷ v 8 smooth (clothes or fabric) with an iron **iron out** v settle (a problem) through discussion **Iron Age** era when iron tools were used **ironing** n clothes to be ironed **ironing board** long cloth-covered board, usu. with folding legs, on which to iron clothes

ironic, ironical adj using irony **ironically** adv

ironmonger n Brit shopkeeper or shop dealing in hardware **ironmongery** n

ironstone n 1 rock consisting mainly of iron ore 2 tough durable earthenware

irony n, pl -**nies** 1 mildly sarcastic use of words to imply the opposite of what is said 2 event or situation that is the opposite of what is expected

irradiate v subject to or treat with radiation **irradiation** n

irrational adj not based on logical reasoning

irredeemable adj 1 not able to be reformed, improved, or corrected 2 not able to be recovered, bought back, or converted into coin

irreducible adj impossible to put in a reduced or simpler form

irrefutable adj impossible to deny or disprove

irregular adj 1 not regular or even 2 unconventional 3 (of a word) not following the typical pattern of formation in a language **irregularly** adv **irregularity** n

irrelevant adj not connected with the matter in hand **irrelevantly** adv **irrelevance** n

irreparable adj not able to be put right or repaired **irreparably** adv

irreproachable adj blameless, faultless **irreproachably** adv

irresistible adj too attractive or strong to resist **irresistibly** adv

irrespective of prep without taking account of

irreverence n 1 lack of due respect 2 disrespectful remark or act **irreverent** adj

irrevocable adj not possible to change or undo **irrevocably** adv

irrigate v water by artificial channels or pipes **irrigation** n

irritate v 1 annoy or anger 2 cause (a body part) to itch or become inflamed **irritable** adj easily annoyed **irritably** adv **irritant** n, adj (person or thing) causing irritation **irritation** n

irrupt v enter forcibly or suddenly **irruption** n

is v third person singular present tense of **be**

isinglass [ize-ing-glass] n kind of gelatine obtained from some freshwater fish

Islam n 1 Muslim religion teaching that there is one God and that Mohammed is his prophet 2 Muslim countries and civilization **Islamic** adj

island n piece of land surrounded by water **islander** n person who lives on an island

isle *n* island **islet** *n* little island

isobar [**ice**-oh-bar] *n* line on a map connecting places of equal barometric pressure **isobaric** *adj*

isolate *v* **1** place apart or alone **2** *chem* obtain (a substance) in uncombined form **isolation** *n* **isolationism** *n* policy of not participating in international affairs **isolationist** *n, adj*

isomer [**ice**-oh-mer] *n* substance whose molecules contain the same atoms as another but in a different arrangement **isomeric** *adj* **isomerism** *n*

isometric *adj* **1** having equal dimensions **2** relating to muscular contraction without movement **3** (of a three-dimensional drawing) having three equally inclined axes and drawn to scale in every direction **isometrics** *pl n* system of isometric exercises

isosceles triangle [ice-**soss**-ill-eez] *n* triangle with two sides of equal length

isotherm [**ice**-oh-therm] *n* line on a map connecting points of equal mean temperature

isotope [**ice**-oh-tope] *n* one of two or more atoms with the same number of protons in the nucleus but a different number of neutrons

issue *n* **1** topic of interest or discussion **2** question requiring a decision **3** particular edition of a magazine or newspaper **4** outcome or result **5** *law* children ▷ *v* **6** make (a statement etc.) publicly

7 officially supply (with) **8** send out or distribute **9** publish **take issue** disagree

isthmus [**iss**-muss] *n, pl* **-muses** narrow strip of land connecting two areas of land

it *pron* **1** refers to a nonhuman, animal, plant, or inanimate object **2** refers to the thing mentioned or being discussed **3** used as the subject of impersonal verbs: *it is snowing* **4** *informal* crucial or ultimate point **its** *adj* belonging to it **it's 1** it is **2** it has **itself** *pron* emphatic form of **it**

IT information technology

italic *adj* (of printing type) sloping to the right **italics** *pl n* this type, now used for emphasis etc. **italicize** *v* put in italics

itch *n* **1** skin irritation causing a desire to scratch **2** restless desire ▷ *v* **3** have an itch **itchy** *adj*

item *n* **1** single thing in a list or collection **2** piece of information **itemize** *v* **1** put on a list **2** make a list of

iterate *v* repeat **iteration** *n*

itinerant *adj* travelling from place to place

itinerary *n, pl* **-aries 1** detailed plan of a journey **2** route

IUD intrauterine device: coil-shaped contraceptive fitted into the womb

IVF in vitro fertilization

ivory *n, pl* **-ries 1** hard white bony substance forming the tusks of elephants ▷ *adj* **2** yellowish-white **ivory tower** remoteness from the realities of everyday life

ivy *n, pl* **ivies** climbing evergreen plant

Jj

jab *v* **jabbing, jabbed 1** poke roughly ▷ *n* **2** quick short punch **3** *informal* injection

jabber *v* talk rapidly or incoherently

jacaranda *n* tropical tree with sweet-smelling wood

jacinth *n* reddish-orange precious stone

jack *n* **1** device for raising an automobile or other heavy object **2** playing card with a picture of a pageboy **3** *bowls* small white ball aimed at by the players **4** socket in electrical equipment into which a plug fits **5** flag flown at the bow of a ship, showing nationality **jack up** *v* lift with a jack

jackal *n* doglike wild animal of Asia and Africa

jackass *n* **1** male of the ass **2** fool **laughing jackass** same as **kookaburra**

jackboot *n* high military boot

jackdaw *n* black-and-grey bird of the crow family

jacket *n* **1** short coat **2** outer paper cover on a hardback book **3** skin of a baked potato

jackknife *n* **1** large clasp knife **2** dive with a sharp bend at the waist in mid-air ▷ *v* **3** (of a tractor-trailer) go out of control so that the trailer swings round at a sharp angle to the cab

jackpot *n* large prize or accumulated stake that may be won in a game **hit the jackpot** be very successful through luck

Jacobean [jak-a-**bee**-an] *adj* of the reign of James I of England

Jacobite *n* supporter of the exiled Stuarts after the overthrow of James II of England

Jacquard [**jak**-ard] *n* fabric in which the design is incorporated into the weave

Jacuzzi [jak-**oo**-zee] *n* ® circular bath with a device that swirls the water

jade *n* **1** ornamental semiprecious stone, usu. dark green ▷ *adj* **2** bluish-green

jaded *adj* tired and unenthusiastic

jag¹ *n* **1** sharp or ragged projection **2** *informal* injection **jagged** [**jag**-gid] *adj*

jag² *n* spree or drinking bout

jaguar *n* large S American spotted cat

jail *n* **1** building for confinement of criminals or suspects ▷ *v* **2** send to jail **jailer** *n* **jailbird** *n informal* person who is or has often been in jail

jalopy [jal-**lop**-ee] *n, pl* **-lopies** *informal* old automobile

jam¹ *n* spread made from fruit boiled with sugar

jam² *v* **jamming, jammed 1** pack tightly into a place **2** crowd or congest **3** make or become stuck **4** *radio* block (another station) with impulses of equal wavelength ▷ *n* **5** hold-up of traffic **6** *informal* awkward situation **jam on** *v* apply (brakes) fiercely **jam-packed** *adj* filled to capacity **jam session** informal rock or jazz performance

jamb *n* side post of a door or window frame

jamboree *n* **1** large rally of Scouts **2** large celebration

Jan. January

jangle *v* **1** (cause to) make a harsh ringing noise **2** (of nerves) be upset or irritated

janitor *n* caretaker of a school or other building

January *n* first month of the year

japan *n* **1** very hard varnish, usu. black ▷ *v* **-panning, -panned 2** cover with this varnish

jape *n old-fashioned* joke or prank

japonica *n* shrub with red flowers

jar¹ *n* wide-mouthed container, usu. cylindrical and made of glass

jar² *v* **jarring, jarred 1** have a disturbing or unpleasant effect on **2** (cause to) vibrate suddenly or violently ▷ *n* **3** jolt or shock

jardinière *n* ornamental plant pot

jargon *n* specialized technical language of a particular subject

jasmine *n* shrub with sweet-smelling yellow or white flowers

jasper *n* red, yellow, dark green, or brown variety of quartz

jaundice *n* disease marked by yellowness of the skin **jaundiced** *adj* **1** (of an attitude or opinion) bitter or cynical **2** having jaundice

jaunt *n* **1** short journey for pleasure ▷ *v* **2** make such a journey

jaunty *adj* **-tier, -tiest 1** sprightly and cheerful **2** smart **jauntily** *adv*

javelin *n* light spear thrown in sports competitions

Javex *n* ® chlorine bleach

jaw *n* **1** one of the bones in which the teeth are set **2** lower part of the face below the mouth **3** *slang* long chat ▷ *v* **4** *slang* have a long chat

jay *n* bird of crow family in Europe and N America

jaywalking *n* crossing the road in a careless or dangerous manner **jaywalker** *n*

jazz *n* rhythmic music of African-American origin **jazzy** *adj* flashy or showy **jazz up** *v* make more lively

jealous *adj* **1** fearful of losing a partner or possession to a rival **2** envious **3** resulting from jealousy: *jealous rage* **jealously** *adv* **jealousy** *n*

jeans *pl n* casual denim trousers

Jeep *n* ® four-wheel-drive motor vehicle

jeer *v* **1** scoff or deride ▷ *n* **2** cry of derision

jeezly *adj Canad slang* (intensifier): *a jeezly idiot*

Jehovah *n* God

jejune *adj* **1** simple or naive **2** dull or boring

jell *v* **1** take on a definite form **2** form a gel

jelly *n, pl* **-lies 1** fruit-flavoured dessert set with gelatine **2** jam made from fruit juice and sugar **jellied** *adj* prepared in a jelly

jellyfish *n* small jelly-like sea animal

jemmy *n, pl* **-mies** short steel crowbar used by burglars

jenny *n, pl* **-nies 1** female ass **2** female wren

jeopardy *n* danger
jeopardize *v* place in danger
jerboa *n* small mouselike African rodent with long hind legs
jeremiad *n* long lamenting complaint
jerk *n* **1** sharp or abruptly stopped movement **2** sharp pull **3** *slang* contemptible person ▷ *v* **4** move or throw with a jerk **jerky** *adj* sudden or abrupt **jerkily** *adv* **jerkiness** *n*
jerkin *n* sleeveless jacket
jerry-built *adj* built badly using flimsy materials
jerry can *n* flat-sided can for carrying gasoline etc.
jersey *n* **1** knitted jumper **2** machine-knitted fabric **3** **Jersey** breed of cow
Jerusalem artichoke *n* small yellowish-white root vegetable
jest *n, v* joke **jester** *n* **1** joker **2** *hist* professional clown at court
Jesuit [jezz-yoo-it] *n* member of the Society of Jesus, a Roman Catholic order **jesuitical** *adj* crafty through using oversubtle reasoning
jet¹ *n* **1** aircraft driven by jet propulsion **2** stream of liquid or gas, esp. one forced from a small hole **3** nozzle from which gas or liquid is forced **4** burner on a gas fire ▷ *v* **jetting, jetted 5** travel by jet aircraft **jet lag** fatigue caused by crossing time zones in an aircraft **jet propulsion** propulsion by thrust provided by a jet of gas or liquid **jet-propelled** *adj* **jet set** rich and fashionable people who travel the world for pleasure
jet² *n* hard black mineral **jet-black** *adj* glossy black
jetsam *n* goods thrown overboard to lighten a ship

and later washed ashore
jettison *v* **-soning, -soned 1** abandon **2** throw overboard
jetty *n, pl* **-ties** small pier
Jew *n* **1** person whose religion is Judaism **2** descendant of the ancient Hebrews **Jewish** *adj* **Jewry** *n* Jews collectively **jew's-harp** *n* musical instrument held between the teeth and played by plucking a metal strip with one's finger
jewel *n* **1** precious stone **2** special person or thing **jeweller** *n* dealer in jewels **jewellery** *n*
jib¹ *n* **jibbing, jibbed** (of a horse, person, etc.) stop and refuse to go on **jib at** *v* object to (a proposal etc.)
jib² *n* **1** projecting arm of a crane or derrick **2** triangular sail set in front of a mast
jibe¹ *n* **1** insulting remark ▷ *v* **2** make insulting remarks
jibe² *v informal* be consistent
jiffy *n, pl* **-fies** *informal* very short period of time
jig *n* **1** type of lively dance **2** music for it **3** device that holds a component in place for cutting etc. ▷ *v* **jigging, jigged 4** make jerky up-and-down movements
jigger *n* small glass for spirits
jiggery-pokery *n informal* trickery or mischief
jiggle *v* move up and down with short jerky movements
jigsaw *n* **1** machine fret saw **2** Also **jigsaw puzzle** picture cut into interlocking pieces, which the user tries to fit together again
jihad *n* Islamic holy war against unbelievers
jilt *v* leave or reject (one's lover)
jingle *n* **1** short catchy song used to advertise a product **2** gentle ringing sound ▷ *v* **3** make a jingling sound

jingoism n aggressive nationalism **jingoist** n **jingoistic** adj

jinks pl n **high jinks** boisterous merrymaking

jinni n, pl **jinn** spirit in Muslim mythology

jinx n 1 person or thing bringing bad luck ▷ v 2 be or put a jinx on

jitters pl n worried nervousness **jittery** adj nervous

jiujitsu n same as **jujitsu**

jive n 1 lively dance of the 1940s and '50s ▷ v 2 dance the jive

job n 1 task to be done 2 occupation or paid employment 3 informal difficult task 4 informal crime, esp. robbery **jobbing** adj doing individual jobs for payment **jobless** adj, pl n unemployed (people) **job lot** assortment sold together **job sharing** splitting of one post between two people working part-time

jock n 1 same as **jockstrap** 2 informal male athlete 3 informal an enthusiast

jockey n 1 (professional) rider of racehorses ▷ v 2 **jockey for position** manoeuvre to obtain an advantage

jockstrap n belt with a pouch to support the genitals, worn by male athletes

jocose [joke-**kohss**] adj playful or humorous **jocosely** adv

jocular adj 1 joking 2 fond of joking **jocularly** adv **jocularity** n

jocund [jok-kund] adj lit merry or cheerful

jodhpurs pl n riding breeches, stretchy or loose-fitting above the knee but tight below

Joe Blow, Joe Six-Pack n sometimes not capitals, slang an average or typical man

jog v **jogging, jogged** 1 run at a gentle pace, esp. for exercise 2 nudge slightly ▷ n 3 jogging **jogger** n **jogging** n

joggle v 1 move to and fro in jerks 2 shake

Johnny Canuck n informal 1 a Canadian 2 Canada

joie de vivre [jwah de **veev**-ra] n French enjoyment of life

join v 1 come or bring together 2 become a member (of) 3 come into someone's company 4 take part (in) ▷ n 5 place of joining **join up** v enlist in the armed services **joined-up** adj integrated by an overall strategy: joined-up government

joiner n maker of finished woodwork **joinery** n joiner's work

joint adj 1 shared by two or more ▷ n 2 place where bones meet but can move 3 junction of two or more parts or objects 4 piece of meat for roasting 5 slang house or place, esp. a disreputable bar or nightclub 6 slang cannabis cigarette ▷ v 7 divide meat into joints **out of joint** 1 dislocated 2 disorganized **jointed** adj **jointly** adv **joint-stock company** firm whose capital is jointly owned by shareholders

jointure n property settled on a wife for her use after her husband's death

joist n horizontal beam that helps support a floor or ceiling

jojoba [hoe-**hoe**-ba] n shrub whose seeds yield oil used in cosmetics

joke n 1 thing said or done to cause laughter 2 amusing or ridiculous person or thing ▷ v 3 make jokes **jokey** adj **jokingly** adv **joker** n 1 person who jokes 2 slang fellow 3 extra card in a pack, counted as any other in some games

jolly *adj* **-lier**, **-liest 1** full of good humour **2** involving a lot of fun ▷ *v* **-lying**, **-lied 3 jolly along** try to keep (someone) cheerful by flattery or coaxing **jolliness** *n* **jollity** *n* **jollification** *n* merrymaking

jolt *n* **1** sudden jerk or bump **2** unpleasant surprise or shock ▷ *v* **3** move or shake with jolts **4** surprise or shock

jonquil *n* fragrant narcissus

josh *v slang* joke or tease

joss stick *n* stick of incense giving off a sweet smell when burnt

jostle *v* **1** knock or push against **2** compete

jot *n* **1** very small amount ▷ *v* **jotting**, **jotted 2** write briefly **3** make a note of **jotter** *n* notebook **jottings** *pl n* notes jotted down

joual *n* French Quebec working-class dialect

joule [jool] *n physics* unit of work or energy

journal *n* **1** daily newspaper or other periodical **2** daily record of events **journalese** *n* superficial and clichéd writing, as found in newspapers **journalism** *n* writing in or editing of periodicals **journalist** *n* **journalistic** *adj*

journey *n* **1** act or process of travelling from one place to another ▷ *v* **3** travel

journeyman *n* qualified craftsman employed by another

joust *hist* ▷ *n* **1** combat with lances between two mounted knights ▷ *v* **2** fight on horseback using lances

jovial *adj* happy and cheerful **jovially** *adv* **joviality** *n*

jowl *n* **1** lower jaw **2** fatty flesh hanging from the lower jaw **jowls** *pl n* cheeks

joy *n* **1** feeling of great delight or pleasure **2** cause of this feeling **joyful** *adj* **joyless** *adj* **joyous** *adj* extremely happy and enthusiastic **joyriding** *n* driving for pleasure, esp. in a stolen vehicle **joyride** *n* **joystick** *n informal* control device for an aircraft or computer

JP Justice of the Peace

JPEG [jay-peg] *computers* **1** standard compressed file format used for pictures **2** picture held in this file format

Jr Junior

jubilant *adj* feeling or expressing great joy **jubilantly** *adv* **jubilation** *n*

jubilee *n* special anniversary, esp. 25th (**silver jubilee**) or 50th (**golden jubilee**)

Judaism *n* religion of the Jews, having only one God and based on the teachings of the Old Testament and the Talmud **Judaic** *adj*

judder *v* **1** vibrate violently ▷ *n* **2** violent vibration

judge *n* **1** public official who hears cases and passes sentence in a court of law **2** person who decides the result of a competition ▷ *v* **3** act as a judge **4** decide the result of (a competition) **5** appraise critically **6** consider something to be the case **judgment** *or* **judgement** *n* **1** opinion reached after careful thought **2** sentence of a court **3** faculty of judging **judgmental** *or* **judgemental** *adj*

judicature *n* **1** administration of justice **2** body of judges

judicial *adj* **1** of or by a court or judge **2** showing or using judgment **judicially** *adv*

judiciary *n* system of courts and judges

judicious *adj* well-judged,

sensible **judiciously** adv

judo n modern sport derived from jujitsu, where the opponent must be defeated using the minimum physical effort

jug n 1 container for liquids, with a handle and small spout 2 its contents 3 slang prison **jugged hare** Brit hare stewed in an earthenware pot

juggernaut n 1 large heavy truck 2 any irresistible destructive force

juggle v 1 throw and catch (several objects) so that most are in the air at the same time 2 manipulate (figures, situations, etc.) to suit one's purposes **juggler** n

jugular vein n one of three large veins of the neck returning blood from the head

juice n 1 liquid part of vegetables, fruit, or meat 2 fluid secreted by an organ of the body 3 informal gasoline **juicy** adj 1 succulent 2 interesting

jujitsu n Japanese art of wrestling and self-defence

juju n W African magic charm or fetish

jujube n chewy candy of flavoured gelatine

jukebox n automatic coin-operated record player

Jul. July

julep n sweet alcoholic drink

julienne n clear soup containing thinly shredded vegetables

July n seventh month of the year

jumble v 1 mix in a disordered way ▷ n 2 confused heap or state 3 articles for a jumble sale **jumble sale** sale of miscellaneous second-hand items

jumbo adj informal very large

jumbo jet large jet airliner

jump v 1 leap or spring into the air using the leg muscles 2 leap over (an obstacle) 3 move quickly and suddenly 4 jerk with surprise 5 increase suddenly 6 pass over or miss out (intervening material) 7 change the subject abruptly 8 come off (tracks, rails, etc.) 9 informal attack without warning 10 informal pass through (a red traffic light) ▷ n 11 jumping 12 obstacle to be jumped 13 sudden nervous jerk 14 sudden rise in prices 15 break in continuity **jump the gun** act prematurely **jump the queue** not wait one's turn **jumpy** adj nervous **jump at** v accept (a chance etc.) gladly **jumper cables** electric cables to connect a discharged automobile battery to an external battery to aid starting an engine **jump jet** fixed-wing jet that can take off and land vertically **jump on** v criticize suddenly and forcefully **jump shot** basketball shot made as a player jumps **jump suit** one-piece garment of trousers and top

jumper[1] n 1 person or animal that jumps 2 basketball a jump shot

jumper[2] n sleeveless dress worn over a blouse etc.

junction n 1 place where routes, railway lines, or roads meet 2 point where traffic can leave or enter a highway 3 join

juncture n point in time, esp. a critical one

June n sixth month of the year

jungle n 1 tropical forest of dense tangled vegetation 2 tangled mass 3 place of intense struggle for survival

junior adj 1 of lower standing 2 younger ▷ n 3 junior person

juniper *n* evergreen shrub with berries yielding oil

junk[1] *n* **1** discarded or useless objects **2** *informal* rubbish **3** *slang* narcotic drug, esp. heroin **junkie** *n slang* drug addict **junk food** snack food of low nutritional value **junk mail** unsolicited mail advertising goods and services

junk[2] *n* flat-bottomed Chinese sailing vessel

junket *n* **1** excursion by public officials paid for from public funds **2** dessert made of milk set with rennet **junketing** *n*

junta *n* group of military officers holding power in a country after a revolution

Jupiter *n* **1** Roman chief of the gods **2** largest of the planets

juridical *adj* of law or the administration of justice

jurisdiction *n* **1** right or power to administer justice and apply laws **2** extent of this right or power

jurisprudence *n* science or philosophy of law

jurist *n* expert in law

jury *n*, *pl* **-ries** group of people sworn to deliver a verdict in a court of law **juror**, **juryman**, *or* **jurywoman** *n*

just *adv* **1** very recently **2** exactly **3** barely **4** at this instant **5** merely, only **6** really ▷ *adj* **7** fair or impartial in action or judgment **8** proper or right **9** well-founded **justly** *adv* **justness** *n*

justice *n* **1** quality of being just **2** fairness **3** judicial proceedings **4** judge or magistrate **justice of the peace** person who is authorized to act as a judge in a local court of law

justify *v* **-fying**, **-fied 1** prove right or reasonable **2** show to be free from blame or guilt **3** align (text) so the margins are straight **justifiable** *adj* **justifiably** *adv* **justification** *n*

jut *v* **jutting**, **jutted** project or stick out

jute *n* fibre of certain plants, used for rope, canvas, etc.

juvenile *adj* **1** young **2** suitable for young people **3** immature and rather silly ▷ *n* **4** young person or child **juvenilia** *pl n* works produced in an author's youth **juvenile delinquent** young person guilty of a crime

juxtapose *v* put side by side **juxtaposition** *n*

j

Kk

K 1 kelvin **2** *chem* potassium **3** *informal* thousand(s)

Kabloona *n* person who is not of Inuit ancestry, esp. a White person

Kaffir [**kaf**-fer] *n S Afr offensive, obsolete* a Black African

kaftan *n* **1** long loose Eastern garment **2** woman's dress resembling this

kail *n* same as **kale**

kaiser [**kize**-er] *n hist* German or Austro-Hungarian emperor

Kalashnikov *n* Russian-made automatic rifle

kale *n* cabbage with crinkled leaves

kaleidoscope *n* tube-shaped toy containing loose pieces of coloured glass reflected by mirrors so that various symmetrical patterns form when the tube is twisted **kaleidoscopic** *adj*

kamik *n* traditional Inuit boot made of caribou hide or sealskin

kamikaze [kam-mee-**kah**-zee] *n* **1** (in World War II) Japanese pilot who performed a suicide mission ▷ *adj* **2** (of an action) undertaken in the knowledge that it will kill or injure the person performing it

kangaroo *n, pl* **-roos** Aust. marsupial which moves by jumping with its powerful hind legs **kangaroo court** unofficial court set up by a group to discipline its members

kaolin *n* fine white clay used to make porcelain and in some medicines

kapok *n* fluffy fibre from a tropical tree, used to stuff cushions etc.

kaput [kap-**poot**] *adj informal* ruined or broken

karaoke [kar-a-**oh**-kee] *n* kind of entertainment in which members of the public sing well-known songs over a prerecorded backing tape

karate *n* Japanese system of unarmed combat using blows with feet, hands, elbows, and legs

karma *n Buddhism, Hinduism* person's actions affecting his or her fate for his or her next reincarnation

karoo *n S Afr* high arid plateau

kasbah *n* citadel of N African town

kayak *n* **1** Inuit canoe made of sealskins stretched over a frame **2** fibreglass or canvas-covered canoe of this design

kbyte *computers* kilobyte

kebab *n* dish of small pieces of meat grilled on skewers

kedge *n* **1** small anchor ▷ *v* **2** move (a ship) by hauling on a cable attached to a kedge

kedgeree *n* dish of fish with rice and eggs

keel *n* main lengthways timber or steel support along the base of a ship **keel over** *v* **1** turn upside down **2** *informal* collapse suddenly

keen¹ *adj* **1** eager or

enthusiastic **2** intense or strong **3** intellectually acute **4** (of the senses) capable of recognizing small distinctions **5** sharp **6** cold and penetrating **7** competitive **keenly** adv **keenness** n

keen² v **1** wail over the dead ▷ n **2** funeral lament

keep v **keeping, kept 1** have or retain possession of **2** take temporary charge of **3** store **4** look after or maintain **5** stay (in, on, or at a place or position) **6** detain (someone) **7** support financially **8** continue or persist **9** remain good ▷ n **10** cost of food and everyday expenses **11** central tower of a castle **keeper** n **1** person who looks after animals in a zoo **2** person in charge of a museum or collection **3** short for **goalkeeper** ▸ **keeping** n care or charge **in** or **out of keeping with** appropriate or inappropriate for **keep fit** exercises designed to promote physical fitness **keepsake** n gift treasured for the sake of the giver **keep up** v maintain at the current level **keep up with** maintain a pace set by (someone)

keg n small metal beer barrel

kelp n large brown seaweed

kelvin n SI unit of temperature **Kelvin scale** temperature scale starting at absolute zero (−273.15° Celsius)

ken n **1** range of knowledge ▷ v **kenning, kenned** or **kent 2** Scot know

kendo n Japanese sport of fencing using wooden staves

kennel n **1** hutlike shelter for a dog **kennels 2** place for breeding, boarding, or training dogs

kepi n French military cap

with a flat top and horizontal peak

kept v past of **keep**

keratin n fibrous protein found in the hair and nails

kerb n Brit curb

kerchief n piece of cloth worn over the head or round the neck

kerfuffle n informal commotion or disorder

kermes [kur-meez] n red dyestuff obtained from dried insects

kernel n **1** inner seed of a nut or fruit stone **2** central and essential part of something

kerosene n paraffin oil distilled from petroleum or coal and shale and used as fuel, solvent, etc.

kestrel n small falcon

ketch n two-masted sailing ship

ketchup n thick cold sauce, usu. of tomatoes

kettle n container with a spout and handle used for boiling water **a different kettle of fish** a different matter entirely

kettledrum n large metal drum with a brass bottom

key n **1** device for operating a lock by moving a bolt **2** device turned to wind a clock, operate a machine, etc. **3** any of a set of levers or buttons pressed to operate a piano, typewriter, etc. **4** music set of related notes **5** list of explanations of codes, symbols, etc. **6** something crucial in providing an explanation or interpretation **7** means of achieving a desired end **8** basketball area of the court under the basket from the end line to the circle around the free throw line ▷ adj **9** of great importance ▷ v **10** (foll. by to) adjust to **keyed**

k

up very excited or nervous
key in v keyboard

keyboard n **1** set of keys on
a piano, typewriter, etc.
2 musical instrument played
using a keyboard ▷ v **3** enter
(text) using a keyboard

keyhole n opening for
inserting a key into a lock

keynote n **1** dominant idea of
a speech etc. **2** basic note of a
musical key

keypad n panel with a set
of buttons for operating an
electronic device

keystone n central stone of
an arch which locks others in
position

kg kilogram(s)

KGB n formerly, the Soviet
secret police

khaki adj **1** dull yellowish-
brown ▷ n **2** hard-wearing
fabric of this colour used for
military uniforms

kHz kilohertz

kibbutz n, pl **kibbutzim**
communal farm or factory in
Israel

kibosh n **put the kibosh on**
slang put a stop to

kick v **1** drive, push, or strike
with the foot **2** score with a
kick **3** (of a gun) recoil when
fired **4** informal object or resist
5 informal free oneself of (an
addiction) ▷ n **6** thrust or
blow with the foot **7** recoil
8 informal excitement or thrill
kickback n money paid
illegally for favours done **kick
off** v **1** start a game of football
2 informal begin **kick out** v
dismiss or expel forcibly
kick-start v start a motorcycle
engine by kicking a pedal **kick
up** v informal create (a fuss)

kid[1] n **1** informal child **2** young
goat **3** leather made from the
skin of a kid

kid[2] v **kidding, kidded** informal
tease or deceive (someone)

kidnap v **-napping, -napped**
seize and hold (a person) to
ransom **kidnapper** n

kidney n **1** either of the pair
of organs which filter waste
products from the blood
to produce urine **2** animal
kidney used as food **kidney
bean** reddish-brown kidney-
shaped bean, edible when
cooked

kill v **1** cause the death of
2 informal cause (someone)
pain or discomfort **3** put
an end to **4** pass (time) ▷ n
5 act of killing **6** animals or
birds killed in a hunt **killer**
n **killing** informal ▷ adj **1** very
tiring **2** very funny ▷ n
3 sudden financial success
killjoy n person who spoils
others' pleasure

kiln n oven for baking, drying,
or processing pottery, bricks,
etc.

kilo n short for **kilogram(me)**

kilo- combining form one
thousand: kilolitre

kilobyte n computers 1000 or
1024 units of information

kilogram, kilogramme n one
thousand grams

kilohertz n one thousand
hertz

kilometre, kilometer n one
thousand metres

kilowatt n electricity one
thousand watts

kilt n knee-length pleated
tartan skirt worn orig. by
Scottish Highlanders **kilted**
adj

kimono [kim-**moan**-no] n,
pl **-nos 1** loose wide-sleeved
Japanese robe, fastened
with a sash **2** European
dressing gown like this

kin n Also **kinsfolk** person's
relatives collectively **kinship** n

kind[1] adj considerate, friendly,
and helpful **kindness** n
kindly adj **-lier, -liest**

1 having a warm-hearted nature **2** pleasant or agreeable ▷ adv **3** in a considerate way **4** please: will you kindly be quiet! **kindliness** n **kind-hearted** adj

kind² n **1** class or group having common characteristics **2** essential nature or character **in kind 1** (of payment) in goods rather than money **2** with something similar **kind of** to a certain extent

kindergarten n class or school for children of about four to six years old

kindle v **1** set (a fire) alight **2** (of a fire) start to burn **3** arouse or be aroused **kindling** n dry wood or straw for starting fires

kindred adj **1** having similar qualities **2** related ▷ n **3** person's relatives collectively

kine pl n obsolete cows or cattle

kinetic [kin-net-ik] adj relating to or caused by motion

king n **1** male ruler of a monarchy **2** ruler or chief **3** best or most important of its kind **4** most important piece in chess **5** playing card with a picture of a king on it **kingly** adj **kingship** n **kingdom** n **1** state ruled by a king or queen **2** division of the natural world **king-size** or **king-sized** adj informal larger than standard size

kingfisher n small bird with a bright plumage that dives for fish

kingpin n most important person in an organization

kink n **1** twist or bend in rope, wire, hair, etc. **2** informal quirk in personality **kinky** adj **1** full of kinks **2** slang given to deviant or unusual sexual practices

kiosk n **1** small booth selling drinks, cigarettes, newspapers, etc. **2** public telephone box

kip n, v **kipping, kipped** informal sleep

kipper n cleaned, salted, and smoked herring

kirk n Scot church

Kirsch n brandy made from cherries

kismet n fate or destiny

kiss v **1** touch with the lips in affection or greeting **2** join lips with a person in love or desire ▷ n **3** touch with the lips **kisser** n slang mouth or face **kiss of life** mouth-to-mouth resuscitation

kit n **1** outfit or equipment for a specific purpose **2** set of pieces of equipment sold ready to be assembled **kitbag** n bag for a soldier's or traveller's belongings **kit out** v **kitting, kitted** provide with clothes or equipment needed for a particular activity

kitchen n room used for cooking **kitchenette** n small kitchen **kitchen garden** garden for growing vegetables, herbs, etc.

kite n **1** light frame covered with a thin material flown on a string in the wind **2** large hawk with a forked tail

kith n **kith and kin** friends and relatives

kitsch n vulgarized or pretentious art or literature with popular sentimental appeal

kitten n young cat **kittenish** adj lively and flirtatious

kittiwake n type of seagull

kitty n, pl **-ties 1** communal fund for buying drinks etc. **2** pool in certain gambling games

kiwi n **1** NZ flightless bird with a stout beak and no tail

2 *informal* a New Zealander
kiwi fruit edible fruit with a fuzzy brown skin and green flesh

klaxon *n* loud horn used on emergency vehicles as a warning signal

kleptomania *n* compulsive tendency to steal **kleptomaniac** *n*

klick *n informal* kilometre

km kilometre(s)

knack *n* **1** skilful way of doing something **2** innate ability

knacker *n* buyer of old horses for killing

knapsack *n* soldier's or traveller's bag worn strapped on the back

knave *n* **1** jack at cards **2** *obsolete* rogue **knavish** *adj* **knavery** *n* dishonest behaviour

knead *v* **1** work (flour) into dough using the hands **2** squeeze or press with the hands

knee *n* **1** joint between thigh and lower leg **2** part of a garment covering the knee **3** lap ▷ *v* **kneeing, kneed** **4** strike or push with the knee **kneecap** *n* **1** bone in front of the knee ▷ *v* **2** shoot in the kneecap **kneejerk** *adj* (of a reply or reaction) automatic and predictable

kneel *v* **kneeling, kneeled** *or* **knelt** fall or rest on one's knees

knell *n* **1** sound of a bell, esp. at a funeral or death **2** portent of doom

knew *v* past tense of **know**

knickerbockers *pl n* loose-fitting short trousers gathered in at the knee

knickers *pl n* woman's or girl's undergarment covering the lower trunk and having legs or leg holes

knick-knack *n* trifle or trinket

knife *n, pl* **knives** **1** cutting tool or weapon consisting of a sharp-edged blade with a handle ▷ *v* **2** cut or stab with a knife

knight *n* **1** honorary title given to a man by the British sovereign **2** *hist* man who served his lord as a mounted armoured soldier **3** chess piece shaped like a horse's head ▷ *v* **4** award a knighthood to **knighthood** *n* **knightly** *adj*

knit *v* **knitting, knitted** *or* **knit** **1** make (a garment) by interlocking a series of loops in wool or other yarn **2** draw (one's eyebrows) together **3** join closely together **knitter** *n* **knitting** *n* **knitwear** *n* knitted clothes, such as sweaters

knob *n* **1** rounded projection, such as a switch on a radio **2** rounded handle on a door or drawer **3** small amount of butter **knobbly** *adj* covered with small bumps

knock *v* **1** give a blow or push to **2** rap sharply with the knuckles **3** make or drive by striking **4** *informal* criticize adversely **5** (of an engine) make a regular banging noise as a result of a fault ▷ *n* **6** blow or rap **7** knocking sound **knocker** *n* metal fitting for knocking on a door **knock about** *or* **knock around** *v* **1** travel or wander **2** hit or kick brutally **knockabout** *adj* (of comedy) boisterous **knock back** *v informal* **1** drink quickly **2** cost **3** reject or refuse **knock down** *v* reduce the price of **knockdown** *adj* (of a price) very low **knock-knees** *pl n* legs that curve in at the knees **knock off** *v* **1** take (a specified amount) off a price **2** *informal* make or do (something) hurriedly or easily **3** *informal* cease work **4** *informal* steal **knock out** *v* **1** render (someone) unconscious **2** *informal* overwhelm or amaze **3** defeat in a knockout competition **knockout** *n* **1** blow that renders an opponent unconscious **2** competition from which competitors are progressively eliminated **3** *informal* overwhelmingly attractive person or thing **knock up** *v* **1** *slang* make pregnant **2** *Brit informal* waken

knoll *n* small rounded hill

knot *n* **1** fastening made by looping and pulling tight strands of string, cord, or rope **2** tangle, as of hair **3** small cluster or huddled group **4** round lump or spot in timber **5** unit of speed used by ships, equal to one nautical mile per hour ▷ *v* **knotting, knotted 6** tie with or into a knot **knotty** *adj* **1** full of knots **2** puzzling or difficult

know *v* **knowing, knew, known 1** be aware of **2** be or feel certain of the truth of (information etc.) **3** be acquainted with **4** have a grasp of or understand (a skill or language) **in the know** *informal* informed or aware **knowable** *adj* **knowing** *adj* cunning or shrewd **knowingly** *adv* **1** shrewdly **2** deliberately **know-all** *n* *offensive* person who acts as if knowing more than other people **know-how** *n* *informal* ingenuity, aptitude, or skill

knowledge *n* **1** facts or experiences known by a person **2** state of knowing **3** specific information on a subject **knowledgeable** or **knowledgable** *adj* intelligent or well-informed

knuckle *n* **1** bone at the finger joint **2** knee joint of a calf or pig **near the knuckle** *informal* approaching indecency **knuckle ball** Also **knuckler** *baseball* pitch that moves slowly and erratically, delivered by gripping the ball with the knuckles **knuckle-duster** *n* metal appliance worn on the knuckles to add force to a blow **knuckle under** *v* yield or submit

KO knockout

koala *n* tree-dwelling Aust. marsupial with dense grey fur

kohl *n* cosmetic powder used to darken the edges of the eyelids

kohlrabi [kole-**rah**-bee] *n, pl* -**bies** type of cabbage with an edible stem

kokanee [koh-**kah**-nee] *n* salmon of N American lakes

kookaburra *n* large Aust. kingfisher with a cackling cry

kopeck *n* monetary unit of the former Soviet republics, one hundredth of a rouble

kopje, koppie *n S Afr* small hill

Koran *n* sacred book of Islam

kosher [**koh**-sher] *adj* **1** conforming to Jewish religious law, esp. (of food) to Jewish dietary law **2** *informal* legitimate or authentic ▷ *n* **3** kosher food

kowtow *v* **1** touch one's forehead to the ground in deference **2** be humble and servile (towards)

kph kilometres per hour

kraal *n S* African village surrounded by a strong fence

kraken *n* mythical Norwegian sea monster

Kremlin *n* central government of Russia and, formerly, of the Soviet Union

krill *n, pl* **krill** small shrimplike sea creature

krypton *n* colourless gas present in the atmosphere and used in fluorescent lights and lasers

kudos [kyoo-doss] *n* fame or credit

kulak *n hist* independent well-to-do Russian peasant

kümmel *n* German liqueur flavoured with caraway seeds

kumquat *n* citrus fruit resembling a tiny orange

kung fu *n* Chinese martial art combining hand, foot, and weapon techniques

kW kilowatt

kWh kilowatt-hour

k

Ll

l litre

L 1 large **2** Latin **3** learner (driver)

laager *n SAfr* camp defended by a circle of wagons

lab *n informal* short for **laboratory**

label *n* **1** piece of card or other material fixed to an object to show its ownership, destination, etc. ▷ *v* **-elling, -elled 2** give a label to

labia *pl n, sing.* **labium** four liplike folds of skin forming part of the female genitals **labial** [**lay**-bee-al] *adj* **1** of the lips **2** pronounced with the lips

laboratory *n, pl* **-ries** building or room designed for scientific research or for the teaching of practical science

laborious *adj* involving great prolonged effort **laboriously** *adv*

labour *n* **1** physical work or exertion **2** workers in industry **3** final stage of pregnancy, leading to childbirth ▷ *v* **4** work hard **5** stress to excess or too persistently **6** be at a disadvantage because of a mistake or false belief **laboured** *adj* uttered or done with difficulty **labourer** *n* person who labours, esp. someone doing manual work for wages

labrador *n* large retriever dog with a yellow or black coat

laburnum *n* ornamental tree with yellow hanging flowers

labyrinth [**lab**-er-inth] *n* **1** network of tortuous passages, maze **2** interconnecting cavities in the internal ear **labyrinthine** *adj*

lace *n* **1** delicate decorative fabric made from threads woven into an open weblike pattern **2** cord drawn through eyelets and tied ▷ *v* **3** fasten with laces **4** thread a cord or string through holes in something **5** add a small amount of alcohol or drug to (food or drink) **lacy** *adj* fine, like lace **lace-ups** *pl n* shoes which fasten with laces

lacerate [**lass**-er-rate] *v* **1** tear (flesh) jaggedly **2** wound (feelings) **laceration** *n*

lachrymose *adj* **1** tearful **2** sad

lack *n* **1** shortage or absence of something needed or wanted ▷ *v* **2** need or be short of (something)

lackadaisical *adj* **1** lacking vitality and purpose **2** lazy and careless in a dreamy way

lackey *n* **1** servile follower **2** uniformed male servant

lacklustre *adj* lacking brilliance or vitality

laconic *adj* using only a few words, terse **laconically** *adv*

lacquer *n* **1** hard varnish for wood or metal **2** clear sticky substance sprayed onto the hair to hold it in place ▷ *v* **3** apply lacquer to

lacrimal, lachrymal *adj* of tears or the glands which

produce them

lacrosse *n* sport in which teams catch and throw a ball using long sticks with a pouched net at the end, in an attempt to score goals

lactation *n* secretion of milk by female mammals to feed young **lactic** *adj* of or derived from milk **lactose** *n* white crystalline sugar found in milk

lacuna [lak-**kew**-na] *n, pl* -**nae**, -**nas** gap or missing part, esp. in a document or series

lad *n* boy or young fellow

ladder *n* **1** frame of two poles connected by horizontal steps used for climbing **2** line of stitches that have come undone in a stocking or tights ▷ *v* **3** have or cause to have such a line of undone stitches

laden *adj* **1** loaded **2** burdened

la-di-da, lah-di-dah *adj informal* affected or pretentious

ladle *n* **1** spoon with a long handle and a large bowl, used for serving soup etc. ▷ *v* **2** serve out liquid with a ladle

lady *n, pl* -**dies** **1** polite term of address for a woman **2** woman regarded as having characteristics of good breeding or high rank **3 Lady** title of some women of rank **Our Lady** the Virgin Mary **lady-in-waiting** *n, pl* **ladies-in-waiting** female servant of a queen or princess **ladykiller** *n informal* man who is or thinks he is irresistible to women **ladylike** *adj* polite, well-mannered

ladybug *n* small red beetle with black spots

lag¹ *v* **lagging, lagged** **1** go too slowly, fall behind ▷ *n* **2** delay between events **laggard** *n* person who lags behind

lag² *v* **lagging, lagged** wrap (a boiler, pipes, etc.) with insulating material **lagging** *n* insulating material

lager *n* light-bodied type of beer

lagoon *n* saltwater lake enclosed by an atoll or separated by a sandbank from the sea

laid *v* past of **lay¹** ▸ **laid-back** *adj informal* relaxed

lain *v* past participle of **lie²**

lair *n* resting place of an animal

laird *n* Scottish landowner

laissez-faire [less-ay-**fair**] *n* principle of nonintervention, esp. by a government in commercial affairs

laity [**lay**-it-ee] *n* people who are not members of the clergy

lake¹ *n* expanse of water entirely surrounded by land **lakeside** *n*

lake² *n* red pigment

lam *v* **lamming, lammed** *slang* beat or hit

lama *n* Buddhist priest in Tibet or Mongolia **lamasery** *n* monastery of lamas

lamb *n* **1** young of sheep **2** its meat **3** innocent or helpless creature ▷ *v* **4** (of sheep) give birth to a lamb or lambs **lambskin** *n* **lambswool** *n*

lambaste, lambast *v* **1** beat or thrash **2** reprimand severely

lambent *adj lit* (of a flame) flickering softly

lame *adj* **1** having an injured or disabled leg or foot **2** (of an excuse) unconvincing ▷ *v* **3** make lame **lamely** *adv* **lameness** *n* **lame duck** person or thing unable to cope without help

lamé [**lah**-may] *n, adj* (fabric) interwoven with gold or silver thread

lament *v* **1** feel or express sorrow (for) ▷ *n* **2** passionate expression of grief **3** song of grief **lamentable** *adj* deplorable **lamentation** *n* **lamented** *adj* grieved for

laminate *v* **1** make (a sheet of material) by bonding together two or more thin sheets **2** cover with a thin sheet of material ▷ *n* **3** laminated sheet **laminated** *adj* **lamination** *n*

lamp *n* device which produces light from electricity, oil, or gas **lampblack** *n* pigment made from soot **lamppost** *n* post supporting a lamp in the street **lampshade** *n*

lampoon *n* **1** humorous satire ridiculing someone ▷ *v* **2** satirize or ridicule

lamprey *n* eel-like fish with a round sucking mouth

lance *n* **1** long spear used by a mounted soldier ▷ *v* **2** pierce (a boil or abscess) with a lancet **lancer** *n* formerly, cavalry soldier armed with a lance **lance corporal** lowest non-commissioned rank in the army

lanceolate *adj* narrow and tapering to a point at each end

lancet *n* **1** pointed two-edged surgical knife **2** narrow window in the shape of a pointed arch

land *n* **1** solid part of the earth's surface **2** ground, esp. with reference to its type or use **3** rural or agricultural area **4** property consisting of land **5** country or region ▷ *v* **6** come or bring to earth after a flight, jump, or fall **7** go or take from a ship at the end of a voyage **8** come to or touch shore **9** come or bring to some point or condition **10** *informal* obtain **11** take (a hooked fish) from the water **12** *informal* deliver (a punch) **landed** *adj* possessing or consisting of lands **landed immigrant** former name for Canadian permanent resident **landless** *adj* **landward** *adj* nearest to or facing the land **land up** *v* arrive at a final point or condition

landau [**lan**-daw] *n* four-wheeled carriage with a folding hood

landfall *n* ship's first landing after a voyage

landing *n* **1** floor area at the top of a flight of stairs **2** bringing or coming to land **3** Also **landing stage** place where people or goods go onto or come off a boat

landline *n* fixed telephone communications cable

landlocked *adj* completely surrounded by land

landlord, landlady *n* **1** person who rents out land, houses, etc. **2** owner or manager of a pub or boarding house

landlubber *n* person who is not experienced at sea

landmark *n* **1** prominent object in or feature of a landscape **2** event, decision, etc. considered as an important development

landscape *n* **1** extensive piece of inland scenery seen from one place **2** picture of it ▷ *v* **3** improve natural features of (a piece of land)

landslide *n* **1** Also **landslip** falling of soil, rock, etc. down the side of a mountain **2** overwhelming electoral victory

lane *n* **1** narrow road **2** area of road for one stream of traffic **3** specified route followed by ships or aircraft **4** strip of a running track or swimming pool for use by one competitor

language *n* **1** system of sounds, symbols, etc. for communicating thought **2** particular system used by a nation or people **3** system of words and symbols for computer programming

languid adj lacking energy or enthusiasm **languidly** adv

languish v 1 suffer neglect or hardship 2 lose or diminish in strength or vigour 3 pine (for) **languishing** adj

languor [**lang**-ger] n 1 laziness or weariness 2 dreamy relaxation 3 oppressive stillness **languorous** adj

lank adj 1 (of hair) greasy and limp 2 lean and tall **lanky** adj ungracefully tall and thin **lankiness** n

lanolin n grease from sheep's wool used in ointments etc.

lantern n light in a transparent protective case **lantern jaw** long thin jaw **lantern-jawed** adj

lanthanum n silvery-white metallic element **lanthanide series** class of 15 elements chemically related to lanthanum

lanyard n 1 short cord worn round the neck to hold a knife or whistle 2 naut short rope

lap[1] n part between the waist and knees of a person when sitting **lapdog** n small pet dog **laptop** adj (of a computer) small enough to fit on a user's lap

lap[2] n 1 single circuit of a racecourse or track 2 stage of a journey 3 overlap ▷ v **lapping, lapped** 4 overtake an opponent so as to be one or more circuits ahead 5 enfold or wrap around

lap[3] v **lapping, lapped** (of waves) beat softly against (a shore etc.) **lap up** v 1 drink by scooping up with the tongue 2 accept (information or attention) eagerly

lapel [lap-**pel**] n part of the front of a coat or jacket folded back towards the shoulders

lapidary adj of stones, esp. gemstones

lapis lazuli [**lap**-iss **lazz**-yoo-lie] n bright blue gemstone

lapse n 1 temporary drop in a standard, esp. through forgetfulness or carelessness 2 instance of bad behaviour by someone usually well-behaved 3 break in occurrence or usage ▷ v 4 drop in standard 5 end or become invalid, esp. through disuse 6 (of time) slip away 7 abandon religious faith **lapsed** adj

lapwing n plover with a tuft of feathers on the head

larboard adj, n old-fashioned port (side of a ship)

larceny n, pl -nies theft

larch n deciduous coniferous tree

lard n 1 soft white fat obtained from a pig ▷ v 2 insert strips of bacon in (meat) before cooking 3 decorate (speech or writing) with strange words unnecessarily

larder n storeroom for food

large adj great in size, number, or extent **at large** 1 in general 2 free, not confined **largely** adv **largish** adj **large-scale** adj wide-ranging or extensive

largesse, largess [lar-**jess**] n generous giving, esp. of money

largo adv music in a slow and dignified manner

lariat n 1 lasso

lark[1] n small brown songbird, skylark

lark[2] n informal 1 harmless piece of mischief 2 unnecessary activity or job **lark about** v play pranks

larkspur n plant with spikes of blue, pink, or white flowers with spurs

larva n, pl -vae insect in an immature stage, often

resembling a worm **larval** adj

larynx n, pl **larynges** part of the throat containing the vocal cords **laryngeal** adj **laryngitis** n inflammation of the larynx

lasagne, lasagna [laz-**zan**-ya] n **1** pasta in wide flat sheets **2** dish made from layers of lasagne, meat, vegetables, etc.

lascivious [lass-**iv**-ee-uss] adj lustful **lasciviously** adv

laser [**lay**-zer] n device that produces a very narrow intense beam of light, used for cutting very hard materials and in surgery etc.

lash¹ n **1** eyelash **2** sharp blow with a whip ▷ v **3** hit with a whip **4** (of rain or waves) beat forcefully against **5** attack verbally, scold **6** flick or wave sharply to and fro **lash out** v **1** make a sudden physical or verbal attack **2** informal spend (money) extravagantly

lash² v fasten or bind tightly with cord etc.

lashings pl n Brit informal large amount

lass, lassie n girl

lassitude n physical or mental weariness

lasso [lass-**oo**] n, pl **-sos, -soes 1** rope with a noose for catching cattle and horses ▷ v **-soing, -soed 2** catch with a lasso

last¹ adj, adv **1** coming at the end or after all others **2** most recent(ly) ▷ adj **3** only remaining ▷ n **4** last person or thing **lastly** adv finally **last-ditch** adj done as a final resort **last post** army bugle-call played at sunset or funerals **last straw** small irritation or setback that, coming after others, is too much to bear **last word 1** final comment in an argument **2** most recent or best example of something

last² v **1** continue **2** be sufficient for (a specified amount of time) **3** remain fresh, uninjured, or unaltered **lasting** adj

last³ n model of a foot on which shoes and boots are made or repaired

latch n **1** fastening for a door with a bar and lever **2** lock which can only be opened from the outside with a key ▷ v **3** fasten with a latch **latchkey** n key for a latch **latch onto** v become attached to (a person or idea)

late adj **1** arriving or occurring after the normal or expected time **2** towards the end of (a period of time) **3** being at an advanced time **4** recently dead **5** recent **6** former ▷ adv **7** after the normal or expected time **8** at a relatively advanced age **9** recently **lately** adv not long since **lateness** n **latish** adj, adv **latecomer** n

lateen sail n triangular sail on a long yard hoisted to the head of a mast

latent adj hidden and not yet developed **latency** n

lateral [**lat**-ter-al] adj **1** of, at, to, or from the side ▷ n **2** football pass thrown sideways **laterally** adv

latex n milky sap found in some plants, esp. the rubber tree, used in making rubber and glue

lath n thin strip of wood used to support plaster, tiles, etc.

lathe n machine for turning wood or metal while it is being shaped

lather n **1** froth of soap and water **2** frothy sweat **3** informal state of agitation ▷ v **4** make frothy **5** rub with soap until lather appears

Latin n **1** language of the ancient Romans ▷ adj **2** of or in Latin **3** of a people whose language derives from Latin **Latin America** parts of South and Central America whose official language is Spanish or Portuguese **Latin American** n, adj

latitude n **1** angular distance measured in degrees N or S of the equator **2** scope for freedom of action or thought **latitudes 3** regions considered in relation to their distance from the equator **latitudinal** adj

latitudinarian adj liberal, esp. in religious matters

latrine n toilet in a barracks or camp

latter adj **1** second of two **2** near or nearer the end **3** more recent **latterly** adv **latter-day** adj modern

lattice [**lat**-iss] n **1** framework of intersecting strips of wood, metal, etc. **2** gate, screen, etc. formed of such a framework **latticed** adj

laud v praise or glorify **laudable** adj praiseworthy **laudably** adv **laudatory** adj praising or glorifying

laudanum [**lawd**-a-num] n opium-based sedative

laugh v **1** make inarticulate sounds with the voice expressing amusement, merriment, or scorn **2** utter or express with laughter ▷ n **3** laughing **4** manner of laughing **5** informal person or thing causing amusement **laughable** adj ludicrous **laughter** n sound or action of laughing **laughing gas** nitrous oxide as an anesthetic **laughing stock** object of general derision **laugh off** v treat (something serious or difficult) lightly

launch¹ v **1** put (a ship or boat) into the water, esp.

for the first time **2** begin (a campaign, project, etc.) **3** put a new product on the market **4** send (a missile or spacecraft) into space or the air ▷ n **5** launching **launcher** n **launch into** v start doing something enthusiastically **launch out** v start doing something new

launch² n large open motorboat

launder v **1** wash and iron (clothes and linen) **2** make (illegally obtained money) seem legal by passing it through foreign banks or legitimate businesses **laundry** n, pl **-dries 1** place for washing clothes and linen, esp. as a business **2** clothes etc. for washing or which have recently been washed **Laundromat** n ® shop with coin-operated washing and drying machines **laundry list** US & Canad long list of things to be done

laureate [**lor**-ee-at] adj **poet laureate** poet appointed by the British sovereign to write poems on important occasions

laurel n **1** glossy-leaved shrub, bay tree **laurels 2** wreath of laurel, an emblem of victory or merit

lava n molten rock thrown out by volcanoes, which hardens as it cools

lavatory n, pl **-ries** toilet

lavender n **1** shrub with fragrant flowers ▷ adj **2** bluish-purple **lavender water** light perfume made from lavender

lavish adj **1** great in quantity or richness **2** giving or spending generously **3** extravagant ▷ v **4** give or spend generously **lavishly** adv

law n **1** rule binding on a

community **2** system of such rules **3** *informal* police **4** general principle deduced from facts **lawful** *adj* allowed by law **lawfully** *adv* **lawless** *adj* breaking the law, esp. in a violent way **lawlessly** *adv* **lawlessness** *n* **law-abiding** *adj* adhering to the laws **law-breaker** *n* **lawsuit** *n* court case brought by one person or group against another

lawn[1] *n* area of tended and mown grass **lawn mower** machine for cutting grass **lawn tennis** tennis, esp. when played on a grass court

lawn[2] *n* fine linen or cotton fabric

lawyer *n* professionally qualified legal expert

lax *adj* not strict **laxity** *n* **laxly** *adv*

laxative *n, adj* (medicine) having a loosening effect on the bowels

lay[1] *v* **laying, laid 1** cause to lie **2** set in a particular place or position **3** arrange (a table) for a meal **4** put forward (a plan, argument, etc.) **5** attribute (blame) **6** (of a bird or reptile) produce eggs **7** devise or prepare **8** place (a bet) **lay waste** devastate **lay-by** *n* *Brit* stopping place for traffic beside a road **lay off** *v* dismiss staff during a slack period **lay-off** *n* **lay on** *v* provide or supply **lay out** *v* **1** arrange or spread out **2** prepare (a corpse) for burial **3** *informal* spend money, esp. lavishly **4** *slang* knock unconscious **layout** *n* arrangement, esp. of matter for printing or of a building

lay[2] *v* past tense of **lie**[2] ▸ **layabout** *n* lazy person, loafer

lay[3] *adj* **1** of or involving people who are not clergymen **2** nonspecialist **layman** *n* ordinary person

lay[4] *n* short narrative poem designed to be sung

layer *n* **1** single thickness of some substance, as a stratum or coating on a surface **2** laying hen ▷ *v* **3** form a layer **layered** *adj*

layette *n* clothes for a newborn baby

lay figure *n* **1** jointed figure of the body used by artists **2** nonentity

laze *v* **1** be idle or lazy ▷ *n* **2** lazing

lazy *adj* **lazier, laziest 1** not inclined to work or exert oneself **2** done in a relaxed manner with little effort **3** (of a movement) slow and gentle **lazily** *adv* **laziness** *n* **lazybones** *n* *informal* lazy person

lb pound (weight)

lea *n* *poetic* meadow

leach *v* remove or be removed from a substance by a liquid passing through it

lead[1] *v* **leading, led 1** guide or conduct **2** cause to feel, think, or behave in a certain way **3** control or direct **4** be the most important person or thing in **5** be, go, or play first **6** (of a road, path, etc.) go towards **7** pass or spend (one's life) **8** result in ▷ *n* **9** first or most prominent place **10** example or leadership **11** amount by which a person or group is ahead of another **12** clue **13** length of leather or chain attached to a dog's collar to control it **14** principal role or actor in a film, play, etc. **15** cable bringing current to an electrical device ▷ *adj* **16** acting as a leader or lead **leading** *adj* **leading question** question worded to prompt the answer desired **lead-in** *n* introduction to a subject

lead² n 1 soft heavy grey metal 2 (in a pencil) graphite 3 lead weight on a line, used for sounding depths of water **leaded** adj (of windows) made from many small panes of glass held together by lead strips **leaden** adj 1 heavy or sluggish 2 dull grey 3 made from lead

leader n 1 person who leads or guides others 2 Also **leading article** article in a newspaper expressing editorial views **leadership** n

leaf n, pl **leaves** 1 flat usu. green blade attached to the stem of a plant 2 single sheet of paper in a book 3 very thin sheet of metal 4 extending flap on a table **leafy** adj **leafless** adj **leaf mould** rich soil composed of decayed leaves **leaf through** v turn pages without reading them

leaflet n 1 sheet of printed matter for distribution 2 small leaf

league¹ n 1 association promoting the interests of its members 2 association of sports clubs organizing competitions between its members 3 informal class or level

league² n obsolete measure of distance, about three miles

leak n 1 hole or defect that allows the escape or entrance of liquid, gas, radiation, etc. 2 liquid etc. that escapes or enters 3 disclosure of secrets ▷ v 4 let fluid etc. in or out 5 (of fluid etc.) find its way through a leak 6 disclose secret information **leakage** n 1 leaking 2 gradual escape or loss **leaky** adj

lean¹ v **leaning, leant** or **leaned** 1 rest against 2 bend or slope from an upright

position 3 tend (towards) **leaning** n tendency **lean on** v 1 informal threaten or intimidate 2 depend on for help or advice **lean-to** n shed built against an existing wall

lean² adj 1 thin but healthy-looking 2 (of meat) lacking fat 3 unproductive ▷ n 4 lean part of meat **leanness** n

leap v **leaping, leapt** or **leaped** 1 make a sudden powerful jump ▷ n 2 sudden powerful jump 3 abrupt increase, as in costs or prices **leapfrog** n game in which a player vaults over another bending down **leap year** year with February 29th as an extra day

learn v **learning, learnt** or **learned** 1 gain skill or knowledge by study, practice, or teaching 2 memorize (something) 3 find out or discover **learned** adj 1 erudite, deeply read 2 showing much learning **learner** n **learning** n knowledge got by study

lease n 1 contract by which land or property is rented for a stated time by the owner to a tenant ▷ v 2 let or rent on lease **leasehold** adj held on lease **leaseholder** n

leash n lead for a dog

least adj 1 smallest 2 superlative of **little** ▷ n 3 smallest one ▷ adv 4 in the smallest degree

leather n 1 material made from specially treated animal skins ▷ adj 2 made of leather ▷ v 3 beat or thrash **leathery** adj like leather, tough

leave¹ v **leaving, left** 1 go away from 2 discontinue membership of 3 allow to remain, accidentally or deliberately 4 cause to be or remain in a specified state 5 permit 6 deposit 7 entrust

8 bequeath **leave out** v exclude or omit

leave² n **1** permission to be absent from work or duty **2** period of such absence **3** permission to do something **4** formal parting

leaven [lev-ven] n **1** yeast **2** influence that produces a gradual change ▷ v **3** raise with leaven **4** spread through and influence (something)

lecher n lecherous man **lechery** n

lecherous [letch-er-uss] adj (of a man) having or showing excessive sexual desire **lecherously** adv **lecherousness** n

lectern n sloping reading desk, esp. in a church

lecture n **1** informative talk to an audience on a subject **2** lengthy rebuke or scolding ▷ v **3** give a talk **4** reprove **lecturer** n **lectureship** n appointment as a lecturer

ledge n **1** narrow shelf sticking out from a wall **2** shelflike projection from a cliff etc.

ledger n book of debit and credit accounts of a firm

lee n **1** sheltered part or side **2** side away from the wind **leeward** adj, n **1** (on) the lee side ▷ adv **2** towards this side **leeway** n room for free movement within limits

leech n **1** species of bloodsucking worm **2** person who lives off others

leek n vegetable of the onion family with a long bulb and thick stem

leer v **1** look or grin at in a sneering or suggestive manner ▷ n **2** sneering or suggestive look or grin

leery adj informal suspicious or wary (of)

lees pl n sediment of wine

left¹ adj **1** denotes the side that faces west when the front faces north **2** opposite to right ▷ n **3** left hand or part **4** politics people supporting socialism rather than capitalism ▷ adv **5** on or towards the left **leftist** n, adj (person) of the political left **left-handed** adj more adept with the left hand than with the right **left-wing** adj **1** socialist **2** belonging to the more radical part of a political party **lefty** n informal **1** left-handed person **2** baseball left-handed pitcher **3** a leftist

left² v past of **leave¹**

left field n baseball area of the outfield to the batter's left **out of left field** unexpected or surprising: their proposal came out of left field **left fielder** baseball fielder who covers left field

leftover n unused portion of food or material

leg n **1** one of the limbs on which a person or animal walks, runs, or stands **2** part of a garment covering the leg **3** structure that supports, such as one of the legs of a table **4** stage of a journey **5** sports (part of) one game or race in a series **pull someone's leg** tease someone **leggy** adj long-legged **legless** adj **1** without legs **2** slang very drunk **leggings** pl n **1** covering of leather or other material for the legs **2** close-fitting trousers for women or children

legacy n, pl **-cies 1** thing left in a will **2** thing handed down to a successor

legal adj **1** established or permitted by law **2** relating to law or lawyers **legally** adv **legalize** v make legal **legalization** n **legality** n

legate n messenger or representative, esp. from the

Pope **legation** n **1** diplomatic minister and his staff **2** official residence of a diplomatic minister

legatee n recipient of a legacy

legato [leg-**ah**-toe] adv music smoothly

legend n **1** traditional story or myth **2** traditional literature **3** famous person or event **4** stories about such a person or event **5** inscription **legendary** adj **1** famous **2** of or in legend

legerdemain [lej-er-de-**main**] n **1** sleight of hand **2** cunning deception

legible adj easily read **legibility** n **legibly** adv

legion n **1** large military force **2** large number **3** association of veterans **4** infantry unit in the Roman army **legionary** adj, n **legionnaire** n member of a legion **legionnaire's disease** serious bacterial disease similar to pneumonia

legislate v make laws **legislation** n **1** legislating **2** laws made **legislative** adj **legislator** n maker of laws **legislature** n body of persons that makes, amends, or repeals the laws of a state

legitimate adj **1** authorized by or in accordance with law **2** fairly deduced **3** born to parents married to each other ▷ v **4** make legitimate **legitimately** adv **legitimacy** n **legitimize** v make legitimate, legalize **legitimization** n

Lego n ® construction toy of plastic bricks fitted together by studs

legume n **1** pod of a plant of the pea or bean family **legumes 2** peas or beans **leguminous** adj (of plants) pod-bearing

lei n (in Hawaii) garland of flowers

leisure n time for relaxation or hobbies **at one's leisure** when one has time **leisurely** adj **1** deliberate, unhurried ▷ adv **2** slowly **leisured** adj with plenty of spare time **leisure centre** building with facilities such as a swimming pool, gymnasium, and café

leitmotif [lite-mote-eef] n music recurring theme associated with a person, situation, or thought

lemming n rodent of Arctic regions, reputed to run into the sea and drown during mass migrations

lemon n **1** yellow acid fruit that grows on trees **2** slang useless or defective person or thing ▷ adj **3** pale-yellow **lemonade** n lemon-flavoured soft drink, often fizzy **lemon curd** creamy spread made of lemons, butter, etc. **lemon sole** edible flatfish

lemur n nocturnal animal like a small monkey, found on Madagascar

lend v **lending, lent 1** give the temporary use of **2** provide (money) temporarily, often for interest **3** add (a quality or effect): her presence lent beauty to the scene **lend itself to** be suitable for **lender** n

length n **1** extent or measurement from end to end **2** duration **3** quality of being long **4** piece of something narrow and long **at length 1** in full detail **2** at last **lengthy** adj very long or tiresome **lengthily** adv **lengthen** v make or become longer **lengthways** or **lengthwise** adj, adv

lenient [lee-nee-ent] adj tolerant, not strict or severe **leniency** n **leniently** adv

lenity n, pl -ties mercy or clemency

lens *n, pl* **lenses 1** piece of glass or similar material with one or both sides curved, used to converge or diverge light rays in cameras, spectacles, telescopes, etc. **2** transparent structure in the eye that focuses light

lent *v* past of **lend**

Lent *n* period from Ash Wednesday to Easter Eve **Lenten** *adj* of, in, or suitable to Lent

lentil *n* edible seed of a leguminous Asian plant

lento *adv* music slowly

leonine *adj* like a lion

leopard *n* large spotted carnivorous animal of the cat family **leopardess** *n fem*

leotard *n* tight-fitting garment covering most of the body, worn by acrobats, dancers, etc.

leper *n* **1** offensive person suffering from leprosy **2** ignored or despised person

lepidoptera *pl n* order of insects with four wings covered with fine gossamer scales, as moths and butterflies **lepidopterist** *n* person who studies or collects butterflies or moths **lepidopterous** *adj*

leprechaun *n* mischievous elf of Irish folklore

leprosy *n* disease attacking the nerves and skin, resulting in loss of feeling in the affected parts **leprous** *adj*

lesbian *n* **1** homosexual woman ▷ *adj* **2** of homosexual women **lesbianism** *n*

lese-majesty [lezz-**maj**-est-ee] *n* **1** treason **2** taking of liberties against people in authority

lesion *n* **1** structural change in an organ of the body caused by illness or injury **2** injury or wound

less *adj* **1** smaller in extent, degree, or duration **2** not so much **3** comparative of **little** ▷ *n* **4** smaller part or quantity **5** lesser amount ▷ *adv* **6** to a smaller extent or degree ▷ *prep* **7** after deducting, minus **lessen** *v* make or become smaller or not as much **lesser** *adj* not as great in quantity, size, or worth

lessee *n* person to whom a lease is granted

lesson *n* **1** single period of instruction in a subject **2** content of this **3** experience that teaches **4** portion of Scripture read in church

lessor *n* person who grants a lease

lest *conj* **1** so as to prevent any possibility that **2** for fear that

let¹ *v* **letting**, **let 1** allow, enable, or cause **2** allow to escape **3** grant use of for rent, lease **4** used as an auxiliary to express a proposal, command, threat, or assumption **let alone** not to mention **let down** *v* **1** disappoint **2** lower **3** deflate **letdown** *n* disappointment **let off** *v* **1** excuse from (a duty or punishment) **2** fire or explode (a weapon) **3** emit (gas, steam, etc.) **let on** *v* informal reveal (a secret) **let out** *v* **1** emit **2** release **let up** *v* diminish or stop **let-up** *n* lessening

let² *n* **1** hindrance **2** tennis minor infringement or obstruction of the ball requiring a replay of the point

lethal *adj* deadly

lethargy *n* **1** sluggishness or dullness **2** abnormal lack of energy **lethargic** *adj* **lethargically** *adv*

letter *n* **1** alphabetical symbol **2** written message, usu. sent by post **3** strict meaning (of a law etc.) ▷ *pl n* **4** literary knowledge or ability **lettered** *adj* learned **lettering** *n* **letter bomb** explosive device in a parcel or letter that explodes when it is opened **letter box 1** slot in a door through which letters are delivered **2** box in a street or post office where letters are posted **letterhead** *n* printed heading on stationery giving the sender's name and address

lettuce *n* plant with large green leaves used in salads

leucocyte [**loo**-koh-site] *n* white blood corpuscle

leukemia, leukaemia [loo-**kee**-mee-a] *n* disease caused by uncontrolled overproduction of white blood corpuscles

levee[1] *n* **1** natural or artificial river embankment **2** landing-place

levee[2] *n* formal reception for visitors, orig. held by a sovereign on rising

level *adj* **1** horizontal **2** having an even surface **3** of the same height as something else **4** equal to or even with (someone or something else) **5** not going above the top edge of (a spoon etc.) ▷ *v* -**elling,** -**elled 6** make even or horizontal **7** make equal in position or status **8** direct (a gun, accusation, etc.) at **9** raze to the ground ▷ *n* **10** horizontal line or surface **11** device for showing or testing if something is horizontal **12** position on a scale **13** standard or grade **14** flat area of land **on the level** *informal* honest or trustworthy **level crossing** point where a railway line and road cross **level-headed** *adj* not apt to be carried away by emotion

lever *n* **1** rigid bar pivoted about a fulcrum to transfer a force with mechanical advantage **2** bar used to move a heavy object or to open something **3** handle pressed, pulled, etc. to operate machinery **4** means of exerting pressure to achieve an aim ▷ *v* **5** prise or move with a lever **leverage** *n* **1** action or power of a lever **2** influence or strategic advantage

leviathan [lev-**vie**-ath-an] *n* **1** sea monster **2** anything huge or formidable

Levis *pl n* ® denim jeans

levitation *n* raising of a solid body into the air supernaturally **levitate** *v* rise or cause to rise into the air

levity *n, pl* -**ties** inclination to make a joke of serious matters

levy [**lev**-vee] *v* **levying, levied 1** impose and collect (a tax) **2** raise (troops) ▷ *n, pl* **levies 3** imposition or collection of taxes **4** enrolling of troops **5** amount or number levied

lewd *adj* lustful or indecent **lewdly** *adv* **lewdness** *n*

lexicon *n* **1** dictionary **2** vocabulary of a language **lexical** *adj* relating to the vocabulary of a language **lexicographer** *n* writer of dictionaries **lexicography** *n*

LGBT lesbian, gay, bisexual, and transgender

liable *adj* **1** legally obliged or responsible **2** given to or at risk from a condition **liability** *n* **1** state of being liable **2** financial obligation **3** hindrance or disadvantage

liaise *v* establish and maintain communication (with) **liaison** *n* **1** communication and cooperation between groups **2** secret or adulterous relationship

liana *n* climbing plant in tropical forests

liar *n* person who tells lies

lib *n informal* short for **liberation**

libation [lie-**bay**-shun] *n* drink poured as an offering to the gods

libel *n* **1** published statement falsely damaging a person's reputation ▷ *v* -**belling,** -**belled 2** defame falsely **libellous** *adj* defamatory

liberal *adj* **1** having political views that favour progress and reform **2** generous in behaviour or temperament **3** tolerant **4** abundant **5** (of education) designed to develop general cultural interests ▷ *n* **6** person who has liberal ideas or opinions **liberally** *adv* **liberalism** *n* belief in democratic reforms and individual freedom **liberality** *n* generosity **liberalize** *v* make (laws, a country, etc.) less restrictive **liberalization** *n* **Liberal Party** major political party with viewpoints between those of the Progressive Conservative Party and the New Democratic Party

liberate *v* set free **liberation** *n* **liberator** *n*

libertarian *n* **1** believer in freedom of thought and action ▷ *adj* **2** having such a belief

libertine [**lib**-er-teen] *n* morally dissolute person

liberty *n, pl* -**ties 1** freedom **2** act or comment regarded as forward or socially unacceptable **at liberty 1** free **2** having the right **take liberties** be presumptuous

libido [lib-**ee**-doe] *n, pl* -**dos 1** life force **2** emotional drive, esp. of sexual origin **libidinous** *adj* lustful

library *n, pl* -**braries 1** room or building where books are kept **2** collection of books, records, etc. for consultation or borrowing **librarian** *n* keeper of or worker in a library **librarianship** *n*

libretto *n, pl* -**tos,** -**ti** words of an opera **librettist** *n*

Librium *n* ® drug used as a tranquillizer

lice *n* a plural of **louse**

licence *n* **1** document giving official permission to do something **2** formal permission **3** excessive liberty **4** disregard of conventions for effect: *poetic licence* **licence number** numbers and letters displayed on a vehicle to identify it **licence plate** plate mounted on front and back of motor vehicle showing the licence number **license** *v* grant a licence to **licensed** *adj* **licensee** *n* holder of a licence, esp. to sell alcohol

licentiate *n* person licensed as competent to practise a profession

licentious *adj* sexually immoral, dissolute **licentiously** *adv*

lichen *n* small flowerless plant forming a crust on rocks, trees, etc.

licit *adj* lawful, permitted

lick *v* **1** pass the tongue over **2** touch lightly or flicker round **3** *slang* defeat ▷ *n* **4** licking **5** small amount (of paint etc.) **6** *informal* fast pace

licorice *n* same as **liquorice**

lid *n* **1** movable cover **2** short for **eyelid**

lie¹ *v* **lying, lied 1** make a deliberately false statement ▷ *n* **2** deliberate falsehood **white lie** untruth said without evil intent

lie² *v* **lying, lay, lain 1** place oneself or be in a horizontal position **2** be situated **3** be or remain in a certain state or position **4** exist or be found ▷ *n* **5** way something lies **lie-down** *n* rest **lie in** *v* remain in bed late into the morning **lie-in** *n* long stay in bed in the morning

lied [leed] *n*, *pl* **lieder** *music* setting for voice and piano of a romantic poem

lief *adv obsolete* gladly, willingly

liege [leej] *n* **1** lord **2** vassal or subject ▷ *adj* **3** bound to give or receive feudal service **4** faithful

lien *n* right to hold another's property until a debt is paid

lieu [lyew] *n* **in lieu of** instead of

lieutenant [lef-ten-ant] *n* **1** junior officer in the army or navy **2** main assistant **lieutenant governor** representative of the Crown in a province

life *n*, *pl* **lives 1** state of living beings, characterized by growth, reproduction, and response to stimuli **2** period between birth and death or between birth and the present time **3** amount of time something is active or functions **4** way of living **5** biography **6** liveliness or high spirits **7** living beings collectively **lifeless** *adj* **1** dead **2** inert **3** dull **lifelike** *adj* **lifelong** *adj* lasting all of a person's life **life belt** *or* **life jacket** buoyant device to keep afloat a person in danger of drowning **life cycle** series of changes undergone by each generation of an animal or plant **lifeline** *n* **1** means of contact or support **2** rope used in rescuing a person in danger **life science** any science concerned with living

organisms, such as biology, botany, or zoology **lifestyle** *n* particular attitudes, habits, etc. **life-support** *adj* (of equipment or treatment) necessary to keep a person alive **lifetime** *n* length of time a person is alive

lift *v* **1** move upwards in position, status, volume, etc. **2** revoke or cancel **3** take (plants) out of the ground for harvesting **4** disappear **5** make or become more cheerful ▷ *n* **6** lifting **7** *Brit* elevator **8** ride in an automobile etc. as a passenger **9** *informal* feeling of cheerfulness **liftoff** *n* moment a rocket leaves the ground

ligament *n* band of tissue joining bones

ligature *n* **1** link, bond, or tie **2** *printing* two or more joined letters

light¹ *n* **1** electromagnetic radiation by which things are visible **2** source of this, lamp **3** anything that lets in light, such as a window **4** mental vision **5** light part of a photograph etc. **6** means of setting fire to **7** understanding **lights 8** traffic lights ▷ *adj* **9** bright **10** (of a colour) pale ▷ *v* **lighting, lighted** *or* **lit 11** ignite **12** illuminate or cause to illuminate **lighten** *v* make less dark **lighting** *n* **1** apparatus for supplying artificial light **2** use of artificial light in theatres, films, etc. **light bulb** glass part of an electric lamp **lighthouse** *n* tower with a light to guide ships **light year** *astronomy* distance light travels in one year, about six million million miles

light² *adj* **1** not heavy, weighing relatively little

2 relatively low in strength, amount, density, etc. **3** not serious or profound **4** not clumsy **5** easily digested **6** carrying light arms or equipment **7** (of industry) producing small goods, using light machinery ▷ *adv* **8** with little equipment or luggage ▷ *v* **lighting, lighted** *or* **lit 9** (esp. of birds) settle after flight **10** come (upon) by chance **lightly** *adv* **lightness** *n* **lighten** *v* **1** make less heavy or burdensome **2** make more cheerful or lively **light-fingered** *adj* liable to steal **light-headed** *adj* **1** feeling faint, dizzy **2** frivolous **light-hearted** *adj* carefree **lightweight** *n, adj* **1** (person) of little importance ▷ *n* **2** boxer weighing up to 135lb (professional) or 60kg (amateur)

lighter[1] *n* device for lighting cigarettes etc.

lighter[2] *n* flat-bottomed boat for unloading ships

lightning *n* **1** visible discharge of electricity in the atmosphere ▷ *adj* **2** fast and sudden

lights *pl n* lungs of animals as animal food

ligneous *adj* of or like wood

lignite [**lig**-nite] *n* woody textured rock used as fuel

like[1] *adj* **1** resembling **2** similar **3** characteristic of ▷ *prep* **4** in the manner of **5** such as ▷ *adv* **6** in the manner of ▷ *pron* **7** similar thing **liken** *v* compare **likeness** *n* **1** resemblance **2** portrait **likewise** *adv* in a similar manner

like[2] *v* **1** find enjoyable **2** be fond of **3** prefer, choose, or wish **likeable** *or* **likable** *adj* **liking** *n* **1** fondness **2** preference

likely *adj* **1** probable **2** tending or inclined **3** hopeful, promising ▷ *adv* **4** probably **not likely** *informal* definitely not **likelihood** *n* probability

lilac *n* **1** shrub bearing pale mauve or white flowers ▷ *adj* **2** light purple

Lilliputian [lil-lip-**pew**-shun] *adj* tiny

lilt *n* **1** pleasing musical quality in speaking **2** jaunty rhythm **3** graceful rhythmic motion **lilting** *adj*

lily *n, pl* **lilies** plant which grows from a bulb and has large, often white, flowers

limb *n* **1** arm or leg **2** wing **3** main branch of a tree

limber *adj* pliant or supple **limber up** *v* loosen stiff muscles by exercising

limbo[1] *n, pl* **-bos 1** supposed region intermediate between Heaven and Hell for the unbaptized **2** unknown intermediate place or state

limbo[2] *n, pl* **-bos** West Indian dance in which dancers lean backwards to pass under a bar

lime[1] calcium compound used as a fertilizer or in making cement **limelight** *n* glare of publicity **limestone** *n* sedimentary rock used in building

lime[2] *n* small green citrus fruit **lime-green** *adj* greenish-yellow

lime[3] *n* linden tree

limerick [**lim**-mer-ik] *n* nonsensical humorous verse of five lines

limey *n slang* British person

limit *n* **1** ultimate extent, degree, or amount of something **2** boundary or edge ▷ *v* **-iting, -ited 3** restrict or confine **limitation** *n* **limitless** *adj* **limited company** company whose shareholders' liability is restricted

limousine n large luxurious automobile

limp[1] adj without firmness or stiffness **limply** adv

limp[2] v 1 walk lamely ▷ n 2 limping gait

limpet n shellfish which sticks tightly to rocks

limpid adj 1 clear or transparent 2 easy to understand **limpidity** n

linchpin n 1 pin to hold a wheel on its axle 2 essential person or thing

linctus n, pl **-tuses** syrupy cough medicine

linden n large deciduous tree with heart-shaped leaves and fragrant yellowish flowers, the lime

line n 1 long narrow mark 2 indented mark or wrinkle 3 continuous length without breadth 4 row of words 5 queue of people 6 boundary or limit 7 mark on a sports ground showing divisions of a field or track 8 string or wire for a particular use 9 telephone connection 10 wire or cable for transmitting electricity 11 shipping company 12 railway track 13 course or direction of movement 14 class of goods 15 prescribed way of thinking 16 field of interest or activity 17 ancestors collectively **lines** 18 words of a theatrical part 19 school punishment of writing out a sentence a specified number of times 20 protected boundary of an area occupied by an army ▷ v 21 mark with lines 22 bring into line 23 be or form a border or edge 24 give a lining to 25 cover the inside of **in line for** candidate for **in line**

with in accordance with **line dancing** form of dancing performed by rows of people to country and western music **line drive** baseball ball hit hard and travelling low above the ground **line-up** n people or things assembled for a particular purpose

lineage [lin-ee-ij] n descent from or descendants of an ancestor **lineal** adj in direct line of descent

lineament n facial feature

linear [lin-ee-er] adj of or in lines

lineman n, pl **-men** 1 football player who lines up in the row closest to the line of scrimmage 2 person who maintains railway, electricity, or telephone lines

linen n 1 cloth or thread made from flax 2 sheets, tablecloths, etc.

liner n 1 large passenger ship 2 something used as a lining

linesman n 1 (in some sports) official who helps the referee or umpire 2 hockey official who makes offside decisions, breaks up fights, etc.

ling n slender food fish

linger v 1 delay or prolong departure 2 continue in a weakened state for a long time before dying or disappearing 3 spend a long time doing something **lingering** adj

lingerie [lan-zher-ee] n women's underwear or nightwear

lingo n, pl **-goes** informal foreign or unfamiliar language or jargon

lingua franca n, pl **lingua francas, linguae francae** language used for communication between people of different mother tongues

lingual *adj* **1** of the tongue **2** made by the tongue

linguist *n* **1** person skilled in foreign languages **2** person who studies linguistics **linguistic** *adj* **1** of languages **2** of linguistics **linguistics** *pl n* scientific study of language

liniment *n* medicated liquid rubbed on the skin to relieve pain or stiffness

lining *n* **1** layer of cloth attached to the inside of a garment etc. **2** inner covering of anything

link *n* **1** any of the rings forming a chain **2** person or thing forming a connection ▷ *v* **3** connect with or as if with links **4** connect by association **linkage** *n* **link-up** *n* joining together of two systems or groups

links *pl n* golf course, esp. one by the sea

linnet *n* songbird of the finch family

lino *n* short for **linoleum**

linocut *n* **1** design cut in relief on a block of linoleum **2** print from such a block

linoleum *n* floor covering of hessian or jute with a smooth decorative coating of powdered cork

Linotype *n* ® typesetting machine which casts lines of words in one piece

linseed *n* seed of the flax plant

lint *n* soft material for dressing a wound

lintel *n* horizontal beam at the top of a door or window

lion *n* large animal of the cat family, the male of which has a shaggy mane **lioness** *n fem* **the lion's share** the biggest part **lionize** *v* treat as a celebrity **lion-hearted** *adj* brave

lip *n* **1** either of the fleshy edges of the mouth **2** rim of a jug etc. **3** *slang* impudence

lip-reading *n* method of understanding speech by interpreting lip movements **lip service** insincere tribute or respect **lipstick** *n* cosmetic in stick form, for colouring the lips

liquefy *v* **-fying, -fied** make or become liquid **liquefaction** *n*

liqueur [lik-**cure**] *n* flavoured and sweetened alcoholic spirit

liquid *n* **1** substance in a physical state which can change shape but not size ▷ *adj* **2** of or being a liquid **3** flowing smoothly **4** (of assets) in the form of money or easily converted into money **liquidize** *v* make or become liquid **liquidity** *n* state of being able to meet financial obligations

liquidate *v* **1** pay (a debt) **2** dissolve a company and share its assets between creditors **3** wipe out or kill **liquidation** *n* **liquidator** *n* official appointed to liquidate a business

liquor *n* **1** alcoholic drink, esp. spirits **2** liquid in which food has been cooked

liquorice [lik-ker-iss] *n* black substance used in medicine and as candy

lira *n, pl* **-re, -ras** monetary unit of Turkey

lisle [rhymes with **mile**] *n* strong fine cotton thread or fabric

lisp *n* **1** speech defect in which 's' and 'z' are pronounced 'th' ▷ *v* **2** speak or utter with a lisp

lissom, lissome *adj* supple, agile

list¹ *n* **1** item-by-item record of names or things, usu. written one below another ▷ *v* **2** make a list of **3** include in a list

list² v **1** (of a ship) lean to one side ▷ n **2** leaning to one side

listen v **1** concentrate on hearing something **2** heed or pay attention to **listener** n **listen in** v listen secretly, eavesdrop

listeriosis n dangerous form of food poisoning

listless adj lacking interest or energy **listlessly** adv

lit v a past of **light¹**, **light²**

litany n, pl -**nies 1** prayer with responses from the congregation **2** any tedious recital

literacy n ability to read and write

literal adj **1** according to the explicit meaning of a word or text, not figurative **2** (of a translation) word for word **3** actual, true **literally** adv

literary adj **1** of or learned in literature **2** (of a word) formal, not colloquial **literariness** n

literate adj **1** able to read and write **2** educated **literati** pl n literary people

literature n **1** written works such as novels, plays, and poetry **2** books and writings of a country, period, or subject

lithe adj flexible or supple, pliant

lithium n chemical element, the lightest known metal

litho n, pl -**thos 1** short for **lithograph** ▷ adj **2** short for **lithographic**

lithography [lith-**og**-ra-fee] n method of printing from a metal or stone surface in which the printing areas are made receptive to ink **lithograph** n **1** print made by lithography ▷ v **2** reproduce by lithography **lithographer** n **lithographic** adj

litigate v **1** bring or contest a law suit **2** engage in legal action **litigant** n person

involved in a lawsuit **litigation** n lawsuit **litigious** [lit-**ij**-uss] adj **1** frequently going to law **2** argumentative

litmus n blue dye turned red by acids and restored to blue by alkali **litmus paper** paper impregnated with litmus **litmus test** something which is regarded as a simple and accurate test of a particular thing

litotes n ironical understatement for rhetorical effect

litre n unit of liquid measure equal to 1.76 pints

litter n **1** untidy rubbish dropped in public places **2** group of young animals produced at one birth **3** straw etc. as bedding for an animal **4** dry material to absorb a cat's excrement ▷ v **5** strew with litter **6** scatter or be scattered about untidily **7** give birth to young

little adj **1** small or smaller than average **2** young ▷ n **3** small amount, extent, or duration ▷ adv **4** not a lot **5** hardly **6** not much or often **Little League** baseball league for children

littoral adj **1** of or by the seashore ▷ n **2** coastal district

liturgy n, pl -**gies** prescribed form of public worship **liturgical** adj

live¹ v **1** be alive **2** remain in life or existence **3** exist in a specified way: *we live well* **4** reside **5** continue or last **6** subsist **7** enjoy life to the full **live down** v wait till people forget a past mistake or misdeed **live-in** adj sharing a house with one's sexual partner **live together** v (of an unmarried couple) share a house and have a sexual relationship **live up to** v meet (expectations) **live with** v tolerate

live² adj **1** living, alive **2** (of a broadcast) transmitted during the actual performance **3** (of a performance) done in front of an audience **4** (of a wire, circuit, etc.) carrying an electric current **5** current **6** glowing or burning **7** capable of exploding ▷ adv **8** in the form of a live performance **lively** adj **1** full of life or vigour **2** animated **3** vivid **liveliness** n **liven up** v make (more) lively

livelihood n occupation or employment

livelong [liv-long] adj lit long

liver n **1** organ secreting bile **2** animal liver as food **liverish** adj **1** unwell **2** touchy or irritable

livery n, pl **-eries** distinctive dress, esp. of a servant or servants **liveried** adj **livery stable** stable where horses are kept at a charge or hired out

livestock n farm animals

livid adj **1** informal angry or furious **2** bluish-grey

living adj **1** possessing life, not dead or inanimate **2** currently in use or existing **3** of everyday life: living conditions ▷ n **4** condition of being alive **5** manner of life **6** financial means **7** church benefice **living room** room in a house used for relaxation and entertainment

lizard n four-footed reptile with a long body and tail

llama n woolly animal of the camel family used as a beast of burden in S America

LLB Bachelor of Laws

loach n carplike freshwater fish

load n **1** burden or weight **2** amount carried **3** amount of electrical energy drawn from a source **4** source of worry **loads 5** informal lots ▷ v **6** put a load on or into **7** burden or oppress **8** cause to be biased **9** put ammunition into a weapon **10** put film into a camera **11** transfer (a program) into computer memory **loaded** adj **1** (of a question) containing a hidden trap or implication **2** slang wealthy **3** (of dice) dishonestly weighted

loadstar n same as **lodestar**

loaf¹ n, pl **loaves 1** shaped mass of baked bread **2** shaped mass of food **3** slang common sense: use your loaf

loaf² v idle, loiter **loafer** n

loam n fertile soil

loan n **1** money borrowed at interest **2** lending **3** thing lent ▷ v **4** lend, grant a loan of **loan shark** person who lends money at an extremely high interest rate

loath, loth [rhymes with **both**] adj unwilling or reluctant (to)

loathe v hate, be disgusted by **loathing** n **loathsome** adj

lob sports ▷ n **1** ball struck or thrown high in the air ▷ v **lobbing, lobbed 2** strike or throw (a ball) high in the air

lobby n, pl **-bies 1** corridor into which rooms open **2** group which tries to influence legislators **3** hall in a legislative building to which the public has access ▷ v **-bying, -bied 4** try to influence (legislators) in the formulation of policy **lobbyist** n

lobe n **1** rounded projection **2** soft hanging part of the ear **3** subdivision of a body organ **lobed** adj **lobar** [loh-ber] adj of or affecting a lobe

lobelia n garden plant with

blue, red, or white lobed flowers

lobotomy *n, pl* **-mies** surgical incision into a lobe of the brain

lobster *n* shellfish with a long tail and claws, which turns red when boiled **lobster pot** basket-like trap for catching lobsters

local *adj* **1** of or existing in a particular place **2** confined to a particular place ▷ *n* **3** person belonging to a particular district **4** *Brit informal* nearby pub **locally** *adv* **locality** *n* neighbourhood or area **localize** *v* restrict to a definite place **locale** [loh-**kahl**] *n* scene of an event **local anesthetic** anesthetic which produces insensibility in one part of the body **local authority** governing body of a county or district **local government** government of towns, counties, and districts by locally elected political bodies

locate *v* **1** discover the whereabouts of **2** situate or place **location** *n* **1** site or position **2** site of a film production away from the studio

loch *n Scot* **1** lake **2** long narrow bay

lock¹ *n* **1** appliance for fastening a door, case, etc. **2** section of a canal shut off by gates between which the water level can be altered to aid boats moving from one level to another **3** extent to which a vehicle's front wheels will turn **4** interlocking of parts **5** mechanism for firing a gun **6** wrestling hold ▷ *v* **7** fasten or become fastened securely **8** become or cause to become immovable **9** become or cause to become

fixed or united **10** embrace closely **lockdown** *n US & Canad* security measure in which people are temporarily confined to a building

lockout *n* exclusion of workers by an employer as a means of coercion **locksmith** *n* person who makes and mends locks **lockstep** *n* standard procedure that is closely, often mindlessly, followed **lockup** *n* **1** prison **2** garage or storage place away from the main premises

lock² *n* tress of hair

locker *n* small cupboard with a lock

locket *n* small hinged pendant for a portrait etc.

lockjaw *n* tetanus

locomotive *n* **1** self-propelled engine for pulling trains ▷ *adj* **2** of locomotion **locomotion** *n* action or power of moving

locum *n* temporary stand-in for a doctor or clergyman

locus *n, pl* **loci 1** area or place where something happens **2** *math* set of points or lines satisfying one or more specified conditions

locust *n* destructive African insect that flies in swarms and eats crops

locution *n* word or phrase

lode *n* vein of ore **lodestar** *n* Pole Star **lodestone** *n* magnetic iron ore

lodge *n* **1** house or cabin used occasionally by hunters, skiers, etc. **2** gatekeeper's house **3** porters' room in a university or college **4** local branch of some societies ▷ *v* **5** live in another's house at a fixed charge **6** stick or become stuck (in a place) **7** deposit for safety or storage **8** make (a complaint etc.) formally **lodger** *n* **lodgings** *pl n* rented room or rooms in another person's house

loft *n* **1** space between the top storey and roof of a building **2** gallery in a church etc. ▷ *v* **3** *sports* strike, throw, or kick (a ball) high into the air

lofty *adj* **loftier**, **loftiest** **1** of great height **2** exalted or noble **3** haughty **loftily** *adv* haughtily **loftiness** *n*

log¹ *n* **1** portion of a felled tree stripped of branches **2** detailed record of a journey of a ship, aircraft, etc. ▷ *v* **logging**, **logged 3** record in a log **4** saw logs from a tree **logging** *n* work of cutting and transporting logs **logbook** *n* **log in** *or* **log out** *v* gain entrance to or leave a computer system by keying in a special command

log² *n* short for **logarithm**

loganberry *n* purplish-red fruit, a cross between a raspberry and a blackberry

logarithm *n* one of a series of arithmetical functions used to make certain calculations easier **logarithmic** *adj*

loggerheads *pl n* **at loggerheads** quarrelling, disputing

loggia [**loj**-ya] *n* covered gallery at the side of a building

logic *n* **1** philosophy of reasoning **2** reasoned thought or argument **logical** *adj* **1** of logic **2** reasonable **3** capable of or using clear valid reasoning **logically** *adv* **logician** *n*

logistics *pl n* detailed planning and organization of a large, esp. military, operation **logistical** *adj*

logo [**loh**-go] *n, pl* **-os** company emblem or similar device

loin *n* **1** part of the body between the ribs and the hips **2** cut of meat from this part

of an animal **loins 3** hips and inner thighs **loincloth** *n* piece of cloth covering the loins only

loiter *v* stand or wait aimlessly or idly **loiterer** *n*

loll *v* **1** lounge lazily **2** (esp. of the tongue) hang out

lollipop *n* boiled candy on a small wooden stick

lolly *n, pl* **-ies 1** *Brit informal* lollipop or ice lolly **2** *Brit slang* money

lone *adj* solitary **lonely** *adj* **1** sad because alone **2** unfrequented **3** resulting from being alone **loneliness** *n* **loner** *n informal* person who prefers to be alone **lonesome** *adj* lonely

long¹ *adj* **1** having length, esp. great length, in space or time ▷ *adv* **2** for a long time **long-distance** *adj* going between places far apart **long-drawn-out** *adj* lasting too long **long face** glum expression **longhand** *n* ordinary writing, not shorthand or typing **long johns** *informal* long underpants **long-life** *adj* (of milk, batteries, etc.) lasting longer than the regular kind **long-lived** *adj* living or lasting for a long time **long-range** *adj* **1** (of weapons) designed to hit a distant target **2** into the future **long shot** competitor, undertaking, or bet with little chance of success **long-standing** *adj* existing for a long time **long-suffering** *adj* enduring trouble or unhappiness without complaint **long-term** *adj* lasting or effective for a long time **long wave** radio wave with a wavelength of over 1000 metres **long-winded** *adj* speaking or writing at tedious length

long² *v* (foll. by *for*) have a

strong desire for **longing** n
yearning **longingly** adv
longevity [lon-**jev**-it-ee] n
long existence or life
longitude n distance east
or west from a standard
meridian **longitudinal**
adj **1** of length or longitude
2 lengthwise
longshoreman n docker
loo n Brit informal lavatory
loofah n dried pod of a gourd,
used as a sponge
look v **1** direct the eyes or
attention (towards) **2** seem
3 face in a particular direction
4 search (for) **5** hope (for) ▷ n
6 looking **7** search **8** often
pl appearance **look after**
v take care of **lookalike** n
person who is the double of
another **look down on** v treat
as inferior or unimportant
look forward to v anticipate
with pleasure **look on** v **1** be
an onlooker **2** consider or
regard **lookout** n **1** guard
2 place for watching **3** chances
or prospect **4** informal worry
or concern **look out** v be
careful **look up** v **1** discover or
confirm by checking in a book
2 visit **3** improve **look up to**
v respect
loom[1] n machine for weaving
cloth
loom[2] v **1** appear dimly **2** seem
ominously close **3** assume
great importance
loon n N American diving
bird **loonie** or **loony** n informal
Canadian dollar coin
loony slang ▷ n, pl **loonies**
1 foolish or insane person
▷ adj **loonier, looniest**
2 foolish or insane **loony bin**
slang psychiatric hospital
loop n **1** rounded shape made
by a curved line or rope
crossing itself ▷ v **2** form a
loop **loop the loop** fly or be
flown in a complete vertical

circle **loophole** n means
of evading a rule without
breaking it
loose adj **1** not tight, fastened,
fixed, or tense **2** slack **3** vague
4 dissolute or promiscuous
▷ adv **5** in a loose manner ▷ v
6 free **7** unfasten **8** slacken
9 let fly (an arrow, bullet,
etc.) **at a loose end** bored,
with nothing to do **loosely**
adv **looseness** n **loosen** v
make loose **loosen up** v relax,
stop worrying **loose-leaf**
adj allowing the addition or
removal of pages
loot n, v plunder **looter** n
looting n
lop v **lopping, lopped 1** cut
away twigs and branches
2 chop off
lope v run with long easy
strides
lop-eared adj having
drooping ears
lopsided adj greater in height,
weight, or size on one side
loquacious adj talkative
loquacity n
lord n **1** person with power over
others, such as a monarch or
master **2** male member of the
nobility **3** hist feudal superior
4 Lord God **5 Lord** title given
to certain male officials
and peers **House of Lords**
unelected upper chamber
of the British parliament
lord it over act in a superior
manner towards **the Lord's
Prayer** prayer taught by
Christ to his disciples
lordly adj imperious, proud
Lordship n title of some male
officials and peers
lore n body of traditions on a
subject
lorgnette [lor-**nyet**] n pair of
spectacles mounted on a long
handle
lorry n Brit truck
lose v **losing, lost 1** come to

be without, as by accident or carelessness **2** fail to keep or maintain **3** be deprived of **4** fail to get or make use of **5** have an income less than one's expenditure **6** fail to perceive or understand **7** be defeated in a competition etc. **8** be or become engrossed: *lost in thought* **9** go astray or allow to go astray **10** die or be destroyed **11** (of a clock etc.) run slow (by a specified amount) **loser** *n*

loss *n* **1** losing **2** that which is lost **3** damage resulting from losing **at a loss 1** confused or bewildered **2** not earning enough to cover costs **loss leader** item sold at a loss to attract customers

lot *pron* **1** great number ▷ *n* **2** collection of people or things **3** large quantity **4** fate or destiny **5** item at auction **6** one of a set of objects drawn at random to make a selection or choice **lots 7** *informal* great numbers or quantities **a lot** *adv informal* a great deal

loth *adj* same as **loath**

lotion *n* medical or cosmetic liquid for use on the skin

lottery *n, pl* **-teries 1** method of raising funds by selling tickets that win prizes by chance **2** gamble

lotto *n* game of chance like bingo

lotus *n* **1** legendary plant whose fruit induces forgetfulness **2** Egyptian water lily

loud *adj* **1** relatively great in volume **2** capable of making much noise **3** insistent and emphatic **4** unpleasantly patterned or colourful **loudly** *adv* **loudness** *n* **loudspeaker** *n* instrument for converting electrical signals into sound

lough *n Irish* loch

lounge *n* **1** living room in a private house **2** area for waiting in an airport **3** more comfortable bar in a pub ▷ *v* **4** sit, lie, or stand in a relaxed manner **5** pass time idly **lounge suit** man's suit for daytime wear

lour *v* same as **lower**²

louse *n* **1** *pl* **lice** wingless parasitic insect **2** *pl* **louses** unpleasant person **lousy** *adj* *slang* **1** very bad or unpleasant **2** bad, inferior **3** unwell

lout *n* crude, oafish, or aggressive person **loutish** *adj*

louvre [**loo**-ver] *n* one of a set of parallel slats slanted to admit air but not rain **louvred** *adj*

love *n* **1** warm affection **2** sexual passion **3** wholehearted liking for something **4** beloved person **5** *tennis, squash, etc.* score of nothing ▷ *v* **6** have a great affection for **7** feel sexual passion for **8** enjoy (something) very much **fall in love** become in love **in love (with)** feeling a strong emotional (and sexual) attraction (for) **make love (to)** have sexual intercourse (with) **lovable** *adj* **loveless** *adj* **lovely** *adj* **1** very attractive **2** highly enjoyable **lover** *n* **loving** *adj* affectionate, tender **lovingly** *adv* **love affair** romantic or sexual relationship between two people who are not married to each other **lovebird** *n* small parrot **love life** person's romantic or sexual relationships **lovelorn** *adj* forsaken by or pining for a lover **lovemaking** *n*

low¹ *adj* **1** not tall, high, or elevated **2** of little or less than the usual amount, degree, quality, or cost **3** coarse or vulgar **4** dejected **5** ill **6** not loud **7** deep in pitch **8** (of a gear) providing a relatively low speed ▷ n **9** low position, level, or degree **10** area of low atmospheric pressure, depression ▷ adv **11** in or to a low position, level, or degree **lowly** adj modest, humble **lowliness** n **lowbrow** n, adj (person) with nonintellectual tastes and interests **Low Church** section of the Anglican Church stressing evangelical beliefs and practices **lowdown** n informal inside information **low-down** adj informal mean, shabby, or dishonest **low-key** adj subdued, restrained, not intense **lowland** n **1** low-lying country **lowlands 2 Lowlands** less mountainous parts of Scotland **low post** basketball area of the court beneath the opposing team's basket **low profile** position or attitude avoiding prominence or publicity **low-spirited** adj depressed

low² n **1** cry of cattle, moo ▷ v **2** moo

lower¹ v **1** cause or allow to move down **2** diminish or degrade **3** lessen ▷ adj **4** below one or more other things **5** smaller or reduced in amount or value **lower case** small, as distinct from capital, letters

lower², lour v (of the sky or weather) look gloomy or threatening **lowering** adj

loyal adj faithful to one's friends, country, or government **loyally** adv **loyalty** n **loyalist** n **loyalty card** swipe card issued by a supermarket or chain store to a customer, used to record credit points awarded for money spent in the store

lozenge n **1** medicated tablet held in the mouth until it dissolves **2** four-sided diamond-shaped figure

LP n record playing approximately 20–25 minutes each side

LSD lysergic acid diethylamide, a hallucinogenic drug

Lt Lieutenant

Ltd Limited (Liability)

lubricate [loo-brik-ate] v oil or grease to lessen friction **lubricant** n lubricating substance such as oil **lubrication** n

lubricious [loo-**brish**-uss] adj lit lewd

lucerne n fodder plant like clover, alfalfa

lucid adj **1** clear and easily understood **2** able to think clearly **3** bright and clear **lucidly** adv **lucidity** n

Lucifer n Satan

luck n **1** fortune, good or bad **2** good fortune **3** chance **lucky** adj having good luck **luckily** adv fortunately **luckless** adj having bad luck

lucrative adj very profitable

lucre [loo-ker] n filthy lucre informal, (usu.) facetious money

Luddite n person opposed to change in industrial methods

ludicrous adj absurd or ridiculous **ludicrously** adv

lug¹ v **lugging, lugged** carry or drag with great effort

lug² n **1** projection serving as a handle **2** informal ear

luggage n traveller's cases, bags, etc.

lugger n working boat rigged with an oblong sail

lugubrious [loo-**goo**-bree-uss] adj mournful, gloomy **lugubriously** adv

lugworm n large worm used as bait

lukewarm adj **1** moderately

warm, tepid **2** indifferent or half-hearted

lull *n* **1** brief time of quiet in a storm etc. ▷ *v* **2** soothe (someone) by soft sounds or motions **3** calm (fears or suspicions) by deception

lullaby *n, pl* **-bies** quiet song to send a child to sleep

lumbago [lum-**bay**-go] *n* pain in the lower back **lumbar** *adj* relating to the lower back

lumber¹ *n* **1** useless disused articles, such as old furniture **2** sawn timber ▷ *v* **3** *informal* burden with something unpleasant **lumberjack** *n* man who fells trees and prepares logs for transport

lumber² *v* move heavily and awkwardly **lumbering** *adj*

luminous *adj* reflecting or giving off light **luminosity** *n* **luminary** *n* **1** famous person **2** *lit* heavenly body giving off light **luminescence** *n* emission of light at low temperatures by any process other than burning **luminescent** *adj*

lump¹ *n* **1** shapeless piece or mass **2** swelling **3** *informal* awkward or stupid person ▷ *v* **4** consider as a single group **lump in one's throat** tight dry feeling in one's throat, usu. caused by great emotion **lumpy** *adj* **lump sum** relatively large sum of money paid at one time

lump² *v* **lump it** *informal* tolerate or put up with it

lunar *adj* relating to the moon **lunar month** *or* **lunation** *n* time taken for the moon to go once round the earth, approx. 29½ days

lunatic *adj* **1** foolish and irresponsible ▷ *n* **2** foolish or annoying person **3** *old-fashioned* insane person **lunacy** *n*

lunch *n* **1** meal taken in the middle of the day ▷ *v* **2** eat lunch **luncheon** *n* formal lunch **luncheon meat** canned ground mixture of meat and cereal **luncheon voucher** voucher for a certain amount, given to an employee and accepted by some restaurants as payment for a meal

lung *n* organ that allows an animal or bird to breathe air: humans have two lungs in the chest

lunge *n* **1** sudden forward motion **2** thrust with a sword ▷ *v* **3** move with or make a lunge

lupin *n* garden plant with tall spikes of flowers

lupine *adj* like a wolf

lupus *n* ulcerous skin disease

lurch¹ *v* **1** tilt or lean suddenly to one side **2** stagger ▷ *n* **3** lurching movement

lurch² *n* **leave someone in the lurch** abandon someone in difficulties

lurcher *n* crossbred dog trained to hunt silently

lure *v* **1** tempt or attract by the promise of reward ▷ *n* **2** person or thing that lures **3** brightly coloured artificial angling bait

lurid *adj* **1** vivid in shocking detail, sensational **2** glaring in colour **luridly** *adv*

lurk *v* **1** lie hidden or move stealthily, esp. for sinister purposes **2** be latent

luscious [**lush**-uss] *adj* **1** extremely pleasurable to taste or smell **2** very attractive

lush¹ *adj* **1** (of grass etc.) growing thickly and healthily **2** opulent **lushly** *adv* **lushness** *n*

lush² *n* *slang* alcoholic

lust *n* **1** strong sexual desire **2** any strong desire ▷ *v*

3 have passionate desire (for) **lustful** adj **lusty** adj vigorous, healthy **lustily** adv

lustre n **1** gloss, sheen **2** splendour or glory **3** metallic pottery glaze **lustrous** adj shining, luminous

lute n ancient guitar-like musical instrument with a body shaped like a half pear **lutenist** n person who plays a lute

Lutheran adj of Martin Luther (1483–1546), German Reformation leader, his doctrines, or a Church following these doctrines

lux n, pl **lux** unit of illumination

luxuriant adj **1** rich and abundant **2** very elaborate **luxuriantly** adv **luxuriance** n

luxuriate v **1** take self-indulgent pleasure (in) **2** flourish

luxury n, pl **-ries 1** enjoyment of rich, very comfortable living **2** enjoyable but not essential thing ▷ adj **3** of or providing luxury **luxurious** adj full of luxury, sumptuous **luxuriously** adv

lychee [lie-**chee**] n Chinese fruit with a whitish juicy pulp

Lycra n ® elastic fabric used for tight-fitting garments, such as swimming costumes

lye n water made alkaline with wood ashes etc., esp. as formerly used for washing

lying v present participle of **lie**[1] and **lie**[2] **lying-in** n old-fashioned period of confinement during childbirth

lymph n colourless bodily fluid consisting mainly of white blood cells **lymphatic** adj

lymphocyte n type of white blood cell

lynch v put to death without a trial

lynx n animal of the cat family with tufted ears and a short tail

lyre n ancient musical instrument like a U-shaped harp

lyric n **1** short poem expressing personal emotion in a songlike style **lyrics 2** words of a popular song ▷ adj **3** of such poems **4** in the style of a song **lyrical** adj **1** lyric **2** enthusiastic **lyricist** n person who writes the words of songs or musicals

Mm

m 1 metre(s) 2 mile(s)
3 minute(s)

M 1 Monsieur 2 Motorway

m. 1 male 2 married
3 masculine 4 meridian
5 month

ma *n informal* mother

MA Master of Arts

ma'am *n* madam

mac *n informal* mackintosh

macabre [mak-**kahb**-ra]
adj strange and horrible,
gruesome

macadam *n* road surface of
pressed layers of small broken
stones **macadamize** *v* pave a
road with macadam

macaroni *n* pasta in short
tubes

macaroon *n* small cookie
or cake made with ground
almonds

macaw *n* large tropical
American parrot

mace[1] *n* 1 ceremonial staff
of office 2 medieval weapon
with a spiked metal head

mace[2] *n* spice made from the
dried husk of the nutmeg

macerate [**mass**-a-
rate] *v* soften by soaking
maceration *n*

machete [mash-**ett**-ee] *n*
broad heavy knife used for
cutting or as a weapon

Machiavellian [mak-ya-**vel**-
ee-yan] *adj* unprincipled,
crafty, and opportunist

machinations [mak-in-**nay**-
shunz] *pl n* cunning plots and
ploys

machine *n* 1 apparatus,
usu. powered by electricity,
designed to perform a
particular task 2 vehicle, such
as an automobile or aircraft
3 controlling system of an
organization ▷ *v* 4 make
or produce by machine

machinery *n* machines or
machine parts collectively

machinist *n* person who
operates a machine **machine
gun** automatic gun that fires
rapidly and continuously
machine-gun *v* fire at
with such a gun **machine-
readable** *adj* (of data) in a
form suitable for processing
by a computer

machismo [mak-**izz**-mow]
n strong or exaggerated
masculinity

Mach number [**mak**] *n*
ratio of the speed of a body
in a particular medium to
the speed of sound in that
medium

macho [**match**-oh] *adj*
strongly or exaggeratedly
masculine

mackerel *n* edible sea fish
with blue and silver stripes

mackinaw coat *n* thick, short
plaid coat

mackintosh *n* 1 waterproof
raincoat of rubberized cloth
2 any raincoat

macramé [mak-**rah**-mee] *n*
ornamental work of knotted
cord

macrobiotics *n* dietary
system advocating whole
grains and vegetables grown

without chemical additives **macrobiotic** *adj*

macrocosm *n* **1** the universe **2** any large complete system

mad *adj* **madder, maddest** **1** mentally deranged, insane **2** very foolish **3** (foll. by *about* or *on*) very enthusiastic (about) **4** frantic **5** *informal* angry **like mad** *informal* with great energy, enthusiasm, or haste **madly** *adv* **madness** *n* **madden** *v* infuriate or irritate **maddening** *adj* **madman** (**madwoman**) *n*

madam *n* **1** polite form of address to a woman **2** *informal* spoilt or conceited girl

madame [mad-**dam**] *n*, *pl* **mesdames** [may-**dam**] French title equivalent to *Mrs*

madcap *adj*, *n* reckless (person)

madder *n* **1** climbing plant **2** red dye made from its root

made *v* past of **make**

Madeira [mad-**deer**-a] *n* fortified white wine **Madeira cake** rich sponge cake

mademoiselle [mad-mwah-zel] *n*, *pl* **mesdemoiselles** [maid-mwah-**zel**] French title equivalent to *Miss*

Madonna *n* **1** the Virgin Mary **2** picture or statue of her

madrigal *n* 16th–17th century part song for unaccompanied voices

maelstrom [**male**-strom] *n* **1** great whirlpool **2** turmoil

maestro [**my**-stroh] *n*, *pl* **-tri, -tros** **1** outstanding musician or conductor **2** any master of an art

Mafia *n* international secret criminal organization founded in Sicily **mafioso** *n* member of the Mafia

magazine *n* **1** periodical publication with articles by different writers **2** television or radio programme made up

of short nonfictional items **3** appliance for automatically supplying cartridges to a gun or slides to a projector **4** storehouse for explosives or arms

magenta [maj-**jen**-ta] *adj* deep purplish-red

maggot *n* larva of an insect, esp. the blowfly **maggoty** *adj*

Magi [**maje**-eye] *pl n* wise men from the East at the Nativity

magic *n* **1** supposed art of invoking supernatural powers to influence events **2** mysterious quality or power ▷ *adj* **3** Also **magical** of, using, or like magic **magically** *adv* **magician** *n* **1** conjurer **2** person with magic powers

magistrate *n* **1** public officer administering the law **2** justice of the peace **magisterial** *adj* **1** commanding or authoritative **2** of a magistrate

magma *n* molten rock inside the earth's crust

magnanimous *adj* noble and generous **magnanimously** *adv* **magnanimity** *n*

magnate *n* influential or wealthy person, esp. in industry

magnesium *n* silvery-white metallic element **magnesia** *n* compound of magnesium used in medicine

magnet *n* piece of iron or steel capable of attracting iron and pointing north when suspended **magnetic** *adj* **1** having the properties of a magnet **2** powerfully attractive **magnetic tape** plastic strip coated with a magnetic substance for recording sound or video signals **magnetically** *adv* **magnetism** *n* **1** magnetic property **2** science of this

3 powerful personal charm
magnetize v **1** make into a magnet **2** attract strongly **magnetization** n
magneto [mag-**nee**-toe] n, pl **-tos** apparatus for ignition in an internal-combustion engine
magnificent adj **1** splendid or impressive **2** excellent **magnificently** adv **magnificence** n
magnify v **-fying, -fied 1** increase in apparent size, as with a lens **2** exaggerate **magnification** n
magniloquent adj speaking pompously **magniloquence** n
magnitude n **1** relative importance **2** relative size or extent
magnolia n shrub or tree with showy white or pink flowers
magnum n large wine bottle holding about 1.5 litres
magpie n black-and-white bird
Magyar n **1** member of the main ethnic group in Hungary **2** Hungarian language ▷ adj **3** of the Magyars or their language
maharajah n former title of some Indian princes **maharanee** n fem
maharishi n Hindu religious teacher or mystic
mahatma n Hinduism person revered for holiness and wisdom
mahjong, mahjongg n Chinese table game for four, played with tiles bearing different designs
mahogany n, pl **-nies** hard reddish-brown wood of several tropical trees
mahout [ma-**howt**] n elephant driver or keeper
maid n **1** Also **maidservant** female servant **2** lit young unmarried woman

maiden n **1** lit young unmarried woman ▷ adj **2** unmarried **3** first: maiden voyage **maidenly** adj modest **maidenhood** n **maidenhair** n fern with delicate fronds **maidenhead** n virginity **maiden name** woman's surname before marriage
mail[1] n **1** letters and packages transported and delivered by the post office **2** postal system **3** single collection or delivery of mail **4** train, ship, or aircraft carrying mail ▷ v **5** send by post **mailbox** n **1** public box into which letters are put for collection and delivery **2** private box outside house where occupant's mail is delivered **3** (on a computer) the directory in which e-mail messages are stored **mail drop** receptacle or chute for mail **mailman** n person who collects or delivers mail **mail order** system of buying goods by post
mail[2] n flexible armour of interlaced rings or links **mailed** adj
maim v cripple or mutilate
main adj **1** chief or principal ▷ n **2** principal pipe or line carrying water, gas, or electricity **in the main** on the whole **mainly** adv for the most part, chiefly **mainframe** n, adj computers (denoting) a high-speed general-purpose computer **mainland** n stretch of land which forms the main part of a country **mainmast** n chief mast in a ship **mainsail** n largest sail on a mainmast **mainspring** n **1** chief spring of a watch or clock **2** chief cause or motive **mainstay** n **1** chief support **2** rope securing a mainmast **mainstream** n prevailing cultural trend
maintain v **1** continue or keep in existence **2** keep up or

m

preserve **3** support financially **4** assert **maintenance** n **1** maintaining **2** upkeep of a building, automobile, etc. **3** provision of money for a separated or divorced spouse

maître d'hôtel [met-ra dote-**tell**] n French head waiter

maize n type of corn with spikes of yellow grains

majesty n, pl -**ties 1** stateliness or grandeur **2** supreme power **majestic** adj **majestically** adv

major adj **1** greater in number, quality, or extent **2** significant or serious ▷ n **3** middle-ranking army officer **4** scale in music **5** principal field of study at a university etc. ▷ v **6** (foll. by in) do one's principal study in (a particular subject) **major-domo** n chief steward of a great household **major junior** hockey highest level in junior amateur competition **major penalty** hockey penalty in which a player is sent off for five minutes

majority n, pl -**ties 1** greater number **2** largest party voting together **3** number by which the votes on one side exceed those on the other **4** full legal age

make v **making, made 1** create, construct, or establish **2** cause to do or be **3** bring about or produce **4** perform (an action) **5** amount to **6** earn **7** serve as or become ▷ n **8** brand, type, or style **make do** manage with an inferior alternative **make it** informal be successful **on the make** informal intent on gain **maker** n **making** n **1** creation or production **makings 2** necessary requirements or qualities **make-believe** n fantasy or pretence **make for** v head towards **make off with** v

steal or abduct **makeshift** adj serving as a temporary substitute **make up** v **1** form or constitute **2** prepare **3** invent **4** supply what is lacking, complete **5** (foll. by for) compensate (for) **6** settle a quarrel **7** apply cosmetics **make-up** n **1** cosmetics **2** mental or physical constitution **3** way something is made **makeweight** n something unimportant added to make up a lack

mal- combining form bad or badly: malformation; malfunction

malachite [mal-a-kite] n green mineral

maladjusted adj psychol unable to meet the demands of society **maladjustment** n

maladministration n inefficient or dishonest administration

maladroit [mal-a-**droyt**] adj clumsy or awkward

malady [**mal**-a-dee] n, pl -**dies** disease or illness

malaise [mal-**laze**] n vague feeling of illness or unease

malapropism n comical misuse of a word by confusion with one which sounds similar

malaria n infectious disease caused by the bite of some mosquitoes **malarial** adj

Malay n **1** member of a people of Malaysia or Indonesia **2** language of this people **Malayan** adj, n

malcontent n discontented person

male adj **1** of the sex which can fertilize female reproductive cells ▷ n **2** male person or animal

malediction [mal-lid-**dik**-shun] n curse

malefactor [**mal**-if-act-or] n criminal or wrongdoer

malevolent [mal-**lev**-alent] *adj* wishing evil to others **malevolently** *adv* **malevolence** *n*

malfeasance [mal-**fee**-zanss] *n* misconduct, esp. by a public official

malformed *adj* misshapen or deformed **malformation** *n*

malfunction *v* **1** function imperfectly or fail to function ▷ *n* **2** defective functioning or failure to function

malice [**mal**-iss] *n* desire to cause harm to others **malicious** *adj* **maliciously** *adv*

malign [mal-**line**] *v* **1** slander or defame ▷ *adj* **2** evil in influence or effect **malignity** *n* evil disposition

malignant [mal-**lig**-nant] *adj* **1** seeking to harm others **2** (of a tumour) harmful and uncontrollable **malignancy** *n*

malinger [mal-**ling**-ger] *v* feign illness to avoid work **malingerer** *n*

mall *n* street or shopping centre closed to vehicles

mallard *n* wild duck

malleable [**mal**-lee-a-bl] *adj* **1** capable of being hammered or pressed into shape **2** easily influenced **malleability** *n*

mallet *n* **1** (wooden) hammer **2** stick with a head like a hammer, used in croquet or polo

mallow *n* plant with pink or purple flowers

malmsey *n* kind of strong sweet wine

malnutrition *n* inadequate nutrition

malodorous [mal-**lode**-or-uss] *adj* bad-smelling

malpractice *n* immoral, illegal, or unethical professional conduct

malt *n* **1** grain, such as barley, prepared for use in making beer or whisky

maltreat *v* treat badly

maltreatment *n*

malware *n computers* program designed specifically to damage or disrupt a system, such as a virus

mama, mamma [mam-ma] *n old-fashioned* mother

mamba *n* deadly S African snake

mammal *n* animal of the type that suckles its young **mammalian** *adj*

mammary *adj* of the breasts or milk-producing glands

mammon *n* **1** wealth regarded as a source of evil **2 Mammon** wealth personified in the New Testament as a false god

mammoth *n* **1** extinct animal like an elephant ▷ *adj* **2** colossal

man *n, pl* **men 1** adult male **2** human being or person **3** mankind **4** manservant **5** piece used in chess etc. ▷ *v* **manning, manned 6** supply with sufficient people for operation or defence **manful** *adj* determined and brave **manfully** *adv* **manhood** *n* **mankind** *n* human beings collectively **manly** *adj* (possessing qualities) appropriate to a man **manliness** *n* **mannish** *adj* like a man **manhandle** *v* treat roughly **manhole** *n* hole with a cover, through which a person can enter a drain or sewer **man-hour** *n* work done by one person in one hour **man-made** *adj* synthetic **manpower** *n* available number of workers **manservant** *n* male servant, esp. a valet **manslaughter** *n* unlawful but unintentional killing of a person

Man. Manitoba

manacle [**man**-a-kl] *n, v* handcuff or fetter

manage *v* **1** succeed in

doing **2** be in charge of, administer **3** handle or control **4** cope with (financial) difficulties **manageable** adj **management** n **1** managers collectively **2** administration or organization **manager** (**manageress**) n person in charge of a business, institution, actor, sports team, etc. **managerial** adj

manatee n large tropical plant-eating aquatic mammal

mandarin n **1** high-ranking government official **2** kind of small orange

mandate n **1** official or authoritative command **2** authorization or instruction from an electorate to its representative or government ▷ v **3** give authority to **mandatory** adj compulsory

mandible n lower jawbone or jawlike part

mandolin n musical instrument with four pairs of strings

mandrake n plant with a forked root, formerly used as a narcotic

mandrel n shaft on which work is held in a lathe

mandrill n large blue-faced baboon

mane n long hair on the neck of a horse, lion, etc.

manganese n brittle greyish-white metallic element

mange n skin disease of domestic animals **mangy** adj **1** having mange **2** scruffy or shabby

mangelwurzel n Brit variety of beet used as cattle food

manger n eating trough in a stable or barn

mangetout [mawnzh-too] n Brit snow pea

mangle¹ v **1** destroy by crushing and twisting **2** spoil

mangle² n **1** machine with rollers for squeezing water from washed clothes ▷ v **2** put through a mangle

mango n, pl **-goes**, **-gos** tropical fruit with sweet juicy yellow flesh

mangrove n tropical tree with exposed roots, which grows beside water

mania n **1** madness **2** extreme enthusiasm **maniac** n **1** mad person **2** informal person who has an extreme enthusiasm for something **maniacal** [man-**eye**-a-kl], **manic** adj affected by mania

manicure n **1** cosmetic care of the fingernails and hands ▷ v **2** care for (the hands and fingernails) in this way **manicurist** n

manifest adj **1** easily noticed, obvious ▷ v **2** show plainly **3** be evidence of ▷ n **4** list of cargo or passengers for customs **manifestation** n

manifesto n, pl **-toes**, **-tos** declaration of policy as issued by a political party

manifold adj **1** numerous and varied ▷ n **2** pipe with several outlets, esp. in an internal-combustion engine

manikin n **1** little man or dwarf **2** model of the human body

manila, manilla n strong brown paper used for envelopes

manipulate v **1** handle skilfully **2** control cleverly or deviously **manipulation** n **manipulative** adj **manipulator** n

manitou, manito n spirit of good or evil among N American Indians

manna n **1** Bible miraculous food which sustained the Israelites in the wilderness **2** windfall

m

mannequin *n* **1** woman who models clothes at a fashion show **2** life-size dummy of the human body used to fit or display clothes

manner *n* **1** way a thing happens or is done **2** person's bearing or behaviour **3** type or kind **4** custom or style **manners 5** (polite) social behaviour **mannered** *adj* affected **mannerism** *n* person's distinctive habit or trait

mannikin *n* same as **manikin**

manoeuvre [man-**noo**-ver] *v* **1** move or do something with skill **2** manipulate a situation to gain some advantage **3** perform manoeuvres ▷ *n* **4** skilful movement **5** contrived, complicated, and possibly deceptive plan or action **manoeuvres 6** military or naval exercises **manoeuvrable** *adj*

manor *n* large country house and its lands **manorial** *adj*

manqué [**mong**-kay] *adj* would-be: *an actor manqué*

mansard roof *n* roof with a break in its slope, the lower part being steeper than the upper

manse *n* minister's house in some religious denominations

mansion *n* large house

mantel *n* structure round a fireplace **mantelpiece** *or* **mantel shelf** *n* shelf above a fireplace

mantilla *n* (in Spain) lace scarf covering a woman's head and shoulders

mantis *n, pl* **-tises, -tes** carnivorous insect like a grasshopper

mantle *n* **1** loose cloak **2** covering **3** responsibilities and duties that go with a particular job or position **4** incandescent gauze round a gas jet

mantra *n Hinduism, Buddhism* any sacred word or syllable used as an object of concentration

manual *adj* **1** of or done with the hands **2** by human labour rather than automatic means ▷ *n* **3** handbook **4** organ keyboard **manually** *adv*

manufacture *v* **1** process or make (goods) on a large scale using machinery **2** invent or concoct (an excuse etc.) ▷ *n* **3** process of manufacturing goods **manufacturer** *n*

manure *n* **1** animal excrement used as a fertilizer ▷ *v* **2** fertilize (land) with this

manuscript *n* **1** book or document, orig. one written by hand **2** copy for printing

Manx *adj* **1** of the Isle of Man or its inhabitants ▷ *n* **2** Manx language **Manx cat** tailless breed of cat

many *adj* **more, most 1** numerous ▷ *n* **2** large number

Maoism *n* form of Marxism advanced by Mao Tse-tung in China **Maoist** *n, adj*

Maori *n* **1** member of the indigenous race of New Zealand **2** Maori language ▷ *adj* **3** of the Maoris or their language

map *n* **1** representation of the earth's surface or some part of it, showing geographical features ▷ *v* **mapping, mapped 2** make a map of **map out** *v* plan

maple *n* tree with broad leaves, a variety of which yields sugar **maple syrup** syrup made from the sap of the sugar maple

mar *v* **marring, marred** spoil or impair

Mar. March

marabou n **1** kind of African stork **2** its soft white down, used to trim hats etc.

maraca [mar-**rak**-a] n shaken percussion instrument made from a gourd containing dried seeds etc.

maraschino cherry [mar-rass-**kee**-no] n cherry preserved in a cherry liqueur with a taste like bitter almonds

marathon n **1** long-distance race of just over 26 miles **2** long or arduous task

marauding adj **1** hunting for plunder **2** pillaging **marauder** n

marble n **1** kind of limestone with a mottled appearance, which can be highly polished **2** slab of or sculpture in this **3** small glass ball used in playing marbles **marbles** **4** game of rolling these **marbled** adj having a mottled appearance like marble

march¹ v **1** walk with a military step **2** make (a person or group) proceed **3** progress steadily ▷ n **4** action of marching **5** distance covered by marching **6** steady progress **7** piece of music, as for a march **marcher** n

march² n border or frontier

March n third month of the year

marchioness [marsh-on-**ness**] n **1** woman holding the rank of marquis **2** wife or widow of a marquis

mare n female horse **mare's nest 1** discovery which proves worthless **2** badly disordered situation or thing

margarine n butter substitute made from animal or vegetable fats

marge n informal margarine

margin n **1** edge or border **2** blank space round a printed page **3** additional amount or one greater than necessary **4** limit **marginal** adj **1** insignificant, unimportant **2** near a limit **3** (of a constituency) won by only a small margin ▷ n **4** marginal constituency **marginally** adv

marguerite n large daisy

marigold n plant with yellow flowers

marijuana [mar-ree-**wah**-na] n dried flowers and leaves of the hemp plant, used as a drug, esp. in cigarettes

marina n harbour for yachts and other pleasure boats

marinade n seasoned liquid in which fish or meat is soaked before cooking ▷ v Also **marinate** soak in marinade

marine adj **1** of the sea or shipping **2** used at or found in the sea ▷ n **3** soldier trained for land or sea combat **4** country's shipping or fleet **mariner** n sailor

marionette n puppet worked with strings

marital adj relating to marriage

maritime adj **1** relating to shipping **2** of, near, or living in the sea

marjoram n aromatic herb

mark¹ n **1** line, dot, scar, etc. visible on a surface **2** distinguishing sign or symbol **3** written or printed symbol **4** letter or number used to grade academic work **5** indication of position **6** indication of some quality **7** target or goal ▷ v **8** make a mark on **9** be a distinguishing mark of **10** indicate **11** pay attention to **12** notice or watch **13** grade (academic work) **14** stay close to (a sporting opponent) to hamper his play **marked** adj noticeable **markedly**

[**mark**-id-lee] adv **marker** n
mark² n same as
Deutschmark
market n 1 assembly or
place for buying and selling
2 demand for goods ▷ v
-**keting**, -**keted** 3 offer or
produce for sale **on the
market** for sale **marketable**
adj **marketing** n part of a
business that controls the
way that goods or services
are sold **market garden**
place where fruit and
vegetables are grown for
sale **marketing board** board
that regulates the price of
agricultural commodities
market maker Stock Exchange
person who uses a firm's
money to create a market
for a stock **marketplace** n
1 market 2 commercial world
market research research
into consumers' needs and
purchases
marksman n person skilled at
shooting **marksmanship** n
marl n soil formed of clay and
lime, used as fertilizer
marlinespike, marlinspike
n pointed hook used to
separate strands of rope
marmalade n jam made from
citrus fruits
marmoreal [mar-**more**-ee-al]
adj of or like marble
marmoset n small bushy-
tailed monkey
marmot n burrowing rodent
maroon¹ adj reddish-purple
maroon² v 1 abandon ashore,
esp. on an island 2 isolate
without resources
marquee n large tent used for
a party or exhibition
marquess [mar-kwiss] n
nobleman of the rank below
a duke
marquetry n, pl -**quetries**
ornamental inlaid work of
wood

marquis n, pl -**quises**,
-**quis** (in various countries)
nobleman of the rank above
a count
marram grass n grass that
grows on sandy shores
marrow n 1 fatty substance
inside bones 2 oblong green
striped vegetable
marry v -**rying**, -**ried** 1 take
as a husband or wife 2 join
or give in marriage 3 unite
closely **marriage** n 1 state
of being married 2 wedding
marriageable adj
Mars n 1 Roman god of war
2 fourth planet from the sun
Martian adj 1 of Mars ▷ n
2 supposed inhabitant of Mars
Marsala [mar-**sah**-la] n dark
sweet wine
marsh n low-lying wet land
marshy adj
marshal n 1 officer of the
highest rank 2 official who
organizes ceremonies or
events 3 US law officer ▷ v
-**shalling**, -**shalled** 4 arrange
in order 5 assemble 6 conduct
with ceremony **marshalling
yard** railway depot for goods
trains
marshmallow n spongy pink
or white candy
marsupial [mar-**soop**-ee-
yal] n animal that carries its
young in a pouch, such as a
kangaroo
mart n market
Martello tower n round
tower for coastal defence
marten n 1 weasel-like animal
2 its fur
martial adj of war, warlike
martial art any of various
philosophies and techniques
of self-defence, orig. Eastern,
such as karate **martial law**
law enforced by military
authorities in times of danger
or emergency
martin n bird with a

m

slightly forked tail

martinet *n* strict disciplinarian

martini *n* cocktail of vermouth and gin

martyr *n* 1 person who dies or suffers for his or her beliefs ▷ *v* 2 make a martyr of **be a martyr to** be constantly suffering from **martyrdom** *n*

marvel *v* **-velling, -velled** 1 be filled with wonder ▷ *n* 2 wonderful thing **marvellous** *adj* 1 excellent 2 causing great surprise

Marxism *n* socialism as conceived by Karl Marx **Marxist** *n, adj*

marzipan *n* paste of ground almonds, sugar, and egg whites

masc. masculine

mascara *n* cosmetic for darkening the eyelashes

mascot *n* thing supposed to bring good luck

masculine *adj* 1 relating to males 2 manly 3 *grammar* of the gender of nouns that includes some male animate things **masculinity** *n*

mash *n* 1 bran or meal mixed with warm water as food for horses etc. 2 *informal* mashed potatoes ▷ *v* 3 crush into a soft mass

mask *n* 1 covering for the face, as a disguise or protection 2 behaviour that hides one's true feelings ▷ *v* 3 cover with a mask 4 hide or disguise

masochism [**mass**-oh-kiz-zum] *n* form of (sexual) perversion marked by love of pain or of being humiliated **masochist** *n* **masochistic** *adj*

mason *n* 1 person who works with stone 2 **Mason** Freemason **Masonic** *adj* of Freemasonry **masonry** *n* 1 stonework 2 **Masonry** Freemasonry

masque [**mask**] *n hist* 16th–17th-century form of dramatic entertainment

masquerade [mask-a-**raid**] *n* 1 deceptive show or pretence 2 party at which masks and costumes are worn ▷ *v* 3 pretend to be someone or something else

mass *n* 1 coherent body of matter 2 large quantity or number 3 *physics* amount of matter in a body ▷ *adj* 4 large-scale 5 involving many people ▷ *v* 6 form into a mass **the masses** ordinary people **massive** *adj* large and heavy **mass-market** *adj* for or appealing to a large number of people **mass media** means of communication to many people, such as television and newspapers **mass-produce** *v* manufacture standardized goods in large quantities

Mass *n* service of the Eucharist, esp. in the RC Church

massacre [**mass**-a-ker] *n* 1 indiscriminate killing of large numbers of people ▷ *v* 2 kill in large numbers

massage [**mass**-ahzh] *n* 1 rubbing and kneading of parts of the body to reduce pain or stiffness ▷ *v* 2 give a massage to **masseur** [mass-**ur**], **masseuse** [mass-**urz**] *n* person who gives massages

massif [**mass**-seef] *n* connected group of mountains

mast[1] *n* tall pole for supporting something, esp. a ship's sails

mast[2] *n* fruit of the beech, oak, etc., used as pig fodder

mastectomy [mass-**tek**-tom-ee] *n, pl* **-mies** surgical removal of a breast

master *n* 1 person in control, such as an employer or an

owner of slaves or animals
2 expert **3** great artist
4 original thing from which
copies are made **5** male
teacher ▷ *adj* **6** overall
or controlling **7** main or
principal ▷ *v* **8** overcome
9 acquire knowledge of
or skill in **masterful** *adj*
1 domineering **2** showing
great skill **masterly** *adj*
showing great skill **mastery**
n **1** expertise **2** control or
command **master key** key
that opens all the locks of
a set **mastermind** *v* **1** plan
and direct (a complex task)
▷ *n* **2** person who plans
and directs a complex task
masterpiece *n* outstanding
work of art

mastic *n* **1** gum obtained from
certain trees **2** putty-like
substance used as a filler,
adhesive, or seal

masticate *v* chew
mastication *n*

mastiff *n* large dog

mastitis *n* inflammation of a
breast or udder

mastodon *n* extinct elephant-
like mammal

mastoid *n* projection of
the bone behind the ear
mastoiditis *n* inflammation
of this area

masturbate *v* caress the
genitals (of) **masturbation** *n*

mat *n* **1** piece of fabric used as
a floor covering or to protect a
surface ▷ *v* **matting, matted**
2 become tangled **on the
mat** *informal* summoned for a
reprimand

matador *n* man who kills the
bull in bullfights

match[1] *n* **1** contest in a game or
sport **2** person or thing exactly
like, equal to, or in harmony
with another **3** marriage ▷ *v*
4 be exactly like, equal to,
or in harmony with **5** put in

competition (with) **6** find a
match for **7** join (in marriage)
matchless *adj* unequalled
matchmaker *n* person who
schemes to bring about a
marriage **matchmaking** *n*

match[2] *n* small stick with a tip
which ignites when scraped
on a rough surface **matchbox**
n **matchstick** *n* **1** wooden part
of a match ▷ *adj* **2** (of drawn
figures) thin and straight
matchwood *n* small splinters

mate[1] *n* **1** sexual partner
of an animal **2** officer in a
merchant ship **3** tradesman's
assistant **4** *Brit informal* friend
or associate **5** *informal* common
Brit. and Aust. term of address
between males ▷ *v* **6** pair
(animals) or (of animals)
be paired for reproduction
matey *adj informal* friendly or
intimate

mate[2] *n, v chess* checkmate

material *n* **1** substance of
which a thing is made **2** cloth
3 information on which a
piece of work may be based
materials 4 things needed for
an activity ▷ *adj* **5** of matter or
substance **6** affecting physical
wellbeing **7** unspiritual
8 relevant **materially** *adv*
considerably **materialism** *n*
1 excessive interest in or desire
for money and possessions
2 belief that only the material
world exists **materialist**
adj, n **materialistic** *adj*
materialize *v* **1** come into
existence or view **2** actually
happen **materialization** *n*

maternal *adj* **1** of a mother
2 related through one's
mother **maternity** *n*
1 motherhood ▷ *adj* **2** of or for
pregnant women

math *n informal* mathematics

mathematics *n* science of
number, quantity, shape,
and space **mathematical**

adj **mathematically** *adv*
mathematician *n*

maths *n Brit informal*
mathematics

matinée [mat-in-nay] *n*
afternoon performance in a
theatre

matins *pl n* early morning
service in various Christian
churches

matriarch [mate-ree-ark]
n female head of a tribe or
family **matriarchal** *adj*
matriarchy *n* society with
matriarchal government and
descent traced through the
female line

matricide *n* 1 crime of killing
one's mother 2 person who
commits this crime

matriculate *v* enrol or
be enrolled in a college or
university **matriculation** *n*

matrimony *n* marriage
matrimonial *adj*

matrix [may-trix] *n, pl*
matrices [may-triss-eez]
1 substance or situation in
which something originates,
takes form, or is enclosed
2 mould for casting 3 *math*
rectangular array of numbers
or elements

matron *n* 1 staid or dignified
married woman 2 woman
who supervises the domestic
or medical arrangements of
an institution **matronly** *adj*

matt *adj* dull, not shiny

matter *n* 1 substance of which
something is made 2 physical
substance 3 event, situation,
or subject 4 written material
in general 5 pus ▷ *v* 6 be
of importance **what's the
matter?** what is wrong?

mattock *n* large pick with one
of its blade ends flattened for
loosening soil

mattress *n* large stuffed flat
case, often with springs, used
on or as a bed

mature *adj* 1 fully developed
or grown-up 2 ripe ▷ *v* 3 make
or become mature 4 (of a
bill or bond) become due
for payment **maturity** *n*
maturation *n*

maudlin *adj* foolishly or
tearfully sentimental

maul *v* 1 handle roughly 2 beat
or tear

maunder *v* talk or act
aimlessly or idly

mausoleum [maw-so-lee-
um] *n* stately tomb

mauve *adj* pale purple

maverick *n* independent
unorthodox person

maw *n* animal's mouth,
throat, or stomach

mawkish *adj* foolishly
sentimental

maxim *n* general truth or
principle

maximum *n, pl* -**mums**, -**ma**
1 greatest possible amount
or number ▷ *adj* 2 greatest
maximal *adj* **maximize** *v*
increase to a maximum

may *v, past tense* **might** used
as an auxiliary to express
possibility, permission,
opportunity, etc.

May *n* 1 fifth month of the year
2 **may** same as **hawthorn**
▸ **mayfly** *n* short-lived aquatic
insect **maypole** *n* pole set up
for dancing round on the first
day of May (**May Day**)

maybe *adv* 1 perhaps
2 possibly

Mayday *n* international
radiotelephone distress signal

mayhem *n* violent destruction
or confusion

mayonnaise *n* creamy sauce
of egg yolks, oil, and vinegar

mayor *n* head of a
municipality **mayoress** *n*
1 mayor's wife 2 lady mayor
mayoral *adj* **mayoralty** *n*
(term of) office of a mayor

maze *n* 1 complex network

of paths or lines designed to puzzle **2** confusing network or system

mazurka *n* **1** lively Polish dance **2** music for this

MB 1 Bachelor of Medicine **2** Manitoba

MBE Member of the Order of the British Empire

MC Master of Ceremonies

MD Doctor of Medicine

MDT Mountain Daylight Time

me *pron* the objective form of **I**

ME myalgic encephalomyelitis, postviral syndrome

mead *n* alcoholic drink made from honey

meadow *n* piece of grassland **meadowsweet** *n* plant with dense heads of small fragrant flowers

meagre *adj* scanty or insufficient

meal¹ *n* **1** occasion when food is served and eaten **2** the food itself

meal² *n* grain ground to powder **mealy** *adj* **mealy-mouthed** *adj* not outspoken enough

mean¹ *v* **meaning, meant 1** intend to convey or express **2** signify, denote, or portend **3** intend **4** have importance as specified **meaning** *n* **1** sense, significance ▷ *adj* **2** expressive **meaningful** *adj* **meaningless** *adj*

mean² *adj* **1** miserly, ungenerous, or petty **2** despicable or callous **3** *informal* bad-tempered **meanly** *adv* **meanness** *n* **meanie** *or* **meany** *n* miserly person

mean³ *n* **1** middle point between two extremes **2** average **means 3** that by which something is done **4** money ▷ *adj* **5** intermediate in size or quantity **6** average

by all means certainly **by no means** not at all **means test** enquiry into a person's means to decide eligibility for financial aid **meantime** *n* **1** intervening period ▷ *adv* **2** meanwhile **meanwhile** *adv* **1** during the intervening period **2** at the same time

meander [mee-**and**-er] *v* **1** follow a winding course **2** wander aimlessly ▷ *n* **3** winding course

measles *n* infectious disease producing red spots **measly** *adj informal* meagre

measure *n* **1** size or quantity **2** graduated scale etc. for measuring size or quantity **3** unit of size or quantity **4** extent **5** action taken **6** law **7** poetical rhythm ▷ *v* **8** determine the size or quantity of **9** be (a specified amount) in size or quantity **measurable** *adj* **measured** *adj* **1** slow and steady **2** carefully considered **measurement** *n* **1** measuring **2** size **measure up to** *v* fulfil (expectations or requirements)

meat *n* animal flesh as food **meaty** *adj* **1** (tasting) of or like meat **2** brawny **3** full of significance or interest

Mecca *n* **1** holy city of Islam **2** place that attracts visitors

mechanic *n* person skilled in repairing or operating machinery **mechanics** scientific study of motion and force **mechanical** *adj* **1** of or done by machines **2** (of an action) without thought or feeling **mechanically** *adv*

mechanism *n* **1** way a machine works **2** piece of machinery **3** process or technique: *defence mechanism* **mechanize** *v* **1** equip with machinery **2** make mechanical or automatic

3 *mil* equip (an army) with armoured vehicles **mechanization** *n*

med. **1** medical **2** medicine **3** medieval **4** medium

medal *n* piece of metal with an inscription etc., given as a reward or memento **medallion** *n* **1** disc-shaped ornament worn on a chain round the neck **2** large medal **3** circular decorative device in architecture **medallist** *n* winner of a medal

meddle *v* interfere annoyingly **meddler** *n* **meddlesome** *adj*

media *n* **1** a plural of **medium 2** the mass media collectively

mediaeval [med-**eve**-al] *adj* same as **medieval**

medial [**mee**-dee-al] *adj* of or in the middle **median** *adj, n* middle (point or line)

mediate [**mee**-dee-ate] *v* **1** intervene to bring about agreement **2** resolve (a dispute) by mediation **mediation** *n* **mediator** *n*

medic *n informal* doctor or medical student

Medicare *n* system of national medical services financed mainly by taxation

medicine *n* **1** substance used to treat disease **2** science of preventing, diagnosing, or curing disease **medical** *adj* **1** of the science of medicine ▷ *n* **2** *informal* medical examination **medically** *adv* **medicament** *n* a medicine **medicate** *v* treat with a medicine **medication** *n* (treatment with) a medicinal substance **medicinal** [med-**diss**-in-al] *adj* having therapeutic properties **medicine man** witch doctor

medieval, mediaeval [med-**eve**-al] *adj* of the Middle Ages

mediocre [mee-dee-**oak**-er] *adj* **1** average in quality **2** second-rate **mediocrity** [mee-dee-**ok**-rit-ee] *n*

meditate *v* **1** reflect deeply, esp. on spiritual matters **2** think about or plan **meditation** *n* meditating **meditative** *adj* **meditatively** *adv* **meditator** *n*

medium *adj* **1** midway between extremes, average ▷ *n, pl* **-dia, -diums 2** middle state, degree, or condition **3** intervening substance producing an effect **4** means of communicating news or information to the public, such as radio or newspapers **5** person who can supposedly communicate with the dead **6** surroundings or environment **7** category of art according to the material used **medium wave** radio wave with a wavelength between 100 and 1000 metres

medlar *n* apple-like fruit of a small tree, eaten when it begins to decay

medley *n* **1** miscellaneous mixture **2** musical sequence of different tunes

meds [medz] *pl n informal* medicinal substances

medulla [mid-**dull**-la] *n, pl* **-las, -lae** marrow, pith, or inner tissue **medullary** *adj*

meek *adj* submissive or humble **meekly** *adv* **meekness** *n*

meerschaum [**meer**-shum] *n* **1** white substance like clay **2** tobacco pipe with a bowl made of this

meet[1] *v* **meeting, met 1** come together (with) **2** come into contact (with) **3** be at the place of arrival of **4** make the acquaintance of **5** satisfy (a need etc.) **6** experience ▷ *n* **7** sports meeting **8** assembly of a hunt **meeting** n **1** coming together **2** assembly

meet[2] adj obsolete fit or suitable

mega- combining form **1** denoting one million: megawatt **2** very great: megastar

megabyte n computers 2^{20} or 1 048 576 bytes

megalith n great stone, esp. as part of a prehistoric monument **megalithic** adj

megalomania n craving for or mental delusions of power **megalomaniac** adj, n

megaphone n cone-shaped instrument used to amplify the voice

megaton n explosive power equal to that of one million tons of TNT

melancholy [mel-an-kol-lee] n **1** sadness or gloom ▷ adj **2** sad or gloomy **melancholia** [mel-an-**kole**-ya] n old name for depression **melancholic** adj, n

melange [**may**-lahnzh] n mixture

melanin n dark pigment found in the hair, skin, and eyes of man and animals

mêlée [**mel**-lay] n noisy confused fight or crowd

mellifluous [mel-**lif**-flew-uss] adj (of sound) smooth and sweet

mellow adj **1** soft, not harsh **2** kind-hearted, esp. through maturity **3** (of fruit) ripe ▷ v **4** make or become mellow

melodrama n **1** play full of extravagant action and emotion **2** overdramatic behaviour or emotion **melodramatic** adj

melody n, pl -**dies 1** series of musical notes which make a tune **2** sweet sound **melodic** [mel-**lod**-ik] adj **1** of melody **2** melodious **melodious** [mel-**lode**-ee-uss] adj **1** pleasing to the ear **2** tuneful

melon n large round juicy

fruit with a hard rind

melt v **1** (cause to) become liquid by heat **2** dissolve **3** soften through emotion **4** blend (into) **5** disappear **meltdown** n (in a nuclear reactor) melting of the fuel rods, with the possible release of radiation

member n **1** individual making up a body or society **2** limb **membership** n **Member of Parliament** person elected to parliament

membrane n thin flexible tissue in a plant or animal body **membranous** adj

meme n video, photo, or story that is viewed by many internet users in a short time

memento n, pl -**tos**, -**toes** thing serving to remind, souvenir

memo n, pl **memos** short for **memorandum**

memoir [**mem**-wahr] n **1** biography or historical account based on personal knowledge **memoirs 2** collection of these **3** autobiography

memory n, pl -**ries 1** ability to remember **2** sum of things remembered **3** particular recollection **4** length of time one can remember **5** commemoration **6** part of a computer which stores information **memorial** n **1** something serving to commemorate a person or thing ▷ adj **2** serving as a memorial **memorable** adj worth remembering, noteworthy **memorably** adv **memorandum** n **1** written record or communication within a business **2** note of things to be remembered **memorize** v commit to memory **memory card** small removable data storage device

men n plural of **man**

menace n 1 threat 2 informal nuisance ▷ v 3 threaten, endanger **menacing** adj

ménage [may-nahzh] n household

menagerie [min-**naj**-er-ee] n collection of wild animals for exhibition

mend v 1 repair or patch 2 make or become better 3 recover or heal ▷ n 4 mended area **on the mend** regaining health

mendacity n (tendency to) untruthfulness **mendacious** adj

mendicant adj 1 begging ▷ n 2 beggar

menhir [**men**-hear] n single upright prehistoric stone

menial [**mean**-ee-yal] adj 1 involving boring work of low status ▷ n 2 domestic servant

meningitis [men-in-**jite**-iss] n inflammation of the membranes of the brain

meniscus n, pl **-nisci, -niscuses** 1 curved surface of a liquid 2 crescent-shaped lens

menopause n time when a woman's menstrual cycle ceases **menopausal** adj

menstruation n approximately monthly discharge of blood and cellular debris from the womb of a nonpregnant woman **menstruate** v **menstrual** adj

mensuration n measuring, esp. in geometry

mental adj 1 of, in, or done by the mind 2 of or for mental illness 3 informal insane **mentally** adv **mentality** n way of thinking

menthol n organic compound found in peppermint, used medicinally

mention v 1 refer to briefly 2 acknowledge ▷ n 3 acknowledgment 4 brief reference to a person or thing

mentor n adviser or guide

menu n 1 list of dishes to be served, or from which to order 2 computers list of options displayed on a screen

mercantile adj of trade or traders

Mercator projection [mer-**kate**-er] n method of map-making in which latitude and longitude form a rectangular grid

mercenary adj 1 influenced by greed 2 working merely for reward ▷ n, pl **-aries** 3 hired soldier

mercerized adj (of cotton) given lustre by treating with chemicals

merchant n person engaged in trade, wholesale trader **merchandise** n commodities **merchant bank** bank dealing mainly with businesses and investment **merchantman** n trading ship **merchant navy** ships or crew engaged in a nation's commercial shipping

mercury n 1 silvery liquid metal 2 **Mercury** Roman myth messenger of the gods 3 **Mercury** planet nearest the sun **mercurial** [mer-**cure**-ee-al] adj lively, changeable

mercy n, pl **-cies** 1 compassionate treatment of an offender or enemy who is in one's power 2 merciful act **merciful** adj 1 compassionate 2 giving relief **merciless** adj

mere[1] adj nothing more than: mere chance **merely** adv

mere[2] n obsolete lake

meretricious adj superficially or garishly attractive but of no real value

merganser [mer-**gan**-ser] n large crested diving duck

merge v (cause to) combine or blend **merger** n combination of business firms into one

meridian n 1 imaginary circle

of the earth passing through both poles **2** peak or zenith

meringue [mer-**rang**] *n* **1** baked mixture of egg whites and sugar **2** small cake of this

merino *n, pl* -**nos 1** breed of sheep with fine soft wool **2** this wool

merit *n* **1** excellence or worth **merits 2** admirable qualities ▷ *v* -**iting**, -**ited 3** deserve **meritorious** *adj* deserving praise **meritocracy** [mer-it-**tok**-rass-ee] *n* rule by people of superior talent or intellect

merlin *n* small falcon

mermaid *n* imaginary sea creature with the upper part of a woman and the lower part of a fish

merry *adj* -**rier**, -**riest 1** cheerful or jolly **2** *informal* slightly drunk **merrily** *adv* **merriment** *n* **merry-go-round** *n* revolving circular platform on which people ride for amusement **merrymaking** *n* revelry

mesdames *n* plural of **madame**

mesdemoiselles *n* plural of **mademoiselle**

mesh *n* **1** network or net **2** (open space between) strands forming a network ▷ *v* **3** (of gear teeth) engage

mesmerize *v* **1** hold spellbound **2** *obsolete* hypnotize

meson [**mee**-zon] *n* elementary atomic particle

mess *n* **1** untidy or dirty confusion **2** trouble or difficulty **3** group of servicemen who regularly eat together **4** place where they eat ▷ *v* **5** muddle or dirty **6** (foll. by *about*) potter about **7** (foll. by *with*) interfere with **8** (of servicemen) eat in a group

message *n* **1** communication **2** meaning or moral **messenger** *n* bearer of a message **message board** internet discussion forum

Messiah *n* **1** Jews' promised deliverer **2** Christ **Messianic** *adj*

messieurs *n* plural of **monsieur**

Messrs [**mess**-erz] *n* plural of **Mr**

messy *adj* **messier**, **messiest** dirty, confused, or untidy **messily** *adv* **messiness** *n*

met *v* past of **meet**[1]

metabolism [met-**tab**-oh-liz-zum] *n* chemical processes of a living body **metabolic** *adj* **metabolic syndrome** condition associated with obesity, which increases the risk of cardiovascular disease and diabetes **metabolize** *v* produce or be produced by metabolism

metal *n* **1** mineral substance, such as iron or copper, that is malleable and capable of conducting heat and electricity **2** short for **road metal** ▶ **metallic** *adj* **metallurgy** *n* scientific study of the structure, properties, extraction, and refining of metals **metallurgical** *adj* **metallurgist** *n*

metamorphosis [met-a-**more**-foss-is] *n, pl* -**phoses** [-foss-eez] change of form or character **metamorphic** *adj* (of rocks) changed in texture or structure by heat and pressure **metamorphose** *v* transform

metaphor *n* figure of speech in which a term is applied to something it does not literally denote in order to imply a resemblance, such as *he is a lion in battle* **metaphorical** *adj* **metaphorically** *adv*

metaphysics *n* branch

of philosophy concerned
with being and knowing
metaphysical adj

mete v (usu. foll. by out) deal
out as punishment

meteor n small fast-moving
heavenly body, visible as a
streak of incandescence if it
enters the earth's atmosphere
meteoric [meet-ee-**or**-rik]
adj **1** of a meteor **2** brilliant
but short-lived **meteorite**
n meteor that has fallen to
earth

meteorology n study of
the earth's atmosphere,
esp. for weather forecasting
meteorological adj
meteorologist n

meter n **1** instrument for
measuring and recording
something, such as the
consumption of gas or
electricity ▷ v **2** measure by
meter

methamphetamine n
variety of amphetamine used
for its stimulant action

methane n colourless
inflammable gas

methanol n colourless
poisonous liquid used as a
solvent and fuel (Also **methyl
alcohol**)

methinks v, past tense
methought obsolete it seems
to me

method n **1** way or
manner **2** technique
3 orderliness **methodical**
adj orderly **methodically** adv
methodology n particular
method or procedure

Methodist n **1** member of any
of the Protestant churches
originated by Wesley and
his followers ▷ adj **2** of
Methodists or their Church
Methodism n

methyl n (compound
containing) a saturated
hydrocarbon group of atoms

methylated spirits alcohol
with methanol added, used as
a solvent and for heating

meticulous adj very careful
about details **meticulously**
adv

métier [**met**-ee-ay] n
1 profession or trade **2** one's
strong point

metonymy [mit-**on**-im-ee] n
figure of speech in which one
thing is replaced by another
associated with it, such as
'the Crown' for 'the king'

metre n **1** basic unit of length
equal to about 1.094 yards
2 rhythm of poetry **metric**
adj of the decimal system
of weights and measures
based on the metre **metrical**
adj **1** of measurement **2** of
poetic metre **metrication**
n conversion to the metric
system

Metro n metropolitan city
administration

metronome n instrument
which marks musical time by
means of a ticking pendulum

metropolis [mit-**trop**-oh-liss]
n chief city of a country or
region **metropolitan** adj of a
metropolis

mettle n courage or spirit

mew n **1** cry of a cat ▷ v **2** utter
this cry

mews n Brit yard or street
orig. of stables, now often
converted to houses

mezzanine [**mez**-zan-een]
n intermediate storey, esp.
between the ground and first
floor

mezzo-soprano [**met**-so-]
n voice or singer between a
soprano and contralto

mezzotint [**met**-so-tint] n
1 method of engraving by
scraping the roughened
surface of a metal plate **2** print
so made

mg milligram(s)

Mg *chem* magnesium

MHz megahertz

miaow [mee-**ow**] *n, v* same as **mew**

miasma [mee-**azz**-ma] *n* unwholesome or foreboding atmosphere

mica [**my**-ka] *n* glasslike mineral used as an electrical insulator

mice *n* plural of **mouse**

Michaelmas [**mik**-kl-mass] *n* Sept. 29th, feast of St Michael the archangel

mickey¹ *n* half bottle of alcoholic liquor

mickey² *n* **take the mickey (out of)** *informal* tease

micro *n, pl* -**cros** short for **microcomputer, microprocessor**

microbe *n* minute organism, esp. one causing disease **microbial** *adj*

microblog *n* **1** social networking site consisting only of updates ▷ *v* **microblogging, microblogged** **2** post on a microblog **microblogger** *n*

microchip *n* small wafer of silicon containing electronic circuits

microcomputer *n* computer having a central processing unit contained in one or more silicon chips

microcosm *n* **1** miniature representation of something **2** man regarded as epitomizing the universe

microfiche [**my**-crow-feesh] *n* microfilm in sheet form

microfilm *n* miniaturized recording of books or documents on a roll of film

microlight *n* very small light private aircraft with large wings

micrometer [my-**krom**-it-er] *n* instrument for measuring very small distances or angles

micron [**my**-kron] *n* one millionth of a metre

microorganism *n* organism of microscopic size

microphone *n* instrument for amplifying or transmitting sounds

microprocessor *n* integrated circuit acting as the central processing unit in a small computer

microscope *n* instrument with lens(es) which produces a magnified image of a very small body **microscopic** *adj* **1** too small to be seen except with a microscope **2** very small **3** of a microscope **microscopically** *adv* **microscopy** *n* use of a microscope

microsurgery *n* intricate surgery using a special microscope and miniature precision instruments

microwave *n* **1** electromagnetic wave with a wavelength of a few centimetres, used in radar and cooking **2** microwave oven ▷ *v* **3** cook in a microwave oven **microwave oven** oven using microwaves to cook food quickly

mid *adj* intermediate, middle **midday** *n* noon **midland** *n* middle part of a country **midnight** *n* twelve o'clock at night **midshipman** *n* naval officer of the lowest commissioned rank **midsummer** *n* **1** middle of summer **2** summer solstice **Midsummer Day** June 24th **midtown** *n* the centre of a town **midway** *adj, adv* **1** halfway ▷ *n* **2** place for games, rides, etc. at a fair **midwinter** *n* **1** middle or depth of winter **2** winter solstice

midden *n* dunghill or rubbish heap

m

middle n **1** point or part
equidistant from two
extremes ▷ adj **2** equidistant
from two extremes **3** medium,
intermediate **middle age**
period of life between youth
and old age **middle-aged**
adj **Middle Ages** period
from about 1000 AD to the
15th century **middle class**
social class of businessmen
and professional people
middle-class adj **Middle
East** area around the eastern
Mediterranean up to and
including Iran **middleman**
n trader who buys from the
producer and sells to the
consumer **middle-of-the-
road** adj **1** politically moderate
2 (of music) generally
popular **middleweight**
n boxer weighing up to
160lb (professional) or 75kg
(amateur)

middling adj **1** mediocre
2 moderate ▷ adv
3 moderately

midge n small mosquito-like
insect

midget n very small person or
thing

midriff n middle part of the
body

midst n **in the midst of**
1 surrounded by **2** at a point
during

midwife n trained person
who assists at childbirth
midwifery n

mien [mean] n lit person's
bearing, demeanour, or
appearance

miffed adj informal offended or
upset

might[1] v past tense of **may**

might[2] n power or strength
with might and main
energetically or forcefully
mighty adj **1** powerful
2 important ▷ adv **3** informal
very **mightily** adv

mignonette [min-yon-**net**] n
grey-green plant with sweet-
smelling flowers

migraine [**mee**-grain] n severe
headache, often with nausea
and other symptoms

migrate v **1** move from one
place to settle in another
2 (of animals) journey
between different habitats at
specific seasons **migration**
n **migrant** n, adj (person
or animal) that migrates
migratory adj

mike n informal microphone

milch [miltch] adj (of a cow)
giving milk

mild adj **1** not strongly
flavoured **2** gentle **3** calm
or temperate **mildly** adv
mildness n

mildew n destructive fungus
on plants or things exposed to
damp **mildewed** adj

mile n unit of length equal
to 1760 yards or 1.609 km
mileage n **1** distance travelled
in miles **2** miles travelled by
a motor vehicle per gallon of
gasoline **3** informal usefulness
of something **milestone** n
1 stone marker showing the
distance to a certain place
2 significant event

milieu [meal-yoo] n, pl
milieus, milieux [meal-yooz]
environment or surroundings

militant adj aggressive or
vigorous in support of a cause
militancy n

military adj **1** of or for soldiers,
armies, or war ▷ n **2** armed
services **militarism** n belief
in the use of military force
and methods **militarist**
n **militarized** adj **militia**
[mill-**ish**-a] n military force
of trained citizens for use in
emergency only

militate v (usu. foll. by against
or for) have a strong influence
or effect

milk n **1** white fluid produced by female mammals to feed their young **2** milk of cows, goats, etc. used by man as food **3** fluid in some plants. ▷ v **4** draw milk from **5** exploit (a person or situation) **milky** adj **Milky Way** luminous band of stars stretching across the night sky **milkmaid** n (esp. formerly) woman who milks cows **milkman** n man who delivers milk to people's houses. **milkshake** n frothy flavoured cold milk drink **milksop** n feeble man **milk teeth** first set of teeth in young mammals

mill[1] n **1** factory **2** machine for grinding, processing, or rolling ▷ v **3** put through a mill **4** move in a confused manner **5** cut fine grooves across the edges of (coins) **miller** n person who works in a mill **millstone** n flat circular stone for grinding corn **mill wheel** water wheel that drives a mill

mill[2] n one thousandth of a dollar

millennium [mill-en-ee-yum] n, pl **-niums**, **-nia 1** period of a thousand years **2** future period of peace and happiness

millet n a cereal grass

milli- combining form denoting a thousandth part: millisecond

millibar n unit of atmospheric pressure

milliner n maker or seller of women's hats **millinery** n

million n one thousand thousands **millionth** adj, n **millionaire** n person who owns at least a million pounds, dollars, etc.

millipede, millepede [mill-lip-peed] n small animal with a jointed body and many pairs of legs

milt n sperm of fish

mime n **1** acting without the use of words **2** performer who does this ▷ v **3** act in mime

mimic v **-icking**, **-icked 1** imitate (a person or manner), esp. for satirical effect ▷ n **2** person or animal clever at mimicking **mimicry** n

mimosa n shrub with fluffy yellow flowers and sensitive leaves

min. **1** minimum **2** minute(s)

minaret n tall slender tower of a mosque

mince Brit ▷ v **1** cut or grind into very small pieces **2** soften or moderate (one's words) **3** walk or speak in an affected manner ▷ n **4** minced meat **mincer** n machine for mincing meat **mincing** adj affected in manner **mincemeat** n sweet mixture of dried fruit and spices **mince pie** pie containing mincemeat

mind n **1** thinking faculties **2** memory or attention **3** intention **4** sanity ▷ v **5** take offence at **6** take care of **7** pay attention to **8** be cautious or careful about (something) **minded** adj having an inclination as specified: politically minded **minder** n Brit slang aide or bodyguard **mindful** adj **1** keeping aware **2** heedful **mindless** adj **1** stupid **2** requiring no thought **3** careless

mine[1] pron belonging to me

mine[2] n **1** deep hole for digging out coal, ores, etc. **2** bomb placed under the ground or in water **3** profitable source ▷ v **4** dig for minerals **5** dig (minerals) from a mine **6** place explosive mines in or on **miner** n person who works in a mine **minefield** n area of land or water containing

m

mines **minesweeper** n ship for clearing away mines

mineral n 1 naturally occurring inorganic substance, such as metal or coal ▷ adj 2 of, containing, or like minerals **mineralogy** [min-er-**al**-a-jee] n study of minerals **mineralogist** n **mineral water** water containing dissolved mineral salts or gases

minestrone [min-ness-**strone**-ee] n soup containing vegetables and pasta

mingle v 1 mix or blend 2 come into association (with)

mingy adj -gier, -giest informal miserly

mini n, adj 1 (something) small or miniature 2 short (skirt)

miniature n 1 small portrait, model, or copy ▷ adj 2 small-scale **miniaturist** n **miniaturize** v make to a very small scale

minibus n small bus

minicab n Brit ordinary automobile used as a taxi

minicomputer n computer smaller than a mainframe but more powerful than a microcomputer

minidisc n small recordable compact disc

minim n Brit half note

minimum adj, n least possible (amount or quantity) **minimal** adj minimum **minimize** v 1 reduce to a minimum 2 belittle

minion n servile assistant

miniseries n TV programme shown in several parts, often on consecutive days

minister n 1 head of a government department 2 diplomatic representative 3 member of the clergy ▷ v 4 (foll. by to) attend to the needs of **ministerial** adj **ministration** n giving of help

ministry n 1 profession or duties of a cleric 2 ministers collectively 3 government department

mink n 1 stoatlike animal 2 its highly valued fur

minnow n small freshwater fish

minor adj 1 lesser 2 under age 3 music (of a scale) having a semitone above the second note ▷ n 4 person below the age of legal majority 5 music minor scale **minority** n 1 lesser number 2 smaller party voting together 3 group in a minority in any state 4 state of being a minor **minority government** (in parliamentary democracies) government that has fewer elected representatives than the combined total of the other parties **minor penalty** hockey penalty in which a player is sent off for two minutes

minster n cathedral or large church

minstrel n medieval singer or musician

mint[1] n 1 place where money is coined ▷ v 2 make (coins)

mint[2] n 1 aromatic herb 2 peppermint 3 candy flavoured with this

minuet [min-new-**wet**] n 1 stately dance 2 music for this

minus prep, adj 1 reduced by the subtraction of 2 informal without 3 less than zero ▷ n 4 sign (–) denoting subtraction or a number less than zero

minuscule [**min**-niss-skyool] adj very small

minute[1] [**min**-it] n 1 60th part of an hour or degree 2 moment **minutes** 3 record of the proceedings of a meeting ▷ v 4 record in the minutes

minute[2] [my-**newt**] *adj* **1** very small **2** precise **minutely** *adv* **minutiae** [my-**new**-shee-eye] *pl n* trifling or precise details

minx *n* bold or flirtatious girl

miracle *n* **1** wonderful supernatural event **2** marvel **miraculous** *adj* **miraculously** *adv* **miracle play** medieval play based on a sacred subject

mirage [mir-**rahzh**] *n* optical illusion, esp. one caused by hot air

mire *n* **1** swampy ground **2** mud

mirror *n* **1** coated glass surface for reflecting images ▷ *v* **2** reflect in or as if in a mirror

mirth *n* laughter, merriment, or gaiety **mirthful** *adj* **mirthless** *adj*

mis- *prefix* wrong(ly), bad(ly)

misadventure *n* unlucky chance

misanthrope [**miz**-zan-thrope], **misanthropist** [miz-**zan**-thrope-ist] *n* person who dislikes people in general **misanthropic** [miz-zan-**throp**-ik] *adj* **misanthropy** [miz-**zan**-throp-ee] *n*

misapprehend *v* misunderstand **misapprehension** *n*

misappropriate *v* take and use (money) dishonestly **misappropriation** *n*

miscarriage *n* **1** spontaneous premature expulsion of a fetus from the womb **2** failure: *a miscarriage of justice* **miscarry** *v* **1** have a miscarriage **2** fail

miscast *v* -**casting**, -**cast** cast (a role or actor) in (a play or film) inappropriately

miscegenation [miss-ij-in-**nay**-shun] *n* interbreeding of races

miscellaneous [miss-sell-**lane**-ee-uss] *adj* mixed or assorted **miscellany** [miss-**sell**-a-nee] *n* mixed assortment

mischance *n* unlucky event

mischief *n* **1** annoying but not malicious behaviour **2** inclination to tease **3** harm **mischievous** [**miss**-chiv-uss] *adj* **1** full of mischief **2** intended to cause harm **mischievously** *adv*

miscible [**miss**-sib-bl] *adj* able to be mixed

misconception *n* wrong idea or belief

misconduct *n* **1** immoral or unethical behaviour **2** *hockey* penalty in which a player is usually sent off for 10 minutes

miscreant [**miss**-kree-ant] *n* wrongdoer

misdeed *n* wrongful act

misdemeanour *n* minor wrongdoing

miser *n* person who hoards money and hates spending it **miserly** *adj*

miserable *adj* **1** very unhappy, wretched **2** causing misery **3** squalid **4** mean **misery** *n* **1** great unhappiness **2** *informal* complaining person

misfire *v* **1** (of a firearm or engine) fail to fire correctly **2** (of a plan) fail to turn out as intended

misfit *n* person not suited to his or her environment

misfortune *n* (piece of) bad luck

misgiving *n* feeling of fear or doubt

misguided *adj* mistaken or unwise

mishandle *v* handle or treat badly or inefficiently

mishap *n* minor accident

misinform *v* give incorrect information to **misinformation** *n*

misjudge *v* judge wrongly or unfairly **misjudgment** *or* **misjudgement** *n*

mislay v lose (something) temporarily

mislead v give false or confusing information to **misleading** adj

mismanage v organize or run (something) badly **mismanagement** n

misnomer [miss-**no**-mer] n 1 wrongly applied name 2 use of this

misogyny [miss-**oj**-in-ee] n hatred of women **misogynist** n

misplace v 1 put in the wrong place 2 mislay 3 give (trust or affection) inappropriately

misprint n printing error

misrepresent v represent wrongly or inaccurately

miss v 1 fail to hit, reach, find, catch, or notice 2 not be in time for 3 notice or regret the absence of 4 avoid 5 fail to take advantage of ▷ n 6 fact or instance of missing **missing** adj lost or absent

Miss n title of a girl or unmarried woman

missal n book containing the prayers and rites of the Mass

misshapen adj badly shaped, deformed

missile n object or weapon thrown, shot, or launched at a target

mission n 1 specific task or duty 2 group of people sent on a mission 3 building in which missionaries work 4 military expedition or operation for a specific purpose **missionary** n, pl **-aries** person sent abroad to spread religion

missive n letter

misspent adj wasted or misused

missus, missis n informal one's wife or the wife of the person addressed or referred to

mist n 1 thin fog 2 fine spray of liquid **misty** adj 1 full of mist

2 dim or obscure **mistiness** n

mistake n 1 error or blunder ▷ v **-taking, -took, -taken** 2 misunderstand 3 confuse (a person or thing) with another

Mister n polite form of address to a man

mistletoe n evergreen plant with white berries growing as a parasite on trees

mistral n strong dry northerly wind of S France

mistress n 1 woman who is the illicit lover of a married man 2 woman in control of people or things 3 female teacher

mistrial n law trial which is invalid because of some error

mistrust v 1 not trust ▷ n 2 lack of trust **mistrustful** adj

misunderstand v fail to understand properly **misunderstanding** n

misuse n 1 incorrect, improper, or careless use ▷ v 2 use wrongly 3 treat badly

mite n 1 very small spider-like animal 2 very small thing or amount

mitigate v make less severe **mitigation** n

mitre [**my**-ter] n 1 bishop's pointed headdress 2 joint between two pieces of wood bevelled to meet at right angles ▷ v 3 join with a mitre joint

mitt n 1 short for **mitten** 2 baseball catcher's glove

mitten n glove with one section for the thumb and one for the four fingers together

mix v 1 combine or blend into one mass 2 form (something) by mixing 3 be sociable ▷ n 4 mixture **mixed** adj **mix up** v 1 confuse 2 make into a mixture **mixer** n **mixture** n 1 something mixed 2 combination **mix-up** n confused situation **mixed-up** *adj informal* confused

mizzenmast *n* mast nearest the stern of a full-rigged ship

mks units *pl n* metric system of units based on the metre, kilogram, and second

ml millilitre(s)

MLA Member of the Legislative Assembly

mm millimetre(s)

Mn *chem* manganese

MNA Member of the National Assembly (of Quebec)

mnemonic [nim-on-ik] *n, adj* (rhyme etc.) intended to help the memory

mo *n Brit informal* short for **moment**

MO Medical Officer

moan *n* **1** low cry of pain **2** *informal* grumble ▷ *v* **3** make or utter with a moan **4** *informal* grumble

moat *n* deep wide ditch, esp. round a castle

mob *n* **1** disorderly crowd **2** *slang* gang ▷ *v* **mobbing, mobbed 3** surround in a mob to acclaim or attack

mobile *adj* **1** able to move ▷ *n* **2** hanging structure designed to move in air currents **mobility** *n* **mobile phone** cordless phone powered by batteries

mobilize *v* **1** (of the armed services) prepare for active service **2** organize for a purpose **mobilization** *n*

moccasin *n* soft leather shoe

mocha [**mock**-a] *n* **1** kind of strong dark coffee **2** flavouring made from coffee and chocolate

mock *v* **1** make fun of **2** mimic ▷ *n* **3** imitation **mocks 4** *informal* practice exams taken before public exams ▷ *adj* **5** sham or imitation **put the mockers on** *informal* ruin the chances of success

of **mockery** *n* **1** derision **2** inadequate attempt

mocking bird N American bird which imitates other birds' songs **mock orange** shrub with white fragrant flowers **mock-up** *n* full-scale model for test or study

mod. **1** moderate **2** modern

mode *n* **1** method or manner **2** particular fashion **modish** [**mow**-dish] *adj* in fashion

model *n* **1** (miniature) representation **2** pattern **3** person or thing worthy of imitation **4** person who poses for an artist or photographer **5** person who wears clothes to display them to prospective buyers ▷ *v* **-elling, -elled 7** make a model of **8** mould **9** display (clothing) as a model

modem [**mow**-dem] *n* device for connecting two computers by a telephone line

moderate *adj* **1** not extreme **2** temperate **3** average ▷ *n* **4** person of moderate views ▷ *v* **5** make or become less violent or extreme **6** preside over a meeting etc. **moderately** *adv* **moderation** *n* **moderator** *n* **1** president of a Presbyterian body **2** arbitrator

modern *adj* **1** of present or recent times **2** in current fashion **modernity** *n* **modernism** *n* (support of) modern tendencies, thoughts, or styles **modernist** *n* **modernize** *v* bring up to date **modernization** *n*

modest *adj* **1** not vain or boastful **2** shy **3** not excessive **4** not showy or pretentious **modestly** *adv* **modesty** *n*

modicum *n* small quantity

modify *v* **-fying, -fied 1** change slightly **2** tone down **3** (of a word) qualify (another word) **modifier** *n* word that qualifies another **modification** n

modulate v 1 vary in tone 2 adjust 3 change the key of (music) **modulation** n 1 modulating 2 electronics superimposing of a wave or signal on to another wave or signal **modulator** n

module n self-contained unit, section, or component with a specific function

modus operandi [mow-duss op-er-**an**-die] n Latin method of operating

mogul [**mow**-gl] n important or powerful person

mohair n 1 fine hair of the Angora goat 2 yarn or fabric made from this

Mohammedan adj, n (not in Muslim use) same as **Muslim**

mohawk n punk hairstyle with shaved sides and a stiff central strip of hair, often brightly coloured

mohican n esp. Brit mohawk

moiety [**moy**-it-ee] n, pl -ties half

moist adj slightly wet **moisten** v make or become moist **moisture** n liquid diffused as vapour or condensed in drops **moisturize** v add moisture to (the skin etc.)

molar n large back tooth used for grinding

molasses n dark syrup, a by-product of sugar refining

mold n same as **mould**

mole[1] n small dark raised spot on the skin

mole[2] n 1 small burrowing mammal 2 informal spy who has infiltrated and become a trusted member of an organization

mole[3] n 1 breakwater 2 harbour protected by this

mole[4] n unit of amount of substance

molecule [**mol**-lik-kyool] n 1 simplest freely existing chemical unit, composed of two or more atoms 2 very small particle **molecular** [mol-**lek**-yew-lar] adj

molest v 1 interfere with sexually 2 annoy or injure **molester** n **molestation** n

moll n slang 1 gangster's female accomplice 2 prostitute

mollify v -fying, -fied pacify or soothe **mollification** n

mollusc n soft-bodied, usu. hard-shelled animal such as a snail or oyster

mollycoddle v pamper

Molotov cocktail n gasoline bomb

molten adj liquefied or melted

molybdenum [mol-**lib**-din-um] n silver-white metallic element

mom n an informal word for **mother**

moment n 1 short space of time 2 (present) point in time **momentary** adj lasting only a moment **momentarily** adv

momentous [mow-**men**-tuss] adj of great significance

momentum [mow-**men**-tum] n, pl -ta, -tums 1 product of a body's mass and velocity 2 impetus of a moving body

monarch n sovereign ruler of a state **monarchical** adj **monarchist** n supporter of monarchy **monarchy** n government by or a state ruled by a sovereign

monastery n, pl -teries residence of a religious order **monastic** adj 1 of monks, nuns, or monasteries 2 ascetic **monasticism** n

Monday n second day of the week

money n medium of exchange, coins or banknotes **moneyed** or **monied** adj rich **monetary** adj of money or currency **monetarism** n theory that inflation is caused by an increase in the money supply **monetarist** n, adj

Mongolian n 1 person from Mongolia 2 language of Mongolia ▷ adj 3 of Mongolia or its language

mongolism n offensive Down's syndrome **mongol** n, adj offensive (person) affected by this

mongoose n, pl -**gooses** stoatlike mammal of Asia and Africa that kills snakes

mongrel n 1 animal, esp. a dog, of mixed breed 2 hybrid ▷ adj 3 of mixed breed

monitor n 1 person or device that checks, controls, warns, or keeps a record of something 2 pupil assisting a teacher with duties 3 television set used in a studio to check what is being transmitted 4 type of large lizard ▷ v 5 watch and check on

monk n member of an all-male religious community bound by vows **monkish** adj **monkshood** n poisonous plant with hooded flowers

monkey n 1 long-tailed primate 2 mischievous child ▷ v 3 (usu. foll. by about or around) meddle or fool **monkey puzzle** coniferous tree with sharp stiff leaves **monkey wrench** wrench with adjustable jaws

mono- combining form single: monolingual

monochrome adj 1 in only one colour 2 black-and-white

monocle [**mon**-a-kl] n eyeglass for one eye only

monocular adj having or for one eye only

monogamy n custom of being married to one person at a time

monogram n design of combined letters, esp. a person's initials

monograph n book or paper on a single subject

monolith n large upright block of stone **monolithic** adj

monologue n 1 dramatic piece for one performer 2 long speech by one person

monomania n obsession with one thing **monomaniac** n, adj

monoplane n airplane with one pair of wings

monopoly n 1 pl -**lies** exclusive possession of or right to do something **monopolist** n **monopolize** v have or take exclusive possession of

monorail n single-rail railway

monotheism n belief in only one God **monotheist** n **monotheistic** adj

monotone n unvaried pitch in speech or sound **monotonous** adj tedious due to lack of variety **monotonously** adv **monotony** n

Monseigneur [mon-sen-**nyur**] n, pl **Messeigneurs** [may-sen-**nyur**] title of French prelates

monsieur [muss-**syur**] n, pl **messieurs** [may-**syur**] French title of address equivalent to sir or Mr

Monsignor n RC Church title attached to certain offices

monsoon n 1 seasonal wind of SE Asia 2 rainy season accompanying this

monster n 1 imaginary, usu. frightening beast 2 very wicked person 3 huge person, animal, or thing ▷ adj 4 huge **monstrosity** n large ugly thing **monstrous** adj 1 unnatural or ugly 2 shocking or unjust 3 huge **monstrously** adv

monstrance n RC Church

container in which the consecrated Host is exposed for adoration

montage [mon-tahzh] *n* **1** (making of) a picture composed from pieces of others **2** method of film editing incorporating several shots to form a single image

month *n* **1** one of the twelve divisions of the calendar year **2** period of four weeks **monthly** *adj* **1** happening or payable once a month ▷ *adv* **2** once a month ▷ *n* **3** monthly periodical

monument *n* something that commemorates, esp. a building or statue **monumental** *adj* **1** large, impressive, or lasting **2** of or being a monument **3** *informal* extreme **monumentally** *adv*

moo *n* **1** long deep cry of a cow ▷ *v* **2** make this noise

mooch *v slang* loiter about aimlessly

mood¹ *n* temporary (gloomy) state of mind **moody** *adj* **1** gloomy or sullen **2** changeable in mood **moodily** *adv*

mood² *n grammar* form of a verb indicating whether it expresses a fact, wish, supposition, or command

moon *n* **1** natural satellite of the earth **2** natural satellite of any planet ▷ *v* **3** (foll. by *about* or *around*) be idle in a listless or dreamy way **moonlight** *n* **1** light from the moon ▷ *v* **2** *informal* work at a secondary job, esp. illegally **moonshine** *n* **1** illicitly distilled whisky **2** nonsense **moonstone** *n* translucent semiprecious stone **moonstruck** *adj* deranged

moor¹ *n* tract of open uncultivated ground covered with grass and heather

moorhen *n* small black water bird

moor² *v* secure (a ship) with ropes etc. **mooring** *n* **1** place for mooring a ship **moorings** **2** ropes etc. used in mooring a ship

Moor *n* member of a Muslim people of NW Africa who ruled Spain between the 8th and 15th centuries **Moorish** *adj*

moose *n* large N American deer **moose pasture** *slang* worthless mining claim

moot *adj* **1** debatable: *a moot point* ▷ *v* **2** bring up for discussion

mop *n* **1** long stick with twists of cotton or a sponge on the end, used for cleaning **2** thick mass of hair ▷ *v* **mopping, mopped 3** clean or soak up with or as if with a mop

mope *v* be gloomy and apathetic

moped [mow-ped] *n* light motorcycle not over 50cc

moraine *n* accumulated mass of debris deposited by a glacier

moral *adj* **1** concerned with right and wrong conduct **2** based on a sense of right and wrong **3** (of support or a victory) psychological rather than practical ▷ *n* **4** lesson to be obtained from a story or event **morals 5** behaviour with respect to right and wrong **morally** *adv* **moralist** *n* person who lives by or expresses moral principles **morality** *n* **1** good moral conduct **2** moral goodness or badness **morality play** medieval play with a moral lesson **morality squad** *Canad* police unit enforcing laws concerning drugs, gambling, prostitution, pornography, etc. **moralize** *v* make moral pronouncements

morale [mor-**rahl**] n degree of confidence or hope of a person or group

morass n 1 marsh 2 mess

moratorium n, pl -ria, -riums legally authorized ban or delay

moray n large voracious eel

morbid adj 1 unduly interested in death or unpleasant events 2 gruesome

mordant adj 1 sarcastic or scathing ▷ n 2 substance used to fix dyes

more adj 1 greater in amount or degree 2 comparative of **much, many** 3 additional or further ▷ adv 4 to a greater extent 5 in addition ▷ pron 6 greater or additional amount or number **moreover** adv besides

mores [**more**-rayz] pl n customs and conventions embodying the fundamental values of a community

morganatic marriage n marriage of a person of high rank to a lower-ranking person whose status remains unchanged

morgue n mortuary

moribund adj without force or vitality

Mormon n member of a religious sect founded in the USA **Mormonism** n

morn n poetic morning

morning n part of the day before noon **morning-glory** n plant with trumpet-shaped flowers which close in the late afternoon

morocco n goatskin leather

moron n 1 obsolete mentally deficient person 2 informal fool **moronic** adj

morose [mor-**rohss**] adj sullen or moody

morphine, morphia n drug extracted from opium, used as an anesthetic and sedative

morphology n science of forms and structures of organisms or words **morphological** adj

morris dance n traditional English folk dance performed by men

morrow n poetic next day

Morse n system of signalling in which letters of the alphabet are represented by combinations of short and long signals

morsel n small piece, esp. of food

mortal adj 1 subject to death 2 causing death ▷ n 3 mortal creature **mortally** adv **mortality** n 1 state of being mortal 2 great loss of life 3 death rate **mortal sin** RC Church sin meriting damnation

mortar n 1 mixture of lime, sand, and water for holding bricks and stones together 2 small cannon with a short range 3 bowl in which substances are pounded **mortarboard** n square academic cap

mortgage n 1 conditional pledging of property, esp. a house, as security for the repayment of a loan 2 the loan itself ▷ v 3 pledge (property) as security thus **mortgagee** n creditor in a mortgage **mortgagor** or **mortgager** n debtor in a mortgage

mortify v -fying, -fied 1 humiliate 2 subdue by self-denial 3 (of flesh) become gangrenous **mortification** n

mortise, mortice [**more**-tiss] n hole in a piece of wood or stone shaped to receive a matching projection on another piece **mortise lock** lock set into a door

mortuary n, pl -aries building where corpses

m

are kept before burial or cremation

mosaic [mow-**zay**-ik] n design or decoration using small bits of coloured stone or glass

Mosaic adj of Moses

Moselle n light white wine

Moslem n, adj same as **Muslim**

mosque n Muslim temple

mosquito n, pl -**toes**, -**tos** blood-sucking flying insect

moss n small flowerless plant growing in masses on moist surfaces **mossy** adj

most adj **1** greatest in number or degree **2** superlative of **much, many** ▷ n **3** greatest number or degree ▷ adv **4** in the greatest degree **mostly** adv for the most part, generally

motel n roadside hotel for motorists

motet [mow-**tet**] n short sacred choral song

moth n nocturnal insect like a butterfly **mothball** n **1** small ball of camphor or naphthalene used to repel moths from stored clothes ▷ v **2** store (something operational) for future use **3** postpone (a project etc.) **moth-eaten** adj **1** eaten or damaged by moth larvae **2** decayed or scruffy

mother n **1** female parent **2** head of a female religious community ▷ adj **3** native or inborn: mother wit ▷ v **4** look after as a mother **motherhood** n **motherly** adj **motherless** adj **mother-in-law** n mother of one's husband or wife **mother of pearl** iridescent lining of certain shells **mother tongue** one's native language

motif [mow-**teef**] n (recurring) theme or design

motion n **1** process, action, or

way of moving **2** proposal in a meeting **3** Brit evacuation of the bowels ▷ v **4** direct (someone) by gesture **motionless** adj not moving **motion picture** film

motive n **1** reason for a course of action ▷ adj **2** causing motion **motivate** v give incentive to **motivation** n

motley adj **1** miscellaneous **2** multicoloured ▷ n **3** hist jester's costume

motocross n motorcycle race over a rough course

motor n **1** engine, esp. of a vehicle **2** machine that converts electrical energy into mechanical energy **3** automobile ▷ v **4** travel by automobile **motorist** n driver of an automobile **motorize** v equip with a motor or motor transport **motorbike** n **motorboat** n **motorcar** n **motorcycle** n **motorcyclist** n **motorhome** n large motor vehicle designed for living in while travelling **motor scooter** a light motorcycle with small wheels and an enclosed engine **motorway** n Brit highway

mottled adj marked with blotches

motto n, pl -**toes**, -**tos 1** saying expressing an ideal or rule of conduct **2** verse or maxim in a paper cracker

mould¹, mold n **1** hollow container in which metal etc. is cast **2** shape, form, or pattern **3** nature or character ▷ v **4** shape **5** influence or direct **moulding** n moulded ornamental edging

mould², mold n fungal growth caused by dampness **mouldy** adj **1** stale or musty **2** dull or boring

mould³, mold n loose soil **moulder** v decay into dust

moult *v* **1** shed feathers, hair, or skin to make way for new growth ▷ *n* **2** process of moulting

mound *n* **1** heap, esp. of earth or stones **2** small hill

mount *v* **1** climb or ascend **2** get up on (a horse etc.) **3** organize: *mount a campaign* **4** increase **5** fix on a support or backing ▷ *n* **6** backing or support on which something is fixed **7** horse for riding **8** hill

mountain *n* **1** hill of great size **2** large heap **mountainous** *adj* **1** full of mountains **2** huge **mountaineer** *n* person who climbs mountains **mountaineering** *n* **mountain bike** bicycle with straight handlebars and heavy-duty tires

Mountain Daylight Time *n* one of the standard times used in North America, six hours behind Greenwich Mean Time **Abbreviation: MDT**

Mountain Standard Time *n* one of the standard times used in North America, seven hours behind Greenwich Mean Time **Abbreviation: MST**

mountebank *n* charlatan or fake

Mountie *n informal* member of the Royal Canadian Mounted Police

mourn *v* feel or express sorrow for (a dead person or lost thing) **mourner** *n* **mournful** *adj* sad or dismal **mournfully** *adv* **mourning** *n* **1** grieving **2** conventional symbols of grief for death, such as the wearing of black

mouse *n, pl* **mice 1** small long-tailed rodent **2** timid person **3** *computers* hand-held device for moving the cursor without

keying **mouser** *n* cat used to catch mice **mousy** *adj* **1** like a mouse, esp. in hair colour **2** meek and shy

mousse *n* **1** dish of flavoured cream whipped and set

moustache *n* hair on the upper lip

mouth *n* **1** opening in the head for eating and issuing sounds **2** opening **3** entrance **4** point where a river enters the sea ▷ *v* **5** speak or utter insincerely, esp. in public **6** form (words) with the lips without speaking **mouth organ** small musical instrument played by sucking and blowing **mouthpiece** *n* **1** part of a telephone into which a person speaks **2** part of a wind instrument into which the player blows **3** spokesman

move *v* **1** change in place or position **2** change (one's house etc.) **3** take action **4** stir the emotions of **5** incite **6** suggest (a proposal) formally ▷ *n* **7** moving **8** action towards some goal **movable** *or* **moveable** *adj*, *n* **movement** *n* **1** action or process of moving **2** moving parts of a machine **3** group with a common aim **4** division of a piece of music

movie *n informal* film

mow *v* **mowing, mowed, mowed** *or* **mown** cut (grass or crops) **mower** *n* **mow down** *v* kill in large numbers

mozzarella [mot-sa-**rel**-la] *n* moist white cheese originally made in Italy from buffalo milk

MP 1 Member of Parliament **2** Military Police

MP3 *computing* Motion Picture Expert Group-1, Audio Layer-3: a digital compression format used to compress audio files to a fraction of their original size without loss of sound quality

MPEG [em-peg] *computing* Motion Picture Expert Group: standard compressed file format used for audio and video files

mpg miles per gallon

mph miles per hour

MPP Member of the Provincial Parliament

Mr Mister

Mrs *n* title of a married woman

Ms [mizz] *n* title used instead of Miss or Mrs

MS 1 manuscript 2 multiple sclerosis

MSc Master of Science

MSS manuscripts

MST Mountain Standard Time

Mt Mount

much *adj* **more, most** 1 existing in quantity ▷ *n* 2 large amount or degree ▷ *adv* **more, most** 3 to a great degree 4 nearly

mucilage [mew-sill-ij] *n* gum or glue

muck *n* 1 dirt, filth 2 manure ▷ *v* 3 *hockey* play tenaciously in attempting to win the puck **mucky** *adj* **mucker** *n* *hockey* player who is physically aggressive and tenacious rather than highly talented

muckamuck *n* **high muckamuck** *informal* important person

mucus [mew-kuss] *n* slimy secretion of the mucous membranes **mucous membrane** membrane lining body cavities or passages

mud *n* wet soft earth **muddy** *adj* **mudguard** *n* cover over a wheel to prevent mud or water being thrown up by it **mudpack** *n* cosmetic paste to improve the complexion

muddle *n* 1 state of confusion

▷ *v* (often foll. by *up*) 2 confuse 3 mix up

muesli [mewz-lee] *n* mixture of grain, nuts, and dried fruit eaten with milk

muezzin [moo-ezz-in] *n* official who summons Muslims to prayer

muff[1] *n* tube-shaped covering to keep the hands warm

muff[2] *v* bungle (an action)

muffin *n* 1 small cup-shaped sweet bread roll 2 see **English muffin**

muffle *v* wrap up for warmth or to deaden sound **muffler** *n* scarf

mufti *n* civilian clothes worn by a person who usually wears a uniform

mug[1] *n* large drinking cup

mug[2] *n* 1 *slang* face 2 *Brit slang* person who is easily swindled ▷ *v* **mugging, mugged** 3 *informal* rob violently **mugger** *n*

mug[3] *v* **mugging, mugged** (esp. foll. by *up*) *Brit informal* study hard

muggy *adj* **-gier, -giest** (of weather) damp and stifling

mukluk *n* Inuit's soft (sealskin) boot

mulatto [mew-lat-toe] *n*, *pl* **-tos, -toes** *offensive* child of one Black and one White parent

mulberry *n* 1 tree whose leaves are used to feed silkworms 2 purple fruit of this tree

mulch *n* 1 mixture of wet straw, leaves, etc., used to protect the roots of plants ▷ *v* 2 cover (land) with mulch

mulct *v* fine (a person)

mule[1] *n* offspring of a horse and a donkey **mulish** *adj* obstinate **muleteer** *n* mule driver

mule[2] *n* backless shoe or slipper

mull *v* 1 heat (wine) with sugar

and spices **2** think (over) or ponder

mullah n Muslim theologian

mullet n edible sea fish

mulligatawny n soup made with curry powder

mullion n upright dividing bar in a window **mullioned** adj

multi- combining form many: multicultural

multifarious [mull-tiff-**fare**-ee-uss] adj having many various parts

multilateral adj of or involving more than two nations or parties

multiple adj **1** having many parts ▷ n **2** quantity which contains another an exact number of times

multiplex adj **2** having many elements, complex

multiplicity n, pl -**ties** large number or great variety

multiply v -**plying**, -**plied** **1** (cause to) increase in number, quantity, or degree **2** add (a number or quantity) to itself a given number of times **3** increase in number by reproduction **multiplication** n **multiplicand** n math number to be multiplied

multitude n **1** great number **2** great crowd **multitudinous** adj very numerous

mum[1] n informal mother

mum[2] adj silent: keep mum

mumble v speak indistinctly, mutter

mumbo jumbo n **1** meaningless religious ritual **2** deliberately complicated language

mummer n actor in a folk play or mime

mummy[1] n, pl -**mies** body embalmed and wrapped for burial in ancient Egypt **mummify** v -**fying**, -**fied** preserve (a body) as a mummy

mummy[2] n, pl -**mies** child's word for **mother**

mumps n infectious disease with swelling in the glands of the neck

munch v chew noisily and steadily

mundane adj **1** everyday **2** earthly

municipal adj relating to a city or town **municipality** n **1** city or town with local self-government **2** governing body of this

munificent [mew-**niff**-fiss-sent] adj very generous **munificence** n

muniments [mew-nim-ments] pl n title deeds or similar documents

munitions [mew-**nish**-unz] pl n military stores

mural [**myoor**-al] n **1** painting on a wall ▷ adj **2** of or on a wall

murder n **1** unlawful intentional killing of a human being ▷ v **2** kill thus **murderer** (**murderess**) n **murderous** adj

murk n thick darkness **murky** adj dark or gloomy

murmur v -**muring**, -**mured** **1** speak in a quiet indistinct way **2** complain ▷ n **3** continuous low indistinct sound

murrain [**murr**-rin] n cattle plague

muscat n sweet white grape **muscatel** [musk-a-**tell**] n **1** wine from muscat grapes **2** muscat grape or raisin

muscle n **1** tissue in the body which produces movement by contracting **2** strength or power **muscular** adj **1** with well-developed muscles **2** of muscles **muscular dystrophy** disease with wasting of the muscles **muscle in** v informal force one's way in

m

muse v ponder
Muse n 1 *Greek myth* one of nine goddesses, each of whom inspired an art or science 2 **muse** force that inspires a creative artist
museum n building where natural, artistic, historical, or scientific objects are exhibited and preserved
mush¹ n 1 soft pulpy mass 2 *informal* cloying sentimentality **mushy** adj
mush² interj 1 order to dogs in sled team to advance ▷ v 2 travel by or drive dogsled ▷ n 3 journey with dogsled
mushroom n 1 edible fungus with a stem and cap ▷ v 2 grow rapidly
music n 1 art form using a melodious and harmonious combination of notes 2 written or printed form of this **musical** adj 1 of or like music 2 talented in or fond of music 3 pleasant-sounding ▷ n 4 play or film with songs and dancing **musically** adv **musician** n **musicology** n scientific study of music **musicologist** n **music hall** variety theatre
musk n scent obtained from a gland of the musk deer or produced synthetically **musky** adj **muskrat** n 1 N American beaver-like rodent 2 its fur
muskeg n bog or swamp
muskellunge n N American freshwater game fish
musket n *hist* long-barrelled gun **musketeer** n **musketry** n (use of) muskets
Muslim n 1 follower of the religion of Islam ▷ adj 2 of or relating to Islam
muslin n fine cotton fabric
muss v *informal* make untidy
mussel n kind of bivalve mollusc

must¹ v 1 used as an auxiliary to express obligation, certainty, or resolution ▷ n 2 something one must do
must² n newly pressed grape juice
mustang n wild horse of SW America
mustard n 1 paste made from the powdered seeds of a plant, used as a condiment 2 the plant **mustard gas** poisonous gas causing blistering
muster v 1 assemble ▷ n 2 assembly
musty adj **-tier, -tiest** smelling mouldy and stale **mustiness** n
mutable [mew-tab-bl] adj liable to change **mutability** n
mutation [mew-**tay**-shun] n (genetic) change **mutate** [mew-**tate**] v (cause to) undergo mutation **mutant** [**mew**-tant] n mutated animal, plant, etc.
mute adj 1 *offensive* unable to speak 2 silent ▷ n 3 *offensive* person unable to speak 4 *music* device to soften the tone of an instrument **muted** adj 1 (of a reaction) subdued 2 (of sound or colour) softened **mutely** adv
mutilate [mew-till-ate] v 1 deprive of a limb or other part 2 damage (a book or text) **mutilation** n
mutiny [mew-tin-ee] n, pl **-nies** 1 rebellion against authority, esp. by soldiers or sailors ▷ v **-nying, -nied** 2 commit mutiny **mutineer** n **mutinous** adj
mutt n *slang* 1 stupid person 2 mongrel dog
mutter v 1 utter or speak indistinctly 2 grumble ▷ n 3 muttered sound or grumble
mutton n flesh of sheep, used as food
mutual [mew-chew-al] adj

m

1 felt or expressed by each of two people about the other **2** *informal* common to both or all **mutually** *adv*

Muzak *n* ® recorded light music played in shops etc.

muzzle *n* **1** animal's mouth and nose **2** cover for these to prevent biting **3** open end of a gun ▷ *v* **4** put a muzzle on **5** force to keep silent

muzzy *adj* **-zier, -ziest 1** confused or muddled **2** blurred or hazy **muzziness** *n*

mW milliwatt(s)

MW megawatt(s)

my *adj* belonging to me

mycology *n* study of fungi

myna, mynah *n* Indian bird which can mimic human speech

myocardium *n, pl* **-dia** the muscular tissue of the heart **myocardial** *adj*

myopia [my-oh-pee-a] *n* short-sightedness **myopic** [my-op-ic] *adj*

myriad [mir-ree-ad] *adj* **1** innumerable ▷ *n* **2** large indefinite number

myriapod *n* invertebrate with a long segmented body and many legs, such as a centipede

myrrh [mur] *n* aromatic gum, formerly used in incense

myrtle [mur-tl] *n* flowering evergreen shrub

myself *pron* emphatic or reflexive form of **I, me**

mystery *n, pl* **-teries 1** strange or inexplicable event or phenomenon **2** obscure or secret thing **3** story or film that arouses suspense **mysterious** *adj* **mysteriously** *adv*

mystic *n* **1** person who seeks spiritual knowledge ▷ *adj* **2** having a spiritual or religious significance beyond human understanding **mystical** *adj* mystic **mysticism** *n*

mystify *v* **-fying, -fied** bewilder or puzzle **mystification** *n*

mystique [miss-**steek**] *n* aura of mystery or power

myth *n* **1** tale with supernatural characters, usu. of how the world and mankind began **2** untrue idea or explanation **3** imaginary person or object **mythical** *adj* **mythology** *n* **1** myths collectively **2** study of myths **mythological** *adj*

myxomatosis [mix-a-mat-oh-siss] *n* contagious fatal viral disease of rabbits

m

Nn

N 1 *chess* knight **2** *chem* nitrogen **3** *physics* newton(s) **4** north(ern)

n. 1 neuter **2** noun **3** number

Na *chem* sodium

naan *n* same as **nan bread**

nab *v* **nabbing, nabbed** *informal* **1** arrest (someone) **2** catch (someone) in wrongdoing

nadir *n* **1** point in the sky opposite the zenith **2** lowest point

naevus [nee-vuss] *n, pl* -**vi** birthmark or mole

naff *adj slang* inferior or useless

NAFTA North American Free Trade Agreement

nag[1] *v* **nagging, nagged** **1** scold or find fault (with) constantly **2** be a constant source of discomfort, pain, or worry (to) ▷ *n* **3** person who nags **nagging** *adj, n*

nag[2] *n informal* (old) horse

naiad [nye-ad] *n Greek myth* water nymph

nail *n* **1** hard covering of the upper tips of the fingers and toes **2** pointed piece of metal with a head, hit with a hammer to join two objects together ▷ *v* **3** attach (something) with nails **4** *informal* catch or arrest **hit the nail on the head** say something exactly correct **nailfile** *n* small metal file used to smooth or shape the finger or toe nails **nail polish** *or* **nail varnish** cosmetic

lacquer applied to the finger or toe nails

naive [nye-**eev**] *adj* **1** innocent and credulous **2** lacking developed powers of reasoning and criticism **naively** *adv* **naivety** *or* **naiveté** [nye-**eev**-tee] *n*

naked *adj* without clothes or covering **the naked eye** the eye unassisted by any optical instrument **nakedness** *n*

namby-pamby *adj* sentimental or insipid

name *n* **1** word by which a person or thing is known **2** reputation, esp. a good one **3** abusive word or description ▷ *v* **4** give a name to **5** refer to by name **6** specify **nameless** *adj* **1** without a name **2** unspecified **3** too horrible to be mentioned **namely** *adv* that is to say **namesake** *n* person with the same name as another

nan bread *n* slightly leavened Indian bread in a large flat leaf shape

nanny *n, pl* -**nies** woman whose job is looking after young children **nanny goat** female goat

nap[1] *n* **1** short sleep ▷ *v* **napping, napped** **2** have a short sleep

nap[2] *n* raised fibres of velvet or similar cloth

nap[3] *n* card game similar to whist

napalm *n* highly inflammable gasoline, used in bombs

nape n back of the neck

naphtha n liquid mixture distilled from coal tar or petroleum, used as a solvent and in petrol **naphthalene** n white crystalline product distilled from coal tar or petroleum, used in disinfectants, mothballs, and explosives

napkin n piece of cloth or paper for wiping the mouth or protecting the clothes while eating

nappy n, pl -pies Brit diaper

narcissism n abnormal love and admiration for oneself **narcissistic** adj

narcissus n, pl -cissi yellow, orange, or white flower related to the daffodil

narcotic n, adj (of) a drug, such as morphine or opium, which produces numbness and drowsiness, used medicinally but addictive **narcosis** n effect of a narcotic

nark Brit slang ▷ v **1** annoy ▷ n **2** someone who complains in an irritating manner **3** informer **narky** adj slang irritable or complaining

narrate v **1** tell (a story) **2** speak the words accompanying and telling what is happening in a film or TV programme **narration** n **narrator** n **narrative** n account, story

narrow adj **1** of little breadth in comparison to length **2** limited in range, extent, or outlook **3** with little margin: a narrow escape ▷ v **4** make or become narrow **5** (often foll. by down) limit or restrict **narrows** pl n narrow part of a strait, river, or current **narrowly** adv **narrowness** n **narrow-minded** adj intolerant or bigoted

narwhal n arctic porpoise with a long spiral tusk

NASA US National Aeronautics and Space Administration

nasal adj **1** of the nose **2** pronounced with air passing through the nose **nasally** adv

nascent adj starting to grow or develop

nasturtium n plant with yellow, red, or orange trumpet-shaped flowers

nasty adj -tier, -tiest **1** unpleasant **2** (of an injury) dangerous or painful **3** spiteful or unkind **nastily** adv **nastiness** n

natal [**nay**-tal] adj of or relating to birth

nation n people of one or more cultures or races organized as a single state **national** adj **1** of or characteristic of a nation ▷ n **2** citizen of a nation **nationally** adv **nationalism** n **1** policy of national independence **2** patriotism **nationalist** n, adj **nationality** n **1** fact of being a citizen of a particular nation **2** nation **nationalize** v put (an industry or a company) under state control **nationalization** n **national insurance** state insurance scheme providing payments to the unemployed, sick, and retired **national park** area of countryside protected by a government for its natural or environmental importance

native adj **1** relating to a place where a person was born **2** born in a specified place **3** (foll. by to) originating (in) **4** inborn ▷ n **5** person born in a specified place **6** member of the original race of a country **7** indigenous animal or plant **Native Canadian** Canadian Inuit, Indian, or Metis

Nativity n Christianity birth of Jesus Christ

NATO North Atlantic Treaty
Organization
natter *informal* ▷ *v* **1** talk idly
or chatter ▷ *n* **2** long idle chat
natty *adj* **-tier, -tiest** *informal*
smart and spruce
natural *adj* **1** normal
2 genuine, not affected
3 of, according to, existing
in, or produced by nature
4 not created by human
beings **5** not synthetic
6 (of a parent) not adoptive
7 (of a child) illegitimate
8 *music* not sharp or flat ▷ *n*
9 person with an inborn
talent or skill **naturally** *adv*
1 of course **2** in a natural or
normal way **3** instinctively
naturalist *n* student of
natural history **naturalism**
n movement in art and
literature advocating detailed
realism **naturalistic** *adj*
naturalize *v* give citizenship
to (a person born in another
country) **naturalization** *n*
natural gas gas found below
the ground, used mainly as a
fuel **natural history** study of
animals and plants **natural
selection** process by which
only creatures and plants well
adapted to their environment
survive
nature *n* **1** whole system of the
existence, forces, and events
of the physical world that
are not controlled by human
beings **2** fundamental or
essential qualities of a person
or thing **3** kind or sort
naturism *n* nudism **naturist**
n
naught *n* **1** *obsolete* nothing
2 figure o
naughty *adj* **-tier, -tiest**
1 disobedient or mischievous
2 mildly indecent **naughtily**
adv **naughtiness** *n*
nausea [naw-zee-a] *n* feeling
of being about to vomit

nauseate *v* **1** make (someone)
feel sick **2** disgust **nauseous**
adj **1** as if about to vomit
2 sickening
nautical *adj* of the sea or ships
nautical mile 1852 metres
nautilus *n, pl* **-luses, -li**
shellfish with many tentacles
naval *adj* see **navy**
nave *n* main part of a church
navel *n* hollow in the middle
of the abdomen where the
umbilical cord was attached
navigate *v* **1** direct or plot
the path or position of a
ship, aircraft, or automobile
2 travel over or through
navigation *n* **navigator** *n*
navigable *adj* **1** wide, deep,
or safe enough to be sailed
through **2** able to be steered
navvy *n, pl* **-vies** *Brit* labourer
employed on a road or a
building site
navy *n, pl* **-vies 1** branch of
a country's armed services
comprising warships with
their crews and organization
2 warships of a nation ▷ *adj*
3 navy-blue **naval** *adj* of or
relating to a navy or ships
navy-blue *adj* very dark blue
nay *interj obsolete* no
Nazi *n* **1** member of the
National Socialist Party,
which seized political control
in Germany in 1933 under
Adolf Hitler ▷ *adj* **2** of or
relating to the Nazis **Nazism**
n
NB 1 note well **2** Also **N.B.** New
Brunswick
NCO non-commissioned
officer
NDP New Democratic Party
NDT Newfoundland Daylight
Time
Ne *chem* neon
NE northeast(ern)
Neanderthal [nee-**ann**-der-
tahl] *adj* of a type of primitive
man that lived in Europe

before 12 000 BC

neap tide n tide at the first and last quarters of the moon when there is the smallest rise and fall in tidal level

near prep **1** close to, not far from ▷ adv **2** at or to a place or time not far away ▷ adj **3** (situated) at or in a place or time not far away **4** (of people) closely related **5** almost being the thing specified: a near tragedy ▷ v **6** approach and be about to reach **nearly** adv almost **nearness** n **nearby** adj not far away **nearside** n side of a vehicle that is nearer the curb

neat adj **1** tidy and clean **2** smoothly or competently done **3** undiluted **neatly** adv **neatness** n

nebula [**neb**-yew-la] n astronomy hazy cloud of particles and gases **nebulous** adj vague, indistinct

necessary adj **1** indispensable or required: the necessary skills **2** certain or unavoidable: the necessary consequences **necessarily** adv **necessitate** v compel or require **necessitous** adj very needy **necessity** n **1** something needed **2** compulsion

neck n **1** part of the body joining the head to the shoulders **2** part of a garment round the neck **3** narrow part of a bottle or violin ▷ v **4** slang kiss and cuddle **neck and neck** absolutely level in a race or competition **neckerchief** n piece of cloth worn tied round the neck **necklace** n decorative piece of jewellery worn around the neck

necromancy [**neck**-rome-man-see] n **1** communication with the dead **2** sorcery

necropolis [neck-**rop**-pol-liss] n cemetery

nectar n **1** sweet liquid collected from flowers by bees **2** drink of the gods

nectarine n smooth-skinned peach

née [**nay**] prep indicating the maiden name of a married woman

need v **1** want or require **2** be obliged (to do something) ▷ n **3** condition of lacking something **4** requirement, necessity **5** poverty **needs** adv (foll. by must) necessarily **needy** adj poor, in need of financial support **needful** adj necessary or required **needless** adj unnecessary

needle n **1** thin pointed piece of metal with an eye through which thread is passed for sewing **2** long pointed rod used in knitting **3** pointed part of a hypodermic syringe **4** small pointed part in a record player that touches the record and picks up the sound signals **5** pointer on a measuring instrument or compass **6** long narrow stiff leaf ▷ v **7** informal goad or provoke **needlework** n sewing and embroidery

ne'er adv lit never **ne'er-do-well** n useless or lazy person

nefarious [nif-**fair**-ee-uss] adj wicked

negate v **1** invalidate **2** deny **negation** n

negative adj **1** expressing a denial or refusal **2** lacking positive qualities **3** (of an electrical charge) having the same electrical charge as an electron ▷ n **4** negative word or statement **5** photog image with a reversal of tones or colours from which positive prints are made

neglect v **1** take no care of **2** disregard **3** fail (to do something) through carelessness ▷ n **4** neglecting or being neglected **neglectful** adj

negligee [neg-lee-zhay] n woman's lightweight usu. lace-trimmed dressing gown

negligence n neglect or carelessness **negligent** adj **negligently** adv

negligible adj so small or unimportant as to be not worth considering

negotiate v **1** discuss in order to reach (an agreement) **2** succeed in passing round or over (a place or problem) **negotiation** n **negotiator** n **negotiable** adj

Negro n, pl **-groes** offensive member of any of the Black peoples originating in Africa **Negroid** adj of or relating to a Black people

neigh n **1** loud high-pitched sound made by a horse ▷ v **2** make this sound

neighbour, neighbor n one who lives or is situated near another **neighbouring** or **neighboring** adj situated nearby **neighbourhood** or **neighborhood** n **1** district where people live **2** surroundings **neighbourly** or **neighborly** adj kind, friendly, and helpful

neither adj, pron **1** not one nor the other ▷ conj **2** not

nemesis [nem-miss-iss] n, pl **-ses** retribution or vengeance

neo- combining form new, recent, or a modern form of: neoclassicism

neolithic adj of the later Stone Age

neologism [nee-ol-a-jiz-zum] n new-coined word or an established word used in a new sense

neon n colourless odourless gaseous element used in illuminated signs and lights

neonatal adj relating to the first few weeks of a baby's life

neophyte n **1** beginner or novice **2** new convert

nephew n son of one's sister or brother

nephritis [nif-frite-tiss] n inflammation of a kidney

nepotism [nep-a-tiz-zum] n favouritism in business shown to relatives and friends

Neptune n **1** Roman god of the sea **2** eighth planet from the sun

neptunium n synthetic metallic element

nerd, nurd n slang **1** boring person obsessed with a particular subject **2** stupid and feeble person

nerve n **1** cordlike bundle of fibres that conducts impulses between the brain and other parts of the body **2** bravery and determination **3** impudence **nerves 4** anxiety or tension **5** ability or inability to remain calm in a difficult situation **get on someone's nerves** irritate someone **nerve oneself** prepare oneself (to do something difficult or unpleasant) **nerveless** adj **1** fearless **2** numb, without feeling **nervy** adj informal brash or cheeky **nerve centre** place from which a system or organization is controlled **nerve-racking** adj very distressing or harrowing

nervous adj **1** apprehensive or worried **2** of or relating to the nerves **nervously** adv **nervousness** n **nervous breakdown** mental illness in which the sufferer ceases to function properly

nest n **1** place or structure in which birds or certain animals lay eggs or give birth to young **2** snug retreat **3** set of things of graduated sizes designed to fit together ▷ v **4** make or inhabit a nest **nest egg** fund of money kept in reserve

nestle v **1** snuggle **2** be in a sheltered position

nestling n bird too young to leave the nest

net[1] n **1** openwork fabric of meshes of string, thread, or wire **2** piece of net used to protect or hold things or to trap animals ▷ v **netting, netted 3** cover with or catch in a net **netting** n material made of net

net[2], **nett** adj **1** left after all deductions **2** (of weight) excluding the wrapping or container ▷ v **netting, netted 3** yield or earn as a clear profit

nether adj lower

nettle n **1** plant with stinging hairs on the leaves ▷ v **2** irritate

network n **1** system of intersecting lines, roads, etc. **2** interconnecting group or system **3** (in broadcasting) group of stations that all transmit the same programmes simultaneously

neural adj of a nerve or the nervous system

neuralgia n severe pain along a nerve

neuritis [nyoor-**rite**-tiss] n inflammation of a nerve or nerves

neurology n scientific study of the nervous system **neurologist** n

neurosis n, pl -**ses** mental illness producing hysteria, anxiety, depression, or obsessive behaviour **neurotic** adj **1** abnormally sensitive **2** suffering from neurosis ▷ n **3** neurotic person

neuter adj **1** belonging to a particular class of grammatical inflections in some languages ▷ v **2** castrate (an animal)

neutral adj **1** taking neither side in a war or dispute **2** of or belonging to a neutral party or country **3** (of a colour) not definite or striking **4** of no distinctive quality or type ▷ n **5** neutral person or nation **6** neutral gear **neutrality** n **neutralize** v **1** make ineffective or neutral **2** mil euphemistic kill or render harmless **neutralization** n **neutral gear** position of the controls of a gearbox that leaves the gears unconnected to the engine **neutral zone** hockey area between the two blue lines

neutrino [new-**tree**-no] n, pl -**nos** elementary particle with no mass or electrical charge

neutron n electrically neutral elementary particle of about the same mass as a proton **neutron bomb** nuclear bomb designed to kill people and animals while leaving buildings virtually undamaged

never adv at no time **nevertheless** adv in spite of that

new adj **1** not existing before **2** having lately come into some state **3** additional **4** (foll. by to) unfamiliar ▷ adv **5** recently **newness** n **New Age** philosophy characterized by a belief in alternative medicine and spiritualism **newbie** n informal person new to a job, club, etc. **newborn** adj recently or just born **newcomer** n recent arrival or participant **New Democrat** Canad member of the New Democratic Party **New Democratic**

n

Party major political party with policies to the left of Liberal and Progressive Conservative Parties **new-fangled** adj objectionably or unnecessarily modern **new moon** moon when it appears as a narrow crescent at the beginning of its cycle

newel n post at the top or bottom of a flight of stairs that supports the handrail

Newfie n informal person from Newfoundland

Newfoundland Daylight Time n standard time used only in Newfoundland and Labrador, 2½ hours behind Greenwich Mean Time **Abbreviation: NDT**

Newfoundland Time n standard time used only in Newfoundland and Labrador, 3½ hours behind Greenwich Mean Time **Abbreviation: NT**

news n 1 important or interesting recent happenings 2 information about such events reported in the mass media **newsy** adj full of news **newsagent** n shopkeeper who sells newspapers and magazines **newscaster** n person who reads the news on the television or radio **newsflash** n brief important news item, which interrupts a radio or television programme **newsgroup** n electronic discussion group on the internet that is devoted to a specific topic **newsletter** n bulletin issued periodically to members of a group **newspaper** n weekly or daily publication containing news **newsprint** n inexpensive paper used for newspapers **newsroom** n room where news is received and prepared for publication or

broadcasting **newsworthy** adj sufficiently interesting to be reported as news

newt n small amphibious creature with a long slender body and tail

newton n unit of force

next adj, adv 1 immediately following 2 nearest **next-of-kin** n closest relative

nexus n, pl **nexus** connection or link

NF, N.F. Newfoundland

Nfld. Newfoundland

Ni chem nickel

nib n writing point of a pen

nibble v 1 take little bites (of) ▷ n 2 little bite 3 light meal

nibs n **his** or **her nibs** slang mock title of respect

nice adj 1 pleasant 2 kind: a nice gesture 3 good or satisfactory: they made a nice job of it 4 subtle: a nice distinction **nicely** adv **niceness** n **nicety** n 1 subtle point 2 refinement or delicacy

niche [neesh] n 1 hollow area in a wall 2 exactly suitable position for a particular person

nick v 1 make a small cut in 2 slang steal 3 Brit slang arrest ▷ n 4 small cut 5 Brit slang prison or police station **in good nick** informal in good condition **in the nick of time** just in time

nickel n 1 silvery-white metal often used in alloys 2 Canadian and US coin worth five cents

nickelodeon n US early type of jukebox

nickname n 1 familiar name given to a person or place ▷ v 2 call by a nickname

nicotine n poisonous substance found in tobacco

niece n daughter of one's sister or brother

nifty adj -tier, -tiest informal neat or smart

niggard n stingy person
niggardly adj
nigger n offensive Black person
niggle v 1 worry slightly
2 continually find fault (with)
▷ n 3 small worry or doubt
nigh adv, prep lit near
night n time of darkness
between sunset and sunrise
nightly adj, adv (happening)
each night **nightcap** n 1 drink
taken just before bedtime
2 soft cap formerly worn in
bed 3 baseball second game
in a double-header, played
in the evening **nightclub** n
establishment for dancing,
music, etc., open late at night
nightdress n woman's loose
dress worn in bed **nightfall**
n approach of darkness
nightie n informal nightdress
nightingale n small bird with
a musical song usually heard
at night **nightjar** n nocturnal
bird with a harsh cry
nightlife n entertainment
and social activities available
at night in a town or city
nightmare n 1 very bad dream
2 very unpleasant experience
night school place where
adults can attend educational
courses in the evenings
nightshade n plant with
bell-shaped flowers which are
often poisonous **nightshirt** n
man's long loose shirt worn in
bed **night-time** n time from
sunset to sunrise
nihilism [nye-ill-liz-zum] n
rejection of all established
authority and institutions
nihilist n **nihilistic** adj
nil n nothing, zero
nimble adj 1 agile and quick
2 mentally alert or acute
nimbly adv
nimbus n, pl -bi, -buses 1 dark
grey rain cloud 2 halo
nimrod n 1 slang boring social
misfit 2 **Nimrod** person who

is dedicated to or skilled in
hunting
nincompoop n informal
stupid person
nine adj, n one more than eight
ninth adj, n (of) number nine
in a series **nineteen** adj, n ten
and nine **nineteenth** adj, n
ninety adj, n ten times nine
ninetieth adj, n **ninepins**
n game of skittles
nip v **nipping, nipped**
1 informal hurry 2 pinch or
squeeze 3 bite lightly ▷ n
4 pinch 5 light bite 6 small
alcoholic drink 7 sharp
coldness: a nip in the air **nippy**
adj 1 frosty or chilly 2 Brit
informal quick or nimble
nipper n informal small child
nipple n projection in the
centre of a breast
nirvana [near-vah-na] n
Buddhism, Hinduism absolute
spiritual enlightenment and
bliss
nit n 1 egg or larva of a
louse 2 informal short for
nitwit ► **nit-picking** adj
informal overconcerned with
insignificant detail, esp. to
find fault **nitwit** n informal
stupid person
nitrogen [nite-roj-jen] n
colourless odourless gas
that forms four fifths of
the air **nitric, nitrous,**
or **nitrogenous** adj of
or containing nitrogen
nitrate n compound
of nitric acid, used as a
fertilizer **nitroglycerin** or
nitroglycerine n explosive
liquid
nitty-gritty n informal basic
facts
NL Newfoundland and
Labrador
no interj 1 expresses denial,
disagreement, or refusal ▷ adj
2 not any, not a ▷ adv 3 not at
all ▷ n, pl **noes, nos** 4 answer

or vote of 'no' **5** person who answers or votes 'no' **no-go area** district barricaded off so that the police or army can enter only by force **no-hitter** n baseball game in which a team's pitchers allow no base hits **no-man's-land** n land between boundaries, esp. contested land between two opposing forces **no-one** or **no one** pron nobody

no. number

nob n slang person of wealth or social distinction

nobble v slang **1** attract the attention of (someone) in order to talk to him or her **2** bribe or threaten

Nobel Prize [no-**bell**] n prize awarded annually for outstanding achievement in various fields

noble adj **1** showing or having high moral qualities **2** of the nobility **3** impressive and magnificent ▷ n **4** member of the nobility **nobility** n **1** quality of being noble **2** class of people holding titles and high social rank **nobly** adv **nobleman** (**noblewoman**) n

nobody pron **1** no person ▷ n, pl -**bodies 2** person of no importance

nocturnal adj **1** of the night **2** active at night

nocturne n short dreamy piece of music

nod v **nodding, nodded 1** lower and raise (one's head) briefly in agreement or greeting **2** let one's head fall forward with sleep ▷ n **3** act of nodding **nod off** v informal fall asleep

node n **1** point on a plant stem from which leaves grow **2** point at which a curve crosses itself

nodule n **1** small knot or lump

2 rounded mineral growth on the root of a plant

Noel n Christmas

noggin n **1** small quantity of an alcoholic drink **2** informal head

noise n sound, usually a loud or disturbing one **be noised abroad** be rumoured **noisy** adj **1** making a lot of noise **2** full of noise **noisily** adv **noiseless** adj

noisome adj **1** (of smells) offensive **2** harmful or poisonous

nomad n member of a tribe with no fixed dwelling place, wanderer **nomadic** adj

nom de plume n, pl **noms de plume** pen name

nomenclature [no-**men**-klatch-er] n system of names used in a particular subject

nominal adj **1** in name only **2** very small in comparison with real worth **nominally** adv

nominate v **1** suggest as a candidate **2** appoint to an office or position **nomination** n **nominee** n candidate **nominative** n form of a noun indicating subject of a verb

non- prefix **1** indicating negation: nonexistent **2** indicating refusal or failure: noncooperation **3** indicating exclusion from a specified class: nonfiction **4** indicating lack or absence: nonevent

nonagenarian n person aged between ninety and ninety-nine

non-aggression n (of countries) not attacking

nonagon n geometric figure with nine sides **nonagonal** adj

non-alcoholic adj containing no alcohol

non-aligned adj (of a country)

not part of a major alliance or power bloc

nonce *n* **for the nonce** for the present

nonchalant [**non**-shall-ant] *adj* casually unconcerned or indifferent **nonchalantly** *adv* **nonchalance** *n*

non-combatant *n* member of the armed forces whose duties do not include fighting

non-commissioned officer *n* (in the armed forces) a subordinate officer, risen from the ranks

noncommittal *adj* not committing oneself to any particular opinion

non compos mentis *adj* of unsound mind

non-conductor *n* substance that is a poor conductor of heat, electricity, or sound

non-confidence *Canad* ▷ *n* **1** absence of majority support in a legislature for a government ▷ *adj* **2** indicating or arising from an absence of majority support for a government: *a non-confidence motion*

nonconformist *n* **1** person who does not conform to generally accepted patterns of behaviour or thought **2 Nonconformist** member of a Protestant group separated from the Church of England ▷ *adj* **3** (of behaviour or ideas) not conforming to accepted patterns **nonconformity** *n*

non-contributory *adj* denoting a pension scheme for employees, the premiums of which are paid entirely by the employer

nondescript *adj* lacking outstanding features

none *pron* **1** not any **2** no-one **nonetheless** *adv* despite that, however

nonentity [non-**enn**-tit-

tee] *n, pl* **-ties** insignificant person or thing

non-event *n* disappointing or insignificant occurrence

non-flammable *adj* not easily set on fire

non-intervention *n* refusal to intervene in the affairs of others

nonpareil [non-par-**rail**] *n* person or thing that is unsurpassed

nonpayment *n* failure to pay money owed

nonplussed *adj* perplexed

nonsense *n* **1** something that has or makes no sense **2** absurd language **3** foolish behaviour **nonsensical** *adj*

non sequitur [**sek**-wit-tur] *n* statement with little or no relation to what preceded it

non-standard *adj* denoting language that is not regarded as correct by educated native speakers

non-starter *n* person or idea that has little chance of success

non-status *adj Canad* of or relating to any person of Indian ancestry who is not registered as such under the Indian Act

non-stick *adj* coated with a substance that food will not stick to when cooked

non-stop *adj, adv* without a stop

non-toxic *adj* not poisonous

noodle *n* strip of pasta

nook *n* sheltered place

noon *n* twelve o'clock midday **noonday** *n lit* noon

noose *n* loop in the end of a rope, tied with a slipknot

nor *conj* and not

Nordic *adj* of Scandinavia **Nordic skiing** cross-country skiing **Nordic walking** recreational walking using poles to aid movement

norm _n_ standard that is regarded as normal

normal _adj_ **1** usual, regular, or typical **2** free from mental or physical disorder **normally** _adv_ **normality** _n_ **normalize** _v_

Norse _n, adj_ (language) of ancient and medieval Norway

north _n_ **1** direction towards the North Pole, opposite south **2** area lying in or towards the north ▷ _adv_ **3** in, to, or towards the north ▷ _adj_ **4** to or in the north **5** (of a wind) from the north **northerly** _adj_ **northern** _adj_ **northerner** _n_ person from the north of a country or area **northwards** _adv_ **northeast** _n, adj, adv_ (in or to) direction between north and east **northwest** _n, adj, adv_ (in or to) direction between north and west **North Pole** northernmost point on the earth's axis

nos. numbers

nose _n_ **1** organ of smell, used also in breathing **2** front part of a vehicle ▷ _v_ **3** move forward slowly and carefully **4** pry or snoop **nosy** _or_ **nosey** _adj_ _informal_ prying or inquisitive **nosiness** _n_ **nose dive** (of an aircraft) sudden drop **nosegay** _n_ small bunch of flowers

nosh _slang_ ▷ _n_ **1** food ▷ _v_ **2** eat

nostalgia _n_ sentimental longing for the past **nostalgic** _adj_

nostril _n_ one of the two openings at the end of the nose

nostrum _n_ **1** quack medicine **2** favourite remedy

not _adv_ expressing negation, refusal, or denial

notable [note-a-bl] _adj_ **1** worthy of being noted, remarkable ▷ _n_ **2** person of distinction **notably** _adv_

notability [note-a-**bill**-lit-tee] _n_

notary [**note**-a-ree] _n, pl_ -**ries** person authorized to witness the signing of legal documents

notation [no-**tay**-shun] _n_ **1** representation of numbers or quantities in a system by a series of symbols **2** set of such symbols

notch _n_ **1** V-shaped cut **2** _informal_ step or level ▷ _v_ **3** make a notch in

note _n_ **1** short letter **2** brief comment or record **3** banknote **4** (symbol for) a musical sound **5** hint or mood ▷ _v_ **6** notice, pay attention to **7** record in writing **8** remark upon **noted** _adj_ well-known **notebook** _n_ book for writing in **noteworthy** _adj_ worth noting, remarkable

nothing _pron_ **1** not anything **2** matter of no importance **3** figure o ▷ _adv_ **4** not at all **nothingness** _n_ **1** nonexistence **2** insignificance

notice _n_ **1** observation or attention **2** sign giving warning or an announcement **3** advance notification of intention to end a contract of employment ▷ _v_ **4** observe, become aware of **5** point out or remark upon **noticeable** _adj_ easily seen or detected, appreciable

notify _v_ -**fying**, -**fied** inform **notification** _n_ **notifiable** _adj_ having to be reported to the authorities

notion _n_ **1** idea or opinion **2** whim **notional** _adj_ speculative, imaginary, or unreal

notorious _adj_ well known for something bad **notoriously** _adv_ **notoriety** _n_

notwithstanding _prep_ in spite of **notwithstanding**

n

clause clause in the Canadian Charter of Rights and Freedoms allowing provincial legislatures and the federal Parliament to override Charter clauses pertaining to equality and legal rights

nougat n chewy candy containing nuts and fruit

nought n **1** nothing **2** figure 0 **noughties** pl n informal decade from 2000 to 2009

noun n word that refers to a person, place, or thing

nourish v **1** feed **2** encourage or foster (an idea or feeling) **nourishment** n **nourishing** adj providing the food necessary for life and growth

nouvelle cuisine [noo-vell kwee-**zeen**] n style of preparing and presenting food with light sauces and unusual combinations of flavours

Nov. November

nova n, pl **-vae**, **-vas** star that suddenly becomes brighter and then gradually decreases to its original brightness

novel[1] n long fictitious story in book form **novelist** n writer of novels **novella** n, pl **-las**, **-lae** short novel

novel[2] adj fresh, new, or original **novelty** n **1** newness **2** something new or unusual **3** cheap toy or trinket

November n eleventh month of the year

novena [no-**vee**-na] n, pl **-nae** RC Church set of prayers or services on nine consecutive days

novice [**nov**-viss] n **1** beginner **2** person who has entered a religious order but has not yet taken vows

now adv **1** at or for the present time **2** immediately ▷ conj **3** seeing that, since **just now**

very recently **now and again** or **now and then** occasionally **nowadays** adv in these times

nowhere adv not anywhere

noxious adj **1** poisonous or harmful **2** extremely unpleasant

nozzle n projecting spout through which fluid is discharged

NS, N.S. Nova Scotia

NST Newfoundland Standard Time

NT 1 New Testament **2** Newfoundland Time

NU Nunavut

nuance [**new**-ahnss] n subtle difference in colour, meaning, or tone

nub n point or gist (of a story etc.)

nubile [**new**-bile] adj **1** (of a young woman) sexually attractive **2** old enough to get married

nuclear adj **1** of nuclear weapons or energy **2** of a nucleus, esp. the nucleus of an atom **nuclear bomb** bomb whose force is due to uncontrolled nuclear fusion or fission **nuclear energy** energy released as a result of nuclear fission or fusion **nuclear fission** splitting of an atomic nucleus **nuclear fusion** combination of two nuclei to form a heavier nucleus with the release of energy **nuclear power** power produced by a nuclear reactor **nuclear reaction** change in structure and energy content of an atomic nucleus by interaction with another nucleus or particle **nuclear reactor** device in which a nuclear reaction is maintained and controlled to produce nuclear energy **nuclear winter** theoretical period of low temperatures

n

and little light after a nuclear war

nucleic acid n complex compound, such as DNA or RNA, found in all living cells

nucleonics n branch of physics dealing with the applications of nuclear energy

nucleus n, pl -clei 1 centre, esp. of an atom or cell 2 central thing around which others are grouped

nude adj 1 naked ▷ n 2 naked figure in painting, sculpture, or photography **nudity** n **nudism** n practice of not wearing clothes **nudist** n

nudge v 1 push gently, esp. with the elbow ▷ n 2 gentle push or touch

nugatory [new-gat-tree] adj 1 trifling 2 not valid

nugget n 1 small lump of gold in its natural state 2 something small but valuable

nuisance n something or someone that causes annoyance or bother

nuke slang ▷ v 1 attack with nuclear weapons ▷ n 2 nuclear bomb

null adj **null and void** not legally valid **nullity** n **nullify** v 1 make ineffective 2 cancel

numb adj 1 without feeling, as through cold, shock, or fear ▷ v 2 make numb **numbly** adv **numbness** n **numbskull** n same as **numskull**

number n 1 sum or quantity 2 word or symbol used to express a sum or quantity, numeral 3 one of a series, such as a copy of a magazine 4 grammar classification of words depending on how many persons or things are referred to 5 song or piece of music 6 group of people 7 numeral or string of numerals used to identify a person or thing ▷ v 8 count 9 give a number to 10 amount to 11 include in a group

numberless adj too many to be counted **number crunching** computers large-scale processing of numerical data **number one** 1 informal oneself 2 first in importance or quality

numeral n word or symbol used to express a sum or quantity

numerate adj able to do basic arithmetic **numeracy** n

numeration n act or process of numbering or counting

numerator n math number above the line in a fraction

numerical adj measured or expressed in numbers **numerically** adv

numerous adj existing or happening in large numbers

numismatist n coin collector

numskull n stupid person

nun n female member of a religious order **nunnery** n convent

nuncio n RC Church pope's ambassador

nuptial adj relating to marriage **nuptials** pl n wedding

nurse n 1 person employed to look after sick people, usu. in hospital 2 woman employed to look after children ▷ v 3 look after (a sick person) 4 breast-feed (a baby) 5 try to cure (an ailment) 6 harbour or foster (a feeling) **nursery** n 1 room where children sleep or play 2 place where children are taken care of while their parents are at work 3 place where plants are grown for sale **nurseryman** n person who raises plants for sale **nursery school** school for children from 3 to 5 years

409 | NZ

old **nursery slope** gentle ski slope for beginners **nursing home** private hospital or home for old people

nurture n **1** act or process of promoting the development of a child or young plant ▷ v **2** promote or encourage the development of

nut n **1** fruit consisting of a hard shell and a kernel **2** small piece of metal that screws onto a bolt **3** slang head **4** slang eccentric person **nutty** adj **1** containing or resembling nuts **2** slang insane or eccentric **nutter** n slang insane or violent person **nutcracker** n device for cracking the shells of nuts **nuthatch** n small songbird **nutmeg** n spice made from the seed of a tropical tree

nutria [**new**-tree-a] n fur of the coypu

nutrient [**new**-tree-ent] n substance that provides nourishment

nutriment [**new**-tree-ment] n food or nourishment required by all living things to grow and stay healthy

nutrition [new-**trish**-shun] n **1** process of taking in and absorbing nutrients **2** process of being nourished **nutritious** or **nutritive** adj nourishing

nuzzle v push or rub gently with the nose or snout

NW northwest(ern)

NWT, N.W.T. Northwest Territories

nylon n **1** synthetic material used for clothing etc. **nylons 2** stockings made of nylon

nymph n mythical spirit of nature, represented as a beautiful young woman

nymphet n sexually precocious young girl

nymphomaniac n woman with an abnormally intense sexual desire

NZ New Zealand

Oo

oaf *n* stupid or clumsy person **oafish** *adj*

oak *n* **1** deciduous forest tree **2** its wood, used for furniture **oaken** *adj* **oak apple** brownish lump found on oak trees

oakum *n* fibre obtained by unravelling old rope

oar *n* pole with a broad blade, used for rowing a boat

oasis *n, pl* **-ses** fertile area in a desert

oast *n* kiln for drying hops

oath *n* **1** solemn promise, esp. to be truthful in court **2** swearword

oats *pl n* grain of a cereal plant, used for food **sow one's wild oats** have many sexual relationships when young **oaten** *adj* **oatmeal** *adj* pale brownish-cream

obbligato [ob-lig-**gah**-toe] *n music* essential part or accompaniment

obdurate *adj* **1** hardhearted **2** stubborn **obduracy** *n*

OBE Officer of the Order of the British Empire

obedient *adj* obeying or willing to obey **obediently** *adv* **obedience** *n*

obeisance [oh-**bay**-sanss] *n* **1** attitude of respect **2** bow or curtsy

obelisk [**ob**-bill-isk] *n* four-sided stone column tapering to a pyramid at the top

obese [oh-**beess**] *adj* very fat **obesity** *n*

obey *v* **1** carry out the instructions of (someone) **2** comply with (instructions)

obfuscate *v* **1** darken **2** make (something) confusing

obituary *n, pl* **-aries** announcement of someone's death, esp. in a newspaper **obituarist** *n*

object¹ *n* **1** physical thing **2** focus of thoughts or action **3** aim or purpose **4** *grammar* word that a verb or preposition affects **no object** not a hindrance

object² *v* (foll. by *to*) oppose **objection** *n* **objectionable** *adj* unpleasant **objector** *n*

objective *adj* **1** existing in the real world outside the human mind **2** not biased ▷ *n* **3** aim or purpose **objectively** *adv* **objectivity** *n*

objet d'art [ob-zhay **dahr**] *n, pl* **objets d'art** small object of artistic value

oblate *adj* (of a sphere) flattened at the poles

oblation *n* religious offering

oblige *v* **1** compel (someone) morally or by law to do (something) **2** do a favour for (someone) **obliging** *adj* ready to help other people **obligingly** *adv* **obligate** *v* cause (someone) to be obliged to do (something) **obligation** *n* duty **obligatory** *adj* required by a rule or law

oblique [oh-**bleak**] *adj* **1** slanting **2** indirect ▷ *n* **3** the symbol (/) **obliquely** *adv* **obliqueness** *n* **oblique angle**

angle that is not a right angle

obliterate v wipe out, destroy **obliteration** n

oblivious adj (foll. by to or of) unaware (of) **oblivion** n **1** state of being forgotten **2** state of being unaware or unconscious

oblong adj **1** having two long sides, two short sides, and four right angles ▷ n **2** oblong figure

obloquy [ob-lock-wee] n, pl -quies **1** verbal abuse **2** discredit

obnoxious adj offensive **obnoxiousness** n

oboe n double-reeded woodwind instrument **oboist** n

obscene adj **1** portraying sex offensively **2** disgusting **obscenity** n

obscure adj **1** not well known **2** hard to understand **3** indistinct ▷ v **4** make (something) obscure **obscurity** n

obsequies [ob-sick-weez] pl n funeral rites

obsequious [ob-seek-wee-uss] adj too eager to please in order to be liked **obsequiousness** n

observe v **1** watch (someone or something) carefully **2** perceive visually **3** remark **4** act according to (a law or custom) **observation** n **1** action or habit of observing **2** something observed **3** remark **observer** n **observable** adj **observably** adv **observance** n observing of a custom **observant** adj quick to notice things **observatory** n building equipped for astronomical or meteorological observations

obsess v preoccupy (someone) compulsively **obsessed** adj **obsessive** adj **obsession** n

obsidian n dark glassy volcanic rock

obsolete adj no longer in use **obsolescent** adj becoming obsolete **obsolescence** n

obstacle n something that makes progress difficult

obstetrics n branch of medicine concerned with pregnancy and childbirth **obstetric** adj **obstetrician** n

obstinate adj **1** stubborn **2** (of a stain) difficult to remove **obstinately** adv **obstinacy** n

obstreperous adj unruly, noisy

obstruct v block with an obstacle **obstruction** n **obstructionist** n person who deliberately obstructs formal proceedings **obstructive** adj

obtain v **1** acquire intentionally **2** be customary **obtainable** adj

obtrude v push oneself or one's ideas on others **obtrusion** n **obtrusive** adj **obtrusively** adv

obtuse adj **1** mentally slow **2** math (of an angle) between 90° and 180° **3** not pointed **obtusely** adv **obtuseness** n

obverse n **1** opposite way of looking at an idea **2** main side of a coin or medal

obviate v make unnecessary

obvious adj easy to see or understand, evident **obviously** adv

ocarina n small oval wind instrument made of clay

occasion n **1** time at which a particular thing happens **2** special event **3** reason: no occasion for complaint ▷ v **4** cause **occasional** adj **1** happening sometimes **2** for a special event **occasionally** adv

Occident n lit the West **Occidental** adj

occiput [**ox**-sip-put] n back of the head

occlude v 1 obstruct 2 close off **occlusion** n **occlusive** adj **occluded front** meteorol front formed when a cold front overtakes a warm front and warm air rises

occult n 1 **the occult** knowledge or study of the supernatural ▷ adj 2 relating to the supernatural

occupant n person occupying a specified place **occupancy** n (length of a) person's stay in a specified place

occupation n 1 profession 2 activity that occupies one's time 3 control of a country by a foreign military power 4 being occupied **occupational** adj **occupational therapy** treatment of physical, emotional, or social problems by means of purposeful activity

occupy v -pying, -pied 1 live or work in (a building) 2 take up the attention of (someone) 3 take up (space or time) 4 take possession of (a place) by force **occupier** n

occur v -curring, -curred 1 take place 2 exist 3 (foll. by to) come to the mind (of) **occurrence** n 1 something that occurs 2 occurring

ocean n vast area of sea between continents **oceanic** adj **oceanography** n scientific study of the oceans **ocean-going** adj able to sail on the open sea

ocelot [**oss**-ill-lot] n American wild cat with a spotted coat

oche [**ok**-kee] n darts mark on the floor behind which a player must stand

ochre [**oak**-er] adj brownish-yellow

o'clock adv used after a number to specify an hour

Oct. October

octagon n geometric figure with eight sides **octagonal** adj

octahedron [ok-ta-**heed**-ron] n, pl -**drons**, -**dra** three-dimensional geometric figure with eight faces

octane n hydrocarbon found in gasoline **octane rating** measure of gasoline quality

octave n music (interval between the first and) eighth note of a scale

octet n 1 group of eight performers 2 music for such a group

October n tenth month of the year

octogenarian n person aged between eighty and eighty-nine

octopus n, pl -**puses** sea creature with a soft body and eight tentacles

ocular adj relating to the eyes or sight

OD n 1 med overdose ▷ v **OD'ing, OD'd** 2 informal take an overdose

odd adj 1 unusual 2 occasional 3 not divisible by two 4 not part of a set **odds** pl n (ratio showing) the probability of something happening **at odds** in conflict **odds and ends** small miscellaneous items **oddness** n quality of being odd **oddity** n odd person or thing **oddments** pl n things left over

ode n lyric poem, usu. addressed to a particular subject

odium [**oh**-dee-um] n widespread dislike **odious** adj offensive

odometer n device that records the distance a vehicle has travelled

odour, odor n particular smell **odorous** adj **odourless**

or **odorless** *adj* **odoriferous**
adj giving off a pleasant smell
odorize *v* fill (something)
with scent

odyssey [**odd**-iss-ee] *n* long
eventful journey

OECD Organization for
Economic Cooperation and
Development

oedema [id-**deem**-a] *n, pl*
-**mata** abnormal swelling

oesophagus [ee-**soff**-a-guss]
n, pl -**gi** passage between the
mouth and stomach

oestrogen [ee-stra-jen] *n*
female hormone that controls
the reproductive cycle

of *prep* **1** belonging to
2 consisting of **3** connected
with **4** characteristic of

off *prep* **1** away from ▷ *adv*
2 away ▷ *adj* **3** not operating
4 cancelled or postponed
5 (of food) gone bad **6** not
up to the usual standard: *an
off day* **off colour** slightly
ill **off-message** *adj* (esp. of a
politician) not following the
official party line

offal *n* edible organs of an
animal, such as liver or
kidneys

offcut *n* piece remaining after
the required parts have been
cut out

offend *v* **1** hurt the feelings
of, insult **2** commit a crime
offender *n* **offence** *n* **1** (cause
of) hurt feelings or annoyance
2 illegal act **offensive** *adj*
1 insulting **2** aggressive
3 disagreeable ▷ *n* **4** position
or action of attack

offer *v* **1** present (something)
for acceptance or rejection
2 provide **3** be willing (to
do something) **4** propose (a
sum of money) as payment
▷ *n* **5** instance of offering
something **offering** *n* thing
offered **offertory** *n* Christianity
offering of the bread and wine

for Communion

offhand *adj* **1** Also **offhanded**
casual, curt ▷ *adv* **2** without
preparation

office *n* **1** room or building
where people work at desks
2 department of a commercial
organization **3** formal position
of responsibility **4** duty,
function **5** *usu pl* something
done for another **officer** *n*
1 person in authority in the
armed services **2** member of
the police force **3** person with
special responsibility in an
organization

official *adj* **1** approved or
arranged by someone in
authority **2** of a position of
authority ▷ *n* **3** person who
holds a position of authority
officialdom *n offensive*
officials collectively

officiate *v* conduct a
ceremony in an official role

officious *adj* **1** giving
unnecessary instructions
2 interfering

offing *n* area of the sea visible
from the shore **in the offing**
likely to happen soon

off-licence *n* shop licensed to
sell alcohol

offline *adj* not connected to
the internet ▷ *adv* while not
connected to the internet

offset *v* cancel out,
compensate for

offside *adj, adv sports*
(positioned) illegally ahead of
the ball or puck

offspring *n, pl* **offspring**
one's child

often *adv* frequently, much of
the time **oft** *adv poetic* often

ogee arch [**oh**-jee] *n* pointed
arch with an S-shaped curve
on both sides

ogle *v* stare at (someone)
lustfully

ogre *n* giant that eats human
flesh

O

oh *interj* exclamation of surprise, pain, etc.

ohm *n* unit of electrical resistance

oil *n* **1** viscous liquid, insoluble in water and usu. flammable **2** same as **petroleum** **3** petroleum derivative, used as a fuel or lubricant **oils** **4** oil-based paints used in art ▷ *v* **5** lubricate (a machine) with oil **oily** *adj* **oilfield** *n* area containing oil reserves **oil rig** platform constructed for boring oil wells **oilskins** *pl n* waterproof clothing

ointment *n* greasy substance used for healing skin or as a cosmetic

O.K., okay *informal* ▷ *interj* **1** all right ▷ *n* **2** approval ▷ *v* **3** approve (something)

okapi [ok-**kah**-pee] *n* African animal related to the giraffe but with a shorter neck

okra *n* tropical plant with edible green pods

old *adj* **1** having lived or existed for a long time **2** of a specified age: *two years old* **3** former **olden** *adj* old: *in the olden days* **oldie** *n informal* old but popular song or film **old-fashioned** *adj* no longer commonly used or valued **old guard** group of people in an organization who have traditional values **old hat** boring because so familiar **old maid** elderly unmarried woman **old master** European painter or painting from the period 1500–1800 **Old Nick** *informal* the Devil **old school tie** system of mutual help between former pupils of a British public school **Old Testament** part of the Bible recording Hebrew history **Old World** world as it was known before the discovery of the Americas

oleaginous [ol-lee-**aj**-in-uss] *adj* oily, producing oil

oleander [ol-lee-**ann**-der] *n* Mediterranean flowering evergreen shrub

olfactory *adj* relating to the sense of smell

oligarchy [**ol**-lee-gark-ee] *n*, *pl* **-chies 1** government by a small group of people **2** state governed this way **oligarch** *n* member of an oligarchy **oligarchic** *or* **oligarchical** *adj*

olive *n* **1** small green or black fruit used as food or pressed for its oil **2** tree on which this fruit grows ▷ *adj* **3** greyish-green **olive branch** conciliatory gesture

Olympic Games *pl n* four-yearly international sports competition

ombudsman *n* official who investigates complaints against government organizations

omelet *n* dish of eggs beaten and fried

omen *n* happening or object thought to foretell success or misfortune **ominous** *adj* worrying, seeming to foretell of misfortune

omit *v* **omitting, omitted** **1** leave out **2** neglect (to do something) **omission** *n*

omni- *combining form* all, everywhere: *omnidirectional*

omnibus *n* **1** *old-fashioned* bus **2** several books or TV or radio programmes made into one

omnipotent [om-**nip**-a-tent] *adj* having unlimited power **omnipotence** *n*

omnipresent *adj* present everywhere **omnipresence** *n*

omniscient [om-**nish**-yent] *adj* knowing everything **omniscience** *n*

omnivorous [om-**niv**-vor-uss] *adj* eating food obtained from both animals and plants

omnivore n omnivorous animal

on prep 1 above and touching 2 attached to 3 concerning: *an article on slimming* 4 during: *on Monday* 5 through the medium of: *on television* ▷ adv 6 in operation 7 forwards 8 continuing ▷ adj 9 operating 10 taking place: *the party's on* **on-message** adj (esp. of a politician) following the official party line

ON, O.N. Ontario

once adv 1 on one occasion 2 formerly ▷ conj 3 as soon as **at once** 1 immediately 2 simultaneously **once-over** n informal quick examination

oncogene [on-koh-jean] n gene that can cause cancer when abnormally activated

oncoming adj approaching from the front

one adj 1 single, lone ▷ n 2 number or figure 1 3 single unit ▷ pron 4 any person **oneness** n unity **oneself** pron reflexive form of **one** ‣ **one-armed bandit** fruit machine operated by a lever on one side **one-liner** n witty remark **one-night stand** sexual encounter lasting one night **one-sided** adj considering only one point of view **one-way** adj allowing movement in one direction only

onerous [own-er-uss] adj (of a task) difficult to carry out

ongoing adj in progress, continuing

onion n strongly flavoured edible bulb

online adj relating to the internet: *online shopping* ▷ adv while connected to the internet

onlooker n person who watches something happening without taking part

only adj 1 alone of its kind ▷ adv 2 exclusively 3 merely 4 no more than ▷ conj 5 but

onomatopoeia [on-a-mat-a-pee-a] n formation of a word which imitates the sound it represents, such as *hiss* **onomatopoeic** adj

onset n beginning

onslaught n violent attack

Ont. Ontario

onto prep 1 to a position on 2 aware of: *she's onto us*

ontology n philosophy study of existence **ontological** adj

onus [own-uss] n, pl **onuses** responsibility or burden

onward adj 1 directed or moving forward ▷ adv 2 Also **onwards** ahead, forward

onyx n type of quartz with coloured layers

oodles pl n informal great quantities

ooze v 1 flow slowly ▷ n 2 sluggish flow 3 soft mud at the bottom of a lake or river **oozy** adj

opacity [oh-**pass**-it-tee] n state of being opaque

opal n iridescent precious stone **opalescent** adj iridescent like an opal

opaque adj not able to be seen through, not transparent

op. cit. [**op** sit] in the work cited

OPEC Organization of Petroleum Exporting Countries

open adj 1 not closed 2 uncovered 3 unfolded 4 ready for business 5 free from obstruction, accessible 6 unrestricted 7 not finalized 8 frank ▷ v 9 (cause to) become open 10 begin ▷ n 11 sports competition open to everyone **in the open** outdoors **openly** adv without concealment **opening** n 1 hole 2 opportunity ▷ adj 3 first

open-and-shut case problem that is easily solved **open day** day on which a school or college is open to the public **open-handed** *adj* generous **open-hearted** *adj* **1** generous **2** frank **open-heart surgery** surgery on the heart during which the blood circulation is maintained by machine **open house** hospitality to visitors at any time **open letter** letter to an individual that the writer makes public in a newspaper or magazine **open-minded** *adj* receptive to new ideas **open-pit mining** mining at the surface and not underground **open-plan** *adj* (of a house or office) having few interior walls **open source** intellectual property, esp. computer source code, that is made freely available to the general public **openwork** *n* patterns made by leaving spaces in a design

opera[1] *n* drama in which the text is sung to an orchestral accompaniment **operatic** *adj* **operetta** *n* light-hearted comic opera

opera[2] *n* a plural of **opus**

operate *v* **1** (cause to) function **2** direct **3** perform an operation **operator** *n* **operation** *n* **1** method or procedure of working **2** medical procedure in which the body is worked on to repair a damaged part **operational** *adj* **1** in working order **2** relating to a working procedure: *operational difficulties* **operative** [op-rat-tiv] *adj* **1** working ▷ *n* **2** worker with a special skill

ophidian *adj, n* (reptile) of the snake family

ophthalmic *adj* relating to the eyes **ophthalmic optician** see **optician**

▶ **ophthalmology** *n* study of the eye and its diseases **ophthalmologist** *n*

opiate [oh-pee-ate] *n* narcotic drug containing opium

opinion *n* personal belief or judgment **opinion poll** see **poll** ▶ **opinionated** *adj* having strong opinions **opine** *v old-fashioned* express an opinion

opium [oh-pee-um] *n* addictive narcotic drug made from poppy seeds

opossum *n* small marsupial of N America or Australia

opponent *n* person one is working against in a contest, battle, or argument

opportunity *n, pl* -**ties** **1** favourable time or condition **2** good chance **opportune** *adj* happening at a suitable time **opportunist** *n* person who does whatever is advantageous without regard for principles **opportunism** *n*

oppose *v* work against **be opposed to** disagree with or disapprove of **opposition** *n* **1** obstruction or hostility **2** largest political party not in power **3** group opposing another

opposite *adj* **1** situated on the other side **2** facing **3** diametrically different ▷ *n* **4** person or thing that is opposite ▷ *prep, adv* **5** facing **6** on the other side (from)

oppress *v* **1** subjugate by cruelty or force **2** depress **oppression** *n* **oppressor** *n* **oppressive** *adj* **1** tyrannical **2** (of weather) hot and humid **oppressively** *adv*

opprobrium [op-**probe**-ree-um] *n* state of being criticized severely for wrong one has done **opprobrious** *adj*

oppugn [op-**pewn**] *v* **1** dispute **2** question

opt v (foll. by for) show a preference (for), choose

optic adj relating to the eyes or sight **optics** n science of sight and light **optical** adj **optical character reader** device that electronically reads and stores text **optical fibre** fine glass-fibre tube used to transmit information

optician n person who makes or sells glasses **dispensing optician** person who supplies and fits glasses **ophthalmic optician** person qualified to prescribe glasses

optimism n tendency to always take the most hopeful view **optimist** n **optimistic** adj **optimistically** adv

optimum n, pl **-ma**, **-mums** 1 best possible conditions ▷ adj 2 most favourable **optimal** adj **optimize** v make the most of

option n 1 choice 2 thing chosen 3 right to buy or sell something at a specified price within a given time **optional** adj possible but not compulsory

optometrist [op-**tom**-met-trist] n person qualified to prescribe glasses **optometry** n

opulent [op-pew-lent] adj having or indicating wealth **opulence** n

opus [oh-puss] n, pl **opuses**, **opera** artistic creation, esp. a musical work

or conj used to join alternatives: tea or coffee

oracle n 1 shrine of an ancient god 2 prophecy, often obscure, revealed at a shrine 3 person believed to make infallible predictions **oracular** adj

oral adj 1 spoken 2 (of a drug) to be taken by mouth ▷ n 3 spoken examination **orally** adv

orange adj 1 reddish-yellow ▷ n 2 reddish-yellow citrus fruit **orangeade** n orange-flavoured, usu. fizzy drink **orangery** n greenhouse for growing orange trees

orang-utan, orang-outang n large reddish-brown ape with long arms

orator [or-rat-tor] n skilful public speaker **oration** n formal speech **oratorical** adj **oratory** [or-rat-tree] n 1 art of making speeches 2 small private chapel

oratorio [or-rat-**tor**-ee-oh] n, pl **-rios** musical composition for choir and orchestra, usu. with a religious theme

orb n ceremonial decorated sphere with a cross on top, carried by a monarch

orbit n 1 curved path of a planet, satellite, or spacecraft around another heavenly body 2 sphere of influence ▷ v **orbiting, orbited** 3 move in an orbit around 4 put (a satellite or spacecraft) into orbit **orbital** adj

orchard n area where fruit trees are grown

orchestra n large group of musicians, esp. playing a variety of instruments **orchestral** adj **orchestrate** v 1 arrange (music) for orchestra 2 organize (something) to particular effect **orchestration** n **orchestra pit** area of a theatre in front of the stage, for the orchestra

orchid n plant with flowers that have unusual lip-shaped petals

ordain v 1 make (someone) a member of the clergy 2 order or establish with authority

ordeal n painful or difficult experience

order n 1 instruction to be carried out 2 request

O

for goods to be supplied **3** methodical arrangement or sequence **4** established social system **5** condition of a law-abiding society **6** social class **7** group of similar plants or animals **8** kind, sort **9** religious society, usu. of monks or nuns ▷ v **10** give an instruction to **11** request (something) to be supplied **12** arrange methodically **in order** so that it is possible **orderly** adj **1** well organized **2** well behaved ▷ n, pl **-lies 3** male hospital attendant **orderliness** n **Order of Canada** order awarded to Canadians for outstanding achievement

ordinal number n number showing a position in a series: *first; second*

ordinance n official rule or order

ordinary adj **1** usual or normal **2** dull or commonplace **ordinarily** adv

ordination n ordaining

ordnance n weapons and military supplies

ordure n excrement

ore n (rock containing) a mineral which yields metal

oregano [or-rig-**gah**-no] n aromatic herb used in cooking

organ n **1** part of an animal or plant that has a particular function, such as the heart or lungs **2** musical keyboard instrument in which notes are produced by forcing air through pipes **3** means of conveying information, esp. a newspaper **organic** adj **1** of or produced from animals or plants **2** chem relating to compounds of carbon **3** grown without artificial fertilizers or pesticides **4** organized systematically **organically** adv **organism** n any living

animal or plant **organist** n organ player

organdie n fine cotton fabric

organize v **1** make arrangements for **2** arrange systematically **3** unite (people) for a shared purpose **organization** n **1** group of people working together **2** act of organizing **organizational** adj **organizer** n

orgasm n most intense point of sexual pleasure **orgasmic** adj

orgy n, pl **-gies 1** party involving promiscuous sexual activity **2** unrestrained indulgence: *an orgy of destruction*

oriel n upper window built out from a wall

Orient n **the Orient** lit East Asia **Oriental** adj **Orientalist** n specialist in the languages and history of the Far East **orient** or **orientate** v **1** position (oneself) according to one's surroundings **2** position (a map) in relation to the points of the compass **orientation** n **orienteering** n sport in which competitors hike over a course using a compass and map

orifice [**or**-rif-fiss] n opening or hole

origami [or-rig-**gah**-mee] n Japanese decorative art of paper folding

origin n point from which something develops **original** adj **1** earliest **2** new, not copied or based on something else **3** able to think up new ideas ▷ n **4** first version, from which others are copied **original sin** human imperfection and mortality as a result of Adam's disobedience **originally** adv **originality** n **originate** v come or bring into existence

origination n **originator** n

oriole n tropical or N American songbird

ormolu n gold-coloured alloy used for decoration

ornament n **1** decorative object ▷ v **2** decorate **ornamental** adj **ornamentation** n

ornate adj highly decorated, elaborate

ornithology n study of birds **ornithological** adj **ornithologist** n

orotund adj **1** (of a voice) resonant **2** (of language) pompous

orphan n child whose parents are dead **orphanage** n children's home for orphans **orphaned** adj having no living parents

orrery n, pl **-ries** mechanical model of the solar system

orris n **1** kind of iris **2** Also **orrisroot** fragrant root used for perfume

orthodontics n branch of dentistry concerned with correcting irregular teeth **orthodontist** n

orthodox adj conforming to established views **orthodoxy** n **Orthodox Church** dominant Christian Church in Eastern Europe

orthography n correct spelling

orthopedics, orthopaedics n branch of medicine concerned with disorders of the muscles or joints **orthopedic** or **orthopaedic** adj **orthopedist** or **orthopaedist** n

ortolan n small European bird eaten as a delicacy

oryx n large African antelope

Oscar n award in the form of a statuette given for achievements in films

oscillate [**oss**-ill-late] v swing back and forth **oscillation** n **oscillator** n **oscillatory** adj **oscilloscope** [oss-**sill**-oh-scope] n instrument that shows the shape of a wave on a cathode-ray tube

osier [**oh**-zee-er] n **1** willow tree **2** willow branch used in basketwork

osmium n heaviest known metallic element

osmosis n **1** movement of a liquid through a membrane from a lower to a higher concentration **2** process of subtle influence **osmotic** adj

osprey n large fish-eating bird of prey

osseous adj made of or like bone

ossify v **-fying, -fied** **1** (cause to) become bone, harden **2** become inflexible **ossification** n

ostensible adj apparent, seeming **ostensibly** adv

ostentation n pretentious display **ostentatious** adj **ostentatiously** adv

osteopathy n medical treatment involving manipulation of the joints **osteopath** n

osteoporosis n brittleness of the bones, caused by lack of calcium

ostracize v exclude (a person) from a group **ostracism** n

ostrich n large African bird that runs fast but cannot fly

OT Old Testament

other adj **1** remaining in a group of which one or some have been specified **2** different from the ones specified or understood **3** additional ▷ n **4** other person or thing **otherwise** adv **1** differently, in another way ▷ conj **2** or else, if not **otherworldly** adj concerned with spiritual rather than practical matters

otiose [oh-tee-oze] *adj* not useful: *otiose language*

otter *n* small brown freshwater mammal that eats fish

ottoman *n, pl* **-mans** storage chest with a padded lid for use as a seat **Ottoman** *n, adj hist* (member) of the former Turkish empire

ouananiche [wah-ni-**neesh**] *n* variety of Atlantic salmon found only in lakes

oubliette [oo-blee-**ett**] *n* dungeon entered only by a trapdoor

ouch *interj* exclamation of sudden pain

ought *v* (foll. by *to*) **1** *used to express* obligation: *you ought to pay* **2** *used to express* advisability: *you ought to diet* **3** *used to express* probability: *you ought to know by then*

Ouija *n* ® lettered board on which supposed messages from the dead are spelt out

ounce *n* unit of weight equal to one sixteenth of a pound (28.4 grams)

our *adj* belonging to us **ours** *pron* thing(s) belonging to us **ourselves** *pron* emphatic and reflexive form of **we, us**

oust *v* force (someone) out, expel

out *adv, adj* **1** away from inside **2** not at home **3** revealed or made public **4** used up **5** no longer burning or shining **6** not correct: *the calculations were out* **7** not fashionable **8** on strike **9** openly homosexual **10** *sports* dismissed ▷ *v* **11** *informal* name (a public figure) as being homosexual **out of** at or to a point outside **outer** *adj* on the outside **outermost** *adj* furthest out **outing** *n* leisure trip **outward** *adj* **1** apparent ▷ *adv* **2** Also **outwards** away from somewhere **outwardly** *adv*

out- *prefix* surpassing: *outlive; outdistance*

outback *n* remote bush country of Australia

outbid *v* offer a higher price than

outboard motor *n* engine externally attached to the stern of a boat

outbox *n* (on a computer) folder in a mailbox in which outgoing messages are stored and displayed

outbreak *n* sudden occurrence (of something unpleasant)

outburst *n* sudden expression of emotion

outcast *n* person rejected by a particular group

outclass *v* surpass in quality

outcome *n* result

outcrop *n geology* area where bedrock is covered by little or no soil

outcry *n, pl* **-cries** expression of vehement or widespread protest

outdated *adj* out of date, old-fashioned

outdo *v* surpass in performance

outdoors *adv* **1** in(to) the open air ▷ *n* **2** the open air **outdoor** *adj*

outface *v* subdue or disconcert (someone) by staring

outfall *n* mouth of a river or pipe

outfield *n baseball* area beyond home plate and the three bases

outfit *n* **1** matching set of clothes **2** *informal* group of people working together **outfitter** *n old-fashioned* supplier of men's clothes

outflank *v* **1** get round the side of (an enemy army) **2** outdo (someone)

outgoing *adj* **1** leaving **2** sociable **outgoings** *pl n* expenses

outgrow *v* become too large or too old for **outgrowth**

n **1** thing growing out from a main body **2** natural development

outhouse *n* building near a main building

outlandish *adj* extravagantly eccentric

outlaw *n* **1** *hist* criminal deprived of legal protection, bandit ▷ *v* **2** make illegal **3** *hist* make (someone) an outlaw

outlay *n* expenditure

outlet *n* **1** means of expressing emotion **2** market for a product **3** place where a product is sold **4** opening or way out

outline *n* **1** line defining the shape of something **2** short general explanation ▷ *v* **3** draw the outline of **4** summarize

outlook *n* **1** attitude **2** probable outcome

outlying *adj* distant from the main area

outmanoeuvre *v* get an advantage over

outmoded *adj* no longer fashionable or accepted

outnumber *v* exceed in number

outpatient *n* patient who does not stay in hospital overnight

outport *n* isolated fishing village, esp. in Newfoundland

outpost *n* outlying settlement

output *n* **1** amount produced **2** power, voltage, or current delivered by an electrical circuit **3** *computers* data produced ▷ *v* **4** *computers* produce (data) at the end of a process

outrage *n* **1** great moral indignation **2** gross violation of morality ▷ *v* **3** offend morally **outrageous** *adj* **1** shocking **2** offensive **outrageously** *adv*

outré [oo-tray] *adj* shockingly eccentric

outrider *n* motorcyclist acting as an escort

outrigger *n* stabilizing frame projecting from a boat

outright *adj*, *adv* **1** absolute(ly) **2** open(ly) and direct(ly)

outrun *v* **1** run faster than **2** exceed

outset *n* beginning

outshine *v* surpass (someone) in excellence

outside *prep* **1** to the exterior of **2** beyond the limits of ▷ *adj* **3** exterior **4** unlikely: *an outside chance* **5** coming from outside ▷ *adv* **6** on or to the exterior **7** in(to) the open air ▷ *n* **8** external area or surface **outsider** *n* **1** person outside a specific group **2** contestant thought unlikely to win

outsize, outsized *adj* larger than normal

outskirts *pl n* outer areas, esp. of a town

outsmart *v* *informal* outwit

outspoken *adj* **1** tending to say what one thinks **2** said openly

outstanding *adj* **1** excellent **2** still to be dealt with or paid

outstrip *v* **1** go faster than **2** surpass

outtake *n* unreleased take from a recording session, film, or TV programme

outweigh *v* be more important, significant or influential than

outwit *v* get the better of (someone) by cunning

outworks *pl n* secondary external defences of a fort

ouzel, ousel [ooze-el] *n* see **dipper**

ova *n* plural of **ovum**

oval *adj* **1** egg-shaped ▷ *n* **2** anything that is oval in shape

ovary *n*, *pl* **-ries** female egg-producing organ **ovarian** *adj*

o

ovation n enthusiastic round of applause

oven n heated compartment or container for cooking or for drying or firing ceramics

over prep 1 higher than 2 on or across the top of 3 on or to the other side of 4 during 5 more than 6 recovered from ▷ adv 7 above or across something 8 onto its side: *the jug toppled over* 9 in excess ▷ adj 10 finished ▷ n 11 cricket series of six balls bowled from one end **overly** adv excessively

over- prefix 1 too much: *overeat* 2 above: *overlord* 3 on top: *overshoe*

overall n 1 coat-shaped protective garment **overalls** 2 protective garment consisting of trousers with a jacket or bib and braces attached ▷ adj, adv 3 in total

overarm adv, adj (thrown) with the arm above the shoulder

overawe v affect (someone) with an overpowering sense of awe

overbalance v lose balance

overbearing adj domineering

overblown adj inflated or excessive: *overblown pride*

overboard adv from a boat into the water **go overboard** go to extremes, esp. in enthusiasm

overcast adj (of the sky) covered with clouds

overcoat n heavy coat

overcome v 1 gain control over after an effort 2 (of an emotion) affect strongly

overdo v 1 do to excess 2 exaggerate (something) **overdo it** do something to a greater degree than is advisable

overdose n 1 excessive dose of a drug ▷ v 2 take an overdose

overdraft n 1 overdrawing 2 amount overdrawn

overdraw v withdraw more money than is in (one's bank account) **overdrawn** adj 1 having overdrawn one's account 2 (of an account) in debit

overdrive n very high gear in a motor vehicle

overdue adj still due after the time allowed

overgrown adj thickly covered with plants and weeds

overhaul v 1 examine and repair ▷ n 2 examination and repair

overhead adv 1 in the sky ▷ adj 2 over one's head **overheads** pl n general cost of maintaining a business

overhear v hear (a speaker or remark) unintentionally or without the speaker's knowledge

overjoyed adj very pleased

overkill n treatment that is greater than required

overland adj, adv by land

overlap v 1 share part of the same space or period of time (as) ▷ n 2 area overlapping

overleaf adv on the back of the current page

overlook v 1 fail to notice 2 ignore 3 look at from above

overnight adj, adv 1 (taking place) during one night 2 (happening) very quickly

overpower v subdue or overcome (someone)

overreach v **overreach oneself** fail by trying to be too clever

override v 1 overrule 2 replace

overrule v 1 reverse the decision of (a person with less power) 2 reverse (someone else's decision)

overrun v 1 spread over (a place) rapidly 2 extend beyond a set limit

overseas *adj, adv* to, of, or from a distant country

oversee *v* watch over from a position of authority **overseer** *n*

overshadow *v* **1** reduce the significance of (a person or thing) by comparison **2** sadden the atmosphere of

oversight *n* mistake caused by not noticing something

overskate *v* **-skating, -skated** *hockey* inadvertently skate past (the puck)

overspill *n* rehousing of people from crowded cities to smaller towns

overstay *v* **overstay one's welcome** stay longer than one's host or hostess would like

overt *adj* open, not hidden **overtly** *adv*

overtake *v* move past (a vehicle or person) while travelling in the same direction

overthrow *v* **1** defeat and replace ▷ *n* **2** downfall, destruction

overtime *n, adv* (paid work done) in addition to one's normal working hours

overtone *n* additional meaning

overture *n* **1** *music* orchestral introduction **overtures** **2** opening moves in a new relationship

overturn *v* **1** turn upside down **2** overrule (a legal decision) **3** overthrow (a government)

overweight *adj* weighing more than is healthy

overwhelm *v* **1** overpower, esp. emotionally **2** defeat by force **overwhelming** *adj* **overwhelmingly** *adv*

overwrought *adj* nervous and agitated

oviparous [oh-**vip**-par-uss] *adj* producing young by laying eggs

ovoid [**oh**-void] *adj* egg-shaped

ovulate [**ov**-yew-late] *v* release an egg cell from an ovary **ovulation** *n*

ovum [**oh**-vum] *n, pl* **ova** unfertilized egg cell

owe *v* be obliged to pay (a sum of money) to (a person) **owing to** as result of

owl *n* night bird of prey **owlish** *adj* **owlet** *n* young owl

own *adj* **1** used to emphasize possession: *my own idea* ▷ *v* **2** possess **owner** *n* **ownership** *n* **own up** *v* confess

ox *n, pl* **oxen** castrated bull

oxeye *n* plant with daisy-like flowers

oxide *n* compound of oxygen and one other element **oxidize** *v* combine chemically with oxygen, as in burning or rusting

oxygen *n* gaseous element essential to life and combustion **oxygenate** *v* add oxygen to **oxyacetylene** *n* mixture of oxygen and acetylene used in high-temperature welding

oxymoron [ox-see-**more**-on] *n* figure of speech that combines two apparently contradictory ideas, such as *cruel kindness*

oyez *interj hist* (shouted three times by a public crier) listen

oyster *n* edible shellfish **oystercatcher** *n* wading bird with black-and-white feathers

oz. ounce

ozone *n* highly reactive strong-smelling form of oxygen **ozone layer** layer of ozone in the upper atmosphere that filters out ultraviolet radiation

o

Pp

p 1 page 2 *music* piano

P *chem* phosphorus

PA 1 personal assistant 2 public-address system

p.a. per annum

pace *n* 1 single step in walking 2 length of a step 3 rate of progress ▷ *v* 4 walk with regular steps 5 set the speed for (competitors in a race) 6 cross or measure with steps **put someone through his** *or* **her paces** test someone's ability **pacemaker** *n* 1 person who sets the speed of a race 2 electronic device surgically implanted in a person with heart disease to regulate the heartbeat

pachyderm [pak-ee-durm] *n* thick-skinned animal such as an elephant

Pacific Daylight Time *n* one of the standard times used in North America, seven hours behind Greenwich Mean Time **Abbreviation: PDT**

Pacific Standard Time *n* one of the standard times used in North America, eight hours behind Greenwich Mean Time **Abbreviation: PST**

pacifist *n* person who refuses on principle to take part in war **pacifism** *n*

pacify *v* **-fying, -fied** 1 soothe, calm 2 establish peace in **pacification** *n* **pacifier** *n* rubber or plastic teat for a baby to suck

pack *n* 1 load carried on the back 2 set of things sold together 3 container for things sold 4 same as **packet** 5 set of playing cards 6 group of hunting animals ▷ *v* 7 put (clothes etc.) together in a suitcase or bag 8 put (goods) into containers or parcels 9 press tightly together, cram 10 fill with things **packhorse** *n* horse for carrying goods **pack ice** mass of floating ice in the sea **pack in** *v informal* stop doing **pack off** *v* send away

package *n* 1 parcel 2 set of things offered together ▷ *v* 3 put into packages **packaging** *n* **package holiday** holiday in which everything is arranged by one company for a fixed price

packet *n* 1 small parcel 2 small container (and contents) 3 *Brit slang* large sum of money **packet boat** *hist* boat that carried mail, goods, or passengers on a fixed short route

packsack *n* canvas bag carried on the back or shoulder

pact *n* formal agreement

pad *n* 1 piece of soft material used for protection, support, absorption of liquid, etc. 2 block of sheets of paper fastened at the edge 3 fleshy underpart of an animal's paw 4 place for launching rockets 5 *slang* home ▷ *v* **padding, padded** 6 protect or fill in with soft material 7 walk with soft or muffled steps

padding n 1 material used to pad 2 words put in simply to increase length

paddle[1] n 1 short oar with a broad blade at one or each end ▷ v 2 move (a canoe etc.) with a paddle **paddle steamer** ship propelled by paddle wheels **paddle wheel** wheel with crosswise blades that strike the water successively to propel a ship

paddle[2] v walk with bare feet in shallow water

paddock n small field or enclosure for horses

paddy field n field where rice is grown

padlock n detachable lock with a hinged hoop fastened over a ring on the object to be secured

padre [**pah**-dray] n chaplain in the armed forces

paean [**pee**-an] n song of triumph or thanksgiving

paediatrics n same as **pediatrics**

paedophilia n same as **pedophilia**

paella [pie-**ell**-a] n Spanish dish made of rice, chicken, shellfish, and vegetables

pagan adj 1 not belonging to one of the world's main religions ▷ n 2 pagan person

page[1] n (one side of) a sheet of paper forming a book etc.

page[2] n 1 hist boy in training for knighthood 2 attendant ▷ v 3 summon (a person whose whereabouts are unknown), for example by electronic bleeper or loudspeaker announcement

pageant n parade or display of people in costume, usu. illustrating a scene from history **pageantry** n

paginate v number the pages of (a book etc.) **pagination** n

pagoda n pyramid-shaped Asian temple or tower

paid v past of **pay** ▷ **put paid to** informal end, destroy

pail n bucket **pailful** n

pain n 1 bodily or mental suffering **pains** 2 trouble, effort **on pain of** subject to the penalty of **painful** adj **painfully** adv **painless** adj **painlessly** adv **painkiller** n drug that reduces pain

painstaking adj thorough and careful

paint n 1 colouring spread on a surface with a brush or roller ▷ v 2 colour or coat with paint 3 make a picture of **painter** n **painting** n

painter n rope at the bow of a boat for tying it up

pair n 1 set of two things ▷ v 2 group or be grouped in twos

paisley pattern n pattern of small curving shapes

pajamas pl n same as **pyjamas**

pal n informal friend

palace n 1 residence of a king, bishop, etc. 2 large grand building

palatable adj pleasant to eat

palate n 1 roof of the mouth 2 sense of taste

palatial adj 1 like a palace 2 magnificent

palaver [pal-**lah**-ver] n time-wasting fuss

pale[1] adj 1 light, whitish 2 having less colour than normal ▷ v 3 become pale

pale[2] n 1 hist fence 2 boundary **beyond the pale** outside the limits of social convention

paleography, palaeography [pal-ee-**og**-ra-fee] n study of ancient writings

paleolithic, palaeolithic [pal-ee-oh-**lith**-ik] adj of the Old Stone Age

paleontology, palaeontology [pal-ee-on-**tol**-a-jee] n study of past geological periods and fossils **paleontological** or **palaeontological** adj

palette n artist's flat board for mixing colours on

palindrome n word, phrase, or sentence that reads the same backwards as forwards

paling n any of the upright planks in a fence

palisade n fence made of stakes

pall[1] n 1 cloth spread over a coffin 2 depressing oppressive atmosphere 3 dark cloud (of smoke) **pallbearer** n person carrying a coffin at a funeral

pall[2] v become boring

pallet[1] n portable platform for storing and moving goods

pallet[2] n 1 straw mattress 2 small bed

palliasse n straw mattress

palliate v lessen the severity of (something) without curing it **palliative** adj 1 giving temporary or partial relief ▷ n 2 something, for example a drug, that palliates

pallid adj pale, esp. because ill or weak **pallor** n

pally adj -lier, -liest informal on friendly terms

palm n 1 inner surface of the hand 2 tropical tree with a straight trunk crowned with long pointed leaves **palm off** v get rid of (an unwanted thing or person), esp. by deceit **Palm Sunday** the Sunday before Easter **palmtop** n computer small enough to be held in the hand

palmistry n fortune-telling from lines on the palm of the hand **palmist** n

palomino n, pl -nos gold-coloured horse with a white mane and tail

palpable adj 1 obvious 2 able to be touched or felt **palpably** adv

palpate v med examine (an

area of the body) by touching

palpitate v 1 (of the heart) beat rapidly 2 flutter or tremble **palpitation** n

palsy [**pawl**-zee] n paralysis **palsied** adj affected with palsy

paltry adj -trier, -triest worthless, insignificant

pampas pl n vast grassy treeless plains in S America **pampas grass** tall grass with feathery ornamental flower branches

pamper v treat (someone) with great indulgence, spoil

pamphlet n thin paper-covered booklet **pamphleteer** n writer of pamphlets

pan[1] n 1 wide long-handled metal container used in cooking 2 Brit bowl of a lavatory ▷ v **panning, panned** 3 sift gravel from (a riverbed) in a pan to search for gold 4 informal criticize harshly **pan out** v result

pan[2] v panning, panned move a film camera slowly so as to cover a whole scene or follow a moving object

pan- combining form all: pan-African

panacea [pan-a-**see**-a] n remedy for all diseases or problems

panache [pan-**ash**] n confident elegant style

panama n straw hat

panatella n long slender cigar

pancake n thin flat circle of fried batter

panchromatic adj photog sensitive to light of all colours

pancreas [**pang**-kree-ass] n large gland behind the stomach that produces insulin and helps digestion **pancreatic** adj

panda n large black-and-white bearlike mammal from China

pandemic *adj* (of a disease) occurring over a wide area

pandemonium *n* **1** wild confusion **2** uproar

pander *n* person who procures a sexual partner for someone **pander to** *v* indulge (a person or his or her desires)

pane *n* single piece of glass in a window or door

panegyric [pan-ee-**jire**-ik] *n* formal speech or piece of writing in praise of someone or something

panel *n* **1** flat distinct section of a larger surface, such as that in a door **2** group of people as a team in a quiz etc. **3** list of jurors, doctors, etc. ▷ *v* **-elling, -elled 4** decorate or cover with panels **panelling** *n* panels collectively, such as those on a wall **panellist** *n* member of a panel **panel beater** person who repairs damage to car bodies

pang *n* sudden sharp feeling of pain or sadness

pangolin *n* scaly anteater

panic *n* **1** sudden overwhelming fear, often infectious ▷ *v* **-icking, -icked 2** feel or cause to feel panic **panicky** *adj* **panic-stricken** or **panic-struck** *adj*

panini *n, pl* **-ni, -nis** Italian bread usu. served grilled with a variety of fillings

pannier *n* **1** bag fixed on the back of a bike or motorbike **2** basket carried by a beast of burden

panoply [**pan**-a-plee] *n* magnificent array

panorama *n* wide or complete view **panoramic** *adj*

pansy *n, pl* **-sies 1** garden flower with velvety petals **2** *offensive* effeminate or homosexual man

pant *v* breathe quickly and noisily after exertion

pantaloons *pl n* baggy trousers gathered at the ankles

pantechnicon *n* large van for furniture removals

pantheism *n* belief that God is present in everything **pantheist** *n* **pantheistic** *adj*

pantheon *n* (in ancient Greece and Rome) temple to all the gods

panther *n* leopard, esp. a black one

panties *pl n* women's underpants

pantile *n* roofing tile with an S-shaped cross section

pantograph *n* **1** instrument for copying maps etc. to any scale **2** device on the roof of an electric train for picking up the electric current

pantomime *n* play based on a fairy tale, performed in Britain at Christmas time

pantry *n, pl* **-tries** room or cupboard for storing food or cooking utensils

pants *pl n* **1** undergarment for the lower part of the body **2** trousers

pap[1] *n* **1** soft food for babies or invalids **2** worthless or oversimplified ideas

pap[2] *n* obsolete nipple

papacy [**pay**-pa-see] *n, pl* **-cies** the position or term of office of a pope **papal** *adj* of the pope or papacy

paparazzo [pap-a-**rat**-so] *n, pl* **-razzi** photographer specializing in unposed shots of famous people

papaya [pa-**pie**-ya], **papaw** [pa-**paw**] *n* large sweet West Indian fruit

paper *n* **1** material made in sheets from wood pulp or other fibres **2** printed sheet of this **3** newspaper **4** set of examination questions **5** article or essay **papers 6** personal documents ▷ *v* **7** cover (walls) with wallpaper **paperback** *n* book with flexible paper covers **paperweight** *n* heavy decorative object placed on top of loose papers **paperwork** *n* the part of a job that consists of dealing with routine letters, forms, etc.

papier-mâché [**pay**-per mash-**ay** or pap-yay **mash**-ay] *n* material made from paper mixed with paste, shaped by moulding and dried hard

papist *n, adj offensive* Roman Catholic

papoose *n* N American Indian baby or toddler

paprika *n* (powdered seasoning made from) a type of red pepper

papyrus [pap-**ire**-uss] *n, pl* -**ri**, -**ruses 1** tall water plant **2** (manuscript written on) a kind of paper made from this plant

par *n* **1** usual or average condition **2** face value of stocks and shares **3** *golf* expected standard score **on a par with** equal to

parable *n* story that illustrates a religious teaching

parabola [par-**ab**-bol-a] *n* regular curve resembling the course of an object thrown forward and up **parabolic** *adj*

paracetamol *n* mild pain-relieving drug

parachute *n* **1** large fabric canopy that slows the descent of a person or object from an aircraft ▷ *v* **2** land or drop by parachute **parachutist** *n*

parade *n* **1** ordered march or procession **2** public promenade or street of shops **3** blatant display: *parade of one's grief* ▷ *v* **4** display or flaunt

5 march in procession

paradigm [**par**-a-dime] *n* example or model

paradise *n* **1** heaven **2** state of bliss **3** Garden of Eden

paradox *n* statement that seems self-contradictory but may be true **paradoxical** *adj* **paradoxically** *adv*

paraffin *n* waxy substance derived from petroleum and used as a solvent, etc.

paragliding *n* cross-country gliding using a parachute

paragon *n* model of perfection

paragraph *n* section of a piece of writing starting on a new line

parakeet *n* small long-tailed parrot

parallax *n* apparent difference in an object's position or direction as viewed from different points

parallel *adj* **1** separated by equal distance at every point **2** precisely corresponding ▷ *n* **3** line equidistant from another at all points **4** thing with similar features to another **5** line of latitude ▷ *v* **6** be parallel to **7** correspond to **parallelism** *n*

parallelogram *n* four-sided geometric figure with opposite sides parallel

paralysis *n* inability to move or feel, because of damage to the nervous system **paralyse** *v* **1** affect with paralysis **2** make immobile **paralytic** *n, adj* (person) affected with paralysis

paramedic *n* person working in support of the medical profession **paramedical** *adj*

parameter [par-**am**-it-er] *n* limiting factor, boundary

paramilitary *adj* organized on military lines

paramount *adj* of the greatest importance or significance

paramour n obsolete illicit lover, mistress

paranoia n 1 mental illness causing delusions of fame or persecution 2 informal intense fear or suspicion **paranoiac** or **paranoid** adj, n

paranormal adj beyond scientific explanation

parapet n low wall or railing along the edge of a balcony, bridge, etc.

paraphernalia n personal belongings or bits of equipment

paraphrase v express (meaning) in different words

paraplegia [par-a-**pleej**-ya] n paralysis of the lower half of the body **paraplegic** n, adj

parapsychology n study of phenomena outside normal human ability, such as telepathy

parasite n 1 animal or plant living in or on another 2 person who lives at the expense of others, sponger **parasitic** adj

parasol n umbrella-like sunshade

paratroops, -troopers pl n troops trained to attack by descending by parachute

parboil v boil until partly cooked

parcel n 1 something wrapped up, a package ▷ v -**celling**, -**celled** 2 wrap up **parcel out** v divide into parts

parch v 1 make very hot and dry 2 make thirsty

parchment n thick smooth writing material made from animal skin

pardon v 1 forgive or excuse ▷ n 2 forgiveness 3 official release from punishment **pardonable** adj **pardonably** adv

pare v trim or cut the edge of **paring** n piece pared off

parent n father or mother **parental** adj **parenthood** n **parentage** n ancestry or family **parenting** n activity of bringing up children

parenthesis [par-en-**thiss**-iss] n, pl -**ses** 1 word or sentence inserted in a passage, usu. marked off by brackets, dashes, or commas **parentheses** 2 round brackets, ( ) **parenthetical** adj

pargeting n ornamental plasterwork on the outside of a house

pariah [par-**rye**-a] n social outcast

parietal [par-**rye**-it-al] adj of the walls of body cavities such as the skull

parish n area that has its own church and cleric **parishioner** n inhabitant of a parish

parity n equality or equivalence

park n 1 area of open land for recreational use by the public 2 area containing a number of related businesses 3 large enclosed piece of ground attached to a country house ▷ v 4 stop and leave (a vehicle) temporarily **parking lot** area or building where vehicles may be left for a time

parka n warm waterproof hooded jacket

parkade n a building used as a car park

parkette n a small public park

parlance n particular way of speaking, idiom

parley n 1 meeting between leaders or representatives of opposing forces to discuss terms ▷ v 2 have a parley

parliament n law-making assembly of a country **parliamentary** adj

parlour, parlor n old-fashioned

living room for receiving visitors

parlous adj obsolete dangerous

Parmesan n hard strong-flavoured Italian cheese

parochial adj 1 narrow in outlook, provincial 2 of a parish **parochialism** n

parody n, pl -dies 1 exaggerated and amusing imitation of someone else's style ▷ v -dying, -died 2 make a parody of

parole n 1 early freeing of a prisoner on condition that he or she behaves well ▷ v 2 place on parole **on parole** (of a prisoner) released on condition that he or she behaves well

paroxysm n 1 uncontrollable outburst, as of laughter 2 spasm or convulsion, as of pain

parquet [par-kay] n wooden blocks arranged in a pattern and forming a floor **parquetry** n

parricide n 1 person who kills one of his or her parents 2 act of killing either of one's parents

parrot n 1 tropical bird with a short hooked beak, some varieties of which can imitate speaking ▷ v -roting, -roted 2 repeat (words) without thinking

parry v -rying, -ried 1 ward off (an attack) 2 cleverly avoid (an awkward question)

parse [parz] v analyse (a sentence) in terms of grammar

parsec n unit of length used in expressing the distance of stars

parsimony n stinginess **parsimonious** adj

parsley n herb used for seasoning and decorating food

parsnip n long tapering cream-coloured root vegetable

parson n parish priest in the Anglican Church **parsonage** n parson's house **parson's nose** rump of a cooked fowl

part n 1 piece or portion 2 one of several equal divisions 3 actor's role 4 region, area 5 component of a vehicle or machine 6 division between sections of hair on the head ▷ v 7 divide 8 (of people) leave each other **take someone's part** support someone in an argument etc. **take something in good part** respond (to criticism etc.) with good humour **parting** n 1 separation 2 leave-taking **parting shot** hostile remark or gesture delivered while departing **partly** adv not completely **part of speech** particular grammatical class of words, such as noun or verb **part song** song for several voices singing in harmony **part-time** adj occupying or working less than the full working week **part with** v give up ownership of

partake v -taking, -took, -taken 1 (foll. by of) take food or drink 2 (foll. by in) take part in

parterre n formally patterned flower garden

partial adj 1 not general or complete 2 prejudiced **partial to** very fond of **partiality** n 1 favouritism 2 fondness for **partially** adv

participate v become actively involved in **participant** n **participation** n **participator** n

participle n form of a verb used in compound tenses or as an adjective: worried; worrying **participial** adj

particle n 1 extremely small

piece or amount **2** *physics* minute piece of matter, such as a proton or electron

parti-coloured *adj* differently coloured in different parts

particular *adj* **1** relating to one person or thing, not general **2** exceptional or special **3** very exact **4** not easily satisfied, fastidious ▷ *n* **5** detail **6** item of information **particularly** *adv* **particularize** *v* give details about **particularity** *n*

Parti Québécois [par-**tee** kay-beck-**wah**] *n* political party in Quebec originally advocating separation of Quebec from rest of country

partisan *n* **1** strong supporter of a party or group **2** guerrilla, member of a resistance movement ▷ *adj* **3** prejudiced or one-sided

partition *n* **1** screen or thin wall that divides a room **2** division of a country into independent parts ▷ *v* **3** divide with a partition

partner *n* **1** either member of a couple in a relationship or activity **2** member of a business partnership ▷ *v* **3** be the partner of (someone) **partnership** *n* joint business venture between two or more people

partridge *n* game bird of the grouse family

parturition *n* act of giving birth

party *n, pl* **-ties 1** social gathering for pleasure **2** group of people travelling or working together **3** group of people with a common political aim **4** person or people forming one side in a lawsuit etc. **party line** official view of a political party **party wall** common wall separating adjoining buildings

parvenu [**par**-ven-new] *n* person newly risen to a position of power or wealth, upstart

pascal *n* unit of pressure

paschal [**pass**-kal] *adj* of the Passover or Easter

pass *v* **1** go by, beyond, through, etc. **2** be successful in a test etc. **3** spend (time) or (of time) elapse **4** exchange **5** be inherited by **6** bring (a law) into force **7** move onwards or over **8** exceed **9** choose not to take one's turn in a game or quiz **10** discharge (urine etc.) from the body **11** come to an end **12** *sports* transfer (the ball) to another player ▷ *n* **13** successful result in a test **14** *sports* transfer of a ball **15** permit or licence **16** narrow gap through mountains **make a pass at** *informal* try to start a sexual relationship **passable** *adj* **1** (just) acceptable **2** (of a road) capable of being travelled along **passing** *adj* **1** brief or transitory **2** cursory or casual **pass away** *v* die **pass out** *v informal* faint **pass up** *v informal* ignore or reject

passage *n* **1** channel or opening providing a way through **2** hall or corridor **3** section of a book etc. **4** journey by sea **5** right or freedom to pass **passageway** *n* passage or corridor

passé [**pas**-say] *adj* out-of-date

passenger *n* **1** person travelling in a vehicle driven by someone else **2** one of a team who does not pull his or her weight

passer-by *n, pl* **passers-by** person who is walking past something or someone

passerine *adj* belonging to the order of perching birds

passim *adv Latin* everywhere, throughout

passion *n* 1 intense sexual love 2 any strong emotion 3 great enthusiasm 4 **Passion** *Christianity* the suffering of Christ **passionate** *adj* **passionflower** *n* tropical American plant **passion fruit** edible fruit of the passionflower **Passion play** play about Christ's suffering

passive *adj* 1 not playing an active part 2 submissive and receptive to outside forces 3 *grammar* denoting a form of verbs indicating that the subject receives the action, such as *was jeered* in *He was jeered by the crowd* **passive resistance** resistance to a government, law, etc. by nonviolent acts **passive smoking** inhalation of smoke from others' cigarettes by a nonsmoker

Passover *n* Jewish festival commemorating the sparing of the Jews in Egypt

passport *n* official document granting permission to travel abroad

pass-rush *n football* 1 same as **blitz** 2 ▸**pass-rusher** *n* **pass-rushing** *n* tactic of trying to tackle the opposing quarterback before he can pass the ball

password *n* secret word or phrase that ensures admission

past *adj* 1 of the time before the present 2 ended, gone by 3 (of a verb tense) indicating that the action specified took place earlier ▹ *n* 4 bygone times 5 person's past life, esp. an earlier, disreputable period 6 past tense ▹ *adv* 7 by 8 along ▹ *prep* 9 beyond **past it** *informal* unable to do the things one could do

when younger **past master** person with great talent or experience in a particular subject

pasta *n* type of food, such as spaghetti, that is made in different shapes from flour and water

paste *n* 1 moist soft mixture, such as toothpaste 2 adhesive, esp. for paper 3 pastry dough 4 shiny glass used to make imitation jewellery ▹ *v* 5 fasten with paste **pasting** *n slang* 1 defeat 2 strong criticism **pasteboard** *n* stiff thick paper

pastel *n* 1 coloured chalk crayon for drawing 2 picture drawn in pastels 3 pale delicate colour ▹ *adj* 4 pale and delicate in colour

pasteurize *v* sterilize by heat **pasteurization** *n*

pastiche [pass-**teesh**] *n* work of art that mixes styles or copies the style of another artist

pastille *n* small fruit-flavoured and sometimes medicated candy

pastime *n* activity that makes time pass pleasantly

pastor *n* clergyman in charge of a congregation **pastoral** *adj* 1 of or depicting country life 2 of a clergyman or his duties

pastrami *n* highly seasoned smoked beef

pastry *n, pl* -**ries** 1 baking dough made of flour, fat, and water 2 cake or pie

pasture *n* grassy land for farm animals to graze on **pasturage** *n* (right to) pasture

pasty¹ [**pay**-stee] *adj* **pastier**, **pastiest** (of a complexion) pale and unhealthy

pasty² [**pass**-tee] *n, pl* **pasties** round of pastry folded over a savoury filling

pat v patting, patted 1 tap
lightly ▷ n 2 gentle tap or
stroke 3 small shaped mass
of butter etc. ▷ adj 4 quick,
ready, or glib **off pat** learned
thoroughly

patch n 1 piece of material
sewn on a garment 2 small
contrasting section 3 plot
of ground 4 protecting pad
for the eye ▷ v 5 mend with
a patch 6 repair clumsily
patchy adj of uneven quality
or intensity **patch up** v make
up (a quarrel) **patchwork** n
needlework made of pieces
of different materials sewn
together

pate n old-fashioned head

pâté [**pat**-ay] n spread of finely
minced liver etc.

patella n, pl -lae kneecap

paten [**pat**-in] n plate for
bread in Communion

patent n 1 document giving
the exclusive right to make or
sell an invention ▷ adj 2 open
to public inspection: letters
patent 3 obvious 4 protected by
a patent ▷ v 5 obtain a patent
for **patently** adv obviously
patent leather leather
processed to give a hard glossy
surface

paternal adj 1 fatherly
2 related through one's
father **paternity** n 1 relation
of a father to his offspring
2 fatherhood **paternalism**
n authority exercised in a
way that limits individual
responsibility **paternalistic**
adj

Paternoster n RC Church the
Lord's Prayer

path n 1 surfaced walk or track
2 course of action

pathetic adj 1 causing
feelings of pity or sadness
2 distressingly inadequate
pathetically adv

pathogen n thing that causes

disease **pathogenic** adj

pathology n scientific study
of diseases **pathological**
adj 1 of pathology 2 informal
compulsively motivated
pathologist n

pathos n power of arousing
pity or sadness

patient adj 1 enduring
difficulties calmly ▷ n
2 person receiving medical
treatment **patience** n
1 quality of being patient
2 card game for one

patina n 1 fine layer on a
surface 2 sheen of age on
woodwork

patio n, pl -tios paved area
adjoining a house

patois [**pat**-wah] n, pl patois
[**pat**-wahz] regional dialect

patriarch n 1 male head of
a family or tribe 2 highest-
ranking bishop in Orthodox
Churches **patriarchal** adj
patriarchy n society in which
men have most of the power

patriate v pass (powers)
from the control of a colonial
government to that of the
region to which they apply

patrician n 1 member of the
nobility, esp. of ancient
Rome ▷ adj 2 of noble birth

patricide n 1 crime of killing
one's father 2 person who
does this

patrimony n, pl -nies
property inherited from
ancestors

patriot n person who loves his
or her country and supports
its interests **patriotic** adj
patriotism n

patrol n 1 regular circuit by a
guard 2 person or small group
patrolling 3 unit of Scouts or
Guides ▷ v -trolling, -trolled
4 go round on guard, or
reconnoitring

patron n 1 person who
gives (financial) support to

P

charities, artists, etc. **2** regular customer of a shop, pub, etc.
patronage n support given by a patron **patronize** v **1** treat in a condescending way **2** be a patron of **patron saint** saint regarded as the guardian of a country or group

patronymic n name derived from one's father or a male ancestor

patten n hist type of clog

patter v **1** make repeated soft tapping sounds ▷ n **2** quick succession of taps **3** glib rapid speech

pattern n **1** arrangement of repeated parts or decorative designs **2** regular way something is done **3** diagram or shape used as a guide to make something ▷ v **4** (foll. by on) make or do on the model of **patterned** adj decorated with a pattern

patty n, pl -ties **1** small pie **2** minced meat formed into a small disc

paucity n **1** scarcity **2** smallness of amount or number

paunch n belly

pauper n very poor person

pause v **1** stop for a time ▷ n **2** stop or rest

pave v form (a surface) with stone or brick **pavement** n **1** paved surface of road or street **2** Brit sidewalk

pavilion n **1** clubhouse on a playing field etc. **2** building for housing an exhibition etc.

paw n **1** animal's foot with claws and pads ▷ v **2** scrape with the paw or hoof **3** handle roughly **4** stroke in an overfamiliar way

pawn¹ v deposit (an article) as security for money borrowed **in pawn** deposited as security with a pawnbroker **pawnbroker** n lender of money on goods deposited

pawn² n **1** chessman of the lowest value **2** person manipulated by someone else

pay v **paying**, **paid** **1** give (money) in return for goods or services **2** settle (a debt or obligation) **3** compensate (for) **4** give, bestow **5** be profitable to ▷ n **6** wages or salary **payment** n **1** act of paying **2** money paid **payable** adj due to be paid **payee** n person to whom money is paid or due **paying guest** lodger **pay off** v **1** pay (debt) in full **2** turn out successfully **pay out** v **1** spend **2** release (a rope) bit by bit **payroll** n list of employees who receive regular pay **paywall** n system preventing access to part of a website unless a fee is paid

payload n **1** passengers or cargo of an aircraft **2** explosive power of a missile etc.

payola n informal bribe to get special treatment, esp. to promote a commercial product

Pb chem lead

pc **1** per cent **2** postcard

PC **1** personal computer **2** Police Constable **3** politically correct **4** Privy Councillor

PDA personal digital assistant

PDF Portable Document Format: format in which electronic documents may be viewed

PDT Pacific Daylight Time

PE **1** physical education **2** Prince Edward Island

pea n **1** climbing plant with seeds growing in pods **2** its seed, eaten as a vegetable **pea-green** adj yellowish-green **peasouper** n informal thick fog

peace n **1** stillness or silence **2** absence of anxiety **3** freedom from war **4** harmony between people **peaceable** adj inclined towards peace **peaceably** adv **peaceful** adj **peacefully** adv

peach *n* **1** soft juicy fruit with a stone and a downy skin **2** *informal* very pleasing person or thing ▷ *adj* **3** pinkish-orange **peachy** or **peachy-keen** *adj* slang, now usually facetious very good, excellent

peacock *n* large male bird with a brilliantly coloured fanlike tail **peahen** *n fem* **peafowl** *n* peacock or peahen

peak *n* **1** pointed top, esp. of a mountain **2** point of greatest development etc. **3** projecting piece on the front of a cap ▷ *adj* **4** of or at the point of greatest demand ▷ *v* **5** (cause to) form or reach peaks **peaked** *adj* **peaky** *adj informal* looking pale and sickly

peal *n* **1** long loud echoing sound, esp. of bells or thunder ▷ *v* **2** sound with a peal or peals

peanut *n* **1** pea-shaped nut that ripens underground **peanuts 2** *informal* trifling amount of money

pear *n* sweet juicy fruit with a narrow top and rounded base

pearl *n* hard round lustrous object found inside some oyster shells and used as a jewel **pearly** *adj*

peasant *n* (in some countries) farmer or farmworker of a low social class **peasantry** *n* peasants collectively

peat *n* decayed vegetable material found in bogs, used as fertilizer or fuel

pebble *n* small roundish stone **pebbly** *adj*

pecan [pee-kan] *n* edible nut of a N American tree

peccadillo *n, pl* **-los, -loes** trivial misdeed

peccary *n, pl* **-ries** wild pig of American forests

peck *v* **1** strike or pick up with the beak **2** *informal* kiss quickly ▷ *n* **3** pecking movement

peckish *adj informal* hungry **peck at** *v* nibble, eat reluctantly

pectin *n* substance in fruit that makes jam set

pectoral *adj* **1** of the chest or thorax ▷ *n* **2** pectoral muscle or fin

peculation *n* embezzlement, theft

peculiar *adj* **1** strange **2** distinct, special **3** belonging exclusively to **peculiarity** *n* **1** oddity, eccentricity **2** characteristic

pecuniary *adj* relating to, or consisting of, money

pedagogue *n* schoolteacher, esp. a pedantic one

pedal *n* **1** foot-operated lever used to control a vehicle or machine, or to modify the tone of a musical instrument ▷ *v* **-alling, -alled 2** propel (a bicycle) by using its pedals

pedant *n* person who is overconcerned with details and rules, esp. in academic work **pedantic** *adj* **pedantry** *n*

peddle *v* sell (goods) from door to door **peddler** *n* person who sells illegal drugs

pederast *n* man who has homosexual relations with boys **pederasty** *n*

pedestal *n* base supporting a column, statue, etc.

pedestrian *n* **1** person who is walking, esp. in a street ▷ *adj* **2** dull, uninspiring **pedestrian crossing** crosswalk **pedestrian precinct** (shopping) area for pedestrians only

pediatrics, paediatrics *n* branch of medicine concerned with diseases of children **pediatrician** or **paediatrician** *n*

pedicel *n* small short stalk of a leaf, flower, or fruit

pedicure n medical or cosmetic treatment of the feet

pedigree n register of ancestors, esp. of a purebred animal

pediment n triangular part over a door etc.

pedlar n person who sells goods from door to door

pedometer [pid-**dom**-it-er] n instrument which measures the distance walked

pedophilia, paedophilia n condition of being sexually attracted to children **pedophile** or **paedophile** n person who is sexually attracted to children

peduncle n 1 flower stalk 2 anat stalklike structure

pee informal ▷ v **peeing, peed** 1 urinate ▷ n 2 urinating

peek v, n peep or glance

peel v 1 remove the skin or rind of (a vegetable or fruit) 2 (of skin or a surface) come off in flakes 3 curling use a stone to remove another, with both stones going out of play ▷ n 4 rind or skin **peelings** pl n

peep[1] v 1 look slyly or quickly ▷ n 2 peeping look **Peeping Tom** man who furtively watches women undressing

peep[2] v 1 make a small shrill noise ▷ n 2 small shrill noise

peer[1] n 1 (**peeress**) nobleman 2 person of the same status, age, etc. **peerage** n 1 whole body of peers 2 rank of a peer **peerless** adj unequalled, unsurpassed **peer group** group of people of similar age, status, etc. **peer pressure** influence from one's peer group

peer[2] v look closely and intently

peeved adj informal annoyed

peevish adj 1 fretful 2 irritable **peevishly** adv **peevishness** n

peewee Canad ▷ n 1 age level of 12 to 13 in amateur sports, esp. hockey ▷ adj 2 (of amateur sports) comprised of players aged 12 to 13 years: peewee hockey

peewit n same as **lapwing**

peg n 1 pin or clip for joining, fastening, marking, etc. 2 hook or knob for hanging things on ▷ v **pegging, pegged** 3 fasten with pegs 4 stabilize (prices) 5 informal categorize: they think they've got you pegged **off the peg** (of clothes) ready-to-wear, not tailor-made

P.E.I. Prince Edward Island

peignoir [**pay**-nwahr] n woman's light dressing gown

pejorative [pij-**jor**-a-tiv] adj (of words etc.) with an insulting or critical connotation

Pekingese, Pekinese n, pl -**ese** small dog with a short wrinkled muzzle

pelargonium n plant with red, white, or pink flowers

pelican n large water bird with a pouch beneath its bill for storing fish

pellagra n disease caused by lack of vitamin B

pellet n small ball of something

pell-mell adv in utter confusion, headlong

pellucid adj very clear

pelmet n ornamental drapery or board, concealing a curtain rail

pelt[1] v 1 throw missiles at 2 run fast, rush 3 rain heavily **at full pelt** at top speed

pelt[2] n skin of a fur-bearing animal

pelvis n framework of bones at the base of the spine, to which the hips are attached **pelvic** adj

pemmican n dried lean meat and melted fat pounded into

paste and used as food for a long journey

pen¹ n **1** instrument for writing in ink ▷ v **penning, penned 2** write or compose **pen friend** friend with whom a person corresponds without meeting **penknife** n small knife with blade(s) that fold into the handle **pen name** name used by an author instead of his or her real name

pen² n **1** small enclosure for domestic animals ▷ v **penning, penned 2** put or keep in a pen

pen³ n female swan

penal [**pee**-nal] adj of or used in punishment **penalize** v **1** impose a penalty on **2** handicap, hinder **penalty** n **1** punishment for a crime or offence **2** sports handicap or disadvantage imposed for an infringement of a rule

penance n voluntary self-punishment to make amends for wrongdoing

pence n a plural of **penny**

penchant [**pon**-shon] n inclination or liking

pencil n **1** thin cylindrical instrument containing graphite, for writing or drawing ▷ v **-cilling, -cilled 2** draw, write, or mark with a pencil

pendant n ornament worn on a chain round the neck

pendent adj hanging

pending prep **1** while waiting for ▷ adj **2** not yet decided or settled

pendulous adj hanging, swinging

pendulum n suspended weight swinging to and fro, esp. as a regulator for a clock

penetrate v **1** find or force a way into or through **2** arrive at the meaning of **penetrable** adj capable of being

penetrated **penetrating** adj **1** quick to understand **2** (of a sound) loud and unpleasant **penetration** n

penguin n flightless black-and-white Antarctic sea bird

penicillin n antibiotic drug effective against a wide range of diseases and infections

peninsula n strip of land nearly surrounded by water **peninsular** adj

penis n organ of copulation and urination in male mammals

penitent adj **1** feeling sorry for having done wrong ▷ n **2** someone who is penitent **penitence** n **penitentiary** n **1** prison ▷ adj **2** Also **penitential** relating to penance

pennant n long narrow flag

pennon n small triangular or swallow-tailed flag

penny n, pl **pence, pennies 1** one cent **2** Brit bronze coin now worth one hundredth of a pound **penniless** adj **1** having no money **2** poor

penology [pee-**nol**-a-jee] n study of punishment and prison management

pension¹ n regular payment to people above a certain age, retired employees, widows, etc. **pensionable** adj **pensioner** n person receiving a pension **pension off** v force (someone) to retire from a job and pay him or her a pension

pension² [**pon**-syon] n boarding house in Europe

pensive adj deeply thoughtful, often with a tinge of sadness

pentacle, pentagram n five-pointed star

pentagon n **1** geometric figure with five sides **2 Pentagon** headquarters of the US military **pentagonal** adj

P

pentameter [pen-**tam**-it-er] n line of poetry with five metrical feet

Pentateuch [**pent**-a-tyuke] n first five books of the Old Testament

pentathlon n athletic event consisting of five sports

Pentecost n **1** Christian festival celebrating the descent of the Holy Spirit to the apostles, Whitsuntide **2** Jewish harvest festival fifty days after Passover

penthouse n apartment built on the roof or top floor of a building

pent-up adj (of an emotion) not released, repressed

penultimate adj second last

penumbra n, pl -**brae**, -**bras 1** partial shadow **2** (in an eclipse) the partially shadowed region which surrounds the full shadow **penumbral** adj

penury n extreme poverty **penurious** adj

peony n, pl -**nies** garden plant with showy red, pink, or white flowers

people pl n **1** persons generally **2** the community **3** one's family or ancestors ▷ n **4** race or nation ▷ v **5** stock with inhabitants **6** populate

pep n informal high spirits, energy or enthusiasm **pep talk** informal talk designed to increase confidence, enthusiasm, etc. **pep up** v stimulate, invigorate

pepper n **1** sharp hot condiment made from the fruit of an East Indian climbing plant **2** colourful tropical fruit used as a vegetable, capsicum ▷ v **3** season with pepper **4** sprinkle, dot **5** pelt with missiles **peppery** adj **1** tasting of pepper **2** irritable

peppercorn n dried berry of the pepper plant **peppercorn rent** low or nominal rent

pepper spray aerosol spray causing temporary blindness and breathing difficulty, used esp. for self-defence

peppermint n **1** plant that yields an oil with a strong sharp flavour **2** candy flavoured with this

peptic adj relating to digestion or the digestive juices

Péquiste [pay-**keest**] n member or supporter of Parti Québécois

per prep **1** for each **2** in the manner of

perambulate v walk through or about (a place) **perambulation** n **perambulator** n Brit baby carriage

per annum adv Latin in each year

percale n woven cotton used esp. for sheets

per capita adj, adv Latin of or for each person

perceive v **1** become aware of (something) through the senses **2** understand

percentage n proportion or rate per hundred **per cent** in each hundred

perceptible adj discernible, recognizable

perception n **1** act of perceiving **2** intuitive judgment **perceptive** adj

perch¹ n **1** resting place for a bird ▷ v **2** alight, rest, or place on or as if on a perch

perch² n edible freshwater fish

perchance adv old-fashioned perhaps

percipient adj quick to notice things, observant **percipience** n

percolate v **1** pass or filter through small holes

2 permeate **3** make (coffee) or (of coffee) be made in a percolator **percolation** n **percolator** n coffeepot in which boiling water is forced through a tube and filters down through coffee

percussion n striking of one thing against another **percussion instrument** musical instrument played by being struck, such as drums or cymbals

perdition n spiritual ruin

peregrination n travels, roaming

peregrine n falcon with dark upper parts and a light underside

peremptory adj authoritative, imperious

perennial adj **1** lasting through the years **2** recurring perpetually ▷ n **3** plant lasting more than two years **perennially** adv

perestroika n formerly, policy of restructuring the Soviet economy and political system

perfect adj **1** having all the essential elements, complete **2** unspoilt **3** faultless **4** correct, precise **5** excellent ▷ n **6** grammar tense of verb describing an action that has been completed ▷ v **7** improve **8** make fully correct **perfectly** adv **perfection** n state of being perfect **perfectionist** n person who demands the highest standards of excellence **perfectionism** n

perfidy n, pl **-dies** treachery, disloyalty **perfidious** adj

perforate v make holes in **perforation** n

perforce adv of necessity

perform v **1** carry out (an action) **2** fulfil (a request etc.) **3** act, sing, or present a play before an audience **4** work

or function **performance** n **performer** n

perfume n **1** liquid cosmetic worn for its pleasant smell **2** fragrance ▷ v **3** give a pleasant smell to **perfumery** n perfumes in general

perfunctory adj done only as a matter of routine, superficial **perfunctorily** adv

pergola n arch or framework of trellis supporting climbing plants

perhaps adv it may be (so), possibly

pericardium n, pl **-dia** membrane enclosing the heart

perihelion n, pl **-lia** point in the orbit of a planet or comet nearest to the sun

peril n great danger **perilous** adj **perilously** adv

perimeter [per-**rim**-it-er] n (length of) the outer edge of an area

perinatal adj of or in the weeks shortly before or after birth

period n **1** particular portion of time **2** series of years **3** single occurrence of menstruation **4** division of time at school etc. when a particular subject is taught **5** same as **full stop** ▷ adj **6** (of furniture, dress, a play, etc.) dating from or in the style of an earlier time in history **periodic** adj recurring at intervals **periodic table** chart of the elements, arranged to show their relationship to each other **periodical** n **1** magazine issued at regular intervals ▷ adj **2** periodic

peripatetic [per-rip-a-**tet**-ik] adj travelling about from place to place

periphery [per-**if**-er-ee] n, pl **-eries 1** circumference **2** fringes of a field of activity

P

peripheral [per-**if**-er-al] *adj*
1 unimportant, not central
2 of or on the periphery
periphrasis [per-**if**-ra-
siss] *n, pl* -**rases** [-ra-seez]
roundabout speech or
expression **periphrastic** *adj*
periscope *n* instrument used,
esp. in submarines, for giving
a view of objects on a different
level
perish *v* **1** be destroyed or
die **2** decay, rot **perishable**
adj liable to rot quickly
perishing *adj informal* very
cold
peritoneum [per-rit-toe-
nee-um] *n, pl* -**nea**, -**neums**
membrane lining the internal
surface of the abdomen
peritonitis [per-rit-tone-**ite**-
iss] *n* inflammation of the
peritoneum
periwig *n hist* wig
periwinkle[1] *n* small edible
shellfish, the winkle
periwinkle[2] *n* plant with
trailing stems and blue
flowers
perjury [**per**-jer-ee] *n, pl*
-**juries** act or crime of lying
while under oath in a court
perjure *v* **perjure oneself**
commit perjury
perk *n informal* incidental
benefit gained from a job,
such as a company car
perk up *v* cheer up **perky** *adj*
lively or cheerful
perm *n* **1** long-lasting curly
hairstyle produced by treating
the hair with chemicals ▷ *v*
2 give (hair) a perm
permafrost *n* permanently
frozen ground
permanent *adj* lasting
forever **permanently** *adv*
permanence *n* **permanent
resident** immigrant allowed
to live and work in Canada but
who is not yet a citizen
permanganate *n* a salt of an
acid of manganese
permeate *v* pervade or
pass through the whole of
(something) **permeable** *adj*
able to be permeated, esp. by
liquid
permit *v* -**mitting**, -**mitted**
1 give permission **2** allow,
agree to ▷ *n* **3** document
giving permission to do
something **permission**
n authorization to do
something **permissible** *adj*
permissive *adj* (excessively)
tolerant, esp. in sexual
matters
permutation *n* any of the
ways a number of things can
be arranged or combined
pernicious *adj* **1** wicked
2 extremely harmful, deadly
pernickety *adj informal*
(excessively) fussy about
details
peroration *n* concluding part
of a speech, usu. summing up
the main points
peroxide *n* **1** oxide of a given
base containing a high
proportion of oxygen **2** short
for **hydrogen peroxide**
perpendicular *adj* **1** at right
angles to a line or surface
2 upright or vertical ▷ *n* **3** line
at right angles to another line
or plane
perpetrate *v* commit
or be responsible for (a
wrongdoing) **perpetration** *n*
perpetrator *n*
perpetual *adj* **1** lasting
forever **2** continually repeated
perpetually *adv* **perpetuate**
v cause to continue or be
remembered **perpetuation** *n*
in perpetuity forever
perplex *v* puzzle, bewilder
perplexity *n*
perquisite *n* same as **perk**
perry *n, pl* -**ries** alcoholic
drink made from fermented
pears

per se [per **say**] *adv Latin* in itself

persecute *v* **1** treat cruelly because of race, religion, etc. **2** subject to persistent harassment **persecution** *n* **persecutor** *n*

persevere *v* keep making an effort despite difficulties **perseverance** *n*

persiflage [per-sif-flahzh] *n* light frivolous talk or writing

persimmon *n* sweet red tropical fruit

persist *v* **1** continue without interruption **2** continue obstinately despite opposition **persistent** *adj* **persistently** *adv* **persistence** *n*

person *n* **1** human being **2** body of a human being **3** *grammar* form of pronouns and verbs that shows if a person is speaking, spoken to, or spoken of **in person** actually present

persona [per-**soh**-na] *n, pl* **-nae** someone's personality as presented to others

personable *adj* pleasant in appearance and personality

personage *n* important person

personal *adj* **1** individual or private **2** of the body: *personal hygiene* **3** (of a remark etc.) offensive **personally** *adv* **1** in one's own opinion **2** directly, not by delegation to others **personal computer** small computer used for word processing or computer games **personal foul** *basketball* foul awarded against a player who makes bodily contact with an opponent **personal pronoun** pronoun like *I* or *she* that stands for a definite person **personal stereo** very small portable cassette player with headphones

personality *n, pl* **-ties** **1** person's whole character **2** celebrity **personalities** **3** personal remarks

personify *v* **-fying, -fied** **1** give human characteristics to **2** be an example of, typify **personification** *n*

personnel *n* people employed in an organization

perspective *n* **1** mental view **2** method of drawing that gives the effect of solidity and relative distances and sizes

perspicacious *adj* having quick mental insight **perspicacity** *n*

perspire *v* sweat **perspiration** *n* sweat

persuade *v* **1** make (someone) do something by argument, charm, etc. **2** convince **persuasion** *n* **1** act of persuading **2** way of thinking or belief **persuasive** *adj*

pert *adj* bright and cheeky

pertain *v* belong or be relevant (to)

pertinacious *adj* very persistent and determined **pertinacity** *n*

pertinent *adj* relevant **pertinence** *n*

perturb *v* **1** disturb greatly **2** alarm **perturbation** *n*

peruke *n hist* wig

peruse *v* read in a careful or leisurely manner **perusal** *n*

pervade *v* spread right through (something) **pervasive** *adj*

perverse *adj* deliberately doing something different from what is thought normal or proper **perversely** *adv* **perversity** *n*

pervert *v* **1** use or alter for a wrong purpose **2** lead into abnormal (sexual) behaviour ▷ *n* **3** person who practises sexual perversion **perversion** *n* **1** sexual act or desire considered abnormal **2** act of perverting

pervious adj able to be penetrated, permeable

peseta [pa-**say**-ta] n former monetary unit of Spain

pessary n, pl -**ries 1** appliance worn in the vagina, either to prevent conception or to support the womb **2** medicated suppository

pessimism n tendency to expect the worst in all things. **pessimist** n **pessimistic** adj **pessimistically** adv

pest n **1** annoying person **2** insect or animal that damages crops **pesticide** n chemical for killing insect pests

pester v annoy or nag continually

pestilence n deadly epidemic disease **pestilential** adj **1** annoying, troublesome **2** deadly

pestle n club-shaped implement for grinding things to powder in a mortar

pet n **1** animal kept for pleasure and companionship **2** person favoured or indulged ▷ adj **3** kept as a pet **4** particularly cherished ▷ v **petting, petted 5** treat as a pet **6** pat or stroke affectionately **7** informal kiss and caress erotically

petal n one of the white or coloured outer parts of a flower **petalled** adj

petard n hist explosive device **hoist with one's own petard** being the victim of one's own schemes

peter out v gradually come to an end

petite adj (of a woman) small and dainty

petition n **1** formal request, esp. one signed by many people and presented to

parliament ▷ v **2** present a petition to **petitioner** n

petrel n long-winged dark-coloured sea bird

petrify v -**fying, -fied 1** frighten severely **2** turn to stone **petrification** n

petrochemical n a substance, such as acetone, obtained from petroleum

petrol n Brit gasoline

petroleum n thick dark crude oil found underground

petticoat n woman's skirt-shaped undergarment

pettifogging adj overconcerned with unimportant detail

pettish adj fretful, irritable

petty adj -**tier, -tiest 1** unimportant, trivial **2** small-minded **3** on a small scale: petty crime **pettiness** n **petty cash** cash kept by a firm to pay minor expenses **petty officer** non-commissioned officer in the navy

petulant adj childishly irritable or peevish **petulantly** adv **petulance** n

petunia n garden plant with funnel-shaped flowers

pew n **1** fixed benchlike seat in a church **2** Brit informal chair, seat

pewter n greyish metal made of tin and lead

pH chem measure of the acidity of a solution

phalanger n long-tailed Aust. tree-dwelling marsupial

phalanx n, pl **phalanxes, phalanges** closely grouped mass of people

phalarope n small wading bird

phallus n, pl -**li, -luses** penis, esp. as a symbol of reproductive power in primitive rites **phallic** adj

phantasm n unreal vision, illusion **phantasmal** adj

phantasmagoria n shifting medley of dreamlike figures

phantasy n, pl **-sies** same as **fantasy**

phantom n **1** ghost **2** unreal vision

Pharaoh [**fare**-oh] n title of the ancient Egyptian kings

pharisee n self-righteous hypocrite **pharisaic** or **pharisaical** adj

pharmaceutical adj of pharmacy

pharmacology n study of drugs **pharmacological** adj **pharmacologist** n

pharmacopoeia [far-ma-koh-**pee**-a] n book with a list of and directions for the use of drugs

pharmacy n, pl **-cies 1** preparation and dispensing of drugs and medicines **2** pharmacist's shop **pharmacist** n person qualified to prepare and sell drugs and medicines

pharynx [**far**-rinks] n, pl **pharynges, pharynxes** cavity forming the back part of the mouth **pharyngeal** adj **pharyngitis** [far-rin-**jite**-iss] n inflammation of the pharynx

phase n **1** any distinct or characteristic stage in a development or chain of events ▷ v **2** arrange or carry out in stages or to coincide with something else **phase in** or **phase out** v introduce or discontinue gradually

PhD Doctor of Philosophy

pheasant n game bird with bright plumage

phenobarbitone n drug inducing sleep or relaxation

phenol n chemical used in disinfectants and antiseptics

phenomenon n, pl **-ena 1** anything appearing or observed **2** remarkable person or thing **phenomenal** adj extraordinary, outstanding **phenomenally** adv

phial n small bottle for medicine etc.

philadelphus n shrub with sweet-scented flowers

philanderer n man who flirts or has many casual love affairs **philandering** n

philanthropy n practice of helping people less well-off than oneself **philanthropic** adj **philanthropist** n

philately [fill-**lat**-a-lee] n stamp collecting **philatelic** adj **philatelist** n

philharmonic adj (in names of orchestras etc.) music-loving

philistine adj, n boorishly uncultivated (person) **philistinism** n

philology n science of the structure and development of languages **philological** adj **philologist** n

philosophy n, pl **-phies 1** study of the meaning of life, knowledge, thought, etc. **2** theory or set of ideas held by a particular philosopher **3** person's outlook on life **philosopher** n person who studies philosophy **philosophical** adj **1** of philosophy **2** calm in the face of difficulties or disappointments **philosophically** adv **philosophize** v talk in a boring and pretentious manner about basic things

philtre n magic drink supposed to arouse love in the person who drinks it

phlebitis [fleb-**bite**-iss] n inflammation of a vein

phlegm [**flem**] n thick yellowish substance formed in the nose and throat during a cold

phlegmatic [fleg-**mat**-ik] *adj* not easily excited, unemotional **phlegmatically** *adv*

phlox *n, pl* **phlox, phloxes** flowering garden plant

phobia *n* intense and unreasoning fear or dislike

phoenix *n* legendary bird said to set fire to itself and rise anew from its ashes

phone *n, v informal* telephone **phonecard** *n* card used to operate certain public telephones **phone-in** *n* broadcast in which telephone comments or questions from the public are transmitted live

phonetic *adj* **1** of speech sounds **2** (of spelling) written as sounded **phonetics** *pl n* science of speech sounds **phonetically** *adv*

phonograph *n old-fashioned* record player

phonology *n, pl* **-gies** study of the speech sounds in a language **phonological** *adj*

phony, phoney *informal* ▷ *adj* **phonier, phoniest 1** not genuine **2** false **3** insincere ▷ *n, pl* **phonies 4** phony person or thing

phosgene [**foz**-jean] *n* poisonous gas used in warfare

phosphorescence *n* faint glow in the dark **phosphorescent** *adj*

phosphorus *n* toxic flammable nonmetallic element which appears luminous in the dark **phosphate** *n* **1** compound of phosphorus **2** fertilizer containing phosphorus

photo *n, pl* **photos** short for **photograph** ▸ **photo finish** finish of a race in which the contestants are so close that a photo is needed to decide the result **Photoshop** *n*

1 ® software application for managing and editing digital images ▷ *v* **2** *informal* alter (a digital image) using Photoshop or a similar application

photocopy *n, pl* **-copies 1** photographic reproduction ▷ *v* **2** make a photocopy of

photoelectric *adj* using or worked by electricity produced by the action of light

photogenic *adj* always looking attractive in photographs

photograph *n* **1** picture made by the chemical action of light on sensitive film ▷ *v* **2** take a photograph of **photographer** *n* **photographic** *adj* **photography** *n* art of taking photographs

photogravure *n* process in which an etched metal plate for printing is produced by photography

photolithography *n* lithographic printing process using photographically made plates

photometer [foe-**tom**-it-er] *n* instrument for measuring the intensity of light

Photostat *n* **1** ® type of photocopying machine **2** copy made by it

photosynthesis *n* process by which a green plant uses sunlight to build up carbohydrate reserves

phrase *n* **1** group of words forming a unit of meaning, esp. within a sentence **2** short effective expression ▷ *v* **3** express in words **phrasal verb** phrase consisting of a verb and an adverb or preposition, with a meaning different from the parts, such as *take in* meaning *deceive*

phraseology *n, pl* **-gies** way

in which words are used

phut *adv* **go phut** *informal* (of a machine) break down

phylactery *n, pl* **-teries** leather case containing religious texts, worn by Jewish men

physical *adj* **1** of the body, as contrasted with the mind or spirit **2** of material things or nature **3** of physics **physically** *adv* **physical geography** branch of geography dealing with the features of the earth's surface **physical education** training and practice in sports and gymnastics

physician *n* doctor of medicine

physics *n* science of the properties of matter and energy **physicist** *n* person skilled in, or studying, physics

physiognomy [fiz-ee-**on**-om-ee] *n, pl* **-mies** face

physiology *n* science of the normal function of living things **physiological** *adj* **physiologist** *n*

physiotherapy *n* treatment of disease or injury by physical means such as massage, rather than by drugs **physiotherapist** *n*

physique *n* person's bodily build and muscular development

pi *n, pl* **pis** *math* ratio of the circumference of a circle to its diameter

pianissimo *adv music* very quietly

piano[1] *n, pl* **pianos** Also **pianoforte** musical instrument with strings which are struck by hammers worked by a keyboard **pianist** *n* **Pianola** *n* ® mechanically played piano

piano[2] *adv music* quietly

piazza *n* large open square or marketplace, esp. in Italy

pibroch [**pee**-brok] *n* form of bagpipe music

pic *n, pl* **pics, pix** *informal* photograph or illustration

pica [**pie**-ka] *n* **1** printing type of 6 lines to the inch **2** typewriter typesize of 10 letters to the inch

picador *n* mounted bullfighter with a lance

picaresque *adj* denoting a type of fiction in which the hero, a rogue, has a series of adventures

piccalilli *n* pickle of vegetables in mustard sauce

piccaninny *n, pl* **-nies** *offensive* Black child

piccolo *n, pl* **-los** small flute

pick[1] *v* **1** choose **2** remove (flowers or fruit) from a plant **3** remove loose particles from **4** (foll. by *at*) nibble (at) without appetite **5** provoke (a fight etc.) deliberately **6** open (a lock) by means other than a key ▷ *n* **7** choice: *take your pick* **8** best part **pick-me-up** *n informal* **1** tonic **2** stimulating drink **pick on** *v* find fault with **pick out** *v* recognize, distinguish **pickpocket** *n* thief who steals from someone's pocket **pick up** *v* **1** raise, lift **2** obtain or purchase **3** improve, get better **4** collect **5** *informal* become acquainted with for a sexual purpose **6** accelerate **pick-up** *n* **1** small truck **2** *informal* casual acquaintance made for a sexual purpose **3** device for conversion of mechanical energy into electric signals, as in a record player

pick[2] *n* tool with a curved iron crossbar and wooden shaft, for breaking up hard ground or masonry

pickaback *n* same as **piggyback**

pickaxe n large pick
picket n 1 person or group
standing outside a workplace
to deter would-be workers
during a strike 2 sentry
or sentries posted to give
warning of an attack
3 pointed stick used as part
of a fence ▷ v 4 form a picket
outside (a workplace) **picket
line** line of people acting
as pickets
pickings pl n money easily
acquired
pickle n 1 food preserved in
vinegar or salt water 2 informal
awkward situation ▷ v
3 preserve in vinegar or salt
water **pickled** adj informal
drunk
picnic n 1 informal meal out of
doors ▷ v -**nicking, -nicked**
2 have a picnic
Pict n member of an ancient
race of N Britain **Pictish** adj
pictorial adj 1 of or in painting
or pictures 2 illustrated
▷ n 3 newspaper etc. with
many pictures **pictorially** adv
picture n 1 drawing or
painting 2 photograph
3 mental image 4 beautiful
or picturesque object 5 image
on a TV screen **pictures**
6 cinema ▷ v 7 visualize,
imagine 8 represent in a
picture **picturesque** adj 1 (of
a place or view) pleasant
to look at 2 (of language)
forceful, vivid **picture
window** large window made
of a single sheet of glass
piddle v informal urinate
pidgin n language, not a
mother tongue, made up of
elements of two or more other
languages
pie n dish of meat, fruit,
etc. baked in pastry **pie
chart** circular diagram
with sectors representing
quantities

piebald n, adj (horse) with
irregular black-and-white
markings
piece n 1 separate bit or part
2 instance: a piece of luck
3 example, specimen 4 literary
or musical composition
5 coin 6 small object used in
checkers, chess, etc. **piece
together** v make or assemble
bit by bit
pièce de résistance [pyess
de ray-**ziss**-tonss] n French
most impressive item
piecemeal adv a bit at a time
piecework n work paid
for according to the
quantity produced
pied adj having markings of
two or more colours
pied-à-terre [pyay da **tair**] n,
pl **pieds-à-terre** [pyay da **tair**]
small apartment or house for
occasional use
pie-eyed adj slang drunk
pier n 1 platform on stilts
sticking out into the sea
2 pillar, esp. one supporting a
bridge
pierce v 1 make a hole in
or through with a sharp
instrument 2 make a way
through **piercing** adj 1 (of
a sound) shrill and high-
pitched 2 (of wind or cold)
fierce, penetrating
pierrot [**pier**-roe] n
pantomime character, clown
piety n, pl -**ties** deep devotion
to God and religion
piffle n informal nonsense
pig n 1 animal kept and killed
for pork, ham, and bacon
2 informal greedy, dirty, or
rude person **piggish** or **piggy**
adj informal 1 dirty 2 greedy
3 stubborn **piggery** n place
for keeping and breeding pigs
pig-headed adj obstinate **pig
iron** crude iron produced in a
blast furnace
pigeon n 1 bird with a

heavy body and short legs, sometimes trained to carry messages **2** *informal* concern or responsibility **pigeonhole** *n* **1** compartment for papers in a desk etc. ▷ *v* **2** classify **3** put aside and do nothing about

pigeon-toed *adj* with the feet or toes turned inwards

piggyback *n* **1** ride on someone's shoulders ▷ *adv* **2** carried on someone's shoulders ▷ *v* **3** exploit an existing resource, system, or product **4** attach to or mount on an existing piece of equipment or system

pigment *n* colouring matter, paint or dye **pigmentation** *n*

Pigmy *adj, n, pl* -**mies** same as **Pygmy**

pigtail *n* plait of hair hanging from the back or either side of the head

pike[1] *n* large predatory freshwater fish

pike[2] *n hist* long-handled spear

pilaster *n* square column, usu. set in a wall

pilau, pilaf, pilaff *n* Middle Eastern dish of meat or poultry boiled with rice, spices, etc.

pilchard *n* small edible sea fish of the herring family

pile[1] *n* **1** number of things lying on top of each other **2** *informal* large amount **3** large building ▷ *v* **4** collect into a pile **5** (foll. by *in* or *out* or *off*) (etc.) move in a group **pile-up** *n informal* traffic accident involving several vehicles

pile[2] *n* beam driven into the ground, esp. as a foundation for building in water or wet ground

pile[3] *n* fibres of a carpet or a fabric, esp. velvet, that stand up from the weave

piles *pl n* swollen veins in the rectum, hemorrhoids

pilfer *v* steal in small quantities

pilgrim *n* person who journeys to a holy place. **pilgrimage** *n*

pill *n* small ball of medicine swallowed whole **the pill** pill taken by a woman to prevent pregnancy **pillbox** *n* **1** small box for pills **2** small concrete fort

pillage *v* **1** steal property by violence in war ▷ *n* **2** violent seizure of goods, esp. in war

pillar *n* **1** slender upright post, usu. supporting a roof **2** strong supporter **pillar box** red pillar-shaped letter box in the street

pillion *n* seat for a passenger behind the rider of a motorcycle

pillory *n, pl* -**ries 1** *hist* frame with holes for the head and hands in which an offender was locked and exposed to public abuse ▷ *v* -**rying, -ried 2** ridicule publicly

pillow *n* **1** stuffed cloth bag for supporting the head in bed ▷ *v* **2** rest as if on a pillow **pillowcase** *n* removable cover for a pillow

pilot *n* **1** person qualified to fly an aircraft or spacecraft **2** person employed to steer a ship entering or leaving a harbour ▷ *adj* **3** experimental and preliminary ▷ *v* **4** act as the pilot of **5** guide, steer **pilot light** small flame lighting the main one in a gas appliance

pimento *n, pl* -**tos** mild-tasting red pepper

pimp *n* **1** man who gets customers for a prostitute in return for a share of his or her earnings ▷ *v* **2** act as a pimp

pimpernel *n* wild plant with small flowers that close in dull weather

pimple *n* small pus-filled spot

p

on the skin **pimply** *adj*

pin *n* 1 short thin piece of stiff wire with a point and head, for fastening things 2 wooden or metal peg or stake ▷ *v* **pinning, pinned** 3 fasten with a pin 4 seize and hold fast **pin down** *v* 1 force (someone) to make a decision, take action, etc. 2 define clearly **pinball** *n* electrically operated table game, in which a small ball is shot through various hazards **pin money** small amount earned to buy small luxuries **pinpoint** *v* locate or identify exactly **pinstripe** *n* 1 very narrow stripe in fabric 2 the fabric itself **pin-up** *n* picture of a sexually attractive person, esp. (partly) naked

pinafore *n* 1 apron 2 dress with a bib top

pince-nez [panss-**nay**] *n, pl* **pince-nez** glasses kept in place only by a clip on the bridge of the nose

pincers *pl n* 1 tool consisting of two hinged arms, for gripping 2 claws of a lobster etc.

pinch *v* 1 squeeze between finger and thumb 2 cause pain by being too tight 3 *informal* steal 4 *informal* arrest ▷ *n* 5 squeeze or sustained nip 6 as much as can be taken up between the finger and thumb **at a pinch** if absolutely necessary **feel the pinch** have to economize

pinch- *prefix baseball* substitute: *pinch-hitter; pinch-runner*

pinchbeck *n* alloy of zinc and copper, used as imitation gold

pine¹ *n* 1 evergreen coniferous tree 2 its wood **pine cone** woody cone-shaped fruit of the pine tree

pine² *v* 1 (foll. by *for*) feel great longing (for) 2 become thin and ill through grief etc.

pineal gland [**pin**-ee-al] *n* small cone-shaped gland at the base of the brain

pineapple *n* large tropical fruit with juicy yellow flesh and a hard skin

ping *v, n* (make) a short high-pitched sound **pinger** *n* device, esp. a timer, that makes a pinging sound

Ping-Pong *n* ® table tennis

pinion¹ *n* 1 bird's wing ▷ *v* 2 immobilize (someone) by tying or holding his or her arms

pinion² *n* small cogwheel

pink *n* 1 pale reddish colour 2 fragrant garden plant ▷ *adj* 3 of the colour pink ▷ *v* 4 (of an engine) make a metallic noise because not working properly, knock **in the pink** in good health

pinking shears *pl n* scissors with a serrated edge that give a wavy edge to material to prevent fraying

pinnacle *n* 1 highest point of success etc. 2 mountain peak 3 small slender spire

pint *n* liquid measure, half a quart, ⅛ gallon (.568 litre)

Pinyin *n* system for representing Chinese in Roman letters

pioneer *n* 1 explorer or early settler of a new country 2 originator or developer of something new ▷ *v* 3 be the pioneer or leader of

pious *adj* deeply religious, devout

pip¹ *n* small seed in a fruit

pip² *n* 1 high-pitched sound used as a time signal on radio 2 *informal* star on a junior army officer's shoulder showing rank

pip³ *n* **give someone the pip** *slang* annoy someone

pipe *n* 1 tube for conveying

liquid or gas **2** tube with a small bowl at the end for smoking tobacco **3** tubular musical instrument **pipes** **4** bagpipes ▷ *v* **5** play on a pipe **6** utter in a shrill tone **7** convey by pipe **8** decorate with piping **piper** *n* player on a pipe or bagpipes **piping** *n* **1** system of pipes **2** decoration of icing on a cake etc. **3** fancy edging on clothes **piped music** recorded music played as background music in public places **pipe down** *v* *informal* stop talking **pipe dream** fanciful impossible plan etc. **pipeline** *n* **1** long pipe for transporting oil, water, etc. **2** means of communication **in the pipeline** in preparation **pipe up** *v* speak suddenly or shrilly

pipette *n* slender glass tube used to transfer or measure fluids

pipit *n* small brownish bird

pippin *n* type of eating apple

piquant [pee-kant] *adj* **1** having a pleasant spicy taste **2** mentally stimulating **piquancy** *n*

pique [peek] *n* **1** feeling of hurt pride, baffled curiosity, or resentment ▷ *v* **2** hurt the pride of **3** arouse (curiosity)

piqué [pee-kay] *n* stiff ribbed cotton fabric

piquet [pik-ket] *n* card game for two

piranha *n* small fierce freshwater fish of tropical America

pirate *n* **1** sea robber **2** person who illegally publishes or sells work owned by someone else **3** person or company that broadcasts illegally ▷ *v* **4** sell or reproduce (artistic work etc.) illegally **piracy** *n* **piratical** *adj*

pirouette *v*, *n* (make) a spinning turn balanced on the toes of one foot

piscatorial *adj* of fishing or fishes

piss *taboo* ▷ *v* **1** urinate ▷ *n* **2** act of urinating **3** urine

pistachio *n, pl* **-os** edible nut of a Mediterranean tree

piste [peest] *n* ski slope

pistil *n* seed-bearing part of a flower

pistol *n* short-barrelled handgun

piston *n* cylindrical part in an engine that slides to and fro in a cylinder

pit *n* **1** deep hole in the ground **2** coal mine **3** dent or depression **4** servicing and refuelling area on a motor-racing track **5** same as **orchestra pit** ▷ *v* **6** pitting, pitted mark with small dents or scars **pit one's wits against** compete against in a test or contest **pit bull terrier** strong muscular terrier with a short coat

pitch¹ *v* **1** throw, hurl **2** set up (a tent) **3** fall headlong **4** (of a ship or plane) move with the front and back going up and down alternately **5** set the level or tone of **6** *baseball* attempt to throw the ball toward home plate so that it passes through the strike zone without being hit by the batter ▷ *n* **7** degree or angle of slope **8** degree of highness or lowness of a (musical) sound **9** place where a street or market trader regularly sells **10** *baseball* instance of pitching **11** *informal* persuasive sales talk **pitcher** *n* *baseball* player who pitches the ball to the batter **pitch in** *v* join in enthusiastically **pitch into** *v* *informal* attack

pitch² *n* dark sticky substance obtained from tar **pitch-**

P

black or **pitch-dark** adj very dark

pitchblende n mineral composed largely of uranium oxide, yielding radium

pitcher n large jug with a narrow neck

pitchfork n **1** large long-handled fork for lifting hay ▷ v **2** thrust abruptly or violently

pitfall n hidden difficulty or danger

pith n **1** soft white lining of the rind of oranges etc. **2** soft tissue in the stems of certain plants **3** essential part **pithy** adj short and full of meaning

piton [peet-on] n metal spike used in climbing to secure a rope

pittance n very small allowance of money

pituitary n, pl -taries gland at the base of the brain, that helps to control growth (Also **pituitary gland**)

pity n, pl -ties **1** sympathy or sorrow for others' suffering **2** regrettable fact ▷ v **pitying, pitied 3** feel pity for **piteous** or **pitiable** adj arousing pity **pitiful** adj **1** arousing pity **2** woeful, contemptible **pitifully** adv **pitiless** adj feeling no pity, hard, merciless

pivot n **1** central shaft on which something turns ▷ v **2** provide with or turn on a pivot **pivotal** adj of crucial importance

pix n informal a plural of **pic**

pixel n smallest constituent element of an image, as on a visual display unit

pixie n (in folklore) fairy

pizza n flat disc of dough covered with a wide variety of savoury toppings and baked

pizzazz n informal attractive combination of energy and style

pizzicato [pit-see-**kah**-toe] adv music played by plucking the string of a violin etc. with the finger

placard n large board with a slogan on it that is carried or displayed in public

placate v make (someone) stop feeling angry or upset **placatory** adj

place n **1** particular part of an area or space **2** particular town, building, etc. **3** position or point reached **4** usual position **5** duty or right **6** position of employment **7** seat or space ▷ v **8** put in a particular place **9** identify, put in context **10** make (an order, bet, etc.) **be placed** (of a competitor in a race) be among the first three **take place** happen, occur **place-kick** n football kick in which the ball is held in place on the field before it is kicked **place-kicker** n football player who specializes in place-kicks

placebo [plas-**see**-bo] n, pl -bos, -boes sugar pill etc. given to an unsuspecting patient as an active drug

placenta [plass-**ent**-a] n, pl -tas, -tae organ formed in the womb during pregnancy, providing nutrients for the fetus **placental** adj

placid adj calm, not easily excited or upset **placidity** n

placket n opening at the top of a skirt etc. fastened with buttons or a zip

plagiarize [**play**-jer-ize] v steal ideas, passages, etc. from (someone else's work) and present them as one's own **plagiarism** n

plague n **1** fast-spreading fatal disease **2** hist bubonic plague **3** widespread infestation ▷ v

plaguing, plagued 4 trouble or annoy continually

plaice n edible European flatfish

plaid n **1** long piece of tartan cloth worn as part of Highland dress **2** tartan cloth or pattern

plain adj **1** easy to see or understand **2** expressed honestly and clearly **3** without decoration or pattern **4** simple, ordinary ▷ n **5** large stretch of level country **plainly** adv **plainness** n **plain clothes** ordinary clothes, as opposed to uniform **plain sailing** easy progress **plain speaking** saying exactly what one thinks

plainsong n unaccompanied singing, esp. in a medieval church

plaintiff n person who sues in a court of law

plaintive adj sad, mournful **plaintively** adv

plait [platt] v **1** intertwine separate strands to form one ropelike length ▷ n **2** length of hair that has been plaited

plan n **1** way thought out to do or achieve something **2** diagram showing the layout or design of something ▷ v **planning, planned 3** arrange beforehand **4** make a diagram of **Plan B** second tactic to be used when the first fails

plane¹ n **1** an aircraft ▷ v **2** (of a boat) rise and partly skim over water

plane² n **1** math flat surface **2** level of attainment etc. **3** tool for smoothing wood ▷ v **4** smooth (wood) with a plane ▷ adj **5** perfectly flat or level

plane³ n tree with broad leaves

planet n large body in space that revolves round the sun or another star **planetary** adj

planetarium n, pl **-iums,** **-ia** building where the movements of the stars, planets, etc. are shown by projecting lights on the inside of a dome

plangent [**plan**-jent] adj (of sounds) mournful and resounding

plank n long flat piece of sawn timber

plankton n minute animals and plants floating in the surface water of a sea or lake

plant n **1** living organism that grows in the ground and has no power to move **2** equipment or machinery used in industrial processes **3** factory or other industrial premises ▷ v **4** put in the ground to grow **5** place firmly in position **6** informal hide (stolen goods etc.) on a person to make him or her seem guilty **7** informal put (a person) secretly in an organization to spy **planter** n **1** ornamental pot for house plants **2** owner of a plantation

plantain¹ n low-growing wild plant with broad leaves

plantain² n tropical fruit like a green banana

plantation n **1** estate for the cultivation of tea, tobacco, etc. **2** wood of cultivated trees

plaque n **1** inscribed commemorative stone or metal plate fixed to a wall **2** filmy deposit on teeth that causes decay

plasma n clear liquid part of blood **plasma screen** type of high-resolution flat screen on a television or visual display unit

plaster n **1** mixture of lime, sand, etc. for coating walls **2** adhesive strip of material for dressing cuts etc. ▷ v **3** cover with plaster **4** coat thickly **plastered** adj slang drunk **plaster of Paris** white powder which dries to form a hard solid when mixed with water, used for sculptures and casts for broken limbs

plastic n 1 synthetic material that can be moulded when soft but sets in a hard long-lasting shape ▷ adj 2 made of plastic 3 easily moulded, pliant **plasticity** n ability to be moulded **plastic bullet** solid PVC cylinder fired by police in riot control **plastic surgery** repair or reconstruction of missing or malformed parts of the body for medical or cosmetic reasons

Plasticine n ® soft coloured modelling material used esp. by children

plate n 1 shallow round dish for holding food 2 flat thin sheet of metal, glass, etc. 3 thin coating of metal on another metal 4 dishes or cutlery made of gold or silver 5 illustration, usu. on fine quality paper, in a book 6 baseball same as **home plate** ▷ v 7 cover with a thin coating of gold, silver, or other metal **plateful** n **plate glass** kind of thick glass used for mirrors and windows **plate tectonics** study of the structure of the earth's crust, esp. the movement of layers of rocks

plateau n, pl -teaus, -teaux 1 area of level high land 2 stage when there is no change or development

platen n 1 roller of a typewriter, against which the paper is held 2 plate in a printing press by which the paper is pressed against the type

platform n 1 raised floor for speakers 2 raised area

in a station from which passengers board trains 3 programme of a political party 4 structure in the sea which holds machinery, stores, etc. for drilling an oil well

platinum n very valuable silvery-white metal **platinum blonde** woman with silvery-blonde hair

platitude n remark that is true but not interesting or original. **platitudinous** adj

platonic adj friendly or affectionate but not sexual

platoon n 1 subunit of a company of soldiers 2 sports pair of players on a team who take turns playing in the same position ▷ v 3 be part of a platoon on a sports team

platteland n S Afr rural district

platter n large dish

platypus n Aust. egg-laying amphibious mammal, with dense fur, webbed feet, and a ducklike bill (Also **duck-billed platypus**)

plaudit n expression of approval

plausible adj 1 apparently true or reasonable 2 persuasive but insincere **plausibly** adv **plausibility** n

play v 1 occupy oneself in (a game or recreation) 2 compete against in a game or sport 3 fulfil (a particular role) in a team game: he plays in the defence 4 behave carelessly 5 act (a part) on the stage 6 perform (music) on an instrument 7 cause (a radio, record player, etc.) to give out sound 8 move lightly or irregularly, flicker ▷ n 9 story performed on stage or broadcast 10 activities children take part in for amusement 11 playing of a game 12 conduct: fair play

13 (scope for) freedom of movement **player** n **playful** adj lively **play back** v listen to or watch (something recorded) **playboy** n rich man who lives only for pleasure **play down** v minimize the importance of **playgroup** n regular meeting of very young children for supervised play **playhouse** n theatre **playing card** one of a set of 52 cards used in card games **playing fields** extensive piece of ground for open-air games **play off** v set (two people) against each other for one's own ends **play on** v exploit or encourage (someone's sympathy or weakness) **playschool** n nursery group for young children **PlayStation** n ® type of video games console **plaything** n toy **play up** v **1** cause trouble **2** give prominence to **playwright** n author of plays

plaza n **1** modern shopping complex **2** open space or square

PLC, plc Public Limited Company

plea n **1** serious or urgent request, entreaty **2** statement of a prisoner or defendant **3** excuse

plead v **1** ask urgently or with deep feeling **2** give as an excuse **3** law declare oneself to be guilty or innocent of a charge made against one

pleasant adj pleasing, enjoyable **pleasantly** adv **pleasantry** n polite or joking remark

please adv **1** polite word of request ▷ v **2** give pleasure or satisfaction to **please oneself** do as one likes **pleased** adj **pleasing** adj giving pleasure or satisfaction

pleasure n **1** feeling of happiness and satisfaction **2** something that causes this **pleasurable** adj giving pleasure **pleasurably** adv

pleat n **1** fold made by doubling material back on itself ▷ v **2** arrange (material) in pleats

plebeian [pleb-**ee**-an] adj **1** of the lower social classes **2** vulgar or rough ▷ n **3** Also **pleb** member of the lower social classes

plebiscite [**pleb**-iss-ite] n decision by direct voting of the people of a country

plectrum n, pl **-trums, -tra** small implement for plucking the strings of a guitar etc.

pledge n **1** solemn promise **2** something valuable given as a guarantee that a promise will be kept or a debt paid ▷ v **3** promise solemnly **4** bind by or as if by a pledge: pledge to secrecy

plenary adj (of a meeting) attended by all members

plenipotentiary n, pl **-aries 1** diplomat or representative having full powers ▷ adj **2** having full powers

plenitude n completeness, abundance

plenteous adj plentiful

plentiful adj existing in large amounts or numbers **plentifully** adv

plenty n **1** large amount or number **2** quite enough

pleonasm n use of more words than necessary **pleonastic** adj

plethora n oversupply

pleurisy n inflammation of the membrane lining the chest and covering the lungs

pliable adj **1** easily bent **2** easily influenced **pliability** n

pliant adj pliable **pliancy** n

pliers pl n tool with hinged

arms and jaws for gripping

plight¹ _n_ difficult or dangerous situation

plight² _v_ **plight one's troth** _old-fashioned_ promise to marry

Plimsoll line _n_ mark on a ship showing the level water should reach when the ship is fully loaded

plinth _n_ slab forming the base of a column etc.

PLO Palestine Liberation Organization

plod _v_ **plodding, plodded** **1** walk with slow heavy steps **2** work slowly but determinedly **plodder** _n_

plonk¹ _v_ put (something) down heavily and carelessly

plonk² _n_ _informal_ cheap inferior wine

plop _n_ **1** sound of an object falling into water without a splash ▷ _v_ **plopping, plopped 2** make this sound

plot¹ _n_ **1** secret plan to do something illegal or wrong **2** sequence of events on which a film, novel, etc. is based ▷ _v_ **plotting, plotted 3** plan secretly, conspire **4** mark the position or course of (a ship or aircraft) on a map **5** mark and join up (points on a graph)

plot². _n_ small piece of land

plover _n_ shore bird with a straight bill and long pointed wings

plow, plough _n_ **1** agricultural tool for turning over soil ▷ _v_ **2** turn over (earth) with a plow **3** move or work through slowly and laboriously **plowman** _or_ **ploughman** _n_ **plowshare** _or_ **ploughshare** _n_ blade of a plow **plow back** reinvest (money)

ploy _n_ manoeuvre designed to gain an advantage

pluck _v_ **1** pull or pick off **2** pull out the feathers of (a bird for cooking) **3** sound the strings

of (a guitar etc.) with the fingers or a plectrum ▷ _n_ **4** courage **plucky** _adj_ brave **pluckily** _adv_ **pluck up** _v_ summon up (courage)

plug _n_ **1** thing fitting into and filling a hole **2** device connecting an appliance to an electricity supply **3** _informal_ favourable mention of a product etc., designed to encourage people to buy it ▷ _v_ **plugging, plugged 4** block or seal (a hole or gap) with a plug **5** _informal_ advertise (a product etc.) by constant repetition **plug away** _v_ _informal_ work steadily **plugger** _n_ **1** person or thing that plugs **2** _slang_ person who works hard in an unspectacular way **plug in** _v_ connect (an electrical appliance) to a power source by pushing a plug into a socket

plum _n_ **1** oval usu. dark red fruit with a stone in the middle ▷ _adj_ **2** dark purplish-red **3** very desirable

plumage _n_ bird's feathers

plumb _v_ **1** understand (something obscure) **2** test with a plumb line ▷ _adv_ **3** exactly **plumb the depths of** experience the worst extremes of (an unpleasant quality or emotion) **plumber** _n_ person who fits and repairs pipes and fixtures for water and drainage systems **plumbing** _n_ pipes and fixtures used in water and drainage systems **plumb in** _v_ connect (an appliance such as a washing machine) to a water supply **plumb line** string with a weight at the end, used to test the depth of water or to test whether something is vertical

plume _n_ feather, esp. one worn as an ornament **plume**

oneself on be proud of oneself because of

plummet v -meting, -meted plunge downward

plump[1] adj moderately or attractively fat **plumpness** n **plump up** v make (a pillow) fuller or rounded

plump[2] v 1 sit or fall heavily and suddenly ▷ adv 2 suddenly and heavily 3 directly **plump for** v choose, vote only for

plunder v 1 take by force, esp. in time of war ▷ n 2 things plundered, spoils

plunge v 1 put or throw forcibly or suddenly (into) ▷ n 2 plunging, dive **take the plunge** informal 1 embark on a risky enterprise 2 get married **plunger** n rubber suction cup used to clear blocked pipes **plunging** adj (of the neckline of a dress) cut low so as to show the top of the breasts **plunge into** v become deeply involved in

plunk v pluck the strings of (a banjo etc.) to produce a twanging sound

pluperfect adj, n grammar (tense) expressing action completed before a past time, such as had gone in his wife had gone already

plural adj 1 of or consisting of more than one ▷ n 2 a word in its plural form

pluralism n existence and toleration of a variety of peoples, opinions, etc. in a society **pluralist** n **pluralistic** adj

plus prep 1 with the addition of: usu. indicated by the sign (+) ▷ adj 2 more than zero or the number already mentioned 3 positive 4 advantageous ▷ n 5 plus sign 6 advantage **plus-minus** n hockey statistic calculated by adding or subtracting one point for every even-strength goal scored respectively by or against a given player's team while that player is on the ice

plus fours pl n trousers gathered in at the knee

plush n 1 fabric with long velvety pile ▷ adj 2 Also **plushy** luxurious

Pluto n 1 Greek god of the underworld 2 farthest planet from the sun

plutocrat n person who is powerful because of being very rich **plutocratic** adj

plutonium n radioactive metallic element used esp. in nuclear reactors and weapons

pluvial adj of or caused by the action of rain

ply[1] v plying, plied 1 work at (a job or trade) 2 use (a tool) 3 (of a ship) travel regularly along or between **ply with** v supply with or subject to persistently

ply[2] n thickness of wool, fabric, etc.

plywood n board made of thin layers of wood glued together

pm, PM 1 after noon 2 postmortem

PM prime minister

PMT premenstrual tension

pneumatic adj worked by or inflated with wind or air

pneumonia n inflammation of the lungs

PO 1 postal order 2 Post Office

poach[1] v 1 catch (animals) illegally on someone else's land 2 encroach on or steal something belonging to someone else **poacher** n

poach[2] v simmer (food) gently in liquid

pocket n 1 small bag sewn into clothing for carrying things 2 pouchlike container, esp. for catching balls at the edge of a snooker table 3 isolated or distinct group or area 4 football area guarded by blockers from which the quarterback attempts to throw a pass ▷ v **pocketing, pocketed 5** put into one's pocket **6** take secretly or dishonestly ▷ adj **7** small **in** or **out of pocket** having made a profit or loss

pocket money 1 small regular allowance given to children by parents **2** allowance for small personal expenses

pockmarked adj (of the skin) marked with hollow scars where diseased spots have been

pod n long narrow seed case of peas, beans, etc.

POD print on demand

podcast n **1** audio file similar to a radio broadcast which can be downloaded to a computer, iPod®, etc. ▷ v **2** create such files and make them available for downloading

podgy adj **podgier, podgiest** short and fat

podium n, pl **-diums, -dia** small raised platform for a conductor or speaker

poem n imaginative piece of writing in rhythmic lines

poesy n obsolete poetry

poet n writer of poems **poet laureate** see **laureate** ▶ **poetaster** n would-be or inferior poet **poetry** n **1** poems **2** art of writing poems **3** beautiful or pleasing quality **poetic** adj Also **poetical** of or like poetry **poetically** adv **poetic justice** suitable reward or punishment for someone's past actions

pogey n slang **1** unemployment insurance **2** dole

pogrom n organized persecution and massacre

poignant adj sharply painful to the feelings **poignancy** n

poinsettia n Central American shrub widely cultivated for its clusters of scarlet leaves, which resemble petals

point n **1** single idea in a discussion, argument, etc. **2** aim or purpose **3** detail or item **4** main or essential aspect **5** characteristic **6** particular position, stage, or time **7** dot indicating decimals **8** full stop **9** sharp end **10** headland **11** unit for recording a value or score **12** one of the direction marks of a compass **13** electrical socket **points 14** electrical contacts in the distributor of an engine ▷ v **15** show the direction or position of something or draw attention to it by extending a finger or other pointed object towards it **16** direct (a gun etc.) towards **17** finish or repair the joints in brickwork with mortar **18** (of a gun dog) show where game is by standing rigidly with the muzzle towards it **on the point of** very shortly going to **pointed** adj **1** having a sharp end **2** (of a remark) obviously directed at a particular person **pointedly** adv **pointer** n **1** helpful hint **2** indicator on a measuring instrument **3** breed of gun dog **pointless** adj meaningless, irrelevant **point-blank** adj, adv **1** fired at a very close target **2** (of a remark or question) direct, blunt **point duty** policeman's position at a road junction to control traffic **point guard** basketball guard who initiates most of a team's offensive moves **point of view** way of considering something **point-to-point** n horse race across open country

poise n calm dignified manner **poised** adj **1** absolutely ready

2 behaving with or showing poise

poison *n* **1** substance that kills or injures when swallowed or absorbed ▷ *v* **2** give poison to **3** have a harmful or evil effect on, spoil **poisoner** *n* **poisonous** *adj* **poison-pen letter** malicious anonymous letter

poke *v* **1** jab or prod with one's finger, a stick, etc. **2** thrust forward or out ▷ *n* **3** poking **poke-check** *v* hockey steal the puck from an opponent by holding the stick low and poking with it **poky** *adj informal* small and cramped

poker[1] *n* metal rod for stirring a fire to make it burn more brightly

poker[2] *n* card game involving bluff **poker-faced** *adj* expressionless

polar *adj* of or near either of the earth's poles **polar bear** white bear that lives in the regions around the North Pole

polarize *v* **1** form or cause to form into groups with directly opposite views **2** *physics* restrict (light waves) to certain directions of vibration **polarization** *n*

Polaroid *n* ® **1** plastic which polarizes light and so reduces glare **2** camera that develops a print very quickly inside itself

polder *n* land reclaimed from the sea

pole[1] *n* long rounded piece of wood, metal, or other material

pole[2] *n* **1** point furthest north (**North Pole**) or furthest south (**South Pole**) on the earth's axis of rotation **2** either of the opposite ends of a magnet or electric cell **Pole Star** star nearest to the North Pole in the northern hemisphere

poleaxe *v* hit or stun with a heavy blow

polecat *n* small animal of the weasel family

polemic [pol-em-ik] *n* fierce attack on or defence of a particular opinion, belief, etc. **polemical** *adj*

police *n* **1** organized force in a state which keeps law and order ▷ *v* **2** control or watch over with police or a similar body **policeman** (**policewoman**) *n* member of a police force

policy[1] *n, pl* **-cies** plan of action adopted by a person, group, or state

policy[2] *n, pl* **-cies** document containing an insurance contract

polio *n* disease affecting the spinal cord, which often causes paralysis (Also **poliomyelitis**)

polish *v* **1** make smooth and shiny by rubbing **2** make more nearly perfect ▷ *n* **3** liquid, aerosol, etc. for polishing **4** pleasing elegant style **polished** *adj* **1** (of a person) socially sophisticated in manner **2** done or performed well or professionally **polish off** *v* finish completely, dispose of

Politburo *n* decision-making committee in a Communist country

polite *adj* **1** showing consideration for others in one's manners, speech, etc. **2** socially correct or refined **politely** *adv* **politeness** *n*

politic *adj* wise and likely to prove advantageous

politics *n* **1** (study of) the art of government **2** person's beliefs about how a country should be governed **3** winning and using of power to govern society **political** adj of the state, government, or public administration **politically** adv **politically correct** (of language) intended to avoid any implied prejudice **political prisoner** person imprisoned because of his or her political beliefs **politician** n person actively engaged in politics, esp. a Member of Parliament

polka n 1 lively 19th-century dance 2 music for this **polka dots** pattern of bold spots on fabric

poll n 1 Also **opinion poll** questioning of a random sample of people to find out general opinion 2 voting 3 number of votes recorded ▷ v 4 receive (votes) 5 question as part of an opinion poll **pollster** n person who conducts opinion polls **polling station** building where people vote in an election

pollarded adj (of a tree) growing very bushy because its top branches have been cut short

pollen n fine dust produced by flowers that fertilizes other flowers **pollinate** v fertilize with pollen **pollen count** measure of the amount of pollen in the air, esp. as a warning to people with hay fever

pollute v contaminate with something poisonous or harmful **pollution** n **pollutant** n something that pollutes

polo n game like hockey played by teams of players on horseback **polo neck** sweater with tight turned-over collar

polonaise n 1 old stately dance 2 music for this

poltergeist n spirit believed to move furniture and throw objects around

poltroon n obsolete utter coward

poly- combining form many, much

polyandry n practice of having more than one husband at the same time

polyanthus n garden primrose

polychromatic adj many-coloured

polyester n synthetic material used to make plastics and textile fibres

polygamy [pol-**ig**-a-mee] n practice of having more than one husband or wife at the same time **polygamous** adj **polygamist** n

polyglot adj, n (person) able to speak or write several languages

polygon n geometrical figure with three or more angles and sides **polygonal** adj

polygyny n practice of having more than one wife at the same time

polyhedron n, pl -**drons**, -**dra** solid figure with four or more sides

polymer n chemical compound with large molecules made of simple molecules of the same kind **polymerize** v form into polymers **polymerization** n

polyp n 1 small simple sea creature with a hollow cylindrical body 2 small growth on a mucous membrane

polyphonic adj music consisting of several melodies played simultaneously

polystyrene n synthetic material used esp. as white rigid foam for packing and insulation

polytheism n belief in

many gods **polytheist** n
polytheistic adj

polythene n light plastic used for many everyday articles

polyunsaturated adj of a group of fats that do not form cholesterol in the blood

polyurethane n synthetic material used esp. in paints

polyvinyl chloride n see **PVC**

pomander n (container for) a mixture of sweet-smelling petals, herbs, etc.

pomegranate n round tropical fruit with a thick rind containing many seeds in a red pulp

Pomeranian n small dog with long straight hair

pommel n 1 raised part on the front of a saddle 2 knob at the top of a sword hilt

pommy n, pl -ies Aust & NZ slang person from Britain (Also **pom**)

pomp n stately display or ceremony

pompom n decorative ball of tufted wool, silk, etc.

pompous adj foolishly serious and grand, self-important **pompously** adv **pomposity** n

ponce n offensive 1 effeminate man 2 pimp **ponce around** v offensive act stupidly, waste time

poncho n, pl -chos loose circular cloak with a hole for the head

pond n small area of still water **pondweed** n plant that grows in ponds

ponder v think thoroughly or deeply (about)

ponderous adj 1 serious and dull 2 heavy or huge 3 (of movement) slow and clumsy **ponderously** adv

pong n, v informal (give off a) strong unpleasant smell

pontiff n the Pope **pontifical** adj pompous and dogmatic

pontificate v 1 state one's opinions as if they were the only possible correct ones ▷ n 2 period of office of a Pope

pontoon¹ n floating platform supporting a temporary bridge

pontoon² n gambling card game

pony n small horse **ponytail** n long hair tied in one bunch at the back of the head

poodle n dog with curly hair often clipped fancifully

poof n offensive homosexual man

pool¹ n 1 small body of still water 2 puddle of spilt liquid 3 swimming pool

pool² n 1 shared fund or group of workers or resources 2 game like snooker **pools** 3 see **football pools** ▷ v 4 put in a common fund

poop n raised part at the back of a sailing ship

poor adj 1 having little money and few possessions 2 less, smaller, or weaker than is needed or expected 3 unproductive 4 unlucky, pitiable **poorly** adv 1 in a poor manner ▷ adj 2 not in good health **poorness** n

pop¹ v popping, popped 1 make or cause to make a small explosive sound 2 informal go, put, or come unexpectedly or suddenly ▷ n 3 small explosive sound 4 non-alcoholic fizzy drink **popcorn** n corn kernels heated until they puff up and burst **pop fly** baseball ball hit high in the air and not very far, thus easily caught **pop-up** n 1 computers image that appears above the open window on a computer screen 2 same as **pop fly**

pop² n 1 music of general

appeal, esp. to young people
▷ adj **2** popular

pop³ n informal father

POP 1 point of presence: device that enables access to the internet **2** post office protocol: protocol which brings e-mail to and from a mail server **3** persistent organic pollutant

Pope n head of the Roman Catholic Church **popish** adj offensive Roman Catholic

poplar n tall slender tree

poplin n ribbed cotton material

poppadom n thin round crisp Indian bread

poppy n, pl **-ies** plant with a large delicate red flower

Popsicle n flavoured ice on a stick

populace n **1** the ordinary people **2** the masses

popular adj **1** widely liked and admired **2** of or for the public in general **popularly** adv **popularity** n **popularize** v **1** make popular **2** make (something technical or specialist) easily understood

populate v **1** live in, inhabit **2** fill with inhabitants **population** n **1** all the people who live in a particular place **2** the number of people living in a particular place **populous** adj thickly populated

populist n, adj (person) appealing to the interests or prejudices of ordinary people **populism** n

porbeagle n kind of shark

porcelain n **1** fine china **2** objects made of it

porch n covered approach to the entrance of a building

porcine adj of or like a pig

porcupine n animal covered with long pointed quills

pore n tiny opening in the skin or in the surface of a plant

pork n pig meat **porker** n pig raised for food

porn, porno n, adj informal short for **pornography, pornographic**

pornography n writing, films, or pictures designed to be sexually exciting **pornographer** n producer of pornography **pornographic** adj

porous adj allowing liquid to pass through gradually **porosity** n

porphyry [por-fir-ee] n reddish rock with large crystals in it

porpoise n fishlike sea mammal

porridge n **1** breakfast food made of oatmeal cooked in water or milk **2** Brit slang prison term

port¹ n **1** harbour **2** town with a harbour

port² n left side of a ship or aircraft when facing the front of it

port³ n strong sweet wine, usu. red

port⁴ n **1** opening in the side of a ship **2** porthole

portable adj easily carried **portability** n

portage n (place for) transporting boats and supplies overland between navigable waterways

portal n **1** large imposing doorway or gate **2** computers internet site providing links to other sites

portcullis n grating suspended above a castle gateway, that can be lowered to block the entrance

portend v be a sign of

portent n sign of a future event **portentous** adj **1** of great or ominous significance **2** pompous, self-important

porter n **1** man on duty at the entrance to a hotel etc. **2** man who carries luggage **3** hospital worker who transfers patients between rooms etc.

portfolio n, pl **-os 1** (flat case for carrying) examples of an artist's work **2** area of responsibility of a minister of state **3** list of investments held by an investor

porthole n small round window in a ship or aircraft

portico n, pl **-cos, -coes** porch or covered walkway with columns supporting the roof

portion n **1** part or share **2** helping of food for one person **3** destiny or fate **portion out** v divide into shares

portly adj **-lier, -liest** rather fat

portmanteau n, pl **-teaus, -teaux 1** old-fashioned large suitcase that opens into two compartments ▷ adj **2** combining aspects of different things

portrait n **1** picture of a person **2** lifelike description

portray v describe or represent by artistic means, as in writing or film **portrayal** n

Portuguese adj **1** of Portugal or its inhabitants ▷ n **2** person from Portugal **3** language of Portugal and Brazil **Portuguese man-of-war** sea creature resembling a jellyfish, with stinging tentacles

pose v **1** place in or take up a particular position to be photographed or drawn **2** behave in an affected way in order to impress others **3** ask (a question) **4** raise (a problem) ▷ n **5** position while posing **6** behaviour adopted for effect **pose as** pretend to be **poser** n **1** informal person who wears trendy clothes and frequents fashionable places **2** person who poses **3** puzzling

question **poseur** n person who behaves in an affected way to impress others

posh adj informal **1** smart, luxurious **2** affectedly upper-class

posit [pozz-it] v lay down as a basis for argument

position n **1** place **2** usual or expected place **3** way in which something is placed or arranged **4** attitude, point of view **5** social standing **6** state of affairs **7** job ▷ v **8** place

positive adj **1** feeling no doubts, certain **2** helpful, providing encouragement **3** confident, hopeful **4** absolute, downright **5** math greater than zero **6** electricity having a deficiency of electrons **positively** adv **positive discrimination** provision of special opportunities for a disadvantaged group

positron n positive electron

posse [poss-ee] n **1** US group of men organized to maintain law and order **2** informal group or gang

possess v **1** have as one's property **2** (of a feeling, belief, etc.) have complete control of, dominate **possessor** n **possession** n **1** state of possessing, ownership **possessions** n things a person possesses **possessive** adj **1** wanting all the attention or love of another person **2** (of a word) indicating the person or thing that something belongs to **possessiveness** n

possible adj **1** able to exist, happen, or be done **2** worthy of consideration ▷ n **3** person or thing that might be suitable or chosen **possibility** n **possibly** adv perhaps, not necessarily

possum n same as **opossum**

▶ **play possum** pretend to be dead or asleep to deceive an opponent

post¹ n **1** official system of carrying and delivering letters and parcels **2** (single collection or delivery of) letters and parcels sent by this system ▷ v **3** send by post **keep someone posted** inform someone regularly of the latest news **postage** n charge for sending a letter or parcel by post **postal** adj **postal code** n system of letters and numbers used to aid the sorting of mail **postal order** written money order sent by post and cashed at a post office by the person who receives it **postcard** n card for sending a message by post without an envelope **postman** n man who collects and delivers post **postmark** n official mark stamped on letters showing place and date of posting **postmaster** (**postmistress**) n official in charge of a post office **post office** place where postal business is conducted

post² n **1** length of wood, concrete, etc. fixed upright to support or mark something **2** goalpost **3** basketball area near the opposing team's basket ▷ v **4** put up (a notice) in a public place

post³ n **1** job **2** position to which someone, esp. a soldier, is assigned for duty **3** military establishment ▷ v **4** send (a person) to a new place to work **5** put (a guard etc.) on duty

post- prefix after, later than: postwar

postdate v write a date on (a cheque) that is later than the actual date

poster n large picture or notice stuck on a wall

poste restante n Brit general delivery

posterior n **1** buttocks ▷ adj **2** behind, at the back of

posterity n future generations, descendants

postern n small back door or gate

postgraduate n person with a degree who is studying for a more advanced qualification

posthaste adv with great speed

posthumous [poss-tume-uss] adj **1** occurring after one's death **2** born after one's father's death **3** published after the author's death **posthumously** adv

postilion, postillion n hist person riding one of a pair of horses drawing a carriage

postmortem n medical examination of a body to establish the cause of death

postnatal adj occurring after childbirth

postpone v put off to a later time **postponement** n

postprandial adj after dinner

postscript n passage added at the end of a letter

postulant n candidate for admission to a religious order

postulate v assume to be true as the basis of an argument or theory **postulation** n

posture n **1** position or way in which someone stands, walks, etc. ▷ v **2** behave in an exaggerated way to get attention

posy n, pl -sies small bunch of flowers

pot n **1** round deep container **2** teapot **3** slang cannabis **pots 4** informal a lot ▷ v **potting, potted 5** plant in a pot **6** snooker hit (a ball) into a pocket **potted** adj **1** grown in a pot **2** (of meat or fish) preserved in a pot **3** informal abridged **potluck** n whatever is available **potsherd** n broken fragment of pottery **pot shot** shot taken without aiming carefully **potting shed** shed where plants are potted

potable [pote-a-bl] adj drinkable

potash n white powdery substance obtained from ashes and used as fertilizer

potassium n white metallic element

potato n, pl -**toes** roundish starchy vegetable that grows underground **potato chip** very thin slice of potato fried till crunchy

poteen n (in Ireland) illicitly distilled alcoholic drink

potent adj **1** having great power or influence **2** (of a male) capable of having sexual intercourse **potency** n

potentate n ruler or monarch

potential adj **1** possible but not yet actual ▷ n **2** ability or talent not yet fully used **3** electricity level of electric pressure **potentially** adv **potentiality** n

pothole n **1** hole in the surface of a road **2** deep hole in a limestone area **potholing** n sport of exploring underground caves **potholer** n

potion n dose of medicine or poison

potpourri [po-**poor**-ee] n **1** fragrant mixture of dried flower petals **2** musical or literary medley

pottage n thick soup or stew

potter[1] n person who makes pottery

potter[2], **putter** v be busy in a pleasant but aimless way **potterer** or **putterer** n

pottery n, pl -**ries** **1** articles made from baked clay **2** place

where they are made

potty[1] n, pl -**ties** bowl used by a small child as a toilet

potty[2] adj -**tier**, -**tiest** Brit informal crazy or silly

pouch n **1** small bag **2** baglike pocket of skin on an animal

pouf, pouffe [**poof**] n large solid cushion used as a seat

poulterer n person who sells poultry

poultice [**pole**-tiss] n moist dressing, often heated, applied to inflamed skin

poultry n domestic fowls

pounce v **1** spring upon suddenly to attack or capture ▷ n **2** pouncing

pound[1] n **1** monetary unit of Britain and some other countries **2** unit of weight equal to 0.454 kg

pound[2] v **1** hit heavily and repeatedly **2** crush to pieces or powder **3** (of the heart) throb heavily **4** run with heavy steps

pound[3] n enclosure for stray animals or officially removed vehicles

pour v **1** flow or cause to flow out in a stream **2** rain heavily **3** come or go in large numbers

pout v **1** thrust out one's lips, look sulky ▷ n **2** pouting look

pouter n pigeon that can puff out its crop

poutine [poo-**teen**] n dish of French fries with gravy or sauce and cheese curds

poverty n **1** state of being without enough food or money **2** lack of, scarcity

POW prisoner of war

powder n **1** substance in the form of tiny loose particles **2** medicine or cosmetic in this form ▷ v **3** apply powder to **powdered** adj in the form of a powder: powdered milk **powdery** adj **powder room** ladies' lavatory

power n **1** ability to do or

act **2** strength **3** position of authority or control **4** person or thing having authority **5** particular form of energy: *nuclear power* **6** electricity supply **7** *physics* rate at which work is done **8** *math* product from continuous multiplication of a number by itself **powered** *adj* having or operated by mechanical or electrical power **powerful** *adj* **powerless** *adj* **power failure** or **power cut** temporary interruption in the supply of electricity **power play** *hockey* situation in which a team has more players on the ice than its opponent because of penalties **power station** installation for generating and distributing electric power

powwow *n* talk, conference

pox *n* **1** disease in which skin pustules form **2** *informal* syphilis

pp **1** pages

PQ Parti Québécois

PR **1** proportional representation **2** public relations

practicable *adj* capable of being carried out successfully **practicability** *n*

practical *adj* **1** involving experience or actual use rather than theory **2** sensible **3** adapted for use **4** good at making or doing things **5** in effect though not in name ▷ *n* **6** examination in which something has to be done or made **practically** *adv* **practical joke** trick intended to make someone look foolish

practice *n* **1** something done regularly or habitually **2** repetition of something so as to gain skill **3** doctor's or lawyer's place of work **in practice** what actually

happens as distinct from what is supposed to happen **put into practice** carry out, do

practise *v* **1** do repeatedly so as to gain skill **2** take part in, follow (a religion etc.) **3** work at: *practise medicine* **4** do habitually

practitioner *n* person who practises a profession

pragmatic *adj* concerned with practical consequences rather than theory **pragmatism** *n* **pragmatist** *n*

prairie *n* large treeless area of grassland, esp. in N America **Prairies** *pl n* this grassland in Manitoba, Saskatchewan, and Alberta **prairie dog** rodent that lives in burrows in the N American prairies

praise *v* **1** express approval or admiration of (someone or something) **2** express honour and thanks to (one's God) ▷ *n* **3** something said or written to show approval or admiration **sing someone's praises** praise someone highly **praiseworthy** *adj*

praline [**prah**-leen] *n* candy made of nuts and caramelized sugar

pram *n* *Brit* baby carriage

prance *v* walk with exaggerated bouncing steps

prank *n* mischievous trick or escapade, frolic

prattle *v* **1** chatter in a childish or foolish way ▷ *n* **2** childish or foolish talk **prattler** *n*

prawn *n* edible shellfish like a large shrimp

praxis *n* practice as opposed to theory

pray *v* **1** say prayers **2** ask earnestly, entreat **prayer** *n* **1** thanks or appeal addressed to one's God **2** set form of words used in praying

3 earnest request

pre- *prefix* before, beforehand: *prenatal; prerecord; preshrunk*

preach *v* **1** give a talk on a religious theme as part of a church service **2** speak in support of (an idea, principle, etc.) **preacher** *n*

preamble *n* introductory part to something said or written

prearranged *adj* arranged beforehand

prebendary *n, pl* **-daries** clergyman who is a member of the chapter of a cathedral

precarious *adj* insecure, unsafe, likely to fall or collapse. **precariously** *adv*

precaution *n* action taken in advance to prevent something bad happening **precautionary** *adj*

precede *v* go or be before **precedence** [press-ee-denss] *n* formal order of rank or position **take precedence over** be more important than **precedent** *n* previous case or occurrence regarded as an example to be followed

precentor *n* person who leads the singing in a church

precept *n* rule of behaviour

precession *n* **precession of the equinoxes** slightly earlier occurrence of the equinoxes each year

precinct *n* **1** area in a town closed to traffic **2** enclosed area round a building: *cathedral precinct* **3** *US* administrative area of a city **precincts** **4** surrounding region

precious *adj* **1** of great value and importance **2** loved and treasured **3** (of behaviour) affected, unnatural **precious metal** gold, silver, or platinum **precious stone** rare mineral, such as a ruby, valued as a gem

precipice *n* very steep cliff or rockface **precipitous** *adj* sheer

precipitant *adj* hasty or rash

precipitate *v* **1** cause to happen suddenly **2** throw headlong **3** *chem* cause to be deposited in solid form from a solution ▷ *adj* **4** done rashly or hastily ▷ *n* **5** *chem* substance precipitated from a solution **precipitately** *adv* **precipitation** *n* **1** precipitating **2** rain, snow, etc.

précis [**pray**-see] *n, pl* **précis** **1** short written summary of the main points of a longer piece ▷ *v* **2** make a précis of

precise *adj* **1** exact, accurate in every detail **2** strict in observing rules or standards **precisely** *adv* **precision** *n*

preclude *v* make impossible to happen

precocious *adj* having developed or matured early or too soon **precocity** *or* **precociousness** *n*

precognition *n* alleged ability to foretell the future

preconceived *adj* (of an idea) formed without real experience or reliable information **preconception** *n*

precondition *n* something that must happen or exist before something else can

precursor *n* something that precedes and is a signal of something else, forerunner

predate *v* **1** occur at an earlier date than **2** write a date on (a document) that is earlier than the actual date

predatory [**pred**-a-tree] *adj* habitually hunting and killing other animals for food **predator** *n* predatory animal

predecease *v* die before (someone else)

predecessor n 1 person who precedes another in an office or position 2 ancestor

predestination n belief that future events have already been decided by God **predestined** adj

predetermined adj decided in advance

predicament n embarrassing or difficult situation

predicate n 1 part of a sentence in which something is said about the subject, eg went home in I went home ▷ v 2 declare or assert **predicative** adj of or in the predicate of a sentence

predict v tell about in advance, prophesy **predictable** adj **prediction** n **predictive** adj (of a word processer or cell phone) able to complete words after only part of a word has been keyed

predilection n preference or liking

predispose v 1 influence (someone) in favour of something 2 make (someone) susceptible to something **predisposition** n

predominate v be the main or controlling element. **predominance** n **predominant** adj **predominantly** adv

pre-eminent adj excelling all others, outstanding **pre-eminently** adv **pre-eminence** n

pre-empt v get or do in advance of or to the exclusion of others. **pre-emption** n **pre-emptive** adj

preen v (of a bird) clean or trim (its feathers) with its beak **preen oneself** 1 smarten oneself 2 show self-satisfaction

prefab n prefabricated house

prefabricated adj (of a building) manufactured in shaped sections for rapid assembly on site

preface [**pref**-iss] n 1 introduction to a book ▷ v 2 serve as an introduction to (a book, speech, etc.) **prefatory** adj

prefect n 1 senior pupil in a school, with limited power over others 2 senior administrative officer in some countries **prefecture** n office or area of authority of a prefect

prefer v -ferring, -ferred 1 like better 2 law bring (charges) before a court **preferable** adj more desirable **preferably** adv **preference** n **preferential** adj showing preference **preferment** n promotion or advancement

prefigure v represent or suggest in advance

prefix n 1 letter or group of letters put at the beginning of a word to make a new word, such as un in unhappy 2 title before a name ▷ v 3 put as an introduction or prefix (to)

pregnant adj 1 carrying a fetus in the womb 2 full of meaning or significance **pregnancy** n

prehensile adj capable of grasping **prehensility** n

prehistoric adj of the period before written history begins **prehistory** n

prejudice n 1 unreasonable or unfair dislike of someone or something ▷ v 2 cause (someone) to have a prejudice 3 harm, cause disadvantage to **prejudicial** adj harmful, disadvantageous

prelate [**prel**-it] n bishop or other churchman of high rank **prelacy** n

preliminary adj 1 happening before and in preparation,

introductory ▷ *n, pl* **-naries**
2 something that happens
before something else
prelude [**pray**-lood] *n*
1 introductory movement in
music **2** event preceding and
introducing something else
premarital *adj* occurring
before marriage
premature *adj* **1** happening
or done before the normal or
expected time **2** (of a baby)
born before the end of the
normal period of pregnancy
prematurely *adv*
premedication *n* drugs given
to prepare a patient for a
general anesthetic
premeditated *adj* planned in
advance **premeditation** *n*
premenstrual *adj* occurring
or experienced before a
menstrual period: *premenstrual
tension*
premier *n* **1** prime minister
▷ *adj* **2** chief, leading
premiership *n*
première *n* first performance
of a play, film, etc.
premise, premiss *n*
statement assumed to be
true and used as the basis of
reasoning
premises *pl n* house or other
building and its land
premium *n* **1** additional sum
of money, as on a wage or
charge **2** (regular) sum paid
for insurance **at a premium**
in great demand because
scarce
premonition *n* feeling that
something unpleasant
is going to happen
premonitory *adj*
prenatal *adj* **1** before birth
2 during pregnancy
preoccupy *v* -**pying**, -**pied**
fill the thoughts or
attention of (someone)
to the exclusion of other
things **preoccupation** *n*

preordained *adj* decreed or
determined in advance
prep. **1** preparatory
2 preposition
prepacked *adj* sold already
wrapped
prepaid *adj* paid for in
advance
prepare *v* make or get ready
prepared *adj* **1** willing
2 ready **preparation** *n*
1 preparing **2** something done
in readiness for something
else **3** mixture prepared for
use as a cosmetic, medicine,
etc. **preparatory** [prip-
par-a-tree] *adj* preparing for
preparatory school private
school for children going on
to public school
preponderant *adj* greater in
amount, force, or influence.
preponderantly *adv*
preponderance *n*
preposition *n* word used
before a noun or pronoun to
show its relationship with
other words, such as *by* in *go by
bus* **prepositional** *adj*
prepossessing *adj* making
a favourable impression,
attractive
preposterous *adj* utterly
absurd
prep school *n* short for
preparatory school
prepuce [**pree**-pyewss]
n retractable fold of skin
covering the tip of the penis,
foreskin
prerecorded *adj* recorded
in advance to be played or
broadcast later
prerequisite *n, adj*
(something) that must
happen or exist before
something else is possible
prerogative *n* special power
or privilege
presage [**press**-ij] *v* be a sign
or warning of
presbyopia *n* inability of the

eye to focus on nearby objects

Presbyterian *adj, n* (member) of a Protestant church governed by lay elders **Presbyterianism** *n*

presbytery *n, pl* **-teries** **1** *Presbyterian Church* local church court **2** *RC Church* priest's house

prescience [**press**-ee-enss] *n* knowledge of events before they happen **prescient** *adj*

prescribe *v* **1** recommend the use of (a medicine) **2** lay down as a rule **prescription** *n* written instructions from a doctor for the making up and use of a medicine **prescriptive** *adj* laying down rules

presence *n* **1** fact of being in a specified place **2** impressive dignified appearance **presence of mind** ability to act sensibly in a crisis

present[1] *adj* **1** being in a specified place **2** existing or happening now **3** (of a verb tense) indicating that the action specified is taking place now ▷ *n* **4** present time or tense **presently** *adv* **1** soon **2** now

present[2] *n* **1** something given to bring pleasure to another person ▷ *v* **2** introduce formally or publicly **3** introduce and compère (a TV or radio show) **4** cause: *present a difficulty* **5** give, award **presentation** *n* **presentable** *adj* attractive, neat, fit for people to see **presenter** *n* person introducing a TV or radio show

presentiment [pree-**zen**-timent] *n* sense of something usu. unpleasant about to happen

preserve *v* **1** keep from being damaged, changed, or ended **2** treat (food) to prevent it decaying ▷ *n* **3** area of interest restricted to a particular person or group **4** fruit preserved by cooking in sugar **5** area where game is kept for private fishing or shooting **preservation** *n* **preservative** *n* chemical that prevents decay

preshrunk *adj* (of fabric or a garment) having been shrunk during manufacture so that further shrinkage will not occur when washed

preside *v* be in charge, esp. of a meeting

president *n* **1** head of state in countries without a king or queen **2** head of a society, institution, etc. **presidential** *adj* **presidency** *n*

press[1] *v* **1** apply force or weight to **2** squeeze **3** smooth by applying pressure or heat **4** crowd, push **5** urge insistently **6** *basketball* guard opponents closely as a defensive tactic ▷ *n* **7** printing machine **pressed for** short of **pressing** *adj* urgent **press box** room at a sports ground reserved for reporters **press conference** interview for reporters given by a celebrity

press[2] *v* **press into service** force to be involved or used **press gang** *hist* group of men who captured men and boys and forced them to join the navy

pressure *n* **1** force produced by pressing **2** urgent claims or demands: *working under pressure* **3** *physics* force applied to a surface per unit of area **bring pressure to bear on** use influence or authority to persuade **pressure cooker** airtight pot which cooks food quickly by steam under pressure **pressure group** group that tries to influence policies, public opinion, etc.

prestidigitation n skilful quickness with the hands, conjuring

prestige n high status or respect resulting from success or achievements **prestigious** adj

presto adv music very quickly

prestressed adj (of concrete) containing stretched steel wires to strengthen it

presume v 1 suppose to be the case 2 (foll. by to) dare (to), take the liberty (of) **presumably** adv one supposes (that) **presumption** n 1 strong probability 2 bold insolent behaviour **presumptuous** adj doing things one has no right or authority to do **presumptuously** adv **presumptive** adj assumed to be true or valid until the contrary is proved **heir presumptive** heir whose right may be defeated by the birth of a closer relative

presuppose v need as a previous condition in order to be true **presupposition** n

pretend v claim or give the appearance of (something untrue) to deceive or in play **pretender** n person who makes a false or disputed claim to a position of power **pretence** n behaviour intended to deceive, pretending **pretentious** adj making (unjustified) claims to special merit or importance **pretension** n

preterite [pret-er-it] adj, n grammar (expressing) a past tense, such as jumped, swam

preternatural adj beyond what is natural, supernatural

pretext n false reason given to hide the real one

pretty adj -tier, -tiest 1 pleasing to look at ▷ adv 2 fairly, moderately **prettily** adv **prettiness** n

pretzel n brittle salted biscuit

prevail v 1 gain mastery 2 be generally established **prevailing** adj 1 widespread 2 predominant **prevalence** n **prevalent** adj widespread, common

prevaricate v be evasive, avoid giving a direct or truthful answer **prevarication** n

prevent v keep from happening or doing **preventable** adj **prevention** n **preventive** adj, n

preview n advance showing of a film or exhibition before it is shown to the public

previous adj coming or happening before **previously** adv

prey n 1 animal hunted and killed for food by another animal 2 victim **bird of prey** bird that kills and eats other birds or animals **prey on** v 1 hunt and kill for food 2 worry, obsess

price n 1 amount of money for which a thing is bought or sold 2 unpleasant thing that must be endured to get something desirable ▷ v 3 fix or ask the price of **priceless** adj 1 very valuable 2 informal very funny **pricey** or **pricy** adj informal expensive

prick v 1 pierce slightly with a sharp point 2 cause to feel mental pain 3 (of an animal) make (the ears) stand erect ▷ n 4 sudden sharp pain caused by pricking 5 mark made by pricking 6 remorse **prick up one's ears** listen intently

prickle n 1 thorn or spike on a plant ▷ v 2 have a tingling or pricking sensation **prickly** adj **prickly heat** itchy rash occurring in hot moist weather

pride n 1 feeling of pleasure and satisfaction when one has done well 2 too high an opinion of oneself 3 sense of dignity and self-respect 4 something that causes one to feel pride 5 group of lions **pride of place** most important position **pride oneself on** feel pride about

priest n 1 (in the Christian Church) a person who can administer the sacraments and preach 2 (in some other religions) an official who performs religious ceremonies **priestess** n woman priest **priesthood** n **priestly** adj

prig n self-righteous person who acts as if superior to others **priggish** adj **priggishness** n

prim adj **primmer, primmest** formal, proper, and rather prudish **primly** adv **primness** n

prima ballerina n leading female ballet dancer

primacy n, pl -cies 1 state of being first in rank, grade, etc. 2 office of an archbishop

prima donna n 1 leading female opera singer 2 informal temperamental person

primaeval adj same as **primeval**

prima facie [prime-a fay-shee] Latin as it seems at first

primal adj of basic causes or origins

primary adj 1 chief, most important 2 being the first stage, elementary **primarily** adv **primary colours** (in physics) red, green, and blue or (in art) red, yellow, and blue, from which all other colours can be produced by mixing **primary school**

school for children from five to eleven years

primate[1] n archbishop

primate[2] n member of an order of mammals including monkeys and humans

prime adj 1 main, most important 2 of the highest quality ▷ n 3 time when someone is at his or her best or most vigorous ▷ v 4 give (someone) information in advance to prepare them for something 5 prepare (a surface) for painting 6 prepare (a gun, pump, etc.) for use **Prime Minister** leader of a government **prime number** number that can be divided exactly only by itself and one

primer n 1 special paint applied to bare wood etc. before the main paint 2 beginners' school book or manual

primeval, primaeval [prime-ee-val] adj of the earliest age of the world

primitive adj 1 of an early simple stage of development 2 basic, crude: a primitive hut

primogeniture n system under which the eldest son inherits all his parents' property

primordial adj existing at or from the beginning

primrose n pale yellow spring flower

primula n type of primrose with brightly coloured flowers

Primus n ® portable cooking stove used esp. by campers

prince n 1 male member of a royal family, esp. the son of the king or queen 2 male ruler of a small country **princely** adj 1 of or like a prince 2 generous, lavish, or magnificent **prince consort** husband of a reigning queen **Prince of Wales** eldest son of the British sovereign **princess** n female member of a royal family, esp. the daughter of the king or queen **Princess Royal** title sometimes given to the eldest daughter of the British sovereign

principal adj **1** main, most important ▷ n **2** head of a school or college **3** person taking a leading part in something **4** sum of money lent on which interest is paid **principally** adv **principal boy** leading male role in pantomime, played by a woman

principality n, pl -ties territory ruled by a prince

principle n **1** moral rule guiding behaviour **2** general or basic truth: *the principle of equality* **3** scientific law concerning the working of something **in principle** in theory but not always in practice **on principle** because of one's beliefs

print v **1** reproduce (a newspaper, book, etc.) in large quantities by mechanical or electronic means **2** reproduce (text or pictures) by pressing ink onto paper etc. **3** write in letters that are not joined **4** stamp (fabric) with a design **5** *photog* produce (pictures) from negatives ▷ n **6** printed words etc. **7** printed lettering **8** photograph **9** printed copy of a painting **10** mark left on a surface by something that has pressed against it **11** printed fabric **out of print** no longer available from a publisher **printer** n **1** person or company engaged in printing **2** machine that prints **printed circuit** electronic circuit with wiring printed on an insulating base **print-out** n printed information from a computer

prior[1] adj earlier **prior to** before

prior[2] n head monk in a priory **prioress** n deputy head nun in a convent **priory** n place where certain orders of monks or nuns live

priority n, pl -ties **1** most important thing that must be dealt with first **2** right to be or go before others

prise v force open by levering

prism n transparent block usu. with triangular ends and rectangular sides, used to disperse light into a spectrum or refract it in optical instruments **prismatic** adj **1** of or shaped like a prism **2** (of colour) as if produced by refraction through a prism, rainbow-like

prison n building where criminals and accused people are held **prisoner** n person held captive **prisoner of war** serviceman captured by an enemy in wartime

prissy adj -sier, -siest prim, correct, and easily shocked. **prissily** adv

pristine adj completely new, clean, and pure

private adj **1** for the use of one person or group only **2** secret **3** owned or paid for by individuals rather than by the government **4** quiet, not likely to be disturbed **5** personal, unconnected with one's work ▷ n **6** soldier of the lowest rank **privately** adv **privacy** n

privateer n hist **1** privately owned armed vessel authorized by the government to take part in a war **2** captain of such a ship

privation n loss or lack of the necessities of life

privatize v sell (a publicly owned company) to individuals or a private company **privatization** n

privet n bushy evergreen shrub used for hedges

privilege n advantage or favour that only some people have **privileged** adj enjoying a special right or immunity

privy adj **1** sharing knowledge of something secret ▷ n, pl **privies 2** obsolete lavatory, esp. an outside one **privy council** council of state of a monarch

prize¹ n **1** reward given for success in a competition etc. ▷ adj **2** winning or likely to win a prize ▷ v **3** value highly **prizefighter** n boxer who fights for money **prizefight** n

prize² v same as **prise**

pro¹ adj, adv in favour of **pros and cons** arguments for and against

pro² n **1** professional **2** prostitute

pro- prefix **1** in favour of: pro-Russian **2** instead of: pronoun

proactive adj tending to initiate change rather than reacting to events

probable adj likely to happen or be true **probably** adv **probability** n

probate n **1** process of proving the authenticity of a will **2** certificate of this

probation n **1** system of dealing with law-breakers, esp. juvenile ones, by placing them under supervision **2** period when someone is assessed for suitability for a job etc. **probationer** n person on probation

probe v **1** search into or examine closely ▷ n **2** surgical instrument used to examine a wound, cavity, etc.

probiotic n **1** bacterium that protects the body from harmful bacteria ▷ adj **2** relating to probiotics: probiotic yoghurts

probity n honesty, integrity

problem n **1** something difficult to deal with or solve **2** question or puzzle set for solution **problematical** adj

proboscis [pro-**boss**-iss] n **1** elephant's trunk **2** long snout **3** elongated mouthpart of some insects

procedure n way of doing something, esp. the correct or usual one

proceed v **1** start or continue doing **2** formal walk, go **3** start a legal action **4** arise from **proceeds** pl n money obtained from an event or activity **proceedings** pl n **1** organized or related series of events **2** minutes of a meeting **3** legal action

process n **1** series of actions or changes **2** method of doing or producing something ▷ v **3** handle or prepare by a special method of manufacture **4** treat (food) to prevent it decaying **processor** n

procession n line of people or vehicles moving forward together in order

proclaim v declare publicly **proclamation** n

proclivity n, pl -**ties** inclination, tendency

proconsul n hist governor of a province, esp. of the Roman Empire

procrastinate v put off taking action, delay **procrastination** n **procrastinator** n

procreate v formal produce offspring **procreation** n

Procrustean adj ruthlessly enforcing uniformity

procure v **1** get, provide

2 obtain (people) to act as prostitutes **procurement** *n* **procurer** (**procuress**) *n* person who obtains people to act as prostitutes

prod *v* **prodding, prodded 1** poke with something pointed **2** goad (someone) to take action ▷ *n* **3** prodding

prodigal *adj* recklessly extravagant, wasteful **prodigality** *n*

prodigy *n, pl* -**gies 1** person with some marvellous talent **2** wonderful thing **prodigious** *adj* **1** very large, immense **2** wonderful **prodigiously** *adv*

produce *v* **1** bring into existence **2** present to view, show **3** make, manufacture **4** present on stage, film, or television ▷ *n* **5** food grown for sale **producer** *n* **1** person with financial and administrative control of a film etc. **2** *Brit* person responsible for the artistic direction of a play **3** person or company that produces something

product *n* **1** something produced **2** number resulting from multiplication **production** *n* **1** producing **2** things produced **3** presentation of a play, opera, etc. **productive** *adj* **1** producing large quantities **2** useful, profitable **productivity** *n*

profane *adj* **1** showing disrespect for religion or holy things **2** (of language) coarse, blasphemous ▷ *v* **3** treat (something sacred) irreverently, desecrate **profanation** *n* act of profaning **profanity** *n* profane talk or behaviour, blasphemy

profess *v* **1** state or claim (something as true), sometimes falsely **2** have as one's belief or religion **professed** *adj* supposed

profession *n* **1** type of work, such as being a doctor, that needs special training **2** all the people employed in a profession: *the legal profession* **3** declaration of a belief or feeling **professional** *adj* **1** working in a profession **2** taking part in an activity, such as sport or music, for money **3** very competent ▷ *n* **4** person who works in a profession **5** person paid to take part in sport, music, etc. **professionally** *adv* **professionalism** *n*

professor *n* teacher in a university **professorial** *adj* **professorship** *n*

proffer *v* offer

proficient *adj* skilled, expert **proficiency** *n*

profile *n* **1** outline, esp. of the face, as seen from the side **2** brief biographical sketch **profiling** *n* practice of categorizing and predicting the behaviour of people according to certain characteristics: *racial profiling*

profit *n* **1** money gained **2** benefit obtained ▷ *v* **3** gain or benefit **profitable** *adj* making profit **profitably** *adv* **profitability** *n* **profiteer** *n* person who makes excessive profits at the expense of the public **profiteering** *n*

profligate *adj* **1** recklessly extravagant **2** shamelessly immoral ▷ *n* **3** dissolute person **profligacy** *n*

pro forma *Latin* prescribing a set form

profound *adj* **1** showing or needing great knowledge **2** strongly felt, intense **profundity** *n*

profuse *adj* plentiful
profusion *n*
progeny [proj-in-ee] *n, pl*
-**nies** children **progenitor**
[pro-**jen**-it-er] *n* ancestor
progesterone *n* hormone
which prepares the womb
for pregnancy and prevents
further ovulation
prognathous *adj* having a
projecting lower jaw
prognosis *n, pl* -**noses**
1 doctor's forecast about the
progress of an illness **2** any
forecast
prognostication *n* forecast or
prediction
program *n* **1** sequence of coded
instructions for a computer
▷ *v* -**gramming**, -**grammed**
2 arrange (data) so that it can
be processed by a computer
3 feed a program into (a
computer) **programmer** *n*
programmable *adj*
programme *n* **1** planned
series of events **2** broadcast
on radio or television **3** list
of items or performers in an
entertainment
progress *n* **1** improvement,
development **2** movement
forward ▷ *v* **3** become more
advanced or skilful **4** move
forward **in progress** taking
place **progression** *n* **1** act
of progressing, advance
2 sequence of numbers in
which each differs from
the next by a fixed ratio
progressive *adj* **1** favouring
political or social reform
2 happening gradually
progressively *adv*
prohibit *v* forbid or prevent
from happening **prohibition**
n **1** act of forbidding **2** ban on
the sale or drinking of alcohol
prohibitive *adj* (of prices)
too high to be affordable
prohibitively *adv*
project *n* **1** planned scheme

to do or examine something
over a period ▷ *v* **2** make a
forecast based on known data
3 make (a film or slide) appear
on a screen **4** communicate
(an impression) **5** stick out
beyond a surface or edge
projector *n* apparatus for
projecting photographic
images, films, or slides
on a screen **projection** *n*
projectionist *n* person who
operates a projector
projectile *n* object thrown as a
weapon or fired from a gun
prolapse *n* slipping down of
an internal organ of the body
from its normal position
prole *adj, n informal* proletarian
proletariat [pro-lit-**air**-ee-at]
n working class **proletarian**
adj, n
proliferate *v* **1** increase
rapidly in numbers **2** grow or
reproduce (new parts, such as
cells) rapidly **proliferation** *n*
prolific *adj* very productive
prolifically *adv*
prolix *adj* (of speech or a piece
of writing) overlong and
boring **prolixity** *n*
prologue *n* introduction to a
play or book
prolong *v* make (something)
last longer **prolongation** *n*
prom *n* **1** formal dance
at a school **2** short for
**promenade, promenade
concert**
promenade *n* **1** paved
walkway along the seafront
at a holiday resort ▷ *v, n* **2** *old-
fashioned* (take) a leisurely
walk **promenade concert**
concert at which part of the
audience stands rather than
sits
prominent *adj* **1** famous,
widely known **2** very
noticeable **prominently** *adv*
prominence *n*
promiscuous *adj* having

many casual sexual relationships **promiscuity** n

promise v 1 say that one will definitely do or not do something 2 show signs of, seem likely ▷ n 3 undertaking to do or not to do something 4 indication of future success **show promise** seem likely to succeed **promising** adj likely to succeed or turn out well

promo n informal short video film made to promote a pop record

promontory n, pl -ries point of high land jutting out into the sea

promote v 1 help to make (something) happen or increase 2 raise to a higher rank or position 3 encourage the sale of by advertising **promoter** n person who organizes or finances an event etc. **promotion** n **promotional** adj

prompt v 1 cause (an action) 2 remind (an actor or speaker) of words that he or she has forgotten ▷ adj 3 done without delay ▷ adv 4 exactly: six o'clock prompt **promptly** adv immediately, without delay **promptness** n **prompter** n person offstage who prompts actors

promulgate v 1 put (a law etc.) into effect by announcing it officially 2 make widely known **promulgation** n **promulgator** n

prone adj 1 (foll. by to) likely to do or be affected by (something) 2 lying face downwards

prong n one spike of a fork or similar instrument **pronged** adj

pronoun n word, such as she, it, used to replace a noun **pronominal** adj

pronounce v 1 form the sounds of (words or letters), esp. clearly or in a particular way 2 declare formally or officially **pronounceable** adj **pronounced** adj very noticeable **pronouncement** n formal announcement **pronunciation** n way in which a word or language is pronounced

pronto adv informal at once

proof n 1 evidence that shows that something is true or has happened 2 copy of something printed, such as the pages of a book, for checking before final production ▷ adj 3 able to withstand: proof against criticism 4 denoting the strength of an alcoholic drink: seventy proof **proofread** v read and correct (printer's proofs) **proofreader** n

prop[1] v propping, propped 1 support (something) so that it stays upright or in place ▷ n 2 pole, beam, etc. used as a support

prop[2] n movable object used on the set of a film or play

prop[3] n informal propeller

propaganda n (organized promotion of) information to assist or damage the cause of a government or movement **propagandist** n

propagate v 1 spread (information and ideas) 2 reproduce, breed, or grow **propagation** n

propane n flammable gas found in petroleum and used as a fuel

propel v -pelling, -pelled cause to move forward **propellant** n 1 something that provides or causes propulsion 2 gas used in an aerosol spray **propeller** n revolving shaft with blades for driving a ship or aircraft **propulsion**

n **1** propelling or being propelled **2** method by which something is propelled

propensity *n, pl* **-ties** natural tendency

proper *adj* **1** real or genuine **2** appropriate **3** suited to a particular purpose **4** correct in behaviour **5** excessively moral **6** *informal* complete **properly** *adv*

property *n, pl* **-ties** **1** something owned **2** possessions collectively **3** land or buildings owned by somebody **4** quality or attribute

prophet *n* **1** person supposedly chosen by God to spread His word **2** person who predicts the future **prophetic** *adj* **prophetically** *adv* **prophecy** *n* **1** prediction **2** message revealing God's will **prophesy** *v* foretell

prophylactic *n, adj* (drug) used to prevent disease

propinquity *n* nearness in time, place, or relationship

propitiate *v* appease, win the favour of **propitiation** *n* **propitiatory** *adj* intended to appease someone **propitious** *adj* favourable or auspicious

proponent *n* person who argues in favour of something

proportion *n* **1** relative size or extent **2** correct relation between connected parts **3** part considered with respect to the whole **proportions** **4** dimensions or size ▷ *v* **5** adjust in relative amount or size **in proportion** **1** comparable in size, rate of increase, etc. **2** without exaggerating **proportional** *or* **proportionate** *adj* being in proportion **proportionally** *adv*

propose *v* **1** put forward for consideration **2** nominate

3 intend or plan (to do) **4** make an offer of marriage **proposal** *n* **proposition** *n* **1** offer **2** statement or assertion **3** theorem **4** *informal* thing to be dealt with ▷ *v* **5** *informal* ask (someone) to have sexual intercourse with one

propound *v* put forward for consideration

proprietor *n* owner of a business establishment **proprietress** *n fem* **proprietary** *adj* **1** made and distributed under a trade name **2** denoting or suggesting ownership

propriety *n, pl* **-ties** correct conduct

propulsion *n* see **propel**

pro rata *Latin* in proportion

prorogue *v* suspend (parliament) without dissolving it **prorogation** *n*

prosaic [pro-**zay**-ik] *adj* lacking imagination, dull **prosaically** *adv*

proscenium *n, pl* **-niums, -nia** arch in a theatre separating the stage from the auditorium

proscribe *v* prohibit, outlaw **proscription** *n* **proscriptive** *adj*

prose *n* ordinary speech or writing in contrast to poetry

prosecute *v* **1** bring a criminal charge against **2** continue to do **prosecution** *n* **prosecutor** *n*

proselyte [**pross**-ill-ite] *n* recent convert **proselytize** [**pross**-ill-it-ize] *v* attempt to convert

prosody [**pross**-a-dee] *n* study of poetic metre and techniques **prosodic** *adj* **prosodist** *n*

prospect *n* **1** something anticipated: *the prospect of defeat* **2** *old-fashioned* view from a place **prospects**

3 probability of future success ▷ v **4** explore, esp. for gold **prospective** adj **1** expected **2** future **prospector** n person who searches, esp. for gold **prospectus** n booklet giving details of a university, company, etc.

prosper v be successful **prosperity** n success and wealth **prosperous** adj

prostate n gland in male mammals that surrounds the neck of the bladder

prosthesis [pross-**theess**-iss] n, pl -**ses** [-seez] artificial body part, such as a limb or breast **prosthetic** adj

prostitute n **1** person who offers sexual intercourse in return for payment ▷ v **2** make a prostitute of **3** offer (oneself or one's talents) for unworthy purposes **prostitution** n

prostrate adj **1** lying face downwards **2** physically or emotionally exhausted ▷ v **3** lie face downwards **4** exhaust physically or emotionally **prostration** n

protagonist n **1** leading character in a play or a story **2** supporter of a cause

protea [pro-**tee**-a] n African shrub with showy flowers

protean [pro-**tee**-an] adj constantly changing

protect v defend from trouble, harm, or loss **protection** n **protectionism** n policy of protecting industries by taxing competing imports **protectionist** n **protective** adj **1** giving protection: *protective clothing* **2** tending or wishing to protect someone **protector** n **1** person or thing that protects **2** regent **protectorate** n **1** territory largely controlled by a stronger state **2** (period of)

rule of a regent

protégé [**pro**-ti-zhay] n person who is protected and helped by another **protégée** n fem

protein n any of a group of complex organic compounds that are essential for life

pro tempore adv, adj Also **pro tem** for the time being

protest n **1** declaration or demonstration of objection ▷ v **2** object, disagree **3** assert formally **protestation** n strong declaration

Protestant adj **1** of or relating to any of the Christian churches that split from the Roman Catholic Church in the sixteenth century ▷ n **2** member of a Protestant church **Protestantism** n

proto-, prot- *combining form* first: *protohuman*

protocol n **1** rules of behaviour for formal occasions **2** *computers* set of rules for transfer of data, esp. between different systems

proton n positively charged particle in the nucleus of an atom

protoplasm n substance forming the living contents of a cell

prototype n original or model after which something is copied

protozoan [pro-toe-**zoe**-an] n, pl -**zoa** microscopic one-celled creature

protract v lengthen or extend **protracted** adj **protraction** n **protractor** n instrument for measuring angles

protrude v stick out, project **protrusion** n

protuberant adj swelling out, bulging **protuberance** n

proud adj **1** feeling pleasure and satisfaction **2** feeling honoured **3** thinking oneself

superior to other people
4 dignified **proudly** adv
proud flesh flesh growing
around a healing wound

prove v **proving, proved,
proved** or **proven 1** establish
the validity of **2** demonstrate,
test **3** be found to be **proven**
adj known from experience
to work

provenance [**prov**-in-anss] n
place of origin

provender n old-fashioned
fodder

proverb n short saying that
expresses a truth or gives a
warning **proverbial** adj

provide v **1** make available
2 (foll. by for) take precautions
(against) **3** support financially
provider n **provided that** on
condition that

providence n God or nature
seen as a protective force
that arranges people's
lives **provident** adj **1** thrifty
2 showing foresight
providential adj lucky
providentially adv

province n **1** territory
governed as a unit of a
country or empire **2** area
of learning, activity,
etc. **provinces 3** any part
of a country outside the
capital **provincial** adj **1** of
a province or the provinces
2 unsophisticated or narrow-
minded ▷ n **3** unsophisticated
person **4** person from a
province or the provinces
provincialism n narrow-
mindedness and lack of
sophistication

provision n **1** act of supplying
something **2** something
supplied **provisions 3** food
4 law condition incorporated
in a document ▷ v **5** supply
with food **provisional** adj
1 temporary **2** conditional
provisionally adv

proviso [pro-**vize**-oh] n,
pl **-sos, -soes** condition,
stipulation

provoke v **1** deliberately anger
2 cause (an adverse reaction)
provocation n **provocative**
adj

provost n **1** head of certain
university colleges **2** chief
councillor of a Scottish town
provost marshal head of
military police

prow n bow of a vessel

prowess n **1** superior skill or
ability **2** bravery, fearlessness

prowl v **1** move stealthily
around a place as if in
search of prey or plunder ▷ n
2 prowling **prowler** n

proximity n **1** nearness in
space or time **2** nearness
or closeness in a series
proximate adj

proxy n, pl **proxies 1** person
authorized to act on behalf of
someone else **2** authority to
act on behalf of someone else

prude n person who is
excessively modest, prim, or
proper **prudish** adj **prudery** n

prudent adj cautious, discreet,
and sensible **prudence** n
prudential adj old-fashioned
prudent

prune[1] n dried plum

prune[2] v **1** cut out dead parts
or excessive branches from
(a tree or plant) **2** shorten,
reduce

prurient adj excessively
interested in sexual matters
prurience n

pry v **prying, pried** make
an impertinent or uninvited
inquiry into a private matter

PS postscript

psalm n sacred song **psalmist**
n writer of psalms **psalmody**
n singing of sacred music

Psalter n book containing
(a version of) psalms from
the Bible **psaltery** n ancient

instrument played by plucking strings

psephology [sef-**fol**-a-jee] n statistical study of elections

pseud n informal pretentious person

pseudo-, pseud- combining form false, pretending, or unauthentic: pseudo-intellectual

pseudonym n fictitious name adopted, esp. by an author **pseudonymous** adj

psittacosis n disease of parrots that can be transmitted to humans

PST Pacific Standard Time

psyche n human mind or soul

psychedelic adj 1 denoting a drug that causes hallucinations 2 having vivid colours and complex patterns similar to those experienced during hallucinations

psychiatry n branch of medicine concerned with mental illness **psychiatric** adj **psychiatrist** n

psychic adj Also **psychical** 1 having mental powers which cannot be explained by natural laws 2 relating to the mind ▷ n 3 person with psychic powers

psycho n informal short for **psychopath**

psychoanalysis n method of treating mental and emotional disorders by discussion and analysis of one's thoughts and feelings **psychoanalyse** v **psychoanalyst** n

psychology n, pl -gies 1 study of human and animal behaviour 2 informal person's mental make-up **psychological** adj 1 of or affecting the mind 2 of psychology **psychologist** n

psychopath n person with a personality disorder causing him or her to commit antisocial or violent acts **psychopathic** adj

psychosis n, pl -choses severe mental illness in which the sufferer's contact with reality becomes distorted **psychotic** adj, n

psychosomatic adj (of a physical disorder) thought to have psychological causes

psychotherapy n treatment of nervous disorders by psychological methods **psychotherapeutic** adj **psychotherapist** n

psych up v prepare (oneself) mentally for a contest or task

pt 1 part 2 point 3 port

Pt chem platinum

PT old-fashioned physical training

pt. pint

PTA Parent-Teacher Association

ptarmigan [**tar**-mig-an] n bird of the grouse family which turns white in winter

pterodactyl [terr-roe-**dak**-til] n extinct flying reptile with batlike wings

ptomaine [**toe**-main] n any of a group of poisonous alkaloids found in decaying matter

Pu chem plutonium

pub n building with a bar licensed to sell alcoholic drinks

puberty [**pew**-ber-tee] n sexual maturity **pubertal** adj

pubic [**pew**-bik] adj of the lower abdomen

public adj 1 of or concerning the people as a whole 2 for use by everyone 3 well-known 4 performed or made openly ▷ n 5 the community, people in general **publicly** adv **publican** n Brit person who owns or runs a pub **public house** pub **public relations** promotion of a favourable opinion towards an organization among the public **public school** private fee-paying school in Britain **public servant** member of the public service **public service** service responsible for the administration of the government **public-spirited** adj having or showing an active interest in the good of the community

publicity n 1 process or information used to arouse public attention 2 public interest aroused **publicize** v advertise **publicist** n person who publicizes something, such as a press agent or journalist

publish v 1 produce and issue (printed matter) for sale 2 announce formally or in public **publication** n **publisher** n

puce adj purplish-brown

puck[1] n small rubber disc used in ice hockey **puckster** n hockey slang hockey player

puck[2] n mischievous or evil spirit **puckish** adj

pucker v 1 gather into wrinkles ▷ n 2 wrinkle or crease

pudding n 1 dessert, esp. a cooked one served hot 2 savoury dish with pastry or batter: steak-and-kidney pudding 3 sausage-like mass of meat: black pudding

puddle n small pool of water, esp. of rain

puerile adj silly and childish

puerperium [pure-**peer**-ee-um] n period following childbirth **puerperal** [pure-per-al] adj

puff n 1 (sound of) a short blast of breath, wind, etc. 2 instance of breathing in and out 3 act of inhaling cigarette smoke ▷ v 4 blow or breathe in short quick drafts 5 take draws at (a cigarette) 6 send out in small clouds 7 swell **out of puff** out of breath **puffy** adj **puffball** n ball-shaped fungus **puff pastry** light flaky pastry

puffin n black-and-white sea bird with a large brightly-coloured beak

pug n small snub-nosed dog **pug nose** short stubby upturned nose

pugilism [**pew**-jil-iz-zum] n boxing **pugilist** n **pugilistic** adj

pugnacious adj ready and eager to fight **pugnacity** n

puissant [**pew**-iss-sant] adj poetic powerful **puissance** n showjumping competition that tests a horse's ability to jump large obstacles

puke slang ▷ v 1 vomit ▷ n 2 act of vomiting 3 vomited matter

pulchritude n lit beauty

pule v 1 whine 2 whimper

pull v 1 exert force on (an object) to move it towards the source of the force 2 strain or stretch 3 remove or extract 4 attract 5 informal act in a way considered characteristic of a particular person: pull a Greta Garbo ▷ n 6 pulling 7 force used in pulling 8 act of taking in drink or smoke 9 informal power, influence **pull in** v 1 (of a vehicle or driver) draw in to the side of the road or stop 2 reach a destination 3 attract in large numbers 4 slang arrest **pull off** v 1 informal succeed in performing 2 (of a vehicle or driver) move to the side of the road and stop 3 (of a vehicle or driver) start to move away **pull out** v 1 (of a vehicle or driver) move away from the side of the road or move out to overtake 2 (of a train) depart 3 withdraw 4 remove by pulling **pull**

up v 1 (of a vehicle or driver) stop 2 remove by the roots 3 reprimand

pullet n young hen

pulley n wheel with a grooved rim in which a belt, chain, or piece of rope runs in order to lift weights by a downward pull

Pullman n, pl -mans luxurious railway coach

pullover n sweater that is pulled on over the head

pulmonary adj of the lungs

pulp n 1 soft moist plant tissue, such as the material used to make paper 2 flesh of a fruit or vegetable 3 any soft soggy mass 4 poor-quality books and magazines ▷ v 5 reduce to pulp

pulpit n raised platform for a preacher

pulsar n small dense star which emits regular bursts of radio waves

pulse[1] n 1 regular beating of blood through the arteries at each heartbeat which can be felt at the wrists and elsewhere 2 any regular beat or vibration **pulsate** v throb, quiver **pulsation** n

pulse[2] n edible seed of a pod-bearing plant such as a bean or pea

pulverize v 1 reduce to fine pieces 2 destroy completely **pulverization** n

puma n large American cat with a greyish-brown coat

pumice [**pumm**-iss] n light porous stone used for scouring

pummel v -melling, -melled strike repeatedly with or as if with the fists

pump[1] n 1 machine used to force a liquid or gas to move in a particular direction ▷ v 2 raise or drive with a pump 3 supply in large amounts 4 extract information from 5 operate or work in the manner of a pump

pump[2] n light flat-soled shoe

pumpkin n large round fruit with an orange rind, soft flesh, and many seeds

pun n 1 use of words to exploit double meanings for humorous effect ▷ v **punning, punned** 2 make puns **punster** n person fond of making puns

punch[1] v 1 strike at with a clenched fist ▷ n 2 blow with a clenched fist 3 informal effectiveness or vigour **punchy** adj forceful **punch-drunk** adj dazed by or as if by repeated blows to the head

punch[2] n 1 tool or machine for shaping, piercing, or engraving ▷ v 2 pierce, cut, stamp, shape, or drive with a punch

punch[3] n drink made from a mixture of wine, spirits, fruit, sugar, and spices

punctilious adj 1 paying great attention to correctness in etiquette 2 careful about small details

punctual adj arriving or taking place at the correct time **punctuality** n **punctually** adv

punctuate v 1 put punctuation marks in 2 interrupt at frequent intervals **punctuation** n (use of) marks such as commas, colons, etc. in writing, to assist in making the sense clear

puncture n 1 small hole made by a sharp object, esp. in a tire ▷ v 2 pierce a hole in

pundit n expert who speaks publicly on a subject

pungent adj having a strong sharp bitter flavour **pungency** n

punish v cause (someone) to suffer or undergo a penalty for some wrongdoing **punishing** adj harsh or difficult **punishment** n **punitive** [**pew**-nit-tiv] adj relating to punishment

punk n 1 worthless person 2 anti-Establishment youth movement and style of rock music of the late 1970s 3 follower of this music

punnet n small basket for fruit

punt[1] n 1 open flat-bottomed boat propelled by a pole ▷ v 2 travel in a punt

punt[2] sports ▷ v 1 kick (a ball) before it touches the ground when dropped from the hands ▷ n 2 such a kick **punter** n

punt[3] n former monetary unit of the Irish Republic

punter n 1 person who bets 2 any member of the public

puny adj -nier, -niest small and feeble

pup n young of certain animals, such as dogs and seals **pup tent** small triangular tent for one or two people

pupa [**pew**-pa] n, pl -pae, -pas insect at the stage of development between a larva and an adult **pupal** adj

pupil[1] n person who is taught by a teacher

pupil[2] n round dark opening in the centre of the eye

puppet n 1 small doll or figure moved by strings or by the operator's hand 2 person or country controlled by another **puppeteer** n

puppy n, pl -pies young dog

purblind adj partly or nearly blind

purchase v 1 obtain by payment ▷ n 2 buying 3 what is bought 4 leverage, grip **purchaser** n

purdah n Muslim and Hindu custom of keeping women in seclusion, with clothing that conceals them completely when they go out

pure adj 1 unmixed, untainted 2 faultless 3 innocent 4 complete: *pure delight* 5 concerned with theory only: *pure mathematics* **purely** adv **purity** n **purify** v make or become pure **purification** n **purist** n person obsessed with strict obedience to the traditions of a subject

purée [**pure**-ray] n 1 pulp of cooked food ▷ v -**reeing**, -**reed** 2 make into a purée

purgatory n 1 place or state of temporary suffering 2 **Purgatory** RC Church place where souls of the dead undergo punishment for their sins before being admitted to Heaven **purgatorial** adj

purge v 1 rid (a thing or place) of (unwanted things or people) ▷ n 2 purging **purgation** n **purgative** adj, n (medicine) designed to cause defecation

Puritan n 1 hist member of the English Protestant group who wanted simpler church ceremonies 2 **puritan** person with strict moral and religious principles **puritanical** adj **puritanism** n

purl n 1 stitch made by knitting a plain stitch backwards ▷ v 2 knit in purl

purlieus [**per**-lyooz] pl n lit outskirts

purloin v steal

purple adj of a colour between red and blue

purport v 1 claim (to be or do something) ▷ n 2 apparent meaning, significance

purpose n 1 reason for which something is done or exists 2 determination 3 practical advantage or use: *use the time to good purpose* ▷ v **4** old-fashioned intend **purposely** *adv* Also **on purpose** intentionally

purr n **1** low vibrant sound that a cat makes when pleased ▷ v **2** make this sound

purse n **1** small bag for money **2** small bag carried to contain personal articles **3** financial resources **4** prize money ▷ v **5** draw (one's lips) together into a small round shape **purser** n ship's officer who keeps the accounts

pursue v **1** chase **2** follow (a goal) **3** engage in **4** continue to discuss or ask about (something) **pursuer** n **pursuit** n **1** pursuing **2** occupation **pursuance** n carrying out

purulent [pure-yoo-lent] *adj* of or containing pus **purulence** n

purvey v supply (provisions) **purveyance** n **purveyor** n

purview n scope or range of activity or outlook

pus n yellowish matter produced by infected tissue

push v **1** move or try to move by steady force **2** drive or spur (oneself or another person) to do something **3** informal sell (drugs) illegally ▷ n **4** pushing **5** special effort **the push** slang **1** dismissal from a job **2** ending of a relationship **pusher** n person who sells illegal drugs **pushy** *adj* too assertive or ambitious **pushover** n informal **1** something easily achieved **2** person or team easily taken advantage of or defeated

pusillanimous *adj* cowardly **pusillanimity** n

puss, pussy n, pl **pusses, pussies** cat

pussyfoot v informal behave too cautiously

pustule n pimple containing pus **pustular** *adj*

put v **putting, put** **1** cause to be (in a position, state, or place) **2** express **3** throw (the shot) in the shot put ▷ n **4** throw in putting the shot **put across** v express successfully **put off** v **1** postpone **2** disconcert **3** repel **put up** v **1** erect **2** accommodate **3** nominate **put-upon** *adj* taken advantage of

putative [pew-tat-iv] *adj* reputed, supposed

putrid *adj* rotten and foul-smelling **putrefy** v rot and produce an offensive smell **putrefaction** n **putrescent** *adj* **1** becoming putrid **2** rotting

putsch n sudden violent attempt to remove a government from power

putt golf ▷ n **1** stroke on the green with a putter to roll the ball into or near the hole ▷ v **2** strike (the ball) in this way **putter** n golf club with a short shaft for putting

puttee n strip of cloth worn wound around the leg from the ankle to the knee

putter v same as **potter**²

putty n paste used to fix glass into frames and fill cracks in woodwork

puzzle v **1** perplex and confuse or be perplexed or confused ▷ n **2** problem that cannot be easily solved **3** toy, game, or question that requires skill or ingenuity to solve **puzzlement** n **puzzling** *adj*

PVC polyvinyl chloride: synthetic thermoplastic material

pyemia, pyaemia n blood poisoning

Pygmy n, pl **-mies** **1** member

of one of the dwarf peoples of Equatorial Africa ▷ *adj* **2 pygmy** very small

pyjamas, pajamas *pl n* loose-fitting trousers and top worn in bed

pylon *n* **1** plastic orange cone used to mark areas on the ground **2** *Brit* steel tower-like structure supporting electrical cables

pyorrhea, pyorrhoea [pire-**ree**-a] *n* disease of the gums and tooth sockets which causes bleeding of the gums and the formation of pus

pyramid *n* **1** solid figure with a flat base and triangular sides sloping upwards to a point **2** structure of this shape, esp. an ancient Egyptian one **pyramidal** *adj*

pyre *n* pile of wood for burning a dead body on

Pyrex *n* ® heat-resistant glassware

pyrites [pie-**rite**-eez] *n* sulfide of a metal, esp. iron pyrites

pyromania *n* uncontrollable urge to set things on fire **pyromaniac** *n*

pyrotechnics *n* **1** art of making fireworks **2** firework display **pyrotechnic** *adj*

Pyrrhic victory [**pir**-ik] *n* victory in which the victor's losses are as great as those of the defeated

python *n* large nonpoisonous snake that crushes its prey

p

Qq

QB quarterback

QC 1 Quebec 2 Queen's Counsel

QED which was to be shown or proved

QM Quartermaster

qr. 1 quarter 2 quire

qt. quart

qua [kwah] *prep* in the capacity of

quack¹ *v* 1 (of a duck) utter a harsh guttural sound ▷ *n* 2 sound made by a duck

quack² *n* 1 unqualified person who claims medical knowledge 2 *informal* doctor

quad *n* 1 short for **quadrangle** 2 *informal* quadruplet ▷ *adj* 3 short for **quadraphonic** ▶ **quad bike** vehicle like a small motorcycle with four large wheels, designed for agricultural and sporting uses

quadrangle *n* 1 rectangular courtyard with buildings on all four sides 2 geometric figure consisting of four points connected by four lines **quadrangular** *adj*

quadrant *n* 1 quarter of a circle 2 quarter of a circle's circumference 3 instrument for measuring the altitude of the stars

quadraphonic *adj* using four independent channels to reproduce or record sound

quadratic *math* ▷ *n* 1 equation in which the variable is raised to the power of two, but nowhere raised to a higher power ▷ *adj* 2 of the second power

quadrennial *adj* 1 occurring every four years 2 lasting four years

quadri- *combining form* four: *quadrilateral*

quadrilateral *adj* 1 having four sides ▷ *n* 2 polygon with four sides

quadrille *n* square dance for four couples

quadruped [kwod-roo-ped] *n* any animal with four legs

quadruple *v* 1 multiply by four ▷ *adj* 2 four times as much or as many 3 consisting of four parts

quadruplet *n* one of four offspring born at one birth

quaff [kwoff] *v* drink heartily or in one draft

quagmire [kwog-mire] *n* soft wet area of land

quail¹ *n* small game bird of the partridge family

quail² *v* shrink back with fear

quaint *adj* attractively unusual, esp. in an old-fashioned style **quaintly** *adv* **quaintness** *n*

quake *v* 1 shake or tremble with or as if with fear ▷ *n* 2 *informal* earthquake

Quaker *n* member of a Christian sect, the Society of Friends **Quakerism** *n*

qualify *v* -fying, -fied 1 provide or be provided with the abilities necessary for a task, office, or duty 2 moderate or restrict (something, esp. a statement) **qualified** *adj* **qualification** *n*

1 quality or skill needed for a particular activity **2** condition that modifies or limits **3** act of qualifying

quality n, pl **-ties 1** degree or standard of excellence **2** distinguishing characteristic or attribute **3** basic character or nature of something **qualitative** adj of or relating to quality

qualm [**kwahm**] n **1** pang of conscience **2** sudden sensation of misgiving

quandary n, pl **-ries** difficult situation or dilemma

quango n, pl **-gos** partly independent official body, set up by a government

quanta n plural of **quantum**

quantify v **-fying, -fied** discover or express the quantity of **quantifiable** adj **quantification** n

quantity n, pl **-ties 1** specified or definite amount or number **2** aspect of anything that can be measured, weighed, or counted **quantitative** adj of or relating to quantity

quantum n, pl **-ta 1** desired or required amount ▷ adj **2** designating a major breakthrough or sudden advance: quantum leap

quantum theory physics theory based on the idea that energy of electrons is discharged in discrete quanta

quarantine n **1** period of isolation of people or animals to prevent the spread of disease ▷ v **2** isolate in or as if in quarantine

quark n physics particle thought to be the fundamental unit of matter

quarrel n **1** angry disagreement **2** cause of dispute ▷ v **-relling, -relled 3** have a disagreement or dispute **quarrelsome** adj

quarry¹ n, pl **-ries 1** place where stone is dug from the surface of the earth ▷ v **-rying, -ried 2** extract (stone) from a quarry

quarry² n, pl **-ries** person or animal that is being hunted

quart n unit of liquid measure equal to two pints

quarter n **1** one of four equal parts of something **2** fourth part of a year **3** region or district of a town or city **4** coin worth 25 cents **6** mercy or pity, as shown towards a defeated opponent **quarters 7** lodgings ▷ v **8** divide into four equal parts **9** billet or be billeted in lodgings

quarterly adj **1** occurring, due, or issued every three months ▷ adv **2** once every three months **quarterback** n player in football who directs attacking play **quarterdeck** n naut rear part of the upper deck of a ship **quarterfinal** n round before the semifinal in a competition **quarter horse** small powerful breed of horse **quartermaster** n military officer responsible for accommodation, food, and equipment **quarter note** musical note half the length of a half note

quartet n **1** group of four performers **2** music for a quartet

quarto n, pl **-tos** book size in which the sheets are folded into four leaves

quartz n hard glossy mineral, used in making very accurate clocks and watches

quasar [**kway**-zar] n extremely distant starlike object that emits powerful radio waves

quash v **1** annul or make void **2** subdue forcefully and completely

quasi- [**kway**-zie] combining

form almost but not really: *quasi-religious; quasi-scholar*

quatrain *n* stanza or poem of four lines

quaver *v* (of a voice) **1** quiver or tremble ▷ *n* **2** *music* note half the length of a crotchet **3** tremulous sound or note

quay [**kee**] *n* wharf built parallel to the shore

Que. Quebec

queasy *adj* **-sier, -siest 1** having the feeling that one is about to vomit **2** feeling or causing uneasiness **queasily** *adv* **queasiness** *n*

queen *n* **1** female sovereign who is the official ruler or head of state **2** wife of a king **3** woman, place, or thing considered to be the best of her or its kind **4** *slang* effeminate male homosexual **5** only fertile female in a colony of bees, wasps, or ants **6** the most powerful piece in chess **queen it** *informal* behave in an overbearing manner **queenly** *adj* **Queen's Counsel** barrister or advocate appointed Counsel to the Crown

queer *adj* **1** not normal or usual **2** faint, giddy, or queasy **3** *offensive* homosexual ▷ *n* **4** *offensive* homosexual **queer someone's pitch** *informal* spoil someone's chances of something

quell *v* **1** suppress **2** overcome

quench *v* **1** satisfy (one's thirst) **2** put out or extinguish

quern *n* stone hand mill for grinding corn

querulous [**kwer**-yoo-luss] *adj* complaining or peevish **querulously** *adv*

query *n, pl* **-ries 1** question, esp. one raising doubt **2** question mark ▷ *v* **-rying, -ried 3** express uncertainty, doubt, or an objection

concerning (something)

quest *n* **1** long and difficult search ▷ *v* **2** (foll. by *for* or *after*) go in search of

question *n* **1** form of words addressed to a person in order to obtain an answer **2** point at issue **3** difficulty or uncertainty ▷ *v* **4** put a question or questions to (a person) **5** express uncertainty about **in question** under discussion **out of the question** impossible **questionable** *adj* of disputable value or authority **questionably** *adv* **questionnaire** *n* set of questions on a form, used to collect information from people **question mark** punctuation mark (?) written at the end of questions

queue *n* **1** line of people or vehicles waiting for something ▷ *v* **queueing** or **queuing, queued 2** (often foll. by *up*) form or remain in a line while waiting

quibble *v* **1** make trivial objections ▷ *n* **2** trivial objection

quiche [**keesh**] *n* savoury flan with an egg custard filling to which vegetables etc. are added

quick *adj* **1** speedy, fast **2** lasting or taking a short time **3** alert and responsive **4** easily excited or aroused ▷ *n* **5** area of sensitive flesh under a nail ▷ *adv* **6** *informal* in a rapid manner **cut someone to the quick** hurt someone's feelings deeply **quickly** *adv* **quicken** *v* make or become faster or more lively **quicklime** *n* white solid used in the manufacture of glass and steel **quicksand** *n* deep mass of loose wet sand that sucks anything on top of it

q

into it **quicksilver** n mercury
quickstep n fast modern
ballroom dance
quid pro quo n one thing, esp.
an advantage or object, given
in exchange for another
quiescent [kwee-**ess**-ent] adj
quiet, inactive, or dormant
quiescence n
quiet adj **1** with little
noise **2** calm or tranquil
3 untroubled ▷ n **4** quietness
▷ v **5** make or become quiet
on the quiet without other
people knowing, secretly
quietly adv **quietness**
n **quieten** v (often foll. by
down) make or become quiet
quietude n quietness, peace,
or tranquillity
quietism n passivity and
calmness of mind towards
external events **quietist** n, adj
quiff n tuft of hair brushed up
above the forehead
quill n **1** pen made from the
feather of a bird's wing or
tail **2** stiff hollow spine of a
hedgehog or porcupine
quilt n padded covering for a
bed **quilted** adj consisting
of two layers of fabric with a
layer of soft material between
them
quince n acid-tasting pear-
shaped fruit
quinine n bitter drug used as
a tonic and formerly to treat
malaria
quinquennial adj **1** occurring
every five years **2** lasting five
years
quinsy n inflammation of the
throat or tonsils
quint n informal quintuplet
quintessence n most perfect
representation of a quality or
state **quintessential** adj
quintet n **1** group of five
performers **2** music for
such a group
quintuplet n one of five

offspring born at one birth
quip n **1** witty saying ▷ v
quipping, quipped 2 make
a quip
quire n set of 24 or 25 sheets of
paper
quirk n **1** peculiarity of
character **2** unexpected twist
or turn: a quirk of fate **quirky**
adj
quisling n traitor who aids an
occupying enemy force
quit v **quitting, quit 1** depart
from **2** give up (a job)
3 stop (doing something)
quitter n person who lacks
perseverance **quits** adj
informal on an equal footing
quite adv **1** to a greater than
average extent: she's quite pretty
2 absolutely: you're quite right
3 in actuality, truly ▷ interj
4 expression of agreement
quiver¹ v **1** shake with a
tremulous movement ▷ n
2 shaking or trembling
quiver² n case for arrows
quixotic [kwik-**sot**-ik] adj
romantic and unrealistic
quixotically adv
quiz n, pl **quizzes**
1 entertainment in which
the knowledge of the
players is tested by a series
of questions ▷ v **quizzing,
quizzed 2** investigate by close
questioning **quizzical** adj
questioning and mocking: a
quizzical look **quizzically** adv
quoit n **1** large ring used in the
game of quoits **quoits 2** game
in which quoits are tossed
at a stake in the ground in
attempts to encircle it
quorum n minimum number
of people required to be
present at a meeting before
any transactions can take
place **quorate** adj having or
being a quorum
quota n **1** share that is due
from, due to, or allocated to a

group or person **2** prescribed number or quantity allowed, required, or admitted

quote *v* **1** repeat (words) exactly from (an earlier work, speech, or conversation) **2** state (a price) for goods or a job of work ▷ *n* **3** *informal* quotation **quotable** *adj* **quotation** *n* **1** written or spoken passage repeated exactly in a later work, speech, or conversation **2** act of quoting **3** estimate of costs submitted by a contractor to a prospective client

quoth *v obsolete* said

quotidian *adj* **1** daily **2** commonplace

quotient *n* result of the division of one number or quantity by another

q.v. which see: used to refer a reader to another item in the same book

qwerty *n* standard English language typewriter or computer keyboard

q

Rr

r 1 radius 2 ratio 3 right

R 1 Queen 2 King 3 River 4 *chess* rook

Ra *chem* radium

RA 1 Royal Academy 2 Royal Artillery

rabbi [rab-bye] *n, pl* -**bis** Jewish spiritual leader **rabbinical** *adj*

rabbit *n* small burrowing mammal with long ears **rabbit on** *v informal* talk too much

rabble *n* disorderly crowd of noisy people

rabid *adj* 1 fanatical 2 having rabies **rabidly** *adv*

rabies [ray-beez] *n* acute infectious viral disease transmitted by dogs and certain other animals

raccoon *n* small N American mammal with a long striped tail

race[1] *n* 1 contest of speed **races** 2 meeting for horse racing ▷ *v* 3 compete with in a race 4 run swiftly 5 (of an engine) run faster than normal **racer** *n* **racecourse** *n* **racehorse** *n* **racetrack** *n*

race[2] *n* group of people of common ancestry with distinguishing physical features, such as skin colour **racial** *adj* **racism** *or* **racialism** *n* hostile attitude or behaviour to members of other races, based on a belief in the innate superiority of one's own race **racist** *or* **racialist** *adj, n*

raceme [rass-**eem**] *n* cluster of flowers along a central stem, as in the foxglove

rack[1] *n* 1 framework for holding particular articles, such as coats or luggage 2 straight bar with teeth on its edge, to work with a cogwheel 3 *hist* instrument of torture that stretched the victim's body ▷ *v* 4 cause great suffering to **rack one's brains** try very hard to remember

rack[2] *n* **go to rack and ruin** be destroyed

racket[1] *n* 1 noisy disturbance, din 2 occupation by which money is made illegally **racketeer** *n* person making illegal profits

racket[2], **racquet** *n* bat with strings stretched in an oval frame, used in tennis etc. **rackets** *n* ball game played in a paved walled court

raconteur [rak-on-**tur**] *n* skilled storyteller

racy *adj* **racier, raciest** 1 slightly shocking 2 spirited or lively **racily** *adv* **raciness** *n*

radar *n* device for tracking distant objects by bouncing high-frequency radio pulses off them

radial *adj* 1 emanating from a common central point 2 of a radius 3 Also **radial-ply** (of a tire) having flexible sidewalls strengthened with radial cords

radiate *v* 1 emit or be emitted

as radiation **2** spread out from a centre **radiant** adj **1** looking happy **2** shining **3** emitting radiation **radiance** n

radiation n **1** transmission of heat or light from one body to another **2** particles or rays emitted in nuclear decay **3** process of radiating

radiator n **1** arrangement of pipes containing hot water or steam to heat a room **2** tubes containing water as cooling apparatus for an automobile engine

radical adj **1** advocating fundamental change **2** fundamental **3** thorough ▷ n **4** person advocating fundamental (political) change **5** number expressed as the root of another **radically** adv **radicalism** n

radicle n small or developing root

radii n a plural of **radius**

radio n, pl -**dios 1** use of electromagnetic waves for broadcasting, communication, etc. **2** device for receiving and amplifying radio signals **3** sound broadcasting ▷ v **4** transmit (a message) by radio

radio- combining form of rays, radiation, or radium

radioactive adj emitting radiation as a result of nuclear decay **radioactivity** n

radiography [ray-dee-**og**-ra-fee] n production of an image on a film or plate by radiation **radiographer** n

radiology [ray-dee-**ol**-a-jee] n science of using x-rays in medicine **radiologist** n

radiotherapy n treatment of disease, esp. cancer, by radiation **radiotherapist** n

radish n small hot-flavoured root vegetable eaten raw in salads

radium n radioactive metallic element

radius n, pl **radii**, **radiuses 1** (length of) a straight line from the centre to the circumference of a circle **2** outer of two bones in the forearm

radon [**ray**-don] n radioactive gaseous element

raffia n prepared palm fibre for weaving mats etc.

raffish adj disreputable

raffle n **1** lottery with an article as a prize ▷ v **2** offer as a prize in a raffle

raft n floating platform of logs, planks, etc.

rafter n one of the main beams of a roof

rag[1] n **1** fragment of cloth **2** torn piece **3** informal newspaper **rags 4** tattered clothing **ragged** [**rag**-gid] adj **1** dressed in shabby or torn clothes **2** torn **3** lacking smoothness **ragtime** n style of jazz piano music

rag[2] v **ragging, ragged 1** tease **2** play practical jokes on ▷ n **3** carnival with processions etc., organized by students to raise money for charities **rag the puck** hockey deliberately use up time by carefully keeping possession of the puck

ragamuffin n ragged dirty child

rage n **1** violent anger or passion ▷ v **2** speak or act with fury **3** proceed violently and without check: a storm was raging **all the rage** very popular

raglan adj (of a sleeve) joined to a garment by diagonal seams from the neck to the underarm

ragout [**rag**-goo] n richly seasoned stew of meat and vegetables

r

raid n 1 sudden surprise attack or search ▷ v 2 make a raid on **raider** n

rail[1] n 1 horizontal bar, esp. as part of a fence or track 2 railway **railing** n fence made of rails supported by posts **railway** or **railroad** n 1 track of iron rails on which trains run 2 company operating a railway

rail[2] v (foll. by at or against) complain bitterly or loudly **raillery** n teasing or joking

rail[3] n small marsh bird

raiment n obsolete clothing

rain n 1 water falling in drops from the clouds ▷ v 2 fall or pour down as rain **rainy** adj **rainbow** n arch of colours in the sky **raincoat** n water-resistant overcoat **rainfall** n amount of rain **rainforest** n dense forest in the tropics

raise v 1 lift up 2 set upright 3 increase in amount or intensity 4 bring up (a family) 5 put forward for consideration 6 collect or levy 7 build 8 end: raise a siege ▷ n 9 increase, esp. of wages

raisin n dried grape

raison d'être [ray-zon det-ra] n French reason or justification for existence

Raj n the Raj former British rule in India

rajah n Indian prince or ruler

rake[1] n 1 tool with a long handle and a crosspiece with teeth, used for smoothing earth or gathering leaves, hay, etc. ▷ v 2 gather or smooth with a rake 3 search (through) 4 sweep (with gunfire) **rake it in** informal make a large amount of money **rake-off** n slang share of profits, esp. illegal **rake up** v revive memories of (a forgotten unpleasant event)

rake[2] n dissolute or immoral man **rakish** adj

rakish [ray-kish] adj dashing or jaunty

rally n, pl -lies 1 large gathering of people for a (political) meeting 2 marked recovery of strength 3 tennis lively exchange of strokes 4 automobile driving competition on public roads ▷ v **rallying, rallied** 5 bring or come together after dispersal or for a common cause 6 regain health or strength, revive

ram n 1 male sheep 2 hydraulic machine ▷ v **ramming, rammed** 3 strike against with force 4 force or drive 5 cram or stuff 6 government (usually foll. by through) aggressively force the passage of an act, bill, etc. **ram raid** informal raid on a shop in which a stolen automobile is driven into the window **ram raider** person who carries out a ram raid

RAM computers random access memory

Ramadan n 1 9th Muslim month 2 strict fasting observed during this time

ramble v 1 walk without a definite route 2 talk incoherently ▷ v 3 walk, esp. in the country **rambler** n 1 climbing rose 2 person who rambles

ramekin [ram-ik-in] n small ovenproof dish for a single serving of food

ramify v -ifying, -ified 1 become complex 2 spread in branches, subdivide **ramification** n consequence

ramp n 1 slope joining two level surfaces 2 small hump on a road to make traffic slow down

rampage v dash about violently **on the rampage**

behaving violently or destructively

rampant *adj* **1** unrestrained in growth or spread, rife **2** (of a heraldic beast) on its hind legs

rampart *n* mound or wall for defence

ramshackle *adj* tumbledown, rickety, or makeshift

ran *v* past tense of **run**

ranch *n* large cattle farm in the N American West **rancher** *n*

rancid *adj* (of butter, bacon, etc.) stale and having an offensive smell **rancidity** *n*

rancour *n* deep bitter hate **rancorous** *adj*

rand *n* monetary unit of S Africa

random *adj* made or done by chance or without plan **at random** haphazard(ly)

randy *adj* **randier**, **randiest** *slang* sexually aroused

rang *v* past tense of **ring**[1]

range *n* **1** limits of effectiveness or variation **2** distance that a missile or plane can travel **3** distance of a mark shot at **4** whole set of related things **5** place for shooting practice or rocket testing **6** chain of mountains **7** kitchen stove ▷ *v* **8** vary between one point and another **9** cover or extend over **10** roam **ranger** *n* **1** official in charge of a nature reserve etc. **2 Ranger** member of the senior branch of Guides **rangefinder** *n* instrument for finding how far away an object is

rangy [**rain**-jee] *adj* **rangier**, **rangiest** having long slender limbs

rank[1] *n* **1** status **2** relative place or position **3** social class **4** order **5** row or line ▷ *v* **6** have a specific rank or

position **7** arrange in rows or lines **rank and file** ordinary people or members **the ranks** common soldiers **rise through the ranks** or **rise from the ranks 1** *mil* obtain a promotion into the officer class **2** become a success through one's own efforts

rank[2] *adj* **1** complete or absolute: *rank favouritism* **2** smelling offensively strong **3** growing too thickly **rankly** *adv*

rankle *v* continue to cause resentment or bitterness

ransack *v* **1** search thoroughly **2** pillage, plunder

ransom *n* money demanded in return for the release of someone who has been kidnapped

rant *v* talk in a loud and excited way **ranter** *n*

ranunculus *n, pl* **-luses**, **-li** genus of plants including the buttercup

rap *v* **rapping**, **rapped 1** hit with a sharp quick blow **2** utter (a command) abruptly **3** perform a rhythmic monologue with musical backing ▷ *n* **4** sharp quick blow **5** rhythmic monologue performed to music **take the rap** *slang* suffer punishment for something whether guilty or not **rapper** *n* **rap sheet** *chiefly US & Canad informal* police record of an individual's criminal history

rapacious *adj* greedy or grasping **rapacity** *n*

rape[1] *v* **1** force to submit to sexual intercourse ▷ *n* **2** act of raping **3** any violation or abuse **rapist** *n*

rape[2] *n* plant with oil-yielding seeds, also used as fodder

rapid *adj* quick, swift **rapid eye movement** movement of the eyeballs while a person is dreaming **rapids** *pl n* stretch of a river with a fast turbulent current **rapidly** *adv* **rapidity** *n*

rapier [**ray**-pyer] *n* fine-bladed sword

rappel [ra-**pell**] *v* descend a vertical cliff by using a rope fixed at a higher point

rapport [rap-**pore**] *n* harmony or agreement

rapprochement [rap-**prosh**-mong] *n* re-establishment of friendly relations, esp. between nations

rapt *adj* engrossed or spellbound **rapture** *n* ecstasy **rapturous** *adj*

raptorial *adj* 1 predatory 2 of birds of prey

rare[1] *adj* 1 uncommon 2 infrequent 3 of uncommonly high quality 4 (of air at high altitudes) having low density, thin **rarely** *adv* seldom **rarity** *n*

rare[2] *adj* (of meat) lightly cooked

rarebit *n* savoury cheese dish

rarefied [**rare**-if-ide] *adj* 1 highly specialized, exalted 2 (of air) thin

raring *adj* **raring to go** enthusiastic, willing, or ready

rascal *n* 1 rogue 2 naughty (young) person **rascally** *adj*

rash[1] *adj* hasty, reckless, or incautious **rashly** *adv*

rash[2] *n* 1 skin eruption 2 outbreak of (unpleasant) occurrences

rasher *n* thin slice of bacon

rasp *n* 1 harsh grating noise 2 coarse file ▷ *v* 3 speak in a grating voice 4 make a scraping noise

raspberry *n* 1 red juicy edible berry 2 plant which bears it 3 *informal* spluttering noise made with the tongue and lips, to show contempt

Rastafarian *n, adj* (member)

of a cult originating in Jamaica and regarding Haile Selassie as God (Also **Rasta**)

raster *v* use web-based technology to turn a digital image into a picture composed of black and white dots

rat *n* 1 small rodent 2 *informal* contemptible person, esp. a deserter or informer ▷ *v* **ratting, ratted** 3 *informal* inform (on) 4 hunt rats **ratty** *adj slang* bad-tempered, irritable **rat race** continual hectic competitive activity

ratafia [rat-a-**fee**-a] *n* 1 liqueur made from fruit 2 almond-flavoured biscuit

ratatouille [rat-a-**twee**] *n* vegetable casserole of tomatoes, eggplants, etc.

ratchet *n* set of teeth on a bar or wheel allowing motion in one direction only

rate *n* 1 degree of speed or progress 2 proportion between two things 3 charge **rates** 4 local tax on property ▷ *v* 5 consider or value 6 estimate the value of **at any rate** in any case **rateable** *or* **ratable** *adj* 1 able to be rated 2 (of property) liable to payment of rates **ratepayer** *n*

rather *adv* 1 to some extent 2 preferably 3 more willingly

ratify *v* -**ifying, -ified** give formal approval to **ratification** *n*

rating *n* 1 valuation or assessment 2 classification 3 non-commissioned sailor **ratings** 4 size of the audience for a TV programme

ratio *n, pl* -**tios** relationship between two numbers or amounts expressed as a proportion

ratiocinate [rat-ee-**oss**-in-nate] *v* reason or think out **ratiocination** *n*

ration n **1** fixed allowance of food etc. ▷ v **2** limit to a certain amount per person

rational adj **1** reasonable, sensible **2** capable of reasoning **rationally** adv **rationality** n **rationale** [rash-a-**nahl**] n reason for an action or decision **rationalism** n philosophy that regards reason as the only basis for beliefs or actions **rationalist** n **rationalize** v **1** justify by plausible reasoning **2** reorganize to improve efficiency or profitability **rationalization** n

rattan n **1** climbing palm with jointed stems **2** cane from this

rattle v **1** give out a succession of short sharp sounds **2** clatter **3** shake briskly causing sharp sounds **4** informal confuse or fluster ▷ n **5** short sharp sound **6** instrument for making it **rattlesnake** n poisonous snake with loose horny segments on the tail that make a rattling sound

raucous adj hoarse or harsh

raunchy adj **raunchier, raunchiest** slang earthy, sexy

ravage v lit lay waste or plunder **ravages** pl n destruction

rave v **1** talk wildly in delirium or with enthusiasm ▷ n **2** informal enthusiastically good review **raving** adj **1** delirious **2** informal exceptional: a raving beauty

ravel v -**elling, -elled** tangle or become entangled

raven n **1** black bird like a crow ▷ adj **2** (of hair) shiny black

ravenous adj very hungry

ravine [rav-**veen**] n narrow steep-sided valley worn by a stream

ravioli pl n small squares of pasta with a savoury filling

ravish v **1** enrapture **2** lit rape **ravishing** adj lovely or entrancing

raw adj **1** uncooked **2** not manufactured or refined **3** inexperienced: raw recruits **4** chilly **raw deal** unfair or dishonest treatment **rawhide** n untanned hide

ray[1] n **1** single line or narrow beam of light **2** any of a set of radiating lines

ray[2] n large sea fish with a whiplike tail

rayon n (fabric made of) a synthetic fibre

raze v destroy (buildings or a town) completely

razor n sharp instrument for shaving **razorbill** n N Atlantic auk

razzle-dazzle, razzmatazz n slang **1** showy activity **2** spree

RBI baseball runs batted in: runs scored during a player's at-bat

RC 1 Red Cross **2** Roman Catholic

RCAF Royal Canadian Air Force

RCMP Royal Canadian Mounted Police

RCN Royal Canadian Navy

Rd Road

re prep with reference to, concerning

re- prefix again: re-enter; retrial

reach v **1** arrive at **2** make a movement in order to grasp or touch **3** succeed in touching **4** make contact or communication with **5** extend to ▷ n **6** distance that one can reach **7** range of influence **8** stretch of a river between two bends **reachable** adj

react v act in response or opposition (to) **reaction** n **1** physical or emotional response to a stimulus **2** any action resisting another **3** opposition to change

4 chemical or nuclear change, combination, or decomposition **reactionary** n, adj (person) opposed to change, esp. in politics **reactance** n electricity resistance in a coil due to the current reacting on itself **reactive** adj chemically active **reactor** n apparatus in which a nuclear reaction is maintained and controlled to produce nuclear energy

read v reading, read **1** look at and understand or take in (written or printed matter) **2** look at and say aloud **3** understand (an indicating instrument) **4** (of an instrument) register **5** study **6** matter suitable for reading: a good read **reading** n **reader** n **1** person who reads **2** senior university lecturer **3** textbook **readership** n readers of a publication collectively **readable** adj **1** enjoyable to read **2** legible **readability** n

readjust v adapt to a new situation **readjustment** n

ready adj **readier, readiest 1** prepared for use or action **2** willing, prompt **readily** adv **readiness** n **ready-made** adj for immediate use by any customer **ready cash** or **ready money** cash for immediate use

reagent [ree-**age**-ent] n chemical substance that reacts with another, used to detect the presence of the other

real adj **1** existing in fact **2** happening **3** actual **4** genuine **5** (of property) consisting of land and houses **really** adv **1** very **2** truly ▷ interj **3** indeed! **reality** n real existence **reality TV** television programmes focusing on members of the public living in conditions created especially by the programme makers **realtor** n agent, esp. accredited one who sells houses etc. for others **realty** n real estate **real ale** Brit beer allowed to ferment in the barrel **real estate** landed property

realistic adj seeing and accepting things as they really are, practical **realistically** adv **realism** n **realist** n

realize v **1** become aware or grasp the significance of **2** achieve (a plan, hopes, etc.) **3** convert into money **realization** n

realm n **1** kingdom **2** sphere of interest

ream n **1** twenty quires of paper, generally 500 sheets **reams 2** informal large quantity (of written matter)

reap v **1** cut and gather (harvest) **2** receive as the result of a previous activity **reaper** n

reappear v appear again **reappearance** n

rear[1] n **1** back part **2** part of an army, procession, etc. behind the others **bring up the rear** come last **rearmost** adj **rear admiral** high-ranking naval officer

rear[2] v **1** care for and educate (children) **2** breed (animals) **3** (of a horse) rise on its hind feet

rearguard n **1** troops protecting the rear of an army **2** hockey slang defensive player **rearguard action** effort to prevent something unavoidable

rearrange v organize differently, alter **rearrangement** n

reason n **1** ground or motive **2** faculty of rational thought

3 sanity ▷ v **4** think logically in forming conclusions **5** (usu. foll. by *with*) persuade by logical argument into doing something **reasonable** *adj* **1** sensible **2** not excessive **3** suitable **4** logical **reasonably** *adv*

reassess *v* reconsider the value or importance of

reassure *v* restore confidence to **reassurance** *n*

rebate *n* discount or refund

rebel *v* -**belling, -belled 1** revolt against the ruling power **2** reject accepted conventions ▷ *n* **3** person who rebels **rebellion** *n* **1** organized open resistance to authority **2** rejection of conventions **rebellious** *adj*

rebirth *n* revival or renaissance **reborn** *adj* active again after a period of inactivity

rebore, reboring *n* boring of a cylinder to restore its true shape

rebound *v* **1** spring back **2** misfire so as to hurt the perpetrator of a plan or deed **3** (of a ball, puck, etc.) bounce back after a missed or blocked shot **4** *basketball* recover possession of a rebound ▷ *n* **5** a ball or puck that has rebounded **6** *basketball* recovery of a rebound **on the rebound** *informal* while recovering from rejection

rebuff *v* **1** reject or snub ▷ *n* **2** blunt refusal, snub

rebuke *v* **1** scold sternly ▷ *n* **2** stern scolding

rebus [ree-buss] *n, pl* -**buses** puzzle consisting of pictures and symbols representing words or syllables

rebut *v* -**butting, -butted** refute or disprove **rebuttal** *n*

recalcitrant *adj* wilfully disobedient **recalcitrance** *n*

recall *v* **1** recollect or remember **2** order to return **3** annul or cancel ▷ *n* **4** order to return **5** ability to remember

recant *v* withdraw (a statement or belief) publicly **recantation** *n*

recap *informal* ▷ v -**capping, -capped 1** recapitulate ▷ *n* **2** recapitulation

recapitulate *v* state again briefly, repeat **recapitulation** *n*

recapture *v* **1** experience again **2** capture again

recce *slang* ▷ v -**ceing, -ced** or -**ceed 1** reconnoitre ▷ *n* **2** reconnaissance

recede *v* **1** become distant **2** (of the hair) stop growing at the front

receipt *n* **1** written acknowledgment of money or goods received **2** receiving or being received

receive *v* **1** take, accept, or get **2** experience **3** greet (guests) **received** *adj* generally accepted **receiver** *n* **1** detachable part of a telephone that is held to the ear **2** equipment in a telephone, radio, or television that converts electrical signals into sound **3** person appointed by court to manage property of a bankrupt **4** person who handles stolen goods knowing they have been stolen **5** *football* player seeking to catch passes from the quarterback **receivership** *n* **1** state of being or having been received **2** (esp. of a business, company, etc.) state of being administered by a receiver due to bankruptcy

recent *adj* **1** having happened lately **2** new **recently** *adv*

receptacle *n* object used to contain something

reception n 1 area for receiving guests, clients, etc. 2 formal party 3 manner of receiving 4 welcome 5 (in broadcasting) quality of signals received 6 *football* catching of a pass from the quarterback **receptionist** n person who receives guests, clients, etc.

receptive adj willing to receive new ideas, suggestions, etc. **receptivity** n

recess n 1 niche or alcove 2 holiday between sessions of work 3 secret hidden place **recessed** adj hidden or placed in a recess

recession n period of reduction in trade **recessive** adj receding

recherché [rish-**air**-shay] adj 1 of studied elegance 2 choice or rare

recidivist n person who relapses into crime

recipe n 1 directions for cooking a dish 2 method for achieving something

recipient n person who receives something

reciprocal [ris-**sip**-pro-kal] adj 1 mutual 2 given or done in return **reciprocally** adv **reciprocity** n

reciprocate v 1 give or feel in return 2 (of a machine part) move backwards and forwards **reciprocation** n

recite v repeat aloud, esp. to an audience **recital** [ris-**site**-al] n 1 musical performance 2 act of reciting **recitation** n recital, usu. from memory, of poetry or prose **recitative** [ress-it-a-**teev**] n musical narration

reckless adj heedless of danger **recklessly** adv **recklessness** n

reckon v 1 expect 2 consider or think 3 make calculations, count **reckoner** n **reckoning** n

reclaim v 1 regain possession of 2 make fit for cultivation **reclamation** n

recline v rest in a leaning position **reclining** adj

recluse n 1 person avoiding society 2 hermit **reclusive** adj

recognize v 1 identify as (a person or thing) already known 2 accept as true or existing 3 treat as valid 4 notice, show appreciation of **recognition** n **recognizable** adj **recognizance** [rik-**og**-nizz-anss] n undertaking before a court to observe some condition

recoil v 1 jerk or spring back 2 draw back in horror 3 (of an action) go wrong so as to hurt the perpetrator ▷ n 4 backward jerk 5 recoiling

recollect v call back to mind, remember **recollection** n

recommend v 1 advise or counsel 2 praise or commend 3 make acceptable **recommendation** n

recompense v 1 pay or reward 2 compensate or make up for ▷ n 3 compensation 4 reward or remuneration

reconcile v 1 harmonize (conflicting beliefs etc.) 2 bring back into friendship 3 accept or cause to accept (an unpleasant situation) **reconcilable** adj **reconciliation** n

recondite adj difficult to understand, abstruse

recondition v restore to good condition or working order

reconnaissance [rik-**kon**-iss-anss] n survey for military or engineering purposes

reconnoitre [rek-a-**noy**-ter] v make a reconnaissance of

reconsider v think about

again, consider changing

reconstitute v 1 reorganize in a slightly different form 2 restore (food) to its former state, esp. by the addition of water to a concentrate **reconstitution** n

reconstruct v 1 use evidence to re-create 2 rebuild **reconstruction** n

record n 1 document or other thing that preserves information 2 disc with indentations which a record player transforms into sound 3 best recorded achievement 4 known facts about a person's past ▷ v 5 put in writing 6 preserve (sound, TV programmes, etc.) for reproduction on a playback device 7 show or register **off the record** not for publication **recorder** n 1 person or machine that records 2 type of flute, blown at one end 3 judge in certain courts **recording** n **record player** instrument for reproducing sound on records

recount v tell in detail

re-count v 1 count again ▷ n 2 second or subsequent count, esp. of votes

recoup [rik-**koop**] v 1 regain or make good (a loss) 2 recompense or compensate

recourse n 1 (resorting to) a source of help 2 law right of action or appeal

recover v 1 become healthy again 2 get back (a loss or expense) **recovery** n **recoverable** adj

recreant n old-fashioned cowardly or disloyal person

re-create v make happen or exist again

recreation n agreeable or refreshing occupation, relaxation or amusement

recreational adj **recreational vehicle** or **RV** large vanlike vehicle equipped to be lived in

recrimination n mutual blame **recriminatory** adj

recruit n 1 newly enlisted soldier 2 new member or supporter ▷ v 3 enlist (new soldiers, members, etc.) **recruitment** n

rectangle n oblong four-sided figure with four right angles **rectangular** adj

rectify v -fying, -fied 1 put right, correct 2 purify by distillation 3 electricity convert (alternating current) into direct current **rectification** n **rectifier** n

rectilinear [rek-ti-**lin**-ee-er] adj 1 in a straight line 2 characterized by straight lines

rectitude n moral correctness

recto n, pl -tos 1 right-hand page of a book 2 front of a sheet of paper

rector n 1 member of the clergy in charge of a parish 2 head of certain academic institutions **rectory** n rector's house

rectum n, pl -ta final section of the large intestine **rectal** adj

recumbent adj lying down

recuperate v recover from illness **recuperation** n **recuperative** adj

recur v -curring, -curred happen again **recurrence** n repetition **recurrent** adj

recusant [**rek**-yew-zant] n 1 hist person who refused to obey the Church of England 2 person refusing to obey authority

recycle v reprocess (used materials) for further use

red adj redder, reddest 1 of a colour varying from crimson

r

to orange and seen in blood, fire, etc. **2** flushed in the face from anger, shame, etc. ▷ *n* **3** red colour **4 Red** *informal* communist **in the red** *informal* in debt **see red** *informal* be angry **redness** *n* **redden** *v* make or become red **reddish** *adj* **red-blooded** *adj informal* **1** vigorous **2** virile **redbrick** *adj* (of a British university) founded in the late 19th or early 20th century **red carpet** very special welcome for an important guest **Red Chamber** the Canadian Senate **redcoat** *n* *hist* British soldier **Red Cross** international organization providing help for victims of war or natural disasters **Red Ensign** red flag having the Union Jack at the upper corner along the hoist, esp. one used as Canada's national flag until 1965 or those currently used as the provincial flags of Ontario and Manitoba **red-handed** *adj informal* (caught) in the act of doing something wrong or illegal **red herring** something which diverts attention from the main issue **red-hot** *adj* **1** glowing red **2** extremely hot **3** very keen **red light 1** traffic signal to stop **2** danger signal **red meat** dark meat, esp. beef or lamb **red tape** excessive adherence to official rules **red zone** *football* area of the field within 20 yards of the opposing goal line

redeem *v* **1** make up for **2** reinstate (oneself) in someone's good opinion **3** free from sin **4** buy back **5** pay off (a loan or debt) **the Redeemer** Jesus Christ **redeemable** *adj* **redemption** *n* **redemptive** *adj*

redeploy *v* assign to a new position or task
redevelop *v* rebuild or renovate (an area or building) **redevelopment** *n*
redolent *adj* **1** smelling strongly (of) **2** reminiscent (of) **redolence** *n*
redouble *v* increase, multiply, or intensify
redoubt *n* small fort defending a hilltop or pass
redoubtable *adj* formidable
redound *v* cause advantage or disadvantage (to)
redox *n* chemical reaction in which one substance is reduced and the other is oxidized
redress *v* **1** make amends for ▷ *n* **2** compensation or amends
reduce *v* **1** bring down, lower **2** lessen, weaken **3** bring by force or necessity to some state or action **4** slim **5** simplify **6** make (sauce) more concentrated **7** *chem* separate (a substance) from others with which it is combined **reducible** *adj* **reduction** *n*
redundant *adj* **1** (of a worker) no longer needed **2** superfluous **redundancy** *n*
reed *n* **1** tall grass that grows in swamps and shallow water **2** tall straight stem of this plant **3** *music* vibrating cane or metal strip in certain wind instruments **reedy** *adj* **1** full of reeds **2** harsh and thin in tone
reef¹ *n* **1** ridge of rock or coral near the surface of the sea **2** vein of ore
reef² *n* **1** part of a sail which can be rolled up to reduce its area ▷ *v* **2** take in a reef of
reefer *n* **1** short thick jacket worn esp. by sailors **2** *old-fashioned, slang* hand-rolled cigarette containing cannabis

reef knot two overhand knots turned opposite ways

reek *n* **1** strong (unpleasant) smell ▷ *v* **2** smell strongly **3** (foll. by *of*) be full (of)

reel¹ *n* **1** cylindrical object on which film, tape, thread, or wire is wound **2** winding apparatus, as of a fishing rod ▷ *v* **3** wind on a reel **4** draw in by means of a reel **reel off** *v* recite or write fluently or quickly

reel² *v* stagger, sway, or whirl

reel³ *n* lively Scottish dance

reeve *n* **1** president of local (esp. rural) council **2** *hist* manorial steward or official

ref *n* *informal* referee in sport

refectory *n, pl* **-tories** room for meals in a college etc.

refer *v* **-ferring, -ferred** (foll. by *to*) **1** mention or allude (to) **2** be relevant (to) **3** send (to) for information **4** submit (to) for decision **referral** *n* **reference** *n* **1** act of referring **2** citation or direction in a book **3** appeal to the judgment of another **4** testimonial **5** person to whom inquiries as to character etc. may be made **with reference to** concerning

referee *n* **1** umpire in sports, esp. football or boxing **2** person willing to testify to someone's character etc. **3** arbitrator ▷ *v* **-eeing, -eed 4** act as referee of

referendum *n, pl* **-dums, -da** submitting of a question to the electorate

refill *v* **1** fill again ▷ *n* **2** subsequent filling **3** replacement supply of something in a permanent container

refine *v* **1** purify **2** improve **refined** *adj* **1** cultured or polite **2** purified **refinement** *n* **1** improvement or elaboration **2** fineness of taste or manners **3** subtle point or distinction

refinery *n* place where sugar, oil, etc. is refined **refiner** *n*

reflation *n* (steps taken to produce) an increase in the economic activity of a country etc. **reflate** *v* **reflationary** *adj*

reflect *v* **1** throw back, esp. rays of light, heat, etc. **2** form an image of **3** show **4** bring credit or discredit upon **5** consider at length **reflection** *n* **1** act of reflecting **2** return of rays of heat, light, etc. from a surface **3** image of an object given back by a mirror etc. **4** conscious thought or meditation **5** attribution of discredit or blame **reflective** *adj* **1** quiet, contemplative **2** capable of reflecting images **reflector** *n* polished surface for reflecting light etc.

reflex *n* **1** involuntary response to a stimulus or situation ▷ *adj* **2** (of a muscular action) involuntary **3** reflected **4** (of an angle) more than 180° **reflexive** *adj grammar* denoting a verb whose subject is the same as its object: *to dress oneself*

reflexology *n* foot massage as a therapy in alternative medicine

reform *v* **1** improve **2** abandon evil practices ▷ *n* **3** improvement **reformer** *n* **reformation** [ref-fer-**may**-shun] *n* **1** a reforming **2 Reformation** religious movement in 16th-century Europe that resulted in the establishment of the Protestant Churches **reformatory** *n* (formerly) institution for reforming juvenile offenders **Reform Party** major political party with policy of low taxation

refract *v* change the course

of (light etc.) passing from one medium to another **refraction** n **refractive** adj **refractor** n

refractory adj
1 unmanageable or rebellious 2 med resistant to treatment 3 resistant to heat

refrain[1] v (foll. by from) keep oneself from doing

refrain[2] n frequently repeated part of a song

refrangible adj that can be refracted **refrangibility** n

refresh v 1 revive or reinvigorate, as through food, drink, or rest 2 stimulate (the memory) **refresher** n **refreshing** adj 1 having a reviving effect 2 pleasantly different or new **refreshment** n something that refreshes, esp. food or drink

refrigerate v 1 freeze 2 cool **refrigeration** n **refrigerator** n apparatus in which food and drinks are kept cool

refuge n (source of) shelter or protection **refugee** n person who seeks refuge, esp. in a foreign country

refulgent adj shining, radiant **refulgence** n

refund v 1 pay back ▷ n 2 return of money 3 amount returned

refurbish v renovate and brighten up

refuse[1] v decline, deny, or reject **refusal** n denial of anything demanded or offered

refuse[2] n garbage or useless matter

refute v disprove **refutable** adj **refutation** n

regain v 1 get back or recover 2 reach again

regal adj of or like a king or queen **regally** adv **regality** n **regalia** pl n ceremonial emblems of royalty, an order, etc.

regale v (foll. by with) attempt to entertain (someone) with (stories)

regard v 1 look at 2 relate to 3 consider 4 heed ▷ n 5 particular respect 6 attention 7 look 8 esteem **regards** 9 expression of goodwill **as regards** or **regarding** in respect of, concerning **regardless** adj 1 heedless ▷ adv 2 in spite of everything

regatta n meeting for yacht or boat races

regenerate v 1 (cause to) undergo spiritual, moral, or physical renewal 2 reproduce or re-create **regeneration** n **regenerative** adj

regent n 1 ruler of a kingdom during the absence, childhood, or illness of its monarch ▷ adj 2 ruling as a regent: prince regent **regency** n status or period of office of a regent

reggae n style of Jamaican popular music with a strong beat

regicide n 1 person who kills a king 2 killing of a king

regime [ray-zheem] n 1 system of government 2 particular administration

regimen n 1 prescribed system of diet etc. 2 rule

regiment n 1 organized body of troops as a unit of the army ▷ v 2 discipline, organize (too) rigidly **regimental** adj **regimentals** pl n military uniform **regimentation** n

region n 1 administrative division of a country 2 area considered as a unit but with no definite boundaries 3 part of the body **regional** adj

register n 1 (book containing) an official list or record of

r

things **2** range of a voice or instrument ▷ *v* **3** enter in a register, record, or set down in writing **4** show or be shown on a scale or other measuring instrument **registration** *n* **registrar** *n* keeper of official records **register office** *or* **registry office** place where births, marriages, and deaths are recorded

regress *v* revert to a former worse condition **regression** *n* **1** act of regressing **2** *psychol* using an earlier (inappropriate) mode of behaviour **regressive** *adj*

regret *v* -**gretting**, -**gretted** **1** feel sorry about **2** express apology or distress ▷ *n* **3** feeling of repentance, guilt, or sorrow **regretful** *adj* **regrettable** *adj*

regular *adj* **1** normal **2** symmetrical or even **3** habitual **4** done or occurring according to a rule **5** periodical **6** employed continuously in the armed forces **7** straight or level ▷ *n* **8** regular soldier **9** *informal* regular customer **regularity** *n* **regularize** *v*

regulate *v* **1** control, esp. by rules **2** adjust slightly **regulation** *n* **1** rule **2** regulating **regulator** *n* device that automatically controls pressure, temperature, etc.

regurgitate *v* **1** vomit **2** (of some birds and animals) bring back (partly digested food) into the mouth **3** reproduce (ideas, facts, etc.) without understanding them **regurgitation** *n*

rehabilitate *v* **1** help (a person) to readjust to society after illness, imprisonment, etc. **2** restore to a former position or rank **3** restore

the good reputation of **rehabilitation** *n*

rehash *v* **1** rework or reuse ▷ *n* **2** old materials presented in a new form

rehearse *v* **1** practise (a play, concert, etc.) **2** repeat aloud **rehearsal** *n*

rehouse *v* provide with a new (and better) home

reign *n* **1** period of a sovereign's rule ▷ *v* **2** rule (a country) **3** be supreme

reimburse *v* refund, pay back **reimbursement** *n*

rein *n usu pl* **1** narrow strap attached to a bit to guide a horse **2** means of control ▷ *v* **3** check or manage with reins **4** control

reincarnation *n* **1** rebirth of a soul in successive bodies **2** one of a series of such transmigrations **reincarnate** *v*

reindeer *n* deer of arctic regions with large branched antlers

reinforce *v* **1** strengthen with new support, material, or force **2** strengthen with additional troops, ships, etc. **reinforcement** *n*

reinstate *v* restore or re-establish **reinstatement** *n*

reiterate *v* repeat again and again **reiteration** *n*

reject *v* **1** refuse to accept or believe **2** discard as useless **3** rebuff (a person) ▷ *n* **4** person or thing rejected as not up to standard **rejection** *n*

rejig *v* -**jigging**, -**jigged** **1** re-equip (a factory or plant) **2** rearrange

rejoice *v* feel or express great happiness

rejoin *v* **1** reply **2** join again

rejoinder *n* answer, retort

rejuvenate *v* restore youth or vitality to **rejuvenation** *n*

relapse v 1 fall back into bad habits, illness, etc. ▷ n 2 return of bad habits, illness, etc.

relate v 1 establish a relation between 2 have reference or relation to 3 (foll. by *to*) have an understanding (of people or ideas): *inability to relate to others* 4 tell (a story) or describe (an event) **related** *adj*

relation n 1 connection between things 2 relative 3 connection by blood or marriage 4 act of relating (a story) **relations** 5 social or political dealings 6 family 7 *euphemistic* sexual intercourse **relationship** n 1 dealings and feelings between people or countries 2 emotional or sexual affair 3 connection between two things 4 association by blood or marriage, kinship

relative *adj* 1 dependent on relation to something else, not absolute 2 having reference or relation (to) 3 *grammar* referring to a word or clause earlier in the sentence ▷ n 4 person connected by blood or marriage 5 *grammar* relative pronoun or clause **relatively** *adv* **relativity** n 1 state of being relative 2 subject of two theories of Albert Einstein, dealing with relationships of space, time, and motion, and acceleration and gravity

relax v 1 make or become looser, less tense, or less rigid 2 ease up from effort or attention, rest 3 become more friendly 4 be less strict about **relaxing** *adj* **relaxation** n

relay n 1 fresh set of people or animals relieving others 2 *electricity* device for making or breaking a local circuit

3 broadcasting station receiving and retransmitting programmes ▷ v **-laying**, **-layed** 4 pass on (a message) **relay race** race between teams of which each runner races part of the distance

release v 1 set free 2 let go or fall 3 permit public showing of (a film etc.) 4 emit heat, energy, etc. ▷ n 5 setting free 6 written discharge 7 statement to the press 8 act of issuing for sale or publication 9 catch or handle 10 newly issued film, record, etc.

relegate v put in a less important position, demote **relegation** n

relent v give up a harsh intention, become less severe **relentless** *adj* 1 merciless 2 unremitting

relevant *adj* to do with the matter in hand **relevance** n

reliable *adj* see **rely**

reliance n see **rely**

relic n 1 something that has survived from the past 2 body or possession of a saint, regarded as holy **relics** 3 remains or traces **relict** n *obsolete* widow

relief n 1 gladness at the end or removal of pain, distress, etc. 2 money or food given to victims of disaster, poverty, etc. 3 release from monotony or duty 4 person who replaces another at a duty etc. 5 freeing of a besieged city etc. 6 projection of a carved design from the surface 7 distinctness or prominence: *stand out in bold relief* **relieve** v bring relief to **relieve oneself** urinate or defecate **relief map** map showing the shape and height of land by shading **relief pitcher** *baseball* pitcher who replaces another during a game

religion *n* system of belief in and worship of a supernatural power or god **religious** *adj* 1 of religion 2 pious or devout 3 scrupulous or conscientious **religiously** *adv*

relinquish *v* give up or abandon **relinquishment** *n*

reliquary [rel-lik-wer-ee] *n, pl* -ries case or shrine for holy relics

relish *v* 1 enjoy, like very much ▷ *n* 2 liking or gusto 3 appetizing savoury food, such as pickle 4 zestful quality or flavour

relocate *v* move to a new place to live or work **relocation** *n*

reluctant *adj* unwilling or disinclined **reluctantly** *adv* **reluctance** *n*

rely *v* -lying, -lied 1 depend (on) 2 trust **reliable** *adj* able to be trusted, dependable **reliably** *adv* **reliability** *n* **reliance** *n* dependence, confidence, or trust **reliant** *adj*

REM rapid eye movement

remain *v* 1 continue to be 2 stay, be left behind 3 be left (over) 4 be left to be done, said, etc. **remains** *pl n* 1 relics, esp. of ancient buildings 2 dead body **remainder** *n* 1 part which is left 2 amount left over after subtraction or division ▷ *v* 3 offer (copies of a poorly selling book) at reduced prices

remand *v* send back into custody **on remand** in custody **remand centre** place where accused people are detained awaiting trial

remark *v* 1 make casual comment (on) 2 say 3 observe or notice ▷ *n* 4 observation or comment **remarkable** *adj* 1 worthy of note or attention 2 striking or unusual **remarkably** *adv*

remedy *n, pl* -dies 1 means of curing pain or disease 2 means of solving a problem ▷ *v* -edying, -edied 3 put right **remedial** *adj* intended to correct a specific disability, handicap, etc.

remember *v* 1 retain in or recall to one's memory 2 have in mind **remembrance** *n* 1 memory 2 token or souvenir 3 honouring of the memory of a person or event

remind *v* 1 cause to remember 2 put in mind (of) **reminder** *n* 1 something that recalls the past 2 note to remind a person of something not done

reminisce *v* talk or write of past times, experiences, etc. **reminiscence** *n* 1 remembering 2 thing recollected **reminiscences** 3 memoirs **reminiscent** *adj* reminding or suggestive (of)

remiss *adj* negligent or careless

remission *n* 1 reduction in the length of a prison term 2 pardon or forgiveness 3 easing of intensity, as of an illness

remit *v* -mitting, -mitted 1 send (money) for goods, services, etc., esp. by post 2 cancel (a punishment or debt) 3 refer (a decision) to a higher authority or later date ▷ *n* 4 area of competence or authority **remittance** *n* 1 sending of money 2 money sent

remnant *n* 1 small piece, esp. of fabric, left over 2 surviving trace

remonstrate *v* argue in protest **remonstrance** *n*

remorse *n* feeling of sorrow and regret for something one did **remorseful**

r

adj **remorsefully** *adv*
remorseless *adj* **1** pitiless
2 persistent **remorselessly**
adv
remote *adj* **1** far away, distant
2 aloof **3** slight or faint
remotely *adv* **remote control**
control of an apparatus from
a distance by an electrical
device
remould *v* **1** renovate (a worn
tire) ▷ *n* **2** renovated tire
remove *v* **1** take away or off
2 dismiss from office **3** get rid
of ▷ *n* **4** degree of difference
removable *adj* **removal** *n*
removing, esp. changing
residence
remunerate *v* reward
or pay **remuneration** *n*
remunerative *adj*
renaissance *n* revival or
rebirth, esp. **Renaissance**
the revival of learning in the
14th–16th centuries
renal [**ree**-nal] *adj* of the
kidneys
renascent *adj* becoming
active or vigorous again
renascence *n*
rend *v* **rending, rent 1** tear or
wrench apart **2** (of a sound)
break (the silence) violently
render *v* **1** cause to become
2 give or provide (aid, a
service, etc.) **3** submit or
present (a bill) **4** portray or
represent **5** cover with plaster
6 melt down (fat)
rendezvous [**ron**-day-voo]
n, pl **-vous 1** appointment
2 meeting place ▷ *v* **3** meet
as arranged
rendition *n* **1** performance
2 translation
renegade *n* person who
deserts a cause
renege [rin-**nayg**] *v* (usu. foll.
by *on*) go back on (a promise
etc.)
renew *v* **1** begin again
2 reaffirm **3** make valid again

4 grow again **5** restore to
a former state **6** replace (a
worn part) **renewable** *adj*
1 able to be renewed **2** (of
energy or an energy source)
inexhaustible or capable of
being perpetually replenished
renewables *pl n* renewable
energy sources **renewal** *n*
rennet *n* substance for
curdling milk to make cheese
renounce *v* **1** give up (a belief,
habit, etc.) voluntarily **2** give
up (a title or claim) formally
renunciation *n*
renovate *v* restore to good
condition **renovation** *n*
renown *n* widespread good
reputation **renowned** *adj*
famous
rent¹ *n* **1** regular payment
for use of land, a building,
machine, etc. ▷ *v* **2** give or
have use of in return for rent
rental *n* sum payable as rent
rent² *n* **1** tear or fissure ▷ *v*
2 past of **rend**
renunciation *n* see **renounce**
reorganize *v* organize in a
new and more efficient way
reorganization *n*
rep¹ *n* short for **repertory
company**
rep² *n* short for
representative
repair¹ *v* **1** restore to good
condition, mend ▷ *n* **2** act
of repairing **3** repaired
part **4** state or condition: *in
good repair* **repairable** *adj*
reparation *n* something done
or given as compensation
repair² *v* go (to)
repartee *n* **1** interchange of
witty retorts **2** witty retort
repast *n* meal
repatriate *v* send (someone)
back to his or her own country
repatriation *n*
repay *v* **1** pay back, refund
2 make a return for
repayable *adj* **repayment** *n*

repeal v 1 cancel (a law) officially ▷ n 2 act of repealing

repeat v 1 say, write, or do again 2 disclose 3 happen again, recur ▷ n 4 act or instance of repeating 5 programme broadcast again **repeatedly** adv

repeater n firearm that may be discharged many times without reloading

repel v -pelling, -pelled 1 be disgusting to 2 drive back, ward off 3 resist **repellent** adj 1 distasteful 2 resisting water etc. ▷ n 3 something that repels, esp. a chemical to repel insects

repent v feel regret for (a deed or omission) **repentance** n **repentant** adj

repercussion n indirect effect, often unpleasant

repertoire n stock of plays, songs, etc. that a player or company can give

repertory n, pl -ries repertoire **repertory company** permanent theatre company producing a succession of plays

repetition n 1 act of repeating 2 thing repeated **repetitive** or **repetitious** adj full of repetition

rephrase v express in different words

repine v fret or complain

replace v 1 substitute for 2 put back **replacement** n

replay n 1 Also **action replay** immediate reshowing on TV of an incident in sport, esp. in slow motion 2 second sports match, esp. one following an earlier draw ▷ v 3 play (a match, recording, etc.) again

replenish v fill up again, resupply **replenishment** n

replete adj filled or gorged

replica n exact copy **replicate**

v make or be a copy of

reply v -plying, -plied 1 answer or respond ▷ n, pl -plies 2 answer or response

report v 1 give an account of 2 make a report (on) 3 announce or relate 4 make a formal complaint about 5 present oneself (to) 6 be responsible (to) ▷ n 7 account or statement 8 rumour 9 written statement of a child's progress at school 10 bang **reportedly** adv according to rumour

reporter n person who gathers news for a newspaper, TV, etc.

repose n 1 peace 2 composure 3 sleep ▷ v 4 lie or lay at rest

repository n, pl -ries place where valuables are deposited for safekeeping, store

repossess v (of a lender) take back property from a customer who is behind with payments **repossession** n

reprehend v find fault with **reprehensible** adj open to criticism, unworthy

represent v 1 stand for 2 act as a delegate for 3 symbolize 4 make out to be 5 portray, as in art **representation** n **representative** n 1 person chosen to act for or represent a group 2 (travelling) salesperson ▷ adj 3 typical of a class or kind

repress v 1 keep (feelings) under control 2 subjugate **repression** n **repressive** adj

reprieve v 1 postpone the execution of (a condemned person) 2 give temporary relief to ▷ n 3 postponement or cancellation of a punishment 4 temporary relief

reprimand v 1 blame (someone) officially for a fault ▷ n 2 official blame

r

reprint v 1 print further copies of (a book) ▷ n 2 reprinted copy

reprisal n retaliation

reproach v 1 blame or rebuke ▷ n 2 scolding or blame **reproachful** adj **reproachfully** adv

reprobate [**rep**-roh-bate] adj, n depraved or disreputable (person) **reprobation** n disapproval or blame

reproduce v 1 produce a copy of 2 bring new individuals into existence 3 re-create **reproducible** adj **reproduction** n 1 process of reproducing 2 thing that is reproduced 3 facsimile, as of a painting etc. 4 quality of sound from an audio system **reproductive** adj

reprove v speak severely to (someone) about a fault **reproof** n severe blaming of someone for a fault

reptile n cold-blooded air-breathing vertebrate with horny scales or plates, such as a snake or tortoise **reptilian** adj

republic n 1 form of government in which the people or their elected representatives possess the supreme power 2 country in which a president is the head of state **Republican** n, adj 1 (member or supporter) of the Republican Party, the more conservative of the two main political parties in the US **Republicanism** n

repudiate [rip-**pew**-dee-ate] v 1 reject the authority or validity of 2 disown **repudiation** n

repugnant adj offensive or distasteful **repugnance** n

repulse v 1 be disgusting to 2 drive (an army) back 3 rebuff or reject ▷ n 4 driving back

5 rejection 6 rebuff **repulsion** n 1 distaste or aversion 2 physics force separating two objects **repulsive** adj loathsome, disgusting

reputation n estimation in which a person or thing is held **reputable** [**rep**-yoo-tab-bl] adj of good reputation, respectable **repute** n reputation **reputed** adj supposed **reputedly** adv

request n 1 asking 2 thing asked for ▷ v 3 ask or politely demand

Requiem [**rek**-wee-em] n 1 Mass for the dead 2 music for this

require v 1 want or need 2 demand **requirement** n 1 essential condition 2 specific need or want

requisite [**rek**-wizz-it] adj 1 necessary, essential ▷ n 2 an essential

requisition n 1 formal demand, such as for materials or supplies ▷ v 2 demand (supplies)

requite v return to someone (the same treatment or feeling as received) **requital** n

reredos [**rear**-doss] n ornamental screen behind an altar

rescind v annul or repeal

rescue v -cuing, -cued 1 deliver from danger or trouble, save ▷ n 2 rescuing **rescuer** n

research n 1 systematic investigation to discover facts or collect information ▷ v 2 carry out investigations **researcher** n

resemble v be or look like **resemblance** n

resent v feel indignant or bitter about **resentful** adj **resentment** n

reservation n 1 doubt

2 exception or limitation **3** seat etc. that has been reserved **4** area of land reserved for use by a particular group, esp. as a home for Native Americans

reserve v **1** set aside, keep for future use **2** obtain by arranging beforehand, book **3** retain ▷ n **4** something, esp. money or troops, kept for emergencies **5** *sports* substitute **6** area of land reserved for a particular purpose, esp. as a home for Canadian Indians **7** concealment of feelings or friendliness **reserved** *adj* **1** not showing one's feelings, lacking friendliness **2** set aside for use by a particular person **reservist** n member of a military reserve

reservoir n **1** natural or artificial lake storing water for community supplies **2** store or supply of something

reshuffle n **1** reorganization ▷ v **2** reorganize

reside v dwell permanently **residence** n home or house **resident** *adj, n* **residential** *adj* **1** (of part of a town) consisting mainly of houses **2** providing living accommodation

residue n what is left, remainder **residual** *adj*

resign v **1** give up office, a job, etc. **2** reconcile (oneself) to **resigned** *adj* content to endure **resignation** n **1** resigning **2** passive endurance of difficulties

resilient *adj* **1** (of a person) recovering quickly from a shock etc. **2** (of an object) able to return to normal shape after stretching etc. **resilience** n

resin [**rezz**-in] n **1** sticky substance from plants, esp. pines **2** similar synthetic

substance **resinous** *adj*

resist v **1** withstand or oppose **2** refrain from despite temptation **3** be proof against **resistance** n **1** act of resisting **2** opposition **3** *electricity* opposition offered by a circuit to the passage of a current through it **resistant** *adj* **resistible** *adj* **resistivity** n measure of electrical resistance **resistor** n component of an electrical circuit producing resistance

resit v **1** retake (an exam) ▷ n **2** exam that has to be retaken

resolute *adj* firm in purpose **resolutely** *adv* **resolution** n **1** resolving **2** firmness **3** thing resolved upon **4** decision of a court or vote of an assembly

resolve v **1** make up one's mind **2** decide with an effort of will **3** form (a resolution) by a vote **4** separate the component parts of **5** make clear, settle **resolved** *adj* determined

resonance n **1** echoing, esp. with a deep sound **2** sound produced in one object by sound waves coming from another object **resonant** *adj* **resonate** v **resonator** n

resort v **1** have recourse (to) for help etc. ▷ n **2** place for holidays **3** recourse

resound [riz-**zownd**] v echo or ring with sound **resounding** *adj* **1** echoing **2** clear and emphatic

resource n **1** thing resorted to for support **2** expedient **3** ingenuity **resources** **4** sources of economic wealth **5** stock that can be drawn on, funds **resourceful** *adj* **resourcefully** *adv* **resourcefulness** n

respect n **1** consideration **2** deference or esteem **3** point or aspect **4** reference or

relation: *with respect to* ▷ *v*
5 treat with esteem **6** show
consideration for **respecter**
n **respectful** *adj* **respecting**
prep concerning

respectable *adj* **1** worthy
of respect **2** fairly
good **respectably** *adv*
respectability *n*

respective *adj* relating
separately to each of those in
question **respectively** *adv*

respiration [ress-per-**ray**-
shun] *n* breathing **respirator**
n apparatus worn over
the mouth and breathed
through as protection against
dust, poison gas, etc., or to
provide artificial respiration
respiratory *adj* **respire** *v*
breathe

respite *n* **1** pause, interval of
rest **2** delay

resplendent *adj* **1** brilliant
or splendid **2** shining
resplendence *n*

respond *v* **1** answer **2** act in
answer to any stimulus **3** react
favourably **respondent** *n*
law defendant **response**
n **1** answer **2** reaction to a
stimulus **responsive** *adj*
readily reacting to some
influence **responsiveness** *n*

responsible *adj* **1** having
control and authority
2 reporting or accountable
(to) **3** sensible and
dependable **4** involving
responsibility **responsibly**
adv **responsibility** *n, pl* **-ties**
1 state of being responsible
2 person or thing for which
one is responsible

rest¹ *n* **1** repose **2** freedom from
exertion etc. **3** an object used
for support **4** pause, esp. in
music ▷ *v* **5** take a rest **6** give a
rest (to) **7** be supported **8** place
on a support **restful** *adj*
restless *adj*

rest² *n* **1** what is left **2** others

▷ *v* **3** remain, continue to be

restaurant *n* commercial
establishment serving meals
restaurateur [rest-er-a-**tur**]
n person who owns or runs a
restaurant

restitution *n* **1** giving back
2 reparation or compensation

restive *adj* restless or
impatient

restore *v* **1** return (a building,
painting, etc.) to its original
condition **2** re-establish **3** give
back, return **4** cause to recover
health or spirits **restoration**
n **restorative** [rest-**or**-a-tiv]
adj **1** restoring ▷ *n* **2** food or
medicine to strengthen etc.
restorer *n*

restrain *v* **1** hold (someone)
back from action **2** control
or restrict **restraint** *n*
1 restraining **2** control, esp.
self-control **restrained** *adj*
not displaying emotion

restrict *v* confine to certain
limits **restriction** *n*
restrictive *adj*

restructure *v* reorganize

result *n* **1** outcome or
consequence **2** number
obtained from a calculation
3 score **4** exam mark or grade
▷ *v* **5** (foll. by *from*) be the
outcome or consequence
(of) **6** (foll. by *in*) end (in)
resultant *adj* arising as a
result

resume *v* **1** begin again
2 occupy or take again
resumption *n*

résumé [**rez**-yoo-may] *n*
summary

resurgence *n* rising again to
vigour **resurgent** *adj*

resurrect *v* **1** restore to life
2 use once more (something
discarded etc.), revive
resurrection *n* **1** rising
again (esp. from the dead)
2 revival

resuscitate [ris-**suss**-it-tate]

v restore to consciousness **resuscitation** *n*

retail *n* **1** selling of goods to the public ▷ *adv* **2** by retail ▷ *v* **3** sell or be sold retail **4** recount in detail **retailer** *n*

retain *v* **1** keep **2** engage the services of **retainer** *n* **1** fee to retain someone's services **2** old-established servant of a family

retaliate *v* repay (an injury or wrong) in kind **retaliation** *n* **retaliatory** *adj*

retard *v* delay or slow (progress or development) **retarded** *adj offensive* underdeveloped, esp. mentally **retardation** *n*

retch *v* try to vomit

retention *n* **1** retaining **2** ability to remember **3** abnormal holding of something, esp. fluid, in the body **retentive** *adj* capable of retaining or remembering

rethink *v* consider again, esp. with a view to changing one's tactics

reticent *adj* uncommunicative, reserved **reticence** *n*

reticulate *adj* made or arranged like a net **reticulation** *n*

retina *n, pl* **-nas, -nae** light-sensitive membrane at the back of the eye **retinopathy** *n* any of various noninflammatory diseases of the retina

retinue *n* band of attendants

retire *v* **1** (cause to) give up office or work, esp. through age **2** go away or withdraw **3** go to bed **retired** *adj* having given up work etc. **retirement** *n* **retiring** *adj* shy

retort[1] *v* **1** reply quickly, wittily, or angrily ▷ *n* **2** quick, witty, or angry reply

retort[2] *n* glass container with a bent neck used for distilling

retouch *v* restore or improve by new touches, esp. of paint

retrace *v* go back over (a route etc.) again

retract *v* **1** withdraw (a statement etc.) **2** draw in or back **retractable** *or* **retractile** *adj* able to be retracted **retraction** *n*

retread *v, n* same as **remould**

retreat *v* **1** move back from a position, withdraw ▷ *n* **2** act of or military signal for retiring or withdrawal **3** place to which anyone retires, refuge

retrench *v* reduce expenditure, cut back **retrenchment** *n*

retrial *n* second trial of a case or defendant in a court of law

retribution *n* punishment or vengeance for evil deeds **retributive** *adj*

retrieve *v* **1** fetch back again **2** restore to a better state **3** recover (information) from a computer **retrievable** *adj* **retrieval** *n* **retriever** *n* dog trained to retrieve shot game

retro *adj* associated with or revived from the past: *retro fashion*

retroactive *adj* effective from a date in the past

retroflex *adj* bent or curved backwards

retrograde *adj* tending towards an earlier worse condition **retrogression** *n* **retrogressive** *adj*

retrorocket *n* small rocket engine used to slow a spacecraft

retrospect *n* **in retrospect** when looking back on the past **retrospective** *adj* **1** looking back in time **2** applying from a date in the past ▷ *n* **3** exhibition of an artist's life's work

retroussé [rit-**troo**-say] adj (of
a nose) turned upwards
retsina n resinous Greek wine
return v 1 go or come back
2 give, put, or send back
3 reply 4 elect 5 football catch (a
kicked ball) and run forward
with it ▷ n 6 returning
7 being returned 8 profit
9 official report, as of taxable
income 10 Brit return ticket
returnable adj **returning
officer** person in charge of
an election **return ticket**
ticket allowing a passenger to
travel to a place and back
reunion n gathering of people
who have been apart **reunite**
v bring or come together
again after a separation
reuse v use again **reusable**
adj
rev informal ▷ n 1 revolution
(of an engine) ▷ v **revving,
revved** 2 (foll. by up) increase
the speed of revolution of (an
engine)
Rev., Revd. Reverend
revalue v adjust the exchange
value of (a currency) upwards
revaluation n
revamp v renovate or restore
reveal v 1 make known
2 expose or show **revelation** n
reveille [riv-**val**-ee] n morning
bugle call to waken soldiers
revel v -**elling, -elled** 1 take
pleasure (in) 2 make merry
▷ n 3 usu pl merrymaking
reveller n **revelry** n festivity
revenge n 1 retaliation for
wrong done ▷ v 2 avenge
(oneself or another) 3 make
retaliation for **revengeful** adj
revenue n income, esp. of a
state, as taxes
reverberate v echo or
resound **reverberation** n
revere v be in awe of and
respect greatly **reverence** n
awe mingled with respect and
esteem **Reverend** adj (as a

prefix to a clergyman's name)
worthy of reverence **reverent**
adj showing reverence
reverently adv **reverential**
adj marked by reverence
reverie n absent-minded
daydream
reverse v 1 turn upside down
or the other way round
2 change completely 3 move
(a vehicle) backwards ▷ n
4 opposite or contrary
5 back side, obverse 6 defeat
7 reverse gear 8 football play
in which a player gives the
ball to a teammate running
in the opposite direction
▷ adj 9 opposite or contrary
reversal n **reversible** adj
reverse gear mechanism
enabling a vehicle to move
backwards
revert v 1 return to a former
state 2 come back to a subject
3 (of property) return to its
former owner **reversion** n (of
property) rightful passing to
the owner, designated heir,
etc.
revetment n facing of stone,
sandbags, etc. for a wall
review v 1 hold or write
a review of 2 examine,
reconsider, or look back
on 3 inspect formally ▷ n
4 critical assessment of a
book, concert, etc. 5 periodical
with critical articles 6 general
survey 7 inspection of troops
reviewer n writer of reviews
revile v be abusively scornful
of
revise v 1 change or
alter 2 look over and
correct 3 restudy (work)
in preparation for an
examination **revision** n
revive v bring or come
back to life, vigour, use,
etc. **revival** n 1 reviving or
renewal 2 movement seeking
to restore religious faith

revivalism n **revivalist** n
revoke v cancel (a will, agreement, etc.) **revocation** n
revolt n 1 uprising against authority ▷ v 2 rise in rebellion 3 cause to feel disgust **revolting** adj disgusting, horrible
revolution n 1 overthrow of a government by the governed 2 great change 3 complete rotation 4 spinning round **revolutionary** adj, n **revolutionize** v change considerably
revolve v 1 turn round, rotate 2 (foll. by around) be centred (on) **revolver** n repeating pistol
revue n theatrical entertainment with topical sketches and songs
revulsion n strong disgust
reward n 1 something given in return for a service 2 sum of money offered for finding a criminal or missing property ▷ v 3 pay or give something to (someone) for a service, information, etc. **rewarding** adj giving personal satisfaction, worthwhile
rewind v run (a tape or film) back to an earlier point in order to replay
rewire v provide (a house, engine, etc.) with new wiring
rewrite v 1 write again in a different way ▷ n 2 something rewritten
rhapsody n, pl -dies 1 freely structured emotional piece of music 2 expression of ecstatic enthusiasm **rhapsodic** adj **rhapsodize** v speak or write with extravagant enthusiasm
rhea [ree-a] n S American three-toed ostrich
rheostat n instrument for varying the resistance of an electric circuit
rhesus [ree-suss] n small long-tailed monkey of S Asia **rhesus factor** or **Rh factor** feature distinguishing different types of human blood
rhetoric [ret-a-rik] n 1 art of effective speaking or writing 2 artificial or exaggerated language **rhetorical** [rit-tor-ik-kal] adj (of a question) not requiring an answer **rhetorically** adv
rheumatism n painful inflammation of joints or muscles **rheumatic** n, adj (person) affected by rheumatism **rheumatoid** adj of or like rheumatism
Rh factor n see **rhesus**
rhinestone n imitation diamond
rhino n short for **rhinoceros**
rhinoceros n, pl -oses, -os large thick-skinned animal with one or two horns on its nose
rhizome n thick underground stem producing new plants
rhodium n hard metal like platinum
rhododendron n evergreen flowering shrub
rhombus n, pl -buses, -bi parallelogram with sides of equal length but no right angles, diamond-shaped figure **rhomboid** n parallelogram with adjacent sides of unequal length
rhubarb n garden plant of which the fleshy stalks are cooked as fruit
rhyme n 1 sameness of the final sounds at the ends of lines of verse, or in words 2 word or syllable identical in sound to another 3 verse marked by rhyme ▷ v 4 make a rhyme
rhythm n measured beat esp. of words, music, etc. **rhythmic** or **rhythmical** adj

r

rhythmically adv **rhythm and blues** popular music, orig. Black American, influenced by the blues

rib[1] n **1** one of the curved bones forming the framework of the upper part of the body **2** cut of meat including the rib(s) **3** curved supporting part, as in the hull of a boat **4** raised series of rows in knitting ▷ v **ribbing, ribbed 5** provide or mark with ribs **6** knit to form a rib pattern **ribbed** adj **ribbing** n **ribcage** n bony structure of ribs enclosing the lungs

rib[2] v **ribbing, ribbed** informal tease or ridicule **ribbing** n

ribald adj humorously or mockingly rude or obscene **ribaldry** n

ribbon n **1** narrow band of fabric used for trimming, tying, etc. **2** any long strip, for example of inked tape in a typewriter

riboflavin [rye-boe-**flay**-vin] n form of vitamin B

rice n **1** cereal plant grown on wet ground in warm countries **2** its seeds as food

rich adj **1** owning a lot of money or property, wealthy **2** fertile **3** abounding **4** valuable **5** (of food) containing much fat or sugar **6** mellow **7** amusing **riches** pl n wealth **richly** adv **1** elaborately **2** fully **richness** n

rick[1] n stack of hay etc.

rick[2] v, n sprain or wrench

rickets n disease of children marked by softening of the bones, bow legs, etc., caused by vitamin D deficiency **rickety** adj shaky or unstable **rickshaw** n light two-wheeled man-drawn Asian vehicle

ricochet [**rik**-osh-ay] v **1** (of a bullet) rebound from a solid surface ▷ n **2** such a rebound

rid v **ridding, rid** clear or relieve (of) **get rid of** free oneself of (something undesirable) **good riddance** relief at getting rid of something or someone

ridden v **1** past participle of **ride** ▷ adj **2** afflicted or affected by the thing specified: disease-ridden

riddle[1] n **1** question made puzzling to test one's ingenuity **2** puzzling person or thing

riddle[2] v **1** pierce with many holes ▷ n **2** coarse sieve for gravel etc. **riddled with** full of

ride v **riding, rode, ridden 1** sit on and control or propel (a horse, bicycle, etc.) **2** go on horseback or in a vehicle **3** be carried on or across **4** travel over **5** lie at anchor ▷ n **6** journey on a horse etc., or in a vehicle **7** type of movement experienced in a vehicle **rider** n **1** person who rides **2** supplementary clause added to a document **ride up** v (of a garment) move up from the proper position

RIDE (in Ontario) Reduce Impaired Driving Everywhere: program of police spot checks of drivers

ridge n **1** long narrow hill **2** long narrow raised part on a surface **3** line where two sloping surfaces meet **4** elongated area of high pressure **ridged** adj

ridiculous adj deserving to be laughed at, absurd **ridicule** n **1** treatment of a person or thing as ridiculous ▷ v **2** laugh at, make fun of

riding n electoral constituency **riding association** branch of a political party at the riding level

riesling n type of white wine

rife adj widespread or common **rife with** full of

riff n jazz, rock short repeated melodic figure

riffle v flick through (pages etc.) quickly

riffraff n rabble, disreputable people

rifle[1] n firearm with a long barrel

rifle[2] v 1 search and rob 2 ransack

rift n 1 break in friendly relations 2 crack, split, or cleft **rift valley** long narrow valley resulting from subsidence between faults

rig v **rigging, rigged** 1 arrange in a dishonest way 2 (often foll. by up) set up, esp. as a makeshift 3 equip 4 provide (a ship) with spars, ropes, etc. ▷ n 5 apparatus for drilling for oil and gas 6 way a ship's masts and sails are arranged 7 Also **rigout** informal outfit of clothes **rigging** n ship's spars and ropes

right adj 1 just 2 in accordance with truth and duty 3 true 4 correct 5 proper 6 of the side that faces east when the front is turned to the north 7 Also **right-wing** politics conservative or reactionary 8 straight 9 upright 10 of the outer side of a fabric ▷ v 11 bring or come back to a vertical position 12 do justice to ▷ n 13 claim, title, etc. allowed or due 14 what is just or due 15 conservative political party ▷ adv 16 straight 17 properly 18 very 19 on or to the right side **in the right** morally or legally correct **right away** immediately **rightly** adv **rightful** adj **rightist** n, adj (person) on the political right **right angle** angle of 90° **right field** baseball area of the outfield to the batter's right **right fielder** baseball fielder who covers right field **right-handed** adj using or for the right hand **right-hand man** person's most valuable assistant **Right Honourable** (in Canada) title of respect given for life to the Prime Minister, the Governor General, and the Chief Justice of the Supreme Court **right of way** law 1 right of one vehicle to go before another 2 legal right to pass over someone's land **righty** n informal 1 right-handed person 2 baseball right-handed pitcher

righteous [rye-chuss] adj 1 upright, godly, or virtuous 2 morally justified **righteousness** n

rigid adj 1 inflexible or strict 2 unyielding or stiff **rigidly** adv **rigidity** n

rigmarole n 1 meaningless string of words 2 long complicated procedure

rigor mortis n stiffening of the body after death

rigour, rigor n 1 harshness, severity, or strictness 2 hardship **rigorous** adj harsh, severe, or stern

rile v anger or annoy

rill n small stream

rim n 1 edge or border 2 outer ring of a wheel **rimmed** adj

rime n lit hoarfrost

rind n outer coating of fruits, cheese, or bacon

ring[1] v **ringing, rang, rung** 1 give out a clear resonant sound, as a bell 2 resound 3 cause (a bell) to sound 4 Also **ring up** telephone ▷ n 5 ringing 6 telephone call

ring[2] n 1 circle of gold etc., esp. for a finger 2 any circular band, coil, or rim 3 circle

r

of people **4** enclosed area, esp. a circle for a circus or a roped-in square for boxing **5** group operating (illegal) control of a market ▷ *v* **6** put a ring round **7** mark (a bird) with a ring **8** kill (a tree) by cutting the bark round the trunk **ringer** *n slang* person or thing apparently identical to another (Also **dead ringer**) **ringlet** *n* curly lock of hair **ringleader** *n* instigator of a mutiny, riot, etc. **ring road** *Brit* main road that bypasses a town (centre) **ringtone** *n* tune played by a cell phone when it receives a call **ringside** *n* row of seats nearest a boxing or circus ring **ringworm** *n* fungal skin disease in circular patches

ringette *n sports* game similar to hockey, with a rubber ring used instead of a puck

rink *n* **1** sheet of ice for skating or ice hockey **2** floor for roller skating **rink rat** *slang* youth who helps with chores at an ice-hockey rink in return for free admission to games

rinse *v* **1** remove soap from (washed clothes, hair, etc.) by applying clean water **2** wash lightly ▷ *n* **3** rinsing **4** liquid to tint hair

riot *n* **1** disorderly unruly disturbance **2** loud revelry **3** *slang* very amusing person or thing **4** profusion ▷ *v* **5** take part in a riot **read the riot act** reprimand severely **run riot 1** behave without restraint **2** grow profusely **riotous** *adj* **1** unrestrained **2** unruly or rebellious

rip *v* **ripping, ripped 1** tear violently **2** tear away **3** *informal* rush ▷ *n* **4** split or tear **let rip** act or speak without restraint **ripcord** *n* cord pulled to open a parachute **rip off** *v slang*

cheat by overcharging **rip-off** *n slang* cheat or swindle **rip-roaring** *adj informal* boisterous and exciting

RIP rest in peace

riparian [rip-**pair**-ee-an] *adj* of or on the banks of a river

ripe *adj* **1** mature enough to be eaten or used **2** fully developed in mind or body **3** suitable: *wait until the time is ripe* **ripen** *v* **1** grow ripe **2** mature

riposte [rip-**posst**] *n* **1** verbal retort **2** counterattack ▷ *v* **3** make a riposte

ripple *n* **1** slight wave, ruffling of a surface **2** sound like ripples of water ▷ *v* **3** flow or form into little waves (on) **4** (of sounds) rise and fall gently

rise *v* **rising, rose, risen 1** get up **2** move upwards **3** (of the sun or moon) appear above the horizon **4** reach a higher level **5** (of an amount or price) increase **6** rebel **7** (of a court) adjourn **8** have its source ▷ *n* **9** rising **10** upward slope **11** *Brit* raise **get a rise out of** *slang* provoke an angry reaction from **give rise to** cause **riser** *n* **1** person who rises, esp. from bed **2** vertical part of a step **rising** *n* **1** revolt ▷ *adj* **2** increasing in rank or maturity

risible [**riz**-zib-bl] *adj* causing laughter, ridiculous

risk *n* **1** chance of disaster or loss **2** person or thing considered as a potential hazard ▷ *v* **3** act in spite of the possibility of (injury or loss) **4** expose to danger or loss **risky** *adj* full of risk, dangerous **riskily** *adv*

risotto *n, pl* **-tos** dish of rice cooked in stock with vegetables, meat, etc.

risqué [**risk**-ay] *adj* making slightly rude references to sex

rissole n cake of minced meat, coated with breadcrumbs and fried

rite n formal practice or custom, esp. religious **ritual** n 1 prescribed order of rites 2 regular repeated action or behaviour ▷ adj 3 concerning rites **ritually** adv **ritualistic** adj like a ritual

ritzy adj **ritzier, ritziest** slang luxurious or elegant

rival n 1 person or thing that competes with or equals another for favour, success, etc. ▷ adj 2 in the position of a rival ▷ v -**valling, -valled** 3 (try to) equal **rivalry** n keen competition

riven adj split

river n 1 large natural stream of water 2 copious flow

rivet [riv-vit] n 1 bolt for fastening metal plates, the end being put through holes and then beaten flat ▷ v **riveting, riveted** 2 cause to be fixed, as in fascination 3 fasten with rivets **riveter** n **riveting** adj very interesting and exciting

rivulet n small stream

RN Royal Navy

RNA ribonucleic acid: substance in living cells essential for the synthesis of protein

roach n freshwater fish

road n 1 way prepared for passengers, vehicles, etc. 2 way or course: the road to fame 3 street **on the road** travelling **roadie** n informal person who transports and sets up equipment for a band **road apple** slang lump of horse manure **roadblock** n barricade across a road to stop traffic for inspection etc. **road hog** informal selfish aggressive driver **roadhouse** n pub or restaurant on a country road **road metal** broken stones used in building roads **roadside** n, adj **road test** test of a vehicle etc. in actual use **roadway** n the part of a road used by vehicles **roadworks** pl n repairs to a road, esp. blocking part of the road **roadworthy** adj (of a vehicle) mechanically sound

roam v wander about

roan adj 1 (of a horse) having a brown or black coat sprinkled with white hairs ▷ n 2 roan horse

roar v 1 make or utter a loud deep hoarse sound like that of a lion 2 shout (something) as in anger 3 laugh loudly ▷ n 4 such a sound **roaring** adj 1 noisy, boisterous 2 informal brisk and profitable ▷ adv 3 noisily

roast v 1 cook by dry heat, as in an oven 2 make or be very hot ▷ n 3 roasted joint of meat ▷ adj 4 roasted **roasting** informal ▷ adj 1 extremely hot ▷ n 2 severe criticism or scolding **roaster** n 1 roasting tin 2 piece of food that is suitable for roasting

rob v **robbing, robbed** 1 steal from 2 deprive **robber** n **robbery** n

robe n 1 long loose outer garment ▷ v 2 put a robe on

robin n large thrush with a red breast

robot n 1 automated machine, esp. one performing functions in a human manner 2 person of machine-like efficiency **robotic** adj **robotics** n science of designing and using robots

robust adj very strong and healthy **robustly** adv **robustness** n

roc n monstrous bird of Arabian mythology

ROC rest of Canada: the areas outside Quebec

r

rock¹ n 1 hard mineral substance that makes up part of the earth's crust, stone 2 large rugged mass of stone 3 hard candy in sticks 4 *curling* curling stone **on the rocks** 1 (of a marriage) about to end 2 (of an alcoholic drink) served with ice **rocky** adj having many rocks **rockery** n mound of stones in a garden for (alpine) plants **rock bottom** lowest possible level **rock tripe** any of various edible lichens that grow on rocks

rock² v 1 (cause to) sway to and fro ▷ n 2 style of pop music with a heavy beat **rocky** adj shaky or unstable **rock and roll** style of pop music blending rhythm and blues and country music **rocking chair** chair allowing the sitter to rock backwards and forwards

rocker n 1 curved piece of wood etc. on which something may rock 2 rocking chair **off one's rocker** informal insane

rocket n 1 self-propelling device powered by the burning of explosive contents (used as a firework, weapon, etc.) 2 vehicle propelled by a rocket engine, as a weapon or carrying a spacecraft ▷ v **rocketing, rocketed** 3 move fast, esp. upwards, as a rocket. **rocketry** n

rococo [rok-**koe**-koe] adj (of furniture, architecture, etc.) having much elaborate decoration in an early 18th-century French style

rod n 1 slender straight bar, stick 2 cane

rode v past tense of **ride**

rodent n animal with teeth specialized for gnawing, such as a rat

rodeo n, pl **-deos** display of skill by cowboys, such as bareback riding

roe¹ n small species of deer

roe² n mass of eggs in a fish

roentgen [**ront**-gan] n unit measuring a radiation dose

rogue n 1 dishonest or unprincipled person 2 mischief-loving person ▷ adj 3 (of a wild beast) having a savage temper and living apart from the herd **roguery** n **roguish** adj

roister v make merry noisily or boisterously **roisterer** n

role n 1 actor's part 2 task or function

roll v 1 move by turning over and over 2 wind round 3 smooth out with a roller 4 move or sweep along 5 undulate 6 (of a ship or aircraft) turn from side to side about a line from nose to tail ▷ n 7 act of rolling over or from side to side 8 piece of paper etc. rolled up 9 list or register 10 small rounded individually baked piece of bread 11 swaying unsteady movement or gait 12 continuous sound, as of drums, thunder, etc. **rolling pin** cylindrical roller for pastry **rolling stock** locomotives, carriages, etc. of a railway **rolling stone** restless, wandering person **roll call** calling out of a list of names, as in a school or the army, to check who is present **rolled gold** metal coated with a thin layer of gold **roll-on/ roll-off** adj denoting a ship which vehicles can be driven straight onto or off **roll-top** adj (of a desk) having a flexible lid sliding in grooves **roll up** v informal appear or arrive

roller n 1 rotating cylinder used for smoothing or supporting a thing to be

moved, spreading paint,
etc. **2** long wave of the sea
Rollerblade n ® roller skate
with the wheels set in one
straight line **roller coaster**
(at a funfair) narrow railway
with steep slopes **roller
skate** skate with wheels
rollicking adj boisterously
carefree
roly-poly adj round or plump
ROM computers read only
memory
Roman adj of Rome or the
Church of Rome **Roman
Catholic** member of that
section of the Christian
Church that acknowledges
the supremacy of the Pope
Roman numerals the letters
I, V, X, L, C, D, M, used to
represent numbers **roman
type** plain upright letters in
printing
romance n **1** love affair
2 mysterious or exciting
quality **3** novel or film dealing
with love, esp. sentimentally
4 story with scenes remote
from ordinary life ▷ v
5 exaggerate or fantasize
romancer n
Romance adj (of a language)
developed from Latin, such as
French, Spanish, or Italian
Romanesque adj, n (in) a style
of architecture of 9th–12th
centuries characterized by
round arches
romantic adj **1** of or dealing
with love **2** idealistic but
impractical **3** (of literature,
music, etc.) displaying
passion and imagination
rather than order and form
▷ n **4** romantic person or
artist **romantically** adv
romanticism n **romanticist**
n **romanticize** v
Romany n, pl **-nies**, adj Gypsy
romp v **1** play wildly and
joyfully ▷ n **2** spell of romping

romp home win easily
rompers pl n child's overalls
rondeau n, pl **-deaux** short
poem with the opening words
used as a refrain
rondo n, pl **-dos** piece of
music with a leading theme
continually returned to
rood n Christianity **1** the Cross
2 crucifix **rood screen** (in a
church) screen separating the
nave from the choir
roof n, pl **roofs 1** outside
upper covering of a building,
automobile, etc. ▷ v **2** put a
roof on
rook[1] n **1** bird of the crow
family ▷ v **2** old-fashioned, slang
swindle **rookery** n colony of
rooks
rook[2] n piece in chess
rookie n informal recruit, esp.
in the army
room n **1** space **2** space enough
3 division of a house **4** scope
or opportunity **rooms**
5 lodgings **roomy** adj
spacious
roost n **1** perch for fowls ▷ v
2 perch **rooster** n domestic
cock
root n **1** part of a plant that
grows down into the earth
obtaining nourishment
2 plant with an edible root,
such as a carrot **3** part of a
tooth, hair, etc. below the skin
4 source or origin **5** form of a
word from which other words
and forms are derived **6** math
factor of a quantity which,
when multiplied by itself the
number of times indicated,
gives the quantity **roots**
7 person's sense of belonging
▷ v **8** establish a root and
start to grow **9** dig or burrow
rootless adj having no sense
of belonging **root for** v
informal cheer on **root out** v
get rid of completely **root up**
v pull up by the roots

r

rope n thick cord **know the ropes** be thoroughly familiar with an activity **rope in** v persuade to join in

ropy adj **ropier, ropiest** informal **1** inferior or inadequate **2** not well **ropiness** n

rorqual n whalebone whale with a dorsal fin

rosary n, pl **-saries 1** series of prayers **2** string of beads for counting these prayers

rose[1] n **1** shrub or climbing plant with prickly stems and fragrant flowers **2** the flower **3** perforated flat nozzle for a hose **4** pink colour ▷ adj **5** reddish-pink **roseate** [roe-zee-ate] adj rose-coloured **rosy** adj **1** flushed **2** hopeful or promising **rose-coloured** adj unjustifiably optimistic **rose window** circular window with spokes branching from the centre **rosewood** n fragrant wood

rose[2] v past tense of **rise**

rosé [roe-zay] n pink wine

rosehip n berry-like fruit of a rose plant

rosemary n **1** fragrant flowering shrub **2** its leaves as a herb

rosette n rose-shaped ornament, esp. a circular bunch of ribbons

rosin [rozz-in] n resin

roster n list of people and their turns of duty

rostrum n, pl **-trums, -tra** platform or stage

rot v **rotting, rotted 1** decompose or decay **2** slowly deteriorate physically or mentally ▷ n **3** decay **4** informal nonsense

rota n list of people who take it in turn to do a particular task

rotary n **1** traffic circle ▷ adj **2** revolving **3** operated by rotation

rotate v **1** (cause to) move round a centre or on a pivot **2** (cause to) follow a set sequence

rotation n **1** act of rotating **2** regular cycle of events **3** baseball group of pitchers on a team who take turns starting games

rote n mechanical repetition **by rote** by memory

rotisserie n **1** (electrically driven) rotating spit for cooking meat ▷ adj **2** baseball relating to a fantasy baseball league in which participants select real players for an imaginary team, and points are awarded according to the actual performances of the chosen players

rotor n **1** revolving portion of a dynamo, motor, or turbine **2** rotating device with long blades that provides thrust to lift a helicopter

rotten adj **1** decomposed **2** informal very bad **3** corrupt

rotter n slang despicable person

Rottweiler [rawt-vile-er] n large sturdy dog with a smooth black and tan coat and usu. a docked tail

rotund [roe-tund] adj **1** round and plump **2** sonorous **rotundity** n

rotunda n circular building or room, esp. with a dome

rouble [roo-bl] n monetary unit of Russia

roué [roo-ay] n man given to immoral living

rouge n red cosmetic used to colour the cheeks

rough adj **1** not smooth, uneven or irregular **2** violent, stormy, or boisterous **3** approximate **4** incomplete or rudimentary **5** lacking refinement ▷ v **6** make rough **7** plan out approximately ▷ n

r

8 rough state or area **rough it** live without the usual comforts etc. **roughen** v **roughly** adv **roughness** n **roughage** n indigestible constituents of food which aid digestion **rough-and-ready** adj hastily prepared but adequate **rough-and-tumble** n playful fight **rough-hewn** adj roughly shaped

roughcast n **1** mixture of plaster and small stones for outside walls ▷ v **2** coat with this

roughshod adv ride **roughshod over** act with total disregard for

roulette n gambling game played with a revolving wheel and a ball

round adj **1** spherical, cylindrical, circular, or curved **2** complete or whole: *round numbers* **3** plump ▷ adv **4** with a circular or circuitous course **5** on all sides: *books scattered round the room* ▷ n **6** thing round in shape **7** recurrent duties **8** customary course, as of a milkman **9** stage in a competition **10** game (of golf) **11** one of several periods in a boxing match etc. **12** number of drinks bought at one time **13** bullet or shell for a gun **14** part song in which singers join at equal intervals **15** circular movement **16** set of sandwiches ▷ prep **17** surrounding or encircling **18** on or outside the perimeter of **19** on all sides of ▷ v **20** make or become round **21** move round **roundly** adv thoroughly **round robin** petition signed with names in a circle to conceal the order **round-the-clock** adj throughout the day and night **round trip** journey out and back again, esp. by a different route **round up** v gather (people or animals) together **roundup** n

roundabout n Brit **1** traffic circle **2** merry-go-round ▷ adj **3** not straightforward: *a roundabout route*

roundel n **1** small disc **2** rondeau **roundelay** n simple song with a refrain

Roundhead n supporter of Parliament against Charles I in the English Civil War

rouse v **1** wake up **2** provoke or excite **rousing** adj lively, vigorous

roustabout n labourer on an oil rig

rout n **1** overwhelming defeat **2** disorderly retreat ▷ v **3** defeat and put to flight **rout out** v **1** search for **2** drive out

route n **1** choice of roads taken to reach a destination **2** fixed path followed by buses, etc. between two places **3** chosen way or method **routemarch** n long training march

routine n **1** usual or regular method of procedure **2** boring repetition of tasks: *mindless routine* **3** set sequence ▷ adj **4** ordinary **5** regular

roux [roo] n fat and flour cooked together as a basis for sauces

rove v wander **rover** n **1** person who roves **2** pirate **3** small remote-controlled vehicle which roams over rough, esp. extraterrestrial, terrain taking photographs and samples

row¹ n straight line of people or things **in a row** in succession

row² v **1** propel (a boat) by oars ▷ n **2** spell of rowing

row³ informal ▷ n **1** dispute **2** disturbance **3** reprimand ▷ v **4** quarrel noisily

rowan *n* tree producing bright red berries, mountain ash

rowdy *adj* **-dier, -diest 1** disorderly, noisy, and rough ▷ *n, pl* **-dies 2** person like this

rowel [rhymes with **towel**] *n* small spiked wheel on a spur

rowlock *n* device on the gunwale of a boat that holds an oar in place

royal *adj* **1** of, befitting, or supported by a king or queen **2** splendid ▷ *n* **3** informal member of a royal family **royally** *adv* **royalist** *n* supporter of monarchy **royalty** *n* **1** royal people **2** rank or power **3** payment to author, musician, inventor, etc. **royal blue** bright blue

rpm revolutions per minute

RRSP Registered Retirement Savings Plan

RSI repetitive strain injury

RSS Rich Site Summary *or* Really Simple Syndication: a way of allowing web users to receive updates from selected websites on their browsers

RSVP please reply

rub *v* **rubbing, rubbed 1** apply pressure and friction to (something) with a circular or backwards-and-forwards movement **2** clean, polish, or dry by rubbing **3** remove by rubbing **4** chafe or fray through rubbing ▷ *n* **5** act of rubbing **rub it in** emphasize an unpleasant fact **rub out** *v* remove with a rubber

rubato *adv music* with expressive flexibility of tempo

rubber[1] *n* **1** strong waterproof elastic material, orig. made from the dried sap of a tropical tree, now usually synthetic **2** piece of rubber used for erasing mistakes **3** *slang* condom **rubbers 4** rubberized waterproof raincoat, overshoe, etc. ▷ *adj* **5** made of or producing rubber **rubberize** *v* coat or treat with rubber **rubbery** *adj* like rubber, soft or elastic **rubberneck** *v* stare with unthinking curiosity **rubber stamp 1** device for imprinting the date, a name, etc. **2** automatic authorization

rubber[2] *n* match consisting of three games of bridge, whist, etc.

rubbish *n* **1** waste matter **2** anything worthless **3** nonsense **rubbishy** *adj*

rubble *n* fragments of broken stone, brick, etc.

rubella [roo-**bell**-a] *n* same as **German measles**

rubicund [**roo**-bik-kund] *adj* ruddy

rubric [**roo**-brik] *n* heading or explanation inserted in a text

ruby *n, pl* **-bies 1** red precious gemstone ▷ *adj* **2** deep red

ruck[1] *n* rough crowd of common people

ruck[2] *n, v* wrinkle or crease

rucksack *n* large pack carried on the back

ructions *pl n* informal noisy uproar

rudder *n* vertical hinged piece at the stern of a boat or at the rear of an aircraft, for steering

ruddy *adj* **-dier, -diest** of a fresh healthy red colour

rude *adj* **1** impolite or insulting **2** coarse, vulgar, or obscene **3** roughly made **4** robust **5** unexpected and unpleasant **rudely** *adv* **rudeness** *n*

rudiments *pl n* simplest and most basic stages of a subject **rudimentary** *adj* basic, elementary

rue[1] *v* **ruing, rued** feel regret for **rueful** *adj* regretful or sorry **ruefully** *adv*

rue[2] *n* plant with evergreen bitter leaves

ruff *n* **1** starched and frilled

collar **2** natural collar of feathers, fur, etc. on certain birds and animals

ruffian *n* violent lawless person

ruffle *v* **1** disturb the calm of **2** annoy, irritate ▷ *n* **3** frill or pleat

rug *n* **1** small carpet **2** thick woollen blanket

rugby *n* form of football played with an oval ball which may be handled by the players

rugged [**rug**-gid] *adj* **1** rough **2** uneven and jagged **3** strong-featured **4** tough and sturdy

rugger *n informal* rugby

ruin *v* **1** destroy or spoil completely **2** impoverish ▷ *n* **3** destruction or decay **4** loss of wealth, position, etc. **5** broken-down unused building(s) **ruination** *n* **1** act of ruining **2** state of being ruined **3** cause of ruin **ruinous** *adj* **1** causing ruin **2** more expensive than is reasonable **ruinously** *adv*

rule *n* **1** statement of what is allowed, for example in a game or procedure **2** what is usual **3** government, authority, or control **4** measuring device with a straight edge ▷ *v* **5** govern **6** restrain **7** give a formal decision **8** be pre-eminent **9** mark with straight line(s) **as a rule** usually **ruler** *n* **1** person who governs **2** measuring device with a straight edge **ruling** *n* formal decision **rule of thumb** practical but imprecise approach **rule out** *v* exclude

rum *n* alcoholic drink distilled from sugar cane

rumba *n* lively ballroom dance of Cuban origin

rumble¹ *v* **1** (of traffic etc.) make a low continuous

noise ▷ *n* **2** such a noise

rumble² *v informal* discover the (disreputable) truth about

rumbustious *adj* boisterous or unruly

ruminate *v* **1** ponder or meditate **2** chew the cud **ruminant** *adj, n* cud-chewing (animal, such as a cow, sheep, or deer) **rumination** *n* quiet meditation and reflection **ruminative** *adj*

rummage *v* **1** search untidily and at length ▷ *n* **2** untidy search through a collection of things

rummy *n* card game in which players try to collect sets or sequences

rumour *n* **1** gossip or common talk **2** unproved statement **be rumoured** be circulated as a rumour

rump *n* **1** buttocks **2** rear of an animal

rumple *v* make untidy, crumpled, or dishevelled

rumpus *n, pl* -**puses** noisy or confused commotion

run *v* **running, ran, run** **1** move with a more rapid gait than walking **2** go quickly (across) **3** flow **4** compete in a race, election, etc. **5** continue (for a specified period) **6** function **7** travel according to schedule **8** melt **9** spread **10** (of stitches) unravel **11** expose oneself to (a risk) **12** (of a newspaper) publish (a story) **13** smuggle (goods, esp. arms) **14** manage or be in charge of ▷ *n* **15** act or spell of running **16** ride in an automobile **17** unrestricted access **18** tendency or trend: *the run of the market* **19** continuous period: *a run of good luck* **20** sequence **21** heavy demand **22** enclosure for domestic fowls **23** series of unravelled stitches, ladder

24 score of one at baseball **25** steep snow-covered course for skiing **run away** v make one's escape, flee **run down** v **1** be rude about **2** stop working **3** reduce in number or size **rundown** n **run-down** adj exhausted **run into** v meet **run-of-the-mill** adj ordinary **run out** v be completely used up **run over** v knock down (a person) with a moving vehicle **run up** v incur (a debt)

rune n any character of the earliest Germanic alphabet **runic** adj

rung¹ n crossbar on a ladder

rung² v past participle of **ring¹**

runnel n small brook or rivulet

runner n **1** competitor in a race **2** messenger **3** part underneath an ice skate etc., on which it slides **4** slender horizontal stem of a plant, such as a strawberry, running along the ground and forming new roots at intervals **5** long strip of carpet or decorative cloth **runner-up** n person who comes second in a competition

running adj **1** continuous **2** consecutive **3** (of water) flowing ▷ n **4** act of moving or flowing quickly **5** management of a business etc. **in** or **out of the running** having or not having a good chance in a competition **running back** football offensive player whose job is to run with the ball

runny adj **-nier, -niest** **1** tending to flow **2** exuding moisture

runt n **1** smallest animal in a litter **2** offensive undersized person

runway n hard level roadway where aircraft take off and land

rupee n monetary unit of India and Pakistan

rupture n **1** breaking, breach **2** hernia ▷ v **3** break, burst, or sever

rural adj in or of the countryside

ruse [rooz] n stratagem or trick

rush¹ v **1** move or do very quickly **2** force (someone) to act hastily **3** make a sudden attack upon (a person or place) **4** football run forwards with the ball ▷ n **5** sudden quick or violent movement **6** football act of rushing **rushes 7** first unedited prints of a scene for a film ▷ adj **8** done with speed, hasty **rushing** n **rush hour** period at the beginning and end of the working day, when many people are travelling to or from work

rush² n marsh plant with a slender pithy stem **rushy** adj full of rushes

rusk n hard brown crisp biscuit, used esp. for feeding babies

russet adj **1** reddish-brown ▷ n **2** the colour **3** apple with rough reddish-brown skin

rust n **1** reddish-brown coating formed on iron etc. that has been exposed to moisture **2** disease of plants with rust-coloured spots ▷ adj **3** reddish-brown ▷ v **4** become coated with rust **rusty** adj **1** coated with rust **2** of a rust colour **3** out of practice **rustproof** adj

rustic adj **1** of or resembling country people **2** rural **3** crude, awkward, or uncouth **4** (of furniture) made of untrimmed branches ▷ n **5** person from the country **rusticity** n

rusticate v banish temporarily from university

as a punishment **rustication**
n

rustle¹ *v* **1** make a low
whispering sound, as of dry
leaves ▷ *n* **2** this sound

rustle² *v* steal (cattle) **rustler**
n cattle thief **rustle up** *v*
prepare at short notice

rut¹ *n* **1** furrow made by wheels
2 dull settled habits or way of
living

rut² *n* **1** recurrent period of
sexual excitability in male
deer ▷ *v* **rutting, rutted**
2 be in a period of sexual
excitability

rutabaga *n* kind of turnip

ruthless *adj* pitiless, merciless
ruthlessly *adv* **ruthlessness**
n

rye *n* **1** kind of grain used for
fodder and bread **2** whiskey
made from rye

rye-grass *n* any of several
kinds of grass cultivated for
fodder

Ss

S 1 second(s) **2** singular
S 1 Saint **2** South(ern) **3** *chem* sulfur
SA 1 Salvation Army **2** South Africa
Sabbath *n* day of worship and rest: Saturday for Jews, Sunday for Christians **sabbatical** *adj, n* (denoting) leave for study
sable *n* **1** dark fur from a small weasel-like Arctic animal ▷ *adj* **2** black
sabot [**sab**-oh] *n* wooden shoe, clog
sabotage *n* **1** intentional damage done to machinery, systems, etc. ▷ *v* **2** damage intentionally **saboteur** *n* person who commits sabotage
sabre *n* curved cavalry sword
sac *n* pouchlike structure in an animal or plant
saccharin, saccharine *n* artificial sweetener **saccharine** *adj* excessively sweet
sacerdotal *adj* of priests
sachet *n* small envelope or bag containing a single portion
sack *n* **1** large bag made of coarse material **2** plundering of a captured town **3** *informal* dismissal **4** *slang* bed ▷ *v* **5** plunder (a captured town) **6** *informal* dismiss **hit the sack** *slang* go to bed **sackcloth** *n* coarse fabric used for sacks, formerly worn as a penance
sacrament *n* ceremony of the Christian Church, esp. Communion **sacramental** *adj*

sacred *adj* **1** holy **2** set apart, reserved **3** connected with religion
sacrifice *n* **1** giving something up **2** thing given up **3** making of an offering to a god **4** thing offered ▷ *v* **5** offer as a sacrifice **6** give (something) up **sacrificial** *adj*
sacrilege *n* misuse or desecration of something sacred **sacrilegious** *adj*
sacristan *n* person in charge of the contents of a church **sacristy** *n* room in a church where sacred objects are kept
sacrosanct *adj* regarded as sacred, inviolable
sacrum [**say**-krum] *n, pl* **-cra** compound bone at the base of the spine
sad *adj* **sadder, saddest 1** sorrowful, unhappy **2** deplorably bad **3** regrettable **sadden** *v* make (someone) sad **sadly** *adv* **sadness** *n*
saddle *n* **1** rider's seat on a horse or bicycle **2** joint of meat ▷ *v* **3** put a saddle on (a horse) **4** burden (with a responsibility) **saddler** *n* maker or seller of saddles **saddlebag** *n* pouch or small bag attached to the saddle of a horse, bicycle, etc.
sadism [**say**-dizz-um] *n* gaining of (sexual) pleasure from inflicting pain **sadist** *n* **sadistic** *adj* **sadistically** *adv*
sadomasochism *n* combination of sadism and masochism **sadomasochist** *n*

s

s.a.e. stamped addressed envelope

safari *n, pl* -**ris** expedition to hunt or observe wild animals, esp. in Africa **safari park** park where lions, elephants, etc. are kept uncaged so that people can see them from automobiles

safe *adj* **1** secure, protected **2** uninjured, out of danger **3** not involving risk **4** *baseball* having successfully reached a base ▷ *n* **5** strong lockable container **6** *esp. Canad slang* condom **safely** *adv* **safe-conduct** *n* permit allowing travel through a dangerous area **safe deposit** place where valuables can be stored safely **safekeeping** *n* protection

safeguard *n* **1** protection ▷ *v* **2** protect

safety *n, pl* -**ties 1** state of being safe **2** *football* player who defends the area furthest back in the field **3** *football* Also **safety touch** play in which the offensive team causes the ball to cross its own goal line and fails to bring it out, scoring two points for the opposing team **safety net** net to catch performers on a trapeze or high wire if they fall **safety pin** pin with a spring fastening and a guard over the point when closed **safety valve** valve that allows steam etc. to escape if pressure becomes excessive

saffron *n* **1** orange-coloured flavouring obtained from a crocus ▷ *adj* **2** orange

sag *v* **sagging, sagged 1** sink in the middle **2** tire **3** (of clothes) hang loosely ▷ *n* **4** droop

saga [**sah**-ga] *n* **1** legend of Norse heroes **2** any long story

sagacious *adj* wise

sagaciously *adv* **sagacity** *n*

sage[1] *n* aromatic herb with grey-green leaves

sage[2] *n* **1** very wise man ▷ *adj* **2** *lit* wise **sagely** *adv*

sago *n* starchy cereal from the powdered pith of the sago palm tree

said *v* past of **say**

sail *n* **1** sheet of fabric stretched to catch the wind for propelling a sailing boat **2** journey by boat **3** arm of a windmill ▷ *v* **4** travel by water **5** move smoothly **6** begin a voyage **sailor** *n* member of a ship's crew **sailboard** *n* board with a mast and single sail, used for windsurfing

saint *n* **1** *Christianity* person venerated after death as specially holy **2** exceptionally good person **saintly** *adj* **saintliness** *n*

saithe *n* dark-coloured edible sea fish

sake[1] *n* **1** benefit **2** purpose **for the sake of 1** for the purpose of **2** to please or benefit (someone)

sake[2], **saki** [**sah**-kee] *n* Japanese alcoholic drink made from fermented rice

salaam [sal-**ahm**] *n* low bow of greeting among Muslims

salacious *adj* excessively concerned with sex

salad *n* dish of raw vegetables, eaten as a meal or part of a meal

salamander *n* **1** type of lizard **2** mythical reptile supposed to live in fire

salami *n* highly spiced sausage

salary *n, pl* -**ries** fixed regular payment, usu. monthly, to an employee **salaried** *adj*

sale *n* **1** exchange of goods for money **2** selling of goods at unusually low prices

3 auction **saleable** adj fit or likely to be sold **salesman** (**saleswoman**) n person who sells goods **salesmanship** n skill in selling

salient [**say**-lee-ent] adj **1** prominent, noticeable ▷ n **2** mil projecting part of a front line

saline [**say**-line] adj containing salt **salinity** n

saliva [sal-**lie**-va] n liquid that forms in the mouth, spittle **salivary** adj **salivate** v produce saliva

sallow[1] adj of an unhealthy pale or yellowish colour

sallow[2] n tree or shrub related to the willow

sally n, pl -**lies 1** sudden brief attack by troops **2** witty remark ▷ v -**lying**, -**lied** (foll. by forth) **3** rush out **4** go out

salmon n **1** large fish with orange-pink flesh valued as food ▷ adj **2** orange-pink

salmonella n, pl -**lae** bacterium causing food poisoning

salon n **1** commercial premises of a hairdresser, beautician, etc. **2** elegant reception room for guests

saloon n **1** large public room, as on a ship **2** bar serving alcoholic drinks **3** Brit sedan

salsify n plant with a long white edible root

salt n **1** white crystalline substance used to season food **2** chemical compound of acid and metal ▷ v **3** season with salt **old salt** experienced sailor **with a pinch of salt** or **with a grain of salt** allowing for exaggeration **worth one's salt** efficient **salty** adj **saltcellar** n small container for salt at table

saltpetre n compound used in gunpowder and as a preservative

salubrious adj favourable to health **salubrity** n

Saluki n tall hound with a silky coat

salutary adj producing a beneficial result

salute n **1** motion of the arm as a formal military sign of respect **2** firing of guns as a military greeting of honour ▷ v **3** greet with a salute **4** make a salute **5** acknowledge with praise **salutation** n greeting by words or actions

salvage n **1** saving of a ship or other property from destruction **2** property so saved ▷ v **3** save from destruction or waste

salvation n fact or state of being saved from harm or the consequences of sin

salve n **1** healing or soothing ointment ▷ v **2** soothe or appease: salve one's conscience

salver n (silver) tray on which something is presented

salvia n plant with blue or red flowers

salvo n, pl -**vos**, -**voes 1** simultaneous discharge of guns etc. **2** burst of applause or questions

sal volatile [sal vol-**at**-ill-ee] n preparation of ammonia, used to revive a person who feels faint

SAM surface-to-air missile

Samaritan n person who helps people in distress

samba n, pl -**bas** lively Brazilian dance

same adj **1** identical, not different, unchanged **2** just mentioned **sameness** n

samovar n Russian tea urn

Samoyed n dog with a thick white coat and tightly curled tail

sampan n small boat with oars used in China

samphire n plant found on rocks by the seashore

sample n 1 part taken as representative of a whole 2 *music* short extract from an existing recording mixed into a backing track to produce a new recording ▷ v 3 take and test a sample of **sampler** n piece of embroidery showing the embroiderer's skill **sampling** n

samurai n, pl -rai member of an ancient Japanese warrior caste

sanatorium n, pl -riums, -ria 1 institution for invalids or convalescents 2 room for sick pupils at a boarding school

sanctify v -fying, -fied make holy **sanctification** n

sanctimonious adj making a show of piety

sanction n 1 permission, authorization 2 usu pl coercive measure or penalty ▷ v 3 allow, authorize

sanctity n sacredness, inviolability

sanctuary n, pl -aries 1 place of safety for a fugitive 2 place where animals or birds can live undisturbed 3 holy place 4 part of a church nearest the altar

sanctum n, pl -tums, -ta 1 sacred place 2 person's private room

sand n 1 substance consisting of small grains of rock, esp. on a beach or in a desert **sands** 2 stretches of sand forming a beach or desert ▷ v 3 smooth with sandpaper **sander** n power tool for smoothing surfaces **sandy** adj 1 covered with sand 2 (of hair) reddish-fair **sandbag** n bag filled with sand, used as protection against gunfire, floodwater, etc. **sandblast** v, n (clean with) a jet of sand blown from a nozzle under pressure

sandpaper n paper coated with sand for smoothing a surface **sandpiper** n shore bird with a long bill and slender legs **sandstone** n rock composed of sand **sandstorm** n desert wind that whips up clouds of sand

sandal n light shoe consisting of a sole attached by straps

sandalwood n sweet-scented wood

sandwich n 1 two slices of bread with a layer of food between ▷ v 2 insert between two other things **sandwich board** pair of boards hung over a person's shoulders to display advertisements in front and behind

sane adj 1 of sound mind 2 sensible, rational **sanity** n

sang v past tense of **sing**

sang-froid [sahng **frwah**] n composure, self-possession

sanguinary adj 1 accompanied by bloodshed 2 bloodthirsty

sanguine adj cheerful, optimistic

sanitary adj promoting health by getting rid of dirt and germs **sanitation** n sanitary measures, esp. drainage or sewerage

sank v past tense of **sink**

Sanskrit n ancient language of India

sap[1] n 1 moisture that circulates in plants 2 energy 3 *informal* gullible person

sap[2] v sapping, sapped 1 undermine 2 weaken ▷ n 3 trench dug to undermine an enemy position **sapper** n soldier in an engineering unit

sapient [**say**-pee-ent] adj lit wise, shrewd **sapience** n

sapling n young tree

sapphire n 1 blue precious stone ▷ adj 2 deep blue

S

saraband, sarabande n slow stately Spanish dance

Saracen n hist Arab or Muslim who opposed the Crusades

sarcasm n (use of) bitter or wounding ironic language **sarcastic** adj **sarcastically** adv

sarcophagus n, pl -**gi**, -**guses** stone coffin

sardine n small fish of the herring family, usu. preserved in tightly packed cans

sardonic adj mocking or scornful **sardonically** adv

sargassum, sargasso n type of floating seaweed

sari, saree n long piece of cloth draped around the body and over one shoulder, worn by Hindu women

sarong n long piece of cloth tucked around the waist or under the armpits, worn esp. in Malaysia

sarsaparilla n soft drink, orig. made from the root of a tropical American plant

sartorial adj of men's clothes or tailoring

sash[1] n decorative strip of cloth worn round the waist or over one shoulder

sash[2] n wooden frame containing the panes of a window **sash window** window consisting of two sashes that can be opened by sliding one over the other

Sask. Saskatchewan

saskatoon n N American shrub with purplish berries

Sasquatch n same as **Bigfoot**

sassafras n American tree with aromatic bark used medicinally

Sassenach n Scot English person

sat v past of **sit**

Satan n the Devil **satanic** adj **1** of Satan **2** supremely evil **Satanism** n worship of Satan

satay, saté [sat-ay] n Indonesian and Malaysian dish consisting of pieces of chicken, pork, etc. grilled on skewers and served with peanut sauce

satchel n bag, usu. with a shoulder strap, for carrying school books

sate v satisfy (a desire or appetite) fully

satellite n **1** man-made device orbiting in space **2** heavenly body that orbits another **3** country that is dependent on a more powerful one **4** of or used in the transmission of television signals from a satellite to the home

satiate [say-she-ate] v **1** satisfy fully **2** surfeit **satiety** [sat-tie-a-tee] n feeling of having had too much

satin n silky fabric with a glossy surface on one side **satiny** adj of or like satin **satinwood** n tropical tree yielding hard wood

satire n **1** use of ridicule to expose vice or folly **2** poem or other work that does this **satirical** adj **satirist** n **satirize** v ridicule by means of satire

satisfy v -**fying**, -**fied 1** please, content **2** provide amply for (a need or desire) **3** convince, persuade **satisfaction** n **satisfactory** adj

satnav n motoring informal satellite navigation

satsuma n kind of small orange

saturate v **1** soak thoroughly **2** cause to absorb the maximum amount of something **saturation** n

Saturday n seventh day of the week

Saturn n **1** Roman god **2** one of the planets **saturnine** adj gloomy in temperament or appearance **saturnalia** *n* wild revelry

satyr *n* **1** woodland god, part man, part goat **2** lustful man

sauce *n* **1** liquid added to food to enhance flavour **2** *informal* impudence **saucy** *adj* **1** impudent **2** pert, jaunty **saucily** *adv* **saucepan** *n* cooking pot with a long handle

saucer *n* small round dish put under a cup

sauerkraut *n* shredded cabbage fermented in brine

sauna *n* Finnish-style steam bath

saunter *v* **1** walk in a leisurely manner, stroll ▷ *n* **2** leisurely walk

saurian *adj* of or like a lizard

sausage *n* minced meat in an edible tube-shaped skin **sausage roll** skinless sausage covered in pastry

sauté [**so**-tay] *v* fry quickly in a little fat

savage *adj* **1** wild, untamed **2** cruel and violent **3** uncivilized, primitive ▷ *n* **4** uncivilized person ▷ *v* **5** attack ferociously **savagely** *adv* **savagery** *n*

savanna, savannah *n* extensive open grassy plain in Africa

savant *n* learned person

save *v* **1** rescue or preserve from harm, protect **2** keep for the future **3** set aside (money) **4** *sports* prevent the scoring of (a goal) ▷ *n* **5** *sports* act of preventing a goal **6** *baseball* statistical credit awarded to a relief pitcher for keeping his or her team's lead in a winning game **saver** *n* **saving** *n* economy **savings** *pl n* money put by for future use

saveloy *n* spicy smoked sausage

saviour *n* **1** person who

rescues another **2** **Saviour** Christ

savoir-faire [sav-wahr **fair**] *n* *French* ability to do and say the right thing in any situation

savory *n* aromatic herb used in cooking

savour *n* **1** characteristic taste or odour **2** slight but distinctive quality ▷ *v* **3** (foll. by *of*) have a flavour or suggestion of **4** enjoy, relish **savoury** *adj* **1** salty or spicy **2** not sweet ▷ *n* **3** *Brit* savoury dish served before or after a meal

savoy *n* variety of cabbage

savvy *slang* ▷ *v* **-vying,** **-vied 1** understand ▷ *n* **2** understanding, intelligence

saw¹ *n* **1** cutting tool with a toothed metal blade ▷ *v* **sawing, sawed, sawed** *or* **sawn 2** cut with a saw **3** move (something) back and forth **sawyer** *n* person who saws timber for a living **sawdust** *n* fine wood fragments made in sawing **sawfish** *n* fish with a long toothed snout **sawmill** *n* mill where timber is sawn into planks **saw-off** *n slang* compromise or settlement

saw² *v* past tense of **see¹**

saw³ *n* wise saying, proverb

sax *n informal* short for **saxophone**

saxifrage *n* alpine rock plant with small flowers

Saxon *n* **1** member of the W Germanic people who settled widely in Europe in the early Middle Ages ▷ *adj* **2** of the Saxons

saxophone *n* brass wind instrument with keys and a curved body **saxophonist** *n*

say *v* **saying, said 1** speak or utter **2** express (an idea) in words **3** suppose as an example or possibility **4** give as one's opinion ▷ *n* **5** right or chance to speak **6** share in a decision **saying** n maxim, proverb

SC Star of Courage

scab n **1** crust formed over a wound **2** offensive blackleg **scabby** adj **1** covered with scabs **2** informal despicable

scabbard n sheath for a sword or dagger

scabies [**skay**-beez] n itchy skin disease

scabious [**skay**-bee-uss] n plant with globular blue flower heads

scabrous [**skay**-bruss] adj **1** indecent **2** rough and scaly

scaffold n **1** temporary platform for workmen **2** gallows **scaffolding** n (materials for building) scaffolds

scalar n, adj (variable quantity) having magnitude but no direction

scald v **1** burn with hot liquid or steam **2** sterilize with boiling water **3** heat (liquid) almost to boiling point ▷ n **4** injury by scalding

scale¹ n **1** one of the thin overlapping plates covering fishes and reptiles **2** thin flake **3** coating which forms in kettles etc. due to hard water **4** tartar formed on the teeth ▷ v **5** remove scales from **6** come off in scales **scaly** adj

scale² n often pl weighing instrument

scale³ n **1** graduated table or sequence of marks at regular intervals, used as a reference in making measurements **2** fixed series of notes in music **3** ratio of size between a thing and a representation of it **4** relative degree or extent ▷ v **6** climb **scale up** or **scale down** v increase or

decrease proportionately in size

scalene adj (of a triangle) with three unequal sides

scallop n **1** edible shellfish **2** one of a series of small curves along an edge **scalloped** adj decorated with small curves along the edge

scallywag n informal scamp, rascal

scalp n **1** skin and hair on top of the head ▷ v **2** cut off the scalp of

scalpel n small surgical knife

scamp n **1** mischievous child ▷ v **2** do carelessly

scamper v **1** run about hurriedly or in play ▷ n **2** scampering

scampi pl n large prawns

scan v **scanning, scanned** **1** scrutinize carefully **2** glance over quickly **3** examine or search (an area) by passing a radar or sonar beam over it **4** (of verse) conform to metrical rules ▷ n **5** scanning **scanner** n electronic device used for scanning **scansion** n metrical scanning of verse

scandal n **1** disgraceful action or event **2** malicious gossip **scandalize** v shock by scandal **scandalous** adj

scant adj barely sufficient, meagre

scanty adj **scantier, scantiest** barely sufficient or not sufficient **scantily** adv **scantiness** n

scapegoat n person made to bear the blame for others

scapula n, pl **-lae, -las** shoulder blade **scapular** adj of the scapula

scar n **1** mark left by a healed wound **2** permanent emotional damage left by an unpleasant experience ▷ v **scarring, scarred 3** mark or become marked with a scar

scarab n sacred beetle of ancient Egypt

scarce adj 1 not common, rarely found 2 insufficient to meet demand **make oneself scarce** informal go away **scarcely** adv 1 only just 2 not quite 3 definitely or probably not **scarcity** n

scare v 1 frighten or be frightened ▷ n 2 fright, sudden panic **scary** adj informal frightening **scarecrow** n 1 figure dressed in old clothes, set up to scare birds away from crops 2 raggedly dressed person **scaremonger** n person who spreads alarming rumours

scarf¹ n piece of material worn round the neck, head, or shoulders

scarf² n 1 joint between two pieces of timber made by notching the ends and fastening them together ▷ v 2 join in this way

scarify v -fying, -fied 1 scratch or cut slightly all over 2 break up and loosen (topsoil) 3 criticize mercilessly **scarification** n

scarlet adj, n brilliant red **scarlet fever** infectious fever with a scarlet rash

scarp n steep slope

scarper v slang run away

scat¹ v scatting, scatted informal go away

scat² n jazz singing using improvised vocal sounds instead of words

scathing adj harshly critical

scatter v 1 throw about in various directions 2 put here and there 3 disperse **scatterbrain** n empty-headed person

scatty adj -tier, -tiest informal empty-headed

scavenge v search for (anything usable) among discarded material **scavenger** n 1 person who scavenges 2 animal that feeds on decaying matter

scenario n, pl -rios 1 summary of the plot of a play or film 2 imagined sequence of future events

scene n 1 place of action of a real or imaginary event 2 subdivision of a play or film in which the action is continuous 3 view of a place 4 display of emotion 5 informal specific activity or interest: the fashion scene **behind the scenes** 1 backstage 2 in secret **scenery** n 1 natural features of a landscape 2 painted backcloths or screens used on stage to represent the scene of action **scenic** adj picturesque

scent n 1 pleasant smell 2 smell left in passing, by which an animal can be traced 3 series of clues 4 perfume ▷ v 5 detect by smell 6 suspect 7 fill with fragrance

sceptic [skep-tik] n person who habitually doubts generally accepted beliefs **sceptical** adj **sceptically** adv **scepticism** n

sceptre n ornamental rod symbolizing royal power

schedule n 1 plan of procedure for a project 2 timetable 3 list ▷ v 4 plan to occur at a certain time

schema n, pl -mata overall plan or diagram **schematic** adj presented as a plan or diagram **schematize** v arrange in a scheme

scheme n 1 systematic plan 2 secret plot ▷ v 3 plan in an underhand manner **scheming** adj, n

scherzo [skairt-so] n, pl -zos, -zi brisk lively piece of music

schism [skizz-um] n (group

resulting from) division in an organization **schismatic** *adj, n*

schist [skist] *n* crystalline rock which splits into layers

schizoid *adj* **1** abnormally introverted **2** *informal* contradictory ▷ *n offensive* **3** schizoid person

schizophrenia *n* **1** mental illness involving deterioration of or confusion about the personality **2** *informal* contradictory behaviour or attitudes **schizophrenic** *adj, n*

schmaltz *n* excessive sentimentality **schmaltzy** *adj*

schnapps *n* strong alcoholic spirit

schnitzel *n* thin slice of meat, esp. veal

scholar *n* **1** learned person **2** pupil **3** student receiving a scholarship **scholarly** *adj* learned **scholarship** *n* **1** learning **2** financial aid given to a student because of academic merit **scholastic** *adj* of schools or scholars

school[1] *n* **1** place where children are taught or instruction is given in a subject **2** group of artists, thinkers, etc. with shared principles or methods ▷ *v* **3** educate **4** discipline, train

school[2] *n* shoal of fish, whales, etc.

schooner *n* **1** sailing ship rigged fore-and-aft **2** large glass

sciatica *n* severe pain in the large nerve in the back of the leg **sciatic** *adj* **1** of the hip **2** of or afflicted with sciatica

science *n* systematic study and knowledge of natural or physical phenomena **scientific** *adj* **1** of science **2** systematic **scientifically** *adv* **scientist** *n* person who studies or practises a science

science fiction stories making imaginative use of scientific knowledge

sci-fi *n* short for **science fiction**

scimitar *n* curved oriental sword

scintillating *adj* animated or witty

scion [sy-on] *n* **1** descendant or heir **2** shoot of a plant for grafting

scissors *pl n* cutting instrument with two crossed pivoted blades

sclerosis *n, pl* **-ses** abnormal hardening of body tissues

scoff[1] *v* express derision

scoff[2] *v slang* eat rapidly

scold *v* **1** find fault with, reprimand ▷ *n* **2** person who scolds **scolding** *n*

sconce *n* bracket on a wall for holding candles or lights

scone *n* small plain cake baked in an oven or on a griddle

scoop *n* **1** shovel-like tool for ladling or hollowing out **2** news story reported in one newspaper before all its rivals ▷ *v* **3** take up or hollow out with or as if with a scoop **4** beat (rival newspapers) in reporting a news item

scoot *v slang* leave or move quickly **scooter** *n* **1** child's vehicle propelled by pushing on the ground with one foot **2** light motorcycle

scope *n* **1** range of activity **2** opportunity for using abilities

scorch *v* **1** burn on the surface **2** parch or shrivel from heat ▷ *n* **3** slight burn **scorcher** *n* *informal* very hot day

score *n* **1** points gained in a game or competition **2** twenty **3** written version of a piece of music showing parts for each musician **4** mark or cut **5** grievance: *settle old scores* **scores 6** lots ▷ *v* **7** gain points in a game **8** mark or cut **9** (foll. by *out*) cross out **10** arrange music (for) **11** keep a record of points **12** achieve a success

scorn *n* **1** contempt, derision ▷ *v* **2** despise **3** reject with contempt **scornful** *adj* **scornfully** *adv*

scorpion *n* small lobster-shaped animal with a sting at the end of a jointed tail

Scot *n* person from Scotland **Scottish** *adj* of Scotland, its people, or their languages (Also **Scots**) **Scotch** *n* whisky distilled in Scotland **Scotch tape** *n* **1** ® type of adhesive tape ▷ *v* **2** stick with Scotch tape **Scotsman** (**Scotswoman**) *n*

scotch *v* put an end to

scot-free *adj* without harm or punishment

scoundrel *n old-fashioned* villainous person

scour¹ *v* **1** clean or polish by rubbing with something rough **2** clear or flush out **scourer** *n* small rough nylon pad used for cleaning pots and pans

scour² *v* search thoroughly and energetically

scourge *n* **1** person or thing causing severe suffering **2** whip ▷ *v* **3** cause severe suffering to **4** whip

scout *n* **1** person sent out to reconnoitre **2 Scout** member of the Scout Association, an organization for boys which aims to develop character and promotes outdoor activities ▷ *v* **3** act as a scout **4** reconnoitre **Scouter** *n* leader of a troop of Scouts

scow *n* unpowered barge

scowl *v, n* (have) an angry or sullen expression

scrabble *v* scrape at with the hands, feet, or claws

scrag *n* lean end of a neck of mutton **scraggy** *adj* thin, bony

scram *v* **scramming, scrammed 1** (of a nuclear reactor) shut or be shut down in an emergency **2** *informal* go away hastily ▷ *n* **3** emergency shutdown of a nuclear reactor

scramble *v* **1** climb or crawl hastily or awkwardly **2** struggle with others (for) **3** mix up **4** cook (eggs beaten up with milk) **5** render (transmitted speech) unintelligible by an electronic device **6** (of an aircraft or aircrew) take off hurriedly in an emergency ▷ *n* **7** scrambling **8** rough climb **9** disorderly struggle **10** motorcycle race over rough ground **scrambler** *n* electronic device that renders transmitted speech unintelligible

scrap *n* **1** small piece **2** waste metal collected for reprocessing **3** *informal* fight or quarrel **scraps 4** leftover food ▷ *v* **scrapping, scrapped 5** discard as useless **6** *informal* fight or quarrel **scrappy** *adj* badly organized or done **scrapbook** *n* book with blank pages in which newspaper cuttings or pictures are stuck

scrape *v* **1** rub with something rough or sharp **2** clean or smooth thus **3** rub with a harsh noise **4** economize ▷ *n* **5** act or sound of scraping **6** mark or wound caused by scraping **7** *informal* awkward situation **scraper** *n* **scrape through** *v* succeed in or obtain with difficulty

scratch v 1 mark or cut with claws, nails, or anything rough or sharp 2 scrape (skin) with nails or claws to relieve itching 3 withdraw from a race or competition ▷ n 4 wound, mark, or sound made by scratching ▷ adj 5 put together at short notice **from scratch** from the very beginning **up to scratch** up to standard **scratchy** adj

scrawl v 1 write carelessly or hastily ▷ n 2 scribbled writing

scrawny adj **scrawnier, scrawniest** thin and bony

scream v 1 utter a piercing cry, esp. of fear or pain 2 utter with a scream ▷ n 3 shrill piercing cry 4 informal very funny person or thing

scree n slope of loose shifting stones

screech[1] v, n (utter) a shrill cry

screech[2] n slang (esp. in Newfoundland) a type of cheap dark rum

screed n long tedious piece of writing

screen n 1 movable structure used to shelter, divide, or conceal something 2 surface of a television set, VDU, etc., on which an image is formed 3 white surface on which photographs are projected ▷ v 4 shelter or conceal with or as if with a screen 5 show (a film) 6 examine (a person or group) to determine suitability for a task or to detect the presence of disease or weapons **the screen** cinema generally **screen saver** computers changing image on a monitor when the computer is operative but idle

screw n 1 metal pin with a spiral ridge along its length, twisted into materials to fasten them together 2 slang prison guard ▷ v 3 turn (a screw) 4 fasten with screw(s) 5 twist 6 informal extort

screwy adj informal crazy or eccentric **screwball** slang ▷ n 1 odd person 2 baseball pitch that curves towards the side from which it was thrown ▷ adj 3 odd **screwdriver** n tool for turning screws **screw up** v informal 1 bungle 2 distort

scribble v 1 write hastily or illegibly 2 make meaningless or illegible marks ▷ n 3 something scribbled

scribe n 1 person who copied manuscripts before the invention of printing 2 Bible scholar of the Jewish Law **scribal** adj

scrimmage n rough or disorderly struggle

scrimp v be very economical

scrip n certificate representing a claim to stocks or shares

script n 1 text of a film, play, or TV programme 2 particular system of writing: Arabic script 3 handwriting

scripture n sacred writings of a religion **scriptural** adj

scrofula n tuberculosis of the lymphatic glands **scrofulous** adj

scroll n 1 roll of parchment or paper 2 ornamental carving shaped like this ▷ v 3 move (text) up or down on a VDU screen

scrotum n, pl -ta, -tums pouch of skin containing the testicles

scrounge v informal get by cadging or begging **scrounger** n

scrub[1] v scrubbing, scrubbed 1 clean by rubbing, often with a hard brush and water 2 informal delete or cancel ▷ n 3 scrubbing **scrubs** pl n med light, loose clothing worn by hospital staff

scrub² n **1** stunted trees **2** area of land covered with scrub **scrubby** adj **1** covered with scrub **2** stunted **3** informal shabby

scruff n nape (of the neck)

scruffy adj **scruffier, scruffiest** unkempt or shabby

scrum, scrummage n **1** rugby restarting of play in which opposing packs of forwards push against each other to gain possession of the ball **2** disorderly struggle

scrumptious adj informal delicious

scrunch v **1** crumple or crunch or be crumpled or crunched ▷ n **2** act or sound of scrunching **scrunchie** n loop of elastic covered loosely with fabric, used to hold the hair in a ponytail

scruple n **1** doubt produced by one's conscience or morals ▷ v **2** have doubts on moral grounds **scrupulous** adj **1** very conscientious **2** very careful or precise **scrupulously** adv

scrutiny n, pl **-nies** close examination **scrutinize** v examine closely

scuba diving n sport of swimming under water using cylinders containing compressed air attached to breathing apparatus

scud v **scudding, scudded** move along swiftly

scuff v **1** drag (the feet) while walking **2** scrape (one's shoes) by doing so ▷ n **3** mark caused by scuffing

scuffle v **1** fight in a disorderly manner **2** move by shuffling ▷ n **3** disorderly struggle **4** scuffling sound

scull n **1** small oar ▷ v **2** row (a boat) using a scull

scullery n, pl **-leries** small room where washing-up and other kitchen work is done

sculpture n **1** art of making figures or designs in wood, stone, etc. **2** product of this art ▷ v **3** Also **sculpt** represent in sculpture **sculptor** (**sculptress**) n **sculptural** adj

scum n **1** impure or waste matter on the surface of a liquid **2** worthless people **scummy** adj

scupper v informal defeat or ruin

scurf n flaky skin on the scalp **scurfy** adj

scurrilous adj untrue and defamatory **scurrility** n

scurry v **-rying, -ried 1** move hastily ▷ n **2** act or sound of scurrying

scurvy n disease caused by lack of vitamin C

scut n short tail of the hare, rabbit, or deer

scuttle¹ n fireside container for coal

scuttle² v **1** run with short quick steps ▷ n **2** hurried run

scuttle³ v make a hole in (a ship) to sink it

scythe n **1** long-handled tool with a curved blade for cutting grass ▷ v **2** cut with a scythe

SE southeast(ern)

sea n **1** mass of salt water covering three quarters of the earth's surface **2** particular area of this **3** turbulence or swell **4** vast expanse **at sea 1** in a ship on the ocean **2** confused or bewildered **sea anemone** sea animal with suckers like petals **seaboard** n coast **sea dog** experienced sailor **seafaring** adj working or travelling by sea **seafood** n edible saltwater fish or shellfish **sea gull** gull **sea horse** small sea fish with a plated body and horselike head **sea level** average level of the sea's surface in relation to the land **sea lion** kind of large seal **seaman** n sailor **seaplane** n aircraft designed to take off from and land on water **seasick** adj suffering from nausea caused by the motion of a ship **seasickness** n **seaside** n area, esp. a holiday resort, on the coast **sea urchin** sea animal with a round spiky shell **seaweed** n plant growing in the sea **seaworthy** adj (of a ship) in fit condition for a sea voyage

seal¹ n 1 piece of wax, lead, etc. with a special design impressed upon it, attached to a letter or document as a mark of authentication 2 device or material used to close an opening tightly ▷ v 3 make airtight or watertight 4 close with or as if with a seal 5 affix a seal to or stamp with a seal 6 decide (one's fate) irrevocably **sealant** n any substance used for sealing **seal off** v enclose or isolate (a place) completely

seal² n amphibious mammal with flippers as limbs **sealskin** n

seam n 1 line where two edges are joined, as by stitching 2 thin layer of coal or ore ▷ v 3 mark with furrows or wrinkles **seamless** adj **seamy** adj sordid

seamstress n woman who sews

seance [say-anss] n meeting at which spiritualists attempt to communicate with the dead

sear v 1 scorch, burn the surface of 2 cause to wither

search v 1 examine closely in order to find something ▷ n 2 searching **searching** adj

keen or thorough: *a searching look* **search engine** *computers* internet service enabling users to search for items of interest **searchlight** n powerful light with a beam that can be shone in any direction

season n 1 one of four divisions of the year, each of which has characteristic weather conditions 2 period during which a thing happens or is plentiful 3 fitting or proper time ▷ v 4 flavour with salt, herbs, etc. 5 dry (timber) till ready for use **seasonable** adj 1 appropriate for the season 2 timely or opportune **seasonal** adj depending on or varying with the seasons **seasoned** adj experienced **seasoning** n salt, herbs, etc. added to food to enhance flavour **season ticket** ticket for a series of journeys or events within a specified period

seat n 1 thing designed or used for sitting on 2 place to sit in a theatre, esp. one that requires a ticket 3 buttocks 4 membership of a legislative or administrative body 5 country house ▷ v 6 cause to sit 7 provide seating for **seat belt** belt worn in an automobile or aircraft to prevent a person being thrown forward in a crash

sebaceous adj of, like, or secreting fat or oil

secateurs pl n small pruning shears

secede v withdraw formally from a political alliance or federation **secession** n

seclude v keep (a person) from contact with others **secluded** adj private, sheltered **seclusion** n

second[1] *adj* **1** coming directly after the first **2** alternate, additional **3** inferior ▷ *n* **4** person or thing coming second **5** sixtieth part of a minute **6** moment **7** attendant in a duel or boxing match **seconds** **8** inferior goods ▷ *v* **9** express formal support for (a motion proposed in a meeting) **secondly** *adv* **second-class** *adj* **1** inferior **2** cheaper, slower, or less comfortable than first-class **second-hand** *adj* bought after use by another **second nature** something so habitual that it seems part of one's character **second sight** supposed ability to predict events **second thoughts** revised opinion on a matter already considered **second wind** renewed ability to continue effort

second[2] [si-**kawnd**] *v* transfer (a person) temporarily to another job **secondment** *n*

secondary *adj* **1** coming after or derived from what is primary or first **2** of less importance **3** relating to the education of people between the ages of 11 and 18

secret *adj* **1** kept from the knowledge of others ▷ *n* **2** something kept secret **3** mystery **4** underlying explanation: *the secret of my success* **in secret** without other people knowing **secretly** *adv* **secrecy** *n* **secretive** *adj* inclined to keep things secret **secretiveness** *n*

secretariat *n* administrative office or staff of a legislative body

secretary *n, pl* **-ries** **1** person who deals with correspondence and general clerical work **2** head of a state department: *Home Secretary* **secretarial** *adj* **Secretary of State** head of a major government department

secrete *v* **1** hide or conceal **2** (of an organ, gland, etc.) produce and release (a substance) **secretion** *n* **secretory** [sek-**reet**-or-ee] *adj*

sect *n* subdivision of a religious or political group, esp. one with extreme beliefs **sectarian** *adj* **1** of a sect **2** narrow-minded

section *n* **1** part cut off **2** part or subdivision of something **3** distinct part of a country or community **4** cutting **5** drawing of something as if cut through ▷ *v* **6** cut or divide into sections **sectional** *adj*

sector *n* **1** part or subdivision **2** part of a circle enclosed by two radii and the arc which they cut off

secular *adj* **1** worldly, as opposed to sacred **2** not connected with religion or the church

secure *adj* **1** free from danger **2** free from anxiety **3** firmly fixed **4** reliable ▷ *v* **5** obtain **6** make safe **7** make firm **8** guarantee payment of (a loan) by giving something as security **securely** *adv* **security** *n* **1** state of being secure **2** precautions against theft, espionage, or other danger **3** something given or pledged to guarantee payment of a loan **4** certificate of ownership of a share, stock, or bond

sedan *n* automobile with a fixed roof **sedan chair** *hist* enclosed chair for one person, carried on poles by two bearers

sedate[1] *adj* **1** calm and dignified **2** sober or decorous **sedately** *adv*

sedate² v give a sedative drug to **sedation** n **sedative** adj **1** having a soothing or calming effect ▷ n **2** sedative drug

sedentary [sed-en-tree] adj done sitting down, involving little exercise

sedge n coarse grasslike plant growing on wet ground

sediment n **1** matter which settles to the bottom of a liquid **2** material deposited by water, ice, or wind **sedimentary** adj

sedition n speech or action encouraging rebellion against the government **seditious** adj

seduce v **1** persuade into sexual intercourse **2** tempt into wrongdoing **seducer** (**seductress**) n **seduction** n **seductive** adj

sedulous adj diligent or persevering **sedulously** adv

see¹ v **seeing, saw, seen** **1** perceive with the eyes or mind **2** watch **3** find out **4** make sure (of something) **5** consider or decide **6** have experience of **7** meet or visit **8** interview **9** frequent the company of **10** accompany **seeing** conj in view of the fact that

see² n diocese of a bishop

seed n **1** mature fertilized grain of a plant **2** such grains used for sowing **3** origin **4** obsolete offspring **5** sports seeded player ▷ v **6** sow with seed **7** remove seeds from **8** arrange (the draw of a sports tournament) so that the outstanding competitors will not meet in the early rounds **go to seed** or **run to seed 1** (of plants) produce or shed seeds after flowering **2** lose vigour or usefulness **seedling** n young plant raised from a seed **seedy** adj

1 shabby **2** informal unwell

seek v **seeking, sought 1** try to find or obtain **2** try (to do something)

seem v appear to be **seeming** adj apparent but not real **seemingly** adv

seemly adj **-lier, -liest** proper or fitting **seemliness** n

seen v past participle of **see**

seep v trickle through slowly, ooze **seepage** n

seer n prophet

seersucker n light cotton fabric with a slightly crinkled surface

seesaw n **1** plank balanced in the middle so that two people seated on either end ride up and down alternately ▷ v **2** move up and down

seethe v **seething, seethed 1** be very agitated **2** (of a liquid) boil or foam

segment n **1** one of several sections into which something may be divided ▷ v **2** divide into segments **segmentation** n

segregate v set apart **segregation** n

seine [sane] n large fishing net that hangs vertically from floats

seismic adj relating to earthquakes **seismology** n study of earthquakes **seismologic** or **seismological** adj **seismologist** n **seismograph** or **seismometer** n instrument that records the strength of earthquakes

seize v **1** take hold of forcibly or quickly **2** take immediate advantage of **3** (usu. foll. by up) (of mechanical parts) stick tightly through overheating **seizure** n **1** seizing or being seized **2** sudden violent attack of an illness

seldom adv not often, rarely

select v **1** pick out or choose ▷ adj **2** chosen in preference to others **3** restricted to a particular group, exclusive **selection** n **1** selecting **2** things that have been selected **3** range from which something may be selected **selective** adj chosen or choosing carefully **selectively** adv **selectivity** n **selector** n

selenium n nonmetallic element with photoelectric properties

self n, pl **selves 1** distinct individuality or identity of a person or thing **2** one's basic nature **3** one's own welfare or interests **selfie** n photograph taken by pointing camera at oneself **selfish** adj caring too much about oneself and not enough about others **selfishly** adv **selfishness** n **selfless** adj unselfish

self- combining form **1** indicating of oneself or itself **2** indicating by, to, in, due to, for, or from the self **3** indicating automatic(ally) **self-assured** adj confident **self-catering** adj (of accommodation) for people who provide their own food **self-coloured** adj having only a single colour **self-conscious** adj embarrassed at being the object of others' attention **self-contained** adj **1** containing everything needed, complete **2** (of an apartment) having its own facilities **self-determination** n right of a nation to decide its own form of government **self-evident** adj obvious without proof **self-help** n **1** use of one's own abilities to solve problems **2** practice of solving one's problems within a group of people with similar problems **self-interest** n one's own advantage **self-made** adj having achieved wealth or status by one's own efforts **self-possessed** adj having control of one's emotions, calm **self-righteous** adj thinking oneself more virtuous than others **self-rising** adj (of flour) containing a raising agent **selfsame** adj the very same **self-seeking** adj, n seeking to promote only one's own interests **self-service** adj denoting a shop, café, or garage where customers serve themselves and then pay a cashier **self-styled** adj using a title or name that one has taken without right **self-sufficient** adj able to provide for oneself without help **self-willed** adj stubbornly determined to get one's own way

sell v **selling, sold 1** exchange (something) for money **2** stock, deal in **3** (of goods) be sold **4** (foll. by for) have a specified price **5** informal persuade (someone) to accept (something) ▷ n **6** manner of selling **seller** n **sell out** v **1** dispose of (something) completely by selling **2** informal betray **sellout** n **1** performance of a show etc. for which all the tickets are sold **2** informal betrayal

selvage, selvedge n edge of cloth, woven so as to prevent unravelling

selves n plural of **self**

semantic adj relating to the meaning of words **semantics** pl n study of linguistic meaning

semaphore n system of signalling by holding two flags in different positions to represent letters of the alphabet

semblance n outward or

superficial appearance

semen n sperm-carrying fluid produced by male animals

semester n either of two divisions of the academic year

semi n informal semidetached house

semi- prefix **1** indicating half: semidome **2** indicating partly or almost: semiprofessional

semibreve n Brit whole note

semicolon n the punctuation mark (;)

semiconductor n substance with an electrical conductivity that increases with temperature

semidetached adj (of a house) joined to another on one side

semifinal n match or round before the final **semifinalist** n

seminal adj **1** capable of developing **2** original and influential **3** of semen or seed

seminar n meeting of a group of students for discussion

seminary n, pl **-ries** college for priests

semiprecious adj (of gemstones) having less value than precious stones

semiquaver n musical note half the length of a quaver

Semite n member of the group of peoples including Jews and Arabs **Semitic** adj

semitone n smallest interval between two notes in Western music

semolina n hard grains of wheat left after the milling of flour, used to make puddings and pasta

Senate n **1** upper house of some parliaments **2** governing body of some universities **senator** n member of a Senate **senatorial** adj

send v **sending, sent 1** cause (a person or thing) to go to or be taken or transmitted to a place **2** bring into a specified state or condition **sendoff** n demonstration of good wishes at a person's departure **send up** v informal make fun of by imitating **send-up** n informal imitation

senile adj mentally or physically weak because of old age **senility** n

senior adj **1** superior in rank or standing **2** older **3** of or for older pupils ▷ n **4** senior person **seniority** n

senna n **1** tropical plant **2** its dried leaves or pods used as a laxative

señor [sen-**nyor**] n, pl **-ores** Spanish term of address equivalent to sir or Mr **señora** [sen-**nyor**-a] n Spanish term of address equivalent to madam or Mrs **señorita** [sen-nyor-**ee**-ta] n Spanish term of address equivalent to madam or Miss

sensation n **1** ability to feel things physically **2** physical feeling **3** general feeling or awareness **4** state of excitement **5** exciting person or thing **sensational** adj **1** causing intense shock, anger, or excitement **2** informal very good **sensationalism** n deliberate use of sensational language or subject matter **sensationalist** adj, n

sense n **1** any of the faculties of perception or feeling (sight, hearing, touch, taste, or smell) **2** ability to perceive **3** feeling perceived through one of the senses **4** awareness **5** sometimes pl sound practical judgment or intelligence **6** specific meaning ▷ v **7** perceive **senseless** adj

sensible adj **1** having or showing good sense **2** (foll. by *of)* aware **3** practical: *sensible shoes* **sensibly** *adv* **sensibility** *n* ability to experience deep feelings

sensitive *adj* **1** responsive to external stimuli **2** easily hurt or offended **3** (of an instrument) responsive to slight changes **4** (of a subject) liable to arouse controversy or strong feelings **sensitively** *adv* **sensitivity** *n* **sensitize** *v* make sensitive

sensor *n* device that detects or measures the presence of something, such as radiation

sensory *adj* of the senses or sensation

sensual *adj* **1** giving pleasure to the body and senses rather than the mind **2** having a strong liking for physical pleasures **sensually** *adv* **sensuality** *n* **sensualism** *n* **sensualist** *n*

sensuous *adj* pleasing to the senses **sensuously** *adv*

sent *v* past of **send**

sentence *n* **1** sequence of words capable of standing alone as a statement, question, or command **2** punishment passed on a criminal ▷ *v* **3** pass sentence on (a convicted person)

sententious *adj* **1** trying to sound wise **2** pompously moralizing **sententiously** *adv* **sententiousness** *n*

sentient [sen-tee-ent] *adj* capable of feeling **sentience** *n*

sentiment *n* **1** thought, opinion, or attitude **2** feeling expressed in words **3** exaggerated or mawkish emotion **sentimental** *adj* excessively romantic or nostalgic **sentimentalism** *n* **sentimentality** *n* **sentimentalize** *v* make sentimental

sentinel *n* sentry

sentry *n, pl* **-tries** soldier on watch

sepal *n* leaflike division of the calyx of a flower

separate *v* **1** act as a barrier between **2** divide up into parts **3** distinguish between **4** (of a married couple) stop living together ▷ *adj* **5** set apart **6** not the same, different **7** not shared, individual **separately** *adv* **separation** *n* **1** separating or being separated **2** *law* living apart of a married couple without divorce **separable** *adj* **separatist** *n* person who advocates the separation of a group or province from an organization or country, such as Quebec from Canada **separatism** *n* **separate school** school for a large religious minority

sepia *adj, n* reddish-brown (pigment)

sepsis *n* poisoning caused by pus-forming bacteria

Sept. September

September *n* ninth month of the year

septet *n* **1** group of seven performers **2** music for such a group

septic *adj* **1** (of a wound) infected **2** of or caused by harmful bacteria **septic tank** tank in which sewage is decomposed by the action of bacteria

septicemia, septicaemia [sep-tis-**see**-mee-a] *n* blood poisoning

septuagenarian *n, adj* (person) between seventy and seventy-nine years old

sepulchre [**sep**-pull-ker] *n* tomb or burial vault **sepulchral** [sip-**pulk**-ral] *adj* gloomy

sequel *n* **1** novel, play, or film

that continues the story of an earlier one **2** consequence

sequence n **1** arrangement of two or more things in successive order **2** the successive order of two or more things **3** section of a film showing a single uninterrupted episode **sequential** adj

sequester v **1** separate **2** seclude

sequestrate v confiscate (property) until its owner's debts are paid or a court order is complied with **sequestration** n

sequin n small ornamental metal disc on a garment **sequined** adj

sequoia n giant Californian coniferous tree

seraglio [sir-**ah**-lee-oh] n, pl -**raglios 1** harem of a Muslim palace **2** Turkish sultan's palace

seraph n member of the highest order of angels **seraphic** adj

Serbian, Serb adj **1** of Serbia ▷ n **2** person from Serbia **Serbo-Croat** or **Serbo-Croatian** adj, n (of) the chief official language of Serbia and Croatia

serenade n **1** music played or sung to a woman by a lover ▷ v **2** sing or play a serenade to (someone)

serendipity n gift of making fortunate discoveries by accident

serene adj calm, peaceful **serenely** adv **serenity** n

serf n medieval farm labourer who could not leave the land he worked on **serfdom** n

serge n strong woollen fabric

sergeant n **1** non-commissioned officer in the army **2** police officer ranking between constable and inspector **sergeant at arms** parliamentary or court officer with ceremonial duties **sergeant major** highest rank of non-commissioned officer in the army

serial n **1** story or play produced in successive instalments ▷ adj **2** of or forming a series **3** published or presented as a serial **serialize** v publish or present as a serial **serial killer** person who commits a series of murders

seriatim [seer-ree-**ah**-tim] adv one after another

series n, pl -**ries 1** group or succession of related things, usu. arranged in order **2** set of radio or TV programmes about the same subject or characters

serious adj **1** giving cause for concern **2** concerned with important matters **3** not cheerful, grave **4** sincere, not joking **5** informal extreme or remarkable **seriously** adv **seriousness** n

sermon n **1** speech on a religious or moral subject by a member of the clergy in a church service **2** long moralizing speech **sermonize** v make a long moralizing speech

serpent n snake **serpentine** adj twisting like a snake

serrated adj having a notched or sawlike edge **serration** n

serried adj in close formation

serum [**seer**-um] n **1** yellowish watery fluid left after blood has clotted **2** this fluid from the blood of immunized animals used for inoculation or vaccination

servant n person employed to do household work for another

serve v **1** work for (a person,

community, or cause)
2 perform official duties
3 attend to (customers)
4 provide with food or drink
5 present (food or drink)
6 provide with a service **7** be
a member of the armed forces
8 spend (time) in prison **9** be
useful or suitable **10** *tennis
etc* put (the ball) into play
11 deliver (a legal document)
to (a person) ▷ *n* **12** *tennis etc*
act of serving the ball

service *n* **1** serving **2** system
that provides something
needed by the public
3 overhaul of a machine
or vehicle **4** availability
for use **5** department of
public employment and its
employees **6** set of dishes etc.
for serving a meal **7** formal
religious ceremony **8** *tennis
etc* act, manner, or right of
serving the ball **services**
9 armed forces ▷ *v* **10** provide
a service or services to
11 overhaul (a machine or
vehicle) **serviceable** *adj*
1 useful or helpful **2** able
or ready to be used **service
apartment** apartment where
domestic services are provided
serviceberry *n* same as
saskatoon ▸ **serviceman** *n*
member of the armed forces
service road narrow road
giving access to houses and
shops **service station** garage
selling fuel for motor vehicles
serviette *n* table napkin
servile *adj* **1** too eager to obey
people, fawning **2** suitable for
a slave **servility** *n*
servitude *n* bondage or
slavery
servomechanism *n* device
which converts a small force
into a larger force, used esp. in
steering mechanisms
sesame [**sess**-am-ee] *n* plant
cultivated for its seeds and oil,
which are used in cooking

session *n* **1** meeting of a
court, parliament, or council
2 series or period of such
meetings **3** period spent in
an activity **4** academic term
or year
set *v* **setting, set 1** put
in a specified position or
state **2** make ready **3** make
or become firm or rigid
4 put (a broken bone) or
(of a broken bone) be put
into a normal position for
healing **5** establish, arrange
6 prescribe, assign **7** put to
music **8** arrange (hair) while
wet, so that it dries in position
9 (of the sun) go down ▷ *adj*
10 fixed or established
beforehand **11** rigid or
inflexible **12** conventional or
stereotyped **13** determined
(to do something) **14** ready
▷ *n* **15** number of things or
people grouped or belonging
together **16** *math* group of
numbers or objects that
satisfy a given condition or
share a property **17** television
or radio receiver **18** scenery
used in a play or film **19** *tennis
etc* group of games in a
match **setback** *n* anything
that delays progress **set
shot** *basketball* shot made
using both hands while
stationary **set square** flat
right-angled triangular
instrument used for drawing
angles **set theory** branch of
mathematics concerned with
the properties of sets **set up**
v arrange or establish **setup**
n way in which anything is
organized or arranged
sett, set *n* badger's burrow
settee *n* couch
setter *n* long-haired gun dog
setting *n* **1** background or
surroundings **2** time and
place where a film, book, etc.

s

is supposed to have taken place **3** music written for the words of a text **4** decorative metalwork in which a gem is set **5** plates and cutlery for a single place at table **6** descending below the horizon of the sun **7** position or level to which the controls of a machine can be adjusted

settle[1] *v* **1** arrange or put in order **2** establish or become established as a resident **3** colonize **4** make quiet, calm, or stable **5** come to rest **6** dispose of, conclude **7** end (a dispute) **8** pay (a bill) **9** bestow (property) legally **settlement** *n* **1** act of settling **2** place newly colonized **3** property bestowed legally **4** subsidence (of a building) **settler** *n* colonist

settle[2] *n* long wooden bench with high back and arms

seven *adj, n* one more than six **seventh** *adj, n* (of) number seven in a series **seventeen** *adj, n* ten and seven **seventeenth** *adj, n* **seventy** *adj, n* ten times seven **seventieth** *adj, n*

sever *v* **1** separate, divide **2** cut off **severance** *n* **severance pay** compensation paid by a firm to an employee for loss of employment

several *adj* **1** some, a few **2** various, separate ▷ *pron* **3** indefinite small number **severally** *adv* separately

severe *adj* **1** strict or harsh **2** very intense or unpleasant **3** strictly restrained in appearance **severely** *adv* **severity** *n*

sew *v* **sewing, sewed, sewn** or **sewed 1** join with thread repeatedly passed through with a needle **2** make or fasten by sewing

sewage *n* waste matter or

excrement carried away in sewers **sewer** *n* drain to remove waste water and sewage **sewerage** *n* system of sewers

sewn *v* a past participle of **sew**

sex *n* **1** state of being male or female **2** male or female category **3** sexual intercourse **4** sexual feelings or behaviour ▷ *v* **5** ascertain the sex of **sexy** *adj* **1** sexually exciting or attractive **2** *informal* exciting or trendy **sexism** *n* discrimination on the basis of a person's sex **sexist** *adj, n* **sexual** *adj* **sexually** *adv* **sexuality** *n* **sexual intercourse** genital sexual activity between two people **sex up** *v informal* make (something) more exciting

sexagenarian *n, adj* (person) between sixty and sixty-nine years old

sextant *n* navigator's instrument for measuring angles, as between the sun and horizon, to calculate one's position

sextet *n* **1** group of six performers **2** music for such a group

sexton *n* official in charge of a church and churchyard

SF science fiction

shabby *adj* **-bier, -biest 1** worn or dilapidated in appearance **2** mean or unworthy: *shabby treatment* **shabbily** *adv* **shabbiness** *n*

shack *n* rough hut **shack up with** *v slang* live with (one's lover)

shackle *n* **1** one of a pair of metal rings joined by a chain, for securing a person's wrists or ankles ▷ *v* **2** fasten with shackles **3** hamper

shad *n* herring-like fish

shade *n* **1** relative darkness **2** place sheltered from sun

3 depth of colour **4** slight amount **5** *lit* ghost **6** screen or cover used to protect from a direct source of light **shades 7** *slang* sunglasses ▷ v **8** screen from light **9** darken **10** represent (darker areas) in drawing **11** change slightly or by degrees **shady** *adj* **1** situated in or giving shade **2** of doubtful honesty or legality

shadow n **1** dark shape cast on a surface when something stands between a light and the surface **2** patch of shade **3** slight trace **4** threatening influence **5** inseparable companion ▷ v **6** cast a shadow over **7** follow secretly **shadowy** *adj* **shadow-boxing** n boxing against an imaginary opponent for practice **Shadow Cabinet** members of the main opposition party in Parliament who would be ministers if their party were in power

shaft n **1** long narrow straight handle of a tool or weapon **2** ray of light **3** revolving rod that transmits power in a machine **4** vertical passageway, as for an elevator **5** one of the bars between which an animal is harnessed to a vehicle

shag[1] n **1** coarse shredded tobacco ▷ *adj* **2** (of a carpet) having a long pile **shaggy** *adj* **1** covered with rough hair or wool **2** tousled, unkempt **shagginess** n **shaggy-dog story** long anecdote with a humorous twist at the end

shag[2] n kind of cormorant

shag[3] v baseball catch and throw back (fly balls) as practice

shagreen n **1** rough grainy untanned leather **2** sharkskin

shah n formerly, ruler of Iran

shake v **shaking, shook, shaken 1** move quickly up and down or back and forth **2** make unsteady **3** tremble **4** grasp (someone's hand) in greeting or agreement **5** shock or upset ▷ n **6** shaking **7** vibration **8** *informal* short period of time **shaky** *adj* **1** unsteady **2** uncertain or questionable **shakily** *adv*

shale n flaky sedimentary rock

shall v, *past tense* **should** used as an auxiliary to make the future tense or to indicate intention, obligation, or inevitability

shallot [shal-**lot**] n kind of small onion

shallow *adj* **1** not deep **2** lacking depth of character or intellect **shallows** *pl n* area of shallow water **shallowness** n

sham n **1** thing or person that is not genuine ▷ *adj* **2** not real or genuine ▷ v **shamming, shammed 3** fake, feign

shamble v walk in a shuffling awkward way

shambles n disorderly event or place

shame n **1** painful emotion caused by awareness of having done something dishonourable or foolish **2** capacity to feel shame **3** cause of shame **4** cause for regret ▷ v **5** cause to feel shame **6** disgrace **7** compel by shame: *she was shamed into helping* **shameful** *adj* causing or deserving shame **shamefully** *adv* **shameless** *adj* with no sense of shame **shamefaced** *adj* looking ashamed

shampoo n **1** liquid soap for washing hair, carpets,

or upholstery **2** process of shampooing ▷ *v* **3** wash with shampoo

shamrock *n* clover leaf, esp. as the Irish emblem

shandy *n, pl* **-dies** drink made of beer and lemonade

shanghai *v* force or trick (someone) into doing something

shank *n* **1** lower leg **2** shaft or stem

shan't shall not

shantung *n* soft Chinese silk with a knobbly surface

shanty[1] *n, pl* **-ties** shack or crude dwelling **shantytown** *n* slum consisting of shanties

shanty[2] *n, pl* **-ties** sailor's traditional song

shape *n* **1** outward form of an object **2** way in which something is organized **3** pattern or mould **4** condition or state ▷ *v* **5** form or mould **6** devise or develop **shapeless** *adj* **shapely** *adj* having an attractive shape

shard *n* broken piece of pottery

share[1] *n* **1** part of something that belongs to or is contributed by a person **2** one of the equal parts into which the capital stock of a public company is divided ▷ *v* **3** give or take a share of (something) **4** join with others in doing or using (something) **shareholder** *n*

share[2] *n* blade of a plough

shark *n* **1** large usu. predatory sea fish **2** person who cheats others

sharkskin *n* stiff glossy fabric

sharp *adj* **1** having a keen cutting edge or fine point **2** not gradual **3** clearly defined **4** mentally acute **5** clever but underhand **6** shrill **7** bitter or sour in taste **8** (of a note) being one semitone above natural pitch **9** (of an instrument or voice) out of tune by being too high in pitch ▷ *adv* **10** promptly ▷ *n music* **11** symbol raising a note one semitone above natural pitch **12** note raised in this way **sharply** *adv* **sharpness** *n* **sharpen** *v* make or become sharp or sharper **sharpener** *n* **sharpshooter** *n* marksman

shatter *v* **1** break into pieces **2** destroy completely **3** upset (someone) greatly **shattered** *adj informal* completely exhausted

shave *v* **shaving, shaved, shaved** *or* **shaven 1** remove (hair) from (the face, head, or body) with a razor or shaver **2** pare away **3** touch lightly in passing **4** reduce ▷ *n* **5** shaving **close shave** see **close** ▸ **shaver** *n* electric razor **shavings** *pl n* parings

shawl *n* piece of cloth worn over a woman's head or shoulders or wrapped around a baby

she *pron* **1** female person or animal previously mentioned **2** something regarded as female, such as an automobile, ship, or nation

sheaf *n, pl* **sheaves 1** bundle of papers **2** tied bundle of reaped corn

shear *v* **shearing, sheared, sheared** *or* **shorn 1** clip hair or wool from **2** cut through **shears** *pl n* large scissors or a cutting tool shaped like these **shearer** *n*

sheath *n* **1** close-fitting cover, esp. for a knife or sword **2** condom **sheathe** *v* put into a sheath

shed[1] *n* building used for storage or shelter or as a workshop

shed[2] *v* **shedding, shed 1** pour

forth (tears) **2** cast off (skin)
3 lose (hair)

sheen *n* glistening brightness
on the surface of something

sheep *n, pl* **sheep** ruminant
animal bred for wool and
meat **sheep-dip** *n* liquid
disinfectant in which sheep
are immersed **sheepdog** *n*
dog used for herding sheep
sheepskin *n* skin of a sheep
with the fleece still on, used
for clothing or rugs

sheepish *adj* embarrassed
because of feeling foolish
sheepishly *adv*

sheer[1] *adj* **1** absolute,
complete: *sheer folly* **2** (of
material) so fine as to be
transparent **3** perpendicular,
steep

sheer[2] *v* change course
suddenly

sheet[1] *n* **1** large piece of cloth
used as an inner bedcover
2 broad thin piece of any
material **3** large expanse

sheet[2] *n* rope for controlling
the position of a sail **sheet
anchor 1** strong anchor for
use in an emergency **2** person
or thing relied on

sheikh, sheik [shake] *n*
Arab chief **sheikhdom** *or*
sheikdom *n*

sheila *n Aust slang* girl or
woman

shekel *n* **1** monetary unit
of Israel **shekels 2** *informal*
money

shelf *n, pl* **shelves 1** board
fixed horizontally for holding
things **2** ledge **shelf life**
time a packaged product will
remain fresh

shell *n* **1** hard outer covering
of an egg, nut, or certain
animals **2** explosive
projectile fired from a large
gun **3** external frame of
something ▷ *v* **4** take the
shell from **5** fire at with

artillery shells **shellfish** *n*
aquatic mollusc or crustacean
shell out *v informal* pay out
or hand over (money) **shell
shock** nervous disorder
caused by exposure to battle
conditions

shellac *n* **1** resin used in
varnishes ▷ *v* **-lacking,
-lacked 2** coat with shellac

shelter *n* **1** structure providing
protection from danger or
the weather **2** protection ▷ *v*
3 give shelter to **4** take shelter

shelve *v* **1** put aside or
postpone **2** slope **shelving** *n*
(material for) shelves

shenanigans *pl n informal*
1 mischief or nonsense
2 trickery

shepherd *n* **1** person who
tends sheep ▷ *v* **2** guide
or watch over (people)
shepherdess *n fem*
shepherd's pie baked dish of
mince covered with mashed
potato

sherbet *n* fruit-flavoured fizzy
powder

sheriff *n* **1** municipal officer
who enforces court orders etc.
2 (in the US) law enforcement
officer **3** (in England and
Wales) chief executive officer
of the Crown in a county **4** (in
Scotland) chief judge of a
district **sheriffdom** *n*

Sherpa *n* member of a people
of Tibet and Nepal

sherry *n, pl* **-ries** pale or dark
brown fortified wine

shibboleth *n* slogan or
principle, usu. considered
outworn, characteristic of a
particular group

shield *n* **1** piece of armour
carried on the arm to protect
the body from blows or
missiles **2** anything that
protects **3** sports trophy in
the shape of a shield ▷ *v*
4 protect

S

shift v **1** move **2** transfer (blame or responsibility) **3** remove or be removed ▷ n **4** shifting **5** group of workers who work during a specified period **6** period of time during which they work **7** loose-fitting straight underskirt or dress **shiftless** adj lacking in ambition or initiative **shifty** adj evasive or untrustworthy **shiftiness** n

shillelagh [shil-**lay**-lee] n (in Ireland) a cudgel

shilling n former British coin, replaced by the 5p piece

shillyshally v **-lying, -lied** informal be indecisive

shimmer v, n (shine with) a faint unsteady light

shin n **1** front of the lower leg ▷ v **shinning, shinned 2** climb by using the hands or arms and legs **shinbone** n tibia

shindig n informal **1** noisy party **2** brawl

shine v **shining, shone 1** give out or reflect light **2** aim (a light) **3** polish **4** excel ▷ n **5** brightness or lustre **take a shine to** informal take a liking to (someone) **shiny** adj **shiner** n informal black eye

shingle[1] n **1** wooden roof tile ▷ v **2** cover (a roof) with shingles

shingle[2] n coarse gravel found on beaches

shingles n disease causing a rash of small blisters along a nerve

shinny n Canad informal game similar to ice hockey

Shinto n Japanese religion in which ancestors and nature spirits are worshipped **Shintoism** n

shinty n game like hockey

ship n **1** large seagoing vessel ▷ v **shipping, shipped 2** send or transport by carrier, esp. a ship **3** bring or go aboard a ship

shipment n **1** act of shipping cargo **2** consignment of goods shipped **shipping** n **1** freight transport business **2** ships collectively **shipshape** adj orderly or neat **shipwreck** n **1** destruction of a ship through storm or collision ▷ v **2** cause to undergo shipwreck **shipyard** n place where ships are built

shire n county

shire horse n large powerful breed of horse

shirk v avoid (duty or work) **shirker** n

shirt n garment for the upper part of the body

shirty adj **-tier, -tiest** slang annoyed

shish kebab n meat and vegetable dish cooked on a skewer

shiver[1] v **1** tremble, as from cold or fear ▷ n **2** shivering

shiver[2] v splinter into pieces

shoal[1] n large number of fish swimming together

shoal[2] n **1** stretch of shallow water **2** sandbank

shock[1] v **1** horrify, disgust, or astonish ▷ n **2** sudden violent emotional disturbance **3** sudden violent blow or impact **4** something causing this **5** state of bodily collapse caused by physical or mental shock **6** pain and muscular spasm caused by an electric current passing through the body **shocker** n **shocking** adj **1** causing horror, disgust, or astonishment **2** informal very bad

shock[2] n bushy mass (of hair)

shod v past of **shoe**

shoddy adj **-dier, -diest** of poor quality

shoe n **1** outer covering for the foot, ending below the ankle **2** horseshoe ▷ v **shoeing, shod 3** fit with a shoe or shoes **shoehorn** n smooth curved implement inserted at the heel of a shoe to ease the foot into it **shoestring** n **on a shoestring** using a very small amount of money

shone v past of **shine**

shoo interj **1** go away! ▷ v **2** drive away as by saying 'shoo'

shook v past tense of **shake**

shoot v **shooting, shot 1** hit, wound, or kill with a missile fired from a weapon **2** fire (a missile from) a weapon **3** send out or move rapidly **4** hunt **5** (of a plant) sprout **6** photograph or film **7** sports take a shot at goal ▷ n **8** new branch or sprout of a plant **9** hunting expedition **shooting star** meteor **shooting stick** stick with a spike at one end and a folding seat at the other

shop n **1** place for sale of goods and services **2** workshop ▷ v **shopping, shopped 3** visit a shop or shops to buy goods **4** slang inform against (someone) **talk shop** discuss one's work, esp. on a social occasion **shop around** v visit various shops to compare goods and prices **shop floor 1** production area of a factory **2** workers in a factory **shoplifter** n person who steals from a shop **shopsoiled** adj soiled or faded from being displayed in a shop **shop steward** trade-union official elected to represent his or her fellow workers

shore¹ n edge of a sea or lake

shore² v (foll. by up) prop or support

shorn v a past participle of **shear**

short adj **1** not long **2** not tall **3** not lasting long, brief **4** deficient: short of cash **5** abrupt, rude **6** (of a drink) consisting chiefly of a spirit **7** (of pastry) crumbly ▷ adv **8** abruptly ▷ n **9** drink of spirits **10** short film **11** informal short circuit **shorts 12** short trousers **shortage** n deficiency **shorten** v make or become shorter **shortly** adv **1** soon **2** rudely **shortbread** or **shortcake** n crumbly cookie made with butter **short-change** v **1** give (someone) less than the correct amount of change **2** slang swindle **short circuit** faulty or accidental connection in a circuit, which deflects current through a path of low resistance **shortcoming** n failing or defect **short cut** quicker route or method **shortfall** n deficit **shorthand** n system of rapid writing using symbols to represent words **short-handed** adj not having enough workers **short list** selected list of candidates for a job or prize, from which the final choice will be made **short-list** v put on a short list **short shrift** brief and unsympathetic treatment **short-sighted** adj **1** unable to see faraway things clearly **2** lacking in foresight **short wave** radio wave with a wavelength of less than 60 metres

shot n **1** shooting **2** small lead pellets used in a shotgun **3** person with specified skill in shooting **4** slang attempt **5** sports act or instance of hitting, kicking, or throwing the ball **6** photograph **7** uninterrupted film sequence **8** informal injection **9** informal drink of spirits ▷ adj **10** woven so that the colour varies according to the angle of light ▷ *v* **11** past of **shoot** ► **shotgun** *n* gun for firing a charge of shot at short range

shot put *n* athletic event in which contestants hurl a heavy metal ball as far as possible **shot-putter** *n*

should *v* past tense of **shall** used as an auxiliary to make the subjunctive mood or to indicate obligation or possibility

shoulder *n* **1** part of the body to which an arm, foreleg, or wing is attached **2** cut of meat including the upper foreleg **3** part of a garment which covers the shoulder **4** side of a road ▷ *v* **5** bear (a burden or responsibility) **6** put on one's shoulder **7** push with one's shoulder **shoulder blade** large flat triangular bone at the shoulder

shouldn't should not

shout *n* **1** loud cry ▷ *v* **2** cry out loudly **shout down** *v* silence (someone) by shouting

shove *v* **1** push roughly **2** *informal* put ▷ *n* **3** rough push **shove off** *v informal* go away

shovel *n* **1** tool for lifting or moving loose material ▷ *v* **-elling, -elled 2** lift or move as with a shovel

show *v* **showing, showed, shown** *or* **showed 1** make, be, or become noticeable or visible **2** exhibit or display **3** indicate **4** instruct by demonstration **5** prove **6** guide **7** reveal or display (an emotion) ▷ *n* **8** public exhibition **9** theatrical or other entertainment **10** mere display or pretence **showy** *adj* **1** gaudy **2** ostentatious **showily** *adv* **show business** the entertainment industry **showcase** *n* **1** glass case

used to display objects **2** situation in which something is displayed to best advantage **showdown** *n* confrontation that settles a dispute **showjumping** *n* competitive sport of riding horses to demonstrate skill in jumping **showman** *n* man skilled at presenting anything spectacularly **showmanship** *n* **show off** *v* **1** exhibit to invite admiration **2** *informal* behave flamboyantly in order to attract attention **show-off** *n informal* person who shows off **showpiece** *n* excellent specimen shown for display or as an example **showroom** *n* room in which goods for sale are on display **show up** *v* **1** reveal or be revealed clearly **2** expose the faults or defects of **3** *informal* embarrass **4** *informal* arrive

shower *n* **1** kind of bath in which a person stands while being sprayed with water **2** wash in this **3** short period of rain, hail, or snow **4** sudden abundant fall of objects: *shower of sparks* ▷ *v* **5** wash in a shower **6** bestow (things) or present (someone) with things liberally **showery** *adj*

shown *v* a past participle of **show**

shrank *v* a past tense of **shrink**

shrapnel *n* **1** artillery shell filled with pellets which scatter on explosion **2** fragments from this

shred *n* **1** long narrow strip torn from something **2** small amount ▷ *v* **shredding, shredded** *or* **shred 3** tear to shreds

shrew *n* **1** small mouselike animal **2** bad-tempered nagging woman **shrewish** *adj*

shrewd *adj* clever and perceptive **shrewdly** *adv* **shrewdness** *n*

shriek *n* **1** shrill cry ▷ *v* **2** utter (with) a shriek

shrike *n* songbird with a heavy hooked bill

shrill *adj* (of a sound) sharp and high-pitched **shrillness** *n* **shrilly** *adv*

shrimp *n* **1** small edible shellfish **2** *informal* small person **shrimping** *n* fishing for shrimps

shrine *n* place of worship associated with a sacred person or object

shrink *v* **shrinking, shrank** *or* **shrunk, shrunk** *or* **shrunken 1** become or make smaller **2** recoil or withdraw ▷ *n* **3** *slang* psychiatrist **shrinkage** *n* decrease in size, value, or weight

shrive *v* **shriving, shrived** *or* **shrove, shriven** *old-fashioned* give absolution to after hearing confession

shrivel *v* **-elling, -elled** shrink and wither

shroud *n* **1** piece of cloth used to wrap a dead body **2** anything which conceals ▷ *v* **3** conceal

Shrovetide *n* the three days preceding Lent **Shrove Tuesday** day before Ash Wednesday

shrub *n* woody plant smaller than a tree **shrubbery** *n* area planted with shrubs

shrug *v* **shrugging, shrugged 1** raise and then drop (the shoulders) as a sign of indifference, ignorance, or doubt ▷ *n* **2** shrugging **shrug off** *v* dismiss as unimportant

shrunk *v* a past of **shrink**

shrunken *v* a past participle of **shrink**

shudder *v* **1** shake or tremble violently, esp. with horror ▷ *n* **2** shaking or trembling

shuffle *v* **1** walk without lifting the feet **2** rearrange **3** jumble together ▷ *n* **4** shuffling **5** rearrangement

shun *v* **shunning, shunned** avoid

shunt *v* **1** move (objects or people) to a different position **2** move (a train) from one track to another

shush *interj* be quiet!

shut *v* **shutting, shut 1** bring together or fold, close **2** prevent access to **3** (of a shop etc.) stop operating for the day **shutter** *n* **1** hinged doorlike cover for closing off a window **2** device in a camera letting in the light required to expose a film **shut down** *v* close or stop (a factory, machine, or business) **shutdown** *n* **shut out** *v* *sports* prevent (an opponent) from scoring for an entire game **shutout** *n* *sports* game in which the opposing team does not score

shuttle *n* **1** vehicle going to and fro over a short distance **2** instrument which passes the weft thread between the warp threads in weaving ▷ *v* **3** travel by or as if by shuttle

shuttlecock *n* small light cone with feathers stuck in one end, struck to and fro in badminton

shy[1] *adj* **1** not at ease in company **2** timid **3** (foll. by *of*) cautious or wary ▷ *v* **shying, shied 4** start back in fear **5** (foll. by *away from*) avoid (doing something) through fear or lack of confidence **shyly** *adv* **shyness** *n*

shy[2] *v* **shying, shied 1** throw ▷ *n, pl* **shies 2** throw

Si *chem* silicon

SI *French* Système International

(d'Unités), international metric system of units of measurement

Siamese *adj* of Siam, former name of Thailand **Siamese cat** breed of cat with cream fur, dark ears and face, and blue eyes **Siamese twins** twins born joined to each other at some part of the body

sibilant *adj* **1** hissing ▷ *n* **2** consonant pronounced with a hissing sound

sibling *n* brother or sister

sibyl *n* (in ancient Greece and Rome) prophetess **sibylline** *adj*

sic *Latin* thus (used to indicate that an odd spelling or reading is in fact accurate)

sick *adj* **1** vomiting or likely to vomit **2** physically or mentally unwell **3** *informal* amused by something sadistic or morbid **4** (foll. by *of*) *informal* disgusted (by) or weary (of) **sickness** *n* **sicken** *v* **1** make nauseated or disgusted **2** become ill **sickly** *adj* **1** unhealthy, weak **2** causing revulsion or nausea **sickbay** *n* place for sick people, such as that on a ship

sickle *n* tool with a curved blade for cutting grass or grain

side *n* **1** line or surface that borders anything **2** either surface of a flat object **3** either of two halves into which something can be divided **4** area immediately next to a person or thing **5** region **6** aspect or part **7** one of two opposing groups or teams **8** line of descent through one parent **9** *slang* conceit ▷ *adj* **10** at or on the side **11** subordinate **on the side 1** as an extra **2** unofficially **siding** *n* short stretch of railway track on which trains

or cars are shunted from the main line **sideboard** *n* **1** piece of furniture for holding plates, cutlery, etc. in a dining room **sideboards 2** Also **sideburns** man's side whiskers **side-effect** *n* additional undesirable effect **sidekick** *n informal* close friend or associate **sidelight** *n* either of two small lights on the front of a vehicle **sideline** *n* **1** subsidiary interest or source of income **2** *sports* line marking the boundary of a playing area **sidelong** *adj* **1** sideways **2** oblique ▷ *adv* **3** obliquely **side-saddle** *n* saddle designed to allow a woman rider to sit with both legs on the same side of the horse **sidestep** *v* **1** dodge (an issue) **2** avoid by stepping sideways **sidetrack** *v* divert from the main topic **sidewalk** *n* paved path for pedestrians **sideways** *adv* **1** to or from the side **2** obliquely **side with** *v* support (one side in a dispute)

sidereal [side-**eer**-ee-al] *adj* of or determined with reference to the stars

sidle *v* move in a furtive manner

SIDS sudden infant death syndrome, crib death

siege *n* surrounding and blockading of a place

sienna *n* reddish- or yellowish-brown pigment made from natural earth

sierra *n* range of mountains in Spain or America with jagged peaks

siesta *n* afternoon nap, taken in hot countries

sieve [siv] *n* **1** utensil with mesh through which a substance is sifted or strained ▷ *v* **2** sift or strain through a sieve

sift v **1** remove the coarser particles from a substance with a sieve **2** examine (information or evidence) to select what is important

sigh n **1** long audible breath expressing sadness, tiredness, relief, or longing ▷ v **2** utter a sigh

sight n **1** ability to see **2** instance of seeing **3** range of vision **4** thing seen **5** thing worth seeing **6** *informal* unsightly thing **7** device for guiding the eye while using a gun or optical instrument **8** *informal* a lot ▷ v **9** catch sight of **sightless** adj blind **sight-read** v play or sing printed music without previous preparation **sightseeing** n visiting places of interest **sightseer** n

sign n **1** indication of something not immediately or outwardly observable **2** notice displayed to advertise, inform, or warn **3** gesture, mark, or symbol conveying a meaning **4** omen ▷ v **5** write (one's name) on (a document or letter) to show its authenticity or one's agreement **6** communicate using sign language **7** make a sign or gesture **signing** n Also **sign language** system of manual signs used to communicate with deaf people **sign on** v **1** register as unemployed **2** sign a document committing oneself to a job, course, etc. **signpost** n post bearing a sign that shows the way

signal n **1** sign or gesture to convey information **2** sequence of electrical impulses or radio waves transmitted or received ▷ adj **3** remarkable or striking ▷ v **-nalling, -nalled 4** make a signal **5** convey (information) by signal **signally** adv **signal box** building from which railway signals are operated **signalman** n railwayman in charge of signals and points

signatory [**sig**-na-tree] n, pl **-ries** one of the parties who sign a document

signature n **1** person's name written by himself or herself in signing something **2** sign at the start of a piece of music to show the key or tempo **signature tune** tune used to introduce a particular television or radio programme

signet n small seal used to authenticate documents **signet ring** finger ring bearing a signet

significant adj **1** important **2** having or expressing a meaning **significantly** adv **significance** n

signify v **-fying, -fied 1** indicate or suggest **2** be a symbol or sign for **3** be important **signification** n meaning

signor [see-**nyor**] n Italian term of address equivalent to *Sir* or *Mr* **signora** [see-**nyor**-a] n Italian term of address equivalent to *madam* or *Mrs* **signorina** [see-nyor-**ee**-na] n Italian term of address equivalent to *madam* or *Miss*

Sikh [**seek**] n member of an Indian religion having only one God

silage [**sile**-ij] n fodder crop harvested while green and partially fermented in a silo

silence n **1** absence of noise or speech ▷ v **2** make silent **3** put a stop to **silent** adj **silently** adv **silencer** n device to reduce the noise of an engine exhaust or gun

silhouette n **1** outline of a dark shape seen against a light background ▷ v **2** show in silhouette

silica n hard glossy mineral found as quartz and in sandstone **silicosis** n lung disease caused by inhaling silica dust

silicon n brittle nonmetallic element widely used in chemistry and industry **silicone** n tough synthetic substance made from silicon and used in lubricants, paints, and resins **silicon chip** tiny wafer of silicon processed to form an integrated circuit

silk n **1** fibre made by the larva of a moth called the silkworm **2** thread or fabric made from this **silky** or **silken** adj of or like silk

sill n ledge at the bottom of a window

silly adj **-lier, -liest** foolish **silliness** n

silo n, pl **-los 1** pit or airtight tower for storing silage **2** underground structure in which nuclear missiles are kept ready for launching

silt n **1** mud deposited by moving water ▷ v **2** (foll. by up) fill or be choked with silt

silvan adj same as **sylvan**

silver n **1** white precious metal **2** coins or articles made of silver ▷ adj **3** made of or of the colour of silver **silver birch** tree with silvery-white bark **silverfish** n small wingless silver-coloured insect **silverside** n Brit cut of beef from below the rump and above the leg **silver thaw** quick-freezing rain that encrusts trees, rocks, etc. **silver wedding** twenty-fifth wedding anniversary

sim n computer game that simulates an activity such as flying or playing a sport

simian adj, n (of or like) a monkey or ape

similar adj alike but not identical **similarity** n **similarly** adv

simile [sim-ill-ee] n figure of speech comparing one thing to another, using 'as' or 'like'

similitude n similarity, likeness

simmer v **1** cook gently at just below boiling point **2** be in a state of suppressed rage **simmer down** v calm down

simnel cake n fruit cake covered with marzipan

simper v **1** smile in a silly or affected way **2** utter (something) with a simper ▷ n **3** simpering smile

simple adj **1** easy to understand or do **2** plain or unpretentious **3** not combined or complex **4** sincere or frank **5** feeble-minded **simply** adv **simplicity** n **simplify** v **-fying, -fied** make less complicated **simplification** n **simplistic** adj oversimplified or oversimplifying **simpleton** n foolish or half-witted person

simulate v **1** make a pretence of **2** have the appearance of **3** imitate the conditions of (a particular situation) **simulation** n **simulator** n

simultaneous adj occurring at the same time **simultaneity** n **simultaneously** adv

sin¹ n **1** breaking of a religious or moral law **2** offence against a principle or standard ▷ v **sinning, sinned 3** commit a sin **sinful** adj **1** being a sin **2** guilty of sin **sinfully** adv **sinner** n

sin² math sine

SIN Social Insurance Number

since prep **1** during the period

of time after ▷ conj **2** from the time when **3** for the reason that ▷ adv **4** from that time

sincere adj without pretence or deceit **sincerely** adv **sincerity** n

sine n (in trigonometry) ratio of the length of the opposite side to that of the hypotenuse in a right-angled triangle

sinecure [**sin**-ih-cure] n paid job with minimal duties

sine die [**sin**-ay **dee**-ay] adv Latin with no date fixed for future action

sine qua non [**sin**-ay kwah **non**] n Latin essential requirement

sinew n **1** tough fibrous tissue joining muscle to bone **2** muscles or strength **sinewy** adj

sing v **singing, sang, sung 1** make musical sounds with the voice **2** perform (a song) **3** make a humming or whistling sound **singer** n **singsong** n **1** informal singing session ▷ adj **2** (of the voice) repeatedly rising and falling in pitch

singe v **singeing, singed 1** burn the surface of ▷ n **2** superficial burn

single adj **1** one only **2** distinct from others of the same kind **3** unmarried **4** designed for one user **5** formed of only one part **6** (of a ticket) valid for an outward journey only ▷ n **7** single thing **8** thing intended for one person **9** record with one short song or tune on each side **10** baseball hit that enables the batter to run to first base **singles 11** game between two players ▷ v **12** (foll. by out) pick out from others **singly** adv **single file** (of people or things) arranged in one line

single-handed adj without assistance **single-minded** adj having one aim only

singlet n sleeveless vest

singular adj **1** (of a word or form) denoting one person or thing **2** remarkable, unusual ▷ n **3** singular form of a word **singularity** n **singularly** adv

sinister adj threatening or suggesting evil or harm

sink v **sinking, sank** or **sunk, sunk** or **sunken 1** submerge (in liquid) **2** cause (a ship) to submerge by attacking it with bombs, etc. **3** descend or cause to descend **4** decline in value or amount **5** become weaker in health **6** dig or drill (a hole or shaft) **7** invest (money) **8** golf, snooker hit (a ball) into a hole or pocket ▷ n **9** fixed basin with a water supply and drainage pipe **sinker** n **1** weight for a fishing line **2** baseball ball which dips considerably after being pitched or hit **sink in** v penetrate the mind **sinking fund** money set aside regularly to repay a long-term debt

Sino- combining form Chinese

sinuous adj **1** curving **2** lithe **sinuously** adv

sinus [**sine**-uss] n hollow space in a bone, esp. an air passage opening into the nose

sip v **sipping, sipped 1** drink in small mouthfuls ▷ n **2** amount sipped

siphon n **1** bent tube which uses air pressure to draw liquid from a container ▷ v **2** draw off thus **3** redirect (resources)

sir n **1** polite term of address for a man **2 Sir** title of a knight or baronet

sire n **1** male parent of a horse or other domestic animal **2** respectful term of address to a king ▷ *v* **3** father

siren *n* **1** device making a loud wailing noise as a warning **2** dangerously alluring woman

sirloin *n* prime cut of loin of beef

sirocco *n, pl* **-cos** hot wind blowing from N Africa into S Europe

sisal [size-al] *n* (fibre of) plant used in making ropes

siskin *n* yellow-and-black finch

sissy *n, pl* **-sies 1** weak or cowardly person **2** effeminate male

sister *n* **1** girl or woman with the same parents as another person **2** senior nurse **3** nun **4** female fellow-member of a group ▷ *adj* **5** closely related, similar **sisterhood** *n* **1** state of being a sister **2** group of women united by common aims or beliefs **sisterly** *adj* **sister-in-law** *n, pl* **sisters-in-law 1** sister of one's husband or wife **2** wife of one's sibling

sit *v* **sitting, sat 1** rest one's body upright on the buttocks **2** cause to sit **3** perch **4** (of a bird) incubate (eggs) by sitting on them **5** be situated **6** pose for a portrait **7** occupy an official position **8** (of an official body) hold a session **9** take (an examination) **sitting room** room in a house where people sit and relax **sit-in** *n* protest in which demonstrators occupy a place and refuse to move

sitar *n* Indian stringed musical instrument

sitcom *n informal* situation comedy

site *n* **1** place where something is, was, or is intended to be located **2** same as **website** ▷ *v* **3** provide with a site

situate *v* place **situation** *n* **1** location and surroundings **2** state of affairs **3** position of employment **situation comedy** radio or television series involving the same characters in various situations

six *adj, n* one more than five **sixth** *adj, n* (of) number six in a series **sixteen** *adj, n* six and ten **sixteenth** *adj, n* **sixty** *adj, n* six times ten **sixtieth** *adj, n*

size[1] *n* **1** dimensions, bigness **2** one of a series of standard measurements of goods ▷ *v* **3** arrange according to size **sizeable** *or* **sizable** *adj* quite large **size up** *v informal* assess

size[2] *n* gluey substance used as a sealer

sizzle *v* make a hissing sound like frying fat

SK Saskatchewan

skanky *adj slang* dirty or unattractive

skate[1] *n* **1** boot with a steel blade or sets of wheels attached to the sole for gliding over ice or a hard surface ▷ *v* **2** glide on or as if on skates **skateboard** *n* board mounted on small wheels for riding on while standing up **skate over** *or* **skate round** *v* avoid discussing or dealing with (a matter) fully

skate[2] *n* large marine flatfish

skedaddle *v informal* run off

skein *n* **1** yarn wound in a loose coil **2** flock of geese in flight

skeleton *n* **1** framework of bones inside a person's or animal's body **2** essential framework of a structure **3** small steel-frame racing sledge ▷ *adj* **4** reduced to a minimum **skeletal** *adj* **skeleton key** key which can open many different locks

skerry *n, pl* **-ries** rocky island or reef

sketch *n* **1** rough drawing

S

2 brief description **3** short humorous play ▷ v **4** make a sketch (of) **sketchy** *adj* incomplete or inadequate

skew *adj* **1** slanting or crooked ▷ v **2** make slanting or crooked **skewed** *adj* (of an opinion or analysis) distorted or biased because of prejudice or lack of information

skewbald *adj* (of a horse) marked with patches of white and another colour

skewer *n* **1** pin to hold meat together during cooking ▷ v **2** fasten with a skewer

ski *n* **1** one of a pair of long runners fastened to boots for gliding over snow or water ▷ v **skiing, skied** or **ski'd 2** travel on skis **skier** *n*

skid *v* **skidding, skidded 1** (of a moving vehicle) slide sideways uncontrollably ▷ *n* **2** skidding **skid row** *slang* dilapidated part of a city frequented by vagrants

skidoo *n* snowmobile

skiff *n* small boat

skill *n* **1** special ability or expertise **2** something requiring special training or expertise **skilful** *adj* having or showing skill **skilfully** *adv* **skilled** *adj*

skillet *n* small frying pan or shallow cooking pot

skim *v* **skimming, skimmed 1** remove floating matter from the surface of (a liquid) **2** glide smoothly over **3** read quickly **skimmed milk** or **skim milk** milk from which the cream has been removed

skimp *v* not invest enough time, money, material, etc. **skimpy** *adj* scanty or insufficient

skin *n* **1** outer covering of the body **2** complexion **3** outer layer or covering **4** film on a liquid **5** animal skin used as a material or container ▷ v **skinning, skinned 6** remove the skin of **skinless** *adj*

skinny *adj* thin **skin-deep** *adj* superficial **skin diving** underwater swimming using flippers and light breathing apparatus **skin-diver** *n* **skinflint** *n* miser **skinhead** *n* youth with very short hair

skint *adj slang* having no money

skip[1] *v* **skipping, skipped 1** leap lightly from one foot to the other **2** jump over a rope as it is swung under one **3** *informal* pass over, omit ▷ *n* **4** skipping

skip[2] *n* large open container for builders' rubbish

skipper *n, v* captain

skirl *n* sound of bagpipes

skirmish *n* **1** brief or minor fight or argument ▷ v **2** take part in a skirmish

skirt *n* **1** woman's garment hanging from the waist **2** part of a dress or coat below the waist **3** cut of beef from the flank ▷ v **4** border **5** go round **6** avoid dealing with (an issue) **skirting board** narrow board round the bottom of an interior wall

skit *n* brief satirical sketch

skittish *adj* playful or lively

skittle *n* **1** bottle-shaped object used as a target in some games **skittles 2** game in which players try to knock over skittles by rolling a ball at them

skookum *adj* powerful or big

skua *n* large predatory gull

skulduggery *n informal* trickery

skulk *v* **1** move stealthily **2** lurk

skull *n* bony framework of the head **skullcap** *n* close-fitting brimless cap

skunk *n* **1** small black-and-white N American mammal which emits an evil-smelling fluid when attacked **2** *slang* despicable person

sky *n, pl* **skies** upper atmosphere as seen from the earth **skydiving** *n* sport of jumping from an aircraft and performing manoeuvres before opening one's parachute **skylark** *n* lark that sings while soaring at a great height **skylight** *n* window in a roof or ceiling **skyscraper** *n* very tall building

Skype *n* ® software application that allows users to make voice and video calls over the internet

slab *n* broad flat piece

slack¹ *adj* **1** not tight **2** negligent **3** not busy ▷ *n* **4** slack part **slacks 5** *informal* trousers ▷ *v* **6** neglect one's work or duty **slackness** *n* **slacken** *v* make or become slack **slacker** *n*

slack² *n* coal dust or small pieces of coal

slag *n* **1** waste left after metal is smelted ▷ *v* **slagging, slagged 2** *slang* criticize

slain *v* past participle of **slay**

slake *v* **1** satisfy (thirst or desire) **2** combine (quicklime) with water

slalom *n* skiing or canoeing race over a winding course

slam *v* **slamming, slammed 1** shut, put down, or hit violently and noisily **2** *informal* criticize harshly ▷ *n* **3** act or sound of slamming **grand slam** winning of all the games or major tournaments in a sport in one season **slam dunk 1** *basketball* scoring shot in which a player jumps up and forces the ball down through the basket **2** task that is easy to achieve

slander *n* **1** false and malicious statement about a person **2** crime of making

such a statement ▷ *v* **3** utter slander about **slanderous** *adj*

slang *n* very informal language **slangy** *adj* **slanging match** abusive argument

slant *v* **1** lean at an angle, slope **2** present (information) in a biased way ▷ *n* **3** slope **4** point of view, esp. a biased one **slanting** *adj*

slap *n* **1** blow with the open hand or a flat object ▷ *v* **slapping, slapped 2** strike with the open hand or a flat object **3** *informal* place forcefully or carelessly **slapdash** *adj* careless and hasty **slap-happy** *adj informal* cheerfully careless **slapstick** *n* boisterous knockabout comedy **slap-up** *adj* Brit (of a meal) large and luxurious

slash *v* **1** gash **2** cut with a sweeping stroke **3** reduce drastically ▷ *n* **4** gash **5** sweeping stroke

slat *n* narrow strip of wood or metal

slate *n* **1** rock which splits easily into thin layers **2** piece of this for covering a roof or, formerly, for writing on ▷ *v* **3** criticize severely

slattern *n old-fashioned* slovenly woman **slatternly** *adj*

slaughter *v* **1** kill (animals) for food **2** kill (people) savagely or indiscriminately ▷ *n* **3** slaughtering **slaughterhouse** *n* place where animals are killed for food

Slav *n* member of any of the peoples of E Europe or the former Soviet Union who speak a Slavonic language **Slavonic** *n* **1** language group including Russian, Polish, and Czech ▷ *adj* **2** of this language group

slave *n* **1** person owned by another for whom he or she has to work **2** person dominated by another or by a habit **3** drudge ▷ *v* **4** work like a slave **slaver** *n* person or ship engaged in the slave trade **slavery** *n* **1** state or condition of being a slave **2** practice of owning slaves **slavish** *adj* **1** of or like a slave **2** imitative **slave-driver** *n* person who makes others work very hard

slaver *v* dribble saliva from the mouth

slay *v* **slaying, slew, slain** kill

sleazy *adj* **-zier, -ziest** sordid **sleaziness** *n*

sled, sledge *n* **1** carriage on runners for sliding on snow **2** light wooden frame for sliding over snow ▷ *v* **3** travel by sled

sledge, sledgehammer *n* heavy hammer with a long handle

sleek *adj* glossy, smooth, and shiny

sleep *n* **1** state of rest characterized by unconsciousness **2** period of this ▷ *v* **sleeping, slept** **3** be in or as if in a state of sleep **4** have sleeping accommodation for (a specified number) **sleeper** *n* **1** person who sleeps **2** beam supporting the rails of a railway **3** railway car fitted for sleeping in **4** ring worn in a pierced ear to stop the hole from closing up **sleepy** *adj* **sleepily** *adv* **sleepiness** *n* **sleepless** *adj* **sleeping bag** padded bag for sleeping in **sleeping sickness** African disease spread by the tsetse fly **sleepover** *n* occasion when a person stays overnight at a friend's house **sleep with** *or* **sleep together** *v* have sexual intercourse (with)

sleet *n* rain and snow or hail falling together

sleeve *n* **1** part of a garment which covers the arm **2** tubelike cover **3** gramophone record cover **up one's sleeve** secretly ready **sleeveless** *adj*

sleigh *n* sled

sleight of hand [**slite**] *n* skilful use of the hands when performing conjuring tricks

slender *adj* **1** slim **2** small in amount

slept *v* past of **sleep**

sleuth [**slooth**] *n* detective

slew[1] *v* past tense of **slay**

slew[2] *v* twist or swing round

slice *n* **1** thin flat piece cut from something **2** share **3** kitchen tool with a broad flat blade **4** *sports* hitting of a ball so that it travels obliquely ▷ *v* **5** cut into slices **6** *sports* hit (a ball) with a slice

slick *adj* **1** persuasive and glib **2** skilfully devised or carried out **3** well-made and attractive, but superficial ▷ *v* **4** make smooth or sleek ▷ *n* **5** patch of oil on water

slide *v* **sliding, slid 1** slip smoothly along (a surface) **2** pass unobtrusively **3** *baseball* dive feet first or headfirst to catch the ball or reach a base ▷ *n* **4** sliding **5** surface or structure for sliding on or down **6** piece of glass holding an object to be viewed under a microscope **7** photographic transparency **8** ornamental hair clip **9** *baseball* instance of sliding to catch the ball or reach a base **let things slide** allow things to get worse by neglect **slider** *n baseball* fast pitch that breaks sharply away from the batter **sliding scale** variable scale according to which things such as wages fluctuate in response to changes in other factors

slight *adj* **1** small in quantity or extent **2** not important **3** slim and delicate ▷ *v, n* **4** snub **slightly** *adv*

slim *adj* **slimmer, slimmest 1** not heavy or stout, thin **2** slight ▷ *v* **slimming, slimmed 3** make or become slim by diet and exercise **slimmer** *n*

slime *n* unpleasant thick slippery substance **slimy** *adj* **1** of, like, or covered with slime **2** ingratiating

sling¹ *n* **1** bandage hung from the neck to support an injured hand or arm **2** strap with a string at each end for throwing a stone **3** rope or strap for lifting something ▷ *v* **slinging, slung 4** throw **5** carry, hang, or throw with or as if with a sling

sling² *n* sweetened drink with a spirit base: *gin sling*

slink *v* **slinking, slunk** move furtively or guiltily **slinky** *adj* **1** (of clothes) figure-hugging **2** sinuously graceful

slip¹ *v* **slipping, slipped 1** lose balance by sliding **2** move smoothly, easily, or quietly **3** (foll. by *on* or *off*) put on *or* take off easily or quickly **4** pass out of (the mind) ▷ *n* **5** slipping **6** mistake **7** petticoat **8** small piece (of paper) **give someone the slip** escape from someone **slippy** *adj informal* slippery **slipknot** *n* knot tied so that it will slip along the rope round which it is made **slipped disc** painful condition in which one of the discs connecting the bones of the spine becomes displaced **slipshod** *adj* (of an action) careless **slipstream** *n* stream of air forced backwards by a fast-moving object **slip up** *v* make a mistake **slipway**

n launching slope on which ships are built or repaired

slip² *n* clay mixed with water used for decorating pottery

slipper *n* light shoe for indoor wear

slippery *adj* **1** so smooth or wet as to cause slipping or be difficult to hold **2** (of a person) untrustworthy

slit *v* **slitting, slit 1** make a long straight cut in ▷ *n* **2** long narrow cut or opening

slither *v* slide unsteadily

sliver [**sliv**-ver] *n* small thin piece

slob *n informal* lazy and untidy person **slobbish** *adj*

slobber *v* dribble or drool **slobbery** *adj*

sloe *n* sour blue-black fruit

slog *v* **slogging, slogged 1** work hard and steadily **2** make one's way with difficulty **3** hit hard ▷ *n* **4** long and exhausting work or walk

slogan *n* catchword or phrase used in politics or advertising

sloop *n* small single-masted ship

slop *v* **slopping, slopped 1** splash or spill ▷ *n* **2** spilt liquid **3** liquid food **slops 4** liquid refuse and waste food used to feed animals **sloppy** *adj* **1** careless or untidy **2** gushingly sentimental

slope *v* **1** slant ▷ *n* **2** sloping surface **3** degree of inclination **slopes 4** hills **slope off** *v informal* go furtively

slosh *n* **1** splashing sound ▷ *v* **2** splash carelessly **3** *slang* hit hard **sloshed** *adj slang* drunk

slot *n* **1** narrow opening for inserting something **2** *informal* place in a series or scheme **3** *hockey* area in the centre of the offensive zone, directly in front of the net

▷ v **slotting, slotted 4** make a slot or slots in **5** fit into a slot **slot machine** automatic machine worked by placing a coin in a slot

sloth [rhymes with **both**] n **1** slow-moving animal of tropical America **2** laziness **slothful** adj lazy or idle

slouch v **1** sit, stand, or move with a drooping posture ▷ n **2** drooping posture **3** informal incompetent or lazy person

slough[1] [rhymes with **now**] n bog

slough[2] [**sluff**] v (of a snake) shed (its skin) or (of a skin) be shed **slough off** v get rid of (something unwanted or unnecessary)

sloven n habitually dirty or untidy person **slovenly** adj **1** dirty or untidy **2** careless

Slovene, Slovenian adj, n **1** (person) from Slovenia ▷ n **2** language of Slovenia

slow adj **1** taking a longer time than is usual or expected **2** not fast **3** (of a clock or watch) showing a time earlier than the correct one **4** stupid ▷ v **5** reduce the speed (of) **slowly** adv **slowness** n **slowcoach** n informal person who moves or works slowly

sludge n **1** thick mud **2** sewage

slug[1] n **1** land snail with no shell **2** bullet **sluggish** adj slow-moving, lacking energy **sluggishly** adv **sluggishness** n **sluggard** n lazy person

slug[2] v **slugging, slugged 1** hit hard ▷ n **2** heavy blow **3** informal mouthful of an alcoholic drink **slugger** n **1** baseball batter noted for powerful hitting **2** boxer noted for heavy punching

sluice n **1** channel carrying off water **2** sliding gate used to control the flow of water in this **3** water controlled by a sluice ▷ v **4** pour a stream of water over or through

slum n **1** squalid overcrowded house or area ▷ v **slumming, slummed 2** temporarily and deliberately experience poorer places or conditions than usual

slumber v, n lit sleep

slump v **1** sink or fall heavily **2** (of prices or demand) decline suddenly ▷ n **3** sudden decline in prices or demand **4** time of substantial unemployment

slung v past of **sling**[1]

slunk v past of **slink**

slur v **slurring, slurred 1** pronounce or utter (words) indistinctly **2** music sing or play (notes) smoothly without a break ▷ n **3** slurring of words **4** remark intended to discredit someone **5** music slurring of notes **6** curved line indicating notes to be slurred

slurp informal ▷ v **1** eat or drink noisily ▷ n **2** slurping sound

slurry n, pl **-ries** muddy liquid mixture

slush n **1** watery muddy substance **2** sloppy sentimental talk or writing **slushy** adj **slush fund** fund for financing bribery or corruption

slut n dirty or immoral woman **sluttish** adj

sly adj **slyer, slyest** or **slier, sliest 1** crafty **2** secretive and cunning **3** roguish ▷ n **on the sly** secretly **slyly** adv **slyness** n

smack[1] v **1** slap sharply **2** open and close (the lips) loudly in enjoyment or anticipation ▷ n **3** sharp slap **4** slapping sound **5** loud kiss ▷ adv **6** informal squarely or directly: smack in the middle

smacker n slang loud kiss
smack² n 1 slight flavour or trace 2 slang heroin ▷ v 3 have a slight flavour or trace (of)
smack³ n small single-masted fishing boat
small adj 1 not large in size, number, or amount 2 unimportant 3 mean or petty ▷ n 4 narrow part of the lower back **smalls** 5 informal underwear **smallness** n **smallholding** n Brit small area of farming land **small hours** hours just after midnight **small-minded** adj intolerant, petty **smallpox** n contagious disease with blisters that leave scars **small talk** light social conversation **small-time** adj insignificant or minor
smarmy adj smarmier, smarmiest informal unpleasantly suave or flattering
smart adj 1 well-kept and neat 2 astute 3 witty 4 impertinent 5 fashionable 6 brisk 7 (of a system) using computer technology ▷ v 8 feel or cause stinging pain ▷ n 9 stinging pain **smarten** v make or become smart **smartly** adv **smartness** n **smart aleck** informal irritatingly clever person **smartphone** n mobile phone allowing access the internet
smash v 1 break violently and noisily 2 throw (against) violently 3 collide forcefully 4 destroy ▷ n 5 act or sound of smashing 6 violent collision of vehicles 7 informal popular success 8 sports powerful overhead shot **smasher** n informal attractive person or thing **smashing** adj informal excellent
smattering n slight knowledge

smear v 1 spread with a greasy or sticky substance 2 rub so as to produce a dirty mark or smudge 3 slander ▷ n 4 dirty mark or smudge 5 slander 6 med sample of a secretion smeared on to a slide for examination under a microscope
smell v smelling, smelt or smelled 1 perceive (a scent or odour) by means of the nose 2 have or give off a smell 3 have an unpleasant smell 4 detect by instinct ▷ n 5 odour or scent 6 smelling 7 ability to perceive odours by the nose **smelly** adj having a nasty smell **smelling salts** preparation of ammonia used to revive a person who feels faint
smelt¹ v extract (a metal) from (an ore) by heating **smelter** n
smelt² n small fish of the salmon family
smelt³ v a past of smell
smile n 1 turning up of the corners of the mouth to show pleasure, amusement, or friendliness ▷ v 2 give a smile **smile on** or **smile upon** v regard favourably
smirch v, n disgrace
smirk n 1 smug smile ▷ v 2 give a smirk
smite v smiting, smote, smitten old-fashioned 1 strike hard 2 affect severely
smith n worker in metal **smithy** n blacksmith's workshop
smithereens pl n shattered fragments
smitten v past participle of smite
smock n 1 loose overall 2 woman's loose blouselike garment ▷ v 3 gather (material) by sewing in a honeycomb pattern **smocking** n
smog n mixture of smoke and fog

smoke n **1** cloudy mass that rises from something burning **2** spell of smoking tobacco ▷ v **3** give off smoke **4** inhale and expel smoke of (a cigar, cigarette, or pipe) **5** do this habitually **6** cure (meat, fish, or cheese) by treating with smoke **smokeless** adj **smoker** n **smoky** adj **smoke screen** something said or done to hide the truth

smooch informal ▷ v **1** kiss and cuddle ▷ n **2** smooching

smooth adj **1** even in surface, texture, or consistency **2** without obstructions or difficulties **3** charming and polite but possibly insincere **4** free from jolts **5** not harsh in taste ▷ v **6** make smooth **7** calm **smoothly** adv

smorgasbord n buffet meal of assorted dishes

smote v past tense of **smite**

smother v **1** suffocate or stifle **2** cover thickly **3** suppress

smoulder v **1** burn slowly with smoke but no flame **2** (of feelings) exist in a suppressed state

SMS short message system: used for sending data to mobile phones

smudge v **1** make or become smeared or soiled ▷ n **2** dirty mark **3** blurred form **smudgy** adj

smug adj **smugger, smuggest** self-satisfied **smugly** adv **smugness** n

smuggle v **1** import or export (goods) secretly and illegally **2** take somewhere secretly **smuggler** n

smut n **1** speck of soot **2** mark left by this **3** obscene jokes, pictures, etc. **smutty** adj

Sn chem tin

snack n light quick meal **snack bar** place where snacks are sold

snaffle n **1** jointed bit for a horse ▷ v **2** slang steal

snag n **1** difficulty or disadvantage **2** sharp projecting point **3** hole in fabric caused by a sharp object ▷ v **snagging, snagged** **4** catch or tear on a point

snail n slow-moving mollusc with a spiral shell **snail mail** informal conventional post, as opposed to e-mail **snail's pace** very slow speed

snake n **1** long thin scaly limbless reptile ▷ v **2** move in a winding course like a snake **snake in the grass** treacherous person **snaky** adj twisted or winding

snap v **snapping, snapped** **1** break suddenly **2** (cause to) make a sharp cracking sound **3** (of animals) bite (at) suddenly **4** move suddenly **5** speak sharply and angrily **6** take a snapshot of ▷ n **7** act or sound of snapping **8** fastener that closes with a snapping sound **9** informal snapshot **10** sudden brief spell of cold weather **11** card game in which the word 'snap' is called when two similar cards are put down ▷ adj **12** made on the spur of the moment **snapper** n fish of the perch family **snappy** adj **1** irritable **2** slang quick **3** slang smart and fashionable **snapdragon** n plant with flowers that can open and shut like a mouth **snapshot** n informal photograph **snap up** v take eagerly and quickly

snare n **1** trap with a noose ▷ v **2** catch in or as if in a snare

snarl v **1** (of an animal) growl with bared teeth **2** speak or utter fiercely **3** make tangled ▷ n **4** act or sound of snarling **5** tangled mass **snarl-up** n *informal* confused situation such as a traffic jam

snatch *v* **1** seize or try to seize suddenly **2** take (food, rest, etc.) hurriedly ▷ *n* **3** snatching **4** fragment

snazzy *adj* **-zier, -ziest** *informal* stylish and flashy

sneak *v* **1** move furtively **2** bring, take, or put furtively **3** *informal* tell tales ▷ *n* **4** cowardly or underhand person **5** *informal* telltale **sneaking** *adj* **1** secret **2** slight but persistent **sneaky** *adj*

sneakers *pl n* canvas shoes with rubber soles

sneer *n* **1** contemptuous expression or remark ▷ *v* **2** show contempt by a sneer

sneeze *v* **1** expel air from the nose involuntarily and noisily ▷ *n* **2** act or sound of sneezing

snib *n* catch of a door or window

snicker *n, v* same as **snigger**

snide *adj* maliciously derogatory

sniff *v* **1** inhale through the nose in short audible breaths **2** smell by sniffing ▷ *n* **3** act or sound of sniffing **sniffle** *v* **1** sniff repeatedly, as when suffering from a cold ▷ *n* **2** slight cold **sniff at** *v* express contempt for **sniffer dog** *Brit* police dog trained to detect drugs or explosives by smell

snifter *n informal* small quantity of alcoholic drink

snigger *n* **1** sly disrespectful laugh, esp. one partly stifled ▷ *v* **2** utter a snigger

snip *v* **snipping, snipped** **1** cut in small quick strokes with scissors or shears ▷ *n* **2** act or sound of snipping **3** *informal* bargain **snippet** *n* small piece

snipe *n* **1** wading bird with a long straight bill ▷ *v* (foll. by

at) **2** shoot at (a person) from cover **3** make critical remarks about **sniper** *n*

snitch *informal* ▷ *v* **1** act as an informer **2** steal ▷ *n* **3** informer

snivel *v* **-elling, -elled** cry in a whining way

snob *n* **1** person who judges others by social rank **2** person who feels smugly superior in his or her tastes or interests **snobbery** *n* **snobbish** *adj*

snood *n* pouch, often of net, loosely holding a woman's hair at the back

snook *n* **cock a snook at** show contempt for

snooker *n* **1** game played on a billiard table ▷ *v* **2** leave (a snooker opponent) in a position such that another ball blocks the target ball **3** *informal* put (someone) in a position where he or she can do nothing

snoop *informal* ▷ *v* **1** pry ▷ *n* **2** snooping **snooper** *n*

snooty *adj* **snootier, snootiest** *informal* haughty

snooze *informal* ▷ *v* **1** take a brief light sleep ▷ *n* **2** brief light sleep

snore *v* **1** make snorting sounds while sleeping ▷ *n* **2** sound of snoring

snorkel *n* **1** tube allowing a swimmer to breathe while face down on the surface of the water ▷ *v* **-kelling, -kelled 2** swim using a snorkel

snort *v* **1** exhale noisily through the nostrils **2** express contempt or anger by snorting ▷ *n* **3** act or sound of snorting

snot *n taboo* mucus from the nose

snout *n* animal's projecting nose and jaws

snow *n* **1** frozen vapour falling from the sky in flakes

2 *slang* cocaine ▷ *v* **3** fall as or like snow **be snowed under** be overwhelmed, esp. with paperwork **snowy** *adj*

snowball *n* **1** snow pressed into a ball for throwing ▷ *v* **2** increase rapidly **snowbird** *n* small N American songbird that breeds in the Arctic **snowblindness** *n* temporary blindness caused by the reflection of sunlight on snow **snowboard** *n* board on which a person stands to slide across the snow **snowboarding** *n* **snowdrift** *n* bank of deep snow **snowdrop** *n* small white bell-shaped spring flower **snow fence** fence erected in winter to prevent snow drifting across a road **snowflake** *n* single crystal of snow **snow line** (on a mountain) height above which there is permanent snow **snowman** *n* figure shaped out of snow **snowmobile** *n* motor vehicle with caterpillar tracks and front skis **snow pea** variety of pea with an edible pod **snowplow** *or* **snowplough** *n* vehicle for clearing away snow **snowshoes** *pl n* racket-shaped shoes for travelling on snow

snub *v* **snubbing, snubbed 1** insult deliberately ▷ *n* **2** deliberate insult ▷ *adj* **3** (of a nose) short and blunt **snub-nosed** *adj*

snuff[1] *n* powdered tobacco for sniffing up the nostrils

snuff[2] *v* extinguish (a candle) **snuff it** *informal* die

snuffle *v* breathe noisily or with difficulty

snug *adj* **snugger, snuggest 1** warm and comfortable **2** comfortably close-fitting **snugly** *adv*

snuggle *v* nestle into a person or thing for warmth or from affection

so *adv* **1** to such an extent **2** in such a manner **3** very **4** also **5** thereupon ▷ *conj* **6** in order that **7** with the result that **8** therefore ▷ *interj* **9** exclamation of surprise, triumph, or realization **so-and-so** *n informal* **1** person whose name is not specified **2** unpleasant person or thing **so-called** *adj* called (in the speaker's opinion, wrongly) by that name **so long** goodbye **so that** in order that

soak *v* **1** make wet **2** put or lie in liquid so as to become thoroughly wet **3** (of liquid) penetrate ▷ *n* **4** soaking **5** *slang* drunkard **soaking** *n*, *adj* **soak up** *v* absorb

soap *n* **1** compound of alkali and fat, used with water as a cleaning agent **2** *informal* soap opera ▷ *v* **3** apply soap to **soapy** *adj* **soap opera** television or radio serial dealing with domestic themes

soapstone *n* soft mineral used for making table tops and ornaments

soar *v* **1** rise or fly upwards **2** increase suddenly

sob *v* **sobbing, sobbed 1** weep with convulsive gasps **2** utter with sobs ▷ *n* **3** act or sound of sobbing **sob story** tale of personal distress told to arouse sympathy

sober *adj* **1** not drunk **2** serious **3** (of colours) plain and dull ▷ *v* **4** make or become sober **soberly** *adv* **sobriety** *n* state of being sober

sobriquet [so-brik-ay] *n* nickname

soccer *n* football played by two teams of eleven kicking or heading a spherical ball

sociable *adj* **1** friendly

or companionable **2** (of an occasion) providing companionship **sociability** n **sociably** adv

social adj **1** living in a community **2** of society or its organization **3** sociable ▷ n **4** convivial gathering **socially** adv **socialize** v meet others socially **socialite** n member of fashionable society **social media** websites and applications that allow users to interact **social networking site** website that allows subscribers to interact **social science** scientific study of society and its relationships **social security** state provision for the unemployed, aged, or sick **social services** welfare services provided by the local authorities **social work** work which involves helping people with serious financial or family problems

socialism n political system which advocates public ownership of industries, resources, and transport **socialist** n, adj **socialistic** adj

society n, pl **-ties 1** human beings considered as a group **2** organized community **3** structure and institutions of such a community **4** organized group with common aims and interests **5** upper-class or fashionable people collectively **6** companionship

sociology n study of human societies **sociological** adj **sociologist** n

sock¹ n cloth covering for the foot

sock² slang ▷ v **1** hit hard ▷ n **2** hard blow

socket n hole or recess into which something fits

sod n **1** (piece of) turf **2** slang obnoxious person

soda n **1** compound of sodium

2 soda water **soda water** fizzy drink made from water charged with carbon dioxide

sodden adj soaked

sodium n silver-white metallic element **sodium bicarbonate** white soluble compound used in baking powder

sodomy n anal intercourse **sodomite** n person who practises sodomy

sofa n couch

soft adj **1** not hard, rough, or harsh **2** (of a breeze or climate) mild **3** (too) lenient **4** easily influenced or imposed upon **5** feeble or silly **6** not robust **7** informal easy **8** (of water) containing few mineral salts **9** (of drugs) not liable to cause addiction **softly** adv **soften** v make or become soft or softer **soft drink** non-alcoholic drink **soft option** easiest alternative **soft-pedal** v deliberately avoid emphasizing something **soft-soap** v informal flatter **software** n computer programs **softwood** n wood of a coniferous tree

soggy adj **-gier, -giest 1** soaked **2** moist and heavy **sogginess** n

soigné, soignée [swah-nyay] adj well-groomed, elegant

soil¹ n **1** top layer of earth **2** country or territory

soil² v **1** make or become dirty **2** disgrace

soiree [swah-ray] n evening party or gathering

sojourn [soj-urn] v **1** stay temporarily ▷ n **2** temporary stay

solace [sol-iss] n, v comfort in distress

solar adj **1** of the sun **2** using the energy of the sun **solar plexus 1** network of nerves at the pit of the stomach

2 this part of the stomach **solar system** the sun and the heavenly bodies that go round it

solarium *n, pl* **-laria, -lariums** place with beds and ultraviolet lights used for acquiring an artificial suntan

sold *v* past of **sell**

solder *n* **1** soft alloy used to join two metal surfaces ▷ *v* **2** join with solder **soldering iron** tool for melting and applying solder

soldier *n* **1** member of an army ▷ *v* **2** serve in an army **soldierly** *adj* **soldier on** *v* persist doggedly

sole¹ *adj* **1** one and only **2** not shared, exclusive **solely** *adv* **1** only, completely **2** entirely **3** alone

sole² *n* **1** underside of the foot **2** underside of a shoe ▷ *v* **3** provide (a shoe) with a sole

sole³ *n* small edible flatfish

solecism [**sol**-iss-izz-um] *n* **1** minor grammatical mistake **2** breach of etiquette

solemn *adj* **1** serious, deeply sincere **2** formal **solemnly** *adv* **solemnity** *n* **solemnize** *v* **1** celebrate or perform (a ceremony) **2** make solemn **solemnization** *n*

solenoid [**sole**-in-oid] *n* coil of wire magnetized by passing a current through it

sol-fa *n* system of syllables used as names for the notes of a scale

solicit *v* **-iting, -ited 1** request **2** (of a prostitute) offer (a person) sex for money **solicitation** *n*

solicitor *n* lawyer who advises clients and prepares documents and cases

solicitous *adj* anxious about someone's welfare **solicitude** *n*

solid *adj* **1** (of a substance) keeping its shape **2** strong or substantial **3** not liquid or gas **4** not hollow **5** of the same substance throughout **6** sound or reliable **7** having three dimensions ▷ *n* **8** three-dimensional shape **9** solid substance **solidly** *adv* **solidify** *v* make or become solid or firm **solidity** *n*

solidarity *n* agreement in aims or interests, total unity

soliloquy *n, pl* **-quies** speech made by a person while alone, esp. in a play **soliloquize** *v* utter a soliloquy

solipsism *n* doctrine that the self is the only thing known to exist **solipsist** *n*

solitaire *n* **1** game for one person played with pegs set in a board **2** gem set by itself

solitary *adj* **1** alone, single **2** (of a place) lonely **solitude** *n* state of being solitary

solo *n, pl* **-los 1** music for one performer **2** any act done without assistance ▷ *adj* **3** done alone ▷ *adv* **4** by oneself, alone **soloist** *n*

solstice *n* either the shortest (in winter) or longest (in summer) day of the year

soluble *adj* **1** able to be dissolved **2** able to be solved **solubility** *n*

solution *n* **1** answer to a problem **2** act of solving a problem **3** liquid with something dissolved in it **4** process of dissolving

solve *v* find the answer to (a problem) **solvable** *adj*

solvent *adj* **1** able to meet financial obligations ▷ *n* **2** liquid capable of dissolving other substances **solvency** *n* **solvent abuse** deliberate inhaling of intoxicating fumes from certain solvents

sombre *adj* dark, gloomy

S

sombrero *n, pl* **-ros** wide-brimmed Mexican hat

some *adj* **1** unknown or unspecified **2** unknown or unspecified quantity or number of **3** considerable number or amount of **4** *informal* remarkable ▷ *pron* **5** certain unknown or unspecified people or things **6** unknown or unspecified number or quantity **somebody** *pron* **1** some person ▷ *n* **2** important person **somehow** *adv* in some unspecified way **someone** *pron* somebody **something** *pron* **1** unknown or unspecified thing or amount **2** impressive or important thing **sometime** *adv* **1** at some unspecified time ▷ *adj* **2** former **sometimes** *adv* from time to time, now and then **somewhat** *adv* to some extent, rather **somewhere** *adv* in, to, or at some unspecified or unknown place

somersault *n* **1** leap or roll in which the trunk and legs are turned over the head ▷ *v* **2** perform a somersault

somnambulist *n* person who walks in his or her sleep **somnambulism** *n*

somnolent *adj* drowsy **somnolence** *n*

son *n* male child **son-in-law** *n, pl* **sons-in-law** husband of one's child

sonar *n* device for detecting underwater objects by the reflection of sound waves

sonata *n* piece of music in several movements for one instrument with or without piano **sonatina** *n* short sonata

son et lumière [**sawn** eh **loo**-mee-er] *n French* night-time entertainment with lighting and sound effects, telling the story of the place where it is staged

song *n* **1** music for the voice **2** tuneful sound made by certain birds **3** singing **for a song** very cheaply **songster** (**songstress**) *n* singer **songbird** *n* any bird with a musical call

sonic *adj* of or producing sound **sonic boom** loud bang caused by an aircraft flying faster than sound

sonnet *n* fourteen-line poem with a fixed rhyme scheme

sonorous *adj* (of sound) deep or resonant **sonorously** *adv* **sonority** *n*

soon *adv* in a short time **sooner** *adv* rather: *I'd sooner go alone* **sooner or later** eventually

soot *n* black powder formed by the incomplete burning of an organic substance **sooty** *adj*

soothe *v* **1** make calm **2** relieve (pain etc.)

soothsayer *n* seer or prophet

sop *n* **1** concession to pacify someone ▷ *v* **sopping**, **sopped** **2** mop up or absorb (liquid) **sopping** *adj* completely soaked **soppy** *adj* *informal* oversentimental

sophist *n* person who uses clever but invalid arguments **sophism** *or* **sophistry** *n* clever but invalid argument

sophisticate *v* **1** make less natural or innocent **2** make more complex or refined ▷ *n* **3** sophisticated person **sophisticated** *adj* **1** having or appealing to refined or cultured tastes and habits **2** complex and refined **sophistication** *n*

sophomore *n* student in second year at college

soporific *adj* **1** causing sleep ▷ *n* **2** drug that causes sleep

soprano *n, pl* **-pranos**

1 (singer with) the highest female or boy's voice **2** highest pitched of a family of instruments

sorbet n flavoured water ice

sorcerer n magician **sorceress** n fem **sorcery** n witchcraft or magic

sordid adj **1** dirty, squalid **2** base, vile **3** selfish and grasping **sordidly** adv **sordidness** n

sore adj **1** painful **2** causing annoyance **3** resentful **4** (of need) urgent ▷ adv **5** obsolete greatly ▷ n **6** painful area on the body **sorely** adv **1** greatly **2** grievously **soreness** n

sorghum n kind of grass cultivated for grain

sorrel n **1** bitter-tasting plant **2** reddish-brown colour **3** horse of this colour

sorrow n **1** grief or sadness **2** cause of sorrow ▷ v **3** grieve **sorrowful** adj **sorrowfully** adv

sorry adj **-rier, -riest 1** feeling pity or regret **2** pitiful or wretched

sort n **1** group all sharing certain qualities or characteristics **2** informal type of character ▷ v **3** arrange according to kind **4** mend or fix **out of sorts** slightly unwell or bad-tempered

sortie n **1** short return trip **2** operational flight by military aircraft **3** raid into enemy territory

SOS n **1** international code signal of distress **2** call for help

so-so adj informal mediocre

sot n habitual drunkard

sotto voce [sot-toe voe-chay] adv in an undertone

soubriquet n same as **sobriquet**

soufflé [soo-flay] n light fluffy dish made with beaten egg whites and other ingredients

sough [rhymes with **now**] v (of the wind) make a sighing sound

sought [sawt] v past of **seek**

souk [sook] n open-air marketplace in Muslim countries

soul n **1** spiritual and immortal part of a human being **2** essential part or fundamental nature **3** deep and sincere feelings **4** person regarded as typifying some quality **5** person **6** Also **soul music** type of Black music combining blues, pop, and gospel **soulful** adj full of emotion **soulless** adj **1** lacking human qualities, mechanical **2** (of a person) lacking sensitivity

sound¹ n **1** something heard, noise ▷ v **2** make or cause to make a sound **3** seem to be as specified **4** pronounce **sound barrier** informal sudden increase in air resistance against an object as it approaches the speed of sound **soundproof** adj **1** not penetrable by sound ▷ v **2** make soundproof **sound track** recorded sound accompaniment to a film

sound² adj **1** in good condition **2** firm, substantial **3** showing good judgment **4** ethically correct **5** financially reliable **6** thorough **7** (of sleep) deep **soundly** adv

sound³ v **1** find the depth of (water etc.) **2** ascertain the views of **3** examine with a probe **soundings** pl n **1** measurements of depth taken by sounding **2** questions asked of someone to find out his or her opinion **sounding board** person or group used to test a new idea

sound⁴ n channel or strait

soup n liquid food made from

meat, vegetables, etc. **soupy**
adj **soup kitchen** place where
food and drink is served to
needy people **soup up** *v*
modify (an engine) to increase
its power

soupçon [soop-sonn] *n* small
amount

sour *adj* **1** sharp-tasting
2 (of milk) gone bad **3** (of
a person's temperament)
sullen ▷ *v* **4** make or become
sour **sourly** *adv* **sourness**
n **sourpuss** *n informal* sullen
person

source *n* **1** origin or starting
point **2** spring where a river or
stream begins **3** person, book,
etc. providing information

souse *v* **1** plunge (something)
into liquid **2** drench **3** pickle

soutane [soo-**tan**] *n* Roman
Catholic priest's cassock

south *n* **1** direction towards
the South Pole, opposite north
2 area lying in or towards
the south ▷ *adj* **3** to or in
the south **4** (of a wind) from
the south ▷ *adv* **5** in, to, or
towards the south **southerly**
adj **southern** *adj* **southerner**
n person from the south of a
country or area **southward**
adj, adv **southwards** *adv*
southeast *n, adj, adv* (in or to)
direction between south and
east **southwest** *n, adj, adv*
(in or to) direction between
south and west **southpaw** *n
informal* left-handed person,
esp. a boxer **South Pole**
southernmost point on the
earth's axis

souvenir *n* keepsake,
memento

sou'wester *n* seaman's
waterproof hat covering the
head and back of the neck

sovereign *n* **1** king or
queen **2** former British
gold coin worth one pound
▷ *adj* **3** supreme in rank

or authority **4** excellent
5 (of a state) independent
sovereigntist *n, adj* promoter
of, or promoting, sovereignty
for Quebec **sovereignty**
n **sovereignty-association**
n proposal for political
sovereignty for Quebec with
economic association with
the rest of Canada

soviet *n* **1** formerly, elected
council at various levels of
government in the USSR ▷ *adj*
2 Soviet of the former USSR

sow[1] *v* sowing, sowed, sown
or sowed **1** scatter or plant
(seed) in or on (the ground)
2 implant or introduce

sow[2] *n* female adult pig

soya *n* plant whose edible
bean (**soya bean**) is used for
food and as a source of oil
soy sauce sauce made from
fermented soya beans, used in
Chinese and Japanese cookery

sozzled *adj slang* drunk

spa *n* resort with a mineral-
water spring

space *n* **1** unlimited expanse
in which all objects exist
and move **2** interval **3** blank
portion **4** unoccupied area
5 the universe beyond the
earth's atmosphere ▷ *v*
6 place at intervals **spacious**
adj having a large capacity or
area **spacecraft** *or* **spaceship**
n vehicle for travel beyond the
earth's atmosphere **space
shuttle** manned reusable
vehicle for repeated space
flights **spacesuit** *n* sealed
pressurized suit worn by an
astronaut

spade[1] *n* tool for digging
spadework *n* hard
preparatory work

spade[2] *n* playing card of the
suit marked with black leaf-
shaped symbols

spaghetti *n* pasta in the form
of long strings

spam computers slang ▷ v **spamming, spammed** 1 send unsolicited e-mail or text messages to multiple recipients ▷ n 2 unsolicited e-mail or text messages sent in this way

span n 1 space between two points 2 complete extent 3 distance from thumb to little finger of the expanded hand ▷ v **spanning, spanned** 4 stretch or extend across

spangle n 1 small shiny metallic ornament ▷ v 2 decorate with spangles

spaniel n dog with long ears and silky hair

spank v 1 slap with the open hand, esp. on the buttocks ▷ n 2 such a slap **spanking** n 1 series of spanks ▷ adj informal 2 quick 3 outstandingly fine or smart

spanner n tool for gripping and turning a nut or bolt

spar[1] n pole used as a ship's mast, boom, or yard

spar[2] v **sparring, sparred** 1 boxing, martial arts fight using light blows for practice 2 argue (with someone)

spare v 1 refrain from punishing or harming 2 protect (someone) from (something unpleasant) 3 afford to give ▷ adj 4 extra 5 in reserve 6 (of a person) thin ▷ n 7 duplicate kept in case of damage or loss **to spare** in addition to what is needed **sparing** adj economical **spare ribs** pork ribs with most of the meat trimmed off

spark n 1 fiery particle thrown out from a fire or caused by friction 2 flash of light produced by an electrical discharge 3 trace or hint (of a particular quality) ▷ v 4 give off sparks 5 initiate **spark plug** or **sparking plug** device in an engine that ignites the fuel by producing an electric spark

sparkle v 1 glitter with many points of light 2 be vivacious or witty ▷ n 3 sparkling points of light 4 vivacity or wit **sparkler** n hand-held firework that emits sparks **sparkling** adj (of wine or mineral water) slightly fizzy

sparrow n small brownish bird **sparrowhawk** n small hawk

sparse adj thinly scattered **sparsely** adv **sparseness** n

spartan adj strict and austere

spasm n 1 involuntary muscular contraction 2 sudden burst of activity or feeling **spasmodic** adj occurring in spasms **spasmodically** adv

spastic ▷ n 1 offensive person with cerebral palsy ▷ adj 2 offensive suffering from cerebral palsy 3 affected by spasms

spat[1] v past of **spit**[1]

spat[2] n slight quarrel

spat[3] n old-fashioned short gaiter

spate n 1 large number of things happening within a period of time 2 sudden outpouring or flood

spathe n large sheathlike leaf enclosing a flower cluster

spatial adj of or in space

spatter v 1 scatter or be scattered in drops over (something) ▷ n 2 spattering sound 3 something spattered

spatula n utensil with a broad flat blade for spreading or stirring

spawn n 1 jelly-like mass of eggs of fish, frogs, or molluscs ▷ v 2 (of fish, frogs, or molluscs) lay eggs 3 generate

spay v remove the ovaries

from (a female animal)

speak v **speaking, spoke, spoken 1** say words, talk **2** communicate or express in words **3** give a speech or lecture **4** know how to talk in (a specified language) **speaker** n **1** person who speaks, esp. at a formal occasion **2** loudspeaker **3 Speaker** official chairman of a body

spear n **1** weapon consisting of a long shaft with a sharp point **2** slender shoot **3** single stalk of broccoli or asparagus ▷ v **4** pierce with or as if with a spear **5** hockey illegally thrust the blade of a stick at (an opponent) **spearing** n **spearhead** n **1** leading force in an attack or campaign ▷ v **2** lead (an attack or campaign)

spearmint n type of mint

spec n **on spec** informal as a risk or gamble

special adj **1** distinguished from others of its kind **2** for a specific purpose **3** exceptional **4** particular **specially** adv **specialist** n expert in a particular activity or subject **specialty** or **speciality** n **1** special interest or skill **2** product specialized in **specialize** v be a specialist **specialization** n **special interest group** group with a common political goal

specie n coins as distinct from paper money

species n, pl **-cies** group of plants or animals that are related closely enough to interbreed naturally

specific adj **1** particular, definite ▷ n **2** drug used to treat a particular disease **specifics 3** particular details **specifically** adv **specification** n detailed description of something to be made or done **specify** v refer to or state specifically **specific gravity** ratio of the density of a substance to that of water

specimen n **1** individual or part typifying a whole **2** sample of blood etc. taken for analysis

specious [**spee**-shuss] adj apparently true, but actually false

speck n small spot or particle **speckle** n **1** small spot ▷ v **2** mark with speckles

specs pl n informal short for **spectacles**

spectacle n **1** strange, interesting, or ridiculous sight **2** impressive public show **spectacles 3** pair of glasses for correcting faulty vision **spectacular** adj **1** impressive ▷ n **2** spectacular public show **spectacularly** adv

spectate v watch **spectator** n person viewing anything, onlooker

spectre n **1** ghost **2** menacing mental image **spectral** adj

spectrum n, pl **-tra 1** range of different colours, radio waves, etc. in order of their wavelengths **2** entire range of anything **spectroscope** n instrument for producing or examining spectra

speculate v **1** guess, conjecture **2** buy property, shares, etc. in the hope of selling them at a profit **speculation** n **speculative** adj **speculator** n

speculum n, pl **-la, -lums** medical instrument for examining body cavities

sped v a past of **speed**

speech n **1** act, power, or manner of speaking **2** talk given to an audience **3** language or dialect **speechify** v make speeches, esp. boringly **speechless** *adj* unable to speak because of great emotion

speed *n* **1** swiftness **2** rate at which something moves or acts **3** *slang* amphetamine ▷ *v* **speeding, sped** *or* **speeded 4** go quickly **5** drive faster than the legal limit **speedy** *adj* **1** rapid **2** prompt **speedily** *adv* **speedboat** *n* light fast motorboat **speedometer** *n* instrument to show the speed of a vehicle **speed up** *v* accelerate **speedway** *n* track for motorcycle racing **speedwell** *n* plant with small blue flowers

speleology *n* study and exploration of caves **speleological** *adj* **speleologist** *n*

spell[1] *v* **spelling, spelt** *or* **spelled 1** give in correct order the letters that form (a word) **2** (of letters) make up (a word) **3** indicate **spelling** *n* **1** way a word is spelt **2** person's ability to spell **spell out** *v* make explicit

spell[2] *n* **1** formula of words supposed to have magic power **2** effect of a spell **3** fascination **spellbound** *adj* entranced

spell[3] *n* period of time of weather or activity

spelt *v* a past of **spell**[1]

spend *v* **spending, spent 1** pay out (money) **2** use or pass (time) **3** use up completely **spendthrift** *n* person who spends money wastefully

sperm *n* **1** male reproductive cell **2** semen **spermicide** *n* substance that kills sperm **sperm whale** large toothed whale

spermaceti [sper-ma-**set**-ee] *n* waxy solid obtained from the sperm whale

spermatozoon [sper-ma-toe-**zoe**-on] *n, pl* **-zoa** sperm

spew *v* **1** vomit **2** send out in a stream

sphagnum *n* moss found in bogs

sphere *n* **1** perfectly round solid object **2** field of activity **spherical** *adj*

sphincter *n* ring of muscle which controls the opening and closing of a hollow organ

Sphinx *n* **1** statue in Egypt with a lion's body and human head **2 sphinx** enigmatic person

spice *n* **1** aromatic substance used as flavouring **2** something that adds zest or interest ▷ *v* **3** flavour with spices **spicy** *adj* **1** flavoured with spices **2** *informal* slightly scandalous

spick-and-span *adj* neat and clean

spider *n* small eight-legged creature which spins a web to catch insects for food **spidery** *adj*

spiel *n* glib plausible talk

spigot *n* stopper for, or tap fitted to, a cask

spike *n* **1** sharp point **2** sharp pointed metal object ▷ *v* **3** put spikes on **4** pierce or fasten with a spike **5** add alcohol to (a drink) **spike someone's guns** thwart someone **spiky** *adj*

spill[1] *v* **spilling, spilt** *or* **spilled 1** pour from or as if from a container ▷ *n* **2** fall **3** amount spilt **spill the beans** *informal* give away a secret **spillage** *n*

spill[2] *n* thin strip of wood or paper for lighting pipes or fires

spin *v* **spinning, spun 1** revolve or cause to revolve rapidly **2** draw out and twist (fibres) into thread

s

▷ *n* **3** revolving motion **4** continuous spiral descent of an aircraft **5** *informal* short drive for pleasure **6** *informal* presenting of information in a way that creates a favourable impression **spin doctor** *informal* person who provides a favourable slant to a news item or policy on behalf of a politician or a political party **spin a yarn** see **yarn** ▸ **spinner** *n* **spin-dry** *v* dry (clothes) in a spin-dryer **spin-dryer** *n* machine in which washed clothes are spun in a perforated drum to remove excess water **spin-off** *n* incidental benefit **spin out** *v* prolong

spina bifida *n* condition in which part of the spinal cord protrudes through a gap in the backbone, often causing paralysis

spinach *n* dark green leafy vegetable

spindle *n* **1** rotating rod that acts as an axle **2** weighted rod rotated for spinning thread by hand **spindly** *adj* long, slender, and frail

spindrift *n* spray blown along the surface of the sea

spine *n* **1** backbone **2** sharp point on an animal or plant **3** edge of a book, record sleeve, etc. on which the title is printed **spinal** *adj* of the spine **spineless** *adj* lacking courage **spiny** *adj* covered with spines

spinet *n* small harpsichord

spinnaker *n* large sail on a racing yacht

spinney *n* small wood

spinster *n* unmarried woman

spiral *n* **1** continuous curve formed by a point winding about a central axis at an ever-increasing distance from it **2** steadily accelerating increase or decrease ▷ *v* **-ralling, -ralled 3** move in a spiral **4** increase or decrease with steady acceleration ▷ *adj* **5** having the form of a spiral

spire *n* pointed part of a steeple

spirit *n* **1** nonphysical aspect of a person concerned with profound thoughts **2** nonphysical part of a person believed to live on after death **3** prevailing feeling **4** temperament or disposition **5** liveliness **6** courage **7** essential meaning as opposed to literal interpretation **8** ghost **spirits 9** emotional state **10** strong alcoholic drink ▷ *v* **-iting, -ited 11** carry away mysteriously **spirited** *adj* lively **spirituous** *adj* alcoholic **spirit level** glass tube containing a bubble in liquid, used to check whether a surface is level

spiritual *adj* **1** relating to the spirit **2** relating to sacred things ▷ *n* **3** type of religious folk song originating among Black slaves in N America **spiritually** *adv* **spirituality** *n* **spiritualism** *n* belief that the spirits of the dead can communicate with the living **spiritualist** *n*

spit[1] *v* **spitting, spat 1** eject (saliva or food) from the mouth **2** throw out particles explosively **3** rain slightly **4** utter (words) in a violent manner ▷ *n* **5** saliva **spitting image** *informal* person who looks very like another **spittle** *n* fluid produced in the mouth, saliva **spittoon** *n* bowl to spit into

spit[2] *n* **1** sharp rod on which meat is skewered for roasting **2** long strip of land projecting into the sea

spite n **1** deliberate nastiness ▷ v **2** annoy or hurt from spite **in spite of** in defiance of **spiteful** adj **spitefully** adv

spitfire n person with a fiery temper

splake n hybrid trout

splash v **1** scatter (liquid) or (of liquid) be scattered in drops **2** scatter liquid on (something) **3** print (a story or photograph) prominently in a newspaper ▷ n **4** splashing sound **5** patch (of colour or light) **6** extravagant display **7** small amount of liquid added to a drink **splash out** v informal spend extravagantly

splatter v, n splash

splay v **1** spread out **2** slant outwards ▷ adj **3** splayed

spleen n **1** abdominal organ which filters bacteria from the blood **2** bad temper **splenetic** adj spiteful or irritable

splendid adj **1** excellent **2** brilliant in appearance **splendidly** adv **splendour** n

splice v join by interweaving or overlapping ends **get spliced** slang get married

splint n rigid support for a broken bone

splinter n **1** thin sharp piece broken off, esp. from wood ▷ v **2** break into fragments **splinter group** group that has broken away from an organization

split v **splitting, split** **1** break into separate pieces **2** separate **3** share ▷ n **4** crack or division caused by splitting **splits 5** act of sitting with the legs outstretched in opposite directions **split second** very short period of time **split up** v **1** separate (something) into parts **2** (of a couple) end a relationship or marriage

splotch, splodge n, v splash, daub

splurge v **1** spend money extravagantly ▷ n **2** bout of extravagance

splutter v **1** make hissing spitting sounds **2** utter with spitting sounds ▷ n **3** spluttering

spoil v **spoiling, spoilt** or **spoiled 1** damage **2** harm the character of (a child) by giving it all it wants **3** rot, go bad **spoiling for** eager for **spoils** pl n booty **spoilsport** n person who spoils the enjoyment of others

spoke[1] v past tense of **speak**

spoke[2] n bar joining the hub of a wheel to the rim

spoken v past participle of **speak**

spokesman, spokeswoman, spokesperson n person chosen to speak on behalf of a group

spoliation n plundering

sponge n **1** sea animal with a porous absorbent skeleton **2** skeleton of a sponge, or a substance like it, used for cleaning **3** type of light cake ▷ v **4** wipe with a sponge **5** live at the expense of others **sponger** n slang person who sponges on others **spongy** adj

sponsor n **1** person who promotes something **2** person who agrees to give money to a charity on completion of a specified activity by another **3** godparent ▷ v **4** act as a sponsor for **sponsorship** n

spontaneous adj **1** voluntary and unpremeditated **2** occurring through natural processes without outside influence **spontaneously** adv **spontaneity** n

spoof n mildly satirical parody

spook n informal ghost **spooky** adj

spool n cylinder round which something can be wound

spoon n 1 shallow bowl attached to a handle for eating, stirring, or serving food ▷ v 2 lift with a spoon **spoonful** n **spoon-feed** v 1 feed with a spoon 2 give (someone) too much help

spoonerism n accidental changing over of the initial sounds of a pair of words, such as *half-warmed fish* for *half-formed wish*

spoor n trail of an animal

sporadic adj intermittent, scattered **sporadically** adv

spore n minute reproductive body of some plants

sporran n pouch worn in front of a kilt

sport n 1 activity for pleasure, competition, or exercise 2 such activities collectively 3 enjoyment 4 playful joking 5 person who reacts cheerfully ▷ v 6 wear proudly **sporting** adj 1 of sport 2 having a sportsmanlike attitude **sporting chance** reasonable chance of success **sporty** adj **sportive** adj playful **sports car** fast low-built car, usu. open-topped **sports jacket** man's casual jacket **sportsman** (**sportswoman**) n 1 person who plays sports 2 person who plays fair and is good-humoured when losing **sportsmanlike** adj **sportsmanship** n **sport utility vehicle** powerful four-wheel drive vehicle for rough terrain

spot n 1 small mark on a surface 2 pimple 3 location 4 informal awkward situation 5 informal small quantity ▷ v **spotting, spotted** 6 notice 7 watch for and take note of 8 mark with spots **on the spot** 1 at the place in question 2 immediately 3 in an awkward predicament **spotless** adj absolutely clean **spotlessly** adv **spotty** adj with spots **spot check** random examination **spotlight** n 1 powerful light illuminating a small area 2 centre of attention **spot-on** adj informal absolutely accurate

spouse n husband or wife

spout n 1 projecting tube or lip for pouring liquids 2 stream or jet of liquid ▷ v 3 pour out in a stream or jet 4 slang utter (a stream of words) lengthily

sprain v 1 injure (a joint) by a sudden twist ▷ n 2 such an injury

sprang v a past tense of **spring**

sprat n small sea fish

sprawl v 1 lie or sit with the limbs spread out 2 spread out in a straggling manner ▷ n 3 anything that spreads out in an untidy and uncontrolled way: *urban sprawl*

spray[1] n 1 (device for producing) fine drops of liquid ▷ v 2 scatter in fine drops 3 cover with a spray **spray gun** device for spraying paint etc.

spray[2] n 1 branch with buds, leaves, flowers, or berries 2 ornament like this

spread v **spreading, spread** 1 open out or be displayed to the fullest extent 2 extend over a larger expanse 3 apply as a coating 4 send or be sent in all directions 5 distribute or be distributed over a period of time ▷ n 6 spreading 7 extent 8 informal ample meal 9 soft food which can be spread **spread-eagled** adj with arms and legs outstretched

spree n session of overindulgence, usu. in

sprig n 1 twig or shoot
sprightly adj -lier,
-liest lively and brisk
sprightliness n
spring v springing, sprang
or sprung, sprung 1 move
suddenly upwards or forwards
in a single motion, jump
2 develop unexpectedly
3 originate (from) 4 informal
arrange the escape of
(someone) from prison ▷ n
5 season between winter and
summer 6 coil which can
be compressed, stretched,
or bent and returns to its
original shape when released
7 natural pool forming the
source of a stream 8 jump
9 elasticity **springy** adj
elastic **springboard** n flexible
board used to gain height
or momentum in diving or
gymnastics **spring-clean** v
clean (a house) thoroughly
spring tide high tide at new
or full moon
springbok n S African
antelope
springer n small spaniel
sprinkle v scatter (liquid
or powder) in tiny drops or
particles over (something)
sprinkler n **sprinkling** n
small quantity or number
sprint v 1 run a short distance
at top speed ▷ n 2 short race
run at top speed 3 fast run
sprinter n
sprit n small spar set
diagonally across a sail to
extend it **spritsail** n sail
extended by a sprit
sprite n elf
sprocket n wheel with teeth
on the rim, that drives or is
driven by a chain
sprout v 1 put forth shoots
2 begin to grow or develop
▷ n 3 shoot 4 short for
Brussels sprout

spruce[1] n kind of fir
spruce[2] adj neat and smart
spruce up v make neat and
smart
sprung v a past tense of
spring
spry adj spryer, spryest or
sprier, spriest active or
nimble
spud n informal potato
spume n, v froth
spun v past of spin
spunk n informal courage, spirit
spunky adj
spur n 1 spiked wheel on the
heel of a rider's boot used to
urge on a horse 2 stimulus
or incentive 3 projection ▷ v
spurring, spurred 4 urge on,
incite (someone) **on the spur
of the moment** on impulse
spurge n plant with milky sap
spurious adj not genuine
spurn v reject with scorn
spurt v 1 gush or cause to
gush out in a jet ▷ n 2 short
sudden burst of activity or
speed 3 sudden gush
sputnik n early Soviet
artificial satellite
sputter v, n splutter
sputum n, pl -ta spittle, usu.
mixed with mucus
spy n, pl spies 1 person
employed to obtain secret
information 2 person who
secretly watches others ▷ v
spying, spied 3 act as a spy
4 catch sight of **spyware** n
computers software secretly
installed via the internet
to gather and transmit
information about the user
Sq. Square
squabble v, n (engage in) a
petty or noisy quarrel
squad n small group of people
working or training together
squadron n division of an
air force, fleet, or cavalry
regiment
squalid adj 1 dirty and

unpleasant **2** morally sordid
squalor n disgusting dirt and
filth
squall n **1** sudden strong wind
2 harsh cry ▷ v **3** cry noisily,
yell
squander v waste (money or
resources)
square n **1** geometric figure
with four equal sides and four
right angles **2** open area in a
town in this shape **3** product
of a number multiplied by
itself ▷ adj **4** square in
shape **5** denoting a measure
of area **6** straight or level
7 fair and honest **8** with all
accounts or debts settled
▷ v **9** make square
10 multiply (a number) by
itself **11** be or cause to be
consistent ▷ adv **12** squarely,
directly **squarely** adv **1** in a
direct way **2** in an honest and
frank manner **square dance**
formation dance in which
the couples form squares
square meal substantial
meal **square root** number
of which a given number is
the square **square up to** v
prepare to confront (a person
or problem)
squash v **1** crush flat
2 suppress **3** humiliate with
a crushing retort **4** push into
a confined space ▷ n **5** sweet
fruit drink diluted with
water **6** crowd of people in a
confined space **7** Also **squash
rackets** game played in an
enclosed court with a rubber
ball and long-handled rackets
8 marrow-like vegetable
squashy adj
squat v **squatting, squatted**
1 crouch with the knees bent
and the weight on the feet
2 occupy unused premises to
which one has no legal right
▷ n **3** place where squatters
live ▷ adj **4** short and broad

squatter n illegal occupier
of unused premises
squaw n offensive native
American or Canadian Indian
woman
squawk n **1** loud harsh cry ▷ v
2 utter a squawk
squeak n **1** short shrill cry or
sound ▷ v **2** make or utter
a squeak **narrow squeak**
informal narrow escape
squeaky adj
squeal n **1** long shrill cry or
sound ▷ v **2** make or utter
a squeal **3** slang inform on
someone to the police
squeamish adj easily
sickened or shocked
squeegee n tool with a rubber
blade for clearing water from
a surface
squeeze v **1** grip or press
firmly **2** crush or press to
extract liquid **3** push into a
confined space **4** hug **5** obtain
(something) by force or
great effort ▷ n **6** squeezing
7 amount extracted by
squeezing **8** hug **9** crush of
people in a confined space
10 restriction on borrowing
11 baseball see **squeeze
play, suicide squeeze**
▷ **squeeze play** baseball play
in which the batter bunts to
bring home a runner on third
base
squelch v **1** make a wet
sucking sound, as by
walking through mud ▷ n
2 squelching sound
squib n small firework that
hisses before exploding
squid n sea creature with a
torpedo-shaped body and ten
tentacles
squiggle n wavy line
squiggly adj
squint v **1** have eyes which
face in different directions
2 glance sideways ▷ n
3 squinting condition of the

eye **4** *informal* glance ▷ *adj*
5 crooked

squire *n* **1** country gentleman,
usu. the main landowner
in a community **2** *hist*
knight's apprentice

squirm *v* **1** wriggle, writhe
2 feel embarrassed ▷ *n*
3 wriggling movement

squirrel *n* small bushy-tailed
tree-living animal

squirt *v* **1** force (a liquid)
or (of a liquid) be forced
out of a narrow opening
2 squirt liquid at ▷ *n* **3** jet
of liquid **4** *informal* small or
insignificant person

squish *v, n* (make) a soft
squelching sound **squishy** *adj*

Sr *chem* strontium

Sr. **1** Senior **2** Señor

SS **1** Schutzstaffel: Nazi
paramilitary security force
2 steamship

st. stone (weight)

St. **1** Saint **2** Street

stab *v* **stabbing, stabbed**
1 pierce with something
pointed **2** jab (at) ▷ *n*
3 stabbing **4** sudden
unpleasant sensation
5 *informal* attempt

stabilize *v* make or become
stable **stabilization**
n **stabilizer** *n* device for
stabilizing a child's bicycle,
an aircraft, or a ship

stable¹ *n* **1** building in
which horses are kept
2 establishment that breeds
and trains racehorses
3 establishment that
manages or trains several
entertainers or athletes ▷ *v*
4 put or keep (a horse) in a
stable

stable² *adj* **1** firmly fixed
or established **2** firm in
character **3** *science* not subject
to decay or decomposition
stability *n*

staccato [stak-ah-toe] *adj, adv*

1 *music* with the notes sharply
separated ▷ *adj* **2** consisting
of short abrupt sounds

stack *n* **1** ordered pile **2** large
amount **3** chimney ▷ *v* **4** pile
in a stack **5** control (aircraft
waiting to land) so that they
fly at different altitudes

stadium *n, pl* **-diums, -dia**
sports arena with tiered seats
for spectators

staff¹ *n* **1** people employed in
an organization **2** stick used
as a weapon, support, etc. ▷ *v*
3 supply with personnel

staff² *n, pl* **staves** set of five
horizontal lines on which
music is written

stag *n* adult male deer **stag
beetle** beetle with large
branched jaws **stag party** or
stag night party for men only

stage *n* **1** step or period of
development **2** platform
in a theatre where actors
perform **3** portion of a
journey **4** separate unit of a
rocket that can be jettisoned
▷ *v* **5** put (a play) on stage
6 organize and carry out (an
event) **the stage** theatre
as a profession **stagy** *adj*
overtheatrical **stagecoach**
n large horse-drawn vehicle
formerly used to carry
passengers and mail **stage
fright** nervousness felt by
a person about to face an
audience **stage whisper** loud
whisper intended to be heard
by an audience

stagger *v* **1** walk unsteadily
2 astound **3** arrange in
alternating positions or
periods ▷ *n* **4** staggering
staggering *adj*

stagnant *adj* **1** (of water or
air) stale from not moving
2 not growing or developing
stagnate *v* be stagnant
stagnation *n*

staid *adj* sedate, serious,

and rather dull

stain v **1** discolour, mark **2** colour with a penetrating pigment ▷ n **3** discoloration or mark **4** moral blemish or slur **5** penetrating liquid used to colour things **stainless** adj **stainless steel** steel alloy that does not rust

stairs pl n flight of steps between floors, usu. indoors **staircase** or **stairway** n flight of stairs with a handrail or banisters

stake n **1** pointed stick or post driven into the ground as a support or marker **2** money wagered **3** an interest, usu. financial, held in something ▷ v **4** support or mark out with stakes **5** wager, risk **at stake** being risked **stake a claim to** claim a right to **stakeholder** n person who has a concern or interest in something, esp. a business **stake out** v slang (of police) keep (a place) under surveillance

stalactite n lime deposit hanging from the roof of a cave

stalagmite n lime deposit sticking up from the floor of a cave

stale adj **1** not fresh **2** uninteresting from overuse **3** lacking energy or ideas through overwork or monotony **staleness** n

stalemate n **1** chess position in which any of a player's moves would put his or her king in check, resulting in a draw **2** deadlock, impasse

stalk¹ n plant's stem

stalk² v **1** follow or approach stealthily **2** pursue persistently and, sometimes, attack (a person with whom one is obsessed) **3** walk in a stiff or haughty manner

stalking-horse n pretext

stall n **1** small stand for the display and sale of goods **2** ground-floor seat in a theatre or cinema **3** one of a row of seats in a church for the choir or clergy **4** compartment in a stable **5** small room or compartment ▷ v **6** stop (a motor vehicle or engine) or (of a motor vehicle or engine) stop accidentally **7** (of an aircraft) begin to drop because the speed is too low **8** employ delaying tactics

stallion n uncastrated male horse

stalwart [**stawl**-wart] adj **1** strong and sturdy **2** dependable ▷ n **3** stalwart person

stamen n pollen-producing part of a flower

stamina n enduring energy and strength

stammer v **1** speak or say with involuntary pauses or repetition of syllables ▷ n **2** tendency to stammer

stamp v **1** stick a postage stamp on **2** impress (a pattern or mark) on **3** bring (one's foot) down forcefully **4** walk with heavy footsteps **5** characterize ▷ n **6** Also **postage stamp** piece of gummed paper stuck to an envelope or parcel to show that the postage has been paid **7** instrument for stamping a pattern or mark **8** pattern or mark stamped **9** act of stamping the foot **10** characteristic feature **stamping ground** favourite meeting place **stamp out** v suppress by force

stampede n **1** sudden rush of frightened animals or of a crowd ▷ v **2** (cause to) take part in a stampede

stance n **1** manner of

standing **2** attitude

stanch [stahnch] v same as **staunch**[2]

stanchion n upright bar used as a support

stand v **standing, stood** **1** be in, rise to, or place in an upright position **2** be situated **3** be in a specified state or position **4** remain unchanged or valid **5** tolerate **6** offer oneself as a candidate **7** informal treat to ▷ n **8** stall for the sale of goods **9** structure for spectators at a sports ground **10** firmly held opinion **11** US witness box **12** rack or piece of furniture on which things may be placed **standing** n **1** reputation or status **2** duration ▷ adj **3** permanent, lasting **stand for** v **1** represent or mean **2** informal tolerate **stand in** v act as a substitute **stand-in** n substitute **stand-offish** adj reserved or haughty **stand up for** v support or defend

standard n **1** level of quality **2** example against which others are judged or measured **3** moral principle **4** distinctive flag **5** upright pole ▷ adj **6** usual, regular, or average **7** accepted as correct **8** of recognized authority **standardize** v cause to conform to a standard **standardization** n **standard lamp** lamp attached to an upright pole on a base

standpipe n tap attached to a water main to provide a public water supply

standpoint n point of view

standstill n complete halt

stank v a past tense of **stink**

Stanley Cup n trophy awarded annually to the National Hockey League champions

stanza n verse of a poem

staple[1] n **1** U-shaped piece of metal used to fasten papers or secure things ▷ v **2** fasten with staples **stapler** n small device for fastening papers together

staple[2] adj **1** of prime importance, principal ▷ n **2** main constituent of anything

star n **1** hot gaseous mass in space, visible in the night sky as a point of light **2** star-shaped mark used to indicate excellence **3** asterisk **4** celebrity in the entertainment or sports world **stars 5** astrological forecast, horoscope ▷ v **starring, starred 6** mark with a star or stars **7** feature or be featured as a star ▷ adj **8** leading, famous **stardom** n status of a star in the entertainment or sports world **starry** adj full of or like stars **starry-eyed** adj full of naive optimism **starfish** n star-shaped sea creature

starboard n **1** right-hand side of a ship, when facing forward ▷ adj **2** of or on this side

starch n **1** carbohydrate forming the main food element in bread, potatoes, etc., and used mixed with water for stiffening fabric ▷ v **2** stiffen (fabric) with starch **starchy** adj **1** containing starch **2** stiff and formal

stare v **1** look or gaze fixedly (at) ▷ n **2** fixed gaze

stark adj **1** desolate, bare **2** without elaboration **3** absolute ▷ adv **4** completely

starling n songbird with glossy black speckled feathers

start v **1** take the first step, begin **2** set or be set

S

in motion **3** establish or set up **4** make a sudden involuntary movement from fright ▷ *n* **5** first part of something **6** place or time of starting **7** advantage or lead in a competitive activity **8** starting movement from fright **starter** *n* **1** device for starting an automobile's engine **2** person who signals the start of a race **3** *baseball* pitcher who plays at the start of a game **4** first course of a meal, appetizer **start-up** *n* recently launched project or business enterprise

startle *v* slightly surprise or frighten

starve *v* **1** die or suffer or cause to die or suffer from hunger **2** deprive of something needed **starvation** *n*

stash *v informal* store in a secret place

state *n* **1** condition of a person or thing **2** *informal* excited or agitated condition **3** pomp **4** **State** sovereign political power or its territory **5** **State** the government ▷ *adj* **6** of or concerning the State **7** involving ceremony ▷ *v* **8** express in words **stately** *adj* dignified or grand **statement** *n* **1** something stated **2** printed financial account **stateroom** *n* **1** private cabin on a ship **2** large room in a palace, used for ceremonial occasions **statesman** (**stateswoman**) *n* experienced and respected political leader **statesmanship** *n*

static *adj* **1** stationary or inactive **2** (of a force) acting but producing no movement ▷ *n* **3** crackling sound or speckled picture caused by interference in radio or television reception **4** Also **static electricity** electric sparks produced by friction **statics** *n* branch of mechanics dealing with the forces producing a state of equilibrium

station *n* **1** place where trains stop for passengers **2** headquarters of the police **3** building with special equipment for a particular purpose: *power station* **4** television or radio channel **5** position in society ▷ *v* **6** assign (someone) to a particular place **station wagon** automobile with a rear door and luggage space behind the rear seats

stationary *adj* not moving

stationery *n* writing materials such as paper and pens **stationer** *n* dealer in stationery

statistic *n* numerical fact collected and classified systematically **statistics** *n* science of classifying and interpreting numerical information **statistical** *adj* **statistically** *adv* **statistician** *n* person who compiles and studies statistics

statue *n* large sculpture of a human or animal figure **statuary** *n* statues collectively **statuesque** [stat-yoo-**esk**] *adj* (of a woman) tall and well-proportioned **statuette** *n* small statue

stature *n* **1** person's height **2** intellectual or moral greatness

status *n* **1** social position **2** prestige **3** person's legal standing **status quo** existing state of affairs

statute *n* written law **statutory** *adj* required or authorized by law

staunch[1] *adj* loyal, firm

staunch², stanch v stop (a flow of blood)

stave n 1 one of the strips of wood forming a barrel 2 *music* same as **staff** ▷ v **staving, staved** or **stove** 3 burst a hole in **stave off** v ward off

stay¹ v 1 remain in a place or condition 2 reside temporarily 3 endure ▷ n 4 period of staying in a place 5 postponement **staying power** stamina

stay² n 1 prop or buttress **stays** 2 corset

STD sexually transmitted disease

stead n **in someone's stead** in someone's place **stand someone in good stead** be useful to someone

steadfast adj firm, determined **steadfastly** adv

steady adj **steadier, steadiest** 1 not shaky or wavering 2 sensible and dependable 3 regular or continuous ▷ v **steadying, steadied** 4 make steady ▷ adv 5 in a steady manner **steadily** adv **steadiness** n

steak n 1 thick slice of meat, esp. beef 2 slice of fish

steal v **stealing, stole, stolen** 1 take unlawfully or without permission 2 move stealthily 3 *baseball* reach (a base) by running to it while the ball is being pitched to the batter ▷ n 4 *informal* something acquired at little cost 5 *baseball* act of stealing a base **steal the show** (of a performer) draw the audience's attention away from the other performers

stealth n 1 secret or underhand behaviour ▷ adj 2 (of technology) able to render an aircraft almost invisible to radar 3 disguised or hidden: *stealth taxes*

stealthy adj **stealthily** adv

steam n 1 vapour into which water changes when boiled 2 power, energy, or speed ▷ v 3 give off steam 4 (of a vehicle) move by steam power 5 cook or treat with steam **steamer** n 1 steam-propelled ship 2 container used to cook food in steam **steam engine** engine worked by steam **steamroller** n 1 steam-powered vehicle with heavy rollers, used to level road surfaces ▷ v 2 use overpowering force to make (someone) do what one wants

steatite [stee-a-tite] n same as **soapstone**

steed n *lit* horse

steel n 1 hard malleable alloy of iron and carbon 2 steel rod used for sharpening knives 3 hardness of character or attitude ▷ v 4 make (oneself) hard and unfeeling **steely** adj

steep¹ adj 1 sloping sharply 2 *informal* (of a price) unreasonably high **steeply** adv **steepness** n

steep² v soak or be soaked in liquid **steeped in** filled with: *Scotland is steeped in history*

steeple n church tower with a spire **steeplejack** n person who repairs steeples and chimneys

steeplechase n 1 horse race with obstacles to jump 2 track race with hurdles and a water jump

steer¹ v 1 direct the course of (a vehicle or ship) 2 direct (one's course) **steerage** n cheapest accommodation on a passenger ship **steering wheel** wheel turned by the driver of a vehicle in order to steer it

steer² n castrated male ox

stein [stine] n earthenware beer mug

stellar _adj_ of stars

stem[1] _n_ **1** long thin central part of a plant **2** long slender part, as of a wineglass **3** part of a word to which inflections are added ▷ _v_ **stemming, stemmed 4 stem from** originate from

stem[2] _v_ **stemming, stemmed** stop (the flow of something)

stench _n_ foul smell

stencil _n_ **1** thin sheet with cut-out pattern through which ink or paint passes to form the pattern on the surface below **2** pattern made thus ▷ _v_ **-cilling, -cilled 3** make (a pattern) with a stencil

stenography _n_ shorthand **stenographer** _n_ shorthand typist

stentorian _adj_ (of a voice) very loud

step _v_ **stepping, stepped 1** move and set down the foot, as when walking **2** walk a short distance ▷ _n_ **3** stepping **4** distance covered by a step **5** sound made by stepping **6** foot movement in a dance **7** one of a sequence of actions taken in order to achieve a goal **8** degree in a series or scale **9** flat surface for placing the foot on when going up or down **steps 10** stepladder **step in** _v_ intervene **stepladder** _n_ folding portable ladder with supporting frame **stepping stone 1** one of a series of stones for stepping on in crossing a stream **2** means of progress towards a goal **step up** _v_ increase (something) by steps

step- _combining form_ denoting a relationship created by the remarriage of a parent: _stepmother_

steppe _n_ wide grassy treeless plain

stereo _adj_ **1** short for **stereophonic** ▷ _n_ **2** stereophonic record player **3** stereophonic sound

stereophonic _adj_ using two separate loudspeakers to give the effect of naturally distributed sound

stereoscopic _adj_ having a three-dimensional effect

stereotype _n_ **1** standardized idea of a type of person or thing ▷ _v_ **2** form a stereotype of

sterile _adj_ **1** free from germs **2** unable to produce offspring **3** lacking inspiration or vitality **sterility** _n_ **sterilize** _v_ make sterile **sterilization** _n_

sterling _n_ **1** British money system ▷ _adj_ **2** genuine **3** reliable

stern[1] _adj_ severe, strict **sternly** _adv_ **sternness** _n_

stern[2] _n_ rear part of a ship

sternum _n, pl_ **-na, -nums** breast bone

steroid _n_ organic compound containing a carbon ring system, such as many hormones

stertorous _adj_ (of breathing) laboured and noisy

stethoscope _n_ medical instrument for listening to sounds made inside the body

Stetson _n_ ® tall broad-brimmed hat, worn mainly by cowboys

stevedore _n_ person who loads and unloads ships

stew _n_ **1** food cooked slowly in a closed pot **2** _informal_ troubled or worried state ▷ _v_ **3** cook slowly in a closed pot

steward _n_ **1** person who looks after passengers on a ship or aircraft **2** official who helps at a public event such as a race **3** person who administers another's property **stewardess** _n fem_

stick[1] *n* **1** long thin piece of wood **2** such a piece of wood shaped for a special purpose: *hockey stick* **3** something like a stick: *stick of celery* **4** *slang* verbal abuse, criticism **stickhandle** *v* control a puck or ball in hockey, lacrosse, etc.

stick[2] *v* **sticking, stuck** **1** push (a pointed object) into (something) **2** fasten or be fastened by or as if by pins or glue **3** (foll. by *out*) extend beyond something else, protrude **4** *informal* put **5** come to a standstill **6** jam **7** remain for a long time **8** *slang* tolerate, abide **sticker** *n* adhesive label or sign **sticky** *adj* **1** covered with an adhesive substance **2** (of weather) warm and humid **3** *informal* difficult, unpleasant **stick-in-the-mud** *n* person who does not like anything new **stick-up** *n slang* robbery at gunpoint **stick up for** *v informal* support or defend

stickleback *n* small fish with sharp spines on its back

stickler *n* person who insists on something: *stickler for accuracy*

stiff *adj* **1** not easily bent or moved **2** firm in consistency **3** unrelaxed or awkward **4** severe: *stiff punishment* **5** strong: *a stiff drink* ▷ *n* **6** *slang* corpse **stiffly** *adv* **stiffness** *n* **stiffen** *v* make or become stiff **stiff-necked** *adj* haughtily stubborn

stifle *v* **1** suffocate **2** suppress

stigma *n* **1** mark of social disgrace **2** part of a plant that receives pollen **stigmata** *pl n* marks resembling the wounds of the crucified Christ **stigmatize** *v* mark as being shameful

stile *n* set of steps allowing people to climb a fence

stiletto *n, pl* **-tos 1** small slender dagger **2** Also **stiletto heel** high narrow heel on a woman's shoe

still[1] *adv* **1** now or in the future as before **2** up to this or that time **3** even or yet: *still more insults* **4** quietly or without movement ▷ *adj* **5** motionless **6** silent and calm, undisturbed **7** (of a drink) not fizzy ▷ *v* **8** make still ▷ *n* **9** photograph from a film scene **stillness** *n* **stillborn** *adj* born dead **still life** painting of inanimate objects

still[2] *n* apparatus for distilling alcoholic drinks

stilted *adj* stiff and formal in manner

stilts *pl n* **1** pair of poles with footrests for walking raised from the ground **2** long posts supporting a building above ground level

stimulus *n, pl* **-li 1** something that acts as an incentive to (someone) **2** something, such as a drug, capable of causing a response in a person or animal **stimulant** *n* drug, food, etc. that makes the body work faster, increases heart rate, etc. **stimulate** *v* **1** encourage to start or progress further: *methods to stimulate job creation* **2** fill (a person) with ideas or enthusiasm **3** act as a stimulus on **stimulation** *n*

sting *v* **stinging, stung 1** (of certain animals or plants) wound by injecting with poison **2** feel or cause to feel sharp physical or mental pain **3** *slang* cheat (someone) by overcharging ▷ *n* **4** wound or pain caused by or as if by stinging **5** mental pain **6** sharp pointed organ of certain animals or plants by

s

which poison can be injected

stingy adj **-gier, -giest** mean or miserly **stinginess** n

stink v **stinking, stank** or **stunk, stunk 1** give off a strong unpleasant smell **2** slang be very unpleasant ▷ n **3** strong unpleasant smell **4** slang unpleasant fuss

stint v **1** (foll. by on) be miserly with (something) ▷ n **2** allotted amount of work

stipend [**sty**-pend] n regular allowance or salary, esp. that paid to a clergyman **stipendiary** adj receiving a stipend

stipple v paint, draw, or engrave using dots **stippling** n

stipulate v specify as a condition of an agreement **stipulation** n

stir v **stirring, stirred 1** mix up (a liquid) by moving a spoon etc. around in it **2** move **3** excite or stimulate (a person) emotionally ▷ n **4** a stirring **5** strong reaction, usu. of excitement

stirrup n metal loop attached to a saddle for supporting a rider's foot

stitch n **1** link made by drawing thread through material with a needle **2** loop of yarn formed round a needle or hook in knitting or crochet **3** sharp pain in the side ▷ v **4** sew **in stitches** informal laughing uncontrollably **not a stitch** informal no clothes at all

stoat n small mammal of the weasel family, with brown fur that turns white in winter

stock n **1** total amount of goods available for sale in a shop **2** supply stored for future use **3** financial shares in, or capital of, a company **4** lineage **5** livestock

6 handle of a rifle **7** liquid produced by boiling meat, fish, bones, or vegetables **8** fragrant flowering plant **9** standing or status **stocks 10** hist instrument of punishment consisting of a wooden frame with holes into which the hands and feet of the victim were locked ▷ adj **11** kept in stock, standard **12** hackneyed ▷ v **13** keep for sale or future use **14** supply (a farm) with livestock or (a lake etc.) with fish **stockist** n dealer who stocks a particular product **stocky** adj (of a person) broad and sturdy **stockbroker** n person who buys and sells stocks and shares for customers **stock car** standard car modified for racing **stock exchange** or **market** institution for the buying and selling of shares **stockpile** v **1** acquire and store a large quantity of (something) for future use ▷ n **2** accumulated store **stock-still** adj motionless **stocktaking** n counting and valuing of the goods in a shop

stockade n enclosure or barrier made of stakes

stockinet n machine-knitted elastic fabric

stocking n close-fitting covering for the foot and leg **stocking stitch** alternate rows of plain and purl in knitting

stodgy adj **stodgier, stodgiest 1** (of food) heavy and starchy **2** (of a person) serious and boring **stodge** n heavy starchy food

stoic [**stow**-ik] n **1** person who suffers hardship without showing his or her feelings ▷ adj **2** Also **stoical** suffering hardship without showing one's feelings **stoically** adv

stoicism [**stow**-iss-izz-um] n

stoke v feed and tend a (fire or furnace) **stoker** n

stole[1] v past tense of **steal**

stole[2] n long scarf or shawl

stolen v past participle of **steal**

stolid adj showing little emotion or interest **stolidity** n **stolidly** adv

stomach n 1 organ in the body which digests food 2 front of the body around the waist 3 desire or inclination ▷ v 4 put up with

stomp v tread heavily

stone n 1 material of which rocks are made 2 piece of this 3 gem 4 hard central part of a fruit 5 hard deposit formed in the kidney or bladder 6 Brit unit of weight equal to 14 pounds ▷ v 7 throw stones at 8 remove stones from (a fruit) **stoned** adj slang under the influence of alcohol or drugs **stony** adj 1 of or like stone 2 unfeeling or hard **stony-broke** adj slang completely penniless **stonily** adv **Stone Age** prehistoric period when tools were made of stone **stone-cold** adj completely cold **stone-deaf** adj completely deaf **stonewall** v obstruct or hinder discussion **stoneware** n hard kind of pottery fired at a very high temperature

stood v past of **stand**

stooge n 1 actor who feeds lines to a comedian or acts as the butt of his jokes 2 slang person taken advantage of by a superior

stool n 1 chair without arms or back 2 piece of excrement

stool pigeon n informer for the police

stoop v 1 bend (the body) forward and downward 2 carry oneself habitually in this way 3 degrade oneself ▷ n 4 stooping posture

stop v **stopping, stopped** 1 bring to or come to a halt 2 cease or cause to cease from doing (something) 3 prevent or restrain 4 withhold 5 block or plug 6 stay or rest ▷ n 7 place where something stops 8 stopping or being stopped 9 full stop 10 knob on an organ that is pulled out to allow a set of pipes to sound **stoppage** n **stoppage time** same as **injury time** ▸ **stopper** n 1 plug for closing a bottle etc. 2 baseball relief pitcher **stopcock** n valve to control or stop the flow of fluid in a pipe **stopgap** n temporary substitute **stopover** n short break in a journey **stop press** news item put into a newspaper after printing has been started **stopwatch** n watch which can be stopped instantly for exact timing of a sporting event

store n 1 place for sale of goods and services, shop 2 supply kept for future use 3 storage place, such as a warehouse **stores** 4 stock of provisions ▷ v 5 collect and keep (things) for future use 6 put (furniture etc.) in a warehouse for safekeeping 7 stock (goods) 8 computers enter or retain (data) **in store** forthcoming or imminent **set great store by** value greatly **storage** n 1 storing 2 space for storing **storage heater** electric device that can accumulate and radiate heat generated by off-peak electricity

storey n floor or level of a building

stork n large wading bird

storm n 1 violent weather with wind, rain, or snow

2 strongly expressed reaction ▷ v **3** rush violently or angrily **4** rage **5** attack or capture (a place) suddenly **stormy** adj **1** characterized by storms **2** involving violent emotions **stormstayed** adj unable to leave a place because of stormy conditions

story n, pl **-ries 1** description of a series of events told or written for entertainment **2** plot of a book or film **3** newspaper report **4** informal lie

stoup [**stoop**] n small basin for holy water

stout adj **1** fat **2** thick and strong **3** brave and resolute ▷ n **4** strong dark beer **stoutly** adv **stoutness** n

stove[1] n apparatus for cooking or heating

stove[2] v a past of **stave**

stow v pack or store **stow away** v hide as a stowaway **stowaway** n person who hides on a ship or aircraft in order to travel free

straddle v have one leg or part on each side of (something)

strafe v attack (an enemy) with machine guns from the air

straggle v go or spread in a rambling or irregular way **straggler** n **straggly** adj

straight adj **1** not curved or crooked **2** level or upright **3** orderly **4** honest or frank **5** in continuous succession **6** (of spirits) undiluted **7** theatre serious **8** slang heterosexual **9** slang conventional ▷ n **10** straight part ▷ adv **11** in a straight line **12** immediately **13** in a level or upright position **go straight** informal reform after being a criminal **straighten** v **straightaway** adv immediately **straight**

face serious facial expression concealing a desire to laugh **straightforward** adj **1** (of a task) easy **2** honest, frank

strain[1] n **1** great demand on strength or resources **2** force exerted by straining **3** injury from overexertion **4** tension or tiredness **5** melody or theme ▷ v **6** cause (something) to be used or tested beyond its limits **7** make an intense effort **8** injure by overexertion **9** sieve **strained** adj **1** not relaxed, tense **2** not natural, forced **strainer** n sieve

strain[2] n **1** breed or race **2** trace or streak

strait n **1** narrow channel connecting two areas of sea **straits** position of acute difficulty **straitjacket** n strong jacket with long sleeves used to bind the arms of a violent person **strait-laced** adj prudish or puritanical

straitened adj **in straitened circumstances** not having much money

strand[1] v **1** run aground **2** leave in difficulties ▷ n **3** poetic shore

strand[2] n single thread of string, wire, etc.

strange adj **1** odd or unusual **2** not familiar **strange to** inexperienced (in) or unaccustomed (to) **strangely** adv **strangeness** n **stranger** n person who is not known or is new to a place or experience

strangle v **1** kill by squeezing the throat **2** prevent the development of **strangler** n **strangulation** n strangling **stranglehold** n **1** strangling grip in wrestling **2** powerful control

strap n **1** strip of flexible material for lifting, fastening,

or holding in place ▷ v
strapping, strapped
2 fasten with a strap or
straps **strapping** adj tall
and sturdy
strata n plural of **stratum**
stratagem n clever plan,
trick
strategy n, pl **-gies 1** overall
plan **2** art of planning in war
strategic [strat-**ee**-jik] adj
1 advantageous **2** (of
weapons) aimed at an
enemy's homeland
strategically adv **strategist** n
strathspey n Scottish dance
with gliding steps
stratosphere n atmospheric
layer between about 15 and
50 km above the earth
stratum [**strah**-tum] n, pl
strata 1 layer, esp. of rock
2 social class **stratify** v divide
into strata **stratification** n
straw n **1** dried stalks of grain
2 single stalk of straw **3** long
thin tube used to suck up
liquid into the mouth **straw
poll** unofficial poll taken to
determine general opinion
strawberry n sweet fleshy red
fruit with small seeds on the
outside **strawberry mark**
red birthmark
stray v **1** wander **2** digress
3 deviate from certain moral
standards ▷ adj **4** having
strayed **5** scattered, random
▷ n **6** stray animal
streak n **1** long band of
contrasting colour or
substance **2** quality or
characteristic **3** short stretch
(of good or bad luck) ▷ v
4 mark with streaks **5** move
rapidly **6** informal run naked in
public **streaker** n **streaky** adj
stream n **1** small river
2 steady flow, as of liquid,
speech, or people
3 schoolchildren grouped
together because of similar

ability ▷ v **4** flow steadily
5 move in unbroken
succession **6** float in the air
7 group (pupils) in streams
8 send video or audio material
over the internet so that the
receiving system can play it
almost simultaneously
streamer n **1** strip of coloured
paper that unrolls when
tossed **2** long narrow flag
streamline v **1** make more
efficient by removing the
parts that are least useful
or profitable **2** give (an
automobile, plane, etc.) a
smooth even shape to offer
least resistance to the flow
of air or water
street n public road, usu.
lined with buildings **on the
street** Also **on the streets**
homeless **streetcar** n public
transport vehicle powered
by an overhead wire and
running on rails laid in the
road **street hockey** or **road
hockey** sports informal hockey
played on a public street with
a ball and ordinary footwear
streetwalker n prostitute
streetwise adj knowing how
to survive in big cities
strength n **1** quality of being
strong **2** quality or ability
considered an advantage
3 degree of intensity **4** total
number of people in a group
on the strength of on the
basis of **strengthen** v
strenuous adj requiring great
energy or effort **strenuously**
adv
streptococcus [strep-toe-
kok-uss] n, pl **-cocci**
bacterium occurring in
chains, many species of
which cause disease
streptomycin n antibiotic
drug
stress n **1** emphasis **2** tension
or strain **3** stronger sound

in saying a word or syllable **4** *physics* force producing strain ▷ *v* **5** emphasize **6** subject to stress **7** put stress on (a word or syllable)

stretch *v* **1** extend or be extended **2** be able to be stretched **3** extend the limbs or body **4** strain (resources or abilities) to the utmost ▷ *n* **5** stretching **6** continuous expanse **7** period **8** ability to be stretched **9** *informal* term of imprisonment **stretchy** *adj* **stretcher** *n* frame covered with canvas, on which an injured person is carried

strew *v* **strewing, strewed, strewed** or **strewn** scatter (things) over a surface

striation *n* **1** scratch or groove **2** pattern of scratches or grooves **striated** *adj*

stricken *adj* seriously affected by disease, grief, pain, etc.

strict *adj* **1** stern or severe **2** adhering closely to specified rules **3** complete, absolute **strictly** *adv* **strictness** *n*

stricture *n* severe criticism

stride *v* **striding, strode, stridden 1** walk with long steps ▷ *n* **2** long step **3** regular pace **strides 4** progress

strident *adj* loud and harsh **stridently** *adv* **stridency** *n*

strife *n* conflict, quarrelling

strike *v* **striking, struck 1** cease work as a protest **2** hit **3** attack suddenly **4** afflict **5** enter the mind of **6** agree (a bargain) **7** ignite (a match) by friction **8** (of a clock) indicate (a time) by sounding a bell **9** discover (gold, oil, etc.) **10** make (a coin) by stamping it **11** take up (a posture) ▷ *n* **12** stoppage of work as a protest **13** striking **14** *baseball* pitched ball at which the batter either

swings and misses or which passes through the strike zone without the batter swinging **strike camp** dismantle and pack up tents **strike home** have the desired effect **striker** *n* **1** striking worker **2** attacking footballer **striking** *adj* **1** noteworthy **2** impressive **strike off** or **strike out** *v* cross out **strike out** *v baseball* **1** (of a pitcher) put a batter out by means of three strikes **2** (of a batter) be put out by means of three strikes **strike up** *v* **1** begin (a conversation or friendship) **2** begin to play music **strike zone** *baseball* area over home plate at which the pitcher aims and through which a ball must normally pass to count as a strike

string *n* **1** thin cord used for tying **2** set of objects threaded on a string **3** series of things or events **4** stretched wire or cord on a musical instrument that produces sound when vibrated **strings 5** restrictions or conditions **6** section of an orchestra consisting of stringed instruments ▷ *v* **stringing, strung 7** provide with a string or strings **8** thread on a string **pull strings** use one's influence **stringed** *adj* (of a musical instrument) having strings that are plucked or played with a bow **stringy** *adj* **1** like string **2** (of meat) fibrous **string along** *v informal* **1** accompany **2** deceive over a period of time **string up** *v informal* kill by hanging

stringent [**strin**-jent] *adj* strictly controlled or enforced **stringently** *adv* **stringency** *n*

strip *v* **stripping, stripped 1** take (the covering or clothes) off **2** take a title or possession away from (someone) **3** dismantle (an engine) ▷ n **4** long narrow piece **5** clothes a football team plays in **stripper** n person who performs a striptease **strip cartoon** sequence of drawings telling a story **striptease** n entertainment in which a performer undresses to music

stripe n **1** long narrow band of contrasting colour or substance **2** chevron on a uniform to indicate rank **striped** or **stripy** adj

stripling n youth

strive v **striving, strove, striven** make a great effort

strobe n short for **stroboscope**

stroboscope n instrument producing a very bright flashing light

strode v past tense of **stride**

stroke v **1** touch or caress lightly with the hand ▷ n **2** light touch or caress with the hand **3** rupture of a blood vessel in the brain **4** mark made by a pen or paintbrush **5** style or method of swimming **6** blow **7** action or occurrence of the kind specified: *a stroke of luck* **8** chime of a clock

stroll v **1** walk in a leisurely manner ▷ n **2** leisurely walk **stroller** n chair-shaped carriage for a baby

strong adj **1** having physical power **2** not easily broken **3** having an extreme or drastic effect: *strong discipline* **4** great in degree or intensity **5** having moral force **6** (of a drink) containing a lot of alcohol **7** having a specified number: *twenty strong* **strongly** adv **stronghold** n **1** fortress **2** area of

predominance of a particular belief **strongroom** n room designed for the safekeeping of valuables

strontium n silvery-white metallic element **strontium-90** n radioactive isotope present in the fallout of nuclear explosions

strop n leather strap for sharpening razors

stroppy adj **-pier, -piest** slang angry or awkward

strove v past tense of **strive**

struck v past of **strike**

structure n **1** complex construction **2** manner or basis of construction or organization ▷ v **3** give a structure to **structural** adj **structuralism** n approach to literature, social sciences, etc., which sees changes in the subject as caused and organized by a hidden set of universal rules **structuralist** n, adj

strudel n thin sheet of filled dough rolled up and baked, usu. with an apple filling

struggle v **1** work, strive, or make one's way with difficulty **2** move about violently in an attempt to get free **3** fight (with someone) ▷ n **4** striving **5** fight

strum v **strumming, strummed** play (a guitar or banjo) by sweeping the thumb or a plectrum across the strings

strumpet n old-fashioned prostitute

strung v past of **string**

strut v **strutting, strutted** **1** walk pompously, swagger ▷ n **2** bar supporting a structure **3** strutting walk

strychnine [**strik**-neen] n very poisonous drug used in small quantities as a stimulant

S

stub n **1** short piece left after use **2** counterfoil of a cheque or ticket ▷ v **stubbing, stubbed 3** strike (the toe) painfully against an object **4** put out (a cigarette) by pressing the end against a surface **stubby** adj short and broad

stubble n **1** short stalks of grain left in a field after reaping **2** short growth of hair on the chin of a man who has not shaved recently **stubbly** adj **stubble-jumper** n slang prairie grain farmer

stubborn adj **1** refusing to agree or give in **2** difficult to deal with **stubbornly** adv **stubbornness** n

stucco n plaster used for coating or decorating walls **stuccoed** adj

stuck v past of stick². **stuck-up** adj informal conceited or snobbish

stud¹ n **1** small piece of metal attached to a surface for decoration **2** dislike removable fastener for clothes **3** one of several small round objects fixed to the sole of a football boot to give better grip ▷ v **studding, studded 4** set with studs

stud² n **1** male animal, esp. a stallion, kept for breeding **2** Also **stud farm** place where horses are bred **3** slang virile or sexually active man

student n person who studies a subject, esp. at university

studio n, pl **-dios 1** workroom of an artist or photographer **2** room or building in which television or radio programmes, records, or films are made **studio apartment** one-room apartment with a small kitchen and bathroom

study v **studying, studied 1** be engaged in learning (a subject) **2** investigate by observation and research **3** scrutinize ▷ n, pl **studies 4** act or process of studying **5** room for studying in **6** book or paper produced as a result of study **7** sketch done as practice or preparation **8** musical composition designed to improve playing technique **studied** adj carefully practised or planned **studious** [styoo-dee-uss] adj **1** fond of study **2** careful and deliberate **studiously** adv

stuff v **1** pack, cram, or fill completely **2** fill (food) with a seasoned mixture **3** fill (an animal's skin) with material to restore the shape of the live animal **4** fill with padding ▷ n **5** substance or material **6** collection of unnamed things **stuff oneself** informal eat large quantities **stuffing** n **1** seasoned mixture with which food is stuffed **2** padding

stuffy adj **stuffier, stuffiest 1** lacking fresh air **2** informal dull or conventional

stultify v **-fying, -fied** dull the mind of (someone) by boring routine

stumble v **1** trip and nearly fall **2** walk with frequent stumbling **3** make frequent mistakes in speech ▷ n **4** stumbling **stumble across** v discover accidentally **stumbling block** obstacle or difficulty

stump n **1** base of a tree left when the main trunk has been cut away **2** part of a thing left after a larger part has been removed ▷ v **3** baffle **4** walk with heavy steps **stumpy** adj short and stubby

stun v **stunning, stunned 1** knock senseless **2** shock or overwhelm **stunning** *adj* very attractive or impressive

stung *v* past of **sting**

stunk *v* a past of **stink**

stunt[1] *v* prevent or impede the growth of **stunted** *adj*

stunt[2] *n* **1** acrobatic or dangerous action **2** anything spectacular done to gain publicity

stupefy *v* -**fying**, -**fied 1** make insensitive or lethargic **2** astound **stupefaction** *n*

stupendous *adj* **1** astonishing **2** huge **stupendously** *adv*

stupid *adj* **1** lacking intelligence **2** silly **3** in a stupor **stupidity** *n* **stupidly** *adv*

stupor *n* dazed or unconscious state

sturdy *adj* -**dier**, -**diest 1** healthy and robust **2** strongly built **sturdily** *adv* **sturdiness** *n*

sturgeon *n* fish from which caviar is obtained

stutter *v* **1** speak with repetition of initial consonants ▷ *n* **2** tendency to stutter

sty[1] *n, pl* **sties** pen for pigs

sty[2], **stye** *n, pl* **sties**, **styes** inflammation at the base of an eyelash

style *n* **1** manner of writing, speaking, or doing something **2** shape or design **3** elegance, refinement **4** prevailing fashion ▷ *v* **5** shape or design **6** name or call **stylish** *adj* smart, elegant, and fashionable **stylishly** *adv* **stylist** *n* **1** hairdresser **2** designer **3** person who writes with great attention to style **stylistic** *adj* of literary or artistic style **stylize** *v* cause to conform to an established stylistic form **styling mousse** foamy substance applied to hair

before styling to hold the style

stylus *n* needle-like device on a record player that rests in the groove of the record and picks up the sound signals

stymie *v* -**mieing**, -**mied** hinder or thwart

styptic *n, adj* (drug) used to stop bleeding

suave [**swahv**] *adj* smooth and sophisticated in manner **suavely** *adv* **suavity** *n*

sub *n* **1** submarine **2** subscription **3** substitute **4** *informal* advance payment of wages or salary ▷ *v* **subbing**, **subbed 5** act as a substitute **6** grant advance payment to

sub- *prefix* **1** *indicating* under or beneath: *submarine* **2** *indicating* subordinate: *sublieutenant* **3** *indicating* falling short of: *subnormal* **4** *indicating* forming a subdivision: *subheading*

subaltern *n* army officer below the rank of captain

subatomic *adj* of or being one of the particles which make up an atom

subcommittee *n* small committee formed from some members of a larger committee

subconscious *adj* **1** happening or existing without one's awareness ▷ *n* **2** *psychoanalysis* that part of the mind of which one is not aware but which can influence one's behaviour **subconsciously** *adv*

subcontinent *n* large land mass that is a distinct part of a continent

subcontract *n* **1** secondary contract by which the main contractor for a job puts work out to others ▷ *v* **2** put out (work) on a subcontract **subcontractor** *n*

subcutaneous [sub-cute-**ayn**-ee-uss] *adj* under the skin

subdivide v divide (a part of something) into smaller parts **subdivision** n

subdue v **-duing, -dued** **1** overcome **2** make less intense

subeditor n Brit person who checks and edits text for a newspaper or magazine

subject n **1** person or thing being dealt with or studied **2** grammar word or phrase that represents the person or thing performing the action of the verb in a sentence **3** person under the rule of a monarch or government ▷ adj **4** being under the rule of a monarch or government ▷ v **5** (foll. by to) cause to undergo **subject to** **1** liable to **2** conditional upon **subjection** n **subjective** adj based on personal feelings or prejudices **subjectively** adv

sub judice [sub **joo**-diss-ee] adj Latin under judicial consideration

subjugate v bring (a group of people) under one's control **subjugation** n

subjunctive grammar ▷ n **1** mood of verbs used when the content of the clause is doubted, supposed, or wished ▷ adj **2** in or of that mood

sublet v **-letting, -let** rent out (property rented from someone else)

sublimate v psychol direct the energy of (a primitive impulse) into socially acceptable activities **sublimation** n

sublime adj **1** of high moral, intellectual, or spiritual value **2** unparalleled, supreme ▷ v **3** chem change from a solid to a vapour without first melting **sublimely** adv

subliminal adj relating to mental processes of which the individual is not aware

sub-machine-gun n portable machine-gun with a short barrel

submarine n **1** vessel which can operate below the surface of the sea ▷ adj **2** below the surface of the sea

submerge v put or go below the surface of water or other liquid **submersion** n

submit v **-mitting, -mitted** **1** surrender **2** be (voluntarily) subjected to a process or treatment **3** put forward for consideration **submission** n **1** submitting **2** something submitted for consideration **3** state of being submissive **submissive** adj meek and obedient

subordinate adj **1** of lesser rank or importance ▷ n **2** subordinate person or thing ▷ v **3** make or treat as subordinate **subordination** n

suborn v bribe or incite (a person) to commit a wrongful act

subpoena [sub-**pee**-na] n **1** writ requiring a person to appear before a lawcourt ▷ v **2** summon (someone) with a subpoena

subscribe v **1** pay (a subscription) **2** give support or approval (to) **subscriber** n **subscription** n **1** payment for issues of a publication over a period **2** money contributed to a charity etc. **3** membership fees paid to a society

subsection n division of a section

subsequent adj occurring after, succeeding **subsequently** adv

subservient adj submissive, servile **subservience** n

subside v **1** become less intense **2** sink to a lower level **subsidence** n act or process of subsiding

subsidiary *adj* **1** of lesser importance **2** subordinate ▷ *n, pl* -**aries 3** subsidiary person or thing

subsidize *v* help financially **subsidy** *n* financial aid

subsist *v* manage to live **subsistence** *n*

subsonic *adj* moving at a speed less than that of sound

substance *n* **1** solid, powder, liquid, or paste **2** physical composition of something **3** essential meaning of something **4** solid or meaningful quality **5** wealth **substantial** *adj* **1** of considerable size or value **2** (of food or a meal) sufficient and nourishing **3** solid or strong **4** real **substantially** *adv* **substantiate** *v* support (a story) with evidence **substantiation** *n* **substantive** *adj* **1** of or being the essential element of a thing ▷ *n* **2** noun

substitute *v* **1** take the place of or put in place of another ▷ *n* **2** person or thing taking the place of another **substitution** *n*

subsume *v* incorporate (an idea, case, etc.) under a comprehensive classification

subterfuge *n* trick used to achieve an objective

subterranean *adj* underground

subtitle *n* **1** secondary title of a book **subtitles 2** printed translation at the bottom of the picture in a film with foreign dialogue ▷ *v* **3** provide with a subtitle or subtitles

subtle *adj* **1** not immediately obvious **2** having or requiring ingenuity **subtly** *adv* **subtlety** *n*

subtract *v* take (one number

or quantity) from another **subtraction** *n*

subtropical *adj* of the regions bordering on the tropics

suburb *n* residential area on the outskirts of a city **suburban** *adj* **1** of or inhabiting a suburb **2** narrow or unadventurous in outlook **suburbia** *n* suburbs and their inhabitants

subvention *n* subsidy

subvert *v* overthrow the authority of **subversion** *n* **subversive** *adj*

subway *n* **1** passage under a road or railway **2** electric passenger railway operated in underground tunnels

succeed *v* **1** accomplish an aim **2** turn out satisfactorily **3** come next in order after (something) **4** take over a position from (someone) **success** *n* **1** favourable outcome of an attempt **2** attainment of wealth, fame, or position **3** successful person or thing **successful** *adj* having success **successfully** *adv* **succession** *n* **1** series of people or things following one another in order **2** act or right by which one person succeeds another in a position **successive** *adj* consecutive **successively** *adv* **successor** *n* person who succeeds someone in a position

succinct *adj* brief and clear **succinctly** *adv*

succour *v, n* help in distress

succulent *adj* **1** juicy and delicious **2** (of a plant) having thick fleshy leaves ▷ *n* **3** succulent plant **succulence** *n*

succumb *v* (foll. by *to*) **1** give way (to something overpowering) **2** die of (an illness)

such *adj* **1** of the kind specified **2** so great, so much ▷ *pron* **3** such things **such-and-such** *adj* specific, but not known or named **suchlike** *adj informal* of the kind specified

suck *v* **1** draw (liquid or air) into the mouth **2** take (something) into the mouth and moisten, dissolve, or roll it around with the tongue **3** (foll. by *in*) draw in by irresistible force ▷ *n* **4** sucking **suck it up** *informal* face up to something unpleasant **sucker** *n* **1** *slang* person who is easily deceived or swindled **2** organ or device which adheres by suction **3** shoot coming from a plant's root or the base of its main stem **suck up to** *v informal* flatter (someone) for one's own profit

suckle *v* feed at the breast **suckling** *n* unweaned baby or young animal

sucrose [**soo**-kroze] *n* chemical name for sugar

suction *n* **1** sucking **2** force produced by drawing air out of a space to make a vacuum that will suck in a substance from another space

sudden *adj* **1** done or occurring quickly and unexpectedly ▷ *n* **2** **all of a sudden** quickly and unexpectedly **suddenly** *adv* **suddenness** *n* **sudden death** *sports* period of extra time in which the first competitor to score wins

sudorific [syoo-dor-**if**-ik] *n, adj* (drug) causing sweating

suds *pl n* froth of soap and water, lather

sue *v* **suing, sued** start legal proceedings against

suede *n* leather with a velvety finish on one side

suet *n* hard fat obtained from sheep and cattle, used in cooking

suffer *v* **1** undergo or be subjected to **2** tolerate **sufferer** *n* **suffering** *n* **sufferance** *n* **on sufferance** tolerated with reluctance

suffice [suf-**fice**] *v* be enough for a purpose **sufficiency** *n* adequate amount **sufficient** *adj* enough, adequate **sufficiently** *adv*

suffix *n* letter or letters added to the end of a word to form another word

suffocate *v* **1** kill or be killed by deprivation of oxygen **2** feel or cause to feel discomfort from heat and lack of air **suffocation** *n*

suffragan *n* bishop appointed to assist an archbishop or another bishop

suffrage *n* vote or right of voting **suffragist** (**suffragette**) *n* one claiming a right of voting

suffuse *v* spread through or over (something) **suffusion** *n*

sugar *n* **1** sweet crystalline carbohydrate found in many plants and used to sweeten food and drinks ▷ *v* **2** sweeten or cover with sugar **sugary** *adj* **sugar beet** beet cultivated for the sugar obtained from its roots **sugar bush** plantation of sugar maples **sugar cane** tropical grass cultivated for the sugar obtained from its canes **sugar daddy** *slang* elderly man who gives a young woman money and gifts in return for sexual favours **sugar maple** large N American maple tree yielding sweet sap from which sugar and syrup are made **sugar off** *v* reduce maple sap to syrup by boiling

suggest *v* **1** put forward

(an idea) for consideration **2** bring to mind by the association of ideas **3** give a hint of **suggestible** *adj* easily influenced **suggestion** *n* **1** suggesting **2** thing suggested **3** hint or indication **suggestive** *adj* **1** suggesting something indecent **2** conveying a hint (of) **suggestively** *adv*

suicide *n* **1** killing oneself intentionally **2** person who kills himself intentionally **3** self-inflicted ruin of one's own prospects or interests **suicidal** *adj* liable to commit suicide **suicidally** *adv* **suicide bomber** terrorist who carries out a bomb attack, knowing he or she will be killed in the explosion **suicide squeeze** *baseball* play in which a runner on third base runs for home as the ball is pitched

suit *n* **1** set of clothes designed to be worn together **2** outfit worn for a specific purpose **3** one of the four sets into which a pack of cards is divided **4** lawsuit ▷ *v* **5** be appropriate for **6** be acceptable to **suitable** *adj* appropriate or proper **suitably** *adv* **suitability** *n* **suitcase** *n* portable travelling case for clothing

suite *n* **1** set of connected rooms in a hotel **2** matching set of furniture **3** set of musical pieces in the same key

suitor *n old-fashioned* man who is courting a woman

sulfate *n* salt or ester of sulfuric acid

sulfide *n* compound of sulfur with another element

sulfite *n* salt or ester of sulfurous acid

sulfonamide [sulf-**on**-a-mide] *n* any of a class of drugs that prevent the growth of bacteria

sulfur *n* pale yellow nonmetallic element **sulfuric** or **sulfurous** *adj* of or containing sulfur

sulk *v* **1** be silent and sullen because of resentment or bad temper ▷ *n* **2** resentful or sullen mood **sulky** *adj* **sulkily** *adv* **sulkiness** *n*

sullen *adj* **1** unwilling to talk or be sociable **2** dark and dismal **sullenly** *adv* **sullenness** *n*

sully *v* **-lying, -lied 1** make dirty **2** ruin (someone's reputation)

sultan *n* sovereign of a Muslim country **sultana** *n* **1** kind of raisin **2** sultan's wife, mother, or daughter **sultanate** *n* territory of a sultan

sultry *adj* **-trier, -triest 1** (of weather or climate) hot and humid **2** passionate, sensual

sum *n* **1** result of addition, total **2** problem in arithmetic **3** quantity of money **sum total** complete or final total **sum up** *v* **summing, summed 1** summarize **2** form a quick opinion of

summary *n, pl* **-ries 1** brief account giving the main points of something ▷ *adj* **2** done quickly, without formalities **summarily** *adv* **summarize** *v* make or be a summary of (something) **summation** *n* **1** summary **2** adding up

summer *n* warmest season of the year, between spring and fall **summery** *adj* **summertime** *n* period or season of summer

summit *n* **1** highest point **2** top of a mountain or hill

S

3 conference between heads of state

summon v **1** order (someone) to come **2** send for (someone) to appear in court **3** call upon (someone) to do something **4** gather (one's courage, strength, etc.) **summons** n **1** command summoning someone **2** order requiring someone to appear in court ▷ v **3** order (someone) to appear in court

sumo n Japanese style of wrestling

sump n **1** receptacle in an internal-combustion engine into which oil can drain **2** hollow into which liquid drains

sumptuous adj lavish, magnificent **sumptuously** adv **sumptuousness** n

sun n **1** star around which the earth and other planets revolve **2** any star around which planets revolve **3** heat and light from the sun ▷ v **sunning, sunned 4** expose (oneself) to the sun's rays **sunless** adj **sunny** adj **1** full of or exposed to sunlight **2** cheerful **sunbathe** v lie in the sunshine in order to get a suntan **sunbeam** n ray of sun **sunburn** n painful reddening of the skin caused by overexposure to the sun **sunburnt** or **sunburned** adj **sundial** n device showing the time by means of a pointer that casts a shadow on a marked dial **sundown** n sunset **sunflower** n tall plant with large golden flowers **sunrise** n **1** daily appearance of the sun above the horizon **2** time of this **sunset** n **1** daily disappearance of the sun below the horizon **2** time of this **sunshine** n light and warmth from the

sun **sunspot** n dark patch appearing temporarily on the sun's surface **sunstroke** n illness caused by prolonged exposure to intensely hot sunlight **suntan** n browning of the skin caused by exposure to the sun **sun-up** n sunrise

sundae n ice cream topped with fruit etc.

Sunday n first day of the week and the Christian day of worship **Sunday school** school for teaching children about Christianity

sunder v break or tear apart

sundry adj several, various **sundries** pl n miscellaneous unspecified items **all and sundry** everybody

sung v past participle of **sing**

sunk, sunken v past participle of **sink**

sup v **supping, supped 1** take (liquid) by sips **2** obsolete take supper

super adj informal excellent

super- prefix **1** indicating above or over: superimpose **2** indicating outstanding: supergroup **3** indicating greater size or extent: supermarket

superannuation n **1** regular payment by an employee into a pension fund **2** pension paid from this **superannuated** adj discharged with a pension, owing to old age or illness

superb adj excellent, impressive, or splendid **superbly** adv

superbug n informal bacterium resistant to antibiotics

supercharged adj (of an engine) having a supercharger **supercharger** n device that increases the power of an internal-combustion engine by forcing extra air into it

supercilious adj showing

arrogant pride or scorn **superciliousness** n

superconductor n substance which has almost no electrical resistance at very low temperatures **superconductivity** n

superficial adj 1 of or on the surface 2 not careful or thorough 3 (of a person) without depth of character, shallow **superficially** adv **superficiality** n

superfluous [soo-**per**-flew-uss] adj more than is needed **superfluity** n

superhuman adj beyond normal human ability or experience

superimpose v place (something) on or over something else

superintend v supervise (a person or activity) **superintendence** n **superintendent** n 1 senior police officer 2 supervisor

superior adj 1 greater in quality, quantity, or merit 2 higher in position or rank 3 believing oneself to be better than others ▷ n 4 person of greater rank or status **superiority** n

superlative [soo-**per**-lat-iv] adj 1 of outstanding quality 2 grammar denoting the form of an adjective or adverb indicating most ▷ n 3 grammar superlative form of a word

superman n man of apparently superhuman powers

supermarket n large self-service store selling food and household goods

supermodel n famous and highly-paid fashion model

supernatural adj 1 of or relating to things beyond the laws of nature ▷ n 2 **the supernatural** supernatural forces, occurrences, and beings collectively

supernova n, pl -**vae**, -**vas** star that explodes and briefly becomes exceptionally bright

supernumerary adj 1 exceeding the required or regular number ▷ n, pl -**ries** 2 supernumerary person or thing

superphosphate n chemical fertilizer containing phosphates

superpower n extremely powerful nation

superscript adj 1 (of a character) printed or written above the line ▷ n 2 superscript character

supersede v replace, supplant

supersonic adj of or travelling at a speed greater than the speed of sound

superstition n 1 belief in omens, ghosts, etc. 2 idea or practice based on this **superstitious** adj

superstore n large supermarket

superstructure n 1 structure erected on something else 2 part of a ship above the main deck

supervene v occur as an unexpected development **supervention** n

supervise v watch over to direct or check **supervision** n **supervisor** n **supervisory** adj

supine [soo-**pine**] adj lying flat on one's back

supper n light evening meal

supplant v take the place of, oust

supple adj 1 (of a person) moving and bending easily and gracefully 2 bending easily without damage **suppleness** n **supply** adv

supplement n 1 thing added to complete something or make up for a lack 2 magazine inserted into a newspaper **3** section added to a publication to supply further information ▷ v **4** provide or be a supplement to (something) **supplementary** adj

supplication n humble request **supplicant** n person who makes a humble request

supply v -**plying**, -**plied 1** provide with something required **2** make available ▷ n, pl -**plies 3** supplying **4** amount available **5** economics willingness and ability to provide goods and services **supplies 6** food or equipment **supplier** n

support v **1** bear the weight of **2** provide the necessities of life for **3** give practical or emotional help to **4** take an active interest in (a sports team, political principle, etc.) **5** help to prove (a theory etc.) **6** speak in favour of ▷ n **7** supporting **8** means of support **supporter** n person who supports a team, principle, etc. **supportive** adj

suppose v **1** presume to be true **2** consider as a proposal for the sake of discussion **supposed** adj **1** presumed to be true without proof **2** doubtful **supposed to 1** expected or required to: *you were supposed to phone me* **2** permitted to: *we're not supposed to swim here* **supposedly** adv **supposition** n **1** supposing **2** something supposed

suppository n, pl -**ries** solid medication inserted into the rectum or vagina and left to melt

suppress v **1** put an end to **2** restrain (an emotion or response) **3** prevent

publication of (information) **suppression** n

suppurate v (of a wound etc.) produce pus **suppuration** n

supreme adj highest in authority, rank, or degree **supremely** adv extremely **supremacy** n **1** supreme power **2** state of being supreme **supremo** n informal person in overall authority

surcharge n additional charge

surd n math number that cannot be expressed in whole numbers

sure adj **1** free from uncertainty or doubt **2** reliable **3** inevitable ▷ adv, interj **4** informal certainly **surely** adv it must be true that **sure-footed** adj unlikely to slip or stumble

surety n, pl -**ties** person who takes responsibility, or thing given as a guarantee, for the fulfilment of another's obligation

surf n **1** foam caused by waves breaking on the shore ▷ v **2** take part in surfing **3** move quickly through a medium such as the internet **surfing** n sport of riding towards the shore on a surfboard on the crest of a wave **surfer** n **surfboard** n board used in surfing

surface n **1** outside or top of an object **2** material covering the surface of an object **3** superficial appearance ▷ v **4** rise to the surface **5** put a surface on

surfeit n excessive amount

surge n **1** sudden powerful increase **2** strong rolling movement of the sea ▷ v **3** increase suddenly **4** move forward strongly

surgeon n doctor who specializes in surgery

surgery n 1 treatment in which the patient's body is cut open in order to treat the affected part 2 Brit place where, or time when, a doctor, dentist, MP, etc. can be consulted **surgical** adj **surgically** adv

surly adj -lier, -liest ill-tempered and rude **surliness** n

surmise v, n guess, conjecture

surmount v 1 overcome (a problem) 2 be on top of (something) **surmountable** adj

surname n family name

surpass v be greater than or superior to

surplice n loose white robe worn by clergymen and choristers

surplus n amount left over in excess of what is required

surprise n 1 unexpected event 2 amazement and wonder ▷ v 3 cause to feel amazement or wonder 4 come upon, attack, or catch suddenly and unexpectedly **take someone by surprise** catch someone unprepared

surrealism n movement in art and literature involving the combination of incongruous images, as in a dream **surreal** adj **surrealist** n, adj **surrealistic** adj

surrender v 1 give oneself up 2 give (something) up to another 3 yield (to a temptation or influence) ▷ n 4 surrendering

surreptitious adj done secretly or stealthily **surreptitiously** adv

surrogate n substitute **surrogate mother** woman who gives birth to a child on behalf of a couple who cannot have children

surround v 1 be, come, or place all around (a person or thing) ▷ n 2 border or edging

surroundings pl n conditions, scenery, etc. around a person, place, or thing

surtax n extra tax on incomes above a certain level

surveillance n close observation

survey v 1 view or consider in a general way 2 make a map of (an area) 3 inspect (a building) to assess its condition and value 4 find out the incomes, opinions, etc. of (a group of people) ▷ n 5 surveying 6 report produced by a survey **surveyor** n

survive v 1 continue to live or exist after (a difficult experience) 2 live after the death of (another) **survival** n 1 condition of having survived 2 thing that has survived from an earlier time **survivor** n

susceptible adj liable to be influenced or affected by **susceptibility** n

suspect v 1 believe (someone) to be guilty without having any proof 2 think (something) to be false or questionable 3 believe (something) to be the case ▷ adj 4 not to be trusted ▷ n 5 person who is suspected

suspend v 1 hang from a high place 2 cause to remain floating or hanging 3 cause to cease temporarily 4 remove (someone) temporarily from a job or team **suspenders** pl n 1 straps worn over the shoulders to hold up trousers 2 Brit straps for holding up stockings

suspense n state of uncertainty while awaiting news, an event, etc.

suspension n 1 suspending or being suspended 2 system of

suspicion n 1 feeling of not trusting a person or thing 2 belief that something is true without definite proof 3 slight trace **suspicious** adj feeling or causing suspicion **suspiciously** adv

suss out v slang work out using one's intuition

sustain v 1 maintain or prolong 2 suffer (an injury or loss) 3 keep up the vitality or strength of 4 support **sustenance** n food

suture [soo-cher] n stitch joining the edges of a wound

SUV sport utility vehicle

suzerain n state or sovereign with limited authority over another self-governing state **suzerainty** n

svelte adj attractively or gracefully slim

SW southwest(ern)

swab n 1 small piece of cotton batting used to apply medication, clean a wound, etc. ▷ v **swabbing, swabbed** 2 clean (a wound) with a swab 3 clean (the deck of a ship) with a mop

swaddle v wrap (a baby) in swaddling clothes **swaddling clothes** long strips of cloth formerly wrapped round a newborn baby

swag n 1 slang stolen property 2 Aust informal bundle of belongings carried by a swagman **swagman** n Aust tramp who carries his belongings in a bundle on his back

swagger v 1 walk or behave arrogantly ▷ n 2 arrogant walk or manner

swain n poetic 1 suitor 2 country youth

swallow[1] v 1 cause to pass down one's throat 2 make a gulping movement in the throat, as when nervous 3 informal believe (something) gullibly 4 refrain from showing (a feeling) 5 engulf or absorb ▷ n 6 swallowing 7 amount swallowed

swallow[2] n small migratory bird with long pointed wings and a forked tail

swam v past tense of **swim**

swamp n 1 watery area of land, bog ▷ v 2 cause (a boat) to fill with water and sink 3 overwhelm **swampy** adj

swan n large usu. white water bird with a long graceful neck **swan song** person's last performance before retirement or death

swank slang ▷ v 1 show off or boast ▷ n 2 showing off or boasting **swanky** adj slang expensive and showy, stylish

swap v **swapping, swapped** 1 exchange (something) for something else ▷ n 2 exchange

sward n stretch of short grass

swarm[1] n 1 large group of bees or other insects 2 large crowd ▷ v 3 move in a swarm 4 (of a place) be crowded or overrun

swarm[2] v (foll. by up) climb (a ladder or rope) by gripping with the hands and feet

swarthy adj **-thier, -thiest** dark-complexioned

swashbuckler n daredevil adventurer **swashbuckling** adj

swastika n symbol in the shape of a cross with the arms bent at right angles, used as the emblem of Nazi Germany

swat v **swatting, swatted**

1 hit sharply ▷ *n* **2** sharp
blow

swatch *n* sample of cloth

swath [**swawth**] *n* the width
of one sweep of a scythe or
mower

swathe *v* **1** wrap in bandages
or layers of cloth ▷ *n* **2** same
as **swath**

sway *v* **1** swing to and fro or
from side to side **2** waver or
cause to waver in opinion
▷ *n* **3** power or influence
4 swaying motion

swear *v* **swearing, swore,
sworn 1** use obscene or
blasphemous language
2 state earnestly **3** state or
promise on oath **swear by**
v have complete confidence
in **swear in** *v* cause to
take an oath **swearword** *n*
word considered obscene or
blasphemous

sweat *n* **1** salty liquid given
off through the pores of the
skin **2** *slang* drudgery or hard
labour ▷ *v* **3** have sweat
coming through the pores
4 be anxious **5** toil **sweaty**
adj **sweatband** *n* strip of cloth
tied around the forehead
or wrist to absorb sweat
sweatshirt *n* long-sleeved
cotton jersey **sweatshop** *n*
place where employees work
long hours in poor conditions
for low pay

sweater *n* (woollen) garment
for the upper part of the body

swede *n* kind of turnip

sweep *v* **sweeping, swept**
1 remove dirt from (a floor)
with a broom **2** move
smoothly and quickly
3 spread rapidly **4** move
majestically **5** carry away
suddenly or forcefully
6 stretch in a long wide
curve ▷ *n* **7** sweeping
8 sweeping motion **9** wide
expanse **10** person who cleans

chimneys **11** sweepstake
sweeper *n* **1** *curling* player
who uses a broom to sweep
the ice in front of a played
stone **2** *soccer* defensive player
usually positioned in front
of the goalkeeper **sweeping**
adj **1** indiscriminate **2** wide-
ranging **sweepstake** *n* lottery
in which the stakes of the
participants make up the
prize

sweet *adj* **1** tasting of or
like sugar **2** kind and
charming **3** agreeable to
the senses or mind **4** (of
wine) with a high sugar
content ▷ *n Brit* **5** shaped
piece of food consisting
mainly of sugar **6** dessert
sweetly *adv* **sweetness**
n **sweeten** *v* **sweetener** *n*
1 sweetening agent that
does not contain sugar
2 *slang* bribe **sweetbread** *n*
animal's pancreas used as
food **sweetbrier** *n* wild rose
sweet corn type of corn with
sweet yellow kernels, eaten
as a vegetable **sweetheart**
n lover **sweetmeat** *n* old-
fashioned a sweet delicacy such
as a small cake **sweet pea**
climbing plant with bright
fragrant flowers **sweet
potato** tropical root vegetable
with yellow flesh **sweet-talk**
v informal coax or flatter **sweet
tooth** strong liking for sweet
foods **sweet william** garden
plant with flat clusters of
scented flowers

swell *v* **swelling, swelled,
swollen** *or* **swelled 1** expand
or increase **2** be puffed up
with pride or other emotion
3 (of a sound) become
gradually louder ▷ *n*
4 swelling or being swollen
5 movement of waves in
the sea **6** *old-fashioned, slang*
fashionable person ▷ *adj*

7 *slang* excellent or fine
swelling *n* enlargement of part of the body, caused by injury or infection
swelter *v* be oppressed by heat
swept *v* past of **sweep**
swerve *v* **1** turn aside from a course sharply or suddenly ▷ *n* **2** swerving
swift *adj* **1** moving or able to move quickly ▷ *n* **2** fast-flying bird with pointed wings **swiftly** *adv* **swiftness** *n*
swig *n* **1** large mouthful of drink ▷ *v* **swigging, swigged** **2** drink in large mouthfuls
swill *v* **1** drink greedily **2** rinse (something) in large amounts of water ▷ *n* **3** sloppy mixture containing waste food, fed to pigs **4** deep drink **5** rinsing
swim *v* **swimming, swam, swum** **1** move along in water by movements of the limbs **2** be covered or flooded with liquid **3** reel: *her head was swimming* ▷ *n* **4** act or period of swimming **swimmer** *n* **swimmingly** *adv* successfully and effortlessly **swimming pool** (building containing an) artificial pond for swimming in
swindle *v* **1** cheat (someone) out of money ▷ *n* **2** instance of swindling **swindler** *n*
swine *n* **1** contemptible person **2** pig **swinish** *adj*
swing *v* **swinging, swung** **1** move to and fro, sway **2** move in a curve **3** hit out with a sweeping motion **4** (of an opinion or mood) change sharply **5** *slang* be hanged **6** *baseball* attempt to hit a pitched ball ▷ *n* **7** swinging **8** suspended seat on which a child can swing to and fro **9** style of popular dance music played by big bands in the 1930s **10** *baseball* attempted hit **swing by** *v*

informal go (somewhere) to pay a visit
swipe *v* **1** strike (at) with a sweeping blow **2** *slang* steal **3** pass (a credit card or debit card) through a machine that electronically reads information stored in the card **4** activate by moving one's finger across (an item on a screen) ▷ *n* **5** sweeping blow
swirl *v* **1** turn with a whirling motion ▷ *n* **2** whirling motion **3** twisting shape
swish *v* **1** move with a whistling or hissing sound ▷ *n* **2** whistling or hissing sound ▷ *adj* **3** *informal* fashionable, smart
Swiss *adj* **1** of Switzerland or its people ▷ *n, pl* **Swiss** **2** person from Switzerland **swiss roll** sponge cake spread with jam or cream and rolled up
switch *n* **1** device for opening and closing an electric circuit **2** abrupt change **3** exchange or swap **4** movable rail used to change a train to other rails **5** flexible rod or twig ▷ *v* **6** change abruptly **7** exchange or swap **switchback** *n* road or railway with many sharp hills or bends **switchboard** *n* installation in a telephone exchange or office where telephone calls are connected **switch on** or **switch off** *v* turn (a device) on or off by means of a switch
swivel *n* **1** coupling device that allows an attached object to turn freely ▷ *v* **-elling, -elled** **2** turn on or as if on a swivel
swizzle stick *n* small ornamental stick used to stir a cocktail
swollen *v* a past participle of **swell**
swoon *v, n* faint
swoop *v* **1** sweep down or

pounce on suddenly ▷ *n*
2 swooping
swop *v* **swopping, swopped**
1 same as **swap** ▷ *n* **2** same
as **swap**
sword *n* weapon with a long
sharp blade **swordfish** *n* large
fish with a very long upper
jaw **swordsman** *n* person
skilled in the use of a sword
swore *v* past tense of **swear**
sworn *v* **1** past participle of
swear ▷ *adj* **2** bound by or as
if by an oath: *sworn enemies*
swot *informal* ▷ *v* **swotting,**
swotted 1 study hard ▷ *n*
2 person who studies hard
swum *v* past participle of
swim
swung *v* past of **swing**
sybarite [sib-bar-ite] *n* lover
of luxury **sybaritic** *adj*
sycamore *n* tree with five-
pointed leaves and two-
winged fruits
sycophant *n* person who
uses flattery to win favour
from people with power or
influence **sycophantic** *adj*
sycophancy *n*
syllable *n* part of a word
pronounced as a unit
syllabic *adj*
syllabub *n* dessert of beaten
cream, sugar, and wine
syllabus *n* list of subjects for a
course of study
syllogism *n* form of logical
reasoning consisting of two
premises and a conclusion
syllogistic *adj*
sylph *n* **1** imaginary being
supposed to inhabit the air
2 slender graceful girl or
woman **sylphlike** *adj*
sylvan *adj lit* relating to woods
and trees
symbiosis *n* close association
of two species living together
to their mutual benefit
symbiotic *adj*
symbol *n* sign or thing that

stands for something else
symbolic *adj* **symbolically**
adv **symbolism** *n*
1 representation of something
by symbols **2** movement in art
and literature using symbols
to express abstract and
mystical ideas **symbolist** *n*,
adj **symbolize** *v* **1** be a symbol
of **2** represent with a symbol
symmetry *n* state of
having two halves that
are mirror images of each
other **symmetrical** *adj*
symmetrically *adv*
sympathy *n, pl* **-thies**
1 compassion for someone's
pain or distress **2** agreement
with someone's feelings
or interests **sympathetic**
adj **1** feeling or showing
sympathy **2** likeable or
appealing **sympathetically**
adv **sympathize** *v* feel
or express sympathy
sympathizer *n*
symphony *n, pl* **-nies**
composition for orchestra,
with several movements
symphonic *adj*
symposium *n, pl* **-siums, -sia**
conference for discussion of a
particular topic
symptom *n* **1** sign indicating
the presence of an illness
2 sign that something is
wrong **symptomatic** *adj*
synagogue *n* Jewish place
of worship and religious
instruction
sync, synch *n informal*
synchronization
synchromesh *adj* (of a
gearbox) having a device that
synchronizes the speeds of
gears before they engage
synchronize *v* **1** (of two or
more people) perform (an
action) at the same time
2 match (the soundtrack and
action of a film) precisely
3 set (watches) to show the

syncline *n* downward fold of rock strata in the earth's surface

same time **synchronization** *n* **synchronous** or **synchronic** *adj* happening or existing at the same time

syncline *n* downward fold of rock strata in the earth's surface

syncopate *v music* stress the weak beats in (a rhythm) instead of the strong ones **syncopation** *n*

syncope [**sing**-kop-ee] *n med* a faint

syndicate *n* **1** group of people or firms undertaking a joint business project **2** agency that sells material to several newspapers ▷ *v* **3** form a syndicate **4** publish (material) in several newspapers **syndication** *n*

syndrome *n* **1** combination of symptoms indicating a particular disease **2** set of characteristics indicating a particular problem

synod *n* church council

synonym *n* word with the same meaning as another **synonymous** *adj*

synopsis *n, pl* **-ses** summary or outline

syntax *n grammar* way in which words are arranged to form phrases and sentences **syntactic** *adj* **syntactically** *adv*

synthesis *n, pl* **-ses 1** combination of objects or ideas into a whole **2** artificial production of a substance **synthesize** *v* produce by synthesis **synthesizer** *n* electronic musical instrument producing a range of sounds **synthetic** *adj* **1** (of a substance) made artificially **2** not genuine, insincere **synthetically** *adv*

syphilis *n* serious sexually transmitted disease **syphilitic** *adj*

syphon *n, v* same as **siphon**

syringa *n* same as **mock orange, lilac**

syringe *n* **1** device for withdrawing or injecting fluids, consisting of a hollow cylinder, a piston, and a hollow needle ▷ *v* **2** wash out or inject with a syringe

syrup *n* **1** solution of sugar in water **2** thick sweet liquid **3** excessive sentimentality **syrupy** *adj*

system *n* **1** method or set of methods **2** scheme of classification or arrangement **3** network or assembly of parts that form a whole **systematic** *adj* **systematically** *adv* **systematize** *v* organize using a system **systematization** *n* **systemic** *adj* affecting the entire animal or body

systole [**siss**-tol-ee] *n* regular contraction of the heart as it pumps blood **systolic** *adj*

Tt

t tonne

T *n* **to a T 1** in every detail **2** perfectly

t. ton

ta *interj informal* thank you

tab *n* small flap or projecting label **keep tabs on** *informal* watch closely

tabard *n* short sleeveless tunic

Tabasco *n* ® very hot red pepper sauce

tabby *n, pl* **-bies**, *adj* (cat) with dark stripes on a lighter background

tabernacle *n* **1** portable shrine of the Israelites **2** *RC Church* receptacle for the consecrated Host **3** Christian place of worship not called a church

tabla *n, pl* **-blas**, **-bla** one of a pair of Indian drums played with the hands

table *n* **1** piece of furniture with a flat top supported by legs **2** arrangement of information in columns ▷ *v* **3** submit (a motion) for discussion by a meeting **4** *US* suspend discussion of (a proposal) **tableland** *n* high plateau **tablespoon** *n* large spoon for serving food **table tennis** game like tennis played on a table with small bats and a light ball

tableau [**tab**-loh] *n, pl* **-leaux**, **-leaus** silent motionless group arranged to represent some scene

table d'hôte [**tah**-bla **dote**] *n, pl* **tables d'hôte**, *adj* (meal) having a set number of dishes at a fixed price

tablet *n* **1** pill of compressed medicinal substance **2** flattish cake of soap etc. **3** inscribed slab of stone etc. **4** handheld computer operated by touching a screen

tabloid *n* small-sized newspaper with many photographs and a concise, usu. sensational style

taboo *n, pl* **-boos 1** prohibition resulting from religious or social conventions ▷ *adj* **2** forbidden by a taboo

tabular *adj* arranged in a table **tabulate** *v* arrange (information) in a table **tabulation** *n*

tachograph *n* device for recording the speed and distance travelled by a motor vehicle

tachometer *n* device for measuring speed, esp. that of a revolving shaft

tacit [**tass**-it] *adj* implied but not spoken **tacitly** *adv*

taciturn [**tass**-it-turn] *adj* habitually uncommunicative **taciturnity** *n*

tack¹ *n* **1** short nail with a large head **2** long loose stitch ▷ *v* **3** fasten with tacks **4** stitch with tacks **5** append

tack² *n* **1** course of a ship sailing obliquely into the wind **2** course of action ▷ *v* **3** sail into the wind on a zigzag course

tack³ *n* riding harness for horses

tackle n 1 set of ropes and pulleys for lifting heavy weights 2 equipment for a particular activity 3 sports act of tackling an opposing player ▷ v 4 undertake (a task) 5 confront (an opponent) 6 sports attempt to get the ball from (an opposing player)

tacky¹ adj tackier, tackiest slightly sticky **tackiness** n

tacky² adj tackier, tackiest informal 1 vulgar and tasteless 2 shabby

taco [tah-koh] n, pl tacos Mexican cookery tortilla fried until crisp, served with a filling

tact n skill in avoiding giving offence **tactful** adj **tactfully** adv **tactless** adj **tactlessly** adv

tactics pl n 1 art of directing military forces in battle 2 methods or plans to achieve an end **tactical** adj **tactician** n

tactile adj of or having the sense of touch

tadpole n limbless tailed larva of a frog or toad

taffeta n shiny silk or rayon fabric

taffrail n rail at the stern of a ship

tag¹ n 1 label bearing information 2 pointed end of a cord or lace 3 trite quotation ▷ v **tagging, tagged** 4 attach a tag to **tag along** v accompany someone, esp. if uninvited

tag² n 1 children's game where the person being chased becomes the chaser upon being touched ▷ v **tagging, tagged** 2 touch and catch in this game 3 baseball put out (a baserunner) by touching him or her with the ball while he or she is off base

tagliatelle n pasta in long narrow strips

tail n 1 rear part of an animal's body, usu. forming a flexible appendage 2 rear or last part or parts of something 3 informal person employed to follow and spy on another **tails** 4 side of a coin without a portrait of a head on it 5 informal tail coat ▷ v 6 informal follow (someone) secretly ▷ adj 7 at the rear **turn tail** run away **tailless** adj **tailback** n queue of traffic stretching back from an obstruction **tailboard** n removable or hinged rear board on a truck etc. **tail coat** man's coat with a long back split into two below the waist **tail off** or **tail away** v diminish gradually **tailspin** n uncontrolled spinning dive of an aircraft **tailwind** n wind coming from the rear

tailor n 1 person who makes men's clothes ▷ v 2 adapt to suit a purpose **tailor-made** adj 1 made by a tailor 2 perfect for a purpose

taint v 1 spoil with a small amount of decay, contamination, or other bad quality ▷ n 2 something that taints

take v **taking, took, taken** 1 remove from a place 2 get possession of, esp. dishonestly 3 carry or accompany 4 capture 5 require (time, resources, or ability) 6 use 7 assume 8 write down 9 accept 10 subtract or deduct ▷ n 11 one of a series of recordings from which the best will be used **take place** see **place** ▶ **taking** adj charming **takings** pl n money received by a shop **take after** v look or behave like (a parent etc.) **take against** v start to dislike **take away** v subtract **takeaway** n Brit 1 shop or restaurant selling meals for eating elsewhere **2** meal bought at a takeaway **take in** v **1** understand **2** make (clothing) smaller **3** deceive or swindle **take off** v **1** (of an aircraft) leave the ground **2** *informal* depart **3** *informal* parody **take-off** n **takeout** *adj* **1** preparing and selling food for consumption away from the premises ▷ n **2** shop or restaurant that sells such food **3** meal bought at such a shop or restaurant **takeover** n act of taking control of a company by buying a large number of its shares **take up** v **1** occupy or fill (space or time) **2** adopt the study or activity of **3** accept (an offer) **4** shorten (a garment)

talc n **1** soft mineral of magnesium silicate **2** talcum powder **talcum powder** powder, usu. scented, used to dry or perfume the body

tale n **1** story **2** malicious piece of gossip

talent n **1** natural ability **2** ancient unit of weight or money **talented** *adj*

talisman n, pl **-mans** object believed to have magic power **talismanic** *adj*

talk v **1** express ideas or feelings by means of speech **2** utter **3** discuss: *let's talk business* **4** reveal information **5** (be able to) speak in a specified language ▷ n **6** speech or lecture **talker** n **talkative** *adj* fond of talking **talk back** v answer impudently **talking point** something which provokes discussion **talking-to** n *informal* reproof

tall *adj* **1** higher than average **2** of a specified height **tall order** difficult task **tall story** unlikely and probably untrue tale

tallboy n high chest of drawers

tallow n hard animal fat used to make candles

tally v **-lying, -lied 1** (of two things) correspond ▷ n, pl **-lies 2** record of a debt or score

tally-ho *interj* huntsman's cry when the quarry is sighted

Talmud n body of Jewish law **Talmudic** *adj*

talon n bird's hooked claw

tamarind n **1** tropical tree **2** its acid fruit

tamarisk n evergreen shrub with slender branches and feathery flower clusters

tambourine n percussion instrument like a small drum with jingling metal discs attached

tame *adj* **1** (of animals) brought under human control **2** (of animals) not afraid of people **3** meek or submissive **4** uninteresting ▷ v **5** make tame **tamely** *adv* **tamer** n

Tamil n **1** member of a people of Sri Lanka and S India **2** their language

tam-o'-shanter n brimless wool cap with a bobble in the centre

tamp v pack down by repeated blows

tamper v (foll. by *with*) interfere

tampon n absorbent plug of cotton batting inserted into the vagina during menstruation

tan v **tanning, tanned 1** (of skin) go brown from exposure to sunlight **2** convert (a hide) into leather ▷ n **3** brown colour of tanned skin ▷ *adj* **4** yellowish-brown **tannery** n place where hides are tanned **tanner** n

tandem n bicycle for two riders, one behind the other **in tandem** together

tandoor n Indian clay oven **tandoori** adj cooked in a tandoor

tang n 1 strong taste or smell 2 trace or hint **tangy** adj

tangent n 1 line that touches a curve without intersecting it 2 (in trigonometry) ratio of the length of the opposite side to that of the adjacent side of a right-angled triangle **go off at a tangent** suddenly take a completely different line of thought or action **tangential** adj 1 of a tangent 2 of superficial relevance only **tangentially** adv

tangerine n small orange-like fruit of an Asian citrus tree

tangible adj 1 able to be touched 2 clear and definite **tangibly** adv **tangibility** n

tangle n 1 confused mass or situation ▷ v 2 twist together in a tangle 3 (often foll. by with) come into conflict

tango n, pl -gos 1 S American dance ▷ v 2 dance a tango

tank n 1 container for liquids or gases 2 armoured fighting vehicle moving on tracks **tanker** n ship or truck for carrying liquid in bulk

tankard n large beer-mug, often with a hinged lid

tannic acid, tannin n vegetable substance used in tanning

tansy n, pl -sies yellow-flowered plant

tantalize v torment by showing but withholding something desired **tantalizing** adj **tantalizingly** adv

tantalus n case in which bottles can be locked with their contents visible

tantamount adj (foll. by to) equivalent in effect to

tantrum n childish outburst of temper

tap¹ v **tapping, tapped** 1 knock lightly and usu. repeatedly ▷ n 2 light knock **tap dance** dance in which the feet beat out an elaborate rhythm

tap² n 1 valve to control the flow of liquid from a pipe or cask ▷ v **tapping, tapped** 2 listen in on (a telephone) secretly by making an illegal connection 3 fit a tap to (a pipe etc.) 4 draw off with or as if with a tap **on tap 1** informal readily available 2 (of beer etc.) drawn from a cask

tape n 1 narrow long strip of material 2 string stretched across a race track to mark the finish 3 recording made on magnetized tape ▷ v 4 bind or fasten with tape 5 record on magnetized tape **have a person** or **situation taped** informal have full understanding and control of a person or situation **tape measure** tape marked off in centimetres or inches for measuring **tape recorder** device for recording and reproducing sound on magnetized tape **tapeworm** n long flat parasitic worm living in the intestines of vertebrates

taper v 1 become narrower towards one end ▷ n 2 long thin candle 3 narrowing **taper off** v become gradually less

tapestry n, pl -tries fabric decorated with coloured woven designs

tapioca n beadlike starch made from cassava root, used in puddings

tapir [tape-er] n piglike mammal of tropical America and SE Asia, with a long snout

tappet n short steel rod in an engine, transferring motion from one part to another

taproot n main root of a plant, growing straight down

tar n 1 thick black liquid distilled from coal etc. ▷ v **tarring, tarred** 2 coat with tar **tar sands** deposit of bitumen mixed with sand, clay, etc.

taramasalata n creamy pink pâté made from fish roe

tarantella n 1 lively Italian dance 2 music for this

tarantula n, pl **-las, -lae** large poisonous hairy spider

tardy adj **-dier, -diest** slow or late **tardily** adv **tardiness** n

tare[1] n 1 weight of the wrapping or container of goods 2 unladen weight of a vehicle

tare[2] n 1 type of vetch 2 Bible weed

target n 1 object or person a missile is aimed at 2 goal or objective 3 object of criticism ▷ v **-geting, -geted** 4 aim or direct

tariff n 1 tax levied on imports 2 list of fixed prices

Tarmac n 1 ® mixture of tar, bitumen, and crushed stones used for roads etc. 2 **tarmac** airport runway

tarn n small mountain lake

tarnish v 1 make or become stained or less bright 2 damage or taint ▷ n 3 discoloration or blemish

tarot [**tarr**-oh] n special pack of cards used mainly in fortune-telling **tarot card**

tarpaulin n (sheet of) heavy waterproof fabric

tarragon n aromatic herb

tarry v **-rying, -ried** old-fashioned 1 linger or delay 2 stay briefly

tarsier n monkey-like mammal of the E Indies

tarsus n, pl **-si** bones of the heel and ankle collectively

tart[1] n pie or flan with a sweet filling

tart[2] adj sharp or bitter **tartly** adv **tartness** n

tart[3] n informal sexually provocative or promiscuous woman **tart up** v informal dress or decorate in a smart or flashy way

tartan n 1 design of straight lines crossing at right angles, esp. one associated with a Scottish clan 2 cloth with such a pattern

tartar[1] n 1 hard deposit on the teeth 2 deposit formed during the fermentation of wine

tartar[2] n fearsome or formidable person

tartrazine [**tar**-traz-zeen] n artificial yellow dye used in food etc.

task n (difficult or unpleasant) piece of work to be done **take to task** criticize or scold **task force** (military) group formed to carry out a specific task **taskmaster** n person who enforces hard work

tassel n decorative fringed knot of threads **tasselled** adj

taste n 1 sense by which the flavour of a substance is distinguished in the mouth 2 distinctive flavour 3 brief experience of something 4 small amount tasted 5 liking 6 ability to appreciate what is beautiful or excellent ▷ v 7 distinguish the taste of (a substance) 8 take a small amount of (something) into the mouth 9 have a specific taste 10 experience briefly **tasteful** adj having or showing good taste **tastefully** adv **tasteless** adj 1 bland or insipid 2 showing bad taste **tastelessly** adv **tasty** adj pleasantly flavoured **taste bud** small organ on the tongue which perceives flavours

tat n tatty or tasteless article(s)

tattered adj ragged or torn **tatters** pl n ragged pieces

tattle n, v gossip or chatter **tattletale** n a scandalmonger or gossip

tattoo[1] v -tooing, -tooed 1 make (a pattern) on the skin by pricking and staining it with indelible inks ▷ n 2 pattern so made **tattooist** n

tattoo[2] n 1 military display or pageant 2 drumming or tapping

tatty adj -tier, -tiest shabby or worn out **tattiness** n

taught v past of **teach**

taunt v 1 tease with jeers ▷ n 2 jeering remark

taupe adj brownish-grey

taut adj 1 drawn tight, tense 2 showing nervous strain, stressed **tauten** v make or become taut

tautology n, pl -gies use of words which merely repeat something already stated **tautological** adj

tavern n old-fashioned pub

tawdry adj -drier, -driest cheap, showy, and of poor quality **tawdriness** n

tawny adj yellowish-brown

tax n 1 compulsory payment levied by a government on income, property, etc. to raise revenue 2 heavy demand on something ▷ v 3 levy a tax on 4 make heavy demands on **taxable** adj **taxation** n levying of taxes **taxpayer** n **tax return** statement of personal income for tax purposes

taxi n 1 Also **taxicab** automobile with a driver that may be hired to take people to any specified destination ▷ v **taxiing, taxied** 2 (of an aircraft) run along the ground before taking off or after

landing **taximeter** n meter in a taxi that registers the fare

taxi rank place where taxis wait to be hired

taxidermy n art of stuffing and mounting animal skins to give them a lifelike appearance **taxidermist** n

taxonomy n classification of plants and animals into groups **taxonomic** adj **taxonomist** n

TB tuberculosis

T-ball n type of baseball for young children in which the ball is placed on a stand in front of the batter

tbs., tbsp. tablespoon(ful)

tea n 1 dried leaves of an Asian bush 2 drink made by infusing these leaves in boiling water 3 drink made like tea from other plants 4 main evening meal 5 light afternoon meal of tea, cakes, etc. **tea bag** small porous bag of tea leaves **tea cosy** covering for a teapot to keep the tea warm **teapot** n container with a lid, spout, and handle for making and serving tea **teaspoon** n small spoon for stirring tea **tea towel** towel for drying dishes

teach v **teaching, taught** 1 tell or show (someone) how to do something 2 cause to learn or understand 3 give lessons in (a subject) **teacher** n **teaching** n

teak n very hard wood of an E Indian tree

teal n kind of small duck

team n 1 group of people forming one side in a game 2 group of people or animals working together **teamster** n 1 driver of team of draft animals 2 truck driver **team up** v make or join a team **teamwork** n cooperative work by a team

tear¹, teardrop n drop of fluid appearing in and falling from the eye **in tears** weeping **tearful** adj weeping or about to weep **tear gas** gas that stings the eyes and causes temporary blindness **tearjerker** n informal excessively sentimental film or book

tear² v **tearing, tore, torn** 1 rip a hole in 2 rip apart 3 become ripped 4 rush ▷ n 5 hole or split **tearaway** n wild or unruly person **tear down** v demolish

tease v 1 make fun of (someone) in a provoking or playful way 2 separate the fibres of ▷ n 3 person who teases **teasing** adj, n

teasel, teazel, teazle n plant with prickly leaves and flowers

teat n 1 rubber nipple of a feeding bottle 2 nipple of a breast or udder

tech n informal technical college

techie informal ▷ n 1 person who is skilled in the use of technology ▷ adj 2 relating to or skilled in the use of technology

technical adj 1 of or specializing in industrial, practical, or mechanical arts and applied sciences 2 skilled in technical subjects 3 relating to a particular field 4 according to the letter of the law 5 showing technique: technical brilliance **technically** adv **technicality** n petty point based on a strict application of rules **technician** n person skilled in a particular technical field **technical college** higher educational institution with courses in art and technical subjects **technical foul** basketball foul for unsportsman-like conduct, resulting in a free throw for the other team

Technicolor n ® system of colour photography used for the cinema

technique n 1 method or skill used for a particular task 2 technical proficiency

technocracy n, pl -cies government by technical experts **technocrat** n

technology n, pl -gies 1 application of practical or mechanical sciences to industry or commerce 2 sciences applied thus **technological** adj **technologist** n

tectonics pl n study of the earth's crust and the forces affecting it

teddy n, pl -dies 1 teddy bear 2 combined camisole and knickers **teddy bear** soft toy bear

tedious adj causing fatigue or boredom **tediously** adv **tedium** n monotony

tee n 1 small peg supporting a golf ball when teeing off 2 area of a golf course from which the first stroke of a hole is made **tee off** v 1 make the first stroke of a hole in golf 2 slang make angry

teem v 1 abound in 2 rain heavily

teenage adj of the period of life between the ages of 13 and 19 **teenager** n person aged between 13 and 19

teens pl n period of being a teenager

teepee n same as **tepee**

tee-shirt n same as **T-shirt**

teeter v wobble or move unsteadily

teeth n plural of **tooth**

teethe v (of a baby) grow his or her first teeth **teething troubles** problems during the early stages of something

teetotal *adj* drinking no alcohol **teetotaller** *n*

TEFL Teaching of English as a Foreign Language

Teflon *n* ® substance used for nonstick coatings on pans etc.

tele- *prefix* **1** at or over a distance: *telescope* **2** involving television or telephone: *telesales*

telecommunications *pl n* communications using telephone, radio, television, etc.

telegram *n* (formerly) message sent by telegraph

telegraph *n* **1** (formerly) system for sending messages over a distance along a cable ▷ *v* **2** communicate by telegraph **telegraphic** *adj* **telegraphist** *n* person who works a telegraph **telegraphy** *n* science or use of a telegraph

telekinesis *n* movement of objects by thought or willpower

telemeter *n* device for recording or measuring a distant event and transmitting the data to a receiver **telemetry** *n* **telemetric** *adj*

teleology *n* belief that all things have a predetermined purpose **teleological** *adj*

telepathy *n* direct communication between minds **telepathic** *adj* **telepathically** *adv*

telephone *n* **1** device for transmitting sound over a distance along wires ▷ *v* **2** call or talk to (a person) by telephone **telephony** *n* **telephonic** *adj* **telephonist** *n* person operating a telephone switchboard **telephone booth** kiosk for a public telephone

telephoto lens *n* camera lens

producing a magnified image of a distant object

teleprinter *n* apparatus like a typewriter for sending and receiving typed messages by wire

Teleprompter *n* ® device under a television camera enabling a speaker to read the script while appearing to look at the camera

telesales *pl n* selling of a product or service by telephone

telescope *n* **1** optical instrument for magnifying distant objects ▷ *v* **2** shorten by the sliding of each part over the next **3** shorten by crushing **telescopic** *adj*

teletext *n* system which shows information and news on subscribers' television screens

television *n* **1** system of producing a moving image and accompanying sound on a distant screen **2** device for receiving broadcast signals and converting them into sound and pictures **3** content of television programmes **televise** *v* broadcast on television **televisual** *adj*

teleworking *n* use of home computers, telephones, etc., to enable a person to work from home while maintaining contact with colleagues or customers **teleworker** *n*

telex *n* **1** international communication service using teleprinters **2** message sent by telex ▷ *v* **3** transmit by telex

tell *v* **telling, told 1** make known in words **2** order or instruct **3** give an account of **4** discern or distinguish **5** have an effect **6** *informal* reveal secrets **teller** *n*

1 narrator **2** bank cashier **3** person who counts votes

telling adj having a marked effect **tell off** v reprimand **telling-off** n **telltale** n **1** person who reveals secrets ▷ adj **2** revealing

tellurian adj of the earth

telly n, pl **-lies** informal television

temerity [tim-**merr**-it-tee] n boldness or audacity

temp informal ▷ n **1** temporary employee, esp. a secretary ▷ v **2** work as a temp

temp. 1 temperature **2** temporary

temper n **1** outburst of anger **2** tendency to become angry **3** calm mental condition: *I lost my temper* **4** frame of mind ▷ v **5** make less extreme **6** strengthen or toughen (metal)

tempera n painting medium of pigment and egg yolk

temperament n person's character or disposition **temperamental** adj **1** having changeable moods **2** of temperament **3** informal erratic and unreliable **temperamentally** adv

temperate adj **1** (of climate) not extreme **2** self-restrained or moderate **temperance** n **1** moderation **2** abstinence from alcohol

temperature n **1** degree of heat or cold **2** informal abnormally high body temperature

tempest n violent storm **tempestuous** adj violent or stormy **tempestuously** adv

template n pattern used to cut out shapes accurately

temple[1] n building for worship

temple[2] n region on either side of the forehead

tempo n, pl **-pos**, **-pi 1** speed of a piece of music **2** rate or pace

temporal adj **1** of time **2** secular rather than spiritual **3** of the temple(s) of the head

temporary adj lasting only for a short time **temporarily** adv

temporize v **1** gain time by negotiation or evasiveness **2** adapt to circumstances **temporization** n

tempt v **1** (try to) entice (a person) to do something wrong **2** risk provoking: *you're tempting fate* **tempter** (**temptress**) n **temptation** n **1** tempting **2** tempting thing **tempting** adj attractive or inviting

ten adj, n one more than nine **tenth** adj, n (of) number ten in a series

tenable adj able to be held or maintained

tenacious adj **1** holding fast **2** stubborn **tenacity** n

tenant n person who rents land or a building **tenancy** n

tench n, pl **tench** freshwater game fish

tend[1] v **1** be inclined **2** go in the direction of **tendency** n inclination to act in a certain way **tendentious** adj biased, not impartial

tend[2] v take care of

tender[1] adj **1** not tough **2** gentle and affectionate **3** vulnerable or sensitive **tenderly** adv **tenderness** n **tenderize** v soften (meat) by pounding or treatment with a special substance **tenderizer** n **tenderloin** n tender cut of beef or pork from between the sirloin and ribs

tender[2] v **1** offer **2** make a tender ▷ n **3** formal offer to supply goods or services at a stated cost **legal tender** currency that must, by law, be accepted as payment

t

tender³ *n* **1** small boat that brings supplies to a larger ship in a port **2** carriage for fuel and water attached to a steam locomotive

tendon *n* sinew attaching a muscle to a bone

tendril *n* slender stem by which a climbing plant clings

tenement *n* building divided into several apartments

tenet [ten-nit] *n* doctrine or belief

tennis *n* game in which players use rackets to hit a ball back and forth over a net

tenon *n* projecting end on a piece of wood fitting into a slot in another

tenor *n* **1** (singer with) the second highest male voice **2** general meaning ▷ *adj* **3** (of a voice or instrument) between alto and baritone

tenpin bowling *n* game in which players try to knock over ten skittles by rolling a ball at them

tense¹ *n* form of a verb showing the time of action

tense² *adj* **1** stretched tight **2** emotionally strained ▷ *v* **3** make or become tense **tensile** *adj* of tension **tension** *n* **1** degree of stretching **2** emotional strain **3** hostility or suspense **4** *electricity* voltage

tent *n* portable canvas shelter

tentacle *n* flexible organ of many invertebrates, used for grasping, feeding, etc.

tentative *adj* **1** provisional or experimental **2** cautious or hesitant **tentatively** *adv*

tenterhooks *pl n* **on tenterhooks** in anxious suspense

tenuous *adj* slight or flimsy **tenuously** *adv* **tenuousness** *n*

tenure *n* (period of) the holding of an office or position

tepee [tee-pee] *n* N American Indian cone-shaped tent

tepid *adj* **1** slightly warm **2** half-hearted

tequila *n* Mexican alcoholic drink

tercentenary *adj, n, pl* **-naries** (of) a three hundredth anniversary

term *n* **1** word or expression **2** fixed period **3** period of the year when a school etc. is open or a lawcourt holds sessions **terms 4** conditions **5** mutual relationship ▷ *v* **6** name or designate

terminal *adj* **1** at or being an end **2** (of an illness) ending in death ▷ *n* **3** terminating point or place **4** point where current enters or leaves an electrical device **5** keyboard and VDU having input and output links with a computer **6** place where people or vehicles begin or end a journey **terminally** *adv*

terminate *v* **1** bring or come to an end **2** kill (someone) **termination** *n*

terminology *n, pl* **-gies** technical terms relating to a subject **terminological** *adj*

terminus *n, pl* **-ni, -nuses 1** final point **2** railway or bus station at the end of a line

termite *n* white antlike insect destructive to timber

tern *n* gull-like sea bird

ternary *adj* consisting of three parts

Terpsichorean *adj* of dancing

terrace *n* **1** row of houses built as one block **2** paved area next to a building **3** level tier cut out of a hill **terraces 4** Also **terracing** tiered area in a stadium where spectators stand ▷ *v* **5** form into or provide with a terrace

terracotta *adj, n* **1** (made of) brownish-red unglazed pottery ▷ *adj* **2** brownish-red

terra firma *n* dry land or solid ground

terrain *n* area of ground, esp. with reference to its physical character

terrapin *n* kind of aquatic tortoise

terrarium *n, pl* **-rariums, -raria** enclosed container for small plants or animals

terrazzo *n, pl* **-zos** floor of marble chips set in mortar and polished

terrestrial *adj* **1** of the earth **2** of or living on land

terrible *adj* **1** very serious **2** *informal* very bad **3** causing fear **terribly** *adv*

terrier *n* any of various breeds of small active dog

terrific *adj* **1** great or intense **2** *informal* excellent

terrify *v* **-fying, -fied** fill with fear **terrifying** *adj*

terrine [terr-**reen**] *n* **1** pâté or similar food **2** earthenware dish with a lid

territory *n, pl* **-ries 1** district **2** **Territory** *Canad* any of three political divisions of Canada that are not provinces **3** area under the control of a particular government **4** area inhabited and defended by an animal **5** area of knowledge or experience **territorial** *adj*

terror *n* **1** great fear **2** terrifying person or thing **3** *informal* troublesome person or thing **terrorism** *n* use of violence and intimidation to achieve political ends **terrorist** *n, adj* **terrorize** *v* force or oppress by fear or violence

terry *n* fabric with the loops in its pile uncut

terse *adj* **1** concise **2** curt **tersely** *adv*

tertiary [**tur**-shar-ee] *adj* third in degree, order, etc.

Terylene *n* ® synthetic polyester yarn or fabric

tessellated *adj* paved or inlaid with a mosaic of small tiles **tessera** *n, pl* **-serae** small square tile used in mosaics

test *v* **1** try out to ascertain the worth, capability, or endurance of **2** carry out an examination on ▷ *n* **3** critical examination **4** method or standard of judgment **5** test match **testing** *adj* **test case** lawsuit that establishes a precedent **test match** one of a series of international cricket or rugby matches **test tube** narrow cylindrical glass vessel used in scientific experiments **test-tube baby** baby conceived outside the mother's body

testament *n* **1** *law* will **2** proof or tribute **3** **Testament** one of the two main divisions of the Bible **testamentary** *adj*

testate *adj* having left a valid will **testacy** *n* **testator** [test-**tay**-tor] (**testatrix** [test-**tay**-triks]) *n* maker of a will

testicle *n* either of the two male reproductive glands

testify *v* **-fying, -fied 1** give evidence under oath **2** (foll. by *to*) be evidence (of)

testimony *n, pl* **-nies 1** declaration of truth or fact **2** evidence given under oath **testimonial** *n* **1** recommendation of the worth of a person or thing **2** tribute for services or achievement

testis *n, pl* **-tes** testicle

testosterone *n* male sex hormone secreted by the testes

testy *adj* **-tier, -tiest** irritable

t

or touchy **testily** adv
testiness n

tetanus n acute infectious
disease producing muscular
spasms and convulsions

tête-à-tête n, pl **-têtes, -tête**
private conversation

tether n **1** rope or chain for
tying an animal to a spot ▷ v
2 tie up with rope **at the end
of one's tether** at the limit of
one's endurance

tetrahedron [tet-ra-**heed**-
ron] n, pl **-drons, -dra** geom
solid figure with four faces

tetralogy n, pl **-gies** series of
four related works

Teutonic [tew-**tonn**-ik] adj of
or like the (ancient) Germans

text n **1** main body of a book
as distinct from illustrations
etc. **2** passage of the Bible
as the subject of a sermon
3 novel or play needed for
a course **4** text message
▷ v **5** send a text message
to (someone) **textual** adj

textbook n **1** standard book
on a particular subject ▷ adj
2 perfect: a textbook landing
text message message sent
in text form, esp. by means of
a cell phone

textile n fabric or cloth, esp.
woven

texture n structure, feel, or
consistency **textured** adj
textural adj

thalidomide [thal-**lid**-oh-
mide] n drug formerly used as
a sedative, but found to cause
abnormalities in developing
fetuses

thallium n highly toxic
metallic element

than conj used to introduce
the second element of a
comparison

thane n hist Anglo-Saxon or
medieval Scottish nobleman

thank v **1** express gratitude to
2 hold responsible **thanks**

pl n **1** words of gratitude
▷ interj **2** Also **thank
you** polite expression of
gratitude **thanks to** because
of **thankful** adj grateful
thankless adj unrewarding or
unappreciated **Thanksgiving
Day** public holiday on second
Monday of October in Canada
and fourth Thursday in
November in the US

that adj, pron **1** used to refer
to something already
mentioned or familiar, or
further away ▷ conj **2** used
to introduce a noun clause
▷ pron **3** used to introduce a
relative clause

thatch n **1** roofing material
of reeds or straw ▷ v **2** roof
(a house) with reeds or straw
thatcher n

thaw v **1** make or become
unfrozen **2** become more
relaxed or friendly ▷ n
3 thawing **4** weather causing
snow or ice to melt

the adj the definite article

theatre n **1** place where
plays etc. are performed
2 drama and acting in
general **3** hospital operating
room **theatrical** adj **1** of
the theatre **2** exaggerated
or affected **theatricals**
pl n (amateur) dramatic
performances **theatrically**
adv **theatricality** n

thee pron obsolete objective
form of **thou**

theft n stealing

their adj of or associated with
them **theirs** pron (thing or
person) belonging to them

theism [**thee**-iz-zum] n belief
in the creation of the universe
by one God **theist** n, adj
theistic adj

them pron refers to people
or things other than the
speaker or those addressed
themselves pron emphatic

and reflexive form of **they**, **them**

theme n 1 main idea or subject being discussed 2 recurring melodic figure in music **thematic** adj **theme park** leisure area based on a single theme

then adv 1 at that time 2 after that 3 that being so

thence adv 1 from that place or time 2 therefore

theocracy n, pl -cies government by a god or priests **theocratic** adj

theodolite [thee-**odd**-oh-lite] n surveying instrument for measuring angles

theology n, pl -gies study of religions and religious beliefs **theologian** n **theological** adj **theologically** adv

theorem n proposition that can be proved by reasoning

theory n, pl -ries 1 set of ideas to explain something 2 abstract knowledge or reasoning 3 idea or opinion 4 ideal or hypothetical situation **theoretical** adj based on theory rather than practice or fact **theoretically** adv **theorist** n **theorize** v form theories, speculate

theosophy n religious or philosophical system claiming to be based on intuitive insight into the divine nature **theosophical** adj

therapy n, pl -pies curing treatment **therapist** n **therapeutic** [ther-rap-**pew**-tik] adj curing **therapeutics** n art of curing

there adv 1 in or to that place 2 in that respect **thereby** adv by that means **therefore** adv consequently, that being so **thereupon** adv immediately after that

therm n unit of heat **thermal**

adj 1 of heat 2 hot or warm 3 (of clothing) retaining heat ▷ n 4 rising current of warm air

thermionic valve n electronic valve in which electrons are emitted from a heated rather than a cold cathode

thermocouple n device for measuring heat, consisting of two wires of different metals joined at both ends

thermodynamics pl n scientific study of the relationship between heat and other forms of energy

thermometer n instrument for measuring temperature

thermonuclear adj involving nuclear fusion

thermoplastic adj (of a plastic) softening when heated and resetting on cooling

thermos n double-walled flask with a vacuum between the walls that keeps drinks hot or cold

thermosetting adj (of a plastic) remaining hard when heated

thermostat n device for automatically regulating temperature **thermostatic** adj **thermostatically** adv

thesaurus [thiss-**sore**-uss] n, pl -ri, -ruses book containing lists of synonyms and related words

these adj, pron plural of **this**

thesis n, pl **theses** 1 written work submitted for a degree 2 doctrine maintained in argument

Thespian adj 1 of the theatre ▷ n 2 actor or actress

they pron 1 refers to people or things other than the speaker or people addressed 2 refers to people in general 3 informal refers to he or she

thiamine n vitamin found in the outer coat of rice and other grains

thick adj 1 of great or specified extent from one side to the other 2 having a dense consistency 3 full of 4 informal stupid or insensitive 5 (of a voice) throaty 6 informal friendly **a bit thick** informal unfair or unreasonable **the thick** busiest or most intense part **thickly** adv **thickness** n 1 state of being thick 2 dimension through an object 3 layer **thicken** v make or become thick or thicker **thickset** adj 1 stocky in build 2 set closely together

thicket n dense growth of small trees

thief n, pl **thieves** person who steals **thieve** v steal **thieving** adj, n

thigh n upper part of the human leg

thimble n cap protecting the end of the finger when sewing

thin adj **thinner, thinnest** 1 not thick 2 slim or lean 3 sparse or meagre 4 of low density 5 poor or unconvincing ▷ v **thinning, thinned** 6 make or become thin **thinly** adv **thinness** n

thine pron obsolete (something) of or associated with you (thou)

thing n 1 material object 2 object, fact, or idea considered as a separate entity 3 informal obsession **things** 4 possessions, clothes, etc.

think v **thinking, thought** 1 consider, judge, or believe 2 make use of the mind 3 be considerate enough or remember to do something **thinker** n **thinking** adj, n **think-tank** n group of experts

studying specific problems **think up** v invent or devise

third adj 1 of number three in a series 2 rated or graded below the second level ▷ n 3 one of three equal parts **third degree** violent interrogation **third party** (applying to) a person involved by chance or only incidentally in legal proceedings, an accident, etc. **Third World** developing countries of Africa, Asia, and Latin America

thirst n 1 desire to drink 2 craving or yearning ▷ v 3 feel thirst **thirsty** adj **thirstily** adv

thirteen adj, n three plus ten **thirteenth** adj, n

thirty adj, n three times ten **thirtieth** adj, n

this adj, pron 1 used to refer to a thing or person nearby or just mentioned ▷ adj 2 used to refer to the present time: this morning

thistle n prickly plant with dense flower heads

thither adv obsolete to or towards that place

thong n 1 thin strip of leather etc. 2 skimpy article of underwear or beachwear that leaves the buttocks bare

thorax n, pl **thoraxes, thoraces** part of the body between the neck and the abdomen **thoracic** adj

thorium n radioactive metallic element

thorn n 1 prickle on a plant 2 bush with thorns **thorn in one's side** or **thorn in one's flesh** source of irritation **thorny** adj

thorough adj 1 careful or methodical 2 complete **thoroughly** adv **thoroughness** n **thoroughbred** n, adj (animal) of pure breed **thoroughfare** *n* way through from one place to another

those *adj, pron* plural of **that**

thou *pron* obsolete singular form of **you**

though *conj* **1** despite the fact that ▷ *adv* **2** nevertheless

thought *v* **1** past of **think** ▷ *n* **2** thinking **3** concept or idea **4** ideas typical of a time or place **5** consideration **6** intention or expectation **thoughtful** *adj* **1** considerate **2** showing careful thought **3** pensive or reflective **thoughtless** *adj* inconsiderate

thousand *adj, n* **1** ten hundred **2** large but unspecified number **thousandth** *adj, n* (of) number one thousand in a series

thrall, thraldom *n* state of being in the power of another person

thrash *v* **1** beat, esp. with a stick or whip **2** defeat soundly **3** move about wildly **4** thresh **thrashing** *n* severe beating **thrash out** *v* solve by thorough argument

thread *n* **1** fine strand or yarn **2** spiral ridge on a screw, nut, or bolt **3** unifying theme ▷ *v* **4** pass thread through **5** fit (a film, tape, etc.) into a machine **6** pick (one's way etc.) **threadbare** *adj* **1** (of fabric) with the nap worn off **2** hackneyed **3** shabby

threat *n* **1** declaration of intent to harm **2** dangerous person or thing **threaten** *v* **1** make or be a threat to **2** be a menacing indication of

three *adj, n* one more than two **threefold** *adj, adv* (having) three times as many or as much **threesome** *n* group of three **three-dimensional** or **3-D** *adj* having three

dimensions **three-ply** *adj* **1** (of wood) having three layers **2** (of wool) having three strands **three-point** *adj basketball* relating to shots scoring three points **three-pointer** *n basketball* three-point shot

threnody *n, pl* **-dies** lament for the dead

thresh *v* **1** beat (wheat etc.) to separate the grain from the husks and straw **2** move about wildly

threshold *n* **1** bar forming the bottom of a doorway **2** entrance **3** starting point **4** point at which a stimulus produces a response

threw *v* past tense of **throw**

thrice *adv lit* three times

thrift *n* **1** wisdom and caution with money **2** low-growing plant with pink flowers **thrifty** *adj* **thriftily** *adv* **thriftiness** *n* **thriftless** *adj*

thrill *n* **1** sudden feeling of excitement *v* **2** (cause to) feel a thrill **thrilling** *adj* **thriller** *n* book, film, etc. with an atmosphere of mystery or suspense

thrive *v* **thriving, thrived** or **throve, thrived** or **thriven** **1** grow well **2** flourish or prosper

throat *n* **1** front of the neck **2** passage from the mouth and nose to the stomach and lungs **throaty** *adj* (of the voice) hoarse

throb *v* **throbbing, throbbed** **1** pulsate repeatedly **2** vibrate rhythmically ▷ *n* **3** throbbing

throes *pl n* violent pangs or pains **in the throes of** *informal* struggling with difficulty with

thrombosis *n, pl* **-ses** forming of a clot in a blood vessel or the heart

throne *n* **1** ceremonial seat

t

of a monarch or bishop
2 sovereign power

throng *n, v* crowd

throstle *n* song-thrush

throttle *n* **1** device controlling
the amount of fuel entering
an engine ▷ *v* **2** strangle

through *prep* **1** from end
to end or side to side of
2 because of **3** during ▷ *adj*
4 finished **5** (of transport)
going directly to a place **6** (on
a telephone line) connected
through and through
completely **throughout**
adv, prep in every part (of)
throughput *n* amount of
material processed

throve *v* past tense of **thrive**

throw *v* **throwing, threw,
thrown 1** hurl through the
air **2** move or put suddenly
or carelessly **3** bring into a
specified state, esp. suddenly
4 direct (a look, light, etc.)
5 give (a party) **6** project
(the voice) so that it seems
to come from elsewhere
7 shape (pottery) on a wheel
8 move (a switch, lever, etc.)
9 *informal* baffle or disconcert
▷ *n* **10** throwing **11** distance
thrown **throwaway** *adj*
1 designed to be discarded
after use **2** done or said
casually **throwback** *n* person
or thing that reverts to an
earlier type **throw up** *v* vomit

thrush¹ *n* brown songbird

thrush² *n* fungal disease of the
mouth or vagina

thrust *v* **thrusting, thrust
1** push forcefully **2** stab
▷ *n* **3** lunge or stab **4** force
or power **5** intellectual or
emotional drive

thud *n* **1** dull heavy sound ▷ *v*
thudding, thudded 2 make
such a sound

thug *n* violent criminal
thuggery *n* **thuggish** *adj*

thumb *n* **1** short thick finger

set apart from the others ▷ *v*
2 touch or handle with the
thumb **3** flick through (a
book or magazine) **4** signal
with the thumb for (a lift in a
vehicle) **thumbtack** *n* short
tack with a smooth broad
head

thump *n* **1** (sound of) a dull
heavy blow ▷ *v* **2** strike
heavily

thunder *n* **1** loud noise
accompanying lightning
▷ *v* **2** rumble with thunder
3 shout **4** move fast, heavily,
and noisily **thunderous** *adj*
thundery *adj* **thunderbolt** *n*
1 lightning flash **2** something
sudden and unexpected
thunderclap *n* peal of
thunder **thunderstruck** *adj*
amazed

Thursday *n* fifth day of the
week

thus *adv* **1** in this way
2 therefore

thwack *v, n* whack

thwart *v* **1** foil or frustrate
▷ *n* **2** seat across a boat

thy *adj obsolete* of or associated
with you (thou) **thyself** *pron
obsolete* emphatic form of
thou

thyme [**time**] *n* aromatic herb

thymus *n, pl* **-muses, -mi**
small gland at the base of the
neck

thyroid *adj, n* (of) a gland
in the neck controlling
body growth

Ti *chem* titanium

tiara *n* semicircular jewelled
headdress

tibia *n, pl* **tibiae, tibias** inner
bone of the lower leg **tibial**
adj

tic *n* spasmodic muscular
twitch

tick¹ *n* **1** mark ($\sqrt{}$) used to
check off or indicate the
correctness of something
2 recurrent tapping sound, as

of a clock **3** *informal* moment ▷ *v* **4** mark with a tick **5** make a ticking sound **tick off** *v* **1** mark off **2** reprimand **tick over** *v* **1** (of an engine) idle **2** function smoothly **ticktack** *n* bookmakers' sign language

tick² *n* tiny bloodsucking parasitic animal

tick³ *n informal* credit or account

ticket *n* **1** card or paper entitling the holder to admission, travel, etc. **2** label **3** official notification of a parking or traffic offence **4** declared policy of a political party ▷ *v* **-eting, -eted** **5** attach or issue a ticket to

ticking *n* strong cotton fabric used for mattress covers

tickle *v* **1** touch or stroke (a person) to produce laughter **2** please or amuse **3** itch or tingle ▷ *n* **4** tickling **ticklish** *adj* **1** sensitive to tickling **2** requiring care or tact

tiddler *n informal* very small fish **tiddly** *adj* **1** tiny **2** *informal* slightly drunk

tiddlywinks *pl n* game in which players try to flip small plastic discs into a cup

tide *n* **1** rise and fall of the sea caused by the gravitational pull of the sun and moon **2** current caused by this **3** widespread feeling or tendency **tidal** *adj* **tidal wave** huge wave produced by an earthquake **tide over** *v* help (someone) temporarily

tidings *pl n* news

tidy *adj* **-dier, -diest 1** neat and orderly **2** *informal* considerable ▷ *v* **-dying, -died 3** put in order **tidily** *adv* **tidiness** *n*

tie *v* **tying, tied 1** fasten or be fastened with string, rope, etc. **2** make (a knot or bow) in

(something) **3** restrict or limit **4** score the same as another competitor ▷ *n* **5** bond or fastening **6** long narrow piece of material worn knotted round the neck **7** drawn game or contest

tier *n* row, layer, or level

tiff *n* petty quarrel

tiger *n* large yellow-and-black striped Asian cat **tigress** *n* **1** female tiger **2** fierce woman

tight *adj* **1** stretched or drawn taut **2** closely fitting **3** secure or firm **4** cramped **5** *informal* mean **6** *informal* drunk **7** (of a match or game) very close **tights** *pl n* one-piece clinging garment covering the body from the waist to the feet **tightly** *adv* **tighten** *v* make or become tight or tighter **tight end** *football* offensive player who can receive passes or block **tightrope** *n* rope stretched taut on which acrobats perform

tike *n informal* same as **tyke**

tikka *adj Indian cookery* marinated in spices and dry-roasted: *chicken tikka*

tilde *n* accent (~) used in Spanish to indicate that the letter 'n' is to be pronounced in a particular way

tile *n* **1** flat piece of ceramic, plastic, etc. used to cover a roof, floor, or wall ▷ *v* **2** cover with tiles **tiled** *adj* **tiling** *n* tiles collectively

till¹ *prep, conj* until

till² *v* cultivate (land) **tillage** *n* **tiller** *n*

till³ *n* drawer for money, usu. in a cash register

tiller *n* lever used to move the rudder of a boat when steering

tilt *v* **1** slant at an angle **2** compete against in a jousting contest **3** aim or thrust with a lance ▷ *n*

4 slope **5** *hist* jousting contest **at full tilt** at full speed or force

timber *n* **1** wood as a building material **2** trees collectively **3** wooden beam in the frame of a house, boat, etc. **timbered** *adj* **timber line** geographical limit beyond which trees will not grow

timbre [**tam**-bra] *n* distinctive quality of sound of a voice or instrument

time *n* **1** past, present, and future as a continuous whole **2** specific point in time **3** unspecified interval **4** period with specific features **5** instance **6** occasion **7** tempo **8** *slang* imprisonment ▷ *v* **9** note the time taken by **10** choose a time for **timeless** *adj* **1** unaffected by time **2** eternal **timely** *adj* at the appropriate time **time bomb 1** bomb containing a timing mechanism that determines when it will explode **2** situation which, if allowed to continue, will develop into a serious problem **time-honoured** *adj* sanctioned by custom **time-lag** *n* period between cause and effect **timepiece** *n* watch or clock **timeserver** *n* person who changes his or her views to gain support or favour **time sharing 1** system of part ownership of a holiday property for a specified period each year **2** system enabling users at different terminals of a computer to use it at the same time **timetable** *n* plan showing the times when something takes place, the departure and arrival times of trains or buses, etc.

timid *adj* **1** easily frightened **2** shy, not bold **timidly** *adv*

timidity *n* **timorous** [**tim**-mor-uss] *adj* timid

timpani [**tim**-pan-ee] *pl n* set of kettledrums **timpanist** *n*

tin *n* **1** soft metallic element **2** *Brit* airtight metal container **tinned** *adj Brit* (of food) preserved by being sealed in a tin **tinny** *adj* (of sound) thin and metallic **tinpot** *adj informal* worthless or unimportant

tincture *n* medicinal extract in a solution of alcohol

tinder *n* dry easily-burning material used to start a fire **tinderbox** *n*

tine *n* prong of a fork or antler

ting *n* high metallic sound, as of a small bell

tinge *n* **1** slight tint **2** trace ▷ *v* **tingeing, tinged 3** give a slight tint or trace to

tingle *v, n* (feel) a prickling or stinging sensation

tinker *n* **1** travelling mender of pots and pans **2** *Scot & Irish* Gypsy **3** tinkering ▷ *v* **4** fiddle with (an engine etc.) in an attempt to repair it

tinkle *v* **1** ring with a high tinny sound like a small bell ▷ *n* **2** tinkling

tinsel *n* **1** decorative metallic strips or threads **2** anything cheap and gaudy

tint *n* **1** (pale) shade of a colour **2** dye for the hair **3** trace ▷ *v* **4** give a tint to

tiny *adj* **tinier, tiniest** very small

tip¹ *n* **1** narrow or pointed end of anything **2** small piece forming an end ▷ *v* **tipping, tipped 3** put a tip on

tip² *n* **1** money given in return for service **2** helpful hint or warning **3** piece of inside information ▷ *v* **tipping, tipped 4** give a tip to **tipster** *n* person who sells tips about races

tip³ v **tipping, tipped 1** tilt or overturn **2** deflect or lightly tap (a ball or puck) ▷ n **3** act or instance of tipping

tippet n piece of fur worn as a scarf

tipple v **1** drink (alcohol) habitually, esp. in small quantities ▷ n **2** drink **tippler** n

tipsy adj **-sier, -siest** slightly drunk

tiptoe v **-toeing, -toed** walk quietly with the heels off the ground

tiptop adj of the highest quality or condition

tirade n long angry speech

tire¹ v **1** reduce the energy of, as by exertion **2** weary or bore **tired** adj **1** weary **2** hackneyed or stale **tiring** adj **tireless** adj not tiring easily **tiresome** adj boring and irritating

tire² n rubber ring, usu. inflated, over the rim of a vehicle's wheel to grip the road

tissue n **1** substance of an animal body or plant **2** piece of thin soft paper used as a handkerchief etc. **3** interwoven series: a tissue of lies

tit¹ n any of various small songbirds

tit² n slang female breast

titanic adj huge

titanium n strong light metallic element used to make alloys

titbit n **1** tasty piece of food **2** pleasing scrap of scandal

tit for tat n equivalent given in retaliation

tithe n **1** esp. formerly, one tenth of one's income or produce paid to the church as a tax ▷ v **2** charge or pay a tithe

titillate v excite or stimulate

pleasurably **titillating** adj **titillation** n

titivate v smarten up **titivation** n

title n **1** name of a book, film, etc. **2** name signifying rank or position **3** formal designation, such as Mrs **4** sports championship **5** law legal right of possession **titled** adj aristocratic **title deed** legal document of ownership

titter v **1** laugh in a suppressed way ▷ n **2** suppressed laugh

tittle-tattle n, v gossip

titular adj **1** of a title **2** in name only

tizzy n, pl **-zies** informal confused or agitated state

TNT n trinitrotoluene, a powerful explosive

to prep **1** towards **2** as far as **3** used to mark the indirect object or infinitive of a verb **4** used to indicate equality or comparison **5** before the hour of ▷ adv **6** to a closed position: pull the door to **to and fro** back and forth

toad n animal like a large frog **toady** n, pl **toadies** ingratiating person ▷ v **toadying, toadied** be ingratiating **toadstool** n poisonous fungus like a mushroom

toast n **1** slice of bread browned by heat **2** tribute or proposal of health or success marked by people raising glasses and drinking together **3** person or thing so honoured ▷ v **4** brown bread by heat **5** drink a toast to **6** warm or be warmed **toaster** n electrical device for toasting bread

tobacco n, pl **-cos, -coes** plant with large leaves dried for smoking **tobacconist**

n person or shop selling tobacco, cigarettes, etc.

toboggan *n* **1** narrow sledge for sliding over snow ▷ *v* **-ganing, -ganed 2** ride a toboggan

toby jug *n* mug in the form of a stout seated man

toccata [tok-**kah**-ta] *n* rapid piece of music for a keyboard instrument

tocsin *n* alarm signal or bell

today *n* **1** this day **2** the present age ▷ *adv* **3** on this day **4** nowadays

toddle *v* walk with short unsteady steps **toddler** *n* child beginning to walk

toddy *n*, *pl* **-dies** sweetened drink of spirits and hot water

to-do *n*, *pl* **-dos** informal fuss or commotion

toe *n* **1** digit of the foot **2** part of a shoe or sock covering the toes ▷ *v* **toeing, toed 3** touch or kick with the toe **toe the line** conform **toerag** *n* slang contemptible person

toff *n* Brit slang well-dressed or upper-class person

toffee *n* chewy candy made of boiled sugar

tofu *n* soft food made from soya-bean curd

tog *n* **1** unit for measuring the insulating power of duvets **togs 2** informal clothes

toga [**toe**-ga] *n* garment worn by citizens of ancient Rome

together *adv* **1** in company **2** simultaneously ▷ *adj* **3** informal organized

toggle *n* **1** small bar-shaped button inserted through a loop for fastening **2** switch used to turn a machine or computer function on or off

toil *n* **1** hard work ▷ *v* **2** work hard **3** progress with difficulty **toilsome** *adj* requiring hard work

toilet *n* **1** (room with) a bowl connected to a drain for receiving and disposing of urine and feces **2** washing and dressing **toiletry** *n*, *pl* **-ries** object or cosmetic used to clean or groom oneself

toilet water light perfume

token *n* **1** sign or symbol **2** memento **3** disc used as money in a slot machine **4** voucher exchangeable for goods of a specified value ▷ *adj* **5** nominal or slight

tokenism *n* policy of making only a token effort, esp. to comply with a law

told *v* past of **tell**

tolerate *v* **1** put up with **2** permit **toleration** *n* **tolerable** *adj* **1** bearable **2** informal quite good **tolerably** *adv* **tolerance** *n* **1** acceptance of other people's rights to their own opinions or actions **2** ability to endure something **tolerant** *adj* **tolerantly** *adv* **toleration** *n*

toll¹ *v* **1** ring (a bell) slowly and regularly, esp. to announce a death ▷ *n* **2** tolling

toll² *n* **1** charge for the use of a bridge or road **2** total loss or damage from a disaster

tom *n* male cat

tomahawk *n* fighting axe of the N American Indians

tomato *n*, *pl* **-toes** red fruit used in salads and as a vegetable

tomb *n* **1** grave **2** monument over a grave **tombstone** *n* gravestone

tombola *n* lottery with tickets drawn from a revolving drum

tomboy *n* girl who acts or dresses like a boy

tome *n* large heavy book

tomfoolery *n* foolish behaviour

Tommy gun *n* light sub-machine-gun

tomorrow *adv*, *n* **1** (on) the day

after today **2** (in) the future

tom-tom *n* drum beaten with the hands

ton *n* unit of weight equal to 2000 lbs or 907 kg (**short ton**) or, in Britain, 2240 lbs or 1016 kg (**long ton**) **metric ton** same as **tonne ▸ tonnage** *n* weight capacity of a ship

tone *n* **1** sound with reference to its pitch, volume, etc. **2** *music* Also **whole tone** interval of two semitones **3** quality of a colour **4** general character **5** healthy bodily condition ▷ *v* **6** give tone to **7** harmonize (with) **tonal** *adj music* written in a key **tonality** *n* **toneless** *adj* **tone-deaf** *adj* unable to perceive subtle differences in pitch **tone down** *v* make or become more moderate

tongs *pl n* large pincers for grasping and lifting

tongue *n* **1** muscular organ in the mouth, used in speaking and tasting **2** animal tongue as food **3** language **4** flap of leather on a shoe **5** thin projecting strip

tonic *n* **1** medicine to improve body tone **2** *music* first note of a scale ▷ *adj* **3** invigorating **tonic water** mineral water containing quinine

tonight *adv, n* (in or during) the night or evening of this day

tonne [tunn] *n* unit of weight equal to 1000 kg

tonsil *n* small gland in the throat **tonsillectomy** *n* surgical removal of the tonsils **tonsillitis** *n* inflammation of the tonsils

tonsure *n* **1** shaving of all or the top of the head as a religious or monastic practice **2** part shaved **tonsured** *adj*

too *adv* **1** also, as well **2** to excess **3** extremely

took *v* past tense of **take**

tool *n* **1** implement used by hand **2** person used by another to perform unpleasant or dishonourable tasks ▷ *v* **3** work on with a tool **4** equip with tools **toolbar** *n computers* row of buttons displayed on a computer screen, allowing the user to select various functions

toonie, twonie *n informal* Canadian two-dollar coin

toot *n* **1** short hooting sound ▷ *v* **2** (cause to) make such a sound

tooth *n, pl* **teeth 1** bonelike projection in the jaws of most vertebrates for biting and chewing **2** toothlike prong or point **sweet tooth** see **sweet ▸ toothless** *adj* **toothpaste** *n* paste used to clean the teeth **toothpick** *n* small stick for removing scraps of food from between the teeth

top¹ *n* **1** highest point or part **2** lid or cap **3** highest rank **4** garment for the upper part of the body ▷ *adj* **5** at or of the top ▷ *v* **topping, topped 6** form a top on **7** be at the top of **8** exceed or surpass **topping** *n* sauce or garnish for food **topless** *adj* (of a costume or woman) with no covering for the breasts **topmost** *adj* highest or best **top brass** most important officers or leaders **top-dress** *v* spread fertilizer on the surface of the land **top-dressing** *n* **top hat** man's tall cylindrical hat **top-heavy** *adj* unstable through being overloaded at the top **top-notch** *adj* excellent, first-class **topsoil** *n* surface layer of soil

top² *n* toy which spins on a pointed base

topaz [**toe**-pazz] n semiprecious stone in various colours

tope[1] v drink (alcohol) regularly

tope[2] n small European shark

topee, topi [**toe**-pee] n lightweight pith hat

topiary [**tope**-ee-yar-ee] n art of trimming trees and bushes into decorative shapes **topiarist** n

topic n subject of a conversation, book, etc. **topical** adj relating to current events **topicality** n

topography n, pl -**phies** (science of describing) the surface features of a place **topographer** n **topographic** adj

topology n geometry of the properties of a shape which are unaffected by continuous distortion **topological** adj

topple v 1 (cause to) fall over 2 overthrow (a government etc.)

topsy-turvy adj 1 upside down 2 in confusion

toque [**toke**] n small round hat

tor n high rocky hill

Torah n body of traditional Jewish teaching

torch n 1 burning brand carried as a light 2 Brit flashlight ▷ v 3 slang set fire to deliberately

tore v past tense of **tear**[2]

toreador [**torr**-ee-a-dor] n bullfighter

torment v 1 cause (someone) great suffering 2 tease cruelly ▷ n 3 great suffering 4 source of suffering **tormentor** n

torn v past participle of **tear**[2]

tornado n, pl -**does, -dos** violent whirlwind

torpedo n, pl -**does** 1 self-propelled underwater missile ▷ v -**doing, -doed** 2 attack or destroy with or as if with torpedoes

torpid adj sluggish and inactive **torpidity** n **torpor** n torpid state

torque [**tork**] n 1 force causing rotation 2 Celtic necklace or armband of twisted metal

torrent n 1 rushing stream 2 downpour **torrential** adj (of rain) very heavy

torrid adj 1 very hot and dry 2 highly emotional

torsion n twisting

torso n, pl -**sos** 1 trunk of the human body 2 statue of a nude human trunk

tort n law civil wrong or injury for which damages may be claimed

tortilla n thin Mexican pancake

tortoise n slow-moving land reptile with a dome-shaped shell **tortoiseshell** n 1 mottled brown shell of a turtle, used for making ornaments ▷ adj 2 having brown, orange, and black markings

tortuous adj 1 winding or twisting 2 not straightforward

torture v 1 cause (someone) severe pain or mental anguish ▷ n 2 severe physical or mental pain 3 torturing **torturer** n

Tory n, pl **Tories** 1 member or supporter of the Progressive Conservative Party ▷ adj 2 of Tories **Toryism** n

toss v 1 throw lightly 2 fling or be flung about 3 (of a horse) throw (its rider) 4 coat (food) by gentle stirring or mixing 5 throw up (a coin) to decide between alternatives by guessing which side will land uppermost ▷ n 6 tossing **toss up** v toss a coin **toss-up** n even chance or risk

tot[1] *n* **1** small child **2** small drink of spirits

tot[2] *v* **totting, totted** ► **tot up** add (numbers) together

total *n* **1** whole, esp. a sum of parts ▷ *adj* **2** complete **3** of or being a total ▷ *v* **totalling, totalled 4** amount to **5** add up **totally** *adv* **totality** *n* **totalizator** *n* machine operating a betting system in which money is paid out to the winners in proportion to their stakes

totalitarian *adj* of a dictatorial one-party government **totalitarianism** *n*

tote[1] *n* short for **totalizator**

tote[2] *v* haul or carry

totem *n* tribal badge or emblem **totem pole** post carved or painted with totems by N American Indians on the Pacific coast

totter *v* **1** move unsteadily **2** be about to fall

toucan *n* large-billed tropical American bird

touch *n* **1** sense by which an object's qualities are perceived when they come into contact with part of the body **2** gentle tap, push, or caress **3** small amount **4** characteristic style **5** detail ▷ *v* **6** come into contact with **7** tap, feel, or stroke **8** affect **9** move emotionally **10** eat or drink **11** refer to in passing **12** equal or match **13** *slang* ask for money **touch and go** risky or critical **touch base** make contact, renew communication **touched** *adj* **1** emotionally moved **2** slightly mad **touching** *adj* emotionally moving **touchy** *adj* easily offended **touch down** *v* (of an aircraft) land **touchdown** *n* *football* score gained by being in possession of ball behind opponents' goal line **touchline** *n* side line of the field in some games **touchstone** *n* criterion **touch-type** *v* type without looking at the keyboard

touché [too-shay] *interj* acknowledgment of the striking home of a remark or witty reply

tough *adj* **1** strong or resilient **2** difficult to chew or cut **3** hardy and fit **4** rough and violent **5** difficult **6** firm and determined **7** *informal* unlucky or unfair ▷ *n* **8** *informal* rough violent person **toughness** *n* **toughen** *v* make or become tough or tougher

toupee [too-pay] *n* wig

tour *n* **1** journey visiting places of interest along the way **2** trip to perform or play in different places ▷ *v* **3** make a tour (of) **tourism** *n* tourist travel as an industry **tourist** *n* person travelling for pleasure **touristy** *adj* full of tourists or tourist attractions

tour de force *n, pl* **tours de force** *French* brilliant stroke or achievement

tournament *n* **1** sporting competition with several stages to decide the overall winner **2** *hist* Also **tourney** contest between knights on horseback

tourniquet [tour-nick-kay] *n* something twisted round a limb to stop bleeding

tousled *adj* ruffled and untidy

tout [rhymes with **shout**] *v* **1** solicit custom in a persistent manner **2** obtain and sell information about racehorses ▷ *n* **3** person who sells tickets for a popular event at inflated prices

tow[1] *v* **1** drag, esp. by means of a rope ▷ *n* **2** towing **in tow** following closely behind **on**

tow being towed **towbar** n metal bar on an automobile for towing vehicles **towpath** n path beside a canal or river, originally for horses towing boats

tow² n fibre of hemp or flax **tow-headed** adj with blond hair

towards, toward prep **1** in the direction of **2** with regard to **3** as a contribution to

towel n cloth for drying things **towelling** n material used for making towels

tower n **1** tall structure, often forming part of a larger building ▷ v **2** be very tall **3** loom (over) **tower of strength** person who supports or comforts

town n **1** group of buildings larger than a village **2** central part of this **3** people of a town **township** n small town **town hall** large building used for council meetings, concerts, etc.

toxemia, toxaemia [tox-**seem**-ya] n **1** blood poisoning **2** high blood pressure in pregnancy

toxic adj **1** poisonous **2** caused by poison **toxicity** n **toxicology** n study of poisons **toxin** n poison of bacterial origin

toy n **1** something designed to be played with ▷ adj **2** (of a dog) of a variety much smaller than is normal for that breed **toy with** v play or fiddle with

trace¹ n **1** track left by something **2** indication **3** minute quantity ▷ v **4** follow the course of **5** track down and find **6** copy exactly by drawing on a thin sheet of transparent paper set on top of the original **traceable** adj **tracer** n projectile which leaves a visible trail **tracing** n

traced copy **tracery** n pattern of interlacing lines **trace element** chemical element occurring in very small amounts in soil etc.

trace² n strap by which a horse pulls a vehicle **kick over the traces** escape or defy control

trachea [track-**kee**-a] n, pl **tracheae** windpipe **tracheotomy** [track-ee-**ot**-a-mee] n surgical incision into the trachea

track n **1** mark or trail left by the passage of anything **2** rough road or path **3** railway line **4** course of action or thought **5** endless band round the wheels of a tank, bulldozer, etc. **6** course for racing **7** separate section on a record, tape, or CD ▷ v **8** follow the trail or path of **track down** v hunt for and find **track event** athletic sport held on a track **track record** past accomplishments of a person or organization **tracksuit** n warm loose-fitting suit worn by athletes etc., esp. during training

tract¹ n **1** wide area **2** anat system of organs with a particular function

tract² n pamphlet, esp. a religious one

tractable adj easy to manage or control

traction n **1** pulling, esp. by engine power **2** med application of a steady pull on an injured limb by weights and pulleys **3** grip of the wheels of a vehicle on the ground

tractor n motor vehicle with large rear wheels for pulling farm machinery **tractor-trailer** n freight vehicle consisting of a truck with engine and cab pulling an open or closed trailer

trade n 1 buying, selling, or exchange of goods 2 person's job or craft 3 (people engaged in) a particular industry or business ▷ v 4 buy and sell 5 exchange 6 engage in trade **trader** n **trading** n **trade-in** n used article given in part payment for a new one **trademark** or **tradename** n (legally registered) name or symbol used by a firm to distinguish its goods **trade-off** n exchange made as a compromise **tradesman** n 1 skilled worker 2 shopkeeper **trade union** society of workers for the protection of their interests **trade wind** wind blowing steadily towards the equator

tradition n 1 unwritten body of beliefs, customs, etc. handed down from generation to generation 2 custom or practice of long standing **traditional** adj **traditionally** adv

traduce v slander

traffic n 1 vehicles coming and going on a road 2 (illicit) trade ▷ v -**ficking**, -**ficked** 3 trade, usu. illicitly **trafficker** n **traffic circle** road junction at which traffic passes around a central island **traffic cop** informal police officer who directs the movement of traffic **traffic lights** set of coloured lights at a junction to control the traffic flow

tragedy n, pl -**dies** 1 shocking or sad event 2 serious play, film, etc. in which the hero is destroyed by a personal failing in adverse circumstances **tragedian** [traj-**jee**-dee-an] n actor in or writer of tragedies **tragedienne** [traj-jee-dee-**enn**] n actress in tragedies **tragic** adj of or like a tragedy

tragically adv **tragicomedy** n play with both tragic and comic elements

trail v 1 drag along the ground 2 follow the tracks of 3 lag behind 4 (of plants) grow along the ground or hang loosely ▷ n 5 track or trace 6 path, track, or road **trailer** n 1 vehicle designed to be towed by another vehicle 2 extract from a film or programme used to advertise it **trailer park** site for parking mobile homes

train v 1 instruct in a skill 2 learn the skills needed to do a particular job or activity 3 cause (an animal) to perform or (a plant) to grow in a particular way 4 aim (a gun etc.) 5 exercise in preparation for a sports event ▷ n 6 line of railway coaches or wagons drawn by an engine 7 sequence or series 8 long trailing back section of a dress 9 body of attendants **trainee** n person being trained **trainer** n person who trains an athlete, sportsperson, or racehorse 2 sports shoe

traipse v informal walk wearily

trait n characteristic feature

traitor n person guilty of treason or treachery **traitorous** adj

trajectory n, pl -**ries** line of flight, esp. of a projectile

tram n Brit streetcar **tramlines** pl n track for trams

trammel v -**elling**, -**elled** hinder or restrain

tramp v 1 travel on foot, hike 2 walk heavily ▷ n 3 homeless person who travels on foot 4 hike 5 sound of tramping 6 cargo ship available for hire 7 promiscuous woman

trample v tread on and crush

trampoline n 1 tough canvas

sheet attached to a frame by springs, used by acrobats etc. ▷ v **2** bounce on a trampoline

trance n **1** unconscious or dazed state **2** state of ecstasy or total absorption

tranche n portion of something large, esp. a sum of money

tranquil adj calm and quiet **tranquilly** adv **tranquillity** n **tranquillize** v make calm **tranquillizer** n drug which reduces anxiety or tension

trans- prefix across, through, or beyond

transact v conduct or negotiate (a business deal) **transaction** n **1** transacting **2** business deal transacted

transatlantic adj on, from, or to the other side of the Atlantic

transceiver n combined radio transmitter and receiver

transcend v **1** rise above **2** be superior to **transcendence** n **transcendent** adj **transcendental** adj **1** based on intuition rather than experience **2** supernatural or mystical **transcendentalism** n

transcribe v **1** copy out **2** write down (something said) **3** record for a later broadcast **4** arrange (music) for a different instrument **transcript** n copy

transducer n device that converts one form of energy to another

transept n either of the two shorter wings of a cross-shaped church

transfer v -ferring, -ferred **1** move or send from one person or place to another ▷ n **2** transferring **3** design which can be transferred from one surface to another **transferable** adj

transference n transferring

transfigure v change in appearance **transfiguration** n

transfix v **1** astound or stun **2** pierce through

transform v change the shape or character of **transformation** n **transformer** n device for changing the voltage of an alternating current

transfusion n injection of blood into the blood vessels of a patient **transfuse** v **1** give a transfusion to **2** permeate or infuse

transgress v break (a moral law) **transgression** n **transgressor** n

transient adj lasting only for a short time **transience** n

transistor n **1** semiconducting device used to amplify electric currents **2** portable radio using transistors **transistorized** adj

transit n going from one place to another **transition** n change from one state to another **transitional** adj **transitive** adj (of a verb) requiring a direct object **transitory** adj not lasting long

translate v turn from one language into another **translation** n **translator** n

transliterate v convert to the letters of a different alphabet **transliteration** n

translucent adj letting light pass through, but not transparent **translucence** n

transmigrate v (of a soul) pass into another body **transmigration** n

transmit v -mitting, -mitted **1** pass (something) from one person or place to another **2** send out (signals) by radio waves **3** broadcast (a radio or television programme) **transmission** *n* **1** transmitting **2** shafts and gears through which power passes from a vehicle's engine to its wheels **transmittable** *adj* **transmitter** *n*

transmogrify *v* **-fying, -fied** *informal* change completely

transmute *v* change the form or nature of **transmutation** *n*

transom *n* **1** horizontal bar across a window **2** bar separating a door from the window over it

transparent *adj* **1** able to be seen through, clear **2** easily understood or recognized **transparently** *adv* **transparency** *n* **1** transparent quality **2** colour photograph on transparent film, viewed by means of a projector

transpire *v* **1** become known **2** *informal* happen **3** give off water vapour through pores **transpiration** *n*

transplant *v* **1** remove and transfer (a plant) to another place **2** transfer (an organ or tissue) surgically from one part or body to another ▷ *n* **3** surgical transplanting **4** thing transplanted **transplantation** *n*

transport *v* **1** convey from one place to another **2** *hist* exile (a criminal) to a penal colony **3** enrapture ▷ *n* **4** business or system of transporting **5** vehicle used in transport **6** ecstasy or rapture **transportation** *n* **transporter** *n* large goods vehicle

transpose *v* **1** interchange two things **2** put (music) into a different key **transposition** *n*

transsexual *n* **1** person of one sex who believes their true

identity is of the opposite sex **2** person who has had a sex-change operation

transubstantiation *n* *Christianity* doctrine that the bread and wine consecrated in the Eucharist changes into the substance of Christ's body

transuranic [tranz-yoor-**ran**-ik] *adj* (of an element) having an atomic number greater than that of uranium

transverse *adj* crossing from side to side

transvestite *n* person who seeks sexual pleasure by wearing the clothes of the opposite sex **transvestism** *n*

trap *n* **1** device for catching animals **2** plan for tricking or catching a person **3** bend in a pipe containing liquid to prevent the escape of gas **4** *hist* two-wheeled carriage **5** *slang* mouth ▷ *v* **trapping, trapped 6** catch **7** trick **trapper** *n* person who traps animals for their fur **trapdoor** *n* door in a floor or roof

trapeze *n* horizontal bar suspended from two ropes, used by circus acrobats

trapezium *n, pl* **-ziums, -zia 1** quadrilateral with no sides parallel **2** *Brit* trapezoid **trapezoid** [**trap**-piz-zoid] *n* **1** quadrilateral with two parallel sides of unequal length **2** *Brit* trapezium

trappings *pl n* equipment or ornaments

Trappist *n* member of an order of Christian monks who observe strict silence

trash *n* **1** garbage **2** anything worthless ▷ *v* **3** throw away **4** attack or destroy **trashy** *adj*

trauma [**traw**-ma] *n* **1** emotional shock **2** injury or wound **traumatic** *adj* **traumatize** *v*

travail v, n lit labour or toil

travel v **-elling, -elled**
1 go from one place to another, through an area, or for a specified distance ▷ n 2 travelling, esp. as a tourist **travels** 3 (account of) travelling **traveller** n **travelogue** n film or talk about someone's travels

traverse v 1 move over or back and forth over 2 move sideways ▷ n 3 traversing 4 path or road across

travesty n, pl **-ties** 1 grotesque imitation or mockery ▷ v **-tying, -tied** 2 make or be a travesty of

trawl n net dragged at deep levels behind a fishing boat ▷ v 2 fish with such a net **trawler** n trawling boat

tray n 1 flat board, usu. with a rim, for carrying things 2 open receptacle for office correspondence

treachery n, pl **-eries** wilful betrayal **treacherous** adj 1 disloyal 2 unreliable or dangerous **treacherously** adv

treacle n thick dark syrup produced when sugar is refined **treacly** adj

tread v **treading, trod, trodden** or **trod** 1 set one's foot on 2 crush by walking on ▷ n 3 way of walking or dancing 4 treading 5 upper surface of a step 6 part of a tire that touches the ground **treadmill** n 1 hist cylinder turned by treading on steps projecting from it 2 dreary routine

treadle [tred-dl] n lever worked by the foot to turn a wheel

treason n 1 betrayal of one's sovereign or country 2 treachery or disloyalty **treasonable** or **treasonous** adj

treasure n 1 collection of wealth, esp. gold or jewels 2 valued person or thing ▷ v 3 prize or cherish **treasurer** n official in charge of funds **treasury** n 1 storage place for treasure 2 government department in charge of finance **treasure-trove** n treasure found with no evidence of ownership

treat n 1 pleasure, entertainment, etc. given or paid for by someone else ▷ v 2 deal with or regard in a certain manner 3 give medical treatment to 4 subject to a chemical or industrial process 5 provide (someone) with (something) as a treat **treatment** n 1 way of treating a person or thing 2 medical care

treatise [treat-izz] n formal piece of writing on a particular subject

treaty n, pl **-ties** signed contract between states

treble adj 1 threefold, triple 2 music high-pitched ▷ n 3 (singer with or part for) a soprano voice ▷ v 4 increase threefold **trebly** adv

tree n large perennial plant with a woody trunk **treeless** adj **tree surgery** repair of damaged trees **tree surgeon**

trefoil [tref-foil] n 1 plant, such as clover, with a three-lobed leaf 2 carved ornament like this

trek n 1 long difficult journey, esp. on foot ▷ v **trekking, trekked** 2 make such a journey

trellis n framework of horizontal and vertical strips of wood

tremble v 1 shake or quiver 2 feel fear or anxiety ▷ n 3 trembling **trembling** adj

tremendous adj 1 huge

2 *informal* great in quality or amount **tremendously** *adv*

tremolo *n, pl* **-los** *music* quivering effect in singing or playing

tremor *n* **1** involuntary shaking **2** minor earthquake

tremulous *adj* trembling, as from fear or excitement

trench *n* long narrow ditch, esp. one used as a shelter in war **trench coat** double-breasted waterproof coat

trenchant *adj* **1** incisive **2** effective

trencher *n hist* wooden plate for serving food **trencherman** *n* hearty eater

trend *n* **1** general tendency or direction **2** fashion ▷ *v* be widely discussed on a social media site **trendy** *adj, n informal* consciously fashionable (person) **trendiness** *n*

trepidation *n* fear or anxiety

trespass *v* **1** go onto another's property without permission ▷ *n* **2** trespassing **3** *old-fashioned* sin or wrongdoing **trespasser** *n* **trespass on** *v* take unfair advantage of (someone's friendship, patience, etc.)

tress *n* long lock of hair

trestle *n* board fixed on pairs of spreading legs, used as a support

trews *pl n* close-fitting tartan trousers

tri- *prefix* three

triad *n* **1** group of three **2 Triad** Chinese criminal secret society

trial *n* **1** trying or testing **2** *law* investigation of a case before a judge **3** thing or person straining endurance or patience **trials 4** sporting competition for individuals

triangle *n* **1** geometric figure with three sides **2** triangular

percussion instrument **3** situation involving three people **triangular** *adj*

tribe *n* group of clans or families believed to have a common ancestor **tribal** *adj* **tribalism** *n* loyalty to a tribe

tribulation *n* great distress

tribune *n* **1** person who upholds public rights **2** people's representative in ancient Rome **tribunal** *n* lawcourt board appointed to inquire into a specific matter

tributary *n, pl* **-taries 1** stream or river flowing into a larger one ▷ *adj* **2** (of a stream or river) flowing into a larger one

tribute *n* **1** sign of respect or admiration **2** tax paid by one state to another

trice *n* **in a trice** instantly

triceps *n* muscle at the back of the upper arm

trichology [trick-**ol**-a-jee] *n* study and treatment of hair and its diseases **trichologist** *n*

trick *n* **1** deceitful or cunning action or plan **2** joke or prank **3** feat of skill or cunning **4** knack **5** mannerism **6** cards played in one round **7** cheat or deceive **trickery** *n* **trickster** *n* **tricky** *adj* **1** difficult, needing careful handling **2** crafty

trickle *v* **1** (cause to) flow in a thin stream or drops **2** move gradually ▷ *n* **3** gradual flow

tricolour [**trick**-kol-lor] *n* three-coloured striped flag

tricycle *n* three-wheeled cycle

trident *n* three-pronged spear

triennial *adj* happening every three years

trifle *n* **1** insignificant thing **2** small amount **3** dessert of sponge cake, custard, etc. ▷ *v* **4** (usu. foll. by *with*) toy with **trifling** *adj* insignificant

trigger *n* **1** small lever releasing a catch on a gun or machine **2** action that sets off a course of events ▷ *v* **3** (usu. foll. by *off*) set (an action or process) in motion **trigger-happy** *adj* too quick to use guns

trigonometry *n* branch of mathematics dealing with relations of the sides and angles of triangles **trigonometrical** *adj*

trike *n informal* tricycle

trilateral *adj* having three sides

trilby *n, pl* **-bies** man's soft felt hat

trill *n* **1** rapid alternation between two notes **2** shrill warbling sound made by some birds ▷ *v* **3** play or sing a trill

trillion *n* **1** *US & Canad* one million million, 10^{12} **2** *Brit* one million million million, 10^{18}

trilobite [**trile**-oh-bite] *n* small prehistoric sea animal

trilogy [**trill**-a-jee] *n, pl* **-gies** series of three related books, plays, etc.

trim *adj* **trimmer, trimmest** **1** neat and smart **2** slender **3** in good condition ▷ *v* **trimming, trimmed 4** cut or prune into good shape **5** decorate with lace, ribbons, etc. **6** adjust the balance of (a ship or aircraft) by shifting the cargo etc. ▷ *n* **7** decoration **8** upholstery and decorative facings in an automobile **9** trim state **10** haircut that neatens the existing style **trimming** *n* **1** decoration **trimmings** **2** usual accompaniments: *turkey with all the trimmings*

trimaran [**trime**-a-ran] *n* three-hulled boat

trinitrotoluene *n* full name of TNT

trinity *n, pl* **-ties 1** group of three **2 Trinity** *Christianity*

union of three persons, Father, Son, and Holy Spirit, in one God

trinket *n* small or worthless ornament or piece of jewellery

trio *n, pl* **trios 1** group of three **2** piece of music for three performers

trip *n* **1** journey to a place and back, esp. for pleasure **2** stumble **3** switch on a mechanism **4** *informal* hallucinogenic drug experience ▷ *v* **tripping, tripped 5** (cause to) stumble **6** (often foll. by *up*) catch (someone) in a mistake **7** move or tread lightly **8** operate (a switch) **9** *informal* take a hallucinogenic drug **tripper** *n* tourist

tripe *n* **1** stomach of a cow used as food **2** *informal* nonsense

triple *adj* **1** having three parts **2** three times as great or as many ▷ *v* **3** increase threefold ▷ *n* **4** *baseball* hit that enables the batter to run to third base **triplet** *n* one of three babies born at one birth **triple jump** athletics event in which competitors make a hop, a step, and a jump as a continuous movement

triplicate *adj* **1** triple ▷ *n* **2** one of three copies **in triplicate** in three copies

tripod [**tripe**-pod] *n* three-legged stand, stool, etc.

tripos [**tripe**-poss] *n* final examinations for the degree of BA at Cambridge University

triptych [**trip**-tick] *n* painting or carving on three hinged panels, often forming an altarpiece

trite *adj* hackneyed or banal

tritium *n* radioactive isotope of hydrogen

triumph *n* **1** (happiness caused by) victory or

success ▷ v **2** be victorious
or successful **3** rejoice
over a victory **triumphal**
adj celebrating a triumph
triumphant *adj* feeling or
showing triumph

triumvirate [try-**umm**-vir-
rit] *n* group of three people in
joint control

trivet [**triv**-vit] *n* metal stand
for a pot or kettle

trivial *adj* **1** of little
importance **2** everyday, trite
trivially *adv* **trivia** *pl n* trivial
things or details **triviality** *n*
trivialize *v* make (something)
seem less important or
complex than it is

trod *v* past tense and a past
participle of **tread**

trodden *v* a past participle of
tread

troglodyte *n* cave dweller

troika *n* **1** Russian vehicle
drawn by three horses abreast
2 group of three people in
authority

troll *n* giant or dwarf in
Scandinavian folklore

trolley *n* **1** small wheeled table
for food and drink **2** wheeled
cart for moving goods **trolley
car** bus powered by electricity
from an overhead wire but not
running on rails

trollop *n* promiscuous or
slovenly woman

trombone *n* brass musical
instrument with a sliding
tube **trombonist** *n*

troop *n* **1** large group
2 artillery or cavalry unit
3 Scout company **troops**
4 soldiers ▷ v **5** move in
a crowd **trooper** *n* cavalry
soldier

trope *n* figure of speech

trophy *n, pl* **-phies 1** cup,
shield, etc. given as a prize
2 memento of success

tropic *n* **1** either of two lines
of latitude at 23½° N (**tropic**

of Cancer) or 23½° S (**tropic of
Capricorn**) **tropics 2** part of
the earth's surface between
these lines **tropical** *adj* **1** of
or in the tropics **2** (of climate)
very hot

trot *v* **trotting, trotted**
1 move or cause (a horse)
to move at a medium pace,
lifting the feet in diagonal
pairs **2** (of a person) move
at a steady brisk pace ▷ n
3 trotting **trotter** *n* pig's foot
trot out *v* repeat (old ideas
etc.) without fresh thought

troth [rhymes with **growth**]
n pledge of fidelity, esp. a
betrothal

troubadour [**troo**-bad-oor] *n*
medieval travelling poet and
singer

trouble *n* **1** (cause of) distress
or anxiety **2** disease or
malfunctioning **3** state of
disorder or unrest **4** care or
effort ▷ v **5** (cause to) worry
6 cause inconvenience to
7 exert oneself **troubled**
adj **troublesome** *adj*
troubleshooter *n* person
employed to locate and deal
with faults or problems

trough [**troff**] *n* **1** long open
container, esp. for animals'
food or water **2** narrow
channel between two waves
or ridges **3** *meteorol* area of low
pressure

trounce *v* defeat utterly

troupe [**troop**] *n* company of
performers **trouper** *n*

trousers *pl n* two-legged outer
garment with legs reaching
usu. to the ankles **trouser** *adj*
of trousers

trousseau [**troo**-so] *n*,
pl **-seaux, -seaus** bride's
collection of clothing etc. for
her marriage

trout *n* game fish related to
the salmon

trowel *n* hand tool with a

flat wide blade for spreading mortar, lifting plants, etc.

troy weight, troy n system of weights used for gold, silver, and jewels

truant n pupil who stays away from school without permission **play truant** stay away from school without permission **truancy** n

truce n temporary agreement to stop fighting

truck[1] n large vehicle for transporting loads by road **trucker** n truck driver

truck[2] n **have no truck with** refuse to be involved with

truckle v (usu. foll. by to) yield weakly

truculent [**truck**-yew-lent] adj aggressively defiant **truculence** n

trudge v **1** walk heavily or wearily ▷ n **2** long tiring walk

true adj **truer, truest 1** in accordance with facts **2** faithful **3** exact **4** genuine **truly** adv **truism** n self-evident truth **truth** n **1** state of being true **2** something true **truthful** adj **1** honest **2** exact **truthfully** adv

truffle n **1** edible underground fungus **2** candy flavoured with chocolate

trug n long shallow basket used by gardeners

trump[1] n, adj **1** (card) of the suit temporarily outranking the others ▷ v **2** play a trump card on (another card) ▷ pl n **3** trump suit **turn up trumps** end unexpectedly well **trump up** v invent or concoct

trump[2] n lit (sound of) a trumpet

trumpet n **1** valved brass instrument with a flared tube ▷ v -**peting**, -**peted 2** (of an elephant) cry loudly

3 proclaim loudly **trumpeter** n

truncate v cut short

truncheon n small club carried by a policeman

trundle v move heavily on wheels

trunk n **1** main stem of a tree **2** person's body excluding the head and limbs **3** large case or box for clothes etc. **4** elephant's long nose **5** space in an automobile for luggage **trunks 6** man's swimming shorts **trunk call** long-distance telephone call **trunk road** main road

truss v **1** tie or bind up ▷ n **2** device for holding a hernia in place **3** framework supporting a roof, bridge, etc.

trust n **1** confidence in the truth, reliability, etc. of a person or thing **2** obligation arising from responsibility **3** charge or care **4** arrangement in which one person administers property, money, etc. on another's behalf **5** property held for another **6** group of companies joined to control a market ▷ v **7** believe in and rely on **8** expect or hope **9** consign to someone's care **trustee** n person holding property on another's behalf **trusteeship** n **trustful** or **trusting** adj inclined to trust **trustworthy** adj reliable or honest **trusty** adj faithful or reliable

truth n see **true**

try v **trying, tried 1** make an effort or attempt **2** test or sample **3** put strain on: he tries my patience **4** investigate (a case) **5** examine (a person) in a lawcourt ▷ n, pl **tries 6** attempt or effort **7** rugby score gained by touching the ball down over the opponent's goal line **try it on** *informal* try to deceive or fool someone **trying** *adj* difficult or annoying

tryst *n old-fashioned* arrangement to meet

tsar [**zahr**] *n hist* Russian emperor

tsetse [**tset**-see] *n* bloodsucking African fly whose bite transmits disease

T-shirt *n* short-sleeved casual shirt or top

tsp. teaspoon

T-square *n* T-shaped ruler

tsunami *n, pl* **-mis, -mi** tidal wave

tub *n* **1** open, usu. round container **2** bath **tubby** *adj* (of a person) short and fat

tuba [**tube**-a] *n* valved low-pitched brass instrument

tube *n* **1** hollow cylinder **2** flexible cylinder with a cap to hold pastes **the tube** underground railway, esp. the one in London **tubing** [**tube**-ing] *n* **1** length of tube **2** system of tubes **tubular** [**tube**-yew-lar] *adj* of or like a tube

tuber [**tube**-er] *n* fleshy underground root of a plant such as a potato **tuberous** [**tube**-er-uss] *adj*

tubercle [**tube**-er-kl] *n* small rounded swelling

tuberculosis [tube-berk-yew-**lohss**-iss] *n* infectious disease causing tubercles, esp. in the lungs **tubercular** [tube-**berk**-yew-lar] *adj* of tuberculosis **tuberculin** *n* extract from a bacillus used to test for tuberculosis

tuck *v* **1** push or fold into a small space **2** stitch in folds ▷ *n* **3** stitched fold **4** *informal* food **tuck away** *v* store in a safe place

tuckamore *n Canad, esp. Newfoundland* small stunted

evergreen tree or scrub

Tudor *adj* **1** of the English royal house ruling from 1485–1603 **2** in an architectural style characterized by half-timbered buildings

Tuesday *n* third day of the week

tufa [**tew**-fa] *n* porous rock formed as a deposit from springs

tuffet *n* small mound or seat

tuft *n* bunch of feathers, grass, hair, etc. held or growing together at the base

tug *v* **tugging, tugged 1** pull hard ▷ *n* **2** hard pull **3** small ship used to tow other vessels **tug of war** contest in which two teams pull against one another on a rope

tuition *n* instruction, esp. received individually or in a small group

tulip *n* plant with bright cup-shaped flowers

tulle [**tewl**] *n* fine net fabric of silk etc.

tumble *v* **1** (cause to) fall, esp. awkwardly or violently **2** roll or twist, esp. in play **3** rumple ▷ *n* **4** fall **5** somersault **tumbler** *n* **1** stemless drinking glass **2** acrobat **3** spring catch in a lock **tumbledown** *adj* dilapidated **tumble dryer** *or* **tumbler dryer** machine that dries laundry by rotating it in warm air **tumble to** *v informal* realize, understand

tumbrel, tumbril *n* farm cart used during the French Revolution to take prisoners to the guillotine

tumescent [tew-**mess**-ent] *adj* swollen or becoming swollen **tumescence** *n*

tummy *n, pl* **-mies** *informal* stomach

tumour [**tew**-mer] *n* abnormal growth in or on the body

tumult [**tew**-mult] *n* uproar or commotion **tumultuous** [tew-**mull**-tew-uss] *adj*

tumulus [**tew**-mew-luss] *n, pl* **-li** burial mound

tun *n* large beer cask

tuna [**tune**-a] *n* large marine food fish

tundra *n* vast treeless Arctic region with permanently frozen subsoil

tune *n* **1** (pleasing) sequence of musical notes **2** correct musical pitch: *she sang out of tune* ▷ *v* **3** adjust (a musical instrument) so that it is in tune **4** adjust (a machine) to obtain the desired performance **tuneful** *adj* **tunefully** *adv* **tuneless** *adj* **tuner** *n* **tune in** *v* adjust (a radio or television) to receive (a station or programme)

tungsten *n* greyish-white metal

tunic *n* **1** close-fitting jacket forming part of some uniforms **2** loose knee-length garment

tunnel *n* **1** underground passage ▷ *v* **-nelling, -nelled** **2** make a tunnel (through)

tunny *n, pl* **-nies, -ny** same as **tuna**

tup *n* male sheep

tupik, tupek *n* traditional type of Inuit dwelling made of animal skins

tuque [**took**] *n* knitted cap with tapering end

turban *n* Muslim or Sikh man's headcovering made by winding cloth round the head

turbid *adj* muddy, not clear **turbidity** *n*

turbine *n* machine or generator driven by gas, water, etc. turning blades

turbo- *combining form* of or powered by a turbine

turbot *n* large European flatfish

turbulence *n* **1** confusion, movement, or agitation **2** atmospheric instability causing gusty air currents **turbulent** *adj*

tureen *n* serving dish for soup

turf *n, pl* **turfs, turves** **1** short thick even grass **2** square of this with roots and soil attached ▷ *v* **3** cover with turf **the turf 1** horse racing **2** racecourse **turf accountant** bookmaker **turf out** *v* *informal* throw out

turgid [**tur**-jid] *adj* **1** swollen and thick **2** (of language) pompous **turgidity** *n*

turkey *n* large bird bred for food

Turkish *adj* **1** of Turkey, its people, or their language ▷ *n* **2** Turkish language **Turkish bath** steam bath **Turkish delight** jelly-like candy coated with icing sugar

turmeric *n* yellow spice obtained from the root of an Asian plant

turmoil *n* agitation or confusion

turn *v* **1** move around an axis, rotate **2** change the position or direction (of) **3** (usu. foll. by *into*) change in nature or character **4** become sour **5** shape on a lathe **6** go round (a corner) **7** reach or pass in age, time, etc.: *she has just turned twenty* ▷ *n* **8** turning **9** direction or drift **10** opportunity to do something as part of an agreed succession **11** period or spell **12** short theatrical performance **good** *or* **bad turn** helpful *or* unhelpful act **turner** *n* **turning** *n* road or path leading off a main route **turning point** moment when a decisive change occurs **turncoat** *n* person who deserts one party or cause to join another **turn down**

v **1** refuse or reject **2** reduce the volume or brightness (of) **turn in** *v* **1** go to bed **2** hand in **turn off** *v* stop (something) working by using a knob etc. **turn on** *v* **1** start (something) working by using a knob etc. **2** become aggressive towards **3** *informal* excite, esp. sexually **turnout** *n* **1** number of people appearing at a gathering **2** outfit **turnover** *n* **1** total sales made by a business over a certain period **2** rate at which staff leave and are replaced **3** small pastry **turnpike** *n* road where a toll is collected at barriers **turnstile** *n* revolving gate for admitting one person at a time **turntable** *n* revolving platform **turn up** *v* **1** arrive or appear **2** find or be found **3** increase the volume or brightness (of) **turn-up** *n* **1** turned-up fold at the bottom of a trouser leg **2** *informal* unexpected event

turnip *n* root vegetable with orange or white flesh

turpentine *n* (oil made from) the resin of certain trees **turps** *n* turpentine oil

turpitude *n* depravity

turquoise *n* **1** blue-green precious stone ▷ *adj* **2** blue-green

turret *n* **1** small tower **2** revolving gun tower on a warship or tank

turtle *n* sea tortoise **turn turtle** capsize **turtledove** *n* small wild dove **turtleneck** *n* (sweater with) a round high close-fitting neck

tusk *n* long pointed tooth of an elephant, walrus, etc.

tussle *n, v* fight or scuffle

tussock *n* tuft of grass

tutelage [**tew**-till-lij] *n* **1** tuition **2** guardianship **tutelary** [**tew**-till-lar-ee] *adj*

tutor *n* **1** person teaching individuals or small groups ▷ *v* **2** act as a tutor to **tutorial** *n* period of instruction with a tutor

tutu *n* short stiff skirt worn by ballerinas

tuxedo *n, pl* **-dos** dinner jacket

TV television

twaddle *n* nonsense

twain *n obsolete* two

twang *n* **1** sharp ringing sound **2** nasal speech ▷ *v* **3** (cause to) make a twang

tweak *v* **1** pinch or twist sharply ▷ *n* **2** tweaking

twee *adj informal* too sentimental, sweet, or pretty

tweed *n* **1** thick woollen cloth **tweeds 2** suit of tweed **tweedy** *adj*

tween *n* **1** person from about 9 to 13 years old ▷ *adj* **2** intended for tweens: *the tween market*

tweet *v* **1** chirp **2** post short messages on the Twitter website ▷ *n* **3** short message posted on the Twitter website **tweeter** *n* **1** loudspeaker reproducing high-frequency sounds **2** person who uses the Twitter website

tweezers *pl n* small pincer-like tool

twelve *adj, n* two more than ten **twelfth** *adj, n* (of) number twelve in a series

twenty *adj, n* two times ten **twenty-four-seven** or **24/7** *adv informal* all the time **twentieth** *adj, n*

24 Sussex Drive *n* official Ottawa residence of the Prime Minister

twerp *n informal* silly person

twice *adv* two times

twiddle *v* (foll. by *with*) fiddle (with), twirl **twiddle one's thumbs** be bored, have nothing to do

twig[1] n small branch or shoot

twig[2] v **twigging, twigged** informal realize or understand

twilight n soft dim light just after sunset

twill n fabric woven to produce parallel ridges

twin n 1 one of a pair, esp. of two children born at one birth ▷ v **twinning, twinned** 2 pair or be paired **twin bill** baseball same as **double-header**

twine v 1 twist or coil round ▷ n 2 string or cord

twinge n sudden sharp pain or pang

twi-night adj baseball designating a double-header that lasts from the afternoon into the evening

twinkle v 1 shine brightly but intermittently ▷ n 2 flickering brightness **in the twinkling of an eye** in a very short time

twirl v 1 turn or twist around quickly 2 twiddle, esp. idly

twirp n informal same as **twerp**

twist v 1 turn out of the natural position 2 wind or twine 3 distort or pervert ▷ n 4 twisting 5 twisted thing 6 unexpected development in the plot of a film, book, etc. 7 bend or curve 8 distortion **twisted** adj (of a person) cruel or perverted **twister** n informal swindler **twisty** adj

twit[1] v **twitting, twitted** taunt, esp. in jest

twit[2] n informal foolish person

twitch v 1 move spasmodically 2 pull sharply ▷ n 3 nervous muscular spasm 4 sharp pull

twitter v 1 (of birds) utter chirping sounds 2 **Twitter** same as **tweet** 2 ▷ n 3 chirping 4 **Twitter** popular microblogging website

two adj, n one more than one **two-edged** adj (of a remark) having both a favourable and an unfavourable interpretation **two-faced** adj deceitful, hypocritical

twonie n same as **toonie**

▶ **two-time** v informal deceive (a lover) by having an affair with someone else

tycoon n powerful wealthy businessman

tyke n 1 informal small cheeky child 2 small mongrel dog

tympani pl n same as **timpani**

type n 1 class or category 2 informal person, esp. of a specified kind 3 block with a raised character used for printing 4 printed text ▷ v 5 print with a typewriter 6 typify 7 classify **typist** n person who types with a typewriter **typecast** v continually cast (an actor or actress) in similar roles

typewriter n machine which prints a character when the appropriate key is pressed

typhoid fever n acute infectious feverish disease

typhoon n violent tropical storm

typhus n infectious feverish disease

typical adj true to type, characteristic **typically** adv

typify v **-fying, -fied** be typical of

typography n art or style of printing **typographical** adj **typographer** n

tyrant n 1 oppressive or cruel ruler 2 person who exercises authority tyrannically **tyrannical** adj like a tyrant, oppressive **tyrannically** adv **tyrannize** v exert power (over) oppressively or cruelly **tyrannous** adj **tyranny** n tyrannical rule

tyre n Brit tire

tyro n, pl **-ros** novice or beginner

t

Uu

ubiquitous [yew-**bik**-wit-uss] *adj* being or seeming to be everywhere at once **ubiquity** *n*

udder *n* large baglike milk-producing gland of cows, sheep, or goats

UFO unidentified flying object

ugly *adj* **uglier, ugliest 1** of unpleasant appearance **2** ominous or menacing **ugliness** *n*

UHF ultrahigh frequency

UK United Kingdom

ukulele, ukelele [yew-kal-**lay**-lee] *n* small guitar with four strings

ulcer *n* open sore on the surface of the skin or mucous membrane. **ulcerate** *v* make or become ulcerous **ulceration** *n* **ulcerous** *adj* of, like, or characterized by ulcers

ulna *n, pl* **-nae, -nas** inner and longer of the two bones of the human forearm

ulterior [ult-**ear**-ee-or] *adj* lying beyond what is revealed or seen: *ulterior motives*

ultimate *adj* **1** final in a series or process **2** highest or most significant **ultimately** *adv* **ultimatum** [ult-im-**may**-tum] *n* final communication stating that action will be taken unless certain conditions are met

ultra- *prefix* **1** beyond a specified extent, range, or limit: *ultrasonic* **2** extremely: *ultramodern*

ultrahigh frequency *n* radio frequency between 3000 and 300 megahertz

ultramarine *adj* vivid blue

ultrasonic *adj* of or producing sound waves with a higher frequency than the human ear can hear

ultrasound *n* ultrasonic waves used in medical diagnosis and therapy and in echo sounding

ultraviolet *adj, n* (of) light beyond the limit of visibility at the violet end of the spectrum

ulu [**oo**-loo] *n* Inuit domestic knife

ululate [**yewl**-yew-late] *v* howl or wail **ululation** *n*

umber *adj* dark brown to greenish-brown

umbilical [um-**bill**-ik-al] *adj* of the navel **umbilical cord** long flexible tube of blood vessels that connects a fetus with the placenta

umbrage *n* displeasure or resentment **take umbrage** feel offended or upset

umbrella *n* **1** portable device used for protection against rain, consisting of a folding frame covered in material attached to a central rod **2** single organization, idea, etc. that contains or covers many different organizations

ump *informal* ▷ *n* **1** umpire ▷ *v* **2** act as umpire

umpire *n* **1** official who rules on the playing of a game ▷ *v*

u

2 act as umpire in (a game)

umpteen *adj informal* very many **umpteenth** *n, adj*

UN United Nations

un- *prefix* **1** not **2** denoting reversal of an action: *untie* **3** denoting removal from: *unthrone*

unable *adj* (foll. by *to*) lacking the necessary power, ability, or authority to (do something)

unaccountable *adj* **1** that cannot be explained **2** (foll. by *to*) not answerable to **unaccountably** *adv*

unadulterated *adj* with nothing added, pure

unanimous [yew-**nan**-im-uss] *adj* **1** in complete agreement **2** agreed by all **unanimity** *n*

unannounced *adj* **1** not declared or arranged in advance: *an unannounced visit* ▷ *adv* **2** without warning

unarmed *adj* without weapons

unassuming *adj* modest or unpretentious

unaware *adj* not aware or conscious **unawares** *adv* **1** by surprise **2** without knowing

unbalanced *adj* **1** mentally deranged **2** biased or one-sided

unbearable *adj* not able to be endured **unbearably** *adv*

unbeknown *adv* (foll. by *to*) without the knowledge of (a person)

unbend *v informal* become less strict or more informal in one's attitudes or behaviour **unbending** *adj*

unbidden *adj* not ordered or asked

unborn *adj* not yet born

unbosom *v* relieve (oneself) of (secrets or feelings) by telling someone

unbridled *adj* (of feelings or behaviour) not controlled in any way

unburden *v* relieve (one's mind or oneself) of a worry by confiding in someone

uncalled-for *adj* not fair or justified

uncanny *adj* weird or mysterious **uncannily** *adv* **uncanniness** *n*

unceremonious *adj* **1** without ceremony **2** abrupt or rude **unceremoniously** *adv*

uncertain *adj* **1** not able to be accurately known or predicted **2** not able to be depended upon **3** changeable **uncertainty** *n*

un-Christian *adj* not in accordance with Christian principles

uncle *n* **1** brother of one's father or mother **2** husband of one's parent's sibling

unclean *adj* lacking moral, spiritual, or physical cleanliness

uncomfortable *adj* **1** not physically relaxed **2** anxious or uneasy

uncommon *adj* **1** not happening often **2** in excess of what is normal **uncommonly** *adv*

uncompromising *adj* not prepared to compromise

unconcerned *adj* lacking in concern or involvement **unconcernedly** *adv*

unconditional *adj* without conditions or limitations

unconscionable *adj* **1** having no principles, unscrupulous **2** excessive in amount or degree

unconscious *adj* **1** lacking normal awareness through the senses **2** not aware of one's actions or behaviour ▷ *n* **3** part of the mind containing instincts and ideas that exist without one's awareness **unconsciously** adv **unconsciousness** n

uncooperative adj not willing to cooperate, unhelpful

uncouth adj lacking in good manners, refinement, or grace

uncover v 1 remove the cap, top, etc. from 2 reveal or disclose

unction n act of anointing with oil in sacramental ceremonies **unctuous** adj pretending to be kind and concerned

undeceive v reveal the truth to (someone previously misled or deceived)

undecided adj 1 not having made up one's mind 2 (of an issue or problem) not agreed or decided upon

undeniable adj indisputably true **undeniably** adv

under prep 1 on, to, or beneath the underside or base of 2 less than 3 subject to the supervision, control, or influence of 4 subject to (conditions) ▷ adv 5 to a position underneath

under- prefix 1 below: underground 2 insufficient or insufficiently: underrate

underage adj below the required or standard age

underarm sports ▷ adj 1 denoting a style of throwing, bowling, or serving in which the hand is swung below shoulder level ▷ adv 2 in an underarm style

undercarriage n 1 landing gear of an aircraft 2 framework supporting the body of a vehicle

underclass n class consisting of the most disadvantaged people, such as the long-term unemployed

undercoat n coat of paint applied before the final coat

undercover adj done or acting in secret

undercurrent n 1 current that is not apparent at the surface 2 underlying opinion or emotion

undercut v charge less than (a competitor) to obtain trade

underdog n person or team unlikely to win in a competition

underdone adj not cooked enough

underestimate v 1 make too low an estimate of 2 not think highly enough of

underfelt n thick felt laid under a carpet to increase insulation

underfoot adv under the feet

undergarment n any piece of underwear

undergo v experience, endure, or sustain

undergraduate n person studying in a university for a first degree

underground adj 1 occurring, situated, used, or going below ground level 2 secret ▷ n 3 movement dedicated to overthrowing a government or occupation forces 4 Brit subway

undergrowth n small trees and bushes growing beneath taller trees in a wood or forest

underhand adj sly, deceitful, and secretive

underlie v 1 lie or be placed under 2 be the foundation, cause, or basis of **underlying** adj fundamental or basic

underline v 1 draw a line under 2 state forcibly, emphasize

underling n subordinate

undermine v 1 weaken gradually 2 (of the sea or

wind) wear away the base of (cliffs)

underneath *prep, adv* **1** under or beneath ▷ *adj, n* **2** lower (part or surface)

underpants *pl n* man's undergarment for the lower part of the body

underpass *n* section of a road that passes under another road or a railway line

underpin *v* give strength or support to

underprivileged *adj* lacking the rights and advantages of other members of society

underrate *v* underestimate **underrated** *adj*

underseal *n* coating of tar etc. applied to the underside of a motor vehicle to retard corrosion

underside *n* bottom or lower surface

understand *v* **1** know and comprehend the nature or meaning of **2** realize or grasp (something) **3** assume, infer, or believe **understandable** *adj* **understandably** *adv* **understanding** *n* **1** ability to learn, judge, or make decisions **2** personal interpretation of a subject **3** mutual agreement, usu. an informal or private one ▷ *adj* **4** kind and sympathetic

understate *v* **1** describe or represent (something) in restrained terms **2** state that (something, such as a number) is less than it is **understatement** *n*

understudy *n* **1** actor who studies a part in order to be able to replace the usual actor if necessary ▷ *v* **2** act as an understudy for

undertake *v* **1** agree or commit oneself to (something) or (to do something) **2** promise

undertaking *n* **1** task or enterprise **2** agreement to do something

undertaker *n* person whose profession is to prepare corpses for burial and organize funerals

undertone *n* **1** quiet tone of voice **2** underlying quality or feeling

undertow *n* strong undercurrent flowing in a different direction from the surface current

underwater *adj, adv* (situated, occurring, or for use) below the surface of the sea, a lake, or a river

underwear *n* clothing worn under the outer garments and next to the skin

underworld *n* **1** criminals and their associates **2** *classical myth* regions below the earth's surface regarded as the abode of the dead

underwrite *v* **1** accept financial responsibility for (a commercial project) **2** sign and issue (an insurance policy), thus accepting liability **underwriter** *n*

undesirable *adj* **1** not desirable or pleasant, objectionable ▷ *n* **2** objectionable person **undesirably** *adv*

undo *v* **1** open, unwrap **2** reverse the effects of **3** cause the downfall of **undone** *adj* **undoing** *n* cause of someone's downfall

undoubted *adj* certain or indisputable **undoubtedly** *adv*

undue *adj* greater than is reasonable, excessive **unduly** *adv*

undulate *v* move in waves **undulation** *n*

undying *adj* never ending, eternal

unearth v 1 dig up out of the earth 2 reveal or discover

unearthly adj 1 ghostly or eerie 2 ridiculous or unreasonable: *an unearthly hour* **unearthliness** n

uneasy adj 1 (of a person) anxious or apprehensive 2 (of a condition) precarious or uncomfortable **uneasily** adv **uneasiness** n **unease** n

unemployed adj out of work **unemployment** n

unequivocal adj completely clear in meaning **unequivocally** adv

unerring adj never mistaken, consistently accurate

unexceptionable adj beyond criticism or objection

unfailing adj continuous or reliable **unfailingly** adv

unfair adj not right, fair, or just **unfairly** adv **unfairness** n

unfaithful adj 1 guilty of adultery 2 not true to a promise or vow **unfaithfulness** n

unfeeling adj without sympathy

unfit adj 1 (foll. by *for*) unqualified or unsuitable 2 in poor physical condition

unflappable adj informal not easily upset **unflappability** n

unfold v 1 open or spread out from a folded state 2 reveal or be revealed

unforgettable adj impossible to forget, memorable

unfortunate adj 1 unlucky, unsuccessful, or unhappy 2 regrettable or unsuitable **unfortunately** adv

unfounded adj not based on facts or evidence

unfrock v deprive (a priest in holy orders) of his priesthood

ungainly adj -lier, -liest lacking grace when moving **ungainliness** n

ungodly adj 1 wicked or sinful 2 informal unreasonable or outrageous **ungodliness** n

ungrateful adj not grateful or thankful **ungratefully** adv **ungratefulness** n

unguarded adj 1 not protected 2 incautious or careless

unguent [**ung**-gwent] n ointment

unhand v old-fashioned, lit release from one's grasp

unhappy adj 1 sad or depressed 2 unfortunate or wretched **unhappily** adv **unhappiness** n

unhealthy adj 1 likely to cause poor health 2 not fit or well 3 morbid, unnatural

unhinge v derange or unbalance (a person or his or her mind)

uni- combining form of, consisting of, or having only one: *unicellular*

unicorn n imaginary horselike creature with one horn growing from its forehead

uniform n 1 special identifying set of clothes for the members of an organization, such as soldiers ▷ adj 2 unvarying 3 alike or like **uniformly** adv **uniformity** n

unify v -fying, -fied make or become one **unification** n

unilateral adj made or done by only one person or group **unilaterally** adv

unilingual adj 1 knowing only one language ▷ n 2 person who knows only one language

unimpeachable adj completely honest and reliable

uninterested adj having or showing no interest in someone or something

union n 1 uniting or being united 2 short for **trade**

u

union 3 association of individuals or groups for a common purpose **unionist** n member or supporter of a trade union **unionize** v organize (workers) into a trade union **unionization** n **Union Flag** or **Union Jack** national flag of the United Kingdom

unique [yoo-**neek**] adj **1** being the only one of a particular type **2** without equal or like **uniquely** adv

unisex adj designed for use by both sexes

unison n **1** complete agreement **2** music singing or playing the same notes at the same time

unit n **1** single undivided entity or whole **2** group or individual regarded as a basic element of a larger whole **3** fixed quantity etc., used as a standard of measurement **unitary** adj

Unitarian n person who believes that God is one being and rejects the Trinity **Unitarianism** n

unite v **1** make or become an integrated whole **2** form an association or alliance **unity** n **1** state of being one **2** mutual agreement **United Church** Canadian church formed by union of some Presbyterians and Methodists **United Empire Loyalist** American colonist who settled in Canada in the War of American Independence through loyalty to Britain

universe n **1** whole of all existing matter, energy, and space **2** the world **universal** adj **1** of or typical of the whole of mankind or of nature **2** existing everywhere **universally** adv **universality** n

university n, pl **-ties** institution of higher education having the authority to award degrees

unkempt adj **1** (of the hair) not combed **2** slovenly or untidy

unknown adj **1** not known **2** not famous ▷ n **3** unknown person, quantity, or thing

unleaded adj (of gasoline) containing less tetraethyl lead, to reduce environmental pollution

unleash v set loose or cause (something bad)

unless conj except under the circumstances that

unlike adj **1** dissimilar or different ▷ prep **2** not like or typical of **unlikely** adj improbable

unload v **1** remove (cargo) from (a ship, truck, or plane) **2** get rid of **3** remove the ammunition from (a firearm)

unmanned adj having no personnel or crew

unmask v **1** remove the mask or disguise from **2** (cause to) appear in true character

unmentionable adj unsuitable as a topic of conversation

unmistakable, unmistakeable adj not ambiguous, clear **unmistakably** or **unmistakeably** adv

unmitigated adj **1** not reduced or lessened in severity, intensity, etc. **2** total and complete

unmoved adj not affected by emotion, indifferent

unnatural adj **1** strange and frightening because not usual: *an unnatural silence* **2** not in accordance with accepted standards of behaviour

unnerve v cause to lose

courage, confidence, or self-control

unnumbered *adj* **1** countless **2** not counted or given a number

unorthodox *adj* **1** (of ideas, methods, etc.) not conventional and not generally accepted **2** (of a person) having unusual opinions or methods

unpack *v* **1** remove the contents of (a suitcase, trunk, etc.) **2** take (something) out of a packed container

unparalleled *adj* not equalled, supreme

unpick *v* undo (the stitches) of (a piece of sewing)

unpleasant *adj* not pleasant or agreeable **unpleasantly** *adv* **unpleasantness** *n*

unprecedented *adj* never having happened before, unparalleled

unprintable *adj* unsuitable for printing for reasons of obscenity or libel

unprofessional *adj* **1** contrary to the accepted code of a profession **2** not belonging to a profession **unprofessionally** *adv*

unqualified *adj* **1** lacking the necessary qualifications **2** not modified

unravel *v* **-elling**, **-elled** **1** reduce (something knitted or woven) to separate strands **2** become unravelled **3** explain or solve

unremitting *adj* never slackening or stopping

unrest *n* rebellious state of discontent

unrivalled *adj* having no equal

unroll *v* open out or unwind (something rolled or coiled) or (of something rolled or coiled) become opened out or unwound

unruly *adj* **-lier**, **-liest** given to disobedience or indiscipline

unsavoury *adj* distasteful or objectionable

unscathed *adj* not harmed or injured

unscrupulous *adj* unprincipled or without scruples

unseat *v* **1** throw or displace from a seat or saddle **2** depose from an office or position

unsettled *adj* **1** lacking order or stability **2** disturbed and restless **3** constantly changing or moving from place to place

unsightly *adj* unpleasant to look at

unsocial *adj* **1** avoiding the company of other people **2** falling outside the normal working day: *unsocial hours*

unsound *adj* **1** unhealthy or unstable **2** not based on truth or fact

unspeakable *adj* indescribably bad or evil **unspeakably** *adv*

unstable *adj* **1** lacking stability or firmness **2** having abrupt changes of mood or behaviour

unstudied *adj* natural or spontaneous

unsuitable *adj* not right or appropriate for a particular purpose **unsuitably** *adv*

unsuited *adj* not appropriate for a particular task or situation

unsung *adj* not acclaimed or honoured: *unsung heroes*

unswerving *adj* firm, constant, not changing

unthinkable *adj* out of the question, inconceivable

untidy *adj* not neat, slovenly **untidily** *adv* **untidiness** *n*

untie *v* **1** open or free

u

(something that is tied) **2** free from constraint

until *conj* **1** up to the time that ▷ *prep* **2** in or throughout the period before **not until** not before (a time or event)

untimely *adj* **1** occurring before the expected or normal time **2** inappropriate to the occasion or time **untimeliness** *n*

unto *prep old-fashioned* to

untold *adj* **1** incapable of description **2** incalculably great in number or quantity

untouchable *adj* **1** above reproach or suspicion **2** unable to be touched ▷ *n offensive* **3** member of the lowest Hindu caste in India

untoward *adj* causing misfortune or annoyance

untruth *n* statement that is not true, lie

unusual *adj* uncommon or extraordinary **unusually** *adv*

unutterable *adj* incapable of being expressed in words **unutterably** *adv*

unvarnished *adj* not elaborated upon

unveil *v* **1** ceremonially remove the cover from (a new picture, plaque, etc.) **2** make public (a secret) **unveiling** *n*

unwarranted *adj* not justified, not necessary

unwieldy *adj* too heavy, large, or awkward to be easily handled

unwind *v* **1** (cause to) slacken, undo, or unravel **2** make or become relaxed

unwitting *adj* **1** not knowing or conscious **2** not intentional **unwittingly** *adv*

unwonted *adj* out of the ordinary

unworthy *adj* **1** not deserving or worthy **2** (foll. by *of*) beneath the level considered

befitting (to) **3** lacking merit or value

unwrap *v* remove the wrapping from (something) or (of something wrapped) have the covering removed

unwritten *adj* **1** not printed or in writing **2** operating only through custom

up *prep* **1** indicating movement to a higher position **2** at a higher or further level or position in or on ▷ *adv* **3** to an upward, higher, or erect position **4** indicating readiness for an activity: *up and about* **5** indicating intensity or completion of an action **6** to the place referred to or where the speaker is ▷ *adj* **7** of a high or higher position **8** out of bed **9** *baseball* currently batting ▷ *v* **upping, upped 10** increase or raise **11** *informal* do something suddenly: *he upped and left* ▷ *n* **12** *baseball* turn at bat **up against** having to cope with **ups and downs** alternating periods of good and bad luck **uptown** *n* the part of a city that is away from the centre **what's up?** *informal* what is wrong? **upward** *adj* **1** directed or moving towards a higher place or level ▷ *adv* **2** Also **upwards** from a lower to a higher place, level, or condition

upbeat *n* **1** *music* unaccented beat ▷ *adj* **2** *informal* cheerful and optimistic

upbraid *v* scold or reproach

upbringing *n* education of a person during the formative years

update *v* **1** bring up to date ▷ *n* **2** act of updating **3** Also **status update** short message on a social networking site with information about the user's current activities or mood

upend v turn or set or be turned or set on end

upfront adj **1** open and frank ▷ adv, adj **2** (of money) paid out at the beginning of a business arrangement

upgrade v promote (a person or job) to a higher rank

upheaval n strong, sudden, or violent disturbance

uphill adj **1** sloping or leading upwards **2** requiring a great deal of effort ▷ adv **3** up a slope

uphold v **1** maintain or defend against opposition **2** give moral support to **upholder** n

upholster v fit (a chair or sofa) with padding, springs, and covering **upholsterer** n **upholstery** n **1** act of upholstering **2** soft covering on a chair or sofa

upkeep n act, process, or cost of keeping something in good repair

upland n **1** area of high or relatively high ground ▷ adj **2** of or in an upland

uplift v **1** raise or lift up **2** raise morally or spiritually ▷ n **3** act, process, or result of lifting up **uplifting** adj

upon prep **1** on **2** up and on

upper adj **1** higher or highest in physical position, wealth, rank, or status ▷ n **2** part of a shoe above the sole **uppermost** adj **1** highest in position, power, or importance ▷ adv **2** in or into the highest place or position **upper-case** adj denoting capital letters as used in printed or typed matter **upper class** highest social class **upper-class** adj **upper crust** informal upper class **upper hand** position of control

uppish, uppity adj informal snobbish, arrogant, or presumptuous

upright adj **1** vertical or erect **2** honest or just ▷ adv **3** vertically ▷ n **4** vertical support, such as a post **uprightness** n

uprising n rebellion or revolt

uproar n disturbance characterized by loud noise and confusion **uproarious** adj **1** very funny **2** (of laughter) loud and boisterous **uproariously** adv

uproot v **1** pull up by or as if by the roots **2** displace (a person or people) from their native or usual surroundings

upset adj **1** emotionally or physically disturbed or distressed ▷ v **2** tip over **3** disturb the normal state or stability of **4** disturb mentally or emotionally **5** make physically ill ▷ n **6** unexpected defeat or reversal **7** disturbance or disorder of the emotions, mind, or body **upsetting** adj

upshot n final result or conclusion

upside down adj **1** turned over completely **2** informal confused or jumbled ▷ adv **3** in an inverted fashion **4** in a chaotic manner

upstage adj **1** at the back half of the stage ▷ v **2** informal draw attention to oneself from (someone else)

upstairs adv **1** up the stairs ▷ n **2** upper floor ▷ adj **3** situated on an upper floor

upstanding adj of good character

upstart n person who has risen suddenly to a position of power and behaves arrogantly

upstream adv, adj in or towards the higher part of a stream

u

upsurge n rapid rise or swell

uptake n **quick** or **slow on the uptake** informal quick or slow to understand or learn

uptight adj informal nervously tense, irritable, or angry

up-to-date adj modern or fashionable

upturn n **1** upward trend or improvement **2** upheaval

uranium [yew-**rain**-ee-um] n radioactive silvery-white metallic element, used chiefly as a source of nuclear energy

Uranus n **1** Greek god of the sky **2** seventh planet from the sun

urban adj **1** of or living in a city or town **2** denoting modern pop music of African-American origin, such as hip-hop **urbanize** v make (a rural area) more industrialized and urban **urbanization** n

urbane adj characterized by courtesy, elegance, and sophistication **urbanity** n

urchin n mischievous child

urethra [yew-**reeth**-ra] n, pl -**thrae**, -**thras** canal that carries urine from the bladder out of the body

urge n **1** strong impulse, inner drive, or yearning ▷ v **2** plead with or press (a person to do something) **3** advocate earnestly **4** force or drive onwards **urgent** adj requiring speedy action or attention **urgency** n **urgently** adv

urine n pale yellow fluid excreted by the kidneys to the bladder and passed as waste from the body **uric** adj **urinal** n (place with) sanitary fitting(s) used by men for urination **urinary** adj **urinate** v discharge urine **urination** n

URL uniform resource locator: the address of a location on the internet

urn n **1** vase used as a container for the ashes of the dead **2** large metal container with a tap, used for making and holding tea or coffee

ursine adj of or like a bear

us pron objective case of **we**

US, USA United States (of America)

use v **1** put into service or action **2** take advantage of **3** consume or expend ▷ n **4** using or being used **5** ability or permission to use **6** usefulness or advantage **7** purpose for which something is used **user** n **user-friendly** adj easy to familiarize oneself with, understand, and use **usable** adj able to be used **usability** n **usage** n **1** regular or constant use **2** way in which a word is used in a language **used** adj second-hand **used to** adj **1** accustomed to ▷ v **2** used as an auxiliary to express past habitual or accustomed actions: I used to live there **useful** adj **usefully** adv **usefulness** n **useless** adj **uselessly** adv **uselessness** n

usher n **1** official who shows people to their seats, as in a church ▷ v **2** conduct or escort **usherette** n female assistant in a cinema who shows people to their seats

USSR formerly, Union of Soviet Socialist Republics

usual adj of the most normal, frequent, or regular type **usually** adv most often, in most cases

usurp [yewz-**zurp**] v seize (a position or power) without authority **usurpation** n **usurper** n

usury n, pl -**ries** practice of lending money at an

extremely high rate of interest **usurer** [yewz-yoor-er] *n*

utensil *n* tool or container for practical use

uterus [yew-ter-russ] *n* womb **uterine** *adj*

utilitarian *adj* **1** of utilitarianism **2** useful rather than beautiful **utilitarianism** *n* doctrine that the right action is that which brings about the greatest good for the greatest number of people

utility *n, pl* **-ties 1** usefulness **2** public service, such as gas ▷ *adj* **3** designed for use rather than beauty **4** *baseball* designating a substitute who can play in a number of positions **utilize** *v* make practical use of **utilization** *n*

utmost *adj, n* (of the) greatest possible degree or amount

Utopia [yew-**tope**-ee-a] *n* any real or imaginary society, place, or state considered to be ideal **Utopian** *adj*

utter[1] *v* express (something) audibly **utterance** *n* **1** something uttered **2** act or power of uttering

utter[2] *adj* total or absolute **utterly** *adv*

uttermost *adj, n* same as **utmost**

U-turn *n* **1** turn, made by a vehicle, in the shape of a U, resulting in a reversal of direction **2** complete change in policy

UV ultraviolet

uvula [yew-view-la] *n, pl* **-las, -lae** small fleshy part of the soft palate that hangs in the back of the throat **uvular** *adj*

uxorious [ux-or-ee-uss] *adj* excessively fond of or dependent on one's wife

u

Vv

V volt

v. 1 versus **2** very

vacant *adj* **1** (of a lavatory, room, etc.) unoccupied **2** without interest or understanding **vacantly** *adv* **vacancy** *n, pl* **-cies 1** unfilled job **2** unoccupied room in a guesthouse **3** state of being unoccupied

vacate *v* leave (a place or job) **vacation** *n* **1** time when universities and law courts are closed **2** holiday

vaccinate *v* inoculate with a vaccine **vaccination** *n* **vaccine** *n* substance designed to cause a mild form of a disease to make a person immune to the disease itself

vacillate [**vass**-ill-late] *v* waver in one's opinions **vacillation** *n*

vacuous *adj* not expressing intelligent thought **vacuity** *n*

vacuum *n, pl* **vacuums, vacua 1** empty space from which all or most air or gas has been removed ▷ *v* **2** clean with a vacuum cleaner **vacuum cleaner** electrical appliance for removing dust by suction **vacuum-packed** *adj* contained in packaging from which the air has been removed

vagabond *n* person with no fixed home, esp. a beggar

vagaries [**vaig**-a-reez] *pl n* unpredictable changes

vagina [vaj-**jine**-a] *n, pl* **-nas, -nae** (in female mammals)
passage from the womb to the external genitals **vaginal** *adj*

vagrant [**vaig**-rant] *n* **1** person with no settled home ▷ *adj* **2** wandering **vagrancy** *n*

vague *adj* **1** not clearly explained **2** unable to be seen or heard clearly **3** absent-minded **vaguely** *adv*

vain *adj* **1** excessively proud, esp. of one's appearance **2** bound to fail, futile **in vain** unsuccessfully

vainglorious *adj lit* boastful **vainglory** *n*

valance [**val**-lenss] *n* piece of drapery round the edge of a bed

vale *n lit* valley

valediction [val-lid-**dik**-shun] *n* farewell speech **valedictory** *adj*

valence [**vale**-ence] *n* molecular bonding between atoms

valency *n, pl* **-cies** power of an atom to make molecular bonds

valentine *n* (person to whom one sends) a romantic card on Saint Valentine's Day, 14th February

valerian *n* herb used as a sedative

valet *n* man's personal male servant

valetudinarian [val-lit-yew-din-**air**-ee-an] *n* **1** person with a long-term illness **2** hypochondriac

valiant *adj* brave or courageous

valid *adj* **1** soundly reasoned **2** having legal force **validate** *v* make valid **validation** *n* **validity** *n*

valise [val-**leez**] *n old-fashioned* travelling bag

Valium *n* ® drug used as a tranquillizer

valley *n* low area between hills, usu. with a river running through it

valour *n lit* bravery **valorous** *adj*

value *n* **1** importance, usefulness **2** monetary worth **values 3** moral principles ▷ *v* **valuing, valued 4** assess the value of **5** have a high regard for **valuable** *adj* having great worth **valuables** *pl n* valuable personal property **valuation** *n* assessment of worth **valueless** *adj* **valuer** *n* **value-added tax** *Brit* see **VAT** ▶ **value judgment** opinion based on personal belief

valve *n* **1** device to control the movement of fluid through a pipe **2** *anat* flap in a part of the body allowing blood to flow in one direction only **3** *physics* tube containing a vacuum, allowing current to flow from a cathode to an anode **valvular** *adj*

vamoose *v slang* go away

vamp[1] *n informal* woman who seduces men to her own advantage

vamp[2] *v* **1** (foll. by *up*) renovate **2** improvise an accompaniment to (a tune)

vampire *n* (in folklore) a corpse that rises at night to drink the blood of the living **vampire bat** tropical bat that feeds on blood

van[1] *n* **1** motor vehicle for transporting goods **2** *Brit* railway carriage for goods in which the guard travels

van[2] *n* short for **vanguard**

vanadium *n* metallic element, used in steel

vandal *n* person who deliberately damages property **vandalism** *n* **vandalize** *v*

vane *n* flat blade on a rotary device such as a weathercock or propeller

vanguard *n* **1** unit of soldiers leading an army **2** most advanced group or position in a movement or activity

Vanier Cup *n* trophy awarded to the Canadian university football champions

vanilla *n* seed pod of a tropical climbing orchid, used for flavouring

vanish *v* **1** disappear suddenly or mysteriously **2** cease to exist

vanity *n, pl* **-ties** (display of) excessive pride

vanquish *v lit* defeat (someone) utterly **vanquishable** *adj* **vanquisher** *n*

vantage *n* advantage **vantage point** position that gives one an overall view

vape *v informal* inhale vapour from e-cigarette

vapid *adj* lacking character, dull **vapidity** *n*

vapour *n* **1** moisture suspended in air as steam or mist **2** gaseous form of something that is liquid or solid at room temperature **vaporize** *v* **vaporizer** *n* **vaporous** *adj*

variable *adj* **1** not always the same ▷ *n* **2** *math* expression with a range of values **variability** *n*

variant *adj* **1** different or alternative ▷ *n* **2** alternative form **at variance** in disagreement

variation *n* **1** extent to which something varies **2** *music* repetition in different forms of a basic theme **variational** *adj*

V

varicose veins pl n knotted and swollen veins, esp. in the legs

variegated adj having patches or streaks of different colours **variegation** n

variety n, pl -ties 1 state of being various 2 different things of the same kind 3 sort or kind 4 light entertainment composed of unrelated acts

various adj of several kinds **variously** adv

varlet n obsolete rascal

varnish n 1 solution of oil and resin, put on a surface to make it hard and glossy ▷ v 2 apply varnish to

varsity adj informal relating to a sports team or athlete that represents a university, college, or high school

vary v varying, varied 1 change 2 cause differences in **varied** adj

vascular adj biol relating to vessels

vas deferens n, pl vasa deferentia anat sperm-carrying duct in each testicle

vase n ornamental jar, esp. for flowers

vasectomy n, pl -mies (operation for) the removal of part of the vas deferens, as a contraceptive method

Vaseline n ® thick oily cream made from petroleum, used in skin care

vassal n hist man given land in return for allegiance to his lord **vassalage** n

vast adj extremely large **vastly** adv **vastness** n

vat n large container for liquids

VAT Brit value-added tax: tax on the difference between the cost of materials and the selling price

Vatican n the Pope's palace

vaudeville n US variety entertainment in a theatre

vault[1] n 1 secure room for storing valuables 2 underground burial chamber **vaulted** adj having an arched roof

vault[2] v 1 jump over (something) by resting one's hand(s) on it. ▷ n 2 such a jump

vaunt v describe or display (success or possessions) boastfully **vaunted** adj

VC 1 Vice Chancellor 2 Victoria Cross

VCR video cassette recorder

VD venereal disease

VDU visual display unit

veal n calf meat

vector n 1 math quantity that has size and direction, such as force 2 animal, usu. an insect, that carries disease

veer v change direction suddenly

vegan [vee-gan] n 1 person who eats no meat, fish, eggs, or dairy products ▷ adj 2 suitable for a vegan **veganism** n

vegetable n 1 edible plant 2 offensive severely brain-damaged person ▷ adj 3 of or like plants or vegetables

vegetarian n 1 person who eats no meat or fish ▷ adj 2 suitable for a vegetarian **vegetarianism** n

vegetate v live a dull uncreative life

vegetation n plant life of a given place

vehement adj expressing strong feelings **vehemence** n **vehemently** adv

vehicle n 1 machine, esp. with an engine and wheels, for carrying people or objects 2 means of communicating something **vehicular** adj

veil n 1 piece of thin cloth

covering the head or face
2 something that conceals
the truth: *a veil of secrecy* ▷ *v*
3 cover with a veil **take the
veil** become a nun **veiled** *adj*
disguised

vein *n* **1** tube that takes blood
to the heart **2** line in a leaf or
an insect's wing **3** layer of ore
or mineral in rock **4** streak in
marble **5** feature of someone's
writing or speech: *a vein of
humour* **6** mood: *in a lighter vein*
veined *adj*

Velcro *n* ® fastening
consisting of one piece of
fabric with tiny hooked
threads and another with a
coarse surface that adheres
to it

veld, veldt *n* high grassland
in Southern Africa

vellum *n* **1** fine calfskin
parchment **2** type of smooth
paper

velocity [vel-**loss**-it-ee] *n, pl*
-ties speed of movement in a
given direction

velours, velour [vel-**loor**] *n*
velvety fabric

velvet *n* fabric with a thick
pile **velvety** *adj* soft and
smooth **velveteen** *n* cotton
velvet

venal [**vee**-nal] *adj* **1** easily
bribed **2** characterized by
bribery **venally** *adv* **venality**
n

vend *v* sell **vendor** *n* **vending
machine** machine that
dispenses goods when coins
are inserted

vendetta *n* prolonged quarrel
between families, esp. one
involving revenge killings

veneer *n* **1** thin layer of
wood etc. covering a cheaper
material **2** superficial
appearance: *a veneer of
sophistication*

venerable *adj* worthy of deep
respect **venerate** *v* hold

(a person) in deep respect
veneration *n*

venereal disease [ven-**ear**-
ee-al] *n* disease transmitted
sexually

Venetian *adj* of Venice,
port in NE Italy **Venetian
blind** window blind made of
horizontal slats that turn to
let in more or less light

vengeance *n* revenge
vengeful *adj* wanting revenge
vengefully *adv*

venial [**veen**-ee-al] *adj* (of a
sin or fault) easily forgiven
veniality *n*

venison *n* deer meat

venom *n* **1** poison produced by
snakes etc. **2** malice or spite
venomous *adj*

venous [**vee**-nuss] *adj anat* of
veins

vent¹ *n* **1** outlet releasing
fumes or fluid ▷ *v* **2** express
(an emotion) freely

vent² *n* vertical slit in a jacket

ventilate *v* **1** let fresh air into
2 discuss (a complaint) openly
ventilation *n* **ventilator** *n*

ventral *adj* relating to the
front of the body

ventricle *n anat* one of the four
cavities of the heart or brain

ventriloquist *n* entertainer
who can speak without
moving his or her lips, so that
a voice seems to come from
elsewhere **ventriloquism** *n*

venture *n* **1** risky
undertaking, esp. in business
▷ *v* **2** do something risky
3 dare to express (an opinion)
4 go to an unknown place
venturesome *adj* **venture
capitalist** provider of
capital for new commercial
enterprises **venture capital** *n*

venue *n* place where an
organized gathering is held

Venus *n* **1** planet second
nearest to the sun **2** Roman
goddess of love **Venus's**

flytrap or **Venus flytrap** plant that traps and digests insects between hinged leaves

veracious adj habitually truthful **veracity** n

veranda, verandah n open porch attached to a house

verb n word that expresses the idea of action, happening, or being **verbal** adj **1** spoken **2** of a verb **verbally** adv **verbalize** v express (something) in words

verbatim [verb-**bait**-im] adv, adj word for word

verbena n plant with sweet-smelling flowers

verbiage n excessive use of words

verbose [verb-**bohss**] adj long-winded **verbosity** n

verdant adj lit covered in green vegetation

verdict n **1** decision of a jury **2** opinion formed after examining the facts

verdigris [**ver**-dig-riss] n green film on copper, brass, or bronze

verdure n lit flourishing green vegetation

verge n Brit grass border along a road **on the verge of** having almost reached (a point or condition) **verge on** v be near to (a condition)

verger n Anglican church church caretaker

verify v **-ifying, -ified** check the truth or accuracy of **verifiable** adj **verification** n

verily adv obsolete in truth

verisimilitude n appearance of being real

veritable adj rightly called, without exaggeration: a veritable feast **veritably** adv

verity n, pl **-ties** true statement or principle

vermicelli [ver-me-**chell**-ee] n **1** fine strands of pasta **2** tiny strands of chocolate

vermiform adj shaped like a worm **vermiform appendix** anat same as **appendix**

vermilion adj orange-red

vermin pl n animals, esp. insects and rodents, that spread disease or cause damage **verminous** adj

vermouth [**ver**-muth] n wine flavoured with herbs

vernacular [ver-**nak**-yew-lar] n most widely spoken language of a particular people or place

vernal adj occurring in spring

vernier [**ver**-nee-er] n movable scale on a graduated measuring instrument for taking readings in fractions

veronica n plant with small flowers

verruca [ver-**roo**-ka] n, pl **-cae, -cas** wart, usu. on the foot

versatile adj having many skills or uses **versatility** n

verse n **1** group of lines in a song or poem **2** poetry as distinct from prose **3** subdivision of a book of the Bible **versed in** knowledgeable about **versify** v write in verse **versification** n

version n **1** form of something, such as a piece of writing, with some differences from other forms **2** account of an incident from a particular point of view

verso n, pl **-sos 1** left-hand page of a book **2** back of a sheet of paper

versus prep **1** sports, law against **2** in contrast with

vertebra [**ver**-tib-ra] n, pl **vertebrae** [**ver**-tib-ree] one of the bones that form the spine **vertebral** adj **vertebrate** n, adj (animal) having a spine

vertex n math **1** point on a geometric figure where the sides form an angle **2** highest point of a triangle

vertical adj **1** straight up and down ▷ n **2** vertical direction

vertigo n dizziness when looking down from a high place **vertiginous** adj

vervain n plant with spikes of blue, purple, or white flowers

verve n enthusiasm or liveliness

very adv **1** more than usually, extremely ▷ adj **2** absolute, exact: *the very top; the very man*

vesicle n biol sac or small cavity, esp. one containing fluid

vespers pl n RC Church (service of) evening prayer

vessel n **1** ship **2** lit container for liquid **3** biol tubular structure in animals and plants that carries body fluids, such as blood or sap

vest n **1** sleeveless garment worn under a jacket or coat **2** Brit undershirt ▷ v **3** (foll. by in or with) give (authority) to (someone) **vested interest** interest someone has in a matter because he or she might benefit from it **vest-pocket** adj small enough to fit into a vest pocket

vestibule n entrance hall

vestige [vest-ij] n small amount or trace **vestigial** [vest-ij-ee-al] adj

vestments pl n priest's robes

vestry n, pl -tries room in a church used as an office by the priest or minister

vet[1] n **1** short for **veterinarian** ▷ v **vetting, vetted 2** check the suitability of (a candidate)

vet[2] n military veteran

vetch n climbing plant with a beanlike fruit used as fodder

veteran n **1** person with long experience in a particular activity, esp. military service ▷ adj **2** long-serving

veterinarian n medical specialist who treats sick animals **veterinary** adj concerning animal health

veto [**vee**-toe] n, pl -toes **1** official power to cancel a proposal ▷ v -toing, -toed **2** enforce a veto against

vex v frustrate, annoy **vexation** n **1** something annoying **2** being annoyed **vexatious** adj **vexed question** much debated subject

VHF radio very high frequency

via prep by way of

viable adj **1** able to be put into practice **2** biol able to live and grow independently **viability** n

viaduct n bridge over a valley

Viagra [vie-**ag**-ra] n ® drug used to treat impotence in men

vial n same as **phial**

viands pl n obsolete food

vibes pl n informal **1** emotional reactions between people, atmosphere of a place **2** short for **vibraphone**

vibrant [**vibe**-rant] adj **1** vigorous in appearance, energetic **2** (of a voice) resonant **3** (of a colour) strong and bright

vibraphone n musical instrument with metal bars that resonate electronically when hit

vibrate v **1** move back and forth rapidly **2** (cause to) resonate **vibration** n **vibrator** n device that produces vibratory motion, used for massage or as a sex aid **vibratory** adj

vibrato n music rapid fluctuation in the pitch of a note

vicar n Anglican church member of the clergy in charge of a parish **vicarage** n vicar's house

vicarious [vick-**air**-ee-uss] *adj* **1** felt indirectly by imagining what another person experiences **2** delegated **vicariously** *adv*

vice[1] *n* **1** immoral personal quality **2** minor imperfection in someone's character **3** criminal activities, esp. involving sex

vice[2] *n* tool with a screw mechanism for holding an object while working on it

vice[3] *adj* serving in place of

vice chancellor *n* chief executive of a university

viceroy *n* governor of a colony who represents the monarch **viceregal** *adj*

vice versa [**vie**-see **ver**-sa] *adv* Latin conversely, the other way round

vicinity [viss-**in**-it-ee] *n* surrounding area

vicious *adj* cruel and violent **viciously** *adv* **vicious circle** sequence of problems and solutions which always leads back to the original problem

vicissitudes [viss-**iss**-it-yewds] *pl n* changes in fortune

victim *n* **1** person or thing harmed or killed **2** person or animal killed as a sacrifice **victimize** *v* **1** punish unfairly **2** discriminate against **victimization** *n*

victor *n* person who has defeated an opponent, esp. in war or in sport **victorious** *adj* **victory** *n* winning of a battle or contest

Victoria Cross *n* Brit highest award for bravery

Victoria Day annual holiday celebrated on the Monday before May 24

Victorian *adj* **1** of or in the reign of Queen Victoria (1837–1901) **2** characterized by prudery or hypocrisy ▷ *n* **3** person who lived during Victoria's reign

victuals [**vit**-als] *pl n* old-fashioned food **victual** *v* **victualling**, **victualled** supply with or obtain victuals **victualler** *n*

vicuña [vik-**koo**-nya] *n* **1** S American animal like the llama **2** fine cloth made from its wool

video *n* **1** short for **video cassette (recorder)** ▷ *v* **videoing**, **videoed 2** record (a TV programme or event) on video ▷ *adj* **3** relating to or used in producing television images **video cassette** cassette containing video tape **video cassette recorder** tape recorder for recording and playing back TV programmes and films **video tape 1** magnetic tape used to record video-frequency signals in TV production **2** magnetic tape used to record programmes when they are broadcast **videotape** *v* record (a TV programme) on video tape **video tape recorder** tape recorder for vision signals, used in TV production **videotext** *n* means of representing on a TV screen information that is held in a computer

vie *v* **vying**, **vied** compete (with someone)

view *n* **1** opinion **2** everything that can be seen from a given place **3** picture of this ▷ *v* **4** think of (something) in a particular way **in view of** taking into consideration **on view** exhibited to the public **viewer** *n* **1** person who watches television **2** hand-held device for looking at photographic slides **viewfinder** *n* window on a camera showing what will appear in a photograph

vigil [**vij**-ill] *n* night-time

period of staying awake to look after a sick person, pray, etc. **vigilant** *adj* watchful in case of danger **vigilance** *n*

vigilante [vij-ill-**ant**-ee] *n* person, esp. as one of a group, who takes it upon himself or herself to enforce the law

vignette [vin-**yet**] *n* **1** concise description of the typical features of something **2** small decorative illustration in a book

vigour *n* physical or mental energy **vigorous** *adj* **vigorously** *adv*

Viking *n hist* seafaring raider and settler from Scandinavia

vile *adj* **1** very wicked **2** disgusting **vilely** *adv* **vileness** *n*

vilify [**vill**-if-fie] *v* **-ifying, -ified** unjustly attack the character of **vilification** *n*

villa *n* **1** large house with gardens **2** house rented to holiday-makers

village *n* **1** small group of houses in a country area **2** rural community **villager** *n*

villain *n* **1** wicked person **2** main wicked character in a play **villainous** *adj* **villainy** *n*

villein [**vill**-an] *n hist* peasant bound in service to his lord

vinaigrette *n* salad dressing of oil and vinegar

vindicate *v* **1** clear (someone) of guilt **2** justify (someone) whose behaviour has been challenged **vindication** *n*

vindictive *adj* maliciously seeking revenge **vindictiveness** *n* **vindictively** *adv*

vine *n* climbing plant, esp. one producing grapes **vineyard** [**vinn**-yard] *n* plantation of grape vines, esp. for making wine

vinegar *n* acid liquid made from wine, beer, or cider **vinegary** *adj*

vino [**vee**-noh] *n informal* wine

vintage *n* **1** wine from a particular harvest of grapes ▷ *adj* **2** best and most typical **vintage car** high-quality antique car

vintner *n* dealer in wine

vinyl [**vine**-ill] *n* type of plastic used in mock leather and records

viol [**vie**-oll] *n* early stringed instrument preceding the violin

viola[1] [vee-**oh**-la] *n* stringed instrument lower in pitch than a violin

viola[2] [**vie**-ol-la] *n* variety of pansy

violate *v* **1** break (a law or agreement) **2** disturb (someone's privacy) **3** treat (a sacred place) disrespectfully **4** rape **violation** *n* **violator** *n*

violent *adj* **1** using or marked by physical strength that is harmful or destructive **2** aggressively intense **3** using excessive force **violence** *n* **violently** *adv*

violet *n* **1** plant with bluish-purple flowers ▷ *adj* **2** bluish-purple

violin *n* small four-stringed musical instrument played with a bow **violinist** *n*

violoncello [vie-oll-on-**chell**-oh] *n, pl* **-los** same as **cello**

VIP very important person

viper *n* poisonous snake

virago [vir-**rah**-go] *n, pl* **-goes, -gos** aggressive woman

viral [**vie**-ral] *adj* of or caused by a virus ▷ *adv* **go viral** spread quickly and widely among internet users

virgin *n* **1** person, esp. a woman, who has not had sexual intercourse ▷ *adj* **2** not having had sexual intercourse **3** not yet exploited or explored **virginal** *adj* **1** like a virgin ▷ *n* **2** rectangular keyboard

v

instrument like a small harpsichord **virginity** n

virile adj having the traditional male characteristics of physical strength and a high sex drive **virility** n

virology n study of viruses

virtual adj 1 having the effect but not the form of 2 of or relating to virtual reality **virtual reality** computer-generated environment that seems real to the user **virtually** adv practically, almost

virtue n 1 moral goodness 2 positive moral quality 3 merit **by virtue of** by reason of **virtuous** adj morally good **virtuously** adv

virtuoso n, pl -sos, -si person with impressive musical skill **virtuosity** n

virulent [vir-yew-lent] adj 1 extremely hostile 2 very infectious 3 violently harmful

virus n 1 microorganism that causes disease in animals and plants 2 computers program that propagates itself, via disks and electronic networks, to cause disruption

visa n permission to enter a country, granted by its government and shown by a stamp on one's passport

visage [viz-zij] n lit face

vis-à-vis [veez-ah-vee] prep in relation to, regarding

viscera [viss-er-a] pl n large abdominal organs **visceral** adj 1 instinctive 2 of or relating to the viscera

viscid [viss-id] adj sticky **viscidity** n

viscose n synthetic fabric made from cellulose

viscount [vie-count] n British nobleman ranking

between an earl and a baron **viscountcy** n

viscountess [vie-count-iss] n 1 wife or widow of a viscount 2 woman holding the rank of viscount in her own right

viscous adj thick and sticky **viscosity** n

visible adj 1 able to be seen 2 able to be perceived by the mind. **visibly** adv **visibility** n range or clarity of vision

vision n 1 ability to see 2 mental image of something 3 hallucination 4 foresight **visionary** adj 1 showing foresight 2 idealistic but impractical ▷ n, pl -aries 3 visionary person

visit v -iting, -ited 1 go or come to see 2 stay temporarily with 3 (foll. by upon) lit afflict ▷ n 4 instance of visiting 5 official call **visitor** n **visitation** n 1 formal visit or inspection 2 catastrophe seen as divine punishment

visor [vize-or] n 1 part of a helmet that moves up and down over the face 2 eyeshade, esp. in an automobile 3 peak on a cap

vista n (beautiful) extensive view

visual adj 1 done by or used in seeing 2 designed to be looked at **visualize** v form a mental image of **visualization** n **visual display unit** device with a screen for displaying data held in a computer

vital adj 1 essential or highly important 2 lively 3 necessary to maintain life **vitals** pl n body organs **vitally** adv **vitality** n physical or mental energy **vital statistics** 1 statistics of births, deaths, and marriages 2 informal woman's bust, waist, and hip measurements

vitamin n one of a group of

substances that are essential in the diet for specific body processes

vitiate [**vish**-ee-ate] v spoil the effectiveness of **vitiation** n

viticulture n cultivation of grape vines

vitreous adj like or made from glass **vitreous humour** gelatinous substance that fills the eyeball

vitrify v **-ifying, -ified** change or be changed into glass or a glassy substance **vitrification** n

vitriol n **1** language expressing bitterness and hatred **2** sulfuric acid **vitriolic** adj

vituperative [vite-**tyew**-pra-tiv] adj bitterly abusive **vituperation** n

viva[1] interj long live (a person or thing)

viva[2] n examination in the form of an interview

vivace [viv-**vah**-chee] adv music in a lively manner

vivacious adj full of energy and enthusiasm **vivacity** n

vivarium n, pl **-iums, -ia** place where animals are kept in natural conditions

viva voce [vive-a **voh**-chee] adv **1** in spoken words ▷ n **2** same as **viva**[2]

vivid adj **1** very bright **2** conveying images that are true to life **vividly** adv **vividness** n

viviparous [viv-**vip**-a-russ] adj producing live offspring

vivisection n performing surgical experiments on living animals **vivisectionist** n

vixen n **1** female fox **2** informal spiteful woman **vixenish** adj

viz. (introducing specified items) namely

vizier [viz-**zeer**] n (formerly) Muslim high official

vizor n same as **visor**

vocabulary n, pl **-aries 1** all the words that a person knows **2** all the words in a language **3** specialist terms used in a given subject **4** list of words in another language with their translation

vocal adj **1** relating to the voice **2** outspoken **vocals** pl n singing part of a piece of pop music **vocally** adv **vocalist** n singer **vocalize** v express with or use the voice **vocalization** n **vocal cords** membranes in the larynx that vibrate to produce sound

vocation n **1** occupation that someone feels called to **2** profession or trade **vocational** adj directed towards a particular profession or trade

vociferous adj characterized by noisy shouting

vodka n (Russian) spirit distilled from potatoes or grain

vogue n **1** popular style **2** period of popularity

voice n **1** (quality of) sound made when speaking or singing **2** expression of opinion by a person or group **3** property of verbs that makes them active or passive ▷ v **4** express verbally **voiceless** adj **voice mail** electronic system for the storage of telephone messages **voice-over** n film commentary spoken by someone off-camera

void n **1** lonely feeling **2** empty space ▷ adj **3** not legally binding **4** empty ▷ v **5** make invalid **6** empty

voile [**voyl**] n light semitransparent fabric

vol. volume

volatile [**voll**-a-tile] adj **1** liable to sudden change, esp.

in behaviour **2** evaporating quickly **volatility** n

vol-au-vent [voll-oh-von] n small puff-pastry case with a savoury filling

volcano n, pl **-noes, -nos** mountain with a vent through which lava is ejected **volcanic** adj

vole n small rodent

volition n faculty of exercising the will **of one's own volition** through one's own choice

volley n **1** simultaneous discharge of ammunition **2** burst of questions or critical comments **3** sports stroke or kick at a moving ball before it hits the ground ▷ v **4** discharge (ammunition) in a volley **5** sports hit or kick (a ball) in a volley **volleyball** n team game where a ball is hit with the hands over a high net

volt n unit of electric potential **voltaic** adj same as **galvanic** ▶ **voltage** n electric potential difference expressed in volts **voltmeter** n instrument for measuring voltage

volte-face [volt-fass] n reversal of opinion

voluble adj talking easily and at length **volubility** n **volubly** adv

volume n **1** size of the space occupied by something **2** amount **3** loudness of sound **4** control on a radio or TV for adjusting this **5** book, esp. one of a series **voluminous** adj **1** (of clothes) large and roomy **2** (of writings) extensive **volumetric** adj relating to measurement by volume

voluntary adj **1** done by choice **2** done or maintained without payment **3** controlled by the will ▷ n, pl **-taries 4** organ solo in a church

service **voluntarily** adv

volunteer n **1** person who offers voluntarily to do something, esp. military service ▷ v **2** offer one's services **3** offer the services of (another person) **4** give (information) willingly

voluptuous adj **1** (of a woman) sexually alluring through fullness of figure **2** sensually pleasurable **voluptuary** n, pl **-aries** person devoted to sensual pleasures

volute n spiral or twisting turn, form, or object

vomit v **-iting, -ited 1** eject (the contents of the stomach) through the mouth ▷ n **2** matter vomited

voodoo n religion involving ancestor worship and witchcraft

voracious adj **1** craving great quantities of food **2** insatiably eager **voraciously** adv **voracity** n

vortex n, pl **-texes, -tices 1** whirlpool **2** whirling motion

vote n **1** choice made by a participant in a shared decision, esp. in electing a candidate **2** right to this choice **3** total number of votes cast **4** collective voting power of a given group: the Black vote ▷ v **5** make a choice by a vote **6** authorize (something) by vote **voter** n

votive adj done or given to fulfil a vow

vouch v **1** (foll. by for) give one's personal assurance about **2** (foll. by for) be proof of **voucher** n **1** ticket used instead of money to buy specified goods **2** record of a financial transaction, receipt

vouchsafe v old-fashioned

1 give, entrust **2** agree graciously

vow n **1** solemn promise, esp. to a god or saint ▷ v **2** promise solemnly

vowel n **1** speech sound made without obstructing the flow of breath **2** letter representing this

vox pop n interviews with members of the public on TV or radio

vox populi n public opinion

voyage n **1** long journey by sea or in space ▷ v **2** make a voyage **voyager** n **voyageur** [vwah-yah-**zher**] n guide or trapper in N regions

voyeur n person who derives pleasure from watching people undressing or having sex

VQA Vintners Quality Alliance: used of Canadian wines that meet certain strict requirements

vs versus

V-sign n **1** offensive gesture made by sticking up the index and middle fingers with the palm inwards **2** similar gesture, with the palm outwards, meaning victory or peace

VTR video tape recorder

vulcanize v strengthen (rubber) by treating it with sulfur **vulcanization** n **vulcanite** n vulcanized rubber

vulgar adj showing lack of good taste, decency, or refinement **vulgarly** adv **vulgarity** n **vulgarian** n vulgar (rich) person **vulgarism** n coarse word or phrase **vulgar fraction** simple fraction

Vulgate n fourth-century Latin version of the Bible

vulnerable adj **1** able to be physically or emotionally hurt **2** exposed to attack **vulnerability** n

vulpine adj of or like a fox

vulture n large bird that feeds on the flesh of dead animals

vulva n woman's external genitals

vying present participle of **vie**

V

Ww

W 1 *chem* tungsten **2** watt
3 Wednesday **4** west(ern)

wacky *adj* **wackier, wackiest**
informal eccentric or funny
wackiness *n*

wad *n* **1** small mass of soft
material **2** roll or bundle ▷ *v*
wadding, wadded 3 make
into a wad **4** pad or stuff with
wadding **wadding** *n* soft
material used for padding or
stuffing

waddle *v* **1** walk with short
swaying steps ▷ *n* **2** swaying
walk

wade *v* **1** walk with difficulty
through water or mud
2 proceed with difficulty
wader *n* **1** long-legged water
bird **waders 2** angler's long
waterproof boots

wadi [wod-dee] *n, pl* **-dies**
(in N Africa and Arabia)
watercourse which is dry
except in the wet season

wafer *n* **1** thin crisp biscuit
2 thin disc of unleavened
bread used at Communion
3 thin slice

waffle[1] *informal* ▷ *v* **1** speak or
write in a vague wordy way
▷ *n* **2** vague wordy talk or
writing

waffle[2] *n* square crisp pancake
with a grid-like pattern

waft *v* **1** drift or carry gently
through air or water ▷ *n*
2 something wafted

wag *v* **wagging, wagged**
1 move rapidly from side to
side ▷ *n* **2** wagging **3** *informal*
humorous witty person

waggish *adj* **wagtail** *n* small
long-tailed bird

wage *n* **1** *often pl* payment for
work done, esp. when paid
weekly ▷ *v* **2** engage in (an
activity)

wager *n, v* bet on the outcome
of something

waggle *v* wag **waggly** *adj*

wagon, waggon *n* **1** four-
wheeled vehicle for heavy
loads **2** railway freight truck
wagoner *or* **waggoner** *n*

waif *n* homeless child

wail *v* **1** cry out in pain or
misery ▷ *n* **2** mournful cry

wain *n poetic* farm wagon

**wainscot, wainscoting,
wainscotting** *n* wooden
lining of the lower part of the
walls of a room

waist *n* **1** part of the body
between the ribs and hips
2 narrow middle part
waistband *n* band of material
sewn on to the waist of
a garment to strengthen
it **waistcoat** *n Brit* vest
waistline *n* (size of) the waist
of a person or garment

wait *v* **1** remain inactive in
expectation (of something)
2 be ready (for something)
3 delay or be delayed **4** serve
in a restaurant etc. ▷ *n*
5 waiting **waiter** *n* man who
serves in a restaurant etc.
waitress *n fem*

waive *v* refrain from
enforcing (a law, right, etc.)
waiver *n* **1** (written statement
of) this act **2** *US & Canad sports*

team's waiving of its right to sign a player that another team wants to trade, demote, or release

wake[1] v **waking, woke, woken 1** rouse from sleep or inactivity ▷ n **2** vigil beside a corpse the night before burial **waken** v wake **wakeful** adj

wake[2] n track left by a moving ship **in the wake of** following close behind

walk v **1** move on foot with at least one foot always on the ground **2** pass through or over on foot **3** escort or accompany on foot **4** baseball reach first base by receiving four balls from the pitcher **5** baseball allow (a batter) to reach first base by throwing four balls ▷ n **6** walking **7** distance walked **8** manner of walking **9** place or route for walking **10** baseball free pass to first base given to a batter who has received four balls **walk of life** occupation or career **walker** n **1** person or thing that walks **2** device consisting of a light metal frame, used by infirm or disabled people for support for walking **walkabout** n informal walk among the public by royalty etc. **walkie-talkie** n portable radio transmitter and receiver **walking stick** stick used as a support when walking **walk into** v meet with unwittingly **Walkman** n ® small portable cassette player with headphones **walkout** n **1** strike **2** act of leaving as a protest **walkover** n informal easy victory

wall n **1** structure of brick, stone, etc. used to enclose, divide, or support **2** something having the function or effect of a wall ▷ v **3** enclose or seal with a

wall or walls **wallflower** n **1** fragrant garden plant **2** at a dance, a woman who remains seated for lack of a partner

wallpaper n decorative paper to cover interior walls

wallaby n, pl **-bies** marsupial like a small kangaroo

wallet n small folding case for paper money, documents, etc.

walleyed adj having eyes with an abnormal amount of white showing

wallop informal ▷ v **-loping, -loped 1** hit hard ▷ n **2** hard blow **walloping** informal ▷ n **1** thrashing ▷ adj **2** large or great

wallow v **1** roll in liquid or mud **2** revel in an emotion ▷ n **3** wallowing

wally n, pl **-lies** slang stupid person

walnut n **1** edible nut with a wrinkled shell **2** tree it grows on **3** its wood

walrus n, pl **-ruses, -rus** large sea mammal with long tusks

waltz n **1** ballroom dance **2** music for this ▷ v **3** dance a waltz **4** move in a relaxed confident way

wampum [wom-pum] n shells woven together, formerly used by N American Indians for money and ornament

wan [rhymes with **swan**] adj **wanner, wannest** pale and sickly looking

wand n thin rod, esp. one used in doing magic

wander v **1** move about without a definite destination or aim **2** go astray, deviate ▷ n **3** wandering **wanderer** n **wanderlust** n great desire to travel

wane v **1** decrease gradually in size or strength **2** (of the moon) decrease in size **on the wane** in decline

wangle v informal get by

w

devious methods

want v **1** desire **2** lack ▷ n
3 wanting **4** thing wanted
5 lack **6** poverty **wanted** adj
sought by the police **wanting**
adj **1** lacking **2** not good
enough

wanton adj **1** dissolute or
immoral **2** without motive
3 unrestrained

wapiti [wop-pit-tee] n, pl **-tis**
large N American and NZ deer

war n **1** fighting between
nations **2** conflict or contest
▷ adj **3** of, like, or caused by
war ▷ v **warring, warred**
4 make war **warring** adj
warlike adj of, for, or fond of
war **war crime** crime, such
as killing, committed during
a war in violation of accepted
conventions **war criminal**
person who has committed
war crimes **warfare** n
fighting or hostilities
warhead n explosive front
part of a missile **warmonger**
n person who encourages war
warship n ship designed and
equipped for naval combat

warble v sing with trills
warbler n any of various small
songbirds

ward n **1** room in a hospital
for patients needing a similar
kind of care **2** electoral
division of a town **3** child
under the care of a guardian
or court **warder** n prison
officer **wardress** n fem **ward
off** v avert or repel (something
unpleasant) **wardroom**
n officers' quarters on a
warship

warden n **1** person in
charge of a building,
institution, college, etc.
2 official responsible for the
enforcement of regulations
wardenship n

wardrobe n **1** cupboard for
hanging clothes in **2** person's

collection of clothes
3 costumes of a theatrical
company

ware n **1** articles of a specified
type or material: silverware
wares 2 goods for sale
warehouse n building for
storing goods prior to sale or
distribution

warlock n sorcerer

warm adj **1** moderately
hot **2** providing warmth
3 affectionate **4** enthusiastic
5 (of a colour) predominantly
yellow or red ▷ v **6** make
or become warm **warmly**
adv **warmth** n **1** mild heat
2 cordiality **3** intensity of
emotion **warm up** v **1** make
or become warmer **2** do
preliminary exercises before
a race or more strenuous
exercise **3** make or become
more lively **warm-up** n

warn v **1** make aware of
possible danger or harm
2 caution or scold **3** inform
(someone) in advance
warning n **1** something that
warns **2** scolding or caution
warn off v advise (someone)
not to become involved with

warp v **1** twist out of shape
2 pervert ▷ n **3** state of being
warped **4** lengthwise threads
on a loom

warrant n **1** (document
giving) official authorization
▷ v **2** guarantee **3** give
authority or power to
warranty n (document
giving) a guarantee **warrant
officer** officer in certain
armed services with a rank
between a commissioned
and non-commissioned
officer

warren n **1** series of burrows
in which rabbits live
2 overcrowded building or
part of a town with many
narrow passages

warrior n person who fights in a war

wart n small hard growth on the skin **wart hog** kind of African wild pig

wary [ware-ree] adj **warier, wariest** watchful or cautious **warily** adv **wariness** n

was v first and third person singular past tense of **be**

wash v 1 clean (oneself, clothes, etc.) with water and usu. soap 2 be washable 3 flow or sweep over or against 4 informal be believable or acceptable: that excuse won't wash ▷ n 5 washing 6 clothes washed at one time 7 thin coat of paint 8 trail of water left by a moving ship **washable** adj **washer** n 1 ring put under a nut or bolt or in a tap as a seal 2 informal washing machine **washing** n clothes to be washed **wash away** v carry or be carried off by moving water **washout** n informal complete failure **washroom** n lavatory **wash up** v wash one's face and hands

wasp n stinging insect with a black-and-yellow body **waspish** adj bad-tempered

waste v 1 use pointlessly or thoughtlessly 2 fail to take advantage of 3 (foll. by away) lose one's health or strength ▷ n 4 wasting 5 something left over because in excess of requirements **wastes** 6 desert ▷ adj 7 rejected as worthless or surplus to requirements 8 not cultivated or inhabited **wastage** n 1 loss by wear or waste 2 reduction in size of a workforce by not filling vacancies **wasteful** adj extravagant **wastefully** adv **waster** or **wastrel** n layabout **wastepaper basket** container for discarded paper

watch v 1 look at closely 2 wait expectantly (for) 3 guard or supervise ▷ n 4 portable timepiece for the wrist or pocket 5 (period of) watching 6 sailor's spell of duty **watchable** adj **watcher** n **watchful** adj carefully observing everything that happens **watchfully** adv **watchdog** n 1 dog kept to guard property 2 person or group guarding against inefficiency or illegality **watchman** n man employed to guard a building or property **watchword** n slogan or motto

water n 1 clear colourless tasteless liquid that falls as rain and forms rivers etc. 2 body of water, such as a sea or lake 3 level of the tide 4 urine ▷ v 5 put water on or into 6 (of the eyes) fill with tears 7 salivate **watery** adj **water bed** waterproof mattress filled with water **water buffalo** oxlike Asian animal **water closet** old-fashioned lavatory **watercolour** n 1 paint thinned with water 2 painting done in this **watercourse** n stream or river **watercress** n edible plant growing in clear ponds and streams **water down** v dilute, make less strong **waterfall** n place where the waters of a river drop vertically **waterfront** n part of a town alongside a body of water **water lily** water plant with large floating leaves **watermark** n faint translucent design in a sheet of paper **watermelon** n melon with green skin and red flesh **water polo** team game played by swimmers with a ball **waterproof** adj

w

1 not letting water through ▷ v **2** make waterproof ▷ n **3** waterproof garment **watershed** n **1** line separating two river systems **2** dividing line **water-skiing** n sport of riding over water on skis towed by a speedboat **watertight** adj **1** not letting water through **2** with no loopholes or weak points **water wheel** large wheel which is turned by flowing water to drive machinery

watt [**wott**] n unit of power **wattage** n electrical power expressed in watts

wattle [**wott**-tl] n **1** branches woven over sticks to make a fence **2** fold of skin hanging from the neck of certain birds

wave v **1** move the hand to and fro as a greeting or signal **2** move or flap to and fro ▷ n **3** moving ridge on water **4** curve(s) in the hair **5** gesture of waving **6** vibration carrying energy through a medium **7** prolonged spell of something **wavy** adj **wavelength** n distance between the same points of two successive waves

waver v **1** hesitate or be irresolute **2** be or become unsteady **waverer** n

wax[1] n **1** solid shiny fatty or oily substance used for sealing, making candles, etc. **2** similar substance made by bees **3** waxy secretion of the ear ▷ v **4** coat or polish with wax **waxen** adj made of or like wax **waxy** adj **waxwing** n small songbird **waxwork** n **1** lifelike wax model of a (famous) person **waxworks** **2** place exhibiting these

wax[2] v **1** increase in size or strength **2** (of the moon) get gradually larger

way n **1** manner or method **2** route or direction **3** track or path **4** room for movement or activity: *you're in the way* **5** distance **6** passage or journey **7** characteristic manner **8** *informal* state or condition **wayward** adj erratic, selfish, or stubborn **waywardness** n **wayfarer** n traveller **waylay** v lie in wait for and accost or attack **waypoint** n specific location as defined by a GPS **wayside** adj, n (situated by) the side of a road

WC water closet

we pron used as the subject of a verb **1** the speaker or writer and one or more others **2** people in general **3** formal word for 'I' used by editors and monarchs

weak adj **1** lacking strength **2** liable to give way **3** lacking flavour **4** unconvincing **weaken** v make or become weak **weakling** n feeble person or animal **weakly** adj **1** weak or sickly ▷ adv **2** feebly **weakness** n

weal n raised mark left on the skin by a blow

wealth n **1** riches **2** abundance **wealthy** adj **wealthiness** n

wean v **1** accustom to food other than mother's milk **2** (often foll. by *from*) coax away (from)

weapon n **1** object used in fighting **2** anything used to get the better of an opponent **weaponry** n weapons collectively

wear v **wearing, wore, worn** **1** have on the body as clothing or ornament **2** show as one's expression **3** (cause to) deteriorate by constant use or action **4** endure constant use **5** *informal* tolerate ▷ n **6** wearing **7** things to wear:

leisure wear **8** damage caused by use **9** ability to endure constant use **wearer** *n* **wear off** *v* have a gradual decrease in intensity **wear on** *v* (of time) pass slowly

weary *adj* **-rier, -riest 1** tired or exhausted **2** tiring ▷ *v* **-rying, -ried 3** make or become weary **wearily** *adv* **weariness** *n* **wearisome** *adj* tedious

weasel *n* small carnivorous mammal with a long body and short legs

weather *n* **1** day-to-day meteorological conditions of a place ▷ *v* **2** (cause to) be affected by the weather **3** come safely through **under the weather** *informal* slightly ill **weather-beaten** *adj* worn, damaged, or (of skin) tanned by exposure to the weather **weathercock** *or* **weathervane** *n* metal object on a roof showing which way the wind is blowing

weave *v* **weaving, wove** *or* **weaved, woven** *or* **weaved 1** make (fabric) by interlacing (yarn) on a loom **2** compose (a story) **3** move from side to side while going forwards **weaver** *n*

web *n* **1** net spun by a spider **2** anything intricate or complex: *web of deceit* **3** skin between the toes of a duck, frog, etc. **the Web** short for **World Wide Web ▶ Web 2.0** internet viewed as a medium in which interactive experience is more important than accessing information **web address** same as **URL ▶ webbed** *adj* **webbing** *n* strong fabric woven in strips **weblog** *n* person's online journal (Also **blog**) **webmail** *n* system of electronic mail that allows account holders to access their mail via an internet site **website** *n* group of connected pages on the World Wide Web

wed *v* **wedding, wedded** *or* **wed 1** marry **2** unite closely **wedding** *n* act or ceremony of marriage **wedlock** *n* marriage

wedge *n* **1** piece of material thick at one end and thin at the other ▷ *v* **2** fasten or split with a wedge **3** squeeze into a narrow space

Wednesday *n* fourth day of the week

wee *adj* small

weed *n* **1** plant growing where undesired **2** *informal* thin ineffectual person ▷ *v* **3** clear of weeds **weedy** *adj* **1** *informal* thin or weak **2** full of weeds **weed out** *v* remove or eliminate (what is unwanted)

weeds *pl n obsolete* widow's mourning clothes

week *n* **1** period of seven days, esp. one beginning on a Sunday **2** hours or days of work in a week **weekly** *adj, adv* **1** happening, done, etc. once a week ▷ *n, pl* **-lies 2** periodical published once a week **weekday** *n* any day of the week except Saturday or Sunday **weekend** *n* Saturday and Sunday

weep *v* **weeping, wept 1** shed tears **2** grieve or lament **3** ooze liquid **weepy** *adj* **weeping willow** willow with drooping branches

weevil *n* small beetle which eats grain etc.

weft *n* cross threads in weaving

weigh *v* **1** measure the weight of **2** have a specified weight **3** consider carefully **4** be influential **5** be burdensome **weigh anchor** raise a ship's anchor or (of a ship) have its anchor raised

weight *n* **1** heaviness of an object **2** object of known mass used for weighing **3** unit of measurement of weight **4** heavy object **5** importance or influence ▷ *v* **6** add weight to **7** slant (a system) to favour one group **weighting** *n* extra allowance paid in special circumstances **weightless** *adj* **weightlessness** *n* **weighty** *adj* **1** heavy **2** important **3** causing worry **weightily** *adv*

weir *n* river dam

weird *adj* **1** unearthly or eerie **2** strange or bizarre **weirdo** *n informal* peculiar person

welch *v* same as **welsh**

welcome *adj* **1** received gladly **2** freely permitted ▷ *n* **3** kindly greeting ▷ *v* **-coming, -comed 4** greet with pleasure **5** receive gladly

weld *v* **1** join (pieces of metal or plastic) by softening with heat **2** unite closely ▷ *n* **3** welded joint **welder** *n*

welfare *n* **1** wellbeing **2** help given to people in need **welfare state** system in which the government takes responsibility for the wellbeing of its citizens

well[1] *adv* **better, best 1** satisfactorily **2** skilfully **3** completely **4** prosperously **5** suitably **6** intimately **7** favourably **8** considerably ▷ *adj* **10** in good health **11** satisfactory ▷ *interj* **12** exclamation of surprise, interrogation, etc. **wellbeing** *n* state of being well, happy, or prosperous **well-disposed** *adj* inclined to be friendly or sympathetic **well-heeled** *adj informal* wealthy **well-meaning** *adj* having good intentions **well-spoken** *adj* speaking in a polite or articulate way **well-worn** *adj*

1 (of a word or phrase) having lost its meaning through overuse **2** so much used as to show signs of wear

well[2] *n* **1** hole sunk into the earth to reach water, oil, or gas **2** deep open shaft ▷ *v* **3** flow upwards or outwards

wellingtons *pl n* high waterproof rubber boots

welsh *v* fail to pay a debt or fulfil an obligation

Welsh *adj* **1** of Wales ▷ *n* **2** language or people of Wales **Welsh rabbit** *or* **Welsh rarebit** dish of melted cheese on toast

welt *n* **1** raised or strengthened seam **2** weal ▷ *v* **3** provide with a welt

welter *n* jumbled mass

welterweight *n* boxer weighing up to 147lb (professional) or 67kg (amateur)

wen *n* cyst on the scalp

wench *n facetious* young woman

wend *v* go or travel

went *v* past tense of **go**

wept *v* past of **weep**

were *v* **1** form of the past tense of **be** used after *we, you, they,* or a plural noun **2** subjunctive of **be**

we're we are

weren't were not

werewolf *n* (in folklore) person who can turn into a wolf

west *n* **1** (direction towards) the point on the horizon where the sun sets **2** region lying in this direction **3** **West** N America and western Europe ▷ *adj* **4** in, going towards, facing, or (of the wind) blowing from the west ▷ *adv* **5** in or to the west **westerly** *adj* in, towards, or (of the wind) blowing from the west **western** *adj* **1** of or in the west ▷ *n* **2** film or story about cowboys in the western US **westerner** *n* **westernize** *v* adapt to the customs and culture of the West **westward** *adj, adv* **westwards** *adv* **West Coast** Pacific coast of N America

wet *adj* **wetter, wettest** **1** covered or soaked with water or another liquid **2** not yet dry: *wet paint* **3** *informal* (of a person) feeble or foolish ▷ *n* **4** moisture or rain **5** *informal* feeble or foolish person ▷ *v* **wetting, wet** *or* **wetted 6** make wet **wet blanket** *informal* person who has a depressing effect on others **wetland** *n* area of marshy land **wet nurse** woman employed to breast-feed another's child **wet room** waterproofed shower room with a drain in the floor **wet suit** close-fitting rubber suit worn by divers etc.

wether *n* castrated ram

whack *v* **1** strike with a resounding blow ▷ *n* **2** such a blow **3** *informal* share **4** *informal* attempt **whacked** *adj* exhausted **whacking** *adj* *informal* huge

whale *n* large fish-shaped sea mammal **have a whale of a time** *informal* enjoy oneself very much **whaling** *n* hunting of whales **whaler** *n* **whalebone** *n* horny substance hanging from the upper jaw of toothless whales

wharf *n, pl* **wharves, wharfs** platform at a harbour for loading and unloading ships **wharfage** *n* accommodation at or charge for use of a wharf

what *pron* **1** which thing **2** that which **3** request for a statement to be repeated ▷ *adv* **4** in which way, how

much: *what do you care?* ▷ *interj* **5** exclamation of surprise, anger, etc. **what for?** why? **whatever** *pron* **1** everything or anything that **2** no matter what **whatnot** *n* *informal* similar unspecified things **whatsoever** *adj* at all

wheat *n* **1** grain used in making flour, bread, and pasta **2** plant producing this **wheaten** *adj* **wheatear** *n* small songbird **wheatmeal** *adj, n* (made with) brown, but not wholewheat, flour

wheedle *v* coax or cajole

wheel *n* **1** disc that revolves on an axle **2** pivoting movement ▷ *v* **3** push or pull (something with wheels) **4** turn as if on an axis **5** turn round suddenly **wheeling and dealing** use of shrewd and sometimes unscrupulous methods to achieve success **wheeler-dealer** *n* **wheelbarrow** *n* shallow box for carrying loads, with a wheel at the front and two handles **wheelbase** *n* distance between a vehicle's front and back axles **wheelchair** *n* chair mounted on wheels for use by people who cannot walk

wheeze *v* **1** breathe with a hoarse whistling noise ▷ *n* **2** wheezing sound **wheezy** *adj*

whelk *n* edible snail-like shellfish

whelp *n* **1** pup or cub **2** *offensive* youth ▷ *v* **3** produce whelps

when *adv* **1** at what time ▷ *conj* **2** at the time that **3** although **4** considering the fact that ▷ *pron* **5** at which time **whenever** *adv, conj* at whatever time

whence *adv, conj* *obsolete* from what place or source

where *adv* **1** in, at, or to what

place ▷ *pron* **2** in, at, or to which place ▷ *conj* **3** in the place at which **whereabouts** *adv* **1** at what place ▷ *n* **2** present position **whereas** *conj* **1** but on the other hand **2** considering that **whereby** *conj* by which **wherefore** *obsolete* ▷ *adv* **1** why ▷ *conj* **2** consequently **whereupon** *conj* at which point **wherever** *adv* at whatever place **wherewithal** *n* necessary funds, resources, etc.

whet *v* **whetting, whetted 1** sharpen (a tool) **2** increase (appetite or desire) **whetstone** *n* stone for sharpening tools

whether *conj* used to introduce an indirect question or a clause expressing doubt or choice

whey [way] *n* watery liquid that separates from the curd when milk is clotted

which *adj, pron* **1** used to request or refer to a choice from different possibilities ▷ *pron* **2** person or thing referred to **whichever** *adj, pron* **1** any out of several **2** no matter which

whiff *n* **1** puff of air or odour **2** trace or hint

Whig *n* member of a British political party of the 18th–19th centuries that sought limited reform

while *conj* **1** in the time that **2** despite the fact that **3** whereas ▷ *n* **4** period of time **whilst** *conj* while **while away** *v* pass (time) idly but pleasantly

whim *n* sudden fancy **whimsy** or **whimsey** *n* **1** capricious idea **2** light or fanciful humour **whimsical** *adj* **1** fanciful **2** full of whims **whimsicality** *n*

whimper *v* **1** cry in a soft

whining way ▷ *n* **2** soft plaintive whine

whin *n* gorse

whine *n* **1** high-pitched plaintive cry **2** peevish complaint ▷ *v* **3** make such a sound **whining** *n, adj*

whinge *v* **1** complain ▷ *n* **2** complaint

whinny *v* **-nying, -nied 1** neigh softly ▷ *n* **2** soft neigh

whip *n* **1** cord attached to a handle, used for beating animals or people **2** call made on Members of Parliament to attend for important divisions **3** politician responsible for organizing and disciplining fellow party members **4** whipped dessert ▷ *v* **whipping, whipped 5** hit with a whip **6** *informal* pull, remove, or move quickly **7** beat (eggs or cream) to a froth **8** rouse into a particular condition **9** *informal* steal **whipped** *adj* **1** having been whipped **2** exhausted **whiplash injury** neck injury caused by a sudden jerk to the head, as in an automobile crash

whippet *n* racing dog like a small greyhound

whir, whirr *n* **1** prolonged soft buzz ▷ *v* **whirring, whirred 2** (cause to) make a whir

whirl *v* **1** spin or revolve **2** be dizzy or confused **3** drive or move at high speed ▷ *n* **4** whirling movement **5** confusion or giddiness **6** bustling activity **whirlpool** *n* strong circular current of water **whirlwind** *n* **1** column of air whirling violently upwards in a spiral ▷ *adj* **2** much quicker than normal

whisk *v* **1** move or remove quickly **2** brush away lightly **3** beat (eggs or cream) to a froth ▷ *n* **4** light brush **5** egg-beating utensil

whisker *n* **1** any of the long stiff hairs on the face of a cat or other mammal **whiskers 2** hair growing on a man's cheeks **by a whisker** *informal* only just

whisky *n, pl* **-kies** strong alcoholic drink distilled from fermented cereals **whiskey** *n* US or Irish whisky **whiskyjack** *n* Canada jay

whisper *v* **1** speak softly, without vibration of the vocal cords **2** rustle ▷ *n* **3** soft voice **4** something whispered **5** rustling **6** *informal* rumour

whist *n* card game

whistle *v* **1** produce a shrill sound by forcing breath through pursed lips **2** make a similar sound **3** signal by a whistle ▷ *n* **4** whistling sound **5** instrument blown to make a whistling sound **blow the whistle on** *informal* inform on or put a stop to **whistling** *n, adj*

whit *n* **not a whit** not the slightest amount

white *adj* **1** of the colour of snow **2** pale **3** light in colour **4** (of coffee) served with milk ▷ *n* **5** colour of snow **6** clear fluid round the yolk of an egg **7** white part of the eyeball **8** **White** member of the race of people with light-coloured skin **whiten** *v* make or become white or whiter **whiteness** *n* **whitish** *adj* **whitebait** *n* small edible fish **white-collar** *adj* denoting nonmanual salaried workers **white elephant** useless or unwanted possession **white flag** signal of surrender or truce **white-hot** *adj* very hot **white lie** see **lie**[1] ▶ **white-knuckle** *adj* *informal* causing fear or anxiety **white paper**

report by the government, outlining its policy on a matter **whitewash** *n* **1** substance for whitening walls ▷ *v* **2** cover with whitewash **3** *informal* conceal or gloss over faults **white water** rapids

whither *adv* *obsolete* to what place

whiting [**white**-ing] *n* edible sea fish

Whitsun *n* week following Whit Sunday, the seventh Sunday after Easter

whittle *v* cut or carve (wood) with a knife **whittle down** or **whittle away** *v* reduce or wear away gradually

whizz, whiz *v* **whizzing, whizzed 1** move with a loud buzzing sound **2** *informal* move quickly ▷ *n, pl* **whizzes 3** loud buzzing sound **4** *informal* person who is very good at something

who *pron* **1** which or what person **2** used to refer to a person or people already mentioned **whoever** *pron* **1** any person who **2** no matter who

whodunnit [hoo-**dun**-nit] *n* *informal* detective story, play, or film

whole *adj* **1** containing all the elements or parts **2** uninjured or undamaged **3** healthy **4** (of a number) not containing a fraction ▷ *n* **5** complete thing or system **on the whole** taking everything into consideration **wholly** *adv* **wholesome** *adj* physically or morally beneficial **wholefood** *n* food that has been processed as little as possible **wholehearted** *adj* sincere or enthusiastic **whole note** musical note four beats long **wholesale** *adj, adv* **1** of the business

w

of selling goods in large quantities and at lower prices to retailers **2** on a large scale: *wholesale destruction of forests* **wholesaler** n **wholewheat** adj **1** (of flour) made from the whole wheat grain **2** made from wholewheat flour

whom pron objective case of **who**

whoop n, v shout or cry to express excitement

whoopee interj informal cry of joy

whooping cough n infectious disease marked by convulsive coughing and noisy breathing

whopper n informal **1** anything unusually large **2** huge lie **whopping** adj

whore [hore] n prostitute

whorl n **1** ring of leaves or petals **2** one turn of a spiral **3** something coiled

whose pron of who or which

why adv **1** for what reason ▷ pron **2** because of which

wick n cord through a lamp or candle which carries fuel to the flame

wicked adj **1** morally bad **2** mischievous **wickedly** adv **wickedness** n

wicker adj made of woven cane **wickerwork** n

wicket n **1** set of three cricket stumps and two bails **2** cricket pitch **3** small gate

wide adj **1** large from side to side **2** having a specified width **3** spacious or extensive **4** opened fully ▷ adv **5** to the full extent **6** over an extensive area **7** far from the target **widely** adv **widen** v make or become wider **width** n **1** distance from side to side **2** quality of being wide **wide receiver** football player whose function is to catch long passes (Also **wideout**)

widespread adj affecting a wide area or a large number of people

widgeon n same as **wigeon**

widow n woman whose spouse is dead and who has not remarried **widowed** adj **widowhood** n **widower** n man whose spouse is dead and who has not remarried

wield v **1** hold and use (a weapon) **2** have and use (power)

wife n, pl **wives** female partner in marriage

Wi-Fi n system of wireless access to the internet

wig n artificial head of hair **wigged** adj

wigeon n duck found in marshland

wiggle v **1** move jerkily from side to side ▷ n **2** wiggling movement **wiggly** adj

wight n obsolete person

wigwam n N American Indian's tent

wild adj **1** (of animals or birds) not tamed or domesticated **2** (of plants) not cultivated **3** not civilized **4** lacking restraint or control **5** violent or stormy **6** informal excited **7** without reason or substance **8** informal furious **wilds** pl n desolate or uninhabited place **wildly** adv **wildness** n **wildcat** n **1** European wild animal like a large domestic cat ▷ adj **2** (of a strike) sudden and unofficial **wild-goose chase** search that has little chance of success **wildlife** n wild animals and plants collectively

wildebeest n gnu

wilderness n **1** uninhabited uncultivated region **2** state of no longer being in a prominent position

wildfire n **spread like**

wildfire spread quickly and uncontrollably

wile n trick or ploy **wily** adj crafty or sly

wilful adj 1 headstrong or obstinate 2 intentional **wilfully** adv **wilfulness** n

will[1] v, past **would** used as an auxiliary to form the future tense or to indicate intention, ability, or expectation

will[2] n 1 faculty of deciding what one will do 2 directions written for disposal of one's property after death 3 desire or wish ▷ v 4 try to make (something) happen by wishing for it 5 wish or desire 6 leave (property) in one's will **willing** adj 1 ready or inclined (to do something) 2 done or given readily **willingly** adv **willingness** n **willpower** n ability to control oneself and one's actions

will-o'-the-wisp n 1 elusive person or thing 2 pale light sometimes seen over marshes at night

willow n 1 tree with thin flexible branches 2 its wood **willowy** adj slender and graceful

willy-nilly adv whether desired or not

wilt v (cause to) become limp or lose strength

wimp n informal feeble ineffectual person

wimple n garment framing the face, worn by medieval women and now by nuns

win v **winning, won** 1 come first in (a competition, fight, etc.) 2 gain (a prize) in a competition 3 get by effort ▷ n 4 victory, esp. in a game **winner** n **winning** adj 1 gaining victory 2 charming **winnings** pl n money won in gambling or in a competition **win over** v gain the support or consent of (someone)

wince v 1 draw back, as from pain ▷ n 2 wincing

winceyette n cotton fabric with a raised nap

winch n 1 machine for lifting or hauling using a cable wound round a drum ▷ v 2 lift or haul using a winch

wind[1] n 1 current of air 2 trend or tendency 3 breath 4 idle talk 5 flatulence 6 hint or suggestion ▷ v 7 make short of breath 8 make (a baby) bring up wind after feeding **windy** adj **windward** adj, n (of or in) the direction from which the wind is blowing **wind-chill factor** added chilling effect of wind on basic temperature **windfall** n 1 unexpected good luck 2 fallen fruit **wind farm** collection of wind-driven turbines for generating electricity **wind instrument** musical instrument played by blowing **windmill** n machine for grinding or pumping driven by sails turned by the wind **windpipe** n tube linking the throat and the lungs **windscreen** n Brit windshield **windshield** n front window of a motor vehicle **windsock** n cloth cone on a mast at an airfield to indicate wind direction **windsurfing** n sport of riding on water using a surfboard propelled and steered by a sail

wind[2] v **winding, wound** 1 coil or wrap around 2 tighten the spring of (a clock or watch) 3 move in a twisting course ▷ n 4 winding 5 single turn or bend **wind up** v 1 bring to or reach an end 2 tighten the spring of (a clock or watch) 3 informal make tense or agitated

w

windlass n winch worked by a crank

window n 1 opening in a wall or vehicle containing glass, which lets in light or air 2 glass pane or panes fitted in such an opening 3 display area behind the window of a shop 4 area on a computer screen that can be manipulated separately from the rest of the display area 5 period of unbooked time in a diary or schedule **window-dressing** n 1 arrangement of goods in a shop window 2 attempt to make something more attractive than it really is **window-shopping** n looking at goods in shop windows without intending to buy

wine n 1 alcoholic drink made from fermented grapes 2 similar drink made from other fruits ▷ adj 3 of a dark purplish-red colour **wine and dine** entertain or be entertained with fine food and drink

wing n 1 one of the limbs or organs of a bird, insect, or bat that are used for flying 2 one of the winglike supporting parts of an aircraft 3 projecting side part of a building 4 group within a political party 5 Brit fender 6 sports (player on) either side of the field or ice **wings** 7 sides of a stage ▷ v 8 move through the air 9 wound slightly in the wing or arm **winged** adj **winger** n sports player positioned on a wing

wink v 1 close and open (an eye) rapidly as a signal 2 twinkle ▷ n 3 winking 4 smallest amount of sleep

winkle n shellfish with a cone-shaped shell **winkle**

out v informal extract or prise out

winnow v 1 separate (chaff) from (grain) 2 examine to select desirable elements

winsome adj charming or winning

winter n 1 coldest season ▷ v 2 spend the winter **wintry** adj 1 of or like winter 2 cold or unfriendly **winter sports** open-air sports held on snow or ice

wipe v 1 clean or dry by rubbing 2 erase (a tape) ▷ n 3 wiping **wiper** n Also **windshield wiper** device that automatically wipes rain etc. from a windshield **wipe out** v 1 destroy completely 2 slang kill

wire n 1 thin flexible strand of metal 2 length of this used to carry electric current 3 fencing made of wire 4 telegram ▷ v 5 provide with wires 6 send by telegraph **wiring** n system of wires **wiry** adj 1 like wire 2 lean and tough **wire-haired** adj (of a dog) having a stiff wiry coat

wireless n old-fashioned same as **radio**

wise[1] adj possessing or showing wisdom **wisely** adv **wisdom** n 1 good sense and judgment 2 accumulated knowledge **wisdom tooth** any of the four large molar teeth cut usu. after the age of twenty **wiseacre** n person who wishes to seem wise **wisecrack** informal ▷ n 1 flippant or sardonic remark ▷ v 2 make a wisecrack **wise**[2] n obsolete manner

wish v 1 want or desire 2 feel or express a hope about someone's wellbeing, success, etc. ▷ n 3 expression of a desire 4 thing desired

wishful adj too optimistic
wishbone n V-shaped bone above the breastbone of a fowl
wishy-washy adj informal insipid or bland
wisp n 1 light delicate streak 2 small untidy bundle or tuft 3 slight trace **wispy** adj
wisteria n climbing shrub with blue or purple flowers
wistful adj sadly longing **wistfully** adv
wit n 1 ability to use words or ideas in a clever and amusing way 2 person with this ability 3 sometimes pl ability to think and act quickly **witty** adj **wittily** adv **witticism** n witty remark **wittingly** adv intentionally **witless** adj foolish
witch n 1 person, usu. female, who practises (black) magic 2 ugly wicked woman 3 fascinating woman **witchcraft** n use of magic **witch doctor** (in certain societies) a man appearing to cure or cause injury or disease by magic **witch-hunt** n campaign against people with unpopular views
with prep 1 by means of 2 in the company of 3 possessing 4 in relation to 5 in a manner characterized by 6 because of 7 understanding or agreeing with **within** prep, adv in or inside **without** prep 1 not having, accompanied by, or using 2 obsolete outside
withdraw v -drawing, -drew, -drawn take or move out or away **withdrawal** n **withdrawn** adj unsociable
wither v wilt or dry up **withering** adj (of a look or remark) scornful
withers pl n ridge between a horse's shoulder blades
withhold v -holding, -held refrain from giving

withstand v -standing, -stood oppose or resist successfully
witness n 1 person who has seen something happen 2 evidence or testimony 3 person giving evidence in court ▷ v 4 see at first hand 5 give evidence 6 sign (a document) to certify that it is genuine
wives n plural of **wife**
wizard n 1 magician 2 person with outstanding skill in a particular field **wizardry** n
wizened [wiz-zend] adj shrivelled or wrinkled
WMD weapon(s) of mass destruction
wobble v 1 move unsteadily 2 shake ▷ n 3 unsteady movement 4 shake **wobbly** adj
wodge n informal thick lump or chunk
woe n 1 grief **woes** 2 problems **woeful** adj 1 miserable 2 causing woe 3 pitiful **woefully** adv **woebegone** adj looking miserable
wok n bowl-shaped Chinese cooking pan, used esp. for frying
woke v past tense of **wake**[1] ▶ **woken** v past participle of **wake**[1]
wold n open downs
wolf n, pl **wolves** 1 wild predatory canine mammal ▷ v 2 eat ravenously **cry wolf** raise a false alarm **wolf whistle** whistle by a man indicating that he thinks a woman is attractive **wolf willow** shrub with silvery leaves
wolfram n tungsten
wolverine n carnivorous mammal of Arctic regions
woman n, pl **women** 1 adult human female 2 women collectively **womanhood**

w

n **womanish** *adj* (of a man) looking like a woman
womanly *adj* having qualities traditionally associated with a woman **womanizing** *n* (of a man) practice of having casual affairs with women
womanizer *n* **Women's Movement** movement for the removal of social and economic inequalities between women and men
womb *n* hollow organ in female mammals where babies are conceived and develop
wombat *n* small heavily-built burrowing Aust. marsupial
won *v* past of **win**
wonder *n* **1** emotion caused by an amazing or unusual thing **2** wonderful thing ▷ *v* **3** be curious about **4** feel wonder ▷ *adj* **5** spectacularly successful: *a wonder drug* **wonderful** *adj* **1** very fine: *a wonderful job* **2** causing surprise or amazement **wonderfully** *adv* **wonderment** *n* **wondrous** *adj* old-fashioned **1** wonderful **2** strange
wonky *adj* **-kier, -kiest** *informal* **1** shaky or unsteady **2** not working properly
wont [rhymes with **don't**] *n* **1** custom ▷ *adj* **2** accustomed
won't will not
woo *v* **1** try to persuade **2** *old-fashioned* try to gain the love of
wood *n* **1** substance trees are made of, used in building and as fuel **2** *also pl* area where trees grow **wooded** *adj* covered with trees **wooden** *adj* **1** made of wood **2** without expression **woody** *adj* **woodbine** *n* honeysuckle **woodcock** *n* game bird **woodcut** *n* **1** engraved block of wood **2** print made from this **woodland** *n* forest

woodlouse *n* small insect-like creature with many legs
woodpecker *n* bird which searches tree trunks for insects **wood pigeon** large Eurasian pigeon **woodwind** *adj, n* (of) a type of wind instrument made of wood **woodworm** *n* insect larva that bores into wood
woodshed *n* shed made of or used for storing wood **take someone to the woodshed** *informal* reprimand privately
woof[1] *n* cross threads in weaving
woof[2] *n* barking noise made by a dog
woofer *n* loudspeaker for reproducing low-frequency sounds
wool *n* **1** soft hair of sheep, goats, etc. **2** yarn spun from this **woollen** *adj* **woolly** *adj* **1** of or like wool **2** vague or muddled ▷ *n* **3** knitted woollen garment **woolgathering** *n* daydreaming
woozy *adj* **woozier, wooziest** *informal* weak, dizzy, and confused
word *n* **1** smallest single meaningful unit of speech or writing **2** chat or discussion **3** brief remark **4** message **5** promise **6** command ▷ *v* **7** express in words **wordy** *adj* using too many words **wordiness** *n* **wording** *n* choice and arrangement of words **word processor** keyboard, microprocessor, and VDU for electronic organization and storage of text **word processing**
wore *v* past tense of **wear**
work *n* **1** physical or mental effort directed to making or doing something **2** paid employment **3** duty or task **4** something made or done

w

5 decoration of a specified kind: *needlework* **works 6** factory **7** total of a writer's or artist's achievements **8** *informal* full treatment **9** mechanism of a machine ▷ *v* **10** (cause to) do work **11** be employed **12** (cause to) operate **13** cultivate (land) **14** manipulate, shape, or process **15** (cause to) reach a specified condition **16** accomplish ▷ *adj* **17** of or for work **work to rule** adhere strictly to all working regulations to reduce the rate of work as a protest **work-to-rule** *n* **workable** *adj* **worker** *n* **workaholic** *n* person addicted to work **workhouse** *n hist* institution where the poor were given food and lodgings in return for work **working class** social class consisting of wage earners, esp. manual workers **working-class** *adj* **working party** committee investigating a specific problem **workman** *n* manual worker **workmanship** *n* **1** skill of a workman **2** skill exhibited in a finished product **worktop** *n* surface in a kitchen, used for food preparation

world *n* **1** the planet earth **2** mankind **3** society **4** sphere of existence ▷ *adj* **5** of the whole world **worldly** *adj* **1** not spiritual **2** concerned with material things **3** wise in the ways of the world **World Wide Web** global network of linked computer files

worm *n* **1** small limbless invertebrate animal **2** wretched or spineless person **3** shaft with a spiral thread forming part of a gear system **4** *computers* type of virus **worms 5** illness caused by parasitic worms in the

intestines ▷ *v* **6** rid of worms **7** crawl **8** insinuate (oneself) **9** extract (information) craftily **wormy** *adj* **wormcast** *n* coil of earth excreted by a burrowing worm **worm-eaten** *adj* eaten into by worms

wormwood *n* bitter plant

worn *v* past participle of **wear**

worry *v* **-rying, -ried 1** (cause to) be anxious or uneasy **2** annoy or bother **3** (of a dog) bite repeatedly ▷ *n, pl* **-ries 4** (cause of) anxiety or concern **worried** *adj* **worrying** *adj, n*

worse *adj, adv* **1** comparative of **bad, badly** ▷ *n* **2** worse thing **worst** *adj, adv* **1** superlative of **bad, badly** ▷ *n* **2** worst thing **worsen** *v* make or grow worse

worship *v* **-shipping, -shipped 1** show religious devotion to **2** love and admire ▷ *n* **3** worshipping **4 Worship** title for a mayor or magistrate **worshipper** *n* **worshipful** *adj* **1** worshipping **2** (in titles) honourable

worsted [wooss-tid] *n* **1** type of woollen yarn or fabric ▷ *adj* **2** made of worsted

wort [wurt] *n* infusion of malt used to make beer

worth *adj* **1** having a value of **2** meriting or justifying ▷ *n* **3** value or price **4** excellence **5** amount to be had for a given sum **worthless** *adj* **worthy** *adj* **1** having value or merit **2** deserving ▷ *n* **3** *informal* notable person **worthily** *adv* **worthiness** *n* **worthwhile** *adj* worth the time or effort involved

would *v* used as an auxiliary to form the past tense or subjunctive mood of **will**, express a request, or describe a habitual past action **would-be** *adj* wishing or pretending to be

w

wouldn't would not

wound[1] *n* **1** injury caused by violence **2** injury to the feelings ▷ *v* **3** inflict a wound on

wound[2] *v* past of **wind**[2]

wove *v* a past tense of **weave** ▸ **woven** *v* a past participle of **weave**

wow *interj* **1** exclamation of astonishment ▷ *n* **2** *informal* astonishing person or thing

wpm words per minute

wrack *n* seaweed

wraith *n* **1** apparition of a person seen shortly before his or her death **2** ghost

wrangle *v* **1** argue noisily ▷ *n* **2** noisy argument

wrap *v* **wrapping, wrapped** **1** fold (something) round (a person or thing) so as to cover ▷ *n* **2** garment wrapped round the shoulders **3** sandwich made by wrapping a filling in a tortilla **wrapper** *n* **1** cover **2** loose dressing gown **wrapping** *n* material used to wrap **wrap party** party held by cast and crew to celebrate the completion of filming of a TV programme or film **wrap up** *v* **1** fold paper round **2** put warm clothes on **3** *informal* finish or settle (a matter)

wrath [roth] *n* intense anger **wrathful** *adj*

wreak *v* **1** inflict (vengeance) **2** cause (chaos)

wreath *n* twisted ring or band of flowers or leaves used as a memorial or tribute **wreathed** *adj* **1** surrounded (by): *wreathed in pipe smoke* **2** surrounded by a ring (of): *wreathed in geraniums*

wreck *n* **1** accidental destruction of a ship at sea **2** wrecked ship **3** remains of something destroyed **4** person in very poor condition ▷ *v* **5** cause

the wreck of **wrecker** *n* **wreckage** *n* wrecked remains

wren *n* small brown songbird

wrench *v* **1** twist or pull forcefully **2** sprain ▷ *n* **3** forceful twist or pull **4** sprain **5** difficult or painful parting **6** adjustable spanner

wrest *v* **1** take by force **2** twist violently

wrestle *v* **1** fight, esp. as a sport, by grappling with and trying to throw down an opponent **2** struggle hard with **wrestler** *n* **wrestling** *n*

wretch *n* **1** despicable person **2** pitiful person **wretched** [retch-id] *adj* **1** miserable or unhappy **2** worthless **wretchedly** *adv* **wretchedness** *n*

wrier *adj* a comparative of **wry** ▸ **wriest** *adj* a superlative of **wry**

wriggle *v* **1** move with a twisting action **2** manoeuvre oneself by devious means ▷ *n* **3** wriggling movement

wright *n* maker: *playwright*

wring *v* **wringing, wrung** **1** twist, esp. to squeeze liquid out of **2** clasp and twist (the hands) **3** obtain by forceful means

wrinkle *n* **1** slight crease, esp. one in the skin due to age ▷ *v* **2** make or become wrinkled **wrinkly** *adj*

wrist *n* joint between the hand and the arm **wristwatch** *n* watch worn on the wrist

writ *n* written legal command

write *v* **writing, wrote, written** **1** mark paper etc. with symbols or words **2** set down in words **3** be the author or composer of **4** communicate by letter **writing** *n* **writer** *n* **1** author **2** person who has written something specified **write-**

off *n informal* something damaged beyond repair

write-up *n* published account of something

writhe *v* **1** twist or squirm in or as if in pain **2** be very embarrassed

wrong *adj* **1** incorrect or mistaken **2** immoral or bad **3** not intended or suitable **4** not working properly ▷ *adv* **5** in a wrong manner ▷ *n* **6** something immoral or unjust ▷ *v* **7** treat unjustly **8** malign **wrongly** *adv* **wrongful** *adj* **wrongfully** *adv* **wrongdoing** *n* immoral or illegal behaviour

wrote *v* past tense of **write**

wrought [rawt] *v* **1** *lit* past of **work** ▷ *adj* **2** (of metals) shaped by hammering or beating **wrought iron** pure form of iron used for decorative work

wrung *v* past of **wring**

wry *adj* **wrier, wriest** or **wryer, wryest** **1** dryly humorous **2** (of a facial expression) contorted **wryly** *adv*

wt. weight

wuss *n slang* feeble person

WWW World Wide Web

wych-elm *n* elm with large rough leaves

W

Xx

X 1 indicating an error, a choice, or a kiss **2** indicating an unknown, unspecified, or variable factor, number, person, or thing

Xe *chem* xenon

xenon *n* colourless odourless gas found in very small quantities in the air

xenophobia [zen-oh-**fobe**-ee-a] *n* fear or hatred of people from other countries

Xerox [**zeer**-ox] *n* **1** ® machine for copying printed material **2** ® copy made by a Xerox machine ▷ *v* **3** copy (a document) using such a machine

Xmas [**eks**-mass] *n* Christmas

x-ray *n* **1** stream of radiation that can pass through some solid materials **2** picture made by sending x-rays through someone's body to examine internal organs ▷ *v* **3** photograph, treat, or examine using x-rays

xylem [**zy**-lem] *n* plant tissue that conducts water and minerals from the roots to all other parts

xylophone [**zile**-oh-fone] *n* musical instrument made of a row of wooden bars played with hammers

Yy

yacht [yott] *n* large boat with sails or an engine used for racing or pleasure cruising **yachting** *n* **yachtsman** (**yachtswoman**) *n*

yak¹ *n* Tibetan ox with long shaggy hair

yak² *v* **yakking, yakked** *slang* talk continuously about unimportant matters

yam *n* tropical root vegetable

yank *v* 1 pull or jerk suddenly ▷ *n* 2 sudden pull or jerk

Yankee, Yank *adj, n slang* (of) a person from the United States

yap *v* **yapping, yapped** 1 bark with a high-pitched sound 2 *informal* talk continuously ▷ *n* 3 high-pitched bark

yard¹ *n* unit of length equal to 36 inches or about 91.4 centimetres **yardstick** *n* standard against which to judge other people or things

yard² *n* enclosed area, usu. next to a building and often used for a particular purpose: *builder's yard*

yarmulke [yar-mull-ka] *n* skullcap worn by Jewish men

yarn *n* 1 thread used for knitting or making cloth 2 *informal* long involved story **spin a yarn** tell an improbable story

yarrow *n* wild plant with flat clusters of white flowers

yashmak *n* veil worn by a Muslim woman to cover her face in public

yaw *v* (of an aircraft or ship)

turn to one side or from side to side while moving

yawl *n* two-masted sailing boat

yawn *v* 1 open the mouth wide and take in air deeply, often when sleepy or bored 2 (of an opening) be large and wide ▷ *n* 3 act of yawning **yawning** *adj*

yaws *n* infectious tropical skin disease

yd. yard

YDT Yukon Daylight Time

ye [yee] *pron obsolete* you

year *n* 1 time taken for the earth to make one revolution around the sun, about 365 days 2 twelve months from January 1 to December 31 **yearly** *adj, adv* (happening) every year or once a year **yearling** *n* animal between one and two years old

yearn *v* (foll. by *for*) want (something) very much **yearning** *n, adj*

yeast *n* fungus used to make bread rise and to ferment alcoholic drinks **yeasty** *adj*

yell *v* 1 shout or scream in a loud or piercing way ▷ *n* 2 loud cry of pain, anger, or fear

yellow *n* 1 the colour of gold, a lemon, etc. ▷ *adj* 2 of this colour 3 *informal* cowardly ▷ *v* 4 make or become yellow **yellow fever** serious infectious tropical disease **yellowhammer** *n* European songbird with a

y

yellow head and body **yellow pages** telephone directory which lists businesses under the headings of the type of business or service they provide

yelp *v, n* (give) a short, sudden cry

yen[1] *n, pl* **yen** main unit of currency in Japan

yen[2] *n informal* longing or desire

yeoman [**yo**-man] *n, pl* -**men** *hist* farmer owning and farming his own land **yeoman of the guard** member of the ceremonial bodyguard of the British monarchy

yes *interj* 1 expresses consent, agreement, or approval 2 used to answer when one is addressed **yes man** person who always agrees with his or her superior

yesterday *adv, n* 1 (on) the day before today 2 (in) the recent past

yet *adv* 1 up until then or now 2 still ▷ *conj* 3 nevertheless, still

yeti *n* same as **abominable snowman**

yew *n* evergreen tree with needle-like leaves and red berries

Yiddish *adj, n* (of or in) a language of German origin spoken by many Jews in Europe and elsewhere

yield *v* 1 produce or bear 2 give up control of, surrender 3 give in ▷ *n* 4 amount produced **yielding** *adj* 1 submissive 2 soft or flexible

YMCA Young Men's Christian Association

yodel *v* -**delling**, -**delled** 1 sing with abrupt changes between a normal and a falsetto voice ▷ *n* 2 act or sound of yodelling

yoga *n* Hindu method of exercise and discipline aiming at spiritual, mental, and physical wellbeing **yogi** *n* person who practises yoga

yoghurt, yogurt, yoghourt *n* slightly sour custard-like food made from milk that has had bacteria added to it, often sweetened and flavoured with fruit

yoke *n* 1 wooden bar put across the necks of two animals to hold them together 2 frame fitting over a person's shoulders for carrying buckets 3 *lit* oppressive force: *the yoke of the tyrant* 4 fitted part of a garment to which a fuller part is attached ▷ *v* 5 put a yoke on 6 unite or link

yokel *n offensive* person who lives in the country and is usu. simple and old-fashioned

yolk *n* yellow part of an egg that provides food for the developing embryo

Yom Kippur *n* annual Jewish religious holiday

yonder *adv* over there

yore *n lit* the distant past

Yorkshire pudding *n* baked batter made from flour, milk, and eggs and often eaten with roast beef

you *pron* 1 refers to the person or people addressed 2 refers to an unspecified person or people in general

young *adj* 1 in an early stage of life or growth ▷ *n* 2 offspring, esp. young animals 3 young people in general **youngster** *n* young person

your *adj* 1 of, belonging to, or associated with you 2 of, belonging to, or associated with an unspecified person or people in general **yours** *pron* something belonging to you **yourself** *pron*

youth *n* **1** time or condition of being young **2** boy or young man **3** young people as a group **youthful** *adj* **youthfulness** *n* **youth club** club that provides leisure activities for young people **youth hostel** inexpensive lodging place for young people travelling cheaply

yowl *v, n* (produce) a loud mournful cry

yo-yo *n, pl* -**yos** toy consisting of a spool attached to a string, by which it is repeatedly spun out and reeled in

YST Yukon Standard Time

YT, Y.T. Yukon Territory

yucca *n* tropical plant with spikes of white leaves

yucky, yukky *adj* **yuckier, yuckiest** *or* **yukkier, yukkiest** *slang* disgusting, nasty

Yule *n lit* Christmas or the Christmas season

Yupik *n* **1** indigenous people of Alaska, Aleutian Islands, or E Siberia **2** any language of Yupik

Yuppie *n* **1** young highly-paid professional person, esp. one who has a fashionable way of life ▷ *adj* **2** typical of or reflecting the values of Yuppies

YWCA Young Women's Christian Association

y

Zz

Zamboni n ® machine that repairs the surface of ice in a rink

zany [zane-ee] adj **zanier, zaniest** comical in an endearing way

zap v **zapping, zapped** slang **1** kill (by shooting) **2** change television channels rapidly by remote control **3** move quickly

zeal n great enthusiasm or eagerness **zealot** [zel-lot] n fanatic or extreme enthusiast **zealous** [zel-luss] adj extremely eager or enthusiastic **zealously** adv

zebra n black-and-white striped African animal of the horse family **zebra crossing** pedestrian crossing marked by black and white stripes on the road

zebu [zee-boo] n Asian ox with a humped back and long horns

Zen n Japanese form of Buddhism that concentrates on learning through meditation and intuition

zenith n **1** highest point of success or power **2** point in the sky directly above an observer

zephyr [zef-fer] n soft gentle breeze

zeppelin n hist large cylindrical airship

zero n, pl **-ros, -roes 1** (symbol representing) the number o **2** point on a scale of measurement from which the graduations commence **3** lowest point **4** nothing, nil ▷ adj **5** having no measurable quantity or size **zero in on** v **1** aim at **2** informal concentrate on

zest n **1** enjoyment or excitement **2** interest, flavour, or charm **3** peel of an orange or lemon

zigzag n **1** line or course having sharp turns in alternating directions ▷ v **-zagging, -zagged 2** move in a zigzag ▷ adj **3** formed in or proceeding in a zigzag ▷ adv **4** in a zigzag manner

zinc n bluish-white metallic element used in alloys and to coat metal

zing n informal quality in something that makes it lively or interesting

zinnia n garden plant with solitary heads of brightly coloured flowers

Zionism n movement to found and support a Jewish homeland in Israel **Zionist** n, adj

zip n **1** fastener with two rows of teeth that are closed or opened by a small clip pulled between them **2** informal energy, vigour **3** short whizzing sound ▷ v **zipping, zipped 4** fasten with a zip **5** move with a sharp whizzing sound

zircon n mineral used as a gemstone and in industry

zither n musical instrument

z

consisting of strings stretched over a flat box and plucked to produce musical notes

Zn *chem* zinc

zodiac *n* imaginary belt in the sky within which the sun, moon, and planets appear to move, divided into twelve equal areas, called signs of the zodiac, each named after a constellation

zombie, zombi *n* **1** person who appears to be lifeless, apathetic, or totally lacking in independent judgment **2** corpse brought back to life by witchcraft

zone *n* **1** area with particular features or properties **2** one of the divisions of the earth's surface according to temperature ▷ *v* **3** divide into zones **zonal** *adj*

zoo *n, pl* **zoos** place where live animals are kept for show

zoology *n* study of animals **zoologist** *n* **zoological** *adj* **zoological garden** zoo

zoom *v* **1** move or rise very rapidly **2** make or move with a buzzing or humming sound **zoom lens** lens that can make the details of a picture larger or smaller while keeping the picture in focus

zucchini [zoo-**keen**-ee] *n, pl* -**nis, -ni** small type of squash with green peel

Zulu *n* **1** member of a tall Black people of southern Africa **2** language of this people

zygote *n* fertilized egg cell

z

CANADA– PROVINCES AND TERRITORIES

Canada

Confederation: July 1, 1867
Capital: Ottawa

Area of land: 9 984 670km²
Population: 35 141 500

Alberta

Entered Confed.: Sept 1, 1905
Area of land: 661 848km²
Provincial bird: Great horned owl
Provincial tree: Lodgepole pine
Motto: Fortis et Liber – "Strong and free"

Capital: Edmonton
Pop.: 3 965 300 (11.3% of Canada)
Provincial flower: Wild rose

British Columbia

Entered Confed.: July 1, 1867
Area of land: 944 735km²
Provincial bird: Steller's jay
Provincial tree: Western red cedar
Motto: Splendor Sine Occasu – "Splendour without diminishment"

Capital: Victoria
Pop.: 4 650 000 (13.2% of Canada)
Provincial flower: Dogwood

Manitoba

Entered Confed.: July 15, 1870
Area of land: 647 797km²
Provincial bird: Great gray owl
Provincial tree: White spruce
Motto: Gloriosus et Liber – "Glorious and free"

Capital: Winnipeg
Pop.: 1 277 300 (3.6% of Canada)
Provincial flower: Prairie crocus

New Brunswick

Entered Confed.: July 20, 1871
Area of land: 72 908km²
Provincial bird: Black-capped
    chickadee
Provincial tree: Balsam fir
Motto: Spem Reduxit – "Hope was restored"

Capital: Fredericton
Pop.: 754 000 (2.1% of Canada)
Provincial flower: Purple violet

Newfoundland & Labrador

Entered Confed.: March 31, 1949
Area of land: 405 212km²
Provincial bird: Atlantic puffin
Provincial tree: Black spruce
Motto: Quaerite Prime Regnum Dei – "Seek ye first the kingdom of God"

Capital: St John's
Pop.: 513 600 (1.5% of Canada)
Provincial flower: Pitcher plant

Northwest Territories

Entered Confed.: July 15, 1870
Area of land: 1 346 106km²
Provincial bird: Gyrfalcon
Provincial tree: Tamarack
Motto: None

Capital: Yellowknife
Pop.: 43 300 (0.1% of Canada)
Provincial flower: Mountain avens

Nova Scotia
Entered Confed.: July 1, 1867
Area of land: 55 284km²
Provincial bird: Osprey
Provincial tree: Red spruce
Motto: Munit Haec et Altera Vincit – "One defends and the other conquers"

Capital: Halifax
Pop.: 945 000 (2.7% of Canada)
Provincial flower: Mayflower

Nunavut
Entered Confed.: April 1, 1999
Area of land: 2 093 190km²
Provincial bird: Rock ptarmigan
Provincial tree: no official tree
Motto: Nunavut Sanginivut – "Nunavut, our strength"

Capital: Iqaluit (Frobisher Bay)
Pop.: 34 000 (0.1% of Canada)
Provincial flower: Purple saxifrage

Ontario
Entered Confed.: July 1, 1867
Area of land: 1 076 395km²
Provincial bird: Common loon
Provincial tree: Eastern white pine
Motto: Ut Incepit Fidelis Sic Permanet – "Loyal she began, loyal she remains"

Capital: Toronto
Pop.: 13 583 700 (38.7% of Canada)
Provincial flower: White trillium

Prince Edward Island
Entered Confed.: July 1, 1873
Area of land: 5 660km²
Provincial bird: Blue jay
Provincial tree: Red oak
Motto: Parva sub Ingenti – "The small under the protection of the great"

Capital: Charlottetown
Pop.: 145 800 (0.4% of Canada)
Provincial flower: Lady's slipper

Quebec
Entered Confed.: July 1, 1867
Area of land: 1 542 056km²
Provincial bird: Snowy owl
Motto: Je me souviens – "I remember"

Capital: Quebec City
Pop.: 8 099 100 (23% of Canada)
Provincial flower: Blue flag

Saskatchewan
Entered Confed.: Sept 1, 1905
Area of land: 651 036km²
Provincial bird: Sharp-tailed grouse
Provincial tree: White birch
Motto: Multibus e Gentibus Vires – "From many peoples strength"

Capital: Regina
Pop.: 1 093 900 (3.1% of Canada)
Provincial flower: Prairie lily

Yukon
Entered Confed.: July 13, 1898
Area of land: 482 443km²
Provincial bird: Raven
Provincial tree: Sub-alpine fir
Motto: None

Capital: Whitehorse
Pop.: 36 400 (0.1% of Canada)
Provincial flower: Fireweed